432

# A HISTORY OF
# ENGLAND
## AND THE
# BRITISH EMPIRE

*By* WALTER PHELPS HALL

PRINCETON UNIVERSITY

*and* ROBERT GREENHALGH ALBION

HARVARD UNIVERSITY

*With the Collaboration of*
JENNIE BARNES POPE

*THIRD EDITION*

GINN AND COMPANY

BOSTON · NEW YORK · CHICAGO · ATLANTA · DALLAS
COLUMBUS · SAN FRANCISCO · TORONTO · LONDON

# PREFACE

A CLEAR and fresh interpretation of an old and honored theme is the aim of this book. The imperial, social, economic, and literary phases have been emphasized more than in most textbooks, without neglect of the constitutional, political, and other more conventional aspects. Mindful of the needs of the college undergraduate, the authors have constantly endeavored to present an adequate background and clear-cut explanation for each new feature as it has arisen, without confusing the picture by too many facts.

The part from Anglo-Saxon institutions through the peace settlement of 1815, inclusive, was written primarily by Albion and Pope, with the exception of Hall's "Thought and Letters from Newton to Burke" and other sections on literature. The pre-Norman narrative and much of the part since 1815 were written originally by Hall, with extensive collaboration by Albion and Pope, particularly in foreign relations, "Imperial Apathy," and the World War. The bibliography, map arrangements, and tables are the work of Albion; the index, that of Pope. The edition of 1946, with Chapter XXXI, is to be credited to Albion and Pope. The new chapter in the edition of 1953 is the work of all three authors.

The authors express their gratitude to publishers of their former writings for permission to include, without quotation marks, occasional passages from those writings: ALBION, *Forests and Sea Power*, Harvard University Press, 1926; *Introduction to Military History*, D. Appleton-Century Company, 1929; "The Communication Revolution," in Transactions of the Newcomen Society of Great Britain, 1933; *The Rise of New York Port*, Charles Scribner's Sons, 1939. HALL, *British Radicalism, 1791–1797*, Columbia Studies in History, Economics and Public Law, 1912; *Empire to Commonwealth,* Henry Holt and Company, 1928; "The Three Arnolds and Their Bible," in

# A History of England and the British Empire

*Essays in Intellectual History*, Harper & Brothers, 1929; *Mr. Gladstone*, W. W. Norton & Company, Inc., 1931; *World Wars and Revolutions*, D. Appleton-Century Company, 1943; *Iron out of Calvary*, D. Appleton-Century Company, 1946. HALL and BELLER (Eds.), *Historical Readings in Nineteenth Century Thought*, D. Appleton-Century Company, 1928. ALBION and POPE, *Sea Lanes in Wartime*, W. W. Norton & Company, Inc., 1942. POPE, *Early European History*, Oxford Book Company, 1936.

The authors wish to acknowledge their indebtedness to many kind colleagues at Princeton and Harvard Universities and to other friends too numerous to mention.

THE AUTHORS

PRINCETON, NEW JERSEY
CAMBRIDGE, MASSACHUSETTS

# CONTENTS

[ v ]

# A History of England and the British Empire

# LIST OF MAPS

Attention is called to the Political Map of England and Wales, facing page 920. This map shows the counties, principal towns, and chief geographical features. It is so arranged that when unfolded it lies clear of the text and thus may prove helpful if used in connection with any part of the book.

[ vii ]

# A History of England and the British Empire

A HISTORY OF

# ENGLAND

AND THE

# BRITISH EMPIRE

# CHAPTER I

## Roman and Saxon

O FF AN open beach some few miles to the north of Dover lie Roman galleys. From them heavily armed soldiers jump into the shallow water. They fight with blue-eyed native Britons, whose eager leaders drive their lightweight chariots into the sea. The Romans reach land; the Britons disperse. The inevitable fortified camp is constructed; Caesar's first invasion of Britain begins.

Just why Julius Caesar made this attack in 55 B.C. we shall never know. It had been reported to him that certain rebellious Gauls had received aid from Britain, and this had to be stopped. It was also said that certain sundry articles of value which might be of use to him as the political leader of the Roman popular party were to be found across the Channel. Caesar had seen with his own eyes gold coins minted in Britain; and even if he found little gold, there were men and women to enslave. His own popularity at Rome had long been enhanced by a steady inflow of both gold and slaves. Perhaps thoughts like these came to the Roman general as he looked at the chalk cliffs of Albion.

Caesar brought no food; he intended to live on the country. His foraging parties, however, met with ill success, and storms wrecked many of his galleys. Taking a hostage or two, he withdrew to Gaul. The expedition was a failure; but it was not so announced at Rome. The following year Caesar came back with an army twice as large. Powerful British tribes were now his allies; they had been maltreated, so they said, by other Britons, and thirsted for vengeance. On his second coming Caesar cut his way from the southeastern shore to the Thames and signally punished some tribesmen just across that river. The Britons decided to treat with their conqueror, who made peace on easy terms. Threatening revolts in Gaul demanded Caesar's presence, a sufficient number of Britons had been captured for the Roman slave market, and his base camp on the coast was too distant for continued campaigning. Upon promise of a yearly tribute to Rome, Caesar and all his troops departed.

The history of the British Isles as a matter of written record begins with the Roman invasion; but there is a history which makes its record elsewhere, which antedates all written symbols, which leaves its mark either upon the surface of the earth, architecturally, or else below the surface in caves, in the scattered weapons of the chase, in burial mounds, in the skeletal remains of what, once, were men. From the time when we have the first record of man's existence England seems to have shared in almost every one of the various stages of progress from the several stone ages into those of copper, bronze, and iron.

Apparently from earliest times wave upon wave of immigration had swept over Britain. It was an easy land to reach. At first, it would seem, men could walk dry-shod to England; even after the sea came through, forming the Straits of Dover, only twenty-one miles of water separated the island from the mainland. In later years, after England learned that her true defense lay in a guardian fleet, that narrow strip of Channel was to prove a bar to invaders and allow England to develop her own individual civilization unmolested. But in these earlier times the land lay invitingly open. The coast line nearest Europe is indented with harbors, while rivers lead into the interior; in fact, no part of England lies more than seventy miles from the sea. The rich lowlands of southern and eastern England were easily overrun time and again; but when the newcomers advanced toward the west and north, rugged highlands barred their way. Had nature set those inhospitable hills nearer the Channel shore, England would have been less open to invasion and her history might well have run a very different course.

The last of these early invaders were the so-called Celts, the first of five conquerors—Celt, Roman, Saxon, Dane, and Norman—about whom there is some written knowledge. Who the Celts were and what their origin was no one is sure. The Romans, who introduced us to the word "Celt," certainly were not. Julius Caesar referred to part of the barbarians to the north and west of Italy as those "who in their own language are called Celts, and in our language Gauls." The term "Celt," so far as English history is concerned, is more a matter of language and civilization than of race; for we do not know the extent to which the Celtic newcomers may simply have imposed their tongue and their customs upon the men whom they found already there. These Celts seem to have poured into the British Isles, perhaps in several floods. The language of the so-called Goidelic, or Gaelic, Celts, noticeable chiefly in Ireland, differed somewhat from that of the Cymric, or Brythonic, Celts. The latter possibly reached Britain about 500 B.C., near the time when the Greeks were repulsing the Persians at Marathon. These Celts occupied the land, and it was theirs. They knew the use of iron, which the softer bronze of their predecessors could not withstand. The Belgae, apparently a branch of the Brythonic Celts and also closely allied to those Gauls whom Caesar conquered, seem in their turn to have taken the southeast corner of the island, including the valley of the Thames. In addition to their general similarity of language the Celtic peoples of Britain all made the clan, a small family unit, the center of their primitive organization.

By the time of Caesar's coming these Britons, although less advanced culturally than their fellow Celts upon the Continent, had progressed a long way from the life of the yet more primitive peoples they had displaced. In the days long before, when great cities were rising in Egypt and Babylonia, those earlier islanders, as far as we know, had not even dared occupy the lowlands, where wolves and other wild beasts prowled; instead they sought refuge on the uplands, the moors, the treeless places where one could see to fight by night. The Britons encountered by Caesar, however, had driven the beasts to cover and had learned to cultivate the soil. They were expert in working bronze, tin, and iron, and knew something of art also, decorating pottery with curved designs. When fighting, they wore metal helmets beautifully ornamented and inlaid, and those who lived in south Britain had a coinage modeled on that of Macedon in the fourth century before Christ. Nor was this strange, for the British Celts were after all probably the far-western wing of the Celtic family which stretched to the Danube.

In religion a priestly caste, the druids, about whom little has been ascertained, conducted sacrifices and interpreted omens. They were apparently leaders of public opinion and were singled out for punishment by the Romans more because of their political leadership in stimulating patriotic resistance than because of their religion. They seemingly enjoyed many privileges; their persons were sacred, and the mistletoe, grown on the oak, was their emblem. They were the guardians of the law, setting penalties for its violation, determining inheritances, and assessing fines. On the island of Anglesey (Mona), off the northern coast of Wales, was their most sacred shrine. At Stonehenge and Avebury are mysterious structures apparently built before the Celtic invasions, but perhaps connected with druid worship. The hardened Romans reported the druid religious rites to be marked by practices which even to them seemed cruel. The druids, according to tradition, did not hesitate to offer living sacrifices on their altars, incinerating victims in large wicker baskets to propitiate their gods, but this was not a regular practice, as was once thought, and presumably happened only in occasional instances of captives or malefactors.

# A History of England and the British Empire

Such was the island Caesar invaded, and his account of the people remains the chief source of our meager knowledge of them. After his withdrawal the Romans did not return in force for nearly a hundred years—a century which saw the birth of Christ and the Roman Empire at its peak. The friendly attitude of the Britons toward the economic penetration of their island by the Roman traders appears to have staved off trouble. Meanwhile the numerous tribes in Britain had combined into two or three so-called kingdoms, though the organization undoubtedly remained simply tribal. Not long before the renewed invasions by the Romans, the largest and most important of these was ruled by a friend of Rome, the Cymbeline of Shakespeare's play. He encouraged the Roman traders and so helped to prepare his people for Roman ways. Following Roman custom, he offered sacrifices at Rome itself and, if we may judge from the number of coins which bear the inscription "Cunobelinus Rex," grew wealthy.

Thus it was in the days of the eccentric Roman emperor Caligula, who gave orders for a new invasion of Britain, countermanded them before a boat took to the water, but decorated the troops designated for the conquest as though they had won astonishing victories. Then the emperor Claudius succeeded to the imperial purple, and in A.D. 43 the permanent occupation of Britain took place. Claudius had trouble with mutinous Gauls who had revolted at the instigation of the druids, and Britain was the center from which these pernicious priests spread disaffection. Furthermore, Cymbeline in his old age had found his power undermined by certain of his sons. These reasons were sufficient for Claudius, who ordered his general Plautius to conquer the island.

The Britons under Caractacus, a son of Cymbeline, resisted stoutly; but the Romans now knew the terrain and by superior strategy were able to march quickly through what is now Kent and to advance past London to Colchester (Camulodunum) in Essex. Claudius came over in person for the last fight and returned to Rome after a week or two, the accredited victor, leaving Plautius in charge of a new Roman province. Plautius campaigned for four years, carrying the Roman arms north to a line from the Mersey River to the Humber, and as far west as Wales and Cornwall. Caractacus, however, still stayed in the field and, though driven out of England, stirred up the tribes in Wales in the west, while in the east, another tribe, the Iceni, alarmed at Roman threats to disarm them, revolted. Caractacus was captured and sent to Rome, where, if we may believe the Roman historian Tacitus, he made a successful plea for clemency at his public trial.

# Roman and Saxon

Still the Britons would not give over, and general after general was sent against them. Finally a determined Roman governor decided to break their morale by capturing Anglesey, the sacred center of druid mysteries. "Seek your auguries," he told his soldiers, "in the quivering intestines of the druid priests." Simultaneously with the slaughter of the druids came the revolt (A.D. 61) of Queen Boudicca (incorrectly called Boadicea), widow of the late king of the Iceni. She was publicly whipped, and her daughters were violated by Roman officials. Thereupon her tribesmen rose in tremendous fury, marched rapidly on Colchester, a center of the Roman occupation, and massacred the inhabitants. Other disaffected Britons joined Boudicca, who found herself at the head of many thousand rebels. The Roman troops, returning from Anglesey, crushed the revolt; Boudicca took her own life, and thereafter much of southern Britain lay quiescent under Rome.

The victorious Romans rested on their laurels for a while, until another still restless tribe, to the northward, soon necessitated more campaigning. For this work Rome sent Agricola, A.D. 78, a famous general, whose exploits as narrated by his son-in-law, Tacitus, lose nothing in the telling. Agricola seems to have led his army in seven different campaigns far beyond the site of Edinburgh, to have sent a fleet to circumnavigate Britain, and to have won the confidence of the Britons in the south of England. His conquests in Scotland were not permanent; but his conciliatory statesmanship was effective, and in the southern part of the island, where Rome held sway, the Britons began to give up their own way of life for that of the Romans.

In the south, consequently, lay the civilization of Rome. Cities, roads, extensive villas, with plumbing better than in many present-day English villages—all have been revealed by excavation. Unfortunately for our knowledge of this elaborate Roman life transported to this northern land, there are but few written records, and those for the most part military. Britain was an outlying province and made little impression on the Roman world. Yet here rose towns, equipped with forums, columns, baths, and other, less desirable, features of Roman life. The Roman soldiers sent to guard Britain from the still wild tribes near by stayed there long years, often permanently, according to the Roman custom, and married the native women. Soldiers were far from being the only Romans in Britain: officials, merchants, and scores of other civilians came to this northern province for business and sometimes stayed. Most of them probably settled in towns, but some wealthy Romans lived in beautiful country houses, or villas.

# A History of England and the British Empire

There were probably from ten to fifteen towns in Roman Britain (depending on classification), and some were fairly sizable. One of these, London, which was developed, if not founded, by the Romans, was to be one day the greatest city of the world. It was considerably larger in Roman times than either Cologne or Bordeaux. Vessels brought cargoes some forty odd miles up the Thames from the sea to this central spot, whence roads spread out in various directions. Commercially London, then as later, was the chief city of England; but officially it was overshadowed by several administrative centers, such as Colchester (Camulodunum), York (Eburacum), and Chester (Deva). A rather small town, but important archaeologically, is Silchester; for it has been fairly easy to complete the work of excavation there, since no other town has ever been superimposed upon its site. It is laid out in checkerboard fashion and contains the remains of a forum, a temple, public baths, an amphitheater outside the gates, many small houses (perhaps shops), and a number of rather extensive residences. In the latter have been discovered wall plaster painted in conventional Roman design, floors laid in mosaic, and numerous water pipes. The population was apparently well Romanized, both the upper and the lower class. Even the tiles and bricks in Silchester have legible scratches on them—bits from the Aeneid, or Latin words like *fecit* or *satis*, which would seem to indicate that so and so made the brick or that he was *satis*, tired of work.

Scattered throughout the countryside were numerous villas with agricultural estates spread out about them; for England from Roman days to the present has been a land of country houses. Presumably these were occupied by the owners of large rural estates, for the most part native Britons, although doubtless some Roman army officers or civilian officials were among them. We do not know upon what terms they held these estates, or what system of agriculture was practiced upon them, or whether the work was done by slaves or by partially free laborers. If we may judge, however, from Roman analogies in Gaul and from the spacious size of many villas, we may assume that wealthy Romano-Britons lived leisured lives, and, since their villas were not fortified, that they felt secure in the countryside of southeastern Britain under Roman law and order.

Near the villas and elsewhere the spade of the excavator has located many villages. For the most part they seem to be Celtic as far as ground plans are concerned, but in a number of them such minor objects of art as brooches or bits of pottery, which have been unearthed, are Roman in design. In other villages the scattered and fragmentary traces of former life seem to indicate that many Britons were only slightly influenced by Roman ways. In the midlands and

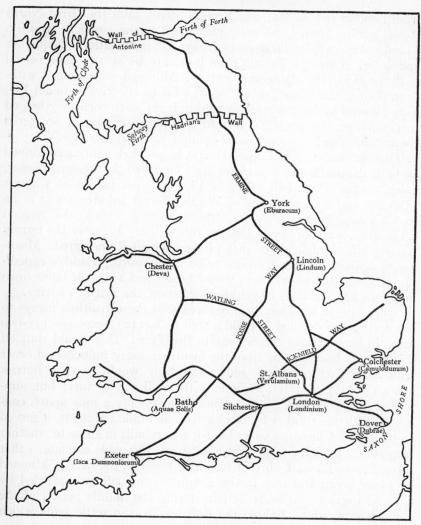

ROMAN BRITAIN

in the north few Roman antiquities, apart from fortifications, are found. The conquerors, it appears, were content simply to fortify the north and west, but preferred to keep to the south and east when it came to permanent settlements of a civilian character.

Even more important, perhaps, to Britain than the Roman town was the construction, for purposes of defense, of substantial military highways. The most famous of these were the Fosse Way, from Exeter in the southwest to Lincoln in the northeast; Watling Street,

# A History of England and the British Empire

from London to Chester; and Ermine Street, later the Great North Road, leading from London up past York to the northern frontier. Thanks to these splendid stone highways, communication was quicker and easier in Roman Britain than it was to be at any later period until the end of the eighteenth century. Although, with Rome's withdrawal from the island, those roads, vital to effective national life, were allowed to degenerate into muddy lanes, even then they helped to counteract the tendency toward complete isolation of scattered communities and thus continued to bind England together.

Though southeastern England might be pacified, fighting continued on both the north and west frontiers. To guard the western border, a legion, the Twentieth (Valeria Victrix), was placed at Chester (Deva); and a continuation of Watling Street led straight as a die to Caerleon, in South Wales, where another legion, the Second (Augusta), was stationed. Beyond this military highway the unruly western tribes might do as they pleased for all Rome cared. Meanwhile, against another fractious tribe in the north, punitive expeditions constantly had to be sent from Chester and York, the latter town being the headquarters of yet another legion, the Sixth (Victrix).

The emperor Hadrian, growing weary of these fruitless forays to the north, then decided to build a wall (A.D. 120), some seventy-two miles in length, from the Solway to the Tyne. This would shut off this restless border tribe from the insurrectionary influence of other tribes still farther north, and particularly would erect a barrier against future invaders. Originally the wall was of turf; but, supported as it was by a large number of forts only a mile apart, connected with one another by blockhouses and military roads, it served its purpose. A hundred years later it was rebuilt in stone by another emperor. This later wall, thirty fee⁺ high, was wide enough so that three men could walk abreast from one tower to the next. "Manned by every breed and race in the Empire," the wall was guarded by most of the legionaries in Britain during the middle period of the Roman occupation. Behind the wall lay Roman settlements which developed, for the amusement of the garrison, "one roaring, rioting, cock-fighting, wolf-baiting, horse-racing town from Ituna on the west to Segedunum on the cold eastern beach." To the north of Hadrian's wall was no man's land. True, another wall, still farther to the north, was built later, thirty-seven miles long and sufficient to cover the distance across the neck of the island, roughly from the modern Edinburgh to Glasgow. But this wall was not the true boundary of the Empire and was soon abandoned. Beyond Hadrian's wall, during most of the Roman occupation, there were only savages, called "Picts" by the Romans, who asserted that their bodies were painted.

# Roman and Saxon

Hadrian's wall was to stand firm for almost three centuries, even when Roman defense was crumbling in Asia and beyond the Danube. Britain was to be in serious danger from only one direction, the sea.

Toward the close of the third century the Empire, after some years of internal disorders and consequent neglect of distant Britain, again came under the rule of strong emperors,—Diocletian and, shortly afterward, the greater Constantine. Both gave close attention to the island. In particular under Constantine, who was proclaimed emperor at York (where he happened to be at the time), Britain prospered. This we may judge from the number of milestones bearing his name, from the quantity of coins inscribed with it, from the fact that grain was shipped from Britain to garrisons on the lower Rhine, and more particularly from the large number of Roman villas dating from this period. Already, however, before the reigns of these emperors, pirates from the region which is now Germany had begun to raid the Channel coast. These were the vanguard of the Saxons who later were to sweep all England before them. As a result, among the imperial reforms the civilian power was separated from the military; Britain was divided into four subprovinces; and the troops were placed under three different high officials. One of these generals was in charge of the north and the wall; another controlled the reserves; while the third, the Count of the Saxon Shore, held the key position in the face of piratical forays, as commander of the fleet and the eastern garrisons.

Not long after the death of Constantine the Roman Empire began to crumble as barbarians from the Germanic regions, pushed on by the Huns, fierce invaders from the east, hewed and hacked at the imperial frontiers. Certain of these Germanic tribesmen not only defeated the imperial legions in the Balkans, A.D. 378, but actually were able to invade Italy itself. From the distant provinces legions were called home, including the Sixth (Victrix), which had been in Britain two hundred years; and one by one these outlying districts were abandoned to their own resources. The collapse of the Rhine barriers brought Germanic tribesmen deep into Gaul and almost severed the line of imperial communication.

As political paralysis at Rome weakened the government in Britain, the settled order of the Roman occupation was shattered by renewed invasions from the north and west, as well as from the sea. From the middle of the fourth century, the Picts—the name was applied rather indiscriminately to the presumably Celtic tribes from north of Hadrian's wall—and the Celtic Scots from northern Ireland made intermittent forays which steadily grew more intensive and alarming. They made such headway that before the fifth century opened the Romans had abandoned the wall and had twice to recommence the conquest of Britain north of London. More serious as an omen for the future, the Nordic pirates, barbarians of the same general stock as those who were harassing other imperial frontiers, were growing bolder in their frequent raids upon the coast. Roman commanders in Britain, intent on their own glory and the emperorship itself, added to the plight of the island. Two such officials, less than thirty years apart, setting out on vain quests for the imperial purple, took many legionaries to the Continent with them; and these troops never came back to Britain, where they were sorely needed to stem the invaders. This second withdrawal of troops occurred in A.D. 407, the traditional date of the end of Rome's long rule in England. Three years later Germanic barbarians sacked Rome itself, and Britain sent to the emperor vain appeals for help against similar foes. This date really signifies nothing except that it happens to be the last fact which our scanty records give us of the Roman occupation. Scattered as the garrisons had become by that year, it is improbable that they all left immediately. Some, perhaps, never left. We know nothing except that the glory of Rome had faded into darkness.

During the next two hundred years Britain became Engia-land. Following the trail of the earlier German pirates, fresh invaders—fair-haired Nordic tribesmen, Jutes, Angles, Saxons—overran the country in the middle of the fifth century and, unlike the Romans, stayed. These incomers hailed from lower Scandinavia and the northwest corner of Germany. The homeland of the Jutes extended from the shores of Sweden across the narrow entrances to the Baltic Sea, into central Denmark; the Angles came from southern Denmark and the adjacent region in Germany; and the Saxons lived on the marshy lowlands which stretched westward to the Elbe River and beyond. All three tribes were closely akin in everything that concerned religion, language, customs, and blood. All three lived on the ocean almost as much as on the land at this early period, although before long they turned to a more settled agricultural life. Perhaps from the first only the more adventurous had spurned the prosaic raising of crops to become "the terror of all neighboring coasts, equally famed for merciless cruelty and destructiveness, sudden as lightning in attack and retreat, of an incredible greed for plunder, laughing and joyous in danger. They chose the tempest in which to sail, that they might find their enemies unprepared, and wherever the winds and waves drove them, there they ravaged."[1]

[1] S. A. Brooke, *English Literature from the Beginning to the Norman Conquest* (1907), p. 38. By permission of the Macmillan Company, Macmillan & Co., Ltd., of London, The Macmillan Company of Canada, Limited, publishers.

# Roman and Saxon

According to legend, in the year 449 their reputed leaders, Hengist and Horsa, invited in by the Britons to aid them against the Picts, soon turned on their hosts with fury. To quote from the history of the Venerable Bede, our best and, at times, only authority, the new-comers "plundered all the neighboring cities and country, spread the conflagration from the eastern to the western sea. . . . Public as well as private structures were overturned; the priests were everywhere slain before the altars; the prelates and the people, without any respect of persons, were destroyed with fire and sword; nor was there anyone to bury those who had been thus cruelly slaughtered."

Roughly speaking, this new conquest continued for more than two centuries, while at the same time the Britons continued to be frequently hard pressed by their old foes, the Picts and the Scots. The Saxon conquest was never carried on systematically. Wandering bands of "Anglo-Saxons" went up the English rivers in their light-draft boats, crossed overland to sack and destroy such villas and towns as they happened upon. Everywhere destruction followed in their wake. They were not city dwellers, and they much preferred to tear down rather than to utilize the stone-constructed Roman villas. The miserable Britons fled before them or hid themselves whenever opportunity offered, sometimes in the heating chambers underneath the hollow floors of Roman villas, whence archaeologists have dragged forth not a few skeletons.

From the little that we can learn of those two "lost centuries" between Roman and Saxon times in Britain, it would seem that the Saxon invaders had a fairly easy time in occupying the civilized southeast but encountered sturdy opposition as they pushed farther inland. At one time in the fifth or sixth century, under a mythical King Arthur, the Britons seem to have made a successful counter-thrust. "Then did Arthur fight against the Saxons in those days along with the leaders of the Britons." Twelve battles were fought by the hero, and "The twelfth was fought at Mount Badon at which 960 men fell in one day at one onslaught by Arthur, and no one felled them but Arthur alone," according to an account probably written some five centuries later. That this writer may have invented the name of Arthur is possible, but that the Britons won at least one major encounter at Mount Badon, apparently near the city of Bath, is highly probable because a monk who wrote long before this tells us that much. If only this monk had been less given to dilating on the wrath of God and the wickedness of his fellow Britons, we should know more about Arthur. The legends about this warrior, as we shall see, strongly appealed to the imagination of his fellow islanders, and kept reappearing in literature down through the centuries.

# A History of England and the British Empire

For the most part the Roman-Celtic people apparently vanished, perhaps into the recesses of the Welsh hills or the tip of Cornwall, or into other remote corners. There they seem to have reverted to the primitive ways of the other Celts in those regions. A few perhaps continued to live in their former homes as wretched slaves, while some may have escaped to the Continent. But the land of England was theirs no longer. Both Celtic and Roman influences were largely swept away by the heathen invaders, as far as the England of the Roman occupation was concerned. Yet throughout English history since that time the Celt has made himself felt, whereas Rome's legacies have been negligible. The four centuries of Roman occupation left little permanent impression on later England; all that definitely survived the Saxon onslaught were the remains of roads and towns and a slight tinge of Christianity, which was apparently carried into Wales by fugitives. On the other hand, in the "Celtic fringe" surrounding England in the British Isles—in Wales, in Ireland, in the Scottish Highlands, and to a lesser degree in Cornwall—have been preserved the language and many of the customs and characteristics of the Celts even into modern times. The organization of the clan, for instance, continued into the eighteenth century in the Scottish Highlands. Risky as it is to generalize, a strain of imagination and quick impulsiveness is found to this day among many of these Celtic people, making the Celt quite different from the average Englishman in both thought and action. Yet even the Englishman probably has in his veins some of the blood of the Celts and their predecessors; for in conquests such as this the victors often took the women, even though the men were driven off or slain.

Scholars still dispute as to just how thoroughgoing this conquest was. At any rate, for several centuries the Saxons dominated the island and in blood, in custom, and in tongue left an indelible imprint on the later history of England and the lives of English-speaking peoples to this day. Most of the population seems to have been displaced by the new Germanic groups. In their piecemeal and long-protracted invasions the Saxons sometimes retreated with their booty and sailed back to their homeland; sometimes they would stay and occupy the land. Then they would send eastward for their wives and children and the less restless of their number, who had stayed behind. They avoided the Roman buildings, which they had easily stormed, and built new crude huts for themselves. Once settled in this new country, the Saxon changed his ways, devoting himself to the soil rather than to the sea. He was now the farmer above all else, rather than the seafarer; but he continued to be a stalwart fighter.

# Roman and Saxon

At that same time other Germans were attacking other parts of the Empire. In the old Roman province of Gaul, for instance, these Germans (the Franks, who were to give their name to France) found the Gallo-Roman civilization more firmly rooted than the Romano-British. The result was that Frenchmen in subsequent centuries represented a more equal mingling of Celtic, Roman, and Teutonic strains than Englishmen, who were overwhelmingly Teutonic. The Goths and Lombards, who invaded Italy, likewise encountered a well-established civilization, which they absorbed rather than supplanted. So the story went: where the Germanic barbarians invaded definitely Romanized parts of the Empire, their imprint was less evident than in the remoter sections.

The Anglo-Saxons found it easy enough to kill Britons, but very difficult to deal with one another. There were no traditions of national unity to which they might appeal; nor did they have a war lord or leader supreme over all. Kings there were in plenty; but kings did not imply kingdoms in the modern sense. Many so-called kingdoms rose and fell in England during these dark ages. Only slowly and almost imperceptibly did seven—of which three were founded by Saxons, three by Angles, and one by Jutes—take on sufficient form and substance to be recognized as such. Of this so-called Heptarchy there were Kent (Jutes), in the extreme southeast; Sussex (South Saxons), to the west of Kent; and Wessex (West Saxons), still farther to the west. The other four were Essex (East Saxons) and East Anglia (Angles), small kingdoms to the north and east of London, fronting on the North Sea; Mercia (Angles), a large central kingdom; and Northumbria (Angles), the largest of all, stretching from south of York to the north beyond Edinburgh (for Scotland, as a separate country did not exist).

Before England could become a nation, these kingdoms somehow must be united; but by what means? One, of course, might grow sufficiently powerful to absorb the other six, and for a time it looked as though this might happen. Northumbria in the seventh century and Mercia in the eighth in turn managed to attain a sort of overlordship over the others; but the forces of decentralization were too strong to be overcome until the rise of Wessex, in the ninth and tenth centuries. Civilization was at a low ebb. These warriors in the early days of the Saxon period had no cities, no commerce, and scarcely any communication with the outside world. Such literature as they possessed was in the form of unwritten songs, passed down from generation to generation; for they could neither read nor write. Furthermore, their religion, aside from a fine appreciation of courage and endurance, was devoid of ethical significance.

# Roman and Saxon

Yet by the commencement of the eleventh century there was to be an England, thanks to Christianity on the one hand and to the Danes on the other. Christianity was to bring England back into the circle of Western civilization, teach manners and morals to the wild tribesmen, make them think, no matter how crudely, about life's meaning. And to the gentler message of the Church there was to be added the menace of a Viking conquest, a fresh attack from overseas by men quite competent to hew and slay.

The Anglo-Saxons, when they came to England, were unacquainted with Christianity. They had a religion of a sort, but not clearly defined. They believed in a group of gods presided over by Thor, the Thunderer, and by Woden, or Odin, God of Magic and Poetry, to whom most of the Anglo-Saxon kings traced their ancestry. There were a number of subdeities, such as Frey, Goddess of Plenty, and Frigg, wife of Odin. The priests were apparently few, and their position was not influential. In Northumbria, where we have mention of them, their social status seems to have been questionable, and they were humiliated by being forbidden to ride any horse but a mare. Their sole duty seems to have been confined to offering sacrifices, originally bloodthirsty in character but by the time of the first Christian missionaries limited apparently to animals. One virtue, valor, was emphasized by this barbaric religion. The Saxons did not fear anything, even their own gods. It was scarcely necessary to propitiate the latter, since they were regarded more as boon companions in the hereafter than as supernatural life-directors. If one was fortunate enough to die fighting, then one went to Valhalla, there to feast and to drink with the gods at a perpetual banquet. The Saxons were much given to drinking. When one met an old friend there was a "greeting ale"; when an illegitimate son was adopted into the family there was a further drinking bout, and likewise another whenever a slave was advanced in status to freeman. Feats of this description were semireligious in character; so also were burial ceremonies. Occasionally bodies were cremated, together with the weapons and the dogs of the departed. More frequently the dead were buried, the heroes having mounds or barrows raised over them. Superheroes became clothed with a kind of divinity; thus the distinction between god and man was made rather shadowy.

Scarcely a trace of any other formal religion has been found among the Saxons. The ideals of life which they cherished were of the simplest, if we may judge from their one great pre-Christian poem, Beowulf. The hero of this epic was a mighty fighter. Usually he and his comrades made the forest their home, but sometimes the "wave-path":

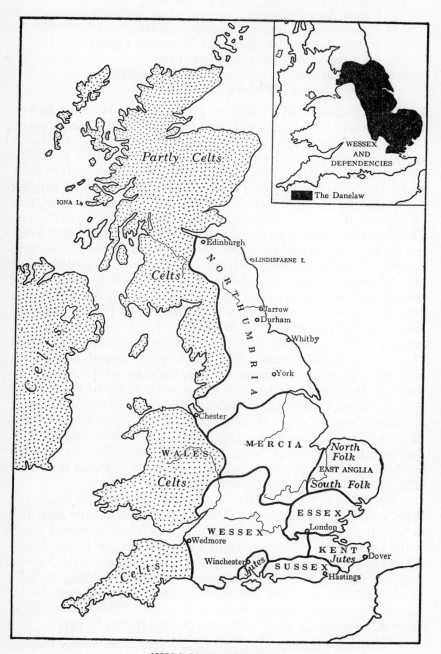

WESSEX
AND
DEPENDENCIES

The Danelaw

Partly Celts

IONA I.

Celts

Edinburgh

LINDISFARNE I.

N
O
R
T
H
U
M
B
R
I
A

Jarrow
Durham

Whitby

York

Chester

Celts

W·A·L·E·S

Celts

M·E·R·C·I·A

North
Folk
EAST ANGLIA
South Folk

E S S E X
London

W E S S E X
Wedmore

K E N T
Jutes    Dover

Winchester  Jutes  S U S S E X

Celts                    Hastings

ANGLO-SAXON ENGLAND

# A History of England and the British Empire

Who are ye of men, having arms in hand,
Covering with your coat of mail, who, your keel a-foaming,
O'er the ocean street, thus have urged along,
Hither on the high-raised sea? Never saw I greater
Earl upon this earth than is one of you.
'Less his looks belie him, he is no home-stayer.
Glorious is his gear of war, aetheling his air.

Thus were Beowulf and his fighters greeted. Most certainly he was no home-stayer. He fought with man and with beast. The monster, Grendel, was subdued by him. Grendel was wont to break the bones and drink the blood of sleeping men. Beowulf waited for him. "In the wan darkness, while the warriors slept, the shadow-stalker drew near from the Moorland; over the misty fells Grendel came ganging on; under the clouds he strode." Beowulf wrestled with him, tore off an arm. There followed then the encounter with Grendel's dam. The fight took place in a cave beneath the sea. Beowulf "saw hanging on the wall an old sword of the Eotens, hallowed by victory, doughty of edges, a pride of warriors, and seizing the gold-charmed hilt, he smote at the sea-wolf's neck. The brand gripped in her throat, broke through the bone into the body." The hero rose through "the bloody sea," and his men acclaimed him. Finally Beowulf, grown old, and now king of his people, came home to stay. A dragon, vomiting fire, terrorized the neighborhood. Beowulf found "his last foe and his death." The hero's sword slipped, and he was at death grips with the dragon. A kinsman came to the rescue, but too late. The dragon got his claw on Beowulf until "the life bubbled forth in waves." The dying man cut the dragon in two with his ax and sang his death song. It epitomized his life,—swearing no oaths which he did not keep, being true to kinsmen; all throughout that time no other ruler dared "greet me with his war friends or press on me the terror of war."[1] Such a man personified the ideal of the Saxon before Christianity entered his life.

It happened in the late sixth century that Gregory the Great, the Pope at Rome, whose intense interest lay in missionary activities to spread Christianity among the pagan peoples, sorrowed much at the anarchy prevalent in western Europe. He knew of the Anglo-Saxons from observing blond youngsters from England in the Roman slave market. Also he was aware that the wife of the king of Kent was a Christian and that through her influence there might be an opportunity for an entering wedge in England. Therefore the Pope selected Augustine, a monk, to head a mission thither in 597.

[1] S. A. Brooke, *English Literature from the Beginning to the Norman Conquest*, pp. 71, 73, 76–78.

# Roman and Saxon

Waving banners and singing litanies, Augustine and forty followers landed in Kent, where the king received them courteously and addressed them as follows: "Because ye are come from afar into my kingdom, and, as I conceive, are desirous to impart to us those things which you believe to be true and most beneficial, we will not molest you, but give you favorable entertainment, and take care to supply you with your necessary sustenance; nor do we forbid you by preaching to gain as many as you can to your religion." The missionaries were given a home in Canterbury and permission to preach. They were successful, converting the king and many of the people. The Pope was delighted; he made Augustine an archbishop and laid plans for further conversion of the English.

The missionaries were not always successful. No sooner did their protector, the king of Kent, die than he was succeeded by a son who insisted on marrying his stepsister, thus putting himself beyond the pale of the Church. In East Anglia also, where Christianity was early adopted, there came a reaction. Certain princes there were much incensed when refused sacramental bread before baptism. They thought the missionaries stingy with their bread and drove them out. Most of the priests left England and sought refuge in France; but one remained, to be visited in the night by Saint Paul, who scourged him soundly. When he showed his wounds the next day to the pagans, they were promptly converted and mended their evil ways.

More immediately successful were the missionaries in the kingdom of Northumbria, which was then at the height of its glory, stretching from Edinburgh on the north almost all the way to London on the south. Again the influence of a woman paved the way. Edwin, king of Northumbria, for whom Edinburgh is named, was married to a princess of Kent, and in her train was Paulinus, a Christian bishop who had been sent to England to further the work of Augustine. Paulinus plied the king hard, and the Pope wrote letters not only to Edwin but also to his wife, urging her active intervention on behalf of the Cross. Edwin finally consented to a conference, just thirty years after Augustine had landed in Kent. It is memorable for a much-quoted speech by one of his chieftains to this effect: "The present life of Man, O King, seems to me, in comparison of that time which is unknown to us, like to the swift flight of a sparrow through the room wherein you sit at supper in winter, with your commanders and ministers, and a good fire in the midst, whilst the storms of rain and snow prevail abroad. The sparrow, I say, flying in at one door, and immediately out at another, whilst he is within is safe from the wintry storm; but after a short space of fair weather, he immediately vanishes out of your sight, from one winter to another. So this life of Man appears for a short space, but of what went before, or what is to follow, we are utterly ignorant. If, therefore, this new doctrine contains something more certain, it seems justly to deserve to be followed." The people apparently took wholesale to the new doctrine with its assurances about the future life. Led by one of their heathen priests, they destroyed their idols and burned them. Rapid now was the success of Paulinus. He traveled everywhere, baptizing thousands, and it was soon reported that "there was then such perfect peace in Britain, wheresoever the dominion of King Edwin extended, that as is now proverbially said, a woman with her new-born babe might walk through the island, from sea to sea, without receiving any harm." The Pope was greatly pleased. He made Paulinus an archbishop, so that now two of these dignitaries resided in Britain, one in the south at Canterbury, one in the north at York.

Doubtless all would have gone well for Christianity had it not been for Penda, king of Mercia, a most redoubtable heathen. Penda waged such successful war against his northern neighbor that Mercia replaced Northumbria as the leading kingdom of the island in the middle of the seventh century. Penda did not persecute Christians, but he had contempt for them; and since they were now without royal patronage, their church went under a partial eclipse. Paulinus, fleeing south, became bishop of Rochester, in Kent.

Shortly afterward the Church was to be revived from another quarter. Christianity had first come to Britain long before Augustine, while the Roman legions were still there. This was not surprising, because Constantine, the emperor who had shown special interest in Britain, was himself a Christian, and edicts in 311 and 313 had placed Christianity on an equal footing with other religions. Naturally, with the spread of Christianity in the Roman Empire, it had reached even so remote a province as Britain. According to contemporary mention, British bishops were attending church councils on the Continent as early as the fourth century. In fact, Christianity was indirectly one of Rome's few lasting legacies to Britain; but with the coming of the pagan Nordic invaders it disappeared from view like most else that was Roman. Some devout souls cherished the Christian belief in Wales, and from there it seems to have spread to Ireland, where, owing to the activity of Saint Patrick and Saint Bridget, it made rapid strides. Just where Patrick was born or in what century he went to Ireland we shall never know, for disputes run high on both these points. But this at least is evident; Ireland, culturally speaking, in the seventh century was one of the most advanced countries in Europe. Although Roman armies had

never brought this island within even the outer rim of Roman civilization, its monks now made it famous. Their enterprise was astonishing,
their illuminated manuscripts artistic, and their scholarship excellent. "The literary output of the seventh century was small throughout western Europe, but there is enough to show that the Irish kept
up the tradition of learning." The monks, indeed, were untiring.
Within Ireland they built many monasteries which were educational
as well as religious centers. Outside of Ireland—in England, in
Scotland, in northern Germany, in France, in Switzerland, and even
in Italy itself—their missionary enterprises were led by men of
ability and wide culture.

Such a man was Columban. With his monks he went to Brittany,
thence to Burgundy, to build a famous monastery in the Vosges
Mountains; and afterward to build another, even more famous, in
Italy. Such a one, also, was that other Irishman, Columba, first abbot
of Iona and the descendant of Irish kings. Although a monk, he
seems in early manhood to have been keenly interested in fighting.
To make amends for the bloodshed which he caused, he was exiled
from Ireland by his fellow monks until he had won for God souls
equal in number to those for whose deaths he had been responsible in
Ireland. Forthwith Columba, at the age of forty-two, embarked with
a number of Irishmen in tiny boats built with a wooden framework
covered with hides. He sailed for the west coast of Scotland, made
his headquarters on the island of Iona, and from thence spread
Christianity in Britain. A genius was Columba, this sailor, soldier,
poet, abbot. He lived austerely in a tiny hut within his monastery,
with a stone for a pillow; but he also lived gently, ever com-
passionate for the poor and the distressed, whether man or beast.
Hardly a day passed but pilgrims came to seek refuge on Iona; and
from that island Columba and his men went on repeated missionary
tours, skimming in their tiny skiffs over the treacherous waters which
surround the northern islands, penetrating deep into the Scottish
lochs, crossing the mountains into the land of the Picts, winning
converts everywhere.

As Northumbria relapsed into barbarism after the victories of
Penda, king of Mercia, it happened that a Northumbrian prince,
Oswald, sought asylum in Iona. Victorious in war, he regained
Northumbria, and, remembering the kindly monks, he asked them
to send him a bishop. On the island of Lindisfarne this Irish
bishop established his see, which was soon to become a center of
learning second only to Iona. And from now on, in the words of a
chronicler, many Irish "came daily into Britain, and with great
devotion preached the word to those provinces over which King

Oswald reigned, and those among them that had received priests' orders administered to them the grace of baptism. Churches were built in several places; the people joyfully flocked together to hear the word; money and lands were given of the king's bounty to build monasteries; the English, great and small, were, by their Scottish [Irish] masters, instructed in the rules and observance of regular discipline, for most of them that came to preach were monks."

Christianity forthwith began to sweep all before it. The much-feared Penda was slain in battle, and Mercia was converted. And as this occurred the Anglo-Saxon kingdoms of the south and east fell under the sway of the new religion. One great question, and one only, called for immediate decision. Was England to acknowledge one Catholic Church alone, or would there be two hierarchies, or organizations? The Celtic monks, instructed at Iona and Lindisfarne, differed in discipline and in the date of the celebration of Easter from the missionaries sent direct from Rome. Also, they shaved their hair from ear to ear instead of in a circle on top of the head. These differences were trivial, but the question involved far more than haircuts and Lenten fasting.

The issue was joined at the Synod of Whitby (664). Over it presided Oswy, king of Northumbria, who said "it behooved those who served only one God to observe the same rule of life; and as they all expected the same kingdom in heaven, so they ought not to differ in the celebration of the Divine mysteries." Thereupon a very long and closely argued debate followed. The bishop who spoke for the Celtic, or Irish, Church was at a disadvantage. He could only quote certain old traditions to which he had been accustomed. On the other hand, the spokesman for Rome had a double advantage: he had traveled widely and could affirm that in Italy, France, Greece, Africa, Asia, and Egypt the Roman date for Easter was the universal practice. He also could argue that Peter had been given the keys of heaven, and that the Pope, as Peter's successor, must be obeyed (the Petrine theory). Since the Irish bishop did not deny Peter's primacy, the king decided against him; and he and his Celtic disciples withdrew, discomfited, to Scotland.

Possibly the king had called the council simply owing to his annoyance at having court life disrupted because some began their Lenten fasting when the rest were completing it. But, however trifling the cause may have been, the results of Whitby were to have a far-reaching significance in English history. The failure of the Irish Church saved England from the danger of stagnant isolation on the outer edge of the civilized world. The decision in favor of Rome bound England more closely to the Continent, with all that it had to offer.

# Roman and Saxon

One particular advantage of the decision was the introduction into England of a system far more clean-cut than anything the Anglo-Saxons themselves produced. The Church throughout the Anglo-Saxon period set the state a shining example of orderly organization. Under the guidance of the Popes, or bishops of Rome, the Roman Church gave western Europe its only practical example of effective international organization during the Dark Ages. However divided into petty jurisdictions Europe might be politically, the Church gave uniformity, not only in belief and religious practices but also in administrative machinery. This far-reaching dominance of the Church was occasioned by the unquestioning faith which it engendered in the people, its universal character, and its elaborate and centralized organization in a period of chaotic disunity.

The Church occupied a tremendous place in the life of the medieval populace. Life after death was a vital tenet of early Christianity, which the Church emphasized in every way. Through the Church alone was salvation to be obtained. It, and it alone, could open the gates of paradise to the true believer or, by closing them, could doom the recalcitrant to hell fire. Consequently the average man of this period had complete faith in his church and never questioned any of its ideas or methods. In a particularly vital way the Church entered the life of every individual from birth to death through the sacraments—baptism, confirmation, marriage, Holy Eucharist, penance, ordination, and extreme unction. The infant was baptized shortly after birth; the youth, by confirmation, became an active communicant and thereafter regularly attended Mass, received Communion, and did penance after confession. When dying, the communicant received extreme unction. Nearly everyone came in contact with six sacraments, but marriage and ordination to the priesthood were normally contradictory, since churchmen were not allowed to wed. This deep connection between the Church and the daily life of the individual explains the effectiveness of the two church weapons for punishing violation of its commands: excommunication, which cut off an individual from the services of the Church, and the interdict, which prohibited most church services within an entire region.

The word "catholic" characterized the universal, or all-embracing, character of the Church throughout western Europe at this period. Everyone belonged to it, as time went on, as a matter of course, or else was branded as an outcast from society, a heretic. The Church stood as the one unified institution in Europe at a time when the barbarian invasions had broken down almost everything else. The medieval people, with their heritage of the Roman Empire, longed for unity in their disrupted life and found it only in the Church.

[ 23 ]

They took comfort in the knowledge that at the same hour, in every Christian hamlet throughout western Europe, priests were chanting the same Latin service.

On the administrative side, Western Christendom was neatly blocked off into definite units, each with its responsible head, subordinate to an immediate higher authority, from the Pope at the head, down through the hierarchy of archbishops and bishops, to the parish priests. There was discipline and control from top to bottom. The members of the religious orders—abbots, monks, and later the friars—were likewise under papal control. In addition, papal ambassadors, known as legates, often represented the Pope in the various countries. Eventually, at a time when the Anglo-Saxon period was drawing to a close, a group of prominent churchmen was organized into the "college of cardinals," to elect the Pope and to act as his advisory body. Occasionally councils, composed of the important churchmen of many regions, were called to discuss special church problems.

The Pope, the bishop of Rome, was the supreme head of this vast network. To what extent this ecclesiastical primacy had been recognized from the beginning it would be difficult to say. Writing as a Roman Catholic, one would advance evidence to show that it existed since Peter was the first bishop of Rome; writing as a Protestant, one would argue that it arose gradually and that at first the bishop of Rome had been no more important than other bishops. Because Rome, however, had long been the capital of the world, churchmen naturally turned toward the bishop there for guidance; and soon he began to give unsolicited advice and even orders. Italy had already turned to him for leadership, since during the barbarian invasions he was often the strongest man there. Two exceptionally able Popes, Leo the Great (about 450) and Gregory the Great, who sent Augustine to England, added immensely to the dignity and prestige of the office. By the so-called Petrine theory, which was cited at Whitby, the Roman bishops claimed that they had succeeded to the power of Saint Peter and that because of this legacy their church had the purest doctrines. By the time of Augustine and his monks no one questioned that Rome was the head of the Church or that the Pope was its leader.

At the time of Whitby most of Europe was under the Roman Church except some parts of the still heathen north. The region of the Balkan Peninsula, in the southeast, however, was beginning to have its separate Christian Church, the Greek Catholic, or the Greek Orthodox, which was to be completely distinct from the Roman Church by the middle of the eleventh century and was to be centered at Constantinople, the capital of the still extant Eastern Roman, or—as it came to be called—the Byzantine, Empire.

The vast area under the sway of Rome was divided into provinces, each of which was controlled by an archbishop. The leading archbishop in each country was called the "primate" and was directly subordinate to the Pope. Each province was divided into dioceses. A bishop managed each diocese, throughout which he administered the sacraments of confirmation and ordination. In its turn the diocese was subdivided into parishes, one for each community, with several in the larger towns. The parish priest administered the sacraments of baptism, Mass, penance, marriage, and extreme unction, as well as attended to other duties among his parishioners. Archbishops, bishops, and priests were called *secular* clergy (from the Latin *saeculum*, "world"), because they came into direct contact with the outside world. Contrasted with them were the *regular* clergy,—the monks and nuns,—so called because they lived according to a "rule" (Latin, *regula*). The three branches of the regular clergy were the monastic orders and the later military and mendicant orders. The idea of the "rule" was introduced by Saint Benedict in the sixth century, when he set up his pioneer monastery at Monte Cassino, in Italy, in 529, thirty-odd years before Columba established the less formal Irish monasticism at Iona. The Benedictine Rule called for the triple vow of poverty, obedience, and chastity in a community life of service and prayer. Each of the scores of monasteries and nunneries, headed by its abbot or abbess, was pretty much a little world in itself, usually claiming independence of the authority of the bishop of the diocese and acknowledging only the superior authority of the Pope. In the tenth century the monks of Cluny, in France, were to strive for more rigid control by establishing subordinate monasteries under their immediate supervision, not only in France but also in England and other lands.

Without the monks the Middle Ages would have been an even harsher period than they were. The service of the monks was fourfold: missionary, economic, social, and cultural. We have already had evidence of the scope of their missionary endeavors in the work of Augustine and the other monks in England. Not only were they frequently first in the work of conversion, but had it not been for their monastic outposts of Christianity in remote regions more than one converted land would quickly have returned to paganism. Their economic service lay in their demonstration of the dignity of labor by themselves working with their hands, particularly in agriculture, during the early days. Their interest in trade sometimes led to the rise of towns around the abbeys. Their social service consisted in caring for the sick, the aged, the poor, the friendless, and the orphaned. The monasteries also served as shelter for the traveler. These communities were a refuge, especially for those men who did not care for the rough life of the times. As monks such men could work and study, in addition to preparing for the future of their souls. The cultural contribution of the monks lay in their preservation of ancient manuscripts during the Dark Ages, when no one else cared about them. The monks copied manuscripts by hand as a religious duty. Later, moreover, nearly all the schools, such as they were, were held in the monasteries.

England was given a more carefully defined place in this system five years after Whitby, when Theodore of Tarsus was sent to be head of the English Church. Born in Asia Minor, educated in Athens, he was at once a splendid scholar and a thorough disciplinarian. Though nearly seventy, he spent twenty energetic years in establishing orderly church organization throughout England. He was Archbishop of Canterbury, and so the "primate," or head, of the English Church. A junior archbishop was continued at York for the northern provinces, but it was made clear that the primacy was Canterbury's. He cut down unwieldy bishoprics; heretofore one had been set up in each kingdom as it embraced Christianity. This step had important political significance, because it identified the Church with England as a whole and helped to pave the way for its unification under a single king. From this time priests ceased to be wandering missionaries and were given definite parishes to administer. Practically every township or group of hamlets was eventually set up as a parish with its own priest.

The Anglo-Saxons were generous in their support of the Church. As in other lands, everyone had to pay the tithe, theoretically a tenth of all he produced each year, for the support of the priest and higher churchmen. In addition, bishoprics and abbeys received rich grants of land from the kings. All this helped to submerge the freemen towards their new status of serfdom; that was the price of the spiritual and cultural leadership which Roman Christianity gave to England. The Church, moreover, was the better able to instill its example of organization into the State because, when the king looked about him for responsible, educated officials, churchmen were practically the only men who could meet those qualifications.

The introduction of Christianity proved of benefit to England in several ways: manners were softened and morals were improved; impetus and direction were given to scholarship and to the growth of English literature; and the unification of the English nation was aided enormously. Of Christianity a famous English historian wrote:

# Roman and Saxon

"From the cradle to the grave it forced on the Englishman a new law of conduct, new habits, new conceptions of life and society. It entered above all into that sphere within which the individual will of the freeman had been until now supreme, the sphere of the home; it curtailed his power over wife and child and slave; it forbade infanticide, the putting away of wives, or cruelty to the serf. It challenged almost every social conception; it denied to the king his heritage of the blood of the gods; it proclaimed slavery an evil, war an evil. . . . It met the feud face to face by denouncing revenge. It held up gluttony and drunkenness, the very essence of the old English 'Feast' as sins. It claimed to control every circumstance of life."[1] These were the ideals of the new religion. They were not always put into practice, it is true. Nevertheless, upon the whole, this tribute to early Christianity was deserved.

During the century and a half after Whitby, Christianity likewise stimulated a literary movement, wherein a curious blending took place between pagan and Christian ideals. This may be seen in the poetry of Cædmon and Cynewulf, who wrote vigorously in Early English. They were both Christian poets, who took their themes either from Holy Writ or from the early traditions of the Church. For all that, they remained men of the north, their imagery copied from that which was familiar to them, their inherited love of heroism and brave deeds making the familiar Bible stories appear in unusual perspective.

Cædmon was a humble monk, apparently a stable boy, who discovered that he could sing. He "was born a heathen and his work bridged the river between the pagan and the Christian poetry." Ascribed to him or to his school is a Saxon version of Genesis. From it we may see how to Saxon eyes appeared the adventures of Abraham, the great earl, as he led his warriors against the men of Sodom.

"Then was hard hand-play, crashing of weapons, storming of death-darts, tumult of battle. From out the sheaths men snatched their ring-decked, keen-edged swords. There might an earl have his fill of fighting, whoso was not yet sated with war. The northmen smote the people of the south." This does not seem altogether like the King James version, nor for that matter does the flight of the children of Israel from Pharaoh. In Cædmon's *Exodus* we read this Saxon account: "Armor gleamed and bucklers glistened as the warriors took their steadfast way. And over the troops and high above the host stood the banner, moving as they moved, even unto the stronghold of the sea and the land's end. And there they pitched a camp and rested, for they were weary. Stewards brought the war-

[1] J. R. Green, *The Conquest of England* (1883), p. 8.

riors food and strengthened them." Then follows the passage of the Red Sea. "Moses bade the earls with brazen trumpets muster the folk, bade warriors rise and don their coats of mail, bear shining arms." Moses parted the waters, and then "proudly marched the seamen, sons of Reuben; the vikings bore their bucklers over the salt sea-marsh, a multitude of men, a mighty legion, advancing unafraid."[1] Thus did Cædmon, in true epic style, picture the Hebrews.

Somewhat later came the poems of Cynewulf, a poet whose name remains shrouded in mystery. He may have lived in the early ninth century or perhaps a century earlier, but that he wrote superbly there are none to question. In his poems was stressed the early Anglo-Saxon love of the sea. Thus in his *Elene*, when the mother of the emperor Constantine set forth to seek the Cross, we read: "Most speedily a band of earls began to hasten down into the deep water. Along the sea's margin stood harnessed ocean-steeds, fettered sea-stallions floating on the sound. Then was the lady's journey to be known, when she sought out the tossing floods with all her train. There stood many a goodly man on the ocean rim. Now and again they hastened over the border paths, one troop behind another; they loaded those stallions of the waves with battle-sarks, with shield and lance and fighting men in burnies, with man and maid." The gentler side of Jesus' life seems to have made but slight impression on these Saxon poets. "Jesus is the victory-child of God, his death a king's death." In *The Dream of the Rood* Cynewulf had the Cross speak thus: "The Hero, young—He was Almighty God—did off His raiment, steadfast, stout of heart, with valor in the sight of many men, He mounted up upon the lofty gallows, when He would fain redeem mankind."[2] Jesus to Cynewulf was merged into the Teutonic hero, and—Rome or no Rome—early Christianity in England, if we may judge from this poem, bore a peculiarly Teutonic impress.

Meanwhile, thanks to the new religion, schools of learning flourished throughout the country. One of the most important was at Canterbury, of which the mighty Archbishop Theodore was patron. Aldhelm, later abbot of Malmesbury and one of Europe's best scholars, was at one time a pupil here. At Canterbury he studied Roman law, metrics, arithmetic, and astronomy. He was well acquainted with sacred as well as classical literature, and in his letters and poems, it has been said, there is a quotation from every book in the Bible.

[1] C. W. Kennedy, *The Cædmon Poems* (1916), p. 109. By permission of E. P. Dutton & Co., Inc., George Routledge and Sons, Ltd., and of the author.

[2] C. W. Kennedy, *The Cynewulf Poems* (1910), p. 307. By permission of E. P. Dutton & Co., Inc., George Routledge and Sons, Ltd., and of the author.

# Roman and Saxon

Another center of learning was the monastery at Jarrow, on the Tyne. At one time in this grim and desolate shipbuilding center of our own day lived and labored for forty years the Venerable Bede, "the Father of English History." Bede wrote textbooks, theological expositions which were extraordinarily learned for his day, and showed a good knowledge of Greek. Above all, his *Ecclesiastical History of the English People* is our foremost, and frequently our only, source for nearly two hundred years of English history. This *Ecclesiastical History* contains numerous miraculous yarns, concerning which doubts may arise; it tells us much about northern England and little about southern England; but none the less it is written in such pure and limpid Latin that even in translation it is a pleasure to read. The feature which makes Bede's history really distinctive, however, in spite of some of his yarns, is the spirit of research, which led him to track down the story of things as they really happened, either from documents or from the participants. In his thoroughness Bede would put to shame many a modern historian.

Finally, there was the cathedral school at York, founded by an archbishop who had been a student of Bede. At this school was one Alcuin, a teacher of grammar, of arts, and of science. So capable was he that even Charlemagne heard of him. This emperor (768-814) of the lands that composed much of western Europe decided to start a school, and Ireland, England, Spain, and Italy were searched for teachers. Alcuin was placed at its head. It was said that "in him were united all the qualifications which Charles desired. A man of Teutonic race, learned with a learning far above the level of the age; a born teacher; pupil and master of York, which was then the greatest school in Europe." Truly the Anglo-Saxons had advanced far since Augustine's singing monks had landed in Kent.

Thus Christianity as an institution paved the way for national unity. The clergy were a caste apart, and continuously they became more and more influential. Not only did they know more than the rough Saxons, but they were armed with spiritual thunderbolts, which all men feared, especially the ignorant, superstitious, and illiterate. And almost every man in England, it must be remembered, fell into that category unless he was either a priest or, in a few cases, educated by priests. The clergy were to use these powers freely. They were stern moralists and would not permit blood feuds; but the only way to end them was to establish law courts, which, in turn, implied central authority. Then, too, altogether aside from morality, there were the estates granted to the clergy, largely for monastic purposes. The clergy could not reap the full economic benefit from these unless there were powerful means to maintain law and order.

[ 29 ]

In consequence clerical influence was cast continuously in favor of consolidating petty kingdoms.

Christianity brought in its train knowledge of the outside world, of law courts, of contracts, of written documents, and, above all, of the Latin alphabet. The crude symbols of the Saxons were of no use as far as written records were concerned, but once the alphabet became general it was possible to draw up written agreements. "A book ceased to be a tablet of beechwood and became a book of parchment." As soon as this took place, the clergy had a new weapon wherewith to coerce wild tribesmen into some semblance of social and political unity. The taxes and tithes which made it possible to start schools, to build churches, to introduce art, architecture, literature, and leisure into England, had to be paid by somebody, and very naturally they were paid partly by the ordinary Saxon freemen. Many of these were submerged as time went on, and the burden of the secular and religious taxes was probably one of the factors responsible for this. On the other hand, had this not happened it is difficult to see how the extraordinarily crude, individualistic, and decentralized Saxons could ever have been whipped into shape as a nation.

Slowly but steadily the pressure of the new religion made its way felt in the world of Anglo-Saxon politics, helping to consolidate, to centralize, and to reduce the number of independent kingdoms until in place of seven there were but three (Northumbria, Mercia, Wessex), and ultimately but one, England.

Northumbria, originally so powerful, never regained its old political pre-eminence. Although strong culturally, politically it became weak, owing to a succession of feeble, inefficient, and short-lived kings.

The star of Mercia, meanwhile, rose in the eighth century, and so strong did this central kingdom become that it seemed for a time as though it might consolidate all England. Two kings of Mercia reigned for a period of nearly eighty years, an almost unparalleled record in those days of rapine and murder. The second, Offa, spreading the boundaries of Mercia in every direction, absorbed East Anglia, gained control of Kent, and built a great dike, or earthen rampart, for a distance of one hundred and thirty miles as a defense against the Welsh. His capital was at Lichfield, and, ambitious for ecclesiastical independence as well as for political power, Offa established there an archbishopric. By the Pope he was greeted as *Rex Anglorum*; and had his successors measured up to him in ability, Mercia might have absorbed the other English kingdoms.

# Roman and Saxon

This role, however, was left for Wessex, the smallest of the three kingdoms which survived as independent states at the opening of the ninth century. Its ruler (802–839) was Egbert, who, when he ascended the throne, found himself surrounded on the north and east by Mercia and on the west by the Welsh. Striking first to the west he conquered West Wales (Cornwall). Then, taking advantage of revolts in Mercia, he swung to the north, defeated the Mercians, and was acknowledged as Bretwalda, or overlord, by all England south of the Humber. Next he turned farther north. The Northumbrians did not fight but "met him and offered him obedience and peace." The north Welsh, meanwhile, were "humbled," and Egbert could regard all England, temporarily at any rate, as under his direct or indirect control.

The supremacy of Wessex was to be a lasting one, owing to a new factor, the Danes. As a centralizing influence Christianity had proved powerful; but it alone might have been incapable of bringing together in one nation these unruly Anglo-Saxons. Added to its influence, however, was another—the absolute necessity of English unity if effective resistance was to be made to new invasions which ominously threatened from Scandinavia.

# CHAPTER II

## King Alfred, Danes, and Dooms

THE comparative serenity of England was again roughly disturbed in 787, when, according to the Anglo-Saxon Chronicle, "first came three ships of Northmen out of Haeretheland [Denmark] and then the reeve [sheriff] rode out to the place and would have driven them to the king's town, because he knew not who they were: and they slew him. These were the first of the Danish men who sought the land of the English nation."

These Danes, Vikings, or Norsemen were of similar blood to the Saxons, but hailed from Scandinavian regions, farther to the north. They loved the sea, craved adventure, had frequent famine in their cold homeland. These or other reasons led them far afield for pillage. They infinitely preferred piracy to peace; and their raids terrified the peoples of the coast communities throughout most of the ninth century and into the eleventh.

If we may judge from name and deed, their ferocity was unbounded. Erik Blood-Ax, Harold Bluetooth, and Thorkill the Skull-Splitter were some of their names; and they were worthy of them. They made a business of war, and on select occasions worked themselves into frenzies of rage, howled like wild wolves, and gnashed their teeth on their iron swords. They took the greatest delight in these psychopathic fits. Not alone did the people of the British Isles have cause to pray, "From the fury of the Northmen, O Lord deliver us." In all directions that oars and wind might carry them they cruised and settled—as far as Greenland, past Gibraltar, and, most significantly, down the North Sea to the coast of France, whence descendants, civilized by centuries in that Romanized region, were later to descend on England as her Norman conquerors (see pages 53–59).

They were as expert in seamanship as in war, and they were skilled shipbuilders—almost of necessity. Commerce was their next thought, after plunder; and both as pirates and as traders they had to have good craft. One of their vessels, a clinker-built ship with the lines of a cup defender, dug up from the sand and mud, may be seen today at Oslo. Generally such a ship had a mast and a square sail for favorable winds. A high prow and stern customarily tapered off into the form of a serpent or a dragon. On a platform at the stern stood the helmsman with a long steer board, whence the English word "starboard." Thwarts on either side of the ship provided for oarsmen, and across the waist a "tilt," or tent, was raised. Since there was not a deep keel, tacking was impossible in contrary winds; so oars were necessarily far oftener in use than the sail. The Northmen were devoted to these ships, or "keels," calling them "Raven of the Wind," "Reindeer of the Breezes," and like titles of affection. In them they descended upon England, to drench that land in blood just at a time when Christianity was beginning to lessen strife.

These Danes, or Vikings, at first merely pillaged, and, successful, they came again and again to strike at England, Scotland, and the east coast of Ireland. They apparently liked the land so much that they commenced to spend their winters there, and then to make permanent settlements. If we trust to their sagas, intermediate between sober history and legend, they harassed England sorely. One of their earlier attacks, on Northumbria, was led by Ragnar Lodbrok, or "Hairy Breeks," who supposedly obtained his name by freezing hairy blankets to his trousers to protect his legs from the serpents which he drove out of his native Sweden. Ragnar's exploits, like those of most of the early heroes, were favorite material for the saga-makers, so that it is almost impossible to disentangle fact and fiction. Ragnar led his men to Constantinople; to Dublin; up the Seine to Paris, which he sacked (845); to the bleak Orkney Islands, north of Britain; and eventually to Northumbria, where, presumably captured by the king thereof, he was thrust into a den of snakes. As he was slowly devoured by them, he sang his death song and recounted his past glories, each stanza beginning, "We hewed with our swords." And so until the end, when he sang: "I willingly depart! See the bright maids brought from the hall of Woden. Lord of hosts, invite me home! There, happy on my high-raised seat among the anses,[1] I'll quaff the mellow ale. The moments of my life are fled, but laughingly I die."

The sons of Ragnar, so the story goes, afterward returned and exacted memorable vengeance for their father's death. All northern England was overrun with Danes, who spread southward and infested the Wessex coast. Egbert spent the last years of his reign (see page 31) in stemming the tide, and apparently this was about all that he was able to do. Driven back, the invaders would reappear from another direction. In 871, so it is said, they rowed up the Thames and attacked Wessex again. They were opposed by

[1] Descendants of Odin.

Egbert's grandson. This king of Wessex engaged in prayer as the Danes struck, but his younger brother, Alfred, led the Wessex fyrd (militia) to a signal victory. This same year, on his brother's death, Alfred, the hero of England's early history, became king of Wessex.

This young ruler, only twenty-two years old, had been unusually well educated. Twice he had traveled to Rome, perhaps because his father had hoped to keep his youngest son out of the never-ending Danish strife. The Pope had made the boy his godson, and Alfred, inclined toward scholarly ways, had learned to read and to write— exceptional accomplishments for a Saxon layman and, for that matter, for most of the clergy. For many years after his accession there was no time for cultural pursuits. The omnipresent Danes won victory after victory, and Alfred had to flee to the wilder parts of his kingdom, where for a short time all the land that remained his was an island in the midst of an impenetrable swamp. Here Alfred prepared for a new war, which was conducted so successfully that in the Peace of Wedmore (878) not only did the Danes agree to retire from Wessex but the Danish king was baptized a Christian.

A broad general division of territory between Dane and Saxon was made by this peace. A line was drawn roughly from near the mouth of the Thames to the north of Liverpool. To the north and east of this line was the "Danelaw," where the Danes, still in part pagan but rapidly becoming Christianized, were to live. South and west was Wessex, English territory ruled by Alfred. Thus the fairer parts of Mercia fell to the Wessex king, also London and the land immediately north of that city (see map, p. 17).

The Danish conversion to Christianity was typical of the way the Viking invader after a while invariably adopted the customs of the lands he originally had plundered. The Saxon, however, was not much more civilized than the Dane at this time, and his antecedents had been very similar, so that the Viking learned less in England than he did in regions which had a civilization more decidedly different from his own and more highly developed. To the Dane, England is indebted for much of her priceless heritage of love for the sea. The Saxon, in the beginning a seafarer too, had lost his maritime interest in his concentration on farming. To the Dane therefore belongs the credit for turning England's eyes seaward. Along with this went commercial enterprise. As the Danes settled down in the Danelaw brisk and active trading undoubtedly began to flourish in the towns there; for such was always the outlet for Viking energy when the first lust for plunder was surfeited.

The Peace of Wedmore did not end all troubles with the Danes, nor did it prevent the ravaging of the Channel coast from time to

# King Alfred, Danes, and Dooms

time by other Norsemen; but there appears to have been a respite until the last years of Alfred's life, when he again had to devote most of his time to war. It has been suggested that Alfred's military reforms (see page 38), his fortification and permanent garrisoning of London and other towns, together with his building of a navy with which to fight the Danes before they might land, made it harder, perhaps, for the Danes to sweep all before them. Yet the navy was an indifferent success; for Alfred built his ships so large that they grounded at low tide, to the joy of his enemies. For whatever reason, Alfred seems to have been comparatively free for some fourteen years to put through many reforms upon which he had set his heart.

Certain of these reforms had to do with raising the general level of culture in England. The English were densely ignorant of the world in which they lived. The Danish wars had destroyed many, if not most, of the monasteries, the only centers of such meager culture as there was. Alfred summoned to his court many men of learning, as had Charlemagne. The king founded a school in which both English and Latin were taught, and his cultured guests helped to conduct it. The pupils, for the most part, were the sons of the nobility, who were compelled to attend. The king ordered that all well-born youths should be taught English, and that important Latin books should be translated for their benefit. Those boys who showed ability were to be trained in both English and Latin, particularly if they desired promotion in his service,—a premium on knowledge such as no Saxon king before Alfred had ever thought to place.

The king meanwhile gave all his spare time to literary pursuits, particularly to the translation into English of certain standard Latin books. He first selected *Pastoral Care*, by Pope Gregory the Great, a book of instructions for priests, copies of which the king ordered sent to all bishops. His purpose is made clear in the preface to his translation. "I remembered," he said, "how the law was first known in Hebrew, and when the Greeks had learned it how they translated the whole of it into their own language, and all other books besides. And again the Romans, when they had learned it, translated the whole of it, through learned interpreters, into their own language. And also other Christian people turned some parts of these books into their own tongue. Therefore it seems better to me, if it seems so also to you, that we too should turn into the tongue which we all can understand certain books which are most necessary for all men to know."

Alfred also translated the Venerable Bede's *Ecclesiastical History*, in order that Englishmen might read their own history in their own language. Further to assist in this patriotic work, he revived and

[ 35 ]

stimulated the writing of the Anglo-Saxon Chronicle. This, like most of the medieval chronicles, originally was simply a monastic table of important happenings made year by year. Alfred enlarged these tables, as kept by the monks at Winchester, so as to make of them a kind of national history. The yearly entries were still made; but their scope was widened, and, under the influence of the king, what originally had been merely dry and scanty notes developed into a chronological history. It was the most important of a series of chronicles, written by the medieval monks, which vary in value as source material with the writer's knowledge and discrimination. Unlike most chronicles, it was written in English instead of Latin. Another historical translation attributed to Alfred was that of the *History of the World,* written several centuries earlier by a Spanish priest, Orosius. Into this inaccurate, rambling work Alfred freely incorporated some sections of his own, such as accounts of the first known exploration north of the Arctic Circle, as told to the king by the explorers themselves.

From the point of view of literature Alfred's translation of the *Consolation of Philosophy* by Boethius was his best work. The writings of this Roman philosopher show the influence of Christianity to such an extent that at times it is difficult to tell whether he was pagan or Christian. But as translated by Alfred he was completely Christian; for the king of England changed the original whenever it suited his fancy, so that it became virtually a confession of his own faith. The following passages, for instance, are not found in Boethius at all but are placed there by the royal translator: "He that will have eternal riches let him build the house of his mind on the foot-stone of lowliness, not on the highest hill where the raging winds of trouble blow or the rain of measureless anxiety." "A man will not be the better because he hath a well-born father, if he himself is naught. The only thing which is good in noble descent is this— that it makes men ashamed of being worse than their elders."

Thus wrote King Alfred, who did his best to bring his crude and rough country within the circle of European civilization—such as there was of it in the ninth century. He kept in constant contact with Rome, and ordered, it was said, English messengers to go all the way to India on a religious mission. "To give money to a school is to give to God," wrote this Saxon king, one of the very few medieval monarchs who regarded culture and education as more important than warfare.

This versatile king also stood far above his contemporaries in the practical administration of his government and in improving the condition of his subjects. His work was probably more a matter of restoring whatever had been weakened or destroyed in the recent invasions than of innovation. While the chronicles, dooms, charters, and wills give considerable information, it is impossible to disentangle Alfred's particular contributions, just as it would be extremely difficult to draw any sort of detailed and accurate picture of the institutional growth in any part of the six centuries between the arrival of the Anglo-Saxons in England and the coming of the Normans. Yet so far-reaching were the effects of the customs and institutions of this Anglo-Saxon period upon the later development of the country that certain significant features must be considered here, although description of the "systems" will be postponed until the coming of the more orderly-minded Normans, in 1066. Since social lines and governmental functions were seldom determined with precision and went through a process of constant evolution, it will be necessary to refer forward to the changes wrought by the Norman Conquest in order to appreciate the lasting effects of the earlier developments.

How extensive is England's institutional heritage from the Anglo-Saxons? Formerly some historians credited the Anglo-Saxons with most of the popular safeguards in law and government, together with the spirit which made England distinctive as a free country. More recent research shows that this enthusiasm for the Anglo-Saxon contributions went too far, because some of the major developments came from other sources. Nevertheless, the Anglo-Saxon influence played a vital part, especially in the field of local government. Some scholars, however, still disagree sharply in their conclusions on doubtful points in this whole matter of Anglo-Saxon institutions. Another difficulty in the way of a definite analysis of the social, economic, or political aspects of the period is the Anglo-Saxon avoidance of any preconceived, clean-cut systems of procedure. Whatever the other heritages from them may have been, they have at any rate bequeathed to later generations of Englishmen this practice of "muddling through." Unwilling and perhaps unable to indulge in rational logic, they went ahead with their continual informal experimenting, apparently trusting that time and common sense would evolve methods which would work. That reluctance to conceive a rigid mold and then to jam everything into it crops up again and again in later English history.

The three principal occupations of the Middle Ages were fighting, praying, and farming. As time went on, the first two became highly paid specialties, supported by forced tribute from the masses who tilled the soil. The Church, as we have already seen, had since Whitby brought England into its system. In addition to the churchmen, there seem to have been four main classes in Anglo-Saxon society. Three were important from the beginning: the noble, or eorl; the ordinary freeman, or ceorl; and the slave, or thrall. The fourth class, the partially free man, later called serf or villein, developed slowly at first, but finally increased so rapidly that it threatened to engulf most of the population. The earliest stages were more democratic than the later, because the ordinary freeman at first made up the bulk of the population, and there was not enough wealth to make inequality obvious.

The hereditary eorls composed the Anglo-Saxon aristocracy at the outset; but gradually a more numerous lower nobility, based at first on services rather than upon birth, developed in the thanes, or thegns. They seem to have been an outgrowth of the German *comitatus*, or band of specialized fighting men, who had originally attached themselves to the king or to some powerful noble. There was a general "fyrd," or militia, which was inadequate in many ways, so that regular fighting men with superior training and with better equipment, such as armor, were found among the thanes. These warriors were rewarded for their military service not only by an honorable social status but, as time went on, by grants of land also. Alfred is said to have inaugurated military reforms particularly in connection with the thanes; he increased the number of those who were equipped to hurry on horseback to the scene of an attack by the fast-moving Danes. On the whole the thanes occupied a position similar to that of the knights of the feudal period and the country gentry of later centuries. In the beginning the honor of thanehood was bestowed only for the particular service of an individual, but gradually it tended to become hereditary. Prosperous merchants trading in foreign parts were also granted the "thane right," as were those freemen who acquired five times the normal amount of land. In the eyes of the law a thane counted, for certain purposes, as much as several ordinary freemen. By the end of the period the aristocracy consisted of three groups: the athelings, or princes of the royal family; the great earls, who dominated whole shires or groups of shires; and the far more numerous thanes.

The freeman was the substantial small farmer, who had his own land, who owed no forced agricultural service to a lord, and who was free to move about as he saw fit. All freemen were liable to military service in the general fyrd, or militia. Alfred appears to have reorganized this more efficiently by dividing the freemen so that, while some did the fighting, others might care for the crops, and still others garrison his newly fortified towns. This method prevented the former danger of being caught unprepared by a sur-

prise attack of the enemy, perhaps when most of the fyrd would
have to be at home reaping the harvest. Yet by Alfred's time the
fyrd was probably not called out much because of its lack of armor
and its primitive weapons, which made it vulnerable to the attack
of the well-equipped Danes. The freeman is an elusive figure in
English history. His was the most common status in the early days
of the Anglo-Saxons, and the freeman was taken as the normal unit
in the rudimentary politics and law. Gradually, however, he became
the exception rather than the rule.

The growth of that large semifree class, which became the serfs
of the Norman period (see page 69), came from several causes,
some of which are obscure. The dread of the Danish invaders may
have led some free communities or individual freemen to place themselves under the protection of a strong man who continued to exact
services long after the danger had passed. The king and his advisers,
too, might have transformed the old free communities into estates,
which were granted as regular property to churchmen or nobles
whom they wished to reward. This loss of independence was the price
which the bulk of ordinary Englishmen had to pay for the leadership
of the nobles and the churchmen,—leadership which perhaps was
to be worth its cost in the long run. The Anglo-Saxons had no
single specific term for these men who sank below the rank of
freemen. Many varying classifications and conditions later were
to be blended into the fairly uniform status of the serf, "tied to
the soil."

If serfdom was to mean a descent for the vast majority, it at least
meant advancement for the lowest of the old English classes—the
thralls, or slaves, who, not long after the close of the Anglo-Saxon
period, gradually merged into the mass of serfs. A slave differed
from a serf in that he could be sold as property and removed to
other land. Some slaves were war captives, some owed their status
to a legal penalty, and, in certain cases, parents even sold their own
children into slavery. The port of Bristol is said to have carried
on a thriving business in selling English slaves, both men and
women, to Ireland.

At least nine out of ten of the people of these various social classes
lived in agricultural villages, which were the commonest economic
and social units in England, not only in Saxon times but down to the
late eighteenth century. The usual village consisted of anywhere
from a dozen to fifty thatched huts ranged along a narrow street
and occupied by peasants, who derived their scanty living from work
on the surrounding land. Generally these bleak, damp hovels were
of the most rude and primitive type, without windows or chimneys.

Other buildings were the mill, the church, and the great house of the local lord or his representative, who dominated the village. Sometimes this residence of the lord was fortified so that all the village might take refuge there in time of danger.

The village lands consisted of the "arable," or plowed, fields for the raising of crops; the meadow for hay; the pasture for the grazing of horses, cattle, and sheep; and a waste woodland which provided acorns for the pigs, as well as firewood. In addition, small garden plots were attached to the various cottages, with a larger garden for the great house. Usually a stream ran through the lands, and sometimes there might be a fish pond. As in many other branches of medieval life, the individual was subordinated to the community. The pastures and wastes were "common" land, undivided among the separate peasants. Even in the arable land and the meadows the distribution of land and the agricultural practices were strongly influenced by this same communal relationship.

One of the most significant features of European history in the medieval and early modern period is the fact that, while most of the inhabitants of England and the Continent thus spent their lives at farming, practically no changes in agricultural methods occurred between Roman days and the eighteenth century. The personal status of the agricultural population underwent certain slow changes, but the methods of raising crops went on in the same time-honored, inefficient manner from century to century. Meanwhile the small, active minority of the population not so engaged was making rapid advances in government, industry, commerce, culture, science, and in other directions. Even if some men may have thought of more effective agricultural methods, the communal situation hampered any deviation from custom. The result was that the rural village remained on a subsistence basis, producing little if any more than was necessary for its own existence. Only when a considerable portion of the population had been lured away to towns and cities did agriculture finally undergo a revolution to increase its productivity. Two of the principal reasons for the inefficiency of medieval agriculture were the "open field" system of land distribution and cultivation, combined with the "three field" (or "two field") system of crude rotation of crops.

Under the "open field" system the average peasant held from fifteen to thirty acres of arable land. They were not, however, in a single, compact, fenced-off block where he could concentrate his energy. Instead, they were scattered widely through several open fields in long, narrow strips of only a half acre or acre each. Nothing but little ridges of turf separated each strip from those on either side. A considerable part of the working day was thus wasted in trudging around among one's various isolated strips. The system doubtless arose from a desire to give each man a fair share of the best, the average, and the poorer soil of the community. Sometimes a redistribution of strips was made each year, and such a transfer of strips discouraged the peasant from improving his holdings because they would soon pass to another. Actually each peasant simply had a fifteen-acre or thirty-acre share in the community arable land. Whether the open-field system came down from the Roman villas or originated in the Saxon free communities is disputed, and there are scholars ready to defend each theory stoutly. Whatever the source, this practice prevailed throughout a considerable part of England and was decidedly wasteful.

The "three field" aspect of medieval agriculture further helps to explain the failure to raise larger crops. Not until the eighteenth century was England finally to realize that turnips and other root crops could restore the nitrogen removed from the soil by the growth of grain; the best the medieval farmers could do was to give the land a complete rest every third year. Consequently the peasant with thirty acres could use only twenty for crops in any given year. All the arable land was divided into three roughly equal fields, in each of which would be a third of each man's strips. A particular field would be sown in the first year with the basic crop of wheat or rye. The next year, in accordance with their partial knowledge of the importance of "rotating" crops, that field would be planted with a different crop, usually barley or oats. The third year it would lie "fallow," or idle. In the cruder stages of development, in fact, there was only a "two field" system, in which half the land remained unproductive each year.

The inefficiency went even further; for implements and field work were crude and inadequate. The wooden plows, generally simply tipped with iron, had to be drawn by eight undersized oxen and, as a peasant seldom owned more than two, it was necessary to co-operate for this work. Seed was scattered broadcast, so that much of it was wasted. Crops were harvested by back-breaking work with short sickles. The result of all this was that, after a year of hard work, an acre yielded only eight or nine bushels of wheat, even in a good season, whereas modern agricultural methods can often produce forty bushels or more. In bad years famine was likely to stalk through the land.

Yet the farmers raised enough at least to survive in a simple manner. From the wheat or rye they had their porridge and bread; from the barley came their principal beverage, beer. From their livestock they could supplement this meager diet with beef, mutton, or pork, usually salted for preservation, as well as with chicken, eggs, and milk. From the sheep, also, came wool, which could be spun and woven into crude cloth; from the cattle came leather for shoes and sometimes jackets.

Altogether, the village was a self-sufficing entity, producing almost everything necessary for its needs. In the early stages it had its own simple industrial specialists, such as a miller, a carpenter, and a smith. Its few outside demands seldom went beyond salt for preserving meat, iron for plows and tools, wax for the church candles, and possibly silk, or other finer textiles than homespun, for the lord and his lady or the priest. Because of this self-sufficiency and because of the formidable obstacles to trade in the matter of robbery, tolls, and bad roads, there was almost no commerce or concentrated industry. Later, as we shall see, the towns began to take over those functions, and the villages, specializing more than ever in agriculture, developed a sufficient surplus to exchange for the wares of the townsmen.

Turning from society to government, we touch upon one of the three things of which the Englishman is particularly proud: his racial blend, his government, and his dominion on the seas and overseas. English history emphasizes in turn these three slightly overlapping developments. At this point, when the first phase, the mingling of Celtic, Roman, Saxon, Danish, and Norman influences is about to reach its climax, the historian picks up the thread of constitutional development, or the growth of English forms of government. That story kept recurring down through the centuries until England finally worked out a unique method of government which was so good that many other nations have copied its essential features. The story of England's success on the seas still lay far in the future.

Compared with the specific, precise document which the American statesmen drew up in 1787 as a constitution for the guidance of their government, the English constitution has always been vague and indefinite. That arises from the Anglo-Saxon unwillingness, which we have mentioned, to define and to confine precisely in words the exact status of their institutions. This has resulted in a desirable flexibility, in which governmental functions can mold themselves to changing circumstances without going through the rigid formality of amendments. Englishmen have always had a fairly clear understanding of just how things stood, and have been willing to let it go at that. The only attempt at a comprehensive written constitution lasted barely five years, and the three documents often piously re-

# King Alfred, Danes, and Dooms

garded in recent centuries as the "bulwarks of English liberty" are mainly negative in character and deal with immediate and specific royal abuses. Even today the king has tremendous theoretical power which has never been taken away by definite enactment; but he himself and all Englishmen understand perfectly that his actual power has been whittled down by custom to almost nothing. Another point must be kept in mind in discussing early constitutional development. The later sharp distinction between legislative, executive, and judicial functions did not exist in men's minds in those days. There was certain public business to be done, and the various individuals or bodies handled it as it came along, without speculating upon whether they were making laws, enforcing laws, or interpreting laws. If they occasionally used terms which now have a very definite meaning, such usage by no means implied that they gave them the present-day clean-cut significance.

The central government of the Anglo-Saxons was so ineffective that the Normans were to transform it almost completely. The local institutions, on the other hand, were permitted in many cases to continue without fundamental change, and consequently were to have permanent importance. The four main political units were in order, the kingdom, the shire, the hundred, and the township, though the functions of that lowest unit remain obscure.

The prestige of the kingship, despite the inadequate machinery for central government, increased during the six centuries of the Anglo-Saxon period. At the outset every little tribe had had its own king, who had either held that office on the Continent or was a temporary war leader raised to permanent leadership. Whatever democratic control may have limited the kingship back in Germany and Denmark disappeared shortly after the arrival in England. After the kings of Wessex had gained leadership over all England, the royal influence grew considerably. The direct acquisition of crown lands from which the king derived a steady income, the influence of royal leadership against the Danes (particularly that of Alfred), and the support of the Church in matters of both theory and practice all probably contributed to this increased prestige. But the royal power fell far short of that which the first Norman king was to wield. England was still far from being a really united country, in spite of the nominal headship of the king. Remains of provincial independence lingered in the outlying regions, which remembered that they had been separate kingdoms, and which were controlled by powerful earls who enjoyed more real authority there than did the king. The services performed by the central government were not extensive or impressive. Local units administered most of the law and were charged with the triple duty (*trinoda necessitas*) of military service in the fyrd, the repair and guarding of fortified places, and the building and repair of bridges. Relatively little fell upon the king's central government except the conduct of foreign affairs and leadership in time of war, together with efforts to supervise the law and, in the case of the specific Danegeld later collected to buy off the Danes, to levy taxes (see page 50). A few "household" officials, such as the butler, chamberlain, marshal, and, later, the chancellor, assisted in administration.

Associated with the king in the central government was the body known as the witan or witenagemot. It was composed of the principal nobles and churchmen of the land, together with certain other prominent men whom the king saw fit to summon. It was not a representative body, for the members were invited because of their personal importance and not as representatives of particular regions. The witan served various purposes. It advised the king on important matters of policy; it served as a high court for certain serious cases, though not as a regular supreme court of appeal; and it co-operated with the king in issuing statements of the law. Ordinarily it did not serve as a check upon the king's authority; for he summoned its members when he saw fit, presided over its meetings, and initiated the business. Under a minor or a weak king, however, this gathering of the "wise men" might take the authority into its own hands. When the king died, the witan elected his successor. Normally it chose one of the royal "athelings," or princes, provided he seemed adequate for the position. At times, however, the witan departed from the regular royal line to select an outsider as king. The example of the witan was important; for the Great Council of the Normans and the subsequent House of Lords may be regarded as its direct descendants.

The most important subdivision of the kingdom, then and ever since, has been the shire, or county, as it came to be called after the Norman Conquest. Yorkshire, the largest of England's shires, has an area greater than the state of Connecticut, but the rest are much smaller. Most of England's forty shires had come into existence by the end of the Anglo-Saxon period. Some of them, like Kent and Sussex, represented former little kingdoms which had been absorbed; others, like Worcestershire and Leicestershire, bear the names of towns which were administrative centers around which they developed. The head man in the shire was the ealdorman, or earl, though that title did not have the same exact significance as "eorl" in the early Anglo-Saxon aristocracy. He was in charge of the military establishment of the shire, presided at its assembly when

# King Alfred, Danes, and Dooms

present, and received the "third penny" of fines levied in the shire court. At first the ealdorman was appointed by the king; but there was a tendency for the office to become hereditary, and hence more independent. Some time after Alfred's reign, moreover, certain earls extended their power over several shires until at one time there were only four earls. Next to the ealdorman in importance came the sheriff, or shire reeve, whose office did not become hereditary and who served as a more direct representative of the king. The office grew out of the functions of the local reeves who collected rents from the crown lands. As time went on, particularly after the earls ceased to confine themselves to a single shire, the authority and duties of the sheriff increased. We shall see that after the Conquest his influence was to be still further augmented; for he was the all-important link between the central and the local government. Those two officials, together with the bishop, presided at the meetings of the shire moot.

This shire moot, which met twice a year, was to prove one of the most significant of the Anglo-Saxon political institutions. It was primarily a court for cases which had not already been settled in the subordinate hundred moots; but in the undivided condition of public business in that day it frequently handled other business of common interest as well. In theory all freemen of the shire were entitled to attend its sessions and participate in its judgments; in practice most of them were too busy to take the time, and attendance was probably confined chiefly to the thanes, together with representatives, perhaps, from the various subdivisions of the shire. Alfred is said to have been specially interested in the administration of justice and to have had both the shire and hundred courts meet with more regularity.

Each shire was divided into several "hundreds," or "wapentakes," as they were called in the region of the Danelaw. The origin of these names is obscure. The hundred moot, which met usually every four weeks, served as a sort of police court and handled the bulk of the ordinary cases. It was more democratic in its actual make-up, having a larger proportion of ordinary freemen, who did not have to travel as far as they would in attending the shire moot.

These moots of shire and hundred embodied the principle of popular participation in government. That principle lasted on after the Norman period and helped to give the English people a practice in political affairs which was lacking in most regions on the Continent. Some have even seen in the shire moot the germs of the national Parliament which later arose.

The older histories told also of tun moots in the various townships, and those were regarded as direct ancestors of the New

England town meetings which still exist. It is quite probable that the men of the township may have gathered occasionally to settle questions of land distribution and other local matters, but there is little evidence of a regular moot which handled law cases, as did the assemblies of hundred and shire. Even if such may have existed, they were absorbed into the courts of the local nobility, which were even to encroach upon the hundred courts. In some of the boroughs, or larger towns, the organization was more definite than in the rural townships, and some may have had regular hundred organization. Towns were the exception in that day, however, and—except for London—were often little more than overgrown villages.

It was not until a full century after the Anglo-Saxon period closed that English law began to take on aspects which are familiar to us, either in the nature of the law itself or in the methods by which it was administered. The justice dispensed in the shire and hundred moots was based on principles strange to us and was arrived at by methods highly unscientific. From time to time the kings and their witans issued "dooms," or rude law codes, which throw considerable, but by no means complete, light on Anglo-Saxon legal principles; for these dooms devoted most of their emphasis to specific penalties or to the announcement of new offenses. Here too there is evidence of Alfred's thoughtful administration; for he was one of those kings who had comprehensive dooms drawn up and proclaimed. Much of the basic law was simply unwritten custom, preserved in the minds of the "wise men" of the community, so that any codification was decidedly useful. Most of the business of the local courts consisted of criminal cases, and the commonest crimes were homicide, assault, and cattle-stealing. Consequently, criminal law loomed far more prominently than civil law, which consists chiefly of private disputes over property. In the latter the royal dooms made one extremely rational provision: that all sales must be made publicly, in town or hundred, in the presence of at least two sworn witnesses who would be bound to testify to the transaction before a court. A third category of moot jurisdiction consisted of religious cases, tried in the presence of the bishop; but separate church courts were not set up in England until after the Norman Conquest.

In the matter of the more emphasized criminal law the striking feature of the early dooms was the principle of cash compensation for crime. The primitive Germans, with their strong ties of family, seem to have handled early criminal offenses by means of personal revenge and to have engaged in bloody feuds. It was a long step toward the preservation of the peace when the injured party or his kinsmen were persuaded to accept cash compensation instead of going out to exact a literal "eye for an eye and tooth for a tooth." As a result the early dooms give a regular list of prices for various forms of physical damage. Compensation for death was known as "wergild," or man money, and was paid to the kinsmen; the "bot" for injuries went to the victim himself; while an additional sum, known as the "wite," often had to be paid to the moot. The laws of Alfred, for instance, are delightfully specific in their details of the cost of bodily damage: "If a man strike off another's nose, let him make bot with LX shillings. If a man strike out another's tooth in the front of his head, let him make bot for it with VIII shillings: if it be the canine tooth, let IV shillings be paid as bot. A man's grinder is worth XV shillings. If the shooting finger be struck off, the bot is XV shillings; for its nail it is IV shillings." There was a separate price for each toe, ranging from twenty shillings for the big toe to five for the little one. The scale did not stop with classifying injuries: there was a separate tariff of prices for each of the social classes. It cost forty times as much to kill an ealdorman or bishop as to kill a ceorl, and the price of king slaughter was prohibitive.

In two particular features the law differed from the present. The wergild, for homicide, was determined without regard to those considerations of motive which now result in varying penalties for first-degree and second-degree murder, manslaughter, and justifiable homicide. Then, too, it was necessary for the injured party to hale the offender into court, to prosecute the case, and to collect the fine. That was frequently difficult, because the very fact of injury implied that the offender was the more aggressive of the two. Only toward the end of the period were certain particularly flagrant offenses regarded as crimes against society in general, to be punished by the king.

The court procedure in the shire and hundred moots seems strangely irrational at the present day, but it is partially explained by two circumstances: that deeply religious age set special faith in oaths and miracles, while the communities were small enough so that the assemblies had a fairly good idea of the relative character of the contesting parties. On those two foundations, rather than on the weighing of evidence in a scientific manner, Anglo-Saxon justice rested. The case was opened before the assembly when the plaintiff, or injured party, swore his complaint under oath. Then the defendant, or accused, swore his denial. The work of the whole assembly consisted in determining which party should proceed to prove his case and by what method. Ordinarily the proof was left to the defendant. There were two ways of proving—compurgation and the ordeal. If the crime was not too serious and if the defendant had some standing in the community, he was allowed to try to clear himself by compurgation. In that, a stipulated number of compurgators, or oath helpers, swore that they believed the defendant's denial was true. They did not attempt to establish an alibi for him or introduce direct evidence bearing on the case; they were simply what would be called today character witnesses. They were under oath, however, and the penalties for false swearing, both immediate and in the next world, were serious enough to make a man think twice before committing perjury. Moreover, the fact that a man could find the necessary number of compurgators indicated that he had a fair standing in the community. If the offense was particularly grave, or if the accused was a stranger or lacking in friends, he was liable to be forced into the grim test of the ordeal, where pain and the probability of adverse judgment awaited the wretch. The ordeal was a religious ceremony, based on the theory that if God considered the man innocent he would perform a miracle to rescue him from otherwise almost certain failure. Three favorite ordeals were by hot iron, hot water, and cold water. The royal doom laid down the procedure in full detail, including the religious ceremonies. In the case of the witnesses to the ordeal, for instance, it was decreed, "Let there go in an equal number of men of either side, and stand on both sides of the ordeal, along the church; and let these all be fasting, and abstinent from their wives on that night; and let the Mass priest sprinkle holy water over them all, and let each of them taste of the holy water, and give them all the book and the image of Christ's rood to kiss." In the first two ordeals the accused had to carry a piece of red-hot iron several paces or pluck a stone out of a kettle of boiling water. "If it be a single accusation, let the hand dive after the stone up to the wrist; and if it be threefold, up to the elbow." Then the hand, inflamed from the iron or the hot water, was tightly bound up. If, on the third day, the skin was not infected, which would be considered a miracle, he was deemed innocent; otherwise he was guilty. The third ordeal consisted of lowering him, bound hand and foot, into cold water; if he floated, he was judged guilty, on the supposition that the water refused to receive anything evil. If the guilty man could not pay the fine or if the crime was too serious to be settled on such a cash basis, there were penalties of death, mutilation, or outlawry; for the Anglo-Saxons had no jails for imprisonment.

Much of this development had come by Alfred's reign, but a few of the features took form only in the century and a half between his death (about 900) and the coming of the Normans. Among these later changes was, in particular, the extension of the Wessex king-

# King Alfred, Danes, and Dooms

ship all over England by Alfred's son and grandson. Alfred's grandfather, Egbert, to be sure, had been acknowledged Bretwalda; but this was only a precarious overlordship, like that wielded by the kings of Northumbria and Mercia in the heyday of those kingdoms. Under a Bretwalda there were still separate kingdoms with their own kings; but in the tenth century the lesser kings had disappeared, their former subordinate kingdoms were administered by earls, and England had only one king, the ruler of Wessex. Unity was thus achieved with this increased prestige of the crown, although, as we have indicated, the machinery of actual government still left much to be desired. Because of this lack in the central government the unification of the kingship paradoxically led to a scattering of administrative functions among the local nobility. It was at this period that it was ruled that "every man must have a lord" to answer for him before the law. Previously his kinsmen had had that responsibility; but England was outgrowing the family stage, yet had not attained the modern conception of the state's full responsibility for law and order.

Alfred's son, Edward the Elder, not only absorbed Danish Mercia, East Anglia, and Northumbria into Wessex but also won the partial, if not complete, submission of Scotland. According to the Anglo-Saxon Chronicle, "The king of Scotland with all his people chose him [Edward] as father and lord," a statement utilized long afterward by Norman kings of England as proof of their alleged suzerainty over Scotland. Athelstan, the grandson, went further. He consolidated his father's victories over Welsh, Danes, and Scots, and was definitely recognized king of all Britain. This reign—unless we include that of Edgar the Peaceful, concerning which the Anglo-Saxon Chronicle tells us practically nothing—marked the peak of the house of Wessex. A succession of weak kings, plots, and counterplots made, for the most part, a sorry tale of England's political history for the rest of the century.

One strong man, and one only, appeared on the horizon,—Dunstan, abbot of Glastonbury, afterward Archbishop of Canterbury. Folklore in regard to Dunstan's miracles are many, but facts in regard to his career are few. This prelate did much to reform English monasticism, purifying it on the model of the contemporary reform movements on the Continent (see page 25). He repaired many monasteries, brought a new influx of Irish monks to England, and wrote a good deal of ecclesiastical music. He was also something of a statesman and did all that he could to uphold the falling fortunes of the Wessex line. Upon the accession of Ethelred the Unready (978), however, he lost influence, and England was now harassed by fresh forays by the Danes. Their ninth-century raids had given them the Danelaw—half of England; these renewed attacks were to put the whole country under Danish rule.

Ethelred did not choose to fight these Danish pirates but bought them off by silver, a practice which led to his undoing. The tax which was levied for this purpose was called the Danegeld. Within a quarter century seven payments of this tribute had totaled more than seventy tons of silver from the thinly settled and impoverished land! Even this did not keep the Danes away; on the contrary, the more Danegeld they received the more frequently they came. In 994 a Danish leader, Sweyn Forkbeard, attacked London, spent the winter near Southampton, and returned to Denmark to fight successfully for the throne; but England was not rid of him for good.

Ethelred, whose "life was cruel in the beginning, wretched in the middle, and disgraceful in the end," now shifted from bribery to blood in his dealings with the Danes. In the year 1002, according to the Anglo-Saxon Chronicle, "the king ordered all the Danish men who were in England to be slain on St. Brice's Day." Since Danes and Saxons had intermarried for generations, the absurdity as well as the viciousness of this command was apparent. It is extremely doubtful, however, if any such wholesale massacre occurred, and perhaps certain Danes in Wessex, who were suspected of plotting against the king, were the only ones slain. The story that among those killed was a sister of Sweyn, beheaded by the special order of the English king, rests on doubtful foundation; at any rate, this time Sweyn, now king of Denmark, vowed vengeance upon the timorous "Unready." Such revenge must have looked easy to him if it is true that he received about this time a letter which read: "The land is a fair land and rich, but the king snores. Devoted to women and wine, he thinks of everything rather than war, and this makes him hateful to his subjects and ridiculous to foreigners. The generals are all jealous of one another; the country folk are weak, and fly from the field at the first crash of battle." A welcome invitation, this, to a Viking!

Sweyn Forkbeard landed in 1013 and within a year held all the north country. London resisted for the time being, and Sweyn rushed past it to Bath, where the English thanes fell over one another in their anxiety to acknowledge his overlordship. Ethelred fled the country, seeking refuge with his wife's relatives in Normandy; and Sweyn presumably would have conquered all England had he not died, after a brief month as king of England.

The witan invited Ethelred back from exile; he returned, worthless as ever. For three years Saxon and Dane engaged in bitter strife for power, under the leadership of two able youths, each barely twenty. One was Edmund Ironside, upholding the cause of his father, Ethelred; the other was Sweyn Forkbeard's son, Canute, whom the witan had passed over in favor of Ethelred. With the death of Ethelred, in 1016, Ironside as king continued to fight valiantly against terrific odds. London alone stoutly resisted the Danish attacks. Treachery helped to end this fitful moment of Saxon resistance; and when Edmund died, after a heroic seven months' reign, Canute became king of all England, at twenty-two.

This plundering young heathen, who had recently sent a group of hostages ashore with hands and noses lopped off, was quickly transformed by responsibility into a wise, efficient, Christian king,— one of the best in English history. From slaughtering and looting the English, he devoted himself to governing them well—so well, in fact, that he soon became popular. Backward as Anglo-Saxon England might be, it was more advanced in many respects than Scandinavia. Coming from that adaptable Viking breed, which would take ideas and practices as readily as they would steal property, Canute respected English laws and customs, partly because they were better than those of his native land. Within a year he had sent his army back to Denmark and had made himself at home within his new country, where he proceeded to build churches on the sites of battlefields, that the latter might be forgotten, and to marry Emma of Normandy, widow of his late rival, Ethelred. He played no favorites; he trusted the Anglo-Saxons and was trusted by them in turn. He published a law code which kept in the main to that laid down by Alfred. Anglo-Saxon prelates were retained in ecclesiastical positions. The welfare of the Church was dear to his heart, if we may judge from a letter written by him from Rome which he visited—the last king of England to do so until Edward VII went there in the twentieth century. In fact, this ex-heathen sent English churchmen to improve the religion of the Danes. Aside from a small body of housecarls (personal retainers), he maintained no military display, and for twenty years he kept the peace, an unusual boon for war-trodden England. But of literary remains of Canute's reign not much survives except one little song:

> Cheerily sungen the monkës in Ely
> When Cnut King rowed thereby.
> Row, cnichts, near the land
> And hear we these monkës sing.

King of England, and soon afterward, at the death of an older brother, of Denmark as well, Canute aspired to further glory. He intrigued with the nobles of Norway and drew many of them away from their ruler. Commanding a great Anglo-Danish armada, he next attempted to conquer Norway. The king's dragon ship was said to have had sixty rowers, and his naval strength was over-powering. None the less he was foiled by the skillful stratagem of the Swedes, allied to the Norwegians. A second try succeeded: the ruler of Norway fled, and Canute added Norway to his English and Danish thrones. Already before this time he had visited Scotland, where he is said to have received the submission of the king. For the time being, it seemed as though a great Scandinavian empire might arise, to be ruled from England.

This was not to be, in that time of difficult communication; but the maritime nature of Canute's dominions was to increase England's interest in her sphere of future greatness, the sea. The Danes, like other Norsemen, were traders, even at their wildest; and for some time, as we have seen, they had been helping to instill maritime energy into England. Canute's wide holdings gave increased opportunity for trade, so that London, which had relapsed from its activity of Roman days, received a powerful impetus toward its future career as a center of commerce.

Canute died in 1035, and his three sons inherited his three king-doms, Denmark going to Hardecanute, Norway to Sweyn, and England to Harold Harefoot. Queen Emma was the mother of Hardecanute only, and she desired England for her son. In consequence, although the majority of the witan voted for Harold Hare-foot, Wessex, where Emma's influence was strong, stood up for Hardecanute.

Neither of these two contestants for the throne measured up to the stature of their father. Harold Harefoot proved to be an extraordinarily bloodthirsty tyrant, who died just as his brother, Harde-canute, prepared to contest the throne with him. This brother proved no better. "He devised no kingly deed during all his reign, and he caused the dead body of Harold to be taken up and shot into the marsh." He increased the Danegeld beyond reason, wrought frightful vengeance with his housecarls on those who refused to pay it, and, only two years a king, died apparently of strong drink. The English now had been surfeited with Danes. They had forgiven or forgotten the iniquities of their old Saxon ruler, Ethelred, and so they welcomed his son, Emma's child by her first marriage, to the English throne. Thus began the strange reign of Edward the Confessor (1042–1066).

# CHAPTER III

## The Coming of the Normans

### 1042-1087

---

O NLY fourteen years after the Danish rule came to a close with the death of Canute's second son, England was to be conquered by another band of former Vikings, the Normans. While the Danes had contributed little that was new to Anglo-Saxon England, these Normans, although originally from the same northern regions, were to transform England so radically as a result of their two centuries of sojourning in France that the date 1066 is a turning point in English history rivaled only by 1485 and 1688.

Who were the Normans and whence did they come? In the beginning the only difference between a Dane of the Danelaw, a Norman of Normandy, a Varangian of Russia, and the other Vikings (or Northmen or Norsemen, as they were variously called) probably depended simply upon the direction from which the wind happened to be blowing upon the day when each group set sail from Scandinavia. A wind from the north or west may well have sent certain of these fierce and restless adventurers to raid the French or Russian coasts, while an easterly breeze may equally have settled the fate of shore communities in England or in Ireland, or even have tempted the earliest explorers past Iceland to Greenland and Vineland (America). The most important streams of these sea raiders headed down the North Sea toward the more settled parts of Europe. Thus it happened that as Alfred strove with the Danes, northern France was ravaged, even to the danger of Paris itself, by other Northmen. Both English and French saved themselves by buying off the invader with grants of territory. The French equivalent of the Danelaw was given in 911 to Rollo (Hrolf), the Norse leader. This, the duchy of Normandy, was a compact region, extending from the coast half-way up the Seine River toward Paris. Here lived the Normans who were to conquer England.

All the Vikings were quick to slough off their own crudeness and to adopt the civilization of those lands in which they settled as a conquering minority. Thus in France they became Roman Catholic in religion and genuinely French in language and in ways of living; in Russia, Greek Orthodox and Slavic; in England, Roman Catholic and Anglo-Saxon. The Northmen found more that was worth imitating in France than in England, where the Anglo-Saxons were not much more advanced than themselves. In consequence Normandy and the Danelaw soon had little in common except Viking ancestry; for France, even in the so-called Dark Ages after Charlemagne's reign, preserved at least a semblance of Latin culture, law, and unity, and was, moreover, working out that unique social system known as feudalism (see page 65).

Owing to this contact and to their own energy the Normans became temporarily the most influential people in all Europe, dominating western and northern France and Sicily, as well as England. They were fully as cruel as the Saxons and perhaps more so, as they were more energetic and more given to wholesale devastation. They were ahead of the rest of the world in their organizing ability, which they learned partly by observing and copying the workings of the Church. (In England they were to find an unusual opportunity to exercise this superlative administrative talent.) Their numbers were small; but, none the less, as noblemen, merchants, and fishermen they lorded it over the older peasant stock of Normandy, a Celtic, Roman, and Germanic mixture. Some were of the shrewd, hard-headed type which made excellent lawyers and administrators. More conspicuous were the restless, proud, and quarrelsome warriors who had been quick to adopt the latest military devices, and who stayed in the pink of condition as a result of constant warfare. While Anglo-Saxons and Danes still hewed at their foes on foot with battle-axes, the Normans were already using horses for their more important warriors, new weapons such as lances and crossbows, and, for defense, fortresses built on mounds. In spirit, ability, and equipment they were pre-eminent.

In 1035 the leadership of Normandy fell to one who was to rise from Duke William the Bastard to King William the Conqueror. His mother was not the duchess but only a tanner's daughter whom Duke Robert (called the Devil by his foes and the Magnificent by his friends) had briefly loved. Duke Robert desired that, in default of a child born in wedlock, this illegitimate son should succeed him. Consequently, before embarking for a pilgrimage to the Holy Land from which he was never to return, he forced all his barons to swear allegiance to the boy. Thus William, eight years old, became duke of the most turbulent baronage in Europe, under the double handicap of being a minor and illegitimate.

Only a person of extraordinary force and ability could have conquered the difficulties which beset William almost from the cradle. "How to deal with men he learned, when to smite and when to spare," at a very early age. First, he had to win his own duchy. The barons, especially in the west, rose to take instant advantage of a boy ruler, and his cousin, with a legitimate claim of his own to the dukedom on the female side, sought to oust the son of a tanner. William was fortunate in his guardians, and although only fourteen when they were murdered, he already knew how to fight. His liege lord, the king of France, assisted him at his decisive victory of Val-ès-Dunes over his barons. Then and there William showed himself for the first time a justly severe but on the whole a merciful conqueror; for after the battle no blood was shed, and the punishments consisted merely of fines, the giving of hostages, the surrender of castles. By nineteen he was the master of his own duchy, which flourished under his intelligent and forceful rule.

William next paid attention to the neighboring counties and duchies,—Anjou, Maine, Brittany, and others. The jealous Count of Anjou persuaded the fickle king to turn against the young duke, whose authority he had just helped to establish, whereupon William, "the Iron-Cutter," proved himself not only a powerful warrior whose blows could cleave horse and man in two but also a skillful strategist. Despite revolts and invasions he kept his duchy intact, and so extended his power that after Anjou's death he became foremost of all vassals in France, stronger even than the king. Flanders became his semi-ally by marriage, and without the friendship of that rich province on the Channel it is doubtful if he could have conquered England. The little county of Maine became his by force of arms; for, although he had some legal claim to it, he was opposed by the people. Certain of them had cause to regret it, particularly the garrison of one town which hung raw oxhides on the walls to taunt the tanner's grandson, who inflicted terrible punishment upon them all. And Brittany meanwhile was "reduced to submission by a single march."

The ability and aggressiveness of the duke as a soldier perhaps were natural inheritances from his pirate forebears, but his exceptional executive power and statesmanship resulted from his own genius. He righted wrongs no matter who the wrongdoer might be, and in consequence much else was easily forgiven him by his subjects, grateful in those unquiet times for law and order. William ever put himself on the right side of the law through craft and cunning, and some of his most oppressive acts were within the bounds of technical legality; for although he respected law he made it his slave. Though short, fat, and bald-headed, William was powerfully built, with broad shoulders and long arms. He had a forbidding eye, which gave indication of violent passion generally held in check. He had all the Northman's brutality when aroused, but he usually kept his raging thoughts to himself. His grim aspect intimidated his court, and his life in many ways was solitary. His marriage to Matilda of Flanders, however, was said to have been a happy one; for, although not always faithful, he was devotedly attached to his wife. Even she, as legend has it, tasted his fierce temper. Scorning his first advances because of his birth, she met her match. According to legend, the duke rode headlong to her father's capital, found Matilda walking in the town with her maids, dragged her about by the hair, and then rode off—an act which apparently won her undying devotion. In his own way William promoted good men, valued education, protected the poor, patronized commerce, and altogether made Normandy into a compact, prosperous state. Because of his absolute authority he became the envy of all contemporary rulers. This was the man who now began to turn interested eyes across the Channel; and in view of his record it is surprising that even slothful England worried so little at his covetous glances and his friendship with her childless king.

But England, in these years between 1042 and 1066, was already experiencing a sort of preliminary Norman Conquest; for the throne was occupied by that much overrated individual Edward the Confessor. Had not Canute's younger sons been so notoriously worthless, the witan would probably have overlooked this colorless son of Ethelred the Unready and Emma of Normandy. Although he came from the old Wessex line in direct descent from his great-great-grandfather, Alfred, the Norman blood seemed to predominate in him. In education, in friends, and in interests he was as Norman as any true-born son of Normandy. His mother had fled with him to her brother's court in Normandy when her husband, Ethelred, had proved himself so notoriously "unready" to deal with the Danish menace. When she returned to England as Canute's bride, Edward remained behind, spending most of his time with those monks who had taught him as a boy and who had ever remained his closest intimates. From these ecclesiastical contacts his personality received so deeply religious an impress that the Church became his main concern, and by it he was later canonized as Saint Edward the Confessor.

Even in the disorganization and stagnation of these twilight years of Saxon England an energetic ruler might have built a firm government out of the chaos left by Danish rule; but this petty-minded and charmless, albeit kindly, "French monk" was not the man for such a task. In after years, when the yoke of Norman kings seemed oppressive, the English, as all people are apt to do, looked back with

# The Coming of the Normans

affection to the "laws of good King Edward"; yet, to quote one authority, "so far as we know he never made a law. Had he made laws, had he even made good use of those that were already made, there might have been no Norman Conquest." In that case, however, "Edward would never have gained his fictitious glories . . . as the last of the English kings of the English."

The Confessor's only policy—if even this could be dignified by such a name—was to introduce Norman ideas into England. Forced in middle age to rule across the Channel, he clung tenaciously to all things Norman. Particularly was this true in the Church. Among the many Norman prelates whom he placed in prominent benefices was Robert of Jumièges, who first was Lord Bishop of London and then Archbishop of Canterbury. So much did Edward rely upon him that it was rumored that if Jumièges "said a black crow was white, the king would rather trust to his mouth than to his own eyes." The Confessor also put the so-called Cinque Ports under Norman control. This was particularly galling; for these seaports— Dover, Sandwich, Romney, Hythe, and Hastings—were proud and, even at this early period, were important for their location on the southeastern coast, nearest the Continent. These ports, to which Rye and Winchelsea were later added, were to furnish most of the ships and men needed for the royal naval service until the end of the Middle Ages, and in return were to receive extensive privileges. Norman barons were also set to guard the important frontier districts known as marches; Norman wine merchants were given a wharf of their own at London; and Edward drew an ever-increasing number of Normans to the royal court.

This peaceful Norman penetration aroused the hostility of many Saxon Englishmen, including certain powerful nobles. They wanted to keep England for the English, without interference from either Dane or Norman; but they were too jealous of one another to act in unison. Foremost among them was Godwin, related by marriage to Canute, who had raised him from simple thane to Earl of Wessex. This vigorous and able Saxon, about whom unfortunately little is known, appears to have had much to do with Edward's elevation to the throne. Apparently hoping to become the power behind the throne, he found himself balked by too many Norman favorites. He succeeded, nevertheless, in marrying his daughter to the king; and from the latter he received so many favors that ultimately he and his sons held so many earldoms that he controlled most of England, except the north country, where the Saxon earls of Northumbria and Mercia were his only real rivals. Chief opponent of Norman influence in England was Earl Godwin.

# A History of England and the British Empire

In 1051 the ill-feeling between Saxon and Norman burst into flame, following hard upon an episode at Dover, where a party of Norman knights, led by a Norman brother-in-law of the king, were returning home from a visit to His Majesty's court at London. Lodgings were denied them; a brawl followed; Normans were killed; and their friend the king ordered Godwin to punish this insult offered his guests. Godwin refused to act, and civil war would have followed had not the earl fled with his sons. The Saxon eclipse was temporary; for within a year public opinion, inflamed by the rumor that the king had made Duke William his heir, brought about the triumphant return of the Godwin clan. Despite the fact that the Godwins sacked the Channel ports on their way home, southern England rose to join them with the cry "Live or die for Earl Godwin!" Terror-stricken Norman favorites fled as Godwin sailed up the Thames to dictate terms at London. For the remainder of the Confessor's reign Saxon interests, or at least those of the Godwin family, were uppermost in England. Robert of Jumièges was replaced as archbishop by a Saxon, Stigand,—a show of power which was to prove a boomerang against the house of Godwin. For the time being, Norman influence was at low ebb.

In the year of his return Godwin died, and for a time his sons succeeded to most of his power. They were an interesting lot. One led his forces into Scotland to dethrone the king, Macbeth, immortalized by Shakespeare; another was responsible for the famous ride of his wife, Lady Godiva; a third, the worthless Tostig, was exiled after kidnaping a nun and misruling his earldom, only to return in the year of the Conquest to distract the Saxon resistance; and finally there was Harold, the oldest surviving son and the ablest of all, who succeeded his father as earl of Wessex. These various earls were virtually independent rulers within their own domains, paying little heed to royal authority, just as William, duke of Normandy, gave scant consideration to the wishes of his overlord, the king of France.

With this submerging of Edward's Norman friends, the Norman Conquest would have probably dwindled to a mere gradual adoption of the more progressive ideas from across the Channel had Edward of England abided by the customary royal duty of providing an heir to his throne. Instead, on his wedding day he followed his marriage vows with an additional oath, one of perpetual chastity. This was rather an unusual act for a bridegroom; but one must remember the king's monastic upbringing. The monk who chronicled this performance praised Edward's pious act, but others in the realm felt that the king was betraying his land by leaving it a prey to rival heirs and covetous Normandy. Primogeniture, to be sure, was not then as firmly established in the English royal line as it was to be later, and Edward's indifference may be extenuated by the fact that real authority in deciding the succession lay with the witan; but, even so, it would seem as though the monk in Edward had triumphed over the king.

Upon the death of King Edward in the first week of 1066 there were several claimants for the throne. The old monarch had named as his heir Harold, who was lucky enough to be at hand, although the next of kin was little Edgar the Atheling, of the old Wessex line. The latter, however, was a mere boy, and in those dangerous days a grown man ordinarily counted for more than blood relationship. Harold was the leading noble; he traced his descent on his mother's side from Scandinavian kings; and, what was most important, he was at once duly named "King" by the witan. No voice appears to have been raised for the dispossessed Atheling; but a clamor arose elsewhere, particularly from Duke William of Normandy. Another possible claimant was Harold Hardrada of Norway, a descendant of Canute. There were those who asserted that Hardrada was in the field rather as a supporter of Normandy than for himself; but, whatever his motives, his activities—as we shall see—occurred at the most propitious moment for the Norman duke. William declared that he himself was the rightful and legitimate king of England, and that, too, on several rather questionable grounds. Although illegitimate, he was related to the English royal family. He insisted that Edward could not make Harold his heir because he had already bestowed that honor long before upon William, at the time of the latter's trip to England. To be sure, it was not legally a gift in Edward's power, and a scantily attended witan had elected Harold; but William, for all his love of legality, ignored that. In addition, Harold once had been shipwrecked on the French coast and, in the custom of those days, became with his ship, cargo, and crew legitimate prize of the shore community. William had taken advantage of this to force Harold to swear to help him gain the English throne; and Harold found to his cost that, unbeknown to himself, he had performed the oath over sacred relics, which made it a serious religious offense should he later break his word. From the modern point of view, William's capitalization of a shipwreck might seem worse than Harold's forswearing of an oath forced under such unfair circumstances; but to the religious mind of the Middle Ages the exploiting of wrecked sailors was a legitimate act, while falseness to an oath, given over relics, was one of the blackest of sins, a fact of which William made good use.

Nevertheless, Harold was not the type to relinquish a crown to escape accusations of perjury. At the start he was able to outplay his rivals, since he was on the spot and had been lawfully elected and crowned as well. But his success was short-lived; he was faced with too many foes, and he had an apathetic England at his back. As the chronicler summed up his nine months' reign, "Little quiet did he enjoy the while he wielded the kingdom." It has been asserted that Harold might have fared better had he been content to be the power behind the Atheling's throne, since the latter, being of the direct Wessex royal line, might have stood a better chance of loyalty from divided England. This disunity of Anglo-Saxon England was to prove its undoing, and it helps to explain why more than a million Englishmen so readily submitted to a few thousand foreign adventurers. Harold could rely only on the earldoms in the south under his direct rule. The earls of Mercia and Northumbria were playing a waiting game, and his own brother Tostig, still enraged at Harold for condoning his exile, was openly aiding Hardrada.

It was from this latter source that trouble first appeared. While Harold was anxiously patrolling the south coast in fear of the rumored arrival of William of Normandy, Hardrada and Tostig, with a fleet of some three hundred ships, landed on the north coast and headed for York. Harold rushed north and offered his brother his old earldom of Northumbria back again, but Tostig asked what Hardrada was to get. "Seven feet of earth, perhaps more, seeing that he is a tall man," came the answer. There was no brotherly reconciliation. At Stamford Bridge, near York, Harold won a smashing victory; both Tostig and Hardrada were slain. The English had no time to celebrate. Three days after Stamford Bridge, William had landed on the unguarded south coast at Pevensey.

The duke was making no haphazard foray upon the English shore. He had put his usual energy and thoroughness into preparations for what was to be one of the most successful military expeditions in history. His first concern had been to win European public opinion by propaganda. He made a pseudo-friendly gesture toward Harold by sending him a message reminding him of his oath, and promising him his daughter and control over a large part of England if he would support William's claims to the throne. The duke expected nothing from this, but it was a good thing to have on record. The active Norman diplomats also told the story of the broken oath in many European courts and denounced Harold's "usurpation" of the crown. Harold was doing little to turn public opinion in his favor. In that superstitious age the opinion of the

# The Coming of the Normans

papacy weighed very heavily, and the Pope was indignant at the irregular ousting of Archbishop Robert of Jumièges in favor of Godwin's Saxon candidate, Stigand. At the instigation of Cardinal Hildebrand, who was soon to succeed to the papacy as the great Gregory VII, the Pope denounced Harold's broken oath and, probably foreseeing that it would be well to be on William's side anyway, gave the Norman duke a banner and a blessing. All this moral support was gratifying, and it bore practical results in stimulating the recruiting of adventurers from many lands. To the spiritual rewards of a "holy war" now were added promises of English estates; for wily William realized that an ordinary feudal levy for the forty days' service, stipulated by the Norman feudal system, would be insufficient. Medieval statistics are notoriously inaccurate, but William's followers probably numbered between three thousand and ten thousand, many of whom were Frenchmen from regions other than Normandy. These men joined the duke in investing a considerable amount to secure the most up-to-date military equipment available and to provide provisions and boats. The conquest has been described not inaptly as "a joint-stock investment," and few investments have paid higher dividends. Prepared to set sail in mid-August, the expedition was delayed by contrary winds during the six weeks when Harold was carefully patrolling the south coast. Then the winds turned favorable just at the unluckiest moment for Harold, when the threat from Scandinavia was drawing him northward.

Upon news of William's landing, Harold hurried his exultant but weary army from Stamford Bridge back to London, two hundred miles, in five days! Meanwhile William acted upon the prime rule of strategy that the proper objective is not a geographical point, such as the enemy capital, but the enemy's main army itself. He remained on the south coast, keeping open his line of retreat by sea and devastating the countryside to entice Harold into premature action. Harold, who up to now had acted with remarkable energy and intelligence, made an error in hastening on through London without resting his men or waiting for reinforcements; but it is possible that apathetic and divided England might never have sent further troops to his assistance anyway.

Harold finally halted his foot-weary men to guard the London road on a steep hill, some eight miles inland from Hastings on the sea. Harold's men were brave; but they were placed under a desperate handicap, since their arms and tactics were hopelessly out of date. At Stamford Bridge they had just fought infantry of their own type, using similar weapons and tactics; at Hastings they were outclassed by the Normans, whose army was the best-equipped in Europe. As in many other ways, Saxon England had been stagnating in military science, still clinging to old methods while the Normans were using cavalry and archers to support the infantry. Harold had a powerful nucleus of real soldiers in his "housecarls," or regulars; but the bulk of the Saxon army was made up of thanes, and of the old regional fyrd, an ill-disciplined and ill-armed militia of farmers, in some cases equipped with nothing better than scythes or clubs. There were probably not more than five or six thousand men on each side. Hastings, as modern battles go, was a trifling affair; but its consequences were to be out of all proportion to its size.

At about nine, on the morning of October 14,—so far as one can reconstruct the story of the battle,—the Normans advanced to the attack, coming down their own hill, crossing a little valley, and struggling up the steep slope where Harold's army waited. First William used archers, but arrows made little impression against the line of Saxon shields. Next came the infantry, no more successful than the archers. Even the first crashing charge of cavalry recoiled, with men and horses gashed and split by the great battle-axes of the housecarls. By that time it was past noon, and a lesser general than William might have given up the attack. His quick eye, however, saw a way to penetrate the unbroken wall of shields. Part of the undisciplined fyrd had broken line to pursue the retreating left wing of William's cavalry. He thereupon launched a new cavalry attack, apparently with orders to feint retreat. The fyrd fell into the trap, broke its line, and was cut to pieces or driven away. The stanch housecarls still stood firm around Harold and his banners of the Dragon and the Fighting Man. They repulsed charge after charge until William finally directed the archers to fire high in the air, so that a galling shower of arrows would fall into the inner ranks. Even at that the gallant band fought almost to the last man. About five o'clock Harold fell with an arrow through his eye, and a few survivors slipped away into the forest behind them. That night the sun set on the last of Anglo-Saxon England.

Once again William paused,—this time, according to the chronicler, for "the nation to make known its submission" or, as it has been more picturesquely put, like a master waiting for a cowed dog to heel. Possibly he simply awaited reinforcements. The delay proved wise; for there was a general scramble to gain the Conqueror's favor, whereas a more rapid advance might have led the northern earls to unite against the small invading force. William moved

# The Coming of the Normans

cautiously against London as the Dover garrison surrendered; he ravaged Kent and Sussex, but spared Canterbury; next he turned westward, making a wide sweep about London to cut off its food supply from the interior. The witan meanwhile, in a panic, had elected the Atheling as Harold's successor; but this stripling prince had the good sense to go to William and offer submission. Finally, since no help was forthcoming from the northern earls, of Northumbria and Mercia, London opened its gates to the Conqueror, and the witan elected its third king that year. On Christmas Day, 1066, while Normans rioted with townspeople, William was crowned in Westminster Abbey, king of England.

Proclaiming himself the true king, who had ousted a usurper, he promised to introduce no foreign law, nor to make arbitrary confiscations except in the case of those who had actively opposed him. He began building the Tower, to keep London in submission, and he felt relatively secure when he saw that the earls in the north showed no stomach for fighting. In the spring he recrossed the Channel to attend to his duchy; for it must be remembered that he remained duke of Normandy and that for the next five centuries the kings of England were to own land in France.

No sooner had he left England than revolts broke out, continuing until 1072. The most serious of all came in the north. Danish fighters from the Continent came over to aid one of these uprisings in the old Danelaw. Exasperated at this reaction to his mild rule, William determined to teach the north country a lesson it would never forget. He and his barons laid waste the region so thoroughly that, as the old chronicler reported, "so great a famine arose that . . . they ate the flesh of human beings, horses, dogs, and cats . . . ; so severe was it that some sold themselves into perpetual slavery. . . . Nor was anyone left to bury the dead, for all were wiped out either by the sword or famine, or had departed from their homes on account of hunger. In the meantime the land was destitute of cultivation, and a broad wilderness existed for nine years. Between York and Durham nowhere was there an inhabited village." Thus at last did William pitilessly play the role of Conqueror. The old Danelaw practically disappeared as a distinct region with this massacre of its inhabitants, and northern and southern England were at last welded into one. All England lay under the grip of the little group of Norman adventurers. Within a generation the great castle and cathedral of Durham arose as a sign of Norman domination of the north country. The native English chafed under the iron heels of their local Norman masters, but no serious revolt was attempted again. The last stand, made by one Hereward the Wake in the swampy fens around Ely, near Cambridge, was finally subdued, and the sullen Saxons settled down under the new regime. William, during this period, had shown himself sparing of death sentences, though he had been callous in ordering the gouging out of eyes and the cutting off of hands. His favorite and practical form of punishment was to confiscate rebel lands, wherewith to reward his followers.

Now, like William, we must turn to the changes to be wrought in quiescent England. This Norman conquest was not like the coming of the Anglo-Saxons six centuries earlier. The Anglo-Saxons had almost completely displaced the earlier peoples, whereas the Normans were never more than a ruling minority of a few thousand in a land of more than a million Anglo-Saxons. The latter had been cheered by William's coronation decree: "This I will and order that all shall have and hold the law of King Edward as to lands and all other things, with these additions which I have established for the good of the English people." This seemed to indicate little intention of making changes, and there were not many as far as new legislation was concerned. William made only three new laws, the most striking dealing with his reservations of vast forests for the royal hunt, for "he loved the tall stags as if he were their father." At these forest reservations and the savage restrictions which accompanied them "the rich complained and the poor murmured, but . . . they must will all that the king willed."

It is difficult to judge the new king's motives at this distance, but it seems likely that he wanted to make only such changes as were needed to reward his Norman followers and to ensure good government in the disorganized land. Instead of making far-reaching theoretical plans for reorganization, his practical mind apparently simply utilized such Norman precedents as seemed applicable as situations arose. His clever statesmanship avoided useless friction by permitting the retention of pre-Conquest customs wherever they did not cross his purposes.

Nevertheless, in spite of this remarkable freedom from the usual mass of restrictive legislation laid down by most conquerors, there were many changes of fundamental importance in the twenty-one years of William's reign. Most salient among the innovations were (1) the introduction of the political feudal system; (2) the tightening and centralizing of the royal power, though local government was left largely as it had been; (3) the Normanizing and improvement of the Church, which was more definitely separated from secular affairs; (4) the importation of a higher culture and a Latinized language which eventually merged with the Anglo-Saxon; and (5) the closer linking of England with the Continent. The

# The Coming of the Normans

coming of the Normans probably did not mean a great deal to the bulk of the population, the lower peasantry, who simply changed from one master to another, though frequently the new Norman barons were harsher than the old Saxon thanes. The upper-class Anglo-Saxon leaders, the thanes and high churchmen, suffered most in the transition; for their lands and their power were William's rewards to his followers.

The most revolutionary of all the Norman changes was the transplanting to England of that system of "land tenure based on military service" which had gradually grown up in Europe during the two centuries following the break-up of Charlemagne's empire,—the so-called *feudal system*. Under it the ablest fighters received estates from the king and higher nobles in return for military service. In the chaotic days which followed the barbarian invasions in Europe, the rulers lacked money but had plenty of land. The only way for a noble to become wealthy and powerful was to secure a vast acreage; for, in the absence of modern industrial and financial capital, land was almost the only source of wealth. The feudal system was associated with, and is often confused with, its economic basis, the *manorial system*, which was the way these landowners managed their own estates. The feudal system was a political and military relationship between the king and the nobility or knights, while the manorial system was primarily an economic relationship between each man in the feudal system and the peasantry on his particular estates. The same men of the upper classes were thus involved in both systems: the noblemen received land from their king in return for military service and subdivided that land on the same terms among other nobles or knights, according to the feudal system. Every one of this fighting aristocracy from the king to the poorest knight was the "lord of the manor" on that part of his land which he kept for his own use and support, and as such had important functions in the manorial system in relation to his serfs. Some writers prefer to call these the political and the economic feudal systems. The latter was already partly developed in Anglo-Saxon England, but the political feudal system was almost a complete innovation. Before showing how it was introduced by William, we must describe its general organization. It is worth studying and remembering in detail; for even the national government was run on a feudal basis for several centuries, and one cannot, for instance, understand the terms of Magna Carta (1215) unless one is familiar with the workings of this political feudal system. The details of feudalism differed in various sections of Europe, but the Norman-French variety is what came to England.

# A History of England and the British Empire

Under the political feudal system all the land of a country belonged in theory to the ruler. He always retained a portion of it as a *demesne* (royal domain, or crown lands), to provide himself with his direct private revenue, while the remainder was divided among his more important followers for military reasons. These retainers, in turn, likewise kept a demesne for themselves, and, if their portion was large enough, parceled out the rest to retainers of their own. This process generally continued down through at least three or four stages, until the pieces of land became so small that they could serve only as a demesne without further subdivision. The land thus transferred was known as a *fief*, which in Latin is *feudum* (hence, "feudal" system). The donor of the fief was always the *lord*, and the recipient the *vassal*; but every man involved in this relationship belonged to the upper classes. A lord might be the vassal of someone else, and as the interchange of land for military purposes became more complicated a vassal might have several different lords. Those who held direct from the king were known as *tenants in chief*. The unit by which the size of the estates was measured was called the *knight's fee*, in return for which the holder furnished one man-at-arms, fully armed and mounted, usually for forty days each year. For example, a lord might grant to A certain holdings valued at thirty knight's fees. Out of these A might keep six as a demesne and grant land worth eight fees each to B, C, and D. B might keep two as a demesne and grant one each to E, F, G, H, I, and J. These last would receive so small a portion that the division could go no further. Although perhaps not originally intended to be inherited, the fiefs by custom soon passed from father to son.

When a vassal received a fief from his lord, he went through the dual ceremony of giving *homage* and swearing *fealty*. In homage the vassal knelt and placed his two hands between those of the lord and promised to be his "man" (Latin, *homo*), in more or less the following words: "I become your man, from this day forward, of life and limb and of earthly worship, and unto you shall be true and faithful and bear to you faith for the tenements that I hold of you." In the ceremony of fealty which followed, the vassal swore on the Bible to be faithful to his lord, with words such as these: "Hear this, my lord, that I shall be faithful and true unto you and faith to you shall bear for the lands that I hold of you, and that I shall lawfully do to you the customs and services which I ought to do, so help me God and his saints." There was a third oath which a vassal took to only *one* of his lords; for as we have seen, a vassal might hold land from several different men, to

# The Coming of the Normans

all of whom he had to pledge homage and fealty. This oath, *allegiance*, a sort of superfealty, was a promise to support this liege lord against all others should a dispute arise among his various lords.

The feudal system was really a contractual relationship, with mutual advantages for both lord and vassal. The lord, in addition to granting the fief, was supposed to protect his vassal's interests, while the vassal had several obligations—the so-called "incidents" which arose only at rare intervals—in addition to the primary and constant one of military service. There were the three feudal *aids*, which were cash payments due upon the knighting of the lord's eldest son, the marriage of the lord's eldest daughter for the first time, and for ransom in case the lord should be captured. *Relief* was a sort of inheritance tax due from an heir before he was allowed to take over his father's fief, and probably it was designed originally to make it clear that, while the custom of inheritance was observed, the land still fundamentally belonged to the lord. By *escheat* a fief was forfeited to the lord if the vassal died without heirs or was convicted of crime. Sometimes the lord, especially if he was the king, had the right of *premier seisin*, which allowed him to enter into possession of a fief, on a vassal's death, and take measures for the satisfaction of all claims against the estate before finally turning it over to the heirs. If the heir was a minor son under twenty-one or a daughter under fourteen, the lord became the guardian; and his *wardship* might be very profitable, since he could keep the fief's revenue over and above the amount needed for the ward's support and education. In addition, the lord controlled the *marriage* of all female wards, and might betroth them to any suitor of equal social rank unless the ward was permitted to pay heavily to escape an unwelcome husband. Again, the vassal had to give his lord *hospitality*, should he travel in the vassal's fief; and, finally, he had to attend the lord's *court*, where he judged and was judged by his fellow vassals. Frequently the lord, particularly the king, abused these privileges, and the vassals brought pressure to have fairly fixed rates established, especially in the case of relief, wardship, marriage, and premier seisin. In fact, the system was far less legal than it appeared, and too often rested on force—as Wordsworth put it:

> . . . the good old rule
> Sufficeth them, the simple plan
> That they should take, who have the power,
> And they should keep, who can.

The military tenure, with its forty-day knight service, was the customary feudal relation, but it was not universal. Some vassals received land on other terms. Most of the church lands were drawn into the system of knight service; but some religious institutions held land in *frankalmoign*, by which they were simply to pray for the souls of the lord's family. High and low officials of the court ordinarily received land in *grand* or *petty sergeanty*, in exchange for civil rather than military duties.

In England, William had a unique opportunity to wipe the slate clean and to modify the Norman-French feudal system to his own liking. It was almost inevitable that he should continue the system, for he and his followers had known no other. Furthermore, the only thing which he possessed wherewith to reward his avaricious men was land; and he needed from them the feudal return of military service, to garrison the conquered country. Consequently he claimed that the Conquest gave him title to the estates of all Anglo-Saxons. Some of the earls and thanes who had not opposed him received back part of their lands, at least temporarily; but those who were at Hastings and in the subsequent rebellions lost everything. Dividing most of this land among his followers on feudal terms, William obtained the service of some five thousand knights and men-at-arms.

King William had been, and still continued to be, as bad a vassal to his liege lord, the king of France, as it was possible to imagine; but he had no intention of being so treated by any of his own vassals. English feudalism consequently became more centralized than the Continental variety. The royal power was strengthened, and much of the troublesome private warfare between nobles, which so distracted medieval Europe, was eliminated. The king seldom granted any vassal very much land in any one locality; and he broke up the old English earldoms, so that no subject in the future would be able to enjoy such power as Godwin had wielded in Wessex. The piecemeal nature of the Conquest, starting in the south and only gradually extending to the north, accounted for the scattering of the holdings which each vassal received. Some historians think that this was a deliberate policy on William's part to prevent anyone from becoming too strong; but there is no proof that it was not a purely accidental occurrence: every time more land was confiscated, it was divided among the Normans. The chief distinction between English and Continental feudalism was that the lower vassals in England came gradually to owe their military service not to their immediate overlord but to the king himself. William, as duke of Normandy, held the allegiance of his vassals and led them "legally" against the French king; William as king of England saw to it that no vassal could do the same to him. In

# The Coming of the Normans

the last year of his reign, 1087, he even is reputed to have called together all his great landowners on Salisbury Plain, where they each and every one gave to him the feudal oath of allegiance, "that they would be faithful to him against all other men, even against their lords." Of late, most historians have felt that this Salisbury Oath has been much overrated, and some have even questioned if it ever occurred.

William did not put entire reliance on the Norman feudal army obtained by this distribution of fiefs. He used the Norman barons to put down Saxon revolts; but he kept the old Saxon militia, or fyrd, as a check on the barons' power. The barons found themselves disappointed at his curtailment of the feudal individualism to which they had been accustomed on the Continent, and revolted in 1075. The king put down the rebellion with the help of the conquered English.

We must now turn to the manorial system, feudalism on its economic side, to understand why the manor was so important. Land was the source of most wealth, because the manorial system was so arranged as to pay the bills of the king, lords, knights, and churchmen involved in the political feudal system. The land unit, the manor, was the whole or part of the private demesne which the vassal kept for his own use. An agricultural unit, with a village, fields, pastures, and woodland, it was in effect the Anglo-Saxon village under new management. Like the Saxon village it was practically self-sufficient, since its inhabitants produced nearly everything they needed (see page 39). The Normans changed this village life very slightly as far as local customs were concerned, except that most of the inhabitants—including many former freemen, together with most of the remaining slaves—were crowded into the common status of serf or villein. Also, the manor, or village, became linked with the feudal system, since its new Norman masters were feudal lords and vassals; so that the distinction between the political feudal system and the economic manorial system must be kept clearly in mind to avoid confusion. The manorial relation, unlike the mutually advantageous political feudal relationship, was most unequal; for it gave almost everything to the lord and almost nothing to the peasant. In return for meager protection, which as times grew more settled was scarcely needed, the peasant was forced to toil all his life on the land for the benefit of the small group of feudal fighting aristocracy. As on the Continent, the English serf with his family was "tied to the soil," and his descendants inherited this bondage. He remained with the land when it changed owners, and could not be sold outside the manor. He was allowed the use of a small bit of land, to raise crops for his family, and he might keep livestock in the common pasture and cut a specified amount of firewood in the wood lot; but all this might be done only in the spare time left from his prime duty of working for the lord. With the extremely inefficient agricultural methods,—in particular the wasteful open-field system, with its scattered plots (see page 40),— the serf, even in years of good harvests, worked from dawn to sundown and was at best able to eke out only a wretched and meager existence for himself. His home was still the bare hut of the Saxon peasant, and in time of war he had to crowd into the manor house or castle for refuge. It is small wonder that landowning was such a source of wealth for the feudal aristocracy when it carried with it such an opportunity for the exploitation of the greater part of the population.

Fortunately, the Conqueror's Domesday Book, a kind of minute census compiled in 1086, enables us to reconstruct manorial conditions with much more accuracy than is possible in most other features of medieval government and society. William wanted to know whether he was getting all that he should in the way of revenue from the country; so his agents went out to every village to inquire the status of all the land and all the people, not only as they stood in that year before William's death but also as they had been on the eve of the Conquest. No other such exhaustive census was made in all Europe for centuries, before or after, since, even if other rulers might have wanted such information, they lacked the Conqueror's power and will to make everyone answer questions. The name Domesday probably came from the "dooms" of Saxon law, though some related it to the day of judgment, or "doom," from which none could escape. As one chronicler remarked, "So narrowly did he cause the survey to be made that there was not one single hide nor rood of land, nor—it is shameful to tell, but he thought it no shame to do—was there ox, cow, or swine that was not set down in the writ." Because of its wealth of detailed information the Domesday Book has been called the most valuable document in English history.

The most startling revelation of the Domesday survey was that about 84 per cent of the rural population, or more than five men out of six, were rated as unfree serfs. Of the rest, 13 per cent were freemen or small landholders. The small remainder—barely one man in thirty—composed the feudal aristocracy of great vassals and lesser vassals who were fighting men and high church officials. From that small group came the lords of the manors, who lived at the expense of the serfs. Not included in the survey were some of the few townsmen and some of the lower clergy.

# The Coming of the Normans

The principal source of revenue for the lord of the manor was the *manorial demesne*. Just as in the political feudal system, where the lord kept out certain demesne manors for his own support before dividing the rest among his vassals as fiefs, so the lord of the manor kept a generous share, often half, of the arable and meadow land when the rest was divided among the freemen and the serfs. Sometimes this was a separate tract, set off by itself; more often it consisted of a portion of the scattered strips in the open fields. Everything produced on that manorial demesne went to the lord, who managed it through his bailiff. Occasionally he might pay for a little of the work, but most of the cultivation came from the required labor of the serfs. The heaviest burden was *week work*, whereby the serf had to spend a certain number of days each week, usually three, working on the lord's land. In emergencies, such as threatening storms or harvest time, the serf must also do extra *boon work*, tending the lord's crop first, even though it might mean the ruin of his own crop and starvation for his family. In addition, the serf had to make still further payments from the produce of his remaining time, which was spent on the portion of land allowed him for his own crops. Extra gifts of chickens or eggs were often required on special occasions, such as Christmas or Easter. The serf, moreover, was mulcted by the manorial *monopolies*: he had to use the lord's mill, oven, bridges, and the like, and to pay a fee each time. When the serf died, his heir had to give the best ox or some other valuable gift as a *heriot*, corresponding to the "relief" in upper feudal circles.

Not only did the serf have to work and pay in these various specified ways, but he had no freedom of action. He and his family could not leave the manor for even a brief time without the lord's permission. That was seldom granted because, since the lord received more than half of the results of the serf's labor, any time a serf was away from the manor the lord suffered a financial loss. The serfs were not allowed to go away to fight. If a serf wanted to marry his daughter to someone on another manor or to send his son to school, he had to pay compensation for the services the lord would lose. A serf had no rights under the law or government outside the manor; for justice he was dependent upon the manor court, under the control of the lord's steward. A runaway serf—such escape was difficult—became automatically free if he reached a town and avoided capture for a year and a day.

Even among the serfs there were varying degrees. The ordinary "villein," the most numerous category, held fifteen to thirty acres and was better off than the "cottar," who had very little land and somewhat different duties. At the time of Domesday Book there were still some bondsmen, or landless laborers, a relic of the Saxon slaves; but they gradually merged with the mass of serfs.

The freemen, whom the Saxons had called ceorls and later centuries were to know as yeomen, stood midway between the feudal aristocracy and the serfs. They were not aristocrats, who enjoyed the prestige and power of feudal vassals; but they differed from the unfree serfs, not only in their landholding but even more conspicuously in their political, legal, and military status. The freemen held their land from the lord of the manor, but they generally gave him rent instead of servile labor. They might have three or four times as much land as the ordinary serf, and sometimes they hired laborers to assist them. Unlike the serfs, they could move to another manor if they saw fit, and without the lord's permission could marry their daughters outside the manor or send their sons to study for the clergy. They could take part in the activity of the hundred and shire courts; later they could carry their grievances to the royal courts and serve as jurors, vote for members of Parliament, and sometimes even sit in the House of Commons. They were eligible and liable for military service in the fyrd. While the feudal aristocracy alone could afford the expensive cavalry equipment, the freemen formed a tough infantry. Three centuries later the longbows of those yeomen would vanquish whole French armies.

A typical manor was Crawley, five miles from the old Wessex capital at Winchester, to whose bishop it had been given early in the Saxon period. The financial accounts of the church were carefully kept and preserved, and from them two scholars, by diligent research, have reconstructed the detailed workings of the village from Alfred's day to modern times. Situated among the undulating hills which made up the manor was the village, "a short winding street of houses and outbuildings running up the hill from the pond to the church." Population remained fairly stationary down through the centuries—about fifty households, or some three hundred souls in all. At the time of the Domesday survey there were no freemen; only six of the heads of households were even ordinary villeins; twenty-five were cottars, and twenty were slaves. Before long, however, all were merged into the general status of serfs. Scarcely a quarter of the manor's thirty-six hundred acres were used for crops; the "home farm," or lord's manorial demesne, comprised about half of that arable land. The soil was chalky, and water was scarce, so that sheep-raising was a particular source of profit. A century and a half after the Conquest each serf had an average of twenty-five sheep, two head of cattle, and ten swine, while half of them owned a horse apiece. In addition to some twelve hundred and fifty sheep owned by the peasants, the lord kept nearly two thousand. Crawley was simply one of the dozens of manors owned by the bishop of Winchester and administered through his seneschal and bailiffs. The bishop's annual income from Crawley during the thirteenth century averaged about £75, ranging from £29 in the poorest year to £130 in the best. A serf, we might deduce from that, was worth about thirty shillings a year to his master.

Turning to the machinery of government, we find that the coming of the Normans introduced new features which were to be developed further by later rulers. Four great English kings of the Middle Ages each made an important contribution to the nation's constitutional development. The feudal system was the particular innovation of the Conqueror. Later, as we shall see, Henry I (1100–1135) built up the machinery of strong central government; Henry II (1154–1189) developed royal courts and the system of common law; and Edward I (1272–1307) further improved the laws and started Parliament on a regular basis.

Although it remained for his son Henry I to perfect the machinery of central government, the Conqueror himself quickly established definite authority over his new realm. Edward the Confessor and numerous other Saxon rulers had been kings in little more than name; for the real power was scattered among the earls (see page 43). After 1066 authority in England lay unquestionably wherever William happened to be. Orders given in his name were treated with respect, because men feared the penalty for disobedience. In his Great Council of nobles and prelates he preserved the functions of the Saxon witan (see page 83). Two of his particular devices for making his authority effective were the Domesday survey, which has already been mentioned, and the sheriff.

Into each county, or shire,—except the border regions, with their special government,—William sent a sheriff to administer government in his name. This official took his name from the old Saxon shire reeve, and some of his functions from the Norman vicomte; but he was, for a century at least, more powerful than any previous district officer. He was endowed with great authority in the administration of law, the collection of taxes, and the raising of armed forces. William thus broke the old local power of the earls, who became little more than figureheads in the shire administration. He preferred to rely upon these new men, who were dependent upon him for favor.

While the Conqueror was strengthening the central power, he left relatively untouched the old machinery of local government (see page 43). Most of the earldoms were broken up; but the Saxon courts of shire and hundred were allowed to continue, as far as the king was concerned. The country had become so thoroughly feudalized, however, that the manorial courts of the barons absorbed most of the local cases and frequently threatened the hundreds. The shire courts, bolstered by the royal authority of the sheriff, had vitality enough to resist most of this feudalizing influence. About a century after the Conquest, as we shall see, the shire courts became partly merged with the new royal courts as a curb upon the barons.

In addition to introducing feudalism and making changes in government, the Conquest also brought new developments to England's century-old relations with the Church. The council of Whitby in 664, we recall, had been of value to England because it joined that remote island to the all-inclusive international system of the Roman Church (see page 22). The Conquest now made those bonds even closer. The somnolent Anglo-Saxon Church received valuable cultural and disciplinary stimulus from this contact, but at the same time the new relationship led to political friction.

The Roman Church, through the sorry centuries of the Dark Ages, had performed an invaluable service in giving Europe a powerful example of unity in a period of general chaos. In the absence of effective political government it had taken over many of the functions of a state, with its regular hierarchy of officials, its courts, its financial system, and its diplomatic corps. By the time of the Conquest, however, this situation was changing. Stronger rulers emerging in France and central Europe, as well as in England, resented what they considered papal interference in their own secular functions. For more than two centuries Europe was to see a series of disputes, sometimes very violent, between Popes and kings. In England the three chief sources of this friction were the power to appoint bishops and abbots, the jurisdiction of courts, and taxation.

One of the strongest men in the whole history of the papacy held sway in Rome during the reign of the Conqueror. Even before he became Pope as Gregory VII in 1073, Hildebrand was for many years the real power in the Holy City. He had been educated in the monastery of Cluny, which had been started to check the general demoralization of the unregulated Benedictine monasteries. This helps to account for the zeal with which he set out to reform not only the monasteries but also the morals, learning, and general tone of the clergy. Gregory was particularly vigorous in his attacks upon the appointment of prelates by political rulers (see page 88). Gregory, moreover, in his *Dictatus* proclaimed that the Pope was

# The Coming of the Normans

superior to any political ruler and that his word was law throughout Christendom.

There have been frequent speculations upon what would happen if an irresistible force should meet an immovable object. The relations between Gregory and William somewhat resembled that situation. The Pope's doctrine of universal power naturally ran counter to William's determination to be supreme authority in England. Both were strong and clever men. Gregory, with his hands full in the Holy Roman Empire, where he was involved in a long and bitter struggle with the emperor over the appointment of prelates, was not eager to engage in a second major fight over this problem. William owed Gregory a debt of gratitude for his support of the Conquest. The result was a compromise. William kept the appointing power in his own hands; but he selected first-rate men to replace the Saxon prelates, who lost their bishoprics and abbeys one by one. He heartily co-operated with Gregory in his efforts to reform the tone of the clergy, but he flatly stated that no papal decree had validity in England without the king's consent. William also helped to take the Church out of politics by removing the bishop from the shire court, where he had sat with the earl and the sheriff. Separate church courts were established to handle ecclesiastical matters. We shall see that within a century these courts were to add their share to the friction between Church and State.

In these church relations William had the able co-operation of the noted Italian scholar Lanfranc, whom he made Archbishop of Canterbury in place of the Saxon, Stigand. Lanfranc had been prior of the Norman abbey of Bec, one of the leading intellectual centers of Christendom. Even before the Conquest he had become William's intimate and able adviser in intricate problems of State and Church. The prior had never degenerated into a "yes man," and on one occasion had so strongly opposed the Duke of Normandy that he was ordered into exile. A lame horse was the best that the monastery could afford for the journey. Overtaken by the angry William, who was impatient at the slow departure, Lanfranc retorted, "Give me a better horse and I shall go quicker." This so amused William that the breach was healed. As Archbishop of Canterbury, Lanfranc worked hand in glove with his king and deserved much credit for the marked improvement in the quality of the Church in England. The bitter conflicts between English kings and Roman Popes still lay in the future.

A fourth important result of the coming of the Normans was the introduction of a new language. The Vikings who had settled on the lower Seine, having profited during their century and a half by contact with the Latinized civilization of that region, came to England speaking their local variety of French. For the next three centuries three different languages were heard in England. The churchmen, the scholars, and sometimes the lawyers used the international language, Latin. English remained the tongue of the bulk of the population; for we must remember that there were perhaps a million native English (Anglo-Saxons) and only a few thousand Normans. The new Norman French was the polite tongue of the royal court and of the dominant feudal minority. Even today, when the royal assent is given to a bill passed by Parliament, one hears the Norman phrase "Le Roy le veult." By the middle of the fourteenth century we shall see that the old English and the Norman French had become blended into a new common English language which could be understood both by the lord of the manor and by the peasant in his fields. Our language today shows traces of both. A farmhand normally uses a larger proportion of old English words than a lawyer, since, on the whole, the simpler, more homely words persisted most strongly among the masses engaged in humble occupations. The French or Latin influence is seen in the words for abstract ideas, the niceties and refinements of life, and in political, military, legal, religious, and artistic fields where the Norman aristocracy was active. As Scott pointed out in *Ivanhoe*, the words for the common domestic animals—cow, calf, sheep, and pig—are Germanic, whereas the meat from those same animals—beef, veal, mutton, and pork—bears French names. The English tended the animals; but the choice roasts found their way to the high table of the manor house.

With their new language the Normans also brought a Continental culture more advanced than that which they found in England. The Confessor's realm had contained nothing which could rival the intellectual activity of the Norman monastery of Bec, whence Lanfranc and other able scholars came to fill church positions. No particular literature of importance was produced in England in the early Norman period. French and Latin, rather than English, were generally used by such few writers as there were. The creative side of Norman culture was to find more prominent expression in the architecture of cathedrals and abbeys (see page 140). The Conquest itself left a unique artistic record in the so-called Bayeux Tapestry, woven possibly under the direction of William's queen, and giving a graphic picture of the stirring events of 1066.

Finally, as a fifth and somewhat less definite consequence of the Conquest, the Normans linked England more closely to the Continent. For many years after the Conquest, barons and churchmen often held lands on both sides of the Channel, and there was constant passing

# The Coming of the Normans

and repassing between England and France. Among the more important results of this stimulus was the beginning of the rise of towns devoted to industry and commerce (see page 130). England was thus brought into contact with the main currents of the day and saved from the stagnant isolation which threatened Scandinavia.

The transition to Norman domination was probably not a happy one for most of the Anglo-Saxons. The earls, thanes, and prelates who were pushed out of their high positions to make room for Normans had particular cause for bitterness. So too did those formerly free peasants who were submerged in serfdom. For the bulk of the peasantry it simply meant the changing of one set of masters for another. We cannot believe that all the Normans were as cruel as Abbot Thurstan, who had his archers shoot down the monks because they refused to sing the new Norman chants, or Robert of Bellême, the able but devilish earl of Shrewsbury, who refused to ransom his prisoners because he preferred to torture them, and who, according to the chronicler, agreed to act as godfather at the baptism of a vassal's infant and then, because the baby cried while he held it in his arms, gouged out the child's eyes (see page 90). These were extreme cases, but it is likely that the average Norman was harder and harsher than his Saxon predecessor. Rough discipline was the price England had to pay for the new efficiency and for the benefits which were to become more obvious as centuries passed.

Altogether, the Norman Conquest did not have the thoroughgoing consequences of the coming of the Saxons six centuries earlier; but it had more permanent influence on later England than had the invasions of the Celts, Romans, or Danes. The Angles, Saxons, and Jutes had pushed aside most of the earlier population and had taken the whole country for themselves. Their descendants were to form the bulk of England's future population, and their speech and customs were to have a lasting importance. The Normans were too few to replace the English, as the English had replaced the Celts; but the Conqueror and his followers had an influence out of all proportion to their numbers. They shook England out of her lethargy and bound that remote island more closely to the Continent; they introduced new elements of language and culture; and, above all, they provided such an efficient, centralized government, based on feudalism, that we can trace the country's constitutional development in orderly fashion from 1066. Hastings marked the last successful hostile invasion of England, and the last wholesale introduction of alien blood and customs. The country finally contained the various major elements which were to make up its distinctive and highly satisfactory blend.

# CHAPTER IV

## *Centralization and Disruption*

### 1087-1154

THE Conqueror died as he had lived—in action. In the summer of 1087 he led from Normandy one of his perennial border raids into the lands of the French king, who had taunted him about his fatness. His horse stumbled in the street of a burning frontier town, and the high iron pommel of the saddle cut deep into its royal rider's stomach. Three weeks later William died at Rouen. His body, stripped by thieving servants while yet warm, was left lying around for days; for everyone had ridden off to protect his own interests in the emergency. A nation has good cause for alarm when a powerful dictator dies. For twenty-one years William's iron will had directed the Normanization of England. The turbulent baronage now saw a chance to strike for liberty, and chaos would have followed had not the Conqueror's deathbed wisdom robbed them of their opportunity and paved the way for nearly a half century more of powerful royal rule.

William's last instructions had been that his second son hurry to England to be crowned by Lanfranc, while the eldest son, Robert, "Curthose," simply became duke of Normandy. Even at that time it was customary for the first-born to succeed his father; but William knew his sons. He had suppressed all three as though they were perpetual children, but he realized that the eldest was not the man to be king of England. Although Robert was brave and superficially chivalrous, he was, at the same time, weak and futile. Because of this he twice missed a chance at the English throne; he even lost Normandy; and he ended his life in imprisonment. Such a man was the natural choice of the self-seeking English barons, but for that very reason his father passed him by. Henry, the third son, wily and somewhat of a scholar, received only a grant of money at his father's death; but later chroniclers maintain that William accompanied the bequest with the cheering prophecy that some day he would win all his father's lands. We shall hear more of him as Henry I.

In the meantime the English crown went to the hard-headed second son, William (1087-1100), usually called Rufus because of the beefy redness of his face. Little that is good can be said of this second William beyond his unquestioned strength, and the fact that, like some of England's other bad kings, he did something for architecture, namely, Westminster Hall. He was fat, with a sneering expression and a noticeable stammer. Evil in character and ugly in temper, with no sense of justice, he had, according to his kindest biographer, already sunk so low in vice at twenty-seven that there was no hope for betterment. It was also said of him that every morning he got up a worse man than he had lain down, and every evening he lay down a worse man than he had got up. The country folk were said to flee to the woods at the approach of this vicious king and his boon companions. Yet if they feared him, so too did the barons. Men said that he wanted to be the heir of every landholder in England, and his extortions would seem to prove this true. He was, withal, a good fighter and a strong ruler, who brooked no interference with the law and kept the nobles in order. England at that moment needed that strength more than she needed nobility of character. Without so strong a king the work of the Conquest might have been undone.

The barons lost no time in trying the mettle of their new ruler. They wanted Robert, with his inability to say No; and, as many of them held fiefs in both England and Normandy, they disliked the idea of two separate suzerains. So they soon revolted under the Conqueror's half brother Odo, bishop of Bayeux and earl of Kent, a man who had swung a lusty mace at Hastings—and only a mace, because a churchman was forbidden to shed blood. Rufus cannily appealed to the Saxon common people against these Norman barons, with all manner of promises for better laws, and, as the chronicle says, "set forth to them his need and prayed their help and promised them the best laws that ever were in this land and that he would forbid all unjust taxation and give them back their woods and hunting." Most of the barons seem to have joined the revolt; but most of the churchmen sided with the English townspeople and peasantry. The uprising failed; and so did a second one, seven years later.

The fine promises made by Rufus in the face of mutiny were not kept. They might have been had Lanfranc lived, but the good old Archbishop of Canterbury died too soon. Rufus left the position vacant for four years, that he might pocket its rich income. He chose as his chief adviser his low-born, unscrupulous, and ingratiating boon companion, Ranulf Flambard, bishop of Durham. This Flambard, the "Fiery Torch," seems to have licked up everything. Justice in the courts depended upon the size of the pocket-book; agriculture was burdened by a species of general land tax; and, as the most lucrative and conspicuous example of irregular revenue, bishoprics and abbacies were left vacant, as Lanfranc's had been, that the king might use their revenue. We are not certain as to the details of Flambard's extortions; possibly they were not much different from the financial control which Henry II exercised later without arousing the same ire.

Rufus, in a fit of remorse on his sickbed, finally appointed an Archbishop of Canterbury. For the second time an Italian abbot of Bec was chosen to head the English Church. Lanfranc's successor was the gentle, unworldly Anselm, sixty years old and perhaps the foremost scholar of his day. He was so reluctant to become archbishop and so loath to leave the contemplative life that he had to be dragged to the king's bedside, where the staff of office was forced into his clenched hand. Once in office, however, Anselm defended his prerogatives with vigor. Lanfranc had been willing to regard the English Church as a branch of the Norman monarchy under the king, but not so Anselm. He considered the English Church as merely a part of the international religious system, and he believed his allegiance due not to the king but to the Pope. Both to Rufus and to his brother Henry, Anselm proved a stumbling block whenever they tried to interfere with his strict version of the rights of the Church. He had a series of squabbles with Rufus, who, as soon as he found out he was not dying, regretted the appointment. In 1097 Anselm finally left England and went to Rome, to lay his case before the Pope. He remained in Italy until after the death of Rufus, who had once more seized the rich Canterbury lands. The appointment of Anselm marked the beginning of the long-standing friction between Crown and Church in England—a friction which eventually led to a complete break from Rome.

England had almost no part in the tremendous wave of religious-military enthusiasm which sent thousands of Europeans to the Holy Land in the First Crusade in 1096; nevertheless Rufus profited from it (see page 115). The Crusade was primarily a French enterprise, and the French were so prominent in it that Europeans for centuries afterward were called "Franks" in the Near East. There were many Normans, some from Sicily and some from Normandy itself, including the romantic, impractical Robert. He had already sold part of his duchy to his younger brother Henry, and had lost a part to Rufus. Now, in order to raise funds for the Crusade, he pawned the remainder to Rufus, and finally returned penniless. There were times, it is said, that Robert had even to stay indoors for want of clothes. Rufus and the Norman barons

# Centralization and Disruption

in England, however, remained at home, distrustful of one another and fearing what might happen during so long an absence. It was not until the Third Crusade, a century later, that England played a conspicuous role under its absentee king, Richard the Lion-Hearted.

Not content with securing control of Normandy, Rufus made further attempts to extend his lands and influence. He launched border raids against Wales and Scotland, and was on the point of seeking further lands in France when an arrow laid him low in 1100. He had been shot by one of his companions on a hunting party in the New Forest, perhaps accidentally.

Two days later, before half of England had learned of Rufus's death, Henry, the Conqueror's third son, was crowned king. He had rushed to seize the royal treasury at Winchester, and his speedy action left no chance to look too closely into his claims. For the second time Robert missed his opportunity to become king of England. He had long since received homage and fealty as heir of Rufus, while as a Crusader his interests were supposedly safe-guarded. Henry, however, was at hand, and that was what counted.

Although Henry I (1100–1135) was one of England's best kings, his work, like that of his grandson, Henry II, was solid rather than of the spectacular sort which leaves a popular reputation. Clearheaded, self-controlled, and painstaking, he was at his best in all that concerned orderly, effective administration. Fattish, like most of his family, black-haired, and rather short, he was prudent, slow, obstinate, and parsimonious. His nickname, "Beauclerc," im-plies he could probably read and write more than most contem-porary rulers. Some say that he had a naturally pleasant disposition, but others say that a man had cause to worry when Henry smiled at him. Now and then traces of the family cruelty might crop out, and once with a taunting remark he pushed a Norman rebel to his death from a high tower. Henry was a good general, but a better diplomat; he avoided fighting whenever this was possible. The machinery of government interested him more than anything else, and good work in the daily business of law or administration was a sure way to his favor. With all his more prosaic qualities, Henry continued the family tradition by ruling with such a strong hand that the chronicler could write, "He made peace for man and beast." He granted a few concessions at the outset, to conciliate his brother's outraged subjects; but at no time did Henry show himself at all weak, nor did he really lessen the crown's central control. The nation might groan under his heavy taxes and savage penalties, but it knew that, unlike his brother Rufus, he usually played fair. The fact that an offender was a great baron did not save him from the same harsh treatment dealt out to lesser men. Henry had not been long on the throne before he was hailed as the "Lion of Justice" whom Merlin, the seer, had predicted.

The king, in his early conciliatory acts, aimed to please all kinds of people: the nobles by the issuance of a Charter of Liberties and the arrest of the rapacious Flambard; the churchmen by recalling Anselm to England and by filling vacant church offices promptly, instead of appropriating their revenue; and the old English populace by marrying Matilda (Edith), niece of the Saxon Atheling, the nearest blood kin of the Wessex line. The Norman nobles might sneer at this Queen "Godiva"; but to the popular mind the marriage fulfilled an old prophecy that England's troubles would end when the green tree (Saxon line), cut from its root and removed for the space of three acres, should be rejoined and bring forth fruit. Anyway, ever since this marriage, all occupants of the English throne have had the blood of both Alfred and the Conqueror in their veins.

The most significant of these conciliatory acts was the Charter of Liberties in which Henry promised to abstain from the worst abuses of Rufus,—the first legal limitation of the virtually absolute royal power established by the Conqueror. The gradual reduction of the king's authority, a process which lasted six centuries, has been the main thread of English constitutional history, which is just the reverse of French history, where the story centers around the gradual increase of royal control. Henry and his immediate successors frequently repeated similar promises. These formed the backbone of the terms which the barons forced upon Henry's great-grandson in the famous Magna Carta, a century later. The process was to go on, through the Petition of Right and the Bill of Rights, until eventually the king had become little more than a figurehead. Henry gave the promises voluntarily, and then did not keep them all; but they are worth remembering, because Englishmen came to look upon them as part of their rights and to feel that there were certain limits beyond which even the king might not go. In this first charter Henry agreed that the king should no longer profit by allowing high church offices to remain vacant; that abnormal exactions in relief and wardship should cease; and that various other sharp practices in connection with the feudal relationship should be modified. Actually, this Charter of Liberties was a strictly feudal document, aimed to secure the support of the powerful barons and churchmen because Henry's claim to the throne was rather shaky. To win more popular support as well, however, Henry urged these lords to treat their subordinates as he promised to treat them.

# Centralization and Disruption

The thirty-five years of his reign left England with an efficient central government. We often think of central government today in connection with structures of stone and mortar, concentrated in a definite capital city, with a palace or White House, halls of Parliament or Congress, and office buildings full of busy bureaucrats. In Norman times, however, the central government was simply a little group of men transacting business wherever they happened to be, as they traveled, often on horseback, around the king's lands in England and France. The Conqueror had gathered the central power into his own hands, but even he needed ministers to conduct his government efficiently. Henry's orderly mind gave definite administrative functions to the men who were closest to the king. In analyzing constitutional development it should be recalled once more that it is difficult, if not impossible, to state definitely when certain institutions first began or what their exact functions were. Scholars are still advancing conflicting theories based on conjectures from meager evidence.

There was no efficiency in that unwieldy body of "advisers" which the Anglo-Saxons had called the witan; which the Normans continued, somewhat feudalized, as the Great Council; and which still exists as the House of Lords. This was only an occasional assembling of the powerful nobles and churchmen to give the king advice, to assent to his decrees, and to choose his successor. Under a weak king such an assemblage of notables might virtually carry on the government; but with men as strong as the first three Norman rulers it was scarcely more than a rubber stamp. One of the duties of a feudal vassal was attendance at the lord's court; so William I, as supreme feudal lord, had summoned his tenants in chief to gather with him three times a year: at Easter in Winchester, the old Wessex capital; at Pentecost in Westminster, now part of London; and at Christmas in Gloucester, in the southwest. He had wanted to keep his eye on restless vassals, who generally regarded attendance as a burden rather than as a privilege. Such a body was too large and too temporary to be of service in managing affairs of state. After the barons and prelates rode home from the periodic meetings of the Great Council, someone had to remain with the king to handle the multitude of details involved in governing a kingdom.

The answer to that problem was the "Curia Regis," or King's Court. This name sometimes had been applied to the Great Council, but from now on it will be used to denote the "permanent standing committee" of the larger body. This smaller group, which took definite form during the reign, remained with the king after the others dispersed. Its functions made it the direct ancestor of three very important parts of the present government. As a little group of intimate advisers to the king the Curia Regis was the forerunner of the Privy Council and the present Cabinet. As a supreme court of justice it was the nucleus out of which grew the principal law courts. Finally, as the "Exchequer" it commenced a formal and regular financial administration which has continued under that name to the present.

With the formation of the Curia Regis came the introduction of three powerful officials as its leaders. The earlier kings, both in England and on the Continent, usually had delegated ministerial duties to "household officials" such as the butler, seneschal, constable, and marshal. Some of these officials continued as members of the Curia Regis; but they were overshadowed in administrative power by three new dignitaries.

Foremost among them was the justiciar, who was chief minister while the king was in the country, and who wielded full authority as viceroy, or regent, when the king was in Normandy or elsewhere. The first to hold this office was Roger, bishop of Salisbury, who had attracted Henry's attention by the speed with which he could rattle through the Mass when the king was impatient to go hunting. He held this position through most of Henry's reign and into the next, and shared with the king credit for the efficient organization of the Curia Regis. For more than a century the justiciar was the most influential government official, but by 1300 the office had been abolished. Next to the justiciar in importance came the chancellor, who was keeper of the great seal and who had charge of all secretarial work, such as the issuing of charters and the conducting of correspondence, both domestic and foreign. Chancellors there had been before, so far as the name went; but now the office became important. Before long the chancellor will be found presiding over a "Chancery Court," which developed a peculiar type of legal jurisdiction that we shall consider later (see page 107). With the disappearance of the office of justiciar the chancellor became for several centuries the chief minister. Even today he holds a position of great dignity and presides over the House of Lords. The third of the new officers was the treasurer, whose functions and importance are obvious from the title. His duties today are performed by the Chancellor of the Exchequer.

These officials and some of the other members of the Curia Regis might meet one month as the "Exchequer," to handle financial matters, and the next month as the supreme court of law. And in the meantime they might serve their third purpose of advising the king on matters of policy. Some of their subordinates might be

# Centralization and Disruption

specialists in financial matters, while others were particularly trained in law. The officials of the Curia Regis were recruited not so much from the headstrong, hot-headed great barons as from that other type of Norman, the shrewd, legalistic, hard-headed kind, to be found among the lesser barons or the clergy.

It was as a financial body that the Curia Regis derived special importance under Henry I. Its members were known as the "Exchequer" when they met to verify the revenue. The name came from the checkered cloth on the table upon which they received the payments from the sheriffs. Calculation of large numbers was a difficult process without the advantage of arabic figures and a decimal system, both unknown to medieval England; so the checkered cloth served the same purpose as the abacus still used by Chinese laundrymen. Each sheriff reported twice a year, bringing with him the money collected from the income of royal estates, court fines, and other sources of revenue. The lower Exchequer officials moved their chips or counters around the squares, verified the total, and cut notches on a stick, which was then split in two, half being given to the sheriff as a receipt. The amounts were also recorded on long sheets of parchment, which were finally rolled up to be saved for future reference. The earliest of these so-called "pipe rolls" which is still preserved dates back to 1130. The Curia Regis, when it met for Exchequer purposes, verified these accounts of the sheriffs and settled disputed cases. This introduction of system into the royal accounting enabled the king to see to it that the sheriffs were collecting and turning in all that they should, and it also made it possible for him to ascertain at a glance the amount of most of his income.

That lone "pipe roll" of Henry I reveals the source of the ten tons of silver collected in 1130 as royal revenue. It accounts for some £25,000, and the few missing counties would bring the total to about £27,000. One tenth of this came from the Danegeld, which was the only equivalent of a regular modern tax, collected on a broad, uniform basis. The remainder came from the king's relation to the feudal and manorial systems as chief feudal lord of England, as though the nation were his private estate. In times of peace the king was expected to "live of his own" from the revenue of the demesne which he controlled directly and from the fiefs allotted to vassals. Under the heading "crown lands and rights" about £11,000 was collected from the demesne manors and towns. This amount could be depended upon regularly; for the sheriff had to turn in the same stipulated amount, or "farm," each year. If he collected somewhat in addition, that was his affair. The almost equal amount derived from the various payments in connection with fiefs was less dependable, since the lucrative dues from relief, escheat, wardship, and marriage were contingent upon the death of vassals. A year when barons and bishops enjoyed uniform good health thus meant a decline in the royal revenue. One of the heaviest individual contributors in 1130 was the widowed Countess of Chester, who paid a relief of £166 for the inheritance of her father's lands, and who also offered £333 that she might not be obliged to marry again within five years. A lesser vassal paid £6 13s. 6d. to be allowed to marry at will. Despite his promise in the Charter of Liberties, Henry collected, as a sort of wardship, £935 from the vacant bishopric of Durham.

The pipe roll reveals some additional sources of revenue which throw little credit on the "Lion of Justice." In addition to the usual fines from the regular and forest courts, Henry accepted bribes to influence court judgments. In a case where a Norman was being sued for a debt by three Jews, the king was offered £133 by the former and got £24 cash down from the latter. We do not know who won the case, but it was understood that the loser's bribe would be returned. The Jewish moneylenders, who began coming to England in the Conqueror's wake, and whose usurious interest rates sometimes reached 86 per cent a year, were called the "king's sponges" because they were tolerated by Henry at the price of frequent heavy fines on trivial pretexts. They had a monopoly of moneylending in the early Middle Ages because the Church forbade Christians to lend money at interest. The Jews of London, in the same year of this pipe roll, were, for instance, fined £2000 because a sick man was said to have died at the hands of a Jewish doctor. Gradually, as we shall see, regular taxes were to replace these feudal and haphazard sources of royal revenue.

The total revenue looks small to us when we think of the pound sterling at its present value. It was then far more than this, because it was literally a pound of silver, the twelve-ounce Troy pound. The only coin in regular circulation was the silver penny, about the size of a very thin dime or sixpence. Twelve pence, as today, were reckoned as a shilling, and two hundred and forty as a pound sterling. The little penny had impressive buying power. For it one could get about four pounds of meat, or six pounds of wheat, or one could hire an ordinary foot soldier for a day. A farm laborer would work all day for twopence, and a fully armed knight's hire was only eightpence a day. A good penny would do all that; but there were too many bad pennies in circulation in Henry's day. It was not until about 1350 that the kings began officially to debase the currency

# Centralization and Disruption

by making the pennies smaller or by increasing the normal one-twelfth-copper alloy. Others, however, were making bad pennies in the time of Henry I. Sometimes this was done by the "moneyers," licensed by the king for a heavy fee to coin official money in some fifty different towns. They might debase the currency by striking more than two hundred and forty pennies from a pound of silver, either by making the coins lighter or by putting in more copper alloy than the legal one-twelfth necessary for toughness. Then, too, the general public did their part by clipping a little silver from the edges of the pennies which passed through their hands or by actual counterfeiting. Finally the situation became so bad, according to the chroniclers, that anyone going to market with a whole pound of pennies could find scarcely twelve acceptable to the merchants. News of this reached Henry in Normandy. It troubled him, for bad coins meant a loss of revenue. He had all the moneyers gathered at Winchester, where each had his right hand amputated in addition to other serious mutilation. Thus Henry upheld the important principle of a sound currency.

In its legal capacity the Curia Regis of Henry I probably took the first steps toward many of the very important reforms which will be considered in detail under Henry II. Historians now feel that the latter owed to his grandfather more than was formerly supposed in the matter of legal reform, but we can be certain of only one of the elder Henry's contributions. This was the introduction of "itinerant justices." The Curia Regis accompanied the king on his travels; and, as it did so, Henry from time to time sent justices out from that body into the counties to inspect the local administration. The justices thus acted a role similar to that of the "King's Eyes and Ears" of the old Persians or of the *missi dominici* of Charlemagne. Probably at first they went primarily on financial business; but, while they were attending the shire courts, they might at times have sat as justices in royal cases. Henry II, as we shall see, established regular circuits for these itinerant justices, and the practice is still followed in England and in the United States.

While perfecting the machinery of his own government, the king ran afoul of that still more extensive organization, the Church. At the very outset there were good prospects for friendly co-operation between Church and State. Henry recalled Anselm and quickly filled a rich vacant bishopric. Anselm aided the king by approving the legality of his marriage, which had been threatened by the charge that Matilda was a nun. The queen, with tears streaming down her face, insisted that she had been forced to wear the veil as a girl by her aunt, an abbess, as a protection in dangerous times, but that whenever she was alone she had angrily pulled it off. Anselm agreed to sanctify the marriage; but on another matter he was adamant.

The investiture problem, like that of taxing church property and of lay versus clerical courts, was one of the chief bones of contention between the Popes and the medieval rulers in England as well as on the Continent. It centered around the question as to whether the Church or the ruler should appoint the prelates and "invest" them with the insignia of office. This selection of bishops and abbots was supposed to lie in the hands of the clergy of the diocese or the monks of the abbey, but ordinarily someone important behind the scenes, such as the Pope or ruler, dictated the choice. Thus, although the word "investiture" referred to the initiation *ceremony*, the real quarrel hinged about the *choice* of the prelates, since the ceremony was of importance only because it implied the right of selection. It was natural that churchmen should feel that it was wrong for a layman, and often a most worldly and ungodly one, to select a man for a spiritual position, and to go through with the traditional elaborate ceremony, which included the bestowing of the pallium, the ring, and the crozier—a ceremony purely religious. The churchmen also considered it wrong that bishoprics and abbacies should be bestowed as political plums to party henchmen. At the same time, the Church had become so deeply enmeshed in the feudal system through gifts of extensive fiefs that a prominent bishop or abbot controlled more land, owed more military service, and enjoyed more income and influence than many feudal lords. In the eyes of the kings the bishops and abbots were in much the same position as earls and counts; for the rich landholdings of the Church carried with them both the powers and the duties of feudal lords and vassals. Many of the highest officials of the Curia Regis were bishops, partly because churchmen alone had the requisite education, and partly because a rich bishopric was an easy way to pay a valuable man without expense to the royal treasury. It is easy to appreciate the strength of both points of view; and it was only natural that they should clash, for the bishops and abbots actually held dual roles: that of the churchman with spiritual duties and that of the feudal lord or vassal with regulation feudal obligations to his king.

The reform movement which had just swept through the Church under the influence of Pope Gregory VII (Hildebrand) (see page 74) placed particular stress upon the evils of lay investiture. Churchmen were strictly forbidden to receive the insignia of office from lay hands. The king, however, had a powerful trump. He need

# Centralization and Disruption

not hand over the church lands, upon which the income of a bishopric or abbey depended, unless the candidate was a man of whom he approved and one who was willing to go through the ceremony of homage as the king's vassal, with all that it entailed. Anselm having made an issue of investiture, both he and the king sent missions to the Pope to present their points of view; and finally Anselm himself, with Henry's approval, once more took the road to Rome. "Know all men present," declared the king's advocate to the Pope on one occasion, "that not to save his kingdom will King Henry lose the investiture of the churches." "And before God," came the sharp reply, "not to save his head will Pope Paschal let him have them." Neither Henry nor Paschal, however, wanted a repetition of the scene twenty-odd years before at Canossa, where the investiture dispute kept the Holy Roman emperor kneeling three days in the snow humbly awaiting Pope Gregory VII's forgiveness. No one except Anselm seems to have wished to carry the matter to a final decision. Henry's hands were fully occupied with Robert's efforts to win the crown, and he did not want Anselm to seem a martyr in the public mind. He and Paschal, without making any important concessions, continued to exchange conciliatory and sometimes contradictory messages. The English bishops, when consulted about the matter, did their best to dodge the ticklish question.

Finally, in 1107, two years before Anselm's death, the opposing parties reached a compromise. The actual terms of this "Compromise of Bec" have not come down to us, but it was apparently a victory for Henry. He relinquished the *ceremony* of investing with ring and crozier; but he kept the *right* to choose the prelate and to receive his homage as a feudal vassal. The Church retained, therefore, little more than an empty ceremony. The king gained what really counted. The Church seems to have been satisfied with this slight victory, or perhaps it decided that the strength of the English monarchy made it necessary to yield. A few years afterward the bitter German investiture struggle ended in a similar compromise. Not until a century later, in the reign of John, was England to be tried by a return of the investiture problem. Another Church-Crown quarrel, however, of longer duration gave indication of starting in this reign,—one that involved the royal "squeezing" of money out of church property, usually through the fiction of demanding "free gifts." The third source of friction between Church and State, the contest for court jurisdiction, still lay a half century in the future, when another stubborn Archbishop of Canterbury carried things so far that he was murdered.

Constitutional changes and the church disputes by no means monopolized all of Henry's attention. There was plenty of fighting in England and Normandy, particularly in the early years of the reign. Henry had not been long on the throne when his luckless, irresponsible elder brother, Robert, returned from the Holy Land, where he had won renown as a Crusader. Robert fully expected to find the English throne awaiting his occupancy. He had not lost title to Normandy, which simply had been pawned as a private debt to Rufus, and the English barons backed him because they wanted an easy-going king. Finally, he was rescued from extreme poverty by the dowry of his new wife, daughter of the famous Norman-Sicilian Crusader, Robert Guiscard, and for once he had money in his pocket. In 1101 Robert invaded England. It is said that victory might have been his had not his kindly chivalry kept him from seizing Winchester, with the royal treasure, because the queen was giving birth to a child there. As it was, Henry had the support of the Saxon English, and even of Anselm. A treaty was struck by which Robert agreed to give up his immediate chances for the English crown for the bait that was ever his undoing—ready money. This time he surrendered his heritage not even for a lump sum but merely for the promise of an annual allowance, and the recognition of himself as heir presumptive. He kept Normandy for a few years more, until Henry got that away from him, too.

This affair made the barons disgruntled; for they had hoped to dislodge Henry. They persisted for a while in their sedition, under that thorn in the side of the king, Robert of Bellême, earl of Shrewsbury, a name which was a byword for cruelty (see page 77). Bellême owned sixty-odd manors in northern and central England and on the Welsh border, with thirty-odd more in Normandy. He finally was ruined, after a persistent struggle, and with him ended the power of the great vassals. The barons thereafter were less powerful as individuals, and could be strong only when united. As the chronicler Orderic Vitalis summed it up, "And so, after Robert of Bellême's flight, the kingdom of Albion was quiet in peace, and King Henry reigned prosperously three and thirty years, during which no man in England dared to rebel or hold any castle against him."

Normandy, however, furnished sufficient rebellion and fighting to keep the reign from dullness. Robert's misrule, or rather lack of rule, had created anarchy there, indicating what would have probably happened had he become king of England. Various motives drew Henry into the Norman situation. The barons with estates overseas urged him to intervene. So did the Church, which always suffered

# Centralization and Disruption

in such disorders and which, despite the Anselm dispute, Henry desired to conciliate. Finally, Henry's own lust for more lands probably made him all the more ready to interfere across the Channel.

To the popular mind the English avenged their defeat at Hastings when Henry's expeditionary force to Normandy crushed his brother's Norman army at Tinchebray, in 1106. This encounter involved more men than any English battle since Hastings and was fought just forty years later to the day. Normandy was thereby reunited with England under Henry's rule. Robert, captured in the fight, remained a prisoner until his death, despite the pleas of the Pope and of many barons. Henry maintained that it was not real imprisonment, but simply a secluded life in utmost comfort. Others gave a different story.

Tinchebray, however, did not bring general peace. The Norman barons rallied around Robert's able son, William "Clito," who was also supported by the king of France and by the adjacent little county of Anjou. But by 1120 Henry had the situation well in hand. He not only had Normandy itself but had re-established the old Norman claims of overlordship over the near-by states of Brittany and Maine. The Count of Anjou cemented an alliance by giving his eldest daughter in marriage to Henry's only son. The Pope intervened in vain. And so it happened that Henry was able to subdue his Norman barons, to block the Pope, and to conciliate the allies of France while the French king abandoned poor Clito.

Then, as everything was going well for the English monarch, came a disaster, after which, it is said, he never smiled again. Young William, his only son, was returning to England after his marriage to the Count of Anjou's daughter. He set sail, with the flower of the young nobility, on the ill-fated "White Ship." So wild was the revelry that the bride was escorted on another ship by her father-in-law. The crew was evidently as drunk as the passengers. A short way from shore the "White Ship" struck a rock and sank with practically all on board. According to the chronicles, only a Rouen butcher survived; but it was said the heir to England might have saved himself had he not tried to rescue an illegitimate half sister.

The king's grief at the loss of his son was coupled with fears for the future of his dynasty. He would still have none of the obvious successor, his nephew, William Clito. One of Henry's bastards, Robert of Gloucester, resembled his father and might have been the wisest choice; but there was prejudice against another illegitimate king in those days of church reform. Henry, long since widowed, remarried, but his wife gave him no heir. In the meantime many intrigues were on foot, with the prospects of a disputed succession.

# A History of England and the British Empire

The Count of Anjou gave his second daughter to William Clito, who had his usual bad luck; for the Pope annulled the marriage.

Matilda, Henry's daughter, was the next pawn in the king's efforts to secure the succession. She had been sent to Germany as the bride of the Holy Roman emperor, Henry V, at the age of nine. Her husband had died shortly after the "White Ship" disaster; and the Germans, it is said, were even ready to bestow upon her the unique honor, for a woman, of the crown of the Holy Roman Empire itself. Reluctantly, at her father's behest, the empress had returned to England where her father forced her to become the bride of Geoffrey, son of that Count of Anjou who had already been marrying his daughters into the Anglo-Norman line. To the shy, proud Matilda of twenty-nine, who for twenty years had occupied the highest position possible for a woman in Christendom, this marriage to a rough, boisterous youth in his middle teens must have been both repulsive and humiliating. The English and the Norman barons too were displeased at this alliance with the despised, loud-mouthed Angevins. By the time Henry I died, six years later, this ill-mated union had produced the coveted grandson; but England was to suffer a long period of anarchy before he finally reigned as Henry II.

The death of Henry I, in 1135, ended a period of nearly seventy years during which the first three Norman kings had been strong enough to consolidate the effects of the Conquest and to establish a firm central government. That system was almost wrecked in the disorders of the next nineteen years. During the anarchy that followed Henry's death, men appreciated that, if he had made heavy exactions, he had at least given something valuable in return. When the news of his death became known, according to the Anglo-Saxon Chronicle, "there was tribulation soon in the land; for every man that could forthwith robbed another." Another chronicler wrote that "no ship was ever so productive of so much misery in England" as the "White Ship"; but, from the tales we have of the evil character of the young drowned son of Henry I, England might have been no better off had he lived to succeed his father. The situation, moreover, was seriously complicated by the dispute for the crown between the "Empress" Matilda and her cousin, Stephen of Blois.

The barons had promised to recognize Matilda as her father's successor; but she was in France when Henry died, and the emergency caught her unawares. Her delay was fatal to her interests; for in those days of slow communication it meant much to get news first. Stephen, who was near the Channel, dashed over to England, where he was immediately crowned. Technically, according to the principles of succession, Matilda, as daughter of the Conqueror's son, had a stronger claim than Stephen, as son of the Conqueror's daughter, Adela, who had married the French count of Blois. But England had already seen the technical rights of the Conqueror's eldest son, Robert, set aside in favor of Rufus and then of Henry. Matilda's sex, her unpopular Angevin marriage, and her personality all told against her; so the barons transferred to Stephen their oaths, which were to prove once again short-lived and worthless. It is doubtful if either Matilda or Stephen could have kept the turbulent baronage in hand, even if there had been no disputed succession. The next nineteen years were, strictly speaking, Stephen's reign; for although Matilda was crowned by the rival faction, he never abdicated.

Stephen, who, according to legend, had slipped off the "White Ship" in port when he saw the drunkenness of the crew, was charming, generous, and chivalrous; but he lacked strength and good sense. He was perhaps the most amiable and likable of England's medieval rulers; but England was soon to learn that "the country of an affable prince" was no man's land. "When the traitors perceived that he was a mild man, and soft, and good, and did no justice, then did they all wonder," states the Anglo-Saxon Chronicle, which goes on to say of the English barons that "they were all forsworn and forfeited their troth, for every powerful man made his castles and held them against him." This illegal castle-building was a sure sign of royal weakness. The conqueror had forbidden his vassals to build castles, except on the borders as defense against the Scots and Welsh. It was not hard to stop the building of a castle; but once it was up, it was much easier to defend than to capture. Even the inflammable wooden structures on huge earthen mounds, which often passed for castles at that time, ordinarily could withstand a siege from a feudal army which melted away after its forty days of military service. So many a petty baron built his unlicensed, or "adulterine," castle, which too often served not only as a place where he could defy the royal forces but also as a lair from which he and his henchmen sallied forth to harass the countryside with robbery and torture.

The whole period (1135–1154) was complicated by an intermittent and none too clearly defined civil war between Stephen and the adherents of Matilda. Prominent among the latter were her bastard half brother, Robert of Gloucester, and her great-uncle, David, king of Scotland. The barons kept constantly shifting from side to side, and one scarcely knew how they stood from day to day. There were fights, sieges, and executions all over the country for nineteen years, since even when the barons were not supporting Matilda they were at least defying the king. The fortunes of war kept shifting. The first major engagement came in 1138, when the Scots under David invaded England. Stephen repulsed them in the so-called "Battle of the Standard," but let the fruits of victory slip through his fingers. The next year Matilda herself landed in England, and the west coast rose to her support. Stephen, in his chivalry, gave up a chance to capture her and was soon taken prisoner himself. Matilda made a triumphal entry into London, Stephen's real stronghold, and was crowned, not as queen but only as "Lady of England." She quickly overplayed her hand. Even her half brother and chief supporter remarked that "when the Empress was in such power so cruel and proud was she that men might suffer it not." Soon no one could endure Matilda's arrogance, and she had to flee. Robert of Gloucester, who had been captured and exchanged for Stephen, soon died. Matilda's fortunes went from bad to worse. Trapped and almost starved in Oxford Castle, she made a spectacular and risky night escape through the snow and left England. Her husband was too busy conquering Normandy to help her in England. For a while, until Matilda's son was old enough to be of assistance in once again turning the scales, Stephen was in the ascendancy; but he could do little to check the anarchy.

The whole nineteen years of Stephen's reign were a period of rapine, pestilence, and general misery, with the possible exception of London and the southeastern part of England, where towns continued to develop. The peasant gave up tilling his field; the townsman fled from his home. "Thou mightest go a whole day's journey," said one chronicle, "and not find a man sitting in a town nor an acre of land tilled."

Grim tales of these days have been preserved by the anonymous author of the *Acts of Stephen*. They are worth quoting, to show what actually happened to a land when law and order disappeared. A particular devil was Geoffrey of Mandeville, who dominated the fen country around Cambridge and Ely. With his "formidable host of mercenary soldiers and freebooters, who flocked to him gladly from all quarters," Geoffrey "devastated the whole country by fire and sword; driving off flocks and herds with insatiable cupidity, sparing neither age nor profession, and freely slaking his thirst for vengeance. The most exquisite cruelties he could invent were instantly executed on his enemies. The town of Cambridge, belonging to the king, was taken by surprise, when the citizens were off their guard, and, being plundered, and the doors of the churches being forced with axes, they were pillaged of their wealth, and whatever the citizens had deposited in them; and the town was set on fire."

# Centralization and Disruption

Meanwhile "all the northern counties were subjected to the tyranny of the Earl of Chester, who subjected the king's barons in the neighborhood to his yoke, surprised their castles by clandestine assaults, and wasted their lands by hostile incursions; and, breathing in his rage nothing but war and devastation, was the terror of all men. John, also, that child of hell, and root of all evil, the lord of Marlborough Castle, was indefatigable in his efforts to create disturbance." Down in the southwest the men of Bristol, "having licence for every sort of villainy," were anticipating the methods of modern gangsters. Having plundered everything available in the immediate region, "they quickly found their way into every part of England where they heard there were men of wealth and substance, and either violently laid hold on them, or got them into their power by fraud; then, bandaging their eyes and stopping their mouths, either by cramming something into them, or inserting a sharp and toothed bit, they conducted their captives, thus blinded, into the middle of Bristol, as we read of the robbers of Elisha, and there, by starvation and torture, mulcted them of their property to the last farthing."

Yet this was a period of extraordinary expansion of monasteries and religious building. It is said that more monasteries were set up in these troublous times than in any previous period of the same length. Perhaps this was because, in such times, men were the more ready to withdraw from this world to contemplate the next; perhaps it was because, in addition to the many pious persons who always contributed gifts eagerly to the Church, bad men in the Middle Ages wanted to leave big monuments for the good of their souls; perhaps it was because general misery sharply reminded men that charity and the relief of suffering were virtues which the Church had ever preached.

Especially significant was the coming to England of the Cistercian monks, with their practices and discipline so much stricter than those of the Benedictine monasteries, of which they were an offshoot. Saint Bernard of Clairvaux, leader of the Second Crusade, was one of the chief Cistercians. At this time also began the first teaching at the incipient university at Oxford. The monks began to go into trade more than ever, and the Cistercians were to make a particular success in raising and gathering wool. Altogether, the Church grew stronger; for, with the strong hand of royal power gone, the Pope interfered more, bringing the English Church more directly under the guidance of Rome.

The years of trouble finally drew to an end. Matilda's son Henry had made one attempt to challenge Stephen's rule at the age of sixteen; that failed. But three years later, in 1153, he returned to

England and was so successful that he secured the compromise known as the Treaty of Wallingford. By this, Stephen was to rule until his death, and then, since his own son was dead, Henry would be accepted as his heir. This long-delayed peace, with its provisions for the destruction of unlicensed castles and other lawless things, was scarcely needed. Stephen died within a year.

Henry II's accession, in 1154, gave England a new line of kings which was to rule until 1399. Sometimes this is called the Angevin line, because Henry was the son of the Count of Anjou; sometimes it is called Plantagenet, because the counts of Anjou had the habit of wearing a sprig of the broom plant (*planta genesta*) as a distinctive sign. Nine generations of these counts, always a Fulk or a Geoffrey, had gradually extended the frontiers of tough little Anjou, lying astride the river Loire, until it had absorbed the rich country of Touraine. The Angevin family, scorned by the Normans as uncouth and provincial, but well known for its vigor and fiery temper, now stepped into power, in the person of its ablest and most energetic member, as probably the chief family of Europe.

Henry II (1154–1189), by inheritance or by marriage, was direct ruler of more than a third of France as well as all of England (see map facing page 104). His title to Normandy, as to England, came through his mother, daughter of Henry I; but his father, Geoffrey of Anjou, had made it doubly sure by conquering Normandy himself. From his father came Anjou, including Touraine, and also the county of Maine. The latter lay as a buffer between Anjou and Normandy, and had been for a long time dominated by one or the other, until it was united to the Angevin lands by a marriage not long before. Greater in area, if not in importance, than Henry's inherited French lands was the duchy of Aquitaine, which he secured for himself by marrying Eleanor, heiress of the tenth duke. Aquitaine comprised most of southwest France and included, from north to south, the three regions of Poitou, Guienne, and Gascony. The high-spirited Eleanor came to Henry with more lands than reputation; for she had just been divorced, not without good reason, by Louis VII of France. She was thirty to Henry's nineteen; but that did not matter when one considered that the extensive region of Aquitaine was thus separated from the French royal domain and added to that of the English king. All these lands were under Henry's direct rule; he also had, like some of his predecessors, shadowy overlordship or suzerainty of the big, barren, Celtic duchy of Brittany, which jutted far out into the Atlantic. These holdings gave him more actual power in France than was enjoyed by the French king, whose authority was pretty well limited to the royal domain, about the size of Normandy, centering on the upper Seine, around Paris. The English king, of course, was vassal to the French king for his French lands; but this did not mean a great deal until the advent of the strong Philip Augustus, in the last years of Henry's reign. Englishmen take pleasure in the fact that English kings once ruled much of France; the French, however, can point out with equal truth that those kings were Frenchmen ruling England. Henry's "Angevin Empire" also extended over much of the British Isles besides England. Like some of his Norman predecessors, he proclaimed a hazy overlordship over Wales and Scotland, just as over Brittany. Even these extensive lands were not enough, and later Henry penetrated into Ireland.

A tremendous task faced the nineteen-year-old Henry in this huge "Angevin Empire." With his lands stretching from Scotland to the Pyrenees, he had the problem of reconciling different people and different ways of doing things; of long distances; jealous neighbors on all sides; a Church grown stronger with appeals to Rome during the unsettled years; an uncontrolled baronage, with its illegal castles; the bitter feelings always left by civil war; serious economic dislocation; and a total breakdown of his grandfather's administrative machinery, with consequent loss of all law and order.

So energetic and eager was Henry that he nearly wore out his court with his dashing about from one place to another. He was so completely master of his own energy, it is said, that he never felt tired night or morning. Like other Angevins, he had a horrible temper which at times almost reached insane rage. He chose priests for their celerity in getting through Mass, and he had no use for anyone who could not keep up with his speed and versatility of accomplishment. So wide a range of territory did he control that his court was cosmopolitan in nature, with men from many places. The itinerary of his movements fills one with amazement, considering the travel conditions in that day—London, Winchester, Gloucester, and York, and then Rouen in Normandy, Le Mans in Maine, Angers or Tours in Anjou, and Bordeaux in Aquitaine.

At a later time England's landholdings in France became a liability, because they distracted the attention, energy, and resources of England's rulers; but in Henry's day that was offset by the fact that, wherever he went in his travels, he noticed what was being done and what needed to be done. He constantly transplanted ideas and methods of government from one region to another. All profited by the interchange, and England was left far richer by Henry's great innovations in the law, a valuable permanent contribution. That, and much else of Henry's work, must be considered further.

# CHAPTER V

## Common Law and Crusading

### 1154-1213

NEARLY every schoolboy is acquainted with the reputations of Richard the Lion-Hearted and the wicked John; but scarcely anyone, until he studies English history, hears of their father, Henry II. Nevertheless, the importance of the second Henry to England transcends that of both these sons; for Henry, by creating an effective legal system, made one of the most valuable permanent contributions to England's development. He has been called "one of the conscious creators of England's greatness." His system of uniform law, under royal control, was so well adapted to the peculiar English needs and tastes that its fundamental features today provide law for some three hundred million people, not only in England itself but also in many lands beyond the seas where Englishmen have gone to settle or to rule. Henry II must have been working from the outset to rebuild the destroyed administrative system, although twelve years elapsed before he issued the first edict for legal reform. These reforms, to be sure, may have arisen from a selfish desire to increase the royal power and revenue; but, whatever their original purpose, they helped to make life and property more secure throughout the kingdom, both then and later.

Henry found English justice in a jumbled condition, partly because of faulty organization and partly because of the anarchy under Stephen. Too many people were striving to administer too many kinds of law. The Conqueror and his sons had kept fairly well their promises to preserve "the laws of good King Edward"; but Saxon legal practices differed widely from region to region and, even at their best, left much to be desired. Already, Norman impatience with the unscientific and too often ineffectual Saxon efforts to achieve justice had brought about some changes, as we have seen, particularly in the foundations laid by Henry I for the greater work of his grandson. Unification is essential for an effective system of law, and herein lay the chief difficulty for the necessary expansion of the royal jurisdiction. Centralization could be achieved only at the expense of three other existing systems of courts,—popular, baronial, and ecclesiastical,—a difficult task, since barons and churchmen were trying to increase the scope of their own tribunals, realizing, like the king, that legal jurisdiction meant power. He who ran the court also pocketed the fees and fines.

Before the Conquest the old Saxon moots of the hundred and shire had conducted most of the legal business; but that was gradually being whittled away by the threefold attack of barons, Church, and king. The shire, or county, court remained as a very important unit in the English legal system, but the private baronial courts had absorbed many of the hundred courts. There was a real danger that the barons might seize an even wider jurisdiction. At that day, and for centuries afterward, many of the feudal lords on the Continent, unchecked by any effective royal power, dispensed "high, low, and middle justice," dealing out penalties all the way from death sentences down to petty fines. Had Henry not overcome the anarchy of Stephen's reign, jurisdiction in England too might have been cut into small pieces.

The baronial courts represented an absence of system; the church courts, on the other hand, threatened to draw most of England's legal business into a uniform international system with its supreme judge at Rome. The Church had built up an elaborate court organization which had provided some kind of unity in the feudal anarchy of the Dark Ages. The Conqueror, in removing the bishop from the shire court, had led to the establishment of separate church tribunals. The Church's canon law, just before Henry's time, had been arranged by one Gratian into a comprehensive code which provided for a wide range of civil and criminal jurisdiction. The churchmen were not modest in their efforts to bring cases into their courts. They claimed the right to try all clerics for all offenses, and all cases as well in which sacraments or oaths were even remotely involved, such as marriage settlements, orphan guardianships, and wills. Their courts were popular, partly because they were well systematized, partly because the penalties set were frequently less harsh than those of royal courts.

Henry took the offensive against these three rival systems of the popular, baronial, and church courts. He drew legal business away from them partly by command and partly by offering a superior method for arriving at justice. Many of his most important reforms were incorporated in decrees which he announced to the assembled barons and prelates of the realm. The most far-reaching of these was the Assize of Clarendon, in 1166, an exact century after the Conquest. In twenty-two articles were outlined most of the basic features of Henry's new legal system, providing for the relation of royal judges to the county courts and the use of the jury as part of the judicial system. This assize is not to be confused with the Constitutions of Clarendon, two years earlier, which dealt with church matters. Less important were Henry's three later decrees, the Inquest of Sheriffs (1170), providing for a closer check-up of those powerful officials; the Assize of Northampton (1176), somewhat modifying the Assize of Clarendon; and the Assize of Woodstock (1184), harshly reaffirming the forest laws. Henry was much aided in establishing his legal system by two able justiciars, Richard de Lucy and, later, Ranulf Glanvill.

A most essential feature of the new reforms was the linking of the royal justices with the old shire courts. The king's grandfather occasionally had sent justices from the Curia Regis out into the counties on financial or legal business. Henry II, by the Assize of Clarendon, made this a regular practice. The shire, or county, court was to meet in its old form, at regular short intervals, for ordinary business (see page 45); but when the king's justices came around to hold their sessions, the king required a full attendance, including not only the barons and clergy of the county but also representatives of all the hundreds and lesser units. This was important in two ways. It preserved the old idea of the Saxon popular assembly, but linked it to the central government through the itinerant justices and the sheriff. It emphasized also the idea of representation; and when Parliament developed later, it had a similar make-up, on a national basis, of barons, churchmen, and representatives of the lesser political units. Henry eventually divided the counties into seven circuits, with three itinerant justices, or "justices in eyre," for each; but the system was too ambitious for the time. Roads were wretched and travel was slow, so that some of the more remote counties often went for long intervals without official visitations. The main body of the Curia Regis, in the meantime, followed the king in his constant travels around the country. As some counties were neglected by the justices and as civil cases could be heard at first only before the Curia Regis, this became a costly nuisance. One man complained that he had trailed the court from town to town and county to county for five years, and that, when he finally was awarded the disputed property, his profits had disappeared in expenses, lawyer's fees, and bribes. To remedy this, five of the justices remained sitting regularly at Westminster, where, not long after Henry's death, the Curia Regis split into three distinct courts: Common Pleas, for private civil cases; Exchequer, for governmental financial cases, largely concerning taxation; and King's Bench, chiefly for criminal cases.

The jury was also a vital part of Henry's reforms. This was the forerunner of the "grand" jury of the present day; the "petty," or trial, jury did not appear until the next century. Formerly historians thought that the jury must have come from Anglo-Saxon origins, since it seemed to resemble the popular legal customs of the early English. Later research indicates that the origins of the jury were not Anglo-Saxon, nor popular, nor even primarily connected with law. The practice apparently was found among the Franks of Charlemagne's time, or even earlier, and was among the French customs which the Normans had adapted. It was originally a special device for fact-finding. The name comes from the Latin for "oath," and the early jury seems to have been a group of men gathered by a royal official and sworn to give truthful information concerning facts which were probably more often financial than legal. This sworn inquest apparently was used by the Conqueror's agents in gathering facts for the Domesday Book. The original juryman, it should be remembered, was more a witness than a passive judge of right and wrong. Witnesses, as distinct from jurors, were not introduced into regular English law trials until nearly 1500. Any facts which they did not know already the old jurors were supposed to find out for themselves, outside of court, from general information or gossip presumably spread through any small community. The modern juror, on the other hand, is expected to base his decision only on what is presented in open court. He is supposed to come with a mind which is open, and which too often is blank. He may be excused or debarred if it is felt that he has too much previous knowledge about the merits of the case. It was the older type of witness-jury which the king applied to both criminal and civil justice.

By Henry's time criminal and civil law were setting out upon the separate paths which they have followed ever since. The layman is apt to associate judges and courts with the sentencing of criminals, but most lawyers are likely to think first of the fat fees in civil cases. A civil case is one in which an individual brings suit against another, usually over a question of property. The state, by furnishing a court, simply acts as umpire. In the Saxon period, criminal cases were usually treated on that same basis. If A cut off B's arm or occupied B's land, either action was regarded simply as an offense against an individual. It rested upon B as plaintiff to bring A as defendant into court. If B won the decision, he was to collect and pocket the damages. In other words, crime was on a cash basis and seldom punished as an offense against the state (see page 46). Gradually, however, the idea developed that cutting off an arm was harmful not only to B but also to society as a whole.

The state therefore accused A as a disturber of the peace. This prosecution of a crime by the state was accomplished by the enlargement of the scope of what was meant by violation of the "king's peace." This had always been an offense to be tried in the royal court. Originally it had applied merely to brawling in the actual presence of the king. Then it was extended to the vicinity of the royal palace, and later to the king's highways. Finally all major crimes committed throughout the land were regarded as violations of the king's peace and came under royal jurisdiction. It was no longer necessary for B to bring the offender into court and conduct the case as a "common plea." It became a "plea of the Crown," when the state became plaintiff as well as umpire, and the case, as the lawyers would cite it, changed from "B v. A." to "Rex v. A." This extension of the king's peace, which had begun late in the Saxon period in connection with very serious crimes, appealed to Henry not only because it promoted peace and order but also because he was now the one to pocket the fine. The state's new relation to criminal cases is seen also in Henry's order that every county provide a jail; but an adequate police system, to make the relationship complete, had to wait for many centuries. Questions of property, on the other hand, still remained "common pleas," with the individual as plaintiff and the state serving merely as umpire.

The jury's first function in the criminal field was to point out what cases should be tried before the king's justices as disturbances of the king's peace. The sheriff of each county was instructed by the Assize of Clarendon to assemble twelve good men from each hundred, together with four from each township, to report all crimes which, in their opinion, ought to be tried. It was felt that any serious crime or any suspicious person naturally would be known to such a group. Under the old system, where the burden of starting a criminal prosecution rested on the injured party, he might be bullied into silence by threats of revenge from the man who had injured him. It was expected that the new jury would be free from such intimidation. This early jury was the forerunner of the present grand jury, whose function is to present cases for trial. Its indictment did not necessarily imply that the defendant was guilty, but simply that the matters seemed worth looking into further. When the royal justices received the jury's "presentments," the question of guilt was at first determined either by the old water ordeal of Saxon days or by "wager of battle," the judicial duel introduced by the Normans. The ordeal, common at the start, was abolished by a church council in 1215. Wager of battle likewise soon fell into disuse, although the English neglected to abolish it officially until 1819, after an ingenious defendant had claimed his right to trial by that almost forgotten practice. Gradually most of the cases came to be settled by a second jury, the direct forerunner of our modern petty, or trial, jury. In cases of mild guilt the justices might settle the cases with fines which found their way into the royal treasury, but for more serious offenses the penalties were savage. In the first regular circuit of the itinerant judges in 1166, in the vicinity of London alone fourteen men were hanged and fourteen mutilated by the loss of hand or foot. Many criminals who escaped hanging were banished from the realm. The king confiscated the property not only of murderers but of the murdered as well, and heavy fines were imposed not only on actual offenders but even on counties and individuals if justice was not handled in exact accordance with the Assize of Clarendon.

Henry II assumed criminal jurisdiction by decree; but the plaintiffs in civil cases for the most part voluntarily shifted from the feudal or regular shire courts to the royal courts because the jury system offered a better chance to secure justice. There were plenty of civil cases in this reign, for much property had been seized by force during the anarchy under Stephen. The complications of feudal land tenure led to many delicate and intricate points of legal dispute. The old system decided these by wager of battle or a development of compurgation known as "wager of law." Even the devout began to question whether God settled fine points of land law through the relative merits of two husky professionals swinging pickaxes at each other, or through a system whereby, as an old Norman chief justice put it, "any dishonest man with six rascals to aid him could swear any honest man out of his goods." Possibly, if one had a weak case and a strong arm, he would prefer the wager of battle; but ordinarily it seemed far more sensible to leave the question to a dozen responsible individuals from the neighborhood, who presumably would have some definite knowledge of the facts.

Henry put his new jury system at the disposal of private litigants and even decreed that certain types of civil cases must be settled through a jury and royal judge. The general use of the jury, however, was still treated as a royal privilege, and it was necessary to ask for specific permission to bring one's case before it. This was done by applying at the chancellor's office for a "writ," a written order directing the sheriff to assemble from a particular locality twelve good men to determine a specific kind of question. The case would be tried before the royal justices, who would render judgment after putting questions of specific fact to the jury. If this body seemed to bring in a false verdict, the verdict might be reviewed and the jurors, if guilty, fined. There was a particular specified writ for each of the principal types of cases which arose in civil law. The most celebrated of the early writs indicate the kind of questions to be settled. If the plaintiff complained that someone had seized land which he himself formerly had occupied, he asked for a writ of *novel disseisin*. If a stranger occupied property upon the death of the plaintiff's parent or close relative, the proper writ was *mort d'ancestor*, while the writ *utrum* was designated for questions of whether particular church lands were held by regular feudal tenure. There was also the *Grand Assize*, which drew into the royal courts cases concerning basic title to land, instead of simply the occupation of it. For a while the chancellor created new writs, defining new types of cases as occasion arose; but gradually the writs became rigidly limited to certain well-defined questions, and we shall see that the chancellor began to settle in his own court and in another way special matters which did not fall into regular categories.

Out of Henry's new legal system grew that distinctive English creation known as common law. The name implied that there was now a uniform law for all England in place of heterogeneous local customs. Other nations, with law of a different type, have also secured legal uniformity, to be sure; but the distinctive feature of the English common law was the development of the so-called "case system." In disputed questions of law or court procedure the judge has been, from Henry's time, governed in his rulings by precedents established in previous cases. The justices of the royal courts drew up written reports of cases tried before them, pointing out their opinions on new features which arose in the trial, or instances where they saw fit to depart from earlier precedents. By the next century the more important of these reports were gathered into "Year Books," which enabled the justices to keep up to date on the decisions of their colleagues. Justice B, for instance, finding an unusual feature in a case of *novel disseisin* in Devonshire, might follow the precedent established by Justice A in Yorkshire five years earlier, or, if his case seemed slightly different, might decide otherwise, whereupon his new decision would serve as a precedent for the rest of the justices. This practice has gone on continuously down through the centuries, making the common law a living organism which gradually can be adapted to changing conditions. From time to time the principles established in the courts might be crystallized into statutes (see page 148), while other statutes might become the subject for common-law interpretation. The citing of precedents has made it necessary for the modern English and American judge and lawyer

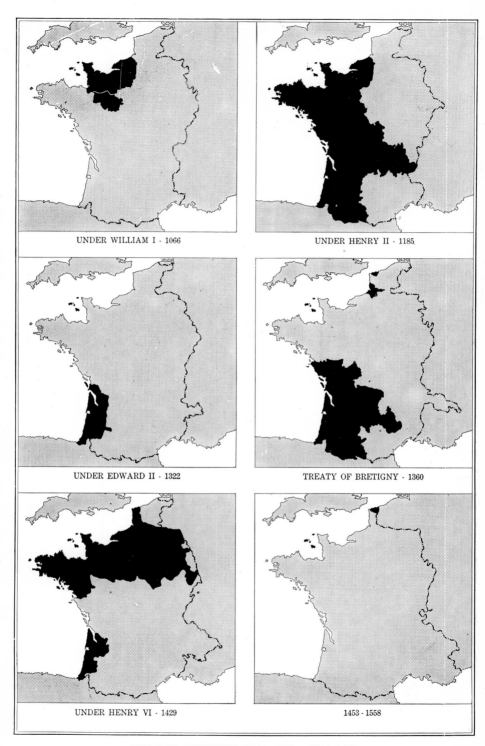

UNDER WILLIAM I · 1066

UNDER HENRY II · 1185

UNDER EDWARD II · 1322

TREATY OF BRETIGNY · 1360

UNDER HENRY VI · 1429

1453 · 1558

ENGLISH HOLDINGS IN FRANCE, 1066–1558

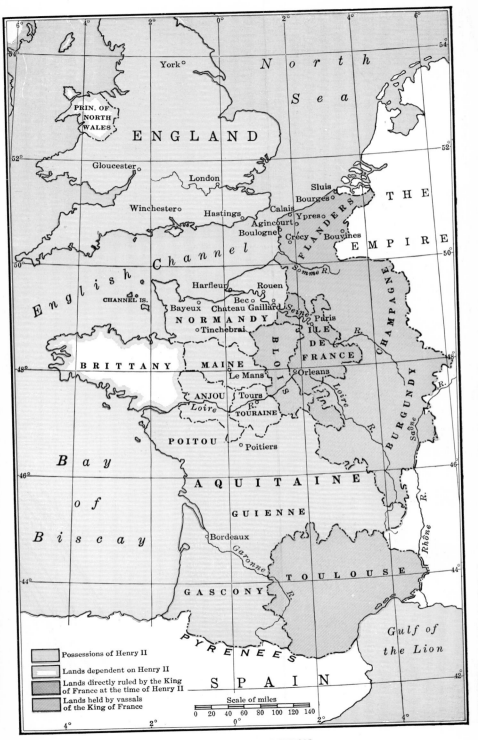

THE ANGEVIN DOMINION

to have access to hundreds of volumes of legal reports. It became increasingly difficult to run back through all the earlier reports for every case, so that digests summing up the principal cases under various headings began to appear. Some of these have been simply mechanical compilations, while a few others have had great influence in molding legal opinion and practice, such as those by Glanvill, the justiciar of Henry II; by Bracton, who by 1250 analyzed some five hundred decisions; by Coke (*c.* 1620); and by Blackstone (*c.* 1770). In addition to analyzing points of law, the English system also developed the forms of court procedure which we have today. A unique feature of criminal practice in this respect is the right to jury trial, and the right of the accused to be faced in open court by his accusers. Finally, the development of the English system led to the theory that the law was supreme, and that even the king and his agents were not free to disregard it.

A well-trained legal profession was one explanation of the unity and permanence of the common law. Even in Henry's time, laymen were replacing churchmen on the bench, and lay lawyers soon began to accompany the justices on their circuits. Training for the common law in the later Middle Ages was to be had at Lincoln's Inn, Gray's Inn and other "Inns of Court" in London. As in a law school at the present day, the students read law by day, and in the evenings, after dinner, held "moots," where they argued intricate hypothetical cases before older lawyers. Three languages usually were necessary to the lawyer's equipment: English for one's clients; Latin for the official records; and, above all, Norman French, which was used both in court and in the reports. Phrases like "oyer and terminer," as well as many common terms such as "plaintiff" and "defendant," still remain as relics of that tongue, which persisted in legal circles long after it was supplanted in common use by English. When the student had shown sufficient ability, he was "called to the bar" of his Inn and became a barrister who might plead in court. The more successful barristers were promoted to the grade of "serjeant," which became a prerequisite for appointment as a royal justice. The whole "bench and bar" of the common-law courts thus became a compact body, all trained in the same fundamentals from generation to generation.

The common law was almost strangled at birth and again in infancy by the rival system of Roman law, which in modified form still prevails on most of the Continent. Legal reform was in the air in the twelfth century, in Italy as well as in England. Gratian, as we saw, organized the Church's canon law, based in part on Roman law, into an orderly system; but the more potent threat came from the slightly earlier work of Irnerius at Bologna. He rescued from virtual oblivion the *Corpus Juris Civilis*, the code of Roman laws, compiled at the order of the Byzantine emperor Justinian about A.D. 530. Thousands flocked to hear Irnerius expound it in the schools, which soon developed into the University of Bologna, and then scattered to teach it throughout Europe. One of these "civilians" had come to England in Stephen's reign. Henry II might easily have adopted it, admiring its systematic efficiency and its support of royal power. For a long time Roman law was a powerful threat to the common law, from which it differed in many ways. It was a "law of the books" rather than a "law of the courts"; its basis was usually a comprehensive code, like that of Justinian, drawn up under the direction of a ruler and covering minutely and definitely the various phases of the law. Emphasizing abstract principles rather than practical experience, it was modified, not by actual case precedents, but by the philosophical opinions of scholars. It was better organized, more clean-cut, and simpler to administer than the English system; but it lacked the popular elements which Englishmen came to consider guarantees of personal security. The final decisions were made, not by the help of a jury, but by judges who were active inquisitors, often hunting up evidence themselves. In place of the open English trial, where the accused must be faced by his accusers, trial under the Roman law was usually one in which the judges gathered evidence from the different parties separately. Finally, Roman law was often made the tool of an absolute ruler who could influence not only the original code but also the work of the judges. It has been estimated that today about an equal number of people, roughly three hundred million, live under the English and under the Roman system of law. The former prevails, with notable exceptions, in most of the British Empire, except Quebec and South Africa, and in the United States, except Louisiana. The latter is used in most of continental Europe except Russia, in Latin America, and in many colonial possessions, and has influenced the law of Scotland.

It has been remarked that the English legal system received the Roman law in occasional small doses, which served as a tonic but which were not strong enough to drug or to kill the distinctive English quality. Men like Bracton helped to systematize the common law and develop its fine points from Roman legal principles, but the influence of Roman law was most marked in the special courts which grew up outside the common-law courts of King's Bench, Common Pleas, and Exchequer. Its effects were noticeable in the Admiralty courts, which arose in the later Middle Ages for

# Common Law and Crusading

maritime questions; and it was closely related to the canon law which was used in the church courts, where matters of probate of wills and cases arising from marriage were tried for many centuries.

Foremost among these outside courts to feel the influence of Roman law was Chancery, which, considerably after Henry's time, grew up under the chancellor. Although Chancery was not established as a regular court until just before 1400, the chancellor had long been exercising a special jurisdiction. This court dispensed "equity," a rather indefinite principle which was applied to situations where the strict letter of the common law could not or did not settle matters in a way which seemed fair. One of its uses was to fill in gaps in the common law. The time came (1258) when the chancellor was restricted in his power to issue new common-law writs to meet new situations. As society became more complex such new situations were bound to arise. Chancery, unfettered by precedents, could advance to meet them more rapidly than Common Pleas. A plaintiff might be told that there was no writ to fit his case for trial in Common Pleas, but that he might get a "bill" which would bring the case directly before the chancellor or his subordinates in Chancery. There the trial, without jury, resembled Roman-law rather than common-law procedure. Chancery could be used also virtually to overrule a common-law decision which to the chancellor, as "keeper of the King's conscience," did not seem "equitable" because of the rigid stiffness of common-law procedure. As time went on, large numbers of cases, starting in Common Pleas, were later carried into Chancery, which would order the winner in the other court not to take advantage of his favorable decision. This practice led to strong protests from the common-law justices and from litigants, but it was extremely profitable to the lawyers. Chancery also had special power through the "injunction." Whereas common-law courts could deal only with accomplished facts, Chancery, on threat of punishment for contempt of court, could "enjoin" an individual from committing an act. If someone, for instance, threatened to cut down a man's valuable old shade trees, Common Pleas could do nothing but award damages after the trees were cut, whereas Chancery might prevent the cutting. This power has been used in recent times, particularly to limit the action of strikers. At first each case in Chancery was supposedly settled on its own merits, but gradually the court developed a body of procedure and precedents of its own. Chancery was influenced both by Roman and by canon law (the early chancellors being bishops or archbishops), and men preparing to practice before Chancery went more often to Oxford to study Roman and canon law than to the Inns of Court, which emphasized common law. Chancery at the outset was supposedly a short cut to justice; in its later years the name became synonymous with tedious and costly delay, since cases sometimes dragged on for years or for generations.

This general survey of the English legal system has carried the development well beyond the time of Henry II, but one can easily appreciate the importance of his contributions. A century after his time we shall see that Edward I crystallized some of the more important legal principles into statutes, and the common law appears later as something with which even the king was warned not to tamper.

Henry's zeal for strong and efficient government was not limited to these legal reforms. Before turning to the dispute which climaxed his reign, it would be well to notice two of his innovations in military policy; for they had a far-reaching influence upon England's social structure as well as upon her fighting efficiency. Both measures tended to curb the dangerous power of the barons and knights whom the Conqueror had richly endowed with lands in return for forty days of military service each year. Such a concentration of undisciplined fighting force was risky, as the reign of Stephen had shown; moreover, it was inefficient. The short-lived armies produced by the feudal system were inadequate for lengthy sieges and for service in France. Early in his reign Henry II extended the practice of *scutage*, or "shield money," with which Henry I had experimented. Instead of calling upon his vassals to furnish so many armed men for forty days, the king at times would demand a certain amount of money for each knight's fee. With that money he then hired mercenaries, either English or foreign, who could be held together long after the brief period of feudal service expired. This may be regarded as the first step in the transformation of the fighting baron into the peaceful country gentleman—a process which was to go on for several centuries. In the north and west, out toward the Scottish and Welsh borders, the fighting tradition continued for more than three centuries; but in the more settled parts of England the claws of the former fighters were clipped, their grim donjon fortresses were transformed into more comfortable country houses, and, still enjoying the rich profits from the manorial system, they gradually devoted themselves more and more to hunting, drinking, politics, local administration, and the supervision of their estates. We shall notice changes in this direction from time to time in the later Middle Ages; not until the sixteenth-century Tudor period would the transformation be fairly complete.

Henry's other military innovation was the *Assize of Arms*, six years before his death. This was a systematic extension of the old

# Common Law and Crusading

Saxon fyrd, or militia. Every freeman, even down to artisans in the towns and the meanest freeholders, was required to maintain certain military equipment and to be ready for the king's service in case of emergency. Henry was inclined to be autocratic and absolute; but he maintained no standing army in England to enforce his will, and his despotism was sufficiently popular so that he dared to trust many men with weapons. By thus extending the number of potential soldiers Henry further weakened the former fighting monopoly of the feudal lords. Within two centuries the bold yeomanry would show their mettle on foreign fields and learn that they could hold their own with the proud knights on horseback.

Henry's military and legal reforms had much in common. In both he was trying to increase the royal power and make it more efficient. In both he played off the lesser freeman against the barons, whom he desired to curb. While the barons were losing their fighting monopoly they were also being deprived of jurisdiction; while the freemen were arming themselves at royal command they were also being given new importance as jurymen.

It was only natural that Henry's efforts, especially toward making the royal courts paramount at the expense of the church and feudal courts, should arouse opposition. The king met the most serious reverse of his career in the dispute over the jurisdiction of church and royal courts. This problem, like lay investiture and taxation, was a fruitful source of church-state quarrels in several countries. In England the conflict degenerated into a personal clash between Henry and his former faithful lieutenant, one Thomas Becket. Becket came from a prosperous family of the merchant class, but family reverses caused young Thomas to be placed at an early age in the household of an important archbishop. Here he learned all the ramifications of church business and rose quickly to a favored position. Henry made Becket chancellor soon after his accession, and they were excellent friends. Hand in glove the two worked together, for Becket's businesslike methods were an asset to Henry's clever statesmanship. In foreign affairs and domestic, even where church privilege was involved, Becket acted as Henry's second self and ally. Perhaps because Pope Adrian IV (1154–1159), the former Nicholas Breakspear, was a native Englishman (the only such Pope in history), and perhaps because the prelates were Henry's own appointees, the king had peaceful relations with the papacy and with his own churchmen during the early years of his reign. Consequently, when the Archbishopric of Canterbury fell vacant, it was only natural that Henry should want to see Becket in that coveted position. Nevertheless, a certain amount of irregularity was involved in Becket's appointment in 1162, as he was merely a Canterbury archdeacon and was rushed within twenty-four hours through all the other church ranks so that he might be invested archbishop.

To the stunned surprise of the king, Thomas came from the investiture a different man. As one chronicler expressed it, "Thomas, then having taken the usual oaths, received the pall from the altar, and reverently put on him the robes of high priest. But this change of habit was preliminary to a change of heart also; for he now renounced secular cares and attended only the spiritual concerns of the church and the gain of souls." The luxury-loving man of the world now went dirty and hungry, with a hair shirt next to his skin. Henry was aghast; for he had envisioned in the appointment of his chancellor to this position the link that would bring the Church closer to the throne. Instead, Thomas resigned the chancellorship and became as unreasonable a die-hard exponent of church privileges as Anselm had been at his worst.

The real trouble between king and primate centered about the clashing jurisdiction of royal and ecclesiastical courts. The ecclesiastical courts, as we have seen, had asserted and had enjoyed complete jurisdiction over many sorts of cases, including the trial and punishment of "criminous clerks" (criminal churchmen), whatever their offenses and their rank might be. This privilege of "benefit of clergy" was claimed not only by regular prelates, priests, and monks but also by thousands of professional men, students, and others, some of whom had no stronger claim to church connection than their ability to patter off a few lines of Latin. Benefit of clergy was decidedly worth while to those who claimed it; for the penalties of the church courts were notoriously more lenient than those of the secular courts. A canon, for instance, had recently cleared himself of murdering a knight by a simple oath in the bishop's court. Henry, in 1164, attempted to bring the clergy under royal law with his Constitutions of Clarendon. This code contained numerous articles defining the relations of Church and State. According to it, a "clerk" accused of a crime was first to be brought into a secular court to plead guilty or not guilty. He was still to be tried, as before, in the church court. If found guilty, he was to be unfrocked and turned over to the king's court, where he would receive the regular punishment for his crime. Becket's bitter stand against this meant that thousands were exempted from the liability to harsh punishment for the worst crimes. The logic of the royal stand that all Englishmen should be subject to the same law ran directly counter to the equally logical claim of the primate that the churchmen should be tried in church courts.

# Common Law and Crusading

After a few months Becket left England; and so acrimonious was the quarrel and so stubborn was the archbishop that even his own bishops were ready to compromise. He stayed abroad six years, until 1170. At that time Henry wanted to have his eldest son crowned king before his own death, and, owing to this absence of the primate, the Archbishop of York, assisted by other bishops, performed the coronation ceremony. This infuriated Becket; but peace of a sort was patched up at a meeting with Henry in France, where no mention was made of the dispute over the courts. Becket came back to England, heralding his approach defiantly by suspending or excommunicating the prelates who had assisted in the coronation. They naturally hurried to Henry in Normandy with their tale of Becket's resumption of hostilities. In one of his not-uncommon moments of sudden Angevin rage the irritated king made a rash exclamation about this troublesome Thomas of whom no one would rid him. Four knights, taking this passionate outburst far too literally, hurried without the king's knowledge to England and made for Canterbury. They burst into the cathedral, where Becket's friends had with difficulty persuaded him to take refuge. In those days, and for long afterward, a church was usually respected as a safe sanctuary, even in the case of red-handed criminals; but on this occasion Canterbury itself was not safe for its own archbishop. The knights called for "the traitor, Thomas Becket"; he stepped down to meet them; bitter words were exchanged; and then they cut him down. One knight even drove his sword into the skull of the dying primate. The spot where he fell became England's most sacred shrine.

Like many people in a temper, Henry had not meant all he had said; but those thoughtlessly rash words cost him a serious loss of prestige and a crushing defeat in his expansion of royal courts against the church courts. The Canterbury murder scandalized and horrified not only the Church but public opinion everywhere. The immediate victory went to the dead archbishop and not to the much-alive king. Henry went to Canterbury as the most groveling of penitents. The chronicler Roger de Hoveden has left us a picture of the way in which Henry, "barefoot and clad in woolen garments, walked the three miles to the tomb of the blessed martyr . . . his tender feet being cut by the hard stones, a great quantity of blood flowed from them to the ground." "When he arrived at the tomb," continues the chronicler, "it was a holy thing to see the affliction which he suffered with sobs and tears, and the discipline to which he submitted from the hands of the bishops and a great number of priests and monks." All of which may have been true; for Henry realized that the murder had seriously hurt his power in that age of faith in Church and sanctuary. He had to withdraw some of the terms of the Constitutions of Clarendon, and, although "benefit of clergy" finally gave way before royal power, the "criminous clerks" continued to get off easily for many years. Henry's efforts, however, blocked the continual expansion of the church courts into new fields, together with the rest of the spreading power of the Church which had so increased during Stephen's years as king.

The murder of Becket coincided with the start of England's relations with Ireland, a sorry and tangled story that has run down through the centuries ever since. In scarcely a year in all that time have relations been satisfactory to both English and Irish. Henry, not content with his immense Plantagenet empire stretching from the Cheviots to the Pyrenees, claimed, like some of his predecessors, overlordship of the Scots and Welsh; and his outstanding contact with the "Celtic fringe" was the start of the Irish problem, between 1169 and 1171.

Ireland had dropped out of English history after 664, when the Council of Whitby had decided in favor of the Roman Church instead of the more informal type of Christianity introduced by the Irish monks. It had continued in a primitive state of civilization, devoted chiefly to the tending or stealing of cattle, together with a little agriculture. The Vikings raided the island at the same time they poured into the Danelaw and Normandy, but they were finally limited to Dublin and a few other towns on the east coast. All through the centuries there had been constant political turmoil, for the Celtic temperament was not as well adapted as the Saxon or the Norman to orderly government beyond the tribal stage. Sometimes seven kings ruled Ireland; sometimes there were more; occasionally a single ruler, like Brian Boru (1002–1014), might gain temporary ascendancy. But the chronicles of Irish history are little more than monotonous annals of feuds and sudden death.

Henry had toyed with the idea of conquering Ireland in the very first year of his reign, and supposedly he had received strong support from the English Pope, Adrian IV, when an ousted king of eastern Ireland appealed for help in regaining his throne. The chief initiative, however, came from a border baron, Richard de Clare, earl of Pembroke, popularly known as "Strongbow," whose Norman-Welsh henchmen, descendants of the charming Nesta, the one-time Welsh mistress of Henry I, invaded Ireland in 1169. Strongbow himself followed in the year of Becket's murder, his knights in chain mail easily overcoming Irish resistance. Henry suddenly realized the dangerous possibility of an independent Norman state in Ireland.

# Common Law and Crusading

Probably anxious to distract public attention from the Becket murder, and perhaps hoping to placate the Church by winning Ireland for stricter Roman rule, he went over in 1171 and received the submission of a good part of the island. The Irish, with their traditions of tribal rule, probably did not realize the significance of the feudal homage which they gave to Strongbow and to Henry. The invading barons, however, took it at its face value and tried to rule accordingly. For the next three or four centuries Ireland fell into three zones, as far as English contact was concerned. The "Pale," extending some thirty miles around Dublin, had fairly effective rule along English lines. Far off in the west there was virtual independence. In between there was a very tangled situation, with the feudalized Norman-Welsh leaders and the old Irish paying only such respect to the king's representative at Dublin as they saw fit. Ireland seems to have had a remarkable capacity for absorbing its invaders. Before long the descendants of these barons—the Fitzgeralds, Lacys, Burkes (De Burgh), and the rest—became "more Irish than the Irish themselves," soon adopting the Celtic customs and point of view. So it was with later waves of invaders, and not until the wholesale plantation of grim Presbyterians in Ulster about 1600 was Ireland to receive newcomers who could not be quickly absorbed.

Of Henry II it has been said that he could rule every house but his own. He and Eleanor had four sons: Henry and Geoffrey, who died before their father, and Richard and John, who succeeded him in turn. The king seems to have been as much too soft in spoiling his sons as William I had been too harsh in repressing his. The Conqueror was at least spared in his last years the sorrow of open and often successful rebellion on the part of his children. The ingratitude of the young Angevins was all the more marked because their father had made generous provision for them during his lifetime. To honor them and to facilitate their inheritance, Henry, the eldest son, was crowned king of England and also received Normandy, Maine, and Anjou; Richard was presented with Aquitaine, which he was to hold as a fief directly from the French king; while Geoffrey, who had married the heiress of Brittany, received that duchy which he was to hold as a fief from his elder brother Henry. John was nicknamed "Lackland" because he was too young to participate in the original distribution, but he later was granted the lordship of Ireland. Not one of the sons was content with these arrangements. They constantly intrigued against their father to make their nominal ownership actual, even in his lifetime. In this they were abetted by their mother, Eleanor, who was notoriously, and perhaps for good cause, hostile to Henry. The younger Henry, in league with the kings of France and Scotland, and supported by many of the barons, led a dangerous revolt in 1173; but the king finally crushed it.

Then came the treachery of Richard. In Philip Augustus (1180–1223), son of Eleanor's first husband by his third wife, France found a strong monarch. At the very beginning of his reign he utilized every chance to make the Plantagenet French lands his own, and Richard, who became heir to the throne after the death of his older brother, joined with him to defeat Henry II. The young prince shamefully humiliated his father, the old king, in the ensuing conference, where all of Richard's claims were perforce accepted. Sick at heart at this, and learning that his favorite son, John, was involved with Richard in this filial disloyalty, Henry died in tragic bitterness in 1189.

The spectacular Richard, called Cœur de Lion, or Lion-Hearted, by his admirers, was anything but an asset to his kingdom. So little did it interest him that he spent less than ten months of his ten-year reign (1189–1199) in England, and his two brief visits were merely money-raising affairs. The rest of the time he spent in quarreling with Philip over French lands, crusading in the Holy Land, or in captivity. Despite the intrigues of his brother John and others during his long absences, his father's work had been so thorough that, for once in medieval England, the government could be safely managed by ministers alone. Governmental details, left uncompleted at Henry's death, were, moreover, so well worked out under the highly capable Hubert Walter, eventually Archbishop of Canterbury and justiciar, that the reign even saw some constitutional advance.

Richard has come down in history and in legend as the embodiment of the romantic medieval knight. Endowed with a magnificent physique, this absentee king was brave, dashing, and at times chivalrous. He was a commander of considerable ability. But he had also some of the characteristic weak points of the medieval knight; he was apt to spend his efforts along unpractical lines; and his subjects paid heavily in taxes for the reflected glory he brought them. Chivalrous as he could be on occasion, ordering that the soldier who gave him his death wound be pardoned, he had also a cruel streak. Once, during the French fighting, he blinded fifteen of Philip's captured knights, leaving a sixteenth with one eye to lead the rest back to their king. Philip, "so that he might not appear inferior to Richard," sent back fifteen of the English king's knights completely blinded and led by a woman.

The motive force of Richard's existence was the crusading move-

# Common Law and Crusading

ment. The Crusades commenced after the Seljuk Turks, sweeping in from central Asia five years after Hastings, had routed an army of the Byzantine Empire and occupied most of Asia Minor and the eastern-Mediterranean lands, including the Holy Land of Palestine. In 1095 the Byzantine emperor at Constantinople begged the Pope, Urban II, to come to his aid. Urban responded at once; for he recognized this as an opportunity to enhance his own power by winning the Holy Land for western Christendom, and hoped at the same time to reunite under his leadership the Eastern (Greek Catholic) with the Western (Roman Catholic) Church. This opportunity to fight for the expansion of Christianity, moreover, might turn the feudal nobility from their civil strife, which for some time the Church had been trying to curb in various ways, such as the "Peace of God," protecting noncombatants from warfare, and the later "Truce of God," forbidding fighting on week ends. The Turkish occupation, moreover, was potentially harmful to European pilgrims to the Holy Land, where formerly the Arabs had been more tolerant.

Passing on the emperor's appeal to the crowds gathered at the church council summoned by him at Clermont, in France, the following year, Urban aroused an amazing response. To gain recruits for the proposed expedition, which was called a "crusade," the Church promised volunteers forgiveness for their sins, protection for their forsaken families, and reduction of their debts. The emperor had hoped for the aid of some well-trained troops, not for the general exodus of western Christendom into his empire. The Pope too was surprised and disturbed when swarms took up the Cross and headed eastward to free Jerusalem from the infidels. People of all sorts flocked to the new adventure. Nobles were eager to gain fame, wealth, and, above all, new lands for themselves; merchants bethought themselves of trade; debtors sought freedom from creditors; criminals hoped to escape punishment; others saw in the Crusade a chance for travel or excitement; and, of course, to the truly devout the rescue of the Holy Sepulcher from infidel hands was a holy duty. Of such stuff were the Crusaders, who dashed eastward, occasionally in roughly organized bands, more frequently in armed expeditions led by knights and princes. The movement became far more significant than merely an answer to the emperor's plea for aid. Regarded in its broadest light, it was the positive expansion of Western Christendom toward the East, under the inspiration of the Roman Catholic Church, the principal creative force of medieval Europe. The Crusades were thus one more act in the frequent resurgence of Europeans and Asiatics into each other's lands, which had been going on for over fifteen hundred years. They occurred midway between the deep inroads by the Mohammedan Arabs into Christian lands in the seventh and eighth centuries and the later conquest of the Byzantine Empire, in the fifteenth century, by the Mohammedan Turks, who thus established a long sway over the Christians of southeastern Europe.

In all, there were several Crusades in the next two centuries, and of these the Third (1189) most concerned England. The First Crusade occurred during the reign of Rufus; but, as we saw, because of his avarice few if any English barons participated in it (see page 81). That initial Crusade consisted of various parts. The first group was composed of devout but poorly equipped pilgrims, led by Peter the Hermit and other religious enthusiasts, who went to what proved certain failure. The main expedition, in which Duke Robert, Rufus's brother, took a minor part, wrested the Holy Land from the Saracens; and for themselves its lucky leaders gained states there which survived for some time despite almost constant fighting among the Crusaders. Edessa, the capital of one of these states, later fell to the Turks. A second Crusade was then called in 1147 by Saint Bernard, leader of the Cistercian reform movement; but this Crusade failed.

Then, in 1187, a brilliant, spirited, and chivalrous leader, Saladin, who had arisen among the Moslems, recaptured Jerusalem, the center of the chief state of the Crusaders. All Christendom was aroused. Henry II himself took the cross,—rather reluctantly,—but rebellion interfered. His decision left one lasting trace in the "Saladin tithe," which was a step toward modern taxation, as contrasted with the usual feudal sources of revenue which we noticed under Henry I. Using the customary church tithe as a model, Henry levied a tax of 10 per cent on the personal property and income of all persons *not* going on the Crusade. This precedent helped to pave the way toward regular taxation. Henry, however, soon died, brokenhearted at the rebellion of Richard, who was a much more spontaneous Crusader.

The Third Crusade was particularly distinguished by the presence of four great leaders. On one side was Saladin, the outstanding commander of the Saracens; on the other side were Richard of England and two of the most celebrated of medieval monarchs: the aged, red-bearded Holy Roman emperor, Frederick Barbarossa, and that astute perennial enemy of the Angevins, Philip Augustus of France. The Christian triumvirate, each of whom was accustomed to the limelight, did not last. Barbarossa lost his life and most of his army during the difficult overland passage through Asia Minor.

Richard, after scraping together all the money he could possibly lay his hands on, made the voyage by sea with Philip Augustus. Relations became strained when, at Cyprus, Richard married the beautiful Berengaria of Navarre, after breaking his engagement to Philip's sister. With real skill Cœur de Lion captured the seaport of Acre, where he massacred nearly three thousand Saracens whose ransom was not forthcoming. Then Philip went home on a plea of ill-health, really in the hope of seizing some of the French lands of Richard, who was left to carry on alone. From Acre, Richard made a grueling march down the coast and inland toward Jerusalem, while the wily Saladin constantly harassed his progress. News came of troubles at home, and Richard, within sight of the Holy City, reluctantly gave up the campaign. On his return he was shipwrecked in the Adriatic and tried to make his way overland through Austria in disguise. He was captured, dressed as a kitchen hand, in an inn near Vienna by followers of the Duke of Austria, who had several old grudges to settle. Richard was imprisoned in a castle, where—as the story goes—his faithful minstrel, Blondel, who had been singing all over Austria hunting for him, finally found his master. It cost England some £100,000, the equivalent of three or four years' normal revenue, to free the king; for ransom was one of the special feudal aids for which vassals were liable.

It might be well, before leaving the Crusades, to mention that, in the Fourth, Christian Constantinople was sacked by the Crusaders themselves; that another was briefly successful under a very reluctant Crusader, Barbarossa's grandson, the Holy Roman emperor Frederick II; while two others, under Saint Louis, grandson of Philip Augustus, were failures. The Holy Land remained under Saracen control until 1917, when, during the World War, the British general, Allenby, captured Jerusalem from the Turks. This campaign has been called "the Last Crusade," Jerusalem, as part of a British mandate, coming again under Christian rule.

The effects of the Crusades have been somewhat disputed among historians, some asserting that the change from medieval to modern Europe began with the Crusades; others claiming much less for them. A leading authority (Munro) has remarked, "Their real significance lay in the fact that they brought people of different nationalities together and caused an interchange of ideas and customs." The present tendency is to question and minimize most of the results once attributed to the stimulus of the Crusading movement, such as improved trade, the growth of towns, the increased use of money, and enlarged scientific knowledge. In the introduction of improved methods of fighting and of luxuries and comforts into

western Europe and hence into England, the direct influence of the
Crusades is, however, generally granted. Politically the kings gained
power by taking over the estates of nobles who died on the Crusades,
and some of the most turbulent and restless of the fighting barons
left their bones in the Holy Land.

Richard spent the last five years of his reign in France, engaged
in constant squabbles with Philip Augustus and with his own French
vassals. While engaged in a petty fight in Aquitaine in 1199, he
was killed by a crossbowman's arrow. As he had no son, the throne
went to his younger brother, John.

Laments at the loss of Henry I's lone son in the "White Ship"
might well have been repeated at this accession; for the people were
soon to realize that Henry II had had too many sons for England's
good. John, the worst of England's kings, undoubtedly had personal
courage and high ability in generalship and political craft; but he
failed because of his unnecessary cruelty, his indolence, his unwillingness to carry things through to conclusions, his utter faithlessness
and lack of reliability, and partly, perhaps, because it was his bad
luck to have as antagonists two of the strongest personalities of
the Middle Ages, Philip Augustus of France and Pope Innocent III.
The darker side of the Plantagenet character appeared in John, but the
fiery Angevin temper and arbitrary will were not balanced in him
by the wisdom, seriousness of purpose, and sustained activity of
his father. Energy he had on occasions, with the old Angevin vim,
and at such times he surmounted seemingly hopeless situations; but
those moments were always soon swamped in his usual self-indulgence
or counterbalanced by deeds of wanton brutality. It has been said
that he was the one English king of a definitely criminal type, and
this may be the explanation of his viciousness and his cunning as
well as of his failures. Sooner or later he alienated nearly everyone,
near or far, high or low, with whom he had any dealings, through
greed, heartlessness, and complete disloyalty.

Three major conflicts dominated the reign and by their consequences made it, in spite of John himself, a significant period. Although the rumblings of these three disputes run throughout the
entire reign, the climax came, first, with Philip Augustus over the
Plantagenet empire, which was largely lost thereby; secondly, with
Pope Innocent III over investiture, after which John gave England
to the papacy as a fief; and, lastly, with the English barons, who
forced the granting of Magna Carta.

Loyalty to no man might well have been John's creed, and nowhere
was it more evident than in his dealings with little Arthur, the son
of Geoffrey, John's deceased older brother. This boy, the rightful

heir according to strict primogeniture, was another victim of the medieval preference for a grown man in a succession. John, however, was designated as heir by Richard, and was also supported in England and Normandy by the aged but still potent Queen Eleanor, and by England's chief men—Hubert Walter, Archbishop of Canterbury; Geoffrey Fitz Peter, justiciar; and William Marshall, earl of Pembroke. On the other hand, Anjou, Maine, and Touraine declared for Arthur, as well as Brittany, which was his anyway through his mother, Constance.

Philip Augustus seized this division in the Plantagenet lands to further his purpose of bringing more of France under his direct control. He played John and Arthur against each other in a long series of petty campaigns in which the mothers, Eleanor and Constance, did their part. The eighty-year-old Eleanor energetically arranged a marriage between her granddaughter, Blanche of Castille, and Philip's son. This brought about a temporary truce in which Philip threw over Arthur's claims in return for the "relief" to be paid by John for Richard's French fiefs, together with some minor cession of territory.

John's own action, as always, quickly canceled this temporary success. He had just secured the annulment of his marriage to the childless heiress of Gloucester; and while awaiting the return of envoys who were seeking the sister of the Portuguese king for his second bride, he suddenly fell in love with a twelve-year-old beauty, Isabel of Angoulême. Isabel, however, was already betrothed to one of John's own vassals in Aquitaine, and a medieval betrothal was a serious matter. Nothing daunted, John married the girl. That crass violation of the feudal code gave the ever-watchful Philip his chance. As John's suzerain, he summoned him to his court to explain this insult to a vassal's honor. John refused to comply because, though he might technically be Philip's vassal for the French lands, he was as king of England equal in rank to Philip. The latter thereupon returned to Arthur all the disputed French fiefs except Normandy, which he wanted for himself. John, during one of his bursts of energy, rescued his mother, who was being besieged by Arthur's forces, and captured his young nephew. That was the last that is known of Arthur. Contemporary rumor convicted John of either ordering the boy's death or—and this seems the more probable from the evidence—slaying him with his own hand one dark night at Rouen. Though simply based on hearsay, the charge of murder seems strengthened by the fact that it was never denied by John or by anyone close to him. These ugly rumors caused Philip to redouble his efforts against John, who was unable to produce Arthur when so ordered by his suzerain; again John ignored Philip's citation to appear at court.

John's energy seemingly was gone for the present, and by the end of 1204 most of his vassals and strongholds were lost to Philip. Even the key to Normandy itself, the Château Gaillard (or Saucy Castle), which Richard had left as his proudest monument, fell with scarcely a struggle to the French forces, although it was the strongest castle in western Europe. It is said that John had plans for defense worthy of a military genius, but he did not bother to carry them out. Thus in five years John lost all the Plantagenet empire north of the river Loire—Normandy, Maine, Anjou, and even part of Poitou, in Aquitaine. They passed forever out of English history, except for a brief interlude in the Hundred Years' War. Although John later made spasmodic efforts to recover these northern French lands, the only overseas heritage that he was able to leave his son was part of his mother's dowry, Aquitaine. By this careless throwing away of half the Plantagenet lands, however, John unwittingly did England an excellent turn. England came more and more to realize that territory on the Continent was a serious liability, causing more trouble than it was worth. After 1204, moreover, the "half-and-half barons," who owned estates in northern France as well as in England, had to choose between France and England. This led to the evolution of a more strictly English baronage, more exclusively concerned with love of England and with interest in her affairs.

The Plantagenet crown was shortly to become more tarnished in the lengthy duel between John and Innocent III over the vacant see of Canterbury. No ruler of his time was the match for that invincible Pope, who compelled even the strong-willed Philip Augustus eventually to take back the Danish bride whom he had rudely repudiated on the morning after the wedding. It had long been customary for the monks of the cathedral chapter of Canterbury to choose the archbishop; but here, as elsewhere, the choice ordinarily was dictated by someone higher up, usually the king. This time some of the younger monks stole a march on the king by secretly selecting one of their number to succeed Hubert Walter, who had died in 1205, and in short order had the new archbishop duly started on his way to Rome for Innocent's approval. Apparently the newly honored young monk could not resist boasting of his promotion. John, naturally desirous of having one of his own men in so important an office, was enraged at the news and insisted upon the election of one John de Gray, bishop of Norwich. Upon the arrival of the two rival archbishops-elect at Rome, Innocent approved neither,

# Common Law and Crusading

but put forward his own candidate, Stephen Langton, for election. Thus everyone concerned violated the correct procedure: the monks by their secrecy, John by his insistence on his personal candidate, and even the great Innocent by his suggestion of the third candidate. But, in justification of Innocent, it must be admitted that Stephen Langton was the best person Canterbury could have. An Englishman born, he had won a great reputation for learning at the University of Paris; he was so gifted that some of his poems are still left us; and he was so able that he had risen to be a cardinal at Rome.

In the duel between John and Innocent each had powerful weapons. The king could seize the church property and make life hard for the clerics as individuals. The Pope had the interdict, which could stop the church services in a nation, and excommunication, which cut off any given individual from contact with the Church and also, supposedly, from society. He used these in turn against John.

The king took the first step, either expelling the Canterbury monks or at least causing them to rush fearfully into exile. He also took over the rich Canterbury lands and threatened reprisals against all the English clergy should Innocent continue his insistence upon Langton. Innocent, who was not one to be defied, placed an interdict upon all England. This weapon was powerful, since, in its strictest interpretation, it would have cut the people off from all public church services and most of the sacraments. It was a devout age, when most of the people had been brought up to believe that very careful participation in all church rites was essential to their future salvation; and an interdict might cause them to rise against their ruler, lest they risk eternal damnation. As a matter of fact, certain sacraments, including baptism, confirmation, penance, and marriage, were continued under restrictions, while Christmas, Easter, and some other church festivals were exempted from the general prohibition. Some monastic orders, such as the Cistercians, were said to have ignored all the restrictions. The feature of the interdict which bore most heavily upon the people was the necessity of burying their dead, without services, in unhallowed ground. John's retaliation was the seizure of the lands not only of most of the bishops but also of the lesser clergy, to whom he left only a bare allowance for a very little food each day. In spite of later modifications in his public utterances, he apparently made no move to save the clergy from persecution. In one instance he is said to have ordered clemency for a highwayman who had murdered a priest because he had slain the "king's enemy." After two years of this, plus some fruitless negotiations, Innocent launched the second church weapon, excommunication, against John himself. Anyone excommunicated was supposed to be shunned by all members of society, high and low; but John took steps to prevent such ostracism by instilling fear of cruel reprisals.

Outside England, John's position seems to have suffered little from this double indignity of interdict and excommunication; for there were three other excommunicated princes at the time, among whom was the Holy Roman emperor. John even had the chance to form an anti-French coalition among certain disaffected princes. Some of the nobles in the former Plantagenet provinces in northern France were chafing under Philip's strict rule and were inclined to prefer the former lax control of a ruler who spent much of his time in England. Nearer home, Scotland, Wales, and Ireland, moreover, were for once fairly quiescent.

Within England itself there was no immediate outburst. The people, as a whole, were accustomed to resent papal interference. The valuable property taken from the clerics momentarily lightened the country's financial burden, so that for a short while there was a less insistent demand for scutage and other feudal dues. The power of John's effective mercenary troops probably had much to do with England's outward calm. Before long, however, the country was seething with discontent, since John created such a reign of terror that, as one chronicler put it, "no one durst speak." The chronicles were discreetly silent about this period; but a few stories, passed around, demonstrate that it was extremely risky to criticize the king. One unfortunate archdeacon was so ill-advised as to wonder, aloud, whether he ought to stay in the service of an excommunicated king. With an appallingly heavy weight of lead fastened to his head, he was incarcerated in a cell, too small for either sitting or standing, until he starved to death. John also used the cruel device of demanding as hostages the children or other dear ones of any noble family whom he suspected of disloyalty. In this connection came one of John's blackest crimes, influential in creating organized resistance to him later. De Braose, a prominent suspect baron, was credited with being one of those who knew what had happened to Arthur of Brittany. His wife, in outspoken manner, refused to trust her son as a hostage to "Arthur's murderer." John thereupon imprisoned the noble lady with her son in Windsor Castle, with only a piece of raw bacon and some uncooked oats for food, until they died. By such methods the king stifled open criticism—for a time.

The despotic power which had been built up and ably used by Henry II was now in the hands of a "disliked and despised man." Arrogant foreigners were installed as sheriffs and overstepped the usual bounds of authority. Increased forest exactions and new illegal tolls made the reign burdensome even to the poorest and least likely objects for royal extortion. The pathetic tale of the Bristol Jew, whose teeth were knocked out one by one each day until, with the eighth day and the eighth tooth, the poor man promised to pay the sum demanded by the king, illustrates John's methods of raising money; although it is only fair to admit that the current pipe rolls proved that the chronicler exaggerated the amount several times over, and possibly the torture too. There is no doubt, however, of the frequency and general illegality of John's demands of money from the noble in scutage and feudal incidents, as well from the Jew, the priest, and the peasant. John went too far in all things. Whispered tales about Arthur, de Braose, and the Bristol Jew passed from mouth to mouth, arousing widespread bitterness; and gradually resistance took form.

Warnings of a conspiracy reached John in 1212 on the western border, where he had summoned the feudal levies for an invasion of now hostile Wales. The situation seemed so threatening that he dropped the idea of invasion and sent home the feudal forces, whose loyalty was in question; but not before he had committed one more act to horrify the nation, by publicly executing twenty-eight boy hostages from prominent Welsh families. John next, with native wit, set out to win the common people with promises of relaxation of the forest laws, lessening of illegal tolls, and royal commissions to hear complaints; but those fair words could not offset the cumulative effect of all his cruelty. Besides, the articulate opposition came, not from the common people, but from the barons, who had suffered from this king even more than the people, both in purse and in honor; for not the least of John's offenses was that, according to report, no woman, no matter how nobly born or well married, was safe from his desire.

In the meantime Innocent, who was not one placidly to accept John's continued defiance, made the clever suggestion to Philip Augustus that he might seize John's throne for himself. Innocent had no desire to build up a powerful Anglo-French monarchy which might threaten the papacy, but he made this threat simply to scare John into submission. Philip, however, took Innocent's idea seriously and, after quick preparations, joyfully made ready for the conquest of England. John, knowing that his baronage was a most uncertain quantity, neatly slid out of the dilemma by fully accepting Innocent's demands in 1213. Considering John's long defiance, these were comparatively moderate: acceptance of Langton, recall of exiled ecclesiastics, compensation for the losses of the clergy, and—an important point with Innocent—John's co-operation in a future Crusade.

John, most sensationally, went even further: he gave England itself to the Pope, and then received it back as a fief, with promises of annual tribute. Humiliating as this sounds, and though later Popes tried occasionally to capitalize the matter financially, the act was of slight importance and was probably done of John's own accord. It was nothing new, as other princes of the time had done likewise. It meant little in the way of sacrifice, beyond a small matter of dignity. On the other hand, it proved an ace of trumps for John, who had the gleeful satisfaction of seeing the disgruntled Philip forbidden by Innocent to invade a papal fief! John's victory, however, was to be short-lived. Serious trouble, as we shall see, was awaiting him at the hands of his barons.

# CHAPTER VI

## Barons and Parliament

### 1214-1297

EXCEPT for the wild years of Stephen's reign, the restless and powerful barons had been kept well under control by a series of iron-handed monarchs for the century and a half since the Conquest. Then, in the last years of John's reign, they commenced a series of more orderly efforts to secure a share in the government, and several times during the next hundred years they were to adopt further measures to curb the formerly absolute royal power. Not one of the purely baronial movements secured lasting results, but they helped to pave the way for the successful rise of Parliament, where barons and commoners together finally gained a major share of the power once monopolized by the king.

John, as we saw in the last chapter, in 1213 once more escaped an apparently hopeless situation when Innocent III forbade Philip Augustus to invade England, the new papal fief. Although the French king had lost his opportunity for an English "crusade," and the Pope was now John's ally, Stephen Langton, the new Archbishop of Canterbury, was, from the moment he landed in England, the guiding spirit of the baronial movement to check royal despotism. On at least one occasion he went so far as to read the Charter of Liberties of Henry I to an assemblage of barons, and to advocate its use to limit the arbitrary actions of John (see page 82). The king, however, was apparently blind to this new danger. Relieved of the threat of French invasion, he decided to take the offensive himself and to regain his lost provinces in northern France. The failure of this further attempt at reconquest overseas, with the resulting additional loss of royal prestige, was the last straw to the baronial impatience with misrule.

John, as usual when he put his mind to it, was an excellent strategist. He had planned to catch Philip Augustus between two fires. John himself would strike from Aquitaine. At the same time the Holy Roman emperor Otto, the son of John's sister, together with several lesser princes in English pay, would attack France from the north and east. The scheme was delayed by the refusal of many English barons to serve overseas, but John finally took over a force composed chiefly of expensive mercenaries. His own campaign failed, and the whole ambitious scheme came to grief in the Flanders marshes in July, 1214, when Philip Augustus routed Otto and his allies at Bouvines. That battle greatly increased the popularity of the king of France; it cost the German emperor his throne; and it also meant serious trouble for the English king.

John, returning to England, soon suffered the consequences. The signs of serious discontent had been multiplying since the refusal of some of the barons to accompany him to France or to pay the scutage which John had levied at a heavier rate than ever before in order to pay his mercenaries and allies. For perhaps the first time since the Conquest the majority of Englishmen sided with the barons against the king; for all classes had felt the burdens imposed by ruthless rule, and not only had John's military exploits been more expensive than Richard's, but the younger brother had given England no glory in return for her money. John at once started north to punish the recalcitrant barons, but was dissuaded by Langton, who was by now the unquestioned leader in the widespread demand for immediate reform. John, who, by the close of 1214, was feeling the loss of prestige at Bouvines, tried unsuccessfully to win over the churchmen and the Londoners with special concessions; but the barons grew constantly more restless. By Easter week in 1215 they gathered in force and a month later occupied London. There was some desultory campaigning, but John soon realized that the odds were too heavy to contest.

On June 12, 1215, one of the most dramatic moments of English history occurred at Runnymede, a meadow on the Thames. The king had ridden over the short distance from Windsor Castle to meet the large force of the barons and their followers who had come up the river the twenty miles from the capital. Stephen Langton, more than anyone else, gave form and direction to the events which followed. The barons brought with them a series of demands, and to this provisional document John set his seal. The next few days were spent in the discussion of details. By the end of the week the two sides had agreed to the sixty-three points of the famous Magna Carta, or Great Charter.

This celebrated document, which has been variously called a treaty, a statute, and a declaration of rights, was drafted in the conventional legal form of a charter or contract such as was used in granting a fief. The modern reader is struck by several strange features of Magna Carta. Unlike the American Declaration of Independence of 1776 and the French Declaration of the Rights of Man of 1789, it did not indulge in political philosophy or in sweeping generalizations about the freedom of the people. Its sixty-three articles, clauses, or "chapters" dealt with immediate, specific problems. They were arranged in a rather haphazard manner, covering a wide range of subjects. The most numerous items centered around questions of feudal dues, law courts, and administrative abuses. One needs to be familiar with technical feudal relations to appreciate those articles designed to keep the king within reasonable bounds in the matter of reliefs, wardships, aids, scutage, and similar points where he had abused his relations with his vassals. The legal articles show that, on the whole, the barons appreciated the value of the new court system established by Henry II, even though it cut into their own jurisdiction. Only in major cases of land title did they object strongly to the new writs. They felt that a royal court should be established permanently in one place for the convenience of litigants; they stipulated that penalties should be reasonable; and they hinted at John's abuse of the legal system in the celebrated fortieth clause, "To no one will we sell, to no one will we refuse or delay, right or justice." The specific attempts to check administrative abuses imply further shortcomings of John. He was to appoint as officials "only such as know the law of the realm and mean to observe it well" (article 45); the sheriffs, who had become very powerful as royal agents, were to be curbed (article 24); committees were to investigate abuses of the forest system (article 48); and royal officials were to be checked in the "purveyance," or commandeering, of property and labor (articles 28, 30, 31). Certain clauses, dealing, for instance, with weights and measures (article 35), fish weirs (article 33), and bridge-building (article 23), seem strangely out of place in company with the weightier ones. Finally, near the end, several clauses dealt with the immediate, temporary situation. John was to return all hostages (articles 49, 56–59); discharge certain unpopular officials and all his mercenaries (articles 50, 51); restore illegal fines and seizures (articles 52, 53, 55); and grant a general pardon (article 62). Langton and the barons, knowing the man with whom they dealt, were giving John no excuse to say that he did not know exactly what they meant.

Scholars have not yet ended their discussion of the exact nature of Magna Carta. One has called it a guarantee of liberty "to every being who breathes English air"; others have termed it a selfish feudal document. The latter view is probably the more correct interpretation. It was natural that the barons, interested in safeguarding their own interests, should give particular prominence to the clauses on feudal dues. A few items, however, definitely extend the privileges of Magna Carta to other classes, in just recognition of the widespread support which the barons had received. All the advantages which the barons gained from the king were definitely extended to their own vassals (article 60). The freedom of the Church was recognized (articles 1, 63), while the men of London and the other towns were promised "all their liberties and free customs" (article 13). In the first clause "all the underwritten liberties" were promised "to all freemen of our kingdom" forever, but this excluded the mass of unfree villeins, or serfs,—roughly four men out of five. The only reference to them in the Charter was the provision that a serf might not be deprived of his growing crops or his plow as legal punishment; he was not to be rendered unable to perform his full services to the lord of the manor.

Two famous articles of Magna Carta were later interpreted as implying far more than presumably was intended. The twelfth article stipulated that, with certain reasonable exceptions, "no scutage nor aid shall be levied in our kingdom, unless by the common consent of our kingdom." This was later stretched to imply the principle of "no taxation without representation" and was considered "the germ of Parliament." The "common consent," as spoken of in the Charter, however, was simply that of the leading barons and prelates, who actually represented no one but themselves, while the scutage and aids were feudal dues rather than taxes. The thirty-ninth article stipulated that no freeman should be arrested or otherwise molested "unless by the lawful judgment of his peers" and "by the law of the land." Although later generations expanded this into a guarantee of jury trial for everyone, it seems to have been originally a reactionary feudal protest against the royal courts. The barons wished to free themselves from trial by juries and royal judges, whom they did not regard as "peers" or social equals.

The real significance of Magna Carta is not to be found in its detailed provisions. They were conservative on the whole, designed to preserve conditions already time-honored. The lasting influence of the Great Charter lay in its general implications rather than in its sixty-three clauses, many of which soon became obsolete. Later generations of Englishmen were to remember particularly that John had given his assent to two principles upon which English constitutional development was based. One of these was that certain laws and customs were of greater authority than the king himself. The other was that, if the king did not observe these laws, the people reserved the right to force him to do so. Regarded in that general light, Magna Carta quite rightly ranks among the most important documents of history.

# Barons and Parliament

Magna Carta had a checkered career in later English history. Its immediate effect in the short remainder of John's reign was slight, as we shall see. Subsequent medieval kings, however, reissued or confirmed it in modified form about forty times (see pages 144, 155). Then it apparently dropped from sight, owing to the popularity of royal absolutism under the Tudors (1485–1603). Shakespeare, around 1595, wrote a whole five-act play about King John and did not make a single reference to Runnymede or to Magna Carta. Some thirty years after that, Magna Carta sprang into prominence when the Parliamentary party used it as a weapon against the Stuart kings and read into it some of those exaggerations which have been noticed. From that time on, it has been regarded as one of the fundamental bulwarks of English liberty. England, of course, has no written constitution of the type drawn up in the United States in 1787, but a famous English statesman once declared that Magna Carta, the Petition of Right (1628), and the Bill of Rights (1689) form "the Bible of the English Constitution." Countless orators during the past three centuries have called upon Magna Carta to strengthen arguments of almost every sort.

Three months after Runnymede the Charter was less effective than it was to be six centuries later. To enforce the terms, the barons had thought of no better device than a committee of twenty-five who could authorize civil war if the king failed to keep his word. Whether the blame lay with John or with some of the more hotheaded barons, civil war soon broke out. Innocent III absolved John from obedience to the terms of Magna Carta, but Langton still strove to maintain the Runnymede settlement. During that last year of his life John waged an energetic, ruthless, and fairly successful war against the barons. They finally called for help from Philip Augustus, who dispatched a considerable force under his son, later Louis VIII. The French occupied London and part of southeastern England while John conducted a campaign all the way from the Welsh border to the eastern counties. While his train was carelessly taking a short cut across an arm of the sea without due regard to the tide, John lost all his baggage and treasure and part of his men in the quicksands. Furious and disheartened, he recklessly overindulged in peaches and new cider, a meal which spared England a long civil war. John struggled on to Newark, where he died in rage in October, 1216, just two months after his great contemporary, Innocent III. John's record was such that no other English sovereign has ever borne that name.

John's death left his nine-year-old son to reign for fifty-six years (1216–1272) as Henry III. For once, the accession of a child to the throne was not only uncontested but actually accepted with enthusiasm by the barons, who forgot their hatred of John, preferring a child to a Frenchman. By necessity, Henry was crowned in the west of England, because Louis and his French army held most of the south and east. Henry was lucky in his regent, the ninety-year-old but still able William Marshall, and within a year the French menace was ended. The energetic English defeated the French on land and also won a signal victory at sea, which, if one excludes Alfred's exploits, has sometimes been termed the beginning of English naval history. Hubert de Burgh, the doughty commander at Dover, appreciated—as have all Englishmen in recent centuries—that the best way to handle invaders was to "drown them in the sea before they ever could set foot on the land." A storm had scattered the defense squadron long enough to let Prince Louis land with part of his French forces, but De Burgh was able to beat off the reinforcements upon which Louis depended. The French, in consequence, soon abandoned the invasion.

For the next forty years the political history of England was relatively uneventful. William Marshall acted as regent for three years, until his death, when the regency was carried on by Hubert de Burgh and three powerful churchmen. At twenty Henry began to rule in his own name. We shall return later to the matter of Henry's weak character and its unfortunate results. Never did the influence of the papacy run so high in England as during these years. Leaving politics for the time being, we must take notice of important developments of another kind.

The boy king was to reign through more than half of the thirteenth century. Many scholars now limit the so-called "Dark Ages" to a period roughly corresponding to the Anglo-Saxon era in England. The darkness began to disappear about the time of the Conquest, and the twelfth and thirteenth centuries—with their awakened interest in the world beyond one's own manor, the growth of towns with their guilds and active artisans, the renewed vigor of the Church through the mendicant orders, the rise of new universities, the building of cathedrals, and all the thriving, busy life of the later medieval period—were really forerunners of what is called the Renaissance.

One of the most significant features of the times was the rising importance of towns, with their trade and industry. During the Dark Ages town life had pretty much disappeared. The manor had been able to supply most of its own simple needs. Some of the manorial workers had taken time off from their farming to spin and weave wool for their clothing, to tan leather, to make shoes, and to do necessary tinkering and the like. About the time of the Conquest, town life began to flourish again on the Continent for the first time since Roman days. This was especially evident in Flanders and in the Rhine valley, as well as in northern Italy, the only locality where town life held its own during the Dark Ages. At this time the towns began to specialize in the making and exchanging of wares. The manors limited themselves, on the whole, to the raising of crops. The surplus food was brought to town to exchange for cloth, shoes, hardware, saddlery, and other articles produced by people who devoted themselves to particular crafts. Most of this industry was still on a local scale, but articles from distant regions began more and more to circulate in trade by way of the towns. This new activity in manufacture and exchange produced a surplus of wealth by which the more successful townsmen became prosperous. They developed into a new middle class; some of them came perhaps from the lower knights, but many of them were recruited from escaped serfs, who became free if they could remain in a town for a year and a day.

Considering her remote, northern position, England had had a fair share of Roman towns, as the names of places like Chester, Worcester, and Gloucester indicate by their derivation from the Roman *castra*, or "camps." Others at the time of the Conquest, when there were about a hundred so-called towns in England, included Saxon and Danish communities which had grown up around fortified places or abbeys and whose names often ended in "ton," "by," or "ham." Most of these towns, such as they were, differed from villages only in size; for few had developed the later functions of industry and trade which made the towns distinctive.

The Conquest gave English towns a temporary setback; for many were burned, and others were partly torn down to make room for castles. The Norman, however, gave more than he took, in this as in most ways. Law and order meant that traders could move about in greater security; in the Conqueror's train came the Jews, who always served as a stimulus to business; and the political union of England with Normandy and Aquitaine meant a lessening of the vexatious tolls and duties which hampered business. The Crusades too may have helped to stimulate trade and industry by increasing the desire for new articles. At any rate, during the eleventh century, in England as well as on the Continent, the rise of towns was slow but sure. Even during the anarchy under Stephen they continued to grow in southeastern England, and after that the increase was rapid. By 1300 the hundred English towns had grown to two hundred, and nearly every one had gained in activity, wealth, and importance.

# A History of England and the British Empire

London was then and for many centuries afterward the only community of any great size in England. It had about forty thousand inhabitants, less than half as many as Paris. It had no rival of more than ten thousand souls; the average town had probably about five thousand; and some contained barely a thousand.

Many of the townsmen may have kept little gardens on the side, but they devoted most of their time to handicrafts or trade. The first stage in an industrial career was apprenticeship. A boy was bound for seven years, more or less, to a master who taught him his trade and fed and clothed him; in return the apprentice worked without pay. Then he became a journeyman, working for the master for wages. If successful, he might become a master himself, with a shop of his own, working alongside his apprentices and journeymen, and selling the goods which he had helped to make. The master thus combined both capital and labor, industry and trade.

In England, as on the Continent, the townsmen organized themselves into guilds, which secured official charters. Some of these might be simply social clubs for friendly drinking, but the two most important types were the merchant guild and the craft guild. The former, which developed first, was a sort of local chamber of commerce, composed of the leading masters in the various crafts. Its chief function was to protect the interests of its members, giving the townsmen a monopoly of the business at the expense of "foreigners," who included all outsiders, even those from the next town. The merchant guilds also acted together in securing special privileges for the town, and often virtually took over the town government. The craft guild was more like a modern labor union, except that it was composed of all men concerned, both employers and employees,—masters, journeymen, and apprentices. Each craft, such as the carpenters, masons, weavers, tanners, shoemakers, goldsmiths, coppersmiths, and blacksmiths, would have its own guild in each town, including all local workers. Each of these guilds would have its own regulations designed primarily to prevent fraudulent work and to ensure the size and quality of the products. Gradually the craft guilds became so rigid in excluding newcomers that the system broke down. In their day, however, the merchant guilds did real service in securing special privileges for the towns, while the craft guilds maintained a high quality of workmanship.

For the exchanging of local goods each town usually held a market at least once a week. The countrymen would bring in their produce and would purchase what they needed from the masters' shops. For the more elaborate articles coming from a distance there would be fairs, held once or twice a year at certain places.

# Barons and Parliament

The most celebrated of these was the Stourbridge Fair near Cambridge, which attracted traders from many lands.

At the outset the political status of the towns was quite indefinite. Some were in little better condition than villages of manorial serfs and were dominated by officials of the king or by some noble or churchman. Gradually, however, the townsmen bargained—usually in the beginning with the king—for special privileges which gave them much greater freedom. There were various things which they desired: the right to pay a lump sum (*firma burgi*) to the king instead of various petty tolls and rents; exemption from tolls throughout the king's lands; the right to a town court, instead of the regular hundred or shire court, for everything outside royal court jurisdiction; the right to elect local officials in place of having a royal official; and, finally, the right to a merchant guild. The borough, if it paid enough, would secure a charter granting one or more of these rights. London had all of them, from a charter given in the reign of Henry I, and could deal directly with the king like a powerful vassal. Its charter privileges were confirmed in Magna Carta. Towns had better luck in securing charters from the king than from barons or churchmen. There is some question about the policy of Henry II toward borough charters; but they were granted in large numbers by Hubert Walter, the justiciar who left no stone unturned to raise money for Richard's costly ventures, and John followed this example in his zeal for more money.

Life was more interesting in the towns than on the isolated manors. Carnivals, pageants, and religious plays were common, as well as brawls and riots. Large sums were spent on the beautification of the churches as well as in alms to the poor. All in all, the towns gave England, as they did the Continent, the busy, creative work of the artisan which did so much to make the Middle Ages memorable. Today, in their picturesque remains, we get an idea, not only of crowded quarters, physical discomforts, and unsanitary conditions, but, withal, of the charm of crooked streets, overhanging houses, busy market places, profusely decorated guildhalls, and imposing churches. The towns, moreover, with their newly acquired wealth, attracted the attention of rulers and barons. The new but increasing middle class, as we shall see, was given its share in the national government during the reigns of Henry III and his son.

The thirteenth century saw the Church at the height of its power; for Innocent III had built it solidly from within while enhancing its external political prestige. The papal hold on England was particularly strong under Henry III. Where previous kings had resisted church encroachments, Henry was thoroughly subservient to

# A History of England and the British Empire

the Pope, who did not hesitate to take full financial advantage of this fact. In return, however, England profited greatly in education, architecture, and other fields where church influence was paramount. To the approximately five hundred monasteries in England by 1200, one hundred and fifty-seven new ones were added during Henry's reign. In the seven centuries since Saint Benedict, however, the monastic system had lost much of its early vigorous simplicity. The early monasteries had served as frontier outposts in carrying Christianity to the barbarians and had fulfilled many valuable social and cultural functions (see page 26). The intellectual, the peaceful, and the weak, as well as the pious, had found valuable refuge in them. The very piety of the monks, however, led to their decline. In England, as on the Continent, dying reprobates were prone to leave much of their wealth to monasteries in order to help win forgiveness for their sins. The monks no longer had to work in the fields, for as the owners of manors they of course had serfs. Therefore many of the Benedictine monks, well provided for in this world's goods, tended to become lazy and sometimes degenerate. The result was that several reform movements started in European monasteries. Foremost among these was the movement at Cluny, as early as the middle of the tenth century, and the one at Clairvaux in the twelfth (see pages 74, 95). The latter establishment was the home of the extremely strict Cistercian order, many of whose members came to England during the reign of Stephen. The trouble was that prospective donors felt that the prayers of the stricter monks might be more effective, so that they left their lands to them, with the result that they too were tempted to become soft, lax, and worldly. It is fair to say that the Cistercians were the least corruptible of the orders, if one may judge from general reports. In the matter of estate management, which became exceedingly important in England's country life, they set an extraordinarily able example, and so effectively developed sheep-raising for the wool trade with Flanders that northern England and Scotland eventually found a valuable source of wealth in wool.

Although few new monastic establishments came into being in England after the thirteenth century, an energetic new type of "regular" clergy appeared early in that century (see page 25). Unlike the monks, who spent their lives shut up in a community, the so-called mendicant or begging orders, or friars, went out among the people, to share in their poverty and distress, to set an example of Christian living, and to teach pure doctrine. Part of the work of Innocent III, who brought the Church to the height of its power and influence, was his sanctioning of these orders of Franciscan

# Barons and Parliament

and Dominican friars. He recognized the need for reform in the wealth and worldliness of many of the upper clergy and the lazy ignorance of many of the lower. He finally sanctioned the proposals of Saint Francis, who had been a rich, pleasure-loving youth in the Italian town of Assisi before he determined to try to reproduce the simple life and the helpful services of Christ. A few years later the Pope gave his approval also to the Dominicans, named after their founder, the Spanish scholar Saint Dominic. Alike in being mendicants, who lived wandering lives in abject poverty, the two orders differed in their aims and activities. The Franciscan "Gray Friars" (later robed in brown) were like social workers in their close contact with the people and in their efforts to supplement the work of negligent parish priests. They were the "jolly friars," and were popular, perhaps, partly because they often did not stay long enough in a parish to see their penances carried out and also because they brought tales of the outside world to isolated places. The more intellectual Dominicans, with their white gowns and black hoods, were "preaching friars" and devoted themselves to combating heresy, especially in southern France, where clever heretics were making fools of ignorant churchmen in debate. These Dominican "Black Friars" never attained the popularity of the Franciscans; for they became the chief agents of the hated Inquisition, and men punned on their name to dub them "the Hounds of God."

In England, where the Dominicans arrived in 1220 and the Franciscans four years later, there was little heresy to combat, and even little feeling against the papacy until Henry III's actions finally aroused it. Yet, as the last of the foreign influences to reach England directly, the work of the friars reached wide proportions. The Franciscans in particular made a tremendous impression upon the lives of the poor. They preached and administered the sacraments in simple language and made themselves always readily accessible to the downtrodden and forlorn. In the towns they were a godsend to the crowded people, especially in the healing of the sick. Unlike the monks, with their isolated communal life and landed wealth, they did not pose as examples to the people but went into their hovels to aid them personally. At this time both orders sided with the people against the king when political troubles arose, and current songs attest the popularity of the friars; but by the time of the religious reformer Wiclif, a century later, they were no longer popular.

The two mendicant orders were also intimately associated with the early history of the two great English universities. The rise of Oxford and Cambridge was part of the general appearance of higher educational institutions throughout Europe at this time. Schools, which had largely disappeared during the barbarian invasions, had been somewhat in evidence in connection with monasteries and cathedrals since the early palace schools of Charlemagne and Alfred; but these were chiefly used for training for the local priesthood. It was not until the eleventh or twelfth century that the first real universities started. They were built almost wholly of men and brains, and lacked almost completely campuses, as well as libraries and other buildings. The very word "university" (from a Latin word meaning "altogether") expressed the idea behind the original institution; for a medieval university at the beginning was simply an informal group of students, who gathered around some teacher with a reputation as a lecturer. Most of the student body might migrate en masse to some other center at any time, and occasionally it did so. The universities were under the protection of the Church, and the teachers at first were clerics. Even the present-day student enjoys a certain amount of "benefit of clergy" in disciplinary matters; for the dean frequently assumes police-court functions. Some of the early universities were guilds of students, as at Bologna (noted for its law), where the students managed everything and paid the teachers. Others were guilds of teachers, as at Paris (noted for its theology), which served as a model for the English universities. The students, whose ages ranged from the teens to middle age, normally listened to lectures and took notes; for books were too scarce and too expensive to be commonly owned. Degrees at first were simply licenses to teach. A full-fledged university, or *studium generale*, had four faculties: theology, civil or canon law, medicine, and the lesser faculty of arts. The term "philosophy" then, and for centuries later, included much that we call science today, and was strongly influenced by the work of the Greek philosopher Aristotle.

Various legends of the early founding of Oxford and Cambridge have grown out of the rival claims of the two places for priority. Because of the indefinite early stages of the medieval universities, which often were in operation many years before they were officially chartered, we cannot fix an exact starting date, as is possible with Harvard and Yale in the United States. Oxford seems to have been the center of some scholarly activity about 1170, when the quarrel between Henry II and Becket led many English students to leave the University of Paris and to settle at Oxford, about fifty miles up the Thames from London. Apparently some years later in origin than Oxford, Cambridge would seem to have received its first big impetus in the thirteenth century when a sanguinary town-and-gown

# Barons and Parliament

riot at Oxford caused large numbers to migrate to the sister institution in the eastern fen country. The connection between the university and the crown was much closer at Oxford than at Cambridge; for there was a royal palace, and several important political events took place in the town. In 1248 Henry III gave Oxford a charter which afforded the students more privileges than the townsmen and gave the university chancellor legal jurisdiction in addition to that of the mayor. The college system within the universities developed because of inadequate living conditions. Three of Oxford's colleges, University, Balliol, and Merton, came into being late in the reign of Henry III. Many of the students came from the lower middle class and went into the Church, which offered the most promising path to advancement.

A few prominent names stand out among the thinkers of Henry's long reign. A pioneer in England's literary and scientific development was Robert Grosseteste, who came from a humble Suffolk home and studied law, medicine, and natural science at Oxford, where he became chancellor. He was the first rector of the school established there by the Franciscans in 1224, and he built up such a reputation that he has been called the foremost mathematician and physicist of his age. He finally became bishop of the large diocese of Lincoln, and we shall hear more of him as a bold, outspoken opponent of the designs of Pope and king to subordinate the English clergy. He was the close friend and patron of another graduate of Oxford. This was the Franciscan friar Roger Bacon, who went from Oxford to Paris and who gained such a high reputation as a scientist that he was suspected of black arts. Twice he was forbidden by the church authorities to spread his radical views and once was even imprisoned, but a more liberal Pope personally asked him to write his celebrated *Opus Majus* about 1267. Like Francis Bacon later, Roger was distinctive as a pioneer in the study of scientific method. He found out a good deal by actual experimentation in regard to chemistry,—or alchemy, as it was called then,—which included the science of weights and the listing of "metals, gems, stones, colors, salts, oils, bitumen, etc." The study of optics also fascinated Bacon, and he became familiar with the use of the convex lens, "both for the magnification of objects [the simple microscope] and as a burning glass." He apparently knew something about gunpowder, and a great deal about geography. Ptolemy's geography was revised by him; and from the letter written by Christopher Columbus from Haiti it would appear that the explorer had relied in part upon Bacon in deciding to go westward to the Indies.

Bacon was not alone in these new interests. Other Englishmen, chiefly Franciscan and Dominican friars, shared these speculations with him. Neither they nor Bacon, however, were revolutionary in their ideas when it came to philosophy and theology. Bacon, it must be remembered, devoted a large part of his writings to grammar and to comments on Holy Scripture, like any other good medieval schoolman.

Outside the work of such scholars, little literature of lasting consequence appeared in England during the three "almost dumb" centuries following the Conquest. Such writing as there was consisted chiefly of chronicles and romances. The Anglo-Saxon Chronicle dwindled away to a disgruntled finish, in very bad English, within a century after Hastings, but various monks, writing almost always in Latin, took up history. The chronicler generally went back to Creation for a running start and boldly adapted previous works until he came down to his own time, where he could make valuable original contributions. William of Malmesbury, who flourished in the reign of Henry I, has been called the first real English historian since Bede. By the reign of Henry III a remarkable center of chronicling was the abbey of St. Albans, situated some thirty miles from London on the Great North Road, where the monks, in entertaining travelers, made the most of their opportunity to find out what was going on. The leaders at St. Albans were Roger of Wendover, whose *Flowers of History* carries the story to 1236, and Matthew Paris, who continued it to 1259.

The literature of the period reflected the refining influence of the new chivalry which was coming more and more into vogue. Chivalry (from the French word for horseman or knight) became the code of the aristocratic military class. Its precepts and practices were drilled into the young men first as pages, then as squires, and finally as knights. There had been an early and very masculine form of chivalry in vogue at the time of the Conquest. Its chief ideals, loyalty and valor, found favorite expression in the *Song of Roland*, which was sung at Hastings and which makes only one casual reference to a woman. By the thirteenth century a strong feminine influence was pervading chivalric thought and deeds. The softening effect may have come partly from the Church, which, in an endeavor to modify the harsh brutality of war, proclaimed the Peace of God, enjoining fighters to spare women and other noncombatants. But far more potent was the pagan influence of the gay regions of southern France. Both Eleanor of Aquitaine and Henry III's wife came from there, and their presence at the English court undoubtedly attracted French minstrels (troubadours, jongleurs, and the like), who were specialists in the new doctrines of romance. Love was uppermost in the new chivalry: every knight must be in "spiritual vassalage" to some fair lady; every lady must have a cavalier lover. One's own husband or wife had little to do with the system. Chivalry led knights to joust for the favor of proud ladies and to seek opportunities to rescue damsels in distress. The songs of chivalry created a world of unreality. The former rough fighting men took on more polished manners under the influence of "courtesy." In the main, the ladies were of their own aristocratic class; chivalry did not extend to townsmen or villeins. The new feminine influence even extended to ecclesiastical fields; for churches were now being dedicated to "Our Lady," in the hope that the Virgin Mary would intercede against harsh divine justice at the Judgment Day.

That new atmosphere of chivalry was particularly receptive to the legends of the mythical King Arthur who had supposedly led the last stand of the Britons against the Saxon invaders. The perennially vivid Celtic imagination had woven about him an amazing collection of tales which began to flourish in this period. Arthur figured prominently not only in the very readable but thoroughly unreliable collection of Celtic legends written in Latin, in the name and form of history, by Geoffrey of Monmouth, a Welsh bishop, but also in the *Brut*, or *History of the Brutons*, a lengthy poem written about 1200 by one Layamon, a parish priest of the west country. The title of the latter work was based on the old legend that the Britons were descended from one Brutus of Troy, a descendant of Aeneas. These tales, together with romances and stories of various sorts which were transmitted by minstrels from one land to another, found eager listeners in thirteenth-century England.

Besides the monkish chronicles and the tales of chivalry, dealing in Latin or French with the affairs of the upper classes, a few scattered fragments of verse in Middle English indicate a love of nature on the part of the middle or lower ranks of society. Perhaps the earliest example of English lyric verse is the "Cuckoo Song," dating from about 1240:

> Sumer is icumen in,
> Lhude sing cuccu!
> Groweth sed, and bloweth med,
> And springth the wood nu—
> Sing cuccu!

and so on for two more verses. By the time of Chaucer, a century and a half later, we shall see how the different languages and the different interests were merging to form a real English literature.

# A History of England and the British Empire

The artistic and creative element in medieval England found its chief outlet not in literature but in magnificent cathedrals and other church buildings. It was appropriate that a period so devout should find its expression in such a form. It was fortunate, too, that the architects so combined technical skill with their art that their creations still last to inspire a more worldly age. Styles in church architecture gradually changed with the centuries, but some features remained fairly constant. The building usually took the form of a cross, the top of which was represented by the choir or the apse, which contained the altar and generally pointed toward the east. The two transepts, at right angles, formed the crossbar, while the lengthy nave, stretching westward, was the main portion. Frequently two towers flanked the western entrance; sometimes a great central tower rose at the junction of nave and transepts.

The earlier churches, until late in the reign of Henry II, were of the type known as Romanesque, which was modeled originally upon the old Roman basilica or law court. The Romanesque type had round arches, massive pillars, thick walls, and small windows. The Anglo-Saxons had built many churches in what is generally called the crudest type of Romanesque in Europe. The Norman bishops and abbots replaced every Saxon cathedral and large church building with a new structure in sturdy Norman Romanesque. Only in the smaller parishes were the Saxon churches spared. The noblest survival of Norman building energy is found in the yellow-stone cathedral, with its adjacent castle, on the river bank at Durham, "half house of God, half castle 'gainst the Scot," as befitted the dual role of the earl-bishop, guardian of the northern border. A famous critic has pointed out that this massive, vigorous, stern Norman Romanesque reflects the distinctly masculine spirit of the eleventh century, just as does the minstrels' *Song of Roland*.

A more graceful type of architecture, known as Gothic, began to appear in northern France about 1150. It was characterized by pointed instead of round arches and by a great increase of window space at the expense of the hitherto massive walls. The most exquisite expression of this new architecture was reached in such French cathedrals as Amiens, Reims, and Chartres; but the influence quickly spread to England, which developed a distinctive Gothic of its own, rather more dignified and restrained than the exuberant French. Gothic passed through three stages in England: the Early English type, with its lancet windows, from about 1180 to 1280; the more elaborate Decorated Gothic, with broader windows, from about 1280 to 1380; and finally, from about 1380 to 1530, the Perpendicular, with flatter-pointed arches and the familiar square towers.

# Barons and Parliament

The pointed arches of the Gothic style reached England late in the reign of Henry II. Canterbury Cathedral was partly destroyed by fire just after Becket's murder, and one William of Sens was brought over from France to direct the rebuilding. After he fell from a scaffold, William the Englishman carried on the work, which was the first important example of Early English Gothic. The beautiful cathedral at Lincoln began to take form in Richard's reign, and by the time of Henry III the graceful new style was well established. This was fortunate; for that long reign was a very active period of building new churches and abbeys, as well as rebuilding the simpler Norman ones. Stonemasons were not the only artisans needed for this work. The enlarged windows were resplendent with colored glass; paintings and mosaics in brilliant hues filled the interiors; and sculptured figures were set in niches both inside and out. This artistic development was quite to the king's taste; for, in contrast to his own colorless personality, Henry himself had a genuine love of fine buildings and beautiful decorations. He undertook at his own expense the rebuilding, in Early English Gothic, of England's most famous church, Westminster Abbey, originally built by the Confessor. Salisbury Cathedral, regarded as one of the most beautiful in all England, came into being, very much as we know it today, between 1220 and 1266. Such rapidity was unique, for most of the cathedrals were not products of any one reign or even any one century. Bishops were constantly being tempted to pull down a transept, nave, or choir and to rebuild in the latest style; and if the body of the church was satisfactory, they could at least add new towers. The "minster," or cathedral, at York, built over the foundations of a seventh-century Saxon church, underwent at least one major operation in rebuilding or addition every fifty years between 1070 and 1472. Despite those constant transformations, most of the cathedrals have maintained a remarkable unity of spirit and design.

Architectural activity, of course, was not limited to churches. During most of the Anglo-Saxon period there was nothing worthy of the name of castle. The characteristic castle of the early Norman period was a wooden tower on an artificial mound of earth, probably surrounded by a ditch and a wooden stockade. The Conqueror, to be sure, built the Tower of London and two other castles of stone, but not until about the time of Henry III did one find the gaunt, square, stone "keep" rising straight from the ground to a considerable height, with walls sometimes as thick as fifteen feet. The Crusaders brought new ideas in castle-building back from the East. The keep was surrounded by outer walls which gave much more protected space and served as first lines of defense. Towers arose at intervals along the walls, and curved lines replaced straight ones, to eliminate "dead space" where the arrows of the defenders could not reach. This new castle architecture reached a climax in Cœur de Lion's Château Gaillard in Normandy and led to several powerful frontier castles in England. The manor houses of barons and knights were at first built with defense strongly in mind, and toward the Scottish border they long retained a resemblance to the castle keep. In the quieter portions of England more comfortable structures, utilizing wood and plaster, gradually replaced the earlier fortress-home. The main feature of all manor houses was the great hall, the center of social activity, used as a dining-room, and often, except for the master's family, as a sleeping-room. At their best the medieval homes of even the proudest barons lacked most of the modern comforts. They were too often smoky and drafty, privacy was lacking, and sanitary arrangements were primitive. A country house underwent even more constant and radical transformations through the centuries than did a cathedral, so that pure medieval examples are very rare today. The poor lived in mean, thatch-roofed hovels or in the crowded, overhanging houses of the towns.

Returning to the sorry and barren political history of Henry's first forty years as king, we find that he was not thoroughly bad, like his father; he resembled more closely, in his piety, his inept weakness, and his un-English sentiments, the flabby Edward the Confessor, whom he unfortunately chose as his model. Refined and cultivated, Henry loved beauty and magnificence; he was extremely devout; he liberally patronized art and religion; and his wife was so beautiful and clever that he let other women alone,—a rather rare virtue among kings. On the other hand, he was recklessly extravagant with his subjects' money; he was thoroughly out of sympathy with everything English; and he was ever ready to sacrifice English interests to Popes or to Frenchmen. Ungrateful to deserving supporters, his "heart of wax" was easily moved by the flattery of intriguing adventurers. Physically brave enough, he was morally a coward. He had that not uncommon combination of obstinacy and indecisiveness which leads to irritability when crossed. Like his father, he was false, shifty, and undependable. Lacking both vision and executive ability, he was nothing of a statesman. Dante, the Italian poet, consigned him to the purgatory of children and simpletons.

Henry's reign very quickly resolved itself into a bitter contest between the English and non-English interests. The latter were represented by four separate waves of foreigners who came over to enjoy high influence and fat offices. During most of the earlier part of the reign these outsiders were in the ascendancy. Prominent in the little group which controlled the kingdom after William Marshall's death was Peter des Roches, an unscrupulous adventurer from that part of Aquitaine called Poitou. John had given him a rich bishopric, and Peter for a while exercised much power. He brought over from Poitou the first wave of the alien parasites. One of Peter's nephews enjoyed an income as sheriff in sixteen different shires and then became treasurer. Those Poitevins were scarcely disposed of when another swarm of Frenchmen came in the train of Henry's charming bride, daughter of the Count of Provence, from southeastern France. Her four uncles all found remunerative posts, one even becoming Archbishop of Canterbury; and many other poor relations of the queen were also well cared for at public expense. A third group from France consisted of Henry's four half brothers. His mother, widowed while still young, had married her original fiancé, from whom John had taken her, and Henry's spoils system provided well for the children of that second marriage.

The fourth swarm of invaders came not from France but from Rome. The Popes were determined to make the most of John's grant of England as a papal fief. Rome had an insatiable thirst for money, and was ready to "milk dry" any land where the ruler did not raise objections. Early in the reign two papal legates took part in governing the country. Heavy financial demands upon the English Church were made, and paid, even up to a fifth of its income. Then the Pope began to fill English church offices with foreigners, chiefly Italians. By the "provisor" system he claimed the right to "provide," or promise to appoint, a man to a church position as soon as it should become vacant. One Pope went so far as to demand that three hundred English positions be reserved for members of Roman families. Many of these alien appointees never bothered to visit England, but drew a goodly income while allowing the actual work to be done by underpaid deputies.

Under the influence of these foreign elements the king was drawn into a foolish, costly, and impractical foreign policy. The papacy persuaded him to chase an alluring but futile will-o'-the-wisp in placing his son Edmund on the throne of the Two Sicilies (Naples and Sicily). This was a matter in which England had no possible interest, but it suited papal political policies in Italy. The English treasury therefore paid heavily for the empty and short-lived honor. Henry's brother, Richard of Cornwall, received an equally hollow title with his election as successor to the Holy Roman emperor. In the meantime the French were closing in on Aquitaine, England's last remaining French province. For a while Henry lost it almost completely. With difficulty and at great expense he finally recovered a part, hereafter known usually as Guienne.

During all this time the "England for the English" party fought the foreign influences with varying success. Their stand closely resembled Godwin's resistance to the Norman favorites of the Confessor. The first strong champion of the English group was Hubert de Burgh, victor of the sea fight off Dover and one of the little group which governed England for the boy king after the death of old William Marshall. For eight years, as justiciar, he stoutly contested Des Roches's power, but was finally dismissed in shameful disgrace. The son of William Marshall led a revolt which was crushed. Des Roches and his Poitevins, however, were finally ejected, only to be replaced in short order by the new queen's Provencal relatives. Three times Henry was forced to reissue Magna Carta, for he was always ready to evade the most solemn oaths. Some of the English prelates stood out against the alliance of king and Pope. Their leader was Robert Grosseteste, bishop of Lincoln, whom we have already noticed as an intellectual and scientific leader. He believed in the normal rights and authority of papacy, but felt that it could command obedience only when its orders were in keeping with the teachings of Christ and his apostles. While rigidly reforming morals and discipline in his own diocese, he fought successfully against the exorbitant financial demands which Henry permitted the Pope to make. Grosseteste pointed out that the foreign churchmen, appointed under the "provisor" system, were annually carrying out of the country 70,000 marks (c. £47,000), at least equal to the regular revenue of the king; and he flatly refused to find a place in his diocese for a nephew of the Pontiff. Rome started to punish him, but hesitated because of his character, influence, and popularity. Meanwhile, the king's foreign ventures were increasing in cost and bringing nothing in return. By 1254 his debts amounted to 350,000 marks (c. £235,000), which was a sum equal to several years of normal income.

Henry's costly rule and his subservience to foreign influences finally resulted in several efforts to set up machinery for the limitation of the royal power and led to the beginnings of Parliament on a broad national basis. There was constant constitutional experimenting from the middle of the thirteenth to the end of the fourteenth century. Chance events, determined by the outcome of a battle or of the political exigencies of the moment, have taken on unusual significance in later days because they marked the obscure beginnings of Parliament, which became the most successful constitutional body in all history.

# Barons and Parliament

The storm first broke early in 1258. Henry summoned to London what was already being called a "parliament," though it still consisted of only the officials, nobles, and churchmen of the old Great Council. "Parliament," which comes from the French for "talk" or "discuss," has been defined as "any meeting of the King's Council that has been solemnly summoned for general business"; and for a half century more there was little uniformity in the elements of its membership. A chronicler dubbed this the "Mad Parliament," and that name was fitting if one uses "mad" in the sense of "angry." Henry always needed money, but at the moment he needed more than usual and proposed an extraordinary levy. The clergy discreetly withdrew, but the barons organized in opposition and defied the king. When, after adjournment, Parliament met again at Oxford that summer, the barons came fully armed. They forced upon Henry the "Provisions of Oxford," which transferred the royal powers to a number of baronial groups. Business was to be conducted in the name of the king through a council named by one baronial committee and constantly checked by another. Several reforms, particularly the expulsion of the foreign favorites, were contemplated. This was a much more thoroughgoing system of baronial control than the inadequate committee set up by Magna Carta, and it has been called the high-water mark of the baronial efforts to rule. The system, however, did not last three years. The barons, though united in opposition to the king, were torn by selfish dissensions when they came to administer the royal power themselves. The Pope annulled the Provisions. The king and barons laid their claims before the French king, Louis IX (Saint Louis), for arbitration, and he also decided in favor of Henry in the so-called "Mise of Amiens" early in 1264.

That led at once to civil war and brought to the foreground a remarkable baron, Simon de Montfort. Strange to say, this new leader of the "England for the English" party was a native Frenchman who had once been one of the most unpopular of the foreign favorites. His father, of the same name, had with cruel thoroughness harried the heretics of southern France for Innocent III. The younger Simon had come to England to secure the lands and high position which went with his title of Earl of Leicester, inherited through his mother. He married the sister of Henry III and served as governor of Aquitaine. Eventually the two brothers-in-law fell out. Simon was harsh, domineering, and impetuous, but he threw his heart, his energy, his common sense, and his real military ability into the fight for political reform. There was some brisk campaigning around the southeast coast, and finally the rival armies met in

May, 1264, at Lewes. Prince Edward, the future Edward I, drove deep into the London infantry in Montfort's center with a sweeping cavalry charge. While the prince was in pursuit, Montfort charged in from the flanks, overcame the rest of the royalists, and took many prisoners, including the king himself. That battle of Lewes made Simon master of England for fifteen months.

This brief period of Simon's rule is memorable because, for the first time, representatives of the towns were summoned to sit in Parliament. On at least one occasion, in 1254, each shire had been directed to send to a parliament a number of knights. Montfort added the final element of the present-day Parliamentary membership when he called for two representatives from each of certain cities and boroughs. It is highly improbable that Simon had any democratic motives for this action, but he did not want to neglect any possible element of strength. Montfort's Parliament was a partisan one, drawn from his own supporters. For this reason, and also because it was not summoned by the king, it did not establish a precedent for future Parliaments. Nevertheless, Montfort's example had much to do with the summoning of a similar "model" Parliament by Edward I thirty years later. Beyond setting that all-important example, Montfort accomplished little that was constructive during his brief period of power.

The royal forces quickly counterattacked with success, under Prince Edward, who had escaped from confinement. Some of Simon's followers deserted him, and his sons were not equal to the military tasks he assigned them. In August, 1265, Edward, with a greatly superior force, trapped Simon at Evesham, in a bend of the river Avon toward the Welsh border. The one-sided fight was quickly over, and Montfort's body was hacked to pieces. To the people he became a martyr, and he was almost worshiped as a saint.

As in the case of Magna Carta, the ultimate influence of the baronial opposition was greater than its immediate result. Neither the people nor the crown forgot that kings had been forcibly called to account for their misrule. The wiser monarchs profited by the lesson. Some of the more foolish suffered deposition and even death because they failed to take into account the teachings of Runnymede, Oxford, and Lewes. The barons had shown themselves unable to set up a satisfactory government of their own. They were torn by too many selfish motives, and their rule did not rest upon a sufficiently broad basis. They had served, however, as indispensable shock troops in the struggle for English liberty; for at that time they were the ones best equipped to offer successful resistance to absolutism.

# Barons and Parliament

Fortunately for England, even before the king died (seven years after Evesham), the control of royal policy had passed from the futile fingers of the aging Henry to the able grasp of his son whom he had named for Edward the Confessor. Montfort's work did not die with him, for the new king was sufficiently intelligent and magnanimous to profit by his able rival's example. Some of the best features of the baronial reforms were incorporated into law two years after Simon's death, and Edward showed an open mind in his continued experimenting with the idea of representative government.

England's four strongest medieval kings each left a lasting contribution to the nation's constitutional development. We have noticed how the Conqueror brought over the political feudal system; Henry I built up a centralized administration; and Henry II organized the legal system. Edward I (1272-1307), the last of this important quartet, contributed further legal reforms and added much to the development of Parliament.

Edward I (numbering started with the Conquest) was the first king since the Conquest to be regarded as primarily English, for his predecessors had been essentially French. Six feet three in height, with a magnificent physique and a strong, attractive personality, "Longshanks" was every inch a king, and not without cause he has been called the greatest of the Plantagenets. Always clear-headed, he drove his tremendous energy along lines best calculated to bring results, and early he overcame those traces of the Angevin impulsiveness which had marred some earlier royal careers in his family. He was an enthusiastic sportsman and a first-rate fighting man; but he was also a statesman, with a realization of the needs of the present and future. Like his father, he led a spotless private life; and he was religious, but without subservience to Rome. He believed strongly in royal power and would never yield until compelled. The tradition of baronial resistance had been built up in the two preceding reigns, however, and Edward stirred up so much opposition with his ambitious projects that he had to give in occasionally. Had such a man followed directly upon Henry II, royal absolutism might well have become firmly entrenched in England.

Edward was absent on the futile last major Crusade when the news of his father's death reached him. Everything was so quiet in England that he spent two years on his leisurely return. On the way he stopped in France to do homage for his fiefs and was received by the king with noticeable coolness, prophetic of future friction. For the first twenty years of his reign he was remarkably successful. Wales was conquered, and he made reforms of lasting value in law and government. Then foreign complications arose on every side, and the barons grew restless. "Longshanks" suffered several setbacks, but he left Parliament as a lasting heritage of the utmost importance. Edward's work in Wales, Scotland, and France will be postponed for later treatment while we analyze his contributions to English constitutional development.

The king was scarcely back in England before he began to make effective use of a very important new device, the statute. This was a kind of legislation issued by the government and intended to be permanent, which had received the assent of both the king and of what was soon to become Parliament. For temporary and minor matters the king and his small council might often issue ordinances, but for matters of fundamental importance it became customary after Edward's time to secure the assent of Parliament to a legislative act. Edward's six great statutes, from "Westminster the First" in 1275 to "Westminster the Third" in 1290, may not all have received the concurrence of the shire knights and the burgesses in that experimental period, but they have come down through the centuries with all the authority of full-fledged acts of Parliament. Only a few in the reign of Henry III antedate them in the long record of "statutes of the realm." Statutes became the law of the land, overriding all previous customs, decrees, or decisions which might conflict with them. The legislation of Edward I, which covered a wide range of matters, was of lasting importance in improving the legal, administrative, and financial work of the government.

Edward has been called the "English Justinian" because of his legal reforms. Henry II had set up the machinery of royal courts which had led to the development of the common law. Edward perfected that machinery, but his more important contributions consisted in defining by statute certain major features of the law itself. In the century since Henry II gave them their start, the royal justices had by their decisions been molding the law and even making new law. The statutes took precedence over this judge-made law. To a certain extent Edward's legislation was a codification of the law as it had thus developed, but in some cases he introduced new features which were an advance upon the existing law. The royal courts, often to their displeasure, had to recognize the superior authority of these statutes. Edward did his work so thoroughly that, in the words of Maitland, one of the leading students of English law, "For ages after Edward's time, king and Parliament left private law and civil procedure, criminal law and criminal procedure, pretty much to themselves."

Edward's legislation left its most permanent traces in the field of land law. His statutes *De Donis* and *Quia Emptores*, known, like papal bulls, by their opening words, dominated the conditions of landholding in England for centuries. They reflected the decline of the old political feudal relationship, already weakened by the introduction of scutage a century earlier. The vassal's duties of fealty, homage, military service, court attendance, and the like were passing into the discard. The fighting men, as we saw, were becoming country gentlemen, and the economic, landholding side of feudalism alone remained important. The relationship of "lord and vassal" was shifting to that of "landlord and tenant." The king and chief barons, as the principal landlords, were interested in retaining all they could of the feudal features which were still profitable—the relief, wardship, and escheat which might come at the death of the vassal-tenant. The new legislation, therefore, was aimed against any transfer of property which would diminish those profits. The statute *De Donis* established the practice of entail. Land would be granted to a tenant and to the "heirs of his body." Such land could not be disposed of as the tenant or the succession of eldest sons saw fit; they had only a life use of it; and if the line of direct heirs ran out, the land reverted by escheat to the lord. This tended, even to modern times, to keep family estates intact and to concentrate the ownership of land in the hands of a relatively small group. The statute *Quia Emptores* was directed against the former practice of subinfeudation by which a vassal could grant part of his land to a subvassal who would owe to him the profitable relief, escheat, or wardship. Such a subvassal now became the direct vassal or tenant of the granter's overlord. This eventually increased the number of tenants who held directly from the king.

In a similar desire to preserve the profits of the landlord, Edward aimed the Statute of Mortmain (1279) against transfers of property to the Church without his consent. The "dead hand" of the Church never relinquished any property which it once received; and as the Church was a perpetual organization, which never died, the overlord lost all hope of future reliefs, wardships, or escheats. The judges and lawyers of the royal courts, who were never enthusiastic about these statutes anyway, quickly developed legal fictions whereby entails could be broken and the Church could receive the benefits of new grants.

In perfecting the legal and administrative machinery established by Henry II, Edward ordered the barons to show by what authority (*Quo warranto*) they were still exercising jurisdiction in their courts. This roused strong opposition; for few barons could show charters, and one stoutly stated that his sword was his authority. Edward did not press the matter too far, but his action led to the gradual decline of baronial jurisdiction except for villeins' cases in the manor courts. Chancery, as a regular court, had not yet come into being, but the separate existence of the courts of King's Bench, Common Pleas, and Exchequer was recognized. These had all sprung from that small body of officials known as the Curia Regis or King's Council, which grew up under Henry I (see pages 83 ff.). This council still retained an important place in giving advice to the king and in settling important or tangled questions which did not fall into the regular business of the law courts or government departments. A new administrative branch known as the "wardrobe" was growing more influential. More directly under the king's eye than the Exchequer or the chancellor's office, it took on an increasing amount of financial and other governmental business. A well-trained corps of civil servants was growing up to handle these various branches of official activity.

Military reform was another feature of Edward's legislation. He systematized and improved upon the Assize of Arms by which Henry II, a century before, had laid the broad foundations of a national militia (see page 108). As in the earlier legislation, Edward stipulated that the lesser freemen maintain the modest equipment for infantry service, while all men with an annual income of at least £20 from land were required to accept knighthood, which involved the more costly paraphernalia of the cavalry.

Finally, innovations in the national finances were instituted because the cost of government was steadily increasing while the king's normal income remained fairly stationary. Henry II had managed with an annual average revenue estimated by Sir James Ramsay at £25,000. Under John this rose to £40,000. The average for the long reign of Edward I was £67,000, and in three different years it exceeded £100,000. With Edward III (1327–1377) the average was to rise to about £140,000. The earlier kings, as we saw in the case of Henry I, had been able to meet most of their expenses from their relation to the manorial and feudal systems. They received roughly £10,000 from the manors and towns of their royal demesne, and about an equal amount from feudal incidents such as reliefs, wardships, escheats, and vacant bishoprics, together with court fees and fines (see page 85). They might at times increase the amount by levying an arbitrary "tallage," or tax, upon the towns or a scutage upon the vassals, but the "hereditary revenues" of the crown remained fairly constant at about £20,000. To meet the steady increase in their expenses, the balance had to be found elsewhere. The year 1275 is a landmark in the history of English revenue, because customs duties then appeared on a permanent, recognized basis. Edward was granted, as a part of his regular revenue, specified export duties on wool and leather. This was welcome to the people, as the burden fell principally upon foreigners. By the end of Edward's reign the king was receiving as much from the customs as from the hereditary revenues, and before long the customs were yielding two or three times as much. Import duties of two shillings on each tun, or cask, of foreign wine, and a penny on each pound's worth of merchandise, were also imposed. Hence these duties came to be known as "tunnage and poundage." Royal efforts to stimulate foreign commerce soon followed (see page 175).

The king meanwhile cut off one old source of royal revenue in 1290, when he banished all Jews from England. The earlier kings had allowed them to make fortunes at lending money and then had fleeced them regularly (see page 86). Edward's edict, which met with popular approval, kept the Jews banished until about 1650. Their place as moneylenders was taken by Italian bankers, and we find the king himself borrowing from Luke of Lucca and other "Lombards."

The combination of hereditary revenues and customs duties was generally enough for normal times of peace; but such occasions were scarce under Edward I, with his costly campaigning in Wales, Scotland, and France. The government finances were still regarded as the king's personal affair, and the people felt that he should "live of his own" from those two regular sources. If he needed more in an emergency, he was no longer to get it by levying arbitrary tallages and scutages but by means of a special direct tax on movables, with the consent of the taxpayers. The chief precedent for such a direct tax lay not so much in the Danegeld as in the Saladin Tithe which Henry II had levied in 1188 upon all who were not going on the Crusade. They were to pay one tenth of the value of their movable goods, which meant generally the surplus produce of a manor or the townsman's stock of wares. This Saladin Tithe opened royal eyes to a rich source of income, and the tax on movables became the basis for later subsidies. There were a few of these under John and Henry III, but the practice became prominent under Edward I, who was granted nine subsidies totaling more than £450,000. Each of the three main taxpaying groups—feudal landowners, churchmen, and townsmen (the villeins were not involved directly)—determined the rate at which it would pay. The normal grant by the laymen was "a tenth and fifteenth," that is, a levy of 10 per cent on the townsmen and of nearly 7 per cent on the landowners. The normal yield of such a grant was about £40,000. The clergy voted a separate "free gift," sometimes a tenth, sometimes a fifteenth. This voting of money became highly important, not only as a financial measure but also as the main cause for the growth of Parliament (see page 145).

During a period of constant experimenting, between 1250 and 1400, England's national assembly was developing, as we have seen, from a Great Council, limited to great barons and churchmen, into a Parliament, where those "Lords Spiritual and Temporal" shared power with a new House of Commons, representing the middle classes of town and country. The first half of the period saw the "commons" gradually admitted to the assembly; the second half saw them organize and gain in influence. The year 1295 is commonly taken as the standard date for the beginning of Parliament. In that year Edward I summoned the so-called "Model Parliament" which contained commons as well as lords. To legal-minded Englishmen, Montfort's Parliament of 1265, it will be recalled, was not a valid body, because it had not been summoned by the king. There is a danger, of course, of attributing too much to the Model Parliament; for though it has been called "more thoroughly representative than any England had yet seen," it by no means had all the functions and features of the modern Parliament, which is clearly divided into a House of Lords and a House of Commons, and which devotes its energy principally to the making of new laws. One of the reasons why Parliament ultimately became so highly successful is that, instead of suddenly being organized in a definite form, it "just grew." Because of constant adjustments and compromises, it became particularly well adapted to the needs of the nation.

The most influential members of the Model Parliament were naturally the barons, bishops, and abbots, who had been summoned for centuries to consult with the king and to give assent to his proposed measures. The witan of Anglo-Saxon times, as we have seen, had been such a body, and so, too, was its feudalized successor, the Great Council of the Norman kings (see pages 44, 73). In the Norman theory these men were the king's chief vassals, whose feudal duties included attendance at their lord's court. This group ultimately developed into the House of Lords, whose members still receive individual summons, not as representatives of any region or group but because of their rank.

The novelty in the Parliament of 1295, as well as in that of 1265, lay in the development of representation. The writs summoning the Model Parliament contained the phrase, which probably did not mean anything definite to the men of those days, "What concerns all should be approved by all" ("all," of course, excluded four men out of five as unfree villeins). In small communities it has often been possible for every free man to have a direct voice in the local government. The Greek city-state and the later New England town meeting are examples of such direct government. It is obviously out of the question, however, to gather all the free men of a whole nation into one place for deliberation. The thirteenth century offered a solution to this problem by having the various scattered districts and communities select representatives, empowered to speak and act for them in the central assembly. Some claim that Parliamentary representation was simply an extension of the practice of the shire courts, where each hundred, town, and village was instructed to send representatives to sit with the nobility, gentry, and clergy of the country. Others see a closer precedent in the national gathering of the Dominican friars, to which each local group sent its representatives. Whatever the inspiration may have been, the effect of representation has been all-important in the government of England and of many other lands.

The representatives of the "commons" fell into two categories which have remained distinct for centuries,—the county members and the borough members. Each of the forty counties, or shires, was directed to send two "knights," while one hundred and fourteen chartered cities, or boroughs, each sent two "burgesses," in addition to London's representatives. Normally only about eighty boroughs sent members during the Middle Ages.

The knights of the shire were more important than the townsmen, not only on account of their social position but also because they represented larger political units. Knights had been summoned to Parliament at least as early as 1254, eleven years before Montfort sent invitations to the townsmen. The knights represented the lower grades of the landholding feudal class. In theory they were fighting men, but actually they were leaving fighting more and more to the professionals and were settling down into peaceful country gentry, or "squires." Such men, belonging to the feudal aristocracy, might have been expected to have more in common with the great barons than with the upstart townsmen. Over on the Continent, men of similar position were rated as part of the nobility, a distinct caste whose "blood" separated them from the commoners by a wide gulf. England never developed such sharp barriers of caste, and one of the sources of her strength was the middle position occupied by this substantial group.

The inclusion of the borough members, a practice which had been employed on more than one occasion during the thirty years since Montfort's Parliament, was a recognition of the rapidly increasing importance of the towns. The townsmen were a comparatively new element in medieval society (see page 130). Their making and selling of goods, while not yet considered fully respectable, was generally recognized as profitable. The more prosperous townsmen could often lay their hands on more ready cash than could the proud barons. The townsmen, however, for a long time did not consider Parliamentary representation a privilege or an honor. To them it was generally a burdensome duty, much as jury service is still regarded. The borough had to pay its representatives for expenses while they were on Parliamentary duty, and at least one borough sought and gained permission to be exempted from the burden of representation. The townsmen probably realized that when their members reached Parliament they would be silenced by a general inferiority complex in the presence of the great men of the land and would probably simply be bullied or cajoled into agreeing to further taxes.

The nobles, the bishops, and the commoners from county and borough still continue as members of Parliament, but there was one group in the "model" body of 1295 which withdrew from later sessions. These were the representatives of the lower clergy. The Church preferred to vote its money to the king through its own body, known as Convocation. The bishops, because of their positions as extensive landholders, continued to sit in Parliament as well as in Convocation, and so did the important abbots until the monasteries were abolished around 1540; but the lower clergy before long sat in Convocation only.

While the members from shire and borough in theory represented the whole country, the huge body of villeins and other lesser workers had no say whatever in the choice of members. Not until the latter part of the nineteenth century was voting for members of Parliament placed on a uniform, democratic basis.

So much for the selection of members. The next problem was their organization after they assembled. The Estates-General, summoned as a French national assembly just seven years after the Model Parliament, remained clearly divided into three separate estates: the clergy, the nobles, and the "third estate," principally townsmen. The result was that the third estate was overshadowed by the two privileged orders and had no effective voice in the government. The Model Parliament probably divided in a similar manner, as each estate voted its own rate of taxation; but before long the English followed a different course from that of the French. The clergy withdrew from Parliament, as we have seen, leaving the landholders and the townsmen. The decision of the "knights of the shire" had far-reaching effects. Had they joined the great barons, the townsmen

# Barons and Parliament

alone might have sunk from view, as they did in France. The knights, however, seem to have felt that they could get along better with the townsmen than with the lords. Their decision was a gradual one, and it was almost half a century before one finds a distinct House of Commons, representing both country and town. The union of the knights with the burgesses gave the Commons a broad enough basis and a substantial enough membership to hold its own against the House of Lords. We shall see that around 1600 the Commons were to overshadow the Lords and that by 1700 they were more important than the king as well.

That "model" gathering in 1295 foreshadowed the basis of Parliament's membership; the "Confirmation of the Charters," two years later, pointed the way by which Parliament was to rise to power. Edward was in immediate need of large amounts for campaigns against both France and Scotland (see page 164). He had managed to antagonize all three of the classes which mattered: the barons were muttering at overseas orders and forest laws; the churchmen were ordered by the Pope not to submit to taxation; and the merchants were exasperated at the king's high-handed seizure of all the wool they were exporting. The result was that Edward, already over in Flanders to start his fighting, reluctantly agreed to the so-called "Confirmation of the Charters," in which he repeated the terms of Magna Carta and other royal concessions and also made an agreement that the crown would abstain from further "maletotes," or irregular exactions (such as the seizure of the wool), "without the common consent of the realm." The significance of this lay in the fact that it gave, by implication, the power of the purse to the new Parliament of Lords and Commons.

By the end of the thirteenth century, therefore, the foundations of Parliamentary development had been laid, both in personnel and in financial control. Parliament's organization, functions, and power were still vague and indefinite; but throughout the fourteenth century it gradually took form, acquired influence, and built up sufficient prestige to become an integral part of the English government.

# CHAPTER VII

## Beyond the Borders

### 1277-1377

EDWARD I won three popular titles: "Longshanks" for his height, "the English Justinian" for his constitutional reforms, and "the Hammer of the Scots" for his aggressive northern policy. He followed in the footsteps of that Roman emperor Justinian in more than lawmaking. Edward too had visions of expanded territory. He undoubtedly realized that the chances of recovering the Plantagenet lands in France, lost through his grandfather's carelessness, were slight. There were, however, the distant reaches of his own British Isles, where conditions were to give him excuse for intervention and invasion—were he wanting excuses.

Had it not been for the inaccessible, rough, and mountainous country of western and northern Britain, each of England's invaders might well have overrun the entire island and absorbed the Celtic strain centuries before. While those remote wildernesses kept the invader away, they likewise blocked national unity for the island. In Wales and also in Scotland lived the primitive descendants of the Celtic predecessors of the Anglo-Saxons, with their own distinctive language, habits of living, and crude tribal or clan organization.

In Wales the inhabitants built no permanent homes but lived in flimsy huts of boughs for a few months at a time as they followed their flocks and herds from valley to mountainside with the seasons. The old racial stock had kept itself sequestered from contact with the Saxons of England; but with the coming of the Normans southern Wales found its seclusion gone. Certain adventurous Norman lords were encouraged by their king to carve out estates for themselves, wherever in Wales they could conquer. As a whole, these Normans made their way up the river valleys of southern Wales; but, even in the lowlands, forest and marsh were barriers against their progress. These "marcher lords"—so called because, in feudal parlance, remote, dangerous border fiefs were generally known as "marches"— built themselves castles and became so well entrenched in power that not until the sixteenth century did they cease to be factors in Welsh affairs, nor until then was this part of Wales brought under close royal control. Though their independence and their private armies

# Beyond the Borders

were sometimes troublesome to the crown, on the other hand they were tremendously useful as buffers between southwestern England and wild Welsh raiders.

Most of the expansion of these marcher lords occurred between the reigns of William I and Edward I. Part of the inhabitants of a region generally fled, at the approach of the barons, to higher places where they might keep their old ways unmolested; but others stayed to live around the new castle and to accept the lord's control. Time, however, was on the invaders' side; for they had constant reserves of people and supplies behind them in England. The marcher lords introduced agriculture, permanent dwellings, and some trade to these communities around the castles, of which there were some one hundred and forty-three; and as time went on, the people represented a mixture of Norman, Saxon, and Welsh blood. For all this, peace did not come with the marcher lords. Even the Welsh of their communities, though they seemingly accepted the Norman rule, clung to their own language (which even today can produce the word "Llanfairpwllgynyllgogerchwyrnydrobwillandisilliogogogoch") and to other distinctive features, such as their own special music, which was sung in parts and rarely in unison. At heart they remained like their brethren in the remote fastnesses of the hills and were inclined to help the latter in their frequent raids upon the marcher lordships. "In the hills, tribe fought against tribe, and in the valleys, baron fought baron, while every baronial valley was at war with its tribal hills."[1]

Such were the conditions on the eve of Edward's Welsh conquest, with South Wales, to this extent, in the hands of Norman marcher lords, but with North Wales utterly primitive. From time to time before this, English kings—Rufus, for instance, and Henry I—had on occasion sent help to the Norman lords in their struggles with the Welsh. During the disorder under Stephen the Welsh regained some territory, and Henry II accepted homage from some of the native Welsh chieftains. It was in his day that the marcher lords from Wales, under Strongbow, undertook the initial conquest of Ireland (see page 112). Independent Wales reached its peak during the long reign (1194–1238) of Llewellyn, "the Great," a prince of North Wales who came close to realizing his ambition of uniting the whole wild western peninsula under his rule. Patronizing the bards liberally, he helped to arouse Welsh patriotism through a revival of poetry and of pride in tradition. He meddled steadily in the turbulent politics of England, siding sometimes with king and sometimes with baronial factions, while the borders suffered from a constant series of

[1] G. M. Trevelyan, *History of England* (1926), p. 208. By permission of Longmans, Green & Co.

raids and reprisals. He married an illegitimate daughter of John, but later broke with that king. John, it will be recalled, hanged his Welsh hostages and was deterred from invasion of Wales only by the temper of his barons on the eve of Magna Carta, some clauses of which were definitely to Llewellyn's advantage. Similar Welsh tactics were continued through the unsettled minority of Henry III.

The grandson of Llewellyn the Great, Llewellyn "ap Griffith," the last native prince of Wales, tried to follow in the same footsteps and to gain prestige in Wales by fishing in the troubled waters of English politics. He sided with Simon de Montfort, whose daughter he later married; but in 1267 the aging Henry III made a generous peace with him. In exchange for rendering homage to the English king, the last Llewellyn was to receive homage from virtually all Wales, even from most of the marcher lords. This success apparently turned his head: brilliant though he was, he saw himself as far stronger than the facts warranted, and seems to have interpreted these lenient concessions after Montfort's defeat as a sign of the fear he inspired in the English. Whatever his motives, Llewellyn rashly refused to render homage to young Edward I or to attend his coronation, stopped paying the indemnity he had promised, and continued the habitual ravaging of the borderlands. Thus Edward was furnished with ample provocation and legal feudal sanction for his attack on Wales in 1277. It was natural that Edward's first outside expedition should be directed against the Welsh; before coming to the throne he had been on the western border as earl of Chester and knew the situation well. While Llewellyn was ignoring his threats, Edward was being told by his Italian bankers that an export duty on wool would give him the money needed for a campaign (see page 151).

The expeditions of Edward into Wales were the usual story of such fighting by trained troops against primitive ones. His first invasion, in 1277, was planned well. He had a broad road torn through the forest in order to avoid ambushes, and he sent his supplies by sea, in ships of the Cinque Ports, to simplify his line of communications. Llewellyn's men retired to their mountain stronghold on the slopes of Snowdon; Edward threatened them with starvation when his ships captured the granary of Wales, the island of Anglesey, off the north shore. By the terms of his submission, Llewellyn's former extensive holdings were whittled down to a small region around Snowdon; and even for that he was required to render homage and to accept the fact that at his death the title of prince would revert to the English crown.

It has been remarked that "whom the gods would destroy, they first make mad." Celtic impatience hastened the complete conquest

# Beyond the Borders

of Wales. The Welsh grew restive under the rough methods by which Edward's officials tried to introduce English law. The match which set this unrest aflame was the sudden capture, in 1282, of the castle of the English justiciar of North Wales, who was badly wounded and kidnaped. This was the work of Llewellyn's brother David, who had sided with Edward in the first war. Edward invaded Wales more ruthlessly than he had done five years before. Llewellyn, in his inaccessible stronghold, might have waited for winter to drive out the English, but again Celtic rashness turned the tide. He made an unwise sally and was killed in a skirmish. His brother David was captured and was hanged, drawn, and quartered. With those two deaths Welsh resistance broke down, and the defeated country was at Edward's disposal.

Edward strengthened his hold on Wales by building powerful new castles of the latest type, with series of outer walls, practically impregnable to the crude siege machinery of the day. At one of these new castles, Carnarvon, his son, later Edward II, was to be born. According to a doubtful legend, Edward made one of his rare jokes by introducing the newborn baby to the Welsh as the prince he had promised them, who would be a native of Wales and could speak no English. However true that tale may be, the eldest sons of England's kings have ever since borne the title "Prince of Wales."

By the Statute of Rhuddlan,—sometimes simply called the Statute of Wales,—in 1284, Wales was definitely declared to be under the English crown and was divided into shires. English courts and law were definitely established. A merchant class was encouraged by England to build up towns and trade, as well as to furnish a prosperous group of taxpayers who could help with revenue problems. The towns became English, but the old Celtic speech and habits lingered on in the wilder regions.

Welsh independence ended in 1284, but the final complete union with England did not come until 1536. In the meantime one Owen Glendower, around 1400, made a spectacular but short-lived attempt to recreate Llewellyn's united Wales under native leadership (see page 201). The settlement at Rhuddlan left the marcher earls relatively undisturbed in their old powers. Their feudal fights, combined with tribal troubles in the hills, made Wales such a land of chronic disorder, pillage, and sudden death that Henry VIII decided to show the lawless land what government really meant. Some well-timed executions, combined with an act of Parliament, did the work. The Act of Union (see page 271) in 1536, a forerunner of similar acts for Scotland in 1707 and for Ireland in 1801, swept away the marcher lordships and other special Welsh features. Wales was incorporated definitely into the English government, with twelve regular shires and twenty-four representatives in Parliament. There will be scant occasion to refer to Wales again as a separate region; but two Welshmen, at least, were to leave their mark on English history: one was Henry VII, founder of the celebrated Tudor dynasty; the other was David Lloyd George, prime minister during the World War.

In summarizing England's relations with the "Celtic fringe," it has been stated with a great deal of truth that Wales was completely conquered; Ireland, partly conquered; and Scotland, never conquered. It is hardly accurate, however, to class Scotland, which was next to receive Edward's attention, as a Celtic nation. In blood and background, to be sure, in so far as any definite statement can be made about the Celts, the majority of Scotland's inhabitants belonged to that race (see page 14). But the Scottish government and dominant society took their form, speech, and spirit not from the examples of Ireland and Wales, with their loose tribal organizations, but from Saxon and Norman England. A relatively small part of Scotland, the southeast, was eventually to give tone to the whole land. This had been overrun by Anglo-Saxons, and Edinburgh, the capital, took its name from one of the great kings of Northumbria (see page 19). The Conquest had driven many Saxons from England into the Lowlands, and after them came various Norman barons who were invited into the country and who established a regular feudal system. The Scottish kings looked to England not only for wives but also for forms of government. Three kings in particular—Malcolm, a contemporary of the Conqueror; David, who ruled in the time of Stephen; and William the Lion, his successor—borrowed freely from the south, copying English shires, English boroughs, and English laws. They freely endowed churches on the English model while their barons were building castles of the English type. From that wealthy and dominant southeast corner, moreover, spread a modified English speech all over the Lowlands. In the northern half of the kingdom, beyond the "Highland line," primitive Celtic tribal customs continued to hold full sway until after the final revolt of 1745; but the Scotland with which Edward and his successors had to deal was a feudal kingdom, built on English lines and able to present a fairly united front.

Edward, fresh from his conquest of Wales, probably visualized, as had Henry II, the mastery of northern Britain. In 1290, the high point of his reign, with power and popularity at their climax, there seemed to be every chance of his achieving this by the easy means of a marriage contract. Scotland's king, falling over the edge of a cliff one dark night on horseback, had left as heir only a three-year-old

# Beyond the Borders

granddaughter, the child of his daughter (who had died at the baby's birth) and of the king of Norway. Scotland ran the risk of being absorbed into either Norway or England. Edward, after four years of negotiation with the Scots and the king of Norway, both of whom were suspicious of his intentions, achieved the engagement of the infant queen to his son, the slightly younger Prince of Wales, in 1290. Edward, by treaties, promised that, in the event of this dual rule of Scotland and England, Scottish laws and customs would be respected. Unfortunately, this peaceful union was not to be realized for another three hundred years, and much blood was to be shed meanwhile in the rivalry of the two nations, because the "Maid of Norway," a delicate girl, died on the rough wintry voyage from her home in her father's country.

In Scotland a divided nation and a disputed succession were the troublesome legacy of the maid. Of some thirteen claimants for the crown, three descendants of the three nieces of King William the Lion were in the foreground, and the choice narrowed down to John Balliol, grandson of the eldest niece, and Robert Bruce, son of her next younger sister. Edward, ever alert, saw a way to capitalize this situation. Before the Conquest there appeared to have been some acknowledgment by Scottish rulers of subservience to the English crown (see page 49). Since the Conquest, homage had been demanded at times by the English king. Except in the case of Henry II, however, this probably was simply for certain fiefs held across the border in England, just as the English kings did homage for their French lands. Henry II, to be sure, had actually received homage for Scotland, but Richard had canceled the claim. Nevertheless, Edward now declared that, as overlord of Scotland, he would take over the government until the rightful king was selected. The Scottish barons, on the brink of civil war, were in no position to resist this ultimatum, but this foreign highhandedness aroused deep resentment among the general run of the people. Balliol and Bruce both hastened to gain Edward's favor by taking the oath of homage to him. Edward referred the claims to a commission chosen by himself and the two rivals, and after the commission's report he eventually announced Balliol as king. This choice, based on primogeniture, apparently satisfied the majority of Scots; and had Edward kept his hands off Scotland after this decision, England might have long retained the nominal suzerainty with little outspoken objection from the Scots.

Edward, however, now treated the northern kingdom as if it were merely his feudal fief, with Balliol his vassal. In particular, he insisted that appeals could be made from the Scottish courts to his jurisdiction, a practice which had started during the interregnum and which was deeply resented by the Scots. In other ways, such as Edward's demands that Scotland furnish troops for English wars, Balliol found himself treated as a subordinate by his southern neighbor, rather than as a brother sovereign on terms of equality. At last, in 1295, goaded by the popular temper and by his barons, who apparently resented England's interference far more than did their weak-willed king, Balliol made an alliance with France, Edward's enemy of the moment. He followed this with a raid across the border, refused Edward's summons to explain these actions at Berwick, and thus renounced homage. It will be recalled that this was the year (1295) in which Edward called together the famous Model Parliament for money to attack these hostile Scots (see page 152).

The English king now acted quickly and openly the role of conqueror of Scotland. The border town of Berwick was captured, and then, in the battle of Dunbar, the Scots were so overwhelmingly defeated that most of their leaders surrendered. The capital, Edinburgh, next surrendered to the victorious English, and so did Balliol—both his crown and himself. Edward took over the government, and appointed English officials to rule in his absence. Adding to Scotland's shame, he carried back with him the historic Stone of Scone, which had long been used in Scotland's coronations. To this day the stone remains under the seat of the coronation chair of England's rulers at Westminster Abbey. In five months of 1296 Scotland had been completely vanquished—for the time being.

Balliol's alliance with France was of more than momentary interest. It was the beginning of nearly three hundred years of close Scottish-French friendship and alliance, a combination that was often to trouble their frequent mutual enemy, England. Philip IV, "the Fair" (1285–1314), like the second Philip, "Augustus," was one of the strongest kings of medieval France. Like the other Philip, who took over so much of the Plantagenet empire from John's loose hold (see page 120), this monarch had his determined eye upon that remaining sore spot, the fief of Aquitaine, still in English hands. Philip, firmly building up his royal power in France on the sure basis of ample royal revenues, took the same attitude toward his vassal Edward as that king had so successfully taken with Balliol. Edward, however, was not the one to endure such a policy of stricter overlordship and interference in Aquitaine. The seagoing French subjects of the two monarchs, Philip's Normans and Edward's Gascons from Aquitaine, had been fighting each other for some time, and Philip summoned his vassal Edward to answer for the Gascon depredations. Upon Edward's ignoring the order, Philip declared Aquitaine forfeit to himself. Edward's answer to this was to construct an anti-

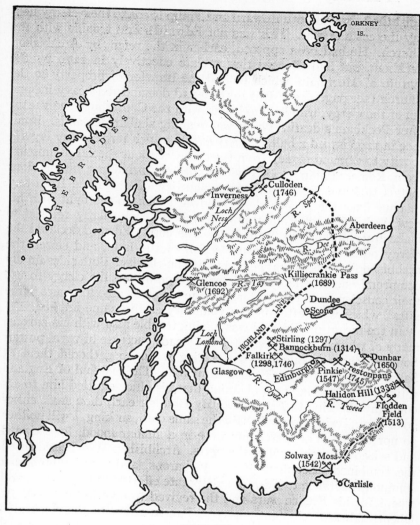

ORKNEY IS.

HEBRIDES

Culloden (1746)
Inverness
Loch Ness
R. Spey
Aberdeen
R. Dee
Killiecrankie Pass (1689)
Glencoe (1692)
R. Tay
Dundee
Scone
HIGHLAND LINE
Loch Lomond
Stirling (1297)
Bannockburn (1314)
Falkirk (1298, 1746)
Glasgow
R. Clyde
Edinburgh
Pinkie (1547)
Dunbar (1650)
Prestonpans (1745)
Halidon Hill (1333)
R. Tweed
Flodden Field (1513)
Solway Moss (1542)
Carlisle

SCOTLAND

French alliance and to declare war in 1294. Philip's alliance with
Scotland, however, gave England more immediate concern at home,
and not until Balliol's collapse, in 1296, was Edward free to turn to
the French troubles again.

By that time another outsider had interfered to postpone the
Anglo-French war. Edward, like John, was pitted not only against
a very strong French king but also against a very powerful Pope.
The newly elected Boniface VIII (1294–1303) began at once to

[ 163 ]

resist the efforts of both Edward and Philip to make their clergy help pay the costs of war. This was not Edward's first trouble with the Church. He had been opposed, earlier in the reign, by Archbishop Peckham, but had silenced that prelate effectively in 1279 by the Statute of Mortmain, which limited the transfer of property to the Church (see page 149). In 1294 Edward demanded a heavy income tax of the clergy, who had no leader with the Canterbury see vacant after Peckham's death. Philip was making similar demands. Boniface in 1296 issued a bull, *Clericis Laicos*, which forbade any lay authority to demand money from the clergy without special permission from Rome. Philip replied with a decree forbidding all precious metals to leave the country, thus shutting off the Pope from any revenue from the French clergy. Edward took up the fight with his new Archbishop of Canterbury, Winchelsea, who flatly refused to make any church grant to the king. Thereupon Edward declared the clergy outlaws, beyond the protection of the laws, and seized the archbishop's lands so that he had to live on charity. Both sides finally compromised. Boniface, in a later bull, permitted the clergy to use their consciences in the matter, and the king was able to secure "free gifts" which were often not as voluntary as the name implied.

In the meantime Edward was having trouble also with his barons, many of whom had long resented the steady increase of royal power. Some of them openly defied the king when he gathered them at Salisbury to discuss the French campaign. The marshal of England refused to go to Gascony, claiming that his office entitled him to accompany the king to Flanders. "By God, sir earl, thou shalt either go or hang," cried Edward. "By the same oath, sir king, I will neither go nor hang." The merchants were in a similar mood, for Edward had seized all their wool at the ports. Archbishop Winchelsea fused the combined discontent of clergy, barons, and merchants into a common resistance to Edward's desperate efforts to raise money and troops for his French wars and the revived trouble in Scotland. At Ghent, Edward reluctantly agreed, late in 1297, to the celebrated "Confirmation of the Charters" (see page 155). The chronic baronial opposition, coupled with the financial demands of foreign wars, pushed England further along the road of its remarkable constitutional development.

Pope Boniface was soon removed from his powerful position, not by Edward but by his rival Philip. Though forced to compromise on financial matters, Boniface in 1302 made an extreme claim of papal power in the bull *Unam Sanctam*, declaring that all were heretics who denied the supremacy of the papacy in temporal matters. The war of words and theories was ended by force. An adviser of

# Beyond the Borders

Philip led a troop of Frenchmen into Italy, where they handled the aged Pope so roughly that he soon died. Shortly thereafter the papacy came for nearly seventy years (1309–1377) under direct French influence. During that so-called "Babylonian Captivity" the Popes were Frenchmen living at Avignon, surrounded by French lands and under French influence, instead of at Rome,—a situation which later had a marked influence on England's attitude toward Saint Peter's successor.

Edward and Philip never came to a conclusive show of strength in the war which they began in 1294. Both were busy with their respective quarrels with the papacy, and both found themselves defeated by nearer and weaker neighbors. Edward had new troubles with Scotland, while Philip was repulsed by the burghers of Flanders who resisted his efforts to conquer them. The two kings finally patched up a peace of sorts, with Aquitaine restored to Edward. Had these energetic rulers, with their expansionist ambitions and their strong governments, been free to fight each other unhampered, the Hundred Years' War between England and France would probably have been under way forty years earlier. As it was, Philip's designs on Aquitaine and on Flanders, with its English wool trade, paved the way for the protracted struggle between the two nations which was to last from 1337 to 1453.

Scotland, in the meantime, had not stayed conquered more than a year after Edward's invasion of 1296. There suddenly arose among the Scots, as if from nowhere, one of those personalities that make for leadership in discontented times. Tall, strong, and magnetic, William Wallace was a guerrilla leader from the class of lairds, or lesser gentry. He quickly stirred Scotland to an intense pitch of democratic nationalism, almost unheard-of in that feudal age except perhaps among the freedom-loving mountaineers of the Swiss Alps. The nobles played doubtful roles: some looked down upon Wallace as an upstart commoner; others, who held land on both sides of the border, were as apt to be for Edward as against him. The feudal lord, as the English crown had already discovered in Normandy and Aquitaine, was frequently either internationally-minded or class-minded, or both, and often put special before national interests. The Scots whom Wallace roused to hot anti-English patriotism were, instead, mostly lairds, like himself, or the more substantial peasantry. Steadier and more determined than the volatile Welsh or Irish, they developed a fighting formation which could repel the armored man on horseback. As infantry pikemen they would form a solid line, bristling with spears, against which the advancing cavalry was liable to impale itself.

In 1297, just a year after Edward had ousted Balliol, Wallace inflicted a spectacular defeat on an English force at Stirling Bridge, at the gateway to the Highlands, his Scots making belts out of the tanned skin of one unpopular English official slain there. Edward's conquest was undone by that single fight. Hurrying back from his French campaign, he led a formidable army northward the following year and met Wallace at Falkirk. Again the hedgehog array of the Scots repulsed the English horsemen, but Edward had brought another infantry device with him for just this situation. This was the longbow, the use of which England had learned from the Welsh and was now to practice on the Scots and later, with devastating effect, on the French. The arrows of Edward's archers cut wide gaps in the stubborn lines of pikemen, so that, when the cavalry charged again, the Scots who escaped slaughter fled in wild disorder. Wallace's brief ascendancy was over, but Scotland was by no means reconquered so easily. That took six patient years, in which Edward made slow, piecemeal gains and held them by scattered castle garrisons, while the Pope interfered and claimed the right to settle the Scottish question himself. At last, in 1304, Edward felt that he had Scotland well enough in hand to begin to transplant English forms of government, as he had done in Wales.

This was not to be. The spirit of Scottish nationalism awakened by Wallace quickly broke out anew, but under a new leader. Wallace, who had escaped death at Falkirk, was betrayed by a Scot into English hands in 1305. Taken to London, he was tried for treason and other crimes, hanged, disemboweled, and quartered; and to four northern towns were sent the gory remains as warnings, while his head was stuck up over London bridge. His fame lived on to inspire his countrymen, who still sing of the "Scots, wha hae wi' Wallace bled." Robert Bruce, grandson of the original claimant of 1290, was a man of another sort, but he carried Wallace's work to a more successful conclusion. Like many Scottish noblemen, Bruce had a past record of much pro-English dealing; but his family position and his royal blood gave him a wider basis of support than Wallace, the commoner, had had. Bruce's temper flung him into sudden prominence, and thence into the role of leader of the disaffected Scots, when in 1306 he stabbed "the Red Comyn," representative of the rival Balliol claim to the throne, before the altar of a church. When his followers completed the murder, Bruce knew himself an outlaw, and realized that his only chance was to throw in his lot with those still fighting Edward's rule. Thereupon the clever Bruce hurried to Scone, ancient seat of Scotland's kings, where he had himself hastily crowned. Then—an outlaw still, even if king—he fled into hiding, where, according to a legend, he was to learn patience from watching a spider spin its web. The Scots, encouraged by the sudden appearance of this new leader, once more broke out in sporadic revolt against England. So sick that he had to be carried in a litter, Edward in 1307 nevertheless started north; but in spite of his doughty spirit his body failed him, and he died before the border was reached. Bruce after this had little to fear from across the border, and he proceeded to build up his anti-English opposition into a powerful force.

One of England's ablest kings, Edward unfortunately left much unfinished work, an empty treasury, restless barons, and various scattered enterprises to a most incapable heir. Edward II (1307–1327) measured up to his illustrious father in his good looks and tall, vigorous athlete's body; in all else that first English Prince of Wales was a sad, even a pitiful, contrast. Edward of Carnarvon, as he was often called from his Welsh birthplace, at times whipped his flaccid will to spurts of energy; but he was incurably lazy and incompetent, perhaps because from boyhood he would never put his mind to anything of serious purport. Primarily the playboy, athlete, and sportsman, he was nevertheless often a coward, and slid away from any risk of personal danger. With his hands he could do much. He might have been a clever artisan; but he never burdened his brain with much exertion. For companionship he always turned to the frivolous, to the dissipated, or to the lower-born; perhaps because of the scorn his shortcomings aroused among his father's friends. In fact, Edward on becoming king seemed intent on reversing much that his father had done and on opposing all whom he had liked. Apparently Edward's one concession was his marriage, according to his father's plan of many years before, to the twelve-year-old Isabella, daughter of Philip IV of France, in the year after his coronation. This young bride, just half his age, was to be the instrument of Edward's undoing; but unscrupulous and faithless though she was, she would have made the better ruler of the two. The marriage incidentally was to be one more step in bringing on the Hundred Years' War, since it was to give the kings of England a claim to the throne of France.

The Scottish policy of the first Edward may have been a mistake, but the weak apathy of his son prevented any chance of its turning into a success. The campaign to vanquish Bruce, begun so resolutely by the dying Edward I in 1307, frittered away to nothing under the son's careless and lukewarm attitude. Not even Longshanks's legendary last command that his bones, boiled clean of flesh, should accompany the troops into Scotland, could furnish a talisman for victory. Young Edward quickly found an excuse for returning home, and the expedition failed.

Bruce, thus left pretty much unmolested for some six years, built up his power from that of a hunted man with a mixed following to that of leader of most of the Scottish factions. He raided the border almost with impunity, and one by one the strongholds, such as Edinburgh, fell into his hands. At last, in 1314, when he laid siege to Stirling, almost the last castle in English hands, Edward and his disaffected barons were stirred into a brief co-operation against the common peril of the Bruce.

This belated activity, however, led to one of the most crushing defeats ever experienced by the English. The armies met at the Bannockburn, a stream just outside Stirling, near the site of Wallace's victory. The English army, though it outnumbered the Scots three to one, was badly directed. The various units became jammed together in a bog; the archers could not discharge their arrows; the reserves could not get into action; and when, finally, some Scotch camp followers feigned a flank attack, the English fled in panic.

Bannockburn won Scotland her freedom. For three centuries the northern kingdom was to be an independent and often troublesome neighbor. Time and again Scotland was to ally herself with the French; time and again Scottish raiders, carrying only a little of the oatmeal which made up their meager diet, swept over the English border to plunder and ravish; time and again English armies struck back in reprisal. England had the geographical advantage in those raids across the border; for the Scots invaded only the barren and sparsely settled northern counties, while the English did not have far to go beyond the border to reach Edinburgh and the most prosperous part of Scotland. But the Scots kept their independence. They were still a free nation when their own Stuart king, James VI, inherited the throne of England in 1603; they remained a separate kingdom even after that for a century and, still independent, joined England voluntarily in 1707 to form the kingdom of Great Britain (see page 420). Those centuries of independence were partly the result of Edward I's faulty policy, which aroused Scottish nationalism under Wallace and which led to successful revolt under Bruce.

At home Edward II was not wholly to blame for the baronial unrest. After a strong king like his father, and with the memory of the halcyon days under weak Henry III still green, the already restless baronage were on the lookout for chances to stir up trouble. It is significant that Parliament and the machinery of government continued to function throughout the disorders not only of this reign but of the whole disturbed period of the fourteenth century and the first half of the fifteenth century. Actually Parliament was strengthened, since both king and barons called upon it from time to time to support their respective positions, and thus the commons were brought into their councils. Under a continuous series of strong rulers, like Henry II and Edward I, an absolute royal autocracy would probably have grown up in England as it did in France. This would have killed, in their feeble youth, the seeds of middle-class supremacy and democracy that were to make England's government distinctive. It has been remarked that "England needed her weak kings to keep her growth well-rounded and to give her special constitutional institutions a chance to develop."

Edward opened the way for his difficulties with his barons by making a clean sweep of his father's experienced ministers. In fact, anyone whom Edward the father had disliked seemed slated for favorable consideration by Edward the son. Chief of the favorites who usurped the king's functions, and who angered the barons by their presumptuous ways, were Piers Gaveston and the two Hugh Despensers, father and son. Gaveston, from Gascony, whom Edward I had exiled as an unfit companion for his son, was an exuberant fellow, not specially wicked, but with the sort of biting wit which makes enemies. Instantly recalled, his head was so completely turned by his new honors that he insisted that all dealings with Edward must come through him. The barons forced his almost immediate return to exile, and Edward made him governor of Ireland. As soon as the king could manage it, Gaveston came back, only to be sent away again because of baronial enmity. Returning once again at Edward's urging in 1312, he was seized and beheaded by his enemies. After this the Despensers, the son and the grandson of a former justiciar, became the royal favorites. So greedy for themselves were these two that they mismanaged the government unnecessarily for their own ends and pushed their king yet faster along his road to personal disaster.

In the meantime, in 1310, only three years after his accession, the government was taken out of Edward's hands by the barons, as in 1258 it had been taken out of Henry III's. The barons put twenty-one so-called "Lords Ordainers" in charge, most of whom were lay barons, with a few ecclesiastical leaders such as former Archbishop Winchelsea, who had come back from exile at Edward I's death. They issued, the next year, the "Ordinances of London," which were much like the "Provisions of Oxford," but, by ignoring the new Commons, were not in line with the constitutional progress of the country. These ordinances provided for the punishment of favorites and forbade any appointment of officials or any declaration of war by the king without the Ordainers' consent. The Ordainers, however, who owed their existence to Edward's personal unpopularity, were to prove only a temporary constitutional innovation. Their main attack was upon the management of the royal household, a heterogeneous mixture of official and semiofficial functionaries, whereby Edward was able to find plenty of loopholes to get his way by varying the functions of the various departments.

In fact, this interference with the king's household was to lead the way to important developments in methods of administration. In theory, at least, the government was regarded as the king's household, and for years certain titles, such as "Steward," "Chamberlain," and "Marshal," had carried with them certain governmental functions. Naturally the men who handled the everyday running of the details of government, together with the collecting and disbursing of money, were in a position of influence, whatever their titles might be. Gradually some of the offices, starting with royal domestic duties, turned into regular public administrative posts. The chancellor, for instance, developed a legal court of equity and was the keeper of the great seal which was attached to official business. The Exchequer was taking over much of the financial business (see page 84). In keeping with the household idea, much was transacted by the "chamber" under the chamberlain. The men who held these offices were conspicuously in the public eye, and their actions, naturally, were closely watched. The result was that this reign saw the marked acceleration of a movement, already begun several reigns before, to start new administrative offices which would not be so much in evidence and which would be more closely under royal control. Thus the "wardrobe," originally simply the little room outside the royal chamber, took over many governmental functions, including war finance, and its keeper began to use a little seal in place of the chancellor's great seal. The barons, attacking the royal administration, in 1312 set up a separate keeper of the Privy Seal. That too became a public and powerful office, so that before long a "secret seal," or signet, was devised for business which the king or his advisers did not want to submit to the chancellor or Privy Seal. Eventually this keeper of the secret seal also became one of the most important administrative officials. There was no orderly defining of what particular sort of business belonged to each office. With this purposely left vague, and with each office carrying with it plenty of potential power, Edward II and other kings could simply "dig underneath" if one part of the royal household were attacked, and could accomplish the same ends through another. A fairly permanent corps of trained underofficials eventually came into existence, so that even when baronial squabblings led to new men in the high offices, the routine business of government continued to function smoothly. It was out of such

# Beyond the Borders

irregular and indefinite beginnings that most of the chief administrative departments of modern government have come.

The barons, with their Lords Ordainers, managed no better than Edward's favorites, partly because their leaders (such as the king's cousin Thomas, earl of Lancaster) were just as self-seeking and no more able. The country was in evil plight, with high taxes, unsuppressed fighting among the baronage, Scottish raiding in the north, and generally poor government. Finally Edward's anger, which had boiled helplessly at Gaveston's execution, pushed him into action in 1322, after the Despensers had been exiled and his queen had been insulted, while traveling, by the refusal of hospitality at the castle of Leeds. With a spurt of energy worthy of his father, Edward defeated the baronial party in battle. Lancaster was executed, many others were exiled, and the Ordinances were revoked, as Edward turned to Parliament and the Commons for co-operation.

Quickly Edward relapsed into his old indolence, the Despensers returned, and once more the king's incapacity alienated everyone. Meantime Queen Isabella had been sent to negotiate with her brother, the king of France, about Aquitaine. This fief had become a bone of contention, because the English vassalage to the crown of France did not grow more acceptable with the need of giving homage at each new coronation, and France was having a series of short-lived kings in the sons of Philip the Fair. In France, Isabella fell in with the disaffected baronial exiles and made herself so notorious as the mistress of one of the leaders, Roger Mortimer, that her brother, the king, asked her to leave. Edward had been writing her for months to come home; consequently she now started, but brought the exiles with her for an invasion of England. Stopping at Hainaut, in the Netherlands, she obtained more troops by betrothing her young son to the daughter of the local count.

Landing in England in 1326 with this escort, Isabella carried all before her. With the Despensers in flight and scarcely a friend left, Edward wandered, a frantic, hunted man, until captured. Parliament was called in, and, most significantly, Edward was told that, unless he abdicated, his son might lose the crown to some Parliamentary candidate. Edward stepped aside in 1327; but the implacable Isabella, who had not forgotten the humiliations placed upon her by Edward and his favorites in the early days of her marriage, had him imprisoned. But she was not content; and when Edward was still living on, after months of abuse, murder, thinly veiled from public knowledge, occurred one night in Berkeley Castle.

Regencies were never welcome in the Middle Ages; and this one, a mere cipher under the domination of such a woman as the queen, might have been worse than most had it not been for the character of the fifteen-year old king, Edward III (1327–1377). For only three years were Isabella and Roger Mortimer able to spend most of the kingdom's revenue on themselves. Then Edward suddenly seized Mortimer for execution, and sent his mother away to spend her days in a very distant castle.

For fifty years this youth was to wear England's crown. Although somewhat below Henry II and Edward I in achievement, he was the third great Plantagenet. He possessed most of the qualities of a king of romantic tales. Handsome, chivalrous, courteous, generous, he reveled in the pomp and glamor of the dying days of feudalism. He dragged England, without adequate reason, into a century of struggle with France, and his armies won amazing but sterile victories. The king himself participated in some of these, a first-rate tactician on the battlefield, but a blundering strategist who had no clear conception of where he was going or why. So Edward, like Richard the Lion-Hearted and Henry V, was the sort of king who lives on in storybooks, but deserves less respect from those who estimate the permanent contributions to England's growth. He had his bad qualities, too: he was immoral, tricky, and vain; he concerned himself little with the welfare of his subjects; and such constitutional advances as were made during his reign were by-products of his flashy war policy rather than any deliberate design of his. His half century on the throne was an extremely significant period of transition, but the most important developments were not the work of the spectacular monarch.

Edward's martial instincts led him quickly to the north, to try to wipe out the stain of Bannockburn. The Bruce was dead, and Scotland in turmoil. Edward whipped the Scots at Halidon Hill, near the border town of Berwick, and helped to establish on the throne another pro-English Balliol. This Edward Balliol, the son of John, lost the respect of the Scots when he rendered homage to the English king, and soon he proved as incapable as his father. In 1342 Bruce's son, David, came home from France, where he had fled as a boy, to gain his father's throne; and thenceforth Scotland remained unmolested.

Before that, however, Edward had encountered a mightier enemy than the Scots in their traditional ally, the French. England and France had had an ancient heritage of hostility, but there were more immediate causes for friction. Foremost among these were the perennial bickerings over the English holdings in France, and the menace to the Flemish wool trade. There were also considerations of maritime rivalry between the ships of the two nations, and finally, more as an excuse than a real cause, there was Edward's hereditary claim to the French throne.

Since the time of John's disastrous dealings with Philip Augustus of France, of the once large Plantagenet empire only a part of Aquitaine was left in English hands. Friction had existed since the Norman Conquest, owing to the fact that across the Channel the king of England was merely a vassal of the king of France. As the French monarchy increased in power and ambition it inevitably encroached upon the remaining English holdings, while the English kings, as their strength also developed, became more reluctant to perform even the ceremonial homage for their French lands. All this had long been evident from the constant bickerings and even fighting between the two prominent rivals, Edward I and Philip IV (see page 165). This situation, which had never cleared, was to help drag the two nations toward a long, exhausting conflict.

Flanders, one of the richest parts of Europe at that time, was another danger; for it was vitally linked with England's economic life. England had played a passive economic role up to that time. A passive region simply produces raw materials; an active region engages in commerce and industry, buying such raw materials, converting them by manufacture into finished products, selling them again, and also bringing outside products which the passive region may want in exchange. Medieval England's chief offering to the world of trade was raw wool. About 1300, of total exports of about £300,000, all but £20,000 came from wool; and the chancellor today sits on the "woolsack," when he presides over the House of Lords, as symbolic of that early economic foundation. But a sack of raw wool was worth only a fraction of the value of that same wool after it had been manufactured into cloth and sold to outside regions which wanted it. The major profits went not to the English woolgrowers but to the foreigners who carried it away, who spun and wove it into cloth, and who sold it again as a finished product.

Three groups of foreigners were particularly active in English trade during the passive period. The Hanseatic League, or Hanse, was a union of Hamburg, Bremen, Lübeck, Danzig, and many other commercial cities of the Baltic and other parts of northern Europe. Allied so effectively that they could bargain for privileges in outside regions, they offered northern products and brought back outside wares in exchange. Their vessels, moreover, conducted an active carrying trade for passive nations which lacked adequate merchant marines of their own. The League was well entrenched in England, where it was granted special privileges and had as its chief post the "Steelyard" in London.

The cities of northern Italy, particularly Venice, were also extremely influential in England's commercial relations at that time. They not only gathered most of the trade of the Mediterranean into their own hands but also established relations with eastern Asia for spices, silks, and other exotic products. These they aggressively peddled throughout the rest of Europe. At least once a year Venice sent northward a trading fleet known as the "Flanders galleys." In the Channel the fleet would split, part of the ships going to Flanders and the rest to England. This Italian trade built up a surplus of capital, and we have noticed that Edward I, like his successors, had frequent occasion to borrow from these "Lombards," who naturally expected trading concessions in return.

But more important than the Hanse or the Italians in the English economic life of that day was Flanders, lying in the southern section of the region known as the "Low Countries," partly in what is today Belgium and partly in the present northeastern corner of France. With its location at the crossroads of the main lines of European commerce and with its flat countryside, this territory was predestined to be the cause of national rivalries and to suffer a constant succession of invasions (see page 406). The lack of definite natural boundaries which would have linked it clearly to either France or Germany was recognized nearly five centuries before this time, when, in the division of Charlemagne's empire among his descendants, one received France and another Germany, whereas the third was given a long middle strip between the two, running from the North Sea to Italy and including the Low Countries, which, like the rest of the middle strip, were in dispute for centuries. Nevertheless, this has been one of the most prosperous regions in all Europe, and its business was particularly flourishing in the fourteenth century. Bruges and, later, Antwerp became the chief centers for the exchange of wares from north, south, east, and west. Not only did those cities reap their percentages of the profits on the goods which passed through their hands but they and the neighboring cities of the Low Countries greatly increased the value of some of the wares by means of manufacture. England and Flanders were brought into close economic interdependence, because Flanders was the chief consumer of the raw wool which constituted England's chief export. Any interruption of the Anglo-Flemish trade meant both loss of revenue to the English sheep-raisers and unemployment to thousands of Flemish workers, whose looms needed the English wool. That trade was now threatened by French attempts to gain control of Flanders.

This situation accelerated the efforts of fourteenth-century English kings and Parliament to divert to English pockets some of the commercial and industrial profits which were going to the foreigners. At the beginning of the century, efforts centered in getting the export of raw wool into English hands; now came measures designed to encourage the weaving of that wool into cloth in England rather than abroad; and by the end of the century steps would be taken to sell the new surplus of woolen cloth abroad in English ships. This legislation, designed to transform England's passive economic role into an active one, was sweeping in its scope and monopolistic in its nature; but frequently the laws were openly evaded.

The rise of the Merchants of the Staple around 1300 facilitated the collection of the new customs duties (see page 151) and gave Englishmen more control of the chief exports, particularly raw wool. It was decreed that all such exports must pass through certain designated "staple" towns. At one time several English seaports were designated for this purpose, but generally the wool was to be sold at a particular place on the Continent—Bruges at first, and later Calais. The English Merchants of the Staple were given a nominal monopoly of this lucrative business.

Now, on the eve of the long war with France, Edward III was successful in introducing a new policy which would serve the dual purpose of stimulating the active role of making cloth in England itself and at the same time taking precautions against the danger that the valuable Flemish wool market would fall into French hands. If the Flemish weavers could be persuaded to come to England, that dependence upon Flanders would be relieved, and England itself would gain the extra profits of industry. At the time, the English woolen industry was in a languishing condition, producing little more than the coarser kinds of cloth. English agents went over to Flanders to recruit weavers, calling attention to their present wretchedness and pointing out "how happy they would be if they would but come into England, bringing their mistery with them, which should provide their welcome in all places. Here they should be fed on beef and mutton, till nothing but their fatness should stint their stomachs." They came over, to the annoyance of the English guildsmen, and the weaving of woolens in England received a decided stimulus. King and Parliament tried to increase the use of English woolens by prohibiting most classes from wearing foreign cloth. The export of raw wool was even flatly prohibited by statute for a while, though the smugglers of the south coast—"owlers" they were called—apparently carried a considerable amount abroad. By the end of the century England would be able to offer finished woolen cloth, instead of simply raw wool, to the world of commerce; but that transition would take time, and meanwhile Edward III was concerned about the security of Flanders, threatened as it was by the French. Flanders, to complicate matters, had a pro-French count for its ruler until the merchants and artisans, dreading the aggression of France and the consequent interruption of the English trade, set up a commoner of Ghent, Jacob van Artevelde, as head of the land in place of the count. Naturally Van Artevelde looked to England and to Edward III for support against France.

The rough mariners of the Channel were a further source of Anglo-French complications. With the expansion of commerce and shipping at this time, their rivalry stopped at nothing. Every clumsy merchantman went heavily armed, not only for defense but also for offense. The border line between peaceful merchantman, warship, and pirate was a hazy one. Even the seaports were not immune from rough raids.

Finally, to crystallize all these latent sources of friction and to protract the war long after all excuse for it had ceased to exist, came the English claim to the French crown. Philip the Fair's three sons, each reigning briefly in turn, died without heirs. Their sister Isabella, who was the mother of Edward III, and a cousin, the son of Philip the Fair's brother, were the next of kin. As in England in the case of Matilda and Stephen, the question of the succession lay between a female claim in the senior line and a male claim in the junior line. The French obviously did not want a foreigner, and particularly the king of England, to rule them, but by strict primogeniture his was the better claim. To save France from an English king, the French courts cited an old rule of the Salian Franks, a tribe in northern France nearly a thousand years before. Extending this "Salic law" from personal to national scope, the French declared that neither might a woman inherit a throne herself nor might her son obtain it through her claim. The nephew of Philip the Fair became king as a result. Under other circumstances these genealogical theories would not have been held sacred by either side, but they served as a pretext whereby the French saved themselves from a foreign king. Before long, however, Edward assumed the title of "King of France," and during most of the next four centuries it was used solemnly and officially by English monarchs.

Underneath all these specific causes lay the fact that England was in an aggressive mood. Although considerably smaller than France in area and population, England was probably the most compact and effective state in the Europe of that day. Henry II and Edward I had built up strong machinery of centralized government, so that royal power could make itself felt throughout the counties in matters of taxation, justice, and military organization.

# Beyond the Borders

In sharp contrast stood the loose feudal structure of France, where power and jurisdiction were still largely in the hands of the feudal nobility. And so, with a king who wanted glory, merchants who wanted secure commerce, and soldiers who wanted plunder, England was ready to utilize genealogy for an attack on her bulky, but disorganized, traditional rival.

For fighting purposes England's social system gave her an advantage over France at this time. The French still relied upon feudal armies of the type which had flourished for centuries. They put their faith in the horses, armor, and lances of the proud, undisciplined nobility, with their stipulated military service. Between those nobility and other ranks there was a wide, impassable gulf. In England the classes shaded off from top to bottom with less clear divisions. England too had her proud barons and her knights, but she had, besides, her less military landholders, the future country gentlemen, and also—very important for the work at hand—the free small farmers, or yeomen. Sturdy, self-reliant, and tough, they were to stiffen the English armies with a rank and file of a quality unequaled in most lands on the Continent. In addition, by the military legislation of Henry II and Edward, the equipment and organization of all these classes had been stipulated and standardized (see pages 108, 150).

Europe was on the edge of a profound revolution in military methods, and England was in a position to take full advantage of it. For nearly a thousand years, since the decay of the Roman legion, the man on horseback had held full sway on the battlefield. Because cavalry equipment was expensive, the feudal armies were generally limited to the landowning caste. The middle of the fourteenth century saw the rise of infantry to the superiority which it has enjoyed ever since over cavalry. In Switzerland rugged mountaineers with long pikes were learning to check their feudal oppressors, while in England the longbow was forging to the fore. This longbow, the crossbow's rival, was of the primitive standard bow design, made of yew wood, about five feet high, and shot arrows a yard long. The English had been developing this for a long time as a distinctive weapon. Every village green had its archery practice, and by 1300 the sturdy yeomen were achieving remarkable speed and accuracy with this new weapon. The longbow in skillful hands could be deadly at two hundred yards, could send off approximately six aimed shots a minute, and could shoot through a full inch of wood or a horseman's armor. Edward I had learned its use from the Welsh and had employed it effectively against the Scots at Falkirk in 1298; but it became generally known—more suddenly than most new weapons—through its deadly work against French horsemen in the early battles of the Hundred Years' War. It thus helped to end the thousand years of unquestioned cavalry superiority. A third arm of military service, artillery, was also just coming into being at this time. It was still too crude to do much more than scare horses on the battlefield, but soon it was to weaken the feudal lord still further by destroying his castle with siege guns.

Yet another military innovation, particularly stimulated by this progress of infantry, was the professional, or mercenary, soldier. Two centuries earlier, when scutage began to appear, Henry II had appreciated the advantage of hiring fighters who would stay under arms for more than the conventional feudal forty days (see page 108). Professionals, therefore, were not a complete novelty; but the system became general during the Hundred Years' War. Contractors— or, as the Italians called them, *condottieri*—would promise to furnish a ruler so many fighters for a certain price. These men were not necessarily of the same nationality. The contractor would then sign up the necessary number of "free companies," or units which were ready to sell their services for ready money. The first armies which England sent to France during the Hundred Years' War were general levies based on the military legislation of Edward I; before long, however, England turned to the professionals of the free companies. During the next three centuries the average free company in Europe might be composed of men of a dozen different lands; they fought for the men who paid them their wages as long as they were paid. The companies in English pay, however, were generally made up largely of Englishmen. During intervals of peace, and consequent unemployment, the companies would live off the country, and any luckless peasant who saw the mercenaries approach knew that neither he himself, his crops, his home, nor his womenfolk were safe. Such bands, both English and French, were to ravage the French countryside year after year in the Hundred Years' War.

The Hundred Years' War was by no means a century of continual heavy fighting. It falls into two periods which were very similar. Each began with an English invasion of France, resulting in one or more crushing English victories, followed by a burst of French patriotism which ousted the invaders. The famous battles—Crécy (1346), Poitiers (1356), and Agincourt (1415)—all went to the English, but the final success was French.

Edward started the war with a fruitless invasion of France in 1339. In the following year he was present at the naval victory off Sluis, the first major sea battle since the time of Christ. In that victory, which was really an infantry fight at sea, a fleet of English merchantmen destroyed the French sea forces so that the English were able to cross the Channel and bother the French whenever the spirit moved,—a role which England has enjoyed most of the time since. The enemy might occasionally raid the ports on the English south coast, but England was not threatened with the sort of serious invasions that she was busily inflicting upon France.

In 1346 England won one of her greatest military victories at Crécy. Here the longbow twanged its way into fame, to make this encounter also a dramatic turning point in general military history. Edward had invaded France with some twenty thousand men. He led them in a blundering, aimless fashion up the Seine on a ravaging expedition, almost to the gates of Paris. The French king, pursuing him, nearly caught him in a strategical trap between the Somme and the sea. As a campaigner Edward did not deserve success but as a battle tactician he was about to win at Crécy a tremendous victory over an army several times the size of his own. He secured a strong defensive position on a crest, with one flank protected by a forest, the other by a stream. Outnumbered three or four to one, the English nevertheless had an advantage in the novelty of their tactical formations. Edward bade the proud horsemen, who had ridden to the fight, dismount in order that they might give a solid defense to the archers with their longbows. Thus armed and lined up, the English awaited the French attack. As at Hastings and at Waterloo, they were standing firm on the defensive against the cavalry attacks of the French. At Hastings the Normans had the advantage of up-to-date methods; at Crécy the French were handicapped by clinging to the traditional disorganized charge of feudal cavalry. It was five in the afternoon when the French approached the English position; good sense called for a halt and a rest for their tired army. The French king, in fact, tried to stop the whole force, but the impatient horsemen would not wait. Rushing headlong, they rode down their own Genoese crossbowmen and in one impulsive mass hurled themselves on the English position. Then the longbow twanged. The English archers, wrote Froissart, the chronicler, "shot their arrows with such force and quickness that it seemed as if it snowed." The French armor was no protection to the riders, while the horses, maddened by pain, charged back into the oncoming mass of French men-at-arms. A few French groups pushed through to the English line, but there the dismounted Englishmen, fighting side by side—king, lord, and commoner—pushed them back. So they fought until dusk, when the French retired, leaving many thousands, including "the flower of French chivalry," dead upon the field. Crécy was the most celebrated victory yet won by English arms; twice more in this war it was to be repeated.

Edward's initial good fortune did not end with Crécy. Two months later an invading army of Scots was routed by the home forces at Neville's Cross, and in 1347, after a long siege, Edward captured the important port of Calais. Just across the Channel from Dover, it was the nearest port to England; and for two centuries, even after all else in France was lost, it was to remain in English hands as a trading post and a jumping-off place for expeditions into France.

Ten years after Crécy, England won an equally striking victory at Poitiers under the "Black Prince," Edward's oldest son. That much-overrated paragon of chivalry had led a raiding force of some six thousand men from the south up toward Tours. The French king started after him with an army ten times as large. Once more French strategy was better, and the English were cut off from retreat to the sea by a vastly superior force. Once more, however, the English triumphed in battle. In a powerful defensive position, protected by hedge and ditch, archers and dismounted men-at-arms cut to pieces the larger French army and even captured the king. In 1360, in the Treaty of Bretigny, Edward received complete sovereignty over the whole of Aquitaine, as well as over Calais and certain adjacent territory. France agreed to pay a crushing indemnity for the release of the king, whom many of his subjects considered not worth ransoming. Edward, in turn, agreed to drop his claims to the French throne.

The war, however, was soon resumed, and dragged on its desultory course for many years. There were minor battles and constant, cruel ravaging of the French countryside by the English free companies, who could scarcely be kept in check. Finally the disgrace and misery aroused a successful patriotic resistance in France. The Black Prince found his match in a tough, able Breton, Bertrand du Guesclin. For a while the French and English shifted their fighting to Spain, where the rivals went to support, respectively, Henry the Bastard and Pedro the Cruel, the contenders for the throne of Castile.

The romantic spirit of the time has come down to us in the chronicles of Jean Froissart, who wrote a thrilling, detailed account of many deeds of valor. The acts and words of kings, earls, knights, and even squires are given at great length. To Froissart they alone were the people who counted,—not the stout yeomanry, whose arrows won Crécy, nor the French peasantry, who went through hell for generations as a result of the war. Froissart is partly responsible for the inflated reputation of the Black Prince. "Wherever true valor and deeds of arms were esteemed, the prince rose in admiration and honor. The Germans, Flemings, and English declared that he was the mirror of knighthood . . . that having gained three glorious victories . . . he was worthy of governing the world." Then Froissart

# Beyond the Borders

gives an example of the prince's chivalry, which led him to sacrifice even military advantage. At one time he called to inquire for the health of his doughty rival, Du Guesclin, whom he was holding as a prisoner at Bordeaux. "My lord," replied Bertrand, "I never was better. Indeed I cannot be otherwise than well, for I am, though in prison, the most honored knight in the world." "How so?" "Why they say in France that you are so much afraid of me, that you dare not set me free, and for this reason I think myself so much valued and honored." "What, Sir Bertrand, do you imagine that we keep you a prisoner for fear of your prowess? By Saint George it is not so; for, my good sir, if you will pay one hundred thousand francs, you shall be free at once." So the Black Prince released the man, who quickly demonstrated his ability to clear France of the English invaders. This chivalry of the Black Prince and his fellows was reserved, like that of Richard the Lion-Hearted, entirely for the well-born. For the common people the prince showed a callous cruelty. For instance, upon hearing of the death of Sir John Chandos, his right-hand man, he assuaged his grief by storming Limoges and having two thousand men, women, and children put to the sword without mercy. There was no Froissart to write the grim story of such forgotten men and women, who suffered murder, pillage, and torture. Even at home the free companies took what they wanted. One expedition, waiting at Southampton two weeks for the arrival of transports to carry them to France, were billeted in a nunnery. There they had their will of all the inmates and carried off a few of the nuns with them when they sailed. The pious chronicler of this cruel episode relates that God finally looked out for "his lambs"; for a storm arose, and, even though the superstitious soldiers threw the nuns overboard, the whole expedition was wrecked.

Even for those who did not suffer physical violence, the war meant a crushing burden in taxes. The desperate French peasantry rose in a brief but savage revolt just after Poitiers; the English peasants twenty-odd years later staged a more orderly but nevertheless dangerous rebellion against their terrific taxation (see page 187). In the earlier stages of the war the English people had not murmured so loudly, for they were receiving the glorious news of Crécy or Poitiers in return for their money; but as the struggle dragged on, its futility became more apparent. By 1377, when Edward died (a year after the Black Prince), the French military revival had been so successful that only the ports of Calais, Bordeaux, and Bayonne remained to England. The Hundred Years' War was to lapse for more than thirty years before a second active and successful invasion ushered in the second stage.

Yet England had achieved something intangible for her effort. The French wars, on top of the Scottish troubles, had brought forth a national spirit in England which for the first time broke down provincial bounds. Men began to think of themselves as Englishmen and grew proud of their country. The news of the prowess of English arms in the victories of Crécy and Poitiers inspired on the Continent a healthy respect for the island. Indirectly, too, the war influenced the political development of the nation: the yeomen, with a longbow in every home, were able to look the barons more squarely in the face, and Parliament was increasing its powers because of the king's constant need for money.

Although the Hundred Years' War was the most spectacular feature of Edward's reign, other forces, which were to have a more fundamental and lasting effect, were at work. Social, economic, cultural, and religious influences were appearing during the last quarter of the century and were to produce results which will be estimated later.

When Edward took his army across the Channel for the Crécy campaign, in 1346, he left about four million subjects in England. Three years later scarcely two and a half million were left; the Black Death had done for the rest. This terrible epidemic, which had somehow slipped in from Asia, swept over France and some other European countries as well as England. It started on the southwest coast of England in 1348 and from there quickly spread through the land. The unsanitary conditions in which men lived— with sewage dumped in the streets, no adequate water supply, and the neglect of bathing—made the people of the Middle Ages vulnerable to disease in normal times and defenseless in epidemics. The Black Death was a sort of bubonic plague. "The pestilence seized especially the young and strong," wrote one chronicler, "commonly sparing the elderly and feeble. Scarcely anyone ventured to touch the sick, and healthy persons shunned the once, and still, precious possessions of the dead as infectious. People perfectly well on one day were found dead on the next. Some were tormented in various parts of their body, and from these many, by means of lancing, or with long suffering, recovered. Others had small black pustules scattered over the whole body, from which very few, nay, scarcely a single person, returned to life and health." "A few noblemen died," he remarks, "but innumerable common people and a multitude of monks and other clerks known to God alone passed away." "After the pestilence," writes another chronicler, "many buildings both great and small in all cities, towns, and boroughs fell into ruins for want of inhabitants, and in the same way many villages and hamlets were depopulated, and there were no houses left in them, all who had lived therein being dead; and it seemed likely that many such hamlets would never again be inhabited. In the following winter there was such a dearth of servants for all sorts of labor as it was believed had never been before. For the sheep and cattle strayed in all directions without herdsmen, and all things were left with none to care for them." Recent research has demonstrated that in some regions, at least, the ravages of the Black Death were by no means as terrible, but it seems likely that about three Englishmen out of every eight perished. Despite this suffering in both England and France from the plague, the war continued without interruption.

Such a tremendous dislocation naturally caused great social and economic readjustments. For the next half century England was to wrestle with the problem caused by the "dearth of servants." Even in Edward's time there was Parliamentary legislation designed to preserve the old economic relationship, but it was futile in the face of such overwhelming changes. The Black Death accelerated the end of serfdom. In the next chapter there will be occasion to discuss more fully the consequences of the epidemic. For later considera-tion, too, will be postponed the religious and constitutional develop-ments of the reign; for both became more prominent in the next. In those eventful years between Crécy and Poitiers, Parliament passed important legislation to curb the power of the Pope, a Frenchman, living virtually in France. About that time, also, Parliament itself split into the two houses of Lords and Commons, and gathered to itself extensive new powers by taking advantage of Edward's need for war funds.

Edward III lived too long for the good of his reputation. His last three years were a sad anticlimax to a reign which had reached its peak at Crécy and Poitiers. He loosened his grip on the reins of government, for his mind and morale were weakened by a senile in-fatuation for one Alice Perrers, who was perhaps the most influential of all English royal mistresses. So secure was her hold on the doting old king that she would enter the law courts to bully the judges, and even the Pope wrote to enlist her co-operation. She was the kind who would abandon her royal lover as he lay dying, after stripping the rings from his fingers.

Only one person was more powerful in these last days of Edward, —his fourth son, John of Gaunt, duke of Lancaster since his mar-riage to the rich Lancastrian heiress. Most of the contemporary accounts pay more tribute to his cleverness than to his character. With all the cunning and methods of a modern political boss, he made himself the strongest man in England. Surrounded by a few confederates of his own sort, he built up a political machine for power and plunder. His older brother, the Black Prince, lay dying, heart-broken and disgusted by the whole situation. It was generally feared that the little son of the Black Prince, the future Richard II, was in grave danger of the same fate which overtook young Arthur, who had been murdered, it will be recalled, probably by his unscrupulous uncle, John.

The situation produced political factions which were to torment England for a century, with rivalry based on lust for power rather than on principles. At the moment all the better elements joined in opposition to John of Gaunt and his clique. The so-called "Good Parliament" of 1376 went so far as to strike at the evil influences, attempting, in the first use of the new weapon of impeachment, to remove John of Gaunt's henchmen from power and to separate Alice Perrers from the king. That last stroke however, went too far for Edward's acquiescence, and he nullified most of Parliament's well-designed legislation.

Edward went to the grave in 1377, a year after the disheartened Black Prince, who missed the crown by that narrow margin. The succession went to the prince's eleven-year-old son, who became the second Richard (1377–1399). It was a sorry heritage. For a while, at least, the royal power would be exercised by some of the grasping group of nobles. At home there were bitter quarrels over religion, and the disgruntled peasantry were about to break forth in revolt. Abroad the invincible reputation of English arms was becoming dimmed by defeat after defeat, and the vast holdings won in the Peace of Bretigny had been whittled away to almost nothing. On the seas Frenchmen harried English shipping and were bold enough to raid the south coast. The future looked black, and was to prove so.

# CHAPTER VIII

## The Twilight of Medieval England

### 1377-1485

BEGINNING in the middle years of Edward III and continuing to the close of the century, changes of far-reaching importance were taking place in England. Some of these, like all significant social or economic developments, shook the security of part of the population while opening up new opportunities for the rest; others, more under the surface, were omens of future change. These pregnant years, from about 1340 to about 1400, saw the first part of the Hundred Years' War; the social and economic discontent of the dying days of serfdom; serious questioning of, and growing hostility to, the authority of the Pope, the clergy, and some of the church doctrines; the emergence of a literature in the new English tongue; and the increasing influence of Parliament, especially the House of Commons.

The shadow of impending strife among the descendants of Edward III did not prevent the peaceful acceptance of his grandson, Richard II, son of the Black Prince, as his successor. That grown men of the caliber of the younger brothers of the Black Prince were passed over so easily for a child of eleven, popular though the boy's father was, shows the growth of the principle of primogeniture since the days of John. The regency for Richard's minority included his mother but none of the uncles. Yet one of these uncles, John of Gaunt, had been the most prominent man in the kingdom in the later days of his father's reign, and probably, from his personal ambitions, was inclined to side with some of the dissatisfied elements. His support of one John Wiclif did much to make the latter's attack on clericals and church beliefs a potent menace toward the end of Edward's reign and especially during the economic unrest of young Richard's difficult kingship.

Brooding discontent among many kinds of people characterized the early reign of this boy king. Economically and socially England had been unable to adjust herself to the tremendous dislocation of labor caused by the Black Death some thirty years earlier. Even before that, there had been signs of modifications of manorial restrictions, together with some rise in prices; and the plague hastened matters. So many serfs or villeins had died of the Black Death that crops lay ungathered, and fully a third of the arable land was left totally uncultivated. Naturally, the remaining workers appreciated the fact that their services were worth more than hitherto. They became more vocally discontented with the demands of the manorial system, and some refused to work at all on the old harsh terms. The owners of the manors, faced with the danger of having vast fields lie untilled, and of the consequent loss of income, began gradually to alter the old manorial terms. Instead of the free days of week work and boon work, during which the serf had to labor on the master's land to the neglect of his own, some were allowed to pay for the use of their own bits of soil as tenants, while others, as regular agricultural laborers, lived on wages which they received by the day for their work on the lord's part of the manorial land. Many serfs, however, fled from their manors; some made for the towns, while others wandered about the country from place to place, seeking the highest wages they could find from the hard-pressed landlords. In the towns the free laborers, whose ranks were being rapidly swelled by these runaway arrivals from the country, were even more aware of the changing circumstances of their employment. The lower groups were becoming so crowded that the opportunities of rising to be a master workman were greatly reduced.

Parliament, composed largely of the landowning employer class, vainly tried to legislate against this tide of increased independence on the part of the workers. Barely had the Black Death receded when the Statute of Laborers was passed (1351). This was an effort to maintain the scale of wages and of prices as they had been on the eve of the plague. On pain of imprisonment, no one might give up his job in order to get higher wages, and all unemployed of both sexes under sixty years of age must take any job offered at the old rate of wages. No able-bodied beggar might longer be given alms. Anyone, moreover, who paid wages above the old level was liable to a heavy fine, which would go to the informer. Also, commodity prices were to be kept down where they had been before the pestilence. Shortly afterward laborers were further forbidden to leave their own communities in search for better jobs. Like many subsequent attempts, this effort to offset economic changes through legislation failed. Stronger than this Parliamentary law was the economic law of supply and demand, which was to make competition, not regulation, the decisive factor in wages and prices. It will readily be seen that as the supply of any commodity, whether goods or labor, diminishes while the demand for it remains the same, the price it can command inevitably increases, while under reverse circumstances the price

# The Twilight of Medieval England

decreases. Consequently, in spite of wholesale arrests and fines, wages and prices continued to go higher, in defiance of the Statute of Laborers.

These manifestations of independence on the part of the hitherto humble led to much bitterness. Naturally the landowning nobility and gentry were shocked at this upheaval in their secure and pleasant manorial life, while in the towns the rich men, such as master workmen or merchants, were equally incensed at the new attitude of their employees. At the same time the poorer classes were losing much of their old deference for their betters. The rhyme

> When Adam delved and Eve span,
> Who was then the gentleman?

which was current at the time aptly sums up the new resentful point of view toward the privileged classes. The government too came in for its share of unpopularity with the poor, who distrusted the dubious role which John of Gaunt was suspected of playing. Furthermore, the renewal of the French war at the beginning of the reign had led only to unsatisfactory campaigning, with French raids on the southern coast, and much expense without the compensation or victories. To pay for the war, Parliament resorted to poll taxes. This proved the spark that set off the general discontent. In Parliament's opinion the normal taxation of the realm fell too heavily on landowners, through the land taxes, and on the merchants, through the customs duties. Since the members of Parliament came mainly from these two groups, they naturally looked for a way to spread out the tax burden to include the whole population. Their eventual poll tax called for one shilling from every man and woman in England over fifteen years of age, except beggars. Direct taxation of this sort was bound to be unpopular, because it was obvious to the person taxed and, being a uniform tax, naturally bore heavily on the poor and was scarcely noticed by the well-to-do. A storm of protest broke out. At first the tax was shamelessly evaded; in one county, for instance, the collections indicated that there had been a sudden drop of 50 per cent in the population. When collectors were sent out to investigate the delinquents, rioting began.

At once (June, 1381) the Peasants' Revolt, often called Wat Tyler's Rebellion, was in full swing. Although concentrated into this one month, it was a grave menace while it lasted. At the same time, it was far more restrained than the terrible rising, after Poitiers, of the French peasantry, with its savage atrocities and reprisals. The English revolt centered in the two eastern counties below London, on the Thames. In Essex it began with the mobbing of the Chief

Justice; in Kent a leader was found in one Wat Tyler, who killed a tax-collector, according to legend, for insulting his young daughter. A "Mad Priest," John Ball, fired the revolutionary spirit with democratic harangues. Manor rolls, with their lists of old peasant obligations, were destroyed, particularly on estates where the landlords were churchmen. Probably by preconcerted arrangement, the men of both counties marched on London, where it was feared the discontented artisans of the capital might join them. The gates were flung open to the mob, and the rebels sent a list of their many grievances to Richard, who had taken refuge in the Tower. The young king, although only in his fifteenth year, bravely kept his head in the crisis and came in person to confer with his aroused peasants. He agreed to their demands, including the abolition of serfdom and other vexatious manorial services. Many rebels, well pleased by this lenient royal attitude, set out for their homes. Others, however, remained in London for a night of rioting, during which the Archbishop-Chancellor and the Lord Treasurer, who to the public mind were most responsible for the hated poll tax, were murdered. Lawyers, clergy, and officials were special targets for the mob's wrath. Again the following day the king rode out from the Tower to meet the rioters. Wat Tyler, flushed with success, was insolent and threatening; the Lord Mayor struck him down, and one of the king's squires killed him. Before the seething mass of peasants could draw their bows on the king's small retinue, the fearless Richard boldly cantered toward them, shouting that he would now be their leader. Won by his courage and by his kindness in granting pardons to all, the remaining rebels dispersed, well satisfied. For all this apparent success, the Peasants' Revolt nevertheless failed, like all similar uprisings of agricultural labor. The king's ready promises, many of which had not been within his power, remained mere words; Parliament answered the revolt by a re-enactment of the Statute of Laborers; and a number of reprisals were inflicted locally upon the peasants.

Revolt or no revolt, however, the old manorial system, with its forced services, was becoming a thing of the past; and serfdom gradually disappeared in England, though it was never formally abolished by Parliament. Changing conditions made that unnecessary. Both the feudal and the manorial relations were now becoming far different from what they had been at the Conqueror's death, three centuries before (see page 65). On the manor, to be sure, the peasant still tilled the soil in the time-honored way, and he still used the common lands for the grazing of animals and the cutting of firewood; but he was gradually achieving a liberty unknown to the earlier serf. For the most part, his former forced services had been commuted to cash payments or he worked as an agricultural laborer for wages. Some of the lords still managed the cultivation of their portion of the farm land, but others found it simpler to lease this manorial demesne to tenants who paid rent. The lord of the manor still enjoyed a generous income from his ownership of the land; but, as we have seen, he gave taxes instead of armed men to the government for its protection, and his other feudal obligations to an overlord were ending (see page 149). In other words, in both the feudal and the manorial system cash was being everywhere substituted for service.

The rebellious poorer classes had a special animus where churchmen were involved. This anticlerical dissatisfaction reached a head in the last years of Edward III and under Richard. Ever since the Conquest there had been a tendency to resent papal interference in English affairs. The episodes of Anselm, Becket, and Langton, and, more recently, the quarrel of Edward I with Pope Boniface VIII over the taxation of church lands were outstanding examples of this. Boniface's death, it will be recalled, was followed by the shifting of the seat of the papacy from Rome to Avignon. For nearly seventy years (1309–1377) the Popes were Frenchmen, living under the domination of the king of France (see page 165). Naturally a French Pope did not inspire any great confidence in England, which, during part of this so-called "Babylonian Captivity" of the papacy, was at war with France! This situation led in England to two important antipapal acts of Parliament under Edward III. The Act of Provisors, in 1351, was directed against the filling of church offices in England by foreign nominees of the Pope (see page 143). The Act of Praemunire, two years later, penalized certain efforts to appeal to the Pope from the decision of an English church court. In 1366 Parliament refused to continue the payment of the annual tribute promised by John when he made England a papal fief; the account was badly in arrears, for England had made no payments since the beginning of the Hundred Years' War. Although the "Babylonian Captivity" ended in 1377, with the decision of a new Pope to return to Rome, the result was to be even more disastrous to the prestige of the papacy, because some of the cardinals preferred to keep its center at Avignon. As a result, in the so-called "Great Schism," from 1378 to 1417, there were two rival popes. The nations of Europe lined up behind either the pope at Rome or the pope at Avignon, with England naturally supporting the one at Rome. Unity, one of the great sources of papal power, was thereby badly weakened.

While thus distrusting many actions of the papacy, many Englishmen were also becoming at this time antagonistic to their own clergy, with their vast lands and increasing wealth. Economic discontent and religious dissatisfaction, indeed, were closely interwoven, and both are evident in the teachings and influence of England's great contemporary religious leader, John Wiclif.

In the year following the Peasants' Revolt the authorities at Oxford were disciplined for permitting the followers of John Wiclif to preach within university walls. Officially, Wiclif was at this time only the humble rector of an insignificant parish in northern England. Yet his voice, slashing at fundamental doctrines of the Catholic Church, of which he was and remained a priest, and urging incessantly the need of a religious revival based directly on the Bible, is the clearest which comes down to us from these troubled times.

Wiclif was a mighty scholar, who wrote in the vernacular as well as in Latin, and with such force and vigor as to make him the foremost contemporary critic of those ecclesiastical and economic relationships which tied England to the papacy. He advocated the disendowment of the Church, poverty as a way of life, and a ban on the export of precious metals to Rome. He was the enemy of ecclesiastical luxury wherever found; he attacked the sloth and ease to be found in the monasteries; he openly defied papal authority in his own country; and he refused to obey an order summoning him to Rome. Meanwhile he was perfectly safe; for he was protected by that able, unscrupulous politician John of Gaunt, who used Wiclif's brain and pen apparently for purposes of consolidating his own power. Only thus can we account for the fact that although after Wiclif's death his bones were dug up and burned by order of the Pope, he remained unmolested throughout his long life.

Two great services Wiclif rendered England: he translated the Bible for the first time into English, and he organized and inspired a religious revival, which unfortunately came to grief as a result of the Peasants' Revolt. The supreme test of authority, according to him, lay not in the Church but in the Bible, "a charter written by God," "the marrow of all laws." Furthermore, according to Wiclif, the New Testament was the common possession of all; therein the simplest and rudest of men might find all that was necessary to salvation. Since this was so, the whole weight of ecclesiastical tradition piled up during the Middle Ages sank into insignificance as compared with the Bible, which ought to be available for everyone. Wiclif therefore arranged its translation, and his friends, with his help, proceeded little by little to render into English the entire Vulgate (the

# The Twilight of Medieval England

Latin Bible of Saint Jerome, an early Church Father). The translators knew neither Hebrew nor Greek, and as Biblical scholars they would be laughed at today; but they did stick manfully to their task at a time when the English language was held little better "than the grunting of pigs and the roaring of lions." Unfortunately, the printing press was not yet invented, and even portions of the Gospels, when copied by hand, cost a good deal; so the influence of the translation was necessarily limited.

It was also Wiclif's inspiration which led to the founding of an order of "poor priests" who went forth to convert and to civilize England, "clad in russet robes of undressed wool reaching to their feet, without sandals, purse or script, a long staff in their hand, dependent for food and shelter on the good will of their neighbors, their only possession a few pages of Wyclif's Bible."[1]

The "poor priests" became known as Lollards, a word of obscure origin meaning either singers or lazy folk. In many ways they resembled the Franciscan friars in their early and more kindly days; but at this time the people were losing faith in the friars and all others associated with the Church. There was, too, always this difference: over the Lollards there was neither bishop nor Pope. They belonged to the lower order of Catholic clergy; but none the less they lacked any kind of official authorization except that of Wiclif, a village rector who, learned though he might be, had opposed the wishes of the Pope's representative in England, his Grace, the Archbishop of Canterbury.

Furthermore, Wiclif was already almost, if not quite, a heretic. He did not deny the miracle of the Mass, but had very queer ideas about it; and he accompanied his acceptance of it by many devious qualifications which mystified everyone and possibly lessened the adoration with which it was heard. He also attacked the abuses of the Church, and so did his Lollards. Both they and he gave credence to the proverb passed around the papal court at Avignon that "the English are good asses, for they carry well all the loads laid upon them," and they grew indignant at the flow of gold from England to Rome. Wiclif derided the idea, quaintly advanced, that the retention of gold in his own country would bring about "petulance, lubricity, and avarice." Monks also attracted his scorn: they had "the religion of fat cows"; he did not believe that they were faithful stewards of their vast properties; he thought perpetual vows unrighteous; he disliked these men with "red and fat cheeks and great bellies," and he did not hesitate to declaim against them.

[1] H. B. Workman, *John Wyclif* (1926), Vol. II, p. 203. By permission of the Clarendon Press.

# A History of England and the British Empire

Just then, as this form of unconventional, simple, evangelical preaching known as Lollardry spread through England, came the Peasants' Revolt. Was there a connection between the rebels and the Lollards? John Ball, the priest-agitator, was said to have confessed that he drew his inspiration from Wiclif, and undoubtedly the latter's foes were able to capitalize the Peasants' Revolt to the discredit of the religious reformer. On the other hand, Ball's confession is not well authenticated, and aside from him there seem to have been very few, if any, priests concerned in the rebellion. That certain of these poor preachers directly or indirectly were involved seems highly probable; for we must remember that they themselves came almost exclusively from the very poor who were revolting. Wiclif personally, we may well assume, was not involved; for he was a quiet and secluded scholar most of his life. He did not denounce the peasants but spoke sympathetically of their cause; nor did he withdraw the Lollards from their work among the poor but urged them on to fresh activity. In the *Short Rule of Life*, written on the eve of the revolt, not only did he advise the peasants "to live in meekness and truly and wilfully to do their labour," but he also urged that lords "govern well their tenants, and maintain them in right and reason, and be merciful to them in their rent, and suffer not their officers to do them wrong or extortions."

Whether the Lollards were in any way responsible for the revolt or not, the very fact of its existence gave the Church an excellent opportunity to suppress heresy. The Archbishop of Canterbury saw his way clear, and by accusing the "poor priests" of stirring up the people he succeeded in practically ending this potentially dangerous movement. From England, it is true, it secretly spread to Bohemia, where the writings of Wiclif made a profound impression on John Huss. Luther (see page 259) took Huss's doctrines and, with certain modifications, made them his own. In his country, however, the following of Wiclif, whether he was a heretic or a prophet of the Protestantism that was to come a century and a half later, grew less and less until it practically ceased to be.

Like other fourteenth-century writers, Wiclif had written his more popular works in what is technically known as Middle English, a halfway house in the development of the language, intermediate between the Old English of the Anglo-Saxon period, which is unintelligible to the average man today, and Early Modern English of the late fifteenth and the sixteenth century, which is intelligible to all. In the neighborhood of 1350, we are told, "John Cornwal, a maystere of gramere, chaunged the lore [teaching] in gramere scole and construction of Freynsch into Englysch," and shortly after-

# The Twilight of Medieval England

ward the law courts followed the precedent set by the schoolteacher and adopted the new English vernacular for pleadings. Poets did likewise; and if we would appreciate the changes taking place in the English language and at the same time endeavor to sense and to feel the undercurrents which were molding English life in the fourteenth century, we cannot do better than to turn to the poetry of William Langland and of Geoffrey Chaucer.

We know next to nothing of the life and career of the poet usually called William Langland. If we may trust his description of himself in the poem *Piers Plowman*, he was a country boy "who yearned up out of the farmyard mire to the cloister and the school."

> For in cloistre cometh no man to chide me to fihte,
> But all is buxumness there and bokes to rede and to lerne.

The poem *Piers Plowman*, one of the most earnest and sincere in English literature, is medieval in form; that is, it is written as a series of allegories, and introduces certain features used on the medieval stage, such as the seven deadly sins. Nevertheless, its spirit is modern; for one feels that the author's main interest lay in the actual life of this world, particularly as it affected the poorer folk. The courts of law, the mendicant friars, disease and pestilence, early and improvident marriages, are what really interested him. Mingled with scorn and satire, however, are some dry and lengthy discourses on theology, which would seem to indicate that Langland was not any too clear in his own mind as to the source of England's troubles. On the other hand, to his credit be it said, there runs throughout his poem a fine spirit of independence and protest, and a most genuine feeling of sympathy for those who find life harsh and cruel. Langland must have been a vigorous fellow; for he seems to have antedated Thomas Carlyle and the gospel of work by five good centuries.

> In dykinge or delvynge, or travailing in prayers—
> Contemplatyf lyf or actyf lyf—cryst wolde men wroughte.

Geoffrey Chaucer (*c.* 1340–1400) was a most prolific and entertaining poet. Although only the son of a wine merchant, fortune shone upon him. His wife was the sister-in-law of John of Gaunt, and he himself, after long experience in the diplomatic service, became, in succession, Comptroller of the Customs and Clerk of the King's Work, a post with varied duties ranging from the custodianship of the king's palaces to the repair of bridges across the Thames and the construction of wooden stands for knightly tournaments.

# A History of England and the British Empire

Both from the standpoint of literary technique and from that of historical significance Chaucer ranks very high among English poets. In his *Canterbury Tales*, his major work, may be found reflected the life of fourteenth-century England, at once curiously medieval and at the same time prophetic of change. A number of pilgrims, on their way to Canterbury, whiled away the time by telling one another stories; and these, loosely connected with sundry occurrences at the tavern or on horseback on the way to Canterbury, comprise the poem.

The company was very mixed; in it were a knight, a miller, a man of law, a pardoner, a shipman, a prioress, a middle-class widow from Bath, and several others. Each spun a yarn. That of the knight was one of old-fashioned chivalry; but it was highly approved.

> In al the route nas there yong ne old
> That he ne seyde it was a noble storie
> And worthy for to drawen to memorie.

The miller's tale was indecent, and Chaucer apologized to all and sundry for telling it.

> For goddes love, demeth nat that I seye
> Of evel entente, but that I moot reherce
> Hir tales alle, be they bettre or werse,
> Or elles falsen som of my matere.
> And therefore, whoso list it nat yhere,
> Turne over the leef, and chese another tale.

On the other hand, the man of law told a most pathetic little story in which may be found these charming lines:

> Hir litel child lay weping in hir arm,
> And kneling, pitously to him she seyde,
> "Pees, litel sone, I wol do thee non harm."

Meanwhile the Wife of Bath had rejoiced in five husbands—"Three of hem were gode and two were badde." The widow discoursed on marriage, attacking with vigor the medieval glorification of celibacy. One should not be too loose in one's conduct, and one should marry; but the number of one's husbands certainly was not limited by divine law.

> But of no nombre mencioun made he,
> Of bigayme or of octogamye.

# The Twilight of Medieval England

Perhaps the best of these stories was that told by the Nun's Priest. Its model went all the way back to Aesop, where, under the guise of animal dialogue, sport is made of human foibles. Dame Partlet was a peasant woman who owned a number of hens, and one cock named Chanticleer, who had various adventures. In the story Chaucer "goes out into the country and paints a peasant's cottage such as must have been a matter of common experience to the readers of his own day—the simple house of two rooms, with its sooty 'hall' serving as kitchen, living-room, hen house, barn and pig-sty, and the smaller 'bower' where slept the widow and her daughters. We are given a view of the every-day peasant life, its hard work and meagre fare, its narrowing interests; all this serving as a sharp contrast to the lordly elegance and wide intellectual scope of Chanticleer,"[1] who

> In al the land of crowing nas his peer.
> His vois was merier than the mery orgon
> On messes-days that in the chirche gon.

The *Canterbury Tales* give a kaleidescopic picture of life as it actually was in fourteenth-century England. Religious dissatisfaction was everywhere in evidence; but as yet there was no indication of any religious upheaval, even if fun was poked at relics. New social classes were beginning to press forward, and people like the Wife of Bath represented a sturdy, independence-loving middle class. English society was in a state of flux. Faith in the accepted order was waning, but not very sharply. What the future had in store nobody seemed to glimpse. There were strong traces of other-worldliness—that major characteristic of the Middle Ages—in Wiclif, Langland, and even to some extent in Chaucer. In all these three men one may find also a new slant on life, a fresh interest in every-day affairs; and in Chaucer this new leaven was predominant.

While Wiclif and Chaucer were writing, English politics were by no means dull. There were several violent episodes in Richard's reign, leading eventually to his deposition. Courageous and clear-headed as he showed himself at the momentary crisis of the Peasants' Revolt, he was to prove too self-willed and impetuous for a successful king. His mother, who had been a restraining influence, died when he was eighteen, and the control of the government fell into the hands of five courtiers, particularly Michael de la Pole, earl of Suffolk, and Robert de Vere, earl of Oxford. The power of such a

[1] R. K. Root, *The Poetry of Chaucer* (1922), p. 214. By permission of Houghton Mifflin Company.

group naturally aroused resentment and jealousy; and an opposition party made headway under one of Richard's uncles, Thomas of Gloucester, who, like the rest of the king's uncles and their equally ambitious sons, were still excluded from all share in the government. The ensuing struggle for control was to result in actual fighting more than once, and was the forerunner of similar conflicts which were to distract England through most of the coming century, when the descendants of Edward III were to continue this selfish scramble for the spoils of power, using high-sounding patriotic aims as the pretext for fighting.

Gloucester and his confederates came to be known as the Lords Appellant because they "appealed," or accused, of treason first Suffolk and then the rest of Richard's courtier group before Parliament. In 1388, after a victory over the royal forces, five Lords Appellant, headed by Gloucester, took over the government. This, like the Provisions of Oxford of 1258 and the Lords Ordainers of 1311, proved to be one more short-lived baronial effort to master England. After a year of this rule, no better nor worse than before, Richard suddenly announced that, being now of age, he would take the reins into his own hands. He did so without bloodshed; and there followed eight good years of what may be termed constitutional government, for Richard ruled well and in harmony with Parliament. He even retained some of the Lords Appellant in his council.

During this period Parliament endeavored to curb a serious evil, revealed in the recent turbulence, by passing an act against "livery and maintenance." This referred to the practice of many a nobleman of maintaining a regular little standing army of his own, which wore his livery with his particular device, or coat of arms, and which was supported in his pay or protected in case of trouble. These bands, sometimes hundreds and even thousands strong, were frequently composed of "free companies" which had been fighting in France. Such groups were different from the feudal vassals who had been their lords' social equals. Despite this act of Parliament, the continued existence of such bands of armed ruffians increased the factious and disturbing role played by the nobility for a full hundred years more. With the threat of their private armies some lords were able to force the election of their henchmen to Parliament and to overawe judges and juries in the shires.

After 1397 Richard's good government suddenly changed into absolutism. This trend toward tyranny has been attributed to that frequent source of discord, Parliamentary criticism of court extravagance. Whatever the cause,—whether this thwarting of his imperious will or the loss of his first wife, Anne of Bohemia, to whom

# The Twilight of Medieval England

he was deeply attached,—Richard showed himself a despot who brooked no curb, even that of English law. He drove the Lords Appellant into exile or to execution; he overawed Parliament with four thousand archers, so that it meekly yielded to his wishes. His forced loans and other arbitrary acts were deeply irritating; but he overstepped himself early in 1399 when, without excuse or provocation, he seized the vast lands of his uncle, John of Gaunt, who had just died. This act, in particular, caused widespread resentment, since it was an attack on private property, which upper-class Englishmen have defended for centuries. Unfortunately for his retention of the crown, Richard sailed at just that time for Ireland, where his deputy had been murdered. Four years before, he had visited there —the first king to cross the Irish Sea since Henry II.

In the meantime John of Gaunt's son, Henry of Lancaster, returning from abroad to take over his father's confiscated estates, landed with a small band. He was an experienced soldier, who had campaigned from the Baltic to Jerusalem; but this time he did not have to fight. Men flocked to the standard of this unjustly despoiled scion of the royal line; and while King Richard remained stormbound in Ireland, Henry discovered that not merely the family lands but the throne itself was his for the taking. Finding that England had gone over to this unsuspected rival, Richard quickly surrendered to the opposing side. Probably reminded of the fate of Edward II, he abdicated, and Parliament at once announced his deposition.

This quick revolution, which made Henry IV king (1399–1413), is taken as the end of the straight Plantagenet line and the beginning of the Lancastrian. Richard had no children, but the next of kin was not this cousin Henry IV, the son of Edward III's fourth son. Another cousin, the eight-year-old Edmund Mortimer, earl of March, as the grandson of Edward III's third son, had a better technical claim. The name of Lancaster came from the family of Henry's mother; and his father, John of Gaunt, had been created Duke of Lancaster after the marriage. England was to have three kings of this Lancastrian line: Henry IV; his son, Henry V; and his insane grandson, Henry VI.

The deposition of the last direct Plantagenet was for two reasons constitutionally far more significant than that of Edward II. In the earlier instance the natural heir apparent became king, while this time Parliament changed the succession by skipping over Edmund Mortimer to select Henry of Lancaster. The events of 1399, moreover, did away with the royal absolutism which was threatening to undo the century of Parliamentary development. The year 1399 may consequently be considered one of the peaks in the growth of

Parliament. The most significant of these steps in the evolution of England's Parliament were concentrated in the fourteenth and the seventeenth century. This transferring of the crown to the Lancastrian line was the climax of the earlier century of development, just as another threatened despotism in 1688 again resulted in Parliament's changing the succession and securing what was to prove a permanent supremacy in England.

Parliament had made great advances since it was last considered, just a century earlier. The Model Parliament of 1295 had contained the essential elements of membership; the Confirmation of the Charters two years later had secured royal assent to the principle that a grant from the prelates, nobles, and commons was essential to the raising of revenue. But Parliament in 1297 had been vague and formless. Its organization, functions, and powers were to evolve during the coming century.

The Hundred Years' War helps to account for this rapid rise of Parliament. The fighting in France meant the constant need for money in large amounts. Increasingly the king was unable to "live of his own," particularly in wartime. No previous king had been forced to ask for such frequent and heavy grants of money as Edward III. To him, moreover, the war was so important that he was ready to make concessions of all sorts to obtain these funds. Probably neither Edward nor his Lords or Commons realized the full future significance of thus yielding to Parliamentary wishes; for henceforth Parliament began to make a regular practice of capitalizing the financial needs of the crown. It learned that here was a way to get whatever it wanted from the king. To the money grants, consequently, were added all sorts of Parliamentary petitions to the king for reforms. The two being thus coupled, the king had to assent to the petitions when he approved the grants of revenue to himself. Parliament also began to appoint committees to check up the collection and expenditure of the funds. These practices became more and more fixed as the century wore on.

The House of Commons was the chief agent in thus coercing the king through his financial needs. It was about 1340, the year of the opening naval battle of Sluis, that the House of Commons as such began to meet as a separate body. The lower clergy had withdrawn to their own Convocation and were no longer part of Parliament. The knights of the shire had taken the all-important step of aligning themselves definitely with the burgesses rather than with the lords, thus greatly strengthening the influence of the commons. From this time the commons began to come into their own as the distinctive feature of the two-bodied Parliament, the lords having long before met as the Great Council. Steadily the House of Commons was to grow to a position of power which far outshadowed the prestige of the House of Lords, with its purely hereditary membership.

While achieving this control of finances by the close of the fourteenth century, Parliament was also endeavoring to secure a similar dominance over legislation. The king, to be sure, had to agree to petitions for reforms in order to get his money grants; but before these reforms were enrolled as statutes, he or his ministers could alter or suppress them. He might also, through his council and independently of Parliament, make ordinances as distinct from statutes (see page 148). It came to be understood that royal ordinances were temporary measures, while Parliamentary statutes were relatively permanent. The Statute of Laborers, for instance, was an emergency ordinance, issued by king and council in 1349, before it became a regular Parliamentary statute in the next year. Gradually Parliament began to submit regular bills to the king, in place of its original petitions. As the system finally evolved, a bill went through three stages before it became a statute, or act of law. It would originate in either the House of Lords or the House of Commons, then be passed by the other House, and, after receiving also the royal assent in the old phrase of Norman French "Le roy le veult," become law. Of course, the other House might kill a bill or the king might veto it by withholding his assent. In either case the bill was finished for that session of Parliament. Ordinances, however, continued to be used for special purposes and in modern times exist as Orders in Council.

In connection with financial grants and lawmaking, Parliament sought also, at times, to direct the policy of the government. It might accomplish this by refusing grants; but it began a more direct and effective method in the "Good Parliament" of 1376, when apparently it first used the weapon of impeachment. Preserving the old idea that the House of Lords, as the successor of the former Great Council, was the highest court in the land, the House of Commons acted as a sort of grand jury in presenting offending ministers to the Upper House for trial for high offenses, particularly treason. Parliament thus kept the view that the king himself could do no wrong, and so avoided open rebellion; but at the same time it evolved the idea that it was an offense to give the king bad advice or even to obey bad orders given by him. The fact that this weapon of impeachment of ministers hung over them often affected the policies of both king and ministers. The net result of the century's development was that by its close Parliament had complete control over finances, a fair hold over legislation, but less direct influence upon policies.

# A History of England and the British Empire

The next sixty years under the three Lancastrian kings have been termed a period of premature constitutional government. The Lancastrian Henries acted hand in glove with Parliament. The fourth Henry owed his title to it; the fifth needed money for French wars; and Henry VI was an infant when his reign began, and insane at its close. No major constitutional changes occurred, but certain details of procedure were rounded out. Among them was an effort to secure freedom of speech in Parliament (Richard II, for instance, had secured a death sentence against a member who criticized his extravagance, although the sentence was not carried into effect); freedom of members from arrest on civil charges while Parliament was in session or even while they were en route between it and their homes; the principle that revenue bills must originate only in the lower house (a practice continued today in national and state governments in the United States); and, finally, a certain control by Parliament itself over the election of members. In 1430 Parliament ruled that knights of the shire were to be elected by all freeholders possessing land worth an annual income of forty shillings. This provision, lasting four centuries, gave considerable importance to the yeomanry, or the lesser freeholders of moderate means; but it kept the great bulk of tenant peasants and agricultural laborers from voting. The borough, or town, on the other hand, chose its members of Parliament on any basis it saw fit, and retained that method until 1832. As we shall see, some of these boroughs continued to send their two members to Parliament even after most of the inhabitants had ceased to live there, while new towns which grew up in other places had no representation at all.

From 1460 to 1603, under the Yorkist and Tudor kings, Parliament did not expand its powers (see page 212). The traditions built up, however, during the earlier period of growth were strong enough to keep alive at least the forms of Parliament, so that in the seventeenth century it was able to forge ahead.

With all these momentous happenings crowded into the latter half of the fourteenth century, the next century stands out in unproductive contrast. England, in fact, was to experience her most sterile period since the Norman Conquest from about 1400 to the coming of the first Tudor king in 1485. During this time the Hundred Years' War, except for the brief splendor of Agincourt, ceased to be a record of English victories and came to an inglorious close. At home the country was torn asunder by a long and bloody dynastic struggle of the descendants of Edward III for the throne. Thus family feuds of little lasting importance in England's history were to dominate

# The Twilight of Medieval England

most of the fifteenth century. Possibly one reason for our low opinion of the period lies in the scarcity of written records. The chronicles were fading out, and the disturbed political conditions diminished the supply of official records. When the men of the next period began to write history, they perhaps overemphasized the contrast between their own glorious achievements and the tumult and brawling of the dying Middle Ages. Underneath the record of battle and intrigue obscure forces were quietly at work preparing for the transition to modern times.

Henry IV, whose crown had come so easily, was to find it another matter to keep it. He had average ability and ample energy (until it was sapped by chronic illness and worry over holding the throne); but revolts and border wars filled the first two thirds of his reign, preventing much constructive work. Parliament continued co-operating with the king, even going so far at first as to nominate the members of his council. The chief piece of legislation of the reign was the statute *De Heretico Comburendo*, which authorized the burning of Lollards or any other heretics (1401); and the first martyr was hurried to the stake just as the law was being enacted.

Once, however, the direct royal line had been broken, there were many candidates for the throne of England, and before Henry had been king a year the revolts began. After the first of these uprisings Richard II, who had been retained in imprisonment, died mysteriously. Rumor, probably unfounded, accused Henry of ordering his murder.

The elimination of Richard did not lessen the revolts. The most serious menace came from Wales. There Owen Glendower, a Welsh gentleman of magnetic personality and dauntless courage, had aroused the spirit of Welsh nationalism to a last fitful flame. For several years Glendower made Wales a virtually independent principality, as the great Llewelyn had done in the thirteenth century (see page 157). Glendower followed the old Welsh policy of taking advantage of English political troubles by allying himself not only with the Scots and the French but also with rebellious English vassals.

The situation became grave for Henry in 1403, when the Percys, one of the great families of the north, made an alliance with Glendower. The head of the Percy clan, the Earl of Northumberland, and his son, known as Harry Hotspur, had helped put Henry on the throne and since then had kept the Scots beaten back. Now they turned against the king, feeling that he had not been sufficiently grateful and not liking his attitude toward the family of the young Earl of March, who was related to Hotspur's wife and whose claim to the throne, we recall, was better than Henry's (see page 197). By a mere matter of minutes the royal army under Henry's young son caught the Percys unexpectedly at Shrewsbury and routed them before they could reach Wales to join Glendower. Not long after this the Scottish threat collapsed when the heir to Scotland, on his way to France, was captured by the English and brought to Henry's court as a hostage. France, which had been decidedly hostile since the death of Richard, who was related to her king, went so far as to dispatch a small expedition to Wales; but the Hundred Years' War was not renewed in force. France was in no position to reopen that contest, since, as we shall see, she was having internal disputes of her own.

By 1408 Henry had the rebellious elements well in hand; but for the remaining five years of his reign he was in very poor health. Popular rumor intimated that he was a leper, but this was never substantiated. He was harassed in these last years by the ambitions of his restless son, whom Shakespeare has portrayed as wild "Prince Hal." When he died, his impatient son eagerly succeeded as Henry V (1413–1422), the ablest of the three Lancastrians, but with all his energies bent on the barren quest of military glory.

In 1415, without provocation and in a most unwarranted fashion, Henry V commenced the second active phase of the Hundred Years' War. Ever since the death of the Black Prince the war had been spasmodic, with minor raids on both sides and with frequent truces. The occasion for Henry's revival of the fighting arose from two circumstances: his own youthful ambitions for military glory and the disrupted condition of France. Henry was a born soldier, an excellent organizer and disciplinarian as well as fighter, and at seventeen had commanded the royal troops at Shrewsbury. In France the strong king Charles V (1364–1380), under whom Du Guesclin had successfully resisted the English, had been followed by an insane son, Charles VI (1380–1422), whose alternating spells of lucidity and madness seriously weakened the monarchy. As a result, for nearly thirty years France was disrupted by the rivalry of two younger branches of the royal house,—a situation similar to that which was to distract England in the latter half of the century. At the head of one faction was the king's able uncle the Duke of Burgundy, who held not only the section of that name in the east but also Flanders and other rich lands in the north. The leader of the other group was the king's attractive younger brother, the Duke of Orleans, with extensive but scattered lands. The quarrel of the original rivals was kept up by their sons. Just as the red rose of Lancaster and the white rose of York were to dispute the control of England, so now Charles VI could not govern his own country, and Frenchmen took sides with the red scarf of Burgundy or the white scarf of Orleans. Such internal dissension naturally prevented France from offering a united front when Henry V rejected all French efforts at conciliation in his energetic reopening of the war.

Henry brought over to the mouth of the Seine a strong expedition and captured the port of Harfleur, near the site of the present Le Havre, the first town ever captured by the English with artillery. Then, with about a third of his force, he decided to strike north to Calais. The ensuing actions closely resembled the Crécy campaign, seventy years earlier. A French army at least five times as strong blocked his way and met him at Agincourt, twenty-five miles from Crécy and an equal distance from Calais. The battle tactics, like the strategy, were also similar to those at Crécy. The French crowded their great army into too small a space and so lost their numerical advantage. The English archers let fly their deadly arrows, and then with axes rushed the enemy lines to kill or capture thousands of Frenchmen too heavily armored to run. Fearing a counterattack, Henry ordered the slaughter of these thousands of prisoners; but that brutality was unnecessary, for the remaining French fled. Many thousands of French dead were, as at Crécy, noblemen. The English losses of all ranks were only a few hundred at most. Agincourt was to be the last great English military victory on the Continent until the achievements of the Duke of Marlborough, three centuries later.

For another fourteen years the war continued to favor the English. In 1417, again invading, they overran Normandy and starved Rouen, the Conqueror's old capital, into surrender. Normandy, which had been French since John lost it in 1204, was to remain in English hands for thirty-odd years. All French hope for unity against the invaders was destroyed in 1419 with the murder of the Duke of Burgundy by the pro-Orleanist heir to the throne (or by his men) as they were about to patch up their quarrel. The resulting alliance of the Burgundians with the English invaders lasted sixteen years. The English successes were sealed in the Treaty of Troyes in 1420. By this Henry was recognized, to the exclusion of the contemporary Dauphin (the name usually applied to heirs of the French throne), as the next king of France upon the death of the insane Charles VI, and was to marry at once the latter's daughter to cement the alliance. In the meantime, as regent of France, Henry was to control Normandy and other lands formerly held by England.

For all the brevity of his reign, Henry had become the most influential prince of Christendom. The striking success of English arms made a profound impression in Europe, where other armies were quick to imitate English methods. Henry enhanced his prestige also by the prominent part he played in bringing to a close the Great Schism, which had kept Europe divided between two popes for forty years (see page 189). Unfortunately for England, most of the glory won by Henry was of a transient military nature, to be completely lost within forty years and to prove the undoing of the Lancastrian house. Perhaps Henry's own untimely death prevented him from making his work more secure. Two years after Troyes, during a third invasion of France for the purpose of consolidating his acquisitions, he died from the effects of exposure during a siege.

The English crown went to an eight-months-old baby, who with the death of his grandfather, Charles VI, three months later, was also proclaimed king of France, in accordance with the terms of Troyes. Thus began the troubled thirty-nine-year reign of Henry VI, who was to be cursed by the inheritance of insanity from his French grandfather. Naturally, others had to rule in his name, not only during his long minority but also in the intervals of his insanity thereafter. In fact, of so retiring and gentle a nature was Henry that he did little actual ruling at any time, even in the decade between the end of his minority and the first appearance of his disease. Other personalities constantly overshadowed him in the government, from the regents of his periods of incapacity to his valiant, strong-minded wife. Henry nevertheless had many fine qualities which in some ways might have fitted him for kingship in a tranquil period; but his kindly, unsuspecting nature, aside from his abnormal mentality, made him a helpless pawn. The founding of the famous boys' school at Eton and of King's College at Cambridge University were evidences of his keen interest in education and letters.

The regency for the infant Henry led, as usual during royal minorities, to keen rivalry for power among several of the grown men of the royal line. Henry V was survived by two younger brothers, of whom the elder, John, duke of Bedford, a man of first-rate ability, was made regent in France, and the other, Humphrey, duke of Gloucester, popular but harebrained, was put in nominal charge at home. An effort was made to keep Gloucester's power within bounds by calling him protector instead of regent. A third man of importance was Bishop, later Cardinal, Beaufort, with good sense and an excellent grasp of foreign affairs. He had had much to do with Henry's successful part in ending the Great Schism. Beaufort was one of four illegitimate children of John of Gaunt. John of Gaunt had eventually married their mother, Catherine Swynford; and the following year Parliament had legitimatized these children.

# The Twilight of Medieval England

The importance of this so-called Beaufort branch of the royal line was to increase during the coming disturbed times.

For seven years, under Bedford's capable leadership, the English continued to have everything their own way in France. Then to the French, from an unforeseen and unusual source, came such mysterious aid that the tide of war was turned dramatically in their favor. Only a few of the southern provinces, to which the city of Orleans was the key, had been opposing the regency of Bedford by recognizing as their king the timid, vacillating Dauphin, who had been disinherited by the Treaty of Troyes. By 1429 Orleans alone stood in the way of the complete subjection of France by the English. Its surrender to the English army at its gates looked imminent when suddenly a young peasant girl, Jeanne d'Arc, or Joan of Arc, appeared at the Dauphin's court. She told impassionedly a strange story of mystic voices in her native woods of Domremy,—voices which had bidden her free France from the invaders. Incredulous at first, the Dauphin was finally persuaded to let her join the army for the rescue of Orleans. She insisted that she could drive out the "goddams," as the English were called, no matter how numerous they might be. Clad in white armor on a white charger, she so inspired the defenders that Orleans was miraculously saved from almost certain doom.

Next this dauntless girl achieved the coronation of the Dauphin, at Reims, as King Charles VII, a step he had not dared risk himself. Joan then seems to have felt that her Heaven-sent mission was over and begged that she be allowed to go home; but, unluckily for her, Charles wanted to keep her inspirational presence with his troops. She was soon captured by the Burgundians, and they sold her to their English allies, who were naturally eager to obtain possession of this menace to their occupation of France. Ungratefully, Charles did not lift a finger to save this girl who was the first of many to account for his epithet "the Well-Served." The unfortunate Joan was charged with bewitching the English troops so that they could not fight, was brought to trial by the church authorities at Rouen, and then was burned at the stake. Some English soldiers, so it is said, were heard to murmur, as she bravely died, "We have burned a saint"; and five centuries later Joan of Arc was made a saint by the Church which had condemned her.

Joan's work lived after her in the renewed energy and in the outburst of national enthusiasm among the French. The English steadily lost ground. Gloucester and later Bedford antagonized the Duke of Burgundy by their marriages, which brought into their hands lands which he had coveted. By 1435, consequently, the Burgundians broke their English alliance to join forces with Charles VII, who, at last aroused, was showing himself to be an excellent leader. In that same year Bedford died and was succeeded in France by a less competent leader, who held out for a while against steadily increasing odds. At home Gloucester wanted to push the war; but Beaufort worked for peace, and finally, in 1444, achieved negotiations by which England was to retain Normandy and part of Aquitaine, while abandoning the rest of the English holdings. Henry VI's marriage was arranged, also, with the fourteen-year-old Margaret of Anjou, niece of the French king. Foolishly the English broke this favorable truce a few years later. In the meantime the French had organized a very efficient army, especially strong in the new artillery. By 1450 Normandy was completely lost, this time for good. The following year England's possessions in Aquitaine crumbled away. In 1453 England sent a last expedition in a vain attempt to recover the lost ground, but the English troops were cut to pieces by the French artillery in what proved the final battle of the war. Bordeaux, which England had held without a break ever since Eleanor had brought it as a dowry three centuries earlier, reverted to France. The Hundred Years' War was over. Of all England's vast holdings in France there now remained only the port of Calais, which had been captured by Edward III. Six weeks before that last battle of the war the Eastern Roman, or Byzantine, Empire had come to an end when Turkish invaders from the east captured its capital, Constantinople. The year 1453 is consequently a very important landmark in European history.

Despite the spectacular English victories at Crécy, Poitiers, and Agincourt, France had finally won the Hundred Years' War. Nevertheless, the loss of the war was to prove a blessing in disguise for England. In earlier years the relation with Normandy and Aquitaine had been an asset because of the cultural contacts which they afforded, but in later years the French lands had become more of a liability. The loss of these possessions freed England from entanglement in many of the petty Continental squabbles into which she had been drawn hitherto. So well did England learn this lesson of the futility of Continental conquests that rarely did she again seek Continental territory as spoils of victory. Centuries later, 1689–1815, England and France were to contend in another "Hundred Years' War," but that time England sought colonies overseas and not land in Europe. Her victories in the second contest led to permanent acquisitions which became valuable parts of the British Empire. Canada and India were to prove more useful than Normandy and Aquitaine. One lasting advantage, aside from this lesson to avoid

# The Twilight of Medieval England

Continental conquests, did England gain from the first Hundred Years' War—the rise of Parliament's power occasioned by the king's need of money for military purposes.

The English of that day, however, did not see these benefits of defeat and turned savagely against the Lancastrian government, which they held responsible. The marriage of Henry to Margaret of Anjou had been unpopular from the start, because the marriage treaty had entailed the loss of land in France instead of the usual gains of territory through a dowry. Besides, Margaret was an exceedingly able person, who never accepted the self-effacing role of compliant nonentity, expected of a king's consort. Her strong will and violent prejudices were frequently to carry her into rash and overarbitrary acts. With her arrival in England (1445) and through her influence, William de la Pole, of the same family as Richard II's favorite, and, like him, eventually duke of Suffolk, supplanted Gloucester and Beaufort as leading minister. Two years later Gloucester was charged with treason in Parliament and almost at once was found dead, presumably murdered, in his bed. Within a few weeks, old Cardinal Beaufort also died. Suffolk was left supreme and alone in power, but was to find himself blamed for all the disasters in France and the troubled conditions at home.

Law and order had been going from bad to worse during these last years of the French war. The legislation against "livery and maintenance" under Richard II had proved ineffectual; great lords, supported by their retainers and tenants, had taken matters into their own hands in defiance of the weak royal authority. Men were ambushed by large armed bands and slain on the highway for incurring the enmity of some local potentate. Disputed lands were seized by force from weak claimants. The justices of the King's Bench and Common Pleas still rode their circuits, but no longer rendered effective justice. Even when armed bands did not terrorize the assizes, these royal judges themselves were openly partisan and not above the suspicion of bribery. The extensive family correspondence, both business and personal, of the Pastons, a substantial middle-class family of Norfolk, has preserved for us a vivid picture of these unruly conditions. The Pastons tell of their difficulty in obtaining a large inheritance left to them by the man who figures as Sir John Falstaff in several of Shakespeare's plays. Trying to secure the property for themselves, three different noblemen with bands of retainers, whose numbers in one case ran as high as three thousand, besieged and captured three different Paston manors. In connection with one of these seizures the sheriff informed Paston that he would gladly accommodate him in most matters, but that the offending lord was too powerful to be defied. Naturally, when defeats in France were coupled with such a state of affairs at home, general discontent threatened the Lancastrian supremacy.

In 1450 Suffolk, the focal point of criticism, was threatened with charges of treason, and for his own safety was sent into exile by the king. On his way to France he was seized from the ship by enemies and murdered. His followers, however, retained control at court for a few months until, when news of the loss of Normandy reached England, the men of Kent and adjacent regions marched on London. This "Jack Cade's Rebellion" was not a revolt of peasantry like that under Wat Tyler. Its leaders included some substantial gentlemen and yeomen; Cade himself was an Irish adventurer, with claims as an illegitimate scion of the royal line. Their demands were for a more efficient government. In London the mob of followers, demoralized by the easy success of their entrance into the city, ran riot, alienating the townspeople, and Cade was among those killed. Although practically nothing immediate was gained, the demonstration nevertheless had some effect. The power wielded by Suffolk passed to another friend of the royal couple, the Duke of Somerset, a Beaufort, who had conducted the recent French campaign badly. This was not the man whom the discontented elements wanted in charge of the government.

Their hopes pointed to Richard, duke of York, who stood next in line to the throne, and whose hereditary claims to it were equal if not superior to those of its present occupant. These rival claims of the Lancastrians and the Yorkists to the throne went back to various sons of Edward III. The line of the eldest son, the Black Prince, had ended with the death of his son, Richard II; the second son of Edward III had died young, without heirs; but the next three sons —Lionel, duke of Clarence; John of Gaunt, duke of Lancaster; and Edmund, duke of York—each had descendants. Ordinarily, by strict primogeniture, which was becoming the rule of the English crown, the children of an older son would have priority over those of a younger one; but in 1399, it will be recalled, Parliament had passed over a boy of the Clarence line to put on the throne John of Gaunt's son, Henry IV, the first of the three Lancastrian Henries. Now, a half century later, in the able Richard of York the malcontents had a candidate for the throne with an exceedingly strong claim because of his descent from Edward III through both father and mother. Whereas the Lancastrian line came only from the fourth son of Edward III, this Yorkist was descended through his mother, the great-granddaughter of Lionel of Clarence, from that third son of Edward III, as well as through his father from the fifth son,

# The Twilight of Medieval England

Edmund of York. Genealogy would not have figured so prominently had it not been for the strength of the Yorkist Richard in contrast to the weakness of the Lancastrian Henry VI. With a good record as a soldier in France to his credit, Richard was also free from all blame in the crisis of affairs, since he had been in Ireland, sent there by the king, undoubtedly in order to get such a popular figure out of the limelight. The influence of Cade's Rebellion, in which Richard's share is disputed, and the attendant confusion brought Richard back from Ireland; and from that time events moved rapidly to open hostility between him and the Lancastrians.

Like Suffolk, Somerset was to bear the brunt of popular hatred as events in France moved toward their humiliating end in 1453. Civil war was almost precipitated in the preceding year through the clamor against Somerset led by York's partisans; but it was averted by Henry's promise (which was not kept) that York would be admitted to a share in the government. Besides, with Richard as the probable heir to the throne, Somerset's retention in power seemed to the Yorkist faction at most only temporary.

In the closing days of the war, however, as England was losing the last of Aquitaine, two events suddenly reversed these brighter prospects for the future: in August, Henry showed the first traces of his French grandfather's mental disease; in October came the birth of a son, which automatically excluded York from the probable succession. With Henry incapacitated, York was placed in charge of the government by the House of Lords; and in spite of his own personal disappointment at the birth of a royal prince, he ruled well. This improved government did not last. One of the unfortunate elements in Henry's illness was its periodic character, and within eighteen months he was suddenly perfectly normal again. With the king's recovery, Queen Margaret, who had always resented York's popularity, showed an unwise tendency to push her advantage too far, which was so often in the future to bring to nothing her deeply loyal and dauntless efforts in her husband's behalf. It has been said of her that she embodied the worst as well as the best of the dynastic spirit; her courage and cleverness probably alone kept alive her husband's interests, yet her lack of moderation and her willingness to call in foreign aid alienated many who normally would have supported their king. Through her vindictiveness at this time, not only was Somerset returned to his old power, but York and his friends were completely excluded from the government. The royal attitude forced York to take to arms, to save himself and his followers from further vengeance, and civil war was thus precipitated.

Barely was the Hundred Years' War over, therefore, when the

rival interests of Lancaster and York were involved in the intermittent thirty-year struggle known as the Wars of the Roses because the white rose was the symbol of York and the red rose, at least in retrospect, was the badge of Lancaster. Unlike the contest between king and Parliament in the Civil War, three centuries later, there were no particular principles or theories of government involved at this time. The Wars of the Roses were simply a conflict for purely personal ends between rival royal lines, each backed by groups of strong noblemen. At times there were some resemblances to the Stephen-Matilda period of anarchy. The nobility were fairly evenly divided between Lancaster and York, and frequently shifted sides as their own interests of the moment seemed to indicate. Under the practice of "livery and maintenance" the lords took into their pay large forces just back from France, and to these added their tenants in such numbers that a nobleman might lead into the field an army of several thousand bearing his own device.

Foremost of this group of nobles and typical of their strength was Richard Neville, earl of Warwick and nephew of Richard of York. The Neville family had practiced on a local scale the policy of obtaining lands by means of marrying heiresses; the same method which at this same time was being used on a national scale by the royal Austrian family of the Hapsburgs to gain control of a large part of Europe. Warwick is said to have held some hundred and fifty manors, in many parts of England but chiefly in the north country. He owned more lands than any subject had ever previously held; his income was even greater than the king's; and as a result many thousands wore his private badge of "the Bear and Ragged Staff." With this private army and these vast resources he was able to play the role of "Kingmaker" in the Wars of the Roses. First he put a Yorkist king on the throne in place of a Lancastrian; and then he lost his life in trying to pull him off again.

These wars were brutal as compared with most other English conflicts. Many of the soldiers employed by the lords were not Englishmen but foreign mercenaries, and the queen showed no hesitation in importing such men for the main part of her army. The mercenaries brought with them many savage practices developed in the wars on the Continent. In regard to the actual fighting, both sides were armed with the longbow, so that neither had any particular advantage. For the bloody work at close range both used the "bill," a broad knife on the end of a staff. In most of the battles the heaviest casualties were suffered by the armored noblemen and mounted knights; for the footmen of the defeated army generally escaped slaughter by running away. Each side was inclined to follow victory

# The Twilight of Medieval England

with the execution of prominent prisoners. London Bridge was decorated with the severed heads of Lancastrian and Yorkist leaders in turn.

Throughout the long struggle the bulk of the people were indifferent to its course. Not a single town was sufficiently interested in either side to withstand a siege, but to avoid trouble opened its gates to whatever force came along, as the easiest way. On the whole, the towns and the more advanced southern counties tended to favor the Yorkist cause, particularly after the plundering excesses of the queen's troops. Of course, London was the chief prize; whoever held it had control of the government for the time being. Consequently a number of the most important battles were fought in the vicinity of the metropolis.

THE WARS OF THE ROSES

The mixture of melodrama, intrigue, genealogy, and homicide which went to make up these Wars of the Roses is not worth following in detail here. The major fighting fell into four distinct parts: the opening battle of St. Albans, in 1455; the nine months in 1460–1461 which placed the Yorkists on the throne; the brief Lancastrian restoration in 1470–1471; and the final battle of Bosworth Field, which brought the Yorkist rule to an end in 1485.

In 1455 the actual fighting began with a Yorkist victory in the old abbey town of St. Albans, thirty miles from London. Somerset was killed. Shortly after the victory York took over again the role of Protector when the king fell ill in another attack of his disease. Before long, however, with the king's recovery, Margaret—who since the death of Somerset was the undisputed leader of the Lancastrian cause—regained the upper hand. Fighting began again in 1459, and after two small battles the leading Yorkists—notably Richard of York, his son Edward, and Warwick—had to flee into exile.

They returned in the summer of 1460, to start nine of the most violent months of the wars. At Northampton, Warwick won a victory, took Henry VI prisoner, and gained control of the government. Richard of York claimed the crown for himself, citing his double descent from Edward III; but Parliament refused to dethrone Henry. It did, however, designate Richard as the king's heir instead of recognizing Henry's son. Two months later Richard was killed in a Lancastrian victory, and his head, derisively decorated with a paper crown, was displayed at York. Margaret, relentlessly bitter at the disinheriting of her son, then led a plundering army of northerners toward London and, in a second battle at St. Albans, rescued the king from his captivity. Then the queen, strangely inactive for once, missed her opportunity. With the capital close at hand, the Lancastrians and their king might have returned to power. Instead, the queen's army retreated up the Great North Road, ravaging all the way.

Thereupon Warwick seized the first of the chances which gave him his title of "Kingmaker." Summoning York's nineteen-year-old son from the Welsh border, where he had just won a victory, Warwick had him crowned by a very irregular assembly at London as Edward IV, early in March, 1461. This substitution of York for Lancaster on the throne was not secure, however, as long as the Red Rose had a powerful army in the field. The southerners, enraged at the way the Lancastrian army had ravaged their lands, were ready to support the new king and joined his army in large numbers to pursue the Lancastrians into the north. Before the end of March the two armies met at Towton, near York, in what has been called the bloodiest battle on English soil. After seven savage hours in a blinding snowstorm the Lancastrians lay dead in thousands upon the field. Henry, Margaret, and their young son fled for safety to a precarious exile in Scotland. Towton placed the Yorkist line firmly upon the throne, and Parliament confirmed to the son the title it had refused to give his father the year before.

After sixty-two years under the three Lancastrian Henrys, England was to have twenty-four years under three Yorkist kings before the White Rose, in turn, gave way to the great century of the Tudors, 1485–1603. Most of the Yorkist period was filled by the reign of this Edward IV (1461–1483); for his young son, Edward V, was king (in name) for only a few months, and his brother, Richard III, ruled only two years.

Edward IV was to give England a more efficient rule than the Lancastrians, at the expense of Parliamentary co-operation. Parliament, it will be recalled, had gained most of its early growth in the fourteenth century, and then had participated in a premature and rather ineffectual constitutional government under the Lancastrians.

# The Twilight of Medieval England

Its last show of independence was its refusal of the crown to Richard of York in 1460. A year later, under his son, it entered upon what was to be a century and a half of relative obscurity. Edward, like his Tudor successors, showed the effects of the new, crafty, calculating methods of statecraft which Europe was beginning to learn from Renaissance Italy (see page 253). By clever financial management and by avoiding costly foreign wars both Edward and the Tudors freed themselves from such constant dependence upon Parliamentary grants as the Hundred Years' War had entailed. Realizing that England would forgive much to a king who would help to restore law, order, and prosperity, they enjoyed much of the power of autocratic rule; but they were wise enough not to boast of it as Richard II had done. Edward, again like the Tudors, knew the art of cultivating popularity among the people in general and among the commercial classes in particular. He realized, too, that occasional high-handed acts against proud nobles would be condoned as long as the people were not constantly nagged with petty vexations. Edward, however, did not attain the Tudor success, partly because too many of the disruptive feudal elements still remained uncrushed in the England of his time, and partly because he did not work hard enough at the job of being king.

A tall and handsome man with a winning personality, Edward was indolent by nature and inordinately fond of a good time. He had real ability as a soldier, and his keen intelligence might have made him equally successful in other fields had he bothered to apply it. Upon his coronation he threw himself into a constant round of pleasure-hunting, dancing, eating, love affairs. Among Edward's many mistresses were the wives of various London citizens; yet by no group was Edward better liked than by the Londoners, with whom he freely mixed and whom he frequently could flatter into making generous loans. Edward's spasmodic bursts of energy quickly gave way to longer spells of laziness, and he would never push himself to spend the necessary long hours on administrative detail. Although guilty of ordering many cold-blooded executions, even of one of his brothers, Edward was not ordinarily a cruel king.

The "Kingmaker" had put Edward on the throne, but before long he was to regret his choice. Warwick wanted an alliance with France, which was making a remarkably thorough recovery from its previous weakness. Edward, appearing to agree, allowed Warwick to negotiate for his marriage to a sister of the French queen. After Warwick had made good progress toward such a betrothal for his king, Edward startled the court with the news that he was already secretly married. He had, it appeared, fallen deeply in love with the widow of a Lancastrian knight, originally Elizabeth Woodville. Indulging in that rare luxury for royalty, a love match, he made her his queen. Politically it was unwise, and Edward was to pay heavily. Not only was Warwick furious, but many other Yorkist supporters were incensed at the honors and riches heaped upon the queen and her numerous upstart relatives, with their Lancastrian connections. Warwick held his peace, however, for five years more, until Edward had defied him continually on foreign policy. Warwick had still been working for a French alliance as the best arrangement for England; but Edward instead allied himself with the rash Duke of Burgundy, the rebellious vassal and archenemy of the crafty French king, Louis XI. This duke was so constantly in difficulties himself with his own bold actions that he would be of little help to an ally and was liable to involve England in his conflicts.

Warwick, his patience at an end, revolted against his king. After a ten-year lull the Wars of the Roses broke out anew. Warwick, after defeat in battle, sought out Queen Margaret, who after long wanderings had taken refuge at the French court. This strange alliance resulted in an invasion which drove Edward temporarily into exile. Poor Henry VI, who had been a prisoner for several years and whose mind was now sadly deranged, was taken from the Tower and replaced upon the throne by the "Kingmaker," who had dethroned him a decade before. His restoration lasted only six months.

In 1471 Edward IV returned from overseas, quickly gathered an army, and won a crushing victory over the Lancastrians at Barnet, near London. Warwick was killed. A few weeks later the Yorkists also routed the queen's army at Tewkesbury, in the west. Margaret was captured and her son, the Lancastrian heir, was killed. Before the month was out, the unfortunate, demented Henry VI had died, presumably murdered, in the Tower, to which he had been returned. The direct Lancastrian line was thus wiped out, and until the death of Edward IV, twelve years later, his Yorkist rule remained scarcely challenged. The Wars of the Roses were over except for the final critical fighting which was to end the Yorkist line in 1485.

The latter half of Edward IV's reign was relatively uneventful, —a welcome relief for harried England. In 1475, in alliance still with the Duke of Burgundy, Edward invaded France; but Louis XI bought him off for some £15,000 cash and payments of £10,000 a year for life. Edward was not the only English king, as we shall see, who was to receive gold instead of glory at the expense of France; for two later monarchs were to copy his example.

Aside from this French expedition, the restoration of order went on in England without outside distractions. Edward now neglected

# The Twilight of Medieval England

his royal duties more and more for gay times with various favorites, particularly one Jane Shore; but so many sources of revenue did he find that he did not have to call upon Parliament for a penny during the last eight years of his reign, and consequently no dissension resulted from Parliamentary criticism of his ways. Not only did he have his handsome allowance from France, but there were also fines from lawbreakers, who were finding royal justice once more active, the confiscation of the rich estates of Warwick and other nobles, and profits from his ownership of merchant ships, with which he traded on his own account. All these helped him to balance his budget and even build up a surplus. On the occasions when he needed more ready money, he resorted to "benevolences" or loans rather than apply to Parliament. The only time he called Parliament during this period was to pass a death sentence upon his troublesome and treacherous brother the Duke of Clarence, who was quarreling with a third brother, Richard, Duke of Gloucester, and who was too ambitious for Edward's peace of mind. Clarence, it is said, had a unique execution, being drowned in a butt of his favorite wine.

Suddenly, in 1483, Edward died, worn out at forty, not by overwork but by overindulgence. His death led to two grim years which spelled the doom of the Yorkist party. Little Edward V, his twelve-year-old son, had the shortest and probably the saddest reign in English history, from the spring until summer only.

The obvious candidates for the regency were Edward's V's unpopular mother, Elizabeth Woodville, and his uncle, Richard of Gloucester. The latter, short and somewhat deformed, with a sad, thin, suspicious face, had a hitherto good record both as soldier and as administrator. Lust for power, however, was suddenly to give him a place among England's few royal villains, second only to that of King John. In this moment of his young nephew's succession Richard acted with promptness, energy, and complete lack of scruple. He won over some of the Council by bribes and executed or imprisoned the others. Declared regent by this method, he secured the custody of Edward by force. Accusing the queen of witchcraft, he announced that her children were illegitimate because her marriage had been irregular. With Edward V thus made ineligible for the crown, Gloucester overawed Parliament with armed forces and had himself declared king as Richard III. All this he accomplished before his brother Edward IV had been three months in the grave.

Had Richard stopped even there, he might have achieved a successful reign; but his next step shocked the whole nation, even in that callous age which had witnessed so much cruelty. The child, Edward V, had been sent to the Tower, where his younger brother was soon confined with him. Some time in August these boys disappeared from their cell. Richard, so rumor whispered, had had them smothered to death by pillows while they slept. Neither the boys' death nor Richard's guilt was certain at the time; but two centuries later some workmen repairing a staircase in the Tower found the bones of two youths. In 1933 a coroner's inquest exhumed the bones and laid the blame upon Richard III, exonerating the next king, Henry VII, whom some had suspected of the crime.

That same autumn (1483) the Wars of the Roses entered their final stage when rebellion broke out in the west against Richard III. The rebels planned to place upon the throne a young Lancastrian, Henry Tudor, earl of Richmond, the future Henry VII. His Tudor grandfather was a Welsh gentleman who had married the young French widow of Henry V; through his other grandfather, a Beaufort, son of John of Gaunt, he inherited an indirect Lancastrian title to the throne. It was proposed to marry him to Elizabeth, the eldest daughter of Edward IV, and thus unite the rival claims of both Lancaster and York. Since the last Lancastrian disaster at Tewkesbury, Henry had been in refuge in Brittany. Richard crushed this revolt even before young Tudor had joined the rebels. Two years were to pass before Henry's second and successful try for the crown.

In the meantime affairs went badly for Richard and gave him little opportunity to show his apparent ability. Rumors of a French invasion led to costly preparations and forced loans. Richard's unpopularity increased, while death carried off his wife and only son. Rumors of his murder of the princes in the Tower dogged his efforts at good government and rendered them worthless. Instead, repression became the order of the day as the reappearance of Henry Tudor grew imminent; a man was executed, for instance, for posting an insulting doggerel couplet about Richard in St. Paul's Cathedral.

Richard's day of reckoning came in the summer of 1485, when Henry Tudor sailed from France with a small force of mercenaries, furnished him by the French queen. Landing on the west coast, Henry flew the banners of both Wales and England. He was joined first by Welshmen and then, as he advanced eastward, by malcontent Englishmen. Richard hurried to meet him with a force twice as large, but reluctant and untrustworthy in spirit. On Bosworth Field, almost in the center of England, the armies met. As battles went, in the Wars of the Roses, it was not a large encounter, but in significant results it outranked all the rest. Richard's half-hearted army broke and ran; but he laid about him bravely with cries of "Treason! Treason!" until the enemy blows brought death. The Wars of the Roses were over; so too, one might say, was medieval England.

# CHAPTER IX

## The Coming of the Renaissance

### 1485-1509

ACCORDING to legend, the battered English crown was picked up at Bosworth Field and placed upon the head of Henry VII, but it was not to prove the crown of old England. Like most of western Europe, England was on the threshold of the tremendous changes which were to transform the Middle Ages into modern times.

In English history the date of this first Tudor's accession is generally taken as the end of medieval and the beginning of modern England. Yet, as has always been true of momentous historical evolutions, most of the changes took place so gradually, and from region to region so unevenly, that not only did the men of the time fail to visualize the significance of what was happening but no historian today, even with the perspective of many centuries, can say with any certainty just where medieval history ends and modern history begins. The division here is even less clear than that between what is called ancient history and medieval. There, at least, one had the deterioration of the Roman world empire and the victorious inroads of the barbarian tribes from the north and east as a focal point.

The present-day historian rejects the positiveness of the earlier textbook writers who printed in large type the dates 476, when the Roman Empire "fell" in the West, and 1453, when Constantinople fell in the East, implying that the light of civilization was suddenly turned off at the earlier date and suddenly turned on again at the latter, leaving the intervening thousand years as stagnant "time out." There have been recent tendencies to push the end of the Middle Ages either farther back or farther ahead. The beginnings of the revival of learning, once the traditional dividing line, have been found to be rooted farther and farther back toward the Dark Ages. One prominent historian has even written about the "twelfth-century Renaissance." Thus some end the Middle Ages proper at some such early date as 1270, that of the last Crusade. Other historians, at the other extreme, insist that the full transition to modern times did not take place until the period of the Industrial and French revolutions, in the late eighteenth century. The main contention of this latter group, justifiable to a large extent, is that agriculture remained the chief occupation, and the manorial system for the most part continued, so that everyday life for the bulk of the people in the sixteenth, the seventeenth, and most of the eighteenth century was closer to that of medieval than of present times.

As a whole, however, the latter part of the fifteenth century is generally accepted by most historians as the period of transition, and a variety of dates explain why. The one-time popular date of 1453 not only marked the end of the Hundred Years' War but, more important, the Turkish capture of Constantinople, which put an end to the Eastern Roman Empire and was credited unduly with stimulating the revival of learning and the age of exploration. Another favorite is 1492, which witnessed not only the discovery of America by Columbus but also the fall of the last Moorish stronghold in Spain and the death of Lorenzo de' Medici, the famous patron of art in Italy. Three nations have their own particular dates within the period: 1479 in Spain for the accession of its joint rulers, Ferdinand and Isabella, who united the nation; 1483 for France, as the date of the death of Louis XI, called France's last medieval and first modern king; and, as we have mentioned for England, 1485, the accession of the first Tudor.

Medieval Europe, as we have seen, had been almost completely contained within itself, with no knowledge of the lands beyond the seas. Most men lived and died within short distances of their village or town. Of trade there was little beyond the local limits, except for a yearly fair and, in the Italian cities, some indirect contact with eastern Asia. Feudalism was the basis of government, with strong nobles, frequently weak kings, and a general lack of the concept of national unity. For most people the manorial system was the basis of economic life. One Christian Church throughout western Europe, with its center at Rome and its closely knit organization, had brought a sense of unity and security to the people. Faith was the keynote of men's intellectual interests—faith in their Church and in their overlord. Learning, such as it was, was pretty much a monopoly of the clergy, and any live interest, scientific or social, in the outside world was lacking.

Gradually, as we have already seen in England (and the same was true throughout western Europe), this state of affairs was giving way to new conditions. First, a new interest in learning was abroad. Secondly, Europe was ceasing to be contained within itself. Voyages of discovery began to spread European peoples and influences overseas, until today this so-called expansion of Europe has brought, with few exceptions, the entire world under the control of Europeans or of their overseas descendants. With the new discoveries, business

# The Coming of the Renaissance

increased, banking developed, and trade routes changed from a Mediterranean to an Atlantic center, which made the location of England far more important. Thirdly, the whole general nature of the governments in western Europe was undergoing a transformation. The loose feudal kingdoms were developing into national states, and along with this went the growth of autocratic royal power. Finally, never recovering the prestige lost through the "Babylonian Captivity" and the Great Schism, and weakened by the new spirit of questioning, the Roman Catholic, or universal, Church, the main power and the one unifying institution of medieval Europe, was about to be broken into many parts by the Reformation, or Protestant Revolt. Each of these changes came sooner or later to England, sometimes in a modified form because of the peculiar circumstances of her separate island position. Sometimes England was ahead of Europe, sometimes she was slower to take the new ways to herself, as we shall see as we take up in the following pages each of the main changes, with particular reference to England, leaving, however, until later the Protestant Revolt.

The word "Renaissance" has a broad and spacious meaning to the modern scholar. An older generation thought of it as meaning rather specifically a rebirth of interest in classical scholarship and Greco-Roman civilization which, widening into a fresh and invigorating interest in affairs of this world rather than the next, led men to cast aside the supposedly confining shackles of medieval thought, to create new cultural patterns, to paint new and glorious pictures, to build new and magnificent palaces. A more recent interpretation, which we shall follow, gives the word a far more inclusive meaning, so that it covers all the outstanding transitions of the period. In other words, the Renaissance may be taken not simply as signifying the revival of interest in the classics but also as comprising the sum total of those changes which culminated in the fifteenth century and made their influence felt in western Europe in literature, philosophy, art, government, geography, and economics.

One aspect of the Renaissance, the Revival of Learning, or renewed interest in Greek and Latin literature, first made its appearance in Italy. Men known as Humanists became absorbed in the study of the classics, began to ferret out from monastic libraries Latin writings which had been forgotten, began to edit and to make numerous copies of old Latin books, and to popularize classical ideas. Enthusiasm spread to the Greek language, the study of which had become practically extinct throughout western Europe. Classical libraries were made; Italian families, becoming wealthy through trade and commerce, such as the celebrated Medici of Florence, acted as patrons; and one of the Popes, Nicholas V, placed himself at the head of the Humanistic movement.

Love of classical literature led to new interest in sculpture, in painting, and in architecture. One phase of this new spirit was the so-called "many-sided man," with interests and ability in several such lines of activity. Pagan as well as Christian subjects began to be chosen by artists, who now enjoyed painting Venus as well as the Madonna. Pagan myths in addition to Biblical subjects served as themes for the imagination of sculptors. The merchant princes of Italy gave a new stimulus to architecture by ordering the construction not of new churches to the greater glory of God but of handsome palaces to their own glory.

There had been traces of the new learning in Chaucer's day; for the model of the *Canterbury Tales* had been Boccaccio's *Decameron*, and Chaucer himself had spent much time in Italy. Humphrey, duke of Gloucester, had also aided the introduction of Humanistic learning (see page 204). Duke Humphrey, as a man and as a prince, was contemptible; but he did have a love for classical lore, and his library, which was the best in England, included Livy, Pliny, Cicero, Ovid, and a number of Greek authors in Latin translations. The duke was a patron of Oxford, and by the time of his death (1447) he had presented that university with nearly three hundred volumes, a very valuable gift, indeed, in those days before there was a single printing press in the land. No wonder the university plied him with fulsome flattery and said that he "was to Oxford what Caesar had been to Rome, what Hector had been to Troy."

The revival of learning came late to England. Anarchy, caused by the Wars of the Roses, meant a serious slowing down of all cultural advance. The printing press, for instance, was invented about 1450, but not until 1477 was one set up in England. The honor of printing the first English book belongs to William Caxton, a London merchant. Caxton went to Bruges in 1464 to negotiate a commercial treaty with the Duke of Burgundy. While there, he became interested in the new art of printing, retired from politics, and spent the latter part of his life printing no less than ninety-six different books in ten years. These were mostly tales of chivalry translated from the French into English. Caxton's press, however, was a commercial venture, and England had to wait for quieter times and the prosperity which the first two Tudors were to give her before scholarship, as such, could receive much attention, either from printers or from anyone else.

Between the revival of learning which took place in Italy, in the fourteenth and fifteenth centuries, and that which occurred north

# The Coming of the Renaissance

of the Alps, particularly in England, from about 1485 to 1525, there was one major difference. In Italy the revival was not directly concerned with religion, except perhaps in a negative sense, whereas in Germany and especially in England it was almost from the beginning quasi-religious in character. A number of the Popes, patrons of the new learning, became less religious in both word and deed as they came in contact with it; but in Germany and England its effect, for some generations at least, seems to have been in the opposite direction. The study of the classics, particularly Greek, tended in northern Europe to make men more serious and more concerned about religion, as we may readily see by studying the careers and the writings of the three exponents of the new learning in early-Renaissance England—Colet, Erasmus, More.

John Colet was a wealthy young Englishman, son of a Lord Mayor of London, a graduate of Oxford, profoundly versed in the classics. He spent considerable time in Italy with the foremost Humanists and returned to Oxford to lecture. His subject was Saint Paul's Epistle to the Romans. Instead of treating it in mystical, allegorical fashion, as was the custom of the medieval scholars, he astonished everyone by a simple analysis. To Colet "the epistles of Saint Paul were not a string of riddles but the real letters of a real man, and he wanted to get at what that man meant."

The freedom, frankness, and passionate earnestness with which Colet spoke at Oxford attracted wide attention, and soon after the turn of the century he became Dean of St. Paul's Cathedral in London. In this capacity he preached to huge congregations. Like Wiclif, he thundered at the corruption of the clergy, and with astonishing boldness he denounced a war upon which young Henry VIII had set his heart. Despite his riches Colet lived modestly, giving away large sums to charity. St. Paul's School, in which both Greek and Latin were to be taught, was founded by him and was his special pride; for it he wrote a celebrated grammar, and to it he left all his wealth.

Among the warm personal friends of Colet was no less a person than Erasmus, most celebrated of all northern Renaissance scholars. Erasmus was an international Humanist. Born at Rotterdam, the illegitimate son of a priest, he lived successively in France, England, Italy, and Switzerland. Of these four countries he praised England the most highly, and England, in turn, adopted Erasmus as a son. A young English nobleman, meeting the young Continental scholar in Paris, introduced him to England, to Oxford, to the English Humanists, and even to the young boy destined to become Henry VIII. Colet at that time urged Erasmus to stay in England permanently, but the brilliant Erasmus was restless, longed for Italy, and departed. Twice again he was to visit England, the second time to remain for five years. It was during this last visit that honors were heaped upon him. He was appointed Lady Margaret's Professor of Divinity at Cambridge; was given a comfortable living in the Church of England; and for the first time in his life had no real financial troubles.

The posts which Erasmus held in England were sinecures; in effect they amounted to an English subsidy, and Erasmus so considered them. He spent no time on the needs of his English parish, but, instead, worked hard at translating the New Testament and the writings of an early Church Father, Saint Jerome. The former task was one of his most important contributions to scholarship. Although not published until the year after he left England, it had been virtually completed in that country. Just as the Church disapproved of Wiclif's translation of the old Vulgate from Latin into English, which could be read by common folk, so, for a somewhat different reason, it did not encourage this translation from the original Greek into Latin (see page 190). Defective as the standardized Vulgate might be, it was the uniform accepted text, and the Church felt that a new translation might stir up talk and imply a challenge to accepted authority. The severely orthodox scented danger: "they felt, and quite truly, that any jarring of the foundations might bring the whole structure of ceremonies and usages in which they were thriving about their ears."

Erasmus was, on the whole, a conservative man, but no reactionary. He advocated reform but not revolt. The temper of his mind, which reflected that of Renaissance England, may best be demonstrated by his own description of a pilgrimage which he made with Colet to the shrine of Saint Thomas Becket. As he wrote in 1523: "In England they expose to be kissed the shoe of Saint Thomas, once Archbishop of Canterbury, which is, perchance, the shoe of some harlequin; and in any case what could be more foolish than to worship the shoe of a man! I have myself seen them showing the linen rags on which he is said to have wiped his nose. When the shrine was opened, the abbot and the rest fell on their knees in worship, raised their hands to heaven, and showed their reverence by their actions. All this seemed to John Colet, who was with me, an unworthy display; I thought it was a thing we must put up with until an opportunity should come to reform it without disturbance."

A friend of both Colet and Erasmus was Sir Thomas More, one of the choicest spirits of the Renaissance. A son of Sir John More, a judge of the King's Bench, More was brought up as a page in the household of the Archbishop of Canterbury. At Oxford he so distinguished himself at his studies that his father, alarmed at his son's literary and religious inclinations, hastily withdrew him from the university. More, following the paternal wishes, studied law; but he never ceased to be interested in the revival of learning, and we find him lecturing at an early age on Saint Augustine, and writing a great deal, in both Latin and Greek, on social and religious topics. More's rise to fame was rapid. When scarcely more than a boy, he opposed the wishes of Henry VII in Parliament, for which act his father was sent temporarily to the Tower. As a young man he won a celebrated lawsuit for the Pope against the crown, thereby attracting the attention of another young man, Henry VIII. The new king, charmed by More's learning and personality, visited him and his family frequently, and became such a nuisance with his attentions that More had to feign stupidity to rid himself of his royal visitor. Henry, however, persisted in heaping honors on More, knighted him, sent him on a diplomatic mission, and finally insisted that he become Lord Chancellor of England, a fatal post for one of Sir Thomas More's character to hold, as we shall see in the next chapter.

Best known of Sir Thomas More's writings is *Utopia*, a book over which scholars still wrangle and dispute, and one which has perhaps converted more Englishmen to socialistic ideas than the later writings of Karl Marx. *Utopia* purports to be a conversation between More and a learned and much-traveled seaman whom he met in Holland. The seaman compares England with the mythical kingdom of Utopia, much to the disadvantage of the former country. He is amazed at the cruelty of the laws in England and suggests that if, instead of hanging men for thievery, the authorities found work for them, such severe punishment would not be necessary. He finds too many idle men of wealth in the country,—men who "not only live in idleness themselves, but also carry about with them at their tails a great flock or train of idle and loitering serving-men, which never learned any craft whereby to get their livings. These men, as soon as their master is dead, or be sick themselves, be incontinent thrust out of doors." He sees that on the farms sheep have taken the place of men (see page 243). "They consume, destroy, and devour whole fields, houses, cities. For look in what parts of the realm doth grow the finest and therefore dearest wool, there noblemen and gentlemen, yea and certain abbots, holy men no doubt, not contenting themselves with the yearly revenues and profits, that were wont to grow to their forefathers and predecessors of their land, nor being content that they live in rest and pleasure nothing profiting, yea much annoying the weal public, leave no ground for tillage, they inclose all into pastures; they throw down houses; they pluck down towns, and leave nothing standing, but only the church to be made a sheep house. And as though you lost no small quantity of ground by forests, chases, lawns and parks, those good holy men turned all dwelling-houses and all glebeland into desolation and wilderness. Therefore that one covetous and insatiable cormorant and very plague of his native country may compass about and inclose many thousand acres of ground together within one pale or hedge."

In Utopia everything was different. There everyone lived a simple life, and everyone had his own craft, both man and woman. A six-hour day sufficed; for all worked and lived without ostentation, sharing their goods in common. None sought fine raiment or jewelry and, to protect their morals from being tempted by gold, they used that metal for punishing criminals. "Finally whosoever for any offense be infamed, by their ears hang rings of gold, and about their necks chains of gold, and in conclusion their heads be tied about with gold."

The Utopians found their major delight in good health and in good conversation. They possessed most of the Greek classical writings and read aloud from them frequently. Invalids, if sufficiently ill, were permitted to take their own lives. Marriages were arranged in accordance with a curious eugenic principle. Wars were avoided; "for with bodily strength (say they) bears, lions, wolves, boars, dogs, and other wild beasts do fight." Nevertheless, the people were not complete pacifists. "If any prince stir up war against them, intending to invade their land, they meet him incontinent out of their own borders with great power and strength."

In religion the Utopians were extraordinarily tolerant. Some worshiped the moon, others the sun, while the more enlightened worshiped an unknown power, "everlasting, incomprehensible." They took rather kindly to the idea of Christianity when told of it by travelers; but when one of their number was baptized and then proceeded to reproach his fellows for their wickedness, they banished him "as a seditious person and as a raiser up of dissensions among the people." The laws of Utopia were both liberal and explicit. Everything was allowed except atheism and the denial of immortality. Many were very religious, but "idleness they utterly forsake and eschew, thinking felicity after this life to be gotten and obtained by busy labours and good exercises. Some therefore of them attend the sick, some amend highways, cleanse ditches, repair bridges, dig turf, gravel, and stones, fell and cleave wood. . . . For whatsoever unpleasant, hard and vile work is anywhere, from the which labour,

# The Coming of the Renaissance

loathesomeness and desperation doth freight other, all that they take upon themselves willingly and gladly." The Utopians, to be sure, had priests (though very few); and they were fond of large, handsome, but dimly lit churches, since "they thought that over much light doth disperse men's cogitations, whereas in dim and doubtful light they be gathered together and more earnestly fixed on religion and devotion." They had other practices which also partook of the psychology of Rome, such as incense and candles. On the other hand, "no image of any kind is seen in the church, to the intent it may be free for every man to conceive God by their religion after what likeness and similitude they will." Unmistakably the church was pagan, for there was no mention of Christ.

This most unusual book was widely popular in Europe. Originally written in Latin, it was translated into French, Italian, and German, and published in four Continental cities before being translated into English. That the writer could remain a Catholic in good standing and afterward become canonized, as a saint, calls for explanation.

Possibly the best that can be given is to remember that the Catholic Church always has distinguished between the four cardinal virtues, wisdom, fortitude, temperance, and justice, and the three theological ones, faith, hope, and charity. Paganism at its best had been characterized by the cardinal virtues, and the Church affirmed them, adding faith, hope, and charity. Utopia was founded on the cardinal virtues; and More, in describing that land, was, in a way, writing a satire on the so-called Christian society of his own day, implying that it fell far short of even the cardinal virtues of his own Church. Not only was there no attack on Catholic dogma in this book but there was emphasis on Catholic practice. He praised the monastic ideals of work and poverty for the sake of religion. As a matter of fact, the medieval Church had placed much stress on the value of the communal life; and, in a sense, Utopia, if it pointed forward to socialism, pointed also backward to earlier and more simple Christian ideals. It was a Renaissance book, since it was critical. Yet it was also a Catholic book, since it denied the worth of individualism, greatly stressed by the Renaissance. Furthermore, we must remember that the author remained assiduous in the exercise of his Catholic faith, not merely externally by attending Mass, but privately by wearing a hair shirt next his skin. In More, indeed, the medieval and the modern were strangely blended.

The revival of learning, however, was but one aspect of the Renaissance. Of equal and perhaps more importance, from the standpoint of English history, were the geographical discoveries of the period. They, as well as the study of the Greek New Testament, were influential in bringing about a revaluation of social ideals. The *Utopia* would never have been written if the imagination of the writer had not been stirred by strange tales of adventure overseas. If the Renaissance led to renewed curiosity and interest in man, it did likewise in regard to the world.

The world map was suddenly unrolled before the eyes of an amazed Europe during the last years of the fifteenth century. In 1485 Europe knew almost nothing of the other continents, except where Asia and Africa touched the Mediterranean. A solid belt of hostile Mohammedans prevented penetration in that direction. Part of the African coast had been explored. Marco Polo, an Italian, had written of his travels to the Far East. The Americas were unknown, for a Viking voyage centuries before had been forgotten. No white man, of course, had ever visited Australia. Fifteen years later, by 1500, Europeans had sailed around Africa and had established direct relations with India. They had discovered and explored the Americas, north and south. Portugal and Spain were laying the foundations of overseas empire. Once started, the movement was to continue until Europeans or their descendants controlled nearly the entire globe.

England played only a minor part in that sudden unrolling of the map, but the story of what the other nations accomplished in exploration is essential here because of its tremendous bearing on later English history. The shift of European maritime activity from the Mediterranean to the Atlantic changed England's relative geographical importance. Hitherto she had lain remote on the outer edge of the European world; now she was to lie directly across the important new lines of sea communications to the new lands. England waited until others had experimented before entering wholeheartedly into the race for maritime and colonial power; but, once she started, she proved more successful than any of her rivals until, at present, she controls a full quarter of the earth's surface and a quarter of the earth's population. Just as the mingling of the races is the significant key to the early chapters of English history, and constitutional development makes distinctive the middle portion, so maritime and colonial activity is England's particularly noteworthy achievement in the modern period.

Few episodes in history have been more fascinating and more far-reaching in their consequences than this expansion. Its high points can be compressed into four short periods of significant changes. The original explorations centered around 1500, when Portugal and Spain opened the new sea routes and commenced their empires.

# The Coming of the Renaissance

Exactly a century later three new rivals—England, Holland, and France—entered the colonial race. Holland took Portugal's best colonies, but was soon left behind. In 1689 England commenced the duel for empire which was to give her most of France's choicest possessions. Finally, the two decades before 1900 saw the feverish spread of a new imperialism into Africa and Asia.

Spices stimulated the remarkable crop of early discoveries. Dreams of gold and glory may have played their part, but the great captains sailed primarily to secure cargoes of the pepper, ginger, cinnamon, and nutmegs which grew on rich islands just southeast of Asia. Europe demanded those spices in the days before refrigeration; for they were necessary to make meat palatable. For centuries the spices had come to Europe by indirect routes. Arab traders had carried them to India and thence, part way by water and the rest of the way by caravan, to the eastern Mediterranean ports. There the Venetians and Genoese had secured the supply and had distributed it throughout Europe, amassing in the process the riches which helped to endow the glories of the Italian Renaissance. After 1400 the spread of Turkish power threatened to close the old caravan routes. The actual fall of Constantinople in 1453 has been overrated in this connection. More important, Europe was growing tired of paying the high prices of the Italians. A direct sea route to the source of the spices would reduce the cost of transportation and cut out the profits of various middlemen. The opening of the new sea routes was to short-circuit the old, indirect Eastern trade and leave Venice and Genoa at one side. Yet, strange to say, the names of Columbus, Vespucius, the Cabots, and others show that some of the most prominent explorers who thus contributed to the decay of Italian trade were themselves Italians sailing under the flags of various Western nations.

It may seem strange that the two out-of-the-way nations, Portugal and Spain, took the lead in overseas enterprise. They were just emerging as compact states after seven centuries of intermittent fighting to drive out the Mohammedan Moors who had occupied their peninsula and who had developed a high degree of civilization there. Little Portugal, remote in the west, was the first to drive out the Moors; following suit came the smaller Christian states of northern Spain, and finally a united Spain ejected the last of the Moors. The restless energy hitherto spent in fighting infidels at home needed a new outlet. These states bordered on the Atlantic, and there lay their future.

If any one man started Europe's overseas expansion, it was Prince Henry "the Navigator," a younger son of the Portuguese king and his English queen. In the very year 1415, when one grandson of John of Gaunt was winning the striking victory of Agincourt, this other grandson was laying the foundations for more lasting achievement. The seagoing English like to think that his maritime initiative came through his English mother. Prince Henry conceived the idea of sending ships around Africa to India. This would mean a further triumph of Christendom over Islam; it would add to the glory of Portugal; it would satisfy geographical curiosity; and, above all, it might prove extremely profitable by bringing spices direct by sea, thus eliminating the expensive freight and the middlemen's profits of the old indirect routes of the Italians. Henry retired in 1415 to a bleak cape, where he devoted the rest of his life to the promotion of exploration. He went at it in a scientific manner, gathering the best available maps, shipbuilders, and mariners. Fortunately, he had ample resources; for exploration then, like polar expeditions and pioneer air flights today, needed financial backing. Henry himself never "navigated," but for half a century he sent captain after captain down the west coast of Africa to find a way around to India.

It was slow work. The superstitious sailors believed the tales of boiling seas and terrific monsters. The actual terrors were bad enough. The invention of the mariner's compass, followed by that of the astrolabe, an ancestor of the sextant, for determining latitude by "shooting the sun," made it no longer necessary to hug the shore; but the clumsy, top-heavy ships were no larger than modern tugs. One captain declared that the sailors continually had the pumps in their hands and the Virgin Mary on their lips. It was a triumph for exploration when one of Henry's captains finally rounded a cape on the Moroccan coast. Thereafter things went a little faster. Gold and slaves were brought home, and merchants sent out expeditions in hope of profit. But Henry wanted more than that. He still urged his captains to make new records. They had nearly reached the equator at his death in 1460.

Henry's work bore rich fruit in the last years of the century. Early in 1488 Bartolomeu Dias worked around the stormy tip of Africa and found himself sailing up the eastern coast. That was only the means toward an end; for the Portuguese were interested in Africa only as the obstacle in their path eastward. For nearly four centuries Europe was to neglect Africa save for the slave trade. But now the way was clear for India, so that the king called that southern cape "Good Hope." Ten years later Vasco da Gama, continuing this route, at last arrived at the center of the spice trade in India. He loaded a heavy cargo of spices in spite of bitter opposition from the Arab merchants, who saw their long-standing trade

# The Coming of the Renaissance

threatened. Da Gama's leaking squadron, absent two years, finally limped back to Portugal. The cargo yielded a sixtyfold profit. Europe was relieved of dependence on the Arabs, caravans, and Italians. Portugal was on the threshold of a brief but brilliant imperial career.

Midway between the voyages of Dias and Da Gama, Christopher Columbus had made the most important of all explorations. This sailor, apparently a Genoese, was a radical. The Portuguese had simply been paid agents, following out the plans laid down by Henry the Navigator. The world might be flat as far as they were concerned. Columbus was one of the minority in Europe who believed that it was round. He was a spice-hunter like the others, but he proposed to get his spices by sailing westward into the Atlantic. He tried persistently to "sell" his idea to someone who would give him the necessary financial backing. The Portuguese, intent upon the African route, rebuffed him. His brother, as the story goes, succeeded in persuading the stingy Henry VII of England to finance the voyage, only to find that Christopher himself had just completed negotiations with Isabella of Spain. Considering the demoralizing effect of the flood of American silver upon Spain, that was perhaps a lucky accident for England. As it was, Isabella enabled Columbus to equip three vessels by advancing the equivalent of five thousand dollars. From the financial standpoint that was to prove the most successful investment in history.

On October 12, 1492, ten weeks out from Spain, Columbus sighted one of the Bahama Islands. America was discovered—by accident. Columbus thought that it was Japan, with the Spice Islands of the Indies not far off. Even today we call our redskins "Indians" and refer to the West Indies because of his error. Spain went wild with joy; her first effort at exploration was a success; and the Spaniards laughed at the Portuguese who had been working nearly eighty years without results. The latter could only point out that Columbus had brought back no spices. The rest of the story of Columbus is an anticlimax. He made three more voyages to the Caribbean, but he lacked the force and tact for successful administration of the new lands he had discovered. Even in the naming of the new continents. he lost out to a second-rate explorer, Americus Vespucius, who had a better flair for publicity. The first voyage of Columbus, however, was probably the most significant in the whole history of exploration.

Two weeks before Da Gama started from Lisbon on his momentous voyage in 1497, the English flag had been planted on the shores of the New World. The initiative in this English exploration came from an Italian, known as Giovanni Caboto back in Genoa and Venice, but called John Cabot by Englishmen. He found financial backing in the seaport of Bristol, on the southwestern coast near Wales. The Bristol merchants were interested in the Atlantic route because of the port's frequent fishing voyages to Iceland. Moreover, at this time successful sales of English woolens in the Baltic had given them surplus money to invest in new adventures. Henry VII gave Cabot and his sons "full and free authority, leave and power, upon their proper costs and charges, to seeke out, discover and finde whatsoever isles, countries, regions or provinces of the heathen and infidels, which before this time have been unknown to all Christians." Cabot sailed from Bristol with eighteen men in the little *Matthew*. Details of the Cabot voyages are vague; for we are dependent largely upon the account written many years later by John's son Sebastian, who seems to have been somewhat of a liar. It appears likely that late in June, 1497, Cabot landed on the tip of Cape Breton Island and also sighted the larger island still known, as it was in his time, as Newfoundland. At any rate, he was back in England that summer a popular hero. "Vast honor is paid him," wrote a Venetian from London, "and he dresses in silk; and the English run after him like mad people." The king, according to this source, promised generous support for another expedition the next year "and has also given him money wherewith to amuse himself till then." The privy-purse accounts of the tight-fisted first Tudor contain the item "To hym that found the New Isle, £10." Henry also granted him a pension of £20 a year, which John seems to have lived only two years to enjoy. In 1498 he and Sebastian made a second voyage, apparently discovering Labrador and penetrating into arctic regions, probably the pioneers in that long, futile, and dangerous quest for a "northwest passage" around the top of America to the Indies. Sebastian himself found a more liberal paymaster in the king of Spain, for whom he helped to open up the Rio de la Plata near the present city of Buenos Aires, in South America. Long afterward he returned to England, and as late as 1551 was promoting explorations of a "northeast passage" around the tip of Europe. Bristol profited from its initiative and investments; for after the American colonies developed, it secured much of their trade and was for many years the second largest city in England. The interesting theory has been advanced that America was named not for Americus Vespucius but for one Richard Amerik, a Bristol merchant who contributed generously to those pioneer voyages of exploration.

In spite of this early start, England quickly dropped out of the expansion race for the time being. The Tudors were too busy with their Continental foreign policy, and the lands which the Cabots discovered were cold and barren, yielding neither spices nor precious

# The Coming of the Renaissance

metals. Yet those Cabot voyages revealed to England something that in the long run was to bring her more wealth than Portugal's pepper trade or Spain's silver mines. In the fogs off the Newfoundland coast lie the shallow Grand Banks, so teeming with cod that they are the best fishing grounds in the world. The Cabots, so Sebastian said, caught them simply by lowering buckets over the side. At any rate, Portuguese and Frenchmen, as well as Englishmen, almost immediately swarmed to the new fishing grounds and, in spite of cold, danger, and hard labor, made huge catches of cod, salted and dried them on the barren shores of Newfoundland, and returned home in the fall with wealth wrested from the sea. When England a century later began to plant colonies in North America, she could claim the rights of discovery because of the Cabot voyages.

The third of the great voyages, ranking with those of Columbus and Da Gama, was the circumnavigation of the earth by one of Magellan's ships between 1519 and 1522. Balboa, a Spaniard, had crossed the Isthmus of Panama in 1513, and was the first European to see the Pacific Ocean. Six years later Spain sent a Portuguese mariner, Ferdinand Magellan, to find out what lay beyond the American continent. He discovered the strait which bears his name, and then pushed across the Pacific. Magellan himself was killed in the Philippines, but one of his ships continued through the East Indies and around the Cape of Good Hope, the first to sail around the world. By that time Europe had unrolled the map enough to realize the extent of the outside world, although there were still plenty of dark corners for later men to explore.

Colonization followed close upon discovery. The nations which had backed the explorers proceeded to establish overseas empires. In other words, they took political and commercial control over the new lands which had been claimed in their names. As soon as Columbus returned in 1493, the Pope, as the highest international authority, divided all the lands beyond the seas between Spain and Portugal. As things worked out, with slight stretchings of this papal "line of demarcation," the Americas —except for Portuguese Brazil—were Spain's, and the East—except for the Spanish Philippines—was Portugal's. This decree theoretically excluded England from a share in overseas territory, but Henry VII disregarded it in authorizing Cabot's voyage, thereby alarming the Spanish envoy at the English court. Within forty more years England was to cast off papal authority, not only in geography but in religion as well. After that the papal decree was to last only as long as the guns of the Portuguese carracks and the Spanish galleons could uphold it.

From that day to this, European expansion in the East and in the West has followed separate courses. The climate and products of the thickly settled East led to colonies of exploitation, where an ever-shifting handful of Europeans dominated vast numbers of natives. The temperate regions of America made possible colonies of settlement (see page 332). To these, European populations migrated to make permanent homes overseas. Men brought their families to the latter type of colonies, but almost never to the former. Some colonies, like part of Spanish America, represented a mixture of the two types.

Spain soon had sway over a vast empire. It included most of Central and South America and even extended into the southern part of the present United States. Ruthless, daring *conquistadores*, with their little bands, overcame the frightened natives, who had never before seen horses or guns. Rich silver and gold mines gave special importance to Mexico and to Peru, where the high-handed work of Cortes in 1519 and Pizarro in 1532 overthrew the semi-civilized states of the Aztec and Inca Indians. The natives died like flies in the unaccustomed forced toil of mining, until a humane official introduced African Negroes in order to save the remaining Indians for Christianity. Spaniards came over by the thousands. Some, in the more temperate regions, managed to preserve a pure European strain down through the generations. But the majority had no scruples about promiscuous interbreeding, which led to a mixture of white, Indian, and Negro blood.

Government and trade were rigidly regulated in the sole interest of the mother country. Powerful viceroys at Lima and at Mexico City passed on to the local governors orders from the king and the Council of the Indies at home. Trade was limited to annual fleets of galleons. A few companies secured control of commerce, to the exclusion of all foreigners and even of Spanish free traders. Silver and gold poured into Spain, the king receiving his royal fifth. This helped to make Spain the leading power of Europe in the sixteenth century; but it led to an abnormal jump in prices, and it made the Spaniards scornful of humdrum domestic industry.

Portugal, in the meantime, was building up a somewhat different sort of empire in the East. That region was populated by races with ancient culture and well-developed civilizations. It was out of the question to dominate them as completely as Spain was dominating the Indians in America. The Portuguese empire therefore became a series of armed trading posts, with little political authority over the interior. The center was at Goa, in western India. Under the stimulus of Alfonso Albuquerque, Portugal's power soon spread all

# The Coming of the Renaissance

along the coasts of India, into the Spice Islands, where the cinnamon and pepper grew, and even to China, where she gained a permanent foothold, in addition to stations along the African coast. This fifteen thousand miles of coast line was held together by sea power and a few garrisons.

The Portuguese people did not settle in India to any extent. There were not men enough; for all Portugal had fewer people than Philadelphia has today. A steady succession of officials spent three-year terms amassing as much money as they could. With them went a swarm of ne'er-do-wells who could live in a style far beyond anything possible at home. Very few Portuguese women migrated to India, so that a race of half-breeds was inevitable. Saint Francis Xavier and other churchmen tried to spread Christianity, but the natives were more impressed by the cruel arrogance of the average Portuguese. Trade, as in the case of Spain, was confined to the annual fleets which carried the spices to Lisbon. The king conducted the entire business as his private monopoly, but dishonest officials pocketed more than half the profits.

Those beginnings overseas were an important part of what has been called the "Commercial Revolution." During the transition from medieval to modern times European economic life underwent several significant changes. Business outgrew its old local character. England and the other western maritime states, as the new centralized monarchies, organized commerce on a national basis, with the government regulating and encouraging it. This led to the decline of those old cities which were unrelated to strong states, especially Venice and the other Italian cities as well as the Hanseatic towns of the north. In order to provide the sinews of war in that day of mercenary soldiers, it was considered essential to have a well-filled treasury, and the more prosperous the population the more it could pay in taxes and customs duties. In alliance with the businessmen, the new monarchs utilized the national resources of legislation, diplomacy, and even war to improve business conditions and to acquire colonies. Out of this grew the so-called "mercantile system," of which we shall hear more when it reaches its prime in the later seventeenth century (see page 329).

The English kings, having achieved a fairly centralized government ahead of their Continental rivals, had for a considerable time been doing this very thing, using the machinery of government to stimulate business on a national basis. This activity began when Edward I was granted customs duties as part of the national revenue. The rulers, to be sure, had not been entirely disinterested in these efforts. Their principal task had been to change England from

[ 233 ]

a passive to an active economic role (see page 175). So successful were these national efforts that by the end of the fourteenth
century England was ready to offer the world of commerce finished
woolen cloth instead of merely raw wool. The attempt to stimulate
the making of cloth in England, partly through the introduction of
Flemish weavers, had been a success. By the end of the fourteenth
century England no longer needed to depend upon Flanders as a
market for her raw wool or as a source of finer cloth for her own
consumption. Her new surplus of woolen cloth of her own manufacture was from that time to be the mainstay of the English export
trade. It was still necessary, however, to find markets in which to
sell the cloth. About 1400 a new group of traders were given export
monopoly rights in cloth and other finished goods, and these rights
soon overshadowed the old privileges of the Staplers, who had been
limited to raw wool, tin, and lead (see page 175). These new Merchant Adventurers began aggressive attempts to peddle English cloth
on the Continent. The best potential markets lay in Germany, on the
Baltic, and in other cold parts of northern Europe; but there the
Merchant Adventurers ran athwart the still powerful monopoly of
the Hanseatic League, which frequently resorted to force to keep out
the intruders. The Englishmen, however, still persisted in forceful
efforts to gain new markets.

By this time England was trying also to secure the additional
profits which come from freight charges paid for carrying exports
and imports. The English merchant marine was small, and even
when Englishmen traded abroad they frequently had to hire foreign
vessels. In 1381, early in the reign of Richard II, Parliament passed
a "navigation act" forbidding exports except in English ships. There
were not enough such ships, however, to handle the trade, and the
law could not be rigidly enforced. Its renewal under the first Tudor
was also not carried out to the letter; but it was the forerunner of the
celebrated Navigation Acts of 1651 and 1660, which finally did much
to build up England's maritime supremacy (see pages 360, 383).
From the fourteenth century also came efforts to establish England's
"sovereignty of the seas," partly so as to reduce piracy and to extend
the king's peace to adjacent waters. Out of these efforts finally came
the practice of forcing foreign vessels in those waters to dip their
flags to the English as a symbol of this authority.

The hectic years of the middle fifteenth century saw little advance
in this economic legislation. Gradually the English extended their,
commerce, however, and Bristol, as we saw, began to grow rich in
selling woolen cloth to Baltic ports. Edward IV did something to
stimulate trade, although he extended still further the privileges of

# The Coming of the Renaissance

the Hanse in return for loans. The first Tudor adopted a positive policy of expanding England's influence on the seas. Besides having been ready to finance Columbus and having encouraged Cabot in his voyages of discovery, he began to develop a regular royal navy, in place of the haphazard gathering of armed merchantmen from the Cinque Ports and elsewhere in wartime. He thus laid the foundations of a fighting force which was to do great things a century later. He likewise showed himself a modern king by his persistent use of legislation and diplomacy to increase England's commerce. A treaty with the king of Denmark promoted trade with Scandinavia and Iceland at the expense of the Hanse. There were treaties with some of the Hanse towns themselves, but more frequently there were reprisals and discriminatory duties. Efforts were made to break the Venetian commercial hold by dealing with rival Italian cities. A treaty with Flanders, known as the "Great Intercourse," removed many of the artificial barriers of trade with that region, which was still a valuable market. Within a hundred years the Flemish, the Venetians, and the Hanseatic League would pass from their old leadership of European commerce; for those city units were overshadowed by the new national economic systems. Altogether, two centuries of national endeavor had transformed England from a passive economic role to an active one, and had pointed the way by which she was to develop into "a nation of shopkeepers," "the workshop of the world," and, most important, "Mistress of the Seas."

The new era saw England, as well as the rest of Europe, coming more and more to a cash basis. In the earlier Middle Ages the relationship between lord and vassal and lord and serf had been on a basis of personal service; now payments were made instead. The influx of precious metals vastly increased the amount of available money. Finance was becoming more important as a separate sphere of economic activity. The earlier functions of the Jews and Lombards were expanding until moneylenders developed on such a scale that they could sometimes determine whether or not a monarch might fight. Antwerp, with its flourishing commerce and its stock exchange, was the important financial center of the sixteenth century, to be followed by Amsterdam and then by London. The Italians had developed drafts and other forms of commercial paper which made it possible to conduct distant transactions without the actual constant transfer of bullion. Previously, borrowed money had not been generally used for productive purposes; men now realized that a judicious use of capital and credit could lead to the production of new wealth. England, however, lagged behind Italy, Germany, and the Low Countries in the development of banking.

# A History of England and the British Empire

A third great change in the transition from medieval to modern times was the growth of national states with strong, centralized monarchical governments. In the Middle Ages, as we have seen, the feudal organizations of the state, wherein the great holdings of the barons sometimes rivaled the royal domain, tended to make the royal power weak and the nobles powerful. This caused decentralization, and men were apt to think of themselves primarily not as Englishmen or Frenchmen but as men of Kent or Cornwall, of Brittany or Anjou. In England this decentralization was not as marked as on the Continent; for William the Conqueror, Henry II, Edward I, and others had set the example of strong central government. The troubled times of the fifteenth century, however, had almost thrown England back into the old feudal disorder.

Gradually, various forces had worked to exalt the monarchs at the expense of the nobles. Many of the feudal lords perished in the Crusades, in the Hundred Years' War, and in such local fighting as the Wars of the Roses. Not only were those troublesome individuals removed but their estates often went to swell the royal domain. The protracted fighting of the Hundred Years' War served, too, to increase the feeling of national patriotism. The victories of Crécy and Poitiers had given Englishmen a national pride; Joan of Arc had done much to produce the same result in France. The long centuries of fighting the Moors had engendered a similar national feeling in Portugal and in the Christian kingdoms of northern Spain. The substitution of professional armies of mercenaries for the inadequate feudal levies had also been accelerated by these long struggles. Thus the original basis of the feudal system, land tenure in return for military service, gradually disappeared. The remaining lords, however, although they had lost the original justification for their generous holdings, clung to their privileges for centuries until, in some cases, dispossessed by revolution. Only an ample royal treasury could afford these new armies of mercenaries, so that one more bulwark was built about the growing royal power. Just as the rise of infantry was diminishing the value of the man on horseback, so the use of gunpowder further weakened the position of the feudal lords; for the new cannon of the royal siege trains could batter down their hitherto almost impregnable castles. As the nobles declined in power the kings found good allies in the men of the rising middle class, who were excellent potential taxpayers and who favored strong government because it was good for business. With the tendency toward increased royal absolutism, national assemblies such as the French Estates-General gradually lost their power; even the English Parliament was to lose its influence temporarily. Administration, military control, justice, and finance passed from feudal into royal hands.

In the late fifteenth century, in addition to England two large European states—France and Spain—and one small one—Portugal —were reaching this status of strong centralized monarchies. The French king Louis XI (1461–1483) had utilized the feeling of nationalism aroused by Joan of Arc and the close of the Hundred Years' War to enhance his power. Using craft and cunning against his barons, he further extended the royal domain so that before his death Brittany, the last of the semi-independent provinces, was brought under the control of the crown. So strong did he leave France that she was ready to look for outside lands to conquer (see page 252). Spain, the leading nation of Europe during the coming century, was united by the marriage of the rulers of her two energetic northern Christian kingdoms, Ferdinand of Aragon and Isabella of Castile, who soon completed the century-old fight against the Moors by capturing their last stronghold in 1492. The Holy Roman Empire, on the other hand, the loose government of the German and Austrian lands, was too decentralized to become a real national state until the nineteenth century; but the emperors, generally chosen from the Hapsburg family, enjoyed a powerful position in Austria and their other hereditary lands which they had built up by judicious marrying of heiresses throughout the centuries. By 1500 one of these marriages was to join these extensive holdings to the strongly centralized Spanish monarchy by the accession of Charles V (see page 254). Likewise Italy was made up of small states and was not united until the nineteenth century. The old Eastern, or Byzantine, Empire was experiencing autocracy from her new Turkish masters, but was too full of diverse peoples for an early rise of nationalism. Russia was just beginning to free herself from centuries of rule by the Tatars in China. The Scandinavian countries were developing into two monarchies: Sweden (by herself) and Denmark (including Norway). Poland, long a powerful state, was following meanwhile a trend quite different from that of the west by disintegrating under an excess of feudalism.

In England, we have already seen that the nationalistic spirit had developed during the long war with France, while the Wars of the Roses had helped to clear out many of the feudal lords. The country, weary of the pointless civil war, craved peace and order, and by this time was ready to forgo some of its liberty to that end. A strong king was needed to accomplish this, and England found him in Henry VII. Although only twenty-eight at the time of his accession, he was old beyond his years, hardened by exile, intrigue, and disappointed hopes. Lean, sharp-featured, hardheaded, Henry had neither the presence nor the personality that makes for popularity; but England did not ask for a popular or romantic king in that hour of disordered confusion.

At this distance we can trace the steps by which Henry VII built up the new royal power; but we must remember that to the men of his day he was for a while simply another temporarily successful dynastic rival who had gained the throne by one battle and might lose it by another. Fifteenth-century England had seen so many rapid rises and falls that it was some time before the Tudor line was accepted as a fixture. In many respects the role played by Henry VII resembled that of Henry II. Both found England in feudal turmoil at their accession; both quickly restored law and order and then proceeded to make lasting contributions to the development of their country. Both have been overshadowed in popular reputation by their sons, whose spectacular achievements were made possible only by the substantial but less showy achievements of the fathers. Like Henry VII, too, in qualities of shrewdness, unromantic realism, and strength, were his Continental contemporaries who also were laying the foundations for the glory of later generations—the kings of France and Spain and, to a lesser degree, the Holy Roman emperor. We have noticed that, so far as policy was concerned, the rule of the Yorkist Edward IV had much in common with that of the Tudors; but England was not quite ready for it then, and Edward IV too often sacrificed business to pleasure (see page 213).

Henry lost no time in establishing his position. Six weeks after Bosworth Field, writs were sent out for a new Parliament. It took time, in those days of wretched roads, for the writs to reach the borders of Scotland and Wales and for lords and commons slowly to assemble, but two months more found the first Tudor Parliament at Westminster. The Tudors were to keep Parliament in the passive role into which it had fallen under the Yorkists. They respected the old forms, but, for a whole century to come, Parliament's role consisted chiefly in acquiescence to royal wishes. The Council, a small group of officials and nobles with important executive and advisory functions, tended to overshadow Parliament in influence throughout the Tudor period. Henry's first Parliament complacently gave him his royal title without saying much about the embarrassing point of hereditary right to the throne. The votes of Lords and Commons simply ratified the verdict of battle, and the *de facto* king became king *de jure*.

Not content with Parliamentary sanction alone, Henry strength-

# The Coming of the Renaissance

ened his position by marriage. Just as Henry I had married into the old Saxon line to widen the hereditary background of the royal house, so, five months after Bosworth, Henry VII, representative of the Red Rose, married a representative of the White Rose, Elizabeth of York, daughter of Edward IV. They had been betrothed during the period when Henry was aiming for the throne. The birth of a son (Arthur) in whose veins flowed the blood of York as well as of Lancaster served to bring the rival factions closer together, although, as we shall see, the reconciliation was not complete.

The three main problems facing Henry, once he had established his own position, were the suppression of the nobles, the filling of the treasury, and the improvement of foreign relations. Sterile as they had been on the whole, the Wars of the Roses had accomplished something by killing or driving into exile many of the turbulent lords. When Henry's first Parliament met, there were only eighteen lay nobles in the House of Lords, whereas there were thirty spiritual peers. Some of these surviving nobles, however, were strong enough to give trouble; for the legislation of a century earlier had been ineffective in suppressing the evils of "livery and maintenance" (see page 196). To break up the private armies of the nobles, Henry set up a special tribunal, composed of the Council together with the two Chief Justices, and authorized to handle cases without any hampering common-law precedents. The most arrogant noble could not browbeat such a court; and it brought to heel one stubborn offender after another. This Court of Star Chamber (so called from the room where it generally met) was the first of several special Tudor tribunals created to meet particular emergencies. The fact that the later abuse of their special powers led to the abolition of those courts should not offset the fact that they were very effective in the immediate situations for which they were designed. Peace gradually settled upon the counties; for the old nobility sank still further in numbers and power. They were lucky who escaped with a simple clipping of their wings; for many were heavily fined and some were executed. Few members of the English peerage can trace their titles farther back than 1485; for the House of Lords was gradually filled with fresh Tudor creations from the "new men," lesser landholders and the middle-class men of business, whose interests coincided more closely with those of the king and whose importance will be discussed later.

Few rulers have been as successful as Henry in building up a treasury surplus. The coffers were bare when he came to the throne; when he died, twenty-four years later, they were so full that their contents were estimated at £1,300,000 to £1,800,000, "the richest

[ 239 ]

treasury in Christendom." It was a strange phenomenon to find a king who could not only balance his budget but also salt away a considerable surplus nearly every year. Henry managed to do this with a minimum of dependence on Parliamentary grants. He did not want to antagonize the middle class, whose support he desired, by asking too much from the House of Commons, where that group was strongly represented. Only five times in his whole reign did he request the Lords and Commons for money—only twice in his last eighteen years. He managed to do this partly by rigid economy, which at times degenerated into stinginess; partly by his regular income from crown lands and customs duties; partly by the acquisition of escheated lands of dead men; and partly by irregular high-pressure methods of extortion which represent the seamy side of the picture. The crown lands now yielded about £100,000 a year. The customs duties, which Parliament granted him for life, were worth about £30,000 a year at the beginning; but Henry so encouraged commerce that the figure had risen to some £40,000 by the end of the reign. The extortions caused bitter complaints. The name of his bishop-chancellor appeared in a tax-collecting device called "Morton's fork," by which, in the words of Francis Bacon, "the sparing were to be pressed for money because they saved, the lavish because they spent." The brunt of the odium fell upon Henry's two over-zealous and unscrupulous lawyers, Sir Richard Empson and Edmund Dudley, who continually dragged out the most flimsy pretexts to fine and confiscate in the king's interest. One of the first popular acts of Henry's son was to execute this hated pair; but without their work the treasury would certainly not have been as full.

While beating down nobles and scraping together gold, Henry constantly had to keep his eyes beyond the borders. The time would come when he would play high politics with France and Spain; but first he had to watch the dangerous pro-Yorkist hostility closer at hand in Scotland and Ireland, as well as in Flanders, where the dowager duchess of Burgundy, Margaret, sister of Edward IV, was an implacable enemy.

These three immediate foes struck at him by launching two Yorkist pretenders, one posing as Edward's nephew, who was Henry's prisoner in the Tower, and the other as Edward's son, the younger of the two princes murdered in the Tower. The first pretender appeared in 1487 in the person of one Lambert Simnel, simple son of an Oxford tradesman. Coached by a priest, he received an enthusiastic reception and coronation in disaffected Ireland, and then crossed to England, backed by a force of German mercenaries sent by the duchess Margaret. Henry crushed the invaders in a single battle

# The Coming of the Renaissance

and sent Simnel to work in the royal kitchens. Five years later a more persistent and dangerous pretender appeared, named Perkin Warbeck, who, with the murder of the princes in the Tower still a debated question, made a natural appeal to the popular mind as the younger of these. With strong Continental backing, Warbeck intrigued for five years. In his name there were one futile attack by sea and two from Scotland, where Warbeck married a high-born lady; and in the meantime general disaffection caused a mob of Cornish miners to march on London. Henry's spies, however, kept close track of the intrigues; and by 1497 Warbeck submitted to the king, who had him executed two years later.

In connection with Scotland and Ireland, Henry took steps which foreshadowed England's later relations with those British neighbors. The Warbeck affair had led to Scottish invasions. Henry tried to relieve this menace by arranging in 1502 a marriage between his elder daughter Margaret and James IV, king of Scotland. Some of his advisers warned him that it might lead to the absorption of England in Scotland; but Henry, citing the case of Normandy, pointed out that "the greater would draw the less." So it resulted; for that marriage brought the great-grandson of James and Margaret southward as England's first Stuart king just a hundred and one years later.

While Scotland was being treated on terms of equality, Ireland was reminded more strongly than ever that she was a dependency of England. Relations had been irregular for many years, and Yorkist Ireland supported both Simnel and Warbeck. Henry sent over a capable soldier, Sir Edward Poynings, who was unsuccessful in subduing the wild Irish in the outlying provinces, but who managed to get some important legislation through the Irish parliament in the "Pale." These "Poynings's Laws" of 1494, later heartily damned by the Irish, made their parliament definitely subordinate to the English crown and to the English Parliament. Ireland's parliament could meet only when the crown agreed, and then could take up only such legislation as the crown approved; whereas all laws passed by the English Parliament were valid in Ireland, even if they ran counter to Irish acts. By the time Henry's granddaughter Elizabeth was on the throne, the Tudors were once more to have their hands full with Scottish and Irish problems.

In foreign affairs Henry dabbled steadily in international diplomacy of the trickiest sort. In 1489 he allied himself with Spain in hostility to France. The crafty Ferdinand wanted English help in acquiring some territory in the Pyrenees from France, and Henry wanted the prestige of a first-class alliance, since, without any

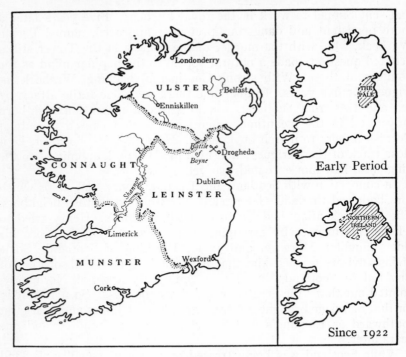

Early Period

Since 1922

IRELAND

apparent good cause, he was meddling in the troubled affairs of the French province of Brittany. The alliance was sealed by the betrothal of two infants, Henry's first-born, Arthur, and Catherine of Aragon, daughter of Ferdinand and Isabella,—a match, like the Scottish, destined to have important consequences. Henry successfully bargained for a heavy dowry. For the remainder of his reign he held his own fairly well against astute rivals, although many of his wily schemes led nowhere in particular.

Only once did matters lead to declared war, and then it was a war of a mercenary, unromantic type that would have made Richard Cœur de Lion and the Black Prince turn in their graves. Of course, twenty years before this, Edward IV had acted in similar fashion (see page 214). The campaign of 1492 was glorified blackmail. Henry secured a very generous war grant from Parliament, and then, in the very week when Columbus reached America, crossed to France with some twenty-seven thousand men. He laid siege to Boulogne, not because he particularly wanted it but because he knew that France was so busy in preparing to invade Italy that she would not want to be bothered with an English war. To the gratification

# The Coming of the Renaissance

of Henry and the disgust of his army, he was bought off before any serious bloodshed occurred. The royal treasury was consequently richer both by the unexpended balance of the Parliamentary grant and by the French bribe. The Middle Ages, with their romantic but impracticable chivalry, were certainly passing.

Whereas the changes of overseas expansion, the new learning, and the strong national monarchies affected other European nations as well as England, two economic innovations which began to be prominent in the first Tudor reign were quite distinctively English and strongly affected the economic life of many Englishmen. One of these was the "enclosure movement"; the other was the "domestic system." Like much else in England's early economic life, both were closely connected with wool.

The increasing demand for wool, both for domestic manufacture and for export, had given great impetus to the enclosure movement, which was to produce grave consequences throughout the Tudor period. Under the old manorial system, which had continued with the simple substitution of cash payments in place of forced service, a considerable part of the manor land, it will be recalled, was used in common (see page 70). This unchanging system of agriculture was so inefficient and wasteful that it produced little more than subsistence for the workers, with a slight surplus for outside sale. Shrewd landowners, who observed the riches which had come to the Cistercian monks through their raising of sheep and selling of wool, realized that the common lands on their estates would be much more productive if given over to sheep grazing instead of agriculture. The word "enclosure" came from the practice of fencing off the former common lands and thus excluding the peasants from their share in the meadows, woods, and even much of the cultivated land. They might be left with small plots for their own cultivation, but no longer could their livestock run at large. A manor which might have had fifty peasants tilling the soil under the old system would need only three or four shepherds to tend the sheep on those same acres; yet the wool from those sheep would be worth much more than the former meager products of the soil.

There had been some enclosures in England as early as the thirteenth century, but with the fifteenth century the process became very general. Sheep-raising was particularly adapted to the barren north country, but the practice spread over much of the nation. By the end of the next century about half the manors of England, it was estimated, had experienced more or less enclosing for sheep-raising. It is easy to understand why the landlords desired enclosures, and it was the landowners who sat in Parliament and dominated local government. But the new process meant a tremendous dis-location of the former agricultural workers, who were rudely displaced with nowhere to go. Tudor England went through a whole century without a satisfactory solution of the problem, while the roads were filled with "lusty beggars" and wandering rogues, and the villages held the weaker unemployed, who had scant means of holding body and soul together. Two centuries later, as we shall see, England was to have another epidemic of enclosures. The process was similar, but the impulse was then to come not from sheep-raising but from the new efficient methods of the so-called Agricultural Revolution.

At this time wool was also helping to bring about another change by which English industry was gradually to burst the bonds of the guild system. England, still continuing her old trade in raw wool, was coming more and more, with her increased raising of wool, to spin and weave at home. With the expansion of industry as well as commerce into new channels, the guilds were simply left neglected at one side. This was largely the fault of the inelastic system itself. At first the craft guilds had rendered valuable service in regulating the conditions of work and the quality of the products (see page 132). They had been a boon to the embryo middle class, had done much to put trade and industry upon a stable foundation, and had protected the workers from abuse by nobles or rulers. As time went on, however, they made many selfish restrictions so that no one might become too rich through higher prices or through soliciting more business. Prices, for instance, were often fixed at a certain supposedly fair amount above the cost of manufacture. The economic law of supply and demand, by which the scarcer article brings the higher price, and vice versa, was not allowed to function. Membership in the guilds was increasingly restricted so that there should not be too many master workmen. This curtailed production and kept prices at a high level. The guilds, as a result of this conservative policy and exclusive membership, became as much a deterrent to the growth of industry as they were originally a help.

It was therefore not surprising that their place was gradually taken by a so-called "domestic," or "putting-out," system, which was the dominant feature in English industry from the late fifteenth to the late eighteenth century. This appeared first and most commonly in the manufacture of woolens and centered in rural villages, which were free from the cramping regulations of the guilds. Enterprising "merchant clothiers" would buy a quantity of raw wool and distribute it among individuals who would carry out the various processes of carding, spinning, or weaving. The clothier would then

# The Coming of the Renaissance

collect the finished product, pay for the work by the piece, and then sell it, receiving most of the profits. The work, especially the weaving, might still be done by a master craftsman, employing a journeyman and an apprentice or two; the spinning was more likely to be done by a family or by a solitary individual. Such a system, which bears a certain resemblance to that of the modern sweatshop, was capable of indefinite expansion. It involved a separation of functions, because the clothier, or entrepreneur, who owned the goods, furnished the capital, and found the market, was a separate person from the master workman, who, under the old guild system, had combined in his person both capital and labor, industry and commerce. No longer was it necessary to gather all the workers under one roof. There was no question of an exclusive guild which would arbitrarily limit the number of workers. Those workers, moreover, had considerable economic freedom: they could work long or short hours as they saw fit, being masters of their own time. They could shift from one employer to another at will. Besides, the domestic workers were not always dependent upon industry alone: they could generally till little gardens, do extra work at harvest time, and perhaps keep a cow, sheep, or geese for food. This new stage in industrial development was prevalent for nearly three centuries, until the further demands of English commerce led to machinery and the factory system in the Industrial Revolution.

These economic developments were partly responsible for certain shifts in the importance and well-being of the various social classes in Tudor England. In the main, the "new men" of the middle groups profited at the expense of the two extremes. The squires, or country gentry, rose in prosperity and power; so too, to a lesser degree, did the "middle class proper, the businessmen of the towns, engaged in trade or industry. Henry VII, on the other hand, was deliberately interested in beating down the power of the great nobles, and did little to prevent the exploitation of the peasantry.

While typical members of these various social groups can easily be identified and described, class lines were not drawn as rigidly in England as they were in France or most other parts of the Continent. In the Middle Ages both England and France had had their fighting feudal aristocracy, their suppressed serfs, and their small group of middle-class townsmen. In France those sharp distinctions still continued; a man was a nobleman or he was not, and a vast gulf in prestige, privilege, and mode of life existed between social classes. The unprivileged paid most of the taxes and did all the work, but were not allowed to participate to any extent in the government. In England, on the other hand, the social frontiers were hazier, gradually blending all the way from dukes down to farm laborers. Those frontiers, too, were easier to cross. There was, to be sure, a difference between "gentle" and "simple" folk; but class lines were not very sharply drawn. England was consequently more of a unit and was better able to escape the terrible revolt against the privileged noble caste which was later to tear France apart.

The difference between the English and French social systems was particularly noticeable and significant in the case of the lower and most numerous ranks of the landed aristocracy. On both sides of the Channel they enjoyed the leisure and social position that came from the family possession of land. In France this lower aristocracy held titles of nobility and as such formed a distinct caste. In England titles were of less consequence. Many of the lesser peers differed little from the squires, or gentlemen, whose acres might be just as extensive. A small group of important Englishmen held the titles of duke, marquess, earl, viscount, or baron, which entitled them to membership in the House of Lords. They alone, strictly speaking, comprised the English nobility, or peerage. The king might create as many new peers as he saw fit; but the power was used sparingly, and the House of Lords never exceeded a few hundred in size. Another influence which kept the peerage small was the fact that the English title descended only to the eldest son,—"the first of the litter," as a later statesman sneered at the House of Lords. Edward I, as we have seen, had helped to crystallize this practice of primogeniture and entail, whereby the family lands as well as the title went intact to the eldest son. The younger sons were commoners, with no automatic social rank or privilege beyond what they might achieve for themselves, and were free to carry their inheritance of class—often their only heritage—into many diverse fields. It was through them in particular that the English social system came to possess more flexible features than the Continental. In France, and elsewhere on the Continent, every son of a nobleman was a nobleman also, rigidly limited by caste in the occupations which he might select. The class thus increased in geometric ratio, until in Poland, as an extreme case, it was estimated that there was a nobleman for every four acres of land.

The bulk of the landed aristocracy in England were known simply as "gentlemen" or "squires." A few might enjoy knighthood and prefix "Sir" to their names; the majority had no official titles and at the most might use "Esquire" or "Gent." after their names. The term "gentleman," however, was not bandied about as carelessly as it is in this democratic age, and generally implied a definite status: good family, a fair amount of property, together with the

# The Coming of the Renaissance

possession of a family coat of arms and the theoretical right to challenge even an earl to a duel.

With the curbing of the Nevilles, the Percys, and the other proud and tempestuous feudal lords, the gentry came into their own in the Tudor period and remained a dominant element in English political as well as social life until well into the twentieth century. Their rise, to be sure, had extended over several centuries, as we have had occasion to notice from time to time (see pages 108, 149). They were counterparts of the Saxon thanes and Norman men at arms who had received land in return for military service. That original reason for their landholding, we recall, had begun to disappear with the introduction of scutage in the twelfth century; but they still retained the power and profit which went with lordship of the manor. The Black Death had accelerated the substitution of cash for service in the manorial relationship. By early Tudor times More, in his *Utopia*, was condemning the greedy thirst for profit which, among other things, stimulated the enclosure movement. The abolition of the monasteries under the second Tudor, moreover, was to give many townsmen, previously engaged in trade or industry, an opportunity to improve their social position by acquiring landed estates and thus buying their way into the ranks of the gentry, bringing with them their business point of view.

These landholders formed a leisure class, for their rents gave them an income without exertion on their part. Both nobility and gentry found various ways of spending that leisure. Then, and for long afterward, some of them formed a lively, ambitious court group; but for a still larger number the normal range of life did not extend beyond the county. Those who aspired to play a conspicuous role in high society were particularly prone in Tudor times to spend a disproportionate amount of their income upon their dress. Under French influence the doublets of the men and the bodices of the ladies became elaborate and costly, sometimes being adorned with gold and jewels. As the century progressed, broad neck ruffs, together with tights for the men, made costumes even more extreme. More than one good grove of oaks was slashed down so that the owner and his wife might cut a proper figure at court. Such outlay might, however, prove a good investment, and Englishmen then as now were good gamblers. The Tudor monarchs favored "new men"; and the experience of the Seymour and Cecil families is an indication of how high country squires might rise if they made the most of their opportunities in the royal presence. Many a family fortune of later days was based upon the cleverness and presence of mind of some ancestor who had used his head at court in Tudor times.

The true habitat of the squire, however, was not the glittering society of London, Windsor, or Hampton Court. The typical country gentleman spent most of his days on his estate, in close contact with his tenants and retainers and with a social circle generally limited to the other "county families." Some squires might take an active interest in the raising of crops on the demesne land with hired laborers; many, however, found it simpler to lease the demesne to tenant farmers. Hunting absorbed a considerable part of the squire's ample leisure—chasing the deer, the hare, or, later, the fox with horse and dogs, or birds with trained hawks. It was a healthy and wholesome, if not elevating, existence, accompanied usually with copious drinking of ale and wine.

The country houses took on a new charm in the Tudor period. The stately "great hall" of the older manor houses gave way to more comfortable and livable quarters in which elaborate staircases and rich oak paneling were prominent features. Glass windows began to come into common use. These Tudor countryseats, often long and rambling, with broad chimneys, were sometimes built of stone or were half-timbered with oak and plaster; but most common was warm, red brick. Altogether they were a happy adaptation of the Renaissance to the spirit of the English squirearchy.

These same hard-hunting, hard-drinking squires controlled England's local government in the rural districts until late in the nineteenth century. In the earlier Middle Ages, we remember, they had enjoyed some local power through their manorial courts; but the kings had relied primarily upon the sheriffs as their direct representatives in running the shires (see page 73). As time went on, however, the functions of the sheriffs were diminished, and the functions of local government passed more and more into the hands of the gentry, who exercised them not as feudal individuals but as unpaid justices of the peace, definitely commissioned by the central government and theoretically subject to the king and his Council. While major legal cases were usually held for the periodic assizes, at which the itinerant royal judges presided, the ordinary run of court work was in the hands of these squire-justices. Such a justice could settle minor cases alone, without a jury, and could bind offenders over for regular court trial, administering bail if he saw fit. For cases too grave for such summary jurisdiction but not weighty enough for the King's Bench assizes, there were the county "quarter sessions" four times a year, presided over by two or more of the justices of the peace. In addition to their legal work, the justices of the peace had supervision of the collection of taxes and served as officers of the militia. In fact, they were the agents for carrying

# The Coming of the Renaissance

out locally nearly everything, affecting the immediate community, enacted by Parliament or decreed by the central government. They had been entrusted with the administration of the old Statute of Laborers and would be given extensive further duties in carrying out the social and economic legislation of the later Tudor period, such as the administration of the Statute of Apprentices. This service was rendered without pay, but sense of duty or love of influence provided an adequate supply of such "J. P.'s." The work, moreover, gave the country gentlemen prestige and experience, not only in local affairs but also for many a national crisis. A trained bureaucracy of royal officials, of the type employed by the kings of France, would doubtless have been more efficient; but England in that case might not have had its unique record of thwarting an absolute monarchy at such an early period.

The Tudors, as we shall see, tended toward autocracy; but it must be remembered that their autocracy prevailed only because it rested upon the approval of the majority of these country gentlemen who administered local government. The crown possessed no standing army or other adequate force under its own control, and its decrees could never have been enforced unless these amateur administrators out in the counties had seen fit to do so. The political role of the gentry was by no means limited to the sphere of local government. Those same squires composed the bulk of the House of Commons, not only as knights of the shire but also as borough representatives. We recall that in the formative days of Parliament it was their decision to take sides with the boroughs rather than with the great barons that gave the House of Commons its strength. Some squires rose even higher in the political system; for the Council, which was the principal administrative body under the Tudors, was composed largely of such "new men."

The preparation for this life of the country gentleman involved more education in Tudor times than it had in previous centuries. An increasing number attended Oxford and Cambridge, and there were protests that the young aristocrats were crowding out the sons of the poor who had formerly sought a university training as preparation for the Church. Many others, too, attended the Inns of Court in preparation for their work as justices of the peace. With some, foreign travel also was a part of the preparation, and already many were taking what would later be called the "Grand Tour," bringing back from France or Italy new ideas of the Renaissance. With the system of primogeniture, only the eldest son, as we have seen, looked forward to inheriting the estates, with the comfortable life of a peer or a squire; and his younger brothers, because of this unique feature of the English social system, had to shift for themselves. The favorite fields for younger sons in later days were army, navy, and Church; but in Tudor times the armed forces were not upon a sufficiently regular basis to give career opportunities. London also offered openings to engage in law or business. Such a process was taboo for the aristocracy on the Continent, but in England it became a regular practice. This did much to break down the class lines between the gentry and the middle class, between manor and town. Just as the squire might have sons in law and business, so many a prosperous townsman of humbler birth was finally able to purchase an estate and become a squire himself. There was also frequent intermarriage between the two classes; for an heiress whose fortune was based on woolens or the Levant trade was no mean match for a young squire.

While the gentry were rising to their position of importance in Tudor times, that same middle class was also steadily improving its position. The "domestic system" of cloth manufacture made possible the accumulation of capital far beyond the normal wealth of a master craftsman of the Middle Ages, while England's constantly expanding foreign commerce led to fortunes in London, Bristol, and other ports. The ambitious middle-class youth had before him several marked examples of such success: "Jack of Newbury," for instance, who was said to have employed a thousand workers in the woolen industry; William Canynge of Bristol, with his scores of ships and hundreds of sailors, extending English commerce into new fields; and, more important in legend than in fact, Dick Whittington, Lord Mayor of London. There had been, to be sure, a Richard Whittington who became a wealthy merchant and Lord Mayor of the City; but he was the son of a prosperous squire rather than the legendary poor orphan whose sole capital was his cat. Nevertheless, the active middle class, interested keenly in the making of money, believed that there was rich opportunity; and the Tudor century proved them right. They were steadily to gain in prosperity and prestige until finally they challenged the squires for control of England in the early nineteenth century.

The last years of Henry's reign were somewhat of an anticlimax. Some attribute this to the death of his wife in 1503. At any rate, most of Henry's constructive work was accomplished before that time, and most of the meaner and more sordid phases of his reign fall within the later years. He made a fool of himself in his fruitless quest for a second wife, even going so far as to talk of marrying his widowed Spanish daughter-in-law; for Arthur had died a few months after that marriage in 1501, and Henry wanted to be sure that the

# The Coming of the Renaissance

dowry remained in England. But, at the worst, Henry was only somewhat ridiculous and somewhat more grasping than before; if England did not continue to go ahead as she had done in his earlier years, at least she did not slip back. The kingdom which he left to his son Henry in 1509 was an immeasurably stronger, happier, and more prosperous country than it had been when he took it over on the day of Bosworth.

What was true of this first Tudor's reign was to be re-enacted in later Tudor reigns, so that it is no exaggeration to call the battle of Bosworth Field a turning point in English history ranking close behind the dates of 1066 and 1688. The three great Tudors— Henry VII, his son Henry VIII (1509–1547), and Elizabeth (1558– 1603), his most successful grandchild and England's greatest queen —managed to combine force with a remarkable tact in understanding and handling people. They gave the English an almost absolute rule and made them like it. Their word was pretty much law, but only because they had sense enough to know what England needed and wanted. Their absolutism was always disguised by respect for traditional forms; for they preserved Parliament, though they were generally able to get the votes they needed from it. Their ability stands out all the more clearly when one contrasts it with the stubborn blundering of the Stuart kings who were to follow them. It is much to the glory of the Tudor family that the first one, on coming to the throne in 1485, found the country disrupted by feudal anarchy, the treasury empty, trade disorganized, and foreign prestige at low ebb, but that when the fifth and last Tudor died, in 1603, England had a stable, powerful government, order and prosperity at home, and deep respect abroad, and was experiencing the greatest period of her history.

# CHAPTER X

## Tudor Politics and Religion

### 1509-1558

T HE cold, calculating Henry VII had never been able to arouse spontaneous enthusiasm, but the reverse was true of his eighteen-year-old son, Henry VIII. The political security, foreign prestige, and financial surplus laboriously built up by the first Tudor, however, made possible a spectacular reign for the second. "Nature could not have done more for him," wrote the Venetian ambassador. "He is much handsomer than any other sovereign in Christendom . . . very fair, and his whole frame admirably proportioned." Young Henry could wear out eight or ten horses without tiring himself; he reveled in jousting and the hunt; he was an enthusiast at tennis. His zest for heavy feasting had not yet begun to ruin his figure. He was a good musician, could speak four languages, and was so able and so enthusiastic a scholar that he roused high hopes among the intellectuals. With his animal vigor and his charm of manner, Henry had a personal magnetism which won loyal support from all sides. England in 1509 did not foresee the later Henry, grown fat and coarse, with an inflexible will which could smash the papal hold on England, and a violent temper which made it equally perilous to serve him as a minister or as a wife. That all lay in the future; and in the meantime the nation cheered the news that one of the young king's first acts was to execute his father's lawyer-ministers, Empson and Dudley, whose legal extortions had helped to amass the royal treasure which Henry was to spend with a lavish hand.

For the time being, the king left most of the details of government in the capable hands of the ministers inherited from his father. Occasionally he spoke with force and authority, but most of his time was spent in sport and revelry. The internal affairs of the kingdom were running smoothly, so that the main interest in the first part of Henry's reign centered in foreign relations.

Italy was in the foreground. Ever since a French invasion in 1494 had shown how easily it might be conquered, there had been a scramble for possession or control of the peninsula. Italy had grown so rich from trade that it was a tempting prize; its many political divisions made it an easy one to grasp, and during the early sixteenth century it merited the name of "the battleground of Europe." As an Austrian minister sneeringly remarked three centuries later, Italy was simply a "geographical expression," cut into numerous states. Foremost among the Italian bones of contention was the rich, strategically located region around Milan, in the north. The maritime republic of Venice also owned enough north-Italian land to excite envy. The Pope, as ruler of a strip running diagonally across central Italy, often seemed more interested in local politics than in religion. Then, too, there was the larger, but poorer, state including Naples, southern Italy, and Sicily, and known as the Kingdom of Naples or the Two Sicilies. It was a glorious but hectic period in Italian history. In the very years when Raphael, Michelangelo, and Leonardo da Vinci were producing immortal masterpieces of art and when Machiavelli was embodying the realistic principles of Renaissance statecraft in his *Prince*, the mercenaries of France and Spain were struggling to bring as much of Italy as possible under foreign domination.

England had no positive interest in securing Italian territory for herself. France and Spain, however, each hoped that an English attack might distract the other from her Italian designs, or that England, with her well-filled treasury, might at least assume the role of "paymaster of the allies," which was to become a familiar British function in the future. In this game young Henry was pitted at first against three elderly, crafty men with whom his father had matched wits. Ferdinand (Isabella had died), who still ruled Aragon and controlled Spain, and Maximilian, the Hapsburg Holy Roman emperor, had both reached sixty; Louis XII of France was prematurely old at fifty. This veteran trio expected to take advantage of the impetuous inexperience of England's new king.

Henry's first foreign venture confirmed their hopes. He still clung to his father's Spanish alliance, which had been cemented by his own marriage to his brother's widow, Catherine, daughter of Ferdinand and Isabella. Ferdinand in 1512 induced Henry to send an expedition to the Bay of Biscay in the hope of regaining some of the lost lands of Guienne. There was mutiny on the expedition; it accomplished nothing; and Henry realized that his foxlike old father-in-law had used him for a cat's-paw.

The next year, however, things went better. Henry in person crossed the Channel, besieged and captured two towns, and won an encounter at Guinegate, called "the Battle of the Spurs" because of the speed with which the French knights fled from the field. Three weeks later, against the Scots, England won an even more decisive victory. Following tradition, the Scots had headed for England as soon as the English sailed for France. Led by their king, they came down the east coast, crossed the Tweed, allowed themselves to be maneuvered out of a strong position, and were crushed on Flodden Field, a battle in which they lost their king and the flower of their nobility. That summer's fighting of 1513 restored England's international prestige. A peace was arranged with France, which included the marriage of Henry's lively eighteen-year-old sister Mary to Louis XII, who died within three months.

Ferdinand and Maximilian followed Louis to the grave by 1519. The places of those three elderly rulers were taken by two men who were even younger than Henry and whose names were to be intimately associated with his for some thirty years. In 1515 the French crown passed to Francis I, who was to wear it until he died in 1547, two months after Henry. Francis, like Henry, was an enthusiastic sportsman and athlete, loved pageantry and dancing, and prided himself upon his physical appearance and prowess. He was brave in battle, a place where Henry, for all the vaunted Tudor courage, never appeared personally. Francis was a liberal patron of the Renaissance arts. He was, however, vacillating and irresolute and much influenced by women, of whom there were, in his debauched career, a larger number than in that of the much-married English king.

Marriages and deaths paved the way for a combination of lands, greater in extent than those of Henry and Francis combined, in the hands of their contemporary Charles V. His vast heritage was the culmination of the marriage policy of the House of Hapsburg, whose diplomats were always on the lookout for eligible heiresses. A single marriage might determine the political destiny of a region for centuries, and it was by a constant succession of those marriages that the Hapsburg family built up its extensive but unnatural empire. One great-grandfather of Charles was the duke of Burgundy, Charles the Bold, whose death in battle left his lands to a daughter Mary. Hapsburg diplomacy secured her as a bride for Maximilian, in spite of her previous engagement to the French heir. For the son of Maximilian and Mary the Hapsburg diplomats found an even richer wife in Joanna, elder daughter of Ferdinand and Isabella and sister of Henry's wife, Catherine of Aragon. With the hand of Joanna, known as the Insane, went the rule of Spain and her possessions. Charles therefore had an extensive inheritance from each of his four grandparents. From Mary came the Netherlands and the county of Burgundy; from Maximilian, Austria and the other hereditary Danubian lands of the Hapsburgs; from Ferdinand, Aragon and parts of Italy; and from Isabella, the rest of Spain, as well as the new colonies in America, with their many silver mines. The Hapsburg tradition, too, made Charles the logical candidate to succeed Maximilian as Holy Roman emperor. His election to that position gave him nominal control of Germany, in addition to these other lands.

Charles, lacking the gay, robust exuberance of Francis and of Henry, was cold, reserved, levelheaded, conservative. His tremendous heritage involved widespread and complex responsibilities. Even in times of peace it was a problem to administer so many countries, held together only by a personal tie and each with its peculiar form of government. But other problems made peace difficult. There was a fourth important contemporary of Henry, Francis, and Charles in Solyman the Magnificent, the "Grande Turke," and it happened that the Ottoman Empire had reached its greatest power and extent in the same years as the Hapsburg empire. Solyman's Janizaries came surging up the Danube valley to the very gates of Vienna, as his corsairs raided and kidnaped along the Mediterranean shores of Charles's domains. Then, again, Charles had to deal with the first outburst of Protestantism in the Reformation, and the Protestants of northern Germany were for years a thorn in his side. Finally, he was drawn into chronic conflict with Francis. The dominions of Charles almost completely surrounded France. Wherever a Frenchman looked outside the country, he saw either Hapsburg territory or the sea. French foreign policy for nearly two centuries consisted in efforts to break that "Hapsburg ring." Francis tried often and in vain; not until the next century was France finally successful. Each side in that conflict sought allies. Solyman was a natural ally of France. The German Protestants might also be counted upon normally to oppose Charles. The doubtful element was England, which might throw in her weight upon either side.

Just before Francis and Charles came upon the scene, Henry found a remarkable minister who was to guide his relations with these rival monarchs. This was Thomas Wolsey, son of middleclass parents and a graduate of Oxford. He had attracted royal attention by unusual speed in traveling to the Continent and back on a diplomatic mission, and he lost no opportunity to demonstrate his usefulness around the court. His organizing and negotiating ability had much to do with the military and diplomatic success against France in 1513 and 1514. From that time on, his rise was meteoric. In addition to receiving several rich bishoprics, he became in short order Archbishop of York, cardinal, and papal legate, and he hoped to become Pope. He was also made chancellor, and in that capacity he gathered most of the threads of administration and justice into his own hands. Impressive in appearance, effective in

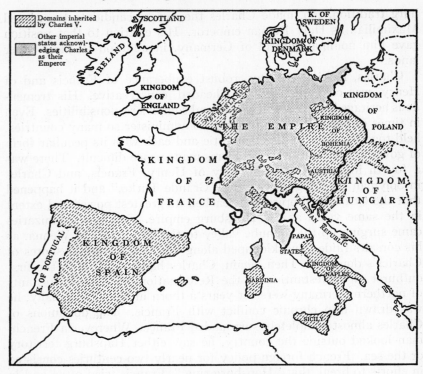

EUROPE IN THE TIME OF HENRY VIII

negotiations, and tireless in industry, Wolsey for fifteen years virtually governed England, in both internal and foreign affairs. He became one of the most powerful subjects in all English history. The "proudest prelate England has ever seen" was well paid for his labors; he enjoyed a magnificent income and lived in almost regal splendor. He referred to "ego et rex meus"; but there were times when even Wolsey had to adjust his policy to the imperious Henry.

Wolsey's special forte was diplomacy. He is credited with leaving England a permanent heritage in his conception of the nation's proper foreign policy. He realized the futility of trying to seize actual Continental territory, as had been attempted in the Hundred Years' War. He believed, instead, that England should exercise the balance of power. According to that principle, England would not seek any territory for herself on the Continent but would throw the influence of her men and money on the weaker side in case any nation or ruler threatened to become too powerful. Ordinarily, it was hoped, the mere threat of this would be enough to maintain peace, and so Wolsey hoped to uphold England's international importance by means of diplomacy rather than war. Since Wolsey's time England has seemed to follow that policy consistently and with general success.

Strange to say, Wolsey's own application of this principle was not a success. He tried to play the arbiter between Charles and Francis, but more than once he backed the wrong horse. Francis no sooner came to the throne, in 1515, than he slipped around the guards of an Alpine pass and made himself master of northern Italy by a crushing victory at Marignano. That victory made him look stronger than Charles, who began to take over his various thrones immediately thereafter. By 1520 Wolsey was intervening in the grand manner. The nobles of England and France nearly bankrupted themselves and "wore their estates upon their backs," because of the extreme pomp and splendor of the meeting between Henry and Francis on the "Field of the Cloth of Gold" near Calais. Negotiations, nevertheless, led to little; for Charles had just visited Henry in England and had made an alliance which was effective when Charles and Francis began their first war the next year. England intervened on the side of Charles and sent a rather ineffectual army to invade France. Wolsey's error was evident in 1525, when Charles overwhelmed the French at Pavia, in Italy, and even captured Francis himself. English aid had helped to make Charles master of Europe, quite contrary to the principle of the balance of power. Even the two million crowns which England received as indemnity from France did not offset the disadvantage of having helped to put Charles securely in the saddle.

In the meantime, while Henry and his fellow rulers, Charles, Francis, and Solyman, were devoting their years to diplomacy and wars, Europe was in the midst of the so-called Reformation, in which considerable portions of western Europe broke away from the Roman Catholic Church. There had been rumblings of this movement, which many scholars call the Protestant Revolt, as early as the twelfth and thirteenth centuries, owing to widespread criticism of certain church abuses, such as simony, broken monastic vows, marriage of the clergy, the general ignorance and laxity of the lower clergy, and the wealth and corruption of the higher clergy. Heretical agitation, notably the Waldensian and Albigensian, had been evidence of this dissatisfaction. Pope Innocent III, about 1200, had made numerous reforms, including the authorization of the mendicant friars (see page 134), and these are said to have helped to postpone the crisis some three centuries. The prestige of the papacy had been badly impaired by its removal to Avignon, under the French influence, it will be recalled; and the English in particular resented this bringing of the head of the universal Church under the apparent control of the king with whom they were at war. That "Babylonian Captivity" led to a further serious blow in the forty years of the Great Schism, when the existence of two or three rival popes shook men's faith in the supremacy of the Pope and his direct spiritual descent from Saint Peter. The Renaissance too did its part in weakening papal prestige, so contrary was the spirit of that movement to the old ideas of faith and submission to the authority of church teachings. The rediscovered pagan classics were full of joy in life and love of beauty—for the most part earthly life and physical beauty, and for that very reason somewhat alien to traditional Christianity and unlike the medieval subordination of the individual and emphasis on the other world.

Even yet, strong, pious Popes might have saved the Church from dismemberment. Instead, the healing of the schism was followed by a series of worldly Popes. Alexander VI, a cruel and debauched Spaniard with a criminal character and notorious children, Caesar and Lucretia Borgia, represented the papacy at its very lowest; Julius II devoted his energy to playing the role of a petty Italian prince; and finally there was Leo X, one of the Florentine Medicis, whose absorption in Renaissance art rather than in spiritual affairs was to bring the issues of dissension to a head in the Reformation in the early sixteenth century.

The expensiveness of Leo's plans for the beautification of Rome, especially for the rebuilding of the church of St. Peter, made essential a drastic increase in papal revenues. For this, Leo turned largely to the old device of the indulgence. A truly penitent sinner might by an indulgence, procured ordinarily by the payment of a sum of money to the Church, reduce the future punishment in purgatory for a sin. One might also purchase an indulgence for a deceased relative or friend. This did not mean that a cash gift to the Church alone won forgiveness for sins; for an indulgence was supposed to be operative only in the case of those already truly penitent. Nevertheless, it was the energetic, careless, and "high-pressure" selling of indulgences in Germany and elsewhere that was the center of the storm.

The sale of indulgences, however, was but one of the sparks that set off the Reformation; for the decline of papal prestige had made more outspoken and dangerous the criticisms which had been muttered for centuries. Of these new critics perhaps the most famous and influential was Erasmus, of whom we have heard as the inspiration of the English Humanists, those Oxford reformers, Grocyn, Linacre, Colet, More, and others. Like most Humanists, Erasmus had the idea of a renaissance of Christianity. No one was more scathing in satirizing clerical abuses than was he in his *Praise of Folly*; but he wanted merely to reform from within and sadly rued the impetus he had unintentionally given to the Protestant Revolt.

Of quite another sort was the German monk Martin Luther, who, because of his unusual and brilliant explanation of Biblical beliefs, was the most popular lecturer at the University of Wittenberg. Luther, after wrestling with personal worry about his own soul's future, stressed the old conclusion that, to win God's forgiveness for sins, men should be justified before God by inner faith—the so-called "justification by faith"—rather than by "good works" and outward acts. He wanted to bring back simple, primitive Christianity where (from the Protestant point of view) man was his own priest and where the clergy were simply guides pointing out the way to God. He had his own interpretation of other church features, such as the Mass, confession, saints' relics, and the marriage of the clergy.

In 1517, when the sale of indulgences was at its scandalous peak, Luther nailed to the local university church door his famous "ninety-five theses." These were merely subjects, posted like any modern university notice, which he intended to discuss; but the list was such a suggestive one, containing the question of indulgences and justification, as well as other of his unconventional ideas, that his hammer blows sounded the break-up of the centuries-old Catholic unity. Within a few months not only Germany, which was seething with all sorts of discontent,—economic, social, and political,—but most of western Europe as well had heard of his theses, which had been translated from Latin into the vernaculars. The sale of indulgences fell off alarmingly. Before long, Luther allowed himself to be argued into decidedly heretical statements. At the same time, he won important German princes to his side by urging them to reform the church within their own borders—in their eyes a God-given chance for more wealth and power in the heterogeneous Empire. The Pope excommunicated the recalcitrant monk, but Luther boldly burned the papal bull. The Church, having thus fired its strongest weapon in vain, appealed to the emperor. Young Charles V summoned Luther before an imperial diet, a sort of parliament, at Worms in 1521, where the ban of the Empire was placed upon him, rendering him an outlaw whom anyone might kill. Luther, however, was spirited away by a powerful noble, in whose castle he remained hidden until the tumult quieted. But he had started far more than he was to approve. All the discontented classes of Germany, from the knights down to the peasants, found this the signal for revolt. They rose in Luther's name, though political and economic considerations were also important causes.

# A History of England and the British Empire

In the meantime another priest, Zwingli of Zurich, was inflaming the people of Switzerland in much the same way and for many of the same reasons as Luther. Zwingli was more radical in some of his religious ideas than Luther and more politically minded; and for a time it looked as though South Germany as well as half of Switzerland might look to him for spiritual leadership. He was killed, however, in one of the first battles between Protestants and Catholics, and most of his followers either turned toward Luther for their religious guidance or toward the Frenchman John Calvin, the third great Reformation pioneer.

Forced to leave France, Calvin made his home in Geneva, a free city which was a willing convert to his teachings and which to all practical purposes was under his control. It speedily became the center of a peculiarly virile and effective form of Protestantism, which spread north through parts of Germany and the Low Countries, into France, across the Channel into England, and especially into Scotland. In England it met with such success that later it came to permeate and dominate English Puritanism. Calvin's teachings were formulated in his *Institutes of Christianity,* published in 1536. In them he stressed above all else the sovereignty of God, who from the beginning had a "definite, individual, and unchanging purpose" for every person. According to this doctrine, which is called predestination, man cannot change his own future, because it is predetermined by God's will. Calvin was a stern man, who emphasized primarily duty, obligations, responsibility, hard work, and discipline rather than forgiveness and gentleness. He laid especial stress upon the Old Testament, and his precepts were both clear and emphatic. From Geneva he issued affirmations and denunciations as though he were a species of Protestant pope, vice-regent on earth to a peculiarly masculine deity.

All northwestern Europe was thus aroused by the middle of the sixteenth century. The Protestant Revolt took a somewhat different form in nearly every country, but region after region was lost to the papacy. Northern and central Germany accepted Lutheranism and later developed some Calvinism. The three Scandinavian kingdoms also went over to Luther. Calvin's ideas spread to France, Holland, and, through the stern John Knox, to Scotland, while England itself did not escape Calvin's influence. Even Bohemia and Poland became Protestant for a while.

There seemed ample evidence to show that the English people were as ready for change as those on the Continent. There was, for instance, the lasting influence of Wiclif's example. The new learning had broadened the people's vision. Colet and other Hu-

# Tudor Politics and Religion

manists had talked freely of reforming church abuses. Furthermore, the Englishman of Henry's day could look back upon four centuries of royal opposition to the Pope. The quarrels which had started with Anselm and Becket had continued into the thirteenth century with King John. The reign of Edward I saw the Statute of Mortmain limiting church landholding; the reign of Edward III saw two more hostile statutes: Provisors, to check the foreign church appointees, and Praemunire, to check appeals to Rome. The Church, however, had found means to avoid some of these laws, and in the early sixteenth century the Pope still enjoyed power and profit from his relationship to England. Every newly appointed bishop and abbot had to pay "annates," or "first fruits," the first year's income of his benefice, into the papal treasury; while the "Peter's pence," an annual contribution of one penny, supposedly voluntary, for every hearth in England, also went to Rome. In spite of the Statute of Praemunire, dispensations from the canon law, especially in the matter of marriage annulments, were still obtained from the papal see; and, despite the Statute of Mortmain, the church lands continued to grow, for the kings granted frequent exceptions to the law. The Church in England was decidedly wealthy: it had an annual income estimated at £320,000 a year, considerably more than the royal treasury normally received. Of that amount about £100,000 was monastic income. There was a growing feeling that the Church did not do enough in return for what it got. Many members of the clergy were reputed to be corrupt; and there was resentment against their special privileges, and their interference in many lay disputes of a legal nature.

"The scene was thus set for change, even if there had been no Henry VIII and no royal divorce problem. The king, with his usual Tudor political sagacity, utilized all these aspects of discontent by making Parliament his instrument in the whole personal matter of the dissolution of his marriage when the Pope refused his assent, and this tended to give a more national aspect to the English Reformation." The importance of Parliament, for once during this Yorkist-Tudor period of neglect, was increased when Henry thus made it his ally, instead of depending solely upon consultation with a church gathering presumably subservient to Rome.

On the other hand, it must be remembered that throughout the early stages of England's participation in the Protestant Revolt, despite criticisms of church abuses, the question was not fundamentally one of belief, and interpretation of the Bible, as on the Continent, but was, rather, the question of the supremacy of the Pope over England. As an illustration of this two-sided aspect of the matter, Henry was so incensed by Luther's ideas that he himself wrote a pamphlet defending the seven sacraments against such an attack; and so grateful was the Pope for this royal literary outburst that he bestowed on Henry the title of "Defender of the Faith." Not only did Henry keep this high-sounding title but even to this day the Protestant ruler of Protestant England adds to his array of titles this papal one! Henry was thus a Catholic in most of his beliefs, and to his deathbed, in spite of his bitter antipapal fight, he apparently retained this faith intact. The result was that in England the Reformation took an extraordinarily middle-of-the-road course, with but brief excursions into either camp.

By 1527, if not a few years earlier, Henry had become seriously obsessed with the necessity of putting aside his wife, Catherine of Aragon, the daughter of Ferdinand and Isabella of Spain. Catherine had been brought to England as the bride of Henry's older brother during the last years of Henry VII's reign; but at the bridegroom's premature death a second marriage was arranged for her with Henry (some five years her junior), in order to save her rich dowry for England. A deceased brother's widow, however, was within the prohibited degrees of marriage in Catholic eyes, so that a special dispensation had been obtained from the Pope to permit the new wedding, which took place soon after Henry's coronation. The reason why it was possible to obtain this permission was that Catherine was said to have been a wife in name only to her sickly young bridegroom of a few months. Catherine's bad marital luck continued; for although in her early years as Henry's wife she bore several children in rapid succession, only a daughter, Mary, survived infancy.

Now, after eighteen years of marriage, Henry began to profess horror because he was living in sin with his widowed sister-in-law. Although the desire to marry her maid in waiting, the black-eyed, vivacious Anne Boleyn, was to hurry Henry's determination, his worry over the lack of a male heir was noticed long before Anne came upon the scene. Heretofore England's one experience with a reigning queen, it must be remembered, had been with the unfortunate Matilda and anarchy. Added weight was given to this aspect of the situation by the fact that had not Henry desired so desperately a legitimate son, he would perhaps not have bothered to lead Anne to the altar, any more than he had her sister or his other mistresses.

Although always referred to as the divorce problem, it was technically something different from the process which we think of today. Divorce was prohibited by the Roman Catholic Church, which claimed sole jurisdiction in all legal matters connected with marriage and other sacraments; consequently it was unheard-of in pre-

# Tudor Politics and Religion

Reformation Europe. Marriage, as one of the seven sacraments, was considered indissoluble except by the hand of God in death. To be sure, annulment of marriage was not uncommon if the Church was shown that some insurmountable impediment, such as too close kinship of the couple or the forcing of one of them, had prevented the marriage in question from being a true sacrament. It was annulment that Henry wanted, on the ground that, since the queen was his brother's widow, they were within the prohibited degrees of kinship. Under ordinary circumstances an annulment would have been granted speedily and easily to one in his regal position, with the need of an heir so obvious and paramount for the good of his kingdom. In Henry's case, however, there was a snag that made annulment virtually impossible. Impediment to the marriage there had seemed to be, but it had been declared nonexistent by the Church in a special dispensation *before* the wedding! Before the present Pope, Clement VII, might annul the marriage, he would first have to show that the earlier papal dispensation, based on affidavits that Catherine had been a wife in name only, was an error. That seemed out of the question. Another technicality occurred in the fact that a dispensation might permit no one to break a law of God but only a law of the Church. Consequently the Church had permitted the marriage with Henry only because all concerned were certain that Catherine was making her first real marriage. Her appearance at this second wedding in virgin white, with her hair hanging down her back, had impressed this vividly upon the public mind. With this unusual complication there were other difficulties. Catherine was the aunt of Charles V, who not only controlled Italy, after an especially savage sack of Rome in 1527, but also even held the Pope as prisoner for a while; and Charles would scarcely countenance the proposed humiliation of his mother's sister. Also, despite the care with which the fact was guarded, many knew that Henry's prospective bride, Anne Boleyn, was herself within the prohibited degrees of kinship because of Henry's past liaison with her older sister. Some of the scandal-mongers carried the relationship even closer. It was obvious that Pope Clement VII was in a tight place when Wolsey began the negotiations to free Henry from his marriage and that the papal approval would be hard to obtain.)

Wolsey made a strenuous effort to help Henry; but, like the Pope, he was in a difficult personal position, since he had his eye on the papal succession for himself. Failure met him on all sides, partly from the oversubtle efforts at compromise to avoid prejudicing his own papal chances; partly from Henry's own premature plans, about which he kept Wolsey in the dark; and partly because of that serious difficulty of the previous dispensation. Henry was ready to accept any expedient, however far-fetched, even to bigamy or the entrance of Catherine and himself into holy orders, with, of course, the assurance of his own later absolution from his vows in order to wed again. But in all these varied plans he was not frank with anyone.

Catherine soon got wind of the divorce plans and made a dignified protest, backed by the whole force of Hapsburg power. Wolsey, in the meantime, continued his efforts, despite his aversion to the Boleyn marriage, which he now recognized was inevitable; but the Pope, caught between the emperor and the king of England, and with church law staring him in the face, procrastinated in the evident hope that time might solve the dilemma if he could not. Finally the upshot of various commissions was that Cardinal Campeggio was sent from Rome to England to act as a legate in conjunction with Wolsey on the question of the validity of Catherine's first marriage. The Pope gave Campeggio a so-called decretal bull, with orders not to let it out of his hands. In the form which Wolsey had asked, this bull would have made the decision final, with no possibility of Catherine's appeal to Rome; but in its final form this was not made clear. Catherine consequently appealed, whereupon the Pope revoked the whole Campeggio-Wolsey mission and summoned the case to Rome in 1529. This spelled doom for Wolsey. Campeggio, whose baggage was searched at Dover in vain for the decretal bull which in English hands might even then have saved the day, sailed for Italy, and on the morrow Wolsey was arrested. He was charged with violating the Statute of Praemunire because he was a legate, a position which he had held at Henry's own special request for fifteen years! The divorce impasse was not the only cause of his fall; Henry had grown impatient at sharing power with the proud prelate and wanted to take more of the ruling into his own hands. Wolsey resigned most of his offices and, with much of his wealth confiscated, was allowed to retire in order to take up his neglected duties as Archbishop of York. Anne's influence was growing, and she hated Wolsey. Late in 1530, at the instigation of enemies who feared that his popularity in the north might return him to favor, Wolsey was arrested again, this time for high treason. Ill and in bitter disgrace, he set out for London to answer the grave charge; but he died en route, thereby probably cheating the block.

Serving Henry as a minister was a thankless and risky task. Two of the men who succeeded to Wolsey's high influence were beheaded by their royal master within the next ten years. One of these was Sir Thomas More, the gentle, high-minded author of *Utopia* (see page 222), who followed Wolsey as chancellor. The other was a man of sterner and coarser fiber, Thomas Cromwell. He had attracted attention by his skillful and loyal work in managing Wolsey's business affairs, and Henry was soon to find him useful for carrying out some of the harsher tasks brought about by the religious changes. More was to die because he was too good a Catholic; Cromwell, because he was to pick out too unattractive a bride for the king.

Henry's next steps in the divorce matter were referred to the universities and the English clergy. Upon the advice of Thomas Cranmer, who was soon to become very helpful as Archbishop of Canterbury, the king asked numerous universities in Europe for their opinions upon the merits of the case. The replies were not conclusive. In 1530 he bullied the English clergy into submission. As they met in their two assemblies, the Convocations of Canterbury and of York, Henry informed them that they, like Wolsey, were guilty of violation of Praemunire, and would be relieved only upon payment of £100,000. Coupled with this, they had to recognize Henry, in this "Submission of the Clergy," as the supreme head of the Church in England. Parliament was to bestow such a title upon Henry four years later. The combined demand was a bitter pill for the clergy. They chose the safer and more practical course—perhaps, too, the more patriotic —in following their king rather than staying loyal to the head of the Church. This stand was to prove decidedly to their advantage in reinstating them in the people's favor and in changing the tone of public opinion, which had been anticlerical. The clergy accepted the king as supreme head, however, only with the evasive clause "as far as the laws of Christ allow."

Henry, however, did not depend upon the churchmen alone for the ratification of his religious program. Late in 1529, just a month after Campeggio had sailed away and Wolsey had fallen from power, one of the most prolific Parliaments in English history met at Westminster,—important not because it increased its own power at the expense of the king but because the king used it as his ally in attaining his religious objectives. Its sessions were to last for seven years and were to be memorable for the legislation which definitely severed the Church of England from Rome. Numerous acts were involved in that process: the most important were the Act of Annates (1532), the Act of Appeals (1533), and the final, decisive Act of Supremacy (1534). That same Parliament was to widen the definition of treason and to legislate on the succession; in fact, it was ready to give the king practically everything he asked, except money.

Parliament's first step, in 1532, was to decree that the annates, or first fruits, were thereafter to be paid to the crown instead of to the

Pope. The papal confirmation of bishops was also ended. At these affronts to the Pope, Sir Thomas More resigned the chancellorship, the first step in his propapal attitude which was to lead to execution.

In 1533 events moved faster. Anne had at last given in to Henry's advances, after cleverly holding out for the title of Queen for nearly five years, so that it became doubly necessary to speed the divorce. Henry found a complaisant Archbishop of Canterbury in the scholarly Thomas Cranmer, who at the end of March gave Henry, through an English church court, the long-desired divorce from Catherine of Aragon. At the same time, Parliament passed an act forbidding appeals to Rome, in even stronger terms than the old Act of Prae-munire, so that the action of Cranmer's court was final. It was none too soon. Henry now married Anne publicly (he had supposedly married her privately about the beginning of the year); but the people were not pleased, and not a cheer enlivened Anne's rather dreary coronation procession. In September, Anne gave birth, not to the hoped-for son, but to the king's second daughter, the future Queen Elizabeth.

Thus Henry, with Parliament passing antipapal laws and the primate of England supporting his ideas, obtained a new queen and defied the Pope. In 1534 Parliament passed the important Act of Supremacy, the climax in the breaking of papal power in England. Parliament also gave Henry an Act of Succession, recognizing the legality of the divorce and securing the crown to Anne's children, at the expense of Catherine's daughter, Mary, who was declared illegitimate. The definition of treason was widely extended, largely to enforce the new legislation and to prevent public criticism. The Act of Supremacy, the most important of all the various pieces of legislation, established the Church of England, or Anglican Church, which is directly related to the Protestant Episcopal Church in the United States. The king, not the Pope, was the head of the Church of England. It was a national church, with all foreign control and interference at an end. It was an "established" church, because of its official connection with the government. To be sure, the Pope excommunicated Henry and declared his English divorce null and void, but most of England regarded this as an idle gesture. In its own words, the act made the king and his successors "Protector and Supreme Head on earth of the Church and Clergy of England," as wrested from the Convocations four years earlier. Every Englishman was required to take the Oath of Supremacy, recognizing the new substitution of king for Pope. Failure to do so was high treason, and there were various executions on this score.

Most prominent among the victims was Sir Thomas More, who,

# Tudor Politics and Religion

as we have seen, had already resigned the chancellorship. By withdrawing from the world and keeping strictly silent on the issue, he hoped to avoid trouble. Others, however, would not hold their tongues. A monk preaching before the king told His Majesty to his face that if he continued on his wicked course "dogs would lick his blood." A nun was so rash as to prophesy the king's imminent death. As a result of such remarks, four monks, one of them the head of the Carthusian order in England, were hanged, cut down alive, and disemboweled, and their heads were stuck up over London Bridge. More, meanwhile, had been lodged in the Tower, together with Bishop Fisher of Rochester. If men such as these two continued their defiance, others might pluck up courage and copy their example; or so, at least, the king feared. Consequently both More and Fisher were tried for high treason and beheaded. More's trial was dramatic. Clever lawyer that he was, his defense was excellent. No one could prove that he had ever uttered a word against the divorce. "For this my silence neither your law, nor any law in the world, is able justly and rightly to punish me." But if the law was on More's side, power abided with the king. Fearful lest More say too much from the scaffold, the command went forth that he speak but briefly. His last words were these: "I die the King's good servant, but God's first."

(Changes were now introduced in the church services, such as the use of English instead of Latin in the Lord's Prayer and other parts of the service.) An English translation of the Bible, probably by one Coverdale, a friend of the Tyndale whose earlier translation in 1526 had been suppressed as heretical, also was adopted. The canon law was overhauled and its study discouraged, which incidentally increased the importance of the lay courts. (Relics and images were destroyed, and the old miracle-working shrines, especially that of Thomas Becket at Canterbury, were discredited.) In dogma, however, the changes were very slight; for Henry was not interested in becoming a Protestant. Two years after the Act of Supremacy the Ten Articles declared the Bible and the creeds to be the sole authority in matters of faith, but this was merely a clerical pronouncement and lacked royal authorization. We shall see that by 1539 Henry was to clamp down on the reformers with the Six Articles, which definitely dragged dogma back into old forms.

Thomas Cromwell had become the king's chief minister since the fall of More. He was not made chancellor, but was given a new title, "Vicar-General of the Church," which gave him power to handle the business end of the new religious situation. As clever a statesman of the Machiavellian school as any king might desire, Cromwell saw further financial possibilities in the break with Rome. Already the royal treasury had been enriched by the diversion of annates, Peter's pence, and other former payments to the Pope. Cromwell's favorite project would lead to even more royal income. The monasteries owned about one sixth of all the land in England. He proposed nothing less than their abolition and the transfer of their wealth to the rapidly emptying royal treasury.

Undoubtedly there was serious corruption in some of the seven hundred monasteries and nunneries. Wolsey had pointed the way by taking the money of certain monasteries to establish a college. In the new spirit of the times monastic foundations which had enjoyed a virtual monopoly of education were giving way to educational institutions with relatively little emphasis on church connections. The impulse which had led men into the monastic life centuries before, to escape from a troubled world, no longer existed. Life was too interesting in the outside world, and few men of energy were willing to isolate themselves. Since the reign of Henry III few new monasteries had been established. The old ones still continued, well endowed by the rich gifts of land which had accumulated through the centuries; but the men and women who occupied them no longer commanded quite the general respect which earlier monks and nuns had enjoyed. The main question was whether the monasteries were still held in high enough esteem to prevent the move which Cromwell had in mind.

This agent of the king ran into no serious opposition when he presented the matter to Parliament. It was ready to sanction the dissolution of the monasteries, in addition to the breach with Rome, because the more money the king could get from the Church the less he would need from Lords and Commons. Parliament consequently authorized a commission to investigate the general condition of the monasteries. Cromwell sent out commissioners who doubtless were told what kind of reports were expected. At any rate, they brought back information of the sort which the vicar-general would find useful. At this distance we cannot tell how far their findings corresponded to the facts. At each monastery and nunnery their questions fell under three main heads: the wealth of the establishment, its superstitious practices, and its immorality. Numerous institutions, even under the circumstances, were reported as satisfactory in the last two respects, but from many came tales of miraculous shirts, girdles, or bones of saints which could cure headaches or relieve the pains of childbirth, while there were a surprising number of pieces of the True Cross. The reports told of monks who had made merry with married and single women and of nuns who had become unwed mothers. There is no question but that the reports blackened and exaggerated the true conditions, but they were sufficient to produce the desired Parliamentary acts. In 1536 Parliament decreed the end of some three hundred and seventy-six lesser monasteries and nunneries which had an annual income of less than £200 each.

Southern and eastern England accepted the abolition quietly, but the conservative Catholic north rose in arms in 1536. There were several reasons for this. Cromwell had identified himself conspicuously with the reformers, and this, added to his low social origin, annoyed many people. The northern monasteries, moreover, were noted for their works of charity among people who were already aroused by the enclosure movement. The revolt started in Lincolnshire, and in Yorkshire it received the name of "the Pilgrimage of Grace." By clever negotiations the first revolt was easily suppressed, but it soon broke out again and this time was repressed harshly. The leaders were executed, but Henry was fairly lenient with their common followers. This revolt led to the establishment of another special Tudor tribunal, which had unusual powers outside the regular courts and laws. This was the Council of the North, composed of powerful officials who were to sit at York and, like the Court of the Star Chamber of Henry VII, were given full authority to handle emergencies.

So far as stopping the suppression of the monasteries was concerned, the rising was a failure. The larger monasteries were dissolved by 1539. A few voluntarily closed their doors, foreseeing their inevitable end; the rest were abolished by royal coercion. By 1540 not a monastic establishment was left in England. The monasteries, as we saw, had an annual income of some £100,000, and this new wealth was a temporary boon to the royal treasury. The actual financial gain to the government, however, was slight; for about two thirds of the lands went by sale to Henry's friends and favorites at bargain prices, and these lands continued as large or medium-sized estates. Many family fortunes date from the sale of monastic lands. Numerous prosperous townsmen took advantage of the opportunity to rise in the social scale by becoming landholders. Among them were the ancestors of Washington, the great American, who spent town-earned money to purchase the manor of Sulgrave, formerly a priory. The poor, moreover, suffered from the change; for the new landlords were generally harder masters than the monks and were more inclined to dispossess tenants in order to enclose the land for sheep-raising. The poor also felt the loss of the social services of the monasteries, which had served as hospitals and centers of charity (see pages 25–26). It was soon necessary for inns to be introduced, to take the place of the former monastic hospitality. The House of Lords was changed by the dissolution. With the abbots removed from membership, the former clerical majority gave way to a lay majority which clearly outnumbered the bishops. Such was the principal work of England's first great Cromwell, who won the epithet of *Malleus Monachorum*, "the Hammer of the Monks."

In 1539, the year the remaining monasteries were abolished, Parliament passed the Six Articles. These were intended to pacify both those who wanted still more church reform and those who wanted to retain as much as possible of the old faith. Cromwell sided with Archbishop Cranmer and Bishop Latimer in the wish to push reform further, but Henry was reluctant. The Six Articles, called the "Whip with the Six Strings," were a victory for those of Henry's persuasion (apparently the majority of Englishmen); for in many ways they reaffirmed the faith, yet emphasized the break with Rome. Unlike the unofficial Ten Articles, they were legally passed by Parliament. These Six Articles insisted upon the death penalty for the denial of the first article, and severe punishment for failure to concur in the others. They decreed that (1) transubstantiation was a fact; (2) confessions and (3) private Masses were essential; but (4) Communion in both kinds was not; (5) priests must not marry; and (6) vows of chastity must be kept. Thus did England separate from the papacy but not essentially from the old faith.

This doctrinal conservatism was a defeat for Cromwell, with his desire for extreme reform, and, added to a diplomatic error in arranging for an alliance with the German Protestants, resulted in his downfall. Henry was again looking for a new wife. Anne Boleyn, after dashing Henry's hopes for a son, lasted less than three years. She was sent to the block in 1536, charged, as an unfaithful wife, with treason to her husband, the king. Directly after her execution Henry married her maid of honor, Jane Seymour, who died the following year when she gave Henry at last his coveted son, the future Edward VI. To cement the Protestant German alliance and to fill the vacant place in the royal bed, Cromwell suggested another Anne, the Protestant sister of the German duke of Cleves. Over-persuaded by Cromwell and by an unduly flattering portrait by Holbein, Henry completed negotiations to marry Anne of Cleves; but suddenly the Protestant alliance no longer seemed essential in the constantly shifting diplomatic scene, and on top of this came the arrival of the unattractive bride. The marriage was carried through by the reluctant Henry, who openly expressed his opinion of the "Flanders mare." Within eight months Cromwell had gone to the block, and Anne, complaisant in the arrangements made for her, retired from court, divorced. That was the last of Henry's political marriages. His fifth wife, Catherine Howard, was soon executed, like her kinswoman Anne Boleyn, for traitorous adultery, while her successor and Henry's last wife, Catherine Parr, was a companion in his sick old age and at his deathbed. Thus it can be said of Henry's wives that two were divorced (the two foreign princesses, Catherine of Aragon and Anne of Cleves); two were executed (Anne Boleyn and Catherine Howard, both of the distinguished Howard family); one died (Jane Seymour); and one was lucky enough to outlive him (Catherine Parr).

After Cromwell's execution Henry trusted no more in ministers but, in his own person,—fat, coarse, diseased, and dangerous,— headed a government more absolute than ever. Parliament had given away some of its own authority by permitting the king to make valid laws simply by proclamation, and it had given a dangerous extension to the scope of treason. It was unsafe to murmur even mild discontent against a ruler who did not hesitate to behead.

Foreign wars, which had been set aside during the years of religious activity, broke out again in 1542. Charles and Francis had been drawn together temporarily by the threat of an English alliance with the German Protestants; but with the repudiation of Anne of Cleves they were free to resume their fighting. There was friction between France and England because Francis was behind in his payments promised in past treaties. The immediate trouble came with Scotland, the perennial French ally. Henry had recently completed the absorption of Wales into the English system of government (see page 159). England had hoped for a peaceful control over Scotland, but that was blocked by the dominant Cardinal Beaton, who hated both England and Protestantism. A series of border raids by both sides led to a decisive but quite bloodless English victory over the Scots at Solway Moss. The news of that reverse killed the Scottish king, James V, son of Henry's sister Margaret. The Scottish throne was left to his week-old daughter, who was to become famous as "Mary Queen of Scots." Two years later an English force attacked Edinburgh from the sea and burned it, an act which served to antagonize Scotland further. In the meantime Henry had allied himself with Charles and had invaded France. The Channel port of Boulogne was captured, but little else was accomplished. Charles made a separate peace, and the French actually sent a fleet to invade England. The French made a temporary landing on the Isle of Wight, but Henry had created a fairly effective navy and had strung a series of forts along the south coast. The French abandoned the attempt, and peace came in 1546. The fighting had given Henry a little temporary glory at a crushing expense to the treasury; but, like Wolsey's earlier meddling in Continental affairs, it was a sterile conflict, without benefit to England.

Henry died on January 28, 1547, two months before his rival Francis I. However much this second Tudor may have degenerated in his later years, he had given England a great reign. His wars and pageantry left no permanent results on the map, but they at least stimulated national pride and for a while raised England in the eyes of Europe. His religious changes, however trivial their causes and however selfish their motives, had permanent and important consequences. Henry may have played the arbitrary despot at times, but it is doubtful whether Parliament and the people would have followed him as they did through such momentous decisions had not the nation as a whole been in general sympathy with what he wanted.

His three children succeeded him in turn. England was to pass through the short and sorry reign of Edward VI (1547–1553), son of Jane Seymour, and that of Mary (1553–1558), daughter of Catherine of Aragon, before reaching the long and glorious rule of Henry's third child, Elizabeth (1558–1603), the daughter of Anne Boleyn. The religious question, initiated by Henry, was to make very stormy the reign of Edward, under whom England went over to extreme Protestantism, and that of Mary, who dragged it back to Catholicism, before Elizabeth quieted the turmoil with a clever compromise. The Tudor line ended with those three children, since— possibly because of the serious venereal disease which he transmitted —Henry had no grandchildren. Edward and Elizabeth never even married, and Mary, fortunately for England, was disappointed in her efforts to continue the Tudor line with a child of her husband, the Catholic Spaniard, Philip.

As Edward VI was a child-king,—nine years old when he came to the throne and not quite sixteen at his death,—his reign was dominated by others. Many were the men ready to enter that dangerous scramble for influence, that desperate gamble for high stakes, during the king's minority. A clever stroke might bring lands, wealth, even the control of England; a single misplay might mean the block. In this period the three outstanding families were the Howards, the Seymours, and the Dudleys. In the course of twelve years two Howards, two Seymours, and two Dudleys were beheaded, including a Seymour and a Dudley who for a short time had each been virtual ruler of England. The habit of referring to a man by his title of nobility is likely to be confusing. One may not realize, for instance, that the Earl of Warwick had recently been Viscount Lisle, and would be heard of later as Duke of Northumberland, or that his "maiden name" was John Dudley; for family relationship is hard to trace through a maze of titles. Of the three families the Howards were the oldest and proudest. They were almost the only family of pre-Tudor nobility to retain both life and power. Howards kept cropping up throughout the Tudor period, generally in high place at court and in command on land or sea, all the way from Flodden Field to the Armada. This conservative and generally Catholic family furnished Henry VIII with his second and fifth wives, both of whom were beheaded. The Howards' bid for supreme power just before Henry's death led Surrey to the block and almost caught his father, Norfolk, too. Compared with the Howards, the Seymours were upstarts. They had been simple country gentry; but after their Jane became queen and gave Henry a son, they rose rapidly to wealth, influence, and high command. Edward Seymour, Earl of Hertford, better known as Duke of Somerset, was the most powerful noble in England at Henry's death; his brother, the admiral, married Henry's widow. Finally, there were three generations of clever, rascally Dudleys. The founder of the house was Edmund, the extortionate tax-gatherer of the first Tudor. Henry VIII executed him, but much of the money he had gathered stayed in the family and contributed to the rise of his son John, successively Viscount Lisle, Earl of Warwick, and Duke of Northumberland. John's son Robert, later Earl of Leicester, played a prominent role at the court of Elizabeth (see page 287).

Henry VIII had intended that a council, composed of men of varying views, should conduct the government during Edward's minority; but Somerset (Seymour-Hertford), the young king's uncle, quickly drew the power into his own hands and assumed the title of Lord Protector. He was ousted late in 1549 by Northumberland (Dudley-Warwick), who continued in control until Edward's death. The two men were radically different in most of their aims and methods; they were alike in their keen desire for wealth and power. Somerset meant well and was a champion of the oppressed classes, but he was ineffectual in getting things accomplished. Northumberland, one of the most desperate political gamblers in English history, was a clever, scheming, hypocritical opportunist. The problems with which both men had to deal were for the most part inherited from Henry's reign.

Their foreign policies were failures. At Henry's death, negotiations were on foot to unite England and Scotland by the marriage of Edward VI to the little Scottish queen, Mary, granddaughter of Henry's older sister. In order to hasten the betrothal, Somerset invaded Scotland. In the battle of Pinkie he killed some ten thousand

Scots and then devastated the region near Edinburgh. Naturally these tactics failed to win the bride for Edward. Instead of becoming queen of England, the little queen of Scots was sent at once to France, where she was soon betrothed to the Dauphin and some years later became queen of France. In the meantime France renewed war against England and succeeded in recovering Boulogne.

Although Henry VIII had inherited from his father an amazingly well-filled treasury, he left an empty one to his son; for the wars of his last years had not only exhausted the church spoils but run the country heavily into debt. Regular taxes could not meet the expenses; Somerset and Northumberland therefore carried to extremes the inflation of the currency started by Henry. Fortunately, the possibilities of paper money were still unknown to the Western world. The worst they could do was to debase the currency to the lowest level in English history, ordering the mints to turn out shillings which were only one-quarter silver and three-quarters alloy. The great influx from the Spanish mines of Mexico and Peru was already beginning to lower the value of silver radically by increasing its supply, even without this deliberate inflation. The result was that prices jumped, and there was widespread distress.

There were other causes for economic and social discontent. The dissolution of the monasteries had resulted in a wholesale change of property titles and conditions. The movement was continued under Edward with the carrying out of a late order by Henry for the abolition of various other religious and semireligious endowments. The religious functions of the guilds were ended, and much of their property was seized, though craft guilds proper still continued, sleepily inactive. The "chantries," endowments for the perpetual saying of prayers for the dead, were also suppressed, on the plea that they increased superstition among the people. To be sure, the chantry priests spent a large part of their time in praying for the dead on special requests; but they frequently had maintained schools in connection with their establishments, and only a few of these were transformed into "King Edward grammar schools." The guilds, moreover, had been exceedingly useful to the poor through their charities, which were now cut off; for the wealth thus confiscated went the way of the monastic riches—chiefly into the pockets of courtiers. The enclosure movement meanwhile still continued to oust many peasants. Altogether, times were bad, and it seemed that the rich were growing richer and the poor poorer. Somerset tried to legislate in the interest of the poor; but he antagonized the upper and middle classes and only aroused false hopes in those he would succor. There were serious uprisings in various parts of England,

and Northumberland crushed them with the help of foreign mercenaries. Then he was able to get rid of Somerset, who, having already sent his own brother to the block, followed him to it.

The most significant feature in the reign of Edward VI was the religious drift toward extreme Protestantism. Somerset began this moderately; but under Northumberland it was pushed much farther. Strange to say, the man who left the strongest lasting influence upon England out of all that period of active, positive men was the timid, vacillating, compromising Thomas Cranmer, Archbishop of Canterbury. From the time he assumed that high office and immediately gave Henry his divorce, his political record was weak and shifting; but this had no ill effect on his rich and mellow scholarship, which, with his remarkable command of language, enabled him to produce an enduring monument in the Book of Common Prayer (1549). Its beautiful phrases still live, with few changes, in the Anglican ritual. Cranmer retained a good deal of the old Catholic prayer book, yet introduced distinctive changes. One of the noticeable breaks with the past was the use of English instead of Latin throughout the service. The new Protestant ideas found in the writings of Cranmer were vigorously reinforced by the able and forceful sermons of Hugh Latimer. With the same outspoken courage which had cost him the bishopric of Chichester under Henry, Latimer harshly denounced the personal profits which politicians were making from church spoils. In 1549 Parliament passed a mild Act of Uniformity, which stipulated that the new prayer book was to go into use throughout England on a particular Sunday. Somerset's aversion to persecution is shown not only in the lack of force in this act but also in the repeal of the "Whip with the Six Strings" and the legitimizing of clerical marriage. This toleration was perhaps premature; for, on the first Sunday the new prayer book was used, thousands rose in protest in the west, and a few elsewhere, to demand the return of the Six Articles and the former service book. The radical Protestants, on the other hand, whitewashed many church frescoes, smashed irreplaceable stained-glass windows, and destroyed beautiful statuary in their desire for Protestant simplicity. All in all, the writings of Cranmer and the sermons of Latimer helped to swing England from the Catholic beliefs and practices which Henry had retained, and planted the ideas of the Reformation so strongly that in the next reign hundreds were ready to die for them.

Under Northumberland the trend toward extreme Protestantism increased markedly, in spite of the hopes that his rise to power had given the Catholics who had supported him against Somerset. Englishmen and foreigners, steeped in the doctrines of Luther, Zwingli, and Calvin, swarmed over from the Continent. These "Hot Gospelers" wanted to push England much farther away from Rome than Cranmer's compromise had carried it. The Reformation in England reached its extreme point in 1553, when the principles of belief were embodied in "Forty-two Articles," following close upon a revision of the Book of Common Prayer, which was still ornamented by Cranmer's beautiful prose. Both these measures showed the marked influence of the teachings of Zwingli and even of Calvin. The revised prayer book did not mention the word "Mass," and the elaborate vestments of the clergy were forbidden. Neither of the prayer books was sanctioned by the body of the clergy, but both had the potent backing of Parliament. Had Edward lived, precocious mentally and strongly Protestant as he was, he might have taken as strong a stand for the new Protestant teachings as his sister Mary was soon to take for the old faith. He probably would have forced the changes upon the people, who perhaps would have reacted as bitterly against Protestantism as they were to turn, under Mary's persecutions, against Catholicism.

The Forty-two Articles, however, were the last legislation signed by the dying Edward. The sickly young king trusted Northumberland and thought him as sincere in religion as he was himself. The people, however, saw that the duke "rang as false on the counter as one of the bad coins issued by his government."[1] Consequently his attempt in 1553 to change the succession was foredoomed. Henry VIII had provided that if Edward should die without heir, the throne should go to Mary, the Catholic daughter of Catherine of Aragon. Northumberland, knowing what his own end would be if that happened, produced a rival for the crown in Lady Jane Grey, a sixteen-year-old girl remarkably well educated and admirable in every way. If one excepted Elizabeth, because of the questionable legitimacy of her birth in the midst of her father's divorce difficulties, Lady Jane was the next Protestant in line for the throne, since she was the granddaughter of Henry's younger sister Mary, who, after her three months as queen of France, had married an English courtier. Northumberland arranged Lady Jane's marriage with his own son, and persuaded Edward, who was fond of his attractive young cousin, to name her possible male heir as successor to the throne in order to avoid the change in religion inevitable should Catholic Mary become queen. Northumberland then altered the will to make Jane queen in her own name, and at Edward's death had her so proclaimed.

[1] G. M. Trevelyan, *History of England* (1926), p. 317. By permission of Longmans, Green & Co.

# Tudor Politics and Religion

Englishmen, however, rallied to Henry's own daughter; for they saw in the little-known Lady Jane only the daughter-in-law of the hated, hypocritical Northumberland. Not yet had the issue between Catholicism and Protestantism reached the point of bitterness where England would let it count in choosing a sovereign; that was to come later. Mary, meanwhile, ignoring Northumberland's summons to the court—and probably to her death—was easily and quickly crowned by her supporters. All England hailed the new ruler, while poor Lady Jane Grey, the "nine-day queen," was imprisoned in the Tower with her young husband. Northumberland tried to save his head, cheered for Mary, and turned Catholic. He had done too much evil, however, and the second Dudley became a victim of the ax.

The spontaneous enthusiasm for England's first reigning queen since the Matilda fiasco did not last long. Unfortunately for herself and for England, Mary, "the most honest" and in many ways "the most merciful of all the Tudors,"[1] was a fanatic in regard to her mother's flouted religion. She seemed never to realize that an England existed beyond the confines of religion. The humiliation of her mother, added to her own anomalous position during the divorce days, was enough to leave a lasting mark on any girl; and to one of Mary's narrow nature the psychological damage was incalculable. Forced, moreover, by her father to deny her faith, she was apparently always seeking to expiate that act. At first she seemed to try to be kind and rather tolerant, but secret opposition and open rebellion soon started her upon that road of persecution which was to give her the undeserved epithet of "Bloody Mary." If the people had distrusted Northumberland, they soon came to hate far more this somber woman of thirty-seven. The six-year reign of Edward may have been ineffectual, but the five years of Mary were to give the English a bitter loathing for Catholicism from which they never recovered. For centuries Mary was to live in the popular imagination, hated for her Spanish husband and her wholesale persecutions. This reaction, from the same people who shortly before had cheered Henry even in his tyrannical last years and were soon to love Elizabeth, whatever she did, can perhaps best be explained by Mary's ignorance of popular opinion, a fault not characteristic of the Tudor family.

Mary's flouting of the people's wishes began, not many months after her coronation, with her betrothal to the bigoted and ardently Catholic son of Charles V. It was natural that Mary, after her difficult young years in England, should have turned with homesick eyes toward her mother's Catholic Spain for a husband; but a long-

---

[1] Conyers Read, *The Tudors* (1936), p. 125.

[ 277 ]

faced Spanish husband accentuated the criticism of the unpopular Spanish characteristics of Mary herself. Unluckily, the queen fell in love with the coldly disdainful Philip, who was to ignore and to humiliate her. He wanted England; the unattractive queen was merely a necessary evil in the bargain. Charles V was soon to abdicate his various thrones and to divide his too burdensome heritage. His brother was to receive the German Hapsburg lands and the imperial title; his son was to become Philip II of Spain, and to inherit along with it the Netherlands, parts of Italy, and the rich Spanish colonies beyond the seas. If a son were to be born of this marriage, England feared that, like the Netherlands, she might perhaps become a hereditary dependency of Spain, to be added to those many other regions drawn into the Hapsburg net by royal marriages. Exhortations that Mary either remain single or marry an Englishman fell on deaf ears. In vain the popular temper showed itself when boys in the London streets pelted the imperial negotiators with snowballs.

Early in 1554 the news of the impending marriage, combined with the threatened restoration of Catholicism in full force, led to a dangerous revolt, known as Wyatt's Rebellion. Various notables of the Northumberland party plotted to put Mary's Protestant sister, Elizabeth, on the throne and to marry her to an Englishman. The revolt in the Midlands failed, but the men of Kent, under Sir Thomas Wyatt, followed much the same course that the rebels from that same county had taken in 1381 under Wat Tyler and in 1450 under Jack Cade. They marched on London, and with a little more boldness might have carried the day. Mary, endowed with the usual Tudor bravery, met the situation with the same coolness that Richard II had shown under similar circumstances. She promised that she would not marry without the consent of Parliament, and the Londoners barred the way to Wyatt's men. Numerous executions followed, including that of Lady Jane Grey, whom Mary might have spared had she not been a focus for plots potentially too dangerous. Even the canny Princess Elizabeth, with her perennially deaf ear to plots and her professed loyalty to Mary, lay in the Tower in the shadow of the block. Parliament, with the usual compliance of such Tudor bodies, finally approved the marriage terms, which, thanks to the efforts of the patriots in the Council, were very favorable to England, imposing careful safeguards against any exercise of royal power on Philip's part. The combination of Philip and Mary was not a legally joint rule like that of William III and another Mary late in the next century.

Had Mary made a moderate return to the faith of her forebears, England undoubtedly would have acquiesced. Moderation, however,

# Tudor Politics and Religion

was not in her nature, and those who would not return to the Roman fold were to be burned as heretics at the stake. When Mary felt that she was serving God, no one could swerve her from her purpose—not even her husband, who saw that England was no place at this time for a blood bath. Three hundred men and women died in agony in the fires of Smithfield and elsewhere because of their Protestant faith—an unusual number of executions even for callous Tudor England. A compliant Parliament sanctioned the repeal of all antipapal statutes since the beginning of Henry's divorce problem, and the revival of the old heresy laws. While Lords and Commons, however, would give their votes to meet new royal ideas in reconciliation with Rome and in dogma, they yielded nothing on the economic side of England's Reformation. There was no vote to restore the seized monastic lands, in which members of Parliament were personally interested. No great spiritual revival accompanied the return to Catholicism. The Venetian ambassador remarked that "with the exception of a few pious Catholics, none of whom are under thirty-five years of age, all the rest make this show of recantation yet do not effectively resume the Catholic faith." Even three quarters of the parish clergy and a few bishops made the change. Lip service was enough to save life and property, and most Englishmen were ready to take that easy way. Some, however, would not do as much. The victims of the Smithfield fires were mostly of humble origin, but attention centered upon three prelates who had been most active in pushing England toward Protestantism. Archbishop Cranmer, with his sensitive nature, at first, in fear of the flames, recanted his Protestantism; but finally he announced his real faith and boldly thrust into the flames the hand that signed the recantation. Latimer and Bishop Ridley of Rochester were burned together at Oxford. "Be of good comfort, Master Ridley, and play the man," said Latimer; "we shall this day light such a candle by God's grace in England as, I trust, shall never be put out." He was right. These executions helped to bring about a tremendous reaction against Catholicism that lasted for centuries. John Foxe's *Book of Martyrs*, written with minute detail and a bitter anti-Catholic bias, played its part in keeping alive the memories of the fires of Smithfield. Mary's open subservience to Spain and the Pope, moreover, injected a patriotic element into the anti-Catholic movement. So strong was this feeling that even a century and a half later England took a stupid German for king simply because he was a Protestant.

In addition to religious persecution, Mary's foreign policy brought her into difficulties. Partnership between Philip and Mary meant that Spain could use English resources without giving England any compensating privileges. English eyes looked longingly at the rich Spanish colonial empire in America, but the royal marriage did not enable the queen's subjects to enter the king's closely guarded pre-serves. That led, in Mary's reign, to the effort to reach the East by way of a northeast passage around the top of Europe, free from Spanish influence. Two captains, Willoughby and Chancellor, under-took the difficult voyage around the North Cape. The former was wrecked and lost; the latter reached the White Sea and opened trade with the semibarbarous Russian state of Muscovy through Archangel. With this attitude of "What's yours is mine and what's mine is mine, too," Philip persuaded Mary to drag England into a war against France, using English men and English money for purely Spanish purposes. A French general boasted that he could capture Calais in seven days; and he did, to a day, in the first week of 1558. That loss ended the five centuries of English ownership of land in France. Since the end of the Hundred Years' War, Calais had been the sole holding, and it was considered a useful commercial outpost, as well as a landing place for expeditions against France. Its loss proved no fundamental detriment to England; but for the time being it was a severe humiliation, and Mary said that at her death the word "Calais" would be found graven on her heart.

Before the year was out she died, and London that night was merry with bonfires and cheering.

# CHAPTER XI

## The Glorious Age

### 1558-1603

Bitter resentment toward Mary made England skeptical about a second Tudor queen. The country could not foresee that Mary's sister, made of different stuff, was about to lead it into the most glorious period of all English history, a half century charged with dramatic action and keen zest for living. Inheriting "the shakiest throne in Europe," Elizabeth gave the nation forty-five years of internal prosperity, high international prestige, and splendid achievement, both on the seas and overseas. Another queen regnant, three centuries later, was to have a reign almost as great; but Victoria scarcely deserved the fame accorded to the imperious virgin daughter of Henry VIII and Anne Boleyn, for the accomplishments of Elizabethan England were in no small measure attributable to the sagacity, tact, and inspiration of "Good Queen Bess" herself.

Elizabeth, at twenty-five, when Mary's death brought her to the precarious throne, was fairly good-looking and rather tall, with an erect carriage. Reddish-gold hair and keen eyes set off somewhat sharpish features, while her olive skin was fine in texture. She had unusually beautiful hands, which she was inclined to display to advantage. It was, however, her mind and her temperament which made her distinctive. An excellent Renaissance scholar, she was at home in French, Italian, and Latin; quick in repartee and brazen in deception, she could more than hold her own in matching wits with the most brilliant; ever the realist, with a clear sense of the practical values of any situation, her shrewd mind proved a dependable brake upon her strong-willed, impulsive nature. Her hectic girlhood, when she had been the natural subject of plots, was a hard school which had sharpened her natural keenness. Thanks to her own native wit and to a caution beyond her years, she had survived those perilous days which once had brought her close to beheading in the Tower. Stripped of illusions and cynical to boot, she had gained the knack of analyzing men and motives. She did not stop here, but, with her father's ability to handle people, knew how to say the right thing at the right moment. Such was her tact that she could rebuff a minister, a suitor, or a Parliament more gracefully than many another would grant a favor. She knew how to enhance the power of the crown by colorful pageantry. Not only did she maintain a gay and glittering court but she showed herself frequently to the cheering Londoners and made numerous lengthy "progresses" out into the counties. Despite this smiling, cheerful surface, there was iron beneath. Never forgetting that she was ruler of England and daughter of Henry VIII, she was often as imperious as her father and, in times of necessity, could show masculine hardness. More than once she sacrificed her own feelings as a woman to what she considered her duty as queen. Before she had been on the throne many months, England knew she had a queen who could and would rule as well as reign.

The success of Elizabeth's reign depended to no small degree on her choice of capable ministers, whom she supported loyally. Almost none of importance were chosen from among the glittering playboys who contributed to the glamour and gaiety of her court. She might flirt with such men and call them by nicknames, but only on rare occasions did she entrust them with serious business.

Her principal adviser for forty years was William Cecil, later Lord Burghley. Although never assuming the pompous magnificence of a Wolsey, Cecil was one of the most capable and useful ministers in all English history. He came from the middle class, like most Tudor ministers; was educated at Cambridge; served as secretary to Somerset and to Northumberland; and managed to keep alive under Mary. Shrewd, practical, and tireless, the cool and cautious Cecil handled a multitude of details and gave the queen excellent advice, which generally she followed. Younger and somewhat more impulsive than Cecil was Francis Walsingham, who first served as ambassador to France and who demonstrated his usefulness by organizing a highly efficient secret service which was all-important in those days of constant plots and of tangled negotiations. Cecil and, later, Walsingham handled much of the major administrative business; but for advice on important matters there was also the Council, in which were some men selected for ability whereas others were included because of family position.

Problems of the gravest sort faced Elizabeth and Cecil as they took stock of the situation in the last days of 1558. Edward and Mary had left their sister a sorry heritage. Religion split the land into hostile and suspicious parties, and feeling ran high and bitter. Finances were in a weak state, with a debased currency, dislocated trade, a heavy national debt, and poor governmental credit. In foreign affairs it was necessary to liquidate as soon as possible the unfortunate French war into which Philip had dragged England and

# The Glorious Age

to make the best of the loss of Calais. Divided as she was, England would be fortunate to escape absorption by Spain or France. To make matters worse, Elizabeth's own title to the throne was none too secure. She had been declared illegitimate by Parliament, and she had in Mary Queen of Scots an influential rival with a good Tudor claim to the crown.

In spite of circumstances, Elizabeth and her ministers brought about a remarkable recovery in all those fields—finance, religion, and foreign affairs—before she had been on the throne two years. Strict economy quickly restored the shattered national finances. Elizabeth in her first six months spent only 40 per cent of what Mary had spent in her last half year. The debased currency was called in, and sound money was issued in its place. Sir Thomas Gresham, who founded the Royal Exchange and whose name is associated with the economic law that "bad money drives out good," was active in the international financial center at Antwerp. He was able to pay off the heavy loans incurred by Mary and to report by 1560 that England enjoyed better credit than any other nation in Europe. Elizabeth throughout her reign fully appreciated the advantages of a balanced budget, and her efforts in that direction brought her, like her grandfather, under charges of stinginess.

Elizabeth also realized that until the religious situation was settled, turmoil would continue at home and England could not present a united front to Europe. Either the Protestant extremes of Edward VI or the Catholic extremes of Mary would leave a great many people bitterly dissatisfied. Her solution was a compromise, which was clever if not noble. Elizabeth herself probably had no strong religious convictions. She was bound closely however, to the antipapal side,— even before she was born, since the intimation of her coming birth had hastened the divorce of Catherine and Henry, thereby accelerating the breach with Rome. Elizabeth herself could not, had she so wished, have been Roman Catholic *and* queen, since in the eyes of Rome she was illegitimate.

The "Elizabethan compromise" was designed to include as many Englishmen, Protestant and Catholic, as possible. The first Parliament of the reign passed most of the legislation essential for this, and a later Parliament ratified the beliefs of the Anglican Church in the Thirty-nine Articles, a modification of Cranmer's Forty-two. In addition, a Parliamentary Act of Uniformity required all Englishmen to conform to the Church of England. The Court of High Commission, a special Tudor tribunal, like the Court of Star Chamber and the Council of the North, was established to handle cases arising under this act. At first, however, the recusants, those who refused to conform, were let off rather easily. Not until after 1569, when the Catholics had become very active with plots and rebellion, was the act enforced at all harshly.

The general lines of the compromise may be stated as follows. Independent of Roman control, as it was, the Church of England was regarded as Protestant, though it still retained some Catholic aspects. As far as doctrinal belief was embodied in the Thirty-nine Articles, it became clearly Protestant; as far as the rubric (the directions for public worship placed in italics in the prayer book) was to be taken into account, it remained to a certain extent Catholic. That the rubric and the Thirty-nine Articles should contradict each other in spirit was illogical. On the other hand, English institutions both then and now have never been noted for logic. What Elizabeth and the English people wanted was a comprehensive church which would include as great a variety of Christians as possible. The Church of England became such an organization. Uncompromising Catholics were dissatisfied, for the Church denied both transubstantiation and the authority of the Pope; the "Hot Gospelers," the more extreme Protestants, also were displeased; and both these minority groups remained outside the Church. The new arrangement, however, was flexible enough to include both the High Church element, which approached Catholic practices in elaborate ritual, and the opposite group of many Protestants who wished to "purify" the Church still further from Romish influence, particularly in regard to vestments and ritual. These "Puritans" comprised the Low Church group in the Elizabethan establishment; and, like the Catholics and extreme Protestants, they were later to cause trouble. For the time being, however, the majority of Englishmen had had quite enough of church broils and were content with the easygoing compromise favored by the queen.

The Church of England was more than a matter of dogma and ritual. From one point of view it was a branch of the government. As an "established" church, its bishops were appointed and its policies were determined by the political authorities. Elizabeth herself, in order to spare the feelings of moderate Catholics, substituted, in enumerating her various titles, the expression "and so forth" where her father and brother had used "Supreme Head of the Church"; but she retained full authority. Parliament even used its religious authority to decree that Wednesday, in addition to Friday, should be a meatless day, in order to encourage the fisheries.

Like most compromises, the Church of England lacked the vital force that goes with more positive settlements. Religious fervor was seldom one of its features, and its services often lapsed into perfunctory formalism. At that price Elizabeth spared England the terrible excesses which were marking religious disputes in many other lands during her day. She had, moreover, a united England at her back when she faced France and Spain, whose principal hopes of aggression lay in finding her subjects divided in a religious civil war.

Elizabeth's foreign problems were not settled so quickly and easily as those of finance and religion. Foreign affairs required the closest attention and cleverest handling during most of the reign. It is no small tribute to her and to Cecil that they gave England a quarter century of nominal peace, the longest such period since Henry III. Peace meant economy in national finances and a breathing spell in which the nation could build up commercial prosperity. Many forces, however, threatened to draw England into open conflict.

European political and diplomatic relations were seriously complicated by the movement which the Protestants call the Counter Reformation and the Catholics call the Catholic Reformation. Rome did not accept without a struggle the terrific dismemberment it had sustained during the first half of the century as a result of Luther and Calvin (see pages 259–260). It sought, partly by cleaning house and partly by intrigue and force, to recover as many as possible of the lands which had turned, or were threatening to turn, to Protestantism. The Church had called a council in 1545 to meet in the Alpine city of Trent to consider prospective reforms. To this the Protestants had been invited in the hope that reform would bring them back to the fold, but they held aloof. For almost twenty years the Council of Trent held its intermittent sessions. It reaffirmed the Catholic belief in the seven sacraments, in papal supremacy, and in other orthodox doctrines. In many ways the council did much to purify the Church of its past abuses. The Counter Reformation found invaluable agents in the new Society of Jesus, an order resembling friars, and commonly known as the Jesuits. It was founded by a former officer in the Spanish army, Ignatius Loyola. The Jesuits received a remarkably thorough training, submitted to an extremely rigid discipline, and often showed fearless devotion in the face of death. They did great work as educators and missionaries and were very energetic in their political activity. Protestant England came to regard this latter phase of their work with grave suspicion, so much so that the word "Jesuitical" came to be used as an adjective synonymous with "tricky" and "deceitful."

The Counter Reformation ensured to the Roman fold Poland, Bohemia, the southern Netherlands (now Belgium), south-central Germany, and most of France. It was the signal for a century of bitter religious wars, which broke out about the time Elizabeth came to the throne. In the name of religion, men indulged in some of the dirtiest fighting Europe has ever seen west of the Balkans. Religion, to be sure, was often only a pretext for political or economic disputes, which might be carried out the more ruthlessly in that name. France and Spain, the two most powerful countries in Europe, might use religion as a cloak for their designs upon English independence; but they, like Scotland, both had their own religious civil wars between the Catholics and the Calvinists. In France, dominated by Catherine de' Medici through her three weak sons as successive kings, troubles with the Calvinist Huguenots distracted the nation from 1562 to 1594 in a long and bewildering series of civil conflicts in which both Catholic and Huguenot partisans were guilty of excessive brutality. The bloody climax occurred in 1572, on Saint Bartholomew's Eve, on the occasion of the wedding of the king's sister and the Protestant Henry of Navarre, when the Catholics, both in Paris and throughout the country, massacred between ten thousand and thirty thousand Huguenots. When this Huguenot leader finally came to the throne as Henry IV, the first Bourbon king, he turned Catholic, because that was necessary to win the support of Paris; but at the same time he granted toleration to the Huguenots in the famous Edict of Nantes. Spain under Philip II was sufficiently Catholic herself to satisfy this archchampion of the Counter Reformation, but he used energetic and cruel means in a vain effort to stamp out Protestantism in the Netherlands. In 1567 a "Council of Blood" under Philip's viceroy there found victims by the hundreds; yet his powerful regiments of Spanish infantry, the best troops in Europe, could not crush the revolt, which continued under William the Silent, prince of Orange. The southern Netherlands (now Belgium) remained Spanish and Catholic; but the northern provinces, commonly called Holland, eventually won their freedom in an "eighty years' war" with Spain, fought vigorously on land and sea. By the close of Elizabeth's reign the Dutch were virtually free and about to enter upon a period of commercial prosperity, though full independence was not recognized until 1648. Scotland, converted thoroughly to Calvinism by John Knox, rebelled against her Catholic regent. During all this period the papacy itself interfered frequently in international and internal affairs.

Faced with this situation, Elizabeth and her ministers followed a course which was bewildering in the details of its tactics but was quite consistent in its general strategy. They kept the country out of open war until it should be strong enough to fight successfully. They accomplished this by means of frequent double-dealing, quick

# The Glorious Age

changes of face, downright lying, and occasional abandonment of allies. Walsingham and the more enthusiastic advisers urged a more heroic course which would make England the active and open champion of Protestantism. Elizabeth and Cecil, however, after one unfortunate venture in France, were too cold and too calculating to be drawn into such activity. They were ready to sneak money and even men to aid the Huguenots, the Dutch, and the Scottish Presbyterians; but, in addition to considerations of economy, Elizabeth did not want openly to encourage rebellion against a lawful monarch. She herself, with the questionable legitimacy of her birth, was too vulnerable to set such an example. The other countries were employing similar, but less successful, methods to bring about a revolt of the English Catholics. Elizabeth also condoned, as we shall see, the raids of her seamen on the Spanish Main—a further example of how far a nation could go without actually declaring open war. Elizabethan England was full of men who were ready to fight papists or to chase galleons, with the clear understanding that if they should fail, Elizabeth and Cecil would disavow their acts to protesting ambassadors. Thus it was that England was steered in a safe but tortuous course, guided by general considerations of balance of power.

Elizabeth's virginity was a very valuable diplomatic asset in these efforts to prevent war. The possibility of sharing the English throne kept more than one foreign prince in line. The suitors were many and varied. During her first two years as queen Elizabeth had fifteen proposals, coming from eight different countries. Philip II tried to continue the advantages he had enjoyed as the husband of Mary. An Austrian archduke and a very persistent Danish prince were also among the early candidates. Even Ivan the Terrible, Czar of Russia, later proposed marriage. To hold France in line, Elizabeth dallied with two royal brothers in turn. Her flirtation with the younger Frenchman, a rather stupid young man with a huge nose, lasted until she was nearly fifty. Some Englishmen too aspired to the honor. Perhaps, as rumor says, the only man Elizabeth ever cared for was Robert Dudley, whom she later made Earl of Leicester. His father, Northumberland, and his grandfather, the tax-collector, had both been beheaded; but that did not seem to injure his career. Elizabeth was showing him marked attentions when news came that his neglected young wife, Amy Robsart, had been found dead of a broken neck. England buzzed with gossip that Lord Robert was clearing his way to the throne. A crop of scandals attached themselves to the queen's reputation, but modern research has cleared her. Parliament, fearing the dangers of a disputed succession if

Elizabeth should die unwed, kept urging her to marry, but she persistently procrastinated. England, she said, was her husband. Londoners kept quoting odds on the prospects of various candidates, domestic and imported, but not one succeeded.

Elizabeth's name is always associated with that of her younger and more attractive cousin and rival for the throne, Mary Stuart, the "Queen of Scots" who for years created complications for Elizabethan England. Queen of Scotland in her own name since babyhood, temporarily queen consort of France, and, as great-granddaughter of Henry VII, enjoying a title to the English throne almost as good as Elizabeth's, Mary was in a powerful position. Tall, with an exquisite pale skin and beautiful dark-brown eyes and hair, Mary had a feminine charm so irresistible that she is ranked as one of the most fascinating women of history. Passion and impulse, however, led her to throw away her many advantages and to be at times incredibly foolish. Her cold English cousin, with her masculine mind, sacrificed the woman to the queen; Mary sacrificed the queen to the woman every time. So it was that eventually Mary lost her life at Elizabeth's order.

Scottish affairs loomed large at the outset of Elizabeth's reign. French influence was strong at Edinburgh; for Mary's French mother, of the strongly Catholic Guise family, was regent of Scotland and placed Frenchmen in important posts. Mary herself, at sixteen, had just married the heir to the French throne, whose brief reign as Francis II was about to begin. England feared a French invasion through her "postern gate," as Scotland was called. Scotland, however, was a restless, poverty-stricken, and far from united land. We shall closely examine the Scots later,—both the Lowlanders, who resembled the English in a backward fashion, and the wild clansmen beyond the Highland line (see pages 418, 452). Religion contributed to the unrest, in which the turbulent nobles were conspicuous. The Calvinism brought over by the stern John Knox appealed strongly to a large proportion of the Lowland Scots, and they were up in arms against the French-Catholic regent. Elizabeth, during the first year of her reign, gave active aid, by land and sea, to the rebels. By 1560 Cecil secured a favorable treaty at Edinburgh, which virtually eliminated the French influence in Scotland.

A year later Mary was back in Scotland, a widow of eighteen, accustomed to French gaiety and stunned by the chill somberness of her northern homeland. She was not content to be simply queen of that barren realm, and she was to spend her remaining years in intrigue for a more impressive title. She was soon in conflict with sober John Knox, who utterly disapproved of everything about her from her sex to her religion. A new husband was deemed essential, and Elizabeth offered her Leicester; but in 1565 Mary married her cousin, Henry Stuart, Lord Darnley, a Protestant who was descended from the second marriage of her grandmother, Henry VII's daughter. With all his notable ancestry, Darnley was a worthless, weak, and drunken debauchee, who quickly turned Mary's ardor into contempt.

The three years following this unhappy marriage were filled with melodrama in which Mary's folly sealed her fate. She was soon paying too much attention to her Italian secretary, David Rizzio. In March, 1566, Darnley and others broke into Mary's sitting-room and murdered Rizzio before her eyes. Three months later Mary had a son, the future James VI of Scotland and James I of England, an extremely prosaic product of such a background. In February, 1567, Darnley was convalescing from an illness at Kirk o' Fields, a little house just outside Edinburgh. One night, after a day in which Mary had visited him, the house was blown up, and Darnley's body was found outside, strangled to death. Letters, which may have been forged, were later found in a silver jewel casket, seriously incriminating Mary in the matter. Scotland was, on the whole, glad to be rid of Darnley, but it was shocked and disgusted three months later when it heard of Mary's marriage to the Earl of Bothwell, a "glorified border ruffian" supposedly involved in Darnley's murder. Bothwell was said to have used force; but there is little evidence to support this contention, and Mary had previously shown him much favor. She may have fallen in love with him, as his dominant personality was the opposite of Darnley's weakness. But, whatever the reason, it is hard to explain such a marriage, even for one as emotionally upset as Mary must have been under the stress of circumstances. At once the nobles revolted under Mary's bastard half brother, the Earl of Murray (or Moray), defeated the queen's supporters, and, ten weeks after her third marriage, forced Mary to abdicate in favor of the infant James. Murray, a pro-English Protestant, ruled as regent. Mary was imprisoned, made a dramatic escape in 1568, was again defeated, and fled to England, where she threw herself on the mercy of Elizabeth. Even at this late date, writers are strongly divided in sympathy between Mary and Elizabeth in analyzing the events which followed.

Elizabeth and her ministers did not know how to dispose of the Scottish queen. As with the man who had the wolf by the ears, there was danger in holding on and danger, too, in letting go. They might have sent her back to Scotland; but they distrusted her word and feared further troubles north of the border. They could foresee that if she remained in England, on the other hand, she would become the center of Catholic plots, domestic and foreign, to win England, by means of her coronation as its queen, back to Rome. This latter risk, however, seemed the lesser of the two evils, and so Mary began her nineteen years of mild imprisonment in England.

Mary's presence was partly responsible in 1569, the year after she arrived, for the one serious threat of rebellion in Elizabeth's reign. There were two separate elements involved in this movement. Part of it was simply a political intrigue on the part of various nobles, headed by the Duke of Norfolk, to oust Cecil. Coupled with this was a Catholic revolt in the north, which, still remaining feudal and conservative, disapproved of the rapid changes going on in southern and eastern England. Led by some of the northern nobles, hundreds of sincere peasants, wearing the red cross of crusaders, took up what crude arms they could find, occupied Durham, discovered a discarded altar in the cathedral, and held Catholic services. It has been remarked that every successful revolution is the result of bad police work at the outset. Elizabeth's government was guilty of no such carelessness. It acted with a speed and vigor which saved the day. Before the rebels could free her, Mary was whisked away to a safer place of confinement, and loyal forces, although outnumbered, dispersed the rebels. Norfolk at the critical moment lost his nerve, went home sick, and was arrested. Until 1569 Elizabeth's reign had not witnessed a single execution for religious or political purposes,—a remarkable contrast to the previous Tudor reigns; but the aftermath of this revolt spoiled this record.

A year later the Pope issued a bull excommunicating Elizabeth, calling her a usurper and releasing her subjects from obedience. In 1571, also, Walsingham discovered a fantastic plot, formed by one Ridolfi, an Italian banker, to put Mary Stuart on the throne with the help of foreign force. The Duke of Norfolk, the ranking peer and last remaining duke in England, was seriously implicated in this plot, as well as in the 1569 rebellion; so he paid for it with his head, thus putting the Howard family ahead of the Dudleys in the matter of executions. Mary was to remain in confinement, at one country estate or another, for seventeen years more, until she became the center of a new crop of plots so serious that her death seemed necessary.

In foreign relations England was shifting from Spain to France. The French were no longer an active menace in Scotland, while Philip II was assuming more and more the role of political champion of the Counter Reformation. Part of his war against Protestantism consisted of support of Mary Stuart for the English throne. England,

# The Glorious Age

therefore, began to give secret aid to the Dutch rebelling against him, opening for a while her ports to the "Sea Beggars" who were making serious depredations upon Spanish shipping. Although the new friendly relationship with France suffered a severe strain in 1572 through the massacre of Saint Bartholomew's Eve, which had caused Elizabeth to receive the French ambassador dressed in deep black, the new diplomatic alignment did not break.

One reason which led to strained relations between England and Spain lay three thousand miles away. Spain had followed up the discoveries of Columbus with conquests which gave her most of the southern part of North America, Central America, and most of South America (see pages 229–232). Spain's chief interest in those American possessions lay in the silver mines of Mexico and Peru, which annually provided the equivalent of millions of dollars. Commerce with those regions was rigidly regulated. Each year a great *flota*, or fleet, set out from Spain. On reaching the West Indies, it generally split, one part sailing to San Juan de Ulloa, the present Veracruz, where the Mexican silver was brought down from the interior, the rest of the ships heading for Nombre de Dios (later to Porto Bello), on the Isthmus of Panama, for the Peruvian silver, which was brought by ship up the Pacific coast to Panama and carried across the Isthmus by mule trains. The Mexican fleet would touch at Havana, in Cuba, and the Panama fleet at Cartagena, the chief city of the Spanish Main, as the coast from Yucatan down to Brazil was called. Then the two divisions would rejoin for the return to Spain, convoyed by warships. The "royal fifth" of the American silver went into the national treasury. Spain neglected the normal economic demands of her colonists, who wanted slaves and other commodities which the mother country failed to provide in adequate quantity. At the same time Spain kept her colonial empire a rigid commercial monopoly and forbade the colonists to trade with any other nation.

This situation strongly appealed to England. Early in Elizabeth's reign we find the beginning of persistent Anglo-Saxon efforts to get a share of the riches of that region which Spain tried to monopolize. Part of those efforts centered in supplying articles to that large but neglected market. The more spectacular feature, however, was the English plundering of the rich plate fleets, and the cities of the Spanish Main where the treasure was collected.

Much of the glamour of Elizabeth's reign comes from the adventures of the most colorful of Elizabeth's subjects, the "sea dogs." These tough mariners, most of whom came from Devon and operated from Plymouth, on the southwest coast, spent part of their energy in exploring arctic wastes and in trying to plant new colonies, and a great deal more in their daring adventures in breaking Spain's monopoly on the seas and in the lands beyond the seas. Until that Spanish grip on so much of the New World was broken, England could not expand into the maritime and colonial field where she was eventually to become the most successful of all nations. Spain had shown that she would permit no peaceful infringement of her colonial monopoly; even when Philip II was married to the English queen, he forbade Mary's subjects to take any share in the rich American commerce which was firing the imagination of all Europe.

Force, then, was England's only pathway to colonial fortune. The sea dogs were eager to apply that force against the galleons, seaports, and treasure trains of His Catholic Majesty. There was one drawback, and the cautious Cecil emphasized it strongly. England needed peace, and inroads on the Spanish colonies might well lead to war with the strongest power in Europe. Elizabeth was more ready to take a chance. She tried to preserve the technical appearances of peace and presented profuse apologies to the Spanish envoys for the rudeness of her unruly subjects even while she winked at their raids, secretly invested in them as commercial ventures, lent them regular warships of the royal navy, and took her very generous share of the profits. The legal status of the sea dogs was anomalous. A monarch at peace could not commission them to command royal vessels or privateers; they were technically pirates, but with royal connivance. For a whole quarter of a century those "pious pirates" harried the Spanish Main before they finally goaded Spain into war. By that time the sea dogs were in a position to smash Spanish sea power and to open the way for the British Empire.

The pioneer of the group was John Hawkins, later Sir John, the son of a prominent Plymouth merchant and shipowner. While trading to the Canaries in one of the family ships he conceived the idea of selling slaves to the Spanish colonists, in spite of the fact that the latter were strictly forbidden to deal with foreigners. In 1562 came the first sea-dog contact with the Spanish Main. Hawkins picked up a cargo of Negroes on the Guinea coast and successfully peddled it in Spanish America. Two years later he set out with a more ambitious expedition in which numerous wealthy Englishmen invested heavily and for which the queen lent a worn-out warship. In view of the Spanish regulations, Hawkins had to resort to various subterfuges; for he always sought to give a cloak of legality to his proceedings and was warned by Elizabeth and Cecil not to provoke the Spaniards with actions too outrageous. He would put into a colonial port, stating that his ships needed refitting or that he was in desperate need of water or supplies. If he could not bribe the authorities, he would stage a mild bombardment or send ashore a landing party so that the local officials could report that they had been trading only under compulsion. The colonists themselves were delighted to have a chance to buy the slaves. Hawkins's second voyage netted a profit of 60 per cent. His third voyage, in 1567–1568, however, came to grief. About the time that Mary Stuart was marrying Bothwell, Hawkins sailed once more; but all along the coast of Spanish America he found that the authorities had strict orders to have nothing to do with him, on penalty of losing their posts. Finally he put in at San Juan de Ulloa (Veracruz), in Mexico, to refit. While he was there a powerful Spanish fleet arrived to convoy the treasure ships, which Hawkins, the "honest trader," had scrupulously left unmolested. There was a desperate, one-sided fight in which only two of the English vessels escaped. Many of Hawkins's men fell into Spanish hands. The more fortunate settled down in Mexico with native wives. Some were imprisoned for years before returning to England. A few were condemned by the Inquisition as heretics and publicly burned at Seville, in Spain.

Hawkins was soon overshadowed in reputation by his stocky, brown-bearded, daredevil young cousin Francis Drake, later Sir Francis. Drake had taken part in that disastrous third voyage and had escaped from San Juan de Ulloa. More impetuous than Hawkins, Drake did not bother with pretenses of "legal" trading but went out boldly for loot. Autocratic, violent in temper, and with an insatiable thirst for glory, Drake had a resolute will and a breezy, magnetic personal charm. Before he was thirty, he was a terror to Spain and an idol to England. After two years of reconnoitering the vulnerable spots of the Spanish Main he sailed from Plymouth in 1572 on a voyage of reckless adventure with two little vessels and a crew of seventy-three, only one of whom had passed the age of thirty. He struck at the Isthmus of Panama, where the treasures of Peru were brought overland. With his handful of men and some Indians who hated the Spaniards, he looted the town of Nombre de Dios, on the Atlantic side, and ambushed a rich treasure train, leaving fifteen tons of silver behind because the other loot was more valuable.

Then Drake conceived an even bolder design. While at Panama, he had climbed to a high hill where he could look out upon the Pacific. He realized that the ports and ships of the Spanish Main were by this time warned and well on guard; but the Spaniards on the Pacific, he thought, probably felt too secure to take similar precautions with their ships bringing Peruvian silver to Panama. Elizabeth made a secret investment in his risky project, warning him to keep Cecil ignorant of the plans. Late in 1577 Drake led one of the most famous expeditions in English history out of Plymouth harbor. Just before he reached the Strait of Magellan, he executed a lieutenant who was fomenting discontent. Then, following Magellan's directions, he led his little squadron through the tortuous and treacherous passage, only to run into a terrific gale on the Pacific side. One vessel was lost, another put back to England, and Drake kept on alone in the *Golden Hind*. The Spaniards, as he anticipated, were caught completely off guard. He raided up the coast and learned that a rich treasure ship had set out for Panama. The unsuspecting craft was overhauled and her cargo of precious metals was transferred to the *Golden Hind* till she could hold no more. That haul made the profits of the voyage. Now came the question of getting home. Drake knew full well that the Spaniards would be waiting for him at the Strait of Magellan; so he pushed on up the coast into the fogs of Vancouver, hoping to find a passage back to the Atlantic. Failing in that, he dropped back to San Francisco Bay, took possession of the region in the name of Elizabeth, and named it New Albion. Then he set out westward across the Pacific. The expedition nearly ended in disaster when, for nearly a whole day, the *Golden Hind* lay fast on a reef in the East Indies. A lucky change of wind and tide finally enabled her to slide off. Once more Drake picked up the course of Magellan's famous voyage fifty years earlier, and came back around the Cape of Good Hope. Finally, after an absence of nearly three years, the *Golden Hind* rode into Plymouth harbor, the first English ship to have circumnavigated the earth. Whole wagonloads of treasure were carried to London; the queen made a personal profit of some £163,000, which was about 40 per cent of the total booty. The other investors made nearly a fiftyfold gain on their shares. The Spanish ambassador protested as usual, but Elizabeth herself knighted Drake on the deck of the *Golden Hind*.

Having tasted so freely of Spanish treasure, the English returned again and again to the Spanish Main; but no subsequent raid yielded either the romance or the profit of Drake's great voyage. While Drake was on his way around the world, another sea dog, Martin Frobisher, tried to find a northwest passage around America, to be used as an English short cut to the East. North of Labrador he discovered the bay which now bears his name. Some ore, optimistically believed to be gold, led to two subsequent returns to the ice fields; but neither wealth nor a passageway was found.

In 1585 English seagoing activity took a more constructive form when Sir Walter Raleigh attempted to plant a colony in Virginia. Raleigh was too versatile and too elegant to be classed simply as a sea dog. He represented, in extreme form, the Elizabethan expression of the many-sided man of the Renaissance who found any single field too narrow for his ambitious ability and who consequently made a considerable mark in several fields. Raleigh was at times explorer, naval officer, and promoter of colonization; but he was also courtier, soldier, poet, historian, economist, and businessman. Like Hawkins and Drake, he was a product of Devonshire, the son of a prominent landholder. He left Oxford to fight in the French religious wars, lived in London for a while as one of the gayest of young bloods, and went to Ireland as an officer in the army sent against the rebels. Several cruel acts marred his record there before he was sent back to court with dispatches. That event marked the beginning of his rapid rise. Adept at intrigue, he made a habit of criticizing his superiors to their superiors and rose rapidly. He soon won the favor of the queen, who from time to time presented him with lucrative monopolies, and sufficient estates in England and Ireland to make him the most extensive landholder in the country. Historians question the familiar story of the cloak and puddle, but it was perhaps typical of the tactics by which he became the chief favorite of Elizabeth in the middle period between Leicester and Essex. Few men of Elizabethan England were more thoroughly hated than Raleigh; he was considered an insolent upstart, untrustworthy and unscrupulous; and even those who admitted his keen ability often hated him the more for it. It was characteristic of Elizabeth that she never entrusted Raleigh with any really serious business of state, although she made him captain of her guard and piled riches upon him, until he married without her knowledge or permission.

Raleigh deserves much credit for his stimulus to colonization. The transplanting of Englishmen into overseas regions was to become a distinctive feature of the country's greatness, and, while the first permanent settlement was not founded until four years after Elizabeth's death, Raleigh was pointing the way by 1585. Several expeditions were sent to the deserted region, north of Spanish Florida, which Raleigh is supposed to have christened Virginia in honor of the queen. Those first settlers, however, were disappointed in their search for gold and silver. One group, on little Roanoke Island, disappeared completely, and other colonists were brought back in a starving condition. Raleigh, meanwhile, was credited with having introduced tobacco and the potato to Europe.

The domestic situation had quieted down after the rebellion of 1569 and the Ridolfi plot two years later. By 1580, however, new Catholic agents were arriving in England. These were the Jesuits, who, after receiving training in seminaries on the Continent, returned to accept the very evident risks involved in attempting to restore England to Rome. Manor houses, especially in the north country, had secret "priest holes" for these devoted men, who not only held surreptitious Mass for those who remained Catholic, but soon became engaged in plots to assassinate Elizabeth and to bring back Catholicism with foreign aid. There was a conspiracy in 1583, but the most serious one came three years later. This was the Babington plot, which aimed to kill Elizabeth and her ministers at court and to rush Mary Stuart to the throne. Philip II sent money, but Walsingham's spies were in the innermost councils of the conspirators. The Scottish queen, still a prisoner after all these years, was the center of the plotting; and that finally sealed her fate. Elizabeth's ministers persuaded her that the security of England demanded the death of Mary. Elizabeth hesitated and finally tried to throw the responsibility on others, but the unfortunate Queen of Scots was beheaded at Fotheringay Castle on a February morning in 1587.

That execution accomplished what Drake's raids had failed to do. Spain at last made ready for open war. Philip and the other Catholics had kept hoping that Mary might yet be queen of England. Now, motivated by both religious and by national interests, Philip began to gather warships for an expedition to crush the obstinate heretics, to make England Catholic, and, incidentally, to put a stop to the humiliating raids of the sea dogs. These mariners, however, acted upon the principle that "the best defense is the offensive." Drake swept down on Cádiz and destroyed a considerable part of the fleet which Philip was assembling. This "singeing of the King of Spain's beard" postponed the final showdown until the following year.

Hawkins, after the San Juan de Ulloa disaster, had gone ashore to undertake a more prosaic but very important task as principal administrative officer of the royal navy. Henry VIII had given the English navy a good start, but Hawkins found and fought conservatism and corruption. His most valuable work lay in encouraging the development of a new type of warship. The Spanish galleons were clumsy craft, with very high forecastles and poops. The old idea of sea fighting was to bring the rival ships alongside each other for an infantry battle at sea. Spain had the best infantry in Europe, and her ships were well designed for these old tactics which the English were about to make obsolete. The sea dogs were experimenting with an improved type of vessel. Its forecastle and poop were sharply cut down, and it was given lines which enabled it to navigate more quickly and efficiently. Even more radical was the new English view of naval tactics. Instead of preparing for close-range boarding action, the English vessels were equipped with plenty of guns which could outrange and pound the enemy from a distance without his being able to come to grips. The royal navy itself was still small; but in those days the line between warship and private ship was not sharply drawn, and there were many sea dogs and other mariners not regularly in the queen's service to assist with their ships in giving effective reinforcement to the regular navy.

By 1588 Philip had repaired the damage of Drake's Cádiz raid and had concentrated most of Spanish sea power in an "Invincible Armada" of some one hundred and thirty vessels and thirty thousand men for the conquest of England. Only eight thousand of his men were sailors; most of the rest were infantry, who were to prove useless against the English long-range tactics. Spain's best admiral, a veteran of fifty years at sea, died just as the preparations were approaching completion. Philip, with incredible folly, chose as his successor the amiable, wealthy young Duke of Medina Sidonia, whose only asset was his high social rank. Medina Sidonia, who was perfectly happy lounging in his orange groves, tried to dodge the responsibility. "The object is of such high importance," he wrote the king, "that the person at the head of it ought to understand navigation and sea fighting, and I know nothing of either." "My health is bad," he added, "and from my small experience of the water I know that I am always seasick." Philip remained stubborn; so the "Golden Duke" took command of the expedition which helped to bring an end to Spanish greatness.

Elizabeth also picked a titled name for command of the defense fleet. She chose Lord Howard of Effingham, a Protestant member of the otherwise Catholic Howard family, and a fairly able naval officer. He, however, deferred in his decisions to the foremost seaman of England, Sir Francis Drake, who served as his vice-admiral. Hawkins was rear admiral, and Frobisher was prominent among the captains. Drake once more wanted to raid Cádiz and the other Spanish ports before the Armada set sail, but the queen's hesitation prevented that stroke. Late in July the Armada appeared off the southwest coast, driven by a wind which held the English bottled up in Plymouth, where Medina Sidonia missed his chance to catch them. By desperate work the English towed their warships out into open water, and then, in a running fight all along the south coast, the Spanish "floating barracks" got a taste of the English tactics, which, to the infantry at least, seemed terribly effective but quite unsportsmanlike. The lighter, faster English ships, about two hundred in number, hammered mercilessly the Spanish craft, which could not reply effectively. Spanish strategy was hampered by the Armada's orders to head for the Netherlands, to pick up an army of the viceroy before attempting the invasion of England. Harried by the English, Medina Sidonia crossed the Channel to Calais, closely followed by the enemy, who had the wind at their backs. To dislodge the Armada, the English let loose blazing fire ships, whereupon the Spaniards in terror cut their moorings and straggled out into the gale. The whole Armada was nearly driven ashore on the Flemish sandbanks, but the wind changed and hurried them into the North Sea. The English followed, although their powder was exhausted. The winds, however, completed England's task. The crippled Spaniards rounded the north end of Scotland, leaving wrecks wherever they were swept. Several of their ships went ashore on the Irish coast, where the crews were massacred. Medina Sidonia finally struggled back to Spain with barely sixty battered ships from his original one hundred and thirty, and with scarce a third of his thirty thousand men. For a full century, from the marriage of Ferdinand and Isabella, Spain had been the first country of Europe; those terrible days of gunnery and gales off the British coasts began her decline.

The open war with Spain continued until 1604, the year after Elizabeth's death. For several years to come the sea dogs were to continue their tormenting of Spain, both at home and on the Spanish Main. Cádiz itself was once more raided under Raleigh, while Drake and Hawkins both died in the Caribbean in 1595 on an unsuccessful expedition. One episode of that post-Armada fighting has become immortal. In 1591 an English fleet was sent to the Azores to intercept the treasure fleet from America. The Spaniards, however, were warned and sent out a greatly superior force of warships which caught the English unawares. To cover the escape of the other English vessels, Raleigh's cousin, Sir Richard Grenville, was posted as a rear guard. Fifteen Spanish warships, each larger than his little *Revenge*, closed in on him; yet he stood off their attacks from mid-afternoon to dawn. With her masts gone and her decks slippery with blood, the *Revenge* was a hopeless wreck; but, with Tudor bravado, Grenville would not surrender. At last the great *St. Philip* came alongside, and Grenville got a taste of Spanish close-range tactics; but even then there was a long grim cutlass fight in which the Spaniards lost heavily. At last, when the situation was beyond hope, Grenville wished to blow up the ship rather than surrender, but his subordinates persuaded him otherwise. Gravely wounded, Grenville was taken to the Spanish flagship and treated with all courtesy; but, after crushing wineglasses and swallowing the fragments in his bitterness and pain, he died before reaching port. The *Revenge*, too, the only English warship captured by Spain in the whole period, sank before reaching port. Raleigh, who up to the last minute was to have sailed in Grenville's place, wrote some of his best prose in telling his cousin's story.

The breaking of Spanish sea power had a tremendous result on later history. The Pope, a century earlier, had divided the lands beyond the seas between Spain and Portugal (see page 231). In 1580 Philip II had seized the Portuguese throne, thus gaining for a short while a complete monopoly of European contact with the other continents. Once his control of the seas had been broken, it was out of the question to keep outsiders from the overseas regions. Spain still had strength enough to preserve the colonies which she had already established in America, from Florida southward, fairly intact for more than two centuries longer; and the silver fleets from America came regularly to Spain until 1804. Two other overseas regions, however, could no longer be defended in view of Spain's reduced naval strength. One of these was the Portuguese empire in the East, centering in the Spice Islands and the coast of India. The other was the American region north of Florida, neglected by the Spaniards because it was "too much like Spain." It was here that Raleigh, just before the Armada, had attempted to plant a colony.

Three newcomers in the colonial field, England, Holland, and France, rushed to take advantage of the possibilities in the two fields which Spain abandoned. The influence of the Armada's defeat is shown by the important dates crowded into the next few years. By 1596, English and Dutch squadrons under Lancaster and Houtman were seeking out the weak points of the rotting Portuguese empire in the East. On December 31, 1600, the last day of the sixteenth century, Elizabeth chartered the English East India Company; two years later the Dutch East India Company came into being. In 1607 the English made their first permanent American settlement at Jamestown; in 1608 the French established Quebec; and in 1609 Henry Hudson, sailing for the Dutch, found the river which bears his name and which shortly became the scene of a Dutch settlement. England, as we shall see, later treated Holland and France as she had treated Spain and Portugal, and secured for herself an easy first place in the race for colonial empire and maritime supremacy.

A more sordid undertone ran throughout Elizabeth's reign in the bloody chapter written into the sorry story of Anglo-Irish relations. We last saw Ireland when it was launching pretenders against the first Tudor, who was finally able to secure "Poynings's Law," which gave England a check on Irish legislation (see page 241). Henry VIII tried to placate the turbulent tribal chieftains by honorary English titles, and tried to hold them in line by a series of able deputies. English authority, however, meant little beyond the "Pale," which was limited, as previously, to about twenty miles around Dublin. The religious reforms were extended to Ireland under Henry VIII and Edward VI; but they were not taken seriously outside the Pale, and the principal effect was felt in the abolition of the monasteries, the only centers of learning and culture in the land. Ireland was to maintain a costly and unattended Anglican Established Church until 1869; but the English religious policy might have caused no particular trouble if the Jesuits had not stirred up religious feeling to embitter the already existing political and racial hatreds. Ireland became one of the most devoted Catholic regions in the world. And, in those days of Elizabeth, with Catholicism went Spanish influence. It became a byword that "England's necessity is Ireland's opportunity"; so Philip II, hoping to open a side door by which to attack England, joined with the Jesuits in arousing the natives of the "other island."

There were three very serious Irish revolts during Elizabeth's reign, one in the early years, another in the middle, and the third ending only a year before her death. The principal centers of the revolts were Ulster, the seat of the O'Neills in the north, and Munster, the stronghold of the Desmonds in the south. English influence was fairly strong in the eastern province of Leinster, while the western province, Connaught, was too remote for serious trouble. The story of those revolts is a monotonous record of treachery and atrocities. Just as before and since that time, England did not use sufficient force to subdue Ireland as thoroughly as she had Wales; and half measures were enough to antagonize and to embitter but not to crush. Englishmen, who were sincerely horrified by Spanish cruelty to Dutchmen and Indians, murdered men, women, and children in cold blood, or so devastated the land that thousands ate weeds or grass until they died of starvation. The Irish, on their part, would generally begin a revolt by a surprise massacre of every "Saxon" in the region. Each revolt was finally drowned in blood or ended by a well-timed assassination. It was remarked, in regard to the Elizabethan forces sent to pacify Ireland, that "the eagles flew to the Spanish Main, while the vultures descended on Ireland"; but even some of the sea dogs hunted the "wild Irish" between voyages. The Irish wars were a heavy drain on the English treasury. Of nearly £5,000,000 of special war expenses throughout the reign, half was spent in Ireland, and most of the other half went to assist the Dutch and French. The repulse of the Armada in 1588 called for only £161,000 in extra expense.

# The Glorious Age

The third Irish revolt was marked by the dramatic fall of Elizabeth's third favorite. This was Leicester's stepson, the Earl of Essex, young, handsome, and chivalrous, but, like Mary Queen of Scots, a fool in matters which required discretion and judgment. Essex, about the time of the Armada, had won the extreme favor of the aging queen, who heaped upon him honors and privileges which went to his head. The spoiled darling of the court tried to push his influence to the limit, and turned petulant and sulky when crossed. He was the magnet for all the exuberantly adventurous young bloods of England, and he led them in several ventures on land and sea, only one of which was successful. Elizabeth departed from her usual rule when she entrusted him with the chief command in Ireland in 1599. He abused his power and neglected his duty. When finally called to account, he conspired with the rebel leader whom he had failed to defeat. Essex returned to England, continued his plots to seize the throne by force, and was executed for treason in 1601. The Irish command, in the meantime, had gone to Lord Mountjoy, a real soldier, who broke the revolt and gave to Elizabeth, in her last year, a control over Ireland which no previous English monarch had enjoyed. The sequel of Mountjoy's victory, the transplanting of thousands of Scots into Ulster, belongs to the next reign.

That next reign, too, was to catch the full force of the Parliamentary protests which began to appear during Elizabeth's last years. The defeat of the Armada brought an increased feeling of security and strong national enthusiasm, but it also produced a new feeling in Parliament. For a century that body had acquiesced in Tudor tactics which sometimes had tended strongly toward absolutism. As long as England was threatened by foreign foes, religious discord, or fears of a disputed succession, Parliament was ready to waive a certain amount of freedom in the interests of security. Now, however, everything seemed secure. The first session of Parliament after the Armada was ready for more fighting, but grumbled even at the moderate cost of that tremendous victory. Its grant was given reluctantly and was collected very slowly. In later sessions Parliament attacked certain royal prerogatives, particularly the granting of monopolies to favorites. Yet, out of respect and gratitude to the old queen, its attacks were not bitter. Parliament was saving them for her successor.

Twice during the reign, however, Parliament tackled social and economic reforms with lasting results, both remaining at least nominally in effect for more than two centuries. For the upper and middle classes Elizabethan England was a particularly happy period. The nobility and gentry, enriched in many cases by monastic loot from previous reigns, built comfortable new homes, long, low, and rambling, with broad chimneys, mullioned windows, and other evidences of increased prosperity, which showed that a man's house was no longer a castle in the military sense. The merchants and tradesmen saw their profits swell during the long period of nominal peace, at a time when rival nations were torn by terrific religious struggle. But for the poor, Elizabethan England, like the previous Tudor reigns, was not so merry. We have seen how the enclosures for sheep grazing had uprooted tens of thousands and emptied whole villages, yet had provided no work for the dispossessed wretches (see page 243). Partly with a view to remedying this matter, Parliament passed early in the reign, in 1563, the Statute of Apprentices (also called the Statute of Artificers). It placed upon a national basis the regulation of industry and labor, which had formerly been handled locally. By requiring a considerable part of the population to remain engaged in agriculture, it tried to check the trend from country to town. While stipulating that everyone must have an occupation, the act limited participation in the town industries to those who had served an apprenticeship of at least seven years, and one was not permitted to become an apprentice in certain fields unless his father possessed an income of a specified amount. Another provision of the act was that each year the justices of the peace in each locality should determine the proper wages for the various industries. Long before the Act of Apprentices was formally repealed in 1814, there was a widespread feeling that it had had a cramping effect upon economic development and that it had outlived its usefulness. Even in Elizabeth's time, however, Parliament was unable to legislate everyone into a job. Multitudes of "valiant and lusty beggars" were elements of disorder during a considerable part of the century, while the "lame, ympotente, olde, blynde, . . . poore and not able to worke" had been in misery, particularly after the dissolution of the monasteries. The early 1590's were a period of grave famine and distress, and Parliament in 1597 and again in 1601 devoted its main energy to the problem thus created. It tried first to strike at the enclosure movement itself; but its act, like the legislation of Somerset, was to prove ineffective (see page 274). If Parliament could not eliminate the root of the evil, its "Poor Laws" at least did something to alleviate the consequences. In brief, these aimed to put an end to wandering and begging, and to make the parish the responsible unit for its own poor. A savage act was aimed at the able-bodied vagrant, who was to be "stripped naked from the middle upwards and shall be openly whipped until his or her body be bloodye." The more serious offenders were to be banished. More constructive was the com-

# The Glorious Age

panion act to improve the "miserable estate of the godly and honest sort of the poor subjects of this Realm." Each parish was to appoint four overseers of the poor, who, with the church wardens, were given the power of compulsory taxation for poor relief. The money thus raised was to be devoted to binding out poor children as apprentices, buying raw materials to give work for the unemployed, and building workhouses for the very poor. This act of 1601 was the basis of subsequent poor relief in England, where it was to remain in force, virtually unchanged, for two centuries. That system of decentralized, local responsibility for care of the poor also spread to America.

With the turn of the century the Elizabethan Age neared its end. In religion and in war, in politics and in economics, and upon the high seas it was a famous era. In literature it was no less distinguished. There was, above all, Shakespeare. As Grenville fought on the *Revenge* Shakespeare was writing his earlier historical plays; as Drake and Hawkins died in the West Indies *A Midsummer Night's Dream* and *Two Gentlemen of Verona* were added to the Shakespearean repertory; and as the East India Company was founded *The Merry Wives of Windsor* and *As You Like It* were performed at the Globe Theatre in London.

William Shakespeare was the most famous of all the Elizabethans, and commentators upon him are next in number to those upon the Bible. Concerning a man of whom we know very little, everything has been demonstrated, even to the extent of proving that he did not write his own poems and plays. In fact, the very scarcity of our information concerning his parentage, education, marriage, and career has increased the number of scholarly volumes about him. The following facts, however, may be verified. He was born in 1564 at Stratford-on-Avon, of old yeoman stock, his father a man of some local importance, his mother a peg or two higher in the social scale. He apparently attended the local "grammar school," and as a young man apparently led a rather reckless life at Stratford. In London, where we next hear of him, he rose slowly from obscurity to a reasonable degree of contemporary fame as poet and playwright, and made sufficient money by 1600 to buy a handsome property in his native town, where he died in 1616.

Every man of letters reflects his own environment, and Shakespeare was an Elizabethan. He held "the mirror up to nature"; but it was an Elizabethan glass which reflected the interests and the enthusiasms of his own generation. Therefore we find in him, as might be expected, a man of the late Renaissance, interested in music, in rural games and pastimes, a sportsman, a man of the world, absorbed in the human drama, fond of society, of adventure, and of all that was new and amazing in the astonishingly fresh and springlike Elizabethan day.

The plays of Shakespeare were presented in a theater very unlike our own. The stage was simply a raised platform, open to the sky, and performances were given only in the daytime. Close to the stage and somewhat below it was the pit, and, unlike our orchestra, admission to it was the cheapest. Socially, to be in the pit corresponded to sitting in the second gallery of a modern theater. Around the stage and the pit were built roofed balconies, and here gathered the élite. There was no scenery. On one side of the stage was a kind of flimsy structure, hollow within. It could be used in various ways: as a cave, a grave, a balcony, battlements, or even as a bed for Desdemona. There were no women actors, and feminine parts were always played by young lads. Here was the rough setting for Shakespeare's glorious portrayal of humanity.

Noticeable in Shakespeare is the warm patriotic fervor with which he praised the house of Tudor and the England which he loved. One has but to read the historical plays, which were freely drawn from the writings of other dramatists and from chronicles, to prove this. It is significant that among the early products from his pen was *Richard III*, in which are celebrated the conclusion of the Wars of the Roses and the ultimate victory of the Tudors, personified in Richmond, afterward Henry VII and grandfather of Shakespeare's queen. Thus, in the last act of *Richard III*, two tents are seen,—in the one, Richard; in the other, Richmond. Between the tents rise ghost after ghost, hurling maledictions on Richard, but wafting blessings upon the queen's sleeping grandfather. The ghost of King Henry VI rises and says to Richard, "Harry the Sixth bids thee despair and die." But to Richmond the ghost says, "Virtuous and holy, be thou conqueror." Other ghosts exalt the Tudor family, while the spirits of the two slain princes of the Tower give this comforting advice to Richmond:

> Live, and beget a happy race of kings!
> Edward's unhappy sons do bid thee flourish.

As for England, Shakespeare's "sceptered isle," he speaks of it as "This blessed spot, this earth, this realm, this England"; and again, in *King John*:

> This England never did, nor never shall,
> Lie at the proud foot of a conqueror.

# The Glorious Age

The Elizabethans were fond of the countryside and of sport, and from Shakespeare's numerous allusions to all kinds of animals certain flattering critics have made him out a great naturalist. This is absurd; for he was a literary man, not a scientific observer of nature. He knew his little rivers that "make sweet music with th' enameled stones." Flowers delighted him,—"Where honeysuckle ripened by the sun,"—and he was also familiar with those two standard forms of sixteenth-century sport, the chase and falconry. "Poor dappled fools" he calls the deer in the Forest of Arden; and again: "Sweep on, you fat and greasy citizens!" as the herd dashes by the injured buck. Over and over again there is mention of falconry, as when Juliet says,

> Hist! Romeo, Hist! O for a falc'ner's voice
> To lure this tassel-gentle back again!

Society in the days of Elizabeth was essentially aristocratic. Mutterings there were in Parliament which became louder in the future; but there was no talk of democracy in Shakespeare's day. Common folk were seldom introduced into his plays, and when they were it was done as a foil or background. His crowds and mobs either were ludicrous or else, as in *Julius Caesar*, they smelled vilely. Clownish characters were now and then described—a drunken porter, Bottom the weaver, Dogberry the constable, and a miscellaneous crew of tapsters and bawds; but Shakespeare had no particular affection for them. His art, his admiration, and his love were reserved for those of higher degree—queens, kings, dukes, and gentlemen.

The most striking way in which Shakespeare reflected Elizabethan England was in the men and women he created. Whatever else may be said of them, they are most distinctly nonmedieval. They do not live according to rules, nor are they restricted by any system of morality, but each, following his or her own natural bent, becomes an individual, not a type. There seems really to have been something in the old grandiloquent definition of the Renaissance as "the self-attainment of the inborn freedom of spirit of the human soul"—at least as applied to the magnificent free lances who crowd the pages of Shakespeare.

Whether or not he was a religious man has been hotly disputed. As Hazlitt writes, "he was in one sense the least moral of all writers; for morality (commonly so-called) is made up of antipathies; and his talent consisted in sympathy with human nature in all its shapes, degrees, depressions and elevations." Even morality in the sense of righteousness does not apparently concern Shakespeare. He displays no interest in ethical standards and codes as such. Both he and the creatures of his imagination cleave fast to their individualism with extraordinary tenacity.

To a considerable degree this was a characteristic of his time. The old standards had faded into dust; the new standards were not yet established. The Renaissance had proved a disruptive force, and the Reformation was as yet too recent to have established its mastery. Historic Christianity seemingly lay dead in England, and Puritanism as yet was only in chrysalis. There was no bourgeois, or middle-class, morality such as the nineteenth century would see. On the other hand, feudalism had made its exit. England, from the point of view of intellectual and psychological freedom, was perhaps freer than ever before in her history, or ever since. To some degree this may account for the superb vitality and striking individualism of Shakespeare's men and women.

As in regard to religion, so in regard to the relative ranking of Shakespeare's plays and of his characters. The critics do not agree; nor do other people. Upon the whole, however, those who fancy tragedy as the higher form of art are apt to select *Othello* or *Hamlet* or *Macbeth*, while those who prefer comedy perhaps take more delight in a character like Falstaff, who reappears in several of the plays. Pompous, vain, egotistical, hilarious Sir John Falstaff! No greater liar ever lived, or more zestful person. First using him in the historical plays named for the Lancastrian Henry IV, even Shakespeare could not get rid of him; he banished his hero from court, killed him, and then brought him back to life in *The Merry Wives of Windsor*, written (according to tradition) especially for Queen Elizabeth, and played before her not long before she died.

Shakespeare, of course, was not the only Elizabethan writer of distinction. Marlowe was an eminent playwright from whom Shakespeare borrowed much. Spenser, considered purely as a poet, takes equal rank with Shakespeare; and Francis Bacon, as a philosophical writer, may be considered Shakespeare's peer, and as a scientist unquestionably his superior. But none of these men can justly contest Shakespeare's right to be considered the representative Elizabethan man of letters.

In addition, he is far more. He belongs to the ages and to the world,—at least to the Anglo-Teutonic world. The French have ever been a little dubious concerning his greatness; but the Germans have no such doubts. Shakespeare's dramas have been as frequently on the boards at Berlin as in New York or London, and Shakespeare himself may well be thought of as the dramatic god of

# The Glorious Age

northern peoples. The finest tribute ever paid him, and the one in which he, personally, would most rejoice, may be found in the writings of Professor Walter Raleigh of Oxford, who says of Shakespeare, "He too learned that in the duel with Fate man is not the hunter, but the game, and that a losing match nobly played is his only possible victory."

Shakespeare was to live on beyond his queen and to write his major tragedies after her death. By the end of the sixteenth century most of the great Elizabethans had gone to the grave. Drake, Hawkins, and Frobisher all died within a single year; Walsingham too was dead. The following year, 1598, saw the death of Philip II and of Cecil, Lord Burghley, who had guided the ship of state so shrewdly for forty years. Part of his skill survived in his son and successor, the hunchbacked Robert, first earl of Salisbury; but of the original group closely associated with the queen scarcely one lived on past the turn of the century. Active, imperious, and tactful to the end, Elizabeth remained mistress of England until death took her, at seventy, on a March morning in 1603 at Richmond. Considering with what she started and what she accomplished, her forty-five years on the throne well deserve the title of "the Golden Age."

# CHAPTER XII

## *Commons and Colonies*

### 1603-1629

O N A Saturday evening late in March, 1603, a young English
courtier galloped into the courtyard of Holyrood Palace at
Edinburgh. By wearing out successive relays of horses in dashing
up the Great North Road at the rate of one hundred and sixty miles
a day he had established a speed record between the English and
Scottish capitals. There was reason for haste. Elizabeth had died
on Thursday, and James VI of Scotland was awaiting with quite
improper impatience the news that he had become James I of England
(1603–1625). Thirty hours later, official messengers of the Council,
sent by Cecil's son, confirmed the tidings that the English crown was
transferred from the House of Tudor to that of Stuart. England
and Scotland were at last joined under a single crown.

At the end of the Elizabethan Era, England was to find herself
involved in a century of civil difficulties and overseas expansion
which were eventually to set her far in advance of her neighbors.
The long-drawn-out conflict between Parliament and the four Stuart
kings, based on money and religious difficulties, was to transform
England into the first modern constitutional monarchy, with the
House of Commons, not the king, the real ruler. The disturbances
brought about by this Parliamentary conflict were to give impetus
to the planting on the Atlantic coast of North America of some of
the sturdiest colonies any nation has ever owned. Ever since the
Norman Conquest, England had been drawn into Continental problems and had developed, despite her insular peculiarities, on the
same general pattern as the rest of western Europe. Now she was
to turn in the opposite direction. In a period which has been called
"the Age of Absolutism" in Continental history, a time when royal
autocracy was reaching its height in the chief European countries,
the English Parliament was to force the crown to submit to its
domination.

Immersed as she was in her particular home problems, England
showed less interest than usual in foreign affairs. France, with
the slogan of "The king first in France; France first in Europe!"
easily forged ahead to front rank on the Continent. The Holy

Roman Empire was nearly wrecked by the prolonged devastation of its politico-religious conflict the Thirty Years' War (1618–1648). Holland and Sweden rose to temporary prominence out of all proportion to their natural capacities. Spain continued to decline from the proud position she had enjoyed before the Armada. France, however, was to sweep along unhindered in her "glorious age" only until England had put her house finally in order on a new constitutional basis; then England was to turn her attention to the humbling of the absolutist French king.

A nightmare had haunted England for many years before Elizabeth died—the question "Who will follow her?" The virgin queen had disliked any talk of her successor and had consistently refused to name one until finally, on her death bed, she is said to have mentioned Mary Stuart's son, James VI of Scotland. He had been commonly considered the logical heir, but there were other legitimate claimants. According to Henry VIII's last Act of Succession, Edward Seymour, Lord Beauchamp, the descendant of Henry's younger sister, Mary, the grandmother of Lady Jane Grey, was favored over the descendants of Henry's older sister Margaret, who had married the king of Scotland in 1503, an exact century before Elizabeth's death. In this latter line, which Henry had probably set aside because it was Scottish, were the thirty-seven-year-old James, king since babyhood, when his mother abdicated the throne, and the unfortunate Arabella Stuart, who, like Darnley, was descended from Margaret's second marriage. When the crucial moment came, however, King James, as he and most others had anticipated, succeeded Elizabeth without disturbance. Robert Cecil, the son of Lord Burghley (who had established Elizabeth upon the throne), proceeded to do a similar service for James.

To serve as Elizabeth's successor was enough to tax the ability of the cleverest and most magnetic person; but in place of such there came to England a singularly unattractive, pudgy, and pedantic Scot. That this uncouth James, with his driveling mouth and overlarge tongue, should have been the true son of the fascinating Mary Stuart and the handsome Lord Darnley seems almost incredible, despite the surprising tricks of inheritance. James was stupid in everyday matters and in many affairs of state, but was learned otherwise. In some ways, such as his desire for peace, his views were ahead of his time; but he was on the whole merely an uninteresting storehouse of facts and theories, with an overweening confidence in his own infallibility. One thing, the King James version of the Bible, did result from his interest in learning; but a contemporary French minister called him the "wisest fool in Christendom," and that about sums up James. Despite his books and writings, and occasional displays of wit, the king seemed incapable of sensible action. Through tactlessness and petty insistence on details he alienated that public opinion which the able Tudors had known how to cajole. On his initial triumphal ride into his new realm, for instance, he showed his inability to understand the long-established English system of justice when, in a self-righteous display of swift retribution for evildoing, he ordered the immediate hanging, without trial, of a pickpocket caught red-handed. In addition to this unfortunate tendency to do the right thing always at the wrong time, James displayed a cowardice and timidity that scarcely inspired respect.

Handicapped as he was by background and character for English leadership, James faced, in a country apparently tranquil and well disposed, a very difficult situation. Ever since the Armada's defeat, the new feeling of security and self-confidence in England was producing a quiet but increasing hostility to strong royal power, which was beginning to seem irksome and unnecessary. The Tudor family had brought law and order to an England torn by civil strife, and its virtual despotism had seemed a safeguard against civil bloodshed and foreign invasion. The people, however, had forgotten the trying years of chaos; the Scots were now harmless and the Spaniards no longer terrifying, while the exactions of royal control became constantly more wearisome. Respect and loyalty for Elizabeth had kept most of this discontent beneath the surface until now.

— To make matters worse, both James and his son Charles talked too much about their rights. One of James's strongest beliefs, and one on which he based his whole theory of kingship, was the belief in the "divine right of kings." God, according to that theory, had placed the monarch on the throne, to rule as his viceroy; and anyone who disobeyed or crossed the king's slightest wish was thus deliberately acting against God himself. This theory was by no means original with James; it was held generally by royalty in that period and was, on the whole, accepted placidly by their subjects. James and his son, by stressing the principle overmuch, were to assist in launching England upon its peculiar seventeenth-century experimentation with limited monarchy. The Tudors had acted upon the principle of divine right, but they had not brought the matter up for discussion. They had received due respect without demanding it. They had been despotic enough; but the two Henrys and Elizabeth were statesmen of note, while outside circumstances had helped to explain the shortcomings under Edward and Mary. The three able Tudors had got what they wanted, but they had kept the surface tranquil and had not unnecessarily irritated the country. They had understood the English mind, and consequently the people had reacted to any tune they chose to play. At the same time, they had respected Parliament as a body with a definite and not unimportant place in the state. James, on the other hand, ignored Parliament's powers and privileges, as his family had long treated its Scottish counterpart; and he alienated one group after another by his stubborn, didactic manner and his bullheaded insistence upon the slightest detail. By overstressing their rights the Stuarts were to cause much trouble for England in this century; but they perhaps saved her from the bloodier revolutions which the Continent later experienced by pushing her, ahead of the times, along the road toward modern democracy.

Even as James came to the throne there was a slight flurry of plots; but they did not reach a serious stage, for Englishmen as a whole were deeply relieved that the dreaded day of Elizabeth's death had come and gone with so little commotion. A so-called "Main Plot" was hatched by Raleigh and some others, to get rid of the younger Cecil because he wanted to end the Spanish war, and the plans even extended to placing Arabella Stuart upon the throne. Closely following upon this, in the same first year of the reign, came the "By-Plot" of certain Roman Catholics to seize James and thus be sure of getting rid of Elizabethan laws against their religion. The net results of all this were a few beheadings and the twelve-year imprisonment of the versatile and illustrious Raleigh. The Catholics, further disappointed at not receiving the favors they had expected from the son of Catholic Mary Stuart, went further. In 1605 a group planned to blow up not only the king but also both houses of Parliament. A gentleman from Warwickshire was leader of the plot; but when one of the conspirators, conscience-stricken or frightened, gave away a clue, it was one Guy Fawkes, a former soldier, who was found with the kegs of powder under the House of Lords. His name has been attached to the "Gunpowder Plot," and November fifth has since been celebrated as a holiday, "Guy Fawkes Day." Catholics in England were now in more disfavor than ever, and the penal code against them was stiffened.

The Puritan element, strong in the House of Commons, expected as much from a king from Calvinistic Scotland as had the Catholics from the son of Mary Stuart. The Elizabethan compromise had been a master stroke because of the number of people it satisfied; but the extreme Protestants on the one side and the inflexible Catholics on the other had been overruled minorities. Throughout Elizabeth's reign both of these factions had remained quiet, though since the Armada they had grumbled more and more audibly. Both groups hoped for recognition from James, and both were to be disappointed.

The nickname "Puritan" had been applied by an archbishop in Elizabeth's reign rather indiscriminately to those left-wing Protestants within the Church of England who demanded simpler church rites and a more Calvinistic theology. The early Puritans grew steadily more radical, became known as "forward" or "advanced" Puritans, regarded bishops with dislike, and, as a whole, generally favored a Presbyterian form of church government. Some of them even became "Separatists," desiring to break with the Church of England. Of the latter a few, called Brownists, set up independent meetings of their own and adopted a Congregationalist form of government, which made the individual congregation an independent unit and even did without the presbyteries. (The presbytery familiar in Presbyterian Scotland was a body composed of both clergy and laymen, governing a certain number of congregations—the Calvinist substitute for the bishop and his diocese.) The Elizabethan Act of Uniformity had kept these extremists either quiet or in hiding. Upon James's accession they proceeded immediately to present the monarch with the "Millenary Petition," named for its supposed signatures of one thousand clergymen, but actually signed by only eight hundred.

The petition was mild enough, but trouble came from it. The king invited the signers to a conference in 1604 at Hampton Court. There was mention of the word "presbytery" which enraged James. Shouting "no bishop, no king," he threatened to harry out of the land all who did not conform to the Established Church. Nothing good resulted from the conference except the King James version of the Holy Scriptures, which for more than three hundred years has been the standard translation of the Bible into the English language. From now on, the Puritans, in many instances wealthy and influential, were to be counted as foes of the king.

James, with all his learning, had neglected to master the significance of the position of Parliament in England. The Scottish Parliament was simply a "court of record," which amounted to little, and the first Stuart failed thoroughly to appreciate the prestige which the English body had accumulated in its three centuries of existence. Exactly two months after he had so violently rebuffed the Puritans at Hampton Court, he again came face to face with Puritans in large numbers when he met his first House of Commons. That first session of 1604 heard the opening guns of the eighty-four-year fight between the Stuart kings and their Parliaments,—a stubborn fight, with varying fortunes, until in 1688, with victorious Parliament in full control, the grandson of James had to flee the country.

Underlying all the particular disputes which marked that long contest was the question of sovereignty. With which side, king or

# Commons and Colonies

Parliament, lay the last word? On that point the unwritten English constitution was characteristically hazy. Both the undefined "prerogatives" of the king and the "rights and liberties" of Parliament might be stretched by the interested side. This was the first time that the rival forces had met openly to settle the issue. In earlier periods there had not been any well-established ascendancy of Parliament over king or of king over Parliament. A satisfactory compromise, dividing sovereignty between the two, was apparently inconsistent with efficient government. With each side vigorously seeking supreme power, a "showdown" was necessary; and it took Parliament nearly the whole seventeenth century to secure victory.

Before resorting to sword and musket in the 1640's, the rivals turned to history for their weapons. Historical research flourished as never before in England when Parliamentary lawyers and royal officials searched musty records to find precedents which could be stretched or twisted to give an aspect of legality to their claims. This search for precedents was natural in a nation accustomed to the procedure of the common law. Parliament, on the whole, had to hunt farther back in history than did the royalists. Magna Carta, which was not even mentioned by Shakespeare when he wrote his *King John*, was dragged from oblivion and set up as a precedent for Parliamentary claims. The Commons could draw heavily upon the experiences of the fourteenth century and the Lancastrian period of the fifteenth, when Parliamentary influence was strong (see page 198). The century and a half of Yorkist and Tudor rule, however, had added little to the increase of Parliamentary power; in fact, Parliament had been fortunate to survive those absolutist tendencies. It had at least been preserved as a matter of form, and at the same time, under the Tudors, had evolved highly effective methods of procedure, such as the committee system. Moreover, the crown had had to take its potential opposition into account; but, for the most part, Parliament had been quite complaisant in agreeing with the will of the ruler.

In Parliament's earlier periods of importance the House of Lords had tended to overshadow the Commons. From 1604 onward, however, the story of Parliament is largely that of the burgesses and knights of the shire rather than of the Lords Spiritual and Temporal. The Upper House had changed in complexion during the Tudor period. The first Parliament of Henry VII had contained two archbishops, nineteen bishops, twenty-eight abbots, and only twenty-nine lay peers. The dissolution of the monasteries, as we have seen, by removing the abbots, gave the Lords Temporal a majority which they have since maintained (see page 270). The first Stuart Parlia-

[ 313 ]

ment had eighty-two lay peers and twenty-six bishops. This Upper House was to play only a minor role in the ensuing struggle. The House of Commons had nearly five hundred members, of whom about four hundred represented boroughs. The bulk of its membership, however, was composed of country gentry; for it was no longer the custom to require a member of Parliament to reside in the constituency which he represented, and, while the boroughs occasionally sent up some of their own merchants or town officials, they were more apt to choose a substantial squire. Another group, however, influential out of all proportion to its numbers, was the lawyers, whose training and technique were all-important for leadership in the work at hand.

Theoretically, the House of Commons perhaps represented all Englishmen and Welshmen, but in practice the franchise was in the hands of a relatively small part of the population. Such public opinion as there was, however lacking in uniformity or logic the basis of franchise may have been, filled the Stuart Lower House with a majority of strong, sober men of Puritan persuasion. Unlike the Commons of the next century, they did not seek seats in order to enrich themselves or their relatives and friends at the public expense. In most cases the members of those early Stuart Parliaments had little to gain personally. It was a strong indication of the politico-religious temper of the Puritan element that that sturdy group, which might have remained comfortably at home, was ready to incur the inconveniences, and even the threat to its liberty and property, which accompanied membership in Parliament.

In 1604 no definitely established rules existed about the particular rights and immunities of members of Parliament nor the frequency of Parliamentary elections and sessions. Part of Parliament's work during the century was to put these matters on a definite basis. In the matter of personal liberties there were questions of freedom of speech in Parliament, freedom from arrest for members, and the right of Parliament to determine the qualification of its members in cases of disputed elections. As for the frequency of elections and sessions, all depended upon the king. He called Parliament only when circumstances forced him. When he had what he wanted, or ran into too stubborn opposition, he might either prorogue that same Parliament for a later session or he might dissolve it completely so that a new House of Commons would have to be elected. James had four separate Parliaments during his reign. The first met in 1604, and held five sessions before it was dissolved in 1611. Then the king went ten years without Parliamentary co-operation; for the "Addled Parliament" of 1614 was dissolved in two months without passing

# Commons and Colonies

an act or voting a penny. The third Parliament, called in 1621, ended its career after two stormy sessions. The fourth and last, in 1624, alone saw king and Commons relatively harmonious.

Linked closely to the Parliamentary situation were the courts of law. The three common-law courts—King's Bench, chiefly for criminal cases; Common Pleas, for private civil suits; and Exchequer, for government financial cases—were all operated upon the basis of precedents which had accumulated since their origin in the Plantagenet period (see page 100). The Court of Chancery, dispensing equity under the chancellor, was more directly under royal control, while the king had even more influence in the special "prerogative" courts, such as Star Chamber and High Commission, which had been established by the Tudors and were given extensive powers unfettered by common-law procedure. The common-law courts were regarded as bulwarks of English liberty, and their judges were supposed to be impartial umpires in cases where the interests of king and subjects might conflict. That role was weakened by the power of the king to dismiss judges at will. The common law found a doughty champion in Sir Edward Coke, Chief Justice of Common Pleas and later of King's Bench. A thoroughly disagreeable person in public and private life, Coke was, nevertheless, remarkably well grounded in the origins of the common law, his one love in life; and he proved a tough fighter in its defense. His chief contention was that the law was superior to the king, whereas James aimed to make the judges agents of royal policy,—"lions under the throne," as Francis Bacon, then his attorney general, expressed it.

The principal key to Parliament's rise to power lay in the king's need for money. Inflated prices seriously affect those who, like the government, depend on fixed incomes; and the influx of Spanish-American silver had increased many items of governmental expenditure while the traditional sources of royal revenue, from the crown lands and the like, remained stationary. Only the customs duties could keep pace with the rising costs because the volume of English commerce increased. Elizabeth had felt the effects of those rising costs, but her rigid economy had kept her budgets well balanced. She had carried England through a highly successful reign, including very grave foreign complications, with an annual income which rarely exceeded £400,000 and frequently fell well below that amount. By her economy she had avoided serious dependence upon Parliament, although she left her successor saddled with a considerable debt. James, however, in spite of occasional instances of thrift, generally threw Elizabethan parsimony to the winds. Anomalous as it may sound for a Scot, he spent like a drunken sailor. In the years of waiting in his barren, impoverished kingdom, he had looked forward eagerly to the day when he should have plenty of money. The wealth of England had impressed Scottish envy just as the wealth of Spain had incited English envy. James was not long on the throne before the regular expenditures jumped to £600,000 a year, even with peace, while income lagged about £150,000 in the rear. A court which was faster and coarser, but less clever, than Elizabeth's helped to account for this unbalanced budget. There were three ways to deal with the constantly mounting debt. One was economy, which James generally failed to practice; a second was dependence upon the hostile Puritans of the House of Commons; and the third was the collecting of money by novel methods beyond Parliament's control. Some of the most energetic work of the Stuart Parliaments lay in their efforts to shut off such outside sources of revenue by which the king might escape from their control.

With these general considerations in mind, we may turn to the narrative of the long encounter. The first clash arose over the question of deciding the qualification of members of the House of Commons in cases of disputed elections. The king had directed that such cases should be referred to the Court of Chancery, but the Commons won the right to settle them themselves. In the course of the dispute, rival views of the status of the Commons were exchanged. The king told the Commons that they "derived all matters of privilege from him and by his grant." They replied that their "privileges and liberties are of right and due inheritance no less than our very lands and goods," and that "they cannot be withheld from us, denied, or impaired, but with apparent wrong to the whole state of the realm."

A cargo of currants from the eastern Mediterranean was the innocent cause of the next encounter. James tried to increase his revenue without Parliament's consent by boosting the customs duties. Like his predecessors, James had received at the beginning of his reign a life grant of "tunnage and poundage," or customs duties, at the regular specified rates. In 1606 he "imposed" an additional duty on currants. John Bate, a merchant in trade with Turkey, carried the case to the Exchequer Court. The judges went out of their way to give James a favorable decision, citing Tudor precedents to demonstrate that the king had full powers in matters of regulation of trade. Thereupon James had a new "Book of Rates" drawn up, increasing the duties on all manner of imports, at a decided advantage to the royal revenue. The House of Commons, aroused to the danger of this flank attack upon its control of the purse, passed a bill against impositions; but it was killed by the Lords, and James continued to collect his increased duties throughout the reign.

# Commons and Colonies

James was trying to do without Parliament not only in the collection of money but also in the making of laws. Henry VIII had been empowered to issue, through his Council, proclamations which had the force of law. Such proclamations, like the earlier ordinances (see page 148), could be—as they still are—a useful and necessary device to meet temporary emergencies, especially at times when Parliament was not in session. If the practice were carried to extremes, however, these royal proclamations might supplant Parliamentary statutes as the law of the land. James showed a tendency in that direction, particularly in defining new offenses which were to be tried in the "prerogative" courts of High Commission or Star Chamber. This brought the House of Commons and the common-law courts into joint opposition to a practice which threatened to injure them both. Coke and three eminent colleagues, when summoned before the Council, boldly stated that the king had no right to create any new offenses by proclamation, and declared that the king had no prerogative but what the law of the land allowed him. This alliance between the Commons and the judges helped to check the threatening practice for some time.

James's first Parliament had thus come into conflict with him on several points during its five sessions between 1604 and 1611. The second Parliament, called in 1614, was dissolved after two stormy months of deadlock. It declared that the king had no right to impose taxes without Parliamentary consent, and it refused to give the king a money grant before discussing its grievances. James consequently dissolved it and sent four members of the Commons to the Tower.

There was no meeting of Parliament now for seven years, nearly a third of the reign. James began in earnest the practice which his son was to carry still further under similar circumstances—the scraping together of money from every possible source in order to keep the government running without Parliament. "Benevolences," or supposedly voluntary contributions, and forced loans were exacted from prosperous individuals, who had little hope of ever seeing their money again. One man, who used strong language of protest in declining to contribute, was sent to the Tower. Altogether, less than £43,000 was raised in three years by this method. Old debts and fines were collected with relentless vigor. Titles were shamelessly put up for sale. One might become a peer, with a seat in the House of Lords, for £10,000, and a new title of hereditary knighthood, baronet, was invented and put on sale at £1000.

In 1616, the year of Shakespeare's death, James struck a powerful blow at the independence of the common-law courts by removing Chief Justice Coke. With Parliament in abeyance, these courts alone were in a position to offer official resistance to the royal policy, by means of decisions which might arise in various sorts of cases. Coke twice strongly resisted the efforts of the king to interfere in trials while these were in progress. He was consequently dismissed; but he was soon to continue his opposition to James from the floor of the Commons. As long as the judges held precarious office, dependent upon royal pleasure rather than upon good behavior, the common-law courts lost their independence. Other chief justices were removed during the Stuart period; but the common-law courts were not perverted as much as they might have been, because the crown preferred to divert cases to Star Chamber and other prerogative courts which were unhampered by past precedents.

If the king could get rid of a chief justice, Parliament could strike back by removing his chancellor. The foreign situation, which will be considered later, made it necessary to summon a Parliament which assembled at Westminster in a loyal and friendly mood. Friction quickly developed, however, and Parliament dragged out the weapon of impeachment, which had been in disuse since the reign of Henry VI (see page 199). A verdict of guilty might simply involve dismissal; so impeachment was less cruel than the favorite Tudor weapon of the bill of attainder, whereby Parliament might vote a man to death without regular trial. The first victims of the revived impeachment were two courtiers who had abused their grants of monopoly, which seemed unjustifiable in the eyes of Parliament. Then, in 1621, the blow fell on the chancellor. This was no less a man than Francis Bacon, the greatest English intellect of his day. Scientist, philosopher, essayist, lawyer, and statesman, Bacon is still believed by some to have written the plays attributed to Shakespeare. He had served as attorney general before his promotion to the chancellorship. Earlier in that same year of his impeachment Bacon had reached the pinnacle of his success with the publication of his scientific theories in the *Novum Organum* and elevation to the peerage as Viscount St. Albans. Like the friar Roger Bacon, in the thirteenth century, he insisted on observation as the foundation of scientific method; and he exercised a wide influence through his writings, notably his *Essays* and the *Advancement of Learning* besides the *Novum Organum*. Later generations have hailed his important pioneer work in arguing for the inductive scientific method; but this work was over the heads of most Englishmen, including the learned James, who said that it resembled the peace of God, which "passeth all understanding." The House of Commons saw in Bacon not the scientist but the royal henchman, and it impeached him for the not uncommon practice of receiving bribes while in office. The Lords found him guilty, and he fell from office. Three years later, impeachment was likewise to remove the Lord Treasurer.

The Parliament of 1621 also ventured into the sphere of foreign relations, where the precedents for its interference were less certain. Relations with Spain and the situation in Germany, as we shall see, were becoming complicated, and the king wanted £900,000 from Parliament, which, however, gave him only £80,000 and tried to give him advice against a Catholic Spanish marriage for his son. Elizabeth, when repeated Parliaments had tried to give her similar advice, had rejected it, but had cleverly smoothed the ruffled feelings of the Houses. James, instead, bluntly told the Commons not to meddle in the mysteries of state, whereof they were ignorant. Parliamentary control over foreign relations has always been a ticklish matter; for any government is loath to reveal, for public discussion, the progress of delicate negotiations. The sturdy squires, to be sure, were quite unversed in the "deep matters of state"; but they answered the king in an outspoken "protestation," reaffirming their privileges and liberties as hereditary rights, and declaring that "the arduous and urgent affairs concerning the king, state and defense of the realm, and of the Church of England . . . are proper subjects and matter of counsel and debate in Parliament." James at once prorogued that body. As soon as the Christmas celebrations were over, he sent for the journals of the Commons and, in the presence of his Council, with his own hands tore out the page with that offensive protestation. As in 1614, several members of the Commons were sent to the Tower, and Parliament was soon dissolved.

The fourth Parliament, in 1624, was more harmonious. It approved of the foreign policy of the moment and gave James £300,000 of the £800,000 he requested. It passed an act against the practice of granting monopolies, which had caused dissatisfaction since the later days of Elizabeth. There was no objection to granting an inventor a monopoly of the sale of his invention for a period of years, but when courtiers received monopolies of the sale of common commodities, such as soap, glass, or coal, in which they did little if anything to stimulate trade, the practice resulted in an unjustifiable tax on the consumer. The impeachment practice, as we have seen, had first been revived in 1621 to punish two men who had abused the inn-licensing monopoly.

That act was the sole piece of constructive legislation resulting from the four Parliaments of the reign. Their importance lay in their defining the points of resistance to the Stuart claims of divine-right absolutism and in paving the way for the more bitter contests of the next reign.

# A History of England and the British Empire

One of the unfortunate tendencies of the first Stuarts was strong dependence upon favorite courtiers, and, unlike Elizabeth's, their choice was generally bad. It was said that any good-looking young man, preferably with a Scottish burr, might go far with James. The gifts lavished upon such favorites did not help the financial situation of this Scottish monarch, so surprisingly thriftless now that he was far from home. At first Lord Salisbury, the younger Cecil, acted as a check upon many of James's foolish tendencies. At Salisbury's death, in 1612, however, James raised to his highest favor a young Scot, Robert Carr, the future earl of Somerset, for his handsome face, it was said, since certainly he had no other qualifications. A scandal soon ended the sway of this first favorite, who fell in love with the Countess of Essex, married her after a divorce which James had ordered the court to grant unfairly, and then was tried, together with his wife, for the murder of a man who threatened blackmail in connection with the divorce proceedings. James, it must be admitted, did nothing to help this pair of favorites beyond sparing them the death penalty after a much publicized trial which advertised, and perhaps exaggerated, the scandals of the court.

There was also the young and good-looking George Villiers, eventually duke of Buckingham, more able than Somerset and exceedingly charming, but one who did not leaven his ambitious ideas with common sense. Rising with extraordinary rapidity under the favor of James, he was the dominant figure in English policy, both foreign and domestic, until his murder early in the next reign. It was unfortunate that James should have taken advice from such a man when he had available the brilliant intellect of Francis Bacon, but Bacon was not the type to have influence with this king.

In foreign affairs James was essentially a pacifist. He gave England peace throughout his entire twenty-two-year reign except for the first year (until the war inherited from Elizabeth could be stopped) and the last year, when Buckingham led the country into a series of mad adventures. James's foreign policy had some strange and unpopular features; but his pacifism, a unique phenomenon, brought the country a more genuine peace than the quarter century of quasi-war under Elizabeth and the elder Cecil.

As far as Scotland was concerned, James brought up the matter of union with England as soon as he came to the throne; but Parliament, perhaps fearing that the wealth of the southern kingdom might be used to relieve the poverty of Scotland, was not even interested in naturalizing Scots as English subjects. A court later ruled that Scots born after 1603—the *postnati*—might enjoy English status; but, except for that, James found that he could not go beyond

# Commons and Colonies

the loose personal union which his accession had brought about. This at least made England more secure by removing the danger of border raids and the old alliances between France and Scotland. It was not until 1707, a full century later, that England and Scotland were to be actually united in the kingdom of Great Britain, with a common Parliament.

England was still engaged in the Spanish war which had opened in the fifteen eighties, but the leaders at court were divided on the advisability of continuing it. Raleigh and other surviving adventurers of the glorious days were determined to humiliate Spain still further, but Salisbury (Cecil) and others were in favor of peace. After Raleigh's arrest following the "Main Plot," Cecil, with the king's support, was the victor, and peace was made.

The Spanish peace was not particularly acceptable to Parliament, but it was even more unpalatable to the seafaring elements of the nation. James alone of the Stuart kings utterly neglected the navy, England's pride for thirty years. The maritime communities consequently smoldered with hostility, which was later to injure the Stuarts when they most needed friends. England no longer insisted that its flag be saluted in home waters, while pirates from the Barbary coast of northern Africa raided ships and towns with impunity. James himself was to find that the degeneration in naval power was to prove costly to the nation's international prestige; for the fact that England was no longer to be feared at sea nullified most of his diplomatic gestures. For those twenty years, however, James did keep his country at peace, though he had what his subjects considered an unfortunate leaning toward Spanish, or at any rate Catholic, alliances. To be sure, as an eminent historian has pointed out, the peace with Spain allowed England to carry out her unique seventeenth-century internal development; for a long war would have strengthened the royal power, kept colonists at home, and drained the nation's resources. Nevertheless, James's policy ran counter to the wishes of his people and of Parliament, and his playing the diplomat made England a joke on the Continent for some time to come.

The long peace brought one strange result. Count Gondomar, a very brilliant grandee, Spanish ambassador to England, was for years one of the most influential men at court. He intrigued James by the tantalizing suggestion of a Spanish infanta for a daughter-in-law, an idea which appealed strongly to the king, while Gondomar himself kept his keen eye upon the prospect of a re-Catholicized England. As a result of his partisanship, life was made easier for the English Catholics, who had suffered severely from the penal code since the Gunpowder Plot. This leniency would have galled the Protestant Englishmen anyway; but Gondomar's presence at court was emphasized by the spectacle of a hundred priests released from prison to escort him on a trip to Spain. The hostile populace retaliated by several angry anti-Catholic demonstrations. The French embassy, hitherto always favored over the Spanish, was no more pleased than were most Englishmen by the spectacle of the haughty grandee strutting about the English court as though he were chief minister, only thirty years after Drake had battered the Armada.

The most spectacular display of Gondomar's power was the execution of Raleigh in 1618. With the fall of Somerset, who had been completely the tool of Gondomar, those who hated Spain as of old seized the chance to precipitate trouble. James was persuaded to release Raleigh for an expedition to seek gold in Guiana. Sent out with strict orders not to fight the Spaniards in that Spanish-infested quarter of the world, and with thoroughly inadequate equipment, Raleigh was to return a beaten man, with no gold. Unavoidably, it would appear, he had attacked a Spanish settlement. The old Elizabethan hero, the hard hater of Spain, was sent to the block by James on an old and ridiculous charge of treasonable relations with that country; and this at the insistence of Gondomar, who was threatening war. Such was the fate of one who had outlived his generation.

In the year of Raleigh's execution the beginning of a long war in Germany further complicated James's already confused foreign policy. Trouble had been brewing in the Germanies since the Protestant Revolt. By a compromise in 1555, permission had been granted the rulers of the various states within the Holy Roman Empire to choose between Lutheranism and Catholicism, but no recognition had been given to Calvinism. Fermenting during the years of the Counter Reformation and the religious wars elsewhere, the bitterness caused by this incomplete settlement broke out in 1618 in the Thirty Years' War, a bloody and devastating conflict which has been called the last of the religious and the first of the political wars. It began when James's son-in-law, a Calvinist prince of the Rhineland, Elector of the Palatinate, accepted the crown of Bohemia in defiance of the traditional rights of the Catholic Holy Roman emperor. This "Winter King" was quickly deposed; and by 1629, four years after James's death, the Catholic imperialists were fully victorious, despite the intervention of Denmark and England. Then Protestant Sweden quickly and permanently turned the tide under her famous king, the "Father of Modern Warfare," Gustavus Adolphus. Politics now definitely overshadowed religion as a war motive; for France, under her two great Catholic cardinal-ministers, Richelieu and Mazarin,

# Commons and Colonies

entering the war on the Protestant side because of French hostility to the Hapsburgs, helped to consolidate Protestant victories and to smash the surrounding ring of Catholic Hapsburg territory. The Spanish Hapsburgs naturally sided with the German Hapsburgs. The war was to end in 1648 with (among other results) France powerful and Holland free, while most of the Germanies were so devastated that it took them a full century to recover.

Elizabeth, the daughter of James, had been married to Frederick of the Palatinate in 1613. That marriage was of subsequent importance, because in 1714 England was to call their German Protestant grandson to the throne as the first of the Hanoverians. For the time being, the match tended to draw England into the war. Protestant England was interested anyway, while James, despite his normal pacifism, had too much family interest to stand aloof. The situation became very complicated when a Spanish invasion threatened to cost Frederick his own territory, the Palatinate. In 1621 it looked as though king and Parliament for once had something upon which they could agree—saving the Palatinate from Spain. Gondomar was in a difficult position; but he met it ably, offsetting the threat of war by continued prospects of a Spanish marriage for Prince Charles.

The threatened war against Spain evaporated; but the Spanish marriage remained to plague England. Prince Charles, the proposed husband, was far more attractive than his father, but fully as unreliable and lacking in good sense. His deceased elder brother had rejected such a marriage, as he did not want "two religions in one bed"; but Charles, as much under the Duke of Buckingham's sway as his father, was attracted by Spanish glamour. The thoughtless, impulsive young prince and the duke now thought it would be a clever stroke, as well as good fun, to dash off to Spain incognito, woo the Infanta, and bring her back a bride, without more protracted negotiations. James privately approved the romantic adventure. England was thoroughly discredited by the antics of the irresponsible pair, Spanish decorum was profoundly shocked, and, despite the extravagant concessions of Charles in the matter of Catholicism, it soon became obvious that Spain had no serious intentions, and that the marriage idea was simply bait to keep James in line. The king, lonely at their absence, recalled the two young men, and they returned to find themselves popular heroes, so glad was England to find its prince "still a live man, a Protestant, and a bachelor"!

Buckingham was so entranced with his own popularity that he turned against Spain, begged for war, and obviously fancied himself the Protestant champion of Europe. The breach with Spain was now an accomplished fact. James, unable to stand out against Charles, Buckingham, and the strong popular sentiment, seemed to lose all interest in his country and to let Buckingham manage everything. The king's death in 1625 and the accession of the prince, as Charles I, made scarcely a ripple.

Between 1624 and 1628 Buckingham was in full control, and he dragged England into a mad orgy of war. One enemy was not enough, though England was in no condition to handle even a single foe. Expeditions were dispatched to Spain, to France, and to Germany,— six expeditions in four years, and every one a miserable failure! Years of unpreparedness and neglect told their story. It always has taken England a considerable time to recover from the military stagnation of a long peace; for the Englishman engaged in civilian pursuits is quite unwarlike. There was no rush to arms; press gangs had to recruit by forced draft. Few communities allowed their better men to be rushed from their homes to what, in a time of unpreparedness, meant probable death by starvation or disease, if not on the battlefield. The army was composed of riffraff; the navy had been allowed to decay. England was small, in comparison with France, Spain, and the Hapsburg empire, and her forces did not make up in quantity what they lacked in quality. Under such circumstances Buckingham's schemes, badly conceived and muddled as they were, were foredoomed. The shameful military inadequacy of this generation of the sons of the Elizabethan fighters, however, was to be redeemed by their sons in Cromwellian victories.

The first of those ill-starred ventures, the most shameful failure in English military history, left early in 1625, two months before the death of James. It was England's sole effort at armed intervention in the Thirty Years' War. Count Mansfield, a swashbuckling German freebooter, was sent to free the Palatinate from Spanish control with twelve thousand English troops. But they were the scum of England, untrained, undisciplined, mutinous, and, because of the lack of funds, ill-clothed and ill-fed. France denied them permission to cross her territory, and the poor wretches were unwelcome guests in Holland, where they had landed. By the time James died, that same year, three quarters of them were dead of disease, exposure, and starvation; the remainder melted away without reaching the Palatinate or striking an honest blow. The navy did no better. In 1625 an expedition was sent against the Spanish port of Cádiz, which had twice been successfully raided by the Elizabethan sea dogs under Drake and Raleigh. It was a hopeless venture for the ill-planned, unequipped, untrained force that set sail in rotten ships. It meant another failure for England, with further loss of prestige.

# Commons and Colonies

In the meantime relations with France were complicated. The proposed Spanish marriage had failed; but Charles I had been on the throne barely ten weeks when Buckingham brought over a devoted Catholic bride for him, Henrietta Maria, the fifteen-year-old sister of Louis XIII of France. The duke knew that a French Catholic queen would be almost as distasteful as a Spanish Catholic one to the members of the House of Commons; so the marriage was rushed through before Parliament met. It was no wonder that Charles and his Parliament started badly; for the deliberate defiance in this accomplished fact deepened the disgust at Buckingham's unsuccessful "statecraft."

Charles I was to have much in common with Louis XVI of France and Nicholas II of Russia, who were also to lose their lives at the hands of revolutionary subjects. These three mediocre men might have been able to hold their thrones under normal conditions; but in the crises which arose, their foreign wives, with their stronger characters, urged their weaker husbands into extreme stands, so that they often turned stubborn on the worst possible occasions. All three kings were good family men. Charles and his young queen, to be sure, had many stormy scenes in their early days when the high-spirited girl resented his autocratic tactics.

The friendship with France was short-lived. Buckingham was no match for the astute and masterful Cardinal Richelieu, the real power in the France of Louis XIII. During the marriage negotiations Buckingham had not only committed indiscretions with the queen of France but also made sweeping promises about improving the condition of the English Catholics. Far from living up to them, Charles declared that the agreement was only a formality and dismissed the French Catholic attendants of Henrietta Maria. Further trouble came when eight English vessels, lent to France for an expedition to Italy, were ordered against the seaport of La Rochelle, the chief stronghold of the French Huguenots, which Richelieu was trying to capture. The English crews mutinied rather than fight against Protestants.

Three English expeditions were now sent to La Rochelle; but they were efforts to relieve the Huguenots from the besieging French royal forces. The troubles with France might have been ironed out; but Buckingham and Charles recklessly added Richelieu to the list of their enemies, as though complications with Spain and the Palatinate were not sufficient. In 1627 Buckingham led an expedition, ill-founded as usual, to the Isle of Ré, just off beleaguered La Rochelle. While awaiting naval reinforcements which never came, his poor devils were attacked by the French and most of them were slaughtered. Early in 1628 a naval expedition was sent to La Rochelle; but the energetic Richelieu had barred the approaches by powerful breakwaters, and the English ships returned in disgrace. Later in 1628, just after Parliament had forced upon Charles the Petition of Right, a third expedition was ready to sail under Buckingham to the relief of the Huguenots, whose situation was daily growing worse. The duke was dead when the fleet sailed, for a disgruntled officer had murdered him at Portsmouth. The nation broke into wild rejoicing at the news, while Charles suffered alone in his palace the loss of his best friend. The Huguenots in La Rochelle were finally starved into surrender while the English fleet made a vain demonstration outside the breakwater. Its return to port marked the end of the brief war activity; it was nearly a quarter of a century before England again was to tackle a foreign foe.

Parliament was linked up with these foreign fiascoes. It had been fairly generous with its money grants in 1624, the only relatively harmonious session under the first two Stuarts. At that time it had trusted Buckingham and had approved his activity on behalf of Protestantism abroad. The three Parliaments crowded into the first four years of the new reign displayed, however, a different temper. They no longer trusted Buckingham, who had tricked them with the French marriage. "Our honor is ruined," they said, "our ships are sunk, our men perished, not by the enemy, not by chance, but by those we trust." They had starved Buckingham's expeditions, and then used his failures as a reason for not granting further funds. The very cost of these expeditions threw the king into dependence upon Parliamentary grants. The House of Commons, realizing its strategic position, went much farther than it had in the preliminary sparring under James. By this time able leadership had appeared among the Puritan squires. Foremost among them was Sir John Eliot, a prosperous Cornishman, who was to guide them through their short, stormy sessions and who, as a result, was to die in prison. Prominent also was Sir Thomas Wentworth, who, although a believer in royal authority and no Puritan, strongly opposed Buckingham. He will be heard of later as Lord Strafford, and because of his activity as a royal minister he was finally to meet his death by the vote of the House of Commons he had once guided. Later prominence was in store for three other country squires in those sessions: John Hampden, John Pym, and Oliver Cromwell.

The first two Parliaments of the new reign were short-lived, since they were determined to discuss abuses and grievances before granting the king the money he needed. Charles angrily dissolved the first Parliament after it granted him tunnage and poundage for only one year, whereas all previous rulers for two centuries had received it for life. He dissolved the second with equal promptness after it impeached Buckingham, whom the king loyally defended.

Finding that he could not get money from Parliament without submitting to humiliating terms, Charles tried to collect it as though it had been voted. "Forced loans," equivalent to the amount of a normal grant, were demanded from the nation. The more prosperous men who refused to pay were imprisoned; the poorer were drafted for the army. The general indignation caused by these measures was increased by the plight of the poor fellows forced into military service. The king, short of funds as he was, could not afford to build barracks for them or to put them up at inns. They were consequently billeted upon private homes, which were forced to receive the unwelcome and unruly guests with little prospect of payment. The troops for the most part represented the scum of England, and from many quarters stories drifted in of looting, rape, and other violence. To check disorder, the king authorized martial law, so that officers in courts-martial, which observed few of the common-law practices, could deal out immediate punishment. Cases involving soldiers with civilians came under this martial law, and the latter complained of unfair treatment.

These circumstances influenced the elections for Charles's third Parliament in 1628, and brought to Westminster a House of Commons unusually high in quality and particularly bitter against Buckingham. Foreign complications made a grant of money absolutely essential, and the Commons took advantage of this to force the king to admit the illegality of the recent acts which had caused such widespread indignation. With the precedent of Magna Carta in mind, they drew up a "Petition of Right," which hit directly at the four main grievances—arbitrary taxation, arbitrary imprisonment, billeting, and martial law; for Parliament refused to be satisfied with a general promise of good behavior upon the part of the king. The petition was passed by Commons and Lords and received specific, formal, royal assent. It thus became virtually, if not technically, a regular statute, a valid part of the law of the land. The Petition of Right, like Magna Carta and the later Bill of Rights of 1689, did not deal in vague generalities but was limited chiefly to stated grievances. The protests of Parliament under James had exerted nothing more than moral influence, and the king might maintain that his prerogative power still enabled him to act as before. The Petition of Right, like its two constitutional companions, contained the royal admission that such acts were illegal. Neither Magna Carta nor the Petition of Right prevented the king from continuing his abuses,

# A History of England and the British Empire

but neither John nor Charles could any longer claim that he had a legal right to do so. The king gave his assent on June 7, 1628, and as a reward received a vote of five subsidies, equivalent to about £350,000. Ten weeks later Buckingham was murdered.

By the time Parliament reassembled for its second session, early in 1629, there was further friction with the king, who still continued to collect tunnage and poundage without a grant. He had even seized the goods of a member of the House of Commons, a merchant who refused to pay the duties. The Court of Star Chamber had ordered a man's ears to be cut off. A serious new complication then arose in Archbishop Laud's efforts to introduce High Church features into the Church of England, the beginning of an activity which thoroughly aroused the Puritans and was to lead to grave further complications. By March 2 the temper of Parliament was such that Charles commanded the Speaker to leave his chair if anyone attempted to speak. The House was determined to register a protest before adjournment was thus forced upon it. The doors were locked to prevent anyone from leaving and to keep out the royal official who was pounding for admission. While several members forcibly held the Speaker in his chair, the Commons passed by acclaim three measures drawn up by John Eliot, condemning the new "Papist innovations" in religion and the illegal customs impositions, and declaring anyone a traitor who paid the latter. Then the Commons voted their own adjournment while the royal serjeant still thundered at the door. That was the last sitting of Parliament for eleven years. Nine members were arrested. Eliot, the leader of the Puritan opposition, died in the Tower in 1632, and two others were still imprisoned there when the next Parliament met in 1640.

Just two days after that last stormy sitting of the Commons, Charles granted a charter to "the Governor and Company of Massachusetts Bay in New England" to establish a new Puritan colony in America. England was about to enter upon a remarkable period of colonial expansion; for during the eleven-year "long vacation" of Parliament the number of Englishmen overseas jumped from some nine thousand to more than sixty-five thousand.

England's empire was already well under way before it received this stimulus. Elizabethan propagandists had argued the value of colonies and had made initial experiments; Elizabethan sea dogs had cleared the way for expansion by crippling Spanish sea power. Under James the actual permanent foundations had been laid, both for colonies of exploitation in the East and for colonies of settlement in North America and the West Indies (see page 232). British colonial activity ever since has fallen into these two distinct

[ 328 ]

# Commons and Colonies

categories, represented today, for instance, by India and Canada. Spain, Portugal, France, and Holland, as well as England, established successful colonies of exploitation, where a handful of Europeans went out to dominate a huge native population of yellows, browns, or blacks, while parts of Spanish America were a combination of exploitation and settlement. England, on the other hand, was unique in attaining success with regular colonies of settlement, where family groups left home permanently to set up a fairly normal European society in some region of temperate climate beyond the seas.

Colonial expansion was stimulated by the doctrines of "mercantilism," which were influential among the European maritime nations from the sixteenth century through the eighteenth. Mercantilism taught that a nation should sell more than it bought in dealing with other nations. In other words, to secure a "favorable balance of trade," exports should exceed imports. The earlier mercantilist writers laid stress upon the "bullionist" theory that such a practice would pile up silver and gold in the nation which had a favorable balance. Climatic conditions prevented the European nations from meeting all their economic needs with home products. Colonies, consequently, were considered desirable in order to produce under one's own flag what otherwise would have to be purchased from foreigners. Colonies of exploitation in tropical regions could provide for exotic needs; colonies of settlement in more temperate zones could not only supply further desirable products but also serve as outlets for the surplus manufactures of the mother country.

Three particular types of desirable products were stressed by the early English writers who urged the planting of colonies. First, there were silver and gold, such as Spain was receiving in tempting quantities from Mexico and Peru. Secondly, spices,—pepper, clove, cinnamon, and nutmeg,—which had served as the original impetus for the great explorations a century earlier and had given Portugal a period of prosperity through her monopoly of the spice-growing islands in the Far East. Thirdly, tar, hemp, and other naval materials, for which England was dependent upon Sweden, Russia, and other lands of northern Europe, were essential to a nation's shipping. The English colonies met with no particular success with any of those three types of products, although sugar, tobacco, indigo, tea, and similar materials eventually did much to round out a self-sufficient empire. The Elizabethans had also pointed out that colonies might serve as a dumping ground for what they considered the surplus population of England. The "sturdy beggars" who had prowled around the land through the whole Tudor period gave the impression that there were too many Englishmen, whereas the population was

# A History of England and the British Empire

simply dislocated by enclosures and other economic changes. The wise legislation of Elizabeth's last years had remedied that trouble, as the slow emigration during the reign of James clearly demonstrated. When Englishmen finally began to swarm overseas under Charles, it was not because there were too many at home but because they were too discontented there.

The pioneer colonial empires of Spain and Portugal had been direct royal ventures in which the crown provided the initiative, capital, and control. Elizabeth and the Stuarts were not disposed to take such full responsibility in colonial expansion, and the cost and risks were too great for successful individual initiative. The result was that most of the early English colonization was carried on by private corporations, known as joint-stock companies. A group of individuals would subscribe to shares in a venture, to provide the necessary capital, and would then divide the profits, if any. A half century before successful English colonization got under way, the joint-stock company had been introduced for trading purposes. In 1553 the Muscovy Company was organized for trade with Russia, with a capital of £6000, divided into shares of £25 each. This first company was successful, and others followed in its wake. In 1581 Elizabeth herself contributed £42,000 from her share of Drake's plunder as half the capital of the Levant Company, formed for trade with Turkey and the East. These were established by members of the Merchant Adventurers, who had grown rich and powerful through the export of English woolen cloth (see page 234). Even the voyages of Drake and Hawkins had been temporary ventures of this type, with various individuals contributing shares of capital and receiving dividends from the profits, which were generally bigger than those of most of the later colonizing companies.

The most successful and long-lived of the English joint-stock companies was the East India Company, or, more fully, "the Governor and Company of the Merchants of London Trading into the East Indies," chartered by Elizabeth on December 31, 1600, the last day of the sixteenth century. The charter gave the company a monopoly of trade in the entire East between the Cape of Good Hope and the Strait of Magellan, with full political and military power in such posts as it might establish. It was formed to exploit the rich but rotten colonial empire which Portugal had built up in India and the East Indies. Portugal was temporarily under the Spanish crown at the time, but after the Armada defeat Spain could do no more than protect her own established colonies in America. England had shown a keen curiosity in the East even before the sea lanes were opened. Anthony Jenkinson, traveling for the Muscovy Company, had explored some of the trade routes of central Asia in the fifteen sixties, while Ralph Fitch, at the time of the Armada, was making an overland trip even deeper into the rich eastern region. Shortly afterward an English sea captain was prowling about the Indian Ocean and exploring the Spice Islands.

The chief problem of the East India Company was not so much the ousting of the Portuguese as the rivalry of the Dutch East India Company, formed in 1602. Holland was entering upon a half century of remarkable maritime success, and rushed into the Eastern trade even more vigorously than England. The Dutch, with their ships outnumbering the English at least three to one in the East, finally secured control over the Spice Islands, the richest part of the Portuguese empire. The English shared this with them for a while, but in 1623 the Dutch tortured and put to death the ten Englishmen on the clove island of Amboina. After that the Dutch had the spice monopoly pretty much to themselves.

The English, unable to seize or share the chief center of Eastern riches, contented themselves with commercial operations on the mainland of India. European contact with India at that time and for a century more was restricted to a few little trading posts, called "factories," on the coast. About the time that Elizabeth came to the throne, a powerful Mohammedan invader gained control over most of the peninsula. He and his five successors, known as the "Mogul" emperors, ruled the land from Delhi, and were so strong that the European posts were maintained only by Mogul sufferance. It was not until after the death of the sixth "Great Mogul" in 1707 that European influence could penetrate into the interior.

By 1613, after a successful fight with the Portuguese, the English East India Company set up a "factory" at Surat, on the northwest coast of India. Diplomatic relations with the Great Mogul once established, an extension of privileges was procured, and before long a ship or two returned each year to England with freight worth about £50,000. Except for some pepper from the Malabar Coast, the English could find little in the way of spices. The principal commodities brought from India in those early years were cotton cloth, which gradually replaced the more expensive linen from Germany; indigo, which was useful for dyeing; and saltpeter, an essential ingredient of gunpowder. There were few English goods which India wanted in return; for the climate was too warm for an extensive use of English woolens, so that most of the payment was in silver. The profits of the East India Company showed a marked jump in the latter half of the century, when annual dividends sometimes reached 20 and even 50 per cent, though the English company could not match the dividend record of its Dutch rival, which averaged 18 per cent for two centuries. In the latter years of the seventeenth century the early post at Surat was overshadowed by later establishments, which have ever since remained the "big three" of British India: Bombay, on the western coast; Madras, on the Coromandel Coast (southeast); and Calcutta, in Bengal (northeast). The East India Company was to last as a commercial monopoly until 1833, and as a nominal political authority until 1858. We can leave it temporarily, until the period of its dramatic struggle with France for control over the interior of India after 1740 (see map, p. 461).

While England was gaining a foothold for her colonies of exploitation in India, she was making a more distinctive experiment with colonies of settlement in North America and the West Indies (see map, p. 443). The defeat of the Armada had thrown open not only the Portuguese East but also the temperate seaboard north of Florida.

The efforts to colonize Virginia, which had begun with Raleigh's abortive effort in 1585, were crowned with success in 1607 with the founding of Jamestown, England's first permanent colony. It was a rather sorry beginning. The hundred and five adventurers who were deposited on a malarial peninsula to commence the little town named for their king were not the kind for a colony of settlement. The pioneer group included no women, and the majority were rated as "gentlemen" who hoped for easy and sudden wealth and who had no taste for hard work. Within four months half of the group were dead, and supplies were nearly gone. Instead of planting crops, the colonists exhausted their strength in factional fights and futile searching for gold. For several years Jamestown dragged out a precarious existence, in constant peril from famine, fever, and Indians. Iron discipline on the part of a few strong leaders alone prevented complete failure. Even at that, permanence hung almost on a matter of hours in 1610, when the discouraged colonists, reduced to a handful by a terrible winter of starvation, had started down the river for home, only to meet a fleet with reinforcements from England. Before long the colony found its economic salvation in tobacco. King James had written a "Counter-Blaste" against smoking; but that did not prevent the popularity of the practice, and the ten tons of tobacco shipped to England in 1617 was the beginning of a lucrative business which gave Virginia a definite niche in the self-sufficient empire. Two years later, a Dutch ship landed "twenty Negars." The gradual introduction of Negro slavery, together with the labor of indentured servants who had to work for several years to pay for their passage, eventually enabled the Virginian planters to lead a comfortable existence with a minimum of physical exertion.

# Commons and Colonies

That same year, 1619, saw the first step toward colonial self-government, a very important and distinctive feature of English colonization. Virginia, which by that time had several thousand colonists, opened its "House of Burgesses," a legislature composed of representatives from its dozen scattered communities. The following year was to see another experiment in self-government in Massachusetts. From that time on, the English colonies of settlement were permitted to manage a considerable portion of their own internal affairs until, in 1926, it was officially announced that the dominions were partners of the mother country within the British Empire. Except to a limited extent in the Dutch settlements in America, such colonial self-government does not appear in the colonial history of the other European nations. It was the natural consequence of the Englishman's willingness to migrate, coupled with his traditional insistence upon his political rights.

By the time Virginia started its legislature it was no longer England's only colony. Part of a squadron headed for Jamestown in 1609 had been wrecked at Bermuda, which became the second permanent English settlement. In 1608 the French established Quebec as the center of their American colonization, which not only included the St. Lawrence valley but spread down the coast to Maine, where it ran into conflict with some abortive English colonial attempts. After the discovery in 1609 by Hudson, an Englishman exploring for Holland, of the river which bears his name, the Dutch founded fur-trading posts on the present sites of New York City and Albany. It was between the French and Dutch spheres of activity that the next English efforts were centered, in the region to be known as New England.

In 1620 an English colony of settlement quite different from Jamestown was planted on the sandy shores of southeastern Massachusetts. The leaders in this new enterprise were extreme Protestant nonconformists, or "Separatists," from eastern England. They had slipped away to Holland in order to worship more freely, but after a dozen years at Leiden some of them determined to migrate to America. Declining an invitation to settle in the new Dutch colony on the Hudson, they secured financial backing from some London merchants who saw possible profits from furs and fish. In September, 1620, one hundred and two "Pilgrims" sailed from Plymouth in the *Mayflower*. Only a third of the group came from Leiden; the rest were gathered from London. The Jamestown pioneers had included only men, and it had been necessary later to send over cargoes of girls for them to marry. The Pilgrims were better adapted to start a normal colony of settlement, for nearly half the *Mayflower's* passengers were women and children. Late in November they reached the tip of Cape Cod, far north of their intended destination. Before anyone went ashore, every man signed the *Mayflower* Compact, an instrument of colonial self-government which all agreed to obey. The dominant Leiden group had drawn this up to keep the restless Londoners in hand, and the colony was spared the factional fights which distracted Jamestown. A settlement, named Plymouth, was soon made on the west shore of Cape Cod Bay. As at Jamestown, almost half the group died during the first few months, but the survivors were of tougher fiber than the Virginians. They resisted starvation and were soon on a self-supporting basis. Plymouth, always a small community, is important chiefly as the initial permanent settlement of the distinctive New England type.

The charter granted by Charles to the Massachusetts Bay Company in 1629 bore quick results. The leaders of the venture were more prosperous than those at Plymouth, and their followers were much more numerous. By the summer of 1630 nearly a thousand settlers had been landed in and about Boston, some thirty-five miles north of Plymouth. A second thousand joined them within a year. By 1640, when Virginia had some eight thousand colonists, Massachusetts Bay alone had about fourteen thousand, while offshoots in Rhode Island and Connecticut, the "old colony" at Plymouth, and scattered settlements up the coast in New Hampshire and Maine brought the New England total to about eighteen thousand.

Massachusetts and Virginia became the outstanding examples of two radically different types of society, which finally came into violent conflict more than two centuries later. This was partly attributable to the types of settlers which each attracted. Occasionally one might find a man like Stephen Hopkins, who started for Virginia in 1609, was shipwrecked at Bermuda, where he became a pioneer colonist, and finally wound up as a *Mayflower* Pilgrim. Generally there was more difference. The New England colonists were a much more homogeneous group than the Virginians, who represented the social extremes, with a few aristocrats and a large number of indentured servants too poor to pay in advance for their passage. The Massachusetts settlers came chiefly from eastern England, the stronghold of Puritanism, and were mostly of the middle classes, either townsmen or small landholders, able to pay their own way. The harsh deputy governor of Virginia complained in 1611 that his colonists were "so profane, so riotous, and so full of mutiny that not many are Christians but in name." The first governor of Massachusetts Bay, on the other hand, wrote proudly that "God sifted a whole nation that he might send the choicest grain into the wilderness." The New Englanders claimed then, and long afterward, that they had come to America in order to worship as they pleased, but it seems likely that free land was an especially strong incentive. The combination of religious, political, and economic conditions in early Stuart England seemed so intolerable that it dislodged many who might never have been willing to take such a chance in normal times.

Whether they came for land or religion, the colonists of Massachusetts Bay got plenty of the latter. The members of the Massachusetts Bay Company, instead of remaining in England, came to America and brought their charter with them, so that they secured even more complete self-government than Virginia or Plymouth. The Puritan element dominated the colony and its numerous towns, showing a harsh intolerance toward all who differed in religion. Only church members, barely a fifth of the total, might take part in the town meetings, where the voters met to settle their political transactions by direct action. The Puritan minority severely regulated not only the beliefs and worship but also the morals of the community, and the "New England conscience," influenced by an overdose of Old Testament "thou shalt not's," lasted on in the region long after the Puritans back in England had become more mellow in thought and habit. The combination of Calvinistic influence, long, rigorous winters, and energetic efforts to wrest a living from the forests, the sea, or rugged farms developed a stern toughness of character, together with shrewdness, clear thinking, and tireless energy. The settlers of each new town quickly built not only a meetinghouse but also a schoolhouse; for every child was to be well grounded in the three R's. Such emphasis was placed on education that Harvard College was founded as early as 1636, and for more than a half century it was the only such institution in the colonies.

From the economic standpoint England regarded New England as the "most prejudicial" of her overseas settlements; for it refused to fit into the scheme of a self-sufficient empire. It might have been extremely useful through the production of naval materials, but it co-operated only to the extent of sending masts. Barely able to sustain themselves with agriculture, the New Englanders devoted their attention to lumbering, fishing, and shipbuilding, and then actively peddled their products wherever they could find markets. Instead of rounding out the needs of England, they were competing with her.

The "great emigration" during those eleven years when England was without Parliament was by no means limited to Virginia and to New England. Some fifteen hundred colonists went to Maryland, established in 1634 under tolerant Catholic auspices, with a feudal form of government under its "proprietor," Lord Baltimore. The West Indian Islands attracted even more settlers than all the mainland colonies together. An unsuccessful expedition to colonize Guiana settled on one of the islands, and before long Englishmen were swarming in great numbers to the Caribbean, the little island of Barbados, only twenty-one miles long and less than fifteen miles wide, having more settlers than all New England. At first these islands raised tobacco; but the Dutch finally demonstrated the advantages of sugar cane, from which sugar, rum, and molasses could be derived. Negro slaves were introduced, and for a long time these few little dots on the map were worth more to England than either the mainland colonies or India.

Along with overseas settlements a colonizing venture was being carried out nearer at hand. After the crushing of the Irish rebellion in the last years of Elizabeth's reign, it was decided to hold Ireland in hand by transplanting thither Englishmen and Scots. Six of the nine counties in Ulster, the northern province, were given over to settlers from Britain. Some of these were English, but a considerable number were Scottish Presbyterians. Hitherto the Celtic Irish had absorbed the Englishmen who had gone among them, but these dour Scotch-Irish of Londonderry, Belfast, and other parts of Ulster have remained sharply distinct and hostile even to the present. A century after their original "plantation" in northern Ireland large numbers of the Scotch-Irish were to go to America, bringing Presbyterianism with them as they moved into the middle colonies and out to the frontier.

Those critical years of the first two Stuarts not only saw England approaching a crisis in its constitutional development but also saw English history spreading out from the little island kingdom into distant regions which must thereafter be taken constantly into account in any history of the English people.

# CHAPTER XIII

## The Puritan Revolt

### 1629-1660

THE contest between king and Parliament reached its height in the middle of the seventeenth century. For eleven years Charles governed England without summoning Parliament. Once it assembled, antagonism was so sharp that both sides soon resorted to arms,—king against Parliament, Cavalier against Puritan. Charles lost his head, and Oliver Cromwell, Parliament's general, in more ways than one kept his. The monarchy of England was submerged beneath the flood; and Cromwell, a species of saint to many, a most decided devil to others, became dictator of an English republic. At his death, chaos almost reigned until Charles's son returned in full glory as King Charles II.

By means of various pretexts, Charles I managed between 1629 and 1640 to scrape together sufficient money without Parliamentary aid. He could collect enough to govern the country on a peace basis, but one drastic economy was necessary. War was a luxury he could not afford. By 1630, peace treaties had ended English meddling in France, Spain, and Germany. It has been remarked that "James made many mistakes, but at least he had a European policy; Charles had no European policy at all." The Thirty Years' War continued its intricate and devastating course; but, much as Charles wanted to help his sister's cause, England was forced to remain aloof. Sweden rose to a brief greatness; Richelieu intervened to smash Hapsburg power; Holland slowly fought her way to complete freedom. But in all that, England stayed at one side, sullenly fermenting with domestic dissensions.

The royal officials left no stone unturned to bring money into the treasury without resorting to Parliamentary grants. No possible source of income was overlooked; even the stumps of oaks in the royal forests were sold. The customs duties were still collected in spite of the recent protests of the Commons and the temporary resistance of the merchants. One merchant, a prosperous London alderman, was thrown into prison and reduced to beggary for refusing to pay. Thereafter the duties were collected. Courtiers formed companies to secure the obnoxious patents which had been denied to individuals, except inventors, by Parliament in 1624. The ancient limits of the royal forests were retraced, and many who had lived for years within the forgotten boundaries were heavily fined under the rigorous forest laws. Fines had to be paid in London before new buildings might be constructed, and in the country before old ones might be demolished. Gentlemen were ordered to leave London for their country estates during certain seasons, and one was fined £1000 for violation of this regulation. One of the most ingenious revivals of ancient laws was the so-called "distraint of knighthood." According to an unrepealed statute of Edward I, all landholders with a stipulated income (originally £20, later £40) were required to become knights (see page 150). In the days of Edward the law had been designed to provide a properly equipped force of armed horsemen. Now, when £40 incomes had become far more common, it was used to mulct a very large group. Men had to pay a heavy fee if they became knights, and they were fined if they refused. By 1631 that device alone had brought £115,000 into the royal coffers.

The most celebrated of these financial attempts was the collection of "ship money." It was an ancient custom that in time of war, when the rest of England was called upon for military service, the seaports of the south coast were to furnish ships for fighting purposes. Now, although the country was at peace, these seaports were asked for money in place of ships. Such an order perhaps might not have been deemed extraordinary had not this ship money also been demanded, in time of peace, from the inland counties as well.

The navy, to be sure, was impoverished. James, as we saw, had allowed it to decay after making peace with Spain, and its low efficiency had been glaringly evident in the ill-starred ventures of Buckingham. Not only was the royal navy ineffective as a weapon of offense; it was unable even to protect the coasts of England. Within half a century after the sea dogs had beaten off the tremendous attack of the Armada, Barbary pirates from Algiers were raiding with impunity the shores of the British Isles. In 1635 they descended one night upon the seacoast town of Baltimore in Ireland and carried away some two hundred of the inhabitants, who were sold in the slave markets at Algiers,—the women for the harems; the men for toil in galleys or in stone quarries. Ten years later England was to send commissioners to Algiers to redeem hundreds of English, Scottish, and Irish men and women at the prices they had fetched in the slave sales. Consequently there was need for money wherewith to construct ships; and the money was well spent when Phineas Pett, one of England's cleverest shipwrights, built, with part of the sums thus collected, the celebrated *Sovereign of the Seas*.

# The Puritan Revolt

But the needs of the navy were one thing, and the methods of collecting ship money another. The former Puritan members of the House of Commons, cut off from normal Parliamentary outlet for expressing their grievances, stiffly resisted this flank attack upon Parliament's power of the purse. John Hampden, one of the foremost Puritan leaders, and one of the wealthiest men in England, refused to pay the twenty shillings of ship money levied upon one of his estates. In his trial, before the twelve justices of the three common-law courts, he vigorously combated the crown. In spite of the past removal of obstinate judges, the king won his decision in 1638 by only a vote of seven to five. Because of the widespread publicity given the case it was a moral victory for Hampden.

By that time another source of irritation was becoming daily more exasperating. Charles had a new chief adviser, the exact opposite of Buckingham. Much of the authority once wielded by that magnificent, harebrained duke was now in the hands of a scholarly little churchman with "prim mouth and sharp, restless eyes." This was William Laud, one-time Oxford don, whose favor with Charles had won him not only the chancellorship of Oxford but also successive promotion through three bishoprics until, in 1633, he became Archbishop of Canterbury. Laud was by nature a disciplinarian; he expected royal authority to back up church discipline, and, in turn, he argued strongly for royal prerogative and sat high in royal courts and councils. He was able, pious, honest, conscientious, and courageous; but his ideas ran counter to those of most Englishmen. He tried to order men rather than to persuade them. By his stubborn persistence in pursuing his unpopular aims he probably did more than any other to bring on the Civil War, which ruined the king whom he so sincerely and energetically tried to serve.

Laud had forced the Oxford students into caps and gowns; now he tried to force England into similar external uniformity in religion. As far as doctrinal beliefs were concerned, Laud was possibly more broad-minded than the Calvinistic Puritans whom he hated. He wanted to link the Church of England with the traditions of the past and to base it upon more than the simple Puritan interpretation of the Scriptures. To achieve this, he sought external uniformity of worship. To Laud it was a matter of utmost importance that the Communion table should be placed in the east end of every church and that all should bow when the name of Jesus was mentioned. His vicar-general made tireless visitations throughout the land to enforce such ceremonial regulations, distasteful to the majority of the clergy and to an even greater proportion of laymen. Milton, the Puritan poet, objected to the emphasis on "palls and mitres, gold

and gewgaws"; Cromwell condemned such "poisonous Papist ceremonies." The Puritans were more interested in the pulpit and in
sermons, but Laud took vigorous measures to suppress the Puritan
preachers. He marked for promotion only those clergy, the minority,
who agreed with his High Church views. This insistence upon ceremonial uniformity caused widespread dissatisfaction; but, Laud,
with his passion for authority, did not stop there. The church courts
during his rule meddled with the morals and daily life of the people,
with expensive and vexatious activity. Laud himself, sitting on the
courts of Star Chamber and High Commission, took a vigorous part
in several savage sentences upon men accused of libel for criticizing
the government and the religious innovations. A preacher was fined
£10,000, sentenced to long imprisonment, flogged, and placed in the
pillory, where his ears were lopped off, his nose slit, and his cheeks
branded "S.S." ("sower of sedition"). Other men received similar
brutal sentences. Such practices help to explain the extensive Puritan migration across the Atlantic during the years in which Laud
held sway.

The archbishop's innovations caused irritation enough in England,
but they produced more immediately violent results when extended
to Scotland. Charles's northern kingdom, with its warlike feudal
nobility and its lowlanders saturated with Presbyterianism, was the
more inflammable of the two countries. When Laud held the work
of John Knox "not a reformation but a defamation," there was
trouble. A new prayer book incorporating Laud's ideas was forced
upon Scotland, ready-made as it came from England, without consulting the Scottish nobles, clergy, or people beyond a few subservient
bishops. Everyone blamed "the pope of Canterbury," and the prayer
book was read in only a few places. On a Sunday morning in June,
1637, the Bishop of Edinburgh tried to use the new service in the
great church of St. Giles. An angry woman hurled a stool at his
head and barely missed the dean; a mob outside shattered the church
windows; and the bishop rode home amid a shower of stones. From
that violent outburst on we can trace a regular and rapid sequence
of events which brought about the Civil War in England.

Seven months later Scotland produced the most famous document
in her history, the National Covenant. In this the Scots declared their
loyalty to the king, but bound themselves to reject all religious innovations which had not first been approved in free assemblies of
the Scottish Church (Kirk). After the clergy, nobility, and gentry
had signed it, the Covenant was spread on a tombstone in the churchyard of Greyfriars' Church in Edinburgh, where thousands of common folk, raised to a high pitch of emotion, added their signatures.

# The Puritan Revolt

The Covenant was circulated around the country and was subscribed to by a large part of the population. A general assembly of the Kirk at Glasgow definitely repudiated bishops and all innovations in religion.

Charles determined to punish his stubborn Scottish subjects, but he had neither the men nor the money necessary for a successful campaign. Nevertheless, in the spring of 1639 he summoned the nobles and the militia of the northern counties, tried to collect some more ship money, and with an ill-led, ill-trained, reluctant army headed for Scotland. At the Tweed, which separates the two kingdoms, he came face to face with a Scottish force better prepared than his own and strengthened by veteran Scots from the Thirty Years' War, who had hastened home to defend the Covenant. There was no fighting, and this "First Bishops' War" soon ended with a peace patched up at Berwick-on-Tweed. Both sides were to disband their forces; but it was only a temporary truce. A year later the Scots were to force Charles to end his long rule without Parliament.

That autumn the king took a new chief adviser, a man of whom we last heard as Sir Thomas Wentworth, better known to history by his new title (1640) of Earl of Strafford. Scion of a prominent family of Yorkshire gentry, Wentworth had gone to Cambridge, had studied law, and had become an experienced parliamentarian. Throughout his life he was loyal to the king; but he disapproved of the arbitrary tendencies under Buckingham, and he wanted to return to earlier Tudor precedents, where the king did the ruling but took Parliament into account. In the stormy session of 1628 he tried his best to work out a compromise between Commons and king, but Charles would not agree. Thereupon the leadership in the Commons passed to Eliot, who pushed through the Petition of Right. Wentworth would not stomach Parliamentary supremacy and was thenceforth one of the stanchest supporters of royal power. In a few months he became Lord Wentworth, and was sent to York as head of the Council of the North. In 1633, when Laud went to Canterbury, Wentworth went to Ireland as deputy. During the next six years he worked hard to improve conditions there. He restored order, remodeled the army, reformed the corrupt civil service, stimulated education, and, by encouraging the linen industry and doubling the volume of trade, did what he could for the Irish. With all that, however, he was a "benevolent despot." He had the natural impatience of the efficient executive at all obstructions. He secured his ends by highhanded methods which he himself described as "thorough," and the experience made him an autocrat. He carried those same principles into his brief but all-powerful period as chief minister of Charles, to whom he offered not only advice but also much of his private fortune and his efficient Irish regiments.

Charles was still bent upon punishing Scotland in 1640; so Wentworth, by that time Strafford, advocated the calling of Parliament as the only means to secure adequate funds. He apparently did not realize that a Parliament could not be manipulated as easily in England as in Ireland. When the Commons assembled, the pent-up grievances of eleven years at last found voice. They would not grant the king a shilling until he listened to them. The king had no intention of doing this, and he dissolved the "Short Parliament," so called because it was in session only three weeks.

Strafford gave England a final brief taste of royal absolutism. There were riots, but the ringleaders were executed. Several members of Parliament were imprisoned. Press gangs rounded up crowds of riffraff for a new army to invade Scotland. But this time, in the "Second Bishops' War," the Scots took the initiative and invaded England. It was a sort of friendly invasion; for they knew that the mass of Englishmen would welcome the forcing of the king's hand. Before Strafford could get his reluctant conscripts to the border, the Scots had advanced as far as Durham. They might have continued on to London; instead they adopted a clever course which must have warmed the heart of every Scot. They simply remained about Durham, running up bills of £850 a day and announcing that they would not leave until Charles paid those bills. This act forced the king to call a new Parliament.

Thus it happened that a new Parliament assembled in November, 1640, the second time in seven months. This one was to go down in history as the "Long Parliament." The presence of the Scots prevented the king from dismissing it as he had its short-lived predecessor, and some of its members were still sitting in 1653. Even in 1660 those of the one hundred and fifty Lords and five hundred members of the Commons who still survived were called together once more for a final settlement of the twenty intervening years.

The Long Parliament had able guidance. When the Petition of Right had been forced on the king in 1628, the leaders of the Commons were Eliot and Wentworth. The former had died in 1632, a prisoner of the king; the latter was now the archenemy of the Commons. The new leader was John Pym, "burly and shaggy and vigilant as a watchdog." A Puritan who "thought it part of a man's religion to see that his country be well governed," he combined breadth of vision, keen ability in political tactics, and the will to transform Parliament from a protesting into a dominating body. Next to him ranked John Hampden, of ship-money fame, with "long, thoughtful face, thin lips, and bright, melancholy eyes," high-minded, clearheaded, and keen-witted. They, with a few other prominent Puritans, had kept in close contact during the eleven-year recess, and they remained together for constant counsel and action in the crisis which approached.

Eight days after the Long Parliament assembled, the Commons impeached Strafford and, shortly afterward, Laud. There was no time to lose. Then, as several times afterward in the coming hectic decade, it was a case of "my head or thy head." If the Commons had not impeached Strafford when they did, he was ready to have Pym and his associates condemned for treasonable relations with the Scots. When the time came for trial in the spring, Parliament substituted for impeachment a speedier and more certain action, namely, an act of attainder, whereby the accused could be voted to death without the formalities of a trial. This had been used against Thomas Cromwell a century before. Strafford had given himself up with the solemn promise of protection from Charles; but howling mobs scared the king into signing the act, which, two days later, sent his faithful, if overzealous, adviser to the block. After remarking, "Put not thy trust in princes," Strafford met his end with dignity. The little archbishop was not executed for four years.

As in the French Revolution, a century and a half later, most of the permanent, constructive work of the English revolution was accomplished in the early months before conditions grew violent. The Long Parliament did away with Star Chamber, High Commission, and other royal-prerogative courts, which had served useful purposes when created by the Tudors, but which had been perverted by the Stuarts into instruments of oppression and ran counter to the ideas of the Puritan gentry. Ship money, distraint of knighthood, and penalties for forest encroachments—the illegal methods by which Charles had raised money—went into the discard and remained permanently abolished. Parliament also passed certain extraordinary measures to prevent the king from dissolving it.

In constitutional legislation against royal absolutism Parliament held together pretty much as a unit; but as Pym steered the business toward religion and control of the army it began to split into distinct parties. The Commons tried to exclude bishops from the House of Lords, and then, in the "root and branch" bills, to abolish bishops altogether. That proposal began to alienate a considerable body of "moderates" who had voted with Pym and his Puritans in purely constitutional controversies.

The breach was widened by terrible news from Ireland in the autumn of 1641. As so often in the sorry story of Anglo-Irish relations, harsh work on one side bred savage reprisals from the other. With Strafford's iron discipline removed, the native Catholic Irish of Ulster determined to expel the Protestants who had been "planted" in that northern province during the preceding quarter century. The pent-up hatred against everything English led to horrible outrages in the evictions. Men and women were stripped and ripped open; children's brains were dashed out; and many who were not actually massacred in the initial outbreak were forced to wander until they froze or starved to death. Probably four thousand perished in the original slaughter and twice as many died later. The wild rumors which horrified England, however, magnified those figures into twenty, fifty, or even a hundred thousand and transformed the widespread contempt for the "wild Irish" into bitter hatred. Everyone wanted to punish the Irish, and plans were made to send an army against them; but neither the king nor Parliament would trust the other with the command of such troops, for fear they might be used in England. Ireland was to wait eight years for the vengeance of the English.

The question of army control, added to that of the bishops, made for exciting days. The new Royalist party in Parliament began to stand out by itself. The closeness of the division was evident in the last days of 1641, when the Puritans introduced the "Grand Remonstrance." This lengthy document, with more than two hundred clauses, was an appeal to the people, reviewing previous evils of the reign, as well as efforts which Parliament had already made to right them. It suggested further reforms, particularly that the royal ministers might be "such as the Parliament may have cause to confide in" and that a body of divines be summoned to consider church reforms. There were long and stormy debates in the Commons on the measure, and it was finally passed only by the narrow margin of eleven votes. That night, as the members were leaving the hall, Oliver Cromwell remarked that if the measure had failed he would have left England forever, probably for New England.

Then Charles blundered. In the first week of 1642 he attempted, illegally, to impeach Pym, Hampden, and three other leaders of the Commons for high treason. The Lords refused to act. The next day Charles himself, at the head of several hundred swaggering, armed "gentlemen," invaded the House of Commons to arrest the five members. Forewarned, however, they had escaped down the Thames by boat. The king, muttering that the birds had flown, retired with much loss of dignity and prestige. The City of London, aroused, took Parliament under its protection to save it from the king's bullies. Hundreds rode in from the adjacent counties to assist in the defense.

# The Puritan Revolt

The king's high-handed action gave Parliament a powerful ally; for London, in addition to its numbers and its wealth, possessed the only adequate armed force in the country in its "trained bands."

A few days later Charles rode north from his capital, which he was not to see again until he returned several years later a prisoner. The Long Parliament suffered the first of the great cuts that were to slash its membership; for many of both houses went northward to join the king. About thirty of the one hundred and fifty Lords and three hundred of the five hundred members of the Commons remained behind to conduct, in the name of Parliament, the government of England.

For eight months both sides prepared for the approaching war between the Royalist "Cavaliers" and the Parliamentarian "Roundheads." Parliament fortified several seacoast towns, took over the command of the militia, and in July organized a force of twenty-four thousand men under the Earl of Essex, the son of Elizabeth's one-time favorite. That same month the navy declared for Parliament,

THE CIVIL WAR

remembering its grievances over Stuart neglect. A considerable number of men rallied around the king, but they lacked discipline and equipment.

Gradually England took sides. For some men, loyalty to king or to Puritanism made the decision easy; many more took their stand reluctantly and with heavy hearts. The Civil War was not primarily a war of section against section nor of class against class. It was more a war of one set of ideas against another. Unlike the French Revolution, no one class stood as a whole for either king or Parliament. There was, however, a tendency for the great nobles and their retainers to side with the king, and for the moderate squires, the sturdy yeomen, and the townsmen to incline toward the Parliamentary cause, though no clean-cut line separated the classes in the struggle. Actually, two minority parties from the upper and middle classes fought the war; the bulk of the peasantry was barely affected. Geographically the division was almost as vague, although a line drawn from Hull to Portsmouth divided roughly and not too accurately the territory of the two sides. The conservative, fairly feudal, sparsely populated north and west of England thus generally supported the king, while Parliament was strongest in the more advanced south and east, which, in addition to agriculture, included most of the nation's commercial and industrial activity. The large counties of Yorkshire and Lancashire, however, were divided. Isolated in the Royalist southwest, Plymouth, the home port of the Elizabethan sea dogs, and the port of Bristol, the second largest city in England, stood for Parliament.

The English Civil War bore several points of resemblance to the American Civil War two centuries later. Both were, on the whole, clean-cut, sportsmanlike fights, with few of the savage atrocities which too frequently marked struggles among other peoples. Only when the Roundheads encountered Celts or Catholics, or the Confederates ran into Negro troops, was there likely to be a massacre. Both wars were fought primarily by amateurs; for neither country maintained a considerable military establishment, and there were relatively few experienced veterans in either war. The position of the Royalists in England in general resembled that of the Confederates in America, while the Roundheads had much in common with the Northerners. The Cavaliers and the Southerners, about whom still clings the glamour of lost causes, were in many ways better prepared for immediate conflict. The Cavalier, writes Morley, was hot, unruly, scornful, with all the feudal readiness for bloodshed, in contrast to the "keen, stubborn, dogged" Roundhead. The king's men and the Confederates, too, produced dashing leaders more rapidly. But every day the war dragged on, the poorer their chances became. Economic considerations gradually wore down their initial advantage. Their opponents not only retained the capital and the machinery of government but also had, in London and New York, the centers of the national commerce and finance, and thus could continue to furnish the golden sinews of war long after the landed aristocrats had sold the last of the family plate. The Roundheads and Northerners both secured the national navy and were able to maintain contact with the outside world, not only bringing in necessary military supplies but actually making money while the contest went on. Both victors, however, had to wait until they could find a military leader who could make full use of their greater potential strength before victory was secure.

# The Puritan Revolt

On August 22, 1642, Charles formally began the war by raising the royal standard at Nottingham in the presence of a rather slender crowd who cheered in the rain. Essex neglected his chance to fall upon the poorly equipped royal forces with his superior numbers; and they slipped off to the west, where the king recruited infantry from the Celtic Welsh and developed a cavalry force under his dashing twenty-three-year-old nephew, Prince Rupert, third son of the late Elector of the Palatinate. Essex followed him, missed him, and the royal army started a race for the unguarded capital. At Edgehill, hard by Stratford-on-Avon, the two armies met in an indecisive encounter; for neither was adequately trained. Charles advanced to the university town of Oxford, sixty miles above London, and made it his gay headquarters during most of the war.

For at least a year after Edgehill the tide of war favored the king. Much of the fighting was on a small scale; for though there were altogether some one hundred and forty thousand men under arms, it was unusual for a single force of fifteen thousand to engage in battle. There were many attacks on towns and on garrisoned country houses; and the larger forces marched and countermarched in surprising ignorance of the enemy's whereabouts. The Royalists evolved a scheme of grand strategy: three separate armies, from the north, the west, and the southwest, were to push aside the Parliamentary forces and to converge below London, thus cutting off the capital from the sea. The battle of Newbury, in which the stubborn London prentices acquitted themselves well, blocked the most threatening Royalist approach to the city. Bristol and other Parliamentary towns fell to the king's men, and nearly two thirds of England was in his hands; but the three armies did not converge as planned.

Parliament, seeing that the fighting was going against it, secured valuable outside aid which helped to redress the balance. In the summer of 1643 it made a "Solemn League and Covenant" with the Scots, who gave military aid which was to neutralize the threat from the north and without which Parliament might never have been victorious. The Scots, however, demanded their price, not only in cash but in religion, and Parliament agreed that England was to become Presbyterian. The latter was a very heavy price, and was the germ of much serious trouble later. A "Committee of the Two Kingdoms" assumed direction of affairs, religious as well as military. That same summer a body of divines, known as the Westminster Assembly, began its thousand wordy sessions, which by 1648 produced a Presbyterian code still important in Scotland and America, but for which, even by that time, England had little use. By the end of 1643 Parliament had lost its two great leaders: Pym was dead of cancer, and Hampden, a colonel, had fallen in battle. For the time being, no man of equal caliber arose to fill their places.

The leader who eventually was to overshadow both was in his middle forties, busily engaged in drilling cavalry. Oliver Cromwell, distantly related to the famous minister of Henry VIII, had grown up in the swampy fen region around Cambridge, in eastern England. For a year, in which his chief interest seems to have been athletic rather than academic, he attended the university; then he settled down as a prosperous landowner, active in farming and the raising of cattle. He went through a religious experience which left him strongly Puritan but with independent views opposed both to the Anglican and to the Presbyterian forms of church government and worship. By 1628 he was in the House of Commons for Huntingdon, and he sat again in the Long Parliament, where Hampden and more than twenty other members were relatives of his. He spoke only occasionally, with more force than grace. With the coming of war he became a cavalry captain and commanded forty men at Edgehill. That battle opened his eyes, and he realized that the principal military need of the Parliamentary forces was effective and dependable cavalry. He told his cousin Hampden that the Parliamentary troopers were mostly "old decayed serving-men and tapsters" who lacked the spirit to encounter gentlemen of resolution such as had participated in the sweeping charges of Prince Rupert. He studied carefully the military innovations of the great Swedish king, Gustavus Adolphus, whose military genius had done much to turn the Thirty Years' War into a Protestant victory. The effectiveness of the heavy cavalry charge had particularly impressed Cromwell, who returned to his eastern counties, the stronghold of Puritan resistance, and within six months after Edgehill was a colonel in command of eleven hundred highly trained troopers. They were substantial and godly men, representing many independent shades of Puritan belief; but along with their prayer meetings they underwent tireless drill and iron discipline. Cromwell wanted a force which not only could deliver a crushing charge, like Rupert's, but, after charging, could so remain under control that it might be used to complete the work in other parts of the battlefield. The fact that his "Ironsides" could do that had a powerful influence upon the history of the period.

Cromwell's Ironsides showed their worth on a long July evening in 1644 at Marston Moor, seven miles west of York. It was the largest gathering of troops on any battlefield of the war: eighteen thousand Royalists faced an army of twenty-seven thousand, half Roundheads and half Scots. Both armies were drawn up in the conventional battle order of the day. In the center of each line were

# The Puritan Revolt

the pikemen and musketeers of the infantry; on either flank was cavalry. Cromwell opened the battle by putting Rupert's cavalry wing to flight, with Scottish aid. Elsewhere, however, matters went badly for the Parliamentary forces; for the Royalists, though outnumbered, fought well. Cromwell, again with Scottish assistance, finally carried the day by keeping his Ironsides in hand and by using them to crush the stubborn infantry regiments of the king. That battle lost northern England to the king, and it made Cromwell.

Marston Moor revealed that the other Parliamentary commanders and troops did not measure up to the high efficiency of Cromwell and his Ironsides. Cromwell himself grew increasingly impatient with Lord Manchester, the supine Parliamentary commander in chief, who obviously did not believe in pushing the war to the limit. In that autumn of 1644 Manchester's inactivity allowed the royal forces, although they were outnumbered two to one, to escape disaster in the second battle of Newbury. A month later, in Parliament, Cromwell launched an open attack upon his inefficient chief, which produced two results. One was the "Self-Denying Ordinance," whereby all members of Parliament in military service were to resign their commissions within forty days. Manchester, Essex, and others accepted this with grace; thus the dead wood at the top was removed. The command was reorganized, with Fairfax appointed at the head and Cromwell second in command, with particular charge of the cavalry. Coupled with this, early in 1645, was the creation of a "New Model Army," based on the efficient discipline of Cromwell's Ironsides. Instead of depending upon sectional armies, maintained by the different regions, Parliament itself took over the control of some twenty-two thousand of its eighty thousand troops and began the intensive training of this body, which, incidentally, was the first to adopt the famous red coat as the regular English uniform.

The New Army soon had a chance to show its mettle. In June, 1645, it blundered into the royal army at Naseby for the decisive battle of the war. The tactics were pretty much a repetition of Marston Moor. Cromwell's charge carried away the opposing cavalry wing; then he turned his disciplined horsemen upon the stubborn Royalist infantry. A thousand Royalists fell; four thousand were captured, and so were the king's private letters. These contained such damaging proof of intrigue that their publication did irreparable harm to Charles. Naseby, to all intents, ended the Civil War. Quickly the remaining royal army was crushed, and one by one the king's isolated strongholds were seized. Charles, reduced almost to the status of a wandering refugee, fled to the Scottish troops. By the spring of 1646 the Roundheads had unquestionably triumphed.

# A History of England and the British Empire

The victorious Parliamentary side was now faced with the problem of reconstruction. The bitterness that was to characterize later Cavalier defeats was scarcely aroused at this time. Religious toleration as a general basis of settlement, with restraint on the part of the victors in making the vanquished pay for the war, might have healed more wounds than anything else and have brought earlier tranquillity to the divided land; but such toleration, unfortunately, for the time being proved impossible, since there were four interests, each determined on its own stubborn way in bigoted fashion: Parliament, the Parliamentary army, the king, and the more or less interested Scots.

The war was won in the name of Parliament; but what did Parliament represent? Never fairly representative of all England, it did not now stand even for dissenting England. At this time it was largely Presbyterian in sentiment, in a country where Anglicans, Independents, and others were very numerous. Yet even the common desire with the Scots to impose the National Covenant on England did not bring these two of the diverse elements into common action, perhaps because of the Scots' lesser interest in the military and political situation and their greater readiness to give Charles what he wished. The army, on the other hand, the winner of the Parliamentary victories, was composed largely of various other sects, some of them extreme in their fanaticism, but chiefly Independents, who wanted self-governing groups to worship freely without outside control and who were almost as ill-disposed to presbyters as to bishops. Since the army had given Parliament its power, it was not to be ignored or snubbed with impunity. These divergent elements on the winning side led Charles, not unnaturally but most unwisely, to try to play off Parliament, army, and Scots one against the other. A dangerous game for the cleverest, this juggling of such inflammable political material; and when the player was a prisoner, and not trusted by any group because of his notorious inability to keep to any promise, the result was foredoomed—failure. Yet the king, in the minds of many, was still the symbol of law and government. His personal disaster made military dictatorship practically inevitable.

Between the various factions stood Oliver Cromwell. That man of contradictions had come to be the focal point of the whole tangled situation. When Charles, on that wintry January morning, had invaded the House of Commons with his soldiers, Cromwell already was forty-three years old and by no means recognized as a leader of men. Yet within four years he forged to the front as a famous soldier, and within four more was to become dictator of his country. Circumstance and not desire made him such; of this we can be reasonably certain. Very little else may be affirmed of him without qualification. He was a Puritan of the Puritans, devoutly religious; but at the same time he, almost alone of his contemporaries, kept a relatively clear head in matters of faith. He was far from radical in his political ideas; but he did not hesitate, roughly and illegally, to execute his king. He did not seek power for himself, and he believed with all his heart in constitutional methods; but he threw three Parliaments out of Westminster by the scruff of the neck because of their ineptitude. He was extraordinarily kind and gentle in his family life; but in his public career he was quick to trample on his enemies. That he was an opportunist none could deny, and that he moved this way and then that among the stubborn, set ideas of Parliament, king, Scots, and army until the decision was in his hands is evident. Nevertheless, when he decided upon action he was always confident that the Almighty had made the decision, a fact which prevented wavering in times of crisis. Tragically enough, Cromwell's way ended for the time being the very constitutional ideas of government for which he had fought. The force of circumstances, combined with his own personal idiosyncrasies, fashioned out of this conscientious opponent of tyranny one of the most absolute rulers England has ever endured.

The first step in the series of futile moves, before Cromwell found himself master of England, was the presentation by Parliament, with the consent of the Scots, of certain peace terms to Charles at Newcastle, in the summer of 1646. These were based, as the Scottish acquiescence would indicate, upon the adoption of official Presbyterianism in England, while the control of the militia—that is, the army—was to be vested for twenty years in Parliament, and the old anti-Catholic penal code was to be enforced. Charles played for time, hoping to widen the breach between the Presbyterians and Independents. Although in the power of the Scots, he remained constant in his hatred of Presbyterianism. He was apparently ready to compromise on the Covenant for three years, pending a religious settlement under the joint auspices of certain Presbyterian clergy and others to be appointed by himself,—a settlement that would obviously be more pleasing to Charles. He wished, in addition, to cut the Parliamentary control of the militia to ten years and not to enforce the penal code. The Scots, disgusted at Charles's stand against the Covenant, permitted Parliament to take him into custody upon payment of certain sums due them for their aid in the war, and withdrew homeward.

Parliament, with Charles as prisoner and with the Scots for the moment out of the picture, embarked upon an arbitrary course of religious persecution and wanton taxation of all and sundry. Not content with driving the Anglican clergy from their parishes and forbidding the prayer book, it began deliberately to persecute the Independents, to sentence certain Baptists to life imprisonment, and to treat other sects harshly. Lasting resentment was aroused among the Royalists over the confiscatory fines charged against them as "rebels," which in numerous cases forced the sale of their family estates. But Parliament in this was only following the easiest way for the conqueror—of making the losers pay the bills of war. Its more conspicuous folly came in its highhanded manner toward the army, which it treated purely as paid employees. Composed, as it was, of many different sects, the army had long been annoyed at Presbyterian dominance, and now it was infuriated by religious persecution. When, in addition, Parliament directed that most of the troops be disbanded without paying them, and ordered that most of the remainder be sent to Ireland,—out of the way,—the patience of the army broke.

The army, acutely aware that it had put into power the very Parliament that was treating it in such a manner, now took the lead in negotiations with Charles, a task made easy by kidnaping His Majesty's person in the summer of 1647. Although Parliament itself had seemed sterile in original ideas for governing the country, political theories were rife in the army. The present day may laugh at the "Fifth-Monarchy Men," who hoped to see the prophecy of Daniel fulfilled by the rule of Christ and the saints as successors to the Assyrian, Persian, Macedonian, and Roman empires; but it can appreciate the prophetic agitation of the "Levelers" and others who clamored for democracy, two centuries before it finally came to England. "The poorest he that is in England hath a life to live as much as the greatest he, and a man is not bound to a government that he has not had a voice to put himself under," declared one of their spokesmen. Although very advanced for the time, such radical suggestions as universal suffrage, equal opportunity for all, and government actually in the hands of the people found ready listeners among the unpaid and religiously dissatisfied soldiery. The radicals began to show, by open personal criticism, an increasing distrust that was to be the ruin of Charles. Nevertheless, Cromwell, who agreed with his son-in-law that "nobody has a right to a share in disposing the affairs of this kingdom unless he has a permanent fixed interest in this kingdom," held the radical elements so well in check that the actual terms sent to Charles, the so-called "Heads of the Proposals," were moderate, tolerant, and less discriminatory against Royalists than any others in those unquiet years. Even religious toleration, except for Catholics, was included, to the extent of guarding against extreme Presbyterianism by the announcement that no one had to accept it, and against too strong Anglicanism by stipulating that the power of the bishops was to be curtailed. Army and state were to be united under Parliamentary control for ten years, but not under the present Long Parliament. A new Parliament was to be elected, with more people allowed to vote for the members.

The king's oversanguine character and impulsive unsteadiness now pushed matters rapidly to the end of the monarchy and his own death, while his acceptance of these comparatively statesmanlike terms would probably have extended the life of both. Not only did Charles foolishly refuse these "Heads of the Proposals," perhaps from the high motive of loyalty to many of his followers who received no amnesty under them, but, late in 1647, he fled to the Isle of Wight. There, however, he was soon to find himself in custody again. The soldiers, under the Levelers' influence, now wholly disgusted at this evidence of the king's instability, could not be controlled longer by the temperate Cromwell. They demanded that the whole settlement be referred to the people in a then unheard-of popular referendum, with the proposal that the monarchy be at once abolished and that one house of Parliament, with no Lords admitted, be substituted for the two houses. While Cromwell was successfully keeping these extreme doctrines from being put into effect, the king again thought that he could get control of the situation into his own hands by playing the various factions one against another. He even called in the Scots. This last piece of stupidity on the king's part convinced England, from Parliament to the patient Cromwell, of Charles's utter duplicity and untrustworthiness.

The Scottish invasion in 1648 opened the Second Civil War, a short affair. A Welsh royalist uprising was put down, as well as others in Kent and Sussex; the attempt of the fleet, for once pro-Stuart, to block the Thames came to nothing; and the invading Scots and their Royalist allies were cut in two by Cromwell at Preston, in the west,—the only major encounter, and a fatal one for the Royalist cause.

The army was now finally and definitely in control. An attempt by Parliament to come to terms with Charles at Newport, a month after Preston, only precipitated Oliver's dictatorship. When the Independents got wind of the pro-Presbyterian, monarchical tone of those negotiations, the army took the king into closer custody. London, upon which Parliament depended for most of its support, was occupied by troops. On the morning of December 6, 1648, one Colonel Pride, on Cromwell's order, stationed armed men at the door of the House of Commons as it was about to meet, and excluded those who were in favor of Presbyterianism or the king. This "Pride's Purge" delivered Parliament into the hands of the army and Cromwell. Of the five hundred members of the Commons who had gathered in 1640, barely a hundred remained. Some humorist dubbed these the "Rump" (the part which was sitting), and that name has ever since been attached to this small but powerful remnant of the Long Parliament.

The army was in possession of the king's person, and what was left of the Long Parliament, the Rump, took orders from the army. But who represented the army? Politically it was divided into two wings. One, the left, was composed of radicals and Levelers, and was bitterly hostile to the monarchy. To this adhered a minority of the officers. The other, the right wing, was conservative in tone, willing to negotiate further with the king. And most of the officers were of this persuasion. Ever since the capitulation of Oxford to the Roundheads, in 1646, there had been conflict open or concealed, between these two wings. From time to time they forgot their differences in the face of common danger, as, for instance, on the occasion of the Windsor Prayer Meeting on the eve of the Second Civil War. At that time officers and men all agreed that "it was our duty, if ever the Lord brought us back in peace, to call Charles Stuart, that man of blood, to an account." No sooner, however, was victory won than unanimity ceased, and the two factions fell to fighting again.

Cromwell's position was enigmatic. Fairfax and not he was commander in chief; but Cromwell's voice was the more influential, and he knew it. His sympathies were divided between the two wings; he had too much sense to be a Leveler, and deep within his heart he was a man of conservative instincts. On the other hand, the radicals had been his best fighting men, and he was loyal to his soldiers. Furthermore, he was a choleric person, and Charles's perpetual evasions had aroused his anger.

Under the circumstances Cromwell, as was his wont, looked to Heaven for a sign. He would give Charles another chance, and God would decide. An envoy was sent to the king with still another offer from the army; His Majesty refused it, and Cromwell hardened his heart. God had spoken. As Cromwell informed the House of Commons, "If any man whatsoever hath carried out the design of deposing the king, and disinheriting his posterity, or if any man hath yet such a design, he should be the greatest traitor and rebel in the world; but since the Providence of God hath cast this upon us, I cannot but submit to Providence, though I am not provided to give you advice." To fathom the psychology of a man who would write thus is not easy.

# The Puritan Revolt

The Rump, with the approval of Cromwell and his friends, now brought the king to trial as a traitor to his country. Treason had hitherto been an offense against the king, but Charles Stuart as an individual was now charged with acting against the safety of England. The handful of Lords objected in vain, for the residual Commons insisted that all power was vested in them. They arranged a court made up of commissioners, among whom was Cromwell, before which Charles was brought. There was a week's trial, which made a farce of justice; for the king was not heard on his own behalf, and the court was illegally constituted. It was charged that Charles had intrigued with the Scots against Parliament, with Parliament against the army, with the army against both Scots and Parliament, and with foreign sympathizers against all three. Nevertheless, the reasons for his death were entirely political; for he had committed no crime recognized by English law. In January, 1649, he went to the block on a balcony at Whitehall. In his last hours he showed himself a man of kingly stature, brave, calm, dignified. No cheers, it is said, greeted this execution,—only deep, pitying sighs. The unfair trial, and the execution at its close of a man not vicious, nor cruel, but merely unstable and untrustworthy did much to turn England back toward the Stuarts even at this time, and more surely during the next kingless eleven years, until Charles's son returned to his rejoicing land. As John Buchan beautifully puts it, "Not to royalists only, but to all who had a care for the human decencies, it seemed that a cruel wrong had been done and that innocence had been outraged. The disturber of England's peace was admitted into the hierarchy of England's saints. More, out of the primeval depths of the folk-heart there welled another feeling, the more perilous because it was intermingled with those ancient things which are beyond reason. It is clear, from contemporary letters and parish records and the diaries of obscure folk, that there fell on the land the horror of a great sacrilege. The priest had been sacrificed, the god slain at the altar. The Middle Ages came to a second birth. That January day in Whitehall did not wash the balm from kingship, but gave it a new anointing."[1]

The army under Cromwell had got its way; but it was to find that the course which the depleted Rump had taken, and which Cromwell had decided was God's will, was not the way of the nation. Many of the Anglicans, Catholics, and even Presbyterians went so far as to wish for a new king. Few people liked the new order; among those who did was the still unpaid army, which wanted a more radical democracy than the Rump was ready to grant. Dangers threatened

[1] J. Buchan, *Oliver Cromwell* (1934), p. 256. By permission of Houghton Mifflin Company, Hodder & Stoughton, Ltd., and the author.

[ 355 ]

on all sides: the Irish, the Scots, and some of the colonies were openly in revolt in the name of the second Charles, for whom there was a growing sentiment in England; foreign powers, deeply disturbed at the execution of a brother monarch in that heyday of absolute royal sovereignty, were so openly hostile that English trade, sea power, and colonial possessions seemed threatened.

The result was the Commonwealth, an experiment in republican government. Cromwell, as always during the coming years, held the reins in his own hands, though for a while with disguised authority. He saw that the extreme sort of republic desired by the army Levelers was absurd. Too much Parliamentary power, considering the personnel of the Rump, was to his mind also undesirable. Yet the immediate dissolution of the Rump, as urged by the army group, might bring dangerous disorder, if not renewed civil war, with the probability of the control being seized by either conservative Royalists or Levelers. Consequently, to ensure order—the first consideration in his opinion—Cromwell for the time being supported the Rump and approved the formation of an executive Council of State, whose members were to be appointed annually by Parliament. The office of king was formally abolished; so also was the House of Lords. For nearly five years the Council of State was the nominal authority in meeting the various crises; but actually the successful restoration of order throughout the British Isles and the restoration of British prestige on the sea and abroad was the work of Cromwell, ably assisted by the great admiral Blake and by John Milton.

John Milton (1608–1674), next to Shakespeare England's greatest poet, had hitherto stayed out of the main vortex of politics. Now he was appointed to the "secretaryship of Foreign Tongues," an important office, for much of the diplomatic correspondence was in Latin, and an able scholar was necessary to conduct it. His sympathies lay with the Puritans, but his life had been dedicated to pure literature. His more famous minor poems, *Il Penseroso*, *L'Allegro*, and *Comus*, had already been written, and he longed for peace and quiet to complete a long epic poem or a tragedy on some subject not yet selected. This ambition he had put aside temporarily in order to attack Episcopal tyranny. His siding thus with the Presbyterians against the king had led to his wife's returning to her Royalist parents, a fact which caused Milton to advocate divorce. The Presbyterians therefore had attacked Milton, and he had deserted them for the Independents, coming to the conclusion that "New Presbyter is but Old Priest, writ large."

Early in the Civil War, Milton had taken his stand for liberty, as he conceived it. "Give me," he wrote, "the liberty to know, to utter,

and to argue freely according to conscience above all other liberties."
This was the theme of the *Areopagitica*, the most important of all his
prose writings. It was an ardent plea for freedom of the press and
not displeasing to Cromwell, who had reasons of his own for disliking Presbyterians. Therefore came Milton's appointment in the
new government, technically that of Latin Secretary, practically that
of pamphleteer at large in defense of Cromwell's administration.
Thus Milton, indeed, conceived it. A flood of pamphlets followed,
in defense of the king's execution and other Cromwellian policies,
until the writer, whose eyes had always been weak, became blind.

Possibly, owing to this latter circumstance, he was permitted to
live quietly in England after the return of Charles II. During that
time he wrote *Paradise Lost*, "the greatest single poetic achievement
in the language." In it are to be found the best qualities of Puritanism:
constant courage, if not mercy; quiet confidence, if not humor; un-
shaken will, even if gloomy; and a spiritual exaltation, mysterious,
overwhelming, which sometimes approaches the sublime.

With the situation in England well in hand, the attention of the
Commonwealth was at once turned to Ireland and Scotland, both of
which seemed dangerous as bases for a Royalist reaction. In two
years and two weeks (August, 1649, to September, 1651) Cromwell
overcame the two regions by force. For the first time all the British
Isles were united under a single powerful authority.

Ireland presented a menacing Royalist front under the Duke of
Ormond, the Lord Lieutenant, who had united both Catholic and
Protestant Ireland in opposition to Parliament. His formidable
forces, strengthened by some English Royalists, threatened to gain
complete control of the island. In August, 1649, Cromwell was
sent over with fifteen thousand men, and in ten months had Ireland
at his feet. But those months left a serious blot on his reputation;
for he went in the vengeful spirit of an Old Testament leader, mindful
of the massacres of 1641, which to him called loudly for reprisals upon
a despised people (see page 344). Quickly after landing, he struck at
the seaport of Drogheda, to improve his communications, and ordered
the massacre of the garrison. The Royalist commander, who had
fought in England all the way from Edgehill to the last little battle
of the war, had his skull smashed with his own wooden leg; hundreds
perished by cold steel in the streets; and when seventy took refuge in
a church steeple, it was set afire. Similar treatment was dealt out to
the garrison at Wexford. There were many scattered operations
against an elusive enemy, and Ireland was well humbled by the
time Oliver returned for his Scottish work.

The name of Cromwell, however, has been hated in Ireland not so much for his cruelty at Drogheda and Wexford as for his land settlement, under which Ireland was to suffer for two centuries and a half. The men whom Cromwell left in charge, his sons-in-law and then his son, carried out a policy which ranks as a very important step in Anglo-Irish relations. It was a different sort of settlement from that of the "plantation of Ulster," where both landowners and peasantry had been moved out of a considerable portion of the northern province to make room for Scottish and English colonists forty years before. Under Cromwell, from two thirds to three quarters of the rest of the land in Ireland passed into the hands of Protestant English landlords. The great majority of the peasants were left in southern Ireland, still predominantly Celtic and Catholic, but were deprived of the natural leadership of a Catholic landed aristocracy; and many were transported overseas, particularly to the West Indies. The new landowners were in part adventurers, who had helped to finance the invasion, and in part officers and soldiers of Cromwell's army. Many of the latter sold their shares to wealthier men, who built up extensive estates. Some of the lesser English landowners ultimately mingled with the native Catholic Irish; but the Protestant aristocrats tended to remain aloof from their oppressed tenantry. They often became absentee landlords, who rarely visited the estates in which their only interest lay in the money which their stewards could squeeze from the tenants. The twentieth century was to come before England finally took effective measures to undo the unfortunate effects of this Cromwellian settlement.

But Oliver did not remain behind to parcel out the land. Late in June, 1650, three weeks after he returned from Ireland, a ship arrived in Scotland bearing a cynical, charming young rake whom the Scots had already hailed as Charles II of Scotland and England, a month after his father's execution. The dour Presbyterians had persuaded Charles to accept their distasteful Covenant as the price of their support in recovering the Stuart thrones. Scotland was preparing to invade England to restore the monarchy. Consequently Parliament decided to strike first, and Cromwell took sixteen thousand men up the Great North Road to Edinburgh. He approached the Scots in a mood quite different from his bitter contempt for the Irish. The army of the Scots was twice the size of his, and he knew from Marston Moor that they were good soldiers. He tried to appeal to the clergy of the Kirk, who controlled the situation; "I beseech you, in the bowels of Christ," he wrote, "think it possible you may be mistaken." But the enemy remained stubborn, and the Scots nearly trapped Cromwell at Dunbar, with his back to the sea. A counterattack, however, in the September dawn brought victory to

# The Puritan Revolt

the Roundheads. Ten thousand Scots were prisoners and three thousand dead, while barely twenty Englishmen had died.

Dunbar broke the ascendancy of the Kirk. Cromwell took Edinburgh and overran the Lowlands; but the Scots rallied a new army on a broader national basis than Calvinism. They held an impregnable position at the gateway to the Highlands, and Cromwell could not dislodge them. Then in the next summer, 1651, he resorted to daring strategy, luring them out by leaving the road to England open. A force of Scots and Royalists started down the west coast under their new king and pushed on far past Preston, where Cromwell had beaten them three years before. He raced down to head them off, and met them, a year to a day after Dunbar, by the old cathedral city of Worcester, far down on the Welsh border. Among the few who escaped was young Charles Stuart. Disguised as a servant, he was spirited from house to house by loyal Royalists. He had many narrow escapes, at one time hiding for hours in an oak while the Roundheads searched the woods. Taking ship, he left England again for nine more years of exile on the Continent. Scotland was soon pacified, and a Cromwellian army of occupation brought relative peace to the unruly Highlands. "The very ruined nation," as Cromwell called it, was not happy under its red-coated masters, but at least it gave England no further serious trouble for many years.

There was trouble enough elsewhere. Five weeks after Worcester, Parliament passed an act which quickly led to foreign war. Under Elizabeth, England and Holland had often worked together in opposition to Spain. The decay of Spanish sea power, however, turned the former allies into rivals. They had raced for the spoils of the Portuguese Indies, and the Dutch had secured the lion's share. The spices from the East were not the only source of Dutch wealth. All sea routes led to Amsterdam, which became the leading seaport and financial center of Europe. It was a case of "he that hath, to him shall be given"; for Amsterdam, with all its wealth, could finance maritime ventures at a low rate of interest, and each venture led to more wealth. The trade of the Baltic, the Mediterranean, and many of the byways of commerce came under Dutch control; and, as one of their lesser ventures, the Dutch had established New Netherland in America for the fur trade.

All this was annoying to England, which had maritime ambitions of her own. The Dutch practice which caused deepest resentment concerned the carrying trade. Holland not only bought and sold in large quantities but also provided ships for the merchants of other nations who wanted to sell their own goods or to buy. If a London merchant wanted to bring wine from Bordeaux or masts from Danzig, he was likely to use Dutch ships, because of lower freight rates. Against this Dutch carrying trade Parliament struck with the first Navigation Act in 1651. Holland was now at the height of her power; for her complete independence from Spain had finally been recognized in 1648, after an eighty-years' struggle, and she had built up a strong navy. Nevertheless, Cromwell defied Holland by this law, which provided that European goods must be imported into England only in English vessels, with crews at least half English, or in vessels of the producing nation. Wine, for instance, might be brought from Bordeaux in English or French vessels, but no longer in the Dutch ships which had been generally employed. In trade with Asia, Africa, and America, however, only English ships could be used.

England now had a navy with which to support this provocative legislation. In 1648 Parliament's control of the seas had been threatened when eleven warships, more than a quarter of the navy, declared for the king in the Second Civil War. Prince Rupert, the erstwhile cavalryman, took them on a far-flung piratical raid. The Commonwealth sent a soldier to sea to catch him,—short, stout Colonel Robert Blake, hero of two sieges in the west country. Fifty years old when he first took command of a warship, Blake in the remaining eight years of his life won a naval reputation which places him with Drake and Nelson among England's greatest seamen. He chased Rupert to Ireland, to Portugal, to Spain, and around into the Mediterranean, demonstrating to England the strategic importance of that sea. Rupert swept over to the colonies, and Barbados and Virginia became temporarily Royalist; but he was pursued, and his squadron dispersed. By 1651 Parliament was powerful on the seas and had re-established its firm hold on the colonies. The fleet was doubled in size. With its eighty warships and its energetic seagoing military commanders, it was ready to challenge the Dutch.

There was no surprise when the Navigation Act led, in 1652, to a two-year naval struggle with Holland. It was the most closely contested of all England's naval wars; for the honors were fairly even in the various stubborn combats which were waged in and around the Channel. Van Tromp and De Ruyter could hold their own with the doughty Blake. But, while the Dutch shared the fighting honors, they were so thoroughly dependent upon sea-borne commerce that its interruption hurt them far more than the English. The harbor of Amsterdam became a forest of masts of idle ships; financial ruin was imminent. Peace was made in 1654, and the Navigation Act remained in force. Two more Dutch wars (1665–1667, 1672–1674) were to be necessary, however, before Holland was eliminated as an active competitor on the high seas.

# The Puritan Revolt

The recurrent crises in the British Isles, with the bold foreign policy, necessitated heavy taxation, considerable censorship, and other rather harsh measures which began to produce a reaction against the Rump and its executive body, the Council of State. In addition, "blue laws," upholding the extreme ascetic Puritan ideals of conduct and morals by repressive restrictions, were a constant, everyday source of irritation. At the same time the army, not even yet paid its arrears, was restive. Cromwell, apparently well aware of the dissatisfaction with the Rump, waited until that body took the unwise step of preparing to fill vacant seats by nomination instead of by election. On April 20, 1653, his impatience produced one of the most dramatic scenes in English history. He rose from his seat and roundly denounced the Rump for its injustice and inefficiency. "I will put an end to your prating," he shouted; "you are no Parliament." He called thirty musketeers into the chamber. Turning to the mace, the symbol of the Commons' authority, he cried: "What are we to do with this bauble? Take it away." As the members crowded out, Cromwell flung individual invectives at them. Then, in characteristic Cromwellian fashion, he called to them, "It's you that have forced me to this, for I have sought the Lord night and day that he would rather slay me than put me upon the doing of this work." He had commented in a similar vein upon the execution of the king. So ended in violence the thirteen years of stress in which at least a portion of the Long Parliament had been sitting regularly.

At last the power of the army was no longer cloaked. A provisional council, composed largely of army officers with Cromwell at its head, replaced the former Council of State. Cromwell still felt that a Parliament was necessary, but one that must be kept under control. Consequently he and the Council selected the members from lists of "suitable" men compiled by the Independent preachers of the country. This new "Nominated Parliament"—or "Barebones Parliament," as it is sometimes known, because one of its members rejoiced in the name "Praise-God Barebones"—naturally was composed of the more extreme religious fanatics. All sorts of measures —some too extreme for the times, like the abolition of tithes—soon alienated every faction in some way or another. The Barebones Parliament lasted from July to December, 1653; then Cromwell again used soldiers to expel such members of this overactive body as did not join in a self-denying motion to dissolve.

This second violent ending of a Parliament led to the Protectorate in place of the Commonwealth (although some use the latter term to include the whole interregnum between the reigns of Charles I and Charles II). The army officers offered England her first and only written constitution, the "Instrument of Government." By this Cromwell was to be Lord Protector for life, while a Parliament was to be elected by a fairly generous franchise, omitting Catholics and those who had borne arms against Parliament. It was to meet for at least five months every three years. The Protector's power and that of Parliament were both to be limited, one by the other.

The first Protectorate Parliament, in 1654, at once debated the Instrument of Government. Parliament was determined to reduce the army and to whittle away the Protector's power. After five months Cromwell's patience ended. "Instead of mercy and truth being brought together," he said, "weeds and nettles, briars and thorns have thriven under your shadow." Again Parliamentary procedure was brought to an end, and the shadow of dictatorship came closer.

As for Cromwell, many expected him to become king; a second Protectorate Parliament requested that he take the crown. The Protector hesitated long before refusing, but he could not bring himself thus to affront his old comrades in arms. The office of Lord Protector, however, he was willing to accept. A new Parliament was elected, and a second House—not called the House of Lords but simply "the other House"—he filled by appointment (1658).

Meanwhile Cromwell's foreign policy continued vigorous and aggressive, although in some ways unusual, since, toward the end of his rule, he ignored the balance of power by his co-operation with France, the strongest nation in Europe. At first it looked even as though the English country squire might become head of a great league of Protestant nations, and Cromwell did his best to unite the Danes, Swedes, Dutch, Protestant Germans, and English against the Catholic powers. This scheme did not succeed; but, on the other hand, Cromwell extended England's prestige among European nations to a point which it had never before attained. His hand fell heavily upon the Spanish empire, and he justly takes title as one of the founders of British naval supremacy. Late in 1654 Admiral Penn, father of the founder of Pennsylvania, took a fleet to the West Indies, and a year later captured Jamaica, soon to become England's richest colony. Blake, under Cromwell's orders, made the Mediterranean all but a British lake. The last dying act of this British admiral was the annihilation of a Spanish treasure fleet. Cromwell made an alliance with Mazarin, France's second great statesman-cardinal; and three thousand redcoats helped to win the battle of the Dunes over the Spaniards, as a result of which the port of Dunkerque fell to England as a prize.

In domestic affairs the Protector was not so fortunate. As a temporary solution, to offset the all-prevailing internal disorders, he

# The Puritan Revolt

parceled England out into wide districts, over each of which he placed a major general with full administrative jurisdiction. A peaceful conforming England was obtained by their harsh rule, but underneath surged a bitter weariness and an increasing desire for a Stuart restoration. The Stuarts at their worst had done nothing as generally unpopular as the enforcement of the blue laws by soldiers. Theaters, cockfighting, church festivals, and other forms of merriment dear to the hearts of the people were prohibited, and England was forced to endure the negations of the harsh, gloomy Puritan Sabbaths. On the Sabbath only grave necessity was an excuse for travel, and then only with formal permission; even walking was deemed an unholy pleasure. Severe morality was enforced; and swearing was forbidden, let alone flirting. But the atmosphere of Massachusetts Bay rested poorly upon England; and Cromwell, who was fond of music, horses, and all field sports, doubtless would have put a stop to this extravagant righteousness had not his own end been near.

Oliver died in September, 1658, on the anniversary of Dunbar and of Worcester; and, his strong hand once removed, England passed through a troubled year and a half during which it seemed likely that a new civil war, this time between soldier and civilian, might break out at any moment. During half this period Cromwell's elder son Richard held nominal authority as Lord Protector; but "Tumbledown Dick" lacked the force and ability for the position and soon dropped from view, while the Rump was recalled and threw its influence behind the civilian discontent as army commanders maneuvered for power. At last, in the first week of 1660, General Monk, who had commanded the army of occupation in Scotland, led his redcoats through the border town of Coldstream (from which the first regiment of the regular army was to take its name) and marched southward to back the civilians in their demand for a free Parliament. All the surviving members of the Long Parliament were called back to join the Rump; the Long Parliament issued a summons for a new election; and the resultant "Convention" Parliament recalled Charles II from his long exile. The turbulence of the interregnum at last gave way to the less heroic gaiety of the Restoration, and the Puritan revolt was at an end.

Its failure for many a long day was to cast a shadow upon Puritanism in general and upon Oliver in particular. The former, at its worst, had been a nightmare; but at its best it had sought, not ignobly, to raise to high and worthy levels the entire life of the English people. As for Oliver, he remains something of an enigma. Like Caesar, like Napoleon, he bent a nation to his will. Unlike them, he was a man most humble of mind, baffled by problems beyond his powers to solve.

# CHAPTER XIV

## Restoration England

### 1660-1688

---

IN MAY, 1660, a dark, slender Stuart celebrated his thirtieth birthday by returning to London as King Charles II. He rode into the capital "with twenty thousand horse and foot, brandishing their swords and shouting with inexpressible joy; the ways strewed with flowers, the bells ringing, the streets hung with tapestry, fountains running with wine." London was madly exuberant. The grim repression of the reign of the saints was over; so, too, was the dread uncertainty which had followed the death of Cromwell. There was gratitude to General Monk, who had made the decision to bring the monarchy back; to the rather irregular Parliament which had extended the invitation; and to Admiral Montague, who had brought the new king over from Holland in a flagship with the name *Naseby* hastily painted out and that of *Royal Charles* substituted.

Just what was this England like to which this son of the Stuarts returned from exile? England's social system, as we have noticed, differed in many ways from that of France, where he had spent many of his impoverished years of exile (see pages 245–247). At the close of the Restoration period a writer made some estimates which are interesting as indications both of the numbers in the various English social classes and occupations and of the average annual income for each group. His guesses were "generally accepted at the time as reasonable," but the money values, of course, must be multiplied several times to reach their modern equivalents. The following list gives the number of heads of families in each group, together with the yearly income per family: 160 temporal lords, £3200; 26 spiritual lords (archbishops and bishops), £1300; 800 baronets, £880; 600 knights, £650; 3000 esquires, £450; 12,000 gentlemen, £450; 5000 persons in greater offices and places, £240; 5000 persons in lesser offices and places, £120; 2000 eminent merchants and traders by sea, £400; 8000 lesser merchants and traders by sea, £198; 10,000 persons in the law, £154; 2000 eminent clergymen, £72; 8000 lesser clergymen, £50; 40,000 freeholders (yeomen) of the better sort, £91; 120,000 freeholders (yeomen) of the lesser sort, £55; 150,000 (tenant) farmers, £42 10s.; 15,000 persons in liberal arts and sciences, £60; 50,000 shopkeepers and tradesmen, £45; 60,000 artisans and handicraftsmen, £38; 5000 naval officers, £80; 4000 military officers, £60; 50,000 common seamen, £20; 35,000 common soldiers, £14; 364,000 laboring people and outservants, £15; 400,000 cottars and paupers, £6 10s.; and an indeterminate number of "vagrants, as gipsies, thieves, beggars, &c." The blanket phrase "gentry" would include the 16,400 baronets, knights, esquires, and gentlemen, while the phrase "middle class" would probably include the group ten times that size, engaged in public office, the professions, commerce, trade, and industry, and as naval and military officers. The yeomen and tenant farmers, some 310,000, formed a sort of agricultural middle class; the remainder, more than half the population, formed the lower classes.

England still had an essentially agricultural economy. There was, of course, the metropolis of London, as well as some smaller towns; but most English wealth was still derived from the ownership of land, and the vast majority of English workers still labored at tilling the soil. The ugliness and efficiency which were to attend England's tremendous industrial development still lay more than a century in the future. The land of England was about half under cultivation, with the remainder pasture, woodland, moor, or fen. The oak forests which had once covered the island were gradually disappearing; many of the huge trees were being devoured as charcoal for the iron furnaces, and the navy was beginning to worry about timber wherewith to build its ships. But much that was still wild and primitive remained in the English landscape, especially in the barren northern and southwestern counties.

Of all the social classes the most conspicuous but the least characteristically English was the court group which surrounded Charles at his Whitehall palace, or which occasionally went to Bath at the proper season for the cures. Among that group were many of those who held the highest titles in the peerage—dukes and earls, not a few created from among the boon companions or loyal supporters of the king. That little group was also, probably, the wealthiest in the land. Aping the new society which the French king was gathering about him at Versailles, and led by a monarch who was a fitting master of revels, the Restoration court lived in a constant round of showy and licentious gaiety. Men with clever, cynical wit and boldness of action strove for the bounties which were lavishly granted by a king too poor to pay his sailors or repair his ships; while maids of honor, whose actions belied their titles, shamelessly sought to make the most of their opportunities, to the scandal of a land just emerging from Puritan repression. Not the least shocking to the nation was the number and prominence of the royal mistresses. Chief among these women, who had no small influence on the course of events, were Barbara Villiers, who became Countess of Castlemaine and eventually Duchess of Cleveland; the French Louise de Querouaille, who was made Duchess of Portsmouth; and "pretty, witty" Nell Gwynne, a vivacious red-headed actress who held first place in the king's affections during the later years of the reign.

But the gay group which surrounded the king at Whitehall was not typical of England, even of upper-class England. Many of the peers and most of the gentry, the true landed aristocracy, seldom visited the capital. The country squires, whom we noticed at the beginning of the Tudor period (see page 246), still held their dominant position in local and national government, though many of them spent a considerable part of their days in hunting the fox, and their nights in emptying the bottle. Harsh game laws, passed by a Parliament of landowners and enforced locally by the justices of the same class, reserved hunting for these gentlemen of fairly high income. The world of the average country gentleman still remained normally limited to his particular county. Seldom did he visit London unless elected to Parliament. Worcester, Leicester, Gloucester, and similar shire towns were to the county families what Whitehall was to the great lords and courtiers; and the quarter sessions of the shire courts were apt to be accompanied by a local social season which brought the neighboring magnates together. This localism helped to produce a stubborn and sometimes ignorant prejudice. The squire, according to Lord Macaulay in his famous picture of various aspects of English life at this period, "hated Frenchmen and Italians, Scotchmen and Irishmen, Papists and Presbyterians, Independents and Baptists, Quakers and Jews. Toward London and Londoners he felt an aversion which more than once produced important political effects." Macaulay further portrayed the squire as an uncouth, crude boor, with little education and with his chief pleasures "commonly derived from field sports and from unrefined sensuality." At the same time, Macaulay admitted that the squire was "essentially a patrician, and had in large measure both the virtues and the vices which flourish among men set from birth in high place, and accustomed to authority, to observance and to self-respect." Macaulay's estimates have of late years been discounted as decidedly too harsh. His prejudices have been explained on the ground that, when rival political parties arose toward the close of the Restoration period, squires and also clergy were generally Tories, whereas Macaulay strongly favored the Whigs. To offset the impression created by the generalities of this "Whig pamphleteer," it must be remembered that Hampden, Eliot, and Pym were among those from this same class of gentry, which had played no small part in the Puritan opposition to the first two Stuart kings and which now gave loyal support to the third.

In the rural classes lower than the gentry were the vast majority of the whole population of England, making what living they could from the soil. In agriculture two groups were about equal in number: the yeomen, who owned their land as freeholders, and the tenant farmers, who rented land to cultivate. Economically there was little difference between the two. They actually worked the land themselves, often with the help of a farm hand or two. In some respects, however, the yeoman could hold his head higher than the tenant farmer. He belonged to that sturdy minority which had maintained independence since Saxon times and which had furnished the archers who won Crécy and Poitiers (see pages 72, 177). As a freeholder with land yielding at least forty shillings a year, he could vote for county members of Parliament. The choice of such members often depended upon the free votes of the yeomen. No landlord could coerce their choice; for they enjoyed an independence greater than the tenant farmer. This class of yeomen, which would begin to dwindle away in the next century, has received high praise as "an eminently manly and true-hearted race," a particularly sturdy and valuable element in English society.

Below the yeomen and the tenant farmers came the great mass of peasantry proper. Some of these were cottars. They lived in the little cottages which made up the rural village, tilling a small strip, or plot, of ground, for which they generally paid rent, keeping a few geese or animals on the common land, and sometimes acting as spinners and weavers for the "clothiers" in the domestic system of industry (see page 244). The cottar made little more than enough to subsist on; £14 a year was a fair average. Still lower in the scale were farm hands, the agricultural laborers who worked for wages, tilling the soil or tending the animals for some lord, gentleman, yeoman, or tenant farmer. It was estimated just after the Restoration that about one third of the whole population made barely enough for subsistence, while another third was unable to live without poor relief. Some of these poor lived in London slums, but most of them were rural.

Yet, with all that, seldom in its history has the land come nearer to being "merry England" than in that period. The per-capita sum of happiness in England's whole population was certainly higher than it was to be in succeeding generations after the Agricultural and Industrial Revolutions had made the nation more efficient at the expense of individual well-being. The peasants, to be sure, toiled hard and lived on the edge of poverty; but they were for the most part wholesome men whose rather slow intellects seldom spent much time in speculation upon their lot. The world of politics and society passed far above them; not for two centuries more would they have a voice in the government. The month-after-month, year-after-year routine of planting, cultivating, and reaping was broken by frequent holidays and festivals in which they could make merry in keeping alive the old customs, some of which ran back into pagan times. All England went into the woods before dawn on May Day; Christmas, Michaelmas, St. Valentine's Day, and many another occasion had its observances to which the peasant as well as his betters could look forward as partial relief from dreary routine.

The remaining "middle class" fifth of England's population were to be found in London and the towns. They were engaged in commerce and industry, which were to become more and more distinctive of modern England. It was estimated that more than one tenth of England's five million inhabitants lived in London, perhaps the largest city of its day. In the vast settlement which had grown up on the Thames, forty miles from the sea, there were then, as now, two centers of particular importance. The "City" proper was the business heart of the nation. A mile or so farther up the Thames, connected with the City by the Strand and Fleet Street, were Westminster and Whitehall, the political center of the nation. Slums stretched to the eastward of the City, where lay the shipping which could not pass above London Bridge. Other parts of the north bank, and to a lesser extent the south bank, already were growing with the steady increase in London's citizens.

The City had once been practically all there was to London. It lay within the lines of the old Roman walls, through which gates led out in various directions. It enjoyed special privileges, some of them dating back to Henry I. The king, for instance, might not enter the City without permission; and a special municipal organization, with a Lord Mayor and other colorful functionaries, extended back into the days of the guilds. Within its walls was transacted most of England's important business. There merchants negotiated for the purchase or sale of goods from all parts of the world, and there most of the major financial transactions were conducted. The port of London was constantly increasing its activity and within a half century would catch up with Amsterdam. The "Pool" below London Bridge was a regular forest of masts. Many of the merchants had their homes within the City; and many lesser buildings, chiefly of timber and plaster, were crowded within the confined space, their

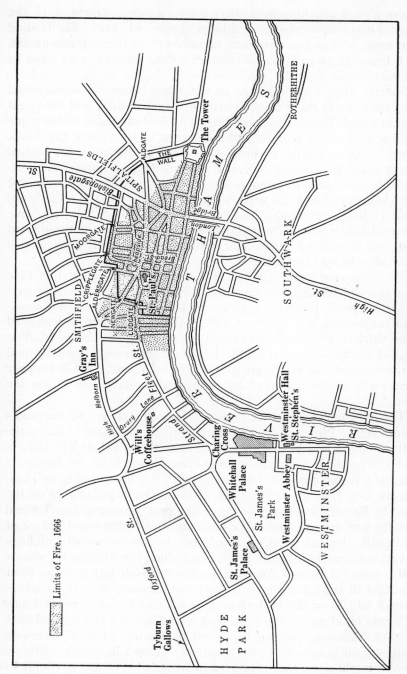

LONDON IN THE RESTORATION PERIOD

gables almost touching over the narrow, winding streets, until the Great Fire of 1666 wiped out a large number of them. The leading merchants of London were men of influence in the nation's affairs, with interests as well as habits often widely distinct from those of the rural squires.

Shortly after Charles came to the throne, London encountered two calamities in rapid succession: the Plague in 1665 and the Great Fire in 1666. The Plague was the last violent outbreak of the same scourge which had cropped out from time to time since the Black Death three centuries earlier. This time its effects were limited pretty much to London, where at least seventy thousand are estimated to have died in a few months. The sturdy Pepys was among the few who stayed at his work while others fled—"little noise heard night or day," he wrote, "but the tolling of bells." The epidemic was probably not much worse than several others in the not-distant past, but it received widespread publicity, particularly through the vivid account by Daniel Defoe.

The following year (1666) London was struck again, this time by a fire which raged five days and cleared out a considerable part of the City. It spared the slums to the eastward, nor did it extend far toward Westminster; but in the City proper it destroyed some thirteen thousand homes and eighty-nine churches, including the old Gothic cathedral of St. Paul's. Fortunately, England had at the moment one of the greatest of her architects, Sir Christopher Wren, who designed a more beautiful and sanitary London on the ruins.

The Westminster district had long been the center of England's government. Within a stone's throw of Westminster Abbey, the national shrine, lay Westminster Hall and St. Stephen's. The highest courts of law had sat for centuries in Westminster Hall. St. Stephen's was the meeting place of Parliament until fire destroyed it in 1834, and the new Parliament buildings which we know today rose on the site. In Restoration times, however, the great center of interest and activity was not in those sober buildings but in the royal palace of Whitehall, close at hand. A conglomerate assemblage of buildings of varying sizes and shapes, it stretched along the Thames for almost half a mile. It housed not only the king himself but also the chief ministers of state and the great array of servants of every kind,— a small edition of the glittering court which Charles's cousin Louis XIV was building for the French at Versailles. In and around that mass of buildings, royalty combined pageantry, play, and serious business, while ministers and courtiers engaged in steady intrigue. Anyone might come to see the king praying in his chapel or dining in

# Restoration England

his stately banqueting hall; anyone might walk in the long stone gallery, where men of all kinds, with errands and schemes of as many sorts, met, chatted, and exchanged rumors. There were more exclusive places to which the king might withdraw: to the anteroom, where he met the foreign ministers; to the great bedchamber overlooking the Thames, where the real business of state was transacted; to the council room; and finally, when he had an opportunity for much-needed solitude, to the "king's closet," where he kept certain prized possessions—clocks, watches, maps, ship models, and "old masters." Beyond Whitehall stretched St. James's Park, where the king sauntered with his spaniels or took his exercise at tennis or "pall mall." The color, glamour, and excitement of Restoration Whitehall have disappeared, save perhaps for the daily guard mount of the Horse Guards or the royal spectacle at the opening of Parliament. Yet in Downing Street, in the Parliament buildings, at the Admiralty, and in other near-by buildings the principal governmental business of the nation and the empire is still transacted in that very region.

There was much more to London than commerce and courts; its half million inhabitants followed a mode of life quite different from that of the rural manor or cottage. We can best see Restoration London through the eyes of Samuel Pepys, who left behind perhaps the most remarkable diary ever written. The middle-class son of a London tailor from Cromwell's fen country, and a graduate of Cambridge, his start toward success came at the Restoration when his cousin, Admiral Montague, secured him a post on the Navy Board, from which he rose to become the secretary of the Admiralty. In his official capacity Pepys has been described as one of the most valuable public servants England ever had; for he managed well a chronically bankrupt navy. Conscientious as he was toward duty, he remembered his cousin's advice that it was not the salary alone which made governmental office profitable. He was ready to accept presents for services rendered, provided they did not run counter to the king's interest; and at the end of every year he remarked with pride upon how his personal fortune had grown.

It was not the description of his official functions, however, that makes the Pepys diary memorable. During the first nine years of the Restoration he confided daily in shorthand to his diary an uncensored and lively account of what he saw, what he did, and what he thought and felt. His complete frankness shows us vividly both the man and the society in which he lived. Between the "up betimes" and the "so to bed" each day he crowded more varied activity than a fox-hunting, hard-drinking squire would encounter in months.

We see the domestic life of a successful middle-class man of the city, and of his wife, "poor wretch," a pretty, rather simple French blonde, who must have found him trying, for he had a roving eye and wrote of his "tousling of wenches" and his more serious amours with a candor which few others would trust to paper. Outside, in the capital, his gregarious disposition and insatiable curiosity about everything left little undescribed. He hobnobbed with peers and high officials; carried drunken admirals home at night; relished the latest gossip about Castlemaine and others of the glittering court; engaged in learned discussions on science, politics, and economics; hunted out hangings and cockfights; and, altogether, missed little of the gay and complex life of the capital. The unwashed denizens of the slums to the eastward seldom appear in his diary; it was they who gave London its importance in quantity, and he was more interested in those who gave it pre-eminence in quality. It is out of the question in brief space to recapture the atmosphere of Restoration London as Pepys saw it; a few delightful hours with the diary itself will do that far more effectively.

Some new features came into London life with the Restoration. Wine and beer were consumed in large quantities as usual, but tea and coffee also made their appearance. The coffeehouse became a daily rendezvous for the Londoner and served as a clearinghouse for rumors and theories of every sort. The theater, too, took on a gayer tone when, in accordance with the new custom, women took the place of boys for feminine roles. Night after night, going cautiously about the unpoliced streets, which were dangerous at night and dirty at all times, Pepys attended plays. *The Slighted Mayde, The Wilde Gallant,* and scores of others were seen by him; for such literary achievement as the Restoration did encourage—and it was not very meritorious—took the form of writing plays which are notorious for licentious dialogue.

Two of the well-known playwrights are William Wycherley and John Dryden. The former, having lived in France, brought a Parisian atmosphere to the English stage. He is noteworthy, among other things, for changing his religion five times, so as to be tactful, and for writing such a graceful poem in praise of harlotry as to win the favor of the king's mistress the Duchess of Cleveland. His later life was more seemly than his early career. Married to a wealthy widow, he was permitted but one public house, and that opposite his home, where he had to sit by an unshaded window in order that Dame Wycherley might note who spoke to him.

As for Dryden, his plays can scarcely be considered an improvement on Wycherley's. Of one of them Pepys wrote, "A very innocent, and most pretty, witty play." The last two adjectives may be applicable, but "innocent" seems a strong word to apply to any theatrical production under the Restoration. Dryden, however, in his latter years abandoned plays for satirical poems. He achieved permanent fame by holding up to scorn the pretensions of Charles's bastard son the Duke of Monmouth and by a poem entitled *The Hind and the Panther*, in which he defended the Catholic Church, of which he became a member to please James II. Religion, it is to be presumed, sat as lightly on Dryden as on his London contemporaries.

There was, however, outside the capital, one of different mold, by name John Bunyan, who wrote at this time. A private in the army of Parliament, an itinerant preacher, a mystic, a fanatic, and a Dissenter of Dissenters, Bunyan had little to recommend him to the Restoration wits. Plenty of other allegories there have been, but none with quite the vividness and stark simplicity of *Pilgrim's Progress*. "Images came crowding on his mind faster than he could put them into words, quagmires and pits, steep hills, dark and gloomy glens, soft vales, sunny pastures, a gloomy castle of which the courtyard was strewn with the skulls and bones of murdered prisoners, a town, all bustle and splendour, like London on Lord Mayor's Day, and the narrow path." There was much emphasis on the "narrow path," as well as the Delectable Mountains, the Enchanted Ground, the Black River, the Shining Gate. Judge Hate-Good, Mrs. Diffidence, and Mr. Great-Heart became in old England and in New England household words. As for their author, released from prison by the king's pardon (His Majesty could not well pardon Catholics without pardoning Dissenters), he became a kind of informal wandering bishop to the lowly. *Pilgrim's Progress*, printed on the roughest of paper and circulating only among the poorer folk, lived on to become a far more celebrated English classic than Dryden's famed translation of Vergil.

Science as well as literature now flourished in England. In the days of Cromwell learned men, interested in "Physick, Anatomy, Geometry, Astronomy, Navigation, Staticks, Magneticks, Chymicles, Mechanicks, and Natural Experiments," had met informally at Oxford,—an "invisible college." These men apparently became the nucleus of the Royal Society, to which Charles II granted a charter in 1662. The king acted as patron, appointed the first officers, and attended at least one meeting, where a special program for His Majesty provided for experiments with a thermometer, with chemicals, and with reflecting pictures on a wall. The Royal Society investigated "soils and clays for making better bricks"; it took note of "all physical receipts and secretes, instrumentes, tools, engines";

it fostered new methods "of brewing ale and beer, manuring with lime, devising a new cider press, and a lamp for hatching eggs." A wide correspondence was begun with foreign scientists; and when Leeuwenhoek, in Holland, invented the microscope, the society sent two of its members there to investigate. The transactions of the society became internationally famous and were published in Latin in different foreign countries. Shortly they filled twelve volumes. A museum and a library were opened. The society grew steadily in influence and authority and has continued to this day, one of the most respected organizations in the world.

London had no rival in England; for Bristol and Norwich, the next two cities in size, each had not quite thirty thousand inhabitants. Bristol, as we have seen, was a busy seaport on the southwest coast, particularly important in the trade with America. Norwich was the center of the East Anglian woolen industry. Below them the population dropped off again sharply to the ten thousand of York, "capital of the north," and to that of Exeter, "capital of the west." The other county towns, centers of the business and social life of the shires, were even smaller. Many of them continued the old forms of the guild organization, although industry had spread out into the country under the domestic system. The future big centers of the Industrial Revolution—Manchester and Leeds, which were to lead in textiles, and Birmingham and Sheffield, the iron centers—still had only a few thousand inhabitants. London, therefore, was clearly *the* city of England.

So much for the general population. In a picture of Restoration England it is desirable also to note certain special branches of activity. Agriculture and industry will be considered later; for they still continued in much the same old medieval ways, though changes lay just around the corner. So too with communication; for there was no novelty in the wretched roads, which only grew worse each spring with their deep ruts and holes. The new stagecoaches did well to travel fifty miles a day, jolting through mire or dust and sticking more commonly than not (see pages 505–511).

The Church of England was settling down into relative apathy after the tense excitement of the earlier part of the century,—an apathy which was to become more marked in the next century. It was opposed to Catholics and Dissenters, but at this time it had little beyond empty formalism to offer. It was "established" as a virtual branch of the government, and its support was compulsory through the collection of tithes. Macaulay's description of the clergy was even more biased than his view of the squires, and has been even more discredited by recent writers. Although there were many able men among the bishops, the London preachers, and the parsons in the more prosperous parishes, he concentrated on the "unemployed" clergy who could not secure a decent living and became domestic chaplains to squires who would use them to say grace at dinner but dismiss them before dessert and, during the rest of the day, treated them as merely handy men around the manor. They were, according to Macaulay, fitting matches for servant girls who were not quite good enough to marry stewards. Yet the country parson certainly had influence in the community second only to the squire, and was to be ranked among the strong elements of Toryism which grew up, late in the Restoration period, in support of royal power. With all its lack of vital force, at this time the Church of England received the loyalty of a large proportion of the country gentlemen.

Connected with the Church were the two universities, Oxford and Cambridge, which had, together, about four thousand students. Neither was a center of vital intellectual activity at the time. Like the Church, they were slipping toward the apathy which was to characterize them in the eighteenth century. Cambridge was generally a little more active and a little less fashionable. The students as a whole fell into two classes. The sons of the nobility and gentry often went to the university simply for the college life as part of their social training. There was, however, a numerous class of "sizars," or self-help students, who either received scholarships or did menial jobs to support themselves, and who generally trained for the ministry. The rules against Dissenters robbed the universities of a supply of excellent potential material.

The standing army was still in its infancy. The English had long had a prejudice against a regular royal force, and the experience of the Cromwellian period had deepened this aversion. The beginning of the regular army dates from 1661, when one of Monk's regiments became the Coldstream Guards (see page 363). Several other guard regiments were gradually formed, but were not popular with Englishmen. Several regiments of Englishmen were in military service in the pay of Holland or other foreign powers, so that a force of trained men might be called upon in an emergency; but domestic military service was not in high repute.

In modern England the royal navy has always enjoyed more prestige and popularity than the army. The country maintained a regular force of fighting ships by this time, no longer depending, as it had done in Tudor times, on using converted merchantmen in an emergency. After the period of neglect under the early Stuarts the navy had risen to high efficiency under Cromwell, and it was kept in fighting trim through the three Dutch wars, in spite of constant financial starvation which it required all the ingenuity of Pepys to offset. Even at that, rotten ships and ill-fed, unpaid crews too often hampered the efficiency of naval operations. The later remarkable breed of professional naval officers had not yet developed. Some were courtier captains, who could barely keep their feet planted on deck in a moderate sea; others were crude, unlettered, but effective "tarpaulins," who had risen from the forecastle. As Macaulay remarked, "there were gentlemen and there were seamen in the navy of Charles the Second. But the seamen were not gentlemen; and the gentlemen were not seamen."

By the next century not only naval officers but much else in England had taken on a more conventional, uniform, and static pattern. The French influences at play during the Restoration period were to assist in transmitting a certain amount of external polish without materially impairing the essential English qualities. While society was thus to settle down into somewhat conventional lines, it was to be but temporarily static. Agriculture and industry were to experience before the end of the eighteenth century as thoroughgoing and as radical transformations as the political and religious upheavals which had convulsed seventeenth-century England.

Charles, who came to this England after long years of exile and hardships which he had borne with good humor, was one of the most astute of all the English kings. Excessive laziness and cynical indifference masked this latent cleverness well. Only in the matter of mental acuteness did Charles have anything in common with the resolute, earnest, hard-hitting, God-fearing Cromwell. Even in national characteristics they differed. Whereas Cromwell was essentially an Englishman born and bred, Charles was foreign in heritage, upbringing, and attitude. Even his grandparents had little English blood—Scottish, Danish, Spanish, and French they were. His mother's French strain, accentuated by his formative years of exile spent principally in France, predominated in Charles. He knew how to capitalize his infectious smile and ready wit to win men to his cause. An assiduous pursuer of pleasure and possessor of a bevy of fascinating mistresses, the "Merry Monarch" was a fit leader for the quarter century of boisterous license into which England lapsed after her overdose of Puritan grimness. His open scandals shocked the more sedate elements in England, who were even more disturbed by his careless neglect of royal duties. A thorough cynic, he took few things seriously and held still fewer sacred. Yet Charles's keen mind kept him safely from playing the fool to any dangerous degree; and whenever matters grew threatening, his ability saved him from his father's fate on the block or his brother's speedy exile. Lacking their determined stubbornness, in emergencies Charles would willingly modify his policy as seemed expedient in the face of opposition. More than once his clever manipulation of hostile situations must have aroused the admiration of his harshest critics. Steady, plodding, everyday attention to his duties was not for him; but brilliant, masterly statecraft he could show on those rare occasions when he bothered to make the effort. One thing he was stubborn about and adhered to in all the tortuous shiftings of his policy: his firm intention to live and die in his own England and not to go on his "travels" again. Though his insidious schemings showed him a traitor, and though by his selfish personal desires he threatened England with the two things the people hated most,—French domination and Catholicism,—he was still to hold the affection of his people on his deathbed. With his remarkable facility for dealing with individuals and with situations, one can only wonder what this astute politician might have done for England had he been less lazy, less selfish, or less cynical.

Yet, for all the wild acclaim, Charles was not restored to all his father's prerogatives—a lesson his stubborn younger brother, James II, never learned. It was a restoration of Parliament as well as of king, after a period of dictatorship. All the lawmaking of the turbulent years since 1642, because it had not gone through all the normal three stages of Commons, Lords, and king, became null and void, except a few laws which were re-enacted through the regular channels. This interesting evidence of the English legal spirit is shown graphically in the collection of Parliamentary acts known as the Statutes at Large. At the top of one page is the last act to which Charles I had given his formal assent; following it, without the skipping of even a line, is the first act to which his son gave royal assent in 1660. While, in the eyes of the law, the whole intervening period was "time out," the lesson of those unsettled years tempered the course of Restoration politics. Therein are to be found all the incipient stages of the modern Parliamentary system, including even the first political parties. Charles himself knew that he was inheriting most of the theoretical powers enjoyed by his father, except those few prerogatives, like the Star Chamber, abolished by the Long Parliament at the end of Charles I's rule (see page 343); but he admitted the increasing authority of Parliament at Breda, in Holland, where he accepted the recall to the throne. He promised that Parliament should decide the religious settlement, provided there should be no persecution of law-abiding sects; he promised to pardon all rebels except those whom Parliament should designate; he promised that Parliament should settle the question of restoring Royalist lands; and he promised to pay the wages of the army, which was about to be disbanded. Also, sensing that part of his father's troubles had come from a tendency to act as his own ministry, Charles avoided many pitfalls by delegating much of his governmental business. This worked out admirably from his point of view: the ministers were blamed when matters went badly, and at the same time the king had more leisure.

First among his ministers there was Sir Edward Hyde, his father's faithful friend of early days and Charles's chief adviser throughout the years of exile. Hyde did much to bring about Charles's return, whereupon he was made Earl of Clarendon, Lord Chancellor, and head of the Privy Council. After seven years of power he ended his days in exile, bearing the brunt of popular disfavor. The next six years saw the five ministers of the so-called "Cabal," who came to grief, as we shall see, on the Test Act, while Charles, profiting by the theory that "the King can do no wrong," escaped much of the odium of his pro-Catholic stand. Then the Earl of Danby barely kept his head on his shoulders in the uproar aroused by his following an order of the king; for Charles dropped his helpers by the road whenever it seemed expedient. Thereafter Charles was pretty much his own chief minister.

The so-called "Convention Parliament," which had called Charles to the throne and had accepted his declaration from Breda, realized that revenge on Roundheads was profitless. England was ready to regard those intervening years as a bad dream, to be forgotten as soon as possible. For the most part, those who had held sway during the kingless years escaped the reprisals which too often accompany restorations. Vengeance was limited to two grim acts. The bodies of Cromwell and of two of his lieutenants were dug up, dragged to Tyburn, where common criminals were executed, publicly hanged until sundown, and then buried at the foot of the gallows. A dozen or so of the "regicides" who had been active in the death sentence of Charles I were carried living to the gallows and there cut to pieces before the crowd, while others fled to precarious exile on the Continent or in America. But for all the rest, an "Act of Indemnity and Oblivion" in 1660 was designed to heal the nation's wounds.

No attempt was made to restore lost Cavalier estates on a wholesale scale. The discontented loyalists dubbed this an act of "Indemnity for the king's enemies and Oblivion for his friends." There was, to be sure, a general restoration of the lands directly confiscated from the crown, the Church, or private owners by the revolutionary governments. Many of the Independents, who had invested heavily in

such property, were ruined. The complaints of the Cavaliers, how·
ever, concerned the more numerous estates which had not been
actually confiscated but which had had to be sold by Royalists in
order to meet the crushing taxes or fines imposed by their enemies.
Most of these now remained in the hands of their new owners, many
of whom were Presbyterians, a group well represented in the Convention Parliament. These Presbyterians thus established themselves
in the gentry, occupying the places of the disgruntled Cavaliers who
had had to part with their cherished ancestral acres.

From this time on, one can more properly refer to land*owners*
instead of simply land*holders*. At the time of the Conquest, we recall, William I had acted upon the principle that all the land in England was his. He had granted most of it to "tenants in chief," or
principal vassals, who owed him in return not only military service
but also the various feudal incidents. We have seen that under the
Conqueror's son nearly half the royal revenue had come from reliefs,
escheats, wardships, and similar payments arising from the king's
position as head of the feudal system. Even after the average tenant
in chief had abandoned military activity and was paying scutage
instead of his forty-day service, Edward I had legislated to preserve
as large a proportion as possible of the old feudal incidents (see
page 149). So matters had continued throughout the intervening
centuries, with persistent relics of those past practices. The squire,
to all intents and purposes, owned his land; but the survival of the
payments of feudal incidents kept alive the theory that the land
really belonged to the king. This ancient practice came to an end
when the Convention Parliament abolished all these old feudal dues.
The squire might still have to pay as much to the government, but his
ownership of the land was now more definite.

The abolition of the feudal dues was part of the well-meaning but
clumsy attempt of the Convention Parliament to place the national
finances upon a more stable basis. There were still heavy debts
from the interregnum; the army, in particular, had to be paid. The
new king urged Parliament to make a satisfactory financial arrangement. Its principal innovation was the substitution of a direct tax
in place of the old feudal dues. We shall see, from time to time, how
this land tax fell most heavily upon the landed aristocracy, while the
men of business escaped. Charles still had his hereditary revenue
from the crown lands, the equivalent of the old demesne of the feudal
system (see page 66), and Parliament granted him for life certain
items from taxation, estimated to give him a regular annual income
of about £1,200,000 for the running of the government. That, however, was not enough even for normal peace-time expenditure; and

the national finances quickly fell into heavy arrears, which became worse during the remaining Dutch wars. Parliament failed to provide an adequate co-ordination between receipts and expenditures, and England had to wait some thirty years longer for a more satisfactory financial system (see page 409).

This Convention Parliament had not been a strictly legal body, because it had not been summoned by the king. In 1661 regular elections were held. A final rising of those military extremists, the Fifth-Monarchy Men, had just been suppressed, and England, in a burst of loyal enthusiasm, returned hundreds of Royalist squires to the House of Commons. The resultant "Cavalier Parliament" was so favorable to Charles that he knew he could never again secure its equal. Consequently, in contrast to the first two Stuarts, who dissolved Parliaments before they had passed a single act, Charles kept this one for eighteen years, long after it had ceased to represent the temper of the nation.

If the Convention Parliament restored the monarchy, the Cavalier Parliament restored the Church of England. It was to prove hostile both to the Dissenters, who represented the military rule and harsh laws of the interregnum, and to the Catholics, who seemed to many to represent the sinister influence of France. Harsh restrictions were placed upon both these minorities which failed to come within the broad compromise of the Elizabethan settlement—restrictions which in some cases lasted nearly two centuries.

The religious legislation was aimed at all non-Anglicans; but the first crop of laws bore particularly upon the Dissenters, while the later Test Act was aimed especially at Catholics. "Dissenters" was a blanket term often used to include Independents, Presbyterians, and numerous other sects (although occasionally they were termed "Nonconformists," a milder expression which later supplanted "Dissenter" in referring to Protestants outside the Church of England). Between 1661 and 1665 Parliament passed the "Clarendon Code," four acts to curb the power of the Presbyterians and others outside the Church of England. The Corporation Act excluded all but Anglicans from the corporations which governed the towns, thereby affecting the election of borough members of Parliament. The Act of Uniformity required that the clergy agree to everything in the prayer book; two thousand Dissenting ministers were expelled for refusing to do this. The Conventicle Act imposed savage penalties for attendance at meetings, or "conventicles," where any but Anglican services were used. Finally, the Five-Mile Act forbade any nonconformist minister to teach school or to come within five miles of any organized town unless he promised that he would not "endeavor

# Restoration England

any alteration in Church or State." Since most of the strength of the Dissenters lay in the towns, this deprived them at once of their religious worship and their education. In Scotland there was a tumult at similar laws against the "Kirk."

In this matter of toleration the king differed from the great majority of the squires and churchmen. The attaching of Clarendon's name to these four acts reflected the popular belief that he was their author; but modern research indicates that Clarendon was more a political opportunist than an ardent Anglican, and that his better judgment opposed such extreme measures. Charles's pro-Catholic leanings led him toward the idea of toleration; for he foresaw that this wave of persecution would turn next against the "papists." Charles tried to compromise by suggesting the exemption of the Presbyterians from this "Clarendon Code"; but Parliament pushed through the program which drove the moderate Dissenters into at least lip service to the Church of England, while many of the others found arrest, hiding, or exile their fate. John Bunyan wrote his famous *Pilgrim's Progress* while imprisoned for violation of the code.

Clarendon, hard-working, morally severe old Stuart friend, paid heavily for this successful dominance of the Established Church. He further alienated Charles by his constant criticism of the court life, the royal mistresses, and the lazy royal neglect of state matters. In addition, the Cavaliers had long been angry because he had not arranged the return of all their lost estates. Parliament resented his rather high-handed demands for money, and, of course, the Dissenters hated him for the code. His daughter's marriage to Charles's younger brother, James, duke of York, which made him father-in-law to the heir to the throne, was called presumptuous by the court, which had always resented the Clarendon prominence. Clarendon, moreover, was exceedingly stiff and pompous, despite his great intellect. He did not belong to this young Restoration generation, and the times had outlived his belief in royal power and the insignificance of the Commons.

Popular suspicion also laid at his door Charles's unpopular marriage to the Portuguese princess Catherine of Braganza, who, surrounded by her nuns and the atmosphere of the cloister, was rather lost and pathetic in the gay court. Clarendon was suspected, no doubt unjustly, of having chosen a princess who he knew was unlikely to have children, in order to ensure the throne to his own grandchildren, James's daughters, the future queens Mary and Anne. As her dowry Catherine brought to England the port of Tangier, in Morocco, just across from Gibraltar, which was retained for twenty years; and, more important, Bombay, which was to become one of the three leading ports of British India. These distant acquisitions did not offset, to the Englishman of the day, the sale to hated France, in 1662, of the near-by Dunkerque, won by Cromwell's redcoats a few years before. Probably unjustly again, Clarendon was blamed for this act and for filling his own pockets in the process. According to an entry in Pepys's diary, his ostentatiously sumptuous new London house was jeered at as "Dunkirk House," while a scurrilous rhyme of the time referred to

> Three things to be seen—
> Dunkirk, Tangier and a barren Queene.

When, on top of all these undercurrents, three major disasters of plague in 1665, fire in 1666, and a victorious Dutch fleet in the Thames in 1667 (see pages 370, 384) descended upon England, a scapegoat was essential. There might be justification for blaming Clarendon for the condition of the navy, but it was less easy to lay the plague and the fire at his door. In fact, some explained those calamities as the work of the French or the papists, while the Puritans proclaimed them the judgment of God for the impious and scandalous actions of the king's wild court. Nevertheless, from the standpoint both of the enraged populace and of Charles himself, Clarendon was the obvious victim, as the most important man in the kingdom next to the king himself. Two months after a mob had howled around his new house in rage at the naval disgrace, he was dismissed, in 1667, and then impeached by Parliament. He fled once again into Continental exile, but a lonely one this time, without his king. That exile left English history richer for the magnificent prose of his autobiography and his history of the Civil War, and his name is appropriately preserved in the Clarendon Press at Oxford.

The next step in ministries, after Clarendon's fall, was the Cabal. Although not the first group of ministers to be called a cabal, this time, by strange coincidence, the initials of the new set of Charles's advisers spelled the word, and since then "Cabal" has generally meant these five particular men. Of them Clifford and Arlington were Roman Catholics; Buckingham was the son of the earlier Stuart favorite; Lauderdale, a Scottish peer and strong Anglican, was governor of the northern kingdom; and Ashley-Cooper, later Earl of Shaftesbury, the most important of the five, was a frequent turncoat during the Stuart period, a clever rascal whose ideas happened to be along the line of England's future development. Theoretically the Cabal was simply a committee of the Privy Council on foreign affairs, and that foreign sphere remained its main interest as well as the chief issue during its period of power. It was, however, as we shall see, upon the rock of religion that the Cabal was to come to grief, through its acquiescence in Charles's ideas of toleration in the interests of Catholicism, just as Clarendon had come to grief with the attachment of his name to the Clarendon Code.

Meantime, in foreign affairs Charles was pursuing a tortuous course between his own friendly inclinations toward Catholic France, the general English hostility toward the traditional French enemy, and the activities of Holland, still in the heyday of her maritime greatness despite Cromwell's naval war and the territorial cupidity of the French king. Parliament, for its part, had its fingers in foreign policies from the beginning and kept them there. In this field Charles and Parliament saw even less eye to eye than in that of religion.

One of the first acts of Parliament in 1660 had been to renew and to amplify as a regular statute the Navigation Act of 1651, and still further to extend it in 1663. The new Navigation Act not only re-affirmed the principle of "English ships with English crews," which had led to the First Dutch War in 1652, but extended the principle more rigidly to the colonies. The latter half of the seventeenth century saw the height of the mercantile system (see page 329), and its principle of "Sell more than you buy in foreign trade" was em-bodied in the new legislation. The ideal function of a colony was to furnish the mother country with materials which could not be pro-duced at home, and in return to purchase its outside necessities from the mother country. The new Navigation Act consequently "enumer-ated" certain articles which must be sent only to England. The principal items on this list, as it gradually expanded, were sugar from the West Indies, rice and indigo from the Carolinas, tobacco from Virginia and Maryland, and masts from New England. The colonies might send their flour, fish, and lumber wherever they pleased, but they could send the enumerated articles only to Bristol, London, or to some other English port, whence the surplus would be sold to the Continent, the extra profits going to English merchants. This colonial code was not altogether a hardship to the colonies: their shipping enjoyed all the privileges of "English ships with English crews," and the Northern colonies were to profit richly thereby. It was, however, a further blow to the Dutch, who had been energetically supplying the English colonies with various necessities and luxuries from abroad and, in turn, disposing of the colonial produce.

This renewed legislation helped to bring on the Second Dutch War (1665–1667). A year before it was officially declared, an Eng-lish squadron swooped down upon a Dutch post on the African coast and then upon New Amsterdam. As a result, New Netherland be-came the English colonies of New York, New Jersey, and, later,

Delaware, thus rounding out the English control of the Atlantic seaboard between the French holdings in the north and the Spanish in the south. For a while the captured region was under the direct proprietorship of the Duke of York, who was Lord High Admiral; hence the name "New York." The war itself was pretty much a repetition of the previous one, with stubborn, hard-fought battles in the North Sea. The English won the first big battle; the second lasted four days and was a sanguinary draw; and then, by 1667, the navy became bankrupt, in spite of all that Pepys could do, and some of the big ships were laid up inactive at Chatham, near the mouth of the Thames. There the Dutch made a raid, caught the English unprepared, burned five men-of-war, and sailed away with the greatest ship of the royal navy as their prize—that very *Royal Charles* which had brought the king home from Holland. Into such disgrace had fallen Blake's sea power! At the peace treaty, however, which quickly followed, England kept her American seizures, although many Englishmen would have preferred the little spice island of Puleroon to all New York.

To Charles, France had been a haven, his mother's country, where his preferred religion was established, and where the one person he is said really to have loved, his young sister "Minette" (Henrietta), was the wife of the Duke of Orléans, younger brother of the French king. To England, almost since the days of the Conquest and certainly in the Hundred Years' War and later rivalry, France was the enemy to watch and to mistrust. France, as no one disputed, was in the seventeenth century the most powerful nation in Europe, just as Spain had been in the sixteenth. France had been raised to this pre-eminence largely by the work of two able cardinal-ministers: Richelieu, who kept his power not only during much of the minority but throughout the reign of Louis XIII (1610–1643), being the real ruler of the country from 1624 to 1642, and Mazarin, the subtle Italian who ruled in the long minority of Louis XIV (reign, 1643–1715). Richelieu's wish to extend France to her "natural boundaries" of the Rhine, the Alps, and the Pyrenees involved the smashing of the "Hapsburg ring," which had surrounded France since Charles V had come into his tremendous inheritance (see page 254). As we have seen, Richelieu, cardinal though he was, attacked the Austrian Hapsburgs in the Thirty Years' War, by bringing France in on the Protestant side, and also fought the Spanish Hapsburgs. Mazarin reaped where Richelieu had sown by taking full advantage of the defeated Austrian Hapsburgs at the Peace of Westphalia, in 1648, and then, aided by Cromwell's army, humbling the Spanish Hapsburgs at the Peace of the Pyrenees in 1659 (see page 362). At the same time these ministers, in the very years when England was struggling to limit royal power, built up royal authority in France. Richelieu crushed the nobles, dismantling their fortified castles, and executing some of the most exalted for treason. The Huguenots too received drastic treatment in losing their fortified towns. In internal affairs Mazarin, despite several factious uprisings, continued Richelieu's policy, so that the young Louis, when he came into his majority in the year following Charles's return, found himself inheriting a kingdom where Richelieu's ambition of "the king first in France and France first in Europe" was realized.

Unhindered, this ambitious young ruler had his own way in Europe during the first part of his long reign, because no other country was in condition to stop him. The Austrians were busy defending themselves from the last outburst of Turkish energy in the Danube valley; most of the German states were still prostrate from the Thirty Years' War; Spain was a beaten nation; and Prussia was barely beginning to rise as a nation. Consequently Louis was free to expand France in the Rhine region and the Spanish Netherlands (present-day Belgium), and even to threaten Holland's independence. One explanation of his victorious progress was that he was remarkably well served. He had exceptional generals and first-rate ministers,—above all, the versatile Colbert, who was almost a whole cabinet in himself. An ardent exponent of mercantilism, Colbert tried to co-ordinate his various departments of finance, industry, commerce, colonies, and navy into a general scheme which, if followed, might have given France an empire as great as that which England later won. Louis, however, preferred banging away at the Low Countries and the Rhine for more territory in Europe.

At home France was enjoying a Golden Age such as England had had under Elizabeth. The center of this was Versailles, with its magnificent new palace, which became the model for courts all over Europe for many generations. Here, too, Louis had completed Richelieu's subjection of the nobility by making it clear that anyone who expected governmental favors must be in constant attendance on the king's person. Consequently the nobles thronged to Versailles to struggle for the privilege of handing the king some article of clothing while he dressed or undressed, instead of plotting revolts on their distant estates. Ultimately this glittering court was to hasten the revolution which convulsed all France in 1789, because it widened the breach between the parasitic nobility and their peasant tenants, who had to pay for the gaiety of their absent masters. For the time being, however, Versailles, with its scintillating life, became the envy of all Europe. France was recognized as the arbiter in matters of letters, art, and society; French became the language of diplomacy and the polite world.

In 1668 the three Protestant maritime nations, England, Holland, and Sweden, joined forces to check the formidable power of France. Within two years, however, Louis had broken up this Triple Alliance by luring away Holland's two allies. The kings of England and Sweden were both bought off.

In the case of Charles this was accomplished by the Treaty of Dover, negotiated in 1670 through his favorite sister "Minette." This treaty was one of the most audacious and un-English in the nation's diplomatic history; it was bound to be unpopular with most Englishmen. In fact, it consisted of two treaties, one more secret than the other. Charles showed to all the Cabal his agreement to help Louis in attacking Holland, in return for cash. But the second agreement was so daring that he showed it to only the two Catholic ministers. In return for more cash, and troops if necessary, Charles would turn Catholic himself and convert England into a Catholic absolutism. Henrietta died soon after achieving this treaty, but the French sent over charming Louise de Querouaille to hold the susceptible monarch in line.

The agreement to help France attack Holland ran counter to two cardinal principles of English foreign policy: the balance of power, and the protection of the Low Countries from falling under the control of a strong nation which could use the position as a menace to England's insular security. Nevertheless, in the spring of 1672 Charles kept his word, and England entered the unpopular Third Dutch War (1672–1674). For the third time in twenty years the rival fleets exchanged broadsides, and the valiant Dutch held their own fairly well against the combined navies of England and France. But Holland had more than navies to worry her. England might safely put all her defense energy into warships, but the Dutch had a vulnerable land frontier over which the most powerful army in Europe was advancing. In the grave crisis of invasion Amsterdam brought to the head of the government a slender, taciturn young man of twenty-two, the third William of Orange to govern Holland. Sixteen years later he was also to be the third William to rule England. By 1673 Parliament refused further funds for the Dutch war, and a year later Charles had to make peace. Although Holland fought the French four years more, she emerged without loss of territory.

The strain, however, of the constant fighting on land and sea dragged Holland down from the proud position which she had held in all things maritime during the earlier part of the century. She still kept her rich spice islands in the East, together with some other

# Restoration England

colonies; Amsterdam remained for some time to come, until overtaken by London, the commercial and financial center of Europe. But the exhaustion of war removed Holland as an active contender for the highest honors on the seas and overseas. Holland joined Portugal and Spain as unsuccessful rivals of England's expansion. The turn of France would come next.

Two days before the Third Dutch War started, in 1672, Charles took his first step toward the other half of the Dover bargain. He tried to lessen the penal restrictions on English Catholics and issued a "Declaration of Indulgence for Tender Consciences." His brother, the Duke of York, turned Catholic, but Charles himself apparently delayed this step until his deathbed. This declaration was an exercise of the "dispensing power" by which the king claimed the right to set aside the operation of certain laws. Not only were Catholics to be relieved from the old penal laws but Dissenters too were included in the act of grace, in order to make toleration seem a general principle and to broaden the support against the inevitable Anglican opposition. The Dissenters, however, suspected that they were included simply as a cloak for the extension of Catholicism and hesitated to take advantage of the favor. The Cavalier Parliament, with its Anglican squires, struck back at the king and the Catholics. In 1673 it passed the Test Act, which excluded from all civil or military office under the crown anyone who refused to take the Sacrament according to the Church of England. This was leveled at the Catholics, just as the Clarendon Code had been aimed at the Dissenters. The latter were included in its terms, but were gradually relieved. The immediate effect was to remove many high officials; in particular, the Duke of York lost his command of the navy. Some of these disabilities lasted until 1828.

Thus, within two years of the Treaty of Dover, Parliament had rendered it null in regard to both the alliance against the Dutch and the Catholic project. Actually traitorous though the whole program was, Charles's point of view was somewhat comprehensible. He was perpetually short of money, partly because of his own extravagance and partly because of a niggardly Parliament; yet he was too wise to resort to his father's illegal money-raising. In addition, as we have seen, he naturally did not share the average Englishman's aversion toward either the French or Catholics. He had, however, badly misjudged the temper of his people on those two points, and, though he quickly learned his lesson and never again tried to help the Catholics, his reign had come to a turning point.

Rebellion and exile Charles safely avoided; but he was about to enter a period of serious dissension with Parliament, lasting until

1681. Hysterical fear of Catholic and French intrigue swept all classes in England, producing a reign of terror which almost became civil war. The "Popish Plot" of 1678, the question of the succession, and the worry over further intrigues between Charles and France were the high points in those unpleasant years of the later seventies, which also saw another important step in constitutional development, the beginning of political parties.

The Test Act had broken up the Cabal, since one of the Catholic members had been forced from office. At about the same time, Charles dismissed Ashley-Cooper, recently promoted to be Earl of Shaftesbury, who soon began to build up a powerful opposition to the king. Charles's chief minister for the rest of the troubled seventies was Thomas Osborne, who held successively six different titles from baronet to duke, but is best known as the Earl of Danby. Danby was most acceptable to the country as the Cabal's successor, for he was known to be strongly Anglican and anti-French. At the same time, he was a shrewd and not particularly honest politician who knew where his interests lay, and who saw to it that, whatever his private inclinations, he pleased his sovereign. An adept at modern party-machine tactics, he got his way in Parliament by buying votes with such a lavish hand that the Cavalier Parliament won the additional nickname of "Pensioned Parliament." Danby's appointment was another milestone toward England's constitutional development, for he was the first chief minister to be appointed because he was the leader of a faction in Parliament. Consequently, he was the real founder of the Tory, or pro-king, party, just as Shaftesbury, as we shall see, became the founder of the Whig, or anti-king, party.

The widespread popular resentment against everything Catholic and French burst into flame in 1678 with the false testimony of a perjured informer, Titus Oates, who revealed what he claimed was a "hellish" Jesuit plot to murder the king, burn London, seize England with French and Irish troops, and massacre all Protestants who refused to turn Catholic. In the panicky temper of the time, men did not question Oates's reliability, and the opposition helped to fan the flames of anti-Catholic hatred. Oates became a popular hero with the London mob and with many other Englishmen. He went so far as to claim that the queen and her physician were plotting to kill Charles. Many Catholics, most of them innocent, were hunted down and dragged into the courts, where several were condemned to death, until Lord Chief Justice Scroggs, in the trial of the queen's physician, had the courage to defy the popular clamor by questioning the flimsy evidence.

The "Popish Plot" gave stimulus to Shaftesbury and his opposition, soon to be known as Whigs. They brought up the question of the succession. Charles himself remarked that he had no fear that anyone would depose him for his brother James, who was an avowed Catholic and whose secretary had just been executed as a result of treasonable correspondence with France. Of the Duke of York it could be said that he was already middle-aged, and that the succession apparently would go to his Protestant daughters, Mary and Anne, the former of whom was married at this time to the Protestant Prince of Orange, her cousin. Yet many favored having Charles divorce his present wife and marry again, or else divert the succession to one of his illegitimate sons, most of whom were dukes. When an obsequious courtier on one occasion remarked to the king, "Sire, you are truly the father of your people," another murmured in an aside, "No, not quite all of them." The Duke of Monmouth, born while Charles was still in exile, with his showy and rather attractive personality, was the favorite of the Protestant opposition in Parliament, which was doing its unsuccessful best at this time to pass an Exclusion Bill to keep Catholic James from the throne.

The year following the Popish Plot saw an end of Danby's ministry, and with him ended the eighteen-year-old Cavalier Parliament. Its members were no longer the enthusiastic loyalists they had been in 1661; a steadily increasing number were following Shaftesbury into opposition. The crisis came with the revelation of a damning letter written by Danby. Charles had been playing fast and loose with Louis as well as with Parliament, taking what money he could from each and then doing as he pleased. The new Dutch marriage of James's daughter had annoyed Louis, so that he revealed a letter from Danby requesting more French funds. Danby had reluctantly written the letter at the king's order, but that fact had been carefully concealed. Parliament, already at fever heat over the Popish Plot, cried for the traitor's impeachment. To save Danby and yet not to incriminate himself, Charles promptly dissolved Parliament for the first time in his reign.

In the midst of these disputes there came into being an all-important device which was to influence strongly the future political life not only of England but also of the United States and many other lands. This was the party system. A political party has been defined as "an organized group of the electorate who attempt to control the action of the government through the election of its candidates to office." The closest approach to a political party in England's previous history had been the organization of the Puritan opposition in the early days of the Long Parliament, under the shrewd and skillful leadership of Pym.

# A History of England and the British Empire

There were bound to be differences of opinion among the five hundred men who composed the House of Commons, as well as among the hundred-odd peers, at any time, but the events of seventeenth-century England seemed to drive them toward more sharply opposing points of view. Then and ever since, men have tended to fall into four different general attitudes toward political policy: reactionary, conservative, liberal, radical. It is well to distinguish carefully among those terms; for they keep recurring and are often misapplied. The reactionary is one who wishes to go back to former conditions; the conservative, usually well contented with things as they exist, is psychologically or economically opposed to any considerable change; the liberal has a broad-minded attitude, ready to preserve whatever seems to him good in the old, but equally ready to make changes which seem to him improvements; while the radical, as the Latin derivation indicates, desires to get at the roots and start anew. Today these viewpoints are often designated by the position in which the various groups arranged themselves in the parliaments which eventually developed on the Continent: reactionaries, extreme right; conservatives, right or right center; liberals, left or left center; radicals, extreme left. With the two extremes, the reactionaries and the radicals, we need not particularly concern ourselves at this time of the birth of political parties; they have, anyway, normally been small minorities, and the terms have generally been flung at opponents as epithets. On the other hand, the two great groups, conservatives and liberals, gave England a normal basis for her two-party system. Such divergent points of view had been reflected in previous Parliamentary debates and actions, of course; but effective results were not to be expected as long as individual members of Parliament acted without any common organization or plan of action. The function of the political party was to provide that necessary cohesion and strategy.

If any one year can be taken as the definite beginning of England's regular party system, it would probably be 1675, when, under the guidance of Shaftesbury, a number of prominent members of both houses formed the Green Ribbon Club, with headquarters at a London tavern, to co-ordinate the liberal "country," or Whig, opposition with the conservative Royalist-Anglican "court," or Tory, element headed by Danby. Numerically this "country" opposition was strong, as the Test Act had shown; but until it built up a machine, it could scarcely hope to compete successfully with the king and Danby, who had all the resources of government for bribery and patronage. Shaftesbury and his colleagues quickly created an effective machine, and during the latter years of the decade we can recognize many of the party devices which have become familiar in later politics. For the purpose of strong appeal to the electorate, the Whigs had a slogan, "No Popery!" They had also a platform: Protestantism, toleration, liberty of the subject, commercial advantages, and Parliamentary supremacy. Their particular source of potential strength lay in the alliance of a few great peers with the men of London and the towns, where dissent was strongest. Some squires also might adhere to this view, though squires and clergy on the whole were inclined to favor the conservative side. The Whig platform, then, was one which would appeal particularly to the middle-class Dissenters. Every election was carefully managed, candidates were selected and supported, and well-timed propaganda was prepared both for the electorate and for the members of Parliament. The new party was even able to call out a London mob to howl for effect at the proper moment. It was important not only to secure a majority but to use it effectively. There was plenty of management of the members already elected. In the sessions of the Green Ribbon Club the next day's course of action was carefully discussed, and, lest there be any slip-up, it was frequently decided just who should propose a measure and who should second it. The Tories were not as well organized as their rivals, but they made ample use of a practice which, like the Whig tricks, was to become a regular feature of party rivalry. This was patronage, or the bestowal of the favors of government—such as offices, pensions, and even bribes —upon those who voted right, a practice which the Whigs would develop even more intensively in the next century (see page 437). The Tories, too, had a platform stressing their support of the Church of England, with a corresponding opposition to toleration of any other faith, together with a preference to let the crown, rather than Parliament, have the last word. Both parties called themselves anti-Catholic, though the Whigs were fiercer in the attack as well as anti-French. Danby was the first leader of the Tories; but when the Whig opposition drove him to the Tower for five years, he was succeeded by others of the king's more conservative advisers, and finally by Charles himself.

The names of the two parties were bestowed by their rivals as insulting epithets. As Trevelyan remarks,[1] "England owes her greatest party names to Titus Oates. He used to croak 'Tory' at any man who dared to question the plot, and his admirers took up the word. And as soon as one side thus called its opponents after the Catholic bandits who waylaid the Saxon settlers among the Irish bogs, it was an

[1] G. M. Trevelyan, *England under the Stuarts* (1926), p. 411. By permission of G. P. Putnam's Sons and Methuen & Co., Ltd.

obvious retort to hurl back the name of the Covenanted 'Whigs' who murdered bishops on the Scottish moors." The creation of the party system was a major step in English political development. For a century and a half the Whigs and Tories were to dispute elections and to sit on opposite sides in Parliament; the names then changed to "Liberal" and "Conservative," but the rivalry went on.

Capitalizing the anti-Catholic feeling during the frenzy of terror, the Whigs now dominated Parliamentary elections. Charles, after keeping one Parliament for eighteen years, reverted to early Stuart tactics and dissolved three short-lived Parliaments within the next two years, because the Whigs had a strong majority in each. The Tories had not contested the elections vigorously; for, while they were normally ready to support the king, they too feared Catholic domination.

The first of these short Whig Parliaments was elected in the spring of 1679, just after the dissolution of the Cavalier Parliament. Shaftesbury, backed by his strong majority, once more pressed for an Exclusion Bill to substitute Monmouth for James in succession to the throne. After four months Charles dissolved this Parliament before it had time to do much harm, but not before it had passed a celebrated act which was to do great good. This was the Habeas Corpus Act, definitely establishing the old practice that anyone arrested had the right to be shown by what authority and for what reason he was being detained. By thus checking arbitrary imprisonment the act was a vital safeguard of English liberty during the next stormy decade, when absolutism was threatening.

Late that summer, elections were held for the third Restoration Parliament, but for more than a year Charles refused to assemble it. England seemed on the verge of civil war. The situation was gravely complicated when Charles himself fell ill and the prospect of a Catholic king seemed imminent. He recovered, and played the risky game of waiting, relying upon the freshness of the memory of civil war in the minds of most Englishmen to avert a serious crisis. When, after vigorous petitions from the Whigs, that third Parliament finally met in the autumn of 1680, Shaftesbury once more pressed for exclusion, and Charles dissolved Parliament before it had granted him any money. There was a fresh election early in 1681, and once again the country returned a Whig majority. Charles summoned this fourth Parliament to Royalist Oxford, where the Whigs would not have the support of a London mob. At Oxford and along the roads to it, he assembled considerable military strength. A week after the Parliament assembled, Charles appeared without warning in the college hall where it was meeting and suddenly dissolved it.

# Restoration England

In the remaining four years of his reign Charles was virtually absolute, ruling by himself without Parliament or even an outstanding minister. His bold coup, which put an end to the brief Whig ascendancy, had taken Shaftesbury and his followers completely by surprise. Mystified at the source of the king's independence of Parliament, they fled in terror from Oxford. The explanation was that by strictly secret negotiations, oral this time, Charles had arranged to receive a new and larger allowance from Louis of France. He consequently no longer needed Parliament. His action in taking matters out of the hands of Parliament met the hearty approval of the Tory clergy and squires, who had feared that the Whigs were pushing the country toward civil strife. Now that the king had dropped Catholicism, they were ready to support him in everything else, even the threat of absolutism. The doctrine of nonresistance spread among them: one Tory went so far as to state that a lawful ruler, even if he were a Nero, should be obeyed in everything. These Tories, it must be remembered, had most of the local government in the shires in their hands; and while the Tory clergy preached nonresistance the Tory justices of the peace harried the Dissenters with renewed vigor. The Whigs, as Charles had foreseen, overplayed their hand. Shut out from legitimate Parliamentary opposition for the next seven years, some of them plotted to assassinate Charles and James and to start an insurrection. Public opinion, which resented any appeal to war, turned against Shaftesbury's partisans. He himself fled to exile on the Continent, where he soon died, and several other prominent Whigs were executed with scant show of justice. Charles then struck at the towns, which were strongholds of Whiggery and Dissent. For centuries no king had ventured to challenge their medieval charters; now Charles called them in on flimsy pretexts, and in their place issued new ones which placed the power in the hands of his Tories. Tory town governments would now send safe borough members to Parliament; Tory sheriffs would now select jurors who would be harsh to Dissenters.

After the troubled middle period of his reign, Charles actually enjoyed these last years. So, too, did most of England, save the Whigs and Dissenters. There was general prosperity; the French subsidy lightened the tax burden; and some of the enthusiasm of the early Restoration once more centered about the king. Charles finally died in 1685. He had safely ridden out several threatening storms and had not "gone on his travels again." He had remained the Anglican king his people required, but as he lay dying he is said to have received the sacraments of the Catholic faith.

That absolutism of Charles's last years might have become permanently fastened upon England had not his successor been a devoted Catholic. Despite the past Whig efforts at exclusion, the Duke of York came to the throne as James II. Probably his age, which was already fifty-three, and the fact that his Protestant daughters were his only heirs, helped to counteract his hated religion and his unpleasant personality. Had he learned the significant lessons from his family's experience, he would have kept his throne more than three years. He inherited much that was favorable: a small standing army, and subjects who were tired of the disturbing results of opposition. Unfortunately for himself, this second James was as tactless as the first, without the latter's erudition; as stubborn as his father, the first Charles, with none of his more attractive qualities; while in politics he was a fool as compared with his older brother. It can be said of James that he had a fixity of purpose in his support of Catholicism, but that was a purpose with which most Englishmen violently disagreed. About the only thing he ever did well was his excellent management of the navy, before the Test Act forced his resignation.

Five months after James came to the throne, Charles's bastard son, the Duke of Monmouth, plunged into a revolt which was hopeless from its inception. Despite his facile charm and popularity, Monmouth was weak and sometimes vicious, doomed to be someone's gullible tool. The Whig exiles on the Continent easily persuaded him that he had but "to show his handsome face among the shouting crowds" and the English crown was his. With only a handful of followers, he landed on the southwest coast, where four or five thousand men, chiefly devoted peasants, flocked to his standard. Most of England held aloof, however, from this ill-equipped and ill-disciplined force. Easily the royal regiments of regulars closed in on Monmouth and quickly crushed his bravely fighting followers at the battle of Sedgemoor. Hopeless and ill-advised as was this "last popular uprising in the old England," the drastic vengeance exacted upon all participants was not deserved. Monmouth was executed after an extremely bungling job by the headsman. More than a thousand others, even persons only remotely involved, were either hanged or sentenced to virtual slavery in Barbados. Lord Chief Justice Jeffreys, later rewarded with the Lord Chancellorship, presided at the "Bloody Assizes" where these unfortunate participants in the unlucky venture were brought to trial. He has been charged with unparalleled brutality, although late research has tended to minimize this greatly. According to some earlier accounts, women seemed to arouse him to his most callous cruelty. One Alice Lisle, a lady of good family, who unwittingly had harbored two starving refugees, was beheaded as a merciful alternative to his original sentence of burning at the stake.

James, with his throne saved, set out to make England Catholic. He did not see that his religion, even kept as a private affair, was a source of general irritation and uneasiness. Everyone had known that he was an avowed Catholic and had attended Mass privately. No sooner was he on the throne, however, than he began to attend Mass publicly. Foolishly, he seems to have thought that the Anglican High Church clergy would aid his plans because they shared his hostility to Dissenters. That, however, was as far as they would go with him in religious policy. It had been one thing for Charles II to persecute the Dissenters, who were a minority; it was one of the most stupid of James's many blunders to antagonize the powerful Anglican Tories by his efforts in behalf of the Catholics. Nine months after James came into power, Englishmen were given a vivid illustration of what Catholic political domination could mean. Louis XIV revoked the Edict of Nantes, which Henry IV had granted to protect the Huguenots, and began such a brutal persecution of those Protestants that as many as possible fled from France.

The religious question cost James an excellent chance for Parliamentary co-operation. Late in the preceding reign the charters had been taken away from London and many other municipalities and new ones issued, designed to curb or eliminate the power of the Whig Dissenters in voting for members of the Commons. The result was that the first Parliament of James's reign was strongly Tory and more loyal than any other since 1661. It was ready to vote the king a generous financial grant if he would only relieve their religious fears. James threw away this opportunity for support by insisting that he had the right to appoint Catholics to any position, Test Act or no Test Act. Since Parliament would do nothing under those conditions, he suddenly dismissed it. Later there was still further tampering with the borough and county officials, in an endeavor to secure members who might be more favorable to the king's Catholic designs; but that second Parliament never met.

Since Parliament would do nothing for him, James proceeded to appoint Catholics to high places, using the so-called "dispensing power" by which he claimed the right to set aside the operation of the laws in the cases of certain individuals (see page 387). A Catholic was placed at the head of the Irish government; another received the command of the fleet; many were made justices of the peace or mayors; others were promoted to the House of Lords, and some were even admitted to the Privy Council, including a Jesuit, Father Petre, who enjoyed considerable influence with the king.

There was particular concern when James began to replace Protestant officers with Catholics in the army; for there were sixteen thousand regulars encamped on Hounslow Heath, just outside London, where they could easily overawe the capital. When Hales, a Catholic, was appointed governor of Dover, the port closest to France, the matter was carried to the courts; but the judges, as in earlier Stuart days, held office at the royal pleasure and gave James a favorable decision in the matter of the dispensing power. Emboldened by such success, James was foolish enough to move against the Church of England itself, proposing to set up a religious court similar in nature to the old Court of High Commission, which had been abolished by the Long Parliament. In spite of the violent protest of the fellows, he also placed a Catholic at the head of Magdalen College at Oxford, a particular stronghold of the Anglicans.

Along with this James tried toleration. In 1687 he issued a Declaration of Indulgence to Dissenters as well as Catholics, similar to that of his brother fifteen years earlier. William Penn, the Quaker founder of Pennsylvania and sometimes called the one good man among James's advisers, urged this action. The Dissenters, released from their prison cells by the hundreds and free once more to worship in their own way, might have forgiven the recent persecutions had not James issued a second Declaration of Indulgence, the next spring (1688), designed to legalize his granting of important civil and military posts to Catholics. Seven bishops were bold enough to protest against this declaration, and James ordered them tried for seditious libel. London cheered loudly in the last days of June when it learned that the jury had acquitted them. This trial of the seven bishops naturally still further infuriated the Anglican Tories.

James was no more intelligent in his foreign than in his religious policy. He steered an indecisive course when his interests called for a close alignment with France. At the same time, his negotiations with Louis XIV surrounded him with all the odium of such an alliance in the minds of the people, ever suspicious of French association; and yet he received none of the advantages his brother had had from French support. He asked Louis for money at the beginning of his reign, but he promised nothing in return. Naturally, his religious policy was in keeping with what Louis himself was doing at the time, and James might have strengthened his position by taking advice from his French cousin. Fortunately for the development of the English constitution, he did not.

The second Declaration of Indulgence, with its warning that England was headed apparently for a purely Catholic personnel in her government while James remained king, was the first of the

# Restoration England

events that were to make 1688 one of the most significant years in English history as the year of the "Bloodless," or "Glorious," Revolution. As has been said, James's heir was his daughter Mary; and a safe Protestant succession seemed thus guaranteed, since James, in the fifteen years of his second marriage, had had no child by his wife, Mary of Modena, an Italian Catholic. This comfort was snatched from England in the early summer of this same year, when a son was born to the royal couple. Of course, this son, certain to be bred a Catholic, would inherit before his half sisters. England now seemed likely to have a succession of Catholic rulers far into the future. The birth of this new Prince of Wales was consequently the spark that ignited the smoldering resentment against the rapid accumulation of grievances of the past three years. The more moderate, who had been inclined to wait out the reign, were now almost as ready as the discontented Whigs for immediate change.

Thus were hastened the negotiations to bring William of Orange from Holland to secure the succession for his wife, Mary. Her claim as the daughter of James II and Anne Hyde far outweighed the fact that William himself was also a grandchild of Charles I, as the son of his daughter. William was the obvious champion for the enemies of James. For sixteen years, ever since he had cut the dikes to save Amsterdam from the invading Frenchmen, he alone had stood up against the tremendous power of Louis XIV. The great end to which he devoted his career was freedom for Europe,—freedom from the danger of French domination. His vision took in something more than Holland alone or England alone, something more than Protestantism alone. He, more than anyone else, deserves the credit for the final realization of that aim.

And now this cold, cautious man was being urged to enter upon a desperate gamble. William had no particular interest in the English crown for its own sake. It appealed to him because it would bind firmly one powerful ally in the league which he was forming against France. He had no intention of following Monmouth to the block; it was not enough to tell him that he had but to land on England's shores and an enthusiastic nation would rally to his standard. He insisted upon a formal invitation from some of the leading men of the nation, so that their fates would be bound up with his. Such a risky but essential document was signed by seven prominent Whigs and Tories on the June day when the seven bishops were acquitted.

Fate or fortune carried William successfully through several narrow escapes during the next few months. If any one of a number of things had gone wrong, England would have missed a "bloodless" revolution. In the first place, Louis XIV was on the point of setting out upon another war of conquest. Had he headed for the Low Countries again, William would have had to stay at home to defend his own land. Instead, however, Louis struck at the middle Rhine region, which suffered terrific devastation. Then William had to secure the consent of the Dutch, with their complex and cumbersome system requiring the approval of the various jealous provinces and cities; with the French menace temporarily removed, they finally agreed. Unlike Monmouth, William went well protected by Dutch warships and regiments. But that too involved risk: if he had to fight the English navy or army, his position, even if he were victorious, would have been that of a foreign conqueror. Fortunately, the command, as well as the rank and file, of both navy and army were not averse to the change of rulers. Even the wind blew in William's favor. The English naval commander saved his face by anchoring his fleet at a point where it was held immobile by wind and tide while William's ships sailed past; then he pursued them at a safe distance. On November 5, Guy Fawkes Day, William landed at Torbay, on the southwest coast, not far from Monmouth's landing place. The remaining hazard was the English army, some thirty thousand strong. The success of the venture was made possible by the defection of the commanders, headed by John Churchill, the future Duke of Marlborough. Though he owed his whole advancement to James, who had placed him in a position of great trust, Churchill wrote the king that under the circumstances he would not oppose the advance of William (see pages 413–414). If James had used his Irish troops, all England would have been exasperated into open revolt.

James, virtually at the mercy of the Dutch invader, might still have saved his throne had he been willing to summon a new Parliament and descend to the role of a limited constitutional monarch. This James would not do. Dropping the Great Seal in the Thames to stay the legality of official action, he hurried to the coast to escape to France. Some zealous fishermen apprehended him and turned him over to the authorities. It was best to have him out of the way,— to say that he had abdicated, instead of having the necessity of deposing him. Consequently, after some fruitless efforts on James's part to negotiate for terms, he was permitted to slip quietly out of the country. Soon the last Stuart king took refuge at the court of his cousin Louis XIV, for the remainder of his life. The way was clear for the "Revolution Settlement," which permanently ended real royal power in England.

# CHAPTER XV

## Limiting the Monarchy

### 1688-1739

THE year 1688 stands as one of the most significant turning points in all English history, almost as important as 1066 and more fundamental than 1485. It marks the final triumph of Parliament in the century-old struggle to limit the royal power. From that time on, the crown abandoned all thoughts of divine right; for it was definitely understood that the king owed his title to Parliament. Within thirty-five years Parliament was to work out a method for exercising its new power in effective form. The resultant system of a limited monarchy with responsible government was England's unique contribution to the field of constitutional development. Other nations by the dozen were to imitate the forms which England had finally achieved in the slow evolution stretching back into the Middle Ages. The English are proud of the revolution of 1688 not only because of its constitutional results but also because of the manner in which it was carried out. They refer to it as the "Glorious" and the "Bloodless" Revolution, comparing it with the savage and lurid episodes which often accompanied political changes in other lands. This was all the more remarkable because the central actor was not an Englishman but William of Orange, the ruler of a foreign nation which only fourteen years earlier had been at war with England. Yet he came, not as did William the Conqueror, after a bloody victory over Englishmen, but as the invited guest of some of the most important men of the island.

By only a narrow margin did the revolution prove bloodless. The departure of James had left England without a lawful government, and anarchy threatened. As soon as the news of the royal flight leaked out, London mobs worked off their anti-Catholic belligerence by two nights of violent rioting. Even the embassies of certain Catholic countries were not spared, while Judge Jeffreys of the "Bloody Assizes," although disguised as a laborer, barely escaped being torn to pieces. Throughout England anxious men patrolled the roads and town walls; for rumor told of marauding bands of armed Catholics. To make matters worse, one of James's last acts was to disband the standing army, and the fear of what these rough soldiers, freed from military discipline, might do added to the popular terror. A dangerous few days were these—some incident might easily have plunged the nation into civil war.

Such disorder scared the responsible elements, Tory as well as Whig, into a common readiness to support the earlier invitation given William of Orange by that small group of prominent men and to accept amicably the summoning of a foreign ruler. Hastily a group of peers and former members of the Commons, together with some London magistrates, gathered. They invited William to take over the administration temporarily, and in his name invitations were sent out for the election of a Commons by the usual methods. This resulted in another irregular "Convention Parliament," similar to that which General Monk and the Long Parliament had proposed in 1660 and, like that body which called in Charles II, not summoned in a legal manner because no king had signed its writs of summons. It met early in 1689 to discuss what should be done with the vacant throne. The precedent of 1399, when another tyrannical king, Richard II, had been deposed in favor of one not in the direct line, was freely discussed. There was also the recollection that at "Bloody Mary's" death, her husband, Philip II of Spain, to England's good fortune, had lost all authority in England's affairs (see pages 279–280). On the whole, opinion veered between asking William of Orange to serve as regent for his absent father-in-law and making his wife, Mary, queen, with William merely administrator of the government during her lifetime. William would have none of either proposal. He would be king himself for life or return at once to his own land. Never would he tolerate the subordinate position of being tied to his wife's apron strings, as Parliament proposed. As a result of this independent attitude, the Convention Parliament declared the throne vacant because James, "having endeavored to subvert the constitution of the kingdom by breaking the original contract between king and people," had "abdicated the government"; and it agreed that William and Mary should be joint sovereigns, with the chief administration in the husband's hands. This was acceptable to William. His wife, as always, supported his views.

Thus did the short, rather sour-faced little Dutchman become the third William to occupy the English throne, in addition to being the third William of the House of Orange to govern Holland. Cold, tight-lipped, taciturn, and discreet, this great-grandson both of William the Silent and of James I made up in character what he lacked in charm (see page 397). From the critical moment of his initiation into power in 1672, when French troops were overrunning Holland, he had shown an indomitable courage, a dogged determina-

tion, and a native shrewdness which were to stand him in good stead
in his new land. As a soldier he lacked the smashing ability of Cromwell, with whom he had something in common; but he was clever
at keeping diverse allies in line. Intellectually he was more mature
and consistent than Cromwell and emotionally more self-controlled.
Mary, with her dull, bovine countenance, was of slight consequence
and was to die after five years as queen; but William, one of the
strongest individuals to occupy the English throne in modern times,
was to continue to rule alone some seven years longer.

Before bestowing the crown upon the new king and queen Parliament ensured its dominant position by the so-called Declaration of
Rights. This was a deathblow to the idea of the "divine right of
kings" in England; for it made it obvious that only Parliamentary
decree had given the crown to William and Mary. Like the two
earlier safeguards of English liberty, Magna Carta and the Petition
of Right, the Declaration of Rights did not deal with broad generalities of political theory but was specific and largely negative in character. The misdeeds of James II were recounted in detail and their
illegality cited. The declaration pronounced illegal, without the consent of Parliament, the making or suspending of laws; the royal
exercise of the dispensing power; the levying of taxes, forced loans,
or other money payments; and the maintenance of a standing army.
The definite rights of subjects were stipulated in regard to petitioning
the sovereign, keeping arms, reasonable bail in case of arrest, and
several other matters. For Parliament itself there were to be frequent sessions, free election of members, and freedom of debate.
Some months later, after the Convention Parliament had been regu-
larized, this Declaration of Rights, with the added specific provision
that the crown of England might never be worn by one of the Roman
Catholic faith, was embodied in the Bill of Rights, a regular statute,
by which name it is more generally known.

This Bill of Rights was further strengthened by several subsequent acts which, together with it, made up the so-called "Revolution
Settlement." The compression of so much in the way of reform into
a comparatively brief period of time was to be typical of much of the
course of English development in the future. In the legislation
following 1688 the liberties of the subject were still further guarded
in the Treasons Act (1696), which protected the accused in treason
trials from arbitrary condemnation, and in that part of the Act
of Settlement (1701) which secured the independence of the bench
by basing the tenure of judges on their good behavior, as decided by
Parliament, instead of on the royal pleasure. Parliament ensured
regular meetings for itself by the Mutiny Act (1689), and regular

elections by the Triennial Act (1694). The Mutiny Act authorized, for a limited period only, the trial of soldiers by court-martial, which had previously been forbidden in the Petition of Right. This act, which has been renewed at least annually ever since, gave Parliament more control of the army. Without such yearly renewal the crown would have no legal way of keeping the armed forces under discipline. Together with the granting of appropriations for one year only, the Mutiny Act prevented the king from ruling long years without calling Parliament, as Charles I had done. The Triennial Act prevented the king from keeping the same Parliament in office year after year without new elections, as Charles II had done for eighteen years with his Cavalier Parliament. The Triennial Act, as its name indicates, stipulated that a new Parliament was to be elected every three years; but before long this was extended to seven years and much later reduced to five.

Finally, in the Act of Settlement (1701), Parliament showed the strength of its new authority by deciding for the future which royal line should be given the succession. It had already indicated that it controlled the choice of the ruler, both in its offer of the throne to William and Mary and in the provision of the Bill of Rights that at their death the crown should pass successively to the children of Mary, to her sister Anne and her children, and, in default of such heirs, to the children of William by a second wife. Before William died, however, it was obvious that Anne would have no surviving children, and William had not remarried after Mary's death. There consequently remained the chance that the throne might go to Anne's half brother James, the "Old Pretender," and his children, who were by strict primogeniture the direct line. Such a possibility being anathema to most of England, with the current hysteria over popish plots and papists, Parliament decided to make the provisions yet more specific. In the Act of Settlement it designated as Anne's successor her next *Protestant* kin, her second cousin Sophia, wife of the Elector of Hanover and granddaughter of James I. England is still ruled under the Act of Settlement; for Sophia's son, as we shall see, was to come to England as the first king of the Hanoverian line.

The Revolution Settlement helped to smooth over religious dissension by the Toleration Act (1689), which granted freedom of worship to most of the Dissenters. Technically the act was more limited in scope than it actually proved in practice. It required that dissenting clergymen accept most of the Thirty-nine Articles, and all political disabilities remained in force. Neither the Clarendon Code nor the Test Act was repealed, nor were the earlier acts of the Tudor period. Catholics and those Dissenters who did not believe in the

Trinity were specifically excluded. Nevertheless, most Dissenters were fairly well satisfied, and most Englishmen from this time on were permitted to worship as they pleased. William and the Whigs had been ready for thoroughgoing religious freedom, with equal political rights regardless of religious belief; but the Tories prevented the extension of toleration as far as that for a long time to come. Dissenters of all sorts, as well as Roman Catholics, were excluded from the higher offices of the state, the army, the navy, and the universities. The Dissenters, however, were permitted to hold some positions, particularly in local government, on the condition that they practice "occasional conformity." To qualify by this occasional conformity merely entailed taking the Anglican Sacrament once a year. Many men were willing to make this slight gesture of conformity in order to obtain office.

William was not accepted in this easy fashion in the other parts of the British Isles. To be sure, the Lowland Scots recognized this break in the Stuart line with equanimity; for not only did they retain their laws as before, but their Parliament, during the confusion of 1688–1689, had even been able to make Presbyterianism the Established Church of Scotland, a blessing which the land of John Knox had long desired. Beyond the Highland line, however, many clans stood loyally behind their old king, "James VII." Viscount Dundee, who, like some of the other Scottish nobles, hated this supremacy of the Presbyterian clergy and the House of Orange, "drew his sword for King James." Certain of the wild clans gathered about him and swept down to crush the regular troops at Killiecrankie (1689). Dundee fell at the moment of victory, however, and the leaderless Highlanders scattered to carry their booty back into the hills. Recognizing the extreme poverty of the Highlanders, William hit on the scheme of buying the support of the chieftains. All but one stubborn, remote clan took the oath of allegiance to the king as specified. This clan, the Macdonalds of Glencoe, delayed their submission until the last day, and then unluckily went to the wrong official. By the time they had trudged through many miles of snow to find the proper one, the legal time limit had been exceeded. The leading royal official in Scotland saw in this an opportunity to display the strong arm of government to the Highlanders, and, with the consent of William, who did not know the full circumstances of the Macdonalds' delay, proceeded to the extermination of this clan. A force of regular soldiers, deliberately selected from among the bitterly hostile Campbells, visited the clan in its wild glen and accepted two weeks of cordial hospitality. Then they suddenly went ahead with their orders to slaughter everyone in the night. This "Massacre of

Glencoe" was not complete, because some of the clansmen escaped into the woods; but it left the blackest stain on William's name.

In Ireland the opposition was far more menacing under the leadership of James's Lord Lieutenant, the Earl of Tyrconnel. The Catholics, bitter at the Cromwellian settlement which had established Protestant landlords over them (see page 358), rose everywhere. James II, supported with funds and with men by Louis XIV, arrived in Ireland early in 1689 to capitalize this uprising in his name and to use Ireland as a back door to regain the English crown. He called an Irish parliament in which the Catholic element predominated. This body passed laws repudiating the Cromwellian settlement and giving the land back to the Catholics. In the meantime the Protestants in the northern province of Ulster, which had been settled by many Scotch Presbyterians in the time of James I (see page 336), took refuge at Londonderry and Enniskillen, where they were at once besieged. The river port of Londonderry put up a valiant fight against starvation, and was saved when the relief ships from William finally broke the boom stretched across the river by the Catholic besiegers. On the same day Enniskillen drove off the army at its gates.

William, aware that any war on the Continent against his enemy Louis XIV would be folly as long as this danger existed in his rear, sent over an army to clear up the situation. This expedition, poorly equipped and ill-managed, as was usual in English military efforts after an interval of peace, fared badly in the face of adverse weather and disease. William himself thereupon went to Ireland. In July, 1690, he met James at the river Boyne. Fording the stream in the face of enemy fire, he routed his father-in-law's army. James threw away his cause in Ireland by fleeing to the Continent after this one defeat. It took William's army another year to run down the last of the opposing forces.

The garrison of Limerick held out until generous terms were granted. This Treaty of Limerick (1691), which closed the campaign, was in future years to become a source of intense Irish bitterness. The terms were indeed generous: Irish Catholics were to retain all the religious privileges which they had been granted in the reign of Charles II, and their estates were not to be sequestered. The treaty, however, was almost immediately repudiated, because William listened to the Protestant clamor for revenge. England now enslaved the Catholic Irish more closely than ever with new and harsh laws, which, among other things, prevented Roman Catholics from teaching in schools and from serving on juries or as constables or in the Irish parliament or in the military or naval forces, forbade their voting, subjected them to a fine if they refused to work on Catholic holy days, and even made it illegal for a Catholic in Ireland to own a horse above the value of £5. The hatred engendered in those years lives on, and there are still free-for-all fights when the Orangemen celebrate the anniversary of the Boyne on July twelfth, northern Ireland's counterpart to the Catholic observance of Saint Patrick's Day on March seventeenth. Many Catholic Irishmen enlisted in the French army, where they could fight England and be paid for it. Even the Protestants of northern Ireland soon found ground for complaint against England's treatment; for selfish trade laws excluded their linen and other products which might have brought them prosperity. Consequently many of them, after 1700, found their way to the American colonies, where they formed the tough, stern "Scotch-Irish" Presbyterian element of the frontier.

William was now ready for the work which had drawn him to accept the English throne—war against Louis XIV. For nearly thirty years that French king, as we have seen, had worked his will on most of his weaker neighbors in Europe. England's king had been in his pay, Austria had had her hands full with Turkish invaders, Spain was too weak to interfere effectively, most of Germany still lay exhausted from the Thirty Years' War; and, finally, the best generals and the ablest ministers of the day were French (see page 385). Only little Holland had stood up to the menace of French aggression, and William had had to flood his land by cutting the dikes to stop the French invaders. William bided his time for revenge. Since about 1682 the picture had been changing. Colbert and the leading French generals were dead; the Turks had been driven from the gates of Vienna; much of Europe had been aroused by Louis's persecution of the Huguenots through the revocation of the Edict of Nantes, which previously had allowed them much religious freedom; and, to cap it all, Louis's bitterest enemy was now no longer merely stadholder of Holland but king of England as well. Undeterred, Louis had already set out for new conquests. This time, luckily for William's purpose, he headed first for the central Rhine valley instead of for the Low Countries; else William, as we saw, would not have been free to try for the throne of England.

The war into which William led England was to be the first of six major encounters between England and France in the next century and a quarter, and for more than half those years the two nations were to be actually engaged in warfare. The series has been called, with some justification, the "Second Hundred Years' War." In the first Hundred Years' War, England had tried to seize and to dominate territory in France herself and had even sought the French crown, only to realize the futility of so doing. This time the conflict developed into a duel for empire, with sea power and colonies as prizes. Each of the six wars in the second series involved fighting beyond the seas, but in the first two wars the colonial aspects were simply side shows in contests which were primarily European. England, throughout the long series, generally paid allies to keep the French busy on the Continent so that she could more readily concentrate her own energies in the maritime and colonial field. The conflict was finally to end, as we shall see, with the choicest of France's overseas possessions in English hands (see Chapter XVI).

In the first war of the series, known variously as the War of the League of Augsburg or the Palatinate War (1689–1697), William was the organizer and mainspring of a widespread anti-French alliance in which England, Holland, and Austria were the chief members, while Spain, Sweden, and several other nations played less active roles. In America, where this was known as King William's War, the fighting was not important. Interest centered in the Spanish Netherlands and in the rivalry of the navies.

This was not the first nor was it to be the last time that English participation in a general European war centered in the region in and around the Spanish Netherlands (Belgium). Here, in the most familiar foreign soil in England's military history, lies the dust of Englishmen who have fallen in battle all the way from Bouvines, in John's reign, to the western front in the World Wars. This region has been a "cockpit of Europe" for centuries, lying, as it does, exposed to France and Germany, and belonging clearly to neither by geography or population. To England the possession of Belgium by a strong power has been a major menace because of the narrowness of the dividing sea; and since the days of the French threats to the Flemish wool trade in the fourteenth century (see page 174) England has more often than not entered a Continental war when Belgium was involved. This critical little region had come into the possession of Spain from the dukes of Burgundy, through the marriages which led to the empire of Charles V (see page 254). In the days of Philip II, it will be recalled, Spanish occupation of Belgium disturbed England because of Spain's strength; now, however, France was the threat, and Spain lacked the strength either to keep out the French invaders or to prevent Louis XIV's permanent absorption of some of the border towns. Holland's interests at this time ran parallel to England's; for the Dutch wanted Belgium to remain a buffer state between them and France.

Not the least of the reasons for such concentration of fighting in the Low Countries was the ideal terrain for military operations. It

# Limiting the Monarchy

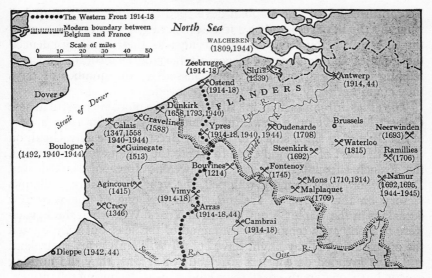

ENGLISH BATTLES IN THE LOW COUNTRIES, 1214–1945

was a flat country with many navigable rivers (particularly the Meuse and Scheldt), connected by canals. In those days of bad roads such waterways were invaluable for moving artillery, munitions, and bulky supplies.

In his fighting against the armies of Louis XIV in this region William pursued much the same course as George Washington, who, like him, was a good but not a brilliant general. Each was finally successful, not through winning startling victories but through being able to hold allies together in spite of defeat. William lost the two major battles of the war, Steenkirk and Neerwinden (or Landen). Fighting in Belgium, however, then and in other wars, was less a matter of pitched battles than of slow siege operations against the fortresses with which every strategic point was guarded. In this siege warfare the French could more than hold their own, because Vauban, the French marshal, had just brought the art of fortification and siegecraft to its peak of perfection. It was said of Vauban, perhaps the greatest military engineer who ever lived, that a fortress which he defended was safe and a fortress which he attacked was doomed. The fortresses of that time were different from the old medieval castles, whose high walls were vulnerable to artillery fire. The new "star-shaped" forts were "sunk in the ground," the stone walls of their scarps so protected by steep outer mounds that only a series of grassy earthworks met the eye. A whole city would be surrounded by such defenses, designed in intricate geometric patterns

[ 407 ]

To capture such places, Vauban developed an attack by "parallels," whereby the besiegers built a successive series of earthworks around the fort, advancing from one to the next as their artillery silenced the guns of the defenders. Siegecraft became an orderly and systematic game, and fortresses were classed by the number of days they could normally hold out unless relieved.

The allies, after a serious initial defeat, were more successful at sea. Colbert had built up a powerful French navy, and in 1690 a fleet of nearly eighty ships sailed forth from Brest. Off Beachy Head, on the south coast of England close to where the Conqueror had landed, the French encountered a somewhat weaker force of English and Dutch whom they roundly whipped, the very day before William's victory on the Boyne in Ireland. This was one of the very few occasions in the whole Second Hundred Years' War when the French were to enjoy even temporary command of the sea; but they wasted the opportunity. They might have cut off William's army in Ireland and have invaded defenseless England; as it was, they did nothing except burn one small coast town and capture some merchantmen. Two years later the battle of La Hogue turned the tables. James was at the Channel port of La Hogue, with a strong force of French regulars and Irish troops ready for an invasion of England. It was necessary for the French to gain command of the Channel; but this time the French admiral ran into a superior force of English and Dutch. In a five-day running encounter the French were driven back; and finally many of their finest ships were run into port, where the English followed in boats and burned them. That was the end of Colbert's magnificent navy. From that time on, the allies were able to move pretty much as they pleased at sea, while the French simply resorted to bold privateering against English and Dutch commerce. It would be more than half a century before the rivals were to meet again in a "full-dress" naval battle.

The English and French colonists in America had meanwhile been fighting their King William's War. At the outbreak of hostilities Count Frontenac, greatest of the governors of New France, was hurriedly sent back to Quebec. He not only saved that colonial capital from an attack by the New Englanders but also devised an effective and devilish system of counterattack. Bands of Indians led by French officers were sent on surprise raids upon the isolated English frontier settlements. Traveling on snowshoes, these stealthy invaders would swoop down at midnight on the luckless community. Then followed war whoops, burning homes, the massacre of some colonists with the tomahawk, and for the rest—men, women, and children—the long, cold route back to Canada, dragged along as prisoners. Schenectady in New York, Deerfield in Massachusetts, Fort Loyal (Portland) in Maine, and various other outlying communities were victims of Frontenac's policy. English settlers disappeared from Maine for a quarter century. Not until the French were finally dislodged from Canada could the pioneers on the outskirts of the English colonies breathe freely once more.

The Peace of Ryswick, in 1697, restored matters very much to the *status quo ante bellum* (that is, the situation before fighting began). While William's victory was not striking, Louis's triumphant spread of French power had been unquestionably checked. William did obtain one significant point, his recognition by Louis as the rightful king of England instead of James II. The peace, however, was to prove only a four-year truce; for new complications arose to embroil Europe again at the turn of the century.

This war cost England even more than previous ones—and war is always an expensive game, as more than one king of England has learned to his cost. In addition to her own heavy military and naval costs, England was starting her familiar role as "paymaster of the allies." The Revolution Settlement survived because it developed a new method of meeting these heavy expenses. This was accomplished in 1693 through the establishment of a permanent national debt, whereby part of the heavy extra war costs were charged to the future. Earlier English kings, with a normal income barely adequate for peacetime purposes, had tried to pay for their wars while these were in progress or soon afterward, partly through extra taxation and partly through short-term loans. Parliament now met about two thirds of this war's costs by taxation, but balked at the heavy taxes which would have been necessary for a completely "pay as you go" policy. As a result the remaining third of the costs was left to future generations by "funding" the debt. In other words, the government borrowed money wherewith to meet its expenses and agreed to pay interest at a specified rate. The nation was like an individual with a fairly fixed income who suddenly incurs heavy extra debts in an emergency. He might keep this a "floating debt" until he could pay the bills of the butcher, the baker, and the doctor bit by bit out of his income; but such a practice works an injustice to his impatient creditors, while his own credit is likely to suffer. Consequently he funds his debt by borrowing the necessary amount from the bank, settling his bills at once, and paying interest to the bank for the use of the money. The bank, to be sure of repayment, takes a mortgage on his house or demands some other "collateral" of value. The collateral for the national debt was the general credit of the government. Nothing was said about paying back the principal of these loans, and the national debt tended to become permanent. When William came to the throne, England had a floating debt of about £1,000,000 in unpaid bills, but with the funding of the debt she owed more than £18,000,000 at his death; and this national debt had risen to some £850,000,000 by the end of the Second Hundred Years' War, in 1815. Some later finance ministers, to be sure, experimented with "sinking funds," whereby money was to be set aside each year for paying off the principal; but these efforts to reduce the debt were generally failures, and England kept on paying interest on money borrowed for wars long past, until interest charges alone came to more than the total annual cost of government in William's time. Considering all that England gained by her ultimate victory over France, that heavy borrowing was a profitable step; but a national debt presented a constant temptation to wage war more frequently and more extravagantly perhaps, since it gave an opportunity to shift a portion of the burden to the shoulders of future generations.

The creation of the national debt led directly to the founding of the Bank of England in 1694. England had lagged behind Italy, Germany, and Holland in the matter of organized banking (see page 235). Jews and Lombards had performed such services in earlier centuries; later the goldsmiths, with whom men deposited their money, carried on banking functions of sorts. Banks could serve two useful purposes: individuals with surplus money might deposit it where it would not only be fairly safe but also pay interest. The bank could pay interest because, on the basis of these deposits, it was able to lend money or discount notes and thus to promote business activity. Underlying the whole financial system was the principle of credit[1]—belief that the money could be repaid. When the government was seeking loans for the national debt, it not only tried to attract the general public with various schemes of annuities and lotteries but also sought to obtain large sums at a single stroke by getting certain companies to take over portions of the debt in place of their capital stock, in return for special privileges. It therefore welcomed the proposals of one William Patterson to organize a Bank of England, which would lend the government £1,200,000 and use the national credit as its capital for doing a general private banking business of deposits, loans, and discounts. The bank was established in London in 1694 and has ever since been a bulwark of the English financial system. It was later given full management of the national debt and the exclusive right to issue bank notes which might pass as currency. In spite of this close relation to the nation's finances, it has remained

[1] "Credit" comes from the Latin word for "believe."

a private institution. Other banks were authorized later, but none had the privileged position of the "Old Lady of Threadneedle Street."

Financial considerations strongly affected the attitude of the two political parties toward the war. When the government determined to pay two thirds of the costs as it went along, its chief device for raising the extra funds was a land tax on the rental income of landowners. Nominally four shillings in the pound, or 20 per cent, it was actually nearer 10 per cent. This tax fell with particular force upon the Tory squires, who complained that the Whig monied interests not only escaped taxation but also gained money through the war, as a result of generous interest on government loans, lucrative war contracts, and the extension of world markets at the expense of French commerce. An income tax was proposed, to make the business and professional men pay their share; but the Treasury was unable to work out an adequate system of collection, and the income tax had to wait a century. The Tories disapproved also of the bank, feeling that such a concentration of money might give undue power to the Whigs and might even render the king too independent of Parliament. The Whigs, on the other hand, became vitally interested in preserving the Revolution Settlement, in which much of their money was invested.

War costs were not the only points of dissension between Whigs and Tories, whose rivalry was sharp and bitter. It was nip and tuck between them during this reign and the next one. No one could foresee with surety how an election would result, nor was there even any certainty as to the outcome of a vote in the closely balanced House of Commons. The absence of a few Whigs or Tories for a cockfight or a party might be enough to change the vote.

Triumphant in its Revolution Settlement, the Commons had yet to work out an orderly way of exercising their new supremacy. Ultimately this was to be achieved by linking the ministers of the cabinet with the party which controlled a majority in the Commons, and there were already gropings in that direction. William was suspicious, and with cause, of his ministers, as well as of his generals and admirals, more than one of whom was in secret correspondence with the exiled James in France, with a view to a possible restoration. Although the king began by choosing ministers from both parties in order to win as broad a support as possible for his government, he soon saw that the Whigs were more inclined to see eye to eye with him on the matter of the French war. By 1694 he had an incipient party cabinet composed entirely of Whigs, hoping that they would assure more unity of action with the majority in the Commons. This group was known as the Whig "Junto," a word like "Cabal," implying a conspiracy of a suspicious nature.

[ 411 ]

# A History of England and the British Empire

With the close of the war, William became more unpopular. His crabbed temper grew worse, and his favoritism toward foreigners in English offices alienated many men. The Tories, winning a majority in the House of Commons, directly flouted him by cutting the army to only seven thousand, despite his request for a force several times that number. The Tories also took away estates which he had granted to some of his Dutch friends. Meanwhile, however, affairs on the Continent grew so threatening to England's security that by 1701 even the Tories were ready for another war against Louis XIV. William lived long enough to organize one more big alliance against Louis, but not to recommence the actual fighting. His wife's sister Anne (1701–1714) peaceably succeeded him on the throne.

Not a murmur was raised against the accession of this younger daughter of James II and Anne Hyde, whatever may have been the private thoughts of those who did not like the Revolution Settlement. Anne's father had died just before William, and those Loyalists who had continued to support their exiled king now transferred their allegiance to his son, Anne's half brother, another James, whose birth, it will be recalled, had brought his father's reign more quickly to its catastrophe in 1688. These Jacobites (so called from *Jacobus,* the Latin for "James") now toasted at their secret meetings the "little gentleman in black velvet" (the mole over whose hole William's horse had stumbled, causing his death), and performed other ceremonies of squeezing an orange and of holding their wine glasses over bowls of water in drinking "To the king over the water." But all this animosity to the Revolution Settlement seldom came into public evidence during the new reign, which, like those of two other queens regnant of England, was to witness much national glory and high literary achievement.

To be sure, only part of the credit for this success can be directly attributed to the dowdy invalid queen, worn out at thirty-six by the births and deaths of "at least fifteen babies," only one of whom survived infancy. Anne's mind has been called "slow as a lowland river"; yet she had more than the usual Stuart share of common sense, and she slaved conscientiously at the details of government in spite of almost steady illness and acute pain. Her stolid husband, Prince George of Denmark, a heavy drinker but withal kindly and devoted to her, was either "too stupid or too shrewd" to interfere with the government and "neither used nor abused his position."[1] All in all, in spite of the dullness of the royal couple and their court, England had much for which to be thankful in this reign.

[1] G. M. Trevelyan, *England under Queen Anne,* Vol. I, pp. 167, 168, 177. By permission of Longmans, Green & Co.

# Limiting the Monarchy

During the first two thirds of the reign three very able persons joined with Anne in governing England: Sarah Churchill, later Duchess of Marlborough, in the queen's chamber; her husband in the field; and Sidney, Lord Godolphin, as chief minister. Sarah, girlhood friend and inseparable companion of Her Majesty until seven years before the queen's death, was as brilliant as Anne was slow. Less clever than the Marlboroughs, but steady, methodical, and thoroughgoing, was Godolphin, whose family wealth had come from Cornish tin mines. Off duty, he enjoyed gambling and horse-racing; his Arabian stallion was one of the three ancestors of most of England's later famous race horses. His son married the Marlboroughs' daughter, and, as Lord Treasurer, Godolphin was to give Marlborough efficient co-operation from home for his military campaigns. Charles II had once said of him, "Little Sidney Godolphin is never in the way and never out of the way"; and this characteristic he retained to the end.

The outstanding member of the trio, John Churchill, was perhaps the greatest military genius who ever fought for England, and certainly the best general since Cromwell's day. Far superior to William III as a general, he was fully his equal in keeping together ill-assorted and jealous allies. In a day of generally static methods of warfare, with siegecraft predominating, Marlborough injected a boldness and originality into strategy, and on the battlefield his keen mind and quick eye seemed always to pick out the best tactical movements. It was not only as a strategist and battle tactician that he excelled. If genius is "the capacity for taking infinite pains," he qualified for that highest distinction. No small part of his success came from his meticulous foresight for every detail: his soldiers always had food, clothing, shelter, and pay, and came to the battlefield in the pink of condition. Whereas there is general agreement about the military ability of the handsome and remarkably gracious Marlborough, such unanimity does not exist about his character. Recent whitewashing has removed much but not all of the black with which he was painted by his contemporary Swift and later by Macaulay. Avarice and disloyalty repeatedly rear their heads as apparent traits. Yet more friendly critics have laid his avarice to his indigent youth, when he had to live on an ensign's meager pay at Charles II's extravagant court, and his apparent disloyalty at times to forethought for England's ultimate advantage rather than for his own. Presumably untrue were many of the charges against him, such as that of sending his officers into dangerous positions in battle so that he might resell their commissions, while the accusations of wholesale graft were often unfair in view of the general custom of the period. Nevertheless, all in all, such charges seem to total a sorry indictment of this famous general. His rise dated from his sister's fall, young John receiving his first commission in the Guards when his sister, Arabella, became the mistress of James II, then Duke of York. The favor of James, coupled with his own ability, quickly raised him to a responsible position. He showed both his mettle and his gratitude by his part in the smashing defeat of the Monmouth rebellion, and in 1688 his shift of allegiance at the last moment from James to William probably did more than anything else to make it a "Bloodless" Revolution. Created Earl of Marlborough by William, but jealous of the favor shown to foreigners in the new regime, he has been accused of going so far in his disloyalty to his new patron as to betray to France a projected naval attack on Brest. Incidentally, the French seem to have already received the same information, possibly from Godolphin. Forced to leave England for a time, Marlborough was called back by William in his last year because the king realized that his new war needed such military talent. Not even his worst enemy accused him of disloyalty to Queen Anne, though some of his intrigues with the enemy during her reign still have a somewhat suspicious look. His military genius rose pre-eminent, however, to win for England some of her greatest victories in the War of the Spanish Succession (1701-1713), which soon ended the short-lived Peace of Ryswick.

England's concern over the lack of a direct heir to the Spanish throne was occasioned by the distinct possibility of the union of France and Spain under a single king, a serious threat to the balance of power. The Spanish king, Charles II, was approaching death at the turn of the century. He had no children, and the marriages of his aunts and sisters into the French Bourbon and Austrian Hapsburg families had made sons of those lines his next of kin. As often happened when a rich and rotten kingdom was unable to look out for itself, other nations were only too ready to intervene. William was particularly determined to prevent the union of Spain with France, because he could foresee that a considerable part of Europe and the New World would then be closed to English and to Dutch trade. Besides, such an aggrandizement of France would seriously threaten the very security of both Holland and England at home, since it would give Belgium to France. An international conference was held, and Louis seemed ready to co-operate with William in the interests of peace. Of the claimants, the French had a somewhat better case than the Austrians, because the Spanish brides who were, respectively, the mother and the wife of Louis XIV were in both cases older than their sisters who had married Hapsburgs at Vienna. This was partially offset by the fact that the Spanish infantas who had come to France had officially given up their claims to the Spanish throne, whereas their younger sisters had not. Such genealogical details may seem decidedly trivial, but they were to lead Europe into a dozen years of war. Both Louis and the emperor claimed the Spanish throne in the names of their second grandson and second son, respectively, both of whom were out of the direct line of inheritance. The conference compromised on the Spanish king's choice of the young son of the Bavarian elector, another grandson of the Austrian line. That solution, which would have left Spain separate from either France or the Empire, came to naught because the young Bavarian died before the aged Charles II of Spain. At a second conference the division of the Spanish lands between the French and Austrian lines was proposed again, but was naturally resented by the Spanish grandees, who wanted to keep Spain's holdings intact and who apparently persuaded Charles, just before he died, to will his entire lands to the second grandson of Louis XIV. Such temptation was too much for Louis, who, disregarding the earlier partition treaties, accepted the bequest for his grandson, who was at once crowned Philip V of Spain. Although this new king, as a younger grandson, was not in direct line for the French throne, England felt that the balance of power was gravely menaced by this double kingship of the Bourbons. Louis at once threw French troops into the Spanish Netherlands in the name of his grandson, and, antagonizing England still further, he also went back on his Ryswick agreement and told the dying James II that he would support his son, James III, for the English throne.

Thereupon, in September, 1701, William organized the Grand Alliance, which included the three chief allies of the preceding war, England, Holland, and Austria, against the Franco-Spanish combination. This began the twelve-year war which was to break the power of Louis.

The war was fought on several fronts. England and Holland were primarily interested in the fighting in the Low Countries. Austria centered her efforts in Italy, where she hoped to recover lands from the Spanish. The defense of the Rhine region was left to those German states which were wheedled onto the side of the allies, Brandenburg-Prussia being bribed by the promotion of her ruler from elector to king, while Hanover, whose ruler in the last war had been bribed by promotion from duke to elector, came in because of the elector's interest in the English throne (see page 402). As a side show, England and Holland, with Portugal, unwisely tried to put the Austrian claimant on the throne of Spain by a campaign there. Except for the Mediterranean, little happened on the sea. The only major naval battle was a draw; but the English and Dutch helped to bring victory by keeping the sea lanes barred to French and Spanish shipping, while they themselves moved troops and cargoes freely. As in the other contests of the Second Hundred Years' War, the War of the Spanish Succession spread to America, where it was known as Queen Anne's War.

The even-numbered years, 1702, 1704, 1706, and 1708, were the fortunate ones for the allies; relatively little happened in the years between. Except for the brief summer campaign in 1704 which produced his masterpiece, Marlborough concentrated his efforts in the Low Countries, where he pushed back the French at the outset of the fighting in 1702 and opened important lines of communication. In 1704 Austria was almost forced out of the war when Vienna itself was threatened by a joint French and Bavarian army, after the entrance of Bavaria into the war. Disguising his intentions from the allies (for he well knew that they would never allow him to leave the Low Countries undefended), Marlborough rushed by secret rapid marches the several hundred miles to the Danube. En route he joined forces with Prince Eugene of Savoy, the Austrian commander, second only to Marlborough himself in military ability, who alone knew of the plans. Together, with some fifty thousand men, they met an equal number of French and Bavarians along a marshy brook which flowed into the Danube at the hamlet of Blenheim. With half the enemy killed, wounded, or prisoners and the rest in disorganized flight, Marlborough won his most spectacular victory. Europe was amazed, for French regiments had been invincible for half a century.

Returning to the Low Countries for the duration of his command, Marlborough cleared the French out of the entire Spanish Netherlands after another smashing victory at Ramillies in 1706. At the same time Prince Eugene drove them out of Italy. In 1708, after the French had recovered part of Belgium, Marlborough inflicted a third decisive defeat upon them at Oudenarde and captured Vauban's masterpiece, the fortress at Lille, in France itself. One more important battle did Marlborough win—at Malplaquet, where he lost three men to the French two, the following year. After that his part was less noticeable. He had won a reputation as the first soldier of Europe; Parliament had voted a huge sum to build him an immense palace; and even two centuries later men still sang, on the Continent, "Malbrouck s'en va t'en guerre" (to the tune "We won't go home till morning").

Already by the time of Ramillies the Grand Alliance had achieved its two chief objectives, the expulsion of the French from the Netherlands and from Italy. The Spanish campaign of the English and Dutch, however, still dragged. Supported by Portugal and the discontented Catalan region of Spain around Barcelona, they tried to oust the Bourbon Philip V in favor of the Austrian claimant. The first allied commander was a rattle-brained English earl who was no match for the Duke of Berwick, Marlborough's nephew and an illegitimate son of James II, who was fighting against England. Despite increasing failures, the allies stubbornly persisted. While the Spanish campaign was a costly blunder, two important by-products came of it. A stipulation of the alliance with Portugal was the exchange of English woolens for Portuguese port and Madeira wine. This tended to replace the use of light French wines and probably increased the goutiness of the eighteenth-century English gentleman. More essential, a week before Blenheim an English fleet captured the weakly defended Rock of Gibraltar, the key to the Mediterranean; and four years later Minorca, in the Balearic Islands, also fell to the English, who made it a permanent winter naval base inside the Mediterranean. Thus did England, which had first seen the value of the Mediterranean in Cromwell's time, and which had come to realize the need of naval protection there after her rich "Smyrna convoy" had been captured in 1693, now come to take her place as a permanent power there.

By 1709 France was bled white and ready for peace. On top of her defeats and an empty treasury from such prolonged warfare, she was faced with famine after an especially bitter winter, the "Great Frost," which froze crops in the ground and peasants in their huts. Louis was ready to concede almost anything for peace and was met with forty demands from the allies. Of these he agreed to all but one, that French armies must join in driving his own grandson from his Spanish throne. Thereupon, with cruel stupidity the blame for which must fall mostly on England, which rallied to the cry of "No peace without Spain!" the war was continued, with the French putting up a stubborn fight.

In the meantime, at home, England and Scotland were uniting to form the kingdom of Great Britain, with a single Parliament, an event which proved of lasting advantage to both countries. James I had tried to achieve this when the two kingdoms had been brought under the same crown in 1603, but England at that time would have none of it. The experiment of one king and two separate Parliaments had not been a very happy one. The rulers were inclined to govern Scotland from London, and the Scots felt, with some justice, that their interests were being sacrificed. Cromwell had joined the two nations by force, but the regime of Monk's redcoats had not endeared the English to the Scots.

# A History of England and the British Empire

On the eve of the union, English writers were calling the Scots "bloody, barbarous, inhuman butchers" and were turning up their noses at their "nastiness and ill manners," while Scots at the same time referred to England as "insolent and proud like hell." Englishmen disliked the bulk of the Scots as Presbyterians or Jacobites, while Scotland still remembered Flodden and Glencoe. Nevertheless, underneath the surface, each nation had a wholesome respect for the other, an attitude quite different from the contempt and bitterness which unfortunately characterized Anglo-Irish relations. Not friendship, then, but a shrewd realization of the mutual advantages of union brought the two together. The act of Union in 1707 embodied a bargain: Scotland gave up her separate parliament and nominal independence in exchange for English trading privileges. And the Scots told the English that the alternative to union might be the installation of the Jacobite Pretender on the Scottish throne; for Scotland had not been a party to the Act of Settlement.

Poverty, more than anything else, drove the Scots to give up the independence they had made secure at Bannockburn (see page 168). The thrift which hundreds of jokes have emphasized as an outstanding Scottish trait was forced upon them by the niggardliness of nature in their bleak north country. Their harsh, dour characteristics had been nourished on a monotonous diet of oatmeal, whisky, and Calvinism. The per-capita wealth of Scotland was reckoned at less than one sixth of that south of the border. Even in the more prosperous Lowlands, an income of £500 a year, regarded as moderate by an English squire, was considered great wealth. Some lairds struggled to keep up appearances as gentlemen on £20 a year, though thousands of English yeomen made twice as much. The peasantry could do little more than exist on the meager crops they gathered from the inhospitable soil by their crude methods; and they lived in little cabins, often with dirt floors and only a single filthy, smoky room, frequently shared with the cattle in winter. There were few towns of account outside Edinburgh, the capital, where a considerable population was crowded into small space, living in gaunt, graystone buildings, seven or eight stories high. Industry and trade were in a feeble state, and the foreign commerce of Leith and Glasgow was negligible.

Beyond the Highland line was another Scotland, wilder, less civilized, and even poorer. The clansmen of the Highlands cared little for the authority of Kirk or king; to them the paternalistic chief, with his power of life and death, was everything. They preserved more of their Celtic inheritance than that, in their speech, in their romantic belief in the supernatural, and in many other ways, while

# Limiting the Monarchy

in religion a large section of them were still Roman Catholic. No Sir Walter Scott had yet appeared to give to Lowlanders and Englishmen a glamorous picture of this Highland life; to the outsiders the kilted clansmen in their plaids were dangerous relics of an older and lower civilization. Physical danger, and the utter absence of roads in those wild hills, discouraged most southerners from venturing beyond the line. But the Act of Union was primarily a Lowland matter; the Highlanders would be heard from later—in 1715 and again in 1745.

The bait which lured Scotland into the union was the commercial and colonial system established by the Navigation Acts, with their exclusive emphasis on English ships and English sailors. England was obviously growing rich: the profits from her commerce were estimated at £2,000,000 a year in 1700, and the contrast was all the sharper because Scotland was staggering from two recent economic blows. A succession of bad crops in William's time had brought famine and widespread death from starvation. To make matters worse, Scotland's solitary venture into the colonial and commercial field in 1698 had been a spectacular failure. Everyone who could scrape together a few pounds had invested them in the "Company for Trading with Africa and the Indies," which had sent a few ships toward India and had planted a colony at Darien, on the Isthmus of Panama. The English East India Company had exercised its monopoly to keep the Scots from India, and William had sided with his English rather than his Scottish subjects in the matter. The Darien colony, planted in the heart of the monopolistic Spanish empire, died a quick and miserable death as the combined result of Spaniards, fever, and dissension, while England did not lift a finger to save it. Thus running afoul of two rigid overseas monopolies, the Scots could appreciate the advantages of being on the inside rather than the outside of such systems. The loss to the investors would have been serious even in England; to the Scots it was a tragedy. England helped to pave the way for the Act of Union by reimbursing the investors, with interest thrown in for good measure.

The price which Scotland paid for commercial rights was the loss of her separate parliament. But that body was even less representative than England's Parliament at Westminster and meant much less to the nation. The real loyalty of the Lowland Scots was to the Kirk, the highly organized Presbyterian system established by John Knox. In its various bodies, ranging from the parish "session" through the presbytery and synod to the annual national General Assembly at Edinburgh, the layman took part as well as the preacher. Scots of all degrees had far more opportunity for actual participation in the Kirk than in the regular political organization. With this valuable democratic influence, the Kirk had "raised the downtrodden people of Scotland to look its political masters in the face." The Scots had risen in 1638 not for political reasons but because Laud was tampering with their Kirk (see page 340). As long as the union left that undisturbed, the Scots would more easily forgo their separate parliament.

After several years of negotiations, during which there was the constant possibility that on Anne's death the Scots might set up an independent kingdom under the Pretender, as "James VIII," thirty-odd commissioners from each kingdom finally met at Whitehall in the spring of 1706. As a result of sharp bargaining, they arrived at the essential terms of the Act of Union. Scotland was not only to retain her own Kirk, which has ever since remained separate from the Church of England, but also to preserve Scotland's particular legal system, based on elements of feudal and Roman law, quite different from the English common law. Scottish ships with Scottish crews would thereafter enjoy the same trading privileges as ships from London and Bristol or colonial Boston and New York. With the abolition of her own parliament, Scotland was to send forty-five members to the House of Commons at Westminster, while the Scottish peers were to select sixteen from their number to sit in the House of Lords. In each case this was less than óne tenth of the number from England and Wales.

The terms were referred first to the Scottish parliament, because approval in England was quite certain. In spite •of protests and riots in various parts of Scotland, the majority favored the measure, and the Scottish parliament signed its own death warrant. On May 1, 1707, the Kingdom of Great Britain came into being. England celebrated that May Day in gay fashion; but in Scotland, it is said, some of the bells played "Why should I be sad on my wedding day?"

The act paved the way for relative prosperity in Scotland. Commerce began to flourish at Glasgow, Leith, and other ports. The canny shrewdness of the Scot had free scope for development in the wider sphere of opportunities and contributed much to the success of the kingdom and the empire. By the end of the century, too, the names of Adam Smith, Robert Burns, and James Watt indicate Scotland's accomplishments in thought, literature, and invention. Only from 1707 on may one properly refer to the "British" government, "British" army, and so on. Within forty years the British army in particular was to become more effective with regiments of those wilder Scots of the Highlands, who in 1707, however, were still untamed troublemakers.

# Limiting the Monarchy

The refusal, soon after the Scottish union, to make peace "without Spain" gave weary Europe four years more of fruitless war. It was largely the result of the party situation in England. The balance between the parties was as close as it had been in William's reign, and feeling ran higher. Anne, moreover, was not the person to keep such a contentious rivalry in hand; for, although she always conscientiously presided at her cabinet meetings, she was not able to control them as William had done. Because of her failure to dominate her ministers, Godolphin for some eight years was virtually a prime minister. Anne wanted a general equable mixture of parties represented in the government; but in vain she declared her constitutional doctrine: "All I desire is my liberty in encouraging and employing all those that concur faithfully in my service, whether they are called Whigs or Tories, not to be tied to one nor the other." Instead, the poor queen expressed her misgivings in 1708 as follows: "The parties are such bugbears that I dare not venture to write my mind freely of either of them without a cypher for fear of any accident. I pray God keep me out of the hands of both of them."[1] To add to the confusion, the Tories were now split into a High Church group,—extreme Anglicans and some of Jacobite persuasion,—determined upon harsh punishment of Nonconformists and the ending of the practice of "occasional conformity," and into a Moderate group, whose name indicated their desire for a middle course. Combined, these Tories at this time would have outnumbered the Whigs; but they did not stay together. As a result of this situation the control of Parliament had gradually changed from united Tories, at the beginning of the reign, to a combination of Moderate Tories and Whigs, and then to Whigs alone. The Whigs, we recall, were the ones who favored vigorous prosecution of the war, and in the election of 1705 large numbers of Whigs came into the Commons. Anne's attitude, however, kept many Tory ministers in office, so that there was combined Tory and Whig control until about 1708, when the Whigs succeeded in obtaining complete domination. This change to Whig ministers had been felt in the conduct of the war, and Marlborough found it expedient to change his professed party affiliation from Tory to Whig. Godolphin, as we have indicated, continued as head of the cabinet through these changes. Between 1708 and 1710, however, as the war dragged on, Whig popularity began to wane in the country at large, and another general shift back to Tory control was obviously pending.

In connection with this coming fall of the Whigs came the eclipse

[1] G. M. Trevelyan, *England under Queen Anne* (1932), Vol. II, pp. 170, 385. By permission of Longmans, Green & Co.

of the trio which had been associated with Anne in governing England during the first part of her reign. Sarah had already lost the queen's friendship in 1707; Godolphin, as we shall see, was dismissed in favor of a Tory in 1710; while the duke fell from power a year later. They had brought England victories abroad and the union with Scotland at home, but they were replaced by three less worthy individuals. Sarah was ousted from favor by Mrs. Abigail Masham, a poor relation of hers, whom she had befriended and introduced into the queen's household. There Abigail's amiable temper, her thoughtfulness for the queen's comfort, and her ingratiating manner helped her to supplant the strong-willed duchess. The steady, dependable Godolphin, as we shall see, was to give way to Robert Harley, whom some called a slippery backstairs politician, "Robin the Trickster." He was a Moderate Tory in policy, careless in administration, and remarkably well informed through his efficient secret service. Mrs. Masham was his tool on more than one occasion. His ally and later archenemy, the third of the newcomers, the High Tory, Henry St. John, later Viscount Bolingbroke, was to come into power along with him. St. John was one of England's most brilliant statesmen, a master of oratory and diplomatic negotiation. Yet he was a profligate debauchee, not to be trusted in matters of finance or loyalty; a man whose desperate gamble in Anne's last hours was to ruin his own future permanently and his party's for half a century. This second trio was to bring England peace, but was to fall out over the question of Anne's successor.

The crisis that brought on this general shift, with the overthrow of the increasingly unpopular Whigs, was hastened by the excessively High Tory sermon of one Dr. Sacheverell, who happened to be preaching at St. Paul's Cathedral, in London, on November 5, 1709, Guy Fawkes Day, and also incidentally the anniversary of the landing of William III. In scathing denunciation Sacheverell virulently attacked not only Godolphin but also the whole Revolution Settlement. Since the Anglican Church was established, the government took action for this bitter attack upon itself. Sacheverell was impeached by the House of Commons and tried by the Lords, who found him guilty by a small majority. His sermon, however, had been in tune with the popular feeling of the moment. The Lords gave him the lightest sentence in their power: he was not to preach for three years, and his sermon was to be burned by the hangman. Some forty thousand copies, however, had already been distributed, and Sacheverell, a popular hero, took triumphal possession of a new and lucrative living. The fickle London mob, which had attacked Catholic chapels in 1688, now turned upon those of the Dissenters.

# Limiting the Monarchy

Then the changes involved in the fall of the Whigs came thick and fast. During the next six months Anne quietly dismissed her ministers one by one, sending even the faithful Godolphin merely a curt note to break his staff of office, without a word of gratitude for his many services. A general election in this same year, 1710, gave the Tories a powerful majority, with the Moderate and High factions temporarily united. It was at this juncture that Harley became chief minister, and that into office came also the more rabid St. John. The latter immediately began to stir up a group of wild young bloods, in the October Club, who were talking of the return of the Pretender.

Plotting permanent confusion to all the Whigs, the Tories now turned to the literary talent of the day to spread their political propaganda. Violent pamphleteering swept the country in 1710 and 1711; rarely if ever has another such collection of able writers been marshaled to use their pens for political purposes. Pre-eminent among the pamphleteers were the violently High Tory Swift, the more moderate Addison and Steele, and Defoe, who had been Harley's ear to the ground and now took money from both sides. The Tories pushed through legislation designed to keep everyone except squires from the House of Commons, to prevent Nonconformists from qualifying for official positions by "occasional conformity" (see page 403), and to close all Dissenting schools. None of those three laws, however, was to have permanent effect.

In the field of foreign affairs St. John was trying with more cleverness than honor to bring about the Tory aim of peace as soon as possible, and "without Spain." Even before the end of the Godolphin regime there had been secret negotiations for peace with France behind the backs of England's allies. Rapidly and shamelessly St. John carried these forward, but Marlborough stood in his way. In the summer of 1711, by a clever move in which he did not lose a man, the duke pierced the French lines and had almost a clear road ahead of him to Paris; but in that very month St. John had completed preliminary peace terms in which England received a great deal at the particular expense of Holland. Marlborough's reputation and popularity had withstood the party changes at home. It was felt necessary to discredit him in order to break his influence; therefore charges were brought against him of accepting £63,000 in bribes from the army bread contractor and of keeping for himself part of the money given him for the hiring of mercenaries, though that was the accepted practice by which generals acquired secret-service funds. Without investigating these charges, Anne dismissed Marlborough as summarily as she had Godolphin. Unfortunately, Marlborough's hands, as we have seen, were not as clean as they might have been in several matters; yet worse graft than his was a common practice, and these charges were much exaggerated, if not untrue. To avoid prosecution, he went into exile abroad for the rest of the queen's life. Becoming captain-general of the forces in the next reign, he kept to his old tricks of accepting office from the new king but making abject approaches to the Pretender for high position in case of a restoration. Marlborough received high rewards from four monarchs, and to Anne alone was he relatively loyal.

The duke was at last out of the way, but there was another obstacle to peace in the attitude of the House of Lords. To ensure a majority to support the Commons' desire for immediate peace, Anne, at a single stroke on New Year's Day of 1712, created twelve new peers, including Mr. Masham. This was an important constitutional development; for it showed a way to override opposition in the House of Lords. The sovereign, of course, was entitled to create as many new peers as he or she should see fit at any time. After this precedent the mere threat of its repetition was to be sufficient to overcome resistance in the Lords on two later occasions.

That same month the peace conference assembled in the quiet Dutch city of Utrecht, but the fighting continued without an armistice. Prince Eugene and the other allied commanders were planning a further invasion of France; but Bolingbroke, to use the better-known name which St. John had just received upon elevation to the Lords, sent secret orders to Marlborough's successor to avoid fighting for the present, stating that a copy of the letter was being despatched to the French court. By the summer of 1712, to the disgust and dismay of the deserted allies, the British troops were hurried back from the front with the soldiers in tears, partly, it is said, from shame and partly because of the loss of anticipated French booty.

By the spring of 1713 the various treaties which bear the name of Utrecht were signed. They reflect shrewd work by Bolingbroke, but England's desertion of her allies won for her the epithet of "Perfidious Albion," which was to be repeated half a century later. Several royal deaths affected the settlement. The Austrian Hapsburg claimant to the Spanish throne had become Emperor Charles VI, and the Spaniards retained as their king the Bourbon Philip V for whom they had been fighting. Both the son and the grandson of Louis XIV, however, had just died, leaving only a great-grandson, the sickly infant who would soon be Louis XV, between Philip V and the French throne. Thus there were now Bourbons on both sides of the Pyrenees, and France need fear no longer the "Hapsburg ring." The agreements stipulated that the same man should never occupy both the French and the Spanish throne; but during the coming century there were to be frequent renewals of a Bourbon "family compact," which forced England to keep her navy as large as the combined French and Spanish fleets.

Both France and Spain, however, paid heavily for this dynastic concession. The Peace of Utrecht marked England's first successful looting of the French colonial empire. While Marlborough had been keeping the French busy on land, English admirals had gained ascendancy on the sea, and the colonies had sustained "Queen Anne's War." England received from France a clear title to the disputed regions of Hudson Bay and Newfoundland and received also part of Acadia, called by the English Nova Scotia. In addition, Louis once again officially recognized the Protestant succession in England at the expense of the direct Stuart line. In the Mediterranean, England kept the island of Minorca and, more important, the key position at Gibraltar, the huge rock fortress which she had also taken from Spain and successfully defended against all the Franco-Spanish attempts to recover it. She also received valuable trading concessions in the hitherto closed preserves of Spanish America, where, in the "Asiento," Spain gave England a thirty-year monopoly of her colonial slave trade and permission to trade with one ship a year (see page 291). England did not share these maritime concessions, obtained in the preliminary secret negotiations, with her ally Holland; and that small nation, exhausted by the long wars and thus abandoned by her ally, dropped from her brief moment in the ranks of the first-class powers to a comfortable berth, where she has since remained, among the lesser nations. For added security against France, Holland was given authority to occupy a string of barrier forts in the Belgium region, though these were far from being the complete safeguards the Dutch desired. Belgium, previously the Spanish Netherlands, now became the Austrian Netherlands, being shifted to the other branch of the Hapsburg house because Austria was too remote to be a menace to either Holland or England. Among other advantages, Austria gained considerable territory in Italy. That did not particularly concern England, whose interest in Continental territory, aside from the security of the Low Countries and the acquisition of Gibraltar, remained a negative one. The quarter century of conflict had removed the French menace and saved the balance of power.

With the Spanish succession out of the way, the question of the English succession loomed larger. It lay between Anne's Protestant cousin of the Hanoverian line, stipulated by the Act of Settlement in 1701, and her Catholic younger half brother, the Jacobite Pretender, whose birth had precipitated the Revolution of 1688.

# A History of England and the British Empire

The Tories had been united on the peace, but they split over the situation involved in the succession. Bolingbroke was steadily building up a High Tory faction to support his own inclination, which was apparently turning more and more toward the Pretender. An urgent crisis seemed imminent at Christmas of 1713, when Anne fell dangerously ill. Oxford (Harley), with his moderate policies, stood in the way of Bolingbroke's plans, which began to materialize feverishly as Anne grew worse. Working in conjunction with the faithless Abigail, who had shifted from Sarah to Oxford and who now intrigued to oust Oxford, Bolingbroke found himself balked; for Oxford clung on, despite increased carelessness and sullen inactivity, in his high post of Lord Treasurer. Bolingbroke pushed through Parliament in June the Schism Act, which closed all Dissenting schools "down to the meanest" (see page 423), hoping to embarrass Oxford and provoke the Nonconformists to revolt, in which case Louis XIV had promised to send over the Pretender with French troops.

At last Oxford was dismissed by Anne, who was disgusted with his strange apathy and neglect, and who was by now too weak to resist the steady pressure exerted by Bolingbroke and Abigail. This was the chance for which Bolingbroke had apparently been working. No one but the dying queen was now his immediate superior. Exactly what his plans were seems far from clear. Whether Bolingbroke was actually plotting a Jacobite restoration, as many of his acts seemed to indicate, or whether he was merely trying to get the power into his own hands, to be in a strong position for the Hanoverian succession, no one knows; but one fact is obvious: he himself intended to be the center of whatever stage he was setting. He had to work quickly, now that the situation was temporarily in his hands; but he did not realize just how short the time was to be. Less than three days did the Lord-Treasurership lie vacant, and Anne did not trust Bolingbroke enough to give him this key position. Oxford had been dismissed late on Tuesday; on Friday the Privy Council hastily met on receiving the grave news that the queen was sinking fast. The Jacobites and Bolingbroke apparently were caught unawares. The Whigs and Moderate Tories were ready with a nominee for Lord Treasurer, a trusted Moderate Tory peer ; and Anne acquiesced. Until midnight this body, whose authority was greater than that of the cabinet alone, worked feverishly, sending orders throughout the land to make ready for the peaceful succession of the Hanoverian heir. Bolingbroke, with his hopes of power dashed to earth, meekly signed the papers with the others. Sunday morning Anne was dead, and with the proclamation at St. James's Palace of the Hanoverian elector as King George I (1714–1727) cheers went up all over London.

# Limiting the Monarchy

That night the city blazed with bonfires before the homes of the prominent peers, not excluding that of Bolingbroke!

Had Anne died a few months earlier, she would have been succeeded by another queen, a lively, clever old lady in her eighties, Sophia, the dowager electress of Hanover. Sophia's mother had been the daughter of James I, and her father that "Winter King" of Bohemia whose aspirations had started the Thirty Years' War (see pages 322–324). Prince Rupert, who had led royal forces on land and sea in the Civil War, was Sophia's brother. Just as the marriage of a Tudor princess to a Scottish king had brought, a century afterward, a Stuart to the English throne, so now the marriage of that first Stuart's daughter to a German duke was to bring the Hanoverian line to the throne just a hundred years later. Sophia had married a rather insignificant German noble, of a branch of the House of Brunswick (whence the name "Brunswick" in colonial towns from Maine to Georgia). In 1692, as the price of his military support, the Hapsburg Holy Roman emperor had raised him to the dignity of Elector of Brunswick-Lüneburg, or, as it has been more generally called, Hanover, from the name of its principal city. Lying in the same general part of northwestern Germany which the Angles and Saxons had left to invade England, Hanover was one of the lesser German states, touching the North Sea near Hamburg and Bremen. Sophia, according to some accounts, intrigued for years to gratify her ambition of having "Queen of England" engraved on her tombstone, and then missed it by four months. Instead, the throne went to her son, who regarded it as something of a nuisance. When the news of Anne's death reached Hanover late in the night, the British minister, it is said, awakened the elector and saluted him as King of Great Britain; but, whereas James of Scotland had restlessly paced the courtyard awaiting the news of Elizabeth's death, George merely grunted and went back to sleep. Nevertheless, the British throne was too important for a mere elector of Hanover to refuse, and before seven weeks had elapsed a reluctant, homesick, and somewhat bewildered George arrived among his new subjects. He was accompanied by two elderly and grasping mistresses, whom the disrespectful dubbed the "Maypole" and the "Elephant." These German countesses became English duchesses, but George's own wife never saw England; she had been divorced and even for a while imprisoned for a youthful indiscretion for which her alleged lover had been murdered.

As individuals the new dynasty possessed none of the glamour or charm of the Tudors or Stuarts. The first two Georges were stolid, stodgy, and colorless German princes; the third George alienated many by his effort to restore royal power and then went insane; the fourth George was probably the coarsest of English monarchs; and his brother, the fourth William, was stupid and uninteresting. England was attached to the Hanoverians not from affection, admiration, or respect but because, with one exception, they interfered little with the running of the government and, by occupying the throne, they kept out a rival line which might have threatened Protestantism and the control of Parliament.

The presence of the Hanoverian kings on the throne frequently complicated foreign policy between 1714 and 1837. They remained electors of Hanover, and their solicitude for this state affected the insular independence of policy which England could otherwise enjoy. The first two Georges in particular took Hanover very seriously into account in their foreign policy. The royal navy could prevent an invasion of England, but it could not defend the frontiers of Hanover from French or Prussian aggression. England was to breathe a sigh of relief when, at Victoria's accession, the tie was broken by German custom, which barred a woman from ruling Hanover.

Georgian England formed a comfortable period in English history. It saw the culmination of the movement for Parliamentary control in the creation of a system of responsible government; but, so far as political history goes, we can almost agree with Carlyle that the eighteenth was "a century which has no history and can have little or none." In England such stagnation served its purpose. It gave the nation a much-needed breathing spell to rest from the struggle which had gone before and to gather strength for the closing years of the century, when, within a few years, it was to run afoul of three revolutions: the American, the Industrial, and the French. During the intervening years much of the interest centers not in England itself but on the fringes of empire. A drowsy atmosphere might hang over the halls of Parliament, but, as we shall see in the next chapter, history was being made in the valleys of the St. Lawrence and the Ohio, in Bengal and the Deccan, and on various parts of the high seas. Even that duel for empire enjoyed its longest breathing spell in the quarter century after Utrecht; England and France remained at peace partly because of war-weariness and partly because of the pacific influence of the ministers in charge of affairs on both sides of the Channel.

The Whigs came into power with George I, who owed them his throne; and so badly discredited were the Tories by Bolingbroke's fiasco and by other events that the Whig regime lasted until the death of the second George, in 1760. Hardly was there a Tory party left. A few die-hard Tories, as a rule, were returned to Parliament; but the moderates turned Whig, and the Tory party as an effective opposition ceased to exist. Much of this Whig power lay in the hands of some seventy great landed families. Under such leadership, which was inclined to raise as few disputed points as possible, England enjoyed a period of sleepy prosperity.

Before settling into that somnolence, however, England was stirred in the year after George's accession by a Jacobite uprising remembered as the "Fifteen." The Jacobites, caught unprepared by Anne's death, were now all ready to fight—the exiles in France, including Bolingbroke; the malcontents in England; and some Scottish chiefs. With better plans and more solidarity among themselves, the Jacobites might well have shaken George's throne. Not only was there woeful bungling, however, but many were still undecided as to whether they wanted to bring "James III" home or retain George; and they determined to keep in the good graces of both sides until they could see how events were shaping themselves. Marlborough, for instance, who had returned from exile to become the nominal head of George's army, was sending money to the Pretender. One Scottish peer betrayed the Jacobite plans to the government, but kept his son in the Pretender's army. The standard was raised prematurely in the Highlands; the government knew the plans through the double-dealers almost as soon as they were formulated. A small band of Highland clansmen was joined by a few Catholics from northern England. Had there been time to rouse the Lowlands, the revolt might have had a different ending; for there were only about eight thousand soldiers stationed in the British Isles. Yet even before the Pretender landed, the Jacobites had been twice defeated. Louis XIV had died on the eve of the Pretender's departure, and the regent for the infant Louis XV made no move to aid James, who fled back to France, where he lived out his life in exile. The rebels were treated with a leniency which was perhaps mistaken; for, thirty years later, James's son, "Bonnie Prince Charlie," the "Young Pretender," was to stir up a similar futile revolt.

The only other serious threat to the new Hanoverian line came not from Highlanders but from the wild financial frenzy of the "South Sea Bubble" in 1720. The South Sea Company was a joint-stock organization formed by Harley in 1711 to handle the trade with Spanish America to be opened by the "Asiento," which he was even then negotiating. In 1720 the company became involved in government high finance. The nation had a large floating debt which it was trying to fund at regular interest rates. It naturally turned to the great companies which had much concentrated wealth at their disposal. The Bank of England and the East India Company had already taken over portions of the national debt in this manner, sub-

stituting government securities for their regular capital (see page
410). Now it was the turn of the South Sea Company, which, by an
act of Parliament, received monopoly privileges and other advantages in exchange for taking over £30,000,000 of the debt. But,
whereas the other two organizations had remained on a conservative
basis, the stock of the South Sea Company was manipulated into an
abnormal boom, all the more easily because, ever since the days of
Elizabeth, Spanish America, with its silver mines of Mexico and
Peru, had suggested fabulous wealth. Within three months after the
act was passed, speculation had driven £100 South Sea shares to a
peak of £1060. Taking advantage of this bull market, unscrupulous
promoters gathered capital for various wildcat schemes; a thousand
gullible fools even subscribed to "a company for carrying on an
undertaking, but nobody to know what it is." As is usual after such
a boom, the bubble suddenly burst; millions in paper profits were
wiped out overnight; sound companies were dragged down with
shaky ones; and thousands were ruined. The public suspected graft
in high places and clamored for victims. The Chancellor of the
Exchequer, who had made some £800,000 by his illegal manipulation,
was expelled by the House of Commons; another high official committed suicide; the royal mistresses were involved. Altogether, it was
a sorry scandal.

As a result of the South Sea Bubble, Sir Robert Walpole was
advanced toward a position of prominence, from a junior capacity
in the ministry. This shrewd, if not brilliant, Norfolk squire, with his
marked financial ability, had advised against the South Sea act;
his hands had remained clean while his colleagues' were besmirched;
and he did an able job in straightening out the tangle afterward.
Even Lord Stanhope, the captor of Minorca, the dominant man in
George's first ministry, who had handled foreign affairs as a secretary
of state with remarkable ability, was acquitted in the Commons by
only three votes, though his part in the "Bubble" was apparently
innocent. He died soon afterward. Lord Townshend, nominally the
senior member of the cabinet, continued in office; but he had been
overshadowed by Stanhope, and now was to be overshadowed again,
even more markedly, by his brother-in-law, Sir Robert Walpole,
until eventually, in annoyance, he retired about 1730 to his estate,
where he won the lasting nickname of "Turnip" Townshend for his
pioneer achievements in agriculture (see page 485).

Walpole was to be hailed in later years as England's first prime
minister. This in effect he was from 1721 to 1742, although he never
had the title and always denied that he was any such thing, for the
phrase had in those days an unpleasant significance, suggesting a

# Limiting the Monarchy

royal favorite. An odd circumstance, arising from the refusal of the German king to learn English, gave Walpole the opportunity to usher in a most important constitutional development. George, with his heart in Hanover, a little state with few problems, where his word was law, without the interference of a troublesome parliament, did not bother to attend the meetings of the cabinet. This was the first time that a monarch had neglected this duty. William had dominated his cabinet through force of personality; and although Anne's influence was less, she had at least gone to the meetings. George, however, refused to sit through long conferences of which he could understand nothing. This indifference left the power and the responsibilities in the hands of ministers, though in the early years of the reign the authority was not concentrated in the hands of a single minister. Walpole had the ability and personality to assume the dual role of control over the cabinet and leadership of the majority in the House of Commons. He thus combined the role of a party leader with that of chief agent for the king, with whom he could communicate in bad Latin. As this worked out in practice, the cabinet ministers, who carried on the government in the king's name, remained in power only as long as they could command support in the House of Commons. This brought about a combination of the executive and legislative; for the executive power came to be directly dependent upon the elected legislature, which, in theory at least, represented the will of the people. Thus arose "responsible government," by which Parliament finally gained the machinery for exercising the control it had won in 1688.

Shortly after this time a French political philosopher, Montesquieu, wrote that the secret of the success of the English government lay in the distinct separation of the executive power as represented by the king and the legislative as represented by Parliament. The United States adopted this in her Constitution at the end of the century, with a sharp separation of function between President and Congress, to which the colonists had become accustomed in the disputes between governors and assemblies. On the other hand, the English government, far from separating those powers in the early eighteenth century, was uniting them more and more in the person of the prime minister through this system of responsible government.

In 1707 England had passed another constitutional landmark, practically unnoticed at the time, but important in retrospect. It will be recalled that before it could become an act, a bill which had passed Commons and Lords must receive the royal assent, as given in the words "Le roy (la reine) le veult." It was within the power of the ruler to withhold assent, with the words "Le roy s'avisera"

(The king will consider the matter). That was equivalent to a veto. William III had withheld his assent from four bills, and the last instance of a "royal veto" occurred when Anne refused assent to a Scottish militia bill. From that time on, every bill which has passed the two houses of Parliament has received the royal assent as a matter of course, though the form is still preserved of making an act the express will of the king. It might be still possible for the crown to exercise the veto power in an emergency, but the fact that the old veto power fell into abeyance gave added importance to the legislative branch of the government in its extension of power into the executive field.

Gradually, during the eighteenth century, Parliament continued to work out the system of making the cabinet responsible to the majority in the Commons. As it finally developed, there were three courses which a cabinet might take in case of an adverse vote there. It might resign at once, whereupon the king would ask the opposition leader to form a new cabinet. It might call for an "appeal to the country," that is, a general election for an entire new House of Commons. Finally, it might disregard a few adverse votes in hope of recovering its majority; but if the Commons voted a "lack of confidence" in the ministers, resignation was necessary. The possibility of an "appeal to the country" at any time theoretically gave the electorate a strong influence on the affairs of government; but that was used sparingly, and the average term of a cabinet during the first two centuries of responsible government was almost identical with the arbitrary four-year term of an administration in the United States. From the period of George I the king tended to become more and more a figurehead, exercising a varying degree of *influence* but little real *power*. Practically the only direct political function left to the crown was the choice of which leader of the opposition to call in as prime minister when a cabinet fell; theoretically, it might be said, of course, that extensive powers and prerogatives still remained to it.

It is characteristically English that this cabinet, which for two centuries has been the mainspring of the government, does not exist in the eyes of the law. The legal authority of its members rests partly on their particular official positions and partly on the fact that they all belong to the Privy Council and can transact business in its name. The Privy Council had been important for centuries, particularly under the Tudors. It had become too large and unwieldy for effective work by the time of William III, who gathered about him some of its most influential members as a Cabinet Council, so called because it met in his cabinet. As a body the members discussed general matters of policy; as individuals most of them were administrative heads of particular departments, transacting business in the king's name. During most of the eighteenth century the cabinet usually consisted of eleven members. The prime minister was never officially known as such, but usually held the office of First Lord of the Treasury. The other members were generally the Lord Chancellor, Lord Privy Seal, Lord President of the Council, two secretaries of state with general administrative authority (particularly in foreign affairs), Chancellor of the Exchequer (for finance), First Lord of the Admiralty, Paymaster-General of the Forces, Lord Lieutenant of Ireland, and Secretary for Scotland. Later there were special secretaries for "home affairs," colonies, war, and India. Other officers were added from time to time, until the cabinet grew so large that in a crisis a small inner group assumed special authority. The meetings of the cabinet have long been held at No. 10 Downing Street, the prime minister's residence, close to Whitehall.

There was nothing unique about the cabinet simply as a group of ministers. Every ruler, even the most absolute, had to have certain men upon whom he could depend for the running of the various branches of the government. The Curia Regis of Henry I had been such a group, and the Cabal of Charles II was a more recent example. There were, however, several distinctive features which gradually developed after Walpole's leadership of the cabinet began in 1721. First, there was the authority of the prime minister, who was ordinarily the definite leader of the cabinet. He selected the members, and the administration was known by his name. At times, however, he might be merely a figurehead, overshadowed by abler colleagues. Secondly, the cabinet was a unit: its members assumed collective responsibility for each others' actions, and resigned in a body in case of defeat, instead of being nibbled away one by one like Godolphin's cabinet. Thirdly, from this it followed that the members of the cabinet generally all belonged to the same party; the experiments of William and Anne with mixed cabinets had not been successful. During the long period of Whig domination, from 1714 to 1760, rivalry among different groups in the Whig party overshadowed opposition from the Tories. Fourthly, unlike the practice in the United States, the cabinet members all belonged to Parliament and sat in either Lords or Commons. A practice grew up by which each of the various departments was represented in each house; if the cabinet minister was a peer, his undersecretary would serve as departmental spokesman in the Commons, and vice versa. The ministers occupied the "Treasury bench," where they sat facing the "Opposition benches."

Since the term of the cabinet rested on the majority in the House of

Commons, how were the prime minister and his colleagues to keep that majority in line? Walpole demonstrated to his successors the methods for maintaining such a mastery of the House of Commons. That was a far simpler matter in his time than it is today, when it depends upon the approval of a democratic electorate numbering some twenty million men and women. In that period we must not think of a majority as resting upon the will of all the people; the electoral system was so arranged that the voice of the people was almost negligible. Scarcely one man in ten of legal age, so it has been estimated, could take part in choosing members of Parliament; and only in a few unusually democratic constituencies were the members really chosen by popular election. A handful of peers, usually from among those seventy-odd prominent Whig families of landowners, who were the real power in the eighteenth century, were very often able to control this majority in the House of Commons. The head of the family in such cases generally sat in the House of Lords, providing seats in the Commons for his sons and for friends who were fairly sure to vote as he wished. This situation naturally simplified the control of Parliament. Walpole had only to placate a sufficient number of those who controlled the seats, and he was then free to do as he pleased. Walpole is credited with the cynical remark, as he once looked over the Commons, "All these have their price." Anything but an idealist or a reformer, he knew how to secure their election and their votes. To understand how such a small group of landowners could control the government, it is worth while to analyze the "unreformed Parliament" as it existed between the Restoration and the Reform Act of 1832 (see page 613). The House of Commons, so imposing in its entirety, loses some of its dignity when we examine the methods by which it could be elected and managed.

The size of the Commons remained stationary at 560 members from the Scottish union in 1707 until 1801, when 100 Irish members were added. Of that total, 45 were from Scotland, 24 from Wales, and the remaining 491 from England proper. The heavy English representation consisted of 82 from the counties and 409 from the boroughs, including the two universities. Normally each county and borough sent two members.

The chief fault in the system lay in the representation of a large number of "rotten" boroughs, which contained few inhabitants or, in one case, none at all. The fact that a Plantagenet, Lancastrian, Yorkist, or Tudor had once given them the right to representation continued them in that right even though they slumbered, almost deserted, in memories of a more important past. Most common in

# Limiting the Monarchy

this class were the decayed seaports along the southern coast. Remote Cornwall, a stronghold of royal influence jutting into the western sea, was most notoriously overrepresented. It sent 44 members to the Commons, only one less than all Scotland. One small Cornish district only twenty-eight miles long and twelve wide, with some 350 voters among its 15,000 inhabitants, returned 18 men to Parliament—more than Middlesex, Westminster, Southwark, and the other populous constituencies which made up London!

Even in the little rotten boroughs the franchise was restricted in strange and devious ways, unlike the counties, where every "forty-shilling freeholder" was entitled to a vote. The two hundred and three English boroughs fell into four general groups, about equally numerous: scot and lot, burgage, corporation, and freeman. The scot and lot, or "pot-walloper," franchise was the nearest approach to a uniform, democratic system; for every householder who had resided in the borough for six months and was not a pauper was generally entitled to a vote. In the burgage boroughs the vote went to the owners of the houses, or sites of houses, of original voting householders. The franchise in the corporation boroughs was limited to the members of the municipal government. In the final category it was restricted to a special group known as "freemen," often members of the trade guilds.

The vote in many of these boroughs could easily be manipulated in return for cash or other valuable considerations. It was no longer the practice in England that the member must be a resident of the constituency which he represented, as is the custom in the United States; consequently anyone with sufficient money or family connection could acquire a seat in the Lower House. Some came so completely under the control of an individual that they were known as "pocket" or "nomination" boroughs. The "scot and lot" boroughs, with their wide franchise, were the most difficult to manipulate, though in little ones a majority of the votes might be purchased at relatively small expense. In those days before secret voting, the candidate who paid for votes at least knew he was getting his money's worth. In the burgage boroughs it was comparatively simple to buy up the real estate which carried the right to vote. Out of the hundred burgages in one borough, a certain peer owned ninety-nine, including one which was deep under water. Ramshackle sheds and pigsties might carry the right to vote if they stood on the proper site. Perhaps the most notorious of all the rotten boroughs was Old Sarum, the "hole in the wall," on the site of the original city of Salisbury. Every one of its inhabitants had moved away, and there was not a single permanent building on the forty acres of plowed land. Yet those

[ 435 ]

acres continued to be represented in Parliament, the owner sending whomsoever he pleased and erecting a tent on the ground for the "election" formalities. The vote in the corporation boroughs was easy to manage because of the small number of voters involved. Some of the more honest corporations contented themselves with extorting from the candidates promises of presents to the town, such as a hall, bridges, or the deepening of a river or harbor. The corporation system was sometimes perverted by the intrusion of outsiders into the corporation, which often became simply a machine for choosing members of Parliament, to the complete neglect of its supposed function of administering the municipal government. Finally, there were the "freeman" boroughs, in some of which there were too many freemen and in others not enough. Some boroughs created a swarm of "honorary freemen," solely for election purposes. Dunwich, which was being eaten away by the North Sea, supplemented its forty-five regular freemen with five hundred outsiders. Some boroughs granted the vote to anyone who had ever been a freeman there, though he might have been absent for years. Candidates would sometimes canvass the London alehouses to gather ex-freemen from the borough in question and transport them to the scene in order to swing the vote. On the other hand, some boroughs went to the opposite extreme, and their freemen were an extremely exclusive group. In Winchelsea there were scarcely a dozen freemen. In the neighboring little decayed port of Rye the election to the House of Commons was at one time in the hands of six men! The right to vote in such places was often handed down to the eldest son or son-in-law, and a freeman's only daughter needed no other dowry than the vote which she would confer upon her husband. He might make enough in one election to support him without further effort until the next.

This system produced a class of men, important in the politics of the time, known as borough patrons and boroughmongers. By using the political arts still practiced by bosses in the United States, and by making judicious expenditures, they could become reasonably sure of controlling the vote in one or more boroughs. Sir James Lowther, for instance, generally had a well-disciplined squad of eight or nine nominees in the Commons, all of whom were supposed to vote as he dictated. If their consciences directed otherwise, it was incumbent upon them to resign, according to the code of Parliamentary honor. The Duke of Newcastle was one of the most powerful of this group of borough patrons.

Patronage was what made boroughmongering profitable and linked it up with the question of the control of Parliament. The control of appointments to government positions, formerly—and still nominally—a function of the crown, passed to the prime minister. He needed votes to keep his majority secure, and the most effective means to that end was the bestowing of the best offices upon those who controlled the votes. The result was a regular spoils system, in which everyone from earls, admirals, and archbishops down to the meanest subordinates in the customs, excise, and dockyard services received appointments in return for or in expectation of political support.

The Commons might also be manipulated in another way— through the House of Lords. The surest way to a peerage was to control votes in the House of Commons. Admirals and generals might occasionally find their way into the House of Lords, but at least two thirds of the peerages were granted to borough patrons like Lowther, for instance, who became Lord Lonsdale in return for the votes of his squad. Even when such a man reached the peerage, it was still possible for the prime minister to influence not only the peer's vote in the Lords but also the votes of his henchmen in the Commons by dangling before him the prospect of promotion from baron to viscount or from viscount to earl.

The borough patron not only could gratify his social ambitions with a peerage but could also make financial profit out of borough-mongering. He might secure fat army or navy contracts, or he might gain the privilege of lending the government money at a high rate of interest. Best of all were the official appointments, where drawing a salary was frequently the only work involved. Some of these, like the post of Master of the King's Buckhounds, were absolute sinecures in which no work was expected. More frequent was the practice of accepting a well-paid position and then appointing a deputy who did all the work for a small fraction of the salary. One George Selwyn, who controlled two or three votes in the Commons, was "at one and the same time, Surveyor-General of Crown Lands, which he never surveyed; Registrar of Chancery at Barbados, which he never visited; and Surveyor of Meltings and Clerk of the Irons at the Mint, where he showed himself once a week, in order to eat a dinner which he ordered but for which the nation paid." Such appointments were sought by the patrons and members not only for themselves but also for sons and relatives and for the families of those whose votes were necessary in the boroughs. If a son was unable to earn a normal living, or if poor relatives clamored for aid, they could be supported at the expense of the government. Members of Parliament spent much of their time bullying or begging for such positions, so that a "patronage secretary" was created to save the time of the department heads. The qualifications of the candidates for office mattered little; newly appointed clerks and copyists sometimes had to be granted leave of absence so that they might learn to write. Outworn offices, no longer necessary to the government, were perpetuated simply to provide more posts. Civil-service reform, in which merit replaced influence, was still a century in the distance.

As for Walpole's own experience, his ministry of twenty-one years reflected his motto "Let sleeping dogs lie." Unlike the Tories in their period of dominance at the end of Anne's reign, the Whigs left undisturbed the Anglican churchmen, Tory and reactionary though most of them were, while the squires, also with Tory traditions, were allowed to manage the local government as justices of the peace without interference. Because of this tolerant attitude toward the potentially dissatisfied elements, coupled with the shrewd methods in bribery and corruption of such a past master of those arts as Walpole, the Whigs, who were really only a minority, went their way virtually unchallenged. Walpole encountered only three serious crises: in 1727 the accession of a new and already hostile king, in 1733 the rejection of his own unpopular excise bill, and in 1739 the declaration, against his will, of war on Spain.

Already a man in his thirties when his father first came to England, the second George (1727–1760) was another dull German whose mind seemed incapable of rising above petty details. He lacked either the intelligence or the ambition to play a more active role in politics than his father had done. There was danger, however, that his accession might be the end of Walpole, simply because Walpole had been the minister of the first George, with whom the second had quarreled most of his life. Luckily the high character and intelligence of the latter's German wife, Caroline, commanded her husband's respect if not his fidelity. Her appreciation of Walpole's ability and her influence kept the minister in office.

Walpole's chief interest lay in economic matters, particularly finance. George I said of him that he could turn stones into gold, and he has been termed "the first great commercial minister since the days of Thomas Cromwell." Early in his public career he had endeavored, with only partial success, to lower the interest rate which the government was paying on the national debt and to use the money thus saved to reduce the principal of the debt itself. He had, as we saw, done much to straighten out the financial confusion caused by the collapse of the South Sea Bubble. In respect to commercial policy his views were advanced, and some of his liberal measures were along the same lines which England was to follow a century later. He announced that his policy was "to make the exportation of our own manufactures and the importation of the commodities used in the manufacturing of them as practicable and as easy as may be." Accordingly, he proposed the removal of export duties on more than a hundred articles of British manufacture and on nearly forty articles of raw materials. Some of the colonial restrictions were specifically relaxed, and in other matters he winked at colonial violations of the existing regulations (see page 468). A considerable part of the national revenue, as we have seen, came from the land tax, which fell most heavily upon the country gentry and nobility. Walpole made a substantial cut in the rate of this tax and hoped to go even further by modifying the revenue laws.

Another major item of governmental income was derived from customs duties. These were collected upon everything brought into British ports,—not only upon the articles imported for consumption in Great Britain but also upon the large quantities which were re-exported to foreign nations. In the latter case the government gave a drawback, or refund, of the customs duties paid. Walpole's logical mind saw wasted effort and wasted money in this cumbersome refunding as well as an additional opportunity for graft. He proposed to simplify this by having duties collected only on those goods which were to remain for internal consumption in England. This would greatly facilitate the re-export trade and incidentally reduce the alarming prevalence of smuggling. Such a step, he said, would "make London a free port and by consequence the market of the world." Before attempting to extend this practice to all articles of importation, he proposed in 1733 to apply it to tobacco and wine. Unfortunately, he called the measure an "excise" bill, which to the popular mind suggested new internal taxes; and consequently that word had an ugly sound to many Englishmen. Walpole's enemies implied that excise officers would soon be snooping into men's homes and that the government might soon be taxing bread and other necessities of life. The popular clamor was so great that Walpole, rather than face an adverse vote in Parliament, withdrew the bill, which might have been passed by any other name.

This was one of the rare instances in eighteenth-century England where public opinion affected governmental action. Another occurred six years later, in 1739, when Walpole's era of peace came to an end, much against his will. The years since Utrecht had not seen England engaged in a major war. France, like England, wanted peace, so that the two traditional rivals for a while had worked together to keep Europe quiet. It was a busy era, however, for the diplomats, who created a constant succession of leagues and alliances; and even the royal navy was at times called upon for service. Year after year squadrons sailed into the Baltic, where

Sweden and Russia were fighting, partly to ensure the safety of England's supply of masts and naval stores from that region and partly to gratify the Hanoverian ambitions of the Georges for more influence in Germany. British warships also entered the Mediterranean, where efforts to curb Spanish ambitions actually led to a desultory war during which British ships of the line destroyed a Spanish fleet off Sicily. Later, however, when many of the Continental powers engaged in a "War of the Polish Succession," Walpole kept aloof and could proudly say to Queen Caroline, "Madam, there are fifty thousand men slain this year in Europe and not one Englishman." But England, bored with smug prosperity, was spoiling for a fight. There were, as we shall see, grievances against Spain arising from conditions in America. The apparently decadent Spanish colonial empire looked like easy loot, and war was started on a very flimsy pretext (see page 450). Walpole worked hard for peace, but his hands were forced by the war party.

The declaration of war was a bitter pill for him. Today a prime minister in such a situation would at once go out of office with his cabinet. There were no precedents at that time for such circumstances. Walpole did twice offer his resignation, but George refused to accept it. So for another three years Walpole remained in power until, conducting a war of which he heartily disapproved, his control of the House of Commons gradually melted away. Finally, two days after receiving a peerage, he retired from office with his cabinet and took his seat in the House of Lords as Earl of Orford.

His great ministry of twenty-one years, however, had laid secure foundations for the new system of responsible government, which enabled Parliament to utilize the supremacy it had achieved in 1688.

# CHAPTER XVI

## The Duel for Empire

### 1739-1783

A RESTLESS England put an end to Walpole's long peace in 1739, and from then until 1815 the nation was to be engaged in war two thirds of the time. France was the principal enemy during that period; for the Second Hundred Years' War (see page 405) was soon revived in full force. The first two wars of that series, between 1689 and 1713, had been primarily European affairs which had only incidentally extended to America. Now the struggle became essentially a "duel for empire." The situation in America and India was to overshadow for a while the affairs of the Continent. England had taken her first colonial loot from France at Utrecht in 1713; exactly fifty years later the French were to be stripped of most of their choicest overseas possessions. But even that was not to end the rivalry.

It might be said that England in those days was doing things by quarter centuries. The period between the Restoration in 1660 and the fall of Napoleon in 1815 falls into six fairly equal periods, of about twenty-five years each, in which England alternated between concentration on domestic concerns and foreign fighting. From 1660 to 1688 the chief interest lay in internal troubles, interrupted only by two Dutch wars. From 1689 to 1713 there was almost continual fighting against Louis XIV. From 1713 to 1739 came the longest interval of real peace, during which the cabinet system came into being and English trade prospered. Now, in this period under consideration, between 1739 and 1763, came fairly steady colonial fighting which resulted in the wreck of the old French empire. Then, in the thirty years from 1763 to 1793, England was to be concerned primarily with internal problems; for even the American Revolution was essentially a private British affair in which the French interfered for revenge. Finally, from 1793 to 1815, was to come the protracted struggle with Revolutionary and Napoleonic France. Since the final act at Waterloo, however, Englishmen and Frenchmen have never officially exchanged hostile shots.

At the outset of the Second Hundred Years' War, France had an overseas empire which looked very impressive on the surface. It occupied more space on the map than the British; its individual leaders were more conspicuous; and it was in no small part the achievement of a single brilliant minister, Colbert. In North America the territory claimed by France almost completely hemmed in the English colonies in their narrow strip between the mountains and the sea. The center of New France was the St. Lawrence valley, with the capital at Quebec and with Montreal as an important post farther up the river. French power was also well entrenched in Acadia, the present Nova Scotia. The explorations of various intrepid Frenchmen had given France title to the region of the Great Lakes and to the valley of the Mississippi and its tributaries. New Orleans was soon to be established, in 1718, to command the outlet to that vast interior region. The ownership of Newfoundland, close to the valuable fishing banks, and the Hudson Bay region, with its fur trade, was disputed between the English and the French.

In the West Indies, France held more islands than Britain. The rich sugar islands of Guadeloupe and Martinique, among the few present relics of that old empire, were the center of French interest; but their richest colony was in Haiti. The Lesser Antilles were a regular rosary of little French sugar islands which were to drop off, bead by bead, under British attacks.

Out in the East, France had arrived on the scene much later than her rival; but Colbert had revived the French East India Company in 1664, and, from that time on, it made aggressive advances. The principal seat of French power was Pondicherry, which France still owns, some seventy miles down the coast from Madras, the chief English post. Chandernagor was established in the northeast, as a counterweight to the English station at Calcutta near by. The French also had a slave-trading post on the Guinea coast of Africa.

But, despite its impressive extent, there were grave elements of weakness in the French colonial empire. In North America, France had more brilliant leaders than England, but they lacked followers. The long record of the English colonies failed to produce such a galaxy of spectacular men as those French explorers whose names still live: Champlain with a lake, La Salle and Cadillac with automobiles, Père Marquette with a railroad, and Joliet with a prison. Nor did any English governor attain the stature of Count Frontenac, whom Louis XIV had sent to America to get him away from the ladies at Versailles. Nevertheless, while the English colonies were rapidly being filled with thousands of substantial middle-class settlers who multiplied so rapidly that their numbers doubled every twenty years, few Frenchmen were willing to migrate to an overseas colony of settlement. France had established Quebec a year after the English founded Jamestown; France was several times larger than

THE AMERICAN COLONIES, WITH INSET SHOWING BRITISH HOLDINGS
IN AMERICA FROM 1713 TO 1783

England; and, unlike England, France made continual official efforts to attract or force settlers to America. Regiments of regulars were disbanded in New France, and land was given to officers and men; cargoes of prostitutes and kidnaped peasants were shipped to the St. Lawrence; bounties were offered for babies. Yet the population remained small. In 1689 there were only about fifteen thousand French settlers in Canada, and even in 1750, after almost a century and a half of effort, there were only some fifty-four thousand; while at both those periods there were some twenty English settlers in America for every Frenchman. Even when French peasants did come over, many were reluctant to settle down as underdogs in the transplanted feudal system; and they were apt to run off into the woods, where they often married Indian wives and became *coureurs de bois*, or forest rangers, trapping for furs and forming an unstable element in the population. No small part of England's colonial population came from her religious malcontents; but France, to keep her colonies safely Roman Catholic, finally forbade her Protestant Huguenots to migrate to them. Consequently that substantial, hard-working commercial class, which might have built up solid colonial prosperity, found its way to the English colonies instead, settling in such places as New Rochelle, near New York.

The unwillingness to migrate was not the only French source of weakness. Despite Colbert's grand visions of co-ordinating industry, commerce, navy, and colonies into a profitable unity (see page 385), the French colonial ventures did not pay. France formed commercial companies, like the English and the Dutch, for her colonial expansion; but whereas Dutch East India stock yielded average dividends of 18 per cent, and English East India stock half that amount, French colonial stock paid no dividends. Since none would invest unless coerced, the government finally had to take over the ventures.

There were also some fundamental strategic considerations in the home countries which help to show the causes of French colonial weakness. As we noticed before (see page 386), England could concentrate most of her fighting energy and appropriations upon a navy which not only would serve as an adequate defense at home but also would be useful as an instrument of aggression on the seas and overseas. The Continental nations had land frontiers to defend, and we have seen how Holland, even though primarily interested in maritime activity, was exhausted by trying to stem French aggression on land. But the French were not even primarily interested in maritime activity. Despite Colbert's pleadings, Louis XIV much preferred to spend his energy banging away at the frontiers, and, throughout the Second Hundred Years' War, Frenchmen, if they could be lured

# The Duel for Empire

into a land fight in the Low Countries or on the Rhine, tended to neglect naval and colonial warfare. England capitalized that French attitude and, by means of generous grants of gold, "hired" Austrians, Prussians, and whoever else would take the money, to keep the French busy on land. Then the royal navy would scour the seas, pick off neglected French colonies, and, without suffering many serious casualties, make more than enough from increased commerce to offset the grants to the allies who suffered the heavy battle losses. It was this system, as we shall see, that caused the Anglo-French duel for colonial empire to become entangled with the Austro-Prussian duel for control of European territory.

Fighting methods remained fairly uniform throughout the period. In these days, when science and invention are constantly adding new instruments and methods in warfare, it is hard to realize the static, unchanging conditions of eighteenth-century fighting. A description of the British ships, regiments, and tactics of 1740 will serve almost equally well for the fighting sixty years later. A warship eighty years old, used in one of the expeditions of the American Revolution, was little different from the newer ships, and the soldiers of Marlborough would have found few essential features changed a century later. War was an orderly and well-regulated game in which everyone knew the common rules until Napoleon on land and Nelson at sea by their originality won surprising victories in the last years of the century. Even they, however, used the same old instruments of war.

England's chief pride and interest, of course, lay in her navy. The royal navy has probably enjoyed a longer record of power and success than any other fighting organization in history except the Roman army. England maintained it on a two-power basis, ordinarily keeping it as large as the combined forces of the French and Spanish Bourbons, who might always be expected to join forces. It consisted during the eighteenth century of three or four hundred vessels, about a hundred of which belonged to the important category known as ships-of-the-line or line-of-battle ships. Counterparts of our modern battleships, they were used in squadrons or fleets to fight the major battles.

Most common among these was the "seventy-four," so called from the number of her guns, arranged in tiers along her two fighting decks. Always a few larger three-decked ships of the line served as flagships, but the seventy-four was the largest that would sail well and fight well under most conditions. She was the favorite instrument of war by sea for more than a century, and by crushing similar seventy-fours from France, Spain, and Holland she contributed much to England's maritime supremacy. Her hull ranged some two hundred feet from the figurehead under the great bowsprit to the ornate windows of the cabin at the stern. She was broad in proportion to her length; for her beams measured more than fifty feet between the bulging sides. This breadth robbed her of the speed of the little frigates, but it gave her strength to withstand terrific buffeting in battle. Much was crowded between the decks of that stout hull. The two fighting decks, flanked with long rows of muzzle-loading guns on wooden trucks, were painted a dull red inside, so that the bloody stains of battle would be less evident. In those cramped quarters some six hundred men lived at sea for months and sometimes years.

Throughout this period the heads of the royal navy worried about the supply of materials wherewith to build such ships. Not only were the woodlands of England becoming less able to supply oak for the hulls of the king's ships, but in all Britain there grew no trees suitable for masts. The "seventy-four" required for the hull some two thousand oak trees, averaging a hundred years old, and England was cutting down her oaks much faster than she was replacing them. There was particular difficulty in securing great trees for the massive sternposts, and crooked timbers for the sixty or seventy ribs of the ship. For the planking of the bulging yellow sides England had to send to Danzig, Riga, or other ports of the Baltic, whence also, from Polish forests, came the masts of middling size. The little spars had generally grown on some Norwegian mountainside; but for the great lower masts, anywhere from two feet to forty inches in diameter, the royal navy depended upon the colonial pines in New Hampshire and Maine. More than once, as we shall see, the navy was to be handicapped when its supply of masts or oak was curtailed.

Next to the ships of the line in importance came the frigates, corresponding to our modern cruisers. Lighter and faster than the heavy ships of the line, they had one fighting deck with some twenty-eight to thirty-eight guns. They served as the "eyes of the fleet" in major operations, and were used also for patrolling, for the protection, regulation, or destroying of commerce, and for the bearing of dispatches. There were various minor types of warships, ranging from sloops and gun brigs down to fire ships. The English were not original as naval architects; it was a byword that the fastest vessels in the navy were the ones captured from the French and Spanish. But, as a famous naval historian remarked, "good men in poor ships are better than poor men in good ships."

The royal navy generally had an excellent personnel. It had been remarked of the Restoration navy, we recall, that among the naval officers the gentlemen were not sailors and the sailors were not

# The Duel for Empire

gentlemen. The eighteenth century developed a type that had both qualities. A naval commission was one of the most attractive goals for a younger son of good family. Boys became midshipmen at twelve or thirteen under the tutelage of a captain who taught them manners as well as seamanship. They spent a good part of their lives afloat. Promotion was fairly rapid at the start, and one was frequently a frigate captain in the twenties; but then there was a long wait until an admiral's flag might be available. The result of this slow promotion by seniority was that admirals were often gouty, choleric, despotic, and hidebound, even if efficient. In those days of slow communication the commander in distant waters frequently had to act on his own judgment in weighty matters, and often served as diplomat as well as admiral. The British naval officer generally developed arrogance, but he usually had ability as well.

Naval life may have seemed attractive to the prospective officer, but there was no enthusiasm for the life of a common sailor. There was a vast gulf between quarter-deck and forecastle. The crew were cramped in stuffy quarters, engaged in laborious and dangerous duties for little pay, and were too often at the mercy of a martinet who could have them lashed for minor infractions of discipline. It is small wonder that the navy did not attract volunteers. To man the fleets, the same Parliament which talked so much of the "fundamental rights of Englishmen" and the "sanctity of private property" time and again authorized impressment, which was virtual kidnaping. Sailors in the merchant marine, looking forward to shore leave after a long voyage, would often find themselves taken off for naval service before they reached land. The men of the coast towns were always on guard against the press gangs which made sailors, willy-nilly, out of anyone upon whom they could lay their hands. Once caught in this way, the poor devils often had to remain in naval service until death or disability released them. The surprising thing is that mutinies were scarce and that these reluctant conscripts generally made excellent seamen.

The naval tactics of the period were rigidly standardized. The opposing squadrons or fleets, ranging ordinarily from eight to thirty ships of the line, fell in behind one another in a long line of battle and lay alongside the enemy line, each ship picking out a single adversary. Then they would blast away at close range until something gave way. The French and Spanish shots were apt to go too high, simply damaging masts and rigging, while the English gunners did more effective work by aiming at the enemy hulls. So conventional was the plan of battle that in one encounter, where the British outnumbered the foe, the extra ships lay at a distance for want of anything better to do. The frigates frequently engaged in single combat, in which the principal trick was to get the "weather gauge," where one could maneuver with the wind at one's back.

While the British navy was the best in the world, the same cannot be said for the British army at this time. The redcoats were brave enough, but the French generally outclassed the British in the size of their military establishment and in their natural genius for leadership. England was inclined to neglect the army, partly from the widespread opposition to the idea of a standing army and partly from the feeling that the navy furnished an adequate defense (see page 375). While the French army was usually kept at one hundred thousand men at least, the English army sometimes dropped as low as fifteen thousand, and had to be expanded with more speed than efficiency in time of war.

As in the navy, there was a wide gap between officers and men. In both instances the officers generally came from the better families. All army commissions up to colonelcies had to be purchased, and this operated as a social restriction. The life of the army officer in time of peace was generally more social than military, and was much less exacting than the naval life. The enlisted men were apt to come from the dregs of society. They were generally lured into service by recruiting officers who slipped the "king's shilling," the symbol of enlistment, into the hand of the prospect while he was too drunk to realize the significance of his act. On occasion, vagabonds were drafted into the army, and more than once the jails were emptied to swell the ranks. The tactics of the day called for "well-drilled marionettes," and it took about two years of hard discipline to whip a recruit into shape. Man for man, the redcoats were as good as any soldiers in Europe. Too often it was a case of "heroes led by fools" or "lions led by asses"; for in battles like Bunker Hill the men executed, with utmost bravery, stupid orders which should never have been given.

The nature of the battle tactics made well-disciplined troops an absolute necessity for effective work. Previously it had been necessary to use a considerable part of the infantry as pikemen who could hold off the enemy while the musketeers reloaded. The introduction of the bayonet at about Marlborough's time made every musketeer his own pikeman and thus greatly increased the fire power of the infantry. It became customary for an army to advance its infantry in two long, thin lines, in parade-ground formation, without firing a shot until within fifty or a hundred yards of the enemy. Then the lines would halt, deliver a series of crushing volleys, and finally, if the enemy still stood fast, charge with the bayonet. Against cavalry charges the infantry formed a square so that there would be no flanks to turn. Such formations would be suicidal in these days of machine guns and quick-firing artillery; but they were thoroughly effective in the era of the "Brown Bess" musket, which was in general use throughout the eighteenth century. The "Brown Bess" musket differed from its present-day successors in several ways. It was smooth-bored instead of rifled; it loaded at the muzzle instead of the breech; it was discharged by a "flintlock" outside the gun instead of by a percussion cap inside; it had to be reloaded after each shot instead of having a repeating mechanism; it could not be fired more than three or four times a minute; it was likely to misfire, especially in the rain; and it was not effective anyway at more than a hundred yards. To save ammunition, soldiers were ordered not to fire "until you see the whites of their eyes." The artillery or cannon were of the same crude, smooth-bore, muzzle-loading type. The gunners simply aimed in a general direction and trusted to luck. Cavalry, much less important than infantry, was used for scouting and to give a heavy shock in battle at the critical moment.

Warfare in the eighteenth century probably disturbed the general population less than it has at any other period. The troops were so severely disciplined that they did not terrorize and loot the noncombatants as they had in earlier wars. They were skilled professionals, generally lacking in religious or nationalistic zeal. The idea of universal military service, which enabled nations to put millions of trained soldiers into the field in 1914, did not gain headway until the French Revolution. The wars, moreover, were generally of a limited nature, designed to gain some special border or colonial objective rather than to crush the enemy completely.

England used a very trivial excuse for ending this quarter century of peace. Ever since the days of Hawkins and Drake the English had cast greedy eyes upon the rigid monopoly with which Spain had guarded the trade of her vast American colonial empire (see page 291). Cromwell's effort to loot the supposedly decaying Spanish empire had resulted only in the capture of Jamaica (see page 362). At Utrecht in 1713, it will be recalled, England had at last made a breach in the exclusive Spanish system. By the "Asiento," England was given monopoly of supplying slaves to Spanish America and was also permitted to send one ship a year to trade at Porto Bello, on the Isthmus of Panama. Keeping within the letter of the law, the English had anchored a ship off that port and had replenished her apparently inexhaustible hold from the cargoes of other ships, thus maintaining almost continuous trade. Some Englishmen took further advantage of the situation for illegal trade and naturally ran afoul of the Spanish coast guards. Finally one Captain Jenkins began to tell a wild tale in the taverns of England. He exhibited a withered ear, which he asserted had been cut off by the Spanish coast guards. Summoned before Parliament, he was asked what he had then done. He replied, "I commended my soul to God and my cause to my country."

In spite of Walpole, that withered ear and the popular restlessness led to a declaration of war against Spain in 1739 (see page 440). London celebrated this with wild enthusiasm. "They now ring the bells," remarked Walpole; "they will soon wring their hands." The navy performed better than the long-disused army. Admiral Vernon immediately seized Porto Bello. Admiral Anson followed Drake's track to the west coast of South America, picked off the Philippine galleon, and circumnavigated the world. The main enterprise was a joint naval and military attack on Cartagena, the key port of the Spanish Main. The bewildered general, taunted by the contemptuous admiral, missed his chance to rush the city. The yellow fever was more deadly than the Spaniards. For weeks the sharks in Cartagena Bay feasted on the corpses of redcoats thrown by thousands from the pestilence-ridden transports. The armament was then turned against Cuba, but felt too weak even to attack. Barely a tenth of the men who had set out to conquer the Spanish Main ever returned home. By 1742 the "War of Jenkins's Ear" had died of inertia, becoming involved in a more general European conflict. England's only worthwhile gain from this effort to loot the Spanish empire was Anson's demonstration that lime juice is an excellent preventive for scurvy, a disease prevalent among sailors deprived of vitamin-bearing fresh foods on long voyages.

While Jenkins had been showing his severed ear in England, two German rulers were approaching death, full of apprehension about what would happen under the rule of their heirs. The Hapsburg emperor, Charles VI, was worried because, having no son, he would be followed by his daughter, Maria Theresa. There was no possibility that she might succeed him in the shadowy title of "Holy Roman Emperor." The question was whether, in view of the old German prejudice, a woman might inherit the family holdings in Austria, Hungary, Bohemia, and the other Hapsburg lands. To forestall, if possible, a partition of those domains among greedy neighbors, Charles had secured by persuasion and concessions the agreement of the other European states to a "Pragmatic Sanction" recognizing Maria Theresa as his rightful successor in those lands.

Meanwhile, Frederick William I was concerned about what would happen to Prussia under his eldest son. Old Frederick William himself was a thoroughgoing militarist. He had devoted his life to the

# The Duel for Empire

building up of a powerful army, gathering tall soldiers from wherever he could and drilling them into a perfect machine. It was irony that such a man should begin his reign in 1713, when one big war ended, and close it in 1740, when another big war began. His son Frederick had literary inclinations and loved to play the flute. Apparently the father's lifework would be thrown away. Little did old Frederick William realize that this rebellious son would become one of the foremost soldiers of history.

In 1740 both Charles VI and Frederick William died. This was the signal for a struggle between Hapsburg and Hohenzollern for first place in Germany, a rivalry which was not finally settled until 1866. Young Frederick II (later to be called "the Great") treated the Pragmatic Sanction like a scrap of paper. He threw his excellent Prussian army into the rich Hapsburg province of Silesia. This private German quarrel spread into the war of the Austrian Succession and was quickly linked up with the Anglo-French colonial rivalry. France, true to her old anti-Hapsburg policy, allied herself with Prussia, Bavaria, and Saxony, hoping to cut Germany into several weak states which would come under French influence. England, with Hanover of course, as well as Holland, backed Austria, taking full credit for supporting the sanctity of the Pragmatic Sanction.

The hostilities lasted from 1740 to 1748. England and France at once sent armies to support their respective allies and were actually battling each other long before their formal declaration of war in 1744. The English campaigns on the Continent were not decisive. The first British commander, a pupil of Marlborough, saw a chance to dash on undefended Paris; but this was too bold a plan for George II, who finally took command himself. The king campaigned aimlessly until, in 1743, the French finally caught his starving army in a trap at Dettingen, near Frankfurt. The French plans went wrong, however, and George won an undeserved victory. His horse, startled by the musketry, bolted far to the rear with the mortified king, who returned and finished the fight on foot. This was the last time an English king personally led an army in battle. The command soon went to his young brother, the Duke of Cumberland, who was outclassed by the able French commander Marshal Saxe, one of the reputed three hundred children of Augustus the Strong, ruler of Saxony and Poland. For five years these two generals fought in the familiar Low Countries. The high point came in 1745 at Fontenoy, on the Scheldt. Cumberland attacked a position strongly fortified by Saxe. The British infantry made one of the most remarkable attacks in its history. Forming under heavy artillery fire, the thin red line marched slowly in perfect order for a half mile, constantly closing up the gaps torn in the ranks. Not firing a shot, the redcoats advanced until within fifty yards of the enemy. A French commander, according to legend, stepped out in front of his line, bowed low, and requested the English gentlemen to fire first; an English officer responded to this courtesy by proposing a toast to the gallant foe. Then the British fired, and several crack regiments of the French army simply melted away under their crushing volleys. But the attack was in vain; for the Dutch and Austrian allies had not cleared away their sections of the French line, and the British had to retire. It was one of the bloodiest battles of the century, the British losing nearly six thousand of their fifteen thousand infantry in killed and wounded, while the French losses were even heavier. From that time on, Saxe generally had the upper hand and gradually gained control of the Austrian Netherlands (Belgium). At least, the French were being kept busy at home.

In the summer of 1745 England was suddenly faced with a serious domestic menace. Less than three months after Fontenoy, the "Young Pretender," grandson of James II and son of the "Old Pretender," who had invaded England in 1715, landed in Scotland with only seven companions. The Highlands rose to support him as they had his father, thirty years before. Edinburgh was occupied, the redcoats in Scotland were roundly whipped, and a small, motley Jacobite army invaded England. Jacobitism had pretty much died out south of the border; but the people were apathetic, and the Pretender's forces penetrated as far as Derby, less than eighty miles from London, which was in panic. A hurried concentration of the scattered troops in England, however, caused the Scottish invaders to retire to their own land. The Duke of Cumberland and some of his regiments, recalled from the Continent, pursued the Scots and finally crushed them the following spring at Culloden in the Highlands. Cumberland won the name of "Butcher" from the ruthless punishment of the vanquished. "Bonnie Prince Charlie," who appealed to the popular imagination much more than his father, was spirited out of the country and off for France by loyal Highlanders. One Flora Macdonald, who disguised him as her maid, won immortality thereby. After that venture he led an aimless, drunken life in Europe until his death, more than forty years later. His younger brother, the "Cardinal York," died in 1807, and with him ended the direct Stuart line.

After the "Forty-five" the Highlands were definitely opened to civilization. England wisely capitalized the martial ardor of the clansmen by enlisting them in her service. Highland regiments were formed in the British army,—the "Black Watch" and many others. Still wearing their distinctive kilts and tartans, they did

# The Duel for Empire

remarkable work in America, in India, and wherever else the empire called them to service.

Meanwhile the War of the Austrian Succession was spreading far afield. The linking of the Austro-Prussian and the Anglo-French rivalries was summed up in an epigram: "Because a monarch robbed a neighbor he had promised to defend, red men scalped each other by the Great Lakes of America, while black men fought on the coast of Coromandel." As soon as England and France formally went to war in 1744, the fighting spread rapidly overseas.

In America the rivals had already clashed in "King William's War" and "Queen Anne's War," as the contests with Louis XIV are frequently called in American colonial history. Frontenac, it will be recalled, had spread terror along the northern English frontiers of settlement by inaugurating the policy of French and Indian raids, which continued as long as France remained in Canada (see page 408). The New England colonists had unsuccessfully attempted to take Quebec in 1690, and twenty years later a British expedition sent for that purpose was wrecked. The British had, however, captured Acadia, and, as "Nova Scotia," it had been ceded to England at Utrecht. The French still retained the adjacent Cape Breton Island. There, at great cost, they erected a powerful fortress at Louisburg, where they were threatening the cod fisheries, which were a vital part of New England's economic existence. In 1745, therefore, a force of New Englanders under Sir William Pepperell, aided by a naval squadron, attacked the French stronghold and captured it after a short siege. This colonial victory, coming as it did just midway between the defeats of the regulars by the French at Fontenoy and by the Highlanders in Scotland, was particularly impressive. The Yankees then urged the conquest of Canada, but England had other uses for her ships and soldiers.

Events of far greater ultimate consequence were taking place in India. Up to that time European contact with India had been limited chiefly to a few trading posts along the coast (see page 331). Shortly after the Portuguese arrived, most of India had come under the sway of Mohammedan invaders, who ruled the land from Delhi. For six generations these Mogul emperors remained strong, and the Europeans stayed in India only at their sufferance.

The charter of the East India Company had granted political and military powers, but these had been restricted to the immediate settlements at Madras, Bombay, and Calcutta, with a few lesser posts. The Company was still essentially a trading corporation, sending to England the cotton cloth of India, together with tea, silks, and other wares brought over from China. There was only a handful of Englishmen in each of those posts, mortality was heavy in that climate, and salaries were ridiculously low; but many of the traders who survived managed to return to England, there to be known as wealthy "nabobs." Two governors of Madras about 1700, in particular, left a lasting influence from their wealth. Elihu Yale contributed part of his gains to construct the first building for a little New England institution founded "to educate ministers in our own way"; and in gratitude the college was named for him. After Yale's successor, who was a Harvard graduate from New England, came Thomas Pitt, who, on an annual salary of £500, managed to buy for £20,000 a famous diamond. This was later sold for several times that amount and firmly established a family which was to give England two of her foremost statesmen. The French posts at Pondicherry, Chandernagor, and elsewhere were also primarily devoted to trade, though their business was only a fraction of that done by the English company.

Then came the beginnings of a fundamental change in the relationship of the Europeans to India. Aurangzeb, the last of the strong Mogul emperors, died in 1707, and, with the control from Delhi relaxed, the various lesser potentates of India engaged in a scramble for power. Freebooting bands plundered far and wide, and India was faced with anarchy. With rival claimants for many of the thrones, intrigue was the order of the day. François Dupleix, the French governor of Pondicherry, saw an opportunity to increase French influence in India by mixing into this maze of intrigue. Older accounts credited him with conceiving this plan as a grand design; more recent writers believe that he was an opportunist, taking advantage of occasions as they arose. At any rate, he developed the practice of supporting one of the pretenders to a disputed throne, in return for special commercial privileges to the French. The few European troops were vastly superior to the huge ordinary armies of the Indian states; so, too, were the "sepoys," Indian troops led by white officers and trained in European methods. It was with such troops that Dupleix planned to set a candidate on a native throne and to keep him there.

Barely had his new scheme begun to take form when the War of the Austrian Succession spread to India at the formal declaration of Anglo-French hostilities in 1744. Both sides had naval forces in those waters, and the presence of a few additional ships of the line on either side could be very important. For a while the French enjoyed superiority under a very energetic admiral who, with Dupleix, managed to capture Madras, England's chief post in India. Some of the English escaped to a smaller post down the coast, and later, when supported by an adequate fleet, even tried to capture Pondicherry.

# The Duel for Empire

The War of the Austrian Succession came to a close in 1748, with the Treaty of Aix-la-Chapelle. Except for the fact that Frederick the Great kept Silesia, which he had wrested from Austria, there was a general return to the *status quo ante*. To the disgust of the New England colonists, Louisburg was returned to the French; to the equal disgust of Dupleix, Madras was returned to the English. Like the Peace of Ryswick, a half century earlier, however, Aix-la-Chapelle was simply a breathing spell between two Anglo-French wars. During the eight years of nominal peace which followed 1748, the French and English were actually fighting for empire both in America and in India. By this time the colonial aspects of the struggle were definitely overshadowing the Continental.

The peace made little difference in India. The English went back to their trading, but Dupleix began more actively than ever to build up his connections with native rulers. The ruler of the Deccan, which covered a considerable part of southern India, died in 1748, and Dupleix supported one pretender while the English supported another. The French candidate won the throne, and another protégé of Dupleix received the subordinate post of nawab of the Carnatic, which included the Coromandel coast, where Pondicherry and Madras both were located. By 1751 the situation at Madras was grave. The English native pretender was closely besieged by the pro-French nawab, with vastly superior forces. If he fell, England's hold in southern India might well be at an end. The officials at Madras were in despair when a young man of twenty-five, destined to be one of the foremost builders of the British Empire, turned the tables. This was Robert Clive, who, having come out to Madras as a clerk for the East India Company, became thoroughly bored by the drudgery of keeping ledgers, and finally managed to secure a commission as captain in the Company's forces. To relieve the pressure upon the besieged English protégé, he hit upon the daring scheme of capturing Arcot, capital of the pro-French nawab. He had only a handful of redcoats and sepoys; but he marched through a violent storm, took Arcot, and then sustained a long and desperate defense against the nawab's numerous forces, who relaxed their original siege to save Arcot instead. Clive's little garrison was nearly starved, but help came from a powerful and hitherto neutral native chieftain. He had watched the rivalry between the French and English. "I never thought till now that the English could fight," he said; "since they can, I will help them." Arcot was saved, and so was Madras. Clive won further victories, and by the time he returned to England, in 1753, English influence was uppermost in southeastern India. Dupleix was recalled in disgrace a year later. Again there was a temporary lull; but Clive and the English soon reappeared to spread their influence in the northeast, around Calcutta.

The French, during this interval between the wars, were also taking the initiative in America. La Salle's discovery of the Mississippi had given them a claim to the valley of that river and its tributaries, and they now energetically proceeded to protect that region with forts. One of these, Fort Duquesne, was erected where two rivers join to form the Ohio, the site of the present Pittsburgh. While the French claimed that region by virtue of the Mississippi explorations, some English colonies also claimed it by virtue of their original charters, which had given them title from sea to sea. In 1753 the governor of Virginia dispatched a letter to the commander of Fort Duquesne warning him that he was trespassing on English territory. Young George Washington, who bore the message, made the long and perilous trip through the wilderness and across the Alleghenies. The French received him courteously, but laughed at the English pretensions. The following year Washington was back there again, this time with a force of colonial militia; he routed one small band of Frenchmen, but was defeated by the forces from Duquesne at Fort Necessity. Then, although the two countries were nominally at peace, England sent over two regular regiments under General Edward Braddock to support her title to the Ohio valley. Braddock marched on Duquesne, but was caught unawares by the French and Indians. He was used to the formal fighting of Flanders and failed even to take customary precautions. His soldiers were lined up in close formation, to be shot down by foes whom they could not see. Braddock himself was killed, and young Washington helped lead back the shattered remnants of the third unsuccessful effort to dislodge the French from the Ohio.

During this interval of nominal peace the British took two steps to protect Nova Scotia and offset the restoration of Louisburg to the French. The first of these measures was the founding of Halifax, in 1749. Several thousand ex-soldiers and their families were settled in the vicinity of an excellent harbor, which became an important naval base. Incidentally, Halifax was the only community in America founded by direct action of the British government. The second measure was the deportation of the Acadians. British security in Nova Scotia was being threatened not only by French and Indian raids upon the English settlers but also by religious propaganda among the French inhabitants of the region. When war became imminent in 1755, the British gathered most of these Acadians into ships and carried them to various colonies to the southward, an event which is celebrated in Longfellow's poem *Evangeline*.

# The Duel for Empire

Many found their way to French Louisiana, where their descendants are still known as "Cajuns."

This peace-time fighting in India and America finally led France and England into open conflict again in the Seven Years' War, 1756–1763. Once more the Anglo-French rivalry was tied up with the Hapsburg-Hohenzollern fight in Germany. Englishmen continued to fight Frenchmen, and Prussians to fight Austrians, as in the previous war; but this time they changed partners. There was a "diplomatic revolution" in which France and Austria became allies, whereupon England made an alliance with Frederick the Great, paying him generously for keeping the French occupied in Europe. This time the best navy (England's) and the best army (Prussia's) were on the same side; consequently the results were far more decisive than in the previous war, where they had been opposed.

At the outset, however, the war went badly for England. The French captured Hanover, and in the Mediterranean they took Minorca. The British admiral whose lack of energy lost the latter was condemned by a court-martial and shot on his quarter-deck. In America the British tried but failed to take Louisburg, while the frontier was once more aflame with French and Indian raids. There was even a fear that the French would invade England.

Then William Pitt came into power and within three years demolished the French colonial empire. To appreciate the situation, it is necessary to explore briefly some of the sordid records of political intrigue. The Whigs remained in undisputed power, but there were various factions within the party. Walpole had finally ended his long ministry in 1742 and for a year was succeeded as prime minister by the colorless Earl of Wilmington, who was overshadowed by Lord Carteret (later Lord Granville) in charge of foreign affairs. Then control passed to the Pelhams—Henry and his older brother, the Duke of Newcastle. Henry, a man of moderate ability and considerable tact and common sense, was prime minister from 1743 to 1754, when he was succeeded by his brother, who had been a secretary of state for thirty years. Newcastle was one of the wealthiest landowners in England, and perhaps the most proficient boroughmonger and Parliamentary manipulator the nation has ever seen. One weakness of responsible government was that high cabinet positions, requiring statesmanship, depended on a majority in the House of Commons, which could be built up simply by the arts of the politician. Newcastle was a master politician, but a ridiculous statesman. A fussy little man, who enjoyed power for its own sake, he bustled around with an air of great importance. One wit remarked that Newcastle always "lost half an hour in the morning and spent the rest of the day in running after it." He could marshal a sizable block of members in the Commons, and through his hands passed the appointments of bishops, judges, admirals, and the many lesser spoils of patronage (see page 437). His anteroom was crowded with job-seekers, and he was the center of attention at every social function. When, just after his fall from power, he was snubbed at a court levee, he looked at the negligent bishops who had formerly been so obsequious. "Even the fathers in God forget their maker," he murmured.

A group of the younger Whigs had commenced an attack on the corrupt methods of governing back in Walpole's time. Foremost among them was William Pitt, a grandson of "Diamond" Pitt, the governor of Madras, who had purchased Old Sarum, the rottenest of the rotten boroughs (see page 435), through which William entered the Commons fresh from Oxford. He quickly demonstrated his unusual powers of oratory. With his commanding presence, flashing eye, and somewhat flowery but impassioned manner of speaking, he was also a master of invective, and soon antagonized the king by his attacks on the influence of Hanover in British foreign policy. He had a burning patriotism, with a desire to make England foremost among the powers, and he was unique in that day in his refusal to join in plundering the public funds. Such a man was disturbing in the somnolent atmosphere of mid-Georgian politics, but he was too insistent to be ignored. The Pelham brothers had had to resign in order to force the reluctant king to accept him in their ministry. The Pelhams were indispensable, and the king was forced to accept Pitt as paymaster of the forces. There was a chance for tremendous profit in that position, by gathering interest on huge sums before they were paid; but Pitt did not take a penny beyond his salary. In spite of the former Pelham support, Pitt finally broke with Newcastle about the time that the opening acts of the Seven Years' War were revealing the incompetence of that archpolitician as a war minister. Pitt, with his desire for England's greatness, was chafing at the bungling mismanagement of the operations. "I am confident," said Pitt, "that I can save the country and that no one else can." In the autumn of 1756 Newcastle was ousted, and the Duke of Devonshire became prime minister, with Pitt as the guiding genius. He began to inject new life into the prosecution of the war, but without Newcastle's well-organized voting power in the Commons the ministry could not make headway. Early in 1757 Pitt was dismissed from office. Immediately a storm of protest arose in all parts of the country, and town after town demonstrated its loyal support of "the Great Commoner." Before the year was out, a compromise was made.

# The Duel for Empire

Pitt, the statesman, joined forces with Newcastle, the politician. The fussy old duke, as prime minister, was allowed to keep control of the patronage and maintain a majority in Commons, while Pitt, as secretary of state, had full control of running the war. Under that arrangement, which lasted four years, the Old Empire was brought to its peak.

Pitt clearly perceived the value of keeping France occupied on the Continent while England gathered in her overseas possessions. He generously financed Frederick the Great, remarking later that he had "won Canada in Germany." Vigorous young men who had demonstrated their ability were given responsible command, in the place of the gouty generals and admirals who had let matters drift. The whole nation, moreover, was roused to a high pitch of national and imperial enthusiasm.

The situation in America reflected the change. Louisburg, which the New Englanders had taken in the previous war only to have it returned to France again, was once more captured in 1758. In that same year a British expedition finally took Fort Duquesne, where Washington and Braddock had failed. It was renamed Fort Pitt and shortly became Pittsburgh. In 1759 three armies were directed to approach from different directions to capture Quebec, the capital of New France, on the St. Lawrence. In general charge of these operations was Sir Jeffrey (later Lord) Amherst, celebrated in the song of the college which was named for him. He was to approach from the south by way of Lake Champlain. A second force was to capture Fort Niagara and approach from the west. A third force, commanded by young James Wolfe, was to attack from the east, going up the St. Lawrence with naval support. The British troops were reinforced by large colonial forces, while Frederick the Great was doing his part in the conquest of Canada by keeping the French so occupied that they did not adequately support the Marquis de Montcalm, their commander in America. The southern and western expeditions captured their initial objectives; but owing to the long distances in the wilderness they could not push through to Quebec, so that the brunt of the attack there fell upon Wolfe and his supporting admiral.

Quebec, situated on a high bluff rising sharply from the river, was a difficult position to attack. One British effort after another failed. Summer passed into autumn, and the time would soon come when the river would freeze, thus necessitating a British withdrawal. Wolfe was not only capable; he was lucky. The French had nearly twenty miles of land above the city exposed to attack. Day after day, boats full of redcoats drifted up the river with the tide and then dropped back again, while the weary French trudged along the shore to prevent a landing. On one of these trips Wolfe spied a narrow path leading up the cliffs to the "Plains of Abraham" above. It seemed the last chance, but complete surprise was essential; if the French had warning, they could defend it easily. One night Wolfe finally prepared his attack and found the path lightly guarded. By daylight the French, to their dismay, found several British regiments lined up on the Plains of Abraham. There was a sharp battle, Wolfe and Montcalm both fell mortally wounded, and the French fleur-de-lis was soon hauled down from the citadel of Quebec, where it had flown for a century and a half. Montreal and the remaining strategic points soon fell, and within a year New France was in British hands.

The British called 1759 the "glorious year" when it simply "rained victories." Nearer home the royal navy won a signal triumph. The French were threatening England once again with invasion and had gathered flatboats at Havre to convey the troops. Three British fleets went out to block the movement. One destroyed the flatboats; another caught the French Mediterranean fleet as it was coming round to join in the attack; while the third, under Admiral Hawke, encountered the main Atlantic fleet at Quiberon Bay, pursued it relentlessly through dangerous rocky channels in a storm, and smashed it as thoroughly as an earlier English fleet had broken up the invading force at La Hogue in 1692. Once more England was clearly mistress of the seas. On land a combined force of British and Hanoverians defeated the French at Minden, and might have routed them if the cavalry commander had not refused to charge. We shall hear more of him later (see page 473).

In the meantime England was laying the foundations of her great empire in India. The rivalry between Clive and Dupleix had centered in southeastern India around Madras and Pondicherry. In 1756 the principal seat of action was suddenly transferred to Bengal, in the northeast. The native ruler of Bengal, Surajah Dowlah, resented the presence of the British at Calcutta and was more favorably inclined toward the French up the river at Chandernagor. The ensuing fight in Bengal was to be primarily a contest between the British and Surajah Dowlah, with the French playing only a subordinate role. The Bengal prince was annoyed at the defenses which the British began to make at Calcutta as soon as they learned of the outbreak of the Seven Years' War. He swooped down on the city, captured it, and herded one hundred and forty-five Englishmen and the half-caste wife of one of them into a little room, the "Black Hole," barely eighteen feet long and fourteen feet wide. All day and all night the

# The Duel for Empire

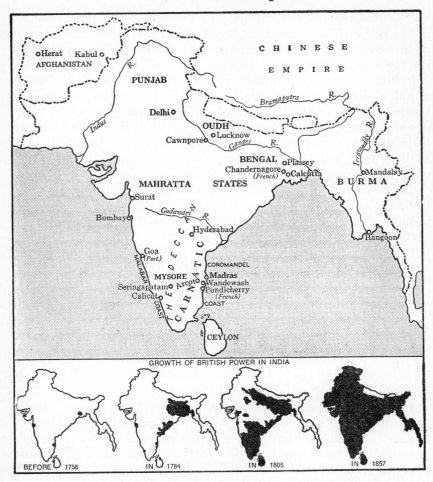

INDIA, WITH MAPS SHOWING DEVELOPMENT OF BRITISH POWER

suffocating group called in vain for more air and for water. On the following morning only twenty-three still remained alive; among these was the woman, who was taken to Surajah Dowlah's harem. Clive was sent up hurriedly from the south to avenge the outrage. Recapturing Calcutta in the first days of 1757, he then moved against Surajah Dowlah. Clive had fewer than a thousand white troops and about two thousand sepoys; his opponent had fifty thousand native troops. Intrigue, however, helped to compensate for that disparity of force. Clive was in agreement with a rascal named Mir Jafar, Surajah Dowlah's second in command, who agreed to betray his master. In perilous dependence on this treacherous Oriental, Clive boldly attacked the Bengali army at Plassey; Mir Jafar remained at one side with his forces until he saw how the battle was going, and at last came to Clive's assistance. That battle of Plassey marked the beginning of England's spread of power into the interior of India. Mir Jafar, as a reward for his work at Plassey, was established as nawab of Bengal, but was required to make a very heavy payment to the British from the state treasury. Clive himself received a grant of some £30,000 a year. For a while the British exerted their influence through this puppet nawab; but Bengal was virtually theirs. We shall see later how Clive and Hastings adapted the East India Company into a ruling force for the millions of inhabitants of Bengal.

Back on the Coromandel Coast around Madras, the British came to final direct grips with the French during the Seven Years' War. Count Lally was sent out to Pondicherry with a strong force of French regulars and with orders to capture Madras. He tried to do so; but early in 1759, that year of English victories, the appearance of a British squadron saved the besieged town. The English, taking the initiative, then wrested from French control the strip of seacoast stretching northward toward Bengal. In 1760 Sir Eyre Coote definitely broke French control in India by defeating Lally at Wandewash, and a year later Pondicherry fell.

Pitt won the war; but he was not in at the finish. For political reasons, which we shall notice shortly, his power was undermined. He learned in 1761 that France and Spain had secretly renewed their Bourbon "family compact" and that Spain would probably declare war on England as soon as her annual plate fleet from America should arrive (see page 232). Pitt urged immediate British declaration of war against Spain in time to capture the silver; but his new colleagues disagreed, and he resigned. Spain duly entered the war, and England promptly punished her. British squadrons captured Havana, in Cuba, and Manila, in the Philippines, and also snapped up several French islands in the West Indies. Pitt had supported Frederick the Great, but that financial and military backing was now withdrawn. The Prussian king continued to battle against heavy odds and managed to retain Silesia, but once more a Continental ally had occasion to complain of the practices of "perfidious Albion."

The Seven Years' War ended with the Treaty of Paris, early in 1763. France withdrew completely from the mainland of North America. England received all of Canada, Cape Breton Island, and the rest of Nova Scotia, together with the region between the Alleghenies and the Mississippi. All that remained to France in the north were the two barren little islands of Saint Pierre and Miquelon off Newfoundland, suitable only for drying fish. In the West Indies,

# The Duel for Empire

France ceded to England four islands (Grenada, Saint Vincent, Dominica, and Tobago), but kept her more important sugar colonies of Guadeloupe, Martinique, and Haiti. In Africa, England took the slaving post at Senegal, but let France keep Gorée. In India the changes were not reflected on the map; for France was permitted to retain Pondicherry and her other trading posts, which she still holds, but the French renounced all political ambitions in connection with the native rulers. Minorca, captured in 1756, was restored to England. Spain ceded Florida to England, and in compensation received from France New Orleans and that portion of "Louisiana" west of the Mississippi.

Altogether, this meant a tremendous extension of overseas power for England and marked the height of the Old Empire. The old French colonial empire had virtually disappeared, and France, moreover, had received a severe setback as a commercial and maritime power. Yet the peace terms were unpopular in England. It was pointed out that Pitt could have won as much in 1761, and there was nothing to show for the additional British successes of the following year. The peace was already signed before the news of the capture of Manila reached Europe. One aspect of the peace discussion reflected clearly the mercantilist conception of colonial values. There were many who argued that it would be better to take the sugar island of Guadeloupe instead of Canada. While the latter would "color the map red" in impressive fashion, its scanty trade in beaver skins would not offset the burden of defense and administration, whereas a sugar island would mean immediate profits, even though it were only a dot on the map. The final decision in favor of Canada is said to have been influenced not only by the desire to remove the French menace to the thirteen colonies but also by a lobby of the powerful British planters of Jamaica, who did not want another sugar colony enjoying imperial privileges. The treaty marked England's victory in the duel for empire.

In the meantime Britain had entered upon a decade of political changes which upset the comfortable and secure domination enjoyed by the Whigs since the accession of the Hanoverian line. George II died in 1760 and was succeeded by his twenty-two-year-old grandson as George III (1760–1820). The new king was, as he proudly stated, a Briton, whereas the first two Georges had been Germans. He was determined from the start to rule as well as to reign. Whereas George II had remarked that the "ministers were king" in England, George III had constantly been urged by his mother, "George, be a king." He was strongly influenced by the book *The Patriot King*, wherein the Tory Bolingbroke, who had overplayed his hand in

# A History of England and the British Empire

Anne's reign, held up the idea of a patriotic king who should be above parties and rule England through ministers of his own choice, preserving, of course, the cabinet system. The young king thoroughly resented the power which had fallen into the hands of the Whig magnates, and determined to break it. His method was to drive wedges between the different factions into which the Whigs were divided, playing off one group against another until he should have time to build up a Tory party of his own. His principal weapon was patronage. Newcastle had maintained his majorities in the Commons by his disposal of appointments, sinecures, and pensions. Therefore George came to the conclusion that since Parliamentary votes were influenced by such awards, and since those awards were granted in the king's name, the king himself might do his own rewarding and punishing.

The consequence was that the Whig control gradually disintegrated from 1760 to 1770, when a Tory ministry of the "King's Friends" came into power for twelve years. In the course of those ten years there were seven different prime ministers, with a resultant lack of controlled and consistent policy at a critical period when the colonial situation in America required intelligent handling. Pitt had resigned in 1761; but Newcastle stubbornly clung on as prime minister for another year, until he was ousted in favor of the king's particular friend Lord Bute, a Scottish peer whose general unpopularity was increased by dissatisfaction with the peace terms. In 1763 he was followed as prime minister by Pitt's brother-in-law, George Grenville, an able man, particularly in finance, but rather stubborn, narrow-minded, and autocratic. He received the support of another Whig group, the "Bedford gang," who had no set principles, but who kept together for bargaining purposes. In 1765 Grenville omitted the king's mother from a proposed regency bill; so George dismissed his ministry and turned to another faction, the "Old Whigs," led by the Marquess of Rockingham. While this group represented the old Whig families, they were ready to depart from the old Whig methods of corruption. They meant well and worked hard; had Pitt joined them, as Rockingham urged, they might have made successful headway against the king. As it was, he dismissed them as soon as he could, in 1766, whereupon Pitt became prime minister at the head of a very ill-assorted cabinet. The "Great Commoner" lost a great deal of popularity by accepting a peerage as Earl of Chatham, the name by which he is often called to avoid confusion with his prominent son, the younger William Pitt. One of Pitt's important assets had been the effect of his oratory in the House of Commons, and that was now lost. He was a complete failure as prime minister; his gout crippled him, and his mind seems to have become affected. As a result his colleagues in the ministry did pretty much as they pleased, particularly his brilliant, erratic Chancellor of the Exchequer, Charles Townshend. By 1767 Chatham virtually retired from public life, and the nominal headship of this individualistic cabinet went to the Duke of Grafton, a descendant of Charles II and Lady Castlemaine. Finally, after a decade which had seen Newcastle, Bute, Grenville, Rockingham, Pitt, and Grafton as prime ministers in rapid succession, George III had so thoroughly broken up the Whig power that he had a sufficient body of "King's Friends" in the Commons to support a Tory ministry of his own. In 1770 his new prime minister was Lord North, an amiable, tactful, and able man who has been severely criticized, but whose chief fault seems to have been excessive devotion to the king. His ministry was to remain in power twelve years, maintained by methods of bribery and corruption learned from Walpole and Newcastle.

The encroachments of the king were highly unpopular, particularly in London. The people, denied adequate representation in the Commons because of the unreasonable methods of electing members, made a popular hero of a clever and courageous rascal. This was John Wilkes, a reprobate member of Parliament who, in 1762, started a review, the *North Briton*, for the express purpose of attacking the royal policy. In the No. 45 issue of the review there were some particularly scathing remarks about a speech by the king. George instructed the ministry to issue a general warrant for the arrest of the authors, printers, and publishers for libel. Wilkes was apprehended and sent to the Tower; but a justice of Common Pleas soon freed him on the ground of his privilege as a member of Parliament and further declared illegal such general warrants, which did not specify by name the individual to be arrested. Thereupon the House of Commons expelled Wilkes as a member, and he was attacked in the Lords for an indecent, but unpublished, "Essay on Woman." Early in 1764, after an adverse judgment in the court of King's Bench, he fled to France and was declared an outlaw.

He returned in 1768, just on the eve of a seven-year general election for Parliament. The county of Middlesex, which included a considerable part of London, was one of the few places in England with a really democratic franchise. It elected Wilkes, popular for his defiance of the king, as one of its representatives, but the Commons expelled him. Three times Middlesex elected him, and the third time, in spite of bitter protests both within and without Parliament, the Commons voted that his opponent, who had received only a few votes, ought to be seated. An anonymous author, presumably

# A History of England and the British Empire

Sir Philip Francis, who was to cause trouble in India, now bitterly attacked the king and his ministers in the *Letters of Junius*, while the London mob howled for "Wilkes and liberty." Wilkes was sentenced on the old libel charge, and the mob tried to rescue him from prison; he was even elected an alderman while in confinement. The irrepressible Wilkes was more popular than ever in England, and the colonists in Pennsylvania even named a town (Wilkes-Barre) for him and for Colonel Barré, another opponent of the royal policy. From this outburst of popular indignation may be dated the commencement of a radical demand for Parliamentary reform which was to culminate in the first of the Reform Bills, in 1832. Even Pitt, who had formerly denounced Wilkes as "the blasphemer of his God and the libeller of his king," now began to realize that an organic change was necessary in the British electoral system. For the time being, however, it remained as it had been. England was not yet a democracy; and no matter how the mobs might howl or Middlesex might vote, the king managed to keep a secure majority in the Commons.

While George III was breaking up the Whigs there were serious rumblings in the American colonies. They were warnings of the approaching conflict that would disrupt the Old Empire, which reached its climax at the Peace of Paris in 1763. In fact, the outcome of the Seven Years' War was linked up closely with the causes of the American Revolution. It is said that Montcalm, when he saw the British closing in on Quebec, predicted that, while France would doubtless lose Canada, England as a result would lose her more populous colonies to the south. In at least three ways the Americans were affected. Ever since Count Frontenac had started the policy of French and Indian raids, in 1689, the English frontier colonists had lived in terror of the French menace to the north and were comforted by the fact that British regulars could help them in an emergency. Now that menace was removed. Experiences such as Braddock's defeat, moreover, had shown the colonial troops that in some types of fighting they were better men than the haughty regulars. Finally, and more immediately, the cost of the Seven Years' War led England to think of measures whereby the colonists might share part of the cost of empire.

In addition to Canada and Nova Scotia, the "continental" colonies had become thirteen in number with the founding of Georgia in 1733. The combination of a high colonial birth rate and constant immigration led to a doubling of the population about every twenty years, until they were almost one third as populous as the mother country herself. They were, moreover, well trained in self-

# The Duel for Empire

government. Every colony had its assembly, with members elected by popular vote, which raised taxes for local purposes and legislated for the needs of the community. The authority of the assembly, to be sure, was not final; for in most of the colonies there was a governor appointed from England, and a council which he nominated. Any acts of the colonial legislature might be overridden by the governor or his council and were subject to review by the Privy Council in England. Nevertheless, the governors used their veto power sparingly, because the assemblies could withhold their salaries, and England was not particularly inclined to interfere in the internal details of colonial affairs. The Board of Trade and Plantations, to be sure, was more apt to check up violations of the Navigation Acts and other trade laws, but during the easygoing period of Walpole and Newcastle the colonists had violated even the commercial regulations with impunity. They had been enjoying a greater degree of self-government than England originally intended.

When Grenville looked over the general matter of imperial finances in 1764, he came to the conclusion that the colonists should bear a share of the cost. The Seven Years' War had increased the national debt by some £130,000,000, and part of that expense had been incurred in defending the American colonists. England did not expect them to pay for that, and had even reimbursed the colonies for their military expenses during the war. At the close of the conflict, however, there was a serious Indian threat in the West which made it seem desirable to keep a considerable force of regulars in America for defense purposes. At least the colonists might pay for their own protection in times of peace. There was no central colonial government in America with which Grenville could deal, and the simplest way, to his mind, seemed to be a stamp tax, whereby all legal documents and similar papers must bear a revenue stamp of specified value. In 1765 Parliament accordingly passed the Stamp Act, which was expected to raise some £100,000 a year. Benjamin Franklin, who was in England at the time as a colonial agent, saw no objection to the scheme. To the general surprise of the English, however, the Americans raised violent objections to the stamps. The cry of "No taxation without representation" resounded through the thirteen colonies, and in several places the stamps were destroyed. Representatives from the seaports gathered in a "Stamp Act Congress" and agreed solemnly to import nothing further from England until the obnoxious act was repealed.

That was an argument which touched deeply the London merchants. The thirteen colonies accounted for about one ninth of all England's commerce, and if this were cut off there would be many failures. The American trade had increased more rapidly than any other branch of England's widespread commerce since 1700. It was not quite as extensive as that of the sugar islands of the British West Indies; but it was about equal to the trade with Ireland, and somewhat greater than the East India Company's business with India and China. In the first seventy years of the century it had jumped nearly eight times as fast as England's trade with Europe. The growth of those various branches of English commerce is shown briefly in the following table, which, except for the final totals, does not include certain minor outside trading regions.

ENGLISH IMPORTS AND EXPORTS, 1701–1770

[Annual averages for decades, in thousands of pounds sterling.]

| Decade | Thirteen Colonies | British West Indies | India | Ireland | Total Empire | Total Europe | Grand Total |
|--------|-------------------|---------------------|-------|---------|--------------|--------------|-------------|
| 1701–1710 | 532 | 942 | 582 | 579 | 2,802 | 7,673 | 11,069 |
| 1711–1720 | 758 | 1346 | 831 | 710 | 3,791 | 8,951 | 13,055 |
| 1721–1730 | 990 | 1699 | 1084 | 817 | 4,923 | 9,911 | 17,081 |
| 1731–1740 | 1330 | 1781 | 1179 | 1045 | 5,751 | 10,555 | 18,919 |
| 1741–1750 | 1521 | 1946 | 1464 | 1484 | 6,766 | 10,912 | 19,715 |
| 1751–1760 | 2380 | 2603 | 1656 | 1803 | 8,974 | 11,071 | 22,400 |
| 1761–1770 | 2807 | 3406 | 2516 | 2850 | 12,651 | 11,740 | 25,930 |

While Grenville's mind was on colonial matters he also checked up the Americans in another way. A considerable part of the exports of the northern and middle colonies consisted of lumber, fish, and flour for which England herself had little use. Consequently the colonists had developed a triangular trade, exchanging their own wares at Jamaica, Barbados, and other West Indian islands for sugar, rum, and molasses, thus creating a surplus with which to purchase English manufactures (see page 335). England had no objection to this as long as the Yankees traded with British islands; but when they extended their operations to Guadeloupe, Martinique, and other foreign sugar islands, it was different. Parliament in 1733 had passed a Molasses Act, which levied an almost prohibitive duty on products of the foreign islands; but in the period of Whig neglect, when Newcastle did not even know where Cape Breton was, smuggling and violations, with official connivance, became the order of the day and contributed much to the building of colonial fortunes. Some of the governors at times protested, but little happened. The Molasses Act was now revised as the Sugar Act (1764), with lower duties, designed to reduce smuggling and to produce revenue rather than to prohibit such trade. Someone has remarked that the American

# The Duel for Empire

Revolution started when George Grenville began to read the colonial dispatches. He tightened up the colonial customs service and ordered a rigid observance of the long-neglected regulations. The colonists considered this an infringement of their "rights."

At any rate, the pressure from the British merchants at the danger of colonial nonimportation was taken into account by the Rockingham administration. In 1766 the Stamp Act was repealed, but, as a face-saving measure, the repeal was accompanied by a declaration that Parliament had a right to tax the colonies. Ever since, there have been lengthy discussions of that theory. It seemed that the colonists had particular objection to the stamps because they represented internal taxation. England therefore tried external taxation. In 1767 Charles Townshend pushed through Parliament an act imposing duties on glass, paint, paper, and tea imported into the colonies. The income from these duties would be devoted to the salaries of colonial governors and judges, thus rendering them independent of the colonial assemblies. Once more the colonies broke out in angry protest. Pitt, whose attitude toward the colonies was favorable, was too ill or too neglectful to prevent this further source of irritation. In 1770 North had the duties removed on everything but tea; the tax was maintained on that, he said, simply to show England's right to tax the colonies.

It is difficult to say at what time the American Revolution became inevitable; but it is likely that a successful compromise might have been achieved if it had not been for two men: George III in England and Samuel Adams in Boston. The king was to display several times in his long reign a pig-headed obstinacy, and he was determined that the colonial defiance should not go unpunished, though many Englishmen were ready to smooth things over. So, too, were many Americans; but Samuel Adams, by continual inflammatory correspondence, strove to keep alive the original indignation engendered by the Stamp Act.

While England and America were slowly drifting toward war the government had to face another imperial problem on the far side of the world. Clive, we recall, had placed his puppet on the throne of Bengal as a result of the battle of Plassey, in 1757. The East India Company had to assume a new function. Hitherto it had been primarily a trading concern, operating through a few posts of limited area. Now it was to become more and more directly the sovereign power in Bengal, a region several times the size of England, with a population of some thirty millions. In 1760 Clive returned to England at the age of thirty-five with a huge fortune, became Lord Clive, and settled down comfortably.

# A History of England and the British Empire

In his absence, the Company's servants shamelessly plundered the natives and built up fortunes for themselves. Clive was sent out in 1765 to clear up the situation. He put the administration on an honest basis and secured from the Mogul emperor the Company's right to the financial administration of Bengal and two adjacent states. Then, after two years, he went home, where an attempt was made to impeach him for a forged treaty and illicit gains. Clive remarked in his defense that when he thought of what he might have taken, he marveled at his moderation. He was only partially cleared of the charges against him, and in 1774 the man who won India for England was found dead, apparently a suicide. By making a scapegoat of Clive, as it was later to do with Warren Hastings, England had salved her conscience about the seizure of Bengal; but no one proposed to give it back to the natives. Indian service was apparently thankless work: Dupleix died in poverty; the admiral who helped him to seize Madras was thrown into prison; and Lally was executed.

In 1773 Parliament took account of the new status of the East India Company. As a trading organization with a royal charter it was not under Parliamentary control, but in view of its new political functions it seemed proper that the government should have more authority. Lord North's India Regulating Act gave the Company a parliamentary title. It combined the three separate presidencies of Bombay, Madras, and Calcutta under the authority of a governor-general who would have his seat at Calcutta. It gave him a council of four men and ruled that all decisions should be made by the majority. The first governor-general appointed under this act was Warren Hastings, already governor at Calcutta. Hastings planned carefully the administration of Bengal and wisely laid the foundations of the remarkable system whereby the British have since ruled India (see page 666). He also had to fight certain native chiefs who were threatening British power. Among his councilors, however, was Sir Philip Francis, who steadily and bitterly opposed him and who frequently was able to overrule him with a majority in the hostile council. In spite of that, Hastings's solid constructive work in Bengal ranks him with Clive as one of the two principal founders of British India.

By the time Parliament was passing the Regulating Act, the East India Company was indirectly causing further complications in America. Its finances were in bad condition, and it had a large quantity of unsold tea on its hands. The government permitted it to sell the tea directly to the colonists without paying the usual duties. Tea was already a sore point with the Americans: they had protested when Townshend taxed it; now they were angered at its cheapness, for the regular merchants could not compete with the Company's special price. At Boston a group of Americans disguised as Indians rowed out to the tea ships and dumped their cargoes into the bay. From that time on, things moved fast toward revolution. Tea had been spilled or sent back at other ports, but Boston from the outset had been the principal source of trouble. In 1774, the same year which saw the very wise and liberal Quebec Act for the new province of Canada (see page 474), Parliament determined to punish the stubborn Bostonians, in spite of pleadings for conciliation from Edmund Burke, the brilliant young Irishman of whom we shall hear more. The Boston Port Act closed that port to all shipping, while companion acts put the Massachusetts government under royal control and prohibited public meetings. A soldier, General Gage, was sent to govern Massachusetts, supported by a strong force of soldiers.

That was enough to stir the Americans into united action. Delegates from most of the colonies met at Philadelphia in the autumn of 1774 in the First Continental Congress. It was agreed to suspend all trade with England until more satisfactory treatment could be secured. There was no intention of war or independence. Each side seemed to be waiting for the other to back down; each remained stubborn; and the drift toward war continued, with no one in apparent control of the situation. Massachusetts organized part of its militia as "minutemen," who would be ready to seize arms at a moment's notice.

The war began on April 19, 1775. Gage sent eight hundred men to destroy some military stores gathered by the colonists at Concord, about twenty miles from Boston. The colonists were warned, and when the British reached Lexington they found a force of minutemen drawn up on the common. The first shots of the war were fired, eight minutemen fell, and the redcoats went on to Concord. There they were stopped by a larger group of "embattled farmers" and had to retire. The British were shot at from behind trees and stone walls; by the time they reached Boston again, they had lost more than a third of their men.

The older American schoolbook accounts of the Revolution pictured it as a struggle in which every American was a "patriot," engaged for eight years of hardship in heroic efforts to eject the British, who were tyrants to a man. The older British accounts, so far as they give more than passing mention to the war, often spoke of the Americans in terms of extreme contempt. Today the majority of American and British historians alike are united in rejecting those extreme views and in agreeing that instead of being primarily a war between America and England, it could more properly be called a civil war within the British Empire. Loyalties were divided on both sides of the Atlantic. It has been estimated that among the American colonists about 20 per cent were active "patriots"; 15 per cent were "Loyalists," or "Tories," who actively favored the king; and the remaining two thirds of the population were relatively indifferent. In England the king and the ministry supported the war; but the Whigs opposed it on the ground that if George III stamped out American liberties, he would next proceed against the liberties of Englishmen, which were already seriously threatened. Such division explains the anomalous facts that New York raised some fifteen thousand Loyalist troops, while in England prominent members of Parliament cheered when the Americans won a victory. It happened that many of the outstanding generals and admirals had Whig loyalties and either declined to fight against the Americans or, like the Howe brothers, fought halfheartedly.

The fighting in America, which began in 1775 at Lexington, continued for six years, until the fall of Yorktown in 1781. But England had far more on her hands than the rebellious colonists alone. France, Spain, and Holland were also finally ranged against her, and most of the rest of Europe was hostile. The navy was engaged not only on the American coast but also in home waters, in the West Indies, in the Mediterranean, and even on the coasts of India. During this contest it was to receive its most serious setbacks.

As far as the situation in America was concerned, each side had certain marked advantages and disadvantages. The British had organization, wealth, and authority on their side. Their experienced troops were well trained, and usually well equipped and well fed. These were assisted by thousands of professional "Hessians," hired from German princes at so much a head. The British navy could move troops rapidly from one part of the coast to another, leaving the Americans guessing where they would strike next. The Americans, on the other hand, lacked money and supplies for even the small regular army which they managed to hold together. They could count on the militia to turn out when their immediate region was in danger; but these untrained men were not dependable in battle, nor were they interested particularly unless near their own homes. There was no adequate central political authority to co-ordinate American activity. Yet all these British advantages were offset by certain other factors. The British had to wage war three thousand miles from home, a fact which entailed problems of supply and control; and they had to subdue a vast region before the rebellion could be crushed. The Americans simply had to make the British so

# The Duel for Empire

weary of the war that they would let the colonies have their own way. When the Americans retired inland, the British would follow and immediately find themselves in trouble. Distances were great, communications were bad, and there was constant danger of being cut off by a rising of local militia. Altogether it developed into an endurance contest, but at times it looked as though the Americans would not hold together long enough to wear out the British.

A few personalities must also be taken into account. Shortly after Lexington, the Continental Congress wisely put the military command in the hands of George Washington, a Virginia planter, one of the wealthiest men in the country. He had, it will be recalled, participated in the events around Fort Duquesne twenty years before (see page 456). Washington was a competent, but not a great, general. He lost many of his battles, but maintained American resistance against disheartening odds: intrigues, apathy, short-term enlistments, local jealousies, and lack of trained men. On the British side the most significant figures were not the generals or admirals but the two ministers of North's cabinet responsible for the direction of the war. It is hard to say whether Lord Sandwich, in charge of the navy, or Lord George Germain, in charge of military affairs, did more damage to the British cause. Sandwich, a cynical debauchee, termed one of the most dissolute men of Georgian England, won immortality of a sort by having meat placed between slices of bread so that he could lunch without having to leave the table and break his luck while gambling. By neglecting the material condition of the ships and by alienating the Whig admirals, Sandwich probably did more damage to the navy entrusted to his care than any hostile French admiral had ever done. Germain was a fitting colleague. At the battle of Minden in the Seven Years' War, it will be recalled, the British cavalry failed to complete the victory when ordered to do so. Germain, the responsible officer, had been court-martialed and forbidden ever again to serve in a military capacity. Yet, because of the king's friendship, here he was in full control of operations! Perhaps the quality of those two men helps to explain why the British neglected to take two steps, either one of which might have won the war in short order. They should have crushed Washington's main army, which was easily possible on several occasions, or they should have made it a purely naval war, with a rigid blockade to cut off the Americans from all outside communications and trade. Instead they engaged in blundering land campaigns combined with naval support.

The main fighting began around Boston and worked south to New York and Philadelphia during the first three years of the war;

then it moved to Georgia and worked up through the Carolinas to Virginia during the next three. There were several varied operations farther west.

The news of Lexington and Concord brought some sixteen thousand colonists to the vicinity of Boston to form an army. Gage lost his chance to nip the revolt in the bud. In June the British lost more than a thousand men in winning the battle of Bunker Hill, across Boston Harbor, where they made a brave but stupid frontal attack on entrenched colonials. That winter an American force, which had made a remarkable march through the wilderness, was defeated in an effort to take Canada. England's wisdom in giving the French Canadians their old religion and law by the Quebec Act, the year before, was now demonstrated; the Canadian settlers surprised and disappointed the Americans by their lack of interest in the contest. In March, 1776, the Americans seized the hills around Boston, and the British evacuated the city by sea. That summer, while the Continental Congress was signing the Declaration of Independence at Philadelphia on July 4, the British were beginning to concentrate against New York, which they captured after defeating Washington on Long Island. New York remained in British hands throughout the rest of the war. Washington's dwindling army was pursued across New Jersey into Pennsylvania; but on Christmas night he crossed the ice-choked Delaware and captured the garrison of Hessian mercenaries at Trenton by surprise. Ten days later, when the British were concentrating on him there, he slipped away from certain defeat by superior forces, and routed the British rear guard at Princeton, thus recovering most of New Jersey and reviving American morale.

Later in 1777 General John Burgoyne, an able playwright who had opened the impeachment attack on Clive, brought an army down from Canada through Lake Champlain to the upper Hudson. There he was surrounded by a swarm of Americans and in the autumn surrendered his army at Saratoga. General Sir William Howe, who should have gone up the Hudson from New York, captured and occupied Philadelphia instead. In the spring of 1778 Sir Henry Clinton, his successor, started across New Jersey for New York. Washington fell upon him at Monmouth; but a jealous subordinate threw away the battle, and Clinton reached New York, where he remained for the rest of the war, with Washington watching him near by for three years.

Meanwhile the news of Saratoga brought France into the war as an ally of the Americans in 1778, the year Pitt died. The French had built up a first-rate navy, which, for once in the Second Hundred Years' War, was to enjoy superiority over the British navy, which

# The Duel for Empire

was suffering from Sandwich's misrule. One after another the best British admirals declined to serve and took their places on the Whig opposition benches in Parliament. Things grew so bad that it was necessary to put an eighty-year-old veteran in command of the Channel fleet. On the American coast, in the West Indies, in India, and even in the Channel, France enjoyed naval superiority. In 1779 France determined to invade England; troops were ready; and a combined fleet of French and Spaniards, who had just come into the war, swept down on the south coast. Allied seasickness and lack of co-operation saved England; her outnumbered naval "first line of defense" had fled for safety.

After the war certain Englishmen asserted that America owed her independence to the winds. "It appeared as if the elements had joined our foes; for storms and hurricanes assisted them to destroy our navy, which by their own strength they were unable to shake," wrote one. Time and again throughout the war came the tale of squadrons scattered and ships rendered useless, while worn-out masts split open and tumbled into the sea. The explanation was that since Cromwell's time the navy had depended on New Hampshire and Maine for its great masts; the colonists had cut off the supply at the opening of the war; and Sandwich neglected to seek substitutes elsewhere. When France entered the war, she dispatched a fleet to America. Admiral Byron, the poet's grandfather, was sent with thirteen ships to head them off. A mild gale struck his squadron in mid-Atlantic, the rotten masts broke, the ships limped away in every direction, and only one reached New York ahead of the French. So it went throughout the war.

England had tried to impose a similar shortage of naval materials upon France by intercepting neutral cargoes from the Baltic. Many of these were being carried in Dutch ships; England forced Holland into the war in order to capture those ships more easily. Under the leadership of Catherine II, empress of Russia, the Baltic nations joined in an armed neutrality to protect their neutral shipping against British attack. It was England against the world: America, France, Spain, and Holland in open war against her, while most of the rest of Europe viewed her with undisguised hostility.

In America active operations had moved to the south. The British took Savannah, Georgia, in 1779; then they captured Charleston, in South Carolina. From that base Lord Cornwallis campaigned with varying success through the Carolinas. Then, for some strange reason, he headed for Virginia and established himself at Yorktown, on a broad river near Chesapeake Bay, while the French and Americans closed in on him. But British generals always felt that, as long as they could remain near the sea, the royal navy would rescue them if they got into trouble. This time the royal navy failed Cornwallis. A French fleet guarded the entrance to Chesapeake Bay and beat off the English fleet. For once in history, England was to feel to her cost the influence of sea power. The French and American siege lines closed in on Cornwallis, and finally he surrendered his army on October 19, 1781. The redcoats marched out with their bands playing "The World Turned Upside Down." That surrender, to all intents and purposes, ended the American fighting and established the independence of the thirteen colonies.

But England in 1782 was able elsewhere to offset some of her earlier misfortunes in the war. In the West Indies, Admiral Rodney, redeemed from the creditors who had been hounding him, tried a new tactical maneuver of cutting through the enemy line instead of lying alongside it. It worked to perfection in the "Battle of the Saints," near Dominica, and undid the effect of some of the earlier British reverses in those waters. Meanwhile France and Spain had been besieging Gibraltar for three years. As the peace negotiations approached they made a final desperate attempt to capture it with powerful floating batteries; but tough old Sir Gilbert Elliot beat them off with red-hot shot, and England kept Gibraltar.

Though the final peace treaties did not come until 1783, negotiations were opened in the fall of 1782. The Americans, French, and Spaniards had agreed not to engage in separate negotiations; but when the Americans learned that the French and Spaniards were working behind their backs to limit American acquisitions, they began their own dealings with the British. Lord North's ministry had fallen after Yorktown (see page 541), and Benjamin Franklin, in charge of the American negotiations, was a friend of the new British prime minister, Lord Shelburne, who was generous in his dealings. In September, 1782, England recognized the independence of her former thirteen colonies as a new republic, the United States of America. Within two months the preliminary terms were all drawn up, and the Americans managed to secure the region between the Alleghenies and the Mississippi up to the Great Lakes, a concession which had not originally been expected. The Americans were granted fishing rights off Newfoundland and in the Gulf of St. Lawrence, as well as free navigation of the Mississippi. The restitution of confiscated estates of Loyalists was to be recommended to the states by Congress, a provision, incidentally, which the states disregarded, so that England herself gave the Loyalists compensation elsewhere (see page 681). These terms were embodied in the final definitive Treaty of Paris on September 3, 1783. On that same day England

# The Duel for Empire

signed the Treaty of Versailles with France and Spain. Minorca, England's naval base in the Mediterranean for three quarters of a century, returned to Spain, as did Florida after twenty years in English hands. France gained little from her costly participation beyond the satisfaction of humbling England. It has been estimated that it cost England some £110,000,000 to lose the American colonies; France spent £55,000,000 to help the Americans gain their independence; and the Americans, who gained most, paid only £20,000,000. That recognition of independence, with the loss of the most populous of the colonies of settlement, marked the end of the Old Empire, which had reached such a proud height just twenty years before. To offset that, it also marked, as we shall see, the end of the last effort of an English king to rule as well as reign.

# CHAPTER XVII

## The New Wealth

THE eighteenth has been called the most comfortable century in English history, because, after the alarm over the Jacobites at the beginning, the country dozed complacently through the long middle years until the specter of the Jacobins arose to cloud the end. On the surface this statement was true, especially for certain people who found it not only comfortable but luxurious. For others, however, it was most decidedly uncomfortable. Economic readjustments were taking place, both in industry and in agriculture, which brought fortunes to many men but which depressed the status of still more. An "Agricultural Revolution" added greatly to the wealth of large landowners and incidentally put money into the purses of their tenant farmers. An "Industrial Revolution" almost simultaneously raised from obscurity many enterprising, hard-working, and sometimes hard-headed men, turning some into petty capitalists, or entrepreneurs, and elevating still others into capitalists on a larger scale. Somebody, as usual, had to pay the piper. As some rose in the social scale, others dropped. Hardships followed for the less enterprising, the more careless, the more stupid, and sometimes for the more kindly and the more generous. Following the changes in agriculture and industry came an equally remarkable development of transportation in the "Communication Revolution." The England which finally emerged from the revolutionary impacts was a more complex and less happy nation. Democracy, nationalism, factories, labor problems, and long trousers all marked the passing of the good old days.

England stood on the threshold of modern capitalism. What that signified in economic and in social terms may well be summarized under the caption "The New Wealth." To understand the nature of this new wealth, its source, and its significance, the three different but nevertheless interlocking revolutions taking place in the world of economics,—one in agriculture, a second in industry, a third in communications,—will be considered in turn. The word "revolution," ordinarily associated with sudden changes in a country's government (such as the American, French, or Russian Revolution),

# The New Wealth

is also used in connection with such economic terms as "industry," "agriculture," or "commerce," and in that sense refers to the changes in the way many of the people at a certain time and place made their living.

In 1750 barely a quarter of the population lived in towns and cities. The village was still the center of English life. The rental of acres, rather than the earnings of factories, ships, or banks, was still the usual and the most respectable source of wealth. The cultivation of those same acres remained the most common form of labor. It was estimated in 1770 that the national income from agriculture was £66,000,000; from industry, £27,000,000; from commerce, £10,000,000; from interest on capital and from the professions or governmental services, about £5,000,000 each. More than half of England's wealth, according to these figures, came from the soil.

The land had been owned for centuries by a surprisingly small part of the population. The vast bulk of Englishmen have been, and still are, tenants paying rent to some landlord. We have no reliable statistics for the ownership in the mid-eighteenth century of England's thirty-six million acres; but in 1688 it was estimated, as we saw, that there were about 175,000 landowners in a population of some 5,000,000 (see page 364), and in 1874 about 1,000,000 landowners in a population of some 23,000,000. Even these figures do not fully indicate the remarkable concentration of landowning in the hands of a favored few. In 1874, 250,000 persons owned nine tenths of the land, while 4200 owned half of it!

How had this little group come into possession of the land? Theoretically it had all belonged to the king. William the Conqueror, it will be recalled, had divided England among his followers, receiving military service and feudal dues in return for the land (see page 68). Gradually the military service became scutage on a cash basis, and finally landowning was divorced from its original military significance. After the Civil War the old feudal dues to the crown disappeared, and the "freeholder," great and small, came into possession. By the early eighteenth century large landowners were taking full advantage of this passing of the royal title. They still continued to derive gain from those below them. Under the medieval manorial system most of the peasantry had been serfs, tied to the land and owing part of their weekly labor to the lord. After the Black Death this labor was placed on a cash basis, some tilling the lord's fields for wages, and others, constantly increasing in number, renting land from the lord to cultivate it themselves (see page 186). The lords gradually abandoned farming on their own account and derived their principal income from this rental, which in the middle of the eighteenth century amounted annually to about ten shillings an acre.

The great landowners of the eighteenth century generally owed their prosperity not to their own efforts but to a series of judicious family marriages in the past, or to the presence of mind of some ancestor at a troubled time of wholesale changes in real estate. The house of Percy, which owned half of Northumberland and much else, could trace back some of its title deeds to the Conqueror's liberality after Hastings. Few other great houses, however, had such an ancient record. The dukes of Bedford, who ranked among the most important of the landlords, received their acres from their Russell ancestor who had happened to be high in royal favor when Henry VIII was handing out lands confiscated from abbeys and nobles. In addition to owning at least a hundred thousand acres in various parts of England, they collected, and still collect, very profitable rent from a large portion of central London. The Cavendish dukes of Devonshire had equal cause to be thankful for the dissolution of the monasteries. The earls of Grosvenor, later dukes of Westminster, owned another large section of London, because a Restoration ancestor had married an eleven-year-old heiress before she had time to change her mind. The dukes of Grafton and Richmond, on the other hand, owed their start to royal love affairs of Charles II.

Few groups in history have been born into pleasanter surroundings than those English aristocrats and gentry of the eighteenth century. Upstarts from the middle class had enjoyed power under the Tudors and to a less extent under the Stuarts, but the landowners reached their zenith under the Georges. No longer subject to the will of a monarch from above, they were not yet at the mercy of a democratic multitude from below.

They formed a compact and homogeneous society with a common background, education, and mode of living (see pages 246, 366). They led, on the whole, a more wholesome and less artificial life than the more polished French nobility of the day, and they had by this period enough education and taste for culture and art to preserve them from the boorishness of the Prussian nobility. Hard drinkers, frequently immoral, sometimes callous and grasping in their treatment of the lower classes, these peers and country squires nevertheless, as a group, utilized their leisure well. Their sense of duty, particularly as justices of the peace (see page 249), also helped them to justify their existence. The calm, strong, handsome faces which look down from the paintings of Gainsborough, Reynolds, and Romney reveal their self-satisfaction and contentment with life in general. It is small wonder that their century of domination wit-

# The New Wealth

nessed only one decade of reform. It naturally seemed folly to tamper with what to them was the best of all possible worlds.

Their closely knit social system is partly explained by the training which many of them underwent as youths. After preliminary tutoring at home the young aristocrat was frequently sent to Eton, Harrow, Winchester, or one of the other great "public" schools, where certain fundamentals of culture and character were drilled into him. Then he often proceeded to Oxford or to Cambridge, which, like the "public" schools, were by this time practically monopolized by the wealthy. The universities were at much lower ebb in the eighteenth century than in the seventeenth. Oxford was described as "steeped in port and prejudice," and Cambridge was not much better. Occasionally a young student like Charles James Fox would develop a real passion for absorbing all the learning he could find; but most of the young aristocrats did little more than grace the university with their presence, receiving at the end a "pass" degree without examination. When Fox left Oxford to travel abroad for a few months, the class in mathematics was suspended until his return, since the others were not interested. Even the idlers, however, developed some taste for the classics, which was sometimes reflected later in their Parliamentary speeches and their libraries.

The "grand tour" finished the young gentleman's education. Armed with letters of introduction and letters of credit, and often accompanied by a tutor, he spent several months or even a couple of years on the Continent, particularly in France, Italy, and Switzerland. The memoirs of the day reveal these young English "milords" at nearly every social gathering, "losing their hearts in one palace and their money in another." Lord Chesterfield's letters to his son show better than anything else the aim of this educational process bent on producing the grand gentleman, who should have "that engaging address, those pleasing manners, those little attentions, that air, and those graces which all conspire to make that first advantageous impression upon people's minds which is of such instant use through the whole course of life." The grand tour did much to give "this most necessary varnish" to Georgian society.

After this common preliminary training there was a parting of the ways. The eldest sons could look forward to inheriting their fathers' acres. Frequently they soon found their way into the House of Commons. If they belonged to the inner circle, they were before long "sailing on a sea of claret from one comfortable official haven to another," passing through undersecretaryships and sinecures to cabinet positions, often with no further recommendation than their family connections. They were members of a fast society which spent much of its time gambling at the clubs,—the Whigs at Brooks's and the Tories at White's. Hours were long and stakes heavy, one young nobleman losing £11,000 at a sitting and winning it back on a single hand. Wit was at a premium, and the first duty of a gentleman was to be amusing. The gossipy letters of Horace Walpole, Sir Robert's son, stand in the front rank of the extremely clever literary products of this group. Its members frequently found their way to Bath, the fashionable watering place in the west, where Beau Nash dictated manners and fashions to English society, as did Beau Brummel later in London.

For younger sons the army, the navy, and the Church offered the principal openings, though many went into government civil service, law, or, occasionally, business. Many of them went through the same educational process as their older brothers, except for the embryo naval officers, who, as we saw, frequently became midshipmen at twelve. The purchase of commissions in the army tended to limit the officers to the upper classes. The churchman gained a more respectable status than he had held the century before (see page 374); for the Church had been dragged into the general "spoils system," and political influence often dictated the filling of lucrative positions. The "two-bottle parson," a gentleman by birth, was often more noted for his hunting prowess than for his spiritual zeal; yet if he had the proper political influence, he might enjoy life to the limit and still become a bishop. The success which an influential family might attain in those three fields is illustrated by Lord Cornwallis and his family. He himself held very high military command and became governor-general of India and viceroy of Ireland; one brother was also a general; another became one of the ranking admirals of the navy; a third attained a bishopric, but was overshadowed by a fourth, who rose to be Archbishop of Canterbury! In the possibility of winning financial success through business the English younger son had an advantage over the French nobleman, who, as we have mentioned before, was automatically barred from such an occupation as degrading. If all other things failed, there was always the government civil service with its thousands of sinecures, the "outdoor relief of the aristocracy" as it was sometimes called. Even though the younger son might go through life with a feeling of grievance at not being the one to inherit his father's lands and wealth, the aristocracy still provided him with ample opportunities to have first call on some highly desirable occupation.

The country house, however, remained the true habitat of the English aristocracy, as we have noticed in the two preceding centuries. The squires were on their estates most of the time. Even the fashion-

# The New Wealth

able London group, with their town houses, were accustomed to spend much time on their country estates. Burgoyne's failure at Saratoga was long attributed to Germain's impatience to get away for a hunting trip. The influence of the grand tour was evident in the architecture of the Georgian country houses. The rambling, gabled features of Tudor and Jacobean days gave way to simple, dignified rectangular lines, with the classical influence often accentuated by pillars. Many of the older mansions and college buildings in the United States show the effects of this architecture. The chaste white interiors, and the furniture designed for them by Chippendale, Heppelwhite, and Adam, were in keeping with the stately Georgian simplicity. The paintings on the walls often included old masters as well as old ancestors. Some of the landed aristocracy, like the dukes of Bedford, took an active interest in the supervision and improvement of agriculture; but the majority of them were to be found more often dressed in scarlet and following the hounds. The stables were an important part of every estate, and the running of the first Derby in 1780 probably aroused much keener interest than the contemporary maneuvers of Cornwallis in the Carolinas. Whether in country house, town house, or London club, the eighteenth-century gentleman consumed a tremendous amount of port, interrupted occasionally by a shift to claret or to sherry. The common habit of downing two or three bottles before making a speech or entering a drawing-room resulted in a painful prevalence of gout, which was one of the very few unpleasant features in a generally delightful life.

The assurance of a steady income without much risk or effort was not the only advantage in landowning; for such an income carried with it much more social and political prestige than money obtained from trade. Besides, it was widely held that landowners were best fitted to control government, since their economic status was more stable. George III would raise no man to the peerage unless he owned land; and a long-standing rule, not strictly enforced, forbade anyone to sit in the Commons unless he had an estate worth at least £300. It is not difficult, therefore, to understand Parliament's vital interest in law, order, and the sanctity of property, especially large landed property. As a result of this prestige, London merchants and bankers, East India "nabobs," and West India planters felt the necessity of purchasing English estates if they expected to count for anything in society and politics.

To understand just how this income was produced we must turn from the ownership to the cultivation of the soil. Except for the communities most severely affected by the Tudor enclosures, the eighteenth-century village differed little from its direct ancestor, the medieval manor (see pages 39, 69). It was still a string of thatched cottages along a single street. At least half the English villages still operated their acres more or less on the old communal basis, according to which no peasant had a permanent interest in any particular portion of the waste, meadow, or tilled land. The whole village might use the waste land for fuel, and as pasture for the indiscriminate wanderings of its cattle, sheep, and geese. The meadow was divided annually by lot into sections; but after the hay was cut the barriers were thrown down, and cattle grazed over the whole tract. The tilled land was still divided into three large hedgeless, open fields, one of which had to rest in fallow every third year in order to recover its fertility. The average single holding of a tenant farmer was about eighteen acres of tilled land, divided evenly among the three fields, in addition to two acres of meadow and common rights for forty sheep and a number of cattle. Each year, therefore, the average small farmer planted twelve acres in the two active fields, most commonly six in wheat and six in rye or barley. His holdings were still scattered widely in long, narrow acres or half-acre strips. On these he sowed broadcast two or three bushels of seed grain to the acre and generally reaped about ten times that amount. That tenfold increase was the object of agricultural labor and the basis of profit. Our typical farmer, then, would have a net gain of about one hundred and fifty bushels of wheat and an equal amount of rye or barley to show for his year's labor in the fields. Out of this he would have to pay his rent, averaging ten shillings an acre, while in addition the tithe proctors of the Church took every tenth sheaf of grain. The farmer, of course, had milk, wool, eggs, and occasionally meat from his livestock. The larger tenant farmers usually hired cottagers to work in their fields at a shilling or so a day. Agriculture is largely a seasonal occupation, requiring special energy at seed time and harvest but allowing some leisure in between. Consequently cottagers and farmers alike had another important source of income in spinning and weaving, as we have seen, in the "domestic system" in industry (see pages 244–245).

By the middle of the eighteenth century England was beginning to feel the first effects of the rural changes known as the "Agricultural Revolution," closely related to and closely followed by the still more sweeping changes which have been termed the "Industrial Revolution." These two movements must be considered together, for they were in a way complementary. Both secured efficiency and increased production at the expense of the workers. The surplus tillers of the soil, uprooted by the Agricultural Revolution, found their way into the new factories of the Industrial Revolution. And, since the factory workers could not themselves produce bread and beef, the agricultural communities underwent still further changes to meet the new demand.

In more than a thousand years of English agriculture no important improvements in methods were developed. A farmer of Alfred's day would probably have noticed little that was unusual either in the practices of Queen Anne's time or in those of ancient Rome. Yet those time-honored methods were wasteful and inefficient in the extreme. Not only was a third of the arable land idle each year, but there was further waste in the broad turf "balks" separating the strips. Even the soil that was used yielded only a fraction of its potential capacity. Labor was squandered as well as land; for the farmer spent a good bit of his working day in moving himself and his crude tools from one strip to another (see pages 40–41).

Then came the Agricultural Revolution. As in many other movements, various obscure pioneers paved the way for persons whose names have been popularly associated with the important innovations. The first such name in agriculture was that of Jethro Tull, an Oxford graduate who had made a close study of European agricultural practices on his grand tour, and who then had settled down to experiment in England. In 1733 he embodied his findings in a volume entitled *Horse-Hoeing Husbandry*. He argued that the soil could be made much more productive by breaking it up into small particles by means of double plowing at the start, followed, even after the grain began to grow, with frequent hoeing by a horse-drawn cultivator. Since this hoeing was out of the question if the seed had been scattered broadcast, it was necessary to plant it in rows, which incidentally saved seed. To the amazement of rural England, Tull showed that a reduced amount of seed would produce more grain to the acre than the traditional tenfold yield of the old method.

Lord Townshend, Walpole's brother-in-law, won the nickname of "Turnip Townshend" by experimenting upon his estate, to which he retired when Walpole began to overshadow him in politics (see page 430). He did valuable, though perhaps not original, work in crop rotation by showing that a usable root crop, like turnips, would restore the fertility of the third field by replacing the missing nitrogen and obviate the necessity of leaving it fallow. The turnips could then be fed to the livestock, which had hitherto often gone hungry in the winter months for want of fodder. The efficacy of manure was also practiced and preached by Townshend. Not only did he urge that barnyard dung be spread on the fields instead of being left piled in unhealthful heaps, but he also advocated lime and marl, a soft, sticky earth which would give increased fertility not merely temporarily, like the manure, but for periods of fifteen or twenty years.

The possibility of thus providing winter fodder from the soil previously wasted turned attention to breeding. The pioneer in this was Robert Bakewell whose findings transformed English sheep and cattle. His object was an increased supply of beef and mutton, whereas farmers had formerly thought primarily of wool from sheep, milk from cows, and hauling from oxen. By constantly inbreeding from chunky, compact animals, well developed in the parts appreciated by butchers, Bakewell helped to supplant the rangy, long-shanked animals which grazed in the village pastures. Sheep and cattle were now much larger in size and fatter. "Symmetry well rounded" was Bakewell's watchword; and visitors came even from the Continent to see his famous ram Twopounder, whose "New Leicester" descendants by the hundreds of thousands were to provide mutton for Englishmen. The records of Smithfield Market at London show that between 1710 and 1795, when Bakewell died at seventy, the average weight of sheep rose from 28 to 80 pounds, while cattle jumped from 370 to 800 pounds.

When the landlords heard that hitherto barren wastes "where two rabbits fought for every blade of grass" were producing rich crops with fourfold and even twelvefold increases in rental value, they developed a lively desire to introduce the new methods, but were balked by the old communal system of village agriculture. Under it the individual small farmer lacked the capital to buy the apparatus required for Tull's "horse hoeing" and to pay for the expensive fertilizing with lime or marl. He could not experiment with rotation of crops by himself; for the village as a whole decided each year what everyone should plant in the two active fields. He could not hope for success in improving the breed of sheep or cattle, since his beasts would have to roam "unchaperoned" among their lanky neighbors on the waste. It was obvious that if these innovations were to be introduced successfully, a farmer would have to shut off his own particular plot of land instead of continuing the old open-field system. Such were the motives leading to the wholesale agricultural enclosures of the Georgian period. These must not be confused with the Tudor enclosures, which were usually intended for sheep-grazing (see page 243).

A village tragedy was enacted on two thousand occasions in the last forty years of the century. The church door one Sunday morning would bear a notice that Parliament was about to be petitioned for an enclosure of the common lands. The lesser villagers might protest or even riot; but with Squire himself or his friends in

# The New Wealth

Parliament, and with that body composed, anyway, largely of landlords, the bill would ordinarily pass. Soon commissioners would appear to put an end to the immemorial communal life of the village. The common waste land would disappear; probably the meadow and tilled land also. Each individual who shared in the old common tillage—and this did not include the cottagers—would be allotted a particular piece of land which he was to fence in, or "enclose," for his own use. The squire and the larger freeholders or tenants would receive enough to make their cultivation more profitable under the new methods; but the lesser tenants, who were losing their free fuel and the pasturage for their livestock, could seldom afford the compulsory cost of enclosing their little allotments and would have to sell out their rights for a song. For them three courses were open. They might go as emigrants to America, where there was a chance to secure plenty of land of their own, or they might become factory hands in the new factories, or they might stay in the village as laborers. No longer their own masters, with no incentive to energy or to thrift, they would try to drown their sorrows in gin as their old freedom disappeared. The cottagers, receiving no land of their own and losing their old common privileges, went the same way. The landlord might argue that "God did not create the earth to be waste for feeding a few geese, but to be cultivated by man." The answer came back, "Parliament may be tender of property; all I know is that I had a cow, and an Act of Parliament has taken it from me."

Such was the Agricultural Revolution. The former happy, inefficient population of the villages dwindled away to a fraction of the old number; yet that small remainder, following the new methods of Tull, Townshend, and Bakewell, made the village acres far more productive than they had ever been before. Bread and beef were thus supplied to meet the demands of the rapidly increasing industrial population. Between 1761 and 1801 there were exactly two thousand enclosure acts, affecting nearly a tenth of the total area of England; and the following forty years saw nearly as many more.

The enclosures were far from being an unmixed evil. Without them it is difficult to see how England could have made good use of the new agricultural discoveries, or how she could have fed a larger population, or even how in later years she could have defeated Napoleon. To some extent, therefore, most Englishmen benefited, but most of all the landlords, who, being rich, became richer still. A certain part of the new wealth percolated down, naturally, to the intelligent farmer, a term always used in England to denote a person who rents a farm and who tills it in person, an agricultural laborer working for wages never being called a farmer. But the lesser folk at the bottom paid the penalty for the advance of science. As the contemporary poet Goldsmith has it in his *Deserted Village,*

> Ill fares the land, to hastening ills a prey,
> Where wealth accumulates, and men decay:
> Princes and lords may flourish, or may fade;
> A breath can make them, as a breath has made;
> But a bold peasantry, their country's pride,
> When once destroy'd, can never be supplied.

Turning to the Industrial Revolution, we shall find what happened to a considerable portion of that bold peasantry, "decaying" in the factories and slums of Manchester, Leeds, and other mushroom centers created by new methods of industry. This Industrial Revolution is perhaps the most striking fact in modern history. Briefly stated, it was the change in human affairs brought about by the application of power machinery to industrial processes. "Manufactured" (derived from the Latin words *manus* and *facio*) originally meant "made by hand." Today it implies the reverse. The Industrial Revolution was the supplanting of the human hand in the making of commodities by the machine. It was to change the very nature of society, politics, and economic life. Starting with this substitution of machinery for handwork, it uprooted a large part of England's population and set it down in another part of the country; it increased population radically; it emphasized two new social classes, the wealthy capitalistic, middle-class bourgeoisie and the landless proletariat of the factory towns; it introduced women and children into industry on a large scale; it brought about a new and hitherto undreamed-of discipline in industrial life; it overthrew the political domination of the landed aristocracy; it substituted the city for the village as the important center of national life; it gave England a position of increased importance in world commerce and finance; and it gave the working class, during the period of change, a half century of extreme misery.

This movement started just before the American Revolution, and the important period of transition lasted about sixty years. It represented the fourth main stage in the development of English industry. It will be recalled that in the early Middle Ages industry, such as it was, centered in the self-sufficient manor, which produced almost everything it needed. Then, about 1100, towns began to arise, and with them the guilds, with their masters, journeymen, and apprentices working together in a shop. The guilds became so rigid and conservative that by 1500 they were being supplanted by the "domes-

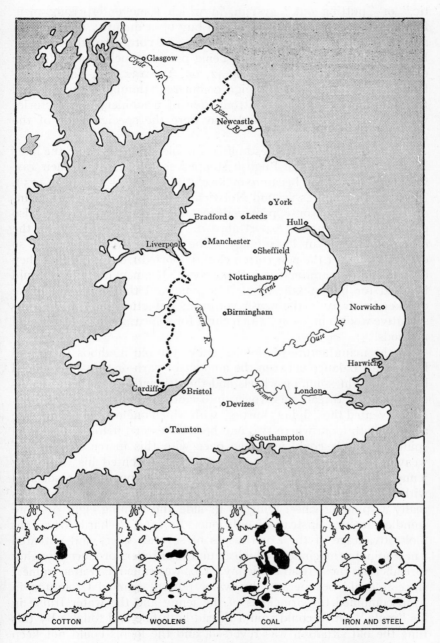

ENGLAND AT THE TIME OF THE INDUSTRIAL REVOLUTION

tic," or "putting out," system, in which some enterprising men, forerunners of the capitalists, would buy up a quantity of raw wool and distribute it among small tenants and cottagers who in their homes would spin and weave it, being paid so much a piece for the cloth they produced (see pages 42, 69, 130–132, 244–245). England's rapidly expanding foreign commerce stimulated the demand for manufactures, and the introduction of machinery and factories was the answer. Textiles and iron were the special fields of the new activity.

England had had a well-established woolen industry from the later Middle Ages, when the English stopped sending most of their raw wool to Flanders and began to make cloth themselves (see page 175). The eastern counties around Norwich were centers of a woolen industry which not only provided for home consumption but also produced a surplus for export abroad. The cotton industry, on the other hand, was in its infancy. The English were becoming so enthusiastic over the new cotton cloth imported from India that they determined to manufacture it themselves. The new machinery could be used for both textiles, but it was natural that it should make quicker headway in the newer cotton manufacture than in the conservative woolen industry, which clung for some time to its traditional methods.

In the manufacture of textiles under the old methods there had been a fair balance between the amount of yarn or thread produced by the upright spinning wheels and the demands of the hand looms on which the thread was woven into cloth. As early as 1733 John Kay invented the "flying shuttle," with which one man could operate a broadcloth loom where two had been necessary before. The hand spinning wheels could not keep pace with this increased speed of weaving until James Hargreaves, in 1764, invented his "spinning jenny," the first of the four big textile inventions popularly associated with the beginning of the Industrial Revolution. This machine was really a spinning wheel lying on its side and turning eight or more spindles at once, instead of only one. In 1769 Richard Arkwright took advantage of the experiments of several others and patented a new spinning machine in which a number of rollers produced tougher threads than those from the jenny. This was called a "water frame," since it could be operated by water power. Samuel Crompton in 1779 combined the principles of the jenny and the water frame in his "mule," which could spin a thread both fine and tough. By this time the old situation was reversed, and the looms could not keep up with the greatly increased supply of thread until, in 1785, the Reverend Edmund Cartwright invented the power loom. This came into general use more slowly than the spinning machinery; but by 1833 there were eighty-five thousand power looms in England, and the original balance between spinning and weaving was restored. The final need was for an adequate supply of raw cotton, which was to come from across the Atlantic as soon as Eli Whitney invented the cotton gin in the United States, about 1793. It quickly separated the fiber from the seeds, and gave to the southern part of the United States its principal source of wealth.

The flying shuttle and the spinning jenny could be used at home under the "domestic system"; but the new looms were too large for this, and they also required water power   This led to the gathering of workers into factories near swift streams and waterfalls, which could turn the wheels. For the most part these were located in lonely valleys in the northwest, especially in Lancashire, with its little streams flowing from the hills into the Ribble and the Mersey. Not until the advent of the steam engine was it possible to concentrate these factories in cities; but that represents another part of the story.

Hand in hand with the textiles went developments in iron. Iron deposits could be found in many parts of England, and for centuries there had been a fairly active iron industry in the southern counties, where the large groves of oaks provided the charcoal necessary for smelting. By the middle of the eighteenth century, however, the industry seemed to be dying a natural death, since the oaks, which took a hundred years to mature, were disappearing so fast that the government was seriously concerned over the future supply of naval timber. But in the Midlands and in the north England had large coal deposits, with plenty of iron close at hand. "Sea coals" had been carried from Newcastle to London for fuel, but it was only gradually that the idea developed of saving the iron industry by using coal instead of oak charcoal for smelting.

Between 1708 and 1754 the Abraham Darbys, father and son, made a series of successful experiments in smelting with coke made from coal, and as a result there was a shift of the iron industry to the coal regions. It was difficult to get the fire hot enough to melt the ore thoroughly, however, until an engineer invented a blowing engine for the coke blast furnaces at the Carron works in Scotland. The blast furnace turned out pig or cast iron containing from 2 to 5 per cent carbon, which made it too brittle for ordinary purposes. The next invention was to produce malleable wrought iron by removing this carbon. Soon, a "reverberatory furnace" was invented for this; but real success came in 1784, when Henry Cort perfected the process of "puddling," which made possible the efficient conversion of pig into wrought iron on a large scale. Cort, working with one

Purnell, also developed the rolling mill, which turned the wrought iron into sheets and other forms needed in industry and engineering. Sheet iron was useful for boilers, tanks, and later for shipbuilding; while bar and other structural iron was used in bridges and canals, and later for rails. The immediate demand for iron led to a wholesale opening of foundries and mines in the "Black Country" of the Midlands and the north.

There still remained the need of producing steel on a large scale. Steel is tougher than cast iron and more easy to work into shape than wrought iron, and because of its strength it is more valuable than iron for many purposes. It must have just the proper proportion of carbon—less than cast iron and more than wrought iron. It was produced in excellent quality but small quantity by the cutlery works of Sheffield and elsewhere, but the production of steel in large quantities had to wait until the inventions of Bessemer and others in the middle of the nineteenth century. Steel thereupon replaced iron in many of its former uses.

More important than either the textile or iron inventions was the development of the steam engine during the mid-eighteenth century. Thomas Newcomen as early as 1705 had invented a steam engine which would work, but not efficiently. It was used to pump water out of mine pits and to work the blowing engines for blast furnaces. James Watt, a young Scot, mathematical instrument-maker at the University of Glasgow, called upon to repair a Newcomen engine, found that too much energy was wasted in heating and cooling the cylinder for every stroke. He developed a separate condenser and made the first practical steam engine, capable of rotary as well as vertical movement, and vastly improved this engine. By closing both ends of the cylinder, he introduced the steam into it by alternate jets. He also added the flywheel, thus making rotary motion possible, an indispensable improvement if the engine was to be of general utility; and later he invented the governor, or speed-regulator. In 1769, four years after Hargreaves invented the "jenny," Watt took out his first patent; and shortly afterward he and Matthew Boulton, a Birmingham manufacturer of note, formed a partnership to manufacture the "Boulton and Watt" engine, particularly for the iron and coal industries. In 1785 one of his engines was first used in a cotton mill; and from that time on, it gradually replaced water power and made possible the concentration of factories in large cities. We shall discuss elsewhere the importance of the steamboat and the locomotive, which were other results of Watt's invention. Until partially replaced by electricity, late in the nineteenth century, steam was the principal source of power for industry and transpor-

# The New Wealth

tation. This invention naturally increased the demand for coal; and hundreds of new mines were opened, in addition to those connected with iron-smelting.

The material results of this age of invention were striking, although some scholars have argued that the influence of the newly invented machinery has been overemphasized and that the revolution was not as sudden as it seemed at first. They point out that there were the beginnings of factories and capitalistic control before that time and that the "great inventors" were preceded by pioneers whose experiments were of equally fundamental importance. The fact remains, however, that England underwent a tremendous transformation, as statistics amply demonstrate. In 1764, the year of the spinning jenny, England imported 1500 tons of raw cotton; in 1833, when we can consider the transition complete, she imported 150,000 tons! The increase in the production of iron was almost as great. In 1740 England had 59 furnaces, producing 17,350 tons. Just a century later, there were 378 furnaces, producing 1,348,000 tons.

Population as well as production was profoundly affected by the Industrial Revolution. Three significant changes came over the people of England: they increased amazingly in numbers, they migrated from the southern and eastern counties to the Midlands and the north, and they shifted from country to city.

As long as most Englishmen were engaged in subsistence agriculture, with its old inefficient methods, population grew very slowly. In nearly seven centuries, between the Domesday survey and 1750, it rose from about 1,500,000 to only about 6,500,000. Then it began to grow by leaps and bounds as industry became increasingly more important: 8,890,000 when the first regular census was taken, in 1801; 13,800,000 in 1831; 17,900,000 in 1851; 22,700,000 in 1871; 32,500,000 in 1901; and 39,947,000 in 1931. Those figures are for England and Wales alone. That rapid rise stands in sharp contrast to the statistics for Scotland and Ireland, which remained more distinctly agricultural, with some 7,000,000 inhabitants in 1801 and only 8,500,000 in 1901, a figure which remained practically stationary for thirty subsequent years, the moderate gains in Scotland having been offset by heavy losses in Ireland. The increase in population cannot, to be sure, be ascribed wholly to increased production. It was caused in part by medical discoveries, which lessened the death rate, such as inoculation against smallpox, and also by improvement in hygiene, which had a like effect, particularly on infant mortality. Nevertheless, these ameliorating circumstances were the result in the long run of the new wealth, which made their inauguration possible.

# A History of England and the British Empire

The geographical shift carried the bulk of the population northward and westward, while the region most severely affected by the Georgian agricultural enclosures, a strip running from near the Isle of Wight northeastward toward Norfolk, suffered most heavily. The cotton industry became located in Lancashire, in the west, northeast of Wales, partly because its moist, even climate prevented the threads from breaking as they would if the air were too dry. The center of the woolen industry moved from Norfolk, in the east, over to the West Riding of Yorkshire. The iron industry converted into a "Black Country" parts of the Midlands and of the north, where, as we have seen, coal was plentiful.

The typical English worker, moreover, became a city dweller instead of a countryman. In 1750 about three quarters of England's population was rural; in 1851 the census showed that the rural and urban populations were almost exactly equal; in 1901 more than three quarters of the population was urban; and in 1931 four fifths. The four most important cities built up by the Industrial Revolution were Manchester and Leeds in the textile industry and Birmingham and Sheffield in iron. These big industrial centers grew at least tenfold in the century following 1760. Towns of about 5000 inhabitants in 1685, they had about 30,000 in 1760 and 300,000 in 1860. Manchester jumped from 17,000 in 1757 to 142,000 in 1833 and continued rapidly toward the half-million mark. Birmingham rose steadily until it was second only to London in size. That distinction had formerly been enjoyed by the seaport of Bristol, which was now completely overshadowed by its rival Liverpool, the outlet for Lancashire. Newcastle-on-Tyne, over on the east coast, waxed great with coal and shipbuilding, while Bradford flourished with the woolen industry. And many another small town grew rapidly into a populous and grimy city.

The social results of the Industrial Revolution were many and profound. In the days before power machinery, class lines between employers and employees were few. That gulf had existed between noble and commoner, landowner and peasant; but under ordinary circumstances an industrious apprentice, who saved his money, had in the early days every expectation of rising in the ranks, turning in course of time into a journeyman, and often becoming a master. Not infrequently he married his former master's daughter, and at any rate lived on terms of intimacy with the master's family during his apprenticeship. The simple, inexpensive, and portable tools were at first the personal property of those who used them. True, under the domestic system a class of middlemen arose between producer and purchaser; but even when this happened, class lines still remained

# The New Wealth

vague. The steam engine ended all this. The new machines were both expensive and bulky; they could not easily be moved; and they belonged to one man, who was called the capitalist. Capital has been defined as wealth which is used to produce more wealth; for instance, the new expensive machines and the factories which housed them. There had been no such thing as capitalism, in the sense that the tools of production belonged to men who did not operate them, until the domestic system, and then the amount involved was very slight as compared with this new concentration of capital in the Industrial Revolution. The capitalist or employer was no longer called by the more personal word "master," and the old social unities began to disappear. The employer did not live with his men; he did not even live at his factory. He "hired and fired" his "hands," and the latter no longer felt bound in personal loyalty to a man whom they saw but seldom. At first, in the smaller factories, this was not so noticeable. When an employer hired only a handful of workingmen, he frequently continued to know each individually; but as factories grew larger and larger this soon ceased to be true. Occasionally a factory hand might rise to the status of employer; but this became the exception rather than the rule. The employers, who owned the tools, became a class apart.

This group of Englishmen, the enterprising and often self-made men who created, owned, and operated the factories, foundries, and mines, profited greatly by the Industrial Revolution. Almost overnight some of them built up fortunes rivaling those of the landed aristocracy. As time went on, they forgot their antecedents and thought of themselves, together with the merchants and middlemen, who also grew richer with the new industry, as men of the middle class. This social stratum was not new in England (see page 250), but never before had it been so prominent. Soon it was to take on a new name and be called by the historian the "bourgeoisie." The bourgeoisie grew steadily more powerful during the nineteenth century, acquiring political power along with their wealth. The Reform Act of 1832 and the repeal of the Corn Laws signalized their victory over the landowners, who had monopolized the government for so long. Under the influence of these capitalists, with their new wealth, the government adopted a *laissez-faire*, or "hands-off," attitude toward business, with the result that for many years little was done to improve the lot of the factory workers. A few factory owners, like Robert Owen (see page 587), tried, it is true, to improve the lot of their workers; but too many others were harsh taskmasters.

Between the bourgeoisie and the working class beneath, a social chasm developed, one difficult but not impossible to bridge. The working class no longer owned the tools with which it worked. Without land, without property, without guarantee of employment, it sank in the social scale, and later came to be known as the "proletariat."

Concurrent with the hardening of class lines came an enormous increase in the employment of women and children in industry. The new machinery, particularly in the manufacture of textiles, made their labor more profitable than in the old days; for a premium was now placed on quickness and agility rather than on strength. Tying broken threads and tending looms was not hard labor from the standpoint of sheer muscle, and most tasks of this description could be done more easily by women and by children than by men. Results were unfortunate. Women, drawn from their homes, competed with men in the labor market, thus depressing the wage scale; and children placed in factories were unable to fend for themselves and were subjected to harsh and inhuman treatment.

In the early factories, operated for the most part by water power, the children were generally orphans or paupers, leased out as apprentices by the guardians of the poor and sent in batches to the north, where they were herded in barracks and forced to work from twelve to fourteen hours a day. On Sundays the machines had to be cleaned and church attended. If the children went to school once a week (on Sunday), that was considered sufficient. By an act of 1747 "an apprentice could appeal to a magistrate against his master's ill-treatment, and if the case was proved, could obtain his or her discharge."[1] In theory this gave protection; but just how a ten-year-old or twelve-year-old boy or girl was to hear of this statute or to avail himself of it was not stated.

As steam succeeded water power the number of child laborers increased. With the congestion of factories in the new industrial towns, it was no longer necessary to hire pauper children, and boys and girls of the working class who lived at home sought jobs in the factories. How they were treated there will be discussed elsewhere (see page 618). It is sufficient to note here that not until 1802 was any act passed by Parliament specifically for their protection. This law was applicable only to the cotton and woolen industries: it limited labor to twelve hours, and called for the appointment of two visitors, a magistrate and a clergyman, who were to inspect the factories. Even this mild proviso annoyed the millowners. "What effects will be produced," they wrote, "in such establishments by the introduc-

---

[1] J. L. Hammond and B. Hammond, *The Town Labourer* (1917), p. 149. By permission of Longmans, Green & Co.

tion of visitors (whom the children will regard as invested with a controlling power over their masters), it is easy to foresee. All subordination will be at an end, let the visitors conduct themselves with what discretion they may; the mills and the factories will become a scene either of idleness and disorder, or of open rebellion; or the masters, harassed and tired out by the incessant complaints of their apprentices, and the perpetual interference of the visitors, will be obliged to give up their works."[1]

These direful prophecies did not come to pass. The children continued to work, doing their bit to defeat Napoleon by adding to England's wealth. An unfounded tradition has accredited William Pitt, the great war prime minister, with advising the millowners, discouraged and disgruntled because of high taxes, to recompense themselves with child labor. Such advice was unnecessary. It was already being followed; and more than one generation of children grew up without education, and with such strenuous labor their daily fare that they were worn out physically far too young, even when they did not lose their jobs, as they became adults, to younger competitors.

The effect on the home life of the working-class family produced by this employment of women and children was not the least of its evils. Long hours in the factory left the women no chance to care for their homes properly. As a result their dark, cheerless rooms were dirty, untidy, and ill-kept. With no time for cooking, the family meals became too largely a matter of baker's bread. The children were dirty and half sick from neglect and the wrong sort òf food. Bad enough as these conditions were for the strong and well, they were the more deplorable for the sick and the aged. The home atmosphere was not improved by the too frequent presence of the unemployed husband and father, spending his days idly in the nearest "pub" or in half-hearted attempts to improve the housekeeping. A by-product of the bad home conditions was the insecurity of the aged. There was, for instance, no room in the crowded tenements for aged parents, nor money to support them.

Before the coming of power machinery the hours of work were as long, sometimes longer; but the worker generally chose those hours as he saw fit, and carried on his work during them as his fancy dictated. To work thus with machines was impossible. No longer did a worker know the creative joy of making à complete article; instead his share was more and more limited to guiding a machine monotonously through some separate part of the process, because this new "division of labor" was found to be more efficient. Machines,

---

[1] Quoted ibid., p. 153.

moreover, were impersonal and never tired; therefore those who tended them were subjected to a necessary but irksome discipline. "The workman was summoned by the factory bell; his daily life was arranged by factory hours; he worked under an overseer imposing a method and precision for which the overseer had in turn to answer to some higher authority; if he broke one of a long series of minute regulations he was fined."[1]

Let us look at a few of the fines on a specimen list:

|  | s. | d. |
|---|---|---|
| Any spinner found with his window open . . . . . . | 1 | 0 |
| Any spinner found dirty at his work . . . . . . . | 1 | 0 |
| Any spinner found washing himself . . . . . . . . | 1 | 0 |
| Any spinner leaving his oil can out of its place . . . . | 1 | 0 |
| Any spinner slipping with his gas lighted . . . . . . | 2 | 0 |
| Any spinner heard whistling . . . . . . . . . | 1 | 0 |
| Any spinner having hard ends hanging on his weights . . | 0 | 6 |
| Any spinner being five minutes after last bell rings . . . | 1 | 0 |
| Any spinner having a little waste on his spindles . . . . | 1 | 0 |

And the foregoing enumerates less than half the fines on the list. When their long day's work was over, the workers had no relief from the new irksome existence; all they had was crowded, unsanitary tenements to which to return.

Finally, the Industrial Revolution brought about the urbanization of life. The new cities grew with astonishing rapidity and without direction. Speculative building went on apace, and "jerry-built" houses were the rule rather than the exception. Since rents must be low and the collection of them was not always easy or regular, it is difficult to see how, in an age of individualism, it could have been otherwise. The little houses in which the industrial proletariat swarmed were built ordinarily either back to back, which economized both space and brick, or else in courts or alleys. In the former case there were, in the back rooms, no windows at all. If the latter method was followed, a number of closely packed houses would front on a tiny court, into which garbage and sometimes sewage was dumped. Frequently both methods of construction were followed at the same time, and the result from a sanitary point of view was alarming.

Two of Britain's great cities illustrate what was taking place in the industrial centers from the end of the eighteenth century down toward the middle of the nineteenth. Thus, for instance, does a British royal commissioner describe the slums of Glasgow in 1839: "The wynds of Glasgow contain a fluctuating population of fifteen

[1] J. L. Hammond and B. Hammond, op. cit., p. 19.

to thirty thousand human beings. This quarter consists wholly of narrow alleys and square courts, in the middle of every one of which there lies a dung heap. . . . In some of the sleeping places . . . we found a complete layer of human beings stretched upon the floor, often fifteen to twenty, some clad, others naked, men and women indiscriminately. Their bed was a litter of moldy straw mixed with rags."

In Manchester the situation was similar. Nassau Senior, a prominent contemporary economist, writes thus about a working-class district in that city: "A carpenter and builder unite to buy a series of building sites (i. e. they lease them for a number of years) and cover them with so-called houses. In one place we found a whole street following the course of a ditch, because in this way deeper cellars could be secured without the cost of digging,—cellars not for storing wares or rubbish, but for dwellings for human beings. *Not one house of this street escaped the cholera.* In general the streets of these suburbs are unpaved, with a dung heap or ditch in the middle; the houses are built back to back, without ventilation or drainage, and the families are limited to a corner of a cellar or garret." Statistics taken from Manchester at approximately this time are illuminating. According to Dr. Kay, who wrote in 1837, out of 6951 houses 6565 needed whitewashing within, 1435 were damp, and 2221 were without even privies. "Of the 687 streets inspected, 248 were unpaved, 53 but partly paved, 112 ill-ventilated, 352 contained standing pools, heaps of débris, refuse, etc."

It is small wonder that men did not flock willingly to the factory towns and wanted nothing more than to continue the old life undisturbed. That was out of the question, of course; for the "domestic" workers, already deprived of their cows and their fuel by the enclosure movement at just this period, could not compete with the new machinery. One man, or even one child, operating a factory machine produced more than several men using the old methods. Textile prices were so reduced by the new large-scale production that the handworkers had their choice—unless they preferred to sink to the level of farm laborers or migrate overseas—of becoming factory hands or else of slowly starving to death upon the reduced income from their spinning and weaving. Exile from familiar surroundings was hard enough in a factory town; but besides that they were only part of the landless proletariat, completely at the mercy of the fluctuations in the demand for labor, with no garden plot, cow, or geese to serve as reserves in times of depression. The medieval serf was pitied because he was tied to the land; the factory worker was to be pitied because he had no land at all. No longer master of his time, he was subject, with his wife and children, to appallingly long hours under severe discipline; and, when his work was done, the filthy slums in which he lived were in sad contrast to the former wholesome village. From a robust, generally contented, though often slow-witted being, many English workers were transformed into sickly, stunted, and disgruntled members of society, potentially dangerous because they had a grievance.

Hard enough as such a life was when there was work to do, it became desperate when the mills shut down in times of depression, which happened frequently and with a certain degree of regularity in the fluctuations of world business. Today such periods of unemployment have become a major problem in the industrialized nations of the world,—a problem that seems to defy solution despite panaceas advanced by theorists. Some blame this unemployment on the continual displacement of workers by labor-saving machinery; others, attribute it to the nature of modern capitalistic society; still others point to the chaos resulting from wartime dislocation of business. Whatever its causes, and they are many and complex, the effect upon the worker and his family is tragic; for it takes away all sense of security.

Such was the growth of industrial England. Yet one must not paint too dark a picture; there were at least some houses built wherein comfort, if not always taste, was to be found. Some men, it must be remembered, became well-to-do if not wealthy; and if luck played a hand in their success, energy and intelligence played more. However, the fact remains that the price paid was heavy.

How did Englishmen react toward these astonishing changes in their economic life,—this physical dislocation of huge numbers of men from southern and eastern England to the north and west; this change from countryside to city, from plow to loom; new wealth for some, new poverty for others?

If we consider first the poorer folk, the depressed classes, it is evident that those who stayed in the country were far more resigned to their fate than their brothers who migrated to the cities. The old economic order very evidently had changed in the village; but this did not mean that the old moral order had disappeared. The squire was still the squire, a justice of the peace; and the aroma of authority still clung round him. The church was still the church; and where, as occasionally happened, the villagers flocked to the ministrations of some itinerant Methodist preacher, they still listened to sermons which stressed obedience to the powers that be. Proposals actually made in Parliament for a minimum wage never had a chance of enactment, but the Poor Law (see page 302) did intervene to some extent to prevent actual death from starvation. With this the dwindling minority who stayed on the farms had to be content.

This was not true of all, for some took to poaching. By an old law of Charles II, persons who were permitted to shoot game must be either freeholders or large leaseholders. This law was held in great favor by those whom the new wealth had enriched. To shoot and to hunt were the perquisites of a gentleman, and there was now more interest in these sports than ever before. There was also more game, of a feathered variety, particularly pheasants, and more gamekeepers. The more daring and perhaps the more unscrupulous among the poor considered the gamekeepers their special enemy, and the game their best chance at a livelihood. "How do you live on half a crown a week?" a countryman was asked. "I don't live on it," came the answer; "I poach."

During the reign of George III poaching increased rapidly. Whipping, imprisonment, and even service in the army and navy were favorite punishments. As for the landlords, they hired and armed gamekeepers, with whom the poachers came frequently into conflict. The landlords (some of them) went farther: "they strewed their woods with spring guns, that dealt death without warning, death without the excitement of battle, death that could catch the nimblest as he slipped and scrambled through the hiding bracken." Even this did not stop poaching; but the spring guns were finally made illegal by Parliament.

Aside, however, from poaching and occasional rick and barn burning, there was general submission on the part of the rural poor. A feeble rebellion flared up in 1830, it is true, as the result of improved threshing machines; but it was quickly suppressed, and the agitators were sent to the penal colonies in Australia. The atmosphere of the village was not conducive to revolt.

Not so the atmosphere of the town. Here the living symbols of traditional authority were lacking,—the squire, the clergyman, perhaps the old grandfather in the chimney corner. In place of them, it is true, were superintendents, overseers, factory owners; but these men carried no traditional, inherited authority. In nearly every instance they had risen from the ranks and were not regarded with awe by those beneath them. Furthermore, in the cities one did not meet simply the men of one's own village. Workers from all over England and Ireland were there thrown together pell-mell. There was a chance here for the agitator to make himself heard. Some of these workers could read, and the pamphlets of Thomas Paine and other radicals were in circulation.

Let us take, for instance, the cotton workers. Arkwright, often called England's first capitalist, was very unpopular with them; and when he set up his first mills in Lancashire, at the time of the American Revolution, "a most riotous and outrageous mob assembled in the Neighborhood, armed in a warlike Manner, and after breaking down the Doors of the Buildings they entered the Rooms, destroying most of the Machinery, and afterwards set fire to and consumed the whole of the Buildings and every Thing contained therein." The mills nevertheless continued to increase in number, and the steam engine supplanted water power. In the year of the French Revolution, 1789, the first Watt engine was started in Manchester. From that time on, for several decades, in that bleak northern city there was intermittently dull misery and bitter hate, which found expression in numerous strikes. The government in alarm introduced soldiers and spoke of French influence. The weavers and spinners alike knew little of France and cared less. They were hungry, ill-fed, ill-clad, and ill-housed, and they wanted higher wages. When they were not striking, or breaking up machinery, they were either drawing up petitions to Parliament for a minimum wage or else attempting to organize themselves into unions, an action forbidden, as we shall see, by the Combination Acts of 1799 and 1800.

With the woolen and worsted workers the situation was somewhat different. In Yorkshire, to which they migrated, there was never quite so decided a concentration either of population or of capital as at Manchester, with its cotton industry. The principal animosity of the workers in Yorkshire was directed against the "gig mill," a machine for raising the nap in cloth. "By hand work it took a man eighty-eight hours to raise the nap on a given piece of cloth: by a gig mill, worked by a man and a boy, the same process was done in twelve hours." Some employers did not dare use the machine, so violent was the feeling against it. Slowly, however, during the first two decades of the nineteenth century it made its way as did the power loom. Nevertheless, so slow was the triumph of power machinery in Bradford that as late as 1836 there were still some fourteen thousand worsted weavers competing against the steam engine.

The same general features characterized the efforts of the Spitalfields silk weavers, workers in the lace trade, and the "stockingers" —namely, strikes, lockouts, arson, troops. In the midst of the Napoleonic Wars riots started in the stocking trade, where unemployment, combined with the high cost of living, led to the destruction of the "frames," as machinery for making stockings was called. Proclamations signed "Ned Ludd, Sherwood Forest" urged this act;

# The New Wealth

and since the frames were widely scattered in small houses, it was difficult to prevent their wreckage. Even when the culprits were caught, so great was local sympathy for them that the government found it necessary from time to time to send soldiers to guard the courthouses where they were tried. The "Luddites," as these bolder and more desperate workers were called, were suppressed in the Mid-land counties, but shortly appeared in Lancashire, burning mills and smashing machinery. The government was quick to act: there were eight death sentences, and Lancashire became quiet. As it did so the same Luddite frenzy broke forth in Yorkshire. Again it was stamped out thoroughly, some fourteen men being hanged for murder, and others transported. Little more was heard of the Luddites. In dealing with them the authorities seem to have acted with decent, albeit harsh, respect for legal rights. They did, it is true, employ spies, whose activities were not above reproach. But England at this time, it must be remembered, was at death grips with Napoleon. It was a time of war; and if the government did secure many convictions, there were many more acquittals.

More intelligent by far than breaking machines were the efforts of the new proletariat to unite in unions, in order to force a higher rate of wages. By joining together, the workmen were able to bargain for better conditions on more equal terms with their employers. Otherwise the cards were all stacked in favor of the employers, with their capital. While the discharge of one employee who tried to get more pay or shorter hours for himself would count for nothing in the running of a factory, the strike, or refusal to work, of all the workers, for the purpose of enforcing their demands, would temporarily disorganize business. This collective bargaining was not possible for a long time, because the workers were prevented from joining in groups or unions by the famous Combination Acts, which stated explicitly that "any workman who combined with any other workman in order to get an increase in wages or a decrease in hours was liable to be brought up before any single magistrate—it might be one of the employers for whom he was working—and on conviction be sent forthwith to jail for three months." Even to attend a meeting for such a purpose, or to urge others to attend, or to help to collect money for holding such a meeting was held a criminal act.

With the repeal of these acts in 1824, the trade union was to become a powerful factor in England. By "trade union" is meant the combination of the workers in a trade, and this was the usual workers' unit in the English movement. It was to use as its most common weapon the strike, or the cessation of workers from their jobs in order to gain some end. Even the more radical "general strike," designed to stop all industry by having all unions strike at the same time, was later advocated and used by the British trade unions. Partly because of the trade unions, the proletariat was to secure more political power in a few generations than the scattered agricultural peasants had gained in centuries. By 1867 a large proportion of the factory workers would secure the vote; and by the end of the century a Labor party would gradually develop, to become more than once after the World War the largest party in the House of Commons. For a long while, however, these Combination Laws were the principal weapon by which the ruling class held the proletariat in subjection. They were rigidly enforced during the Napoleonic Wars and continued in existence twenty-five years.

One may wonder how intelligent and educated men, such as those who governed England during this period, could be so blind to the plight of the workers, to child labor, and to other factory abuses. One explanation is that the ruling class, including the newly rich, were, like everybody else, confused by the sudden impact and onrush of the Industrial Revolution and could not see clearly what was taking place. There were no historic precedents to guide men's actions in regard to the new wealth. The energetic and hard-working business-man, who was rising fast in the economic scale, had little time to reflect on the social significance of what he was doing. When he did think, he ordinarily adopted the prevalent view that the employer or capitalist was beneficial to the community, "whatever the wages he paid or the conditions he imposed. If somebody thought that work people should have a little of the daylight for their own lives, the employer had only to say that all the profits of his industry depended on his last half hour, and the kindest people saw that it was cruel to give the workmen a little leisure at the risk of their livelihood."[1] The leading economic thinkers of the day were in general agreement with such a point of view: Adam Smith, as we shall see, explained and defended the changing economic order, and Malthus emphasized the dangers of overpopulation. For the most part, however, few troubled their heads at this time with pondering over economic theories (see page 531). A second explanation was the panic created by the French Revolution and heightened by Napoleonic victories on the Continent (see page 550). A third might possibly be sheer selfishness, rationalized into devotion to law and order. For a fourth it is necessary to have in mind the religious revival, almost purely evangelical in nature, that characterized the times (see page 526). Strange as it may seem, if we may trust to evidence drawn

[1] J. L. Hammond and B. Hammond, *The Town Labourer* (1917), p. 209. By permission of Longmans, Green & Co.

# The New Wealth

from the writings of that ever-popular writer Hannah More and from the speeches of William Wilberforce, an influential member of the House of Commons, poverty was generally considered to be good for the soul. Workingmen were expected to remain patient under affliction and to look forward for better days to heaven alone. At the same time, private benevolence was considered a duty of the rich, and many of the ruling class did a great deal of humanitarian work in regard to schools, jails, and insane asylums, as well as in spending their money freely in relieving individuals as such. But even men like these failed to see any connection between religion or justice and the necessity for dragging a whole social class out of the gutter. Looking back to the Industrial Revolution, we may perhaps see more easily the significance of what occurred than those who lived in the midst of the hurly-burly. Let us remember that

> then came steam
> And then came everything else. They kicked the lock off
> Pandora's box and turned it upside down.
> And they made everything right and everything wrong:
> Machines that marched the floor with the measured precision of the planetary system,
> And towns that sprawled in muddles of beastliness:
> Had hands as tender as a lover's for yarn and hard as Cain's for the children they enslaved.
> Was there a bargain? They drove it. An ugliness? They made it.
> An obstacle? They cursed at it, and battered at it, and either solved it or botched it,
> Being neither demigods nor heroes,
> But ingenious, hard-working descendants of *homo sapiens,*
> Who had the luck to plant their seedlings in kind weather,
> Not in the frost or the storm, but when the slow ripening of time, the felicitous crossings of circumstance
> Presented unimagined opportunities,
> Which they took. And prospered. And grew tall.[1]

Simultaneously with the Industrial Revolution came the beginning of another great change which, for want of a better name, we might call the "Communication Revolution" or the "Revolution in Communications." Unlike the contemporary transformation of agriculture and industry, its benefits were not secured at the expense of the workers. Developments in transportation and communication have linked the world closer together, have broken down the old provincialism, have facilitated the exchange of commodities and ideas, and have added much to the possible pleasure of life, while

[1] *Manchester Guardian Weekly,* November 13, 1935. By permission.

they have created still further new wealth. They have helped men to explore and settle the wilderness, and to centralize business and government both at home and overseas. This "revolution," which began in the England of George III with canals and turnpikes, later developed the steamboat, railway, telegraph, cable, telephone, automobile, and airplane, and still continues with radio and television.

The changes were certainly revolutionary. Goods, men, and messages did not move as fast in 1760 as they had done in Roman times. The rate of communication on land was determined by the speed of the horse, modified by the variable condition of the roads, which in the eighteenth century were poorer than they had been in the days of Claudius and Hadrian. Every decade since 1760 has seen a greater development in communication than took place in the whole fifteen hundred years before that date. In the England of 1760 a speed of one hundred and fifty miles a day was considered fast even for couriers riding night and day with important messages. The normal rate of travel on the main roads was about forty miles a day, while freight moved at about half that speed. In France, where a start had already been made in improving roads, the rate was somewhat faster, while in America it was slower.

The condition of the roads was responsible for those relatively slow rates of communication. Travelers of the eighteenth century have left most uncomplimentary accounts of the narrow, deeply rutted, and muddy English roads, even on the main lines of communication, where they often followed the track of the splendid Roman highways (see page 9). In some places the roads had been worn ten or twelve feet below the surrounding countryside; in other districts the highways, lacking signposts, pursued an ill-defined course over the moors, so that travelers could scarcely keep on the route. Arthur Young, who traveled thousands of miles over the roads of the late eighteenth century, left vivid accounts of their wretched condition, describing one highway as so narrow that "a mouse cannot pass by any carriage." In 1760 the stagecoach, springless and uncomfortable, had been in use for about a century, and it took two weeks to travel the four hundred miles between the English and Scottish capitals. Many still traveled on horseback, and, except on the main roads, this was often a necessity. For freight, four-wheeled wagons, carrying a ton or two, were in use on the main highways. It took one of these wagons three weeks to cover the distance between London and Edinburgh. Over the poorer roads or paths the pack horse was the common means of transportation, and it took seven of these to carry a ton of coal.

Freight was moved by water whenever this was possible, although

# The New Wealth

freshets, droughts, and mud banks made river traffic unreliable, while coasting voyages were often protracted to unreasonable lengths by the contrary winds. At sea seventy-five miles a day was a fair average. Six weeks was good time for a transatlantic voyage, but head winds might extend this to ten weeks or more. In 1759 it took thirty-three days for London to hear the news of Wolfe's victory at Quebec, which was much nearer England than the other American ports. The East Indiamen required about six months for the voyage to or from Calcutta, while the expedition which first settled Australia was eight months on the way.

Even the maximum speeds attained under such general conditions were not impressive. Ordinarily the best records were made by couriers riding night and day with frequent changes of horses. The quickest time recorded under such circumstances was made by the Pony Express across the Western plains and mountains in the United States in 1861, just before telegraph wires were stretched over that route. President Lincoln's inaugural address was carried by these riders nearly two thousand miles at the average rate of two hundred and fifty-six miles a day. For an approach to such speed one must go back to Roman times. The young courier who had hastened from London to Edinburgh with the news of Elizabeth's death had averaged only one hundred and sixty miles a day. When the first shots of the American Revolution were fired at Lexington, near Boston, on the morning of Wednesday, April 19, 1775, a messenger was dispatched immediately to carry the news southward over the main post road with all possible speed. The message reached New York on Sunday noon, four days after the fighting. A fuller account was sent over the same route two days later. We have a detailed record of its transmission, giving the day and generally the hour, at nearly forty places between New Haven, Connecticut, and Georgetown, South Carolina. It left New Haven on Monday, April 24, at 9.30 A.M.; reached New York, seventy-five miles away, Tuesday at 2 P.M.; Philadelphia, ninety miles farther, Wednesday at noon; and Baltimore, a hundred miles more, on Thursday at 10 P.M. The speed slackened as the message reached the Southern colonies, with their still poorer roads, cut by broad inlets of the sea, so that it took five days to travel some two hundred and fifty miles across Virginia, and six days for a similar distance across North Carolina. This can be taken fairly to represent colonial land communication at its fastest, an average of about fifty-five miles a day for the whole three weeks' run, reaching a maximum rate of about one hundred miles a day across New Jersey. Had the winds been favorable all the way, the message would have traveled faster by water.

# A History of England and the British Empire

Now, as a result of the developments in communication, messages can be sent almost instantaneously around the entire earth, and men have traveled that distance in less than nine days. The progress of the Revolution in Communications can be summarized by recalling a dozen dates when new developments reached a fairly practicable stage. In 1761 the first bargeload of coal was shipped over Brindley's Bridgewater Canal. In 1803 Thomas Telford went to Scotland to inaugurate scientific road construction on a large scale. In 1807 Robert Fulton's *Clermont* steamed up the Hudson from New York to Albany. In 1825 George Stephenson's locomotive opened the Stockton and Darlington Railway in England. In 1844 Samuel F. B. Morse sent from Washington to Baltimore the first long-distance telegraph message. In 1866 transatlantic cable service was permanently established, after an abortive attempt eight years earlier. In 1876 Alexander Graham Bell sent to his assistant the first telephone message. In 1879 a little electric train at the Berlin Exposition foreshadowed electric power on railways and local lines. In 1887 Gottlieb Daimler operated the first gasoline-propelled automobile. In 1901 Count Marconi, in Newfoundland, heard the three dots of the Morse code *S* sent across the Atlantic from his wireless station in Cornwall. In 1903 Wilbur and Orville Wright made the first successful airplane flight at Kitty Hawk, on the Carolina coast. In 1915 the human voice was transmitted from Washington to Hawaii by wireless, paving the way for the rapid development of radio and television.

The coming of the Industrial Revolution, and particularly the necessity of moving iron and coal, called for improved methods of communication. Canals were the first answer to the problem. They had been used on the Continent, but in England the first one was not completed until 1761. This was a short one built by the Duke of Bridgewater to connect his coal mine with Manchester, ten miles away, and later it was extended to Liverpool. The inventive credit goes to James Brindley, who showed great engineering originality. Freight costs were radically reduced, and soon all the important industrial parts of England were linked with a network of canals.

Then came the building of turnpikes. The word "macadamize" has given lasting recognition to the success of Thomas Telford and John McAdam, about 1800, in giving the roads a hard surface of crushed rock. The principal reason for the poor roads of the earlier period was the old duty of each community to maintain the roads which passed through it; now turnpike companies were formed to undertake the costly new construction, and they were permitted to charge tolls to reimburse themselves. Stagecoaches could now travel twelve miles an hour, and freight could be moved much more easily than had been possible under previous conditions.

The chief value of the steamboat lay in relieving shipping from dependence upon the whims of the winds. The effects of this new regularity and dependability were most noticeable in short coasting voyages and in the harbor functions of tugs and ferries, while steamboats could also be used to ascend rivers with swift currents. Steam was not so essential upon the high seas, and it was not until 1838, more than twenty years after the *Clermont's* trip, that steamships began to supplant the swift sailing packets on the transatlantic shuttle. The old sailing square-riggers clung even longer to ordinary ocean freight-carrying, and not until the last quarter of the nineteenth century was the tramp steamer quite generally supplanting them. We shall consider later the beginnings of the railway (see page 607).

Altogether the developments in communication were to have a widespread effect. In the matter of freight the influence was particularly noticeable in the very bulky commodities, such as coal, and the very perishable ones, such as food. In the eighteenth century transportation was so slow that herrings began to smell before they had been carried many miles inland. Now, with the application of refrigeration to railways and ships, the "roast beef of old England" comes fresh from the Argentine or the plains of the United States, while mutton comes from "down under" in Australia and New Zealand. No longer does a community have to depend upon the seasonal supply of fruit and green vegetables from local gardens, and even milk, which spoils quickly, can be brought from long distances.

Business too has felt the effect of improved communications. The term "venture" was aptly applied to the sending forth of a shipment, as it was not known whether it would reach an empty or a glutted market. If one could secure advance information of important matters, even a few hours before the information became public, it might mean a fortune. Financial giants like the Rothschilds maintained an elaborate service of correspondents and couriers; but even they lacked the full and fresh business information that is to be found in any metropolitan daily today. World prices, too, have tended to become equalized. The buyer now can ascertain in a few hours the current prices of a desired commodity, even in different continents. After taking freight and other charges into account, he will normally buy in the cheapest market, thus bringing into close competition commercial centers thousands of miles apart. The financial world also became involved in the various agencies of communication. The coming of the railway meant heavy depreciation of canal and turnpike securities, and for nearly a century the locomotive held full sway on land, moving nearly everything and everybody that had to travel more than a few miles. Profits were good, and transport was an absolute necessity; consequently railroad securities became favorites with conservative as well as with speculative investors. Of late years, however, the railways have been fighting the inroads of the automobile into their former freight and passenger monopoly.

Rapid communication has also made possible the concentration of authority and responsibility, particularly in the field of political control. This is especially evident in colonial and foreign affairs. When an interchange of messages with the home government involved weeks and even months, governors, admirals, generals, and diplomats had to be endowed with wide powers to meet emergencies. The ministers at home frequently had no control in important crises and were furnished long afterward with reports of the accomplished facts. The new methods of communication transformed those in authority on distant stations from plenipotentiaries into "nothing but damned errand boys at the end of a wire." London is in closer communication today with Ottawa, Cape Town, Sydney, and Delhi than it was with Oxford or Portsmouth in 1760. There might have been no spread of British rule in India if there had been a cable to Calcutta and Madras in the formative period. Even in home governments this centralizing effect has been noticeable. It formerly took many weeks to send out writs for a new election to Parliament and to assemble the members from the distant shires; now a new Parliament has gathered at Westminster within a week of the general election. Downing Street can keep its finger at all times upon the course of events, not only all over the British Isles but all over the world as well. This centralization of control has also influenced warfare, which likewise has been affected by the possibility of concentrating armies rapidly in large numbers, of relieving threatened positions quickly, of improving the situation of the wounded, and of extending the campaigning distance from the base of supplies. At sea, steam and wireless have wrought a tremendous change in naval strategy and tactics.

By no means the least important influence of the Revolution in Communications has been the broadening of the horizon of the individual. The people of the eighteenth century "led quiet and uneventful lives, little disturbed by the lust for travel and seldom interrupted by journeys from their place of abode." The average village was practically cut off from the outside world, and news of great events trickled in slowly. Most people never in their lives traveled more than fifty miles from their birthplace, and for many persons twenty miles would be the limit. The railway did much to

# The New Wealth

increase travel; but the motor car has done infinitely more, giving man a new control over his movements while, always available, it creates and gratifies a wanderlust. Even for those who do not travel far from home, cheap and rapid postal service, together with the telephone, have helped to increase outside contacts. Provincialism has been still further broken down by the instruments of mass communication,—the newspaper, the moving picture, and finally the radio. Altogether the age of speed has resulted, as one author remarked, "in a shrunken planet and an expanded humanity." And that has been accomplished without those grim accompaniments— the grinding discipline, the dreary factory towns, the labor problems, and the squalid slums—which marked the companion movement, the Industrial Revolution.

# CHAPTER XVIII

## *Thought and Letters from Newton to Burke*

EIGHTEENTH-CENTURY Englishmen excelled in war, in economics, in thought, and in letters. By land and by sea British arms were victorious. Soldiers and sailors, merchants, colonial administrators, and, more especially, colonial mothers formed and fashioned a fine empire—only to lose the choicest part of it. A host of miners tapped the coal and iron mines of England. The steam engine, noisily if somewhat ineffectually, began its miraculous career. Textile mills appeared in many places in the north. Liverpool began to thrive on the West Indian trade. Bath, the favored watering place of the rich, took pride in its superb and dignified private dwellings, which even today command admiration; and London was changing rapidly into a well-paved and relatively well-illuminated city.

Almost simultaneously with the economic revolutions of the century there was taking place what has been called "a revolution in men's minds." It must not be forgotten that the century was intellectually famous. The printing press, the book store, and the laboratory, as well as the countinghouse and the royal navy, were high in popular esteem. Philosopher and scientist, poet, pamphleteer, and historian were, each from his respective point of view, participating in this intellectual revolution. No fanfare of trumpets announced its arrival, and no bonfires were lighted to celebrate its advent. It seeped in slowly, with just sufficient changes here and there to make it possible to subdivide the story into three chapters, each one associated with a distinguished man of letters—Alexander Pope, Dr. Samuel Johnson, and Edmund Burke. The influence of these three on the life of the time, and the way in which they reflected its ideals, is the principal theme of what follows.

To men of letters and to the social philosopher the eighteenth century will ever remain one of the choicest in English history. It was an era spacious, rational, and tolerant in spirit; interested in things of the mind, but not forgetful of the body; sufficiently static, socially, to permit cultural standards to form, and sufficiently dynamic, intellectually, to keep them alive. The century had a fair heritage in the Revolution of 1688, an event not merely of constitutional importance. The Stuart exit meant more than the death of the divine right of kings: it signified at once the end of Restoration immorality and of Puritanical bigotry. Although weary of dissipated Royalists, England did not yearn for the return of the "saints." Instead good-natured compromise was sought. Its idealized expression may be found in the music of Handel and in the English words which were written in 1740 as a libretto for his *Il Moderato*.

> Kindly teach, how blest are they
> Who nature's equal rule obey;
> Who safely steer two rocks between,
> And prudent keep the golden mean.

The era of the coffeehouse and the tavern was at hand. The cessation of political turmoil had been accompanied by prosperity, largely the result of foreign and colonial trade. London, the commercial and political center, drew like a magnet the English world of fashion, of wealth, and of culture. "Pretty fellows," as they were called, hied hither to dazzle society and themselves by the gaiety of their waistcoats and the expensiveness of their wigs; and to dine and to gamble at White's or, later, at Brooks's. Solid merchants met to exchange gossip and to hear the latest maritime news at Lloyd's. Literary folk foregathered at Will's to listen to the serious-minded Addison or to laugh with "Dick" Steele.

In its opening decades the century was far from introspective. Men did not wear their hearts upon their sleeves nor did they worry much about their souls. Literature was "urban and urbane," conversational in tone, devoted primarily to one theme, man—his foibles, prejudices, and behavior. *The Spectator*, with its "Sir Roger de Coverley Papers" and famous essays, was a successful as well as an original venture in periodical literature, selling occasionally as many as ten thousand copies of a single issue. Swift, Addison, Steele, Defoe, and Pope were in their glory. England was a cheerful place for the "Queen Anne wits." It was difficult, then as now, to make a living by the pen, but politics helped. Sinecures of one kind or another were to be had; for Whig and Tory bigwigs freely bestowed them in return for service rendered and pamphlets written. The Drury Lane Theater helped to fill the bottomless pockets of Mr. Richard Steele. There was the Church of England and its sister, the Church of Ireland, with a deanship for Jonathan Swift. The writers of the "Augustan Age," as the first three or four decades of the eighteenth century are aptly called, did not complain of an unappreciative world.

# A History of England and the British Empire

Literary men in general turned to the classics, because Greco-Roman civilization had been stable and not given to emotional vagaries. Style and diction then had been formalized, with the grooves made, the channels cut, and authority established. The eighteenth-century man liked this; for it was quiet, peaceful, and, above all, reasonable. He was, on the whole, more Roman than Greek. There was somewhat too fanciful and too light a suggestion about Greek life and thought. The eighteenth century believed that it had found certain finalities, and it preferred a model at once more permanent and more substantial, such as was offered by the Augustan Age of Rome.

If the Revolution Settlement which had brought William and Mary and then Anne to the throne had laid stress on classical values merely as the result of sheer exhaustion from the turmoil of the seventeenth century, the cultural expression of the new age would have been purely imitative and probably second-rate. This was not the case. The early eighteenth century imitated only the form, not the substance, of classicism; for it possessed distinct values of its own. Its foundations were laid in certain new ideas, the key to which may be found in the mathematics of Sir Isaac Newton and in the philosophy of John Locke. Their influence upon the thought of the entire eighteenth century is difficult to exaggerate, not simply in England but also upon the Continent and in America.

Sir Isaac Newton (1642–1727) was a modest man of science, retiring by nature, content to ponder twenty-one years over his discoveries before publishing them. He was so brilliant that he was elected to a professorship at Cambridge when only twenty-seven. In that position he became indignant at the efforts of James II to interfere with the universities, and he entered Parliament to fight on their behalf, remaining more or less in political life until his death. In 1687 appeared his major work, *Principia*, which almost instantly made him famous. A few years later he was elected president of the Royal Society and afterward knighted. His fame spread to the Continent, and the king of France offered him a pension, which he refused. Upon his death he was buried in Westminster Abbey, as one of England's greatest men.

The *Principia* explained the Newtonian law of gravitation, which states that "the forces which keep the planets in their orbits must be reciprocally as the squares of their distance from the centers upon which they revolve." From this mathematical formula it followed as the night the day that the sun, moon, stars, earth, planets, and comets —indeed, the universe itself—are controlled, directed, and kept in place by a universal law of gravitation certain, unchanging, enduring, inflexible. Far beyond the realms of astronomy were the implications of this new theory. The Newtonian laws made it possible to weigh and to estimate the size of the celestial bodies, scientific facts of importance; but they also led man to revolutionize his social and religious ideas. The law of gravitation did not abolish the Almighty, but seemingly it did make him decidedly less personal, a kind of glorified watchmaker who wound up the universe and then retired to the background. It led also to a firm and implicit belief in natural law, applicable to all life as well as to astronomy. Nature meant natural law. The birds of the air, the beasts of the field, and even man lived in accordance with it; and should man try to revolt therefrom, so much the worse for him. A scientific sanction was thus given to the compromises of Greco-Roman civilization. Throughout all the eighteenth century and down to the fall of Napoleon, this Newtonian concept met with favor. By the time of the French Revolution fifty books had already been written in English alone on the significance of the *Principia*, to say nothing of many more in other languages.

Complementing the work of Newton on the political side was that of John Locke (1632–1704), who became so influential that English and American statesmen both drew heavily on his ideas for political and constitutional arguments. Locke came of Puritan ancestry. He was a student at Christ Church, Oxford, during the Commonwealth; but so disgusted did he become over the theological wranglings of Presbyterians with the more radical Independents (afterward known as Congregationalists) that he chose to enter the Anglican Church. Even in that, however, he was an extreme latitudinarian, or tolerant liberal, in his views, much more interested in chemistry and in meteorology than in dogma. Locke practiced medicine for a while, but showed so much interest in politics that he found it expedient during the reign of Charles II to live in France. He returned to Oxford, incurred the displeasure of James II, went into exile in Holland, and came back with William and Mary. Although always an eager writer, he published nothing before he was fifty-four years old, and then only minor articles. His famous essays on *Toleration*, on *Human Understanding*, and on *Government* did not appear until the final decade of the seventeenth century. The last recorded words of John Locke represent the eighteenth century at its best. "I die," he said, "in perfect charity with all men and in sincere communion with the whole church of Christ by whatever names we followers call ourselves."

Key words to an understanding of Locke are these: "probability," "reasonable," "compromise." And a key sentence in his essay on

*Civil Government* runs thus: "Man . . . hath by nature a power to preserve his property—that is his life, liberty and estate—against the injuries and attempts of other men." In other words, there must be government; but it must not be confiscatory, tyrannical, or illiberal. Locke argued further that such a government may best be secured by a system of checks and balances. Liberty can be had only by limiting the power of both king and legislature. Kings, lords, commons, and likewise a judicial system calling for independent judges and for juries, should balance off against each other in a way reminiscent of Newtonian natural law. In fact, Locke's whole idea of government was Newtonian. If a balance were found between governmental functions, a reasonable civic society would flourish. In his opinion, if the balance were destroyed, disaster would result. Revolution might also occur. "Whenever law ends," he wrote, "tyranny begins, if the law be transgressed, to another's harm; and whosoever in authority exceeds the power given him by the law, and makes use of the force he has under his command, to compass that upon the subject which the law allows not, ceases in that to be a magistrate, and acting without authority may be opposed, as any other man who by force invades the right of another." Here surely was a justification of revolutions in general, but just how or when they were to be brought about in particular, Locke does not tell us. He was more intent upon justifying the Revolution Settlement of 1688 than in proposing new ones. In fact, he was a good Whig; but, as time passed, both Whigs and Tories accepted his main conclusions.

The major currents of early-eighteenth-century thought flow from these scientific and philosophic ideas and find their best reflection in literature in the works of Alexander Pope and of Joseph Addison. The premier poet of the period was "Mr. Pope of Twickenham" (1688–1744), a writer vastly popular in his own day, much derided in the nineteenth century, and now returning once more to his own.

Pope, a Roman Catholic, without political privilege, a malformed cripple unduly sensitive to ridicule, was so precocious and so brilliant that he was virtually subsidized as a young man to translate Homer. By this literary venture he made £8000, a fabulous achievement in those days of pirated copyrights, when the purchasing value of the pound was far greater than in the twentieth century. Augmented by an inheritance from his father by no means inconsiderable, it made Pope financially independent, freed from the necessity of selling his pen for political purposes. Pope knew almost everyone worth knowing. His country place at Twickenham on the Thames, near London, was for years the Mecca of the learned. Here in his famous grotto he entertained the élite, gossiped freely and sometimes venomously (for he was a good hater), and wrote and rewrote and polished and repolished his poems in his own inimitable manner.

He was and is an authority on the technique of poetry and poetical forms; but not on that account does the historian primarily value him. The reason why he is justly renowned as a historic figure is that his writings sum up an epoch. He is as truly representative of the early eighteenth century as is Shakespeare of Elizabethan England or Tennyson of Victoria's reign. And that is equivalent in part to saying that the poetry of Pope popularized the ideas of Newton and of Locke.

One of the clearest landmarks in the intellectual history of Britain is the year 1733–1734, the date of the publication of Pope's *Essay on Man*, a long poem written in the form of the heroic couplet and divided logically into four epistles, each dealing with certain philosophic questions which long have perplexed humanity. The first epistle treats of man's relation to the universe and implies that it is foolish to fuss too much about trying to discover God's purposes.

> Heaven from all creatures hides the book of fate!

It is just as well that this is so. "Lo, the poor Indian!" He is happy living in accordance with Nature's laws. Every animal is provided for by Providence (the eighteenth century liked the word "Providence"; it was much less personal than God). Strength is given to bulls, fur to bears, mind to man.

> Each beast, each insect, happy in its own:
> Is Heaven unkind to man, and man alone?

It is unreasonable to presume that such should be the case. The next epistle takes up man's knowledge of himself.

> Know then thyself, presume not God to scan;
> The proper study of mankind is man.

That study should be undertaken with due respect for Newtonian principles of balance, weight and counterweight, attraction and counterattraction. Thus, for instance:

> Love, Hope, and Joy, fair pleasure's smiling train,
> Hate, Fear, and Grief, the family of pain,
> These mixed with art, and to due bounds confined,
> Make and maintain the balance of the mind.

Ease and toil, humility and pride, avarice and prudence, sloth and philosophy—all are in evidence. But this is not contradictory to beneficent natural law. It is desirable that the hero should have pride, that the merchant should toil; so does Nature provide by a kind of law of social gravitation. Rightly understood, this means that all may be happy.

> The learned is happy, nature to explore,
> The fool is happy that he knows no more;
> The rich is happy in the plenty given,
> The poor contents him with the care of Heaven.

Then follow the two remaining epistles, one on man's relation to society, the other on happiness. Pope, like most eighteenth-century men, is very much concerned about happiness. "WHATEVER IS, IS RIGHT" he puts in large type. If you would be happy, do not question but accept. There are rich people, there are poor people; some are of elevated station, some of low; but all have an equal right to happiness, and may obtain it only by a recognition of the fact that

> Reason's whole pleasure, all the joys of sense,
> Lie in three words, health, peace, and competence.

Now it was evident that health, peace, and competence, to say nothing of reason, had but remote resemblance to the three virtues of the Catholic Church and of Christianity, namely, faith, hope, and charity. Furthermore, an abstract first cause, called by courtesy "God," who never interfered with the cold, passionless laws of Nature, did not resemble to any striking degree the God of historic Christianity. Pope was moralizing throughout in this poem, and some there were who intimated that the morality taught was dubious and that the author did not believe in God.

Whereupon, to answer this charge, Pope wrote a hymn. Three stanzas of it show his point of view and that of his generation.

> Father of all! in every age,
> In every clime adored,
> By saint, by savage, and by sage,
> Jehovah, Jove, or Lord!

This opening stanza would seem to indicate that the Roman, the Hebrew, and the Christian were on an equal footing.

> This day, be bread and peace my lot:
> All else beneath the sun
> Thou know'st if best bestowed or not,
> And let Thy will be done.

[ 518 ]

# Thought and Letters from Newton to Burke

Here we find a spiritual truth not confined to Christianity. It might imply the fatalism of the "kismet" of the Moslem or of the "karma" of the Hindu; and the last stanza indicates an impersonal deity, some distance from both the Mass of the Roman Catholic and the indwelling spirit of the Quaker.

> To Thee, whose temple is all space,
> Whose altar earth, sea, skies,
> One chorus let all being raise,
> All nature's incense rise!

A new kind of Christianity seemingly was coming in with the eighteenth century.

This "civilized and sophisticated society," where reason reigned, was noted for its prose as well as for its poetry. The prose was characterized by wit, kindliness, taste, and judgment rather than by warmth and enthusiasm; comedy was preferred to tragedy, laughter to seriousness, and smiles to laughter. Two of its best-known representatives were Joseph Addison (1672-1719) and Richard Steele (1672-1729). These two friends collaborated closely in bringing out first *The Tatler* and then *The Spectator*, the simple and unpretentious forerunners of the modern magazine. Addison was the more serious of the two, and his style was somewhat more polished; Steele was the more lovable, the more irresponsible, and his style was lighter. Both were, however, fundamentally alike in their approach to life, determined like Pope to make the best of what was, content with their lot and with the world.

Together they invented a group of imaginary characters headed by the squire Sir Roger de Coverley, and first one and then the other of the two authors discoursed upon their fictitious heroes. Sir Roger, according to Steele, was in "his fifty-sixth year, cheerful, gay and hearty, keeping a good house both in town and country." One of his friends is Sir Andrew Freeport, a merchant, whose "notions of trade are free and generous." Side by side with "Sir Andrew in the club-room sits Captain Sentry, a gentleman of great courage, good understanding, but invincible modesty." Also there is "the gallant Will Honeycomb, a gentleman who according to his years should be in the decline of his life, but having ever been very careful of his person, and always having had a very easy fortune, time had made but little impression, either by wrinkles on his forehead or traces in his brain." The sayings of these mythical gentlemen and of their numerous friends fill no inconsiderable part of *The Spectator*. Addison takes up the tale of Honeycomb and satirizes him in very gentle fashion, saying that he himself "is more at ease in Sir Roger's family." He rings the changes on that "good old knight," tells of his kindly behavior to his servants and of "the affection and good will which are paid him by every one who lives in the neighborhood." Steele thereupon exalts Sir Andrew Freeport, his business acumen and rigid honesty, possibly with his tongue slightly in his cheek, for Steele was no prudent soul. Steele finally leads Sir Roger into paths which seem not altogether respectable to the more prudish Addison, and the latter ends the life of his hero lest he die with blemished character. *The Spectator* was compounded of such trivial sketches, interspersed with essays on taste, on the theater, on poetry, on the passing show, now serious, now tragicomic, but never boisterous, extreme, passionate, or partisan. Politics were excluded, and in place of controversy there was kindly comment and subdued humor.

Different in approach was Jonathan Swift (1667–1745), a man whose life was a tragedy and whose writings reflect it. To Thackeray, Swift was a species of ogre; but to the more sensitive critics of our own day "his misanthropy is a kind of perverted philanthropy." Swift was an ambitious man of talent, a Tory pamphleteer whose career was checked by a long period of Whig ascendancy, whose love was thwarted by adverse circumstances, and whose health grew steadily worse and worse. Much of his life was spent in virtual exile in Dublin, where he suffered intensely from ill-health and deafness.

*Gulliver's Travels*, Swift's best-known book, is the most celebrated satire in the English language. In certain respects it is not at all characteristic of its age,—for instance, in its savage invective and in its belittlement of man, "the most pernicious race of little odious vermin that nature ever suffered to crawl upon this earth." On the other hand, Gulliver has distinctively eighteenth-century earmarks. It is in no way sentimental, and is so realistic as to describe imaginary minutiae with the utmost plausibility. It is also a distinctly non-theological, impersonal work of art, wherein life is faced as it is, without hope and without remedy, its hero being noted for his literal truthfulness and common sense.

By the fourth decade of the century the Augustan Age of English literature was well-nigh over. A change was coming over English thought and letters. Philosophers and thinkers began to question the pleasant, easygoing compromise by which Pope and his friends had simply accepted the universe without thinking very much about it. Literary men began to break away from the correct but formalized modes of expression and to feel the need of more emotional warmth. The Augustan Age had specialized, perhaps overspecialized, in wit;

and to appreciate wit one must be highly cultured. The rapidly rising middle class, which the new wealth was bringing to the fore, was not; but many members of it had intellectual interests and were not content with simply making money. They too, as well as the aristocracy, wanted to read books and to talk about them. They were at one and the same time interested in the why and wherefore of life and in reading which would not unduly tax their intellectual capacity but which might satisfy their desire to escape the monotony of everyday existence.

In consequence a shift of emphasis may now be noted, and the intellectual and literary history of the century may be considered as entering a second stage. The first, occupied by the Augustans, had, as we have seen, certain distinctive ideals. These were now challenged both by the advocates of the cult of sensibility, who were the forerunners of English romanticism, and by the Methodists and evangelical leaders in the Church of England, who advocated a more emotional type of religion. This new chapter, or stage, in the intellectual life of the eighteenth century was to run approximately from 1740 to 1789, the date of the outbreak of the French Revolution. It was a period in which Augustan ideals were largely on the defensive but were defended so well and so stanchly by Dr. Samuel Johnson as to weather the attack in large measure. Dr. Johnson, as we shall see, was a fighter who believed that a good offensive was the best defense. He held the fortress of the accepted order, and it never surrendered. Nevertheless, breaches were made in the ramparts, and to them we shall turn our attention.

The first major challenge to the Augustan conception of life, that of the sentimentalist writer with his cult of sensibility, may best be studied in the writings of the Reverend Laurence Sterne (1713-1768). He was born in Ireland, the son of a poor army officer who had influential relations. Owing to their help and to his natural wit, Sterne was graduated at Cambridge, took holy orders, and received a living near York, as well as a lucrative connection with York Cathedral. He was an unusual clergyman, even for the easygoing Church of England. Much of his early manhood was spent at "Crazy Castle," where a club, the "Demoniacs," held sway and where

> Some fell to fiddling, some to fluting,
> Some to shooting, some to fishing,
> Others to pishing and disputing.

In 1759 Sterne published at York *Tristram Shandy*, which greatly scandalized the cathedral city. Soon afterward the book appeared in London, where it instantly made Sterne famous. He became an international figure; France welcomed him with open arms, and Italy likewise. In 1768, three weeks before his death, was published his *Sentimental Journey*, a book even more widely read.

This clergyman was far from pious. At York Cathedral he preached once on the text "It is better to go to the house of mourning than to the house of feasting." His sermon began thus: "That I deny. . . . For a crackbrained order of Carthusian monks, I grant, but not for a man of the world." Sterne was indeed a man of the world, but in a way different from the "Queen Anne wits," who believed in quiet self-restraint. There was nothing controlled about the emotions of Sterne; he reveled in them. Man was by nature warmhearted, good, and benevolent; so his natural feelings should have free play. The heart was what mattered, not the head. The traveler in the *Sentimental Journey*, who was Sterne himself, delighted in his feelings, glowed with sympathy toward old peasants, old donkeys, and even toward old traveling carriages because of the charming experiences which must have taken place within them. He felt so much compassion for a starling in a cage that he could not bear to release the bird, because by so doing he would cease to see the object of his sympathy. As for love and ladies, there could not be too much of the one or too many of the other. A man of sensibility would expect and enjoy many love affairs. If they ended in tears, so much the better; for the mere falling of tears was evidence of warm feeling. Sterne shed them often, and he was equally moved when he saw other people shed them. But Sterne also laughed. As Mr. Yorick, the king's jester, he delighted in telling stories, frequently indecorous ones. In the *Sentimental Journey* and in *The Life and Opinions of Tristram Shandy, Gent.* there are many such stories, which are humorous not so much because of their suggestiveness as because of their whimsicalities, or "shandyisms," as they came to be called.

*Tristram Shandy*, although seemingly without plan or plot, did have a purpose: to reveal character by dialogue, and incidentally to poke fun at all prigs and pretentious persons. Mr. and Mrs. Shandy, Uncle Toby, Corporal Trim, and Dr. Slop converse wittily on all kinds of topics from noses and baptismal names to varieties of cursing. This book in which they do so is unique in literary history.

Contemporaneous with the cult of sensibility, and a part of it, was the cult of the natural man. Writers in the mid-eighteenth century were accustomed fancifully to idealize the residents of the South Sea Islands, of Lapland, and even of Chile as noble savages. They knew nothing of those distant regions, but in their imagination they peopled them with excellent creatures, bold, simple, free. A few Eskimos brought to London were widely acclaimed as representatives of these uncontaminated folk, and Omai, a Polynesian, became for a time the hero of London drawing-rooms. Of Omai's native Tahiti an anonymous writer wrote:

> Beneath their shades the gentle tribes repose;
> Each bending branch their frugal feast bestows.
> For them the cocoa yields its milky flood
> To slake their thirst, and feed their temperate blood.

A wonderful land, indeed, where bread grew on trees, where no one bothered about property, or clothes, or anything else. The natural man was found also nearer home. In Wales and in the Scottish Highlands his descendants might be discerned, living simple and virtuous lives. True, they were expected to be different from the average man—to delight in bards rather than in neoclassic poets, and to take pleasure in gloomy shades and wild, desolate forests; but none the less they led lives of chivalrous honor. Nearer home yet came this idealization of simplicity. The humble crofter, the peasant, the village laborer, were crowned ultimately with Nature's olive wreath; and the farm rather than the city was the stage set for these new heroes.

These notions, stressed by the forerunners of the Romantic school of English writers (see pages 604–606), found their reflection principally in the poetry of the eighteenth century. They came to light in Gray's "Elegy in a Country Churchyard," which intimates democratically that there may lie, unknown to fame, "mute inglorious Miltons." These same ideas found expression in the less popular Collins, Gray's friend and contemporary, whose "Ode to Evening" is held by some competent critics to be quite as good as the popular "Elegy," if not better; and more particularly they were represented in the prose of Macpherson and verse of William Cowper.

James Macpherson (1736–1796) was the perpetrator of perhaps the biggest fraud in the history of English letters. In *Ossian* he pretended to have unearthed a Scottish saga of the third century. The forgery was accepted at its face value by almost everyone. The work was heralded as "exquisite," "in native majesty of passion as equal to Homer or Vergil." On the basis of a few local songs Macpherson had fabricated an epic which did not exist. The original, he said, was in Gaelic, and he had translated it. For a time no one thought to demand the original, until the poet Gray detected traces of his own poetry in the epic. Interest in the original was whetted. To satisfy this, Macpherson translated his English "translation" into Gaelic and did it so clumsily that his forgery was discovered.

This double cult of sensibility and of the natural man was easier to describe than to explain. How did it happen that in the middle of the century so much interest was displayed in these ideas? It was no answer to say that the English derived them from the contemporary French philosopher Rousseau; for, in the first place, where did Rousseau get them? Secondly, it was evident that they blossomed forth in English literature before Rousseau wrote. The best explanation that can be given would probably be this: Newtonian philosophy led to the exaltation of reason, and it is difficult for man to live by reason alone. Furthermore, reason led to further reasoning, particularly concerning God. "Is he willing to prevent evil but not able? Then he is impotent. Is he able, but not willing? Then he is malevolent. Is he both able and willing? Whence then is evil?" These questions were asked by David Hume, contemporary philosopher and historian. To be sure, the *Dialogues* from which this is quoted were safely locked up by the author; but thoughts like these were widely current and headed straight toward skepticism. The eighteenth century, not wishing to follow reason to that logical end, invented something new: the reason of the heart, delight in emotional reaction. For the time being, this cult of the heart satisfied and stifled lurking doubts. As long as it continued, the ultimate logical consequences of Newtonian reasoning and skepticism might be avoided. Presumably these sentimental emotions in their purest form would be felt by simple people. Hence the return to nature. If we add to this argument the inborn pleasure which humanity feels in contemplating that which is contrary to its common experience, the cult of nature is explained further. Eighteenth-century England, relatively speaking, was a wealthy and civilized society, and therefore liked its opposite. In consequence the new, the bizarre, and the strange made an added appeal.

Another reaction to Newtonian philosophy was Methodism. For better or for worse it seemed inevitable to many that there were only two alternatives, the skepticism of Hume and a return to historic Christianity. A large number chose the old trail rather than the new. This, more than any other reason, explains the contemporary evangelical movement within the Church of England, which stressed personal salvation, and likewise the Methodist revival.

The Church of England in the middle of the eighteenth century had become, more or less, an intellectual backwater, losing steadily in influence and power. Its clergy, poisoned by the contemporary deism (belief in an inactive and remote deity), did not pay much attention to their duties. Enthusiasm was frowned upon, and, while outward respect was shown, there was little inner zeal. Thus lay

# Thought and Letters from Newton to Burke

the situation until the arrival of John Wesley (1703–1791), the founder of English Methodism.

John Wesley and his brother Charles, while at Oxford, sought to re-establish the simplicity of life and the spiritual fervor of the Christian Church in its first century. They organized a little group of about twenty-five, who became known as "Methodists," a term of obscure origin. For some time their activity was confined to members of the Church of England, in which John became an ordained clergyman. So orthodox was he at first that on a missionary tour in the American colonies he refused Communion to those not blessed by episcopal hands.

In 1738, on a May evening "about a quarter before nine," John Wesley wrote, "I felt my heart strongly warmed. I felt I did trust in Christ and Christ alone for salvation." This experience was the real commencement of Methodism. Wesley began to preach with such warmth and abandon that his own church would have none of him. He then went forth like an apostle all over England and many times to Ireland, traveling five thousand miles a year and preaching fifteen sermons weekly. As his followers grew in number he assumed one function of a bishop in appointing ministers in his own right. His brother wrote hymns by the dozen.

The peculiar character of this religious movement may best be studied by two or three extracts from Wesley's journals. For instance, let us take the first part of his entry for "Sun. 30th May, 1742."

"At seven I walked down to Sandgate, the poorest and most contemptible part of the town, and, standing at the end of the street with John Taylor, began to sing the hundredth psalm. Three or four people came out to see, who soon increased to three or four hundred. I suppose there might be twelve to fifteen hundred before I had done preaching; to whom I applied these solemn words: 'He was wounded for our transgressions, He was bruised for our iniquities; the chastisement of our peace was upon Him; and by His stripes we are healed.' Observing the people, when I had done, to stand gaping and staring upon me with the most profound astonishment, I told them, 'If you desire to know who I am, I am John Wesley. At five in the evening, with God's help, I design to preach here again.'"

Wesley did not preach thus without violent opposition, particularly from mobs. His life was threatened again and again. Frequently he was brought before magistrates, charged with making a disturbance; but inasmuch as the latter consisted simply in getting people to rise in the early morning, to sing hymns, and to convert others, the magistrates were forced to release the prisoner. Wesley thrived on excitement. "'No, no, knock his brains out; down with him, kill him at once.' Others said, 'Nay, but we will hear him first.' I began asking, 'What evil have I done? Which of you have I wronged in word or deed?' and continued speaking for above a quarter of an hour, till my voice suddenly failed. Then the floods began to lift up their voice again, many crying out, 'Bring him away! Bring him away.'"

Even so did Methodism originate, and the author of it continued in the active service of his new church until his eighty-eighth year. His followers, for the most part, were of lowly rank; but the movement which he started was instantly felt in the Church of England, where, in the middle of the century, evangelicalism, or emotional conversion, became strong. It included within its ranks such literary celebrities as Cowper and Hannah More.

As literary England turned first toward one of these paths and then toward another—toward sentimentalism, toward the nature cult, toward religion, and occasionally toward agnosticism (refusal to affirm or deny the existence of God)—one man of letters, Samuel Johnson (1709–1784) never veered an inch from the old loyalties. The evangelicals might turn to the right, the skeptics to the left, and the sentimentalists to an unmarked path; but Johnson kept to the old road. Possibly on that account, and because of his sturdy loyalty, Dr. Johnson has become to many the eighteenth century incarnate.

The son of a provincial bookseller, he was used to poverty from youth. His rise to fame was slow but steady; and after his dictionary was completed, in 1755, he became the foremost star in the English literary firmament. He was very much of a fixed star, a sturdy fighter for the old cause of common sense, neoclassical literary standards, a Christianity not too fervent, not too cold, suspicious of all "isms" and all cults, devoted to old England as it had been.

The famous Doctor scarcely can be considered in the first rank as a writer. His novel, *Rasselas*, was better philosophy than fiction; his articles in *The Rambler* and *The Idler* do not match the better essays of Addison and Swift; his life of the poet Savage is a good biography of a second-rate poet, and not noteworthy. As a dictionary-maker Johnson was an eminent figure, but it is not for that he is remembered. His conversations, as recorded by his faithful friend and devotee James Boswell, the "perfect biographer," have made an everlasting niche for him in the annals of history. In Boswell's *Life of Johnson* the character of this great man stands out in clear and complete relief. The hero, as his well-known letter on patrons to Lord Chesterfield bears witness, is no toady; on the other hand, he is not a rebel, for he received and gratefully accepted a pension from his sovereign, King George III. He is a sincere and honest, gruff, and hearty fighter in defense of the old order and of the old ways of thinking. Dr. Johnson had no use for those who spoke in sentimental vein of distant lands. England was good enough for him. He hated America and Americans, and he disliked Scotland almost as heartily. "Let me tell you," he says to Boswell, "the noblest prospect which a Scotchman ever sees is the high road that leads him to England." Johnson also treats with disdain the idea that crude living in the wilds made for happiness. "Do not allow yourself, Sir," he says to Boswell, "to be imposed upon by such absurdity. It is sad stuff; it is brutish. If a bull could speak he might as well exclaim, 'Here am I with this cow and this grass; what being can enjoy greater felicity?'" Johnson did not like sentimental talk. "Sir," he repeats, "it is an affectation to pretend to feel the distress of others as much as they do themselves." Known for his own kind heart, he always went out of his way to conceal its existence. "They pay you by feeling," he once remarked, to Boswell, of persons who gushed with sympathy.

On matters of religion and politics the opinions of Dr. Johnson were equally frank. He was a stanch upholder of the Church of England and genuinely devout, as a number of his written prayers amply attest. He disliked Voltaire, the cynical and bitingly sarcastic contemporary French philosopher, and his fellow agnostics; he disliked even more Rousseau, with his ideas of a "social contract" between the ruler and the "sovereign people," and the other sentimentalists. Quakers and women preachers annoyed the Doctor greatly. "Sir," he observed, "a woman preaching is like a dog walking on his hinder legs. It it not done well; but you are surprised to find it done at all." The Methodists also annoyed him with their belief in the inward light, "a principle utterly incompatible with social or civil security." Incited by Boswell, Oliver Goldsmith, and other friends, Dr. Johnson continued to lay down the law in this fashion. He knew very little about economics, politics, or government, but he spoke as freely on such topics as he did on literature. No man could be more positive in regard to *Ossian*. "Sir, a man might write such stuff forever if he would but abandon his mind to it." On the other hand, he was just as positive in regard to the desirability of public executions, which were not abolished until a century later. "The old method," he said, "was most satisfactory to all parties: the public was gratified by the procession; the criminal was supported by it."

He was an ardent Tory and abominated Whigs. "Sir," he declared, "I perceive you are a vile Whig." The Whigs, in reality, were aristocratic enough; but from Johnson's point of view they were jealous of the power of the crown and on that account to be condemned. This did not mean that he advocated an absolute king. On the contrary, all that he had in mind was a perfect balance of power, that liberty might be guaranteed. He was not much of a politician, and he never sat in Parliament. What he loathed was anything in the way of a leveling principle. Society should be divided into social classes. He wanted for himself both superiors and subordinates, and fixed, invariable rules for the distinction of rank. "Madam," he once remarked to Mrs. Thrale, "were I a man of rank, I would not let a daughter starve who had made a mean marriage; but having voluntarily degraded herself from the station which she was originally entitled to hold, I would support her only in that which she herself had chosen; and would not put her on a level with my other daughters."

No one could defend the thesis that Dr. Johnson was an original thinker. Rather was he a great bear of a man, whose honesty, loud noise, deep growls, made such an impression on his contemporaries that he was regarded as the principal bulwark of the established regime in Church, State, education, and society. His fame rests, it is true, to no inconsiderable degree on Boswell's hero-worshiping biography. Had it not been written, however, there is sufficient evidence to be gleaned from Johnson's friends to prove that no man was held in higher esteem in England in the middle of the eighteenth century.

Among those who gathered in friendly intercourse with the mighty Doctor at the Turk's Head Tavern were Reynolds, the portrait painter; Sheridan, the playwright; Burke, the rising young politician; Garrick, the actor; and Goldsmith, the novelist. The last mentioned was especially protected by the favor of Johnson and was made the special butt of Boswell and of others who showed little appreciation for the unfortunate Irishman.

Oliver Goldsmith (1728–1774) occupies a place in English literature intermediate between the sturdy Johnson and the sentimentalists. He is like the former in his praise and approbation of wealth and civilization; he resembles the latter in his tender-heartedness and simplicity. Otherwise how did he create *The Vicar of Wakefield* or write *The Deserted Village*? Many of the ideas found in the satiric writings of Voltaire appear faintly in what he wrote,—the attack upon pompous authority, the absurdity of certain customs, the unfair treatment meted out to the poor. But in Goldsmith, the sentimentalist, the sting is missing from the satire. Despite the poverty, neglect, and suffering which that Irishman endured, he could not avoid being mellow. In his way he was a kind of universal genius with his pen. Dr. Johnson stuck rather close to literary criticism, venturing now and again into the realms of biography and of novel-writing; but Goldsmith included history in his repertoire and made very tidy sums from hastily compiled histories which were used freely in the schools of both England and the United States for many decades. The money speedily evaporated, for Goldsmith was generous. This, combined with the fact that he worshiped Johnson, probably accounts for the famous Doctor's including him in his list of intimates.

There were many other notable writers in the middle years of the eighteenth century, among them Fielding, the author of *Tom Jones*, said to be the most perfect novel in the English language, and Richardson, who described at interminable length in *Pamela* the adventures of a poor servant girl in defense of her chastity. Since mere cataloguing, however, is useless, we shall conclude this middle period of eighteenth-century intellectual achievement with a brief survey of history, economic thought, and pure science.

History, indeed, was extraordinarily popular with the average reader—far more so than in the twentieth century; and many thousands of pounds were paid in royalties to the three important historians of the period: Hume, Robertson, and Gibbon. History, as popularly conceived, was a branch of literature, not a science. It was written in the grand manner; that is to say, it portrayed the past on a broad canvas, with a big brush. Rarely did the eighteenth-century historian attempt details. Even had he chosen to do so, he would have failed; for collected material in the way of sources was lacking. On the other hand, he read more widely than his modern confrere, devoted more attention to form and style, and in consequence was more readable.

David Hume (1711–1776) and William Robertson (1721–1793) were Scotland's eighteenth-century historians. Both were of rather humble parentage, both attended Edinburgh University, both made much money by writing history and were read widely.

By a strange irony of fate, Hume won more contemporary renown as historian than as philosopher, although his early ambitions lay all the other way. Educated for the law, he abandoned it for philosophy, secluded himself for years in France to write philosophy, and sought in his *Treatise of Human Nature* "to produce almost the total alteration of philosophy." It was no use; people refused to buy his books. He failed to win the Professorship of Ethics and Pneumatic Philosophy at Edinburgh because of accusations of skepticism; and so he became a historian.

The history of England was his field, his first two volumes dealing with that country from the accession of James I to 1688; his second two volumes, the Tudor period, and the last two, England from Caesar to Henry VII. Hume sought to be "instructive and amusing," and was both. Imbued with the eighteenth-century belief in natural laws, his psychology was at fault; and his analysis of historical characters, like Luther and Joan of Arc, was based on the assumption that their reactions were the same as his own. On the other hand, Hume's style was easy and flowing, and his scholarship was much better in the periods nearer to his own day. He loved intellectual processes, and he had a genuine appreciation of culture. For the first time the English people found in his history a clear and readable account of their own past from its early origins.

Robertson, a Presbyterian clergyman, was an even more distinguished historian. He rose to fame early by writing a history of Scotland which won the warmest praise from such distinguished men of letters as Lord Chesterfield, Burke, and Horace Walpole. He was appointed official historian of Scotland, and in addition had other honors bestowed upon him. His *Scotland* was a dignified history. It would be called a trifle ponderous at present; but the eighteenth century was a leisurely time, which placed no premium on brevity or conciseness. It also possessed "a certain tonelessness, which resembled nothing so much as the appearance of his beloved Edinburgh under the grey caress of an east wind"; but that did not diminish his popularity.

Robertson next wrote a massive biography of Emperor Charles V, for which he was paid £4500. The book was hailed with enthusiasm from America to Russia, and so also was his *History of America*, which had to do mainly with the voyages of discovery and the Spanish conquests. Here Robertson is at his best. His accounts of Columbus and of Cortes are not only excellent history but excellent literature, since, for the most part, they are simple and rather literal translations of contemporary chronicles.

Finally, of course, there was Edward Gibbon (1737–1794), ablest of all English historians, possibly premier historian of all time. Gibbon was the grandson of a wealthy army contractor and therefore, fortunately enough, excused from the necessity of earning a living. He was educated largely at home, owing to his poor health. He went to Oxford, but learned nothing much there except to become a Roman Catholic. His horrified father dispatched him forthwith to Switzerland, to study other doctrines. The young Gibbon spent five years there, reading omnivorously. He became a Protestant again, but a lukewarm one, his studies tending rather toward agnosticism than toward a rejuvenated faith. He returned to England, took some insignificant part in public affairs, and became a member of

# Thought and Letters from Newton to Burke

Johnson's club. According to Boswell, he was "an ugly, disgusting fellow." The worthy Boswell doubtless was jealous. With the exception of Dr. Johnson, Gibbon towered high above his contemporaries, and he preferred to be isolated like an Alpine peak, thus in a way resembling his famous history.

For a long time Gibbon hesitated in regard to a subject for his projected lifework. His final choice was *The Decline and Fall of the Roman Empire*. To prepare himself for this task, he traveled extensively in Italy and read every scrap of the original Greek and Latin that he could find. With tremendous and loving energy he wrote and rewrote his more important chapters. He finished his first volume in 1776, the year of American independence, and his last in 1787, two years before the French Revolution. His greatness lay in his mastery of form. Every event and every actor in this majestic enterprise falls into its proper place. His style is brilliant, but inclined to be rather too ostentatious. Since his day *The Decline and Fall* has been assailed because of the unreliablity of many of the authorities upon which he depended and the unfairness of his treatment of the early history of the Christian Church. Despite such blemishes no one can cavil at the completed work, which is so dignified and comprehensive as to merit the name "Roman." Certainly no historian has ever written in the English language with more sustained eloquence and power.

Economic thought in the eighteenth century was both stimulated and transformed by the new wealth. The prevailing economic doctrines at the beginning of that era were those of the mercantilist school, which upheld the omnipotence of the state and the subordination of the individual to it. Ever since the advent of the Tudors, in economics "as in politics, the movement was away from the small unit, the guild and the town, and toward intensified competition along national lines." The prosperity of a country was thought to depend upon governmental regulation of trade and industry. Wealth was generally thought of in terms of bullion, actual gold and silver; and governments strove to stimulate exports but to keep imports to a minimum. In consequence there was a very strict regulation of trade, especially foreign trade. Nations competed against nations rather than individuals against individuals. Such were the mercantilist ideas, which were destined to be overthrown in the nineteenth century, only to reappear in new guise in the neomercantilist practices of European dictators in the twentieth (see pages 233, 329).

The first attack on mercantilism developed in France in the eighteenth century. Men known as physiocrats began to argue that governments would do well to leave business alone. Deducing their ideas from the Newtonian faith in natural law, they believed that there were natural laws in economics, which were as immutable as the natural laws of astronomy. Laissez faire (let things alone),—let nature run its course,—and all will be well, these men proclaimed. The physiocrats were very theoretical in their beliefs, and, living in an agricultural country, they considered agriculture to be the principal source of all wealth.

In Scotland a more practical man, Adam Smith, gave expression to the ideas of the physiocrats in somewhat different form in 1776 in his *Wealth of Nations*. This book, a landmark in economic thought, was destined to become almost an economic Bible in years to come. Since its major political and economic influence was not felt in England until the nineteenth century, an analysis of its contents is postponed for a few chapters (see page 628). Suffice it to say here that Adam Smith agreed with the physiocrats in their main idea concerning natural law and laissez faire. He differed from them principally in stressing trade and commerce rather than agriculture as the source of wealth, and in favoring a tax on income rather than a tax on land. England in his day was, of course, still an agricultural country to a large extent; nevertheless, the commercial and manufacturing class was much larger than that in France, and in consequence Smith thought in terms of trade rather than in those of agriculture.

Experimental science, called in the old days "natural history," had a wide vogue in the eighteenth century. Cabinets containing stuffed birds, rocks, and plants were popular; amateur laboratory experiments were common; and the "enlightened" man of the day was intensely interested in the new discoveries, particularly those relating to physics and chemistry. In general, it may be said that the major scientific discoveries of the century were made by German, French, and English scientists, with some collaboration from other countries; but it is impossible to award the palm for scientific research to any one country, since different scientists sometimes happen upon the same scientific truths almost simultaneously.

Nevertheless, England holds a very high place in the scientific discoveries of the age. Besides the great Newton, there was, for instance, Edward Jenner (1749–1823), doctor and naturalist, who set the world free from smallpox. Jenner, already well known as a scientist, had charge of the zoological specimens brought back by Captain Cook from his famous first voyage (see page 659). As early as 1775 Jenner had begun his investigation in regard to cowpox, and before long he was able to prepare from a sick cow a serum which, injected into the human blood, made man immune to smallpox. By the end of the century his discovery was accepted everywhere by intelligent doctors, and a grateful government twice honored him with large grants of money.

Then there was Henry Cavendish (1731–1810), a wealthy nobleman and a recluse, who dabbled in all sorts of scientific experiments. He took to examining water drawn from London pumps; he investigated heat, light, and electricity; and "he was the first who, by purely inductive experiments, converted oxygen and hydrogen into water, and who taught that water consisted of these gases." Even better known for chemistry experiments was Joseph Priestley (1733–1804), a famous Unitarian clergyman and political radical (see page 537). Priestley was a poor man, but he was aided, after the eighteenth-century fashion, by wealthy patrons, among whom were the Earl of Shelburne and Josiah Wedgwood, the manufacturer of fine china. Priestley specialized in gases, which he studied carefully in English breweries and elsewhere. He proved that the theory that "combustible bodies are composed in part of an invisible and highly combustible substance" was impossible. He must be credited also with the discovery of oxygen, while he and Cavendish between them made possible the later work of the Frenchman Lavoisier, the founder of quantitative chemistry. Later in life Priestley, because of his radical political ideas, was to flee from England to spend his last years in Pennsylvania.

A third and final chapter in the intellectual history of the century began almost simultaneously with the French Revolution of 1789. The fall of the Bastille in Paris made an astonishing impression on English minds. English writers as well as English statesmen began to take sides both for and against the new ideas so boldly proclaimed across the Channel (see page 549). The England of Newton, Locke, and Alexander Pope had withstood with some degree of success the attack made upon it by the cult of sensibility, by the nature-worshipers, by the Methodists, and by the rather mild agnosticism of men like Hume. Now that same old England faced a fresh assault, more vigorous and more threatening. In the England of 1770 one might favor the democratic doctrines of Rousseau or the skepticism of Voltaire without appearing to threaten British institutions; to do so in 1790 was a somewhat different matter. By the latter date the old order of society was dashing to destruction in France, and many suspected that the wild storm might spread from that country into England. There were some Englishmen who hoped that it would. The "new wealth," as we have seen, had created new areas of social and economic friction and had accentuated many that were old. Compromises that seemed reasonable in 1700 wore the appearance of illogical, if not tyrannical, maladjustments by 1790. "Liberty, equality, and fraternity" was a French slogan; but it was heard also in London, even within the halls of Parliament.

The spread of the new French ideas was checked in England by a number of factors, predominant among which was the long war which England waged against the French Revolution and Napoleon. This conflict, however, was not waged entirely by ships and men. It was a literary and an intellectual war as well, in which England had a redoubtable champion, in his own way as famous as Lord Nelson or the Duke of Wellington. His name was Edmund Burke, and his role in English letters at the end of the century, in certain respects, was like that of Dr. Johnson in the middle decades, namely, to inspire his countrymen with a love of English ways and to defend the established institutions of his country against revolutionary criticism.

Burke (1729–1797) was Dublin-born and, like Swift and Goldsmith, a graduate of Dublin's famous Trinity College. The years of his early manhood were spent in comparative obscurity in London, where he supported himself, after a fashion, as a hack writer. Slowly he emerged as a literary free lance, became private secretary to a peer, and then entered Parliament, in the Whig interest, from a rotten borough. Within little more than a decade he was one of the foremost statesmen of England,—an astonishing fact when we remember that he inherited neither a great name nor a fortune, that he was an Irishman, that his wife was a Roman Catholic, that his relatives, who were always pestering him, were not to the aristocratic manner born. On the other hand, there were assets. Like Disraeli in the century to follow, Burke knew how to charm his friends. Even Dr. Johnson, who despised all Whigs, made an exception in Burke's favor and said of him, "I love his knowledge, his genius, his diffusion and affluence of conversation." And as Burke talked, so did he write, glowing with imagination, clothing general principles with such a wealth of imagery and sustained enthusiasm as to seem lifted far above everything mean and commonplace.

These qualities were to carry Burke far. He never rose to high rank as a practical statesman, nor did he ever enter a British cabinet; but his pen and his voice were the most influential in Britain as the century closed. He took a leading part in three great controversies: in the American Revolution, in the investigation of alleged scandals connected with British rule in India, and in Britain's relations to the French Revolution (see pages 471, 666, 549). The culminating effect was to procure for him a permanent and honored niche in British history. His name has become traditional as the distinguished foe of the French Revolution. In him conservatism, both then and now, finds its ablest expression.

Within two years, 1774 and 1775, Burke wrote one letter and composed and delivered two speeches which laid the foundations for his fame as a leading exponent of British political philosophy. The letter was written to the electors of Bristol, a city which he then represented in Parliament. In it he made clear that he was not elected merely to act as their delegate. "Your representative owes you," he said, "not his industry alone, but his judgment; and he betrays it, instead of serving you, if he sacrifices it to your opinion." In other words, Burke refused to be an automaton, scorning, as he did, the idea that true wisdom lay in local loyalties.

The two speeches, on taxation and on American reconciliation, dealt with the approaching revolution overseas, and are packed with phrases which came later to be recognized in England as the quintessence of good statesmanship. Burke refused to discuss theoretical rights. "What is the use of discussing a man's abstract right to food or medicine? The question is, What is the method of procuring and administering them." The author was for taking a practical yet at the same time a long view of the American controversy. "The question with me is not whether you have a right to render people miserable; but whether it is not your interest to make them happy. It is not what a lawyer tells me I may do, but what humanity, reason, and justice tell me I ought to do." Throughout, Burke was determined to ignore complicated legalities. He insisted that the fact that the Americans were sensitive, that their inheritance was nonconformist, and that their religion was "the dissidence of dissent and the Protestantism of the Protestant religion" must be remembered. "An Englishman," said Burke, "is the unfittest person on earth to argue another Englishman into slavery." Then, too, there was, in his opinion, the empire to consider. "Magnanimity in politics is not seldom the truest wisdom; and a great empire and little minds go ill together." Contemporary England recognized to some extent the validity of these views, even if official England was so foolish as not to act in accordance with them. Burke's reputation continued to rise.

Not, however, until 1790, when he publicly broke his friendship with Fox, the Whig champion (see page 549), and when he published his *Reflections on the French Revolution,* did he win recognition as the chief literary and philosophic representative of old England, her ways of thought, her spirit, her temper, and her constitution. The celebrated *Reflections* contained much which was not true in regard to facts, for Burke knew very little about France or French affairs. As a contribution to the history of the French Revolution his book was well-nigh worthless. What raised it to high place in English letters was that it incarnated the political and social traditions of his own countrymen in such an earnest, elevated, and memorable style as to win lasting renown. "People will not look forward to posterity," says Burke, "who never looked backward to their ancestors." Reformers, in his opinion, should always have this in mind. The present should be blended with the past, and the future blended with the present; for it is unwise to hew and to hack at the roots of any society. Among the British roots which Burke cherished were private property, the Established Church, the law of entail (see page 149), and the aristocratic tradition. He had no more confidence in democracy than in absolute monarchy. "Of this I am certain, that in a democracy the majority of the citizens is capable of exercising the most cruel oppression on the minority." Equality of rank was absurd to his mind, because certain occupations are honorable while others are not. Hairdressing, for instance, is not an honorable function. Liberty, furthermore, is an old English ideal, and it may best be secured by relying on the old system of checks and balances. "Property," he affirmed, "is sluggish, inert, and timid, and it never can be safe from the invasions of ability unless it be out of all proportions predominant in the representation." Therefore he thought it fit and proper that the House of Commons in large measure should represent property; kings and Church, Lords, Commons, check, balance, and control one another in the interests of all. This does not make for a perfect state; but Burke was not interested in perfectibility. What captured his imagination and held his respect was a society which is cautious in regard to change. The quintessence of Burke may be found in these words: "Our political system is placed in a just correspondence and symmetry with the order of the world, and with the mode of existence decreed to a permanent body composed of transitory parts; wherein by the disposition of a stupendous wisdom, moulding together the great mysterious incorporation of the human race, the whole, at any one time, is never old, or middle-aged, or young, but, in a condition of unchangeable constancy, moves on through the varied tenor of perpetual decay, fall, renovation, and progression. Thus by preserving the method of nature in the conduct of the state, in what we improve we are never wholly new; in what we retain we are never wholly obsolete."

Now Burke, thus far, had followed mainly in the paths indicated by Locke and Newton. It is true that he stood for traditions; but he was also sensitive to his own day, and in that he differed from Locke and Newton. The Romantic movement in literature (see page 604) was in bud; and Burke was a part of this movement, which is equivalent to saying that he emphasized the validity of the non-rational and mystical, and that he held to a type of religious experience different from that which characterized the age of Pope. At the commencement of the century, Locke had based his philosophy on individualism and on natural rights. Burke, toward the close of the century, based his philosophy on a "religion which so much hates oppression that when the God whom we adore appeared in human form he did not appear in the form of greatness and majesty but in sympathy with the lowest of the people, and thereby made it a firm and ruling principle that their welfare was the object of all government." That these sentiments were expressed by a man who believed in the perpetuation of social classes, ranks, and grades was paradoxical; but it must be remembered that Burke's philosophy was, in a sense, a throwback to earlier centuries, when the natural man was considered evil rather than good and when it was held necessary for strong and powerful forces to save him from the follies inherent in his weakness.

Burke's pamphlet raised the conservative standard, and to it flocked the gentlemen of England. It was to wave victorious until after Napoleon's downfall, and, although it helped to bring about the deadening Tory reaction to all liberal trends (see page 549), much that it stood for still remains victorious in England. On the other hand, it met with a bitter, uncompromising, and by no means negligible radical attack, which likewise was to be interwoven with the history of English thought and letters.

Some thirty-eight printed replies to Burke's *Reflections* indicated that he had many opponents. Prominent among them were Priestley, the scientist; Holcroft, the dramatist; and Thelwall, a popular lecturer and pamphleteer. The three, however, who were possibly the most representative were Mary Wollstonecraft (1759–1797), schoolmistress and later mother-in-law of Percy Bysshe Shelley; Thomas Paine (1737–1809), former excise collector, and pamphleteer extraordinary on two continents; and William Godwin (1756–1836), ex-clergyman, and subsequently the second husband of Mary Wollstonecraft.

First in the field in reply to Burke was a woman. Mary Wollstonecraft's *Vindication of the Rights of Man* opened the radical campaign, as the first of those thirty-eight replies to the famous *Reflections*. "I perceive," she wrote to Burke, "that you have a mortal antipathy to reason, but if there is anything like argument or first principles in your wild declamation, behold the result—that we are to reverence the rust of antiquity, and those unnatural customs which ignorance and self-interest have consolidated into the sage fruit of experience." The schoolmistress had no respect for the British constitution. It guaranteed property, no doubt, but at the same time "the liberty of an honest mechanic is often sacrificed to secure the property of the rich." Why should the life of a deer be more prized than the life of a man? Why, under our excellent constitution, should men be kidnaped for the navy? "Why cannot large estates be divided into small farms? Why does the brown waste meet the traveller's view when men want work?" As for the much-praised House of Commons, its members were in her opinion but puppets. "After the effervescence of spirit raised by the opposition and all the little tyrannical acts of canvassing are over—quiet souls!—they only intend to march rank and file, and to say yes or no." "You were," she said to Burke, "behind the curtain. You must have seen the clogged wheels of corruption continually oiled, and the sweat of the labouring poor squeezed out of them by increasing taxation. You must have discovered that the majority of the House of Commons was openly purchased by the Crown, and that the people were oppressed by the influence of their own money. . . . You must have known that a man of talent cannot rise in the Church, the army, or navy unless he had some interest in a borough." Yet, she continued, Burke talked of liberty, and derided the French, and praised the House of Commons, that "dead weight of benumbing opulence where the sheep obsequiously pursue their steps with all the undeviating sagacity of instinct."

Mary Wollstonecraft was well-nigh forgotten amid the bleatings of timidity, exclamations of hatred, and shouts of approval that greeted the writings of Thomas Paine. He embodied the spirit of radicalism as Burke did that of conservatism. This was recognized by everyone of the period, as the discussion of Paine in the contemporary literature and the numerous replies called forth by his pamphlets demonstrate. It was further indicated by the venomous hatred of Paine in certain circles. We are told that it was fashionable to wear Tom Paine shoe nails, that he might be trampled underfoot. Tom Paine pitchers were manufactured, bearing painted serpents with Paine's head and this inscription:

> Observe the wicked and malicious man
> Projecting all the mischief that he can.

The burning of Paine in effigy was a common sight, while, on the other hand, celebrations were held to do him honor.

# Thought and Letters from Newton to Burke

It is rather difficult nowadays to account for the horror with which Paine's *Rights of Man* was received. It is true, his language in defense of France was violent; but his proposals for the reform of England were not particularly immoderate. His principal idea was to make the government more democratic, to abolish entail, to create peasant proprietorship, to lessen expenditure on the court, the army, and the navy, to finance the country by an income tax, to pay old-age pensions, to give bonuses for births and marriages, and to spend a good deal for education. Very likely if he had not included royalty in his diatribes, always calling the king "Mr. Guelph," he would not have been hounded out of England.

Finally there was Godwin, a most unassuming little person who in 1784 had published six sermons devoted to this theme: "God himself has no right to be a tyrant." Godwin thereupon decided to preach no more, but busied himself with writing the most radical book of the decade, more radical than most contemporary French theory. *Political Justice*, published in 1793, was an attack on private property, the greatest evil of the day in the author's opinion, since it was responsible for the lack of an independent spirit. The fawning pauper, the submissive servant, and the obsequious shopkeeper illustrated this. Also the constant projection of property before the vision of mankind as the most desirable of all objects perverted human judgment. This glorification of property Godwin considered much more detrimental than the swollen pension roll of the government, because "hereditary wealth" was "a premium paid to idleness." He held that private property retarded not only the development of genius but the growth of intelligence as well; for property either surfeited those who held it or, by its unequal distribution, compelled others to spend their days in sordid cares. There were few, however, to read Godwin. His book cost three guineas, a prohibitive price; his influence was to lie in the future.

Had it not been for protracted war with France, it is probable that these radical writers would have made more of a dent in English public opinion than they did. There was much which needed reforming: corrupt politics, outrageous penal laws, grave economic injustice brought about by the Industrial Revolution, and still much deep-rooted religious and social bigotry. Furthermore, as we shall see, the younger Pitt was a genuine reformer; and England, after the loss of the American colonies, was in a mood to clean house. The war with France, however, hushed, for the time being, the radical note in England. The country gentry tightened their grip on their country. To be a radical was to be a French sympathizer and therefore unpatriotic. Not until some time after Waterloo was it otherwise.

# A History of England and the British Empire

Taken as a whole the eighteenth century was a comfortable one; consequently literature in general reflected a sense of physical well-being. True, the status quo of the early part of the century was rather sharply criticized toward the middle years, but the attacks upon it were more sentimental than vigorous and were easily rebuffed by Dr. Johnson. By the close of the century these attacks were energetically renewed; but Burke did not stand alone in defending old England, for behind him were practically all the middle and upper classes. Between the days of Newton and those of Burke two British revolutions, the American and the Industrial, intervened, and, in addition, the French Revolution had aroused all Europe. England survived all three, and with increased prestige. When the century had dawned, she had been relatively weak in comparison with France under Louis XIV; when it closed, England was mistress of the ocean and the leading commercial power of the world.

Nevertheless, the tide of human life was changing fast, and the old shibboleths of placid worldliness and contentment seemed no longer valid. The cult of sensibility in literature was deepened and broadening into romanticism. It so happened that in Burke the new Romantic movement showed its conservative side, but with others it took a different form. There was the poetry of Robert Burns, for instance, with its democratic note and its insistence on the value of all human life, even that of the humblest crofter. There was likewise the poetry of William Blake, that strange artist, engraver, and religious mystic. If we began this chapter with the contentment expressed in Pope's *Essay on Man*, perhaps it would be well to end it with the hope expressed by Blake for days to come:

> I will not cease from mental fight,
> Nor shall my sword sleep in my hand,
> Till we have built Jerusalem
> In England's green and pleasant land.

Needless to say, the Jerusalem of Blake's dream has not yet appeared; but there were more Englishmen eager for its coming in 1804, when this poem was published, than there had been a hundred years earlier, when one did not worry about "Jerusalems" but sought instead the measured comfort of the London coffeehouse.

# CHAPTER XIX

## Reaction and Napoleon

### 1783-1815

Not only did the economic and the American Revolution affect England, leaving profound changes in their wake, but the French Revolution as well made its lasting imprint on English life and thought. Twenty-two years of war with France and the postponement of her own reform movement for decades were the immediate effects of the French Revolution upon England, but its results went deeper than that. Europe, including England, was never to be the same after the passionate outburst of the revolutionaries; for democracy and nationalism had torn to shreds the secure existence of the privileged classes of the old regime.

Had it not been for the French Revolution, England would have been ready for an extensive era of reform after the loss of the thirteen colonies. In fact, such a movement was well under way when the significance of the guillotine's toll in France began to seep into English minds. The news of Yorktown in 1781 had at once caused the Whigs, who had opposed the king and his Tory ministers throughout the American war even to the extent of occasionally cheering for the Americans, to attack the luckless ministry with renewed energy. Not only was Germain, whose blundering was in no small measure responsible for the failure, thrown overboard, but Whig efforts did not slacken until the powerful majority which North had built up by bribery and corruption had melted away. Five months after Yorktown the "King's Friends" were out of office with the resignation of North himself, "the genial old man who for twelve years had done the king's dirty work."

After twenty lean years the Whigs now had their chance again; but this time they were not to stay in power for forty years, as under the first two Georges. Within two years they were to be out because of dissension among themselves. Divided more by personalities than by principles, the party split into two strong and jealous groups,— an unfortunate fact for England, who was at last ready for the reforms for which the Whigs had been clamoring and which both factions wanted. One Whig leader, the Earl of Shelburne, later Marquess of Lansdowne, a man of high ability, knowledge, and industry, the intimate friend of Adam Smith, Benjamin Franklin, and other intellectuals of the day, had made exhaustive studies of the existing political and economic ills with an eye to their reform. In spite of all these fine qualities, he gave a certain impression of secretiveness which made men distrust the sincerity of the "Jesuit of Berkeley Square." His rival was the lovable, unselfish, impulsive Charles James Fox, who seldom went to bed before sunrise and who squandered a fortune on cards, women, and horses, amassing debts of some £140,000 before he was twenty-five. Admired by later generations for his fight for all sorts of liberal reforms, not only when reform was popular but long after most others had turned reactionary, it was yet largely his own fault that he was left as a solitary champion of forlorn hopes. Shelburne, a follower of Chatham with little desire for party rule, was content to give the king a reasonable share in the government. Fox, hating George as much as George hated him, wanted the thoroughgoing supremacy of a Whig Parliament. Shelburne and Fox agreed on most of the essential points of policy; yet the latter's jealousy and dislike of Shelburne was to wreck the party almost at once.

The victorious Whigs remained united barely a hundred days. The new prime minister, Lord Rockingham, a high-minded and liberal old Whig aristocrat, who had been prime minister eighteen years before at the time the Stamp Act was repealed, asked both Shelburne and Fox to serve in his ministry, where they quarreled violently over the American peace negotiations. Rockingham died, and the king asked Shelburne to form a new ministry. To the general surprise and disgust of the nation, Fox, refusing to serve under Shelburne, allied himself with North, less than a year after he had been threatening the king's henchman with impeachment. The ratio of power in the Commons was roughly as follows: Shelburne, 7; North, 6; Fox, 5. Hence no one of the three could command a majority by himself. Unable to stand alone against this unnatural alliance, Shelburne resigned in less than nine months when Fox and North carried a vote of disapproval of the peace negotiations as finally completed by Shelburne. Fox and North were finally called in by the king under the nominal leadership of the Duke of Portland. Their ministry lasted a few days less than Shelburne's, being ended by a high-handed royal maneuver. When the Commons passed Fox's bill for a reorganization of the government of India, the king sent word to the Lords that he would regard as a personal enemy anyone who voted for it! It was defeated by thirteen votes. Then, in spite of the majority in the Commons, George took the unconstitutional step of dismissing the ministry and asked young William Pitt to be prime minister.

# Reaction and Napoleon

Probably the king expected to find in the twenty-four-year-old Pitt another docile tool like North; instead he found his master. England's first reaction to the change was mild amusement at

> A sight to make surrounding nations stare—
> A nation trusted to a school-boy's care.

This amusement soon changed to admiration when the "school-boy" showed his ability in "one of the most desperate battles in English Parliamentary history." Today a ministry is expected to resign when it meets defeat in the Commons; but Pitt, backed by the king, continued after a dozen defeats. Taking consistent advantage of Fox's blunders, he at last wore down the hostile majority to one vote! Then he asked for a general election. The voters, still angered at the Fox-North combination, returned a substantial Tory majority, as a result of which one hundred and sixty of Fox's "martyrs" lost their seats. With the backing of the king, of the Lords, of the Commons, and of the people, Pitt was now in a more powerful position than any prime minister had yet enjoyed. This marked the end of the Whigs' power for more than fifty years. England, after the confusion of four changes of ministry in little more than two years, was to wait until 1801 before another shift in party power.

The new prime minister, a son of the "Great Commoner," had inherited his father's brains, his self-assurance, and—for a while at least—his popularity, although to his older brother had gone the title of Chatham. Few cases exist where father and son have both risen to such eminence. Pitt was born in his father's great year, 1759. At Cambridge he studied classics and mathematics and at twenty-one entered Parliament. After his maiden speech a wit remarked, "It's not a chip from the old block; it's the old block itself!" At twenty-three, as Chancellor of the Exchequer under Shelburne, he was vigorously attacking the Fox-North alliance. From twenty-four until his death at forty-six, except for a brief voluntary retirement, he was prime minister, holding that office years longer than anyone else except Walpole. As a speaker Pitt lacked his father's fiery vehemence; but he was never at a loss for the right word and was a master of sarcasm. Unlike his father, he quickly showed himself an adept at Parliamentary tactics and knew how to utilize every major and minor trick to build up and keep in line the essential majority in the Commons. As a war minister he was to find to his cost that he had not inherited his father's ability; but in finance he was a genius. He was always able to assimilate and to use the best ideas of others, and many of his constructive proposals did not originate with him. In marked contrast to the impetuous Fox, Pitt always kept himself under strict control. His very youth made him assume a solemn and haughty austerity. None could penetrate beyond this icy barrier except the chosen few with whom he unbent even to the extent of pillow fights and blackface comedy. Tall and slender, with handsome, clean-cut features, he was distinguished for the purity of his private life. A doctor had prescribed port to build him up as a sickly youth, and he followed this prescription with excessive zeal throughout life, sometimes consuming a whole bottle before entering a debate. But that was his nearest approach to a bad habit. He never married, partly because he could not afford it. His private income was only £300 a year; but, although he ran deeply into debt, he followed his father's example in refusing to take a relatively respectable official sinecure worth £3000 a year. In finance, millions passed through his hands; yet his absolute integrity was never questioned. He created peers by the score, nearly doubling the House of Lords, but took no such honors for himself, remembering, perhaps, that his father's peerage had been a political liability. His thirst was for power, and few men have had a better chance, outside a despotism, to gratify such an ambition.

With Pitt a new Tory party came into being. It was Tory in so far as it supported the king and was aided by the country squires. it was a different party, however, from the Jacobite Toryism of Bolingbroke or the sordid submission of the "King's Friends" under North. Those Tories had put the royal power first; Pitt's Tories saved the crown from complete nullification at the hands of the Whigs and were nevertheless the first positively to establish the prime minister as the most powerful individual in the kingdom (see page 431). Pitt's was a Toryism of the future rather than of the past, and it began with such high promise of liberalism that during his first ten years Pitt has often been claimed by the Whigs. In the course of these forty-odd years of power the Tory party increased in numbers, absorbing ex-Whigs until the rival party diminished to a mere "rump." The Tories, under the influence of the French Revolution, became more and more conservative until finally we shall find the Whigs emerging again, not as a close corporation of great landowners but as the champions of liberalism in the nineteenth century.

Only once after 1784 was Pitt seriously threatened by a Whig return. George III was the victim of insanity, which apparently resembled the same insidious form from which Henry VI had suffered, and which became obvious only intermittently. When George showed the first touch of this malady, in 1788, the Whigs proclaimed that by right the Prince of Wales should immediately become regent, with full royal powers. Since each of the three Hanoverian Princes of Wales had, in turn, identified himself with the opposite political party from his father's, Pitt realized that Fox would be immediately called into office if his friend, that coarse and jovial prince the future George IV, were made regent. Pitt and the Tories consequently upheld the claims of the Commons and the ministry against such a regency in a strange reversal of party roles. The king, however, returned suddenly to apparent sanity before any steps had been taken.

In the meantime, during these years since Yorktown, the movement for reform was making headway. That humiliating defeat by the Americans and the French had created a determination to overhaul the rotten system which had helped to cause so much trouble. In fact, even before the peace, England had begun to put her house in order, and she continued to do it under the leadership of Shelburne, Fox, Pitt, and others, making progress as we shall see along Parliamentary, commercial, financial, and colonial lines.

Parliamentary corruption had existed as far back as Walpole's day under the Whigs; but their majorities had not been purchased quite as crudely and openly as the Tory one under North, nor had their corruption lost wars. After North's resignation the first step was the disfranchisement of the government revenue officers, who comprised about one sixth of the total national electorate. These officials naturally had found it expedient to vote as the Treasury had dictated, and they had helped to swell the ministerial majority. Next, for obvious reasons, contractors for the army and navy were forbidden to sit in Parliament. Then Burke's Economy Act of 1782 saved the government much revenue by making drastic reductions in the number of lucrative sinecures (those government positions which involved little or no work) ; in the number of pensions ; and in the amount of the secret-service funds sometimes used for actual cash bribery of foreign officials. Never again, with these opportunities for promising rich reward to one's supporters thus reduced, was it possible to buy votes as easily as North had done. Here the Parliamentary reforms stopped until the Reform Bill of 1832 (see page 613), although Pitt did his best to eliminate the rotten boroughs. He brought up the question three times, only to meet defeat (once, however, by only twenty votes).

In 1776 Adam Smith, in his *Wealth of Nations* (see page 628), denounced the arbitrary barriers imposed by the mercantile system, and urged a general adoption of international free trade, with each region producing the things for which it was best adapted. "We are all your pupils," Pitt told Smith; and he proceeded to put the Scottish economist's theories into practice. He thus advocated free trade between Great Britain and Ireland. This would have meant prosperity for Ireland, and better relations between the two islands; but the mercantile interests in Parliament killed the proposal. Pitt was more successful in his reciprocity treaty with France in 1786, which opened rich new markets for English manufactures in France and set up French claret as a rival to Portuguese port in England. It was a short-lived treaty, however; for England and France were about to settle down to their last great war, and free trade, like Parliamentary reform, was to lie dormant for many years.

In the financial field Pitt's achievements resembled those of Alexander Hamilton, the American, somewhat later. The American Revolution had nearly doubled England's national debt, increasing it from £126,000,000 to £240,000,000. In addition to the funded debt (see page 409), there was a considerable floating debt as well, because many salaries and bills for supplies had remained unpaid for several years; and credit was so low that governmental securities sold for only about 57, little more than half their nominal value. Pitt soon raised them to 96 by a series of intelligent measures. He funded the floating debt and introduced a valuable reform by disposing of the equivalent of present-day "bonds" in open sale to the highest bidders, instead of allotting them at special rates to political supporters, as North had done. The next step consisted of arrangements to pay back the principal on the national debt. This, it will be recalled, had tended from the outset to become permanent, with consequent heavy interest charges to be met each year. Pitt hoped to wipe out the national debt by means of a sinking fund, for which a certain amount was to be set aside each year. This, he predicted, would accumulate at compound interest until it would automatically pay off the debt. The plan might have worked if there had always been a surplus to set aside; but it broke down when the government borrowed money at 5 per cent to gather interest at 3 per cent in the sinking fund! Hamilton soon fell into the same trap.

Pitt was also determined that England should learn to pay as she went, instead of charging so much to the future. He consequently tried to balance the budget by increasing the government's income and reducing its expenditures. There had been a tremendous loss in customs duties through the widespread smuggling which was conducted shamelessly all along the coast, especially in tea, silk, tobacco, and wine. To make smuggling less worth while, he had the duty on tea reduced to a bare tenth of the former amount; he also secured legislation which authorized the seizure of any vessel "hovering" off the coast in a suspicious manner. To offset the possible loss in

# Reaction and Napoleon

customs, he laid excise, or internal, taxes on a queer assortment of articles, chiefly luxuries, including ribbons, race horses, ale licenses, windows, and servants. Finally, he made possible a simplified national balance sheet. Abolishing the bewildering array of special accounts for items of income and expense, which had been so intricate that they encouraged graft, he combined them into one general Consolidated Fund into which everything was paid and from which everything was drawn. Since the "bonds" were secured against this fund, they were popularly known as "consols." Pitt secured a surplus of income over expense during the years of peace. These financial reforms were perhaps his most valuable work, and (combined with the economic strength and prosperity born of the Industrial Revolution) they enabled England to act as "paymaster of the Allies" during the long struggle which was about to begin. At the close of the century, after war costs had once more begun to mount, he introduced an income tax, so that business and professional men would pay their share of the burden, which had fallen heavily on the landowners. Such a tax, we recall, had been proposed a full century before (see page 411).

Various other reforms were suggested at this time. An effort to further religious toleration by removing the disabilities against Dissenters and Catholics came to nothing for another fifty years, but the society organized by Pitt's evangelical friend William Wilberforce for the abolition of the slave trade won its fight in 1807 through the work of Fox. As a result of this decade, then, England had a purer, if still unrepresentative Parliament; a new and more liberal attitude toward the regulation of commerce; an improved financial system; and a public awakened to the need of further reform. Overseas, as we shall see later, better relations existed with India and Canada, through improvements in their government, while beginnings were made in the settlement of the continent of Australia. This reform movement, which began so auspiciously, might have continued to gain momentum had not events across the Channel suddenly hardened England's heart against reform and led to a mixture of fears and suspicions which provoked reaction and set back progress, in that direction at least, thirty years.

In France, with her absolute monarchy and her parasitic nobility, revolution reared its head in 1789. Beginning as a liberal movement, which copied some features of the English government, it grew into a radical upheaval with many lurid episodes and involved Europe in more than twenty years of war. Its legacy of nationalism and democracy continued to ferment during the next century and has altered many aspects of government and society in the world at large.

# A History of England and the British Empire

England, flattered at first by the attempted imitation, finally reacted in alarm and became the most persistent enemy of revolutionary France.

The French Revolution was essentially an effort of the intelligent middle class, such as doctors, lawyers, and merchants, to secure equality of opportunity with the nobility, who—unlike the English aristocracy, as we have seen—did practically nothing to justify the extensive and exclusive privileges which they enjoyed in respect to special rights before the law and virtual exemption from taxation. It was not primarily a revolt of the peasants, who were better off than most peasantry of the day outside of England. The Estates-General, the counterpart of the English Parliament,—with its groupings of first estate, or clergy; second estate, or nobles; and third estate, comprising everybody else,—had not met for one hundred and seventy-five years; and middle-class royal officials appointed by the king fulfilled the duties of the aristocratic English justices of the peace. In other words, whereas in England the aristocracy had power rather than privilege, in France they had privilege rather than power. Consequently this delightful parasitic class, drawn together by Louis XIV, who could manage them, continued to intrigue and make love under the debauched Louis XV, whose careless rule cost France heavily in treasure, territory, and prestige. The reigning king, the well-meaning but incapable Louis XVI (1774–1793), and Marie Antoinette, his spirited Austrian queen, were totally unfitted to exercise command in the approaching crisis.

During the eighteenth century the intelligent members of the ignored middle class were growing increasingly resentful of everything which Versailles represented, and their reading of the works of the contemporary French philosophers gave them ample ammunition in the realm of ideas to bolster their personal grudge. Montesquieu, with his guarded attack on absolute monarchy while stressing the value of separation in governmental powers (see page 431); Voltaire, with his merciless, logical sarcasm directed against all things based upon mere tradition, from monarchy to Church; Diderot, with his provocative definitions of established institutions in his *Encyclopedia*; and, above all, Rousseau, with the new idea that the people were the sovereign power and, as such, could set up a new government if the king failed to keep his "social contract" with them,—all paved the way for the Revolution. The times were ripe for such a movement. England not only set an example by her long record of constitutional development, but, after the loss of the American colonies, was moving steadily in the direction of further reform. The astonishing success of the American Revolution, aided and abetted by French money and forces, was also, no doubt, accelerating the demand for change in France. Consequently the bankruptcy of the government, caused in part by the American Revolution, which had been a luxury France could ill afford on top of all her other wars, together with an extravagant court, gave the middle class their chance. When, as a last resort, Louis XVI called the Estates-General in 1789, the third estate, with its largely middle-class membership, finding that the privileged nobles and clergy would be enabled by the traditional method of group voting to override it with a two-to-one vote on every measure, set itself up as a distinct body. Influenced, perhaps, by the fact that the new American constitution had gone into operation a few months before, it announced that it would not disband until it had given France a constitution.

For a year or so the French Revolution continued to be comparatively respectable, constructive, and "English." France became a limited monarchy; the special feudal privileges of the nobles were renounced; and "liberty, equality, and fraternity" were proclaimed. From across the Channel it looked like an imitation of the "Glorious Revolution" of 1688, with its high principles and lack of bloodshed, so that the English forgot their traditional enmity and felt flattered. Correspondence societies sprang up for the exchange of liberal ideas. Then an increasing number of French noblemen began slipping quietly over to England. The story went round that this revolution was not as roseate as it had appeared at first. It seemed that groups of radicals were getting control of the government, that peasants were sacking the châteaux of the nobles, and that many of the nobility were swarming across the Rhine to Germany or across the Channel to England to save their lives if they could not save their property. The aristocrats who ruled England had made the grand tour and knew those émigré French nobles personally. They thought of the possibility that their own half-starving peasantry might burn looms and tear down enclosures. Long before the real Terror began in France, the English landlords were using their imaginations with unpleasant results.

Then came tragedy for England. Edmund Burke, one of her foremost liberals, who had stood out strongly for American and Irish rights and who had sponsored the movement to reform Parliament, threw his eloquent influence on the conservative side. In November, 1790, appeared Burke's *Reflections on the French Revolution* (see page 535). Not an aristocrat himself, Burke felt that England's security was bound up in the interests of her dominant landed aristocracy. He denounced the French Revolution and predicted that, unless checked, its pernicious ideas would permeate all Europe and that law, order, religion, and society would disappear in democratic anarchy. That settled the question for the mass of the wavering English landowners. They felt firmly convinced, and remained so for forty years, that the success of the French revolutionary ideas meant the destruction of their own class. This view was strengthened, a few months after Burke's *Reflections* appeared, with the publication of Tom Paine's *Rights of Man*, presenting the radical point of view that what England needed was a really representative republican government, with the abolition of the hereditary power of king and Lords. The subsequent events in France—the establishment of the republic, the imprisonment and final execution of the king, the death of thousands on the guillotine, and the excesses of the extreme radicals—simply confirmed the idea that Burke was right.

The effect was evident in Parliament. The Whigs split in two, the majority following Burke over to the Tory camp, and backing the harsh reaction that quickly set in. Pitt himself, who until now had been a liberal, went over to the counterrevolutionary point of view. That was the turning point in his career. His government was turned into an instrument of oppression, crushing not only those who expressed radical sentiments but liberals as well. By the spring of 1792 a proclamation was issued against "seditious" writings, a forerunner of the series of harsh measures which silenced many and punished ruthlessly those who would not keep silent. The next few years saw an Aliens Act, a Seditious Meetings Act, a Treasonable Practices Act, and the Combination Acts, which made trade unions illegal (see page 503). Suspension of habeas corpus, much of the time until 1801, also made possible imprisonment without trial. Government spies sneaked into every sort of gathering, and some excellent men whose views were only a little more liberal than Pitt's had been a few years earlier were transported to Australia for their "treason." Lord Erskine's eloquence persuaded a jury to acquit Thomas Hardy, Horne Tooke, and others when they were tried for high treason for having advocated "representative government, the direct opposite of the government which is established here"; but that was an exception to the repression which was frequently paralleled in other lands during time of war.

Fox, almost alone, kept liberal ideas alive in Parliament during the black reaction of the nineties; otherwise there might have been no revival even at the end of thirty years. When most of the Whigs followed Burke over to the Tories, a few remained with Fox, registering persistent but ineffectual protests against the muzzling of the nation. Gradually most of them slipped away in disgust to their estates, and Fox, with a few of his "young men," was left to carry on.

# Reaction and Napoleon

As a fashionable gentleman and a member of Parliament, he was permitted to express views which would have led to instant arrest had they come from a humbler person. He was able at least to register vehement disapproval of the panicky reaction and to keep alive the ideas of reform, free speech, and the traditional rights of Englishmen; and we shall later see his "young men" successfully reviving the dormant liberalism in 1832.

In the meantime war descended on most of Europe. Revolutionary France was not content to keep her revolutionary ideas to herself; she wanted to convert the world. As one statesman later remarked, "When France sneezes, all Europe catches cold." At the same time the course of events in France and the tales of the émigré nobles had naturally aroused the absolutist states of Europe, particularly Austria, Russia, Prussia, and Spain, more than they had England. France in 1791 was annoyed by a joint declaration from the monarchies of Austria and Prussia expressing the hope that the European rulers would act together to restore Louis XVI to his full powers. By 1792 a French republic had been proclaimed, the moderate revolutionaries were out of the picture, and soon a radical "Convention," with its executive Committee of Public Safety under Robespierre, was entering upon a mad career. For some time to come, French policy was to be determined by heads which one year were totally untrained; the next year were enjoying complete and reckless power; and the third year were rolling into the basket of the guillotine. In the rivalry between parties and between members of the same party the question of war or peace was too often a political football, dependent upon the internal situation. As early as the close of 1791 the revolutionary foreign minister declared that "war is a national benefit; the only calamity to be dreaded is that we should have no war." Relations with Vienna grew constantly more strained, neither side showing any strong desire for peace; and the conflict began on April 20, 1792, when France declared war on Austria. This automatically brought in Austria's ally, Prussia.

The French were in no condition for a fight. Government and finances were shaky. Mutinies were widespread in the old standing army; the new raw volunteers left much to be desired; and most of the titled officers had left or had been ejected. Rochambeau and Lafayette, who had been among the victors at Yorktown eleven years before, led two of the armies toward enemy territory. At the first sight of the foe the French ran. This left the offensive to the allies, who were slowly gathering their forces. Had they marched at once directly against Paris with their well-trained, well-disciplined troops, they could probably have put an end to the French Revolution then and there. But various complications held them back, and the next allied invading army did not find the French running from them. The French had declared the nation in danger and called for volunteers, who came swarming by the thousands, singing the new *Marseillaise* with its ringing revolutionary spirit. At Valmy the French artillery fire caused the invading Prussians to withdraw. That cannonade at Valmy in September, 1792, has been ranked as one of the "decisive battles of the world"; for it saved the French Revolution, and it was on the day following that France was declared a republic. Encouraged by Valmy, the French took the offensive and soon overran the Austrian Netherlands (Belgium), which had been in revolt against its Austrian masters and so was a fertile field for the spreading of revolutionary ideas. The French Convention proclaimed that the river Scheldt, which, with its port of Antwerp, had been closed to navigation by international agreement ever since 1648, was once more open to shipping.

That news profoundly stirred England, and was shortly to bring her into the war. The English have always felt the presence of a strong power in the Low Countries to be a menace to their safety, as we have seen, for instance, in the wars with Louis XIV (see page 406). Pitt called Belgium the "chain which unites England to the Continent" and declared that any powerful nation holding Antwerp and the Scheldt "holds a pistol pointed at the heart of England." Hitherto he had favored peace with France, and at the beginning he had actually reduced the army and navy in the interests of economy. England was by no means unanimous in her reaction. The rains which delayed the allied army in invading France spoiled English crops, and the workers were in an ugly mood. At Sheffield they celebrated the French victory in Belgium by barbecuing an ox and parading ten thousand strong with the revolutionary tricolor. In the Commons, Fox made a strong pro-French speech which at least kept fifty members from voting unanimous support of Pitt's stand.

Both nations, however, pushed steadily toward war, neither being in the mood to give way. The four principal actors were young men who had not yet reached the age of thirty-four. The French foreign minister and the ambassador at London were inexperienced and enthusiastic; Pitt and Grenville, his foreign minister, were so cold and so haughty that their attitude often verged on insolence. Pitt immediately called out part of the militia and put the navy in a state of readiness. In reckless self-confidence, the French Convention had voted to "grant fraternity and assistance to all people who wish to recover their liberty," and later to "revolutionize all

# Reaction and Napoleon

countries where its armies are or shall come." In the meantime it annexed Savoy. England offered to leave the French Revolution alone if it would confine itself to the limits of France. The French refused, and announced their determination to secure their "natural frontiers"—the Alps, the Pyrenees, the Rhine, and the ocean. This, of course, involved Belgium and a part of Holland. Then came, on January 21, 1793, the beheading of Louis XVI by the guillotine. Apparently forgetting the fate of Charles I, England was roused to indignation, denouncing this as "the most odious and atrocious crime in history." Having now a high moral purpose, in addition to her more practical reasons of state, England was ready for war. The French ambassador was given a week to get out of London. The actual declaration of war came from France on February 1, after an all-night session of the Convention.

Within a few weeks the French also declared war on Spain and Holland. Prussia, Austria, and Sardinia were already at war with them, and the other German states of the "Empire," together with several small nations, joined the contest by the end of March. France, in a reckless mood, had taken on all comers and was ringed around with enemies. These numerous foes were known as the "First Coalition." The word "coalition," however, implies a more effective alliance than this really was. All the allies gave lip service to the "cause of kings" and to the fight against nationalism and democracy. Most of them, however, were in the fight for their own special reasons, which outweighed the common cause. Austria and Prussia, for instance, hoped to seize some French frontier territory and were busy with other diplomatic juggling. In England, George III and Burke sincerely wanted to crush the revolutionary ideas, but Pitt's prime interest was the security of the Low Countries. Practically the only strong bond in the whole coalition was the hope of securing gifts or loans from the British treasury, which Pitt had filled so successfully. Pitt, looking at the situation through the eyes of the financier, underestimated the fighting power of France, with her exhausted treasury and demoralized administration. He put too much faith in the power of gold, overlooking the importance of the will to win. He took over his father's policy of "hiring" Continental countries to fight the French; but the recipients were so involved in their own particular intrigues that England did not always get full value for the millions which she poured into their coffers. England was to remain the "paymaster of the allies" throughout the long struggle and to take the initiative in building up a succession of coalitions which the French proceeded to destroy. It was not until 1813, long after Pitt's death, that Austria, Prussia, and Russia, all three at the same time, joined in alliance with England and finally beat the French. Had all these worked together earlier, the conflict would probably not have dragged over so many years.

The intrigues and individual problems of England's allies hindered united action against France so seriously that it is necessary to consider them. Austria, who, next to England, was France's most persistent enemy, bore the brunt of the French attacks. Behind the pomp at Vienna and the imposing armies of whitecoats was not a nation but a heterogeneous conglomeration of regions and races— German, Magyar, Slav, Italian, Belgian—accumulated by Hapsburg marriages and conquests, and also the shadowy Holy Roman Empire. After an overdose of royal reform under two "benevolent despots," Maria Theresa and her son Joseph II,—who recognized the need for change but accomplished it as they saw fit, with no lessening of their absolute control,—Austria had lapsed into stiff-necked conservatism. The new ruler, Francis II, narrow-minded, pedantic, and shy, met all problems by "Let us sleep upon it," with the result that irresponsible court adventurers controlled affairs. As for Prussia, Frederick the Great would have turned in his tomb could he have seen how she had slumped in the twenty years since his death. Frederick William III was weak, and his predecessor had neglected the army and had bankrupted the state. Prussia's role in the coming struggle was marked by apathy and sordid haggling. She was to stay at peace with France from 1795 until 1806, when a crushing defeat shocked her into a thoroughgoing national revival. Russia's Catherine II, on the other hand, established as high a record for ability as for immorality. Whereas Peter the Great was said to have made Russia a European power, Catherine made her a great one. The backward condition of Russia offset the size; but the reason that this country did not play a more decisive role in the French situation was that Catherine's prime interest was in Russia's own expansion against Turkey in the south, Sweden in the north, and especially Poland in the west. Spain, only a shadow of her former greatness, with probably the most worthless of all the contemporary crowned heads for king in Charles IV, used her mediocre forces first on one side, then on the other, in the war. Of the lesser states there were Holland, with civil war recently within her borders; Piedmont, or Sardinia, Italy's chief independent nation, to be the nucleus of a united Italian kingdom in the next century; Sweden, which played no important role in the conflict; Denmark and Portugal, about which none of the allies bothered much; the three hundred and sixty-odd virtually independent units in Germany, loosely held together in the Holy Roman Empire, but acting separately as each selfish interest dictated in the great conflict; and Poland, where the turbulent rule of the nobility gave the neighboring states, Russia, Prussia, and Austria, a chance to intervene, with the result that by 1795, after three partitions, no Poland was left.

This was the heyday of the old secret diplomacy, with double-dealing the rule; and more than one clever foreign minister would draw up a treaty of alliance with one nation when the ink was barely dry on a similar agreement with its rivals. The general system then, as too often now, was that if one or two powers showed an aggressive determination to seize new territory it was incumbent upon the others to bluff them out of it by a show of force, to share in the spoils themselves, or to demand "compensation" elsewhere. For instance, the canny Catherine II, who had urged Austria and Prussia to advance on France, seized that moment in 1792 for the second partition of Poland, so that the suspicious allies, as they marched forward, kept turning back to see what was happening there, and their divided interest did much to save the French Revolution. It would be futile here to attempt to disentangle all the intricate webs of diplomatic intrigues about 1789, but we shall note two or three in which England was concerned. She was too insular and too maritime to play as fast a game as the Continental powers; but Pitt and his foreign minister, Grenville, formed their own alliances and three times prepared the royal navy for action as a threat. Twice the threat was sufficient: in 1786 to keep the Dutch ruler on his throne; and four years later to stop a Spanish attempt to expand on Nootka Sound, near Van-couver Island, on the Pacific coast of North America, where there was an English settlement. The third time, in 1791, Pitt's objection to Catherine's expansion on the Black Sea coast against Turkey —a grave threat in English eyes to the safety of her possessions in India—came to nothing, partly because of the lack of Parliamentary co-operation in appropriating money for the navy. Belgium, of course, was England's prime concern in this diplomatic game, and she balked the Austrian plot to exchange Bavaria for Belgium for fear of Belgium's falling into French hands.

Now, with the long war once under way, England's constant building up and paying of alliances was to be a very important factor in the ultimate French defeat; but her function as a belligerent did not end there. The army and navy were quickly drawn into action in many places—altogether too many places. Pitt lacked his father's distinguished ability as a war minister, and the first few years after 1793 brought disheartening reverses. He showed poor judgment in selecting the ministers who were to share with him the responsibility for guiding the fighting forces. His own elder brother, the second

Earl of Chatham, was quite worthless as First Lord of the Admiralty. Pitt made a grave mistake in entrusting the general supervision of the fighting to his close friend Henry Dundas, the political boss of Scotland, who already had his hands full with the control of Indian and home affairs. Dundas, in his ignorant optimism, frittered away England's military strength in giving the army far more tasks than it could adequately perform. It was 1797 before the navy accomplished anything conspicuous, while the army had to wait eleven years more before it began to meet with real success.

The navy was in fair condition, having benefited by the recent preparations in the Dutch, Spanish, and Russian crises. As soon as the press gangs could kidnap enough wretches to man the ships, these were sent off to the usual stations: twenty-five ships of the line in the Channel, twenty-five in the Mediterranean, ten in the West Indies, and twenty-five in reserve. Instead of clapping down an effective blockade upon the French ports, the Channel fleet remained sheltered at Portsmouth. This allowed several French squadrons to slip out and cause unnecessary alarm and damage. The work of the British navy was facilitated by the demoralization of the French fleets which had been so effective in the last war. As in the army, the titled officers had slipped away or had been ejected by mutineers; lieutenants or merchant-marine officers were raised to high command; discipline disintegrated; and England cut off the supplies of masts and other naval stores needed to put the ships in condition.

The British army was in worse shape than the navy. Widespread abuses flourished, unchecked by its nominal head, old Jeffrey, Lord Amherst, who was nearly eighty. The amiable Duke of York, second son of George III, was to prove an ineffectual field commander, but later showed himself an excellent organizer when he replaced Amherst. Too many of the officers were interested solely in the bottle, to the complete neglect of tactics and strategy. The old rank and file were good, but all too few. When England suddenly tried to expand her little army, she depended on cash alone instead of a patriotic appeal which might have brought good and enthusiastic volunteers. There was little inducement to volunteer in a service which offered inadequate food and clothing, flogging for drunkenness at the orders of officers who were too often drunk themselves, and, in addition to the usual perils of bullets and bayonets, the likelihood of freezing to death in the Low Countries or of perishing of yellow fever in the Caribbean. Consequently a large quantity of human riffraff was dragged into service by methods almost as crude as the kidnaping by the navy. As usual, England supplemented her forces by hiring large numbers of Hessians and Hanoverians.

# Reaction and Napoleon

At the outbreak of hostilities England had fewer than twenty thousand men available for use. That did not prevent Dundas from undertaking tasks which would have required five times that number. There were various fields where England might use her army. Most immediate and obvious was the Belgian front, where the French were threatening Holland. Then, too, there were opportunities to assist the rebellions in various parts of France. Finally, there was the temptation to seize the French West Indian islands. Instead of deciding in which one of these spheres of activity to concentrate his meager forces, Dundas determined to try them all and met with glaring failure in each.

England first sent troops to the Low Countries. There was no time to lose, for the French were starting a dash for Holland. The British and Austrian troops had temporary success, and not only saved Holland for the moment but cleared Belgium as well. The allies again had a clear road to Paris. As in 1792, a determined advance might have ended the French Revolution; but the allies were so busy wrangling over their prospective spoils that they neglected to beat the French first. They were not to have another such opportunity for twenty years. They wasted most of 1793 in trying to capture cities for themselves. The Duke of York was ordered to take Dunkirk, as England's particular booty, but was driven off.

In the meantime the French army was being transformed from a disorganized rabble into an extremely formidable fighting force by Lazare Carnot, a spare, stern, ascetic former captain of engineers, who won for himself the title of "Organizer of Victory." An empty treasury and worthless paper money, insuperable handicaps in the eyes of Pitt, did not deter Carnot. He appealed to the spirit as Pitt utterly failed to do, and marshaled all the resources of the French. Young men were drafted into the fighting ranks, older men made munitions and hauled supplies, women served as nurses and made tents and clothing, children scraped old linen for bandages. Shirts and shoes were requisitioned by the tens of thousands, and every eighth pig in France gave up its life to feed the army. Rigid discipline stamped out mutinies. New tactics were developed to suit the needs of the new armies, which were large and enthusiastic but only partly trained. Great massed columns of infantry were to crush through the thin lines of the enemy. For high command there was a career open to talent, and military commissions no longer remained a monopoly of the nobility; sergeants and privates, Jews and foreigners, might become marshals if they had the ability. The guillotine awaited the commander who failed to crush the enemy. In fact, the general who drove the British away from Dunkirk was beheaded for not having whipped them more decisively. Above all, these French armies fought with a fervor quite lacking among their professional opponents, where commissions depended on social rank and where men were regarded as units hired at so much a head.

The reorganized French forces began to win victories in every direction. On the October day in 1793 when the head of Queen Marie Antoinette fell into the basket of the guillotine, the Austrians sustained a defeat which threw them back on the defensive. By 1794 the French had recovered Belgium, and by 1795 they had Holland as well, after hundreds of British soldiers, neglected by Dundas, had actually frozen to death. The Low Countries were to remain in French hands for twenty years.

The British were no more successful in their efforts to co-operate with the rebellious royalists within France. Late in 1793 the British Mediterranean fleet, at the invitation of the royalists, occupied the great naval base at Toulon; but the allies did not send troops enough to hold the hills commanding the harbor. The French rushed the hills; and a young artillery lieutenant, named Bonaparte, helped to drive out the British ships, which left in too much of a hurry to carry off or destroy half the French navy after it had been at their mercy throughout the autumn. Closer at hand there were appeals for England to co-operate with the strong royalist uprisings in western France near the sea. Dundas, as usual, "sent a boy to do a man's work"; and one inadequate expedition after another failed after raising false hopes among the royalists and exposing them to additional vengeance.

These failures were overshadowed by an even worse mishap in the West Indies. In view of superior British sea power the rich sugar islands still in French hands should have been easy prey; but delays, blunders, and injudicious intervention in Haiti, where the Negroes had risen against the French planters, resulted in lost opportunities and terrific losses from yellow fever.

Aside from the Toulon affair, the principal naval action of the first four years of the war was only a technical victory for the British. In the spring of 1794 France was on the verge of starvation, and depended upon American grain to carry her through the year. A flotilla of one hundred and twenty merchantmen loaded with flour and other essential supplies sailed from Chesapeake Bay for France, protected by only a small convoy of warships. The British might have captured the whole expedition as it left American shores or, failing that, might have blockaded the French ports to prevent its arrival there. As it was, the French fleet put out from Brest and made a sacrifice play, engaging the British Channel fleet while the grain ships slipped safely into port. The French lost seven of their twenty-six ships of the line in that "glorious first of June," as it was called by the British, who under more energetic leadership might have destroyed the French fleet and intercepted the grain convoy as well.

By the summer of 1795 the First Coalition had nearly fallen to pieces. Holland, overrun by the French, not only left the allies but had to join the French. Spain made peace with France and before long also appeared on the French side. Prussia, more interested in the third partition of Poland and quite bankrupt, agreed at Basel to withdraw from the fight provided that the French would not disturb northern Germany. Several of the smaller German states of the Empire followed Prussia into the paths of peace. This left Austria and little Sardinia as England's sole remaining allies.

The year 1795 was a quiet one on nearly all fronts. The British army had withdrawn from the Continent, contenting itself with a single raid on the French coast. The rival naval forces in the Mediterranean engaged in ineffective encounters. Redcoats continued to die like flies in the West Indies, where Negro rebellions complicated the situation. The only new task which the British undertook was the capture of the Dutch colonies, including the Cape of Good Hope and Ceylon, holding them "in trust" for the regular pro-British Dutch ruler. This marked virtually the only real success of British arms in the early period of the conflict.

By 1796 the situation grew worse. The French, after their quiet year, determined to put Austria and Sardinia out of the fight. They decided upon a triple campaign. Two of their most experienced generals were to strike at Austria from the Rhine and the Danube, while, as a diversion, a third force was to strike at Italy; and then all three were to join in a march on Vienna. The two main forces were stopped; but the sideshow revealed the military genius of a young man of twenty-seven who was to occupy the center of the stage for nearly twenty years.

This was Napoleon Bonaparte. His family was of the lesser aristocracy, but very poor. Bonaparte had become an officer of artillery, and first distinguished himself with his batteries in helping to eject the British from Toulon. Intense, quiet, and studious, he almost at once revealed the qualities which were to give him a place among the greatest soldiers of history. A master of strategy and tactics, he could also inspire his men to utter devotion. He knew all the conventional rules practiced by his rivals and was capable of constant originality in developing new movements to surprise them. It was a grave day for England when this short, dark, and, at that time, slender soldier was given the opportunity to show his ability. Approaching by the Riviera, between the Alps and the sea, he rapidly put Sardinia out of the fight and deftly parried the attacks of one Austrian general after another. Northern Italy quickly came under his control, new republics on the French model were set up, and the loot from Italian cities helped to replenish the empty French treasury. By the spring of 1797 he had his sixth Austrian opponent on the run. Finally, when he was only sixty miles from Vienna, Austria made peace, and England was left alone. Napoleon deliberately gave the Austrians lenient terms so that France might be able to concentrate her energies against England.

But those twenty-one miles of Channel put England in an entirely different category from the Continental nations which the invincible French armies had overrun and would continue to overrun for years to come. Infantry, cavalry, and artillery could not bring the British to terms as long as their royal navy held the sea. Yet, while England remained unconquered, her diplomacy and gold would continue to bring together alliances to fight France. In the course of ten years France was to try four different ways of putting England out of the fight: by armed threats at Ireland, at India, and at England herself, and finally by economic pressure.

The royal navy blocked all those attempts; yet that same navy was seething with mutiny in 1797. The sailors had legitimate grievances. Many of them were there against their will, their pay was disgracefully low, and even that was badly in arrears. They were subject, moreover, to an iron discipline, sometimes degenerating into tyranny, which a few years before had led to an isolated case of mutiny on the *Bounty* in the South Seas. Now mutiny became epidemic. Trouble started at Spithead, off Portsmouth. When the Channel fleet was ordered to sea, the crews hoisted the red flag and declared that they would not sail until their pay was raised. Parliament, recognizing the justice of their claims, tardily redressed some of the grievances. That leniency, however, led to a less justifiable and more violent mutiny in the North Sea squadron off the mouth of the Thames. This time the government answered by hanging eighteen ringleaders. Order was restored at home; but mutiny spread to the squadron off Spain, to the West Indies, and even to the Cape of Good Hope.

In spite of the mutinies, however, some of these very ships won two decisive victories that same year. The immediate need of the French was for ships of the line. Their own navy had pretty much gone to pieces, but luck gave them sudden outside reinforcements in the shape of two ready-made navies, those of Spain and Holland.

# Reaction and Napoleon

Spain, which had started as an enemy of France, now became an ally, while Holland was overrun and part of her icebound navy was captured by French cavalry. By the autumn of 1797, however, England had shattered both fleets: the Spaniards off Cape St. Vincent, near Gibraltar, and the Dutch at Camperdown, in the North Sea. France was thrown back on her own depleted naval resources. Part of her vessels were used for fruitless expeditions to discontented Ireland (see page 564), but a more dramatic role was selected for the Mediterranean squadron.

Bonaparte returned from his Italian triumphs a hero. He was urged to overthrow the corrupt government, but felt that "the pear was not yet ripe." He would wait until the politicians had further proved their incapacity, and in the meantime he wanted to be out of the way. He therefore determined to strike at Egypt, an attempt which appealed not only because of its Oriental glamour but also because it might be a threat to British power in India. In 1798 he sailed from Toulon with fifteen ships (all that France could scrape together), narrowly missed the British Mediterranean fleet, and landed in Egypt, which was nominally subject to Turkey but was actually governed by a group of professional soldiers known as Mamelukes. Bonaparte defeated them in the shadow of the pyramids. Then his plans were wrecked by a man who was to be as successful on the sea as the Frenchman on the land.

This was Horatio Nelson, the greatest of England's sea heroes. Son of a clergyman, he had gone to sea at twelve as a midshipman, and had run up through the grades with extraordinary rapidity— a captain at twenty; a rear admiral at thirty-nine, the year just before this. He has been called the least English of prominent Englishmen. In contrast to the average bluff, rugged, and unimaginative British admiral, he had dash, daring, and magnetism, and was highly unconventional in everything from dress to morals. He had burst into fame the previous year when, in a subordinate role at the battle of Cape St. Vincent, where the Spanish fleet was smashed, his bold boarding action had forced the surrender of two of the largest enemy ships. Physically there was not much to this exceedingly vain little man, and he had already lost an eye and an arm in battle; but his officers and men swore by him, and in battle he had that same brilliant advantage over conventional rivals that Bonaparte enjoyed on land.

At Abukir Bay, at one mouth of the Nile, the French were first to experience the "Nelson touch." Their fleet was anchored in a single line fairly close to shore. Any ordinary admiral would have attacked them in the regulation single line, with the ships pairing off one by one for duels. That was what the French admiral expected, but Nelson had an original idea. He found that, with careful steering, his ships could get between the French and the shore; consequently he attacked in two lines, one outside the French, the other inside. Each French ship was thus caught between two fires, and one after another succumbed as Nelson rolled up their line. The great French flagship blew up; most of the rest were captured; and Bonaparte's army was marooned on the wrong side of the Mediterranean. Then Nelson relapsed into the most bizarre episode of his whole unconventional career. Forgetful of his wife back in England, he fell under the spell of Emma, Lady Hamilton, wife of the British minister at Naples, a beautiful blonde who had served as model for some of Romney's paintings. Consequently, for two years Nelson's infatuation kept him around Naples, where he even used his fleet to meddle in Neapolitan affairs, to the neglect of its proper function.

Bonaparte, in the meantime, had started up the Mediterranean coast toward Turkey, but was checked by the fortress of Acre, where the Turks were assisted by a British squadron. Thus thwarted again by the royal navy, he abandoned his army, which was later conquered by British redcoats, and slipped off to France. By that time the "pear was ripe." By a bold stroke in 1799 he overthrew the corrupt government, and for the next fifteen years was to be master of France, for five years as First Consul and for ten as Emperor. While he was busy in Egypt, England had built up a Second Coalition, with Austria, Russia, and Turkey. Those allies had recovered Italy and had undone all his work there. They lay guarding the Riviera route by which he had entered in 1796; but he crossed the Alps by the St. Bernard Pass, got between them and their base, and in a crushing victory at Marengo broke up the Second Coalition in 1800.

Then Bonaparte, in alliance with Russia, planned to join the northern European nations to close the Baltic to England. The "Nelson touch" foiled the plot. Denmark controlled the entrance to the Baltic. Without a declaration of war a British fleet was sent in 1801 against Copenhagen, with Nelson second in command. His superior reluctantly agreed to Nelson's bold plan to attack the Danish fortifications through a shallow channel risky for great ships. Remaining with the reserve, he hoisted the recall signal, generously giving Nelson a chance to retire; for the situation looked serious. Nelson, with the advance force, put his telescope to his blind eye and said he could see no such signal. He thoroughly smashed the Danes; the pro-French Czar of Russia was assassinated as the result of a domestic plot; and the Baltic remained open.

For two years there was a respite in the long struggle between

# Reaction and Napoleon

**France and England.** In 1802 the two countries signed the Peace of Amiens, in which most captured places were restored. Bonaparte demonstrated his genius as a ruler during this breathing spell, accomplishing much of lasting value for France in legal, educational, and religious reforms. At the same time he made active preparations for renewed conflict. England, on the other hand, unwisely let the navy lapse to a peace basis for the sake of economy.

During those last years of fighting England had had serious trouble with her "other island." The ever-smoldering Irish problem had flared up violently, as it almost always did in English emergencies. Only when the English had their hands full with outside problems could Ireland hope to secure anything for herself. The Irish had threatened trouble during the American Revolution, demanding free trade and a free parliament. The leadership was Protestant, with the moral support of the Catholics; for the easygoing atmosphere of the century had quieted religious animosities. There were one hundred thousand Irish Protestants under arms, with only five thousand redcoats to check them. Consequently, less from benevolence than from fear, Parliament in 1782 gave Ireland the most satisfactory government she had had in centuries. Many of the trading restrictions were lifted, and Poynings's Laws, which had subordinated the Irish parliament completely to England for nearly three centuries (see page 241), were repealed. Ireland was given a fair amount of "home rule," with her own parliament at Dublin, a body which was commonly known as "Grattan's Parliament" because Henry Grattan (a Protestant, like many of Ireland's national leaders then and for a century to come) was largely responsible for it. This arrangement, to be sure, left much to be desired. The Irish boroughs were even more "rotten" than those in England, and majorities could easily be manipulated through the landlords. Only Protestants might sit in parliament and, at first, only Protestants were permitted to vote for members of this parliament; the executive power, moreover, was still in the hands of English appointees at Dublin Castle. There was relative prosperity for a time, and in eighteen years the population jumped from fewer than three millions to more than five. England was partly to blame for failing to co-operate more thoroughly with Grattan. The rabid Protestant officials of the "Castle Junto" opposed any reform of Ireland's main grievances—the exclusion of the Catholics from a share in government; the payment of rent to the English landlords, imposed by Cromwell; and the payment of tithes by Catholics to an established Protestant Church which they did not attend.

Nevertheless, for a time the Irish Protestants and Catholics forgot their religious differences and worked together to gain whatever they could for their unhappy island. The penal code was modified, and Catholics were given the vote; but they could not sit in the Irish parliament. Then came the French Revolution, which seemed to be aiming at the very things Ireland wanted; and the Irish radicals decided to seek French help. A revolutionary society was organized by one Wolfe Tone. By 1797, in this emergency, there was mutiny in the fleet, the Bank of England had suspended specie payment, and England's European allies had succumbed one by one to the French. Dublin Castle, unearthing the revolutionary plots, decided to stamp them out by force, but unfortunately chose as its agents the unruly Protestant militia. The latter used the opportunity to settle old scores, and religious intolerance reappeared in its worst form. Men and women were stripped on the streets and punished if they were wearing as much as a ribbon of the revolutionary green; some were flogged, hanged, or shot down in cold blood. These methods prevented rebellion in the north; but in the south it flared out in 1798, and the rebels were as ruthless as the government forces. Militia companies were massacred in their barracks, and a barn containing nearly two hundred men, women, and children was burned to the ground. A powerful French fleet nearly made a landing, but was dispersed by gales; a smaller French force got ashore, but finally was forced to surrender. The main body of the rebels was defeated at Vinegar Hill, and vengeance was once more visited upon them. These events gave rise to the famous Irish song with the refrain

> It's the most distressful country that ever I have seen,
> They're hanging men and women for the wearing of the green.

Having crushed the revolt, Pitt decided that something must be done to remedy the conditions which provoked it. In a time of foreign war, and after the events just described, an independent Irish legislature seemed dangerous; consequently he decided that Ireland should be drawn more closely to the British government, by sending representatives to Westminster instead of to the Dublin parliament. Scotland in 1707 had received trade advantages in exchange for her loss of legislative independence. Ireland's compensation, Pitt agreed, was that full political rights should be given to the Catholics and that they should no longer have to pay for the expenses of a church they did not want. By means of heavy bribes in peerages and gold, Grattan's Parliament was persuaded to terminate its existence and to agree to a legislative union with England.

On the first day of the nineteenth century, January 1, 1801, the Kingdom of Great Britain, which had been formed in 1707 by the inclusion of Scotland, was expanded into the United Kingdom of Great Britain and Ireland, which lasted until 1922. The Irish were to have 32 members in the House of Lords and 100 in the Commons, as compared with 12 in the Lords and 45 in the Commons for Scotland. On a strict basis of population Ireland would have had a good many more members in the House of Commons; for of some 15,500,000 inhabitants in the new United Kingdom, Ireland had more than one quarter and Scotland barely one tenth. Wealth, rather than population, however, was the important consideration. The union was not pleasing to Ireland. The Scots had been granted commercial privileges which had induced them to give up their independence; the Irish did not receive the compensations they had been led to expect. This was primarily the fault of George III. When Pitt proposed to grant new rights to the Irish Catholics, the king opposed the plan, arguing that it would be a violation of his coronation oath; then he extracted a promise from Pitt, and later from other ministers, not to bring up the question again as long as he lived. While the last royal veto had occurred in 1707, this stubborn stand of the intermittently insane monarch amounted to virtually the same thing, and it helped to embitter Anglo-Irish relations for many years to come.

In the face of this royal opposition Pitt resigned, and did not return to office for three years. The dissolution of the Whigs had destroyed the normal two-party rivalry, and the Commons were once more divided into several groups which the king could play against each other. George continued to act thus until he was declared permanently insane and his son, in 1811, became Prince Regent. Pitt was succeeded in 1801 by Henry Addington (later Lord Sidmouth), a dull, well-meaning man who provoked the couplet

> Pitt is to Addington
> As London is to Paddington.

His weak ministry came at the time of the one breathing spell in the French wars; and soon after the contest was resumed with Napoleon, popular demand brought Pitt back to power in 1804.

The Treaty of Amiens gave England barely a year of peace. Its terms were decidedly less favorable to the British, who restored most of their conquests, than to the French, who retained a fairly free hand in Continental matters. The French still held Belgium, which was always a sensitive point in British foreign policy, and were interfering in Italy and Switzerland. As a particular matter of concern to the British, they seemed to have designs upon the independence of Holland, to whom England had restored the Cape of Good Hope. The technical excuse for the resumption of hostilities in 1803, however, was England's failure to restore Malta as agreed at Amiens. That little island, strategically situated where it could dominate the narrow passage between the eastern and the western Mediterranean, had for two and a half centuries belonged to the military crusading order of the Knights of Saint John, to whom it had been given after the Turks drove them from Rhodes. Bonaparte, on his way to Egypt in 1798, had seized the island; but the French had treated the inhabitants so wantonly that they welcomed the British, who occupied it the following year. England realized that its location and its splendid harbor provided an excellent naval base, all the more necessary because Minorca had been lost in 1783. Consequently the British clung to it despite the treaty terms, while Bonaparte, on his side, was threatening the independence of those little neighbors of France.

With the resumption of hostilities England was faced with a grave menace of invasion. Bonaparte had his grand army encamped at Boulogne, just across the Channel, while artisans were hard at work making flatboats in which it could be transported. It remained only for the French navy, strengthened by many new ships, to hold off the British warships long enough to get the troops across those twenty-odd miles of water. Once they were across, England would have no armed forces capable of effective resistance. In naval strategy, however, France had always been under a heavy handicap. She had to have ships on the Atlantic and also on the Mediterranean. For the Atlantic she had a powerful base at Brest, near the Channel; and for the Mediterranean another at Toulon; but between those two lay the whole Spanish peninsula. Bonaparte's plan was to have the Toulon fleet join the Brest fleet in order to gain temporary control of the Channel.

England was faced with a threat as grave as that of 1588; but once again the royal navy rose to the occasion. A close and continuous blockade was clapped down on the enemy ports and, despite terrific difficulties, maintained for twenty grueling months. While the French veterans were practicing getting into flatboats, and panicky land-defense measures were being taken on England's side of the Channel, the squadrons kept their stations. Admiral Cornwallis, whose brother had lost Yorktown, kept guard off Brest while Nelson watched the Toulon fleet. Lesser squadrons cruised before lesser ports, including those of Spain, which came in again as a French ally in 1804. England had fifty-five ships of the line to offset forty-two of the enemy at the start. Such numerical superiority was necessary from the very nature of the work. The enemy had their ships together for use at any favorable moment, whereas the forces outside were liable to be scattered by storms or diminished by the necessity to refit. The blockaders had a negative mission, requiring constant vigilance, and they had to be strong enough to drive the enemy back into port. The constant service on blockade kept the crews well trained, while the enemy lay inactive; but it was a severe test for unsound ships. And there were plenty of unsound ships in the British blockade. They had not been repaired during the interval of peace, and now there was no timber with which to repair them. English oaks were constantly growing scarcer, and even the available supply was in the hands of a powerful monopoly which refused to give any to the navy unless its old graft were restored. Consequently complaints came in from the various stations of British squadrons, which were weakened by wear and tear while the enemy grew stronger in port. "My crazy fleet are getting in a very indifferent state," wrote Nelson off Toulon, "and others will soon follow. The finest ships in the service will be destroyed. I know that if I was to go to Malta, I should save the ships during this bad season; but if I am to watch the French, I must be at sea, and if at sea must have bad weather; and if the ships are not fit to stand bad weather, they are useless." "However," he wrote in closing, "you may rely that all which can be done by ships and men shall be done." He and his ships and his men made good that promise. So did the forces on the other stations, from one of which an admiral wrote, "We have been sailing for months with only a copper sheet between us and eternity." But repairs could not be made because the timber monopoly withheld the oak (it was reported that on a certain day there was not a single four-inch plank in the great dockyard at Portsmouth). By 1805 the Admiralty had yielded to the terms of the monopolists and had hastily patched up some of the decrepit ships. It was none too soon. The enemy now outnumbered the British blockaders by fifteen ships; but still the blockade held fast. "The world has never seen a more impressive demonstration of the influence of sea power upon its history," wrote Mahan in his study of sea power. "Those far-distant, storm-beaten ships, upon which the Grand Army never looked, stood between it and the dominion of the world."[1]

Then, in the summer of 1805, the monotonous siege gave way to rapid and dramatic action. While Nelson's forces were temporarily scattered by a storm, the Toulon fleet slipped out of port and headed for the West Indies, to draw the British away from their sentry duty. Nelson, after a hurried search of the Mediterranean, followed them

[1] A. T. Mahan, *Influence of Sea Power upon the French Revolution and Empire* (1898), Vol. II, p. 118. By permission of Little, Brown & Company and Sampson Low, Marston & Co., Ltd.

to the Caribbean and then back again. The Toulon fleet put into Cádiz, where it joined forces with the Spaniards. Napoleon (for Bonaparte had become emperor in 1804) ordered a more energetic admiral to take command; but before he could reach Cádiz, the combined French and Spanish fleet, in a gesture of despair, sailed out to challenge the British. The result was a decisive battle off Cape Trafalgar, just outside Gibraltar, on October 21, 1805.

The enemy had thirty-three ships of the line. Nelson had only twenty-seven; but his men had been kept in fighting trim, and he inspired a high morale. The enemy were finally sighted, straggling out in the single conventional line in such slovenly fashion that it resembled a crescent. Nelson headed for its center with his ships in two parallel columns, one of which he himself led in the *Victory*. Signal flags were run up from the flagship—not a regular tactical message this time but a characteristic Nelson touch, "England expects every man to do his duty." The lazy breeze brought the fleets together at barely a mile an hour; but at last they joined in a melee, exchanging broadsides at close range. The *Victory* was actually grappled to a French seventy-four when a marine from the enemy ship's fighting top fired at Nelson. He fell, and was carried below to the dark cockpit among the other wounded, where he died a few hours later, after learning that the enemy fleet was routed. Only once in the next hundred years was England's command of the seas to be questioned, and not until 1916, in fact, was England's main fleet again to engage in battle with an enemy of fairly equal strength.

Nelson died thinking that he had saved England from invasion by the Grand Army at Boulogne. But by the time Trafalgar was fought, that army was on the Danube. In order to distract Napoleon, Pitt had persuaded Austria and Russia to join England in a Third Coalition, England, as usual, paying a generous share of the bills. Napoleon learned of this, and, determining to break up the alliance before it could get under way, he abandoned the idea of invading England. Later, to save his face, he declared that he had never really intended to do more than give England a scare. At any rate, as soon as he found out that the Toulon fleet had put into Cádiz instead of clearing the Channel, he secretly withdrew the Grand Army from Boulogne; hurried it eastward across Europe by forced marches, much as Marlborough had done in the Blenheim campaign; and, four days before Trafalgar was fought, caught one whole Austrian army by surprise. Then he entered Vienna and in December crushed an allied Austrian and Russian army at Austerlitz.

That news really killed Pitt. When he saw his Third Coalition crumble away before Napoleon's onslaught, he said, "Roll up the map of Europe; it will not be needed these ten years." Early in 1806 he was dead. He was followed by a succession of very mediocre prime ministers, each of whom was overshadowed by at least one member of his cabinet. His immediate successor was Lord Grenville, the former foreign minister, whose father had pushed through the Stamp Act in 1765. He headed a "Ministry of All the Talents" including several Whigs, particularly Fox, who, with only a few months left to live, crowned his career with the abolition of the slave trade. In 1807 the innocuous Duke of Portland, who had been nominal head of the Fox-North ministry, again became titular head of a cabinet which included the sharp-tongued George Canning, later famous as a liberal Tory, and Lord Castlereagh (later Lord Londonderry), handsome, cold, and competent, who guided England's military policy and foreign relations during most of the ensuing years of war and of peace negotiations and won a name for being a worse reactionary than he really was. By 1809, after these two men had fought a duel and Portland had died, a new ministry was formed by Spencer Perceval, a clever Parliamentary tactician and a good hater of the French. His assassination in 1812 came just too late to avert war with the United States (see page 573). Then politics settled down for a fifteen-year ministry under the "arch mediocrity" Lord Liverpool, who was obscured by Castlereagh and other able subordinates. These men, stubborn, dogged, and level-headed, deserve credit for keeping alive the opposition to Napoleon and for making possible his final downfall. But the distant gunfire from the Continent deafened them to sounds closer at hand—the smashing of looms by the distressed handworkers and the complaints of the starving rural peasantry.

Napoleon, in the meantime, had followed up Austerlitz with further victories. Austria was out of the fight for the third time, and the Russians withdrew; but Prussia, who had kept out of the fray for eleven years, suddenly took up arms. Had she done so a year earlier, when Pitt was desperately urging such a course, the Third Coalition might have been another story. As it was, Prussia's rusty army was routed in a single battle at Jena, in 1806, and Napoleon showed his contempt by imposing humiliating terms. Russia still remained; but after two desperate and bloody battles, Napoleon and Czar Alexander met amicably at Tilsit, in 1807, to "divide the world between them." For the next few years Napoleon's power was at its height. Most of the Continent was to be either under his direct control or, if not controlled by his brothers or his marshals, at least in alliance. Until 1812 there was a lull in the major campaigning, and Europe listened to his commands.

Even though the fleets and the regiments might refrain from battle for a while, Napoleon and England were constantly engaged in economic warfare on a grand scale. Napoleon had determined upon a final effort to bring England to her knees, months before he met Alexander at Tilsit. The thrusts at Ireland, and at India through Egypt, had failed; Trafalgar had demonstrated that direct invasion was out of the question. But as long as England remained untamed, her gold and diplomacy would go on building up coalitions to challenge his power. In an attempt to dry up the source of much of that gold, Napoleon issued at Berlin, in 1806, a decree which nominally closed the ports of his empire and dependencies to all ships from Great Britain, made British goods liable to seizure, and declared the British Isles in a state of blockade. At the Tilsit conference he had secured the adherence of Russia and Prussia to these terms, and Denmark also joined. Napoleon's Milan Decree, of 1807, declared all neutral ships liable to seizure if suspected of trade with the British. England had countered with Orders in Council (similar to the old ordinances and proclamations); the severest of these, issued in 1807, declared Napoleon's coasts in a state of blockade and practically required all neutrals to trade through British ports. These blockades were of the "paper" sort, as neither side had ships enough for a literal one; they simply announced that a port was blockaded and that anyone trading with it was therefore considered liable to capture. Despite all efforts to keep the Tilsit terms secret, even to staging the conference on a raft in the river, England learned of them quickly, because, as legend has it, a Scot was hidden underneath. Within two months a British fleet repeated Nelson's work of six years before by smashing the Danes at Copenhagen without bothering to declare war, and carrying their navy back to England. This prompt, if illegal, action kept the Baltic open.

Either Napoleon's "Continental System" or England's "Continental Blockade" could have practically put an end to European commerce if the original edicts had been enforced at their face value. Each side, however, wished to maintain its own trade while crippling that of the enemy. Out of this situation arose the license system of "trading by exception" through maritime indulgences. Both sides adopted this practice of maritime hypocrisy and sometimes went to ridiculous lengths. Later, when Napoleon was preparing to invade Russia, he bought vast quantities of overcoats in England; and his old mother put the extra money which he gave her into English consols, so that she should be sure of an income whether he won or lost. England, while fighting in Spain, paid the armies by means of drafts which passed through the bankers of

# Reaction and Napoleon

Paris. On the whole, England was the one who profited most as a result of these irregularities.

The function of the royal navy underwent a decided change after Trafalgar. The ships of the line, which had performed their duties in such thorough fashion, were relieved of the long strain and, except for the raid on Copenhagen, had little fighting to do. It was now the turn of the smaller craft to take up the navy's burden in enforcing the Continental Blockade. England gave a remarkable demonstration of "the noiseless, steady, exhausting pressure with which sea power acts, cutting off the resources of the enemy while maintaining its own, supporting war in scenes where it does not appear itself or appears only in the background, and striking open blows only at rare intervals."[1] Frigates and sloops by the hundred were necessary for the exercise of this pressure. Even the little gun brigs were needed; for their ten guns were enough to make a merchantman heave to and prove that its papers and cargo satisfied Britain's commercial regulations.

While thus rendering hazardous the enemy trade, the British constantly sought loopholes in the Continental System. The Public Record Office in London contains hundreds of interesting letters written by British secret-service agents who kept the government informed of the situation in the various ports. The officials, it seems, were frequently negligent or corruptible. One agent, for instance, reported from the Baltic in 1809 that "notwithstanding the many impediments laid in the way of trade, several ships have cleared out from these ports actually bound for Great Britain. . . . The French consul takes a fee of 1 per cent for himself and a *douceur* to his secretary for his certificate." Thereupon scores of merchantmen, under naval convoy up to the last minute, would descend on those ports to sell England's commercial offerings. Europe craved some of the products which England alone could bring from her empire. Scientists found that an adequate substitute for West Indian sugar could be derived from beets; but tea, coffee, chocolate, and tobacco were in high demand, while the landowners of northern Europe wanted an outlet for their grain and timber which lay rotting at the ports. Even if officials were occasionally changed, and some zealous newcomer seized ships and publicly burned cargoes of English woolens in the square, the profits on successful cargoes were enough to offset such losses. Even when the Continental System was enforced most rigidly, there was a certain amount of leakage.

British trade, in fact, actually expanded during this period of the

[1] A. T. Mahan, *Influence of Sea Power upon History, 1660–1783* (1890), p. 209. By permission of Little, Brown & Company, and Sampson Low, Marston & Co., Ltd.

# A History of England and the British Empire

Continental System. In 1805 British exports had amounted to some £50,000,000, and they remained at that level for the next three years. In 1809 they rose to £66,000,000—higher than ever before—and fell off only slightly in 1810. The quantity of exports, to be sure, decreased, but that very scarcity enhanced the price of what was sold. The Industrial Revolution played its part in carrying England through the Napoleonic crisis. The textiles and hardware of Manchester, Birmingham, and the other British factory towns could not be matched elsewhere at equal price. Temporary stoppages of trade during this period might mean failure for individual merchants or factory owners; but the outside world, whenever it was able, bought British manufactures, "because they were better at the price." England did not have to force her wares on unwilling foreigners; her sea power enabled her to set her goods ashore, where they were taken by "the willing hands of the people whom Napoleon claimed to be rescuing from her commercial tyranny." While the looms of Lancashire were helping England to accumulate funds for fighting Napoleon, the improved productivity resulting from the Agricultural Revolution was enabling England to feed not only her peasantry but also, in part, her factory workers and her armed forces.

Neutral flags were absolutely essential for that commerce which survived the edicts of 1806 and 1807. The English flag would be as vulnerable in a Continental port as the French flag would be at sea. Each side had to use neutrals, but each distrusted them. England, in particular, had a long record of opposing the sanctity of neutrality. If the doctrine of "free ships, free goods" were allowed, the whole advantage which command of the seas gave her in cutting off enemy trade would be nullified. For centuries, suspected merchantmen had been brought to by a shot across the bow from a British warship; whereupon the "right of search" would be exercised with cold insolence, and would frequently end with a prize crew's taking the vessel to England for trial in an Admiralty court. There were neutrals and neutrals. Some were legitimate, exporting their own products in their own ships or carrying the wares of others in time of war. There was also a farcical prostitution of neutrality afforded by little free German cities which had their own flags. Their tiny merchant marines were sometimes expanded a hundredfold overnight in time of war by wholesale registration of belligerent ships. A French or British brig might secure shelter behind the sacred protection of neutrality by a mere scratch of the pen and a liberal use of money. Suspicious boarding officers might have the stern of the vessel scraped to see what name and hailing port had been originally painted underneath. Pitt had expressed the British point of view when he asked in the House of Commons "whether we are to suffer neutral nations, by hoisting a flag upon a sloop or a fishing boat, to convey the treasures of South America or the naval stores of the Baltic to Brest or Toulon." But England herself had to use neutral "protective coloring" when she approached the ports of Napoleon's domains during these years. England's point of view, like that of most nations on the subject of neutral ships, depended wholly upon whether she was a neutral who wanted to trade, as in the American Civil War, or—her usual role—a blockading belligerent.

Most conspicuous among the legitimate neutrals was the United States. The outbreak of the Anglo-French war in 1793 had been a boon to the infant republic, whose old colonial commerce had been knocked askew by the Revolution. New ships were built by the score, and did a lively business carrying wares for both England and France. Even in the earlier years of the fighting, many had run afoul of the regulations of one belligerent or the other; but that carrying trade laid the foundations of many a Yankee fortune. The Berlin and Milan Decrees, combined with the Orders in Council, however, made the chances of seizure much greater. The owners and the mariners were ready to take the risk, but President Jefferson pushed through Congress in 1807 an Embargo Act, forbidding all foreign commerce in American vessels. It was soon modified into "nonintercourse," and England and France were told that the Americans would trade with the one which repealed her decrees. Napoleon made a gesture of doing so. There was bitter feeling against England's exercise of the right of search, together with the impressing of seamen from American ships on the charge that they were British deserters. That, combined with irritation over the British relations with the Indians in the Northwest, and a hope that Canada could be easily captured, led the United States to declare war on England in 1812. Had there been a transatlantic cable then, there might have been no war; for after Perceval's assassination the new ministry relaxed the Orders in Council, just before the American declaration of war.

One's impressions of the so-called "War of 1812" depend upon whether one reads an American, Canadian, or English account. The Americans dwell upon the naval exploits. They had devised frigates strong enough to whip most of the British frigates and fast enough to run away from anything stronger, so that the *Constitution* whipped the *Guerrière* and *Java*, and the *United States* crushed the *Macedonian*. These defeats were a blow to British pride; but the fact remained that the royal navy soon blockaded most of the American ports, swept American merchantmen off the seas, and even captured two of the frigates. The Americans also tell of the triumphs of their improvised flotillas on the lakes, and of the smashing defeat of veteran redcoats by backwoods riflemen at New Orleans (a battle fought, incidentally, after the peace had been signed). The Canadian versions are likely to dwell upon the repeated and unsuccessful efforts of large but unprepared American armies to conquer Canada. The British barely mention the indecisive war, treating it as a subordinate "sideshow" to more weighty events on the Continent.

To the Englishmen the War of 1812 was completely overshadowed by the contemporary "Peninsular War" which the redcoats were waging in Spain and Portugal, and in which the army fully offset its lack of accomplishment during the previous fifteen years. Those six years in the Peninsula loom particularly large in English annals. This war had its origin in the Continental System. Napoleon had assumed a crushing burden when, in order to cut off British trade, he undertook to hold all the nations of the Continent in line. He could not afford to countenance a single breach in the wall as long as he clung to that policy. England's old ally Portugal in 1807 was still outside his sphere of influence. Napoleon persuaded the weak Spanish Bourbon government to allow him to send troops through Spain to bring Portugal to terms. He did so; and the Portuguese government took ship to Brazil, where it remained until the storm blew over. The next step was Spain. Using the Portuguese expedition as an excuse, he filled the strategic spots in Spain with French troops. Then, in the spring of 1808, he bullied the weak king and also his worthless son into abdication. Next he persuaded a packed council to accept his brother as king of Spain. Holland had accepted another brother as king; Westphalia, in Germany, had taken a third without trouble; and his stepson had likewise become ruler of Italy. But with Spain it was different. The Spaniards revolted against the Bonaparte king from the beginning; they were loyal to their legitimate ruler, worthless though he was.

Thus Napoleon tasted the first violent reaction of that same fierce national spirit which had enabled France to conquer her neighbors but now was to roll back upon the French and to wreck their superstate. This Spanish war was of a sort which puzzled and annoyed Napoleon. It was not like fighting the Austrians or Prussians, who came out on the battlefield according to the regular rules and could be put out of the fight in a battle or two. A treaty would be signed, a little more land annexed, and that would end the episode. But there were no rules in the sort of war the Spaniards waged—*guerrilla*, they called it, or "little war." Everyone might fight, even priests and women. An army would vanish from sight, and there was no telling where the scattered detachments might turn up next, falling, perhaps, on some isolated outpost or harassing the long lines of communication. Indeed, if a message was to have a reasonable chance of getting back through the Pyrenean passes to France, a whole brigade of cavalry had sometimes to accompany the courier. There was no glory in winning such a war, and there was a very good chance of losing, as Napoleon was to find out. He had to keep some three hundred thousand troops in the Peninsula, but many of them were simply guarding vulnerable communications. He later made the unpleasant but apt comparison of the Spanish war to an ulcer which drained away the strength of his empire. Reverses came quickly. The Bourbons had been ejected in April; in July one of his generals, with eighteen thousand men, was trapped by the Spaniards and forced to surrender. The French were not invincible.

What the Spanish "nation in arms," with its fierce, irregular guerrilla methods, needed was a small, well-disciplined body of troops to serve as a nucleus for its resistance. It was just such a nucleus that England sent in the summer of 1808 and kept there until it had driven the French out of Spain. A century earlier, England had tried to do just such a thing during the War of the Spanish Succession, but the rattle-brained commander had bungled the situation (see page 417). The slender, austere general of thirty-nine who was sent down this time was clear-headed, self-possessed, shrewd, and painstaking. Sir Arthur Wellesley, who would be Lord Wellington next year, and later Duke, was one of England's foremost soldiers. He came from a family of Anglo-Irish aristocrats of that governing caste for which Ireland blames Cromwell. He had served skillfully in India, where his older brother, not yet overshadowed by Arthur, was viceroy. Owing to his cold nature he never won the affection of his officers and men, as Marlborough or Nelson had done; but he did command their entire confidence. Napoleon's men affectionately called their leader the "Little Corporal"; Wellington was to be known as the "Iron Duke."

A month after that French general surrendered his army in Spain, Wellesley landed at Lisbon, which England was always glad to use as a convenient jumping-off place. British generals always felt more secure with their backs to the sea; and seldom did the royal navy let them down as it had Cornwallis at Yorktown. Before long Wellesley ran the French out of Portugal. Spain, however, was a different matter—the French had ten men to his one. Consequently he adopted for several years a "hit and run" policy. He found that he could disconcert the enemy by darting at their lines of communications and then hurrying back to Portugal before they could catch him. To protect himself there, he defended Lisbon with a powerful triple series of field fortifications known as the Torres Vedras Lines. Here, after stripping the countryside of anything the French could eat, he could rest secure after his hide-and-seek. This he did in 1810, to the deep chagrin of the marshal whom Napoleon sent to drive him into the sea. Unlike the generals of the other nations that fought Napoleon, Wellington retained the effective old "thin-line" tactics (see page 448), which enabled every soldier to use his musket against an attacking force. This, combined with his remarkably efficient supply system, gave Wellington a decided advantage over the French, who clung to the vulnerable mass formations devised for green troops early in the Revolution, and who hoped to settle the supply problem by "living off the country," a difficult feat in sun-parched Spain and Portugal. So it went until 1812, when Napoleon began to withdraw troops for his Russian campaign. Wellington grew bolder: he forced, at terrific cost in men, the fortresses which guarded the two mountain gateways from Portugal into Spain, and then "beat forty thousand men in forty minutes" at Salamanca. There was one more winter at Lisbon; then, as the campaigning season of 1813 opened, Wellington said a final farewell to Portugal, took the offensive, and after a month's rapid campaigning smashed the French at Vitoria and drove the Bonaparte government out of Spain. It was still hit and run; but now Wellington was doing all the hitting and the enemy all the running. By autumn he was crossing into France.

The effort to maintain the Continental System had helped to ruin the Corsican genius. Europe had grown more and more restless under its restrictions. Finally Alexander of Russia decided to withdraw from the system. Napoleon thereupon invaded Russia in 1812 with six hundred thousand men, drawn from his many subject regions. Russian armies were often inefficient outside their own borders, but on the defensive they had both the tremendous distances and the terrible weather on their side. Napoleon reached Moscow and started back; winter caught him; and only a pitiful remnant of the Grand Army ever returned. Meanwhile Castlereagh was carrying on Pitt's old work as a coalition-builder. This time almost all joined in the killing—Austria, Russia, Prussia, and many lesser powers. Prussia had been experiencing a remarkable national revival and, thanks to an ingenious system of universal military training, was able to put an effective army into the field. In the fall of 1813, while Wellington was crossing the Pyrenees and an American commodore on Lake Erie was writing, "We have met the enemy and they are ours," these

# Reaction and Napoleon

various allied foes whipped Napoleon in the three-day "Battle of the Nations" at Leipzig. He never recovered from that defeat. Deftly parrying the blows from several different armies, he fought a series of brilliant rearguard actions as he retired toward Paris, ever hoping that his luck would change. It did not; and in April, 1814, he abdicated his power, to become "emperor" of the little Mediterranean island of Elba, off the coast of Italy.

Europe breathed freely. The quarter century of the nightmare of French threats seemed over. The stodgy Bourbon brother of the late Louis XVI was placed on the French throne. A grateful nation made Wellington, the hero of Europe, a duke, and he took his place with Castlereagh as England's spokesman at Vienna, where the potentates of Europe gathered to redraw the map which had been so strangely altered since 1792.

But the fighting was not yet over. Napoleon escaped from Elba in March, 1815, and landed in France, where many of his old soldiers gathered around him. He went back to the throne as emperor, and in the following "Hundred Days" Europe wondered with dread what he might do. But, whichever way he turned, allied armies blocked the roads. England, as usual, was most interested in the Low Countries; so Wellington waited across the road to Brussels with a mixed force of British, Dutch, Hanoverian, and other troops. Near by was rough old Marshal Blücher, with his Prussians. Napoleon turned toward Brussels; and so to Wellington fell the brunt of the defense.

The final battle was fought at Waterloo, near Brussels, in June, 1815. Except for the outcome, Waterloo bore a striking resemblance to Hastings, seven centuries and a half before. In both instances the English took the role best suited to them: a stubborn defensive stand across a road along which their French foes were trying to advance. In each case the enemy tried to dislodge them by repeated charging. At Hastings the English finally broke, but at Waterloo, after resisting terrific punishment, they still held their hill. It was the Peninsular battles over again. The "thin red line of heroes" beat off the massed columns of infantry which Napoleon hurled against them; when the cavalry charged, the British "formed square" and drove them back, too. Thus it went until, late in the day, a large body of troops was seen marching from the east to the sound of the guns. It might be the Prussians under Blücher; it might be a French corps which had gone astray; in either case these fresh forces would probably turn the tide. They came nearer, and it became evident that they wore the Prussian blue. The day was saved. After vainly shattering the "Old Guard," the choicest of his crack regiments, against the stubborn wall, Napoleon got into his coach and drove furiously for the coast. Blücher was after him, swearing to hang his enemy if he caught him. Thereupon Napoleon, finding that he could not escape to America as he had planned, went aboard H. M. S. *Bellerophon* and threw himself on the mercy of the British. It was a dramatic finish to the long struggle between land power and sea power. This time no chances were taken: England carried him to exile on her bleak and lonely island of St. Helena, in the South Atlantic, where he died six years later. The diplomats, the captains, and the kings went back to finish up the peace settlement which he had so rudely disturbed.

# CHAPTER XX

## *The Approach to Reform*

### 1815-1832

IN 1815 England had won her heart's desire, peace with victory. She was mistress of the seven seas; her trade, her shipping, and her wealth seemed impregnably secure. Napoleon was a captive in her hands; Wellington, her Iron Duke, kept watch and ward in northern France; and Castlereagh, her chief representative at Vienna, was obtaining here and there throughout the world a few strategic places which would prove useful in the future of her empire.

England was on the threshhold of a transitional period of seventeen years during which she was gradually to readjust her attitude toward foreign and domestic affairs. Her close co-operation with the Continental powers, which had contributed much to the downfall of Napoleon, was gradually to give way to a policy which would later be described as "splendid isolation," coupled with English support of various nationalistic aspirations for independence. At home England was still more slowly to free herself from the deadening Tory repression, and the period was to end with a liberal political reform of the utmost importance.

The Hundred Days had broken into the midst of the peace negotiations, which nevertheless continued despite the emergency created by Napoleon's spectacular return from Elba. Since the first abdication of the French emperor in 1814, the representatives of the powers had been laboring to establish a lasting peace and, at the same time, to get for their respective countries as much as possible. Most of the work was done at Vienna, where the peace congress lasted from September, 1814, until early in June, 1815, just before Waterloo, though certain important treaties were signed at Paris and elsewhere before and after the Vienna meetings. The Congress of Vienna was carried on in an atmosphere of constant social revelry which nearly bankrupted the Austrian government. Some of the important decisions were made during dinners, balls, or hunts, and formal sessions were rare. During the gay parties intrigue flourished, for the map of Europe was being redrawn. Bullying and bargaining went on feverishly before the frontiers should become fixed; for all realized that the course of events during a single evening might determine the flag under which thousands would live. Hundreds of delegates, representing every European country save Turkey, were present; but, as is usual under such circumstances, the power to make the real decisions rested with a few men representing the great powers.

The dominating figure of the congress was Count Metternich, the Austrian chancellor. Of all the great powers, Austria had probably taken the heaviest punishment during the French wars, having five times challenged France to fight and, on the first four occasions, having been quickly beaten down. Naturally such a record of persistent opposition gave Metternich, as her spokesman, a commanding position. Calculating, cynical, and conceited, a thorough realist and reactionary, Metternich had spent years as a diplomat at various European capitals fighting the ideas of the French Revolution, which filled him with horror and disgust. With characteristic self-glorification, he claimed that his constant intriguing had deliberately caused the downfall of Napoleon. His aim was to restore Europe as far as possible to its condition before the French Revolution. In particular, he was determined to have Germany and Italy so reorganized that Austrian influence would be increased in both regions and the French doctrines of democracy and nationalism stifled.

British interests were in the capable hands of Lord Castlereagh, the most influential man in English politics during the ten years preceding his death in 1822. His reputation is beginning to emerge from the bitter opprobrium many heaped upon him during his lifetime. The rebellious young romantic poets did much to blacken his name for later generations:

> I met Murder on the way,—
> He had a mask like Castlereagh,

wrote Shelley, while Byron assailed him as "the most despotic in intention, the weakest in intellect, that ever tyrannized over a country." Crowds cheered when they learned that he had finally cut his throat with a penknife. Yet ample evidence from sources of better authority indicates that there is no question whatever about the penetrating and straightforward quality of his intellect, and that, while he was cold in public and a poor speaker, he owed much of his diplomatic success to his charm, graciousness, and persuasiveness in intimate company. He steered his way with force and adroitness through the maze of intrigues at Vienna, whither he had even brought his own maidservants to prevent spies from serving in his household. Quietly and efficiently he played an important part in the critical decisions. England had been even more persistently than Austria the foe of France, and her prestige was further enhanced by the recent victories of Wellington, who also attended the congress until called away by the Hundred Days. Since England had no desire for Continental territory, Castlereagh could act in a more disinterested fashion than most of the other delegates. He declared that his policy was "to bring back the world to peaceful habits"; and, although he disapproved of some of Metternich's views, he was inclined to side with Austria against Russia and Prussia, whose ambitions seemed disturbing to European tranquillity and the balance of power.

Czar Alexander of Russia, still in his thirties, played something of a dual role in the peace negotiations. He was the same Alexander who, on the raft at Tilsit, had suddenly changed from stubborn battling to enthusiastic co-operation with Napoleon. Now, on the one hand, as an idealist he injected an atmosphere of religious mysticism into his proposals for a "holy" basis for future peace, and at the same time his ministers were engaged in the most successful land-grabbing at the congress. Russia would continue for several years to threaten European peace with incessant intrigues.

Talleyrand, spokesman for defeated France, overshadowed the representatives of Prussia, the fourth of the victorious great powers. Subtle, dishonest, disloyal, unscrupulous, albeit charming, Talleyrand, always the opportunist, had served France and himself by always moving ahead of others to whatever side was coming into power during the difficult years since 1789 and always landing upon his feet. A member of the nobility and a bishop in pre-Revolutionary France, a moderate during the early Revolution, foreign minister under both the Directory and Napoleon, sponsor of the restoration of the Bourbon king, he now utilized the violent disagreements among the four victors by throwing his weight with Metternich and Castlereagh against Russia and Prussia. Though the influence of this man, whom Napoleon called a "silk stocking filled with mud," has perhaps been overrated, he helped to bring others to the view that Napoleon, not France, was the defeated enemy and that the keynote of the congress should be "legitimacy."

This keynote of the settlement, "legitimacy," meant the restoration of the legitimate prewar monarchs to their thrones. The powers adhered to this policy, however, only in those cases where it suited their interests. The house of Bourbon was restored to three former thrones—a dull king in France, a worse one in Spain, and the worst of all in Naples. More than three hundred "legitimate" political units in Germany, however, were compressed into thirty-nine. The former independent states of Venice and Poland were not revived. In general practice the great powers seemed to take what they wanted, and the medium nations were compensated at the expense of the small ones, whose interests were quite neglected. Russia received Finland and a very generous share of territory formerly Polish; Prussia's gains were chiefly in Germany; while Austria became paramount in Italy and head of the new loose German Confederation, which arose in place of the defunct Holy Roman Empire. Belgium (the former Austrian Netherlands) was joined to Holland under the Dutch king, to form a buffer state on the northern frontier of France. For a like reason the ancient republic of Genoa was granted to the House of Savoy, in order that its kingdom of Sardinia (or Piedmont), the future nucleus of a united Italy, might better guard the French southeastern frontier.

The treatment accorded France was remarkably lenient. Castlereagh and Metternich had been willing to work with Talleyrand to prevent the aggrandizement of Russia and Prussia and to whittle down the demands made for the punishment of France. The French loss of territory was inconsiderable—a few valleys on the frontier only. An indemnity was imposed as punishment for the Hundred Days, and allied troops were to occupy French territory until it was paid. But the amount was light; and when it came to paying, the British made borrowing easy.

As for England, the rival French, Dutch, and Spanish fleets had virtually disappeared, and the royal navy ruled supreme on the seas. In the matter of overseas territory Castlereagh might have taken anything England desired. With real moderation, however, he restored many of the former enemy colonies and kept only a few— the Cape of Good Hope; Ceylon and Mauritius, in the Indian Ocean; Heligoland, in the North Sea; and part of Guiana—and a few others, as we shall note (see page 656), which would make valuable strategic bases. Castlereagh also obtained the assent of the powers to the abolition of the slave trade, which Wilberforce and Fox had secured in England in 1807. The question of freedom of the seas and neutral rights, however, was not discussed.

Before adjourning the congress, the representatives of the great powers arranged to continue their co-operative action for a period of twenty years. England, Austria, Prussia, and Russia late in 1815 signed at Paris a treaty forming the Quadruple Alliance "for the safety of their governments and for the general peace of Europe," and, in view of the fact that "revolutionary principles might again convulse France and endanger the peace of other countries," they guaranteed the territorial and dynastic settlements which they had made. It was arranged to hold occasional congresses to discuss matters. Metternich set considerable store by this, and Castlereagh thought that it was more desirable for the representatives of the

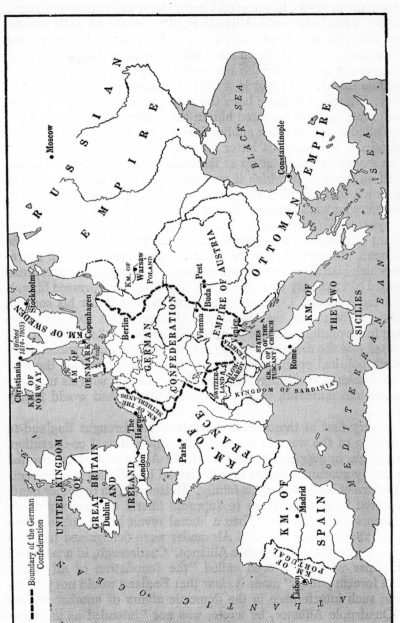

EUROPE IN 1815

- - - - Boundary of the German Confederation

powers thus to sit together around a table and discuss matters openly than to resort to the secret methods of individual diplomatic intrigue. This Quadruple Alliance is often confused with the so-called Holy Alliance, a pet idea of Czar Alexander's for permanent international peace, which he advocated as part of the work of the congress. He wanted all the monarchs of Europe, the small ones as well as the great, to join in a Christian union of peace, love, and charity. He seems to have been the only one who took it seriously, though most of them humored him in the matter. Castlereagh, however, called it a "piece of sublime mysticism and nonsense"; and England did not join this latter alliance.

The machinery thus set up at the close of the Napoleonic period, as well as the way in which it was used, was so much the work of Metternich that the next thirty-odd years are known by his name. There were no wars between the great powers, to be sure, for nearly forty years. To that extent the settlement was satisfactory, but constant political unrest seethed among the liberal elements on the Continent. Metternich led the antirevolutionary, repressive movement which characterized the period from 1815 until the widespread upheaval of 1848. By this "Metternich system" he repressed liberalism in the Austrian, German, and Italian regions under his control, and he sought to use the Quadruple Alliance as his tool for intervening in revolutions outside that zone. The years 1820–1821, 1830, and 1848 saw the main revolts against his system, which successfully set back political progress in Europe. His system survived the first two epidemics of revolution; but the third, in 1848, with its underlying economic upheaval, was to prove too strong and would finally break it.

The very first of those revolutions, however, brought England to the parting of the ways in the matter of international co-operation. Castlereagh, in supporting the Quadruple Alliance, had interpreted it as simply guaranteeing the new territorial boundaries and preventing a return of Napoleon or his family. Metternich, on the other hand, interpreted it as an alliance to suppress liberal and revolutionary movements within states. When a liberal revolt broke out in Spain early in 1820, Metternich and Alexander were determined to crush it in the name of the Quadruple Alliance. Castlereagh, in a powerful state paper which has been called "the foundation of all future British foreign policy," made it clear that England would not participate in such interference in the domestic affairs of another nation. The Quadruple Alliance, he wrote, was not "intended as an union for the government of the world, or for the superintendence of the internal affairs of other states." England, to be sure, had joined in the precautions against revolutionary France; but that, he said, was on account of her military menace, and not directed "against the democratic principles, then as now, but too generally spread throughout Europe." England, unlike the other members of the alliance, had representative government; "Our position, our institutions, the habits of thinking, and the prejudice of our people, render us essentially different." England, he declared, would be found in her place if actual danger menaced the territorial system of Europe; "but this country cannot, and will not, act upon abstract and speculative principles of precaution." In brief, he wanted the Quadruple Alliance kept "within its common-sense limits."

Nevertheless, the rulers of Austria, Russia, and Prussia decided to go ahead, even without England; and at the Congress of Troppau, later in 1820, authorized the Austrian troops to intervene in Italy and suppress the revolts which in the meantime had broken out in Naples and Piedmont. England was simply an interested observer at this congress. Castlereagh refused to participate in the policy of intervention; but at the same time he was careful not to break openly with his old allies. Intervention in Spain remained unsettled until after Castlereagh's death; his successor, Canning, was to make the breach complete, and England's withdrawal, as we shall see, quickly led to the end of the close co-operation through congresses.

Castlereagh also considerably improved relations between England and her former colonies, the United States. The Treaty of Ghent, concluded during the last days of 1814, simply ended the indecisive War of 1812, and did not even mention the questions of neutral rights and impressment of seamen which had caused the Americans to fight. By the Rush-Bagot agreement, in 1817, the two nations agreed to maintain no armed forces on the Great Lakes, where an expensive naval rivalry was continuing after the war. Each side thought the other would have the advantage in such a building race and was ready to abandon it; that probably accounts for what has been called one of the most successful disarmament agreements in history. Several commercial agreements of mutual advantage were also made, as we shall see, during these years. The long frontier between the United States and Canada was retraced. Each side continued to fortify strategic points along this border for a half century; but they were never put to the test, despite serious mutterings of war in the forties over the Maine–New Brunswick boundary in the East and the Oregon territory in the West. Each country was the other's best customer, and the common heritage of Anglo-Saxon backgrounds also counted for something.

Altogether, England's external position seemed enviable at the close of the Napoleonic period. She had fought the good fight with gold, with redcoats, and particularly with ships of the line. She was undisputed mistress of the seas, and her early start with the Industrial Revolution gave her pretty much a monopoly of the world market for manufactures. The new wealth was breeding capital, too; and London, rather than Amsterdam, now became the foremost financial center to which borrowers turned.

Yet almost instantly the fruits of victory tasted sour. The stress and strain of protracted war had taken a heavy toll from Englishmen. With their trade in confusion, their treasury empty, their taxes high, and their national debt colossal, peace found their morale shattered. War, as always, had stimulated British economic life for the time being; for its needs made essential the cultivation of every available acre and the rapid expansion of manufacturing. The government, which had been spending millions of pounds a year in providing for its own fighting men and in subsidizing Continental allies, now, after Waterloo, bought but little, and impoverished Europe proved an equally poor customer. England was consequently overstocked with goods, which, thrown upon the market, drove prices down so rapidly that many firms failed. The resulting widespread unemployment of miner, artisan, and agricultural laborer was made worse by the competition of some three hundred thousand disbanded soldiers and sailors for the fewer jobs. Furthermore, over field and factory and countinghouse hung the shadow of the national debt, by that time some £850,000,000.

The economic aspects of this postwar depression were serious enough, but in addition there was a new spiritual uneasiness abroad in the land. The grit and courage which had buoyed up the British people in the face of many a Napoleonic triumph seemed exhausted in their own hour of victory. The panic aroused by the French Revolution and the fear of French ideas paralyzed those more generous impulses toward social and political reform which had made the eighteenth century bright with hope (see page 547). Now the very word "reform" carried with it the suggestion of something French and therefore sinister. England in 1815 was more "Old England" than she had been just before the French Revolution. Patriotic emotion sanctified old laws, old customs, the old Church, and particularly the old constitution. The suggestion that anything might be unjust or irrational in the established order angered and at the same time frightened the country gentlemen, whose rule had brought the country through more than twenty years of desperate crises. The years, therefore, immediately following the peace were full of

# The Approach to Reform

confusion, and, as is usual at such times, the extremists overshadowed the moderates on the political stage. As a result, the Whigs, with their more moderate policies, were out of the picture for a while. In the foreground were, on the right, the Tories, devoted to the stern maintenance of order, and, on the left, radicals of various sorts, engaged in fomenting economic and political agitation.

The Tory party was still in control of the government, with Lord Liverpool's ministry enjoying an overwhelming majority in the House of Commons. The Tory ideals were peace abroad, and law, order, and discipline at home. For the time being, however, only one idea obsessed the Tory mind—repression. Except for a brief interlude under Fox, the Tories had been in power more than thirty years, and for more than twenty of these they had been engaged in repression. True, the more thoughtful among them, like the poet Southey, admitted "there are too much riches and too much poverty in England, and were there less of the one there would be less of the other"; but even he warned the government that its prime duty was to stop the "contagion"of radical ideas. Such advice the Tory Parliament was quick to accept. It did not hesitate to repeal the Habeas Corpus Act, to bring suit for criminal libel against pamphleteers, to place a heavy stamp tax on newspapers, and to suppress public meetings.

The radicals were divided in their diagnosis of England's ills. Some blamed the new machinery for putting men out of work and, here and there, urged its destruction. Acting on this theory, handicraft workers smashed machinery in the so-called Luddite riots (see page 503). Other theorists, particularly the followers of Thomas Spence, considered that the true remedy lay in national instead of private ownership of land. Francis Place, London tailor and labor leader, busied himself with the organization of trade unions, supplied Sir Francis Burdett with valuable and authentic data on labor conditions, and quietly but effectively proved himself a good political manipulator. "Orator" Hunt, a somewhat shallow but glib person, preached everywhere that hope for England lay in universal suffrage and in annual Parliaments. The best-known of these radicals were Robert Owen, wealthy cotton manufacturer, who urged the protection of factory workers by law, and William Cobbett, the celebrated and caustic editor of a popular political weekly, who advocated the repudiation of the national debt and the devaluation of the currency.

Robert Owen combined shrewd business ability with unselfish idealism. Born of poor Welsh parents, he made a fortune in the early days of the Industrial Revolution; but he became so shocked by the appalling conditions of the factory system that he later impoverished himself in trying to remedy them. Through his marriage he became a large shareholder and, later, manager of the New Lanark Mills in Scotland. There some five hundred children, largely five-and six-year-old "poor house" children, worked from six in the morning to seven at night, while among the fifteen hundred adult employees also conditions were very bad. Owen made New Lanark famous as the first "model" factory and community. He established the first schools for factory children in Great Britain, shortened the hours of all employees, raised wages, improved housing, started a co-operative store,—in short, he attempted much that was far in advance of the social conscience of his time. Not only did he essay reform in his own factory, but he was one of the advocates of the inadequate First Factory Act, of 1802 (see page 618), and was a pioneer in the trade-union movement (see page 598), presiding at the first congress. He also tried to reform the whole basis of society itself. Probably it was in connection with his theories that the term "socialism" was first used; but his was not the later socialism, which was opposed to the private ownership and operation of industries. Owen was known as a Utopian socialist, after the book *Utopia*, by Sir Thomas More (see pages 222–225), and believed that individuals, acting upon their own initiative, could create model co-operative enterprises. Like the other highly idealistic Utopians, of whom there were many in France, he hoped to create in this way such an ideal community that the rest of the world would copy it and that competition would thus give place everywhere to co-operation in a transformed world. His most ambitious attempt, which occurred in the United States, was a dismal failure and swept away much of his fortune. In England his schemes also failed; and when, in later life, Owen went in for curious religious ideas, his influence in his own country became negligible.

More influential among his contemporaries and more in line with his own times was Cobbett, a former plowboy and ex-sergeant-major in the army, who began his public career as a violent Tory pamphleteer. At the beginning of the century, under the pen name of "Peter Porcupine," his defense of the status quo attracted the attention of the cabinet, which subsidized him for his writings; but as the Napoleonic wars drew to a close, he began to attack the government itself. Sentenced to prison, and his papers confiscated, Cobbett sought refuge in the United States. Returning to England, he revived his weekly *Register*, which, with its cheap price and clear, incisive style, soon had a tremendous circulation. Cobbett plunged into the limelight as "an all-round reformer, agitating against placemen, pluralists, German princes, landlords, manufacturers, fundholders, potatoes, and emigration." The vigor of his words frequently made

# The Approach to Reform

him appear more radical than he really was. Interested primarily in the welfare of the peasantry, he rode back and forth through rural England making incendiary attacks on the wealthy. He did not approve of burning ricks or of destroying machines, but the emotional excitement aroused by his speeches and the articles in his paper caused less intelligent men to take the law into their own hands.

On one thing, at least, all radicals were agreed: the need for Parliamentary reform. Even Place and Cobbett were willing to press for a political platform as a first step. The old movement which Pitt had sponsored before the French Revolution for a reform of Parliament had never died (see page 545), despite the fear of the French Revolution and of "Boney." Taking on new vigor with the return of peace, what originally had been a cautious move to readjust inequalities in Parliamentary elections grew rapidly into a demand for universal suffrage and annual elections for Parliament.

In the midst of this agitation the Tories themselves offered reform, of a kind. The duty on imported grain (Corn Laws) (see page 635) was raised to prohibitive heights, to ensure landlords against heavy loss in farm rentals during the depression. The income tax was repealed, to please the well-to-do middle class. The sum of £1,000,000 was voted for the erection of new buildings for the Church of England in the industrial north, where the towns had outgrown the rural parishes. Such a sum for this purpose infuriated many who felt that the money would be spent to teach the poor to be contented with that state of life to which the Almighty supposedly had called them, rather than to succor them in this time of dire necessity.

Altogether, these panaceas aided the Tories little. Although they still controlled the government, they were faced with numerous riots. In 1816 a huge meeting at Spa Fields, on the outskirts of London, was dispersed by force, but not until it had passed a resolution that there were "four million of people on the point of starvation, four million with a bare subsistence, four million in straitened circumstances, and a half million in dazzling luxury." From the north in the following year came the march of the "blanketeers," unemployed workmen tramping to London; and in 1819 a strike of cotton-spinners at Manchester made fertile soil for radical propaganda. A large demonstration was held there in St. Peter's Fields on behalf of universal suffrage, with numerous delegates coming from near-by towns. The local magistrates lost their heads. They neither tried to prevent the meeting nor were willing to leave it in peace, once it was under way. An attempt to arrest the ubiquitous "Orator" Hunt resulted in the so-called "Peterloo Massacre," concerning which many witnesses gave as many divergent accounts. At any rate, cavalry were launched into the milling throng, with the result that eleven persons were killed and several hundred wounded. This "military victory" was dubbed "Peterloo," in derisive comparison with Waterloo.

The "Peterloo Massacre" brought into being the famous "Six Acts," the Tory government's effective if temporary answer to popular agitation. They speeded the trial of offenders, prohibited military drilling without authorization, empowered justices of the peace to search dwellings, authorized the seizure of printed libels, banned public meetings, and, finally, subjected all political publications to a stamp tax. Adverse public opinion was now effectively gagged.

Meanwhile George III, aged, blind, and insane,—a pathetic figure, —wandered aimlessly through the corridors of Windsor, until his death in 1820. His eldest son, in his years as Prince Regent, had already deservedly forfeited the respect of the nation. "He was a debauchee, a gambler, a disobedient son, and a cruel, treacherous friend." His accession as George IV (1820–1830) changed neither his character nor his behavior. He brought divorce proceedings against Queen Caroline, only to make the poor lady a heroine with the masses. The queen's character was not above suspicion, but the public rightly sensed that she was more sinned against than sinning. Popular discontent, restrained from political expression by the Six Acts, took the form of insults to the sovereign. The monarchy had indeed sunk to low estate amid the scandals of the regency.

During the decade which followed, affairs took a turn for the better. Castlereagh, overworked by his combined burden of managing Parliament and foreign affairs, committed suicide in 1822. For ten years he had dominated British politics and, as we saw, had made an excellent record in diplomacy. In the popular mind, however, he was blamed for the domestic repression of the period and was cordially hated. Just as during the period of the Whig ascendancy there had been various groups of Whigs, so now the Tories did not all think alike. A reorganization of Lord Liverpool's cabinet brought forward some of the more liberal and enlightened Tory leaders, particularly George Canning, William Huskisson, and Sir Robert Peel. The government took on a new lease of life, blazing a new trail in foreign policy and inaugurating measure after measure of reform.

At the Foreign Office, Castlereagh was succeeded by Canning, who, during the remaining five years of his life, won a secure place among England's foremost statesmen. Neither the Whigs nor the Tories had fully trusted Canning, since in the course of a tortuous career of nearly thirty years he had not been a regular party man. On the other

# The Approach to Reform

hand, everyone recognized the political ability and brilliance of this self-made man. Unlike the more silent Castlereagh, he was a magnetic orator and, by letting the public know his aims and actions, won widespread popular support for his foreign policy. These two men had once fought a duel, but in foreign affairs Canning continued many of his predecessor's policies and pushed them even further along a distinctively English course. His three particular achievements were a complete separation from the Metternich system and the support of nationalistic efforts for independence in Latin America and in Greece.

Canning was barely in office when he struck a telling blow at the congress system. The Italian revolts, it will be recalled, had already been stamped out by Austria, though Castlereagh had made clear England's nonintervention stand. The liberal Spanish government, set up by the revolt of 1820, was still in operation, however, and at the time of Castlereagh's death the powers were about to assemble to discuss its suppression. Canning had no sympathy with the "European police system" which the three autocratic monarchies, Austria, Russia, and Prussia, were trying to enforce. On Canning's instructions, Wellington announced at Verona that, come what might, England would not take part in measures against Spain. Thereupon the Iron Duke left the congress. That was enough to break up combined action by the powers. Although France alone intervened in 1823 to crush the Spanish revolutionary government, the congress system never recovered from England's abrupt withdrawal. Two further attempts to summon congresses failed, largely because England flatly refused to participate.

Linked with the troubles in Spain was the revolt of her colonies in America. England had good reason to be keenly interested in that matter. Ever since the days when Hawkins had peddled slaves at the cannon's mouth along the Spanish Main, she had sought an entrance into that jealously guarded preserve where the Spaniards, intent on silver and gold, were allowing rich normal commercial opportunities to go to waste. The Asiento at Utrecht had been the first entering wedge into this valuable market, and the "War of Jenkins's Ear" had been an effort to drive it farther in (see pages 425, 450). When Spain's internal troubles grew serious during the Napoleonic Wars, revolts began to break out in all Spanish America except Cuba and the other islands. England had aided and abetted these uprisings: "patriot" expeditions had been openly fitted out in British ports; veterans of Wellington's campaigns held commissions in the revolutionary armies; and the Chilean navy was commanded by Lord Cochrane, formerly of the royal navy. "We are fighting the battles of British commerce," wrote a South American merchant to his English correspondent; and cargoes of Lancashire cottons and Birmingham hardware found their way into ports opened by the revolutionaries. The revolt of 1820 at home further weakened Spain's hold on her colonies; the rebel armies made rapid headway, and republics were set up in various regions from Mexico southward.

The movement was reaching a climax when Canning took over the direction of foreign affairs, and the next two years saw the most important steps toward Spanish-American independence. Canning had a double problem on his hands. He had to keep France and the other European powers from restoring Spanish rule in America. At the same time, in the interest of future commercial relations, he had to keep the United States from stealing all the credit for supporting the new republics. The United States, as a republic, was more free than England to extend diplomatic recognition, but England alone had a navy strong enough to keep the European powers from restoring Spanish rule by force. Canning played his cards extremely well and achieved both ends.

The United States made her first important gesture in 1822, when she recognized some of the new republics as independent states. In 1823 Canning made a partial reply by sending British commercial consuls to certain Spanish-American ports. Then he proposed to the United States minister that their two nations make a joint declaration opposing European intervention; but an agreement upon terms could not be reached. Thereupon Adams, the United States Secretary of State, drew up a powerful single-handed declaration which was included in President Monroe's annual message late in 1823. This "Monroe Doctrine" stated that "the American continents, by the free and independent condition which they have assumed and maintain, are henceforth not to be considered as future subjects for colonization by any European powers" and that any European effort to interfere with the new republics would be regarded as "the manifestation of an unfriendly disposition towards the United States." This was more than Canning had wanted. He may not have foreseen that it would one day be invoked against England herself, but he did fear the formation of an American league of republics. He quickly managed to steal much of the Yankee thunder by publishing the action which he had taken just before Monroe read his message. The French had overrun Spain; their next step might be an expedition to recover Spain's colonies. Canning had delivered an ultimatum that England would fight any such attempt. The Spanish-Americans were given to understand that they owed their liberty more to this threat, backed as it was by the full force of the royal navy, than to the bold words

# The Approach to Reform

from Washington. When the Spanish king asked for a congress to discuss the recovery of the colonies, Canning flatly refused to participate in it. In 1824, while the revolutionists were crushing Spain's last army in America, England at last accorded full diplomatic recognition to several of the new states. Considering how Metternich and his colleagues felt about revolutions and republics, this open recognition of revolutionary republics showed how far Canning had cut loose from England's former allies. He could tell the House of Commons, "I called the New World into existence to redress the balance of the Old." Brazil broke away from Portugal at this time, under the son of the Portuguese king, and Canning soon gave recognition. He became a hero to the Latin Americans, and England received the lion's share of their trade.

The Spanish-American problem was barely settled when the revolt of the Greeks finally drew Canning into active participation in the Near East, which was to loom large in British foreign policy for a full half century. The Eastern Question resulted from the gradual decay of the huge Turkish Empire. Between about 1250 and 1550 a succession of powerful Ottoman Sultans, starting in Asia Minor, had spread their conquests along the eastern and southern shores of the Mediterranean and up into the Danube valley. Their empire fell into four main parts, each of which was to play a different role. The only region with a considerable Turkish population was Asia Minor, where the Ottoman dominion began and to which Turkey is now chiefly restricted. To the south and east lay a vast area peopled largely by Arabs,—like the Turks, Mohammedans, but different in race and background. Egypt and the piratical Barbary States of North Africa had a mongrel population under loose, nominal control, and, one by one, these states would cause international problems as they came under European control. Most important in the eyes of nineteenth-century Europe, there were the Balkan Christians— predominantly Slavs: the semi-independent Rumanians, who prided themselves upon being different from the rest; the Greeks, active by sea as well as by land, and the sharpest traders of the lot; the Serbs and Montenegrins, fierce swineherds of the mountains; and, finally, the Bulgarians, closest to Constantinople and most heavily burdened by Turkish rule. In the course of the nineteenth century these various peoples, beginning with the Serbs, were to break loose from their Turkish masters and set up independent or autonomous states.

This Balkan nationalism in the disintegrating Ottoman Empire became closely entangled with European ambitions. The peninsula became known as the "tinderbox" of Europe, because a constant series of diplomatic crises and several wars, including the World War of 1914, arose here. Russia, whose eyes had long been on Constantinople, with its strategic position on the Straits at the entrance to the Black Sea, abetted these Balkan revolts and claimed to be the natural protector of the Balkan Christians, most of whom, like her own people, were Slavic in race and Greek Orthodox in religion. She thus hoped to obtain her ambition of pushing Turkey out of Europe. Austria, on the other hand, as we shall see later, likewise had Balkan ambitions; but she opposed the revolts, because she feared that victory of those Slavic minorities might lead her own subject Slavic peoples to seek freedom also, and leave her (as she was to become after the World War) bereft of the southern part of her empire. France too and, after her unification in 1871, Germany mixed in Balkan affairs; but their interests were less obvious than those of England, who, although distant from Constantinople, played a major role in most of these crises. England's policy was a purely negative one. She wanted no Turkish territory for herself; but she was vitally concerned with preventing Russia from getting too close to Constantinople, because that might menace British trade in the eastern Mediterranean and especially communications with India. She consequently preferred a weak Turkey at the Straits, even one cruel to her subject Christians, to the powerful Russia, which she was to fear throughout the century. It was said later that Turkey, the "Sick Man of Europe," would probably not have survived the crises of the nineteenth century had it not been for frequent injections of medicine in the form of English support. Already, for more than a century, Russian armies in war after war had been encroaching on Turkish territory around the Black Sea. In 1791 the younger Pitt had wanted to interfere, but Parliament would not empower him to do so. Russia's pretext for interference, the protection of the Balkan Christians, was sanctified by treaty. There was no question about their needing protection; for as the Turks grew weaker, their rule became more brutal, more corrupt, and more inefficient. Russian agents were constantly attempting to stir up revolts, which came frequently after the Serbs rose at the turn of the century.

Europe was too busy with Napoleon to bother with that Serbian uprising; but when the Greeks revolted in 1821, it was a different matter. For a while the powers sought to localize the conflict, to prevent international complications while Greeks and Turks slaughtered one another with the atrocious savagery which marked most Balkan wars. Then, in 1825, the Sultan called in the efficient army of Egypt, which threatened to exterminate the Greeks. The powers could no longer remain indifferent. Russia seemed ready to inter-vene on behalf of the Greeks, however opposed Czar Alexander might be to revolutions elsewhere. Russian intervention was the last thing Canning wanted; for it would bring Russian power unpleasantly close to the Mediterranean. At the same time, he was accustomed to uphold liberalism abroad and wanted particularly to help the Greeks. If Russia wanted to intervene, therefore, England would too. Numerous Englishmen who admired ancient Greece went out to fight for the freedom of the modern Greeks, though these were a far cry from the men who had made Athens glorious. Byron died at Missolonghi, and Admiral Cochrane, with his Chilean job finished, went over to command the Greek navy. British bankers made heavy loans to the Greeks, charging stiffly for their services. But Canning realized that still more was necessary to prevent the Russians from acting alone. After various negotiations England, Russia, and France agreed at London in the summer of 1827 to impose an armistice upon the Turks and Greeks, by peaceful means if possible. A combined fleet of the three powers, under a British admiral, proceeded to blockade the Turkish navy. That autumn there was an "accidental" encounter in Navarino Bay; and when the smoke cleared away, the Sultan's ships were no longer afloat. That virtually ensured Greek independence. Canning had lived just long enough to arrange the London agreement; before its speedy consequence at Navarino he was dead. After protracted delays, during which Russia fought Turkey alone after all, Greece was declared independent. A German prince was selected as her king, and a British frigate bore him to his new realm.

In co-operation with the Board of Trade and the Exchequer, Canning also used diplomacy to push England along the new path toward free trade. The dominant spirit in this movement was William Huskisson, president of the Board of Trade, keen in his grasp of economic principles, broad and far-seeing in his vision, and tireless in pushing his new ideas in the face of business skepticism. In 1776, as we recall, Adam Smith had denounced the artificial restrictions of mercantilism, and within ten years the younger Pitt was beginning to put those new ideas into practice (see page 545). The French wars had interrupted this movement, however, and Huskisson, with the co-operation of Robinson, Chancellor of the Exchequer, now had to begin anew. The principal features in these reforms were modifica-tion of the Navigation Acts, readjustment of colonial regulations, abolition or reduction of tariff duties, and diplomatic pressure through reciprocity or reprisals.

Conditions had undergone great changes since the Navigation Acts and old tariff codes had been enacted. Holland was no longer a rival to be feared; the United States, on the other hand, being no longer a part of the colonial system, threatened lively maritime competition. Latin America was being opened to British commerce. England had made such strides with the Industrial Revolution that, except perhaps in grain, she needed little tariff protection against outsiders, while reduced tariffs would mean a cheaper supply of raw materials. Financial developments also affected the situation, for London was fast becoming the money market of the world. The Rothschilds, Barings, and other great banking houses lent some £100,000,000 overseas during the first quarter of the century. The interest rates were high, but the risks were considerable—fully a quarter of that vast amount was defaulted. Since England was the creditor country, the tariff walls needed to be low enough to admit wares from the debtor foreign nations, as these borrowers would naturally find difficulty, except through building up a surplus by selling goods to England, in paying back interest and capital. Altogether, England was ready for an application of Adam Smith's theories,—that is, all England except the landowners, who wanted protection for their grain.

The old Navigation Acts had required that all goods from America, Africa, and Asia be brought in British bottoms. England still tried to keep those profitable "long hauls" for her own shipping, but had to adjust conditions to the new American republics. The harsh limitations on imports from Holland in the old acts also were relaxed. These old acts had forbidden foreigners to trade with British colonies; but the British West Indies had suffered from the restriction of their supply of food and lumber from the United States, so that there too there were adjustments. Many of the former stipulations about "English ships with English crews," however, were to remain on the statute books until the final abolition of the Navigation Acts in 1849.

In liberalizing the colonial restrictions, Huskisson threw open colonial ports to foreign trade, though keeping in British hands the shipping between England and her colonies. He also introduced a system of "colonial preference" whereby British goods would enter colonial ports at a somewhat lower duty than foreign goods, while, conversely, colonial goods would enjoy a tariff preference in British markets. That principle was not continued by his successors, although, as we shall see, strong efforts were made to revive the system later in the century.

The customs regulations underwent a thorough overhauling. It was here that the Chancellor of the Exchequer had to be called into co-operation; for customs duties formed no small part of the national revenue. More than a thousand acts were scrapped and the whole scale of duties compressed into a compact system. Export duties were completely eliminated, while many import duties were abolished and others reduced. To render less profitable the work of the smugglers of Romney Marsh, the duties on articles of large value in small bulk, wine, brandy, and silks, were reduced with the hope that greater quantities of such goods would enter legally through the customs. Finally, the resources of Canning's diplomacy were used to secure advantages from other countries in the matter of tariffs, port duties, and the like, with reciprocity for the nations which would co-operate and reprisals for those which would not.

In one field, however, rigid protection stood firmly entrenched. British industry and commerce, because of their superior advantages, could well afford to take chances in the removal of restrictions. British agriculture, however, was exposed to the competition of cheap grain and flour from the Baltic and America. The landowners still dominated Parliament; they pointed that they had fed England during the Napoleonic crisis and, to ensure adequate rents from their lands, they had passed the celebrated Corn Laws. The 1815 laws had flatly forbidden the importation of foreign "corn" (which included wheat) until prices in England should have reached a certain fairly high price. Gradually the Corn Laws were made less rigid, and a sliding scale of duties was introduced; but the principle and practice remained until the great battle between agriculture and industry in the middle of the century (see page 635). Huskisson was killed by a locomotive at the opening of the Liverpool and Manchester Railway; but the drive for free trade continued under Peel and Gladstone until, by 1860, only twenty-six tariff duties out of more than twelve hundred still remained.

Outside of the field of commerce a further step toward the abolition of old restrictions was the repeal of the harsh Combination Acts which had been passed during the reaction against the French Revolution. In theory they had been directed against combinations of employers as well as of employees. In practice, however, they bore heavily on the working class alone, making it "illegal for any body of workmen to meet, even peacefully, for the purpose of discussing wages." These laws had proved unenforceable as well as unjust. The repeal was brought about by the skillful manipulation of Francis Place, who secured a favorable member of Commons to call for a committee and act as its chairman. Quietly and efficiently Place procured an array of witnesses who gave overwhelming evidence against the laws, and they were repealed. Immediately many violent strikes broke out. It consequently seemed necessary within a year to pass a new law clipping the wings of the trade unions which were now springing up everywhere. Not until several decades later were the trade unions to obtain full legal recognition. Nevertheless, the trade-union movement was to make rapid progress in England during the century and to become a powerful weapon of the laboring class.

Huskisson's influence had also brought about the repeal of another old and often violated statute, which prohibited the emigration of artisans. British mechanics had been enticed to Prussia, and others had slipped away to aid in the beginning of the cotton industry in the United States. Since it was impossible to prevent such men from carrying the plans of the new machinery in their heads, it ultimately became necessary to repeal another statute which forbade the exportation of machinery.

One cannot tell to what extent the economic advance of Britain during the next few years was occasioned by this reform movement or by a change in the economic cycle. Doubtless trade would have improved even if new laws had not been passed. From both North and South America, as well as from the Continent, came an increased demand for British goods and British capital. Prices began to rise; pig iron doubled in value, as did cotton; new mines were opened; new factories were established; and those who held office received the credit.

Another liberal Tory was Sir Robert Peel, the son of the wealthy calico manufacturer of the same name who had been active in the factory law of 1802, and the grandson of an artisan. Peel was a paragon of both virtue and ability. His ambitious father had sent him to Harrow and to Oxford, where he had made a reputation as a scholar. A seat was then purchased for him in the House of Commons, where he won fame in debate and also the friendship of the younger Pitt. Before Waterloo he served as Chief Secretary for Ireland, and in 1822 he became Home Secretary in Liverpool's cabinet. Peel, by antecedents and by nature, was first of all a man of business and loved order and efficiency, as well as power and prestige. He had risen straight from the middle class, and this fact possibly made him somewhat aloof and self-conscious.

Within certain limits Peel was a true reformer. He improved the prison system, the method of deporting prisoners, and the way in which judges were paid. He also brought an end to the practice of employing spies among workingmen; he stopped the persecution of radical newspapers; and in the metropolis he established the first civilian force of trained police, known as "Peelers" or "Bobbies." Above all, he improved the criminal code, which had long needed overhauling. In the early nineteenth century there were over two

# The Approach to Reform

hundred crimes for which the punishment was death. "It was a capital offense to pick a man's pocket; it was a capital offense to steal five shillings from a shop; it was a capital offense to steal a fish; it was a capital offense to rob a rabbit warren; it was a capital offense to cut down a tree." This state of affairs tended on the one hand to cause occasional oversevere punishment, and on the other to discourage juries from bringing in a verdict of guilty. For a whole decade before Peel became Home Secretary, law reformers tried time after time to revise this barbaric code. Sir Samuel Romilly devoted his life to the cause with small success; and although his successor in this work, Mackintosh, secured a great deal of publicity, it was not until Peel gained power that much was done. Peel built upon the labor of these early reformers and made it his own. Through his agency the death penalty was removed from a hundred offenses.

The Tories approached religious problems in gingerly fashion, but here also was need of reform. Church and State had been closely interwoven socially as well as politically for so long a time that it went against the grain of the ruling class to place the Nonconformists, let alone the Catholics, on a basis of equality with members of the Church of England. The Toleration Act of 1689 had permitted most Nonconforming Protestants to worship as they pleased; but the political disabilities of the Test and Corporation Acts still remained on the statute books, along with certain restrictive laws particularly directed against the Catholics (see page 402). By the strict letter of the law both Nonconformists and Catholics were thus debarred from all civil and military positions under the crown, from municipal corporations, and from the universities.

Opposition to the relaxation of these laws on behalf of the Nonconformists was not particularly strong, as they had tended to lapse in practice. "Occasional conformity," which meant that Nonconformists might qualify for office by partaking of the Anglican Sacrament annually, had been permitted during most of the intervening years. For a long time it had been customary to pass an annual bill of indemnity pardoning them for holding office illegally. Many people feared, however, that an official lowering of the bars in favor of the Nonconformists would encourage Catholics to renew their agitation for the repeal of certain further restrictions which applied to them alone. For this reason the repeal of the Test and Corporation Acts, which would have released the Nonconformists from their nominal disabilities, was delayed until 1828. Then, as many had dreaded, further emancipation followed during the next year, this time for Catholics.

# A History of England and the British Empire

The Elizabethan legislation and the penal code against the Catholics in both England and Ireland still made it illegal to hear Mass, to make Catholic converts, to conduct Catholic schools, or to engage Catholic tutors. In fact, any priest by his mere presence on British soil theoretically risked the death penalty. The worst of these legal discriminations had been removed during the last quarter of the eighteenth century; as a matter of fact, most of them had been a dead letter, as far as England was concerned, long before that. The American Revolution had made it desirable to placate unhappy Irishmen, and the French Revolution, by its attack on the Roman Church, had made that institution more respectable, although hardly popular, in England. Nevertheless, even after the repeal of the Test and Corporation Acts, certain grave restrictions still rested upon all Catholic subjects. In particular, they could not be elected to the House of Commons; they could not serve upon grand juries, in whose hands lay much of the local government of Ireland; and if peers, they could not take their seats in the House of Lords.

Vigorous protests against this state of affairs came not only from Ireland, where Catholics were numerous, but from Great Britain, where they were not more than a hundred thousand in number. The English Catholics were mainly well-to-do, and with the death, in 1807, of the last male heir of the direct Stuart line the last political reason had disappeared for depriving these Englishmen of civil rights. The Irish Catholics, on the other hand, were poor, and most of them were peasants. During the French Revolution and Napoleonic days many had taken up arms against the king (see page 564). Although the younger Pitt had resigned when George III refused to allow the Irish Catholics a share in the government in 1801, at the time of the Act of Union, most Englishmen continued to feel that it was better to play safe and to watch all Catholics. Yet Catholics were almost enfranchised, some years later, when a bill for their emancipation was defeated only because the Irish Catholics, unlike their English brethren, refused to accept a veto power held in reserve by Parliament in the appointment of new bishops. The English Catholics, inclined to oppose further concentration of power in the hands of the Pope, would have accepted this compromise. The Irish would have none of it, and so the bill failed.

Thereupon a new leader, Daniel O'Connell, appeared in Ireland. This Dublin barrister, disliking England and all things English, had been connected with revolutionary Irish societies. He firmly believed that Pitt's Act of Union was iniquitous and that Ireland should be independent or, at least, self-governing. Realizing that it would be impossible at this time to secure repeal of the union, he felt that

# The Approach to Reform

Catholic emancipation might be a step in that direction. Furthermore, O'Connell, politically ambitious, and a powerful speaker with a magnetic personality, determined to gain admission to the Commons, law or no law. Seeing his chance for this, he organized in Ireland the Catholic Association and drew into its membership huge numbers of his countrymen. The association grew like a mushroom. Parish priests joined it, and preached its cause before the altar. Its members marched and countermarched throughout Ireland, contested Parliamentary elections, and elected O'Connell despite the law which would prevent him from taking his seat.

The English authorities were fearful of civil war. They did not dare to advocate openly a change in the law, since George IV, seized with an unusual fit of conscience, affirmed as stoutly as his father had done in 1801 that it would violate his coronation oath to approve such a bill. On the other hand, to exclude O'Connell, duly elected by his constituents, was dangerous. Ireland seethed with economic discontent and was fully capable of starting serious trouble for the landlords. Both in England and in Ireland the landlords formed a class that held together, and, at heart little troubled about religion, disliked Catholics not primarily as such but as Irishmen and peasants.

Canning was favorably inclined toward emancipation, but by 1828 he was dead. Lord Liverpool, the colorless peer who, we recall, had been prime minister for fifteen years, had retired in the spring of 1827, and Canning, succeeding him, had died four months later. Then followed Lord Goderich (Robinson), who had recently served well as Chancellor of the Exchequer, but who as prime minister proved an ineffectual figurehead and lasted only five months. Early in 1828 the Duke of Wellington next agreed to head the government. Thus there were four prime ministers, all Tories, within ten months! Although Wellington had been very vehement in opposition to emancipation, he was a better general than politician and now decided upon one of his strategic retreats. His ministry, moreover, was already seriously weakened by the withdrawal of Canning's friends, who resented his sharp military manner. He realized, too, that the landlord class would not stomach rick-burning and cattle-maiming. Consequently Wellington approached George IV. The king, fortified by much brandy, invoked the memory of his sainted father and dismissed his ministers. He soon changed his mind, however; for he preferred Wellington and Peel to Whigs and radicals, even at the price of surrender. Consequently, by 1829 the Catholics became eligible for most offices under the crown, with a very few exceptions such as the Lord Chancellorship.

Emancipation, however, had a joker concealed within it. As Catholics won the right to elect men of their own religion to Parliament many of them lost the right to vote at all. The forty-shilling free-holders—small landholders, of whom there were some one hundred and ninety thousand—were disenfranchised in Ireland. Wellington had insisted on this minimum safeguard.

This was the last reform of the liberal Tories, who in the majority of cases had been pushed forward by public opinion against their own inclinations. Now, for the most part, they were to line up with the true-blue, more extreme Tories in opposition to constitutional reform, which almost immediately was to become the principal question of the hour.

The British constitution was extraordinarily complex and intricate in regard to Parliamentary government. The political center of gravity rested, we recall, in the House of Commons, as a result of the constitutional struggles of the seventeenth and eighteenth centuries (see pages 313, 431). The Industrial Revolution, with the rapid growth of new towns, especially in the north, had intensified the inequalities in borough representation, which were flagrant enough in the time of Walpole (see page 435). Only two new boroughs had been created since 1625, when great industrial centers like Leeds, Birmingham, and Manchester were only tiny hamlets. In 1830 these great new cities had no representation in Parliament except through the two members elected by the shire, or county, as a whole. On the other hand, many small towns which had decayed, or actually disappeared, were still represented in the Commons by two members each. Because of the ease with which the votes of "pocket" and "rotten" boroughs, with their bewildering lack of franchise uniformity, could be manipulated, the control of the House of Commons remained in the hands of a few. It has been estimated that an actual majority in the Commons could be elected by fewer than fifteen hundred votes. This was the time-honored English system of representation, which had drawn the fire of reformers in the latter part of the eighteenth century and even more after Waterloo. It was not completely undemocratic; for where "pot-wallopers" might vote, there was democracy. But it was archaic and illogical, as well as grossly unfair to precisely those sections of the country, the industrial areas of the Midlands and the north, which had evinced the greatest spirit of progress.

For the first five years after Waterloo no single question was discussed more vigorously in Great Britain than the necessity of reforming the old system. Then, curiously enough, nearly ten years elapsed before public opinion again actively concerned itself with Parliamentary reform. Between 1820 and 1830 one particularly notorious borough, Grampound, to be sure, was disfranchised; but Lord John Russell, second son of the Duke of Bedford, tried in vain to increase the membership of the House of Commons by one hundred, giving sixty new members to the counties and forty to the unrepresented cities.

Parliament, however, gave little heed to Russell; and the public apparently lost interest in Parliamentary reform, only to recover it with increased intensity in 1830. Among the reasons which underlay Britain's apparent contentment with her venerable framework of government were these: the revival of evangelical religion in the early nineteenth century; the character of the country gentry; the state of party politics; and finally the "romantic" reaction of the public mind to the French Revolution and Napoleon.

These years saw a noticeable increase of interest in religion, both within the Church of England and among those outside its fold. The cold and formal deism of the eighteenth century, with its concept of a remote deity never interfering in human affairs, faded away in the white heat of the revolutionary period. In its place came a surging tide of pious sentiment, with tremendous emphasis on other-worldliness, saintly living, and patient endurance. The men who represented this wave of piety in Parliament were known as the "Saints." Not only were they numerous, but many of them were wealthy, particularly the Quakers. They were reformers of a kind. Slavery was their particular bête noire, and they were ever ready to fight vigorously for the emancipation of the blacks in the West Indies. They also urged educational and prison reform; but democracy was something which did not concern them. "Render unto Caesar the things which are Caesar's" was their favorite text; and second to it was "Servants, obey your masters." Thus most of the Nonconformists resembled the Church of England evangelicals (see page 526) in taking no interest in politics. Some were willing, it is true, to bring pressure on Parliament for the repeal of the Test and Corporation Acts, but not until decades later were they willing to organize for Parliamentary reform.

Meanwhile the country gentry were well-nigh unanimous in fighting Parliamentary reform; and they knew how to fight. No matter how narrow their outlook, or how ingrained their selfishness, these men had wielded power for centuries, and they had no intention of surrendering it. Far from being social parasites, like the French nobility of 1789, these squires were, it will be recalled, the mainstay of English society as the backbone of the House of Commons, and as the administrators of the law—justices of the peace—in their local communities. Furthermore, their ranks were not shut against the more wealthy of the middle class. Many a poor boy, having made a fortune in India, in industry or in commerce, bought landed property, intermarried with some poor but socially eligible family, and thus in his own person or in that of his descendants was admitted to the ranks of the favored few who governed England. The elasticity of the British aristocracy enabled it to survive: it bent, but it did not break. It had, however, no intention of bending unless self-preservation so dictated.

Although there was a two-party system in the House of Commons, both parties drew their strength from the same aristocratic class. Lord Grey, the titular leader of the Whigs, was a great landlord in his own right; and the Greys, Russells, and Hollands, famous Whig families and wealthy landowners, were as closely identified with the aristocratic tradition as the Tory families. The Whigs, moreover, since the advent of the French Revolution, had been sharply divided among themselves, although very few in 1815 could be considered radical in any sense. The Whigs in general were comfortably off under the old system, mumbling their old formulas. In fact, party lines between 1820 and 1830 almost melted way, and between the more liberal of the Whigs and the liberal Tories (often called Canningites) there was little to distinguish. Since the Whigs were His Majesty's Opposition, they were willing to criticize those laws which the Tories sponsored; but this did not mean that the Whigs as a party were willing to adopt Parliamentary reform as their child— not yet.

More significant than either the evangelical movement or the party seesaws of Whigs and Tories was the reaction of the public mind to the long struggle with Napoleon. This may perhaps best be studied by an analysis of the literature of the early nineteenth century, which, on the whole, was conservative in trend. English letters at this time were dominated by the brilliant and versatile Romantic school, which, perhaps more than anything else, sought to escape from reality. Twenty years of warfare had been reality enough for most of Europe, and discouraged humanity sought relief in reading books which appealed to the imagination rather than to the critical faculties.

Sir Walter Scott, Britain's leading literary figure, afforded this relief to his fellow citizens. His novels deal with England's past— with old ways, old customs, old virtues. "They set forth a Tory view of life, not a Tory program. It is a view evident in the choice of subjects for the novels and in their settings. Whether the scene be laid in the court of Prince Charlie, or in the England of Richard Cœur de Lion, or in the struggles of the Crusaders, the same glory is cast about the heads of princes, the same tribute is paid to those who serve loyally and without question, the same attempt is made to show man at his best when most conforming to the usages and institutions of society. " 'I am no politician,' says the Major in *Old Mortality*, 'and I do not understand nice distinctions. My sword is the king's, and when he commands I draw it in his cause.' "[1] Here was the essence of the Tory credo—loyalty. Scott was not a political philosopher or, for that matter, a philosopher of any kind. A man of glowing imagination and warm heart, in no wise a dispassionate critic of the contemporary scene, he was a country gentleman, happy in his environment, believing with all his heart in a society of fixed classes.

Also characteristic of the Romantic school was the love of nature. No man personified this more completely than the poet laureate William Wordsworth. Cities to him were obnoxious, and virtue dwelt in the untrodden ways of the countryside, the abode of beauty, truth, and wisdom. Man, according to him, should seek his place in the universe by mystic communion with Nature.

> One impulse from a vernal wood
> May teach you more of man,
> Of moral evil and of good,
> Than all the sages can.

This Wordsworth believed, and therefore he had little confidence in man's capacity to raise himself in the earthly scheme of things by his own efforts. In consequence Wordsworth, although a radical in his youth, grew conservative with the years, a tendency which was accelerated and intensified by his patriotic reaction against Napoleon Bonaparte.

> Perpetual emptiness! unceasing change!
> No single volume paramount, no code,
> No master spirit, no determined road;
> But equally a want of books and men!

Thus Wordsworth wrote of France as early as 1802. Liberty, Equality, and Fraternity were to him false gods, partly because they were French gods.

Coleridge and Southey, England's two other "Lake poets" (a term applied to poets who lived in and wrote of the Lake country of northwestern England), were as disillusioned with the French Revo-

---

[1] Crane Brinton, *Political Ideas of English Romanticists* (1926), p. 109. By permission of the Clarendon Press.

lution as was Wordsworth. Coleridge became more and more a mystic, preoccupied with religion and the glorification of the national Church. Southey is more difficult to place. He was as radical in economic ideas as he was conservative in political theory. There can be no doubt, however, that political democracy was anathema to him and that as contributor to the *Quarterly Review* he fought all proposals to obtain Parliamentary reform.

The influence of these four conservative writers more than offset that of the so-called "Romantic rebels," Lord Byron and Percy Bysshe Shelley. In many ways Lord Byron was not a radical; he was not, for instance, particularly interested in democracy. He exalted liberty, it is true:

> Yet, freedom! yet, thy banner, torn but flying,
> Streams, like the thunder-storm, against the wind.

But it was of freedom in the national sense that he sang,—the freedom of Greece or of Italy from alien tyrannies. Byron attacked Georgian England,—English morals, English domesticities, and English kings; but he was not the sort to lead a mob, nor did he offer any constructive theories for a new society.

Shelley, however, was a true revolutionary, imbued with a flaming idealism which only an untimely death could quench.

> Men of England, wherefore plough,
> For the lords who lay ye low?
> Wherefore weave with toil and care
> The rich robes your tyrants wear?

There is a revolutionary bite and tang to these lines, and to all his political poetry.

Byron's influence was more Continental than British. His fellow countrymen read his poems; but they disapproved of the author, and were in no way inclined to accept him as a radical prophet. As for Shelley, his day was not yet. The weather vane of British literature during the first third of the nineteenth century continued to point rather steadily in the conservative direction. Religion, politics, literature—all three buttressed the old order.

Despite these retarding elements there was at work one unceasing influence which made change inevitable: the economic revolutions in industry and communication. The middle class—the industrial entrepreneurs, the bankers, the manufacturers, the merchants, who were growing wealthier and more numerous—demanded a share in the government. Sooner or later their constant demands for a redis-

# The Approach to Reform

tribution of Parliamentary seats that would recognize the growth of population in the manufacturing cities of the north must be answered.

The Communication Revolution was now entering on a new stage. No matter how good the turnpikes, no matter how efficient the canals, the full force of the new power machinery could not be realized until some cheaper method of transportation was available. George Stephenson and his locomotive made a national market possible, and ensured the ultimate rise of the middle class, by means of its increased wealth, to political power in England. In a sense the locomotive was the harbinger of the Reform Bill of 1832.

The railway came in dramatic fashion. The novelty at this time lay not in the use of rails but in the new motive power. For some time rails had been used to reduce the friction of wheels in hauling coal, but the power had been provided by horses and mules. Occasionally gravity was used, and sometimes empty coal wagons were hauled up steep grades by means of inclined planes. That locomotives could haul long trains for any considerable distance was, before 1825, purely a matter of speculation. A Cornishman, Trevithick, to be sure, had invented what to all practical purposes was a steam automobile, and upon it he had made the long trip from Cornwall to London. His engine, however, had little power and could haul nothing. The same Cornishman also invented a locomotive which performed useful service in the coal districts, pulling coal wagons upon rails. But before the days of England's most famous engineer, George Stephenson, all these inventions had but slight practical value.

Stephenson, son of a poverty-stricken miner, began earning his own living at the age of eight and taught himself to read when he was eighteen. By occupation he was a plugman, that is, a man whose duty it was to watch the old-fashioned pumping engine at work and to plug the suction holes in its pipes when the pit which it drained went dry. Stephenson became an adept at repairing stationary engines, studied Trevithick's invention, improved it, and discovered that flanges on the wheels of both cars and engine would do away with the clumsy rack-and-pinion, or cogwheel, method.

Then came the Stockton and Darlington Railway, begun by enterprising Quakers to carry coal over the forty miles from the mines at Stockton to the sea at Darlington, near Newcastle. The original plan left the question of motive power undecided between horsecars, stationary engines drawing cars by cables, or a "traveling engine." Stephenson was invited to make the latter, and the history of the locomotive dates from its first successful run in 1825. It was a crude affair, but it worked. "A man on horseback rode in front of the train to drive off cows and careless farmers. . . . At times the horseman had to break into a gallop so swift was the speed of the train." The traveling engine hauled passengers as well as freight, and it halved the price of coal at Darlington.

Although this was a mechanical success, another four years elapsed before a better locomotive, also made by Stephenson, demonstrated to the public the possibilities of the modern railway. The cotton-manufacturers of Manchester and the cotton-importers of Liverpool were planning a railway to connect their respective cities, some thirty miles apart, so as to relieve the congestion on the canal between the cities and to break the monopoly of the canal-owners. No decision was made in advance as to the type of motive power to be used. Opposition to locomotives was loud and powerful, and strongly entrenched interests were prepared to fight their introduction. The canal companies feared the loss of their gigantic dividends, and there was an immense amount of capital invested in stage lines, in turnpike companies, in taverns. Engineers testified in Parliament that locomotives would be dangerous, and that the cars would fly off the tracks upon rounding curves. It was confidently stated that "cows would not graze nor hens lay if locomotives were to roar past; that poisoned air would kill birds if they flew over the road; that farm houses near the line would be burned up by the fires which streamed from burning engine stacks; that the air would become polluted with clouds of smoke; that horses would become extinct, and oats and hay unsalable; and that boilers would burst and blow passengers to atoms." Had it not been for the influence of Huskisson and the expenditure of many thousands of pounds, permission to build a railway of any description would have been refused. The railway was completed before the directors faced the question of motive power. Various proposals were made: that the cars might be propelled by hoisting sails or by the use of bottled gas or by stationary engines and cables. A traveling engine, it was argued, once disabled, might hold up the entire line, whereas a stationary engine could not do this, since it would be possible to haul cars past it by the use of horses.

Nevertheless, the directors of the railway advertised a competition with a prize of £500 for the best locomotive. Stephenson had done the preliminary work of building the line, bridging the swamps, and digging the tunnels; and they were willing to give him a chance to accomplish the supposedly impossible. The battle of the engines was held in 1829 and was a sporting event witnessed by thousands. Prominent among the competitors was a Swedish engineer, later the inventor of the screw propeller, Ericsson, who afterward emigrated to the United States, there to help win a victory for the North in

# The Approach to Reform

the Civil War by the invention of the ironclad warship *Monitor*. Ericsson's entry for the prize was a prime favorite, and the handsomest, for it was "covered with copper like a tea urn." Next in esteem was the engine which made the most noise and threw the most sparks. But of the four entries—the *Novelty*, the *Rocket*, the *Perseverance*, and the *Sanspareil*—all broke down under the grueling test except Stephenson's. Crude as his *Rocket* was, it more closely resembled a modern locomotive than the other entries and showed the skilled designing and engineering of its maker.

Thus the railway—or railroad, as it is more generally called in the United States—came to stay. For a time it made slow progress. The first really long one, the London and Birmingham, was not authorized until 1833. From that time, however, the pace quickened, and by 1840 there were no less than 1331 miles of railway in England; by 1850 the "railway mania" had run the total up to 6665; and by 1860, to 10,410 miles. In the United States, where the distances were longer, the first locomotive had made its run a month before the trial of the *Rocket*, and at each successive date the American railway mileage was about double that of the English.

George Stephenson and his railway did not directly precipitate Parliamentary reform, although the railway's very existence called the attention of the British people to the manifest absurdity of allotting two seats in Parliament to the almost unpopulated hamlets through which it passed. Nevertheless, the forces which brought about reform were in the last analysis the same as those which brought the railway into existence—surplus capital seeking investment, and surplus capital in the hands of an unrepresented but proud and self-conscious class of capable men who were knocking insistently at the gates of political privilege. To be sure, the radical agitators wanted votes for everyone; but the money and the organization for their agitation came from the new middle class, which by the Reform Bill of 1832 was to win a measure of political power commensurate with its economic importance.

Two years before that a tidal wave of revolution more widespread than the previous one, of 1820, swept over a large part of Europe and partially disrupted the settlement of 1815. In France the rule of the feudal nobility was abruptly terminated with the overthrow of the king and the elevation to the throne of Louis Philippe, who belonged to another branch of the royal family. With the new king the French middle class rose to power, a fact of which the English middle class, already clamoring for political privilege, speedily took note. The famous Duke of Wellington had proved a thoroughly unpopular prime minister. He was disliked by many Whigs, who had been willing to co-operate with Canning; by his own die-hard Tories, who felt he had given way unnecessarily in the matter of Catholic emancipation; and by other Tories because he ordered them around like noncommissioned officers, instead of treating them with the finesse due their rank and importance. Here, then, was an opportunity for the Parliamentary opposition, the Whigs, to reopen the old question of Parliamentary reform, to take advantage of the ever-increasing pressure of the middle class, to overturn Wellington, and to gain power for themselves.

The duke, less adroit than usual, took the offensive before it was forced upon him. Upon opening Parliament in 1830 he praised the British system of government to the skies. It answered, he said, "all the good purposes of legislation, and this to a greater degree than any legislature had ever answered, in any country whatever." This speech angered the House of Commons, and the duke's majority melted away. Defeated on a minor issue, he resigned, and Lord Grey, the Whig chieftain, came into office.

Apparently the first idea of the Whig cabinet was to keep the old system more or less intact, with some minor changes in representation. But Lord Grey's composite cabinet contained radicals as well as conservatives. The prime minister's son-in-law, Lord Durham, who was later to win fame by recommending responsible government in the colonies (see page 683), was called "Radical Jack" and did not belie his name. Also there was Henry Brougham, a celebrated radical, law-reformer, and advocate of Parliamentary reform. With such members the cabinet might, under sufficient pressure, turn toward the left. That pressure was supplied by popular opinion.

"Orator" Hunt emerged from obscurity and was elected to the new Parliament. Cobbett took up his pen again with unsurpassed bitterness. O'Connell started an antirent campaign in Ireland. At London and at Birmingham huge crowds angrily protested. It was evident that no halfway measure would meet with popular approval. Consequently, early in 1831, Lord John Russell introduced for the Grey ministry a more far-reaching bill than had been originally intended.

Drawn up on comprehensive lines, it proposed to redistribute the seats in the House of Commons and to extend the franchise. The first it would accomplish by taking away representation from boroughs with a population under 2000, and cutting down the representation from two members to one for boroughs with a population of from 2000 to 4000, thus eliminating most of the rotten boroughs. In their place it was proposed to create new seats for some of the industrial cities hitherto inadequately represented and for several

# The Approach to Reform

counties which had grown rapidly in population. The second aim ot the bill was to provide a uniform borough franchise in place of the bewildering and entirely irrational old system. As finally modified the franchise in the boroughs was to be given to all men who owned or rented a house of the annual rental of £10 over and above all taxes. While this extended the franchise to many who had formerly lacked the vote, it disfranchised some of the voters in the more democratic constituencies. In the counties the franchise was retained by the forty-shilling freeholders who actually resided on their freehold. It was extended to men with certain long-term tenures worth £10 a year, and to still others with more precarious tenures at £50 a year, thus enfranchising well-to-do farmers who leased but did not own land.

This was the famous bill which finally, with minor alterations, passed into law after sixteen months of violent agitation. It did not provide for annual or even triennial elections of Parliament; and the ballot, or secret voting, long advocated by reformers, was rejected. Nevertheless, opposition to the measure was vehement. Reverence for the old system was strong, and in its favor three main arguments were advanced. In the first place, the old constitution was said to have stood the test of time, and under it England had become the foremost country in the world. If Parliament, from time to time, had lagged behind in its duty to the country, public opinion in the long run, it was argued, had always been successful in forcing through laws which were really needed. Secondly, the rotten boroughs could be said to have proved their usefulness by introducing early into Parliament young men of great promise, such as Burke, Pitt, Peel, and many others, who owed their start in politics to the nomination of a patron. Under a more democratic system some held it unlikely that men of their caliber would become members of the House in their early twenties. The rotten boroughs served as a training ground for the young; they also provided a safe refuge for elder statesmen of worth and value who were unwilling to go through the hurly-burly of contesting elections. Finally, there was the argument that the House of Commons should represent interests rather than numbers. The English constitution, as it had evolved throughout the centuries, provided for this. The very poor were represented by the vote of the "pot-wallopers" and those who paid "scot and lot." The agricultural interests were directly represented by the counties, and the mercantile and manufacturing interests were represented indirectly, since any man willing to spend sufficient money could buy a borough. "The new bill was a leveling measure. In every constituency throughout the country it created two legally defined classes, the one above, the other below, a definite standard of property. . . . At the very first economic crisis the poor would rise against the rich, and that day would see the end of the monarchy, the nobility, and the middle class itself."

These arguments could not prevail in the face of the actual facts. The evidence of Parliamentary corruption was overwhelming, the unfairness of the failure to recognize that the population of England had shifted was too patent, and the pressure of the inadequately represented middle class was too powerful. The bill passed its second reading, but by a majority of only one.

Then it was defeated, to all intents and purposes, by a successful motion that the representation of England in the Commons be not reduced; and in April, 1831, persuading the king to dissolve Parliament, Grey appealed to the country. Strenuous days followed. "The bill, the whole bill, and nothing but the bill" became the slogan of Whigs and radicals alike. The combined pressure of the middle class and the workingmen, together with the potent influence of government patronage, was irresistible. The Tory strength in the counties was almost wiped out, and in the boroughs it was greatly reduced. Even Scotland had a majority for the bill. Therefore, when reintroduced in the autumn of 1831, it passed the Commons by a sizable majority. But the reformers had yet to reckon with the House of Lords. Wellington, deciding to dig himself in, advised the Lords to reject the bill, and they did so.

All England rang with revolt at the presumption of the peers. The castle of the Duke of Nottingham, a well-known boroughmonger, was destroyed. The jails were opened at Derby and the inmates freed. A mob fired the town hall at Bristol and burned the bishop's palace. The Birmingham Political Union, with its affiliated branches, staged huge demonstrations, and a national union of workingmen was organized to attain universal suffrage. At Oxford young Mr. Gladstone, feeling that the British constitution was in danger, warned other undergraduates against the bill. On the other hand, John Stuart Mill, equally young, wrote "if the ministers flinch or if the peers remain obstinate, I am firmly convinced that within six months a National Convention chosen by universal suffrage will be sitting in London."

In 1832 the bill was introduced for the third time. To conciliate the Tories a few slight changes were made, the most important being that wealth as well as population should be given weight in determining the boroughs to be disfranchised. This time the Commons accepted the bill by a two-to-one vote, but the Lords tried to kill it by amending it. Thereupon Grey sought authority from the new king, William IV (1830–1837), to follow the precedent of 1712 by creating a sufficient number of new peers to pass his bill unamended through the Upper House. Failing to obtain this, the prime minister resigned.

Once more the Tory, Wellington, went to Downing Street; but as he did so the church bells began ringing throughout England, and workmen threw down their tools. The king was hooted in his coach, and a run was started on the Bank of England. "To stop the Duke, go for gold," was the brilliant idea of Francis Place. It was effective. The Iron Duke promptly withdrew, and the king sent once again for Grey.

William IV, the "Sailor King," was not brilliant, but in character he was an improvement upon his elder brother, the late George IV. This time Grey was able to persuade him to create the necessary number of peers, and, fortified by the king's written promise to that effect, Grey accepted office. Wellington could read the writing on the wall and knew the fight was lost. Rather than have the House of Lords swamped by a host of new peers he and a hundred of his Tory followers absented themselves from Parliament, and the bill, passed by a rump of the Lords, became law at last on July 7, 1832. Even after its final passage, it was popularly called the Reform "Bill" because of the prominence it had gained before it had become an act.

Thus did the British people accomplish a kind of revolution. It was a more genuine revolution than that which occurred in France in 1830. It did not dethrone a dynasty; but it did destroy what amounted to a semifeudal monopoly of the British government in the hands of the landed aristocracy. The contemporary revolution in France provided one vote for every two hundred citizens; in England the bill gave the vote to one in every thirty, almost doubling the voters in the counties. The revolution, however, if we may call it such, was characteristically British. It changed old methods and practices somewhat roughly, but it did not end them altogether. The political power of the landlord class was reduced. The act did not put the middle class in the saddle, but it did elevate the upper middle class to a position of approximate equality with the country gentry. Practically nothing was done for the working classes. The laborers were too poor to occupy £10 houses. In cities such as Leeds they lived in houses with rents from £5 to £8, and only about 10 per cent of the artisan class received votes. What the bill gave with one hand it took away with the other: the "pot-wallopers" and the "scot and lot" men lost the franchise which they had once had, and consequently in certain boroughs there were fewer voters after 1832 than before. Furthermore, the extension of the franchise in the counties added in a curious way to the political influence of the wealthy landlords. Before 1832, when only landowners could vote in the counties, the yeomen, or lesser landowners, held the balance of power in a number of constituencies. Now they were heavily outnumbered by the voting tenants who stood in fear of losing their leases if they voted against their landlords; for all voting, it must be remembered, had to be done in the open.

The great Reform Bill of 1832, in short, was a compromise. The poor had supported the middle class mainly by riots, actual or threatened, and had helped it to win a secure footing in the British constitutional system. The bill set a precedent and was an important landmark in the advance toward democracy: it was to be followed by four similar acts (1867, 1884, 1918, 1928) which finally gave England universal suffrage. It strengthened another precedent, equally important. Although the House of Lords had surrendered none of its power in theory, nevertheless the fact remained that when faced with the repetition of Queen Anne's mass creation of new peers it had yielded against its will to the popular demand as expressed in a Parliamentary election. The strategic retreat of Wellington in 1832 was not forgotten, as we shall see, either by Gladstone, later in the nineteenth century, or by Asquith in the twentieth.

The predominance, in the British constitutional system, of the House of Commons, and of the middle class entrenched there along with the aristocracy by the Reform Bill of 1832, was now an established fact which the peers of the realm, in order to preserve the prestige of their class, had recognized with what good grace they could muster.

# CHAPTER XXI

## *The Victorian Compromise*

### 1832-1865

FOR more than thirty years after the Reform Bill of 1832 England enjoyed one of the most prosperous and fruitful periods in her whole history. The era is intimately associated with the name of Queen Victoria, constituting as it did nearly half of her long reign, which commenced in 1837. England was enjoying the fruits of the Industrial Revolution at their richest; for material growth continued, and outside competition was as yet negligible. Abroad British prestige was high; a vigorous spokesman, backed by the royal navy, used, we shall see, no uncertain tones in defending the interests of England and Englishmen, as well as in exerting British influence on behalf of those who struggled to establish new governments on the English model. There was a growing realization of the manifold problems, social and economic, arising out of the Industrial Revolution; and upper-class England, while warding off democracy for the time being, made a moderate effort to adjust the nation to the new conditions. Accompanying all that, there were remarkable achievements in the field of thought.

Moderate men controlled Parliament during this period. The fears of the Duke of Wellington lest the gentlemen of England should no longer serve their country in the House of Commons were groundless. In the first Parliament elected under the Reform Bill the vast majority were gentlemen in the narrowest sense of the word; that is, men who did not have to earn their own living. Parliament had a less conservative complexion than hitherto, but primarily it was drawn from the old social groups. That proportion was only gradually modified during the next thirty years. The electorate evidently preferred to remain loyal to the old tradition.

Party rivalry was in a transitional state during these years. Before 1830 there had been almost a half century of Tory domination, preceded by a similar period of Whig supremacy. After 1860 one began to find relatively compact and disciplined Liberal and Conservative parties. During the intervening years, however, Parliament was divided into several groups, no one of which could command a majority by itself. There were the aristocratic old Whigs, fairly conservative by nature; there were conservative Liberals and liberal Conservatives; there were die-hard Tory squires, who regretted the changes which had already been made; there were the radicals, as they chose to call themselves, clamoring for universal suffrage and the secret ballot; there were liberal reformers, to some of whom "Church Rates, Pensions, Tithes, Offices, Poor Rate Laws, Close Corporations, Slavery, Corn Laws, Game Laws were so many nine-pins which it was their urgent duty to knock down"; and there were usually some independents, whose views and support were at times problematical. The result was that, as in later Continental parliaments, a ministry consisted of an alliance of several such groups—frequently a very unnatural alliance. Each would seek places in the cabinet; each would seek support for certain policies; and some, at least, would not hesitate to shift to the other side upon due provocation. On the whole, the Whig-Liberal combinations had the upper hand, since they were in power three quarters of the time between 1830 and 1867, while for two more years they had a share in a coalition ministry.

The Whigs had pushed through the Reform Bill and, first under Grey and then under Melbourne, were to remain in power for nine more years, save for the five-month ministry of Sir Robert Peel. The Tories, under the latter, proved a chastened group. Many of the die-hards had either retired from politics or been rejected at the polls. Peel, making no effort to repeal the Reform Bill, was determined "to look forward to the future." The Tories apparently would not be a brake on progress, provided it kept within reasonable limits. Grey, in the meantime, presided over a motley group ranging from old Whigs to radicals and including a considerable number of reformers.

Flushed by their victory and invigorated by new blood, the Whigs approached their task with energy. Reform after reform was put through Parliament. By 1835 the Whigs, scarcely knowing themselves, had abolished slavery, enacted factory legislation, revolutionized the Poor Law, and reformed the British municipalities. Then, curiously enough, their zeal abated, and they relapsed into comparative inactivity, seemingly compounded of fear and contentment.

England, as we saw, had already abolished the slave trade in 1807; and, at Vienna, Castlereagh had persuaded the other nations to agree to do likewise. Ever since Waterloo there had been a cry for the emancipation of the slaves, of whom there were some seven hundred and fifty thousand under the British flag, principally in the West Indies and South Africa. Wilberforce led this new fight

with the same energy and enthusiasm which had marked his successful campaign against the slave trade. But to get rid of slavery itself
proved a more difficult task. The West Indian planters were politically
powerful, and they tenaciously resisted all proposals to free the
Negroes.

Wilberforce, worn out by the struggle, was succeeded by Buxton,
a Quaker, who brought forward his motion to free the Negroes as
early as 1822, and who kept on reintroducing it until the victory was
won in 1833. Buxton collected an extraordinary mass of information
to prove that Negroes were brutally treated on British plantations.
It was demonstrated, for instance, that an expectant Negro mother
had been punished for a trivial offense by one hundred and seventy
lashes; also that other Negro women had been branded on their
breasts. "A slave was the property of his master. A slave who ran
away was technically supposed to rob his master. In 1815 a poor
Negro boy ran away to his mother. The lad was hanged for endeavoring to rob his owner; his mother was imprisoned for life for
receiving stolen goods—in other words for sheltering her son." In
the face of facts like these, Buxton's proposals seemed moderate. All
he asked was that Negroes born after a certain date be declared free,
an idea which Canning had approved. Doubtless slavery would have
come to an end even before 1833 had Canning had his way. That
statesman, however, did not care to antagonize too greatly the planters
of Jamaica, who took affront at even the mildest resolutions passed
by the British Parliament. In consequence nothing happened except
in those colonies directly under the crown, where it was not necessary
to deal with strong colonial legislatures as was the case in Jamaica.
In the crown colonies punishment by the whip was strictly limited,
and forbidden altogether for women. Also, the owners were no
longer permitted to separate man from wife, and slaves were to be
allowed to accumulate property.

After the passage of the Reform Bill antislavery agitation began
again, and the Whig government was forced to declare itself. Slaves
were property, and to emancipate all of them at one stroke seemed
unfair to the owners. Parliament, having rejected Buxton's scheme,
proposed instead an apprenticeship stage of twenty years, halfway
between slavery and freedom. During these trial years three quarters
of the Negroes' time was to be at the service of the owners, who were
to receive in addition a loan of £15,000,000. This was the basis of
the bill passed in 1833, in which the term of apprenticeship was
lowered to seven years, and the amount awarded to the planters—a
free gift rather than a loan—was increased from £15,000,000 to
£20,000,000. Slavery throughout the empire officially came to an

end on January 1, 1834, and, despite gloomy prophecies, the day passed everywhere without bloodshed.

In 1833, also, was passed the first effective law for the protection of children in British factories. For some strange reason the evangelical reformers, known as the "Saints,"—men of the type of Buxton and Wilberforce,—had been willing to work hard and faithfully for the welfare of the Negroes while at the same time they remained indifferent to that of the white children employed in factories. Certainly this was not because the factories were new. The early ones, we have seen, antedated the practical application of the steam engine, having been built in the late eighteenth century in the rural districts of the north and west, where water power made possible the use of Arkwright's water frame. The labor employed had been principally that of children; for a child occupied less space on a crowded factory floor than an adult, its little fingers were more flexible when it came to tying broken threads, and, above everything else, child labor was very cheap. The guardians of the poor in southern England had been only too glad to get rid of pauper children, who were sent in large numbers to the north, ostensibly as apprentices, in reality as little better than slaves (see page 496).

Before 1802 Parliament had ignored this situation altogether. In that year, partly through the efforts of Robert Owen and of Sir Robert Peel the Elder, a law was passed ordering the whitewashing of factory buildings for sanitary reasons, forbidding the employment of children for more than twelve hours a day, exclusive of time for meals, and prohibiting night work in certain cases. This law applied only to factories employing apprentices; and since the enforcement of it rested with the local authorities, the resultant benefit was slight.

As the steam engine supplanted the water wheel, the newer factories, as we have seen, were located in large cities, where the laboring classes had children of their own to set to work (see Chapter XVII). The apprenticeship system therefore died out, but the harsh treatment of the juvenile workers continued. The elder Peel again came to their help when he secured an act of Parliament (1819) forbidding the employment of children under nine years of age, and limiting the actual work of those between nine and sixteen to twelve hours. This also availed but little, since it applied only to cotton factories and did not include children employed in the woolen and silk industries. As in the earlier law, there was no machinery for enforcement, the chief essential in factory legislation.

Three men deserve the credit for the factory reform of 1833. The first was Michael Sadler, a Tory member of Parliament who lost his seat in the upheaval of 1832. To Sadler belongs the credit of first

# The Victorian Compromise

awakening the conscience of Parliament to what went on behind factory walls. His fiery denunciations brought about the appointment, in 1831, of a royal commission before which operatives and medical men testified freely. In most mills the children worked from six in the morning until seven at night, with an hour off at noon. In some mills they worked longer. Their factory life began frequently at the age of eight and occasionally at six or younger. Poor ventilation, stunted bodies, consumptive lungs, brutal overseers—the tale of iniquity was long and horrible.

The second man was Richard Oastler, a simple, straightforward Tory, the steward of a wealthy squire whose estates were located in Yorkshire, near factory towns. Oastler, afterward dubbed "king of the factory children," had been keenly interested in the abolition of Negro slavery. When taunted by friends with indifference to what took place within his native England, he hurriedly rode to a near-by factory town, where what he saw infuriated him. Thereafter he fearlessly and loudly cursed conditions in Huddersfield, Manchester, Leeds, Bradford, and other factory cities. The mass meetings at which Oastler spoke added the necessary pressure to Sadler's efforts in the Commons. It was Oastler's custom to watch outside factories before sunrise; to take note of parents carrying their sleeping children to work before daylight; to get evidence as to the use of the whip, of food covered with dust and lint, of arches and insteps broken, of legs supported by iron braces. Oastler knew and could prove a hundred items of this sort.

The conscience of England was now touched, and the prospect of a ten-hour working day for boys and girls under eighteen seemed bright. Then, suddenly, the storm of 1832 struck the nation. Children, factories, slaves, were all forgotten in the scramble for the vote. Sadler was defeated, and the manufacturers held the whip hand in Parliament. Asserting that the royal commission had been ill-advised, they counseled further delay, and spoke wisely of commissioners who should travel, inspect, and report. The work of years seemed lost.

The third advocate for England's children now appeared in the Commons in the person of Lord Ashley, who, like his ancestor the founder of the Whig party, later became Earl of Shaftesbury. Ashley, an aristocrat to his finger tips, was a Tory like Oastler and Sadler, and a convinced opponent of democracy; but he agreed to take over Sadler's work on the understanding that it had nothing to do with trade unions. In 1833 he sponsored the first effective factory act in British history.

The original bill was far more drastic than the law as enacted. Ashley's idea was that no child was to be employed under the age of nine, and that no person under eighteen was to work more than ten hours a day (eight on Saturday). Today this seems a moderate measure of reform, but it was drastic from the point of view of the average M. P. of that time. The opposition, sparring for time, therefore secured the appointment of another royal commission, which made a noteworthy report. It could not well refute the evidence of Sadler's commission two years before; but it could and did denounce the agitation for a ten-hour day and produce medical evidence (of a kind) which seemed to demonstrate that children over thirteen were not in need of special care. According to the commission there was something magical about the thirteenth year. "At that age the period of childhood properly so called ceases, and that of puberty is established, when the body becomes more capable of protracted labor." Supported by this report, the opponents of Ashley proposed to substitute thirteen for eighteen as the age limit, and the House approved the provision by a large majority. The law as finally enacted forbade employment under nine except in silk mills, limited labor between the ages of nine and thirteen to nine hours a day, or a total of forty-eight hours a week, and permitted a twelve-hour day for young workers from thirteen to eighteen. For the work of adults there was no time limit, because it was felt that if there were one it would interfere with the sacred right of free contract. As one and a half hours were to be allowed for meals, the regular factory day for those over the age of twelve was fixed at thirteen and a half hours; and these hours were to be between 5.30 A. M. and 8.30 P. M. This law applied to most textile mills, and inspectors were to be sent out from London to enforce it.

Ashley had won a real victory, but it was a partial one. His original bill had been trimmed to suit the low social ethics of the day; but the provision for inspectors did give teeth to the final law. Since it was passed by Parliament as a nonpartisan measure, and therefore found supporters in both political parties, neither of them could claim entire credit for its passage. Yet, on the whole, the Tories deserved the greater measure of praise. Their economic interests being primarily agricultural, they had welcomed this opportunity to criticize the manufacturing and commercial classes, and as Tories they were less indoctrinated with the laissez-faire principles of Adam Smith than the Whigs. Nevertheless, since in the Commons in 1833 the latter had a huge majority over Tories and radicals combined, it is evident that without Whig support the bill would never have become law.

Factory legislation, begun in earnest in 1833, was to continue at intervals throughout the century, with Lord Ashley for many years as its principal champion. In 1842 he was also foremost among those who strove to improve mining conditions. The situation in the mining industry was reputed worse than in the mills, and it was vividly illustrated in the report of the royal commission of investigation. To cite extreme instances, children of six and seven years were employed as trappers, staying underground twelve hours a day in order to open and shut doors which provided for the ventilation of the mines. They were also used to haul coal wagons through passages too small for adults, and sometimes they "were harnessed like dogs in a go-cart." Women and girls were employed underground with the men, frequently working half naked, the breasts of the young girls so hardened by toil as to make it difficult at times to distinguish one sex from the other. The Parliamentary testimony in regard to the mines was a damning indictment of the industry. Let us read that of Isabel Wilson, thirty-eight years old, coal-putter. "When," she said, "women have children thick [fast] they are compelled to take them down early. I have been married nineteen years and have had ten bairns; seven are in life. When on Sir John's work was a carrier of coals, which caused me to miscarry five times from the strains, and was gai ill after each. Putting is no so oppressive; last child was born on Saturday morning, and I was at work the Friday night. Once met with an accident; a coal brake my cheek bone which kept me idle some weeks. I have wrought below now thirty years and so has the guidman; he is getting touches in the breath now. None of the children read, as the work is no regular. I did read once, but no able to attend to it now; when I go below lassie ten years of age keeps house and makes the broth or stirabout."

Ashley proposed to remedy this state of affairs by a bill forbidding boys under thirteen and women of any age from working in the mines at all. To secure the approval of the House it proved necessary to lower the age limit for boys to ten so as to permit boys from ten to thirteen to work every other day. Even these provisions met with opposition in the Lords, where the mining interests were strongly entrenched. The "every other day" clause was taken from the bill, and, thus amended, the Mines Act became law in 1842. Ashley, now earl of Shaftesbury, continued the fight for the ten-hour day for young workers between thirteen and eighteen in the factories, whose working day had been fixed at twelve hours a day by the Factory Act of 1833. For years the "Ten-Hours Bill" hung fire, finally to become law in 1846. In general, one might say that as a result of these various acts no child under nine was permitted to work in mines or in most textile factories; no woman or girl might work underground in the mines; in the factories children under eighteen might not work more than ten hours a day. But there was still no limit on the hours for boys or men in the mines, nor for men or women in the factories.

The third great reform of the Whig Parliament was the new Poor Law of 1834. The problem of poor relief had grown constantly more perplexing ever since Tudor days, but the basic Elizabethan legislation had been little altered except for the Speenhamland system. Although this was merely a local emergency measure, it was widely copied and continued to be the custom, making the present confusion worse. This system, originating in 1795 with the justices of the peace at Speenhamland, had tried to alleviate the sufferings of the poor, which had been aggravated by the increased cost of bread during the wars. It guaranteed agricultural workers a certain minimum income by supplementing wages out of taxes. Consequently, whether the cost of bread went up or down, a family would get the designated minimum amount of bread, even if the wage-earner of a family did not make enough to buy that quantity. This principle, that all poor persons were entitled to doles, entirely on the basis of need, whether man, woman, or child, legitimate or illegitimate, had resulted in an incredible increase in the number of paupers. Farmers reduced wages, knowing that the laborers could obtain sufficient relief from the poor rates to keep body and soul together, and many manufacturers did likewise. Lower wages forced independent workingmen into the ranks of pauperdom. The greater the number of paupers the higher became the taxes and the more wages fell.

The answer of the reform Parliament was hard and cruel, but in some ways probably salutary. The old methods of relief had failed, poor rates were increasing so rapidly as to become an intolerable burden, and it was true that many persons took advantage of the old law to avoid work. Parliament therefore decided to end all this and to make every individual fend for himself and his family.

It decreed, in the famous new Poor Law of 1834, that the relief of the poor should be centralized at London under three commissioners, who were to curtail drastically all outdoor relief or assistance to the poor in their own homes. Instead the poor were to be herded into large workhouses ("bastilles," the people called them), where they were purposely to be subjected to a lower standard of living than that which prevailed among the lowest-paid independent workingmen. The occupants of the "bastilles" were to be segregated, sex from sex. After entering a "bastille" a man could no longer live with his wife; for to do so might make him comfortable and contented. Food and heat were to be kept at a minimum. Paupers— and this age classed all the poor as such—were not to be buried in parish churchyards. Poverty was to be treated as a crime, and made so unbearable that the individual would put forth every effort to avoid public support.

The violent opposition to the new statute was led in large measure by the same group of philanthropic Tories who labored so unceasingly for the factory acts. These men knew nothing of the new science of economics. The Christian religion taught the reverse of the projected law, and that was enough for them. Once again Oastler stormed through Yorkshire. To his voice was added that of Stephens, a dissenting minister, who spoke in blood-curdling fashion. "If Lord John Russell wanted to know what he thought of the new poor law he would tell him plainly, he thought it was the law of devils." The aged Cobbett denounced the measure as "the poor man's robbery bill," and even *The Times* attacked it. But all this did no good; for public opinion was on the other side, determined to force national economy as well as to prevent graft. Consequently this act, hated by the poor of England for many decades,—if one may judge from Dickens's *Oliver Twist* and Arnold Bennett's *Clayhanger*,—was added to the accomplishments of the new Parliament.

The Municipal Corporations Act of 1835 completed the major legislative program of that august body. This did for the cities what the Reform Bill did, more or less, for the nation. It straightened out a tangled mess of local customs and gave to all British cities (except London, which already enjoyed a considerable degree of self-government) a common form of local government. Before 1835 the control of municipalities had rested in a small self-perpetuating body, the corporation, frequently corrupt and generally negligent, which let out to private companies or left to separate authorities the monopolies of water supply, lighting, and sewerage. The new law wiped out this system. Municipal councilors, according to it, were to be elected for three years by all ratepayers (taxpayers), who included practically anyone who occupied a house. These councilors then elected part of their number as aldermen, to serve six years. Councilors and aldermen comprised the city council, which chose a mayor to serve one year, and which also had power to regulate all public utilities. Thus, in a way, the Municipal Corporations Act was a more thoroughgoing reform than the Reform Bill itself. The latter left a number of rotten boroughs and kept a strictly limited suffrage; the former established uniformity and was far more democratic as far as the suffrage was concerned.

The Antislavery Act, the Factory Act, the new Poor Law, and the Municipal Corporations Act once passed, Parliament rested on its laurels. It was to continue to do so for the next thirty years, with only two major exceptions: further factory legislation and the repeal

of the Corn Laws. This did not mean the cessation of political life—
far from it. Ministries rose and fell. Cabals and party alignments
formed and re-formed; one foreign war and several frontier wars
were fought. Furthermore, this long period of excellent administration led to adjustments here and there in the British political system.
Nevertheless, the fact remains that those who ruled Britain, the
landed aristocracy and the middle class in joint harness, were well
content with their work. Convinced that on the whole this was the
best of all possible worlds, they were unwilling to embark on further
untried paths.

Five years after the Reform Bill a slender, attractive girl of
eighteen, niece of George IV and of William IV, came to the throne
as Queen Victoria (1837–1901). Her reign, the longest in English
history, ranks with that of Elizabeth as one of the most successful
in all fields of activity. But this later queen regnant deserved less
personal credit for such success, for the function of the crown
had changed. Victoria lacked Elizabeth's high intellectual qualities,
though she was sensible, if somewhat stubborn. Perhaps her most
distinctive contribution was the restoration of the crown to a position
of respect which it had lost under the Georges. Victoria was the
personification of respectability, and the term "mid-Victorian" now
connotes the ultrapropriety of "middle-class morality" in that period
when legs were "limbs" and many other things were unmentionable.
Later generations might sneer at such extremes, but they were a
decided improvement over the coarseness which reflected the character of her uncle George IV. An incidental result of Victoria's
accession was the end of England's connection with Hanover, which
had been joined to the British crown since 1714 (see page 428).
Since a woman might not rule there, her uncle became king of Hanover, and England was fortunately rid of that vulnerable point in her
foreign relations.

Victoria herself selected her cousin, the serious, conscientious, and
somewhat stiff Prince Albert of Saxe-Coburg-Gotha for her husband
and Prince Consort. Through his family connections and through
the marriage of some of their nine children, Victoria became closely
related to many of the other rulers of Europe. Theirs was an
unusually devoted marriage; his death twenty-one years later left
her inconsolable, and she was constant during her long widowhood
to all that she knew he would approve. In fact, so long was her
mourning that England keenly missed the pageantry which was one
of the chief remaining functions of the crown.

Although on the whole she accepted the role of constitutional
monarch, the young queen was determined that the crown should

# The Victorian Compromise

have much more than decorative, figurehead importance. This point of view at times seemed almost to threaten the normal workings of the responsible government. Her husband, her uncle, king of Belgium, and her adviser, Baron Stockmar, were all Germans, brought up on political theories quite different from those of English limited monarchy; and those were the three upon whom Victoria leaned most heavily for advice. In 1839 her stubbornness kept the Tories out of office. Sir Robert Peel, doubtless remembering the influence of Sarah Churchill and Mrs. Masham over Queen Anne, refused to form a ministry unless she would replace the Whig ladies of the bedchamber with Tories. Victoria would not, and the Whigs stayed in office, though it was later agreed that "the ladies should retire with the ministers." Most of her interference, however, was in the field of foreign affairs, where her prejudices were Conservative and strongly pro-German. Matters came to a head in 1850, when Victoria was thoroughly, and not without reason, shocked by the way in which Lord Palmerston was conducting foreign affairs (see page 642). Stockmar drew up a constitutional memorandum which met Albert's thorough approval. These Germans agreed that the monarch should be the permanent prime minister "who takes rank above the temporary head of the cabinet and in matters of discipline exercises supreme authority." The detachment of the crown from politics was regarded as a dangerous "constitutional fiction," and it was stated that the ruler might even take part in "the initiation and the maturing of government measures." Foreign affairs were regarded as a particular sphere of royal influence, and Palmerston was presented with a demand that the queen be kept informed of what was happening, that she see important dispatches before they were sent, and that they should not be changed after receiving her approval. When, after agreeing to this, Palmerston went his old way, she was instrumental in bringing about his dismissal. More than once she tried to keep him from becoming foreign secretary or prime minister, but popular pressure was too strong. In the army too, where her cousin became commander in chief, Victoria was inclined to stress royal against Parliamentary control. If such a tendency had been carried to extremes, of course, the whole system of responsible government might have been undermined. It has even been remarked that "Victoria's widowhood saved the British constitution."

Despite those theories and practices involving the relation of the crown to Parliamentary government, Victoria was profoundly in accord with the general sentiment of the time, accepting willingly and graciously the organization of society as she found it,—an organization firmly based on what is known to history as the "Victorian

Compromise." The tacit terms of this compromise were these: the aristocracy and the middle class divided political power between them to the exclusion of the working class. The two dominant classes were willing to compromise on voting privileges, provided that these did not go beyond the ideas of 1832. They did not deny that the act of 1832 might be modified or improved, but in one respect it was held final: it placed the control of Britain exactly where it should be placed—in the hands of trustees, capable, tried, trustworthy representatives of the aristocracy and of the middle class.

The Victorian Compromise had an important corollary which had to do with the welfare of the laboring class. According to it, workingmen were not to be ignored by the government, since England was a Christian country and it would be unseemly to let the poor starve. A moderate amount of protection for the "down-and-out," the inefficient, the pauper, the depressed classes should be given (witness the Factory Acts and the Poor Law); but such protection must be strictly limited or else laziness would be encouraged. Deep in the psychology of the middle class was the conviction that there was a link between poverty and wickedness. The successful Victorian businessmen had worked hard, and in work as such they found virtue. In frugality, hard work, and temperance lay the salvation of the lower classes, so they thought; and these virtues must not be weakened by a paternalistic society that looked out for the less able.

The loosely drawn alliance between the aristocracy and the middle class, which controlled the government of England from 1837 to 1867 and beyond, conformed to a rather definite political and economic philosophy, based largely on the writings of three men; Jeremy Bentham, Thomas Malthus, and Adam Smith.

Tories, Whigs, and radicals were all influenced by the philosophy of Jeremy Bentham,—the Tories to a minor degree, the Whigs to a greater, and the radicals overwhelmingly so. Benthamism—or utilitarianism, to give it its other name—did not sweep over England without stirring strong countercurrents, as we shall see; but Benthamism did, consciously or unconsciously, set the drift and the direction of English politics during the first two thirds of the nineteenth century.

Jeremy Bentham (1748–1832) was a rich recluse who spun out theory after theory in the seclusion of his study. These were not purely abstract concepts based on metaphysical speculation but very tangible ideas covering a vast range of human interests such as law, government, prisons, voting, applied psychology, ethics, and education. The fame of Bentham dates from the eighteenth century, when he upset many conventional legal concepts by a frontal attack on Blackstone, the foremost authority of that period on English jurisprudence. After the French Revolution he interested himself in a number of varied reforms and soon became a recognized authority on constitutions. His influence spread to Russia, Germany, Spain, France, and both the Americas. Few persons ever saw Bentham. For a brief period he emerged into public life as one of the founders of the *Westminster Review,* which was established to advance his ideas. Then he retreated into his shell, there to stay until his death. The public was not surprised to discover that his will provided for the founding of the University of London; but it was amazed to read that Bentham had given orders that his skeleton be placed on display at University College, the first unit of the new university.

Benthamism was based primarily on two concepts, utility and happiness. They were correlated, the value of every human institution or custom depending exclusively on whether or not it furthers human happiness. "Good" and "happiness" according to Bentham were well-nigh interchangeable terms, and were quantitative rather than qualitative; in other words, goodness and happiness might be measured like bushels of wheat or piles of lumber. Bentham further argued that every individual was best fitted to know what was most conducive to his own happiness. Human society was composed exclusively of individual units, each isolated from its neighbor, working for its own advancement. Any interference with any individual retarded that individual's advance, and so lessened his opportunity for personal happiness. Since the welfare of any society was determined by adding up the happiness of the various individuals which comprised it and measuring it in bulk, the goal of every government should be to secure as great a degree of individual freedom as possible.

The second intellectual pillar of the Victorian Compromise was Thomas Malthus (1766–1834), an English clergyman and the first man to occupy a professorial chair of political economy (economics) in Great Britain. Malthus's fame rests on his *Essay on Population* (1798). It met with an extraordinary popularity, which can be explained by the fact that what Malthus had to say fitted in nicely with the psychology of early Victorian England. Malthus held that under normal conditions population increased faster than food, the former in a geometrical, the latter in an arithmetical, progression. This meant that human suffering was inevitable because the population unchecked would outrun the food supply. In the past the natural increase of people had been held back by war and disease. Without these two scourges it was inevitable that there would be too many babies and not enough food unless humanity voluntarily refrained from reproduction. The majority of the early Victorians concurred in this theory. It would have seemed utter madness to them to preach, as some do in the twentieth century, that human beings are hungry because there is too much food, which chokes the markets and helps to bring on economic depression. There was not too much in their day; for population was increasing by leaps and bounds, and with it poverty and starvation in the towns. The Malthusian argument offered a complete explanation of this phenomenon to early Victorian England.

Adam Smith (1723–1790), a Scot who had studied at Glasgow and Oxford before becoming a professor of logic, was the third member of the middle-class trinity of social philosophers, although he had done his writing very much earlier than the others (see pages 532, 545). Resigning his university post, he had published in 1776 his *Wealth of Nations*, which in time came to be accepted as the authority on economics, especially by manufacturers, bankers, and business men. The *Wealth of Nations* may be summed up in one term, *laissez faire*, that is, the absence of most restrictions on trade and industry, in contrast to the narrow economic regulations of the earlier period. Monopolies, the regulation of labor, the fixing of wages, trade unions which limit apprenticeship, tariffs, every kind of restraint on trade, Smith called injurious. Government, in his opinion, should not interfere with business. He thought that taxes should be kept at a minimum and doubted if they should even be used for educational purposes, unless, possibly, in the most elementary branches. Smith, a keen individualist like Bentham, wrote that man "by pursuing his own interests frequently promotes that of society more effectually than when he really intends to promote it. I have never known much good to be done by those who affected to trade for the public good. It is an affectation, indeed, not very common among merchants, and very few words need be employed in dissuading them from it."

If one combines the ideas of Bentham, Malthus, and Smith, one finds what the middle class believed in regard to politics and economics. Briefly summarized, their platform contained seven points. (1) The right of free contract must be safeguarded; for every man knows what is best for his own interests and should be permitted to sell his labor as he sees fit. (2) Free trade is desirable; for it will increase the sum total of national wealth in pounds, shillings, and pence, since to interfere with trade is to reduce its volume and profit. (3) Peace is necessary; for wars are destructive, consume capital, interfere with trade, and give employment and profits to the less worthy representatives of the old aristocracy. (4) Reform is needed in certain institutions (for instance, the Game Laws) which have outlived their usefulness. (5) The sanctity of private property is the foundation stone of civilization. If the suffrage is based upon it, so much the better. (6) Poverty is the result of imprudence, particularly in the matter of having children. (7) Individualism is the right social philosophy; each man for himself, and the devil take the hindmost. In other words, taxation should be low, extravagance should be checked, and governments should confine themselves principally to enforcing contracts and to preserving the peace.

Needless to say, there was not unanimity on the part of the members of the alliance between the middle class and the aristocracy in regard to this platform. A few of the more radical went so far as to advocate universal suffrage, as a logical deduction from Bentham's teachings. Some of the more conservative had their doubts about individualism and harked back to earlier, semifeudal ideas which held the ruling class responsible for the welfare of society and which denied the competence of the individual to look after himself. The majority, however, accepted this seven-point program. Only on one point, that of free trade, did it seem impossible to work out a compromise; and this was to cause serious friction within a decade.

Meanwhile the Commons were ready to enact into law various reforms in harmony with the spirit of the age. Jews were permitted to enter Parliament. The character of the Anglican religious establishment, both in England and in Ireland, was improved by cutting down the number of pluralities, by reducing the enormous incomes of certain bishops, and by making a modest grant of money to a Catholic training college in Ireland. A "Truck Act" was passed making it illegal to pay wages simply in credit at company stores. Cheap postage was introduced. The formation of savings banks was encouraged. Assent to the thirty-nine articles of the Church of England was no longer required for matriculation at Oxford and Cambridge. But the Commons were not willing to extend the suffrage, nor seriously to interfere with laissez faire.

The Victorian Compromise proved so acceptable to English public opinion largely because of the indirect influence of the Oxford Movement, fear of the Chartists, the success of the anti-Corn Law agitation, the popularity and influence of Lord Palmerston, and economic prosperity.

The Oxford Movement was a religious revival which began in 1833 and reached a climax in the conversion to Catholicism, in 1845, of John Henry Newman, a prominent Anglican clergyman. It began as a protest on the part of certain talented Anglican churchmen against what seemed to them dangers threatening the Church. They were particularly disturbed by the prevailing ignorance of the principles upon which the Church of England was founded; by the passage of certain laws by Parliament (such as the repeal of the Test and Corporation Acts, and Catholic emancipation) which undermined the exclusively Anglican character of the government; by what they called "Erastianism," which exalted the State over both Bible and Church; and by a growing demand that the Church do something for the money paid it, which manifested itself in a successful attack on the Irish Church and an unsuccessful one on the English Church.

The leaders of this movement, men like Newman and Pusey, were passionately devoted to the Church as an institution, and as scholars of Oxford they looked to the past of the Church to find inspiration for her future. By so doing they tended to stress more and more the idea of Apostolic succession and of one Holy Catholic Church, broken, unfortunately, into various national groups but none the less one in faith and ecclesiastical order. Their message, which made an eloquent appeal to reason as well as to emotion, was extraordinarily successful at first. In vain did Dr. Arnold of Rugby, England's famous schoolmaster and Low Church champion, contend against it. The Oxford Movement grew rapidly at the expense of both Low Church and Broad Church because of its color, its fervor, its more brilliant preachers, its profound scholarship, and its greater contrast to the lay progressivism of the eighteen thirties, which exalted the steam engine, commercial prosperity, and the accumulation of wealth while manifesting distrust of ancient ways and modes of thought.

This religious revival, the parent of the later High Church movement, was not directly concerned, of course, with the politics and economics of the Victorian Compromise. Nevertheless, it negatively abetted their acceptance by proclaiming religion as something apart from economic and political life. The drift of High Church sentiment in after decades was to reaffirm in no uncertain terms various aspects of the social gospel practiced in the primitive and medieval Church; but this was not true of the original leaders, who were so intent on trying to prove that the Church of England was not Protestant but truly Catholic that they laid too much emphasis on scholarship, ritual, and forms of worship. Intellectually speaking, it is true, they were opposed to all materialistic philosophy; but practically they let the battle go by default in all matters which seemed to them of merely lay concern, or, to judge them more kindly, they were so intent on changing man's spiritual outlook as to consider mere changes in law of minor importance. Furthermore, if they were to persuade the State to leave the Church alone, by that same token the Church must not interfere in what concerned the State. Consequently they were willing to accept tacitly, if not to approve, competition, laissez

# The Victorian Compromise

faire, and all that these implied in the world of business and practical affairs, provided that such acceptance had nothing to do with religion.

The Chartist movement crystallized rapidly in the late thirties, came to a head in 1839–1840, continued with various ups and downs, as a serious threat to the Victorian Compromise as late as 1848, and then, sinking rapidly, virtually disappeared ten years later. Industrial distress was largely responsible for calling it forth. Technical improvements in the textile industry were perfected so slowly that for decades poor weavers competed by handwork against machines. As late as 1838 there were from 120,000 to 150,000 still dependent on hand looms, working some seventy hours a week at an average remuneration of a penny an hour. In the hosiery trade the "stockingers" were at the mercy of middlemen who owned and who rented out at exorbitant rentals the all-essential "frame," or machine by which stockings were made. In the mines the "butties," small contractors, owned the tools used and hired the miners. "They resorted to all sorts of practices: compelled miners to work at certain jobs without pay; increased their daily tasks surreptitiously; abused the labor of children, especially pauper children; and finally and inevitably paid in truck."

The Chartists were radical agitators drawn in about equal proportion from the lower middle class and from workingmen. The London Workingman's Association, led by Francis Place, the radical tailor (see page 587), and William Lovett, a cabinetmaker deeply concerned with the education of the depressed classes, was mainly responsible for the program of the Chartists. Indignant at the compromises of the Reform Bill, this group felt that the workingmen who had fought for reform in 1832 had been used as a cat's-paw by the middle class, a point of view in which they were encouraged by the nucleus of radicals in the Commons. In 1838, at the suggestion of the latter, these London workingmen drew up for presentation to Parliament a form of bill which was published as a pamphlet and called the "People's Charter." It contained six points: universal suffrage, the ballot (or secret voting), equal electoral districts, no property qualification for members of Parliament, payment of members, and annual elections. The organization of this group on a national scale was largely the result of the revival of the Birmingham Political Union by a Birmingham banker, Attwood, who had made the Union effective in 1832. His purpose was inflation of the currency; but to win the support of the workingmen who joined the Union, he subordinated his currency ideas to a demand for universal suffrage. After missionaries of the Union had met with great success in Scottish cities, Attwood proposed a National Convention of Workingmen to meet in London in 1839. Meanwhile copies of the People's Charter and of a Birmingham Union petition to Parliament were widely circulated, particularly in the industrial north, where the Chartists were to enlist their largest membership. In the north, too, the agitation against the new Poor Law was directed in favor of the Charter.

Foremost among the northerners was Feargus O'Connor, ex-member of Parliament, editor of a widely circulated radical newspaper, and an Irishman of revolutionary ancestry, whose father had been a United Irishman (see page 564) and whose uncle had been made a general by Napoleon. A born demagogue, large in stature and bold of speech, he was prodigiously active in addressing meetings and in denouncing the "big-bellied, little-brained, numskull aristocracy." His activities and the idea of the forthcoming "convention" (a name too reminiscent of the terror of the French Revolution) caused serious but, as it happened, unnecessary concern.

The Chartist delegates in London for the convention in 1839 had an absurd idea of their own importance, writing "M. C." after their names and inviting the House of Commons to meet with them. They frittered away weeks in lengthy arguments over abstract rights while awaiting the return of the first of the three national petitions for a charter which they were to prepare. When the petition was ready,— a roll of paper said to have over a million signatures,—the House received it courteously, but rejected it almost six to one. Thereupon the convention, from which many members already had resigned, issued orders for a general strike, which it called "a sacred month." This was never realized; for no money was available, the trade unions held aloof, and no unity of purpose existed among the striking Chartists. Many of them were alarmed at the wild talk of insurrection which emanated from certain of their comrades, and all of them were impressed by the preparations made by the army to nip civil war in the bud. Before the strike was due, the convention ate its own words and canceled it. Fierce quarrels broke out in the ranks. Returning missionaries, particularly those sent through rural England, brought doleful news of failure. A large number of the delegates already had been arrested for incendiary speeches; a larger number were sick of the whole affair. Disheartened, the convention agreed to disband, leaving in the hands of a committee all decisions as to future action.

Chartism, however, was not to die thus easily. It had a long future ahead of it, and might perhaps have been successful in the long run if the Chartists could have agreed upon common tactics. It is difficult to distinguish between the physical-force Chartists and those who believed in peaceful measures. The former started an abortive revolt among the Welsh miners, which was easily put down. The ringleaders were tried for high treason and condemned to die, but instead were transported. O'Connor, despite his violent words, conveniently absented himself in Ireland during this affair. Nevertheless, after Place's resignation he came gradually to control the movement, eliminating first Lovett, who wanted to turn the movement into a campaign for general education, and then O'Brien, who wanted it to oppose the Corn Laws.

In 1842, with O'Connor the undisputed leader, the Chartists prepared their second petition, which was supposed to have over three million signatures. In a procession two miles long it was carried on poles to Parliament, where it had to be broken into segments to get it through the doors. Macaulay, who was among those that led the attack upon it, declared his belief that "universal suffrage would be fatal to all purposes for which government exists, and for which aristocracies and all other things exist, and that it is utterly incompatible with the very existence of civilization. I conceive that civilization rests upon the security of property. . . . I will assert that while property is insecure it is not within the power of the finest soil, or the moral or intellectual constitution of any country, to prevent the country sinking into barbarism." Lord John Russell likewise held that "even to discuss such demands would bring into question the ancient and venerable institutions of the country"— this from the sponsor of the Reform Bill. Even the radicals in the House who believed in universal suffrage were not enthusiastic about the Chartists, and many of them considered O'Connor "a malignant and cowardly demagogue." Under such circumstances it is remarkable that the petition received as many votes as it did, being rejected 289 to 49.

Chartism now entered a new phase, in which O'Connor subordinated its political aims to experiments in land settlement. He planned to buy big estates with the pennies of the poor and establish peasant proprietors upon them. Money came flowing in; there were over forty thousand shareholders in the Chartist Co-operative Land Company; O'Connorville was founded; and Rebecca, the Chartist cow, shared a cottage there for a while with the founder. A lottery decided which of the shareholders should receive the first plots; and as they were taking possession of their holdings the year of revolutions, 1848, approached.

The reverberations of these numerous revolutions on the Continent were now dimly heard in London. There were many exiled

Germans there, as well as French and Italian revolutionaries. With a successful revolution (followed by a Second Republic) in France, with a national parliament assembling in Germany, with Italy up in arms against Austria, and with the Austrian Empire aflame with revolt at home, the old Metternich system of reaction and oppression which had dominated Europe since 1815 was rapidly breaking up. The Chartists decided to take advantage of the general confusion to circulate a third petition and to call a convention again. Once more a spectacle was staged in the streets of London, with O'Connor, now a member of Parliament, presiding over it.

Never, perhaps, was there more alarm with less reason in London. Troops were carefully located in strategic places by the aged commander in chief, the Duke of Wellington. A quarter of a million special constables were sworn in, among them Louis Napoleon Bonaparte, soon to be president of the new French Republic and then, like his uncle, emperor of France. There was, however, no disturbance. O'Connor made a speech to his followers about his revolutionary forebears, and he urged the Chartists to put their faith in the six million signatures supposedly attached to their third petition. The crowd dispersed quietly; and some thirteen clerks, detailed by the suspicious government to count the signatures, discovered that there were only two million signers, and that among them were such names as Victoria, the Duke of Wellington, Pugnose, and No Cheese. All this did not enhance the Chartists' prestige, and this last of their conventions soon faded into oblivion. Soon afterward O'Connor died insane.

With him died the Chartist movement. Probably the only direct good which may be traced to it was the commencement of that highly successful co-operative movement which has dotted England with co-operative retail stores, mainly for the poor. Nevertheless, all but one of the six demands of the Chartists, the annual election of Parliaments, have been granted. Shortly after the debacle of 1848 Parliament voted that pecuniary qualifications should no longer be required from members of the House of Commons. The second Reform Bill, of 1867, further equalized electoral districts, and soon afterward the ballot replaced open voting. Early in the twentieth century members of Commons were granted moderate salaries; and finally the suffrage was made universal, even for women. There was more virtue in the charter, apparently, than in Chartists. Never really dangerous, never really enlisting any clear-cut majority of the working class, they yet succeeded in alarming many Englishmen. They had been numerous and noisy enough to draw widespread attention to the need for reform.

# The Victorian Compromise

To the credit of the Chartists be it stated that if their leaders proved inadequate, they had at least one creditable poet, Ernest Jones, who epitomized Chartism in these lines of blind protest:

> The land, it is the landlord's;
> The trader's is the sea;
> The ore the usurer's coffer fills,
> But what remains for me?

> The camp, the pulpit, and the law,
> For rich men's sons are free.
> Theirs, theirs are learning, arts, and arms;
> But what remains for me?

> The coming hope, the future day,
> When wrong to right shall bow,
> And hearts that have the courage, man
> To make that future now.

A third explanation of the strength of the Victorian Compromise lay in the success of the Anti-Corn-Law League, a well-officered, well-financed association which outbid the Chartists for the support of the workingmen and which revolutionized England's fiscal system. The Corn Laws in 1840 differed little from those of 1815. The act of earlier date prohibited the importation of corn (the term was a general one, which included all grain intended for man or horse) until domestic prices rose to a certain high point, a regulation which had been slightly modified in 1828 by a sliding scale (see page 589). Accordingly the tariff rose sharply as domestic prices fell, thus accomplishing the same result, adequate protection for the landlord. The Corn Laws had been the target of desultory attack for many years, but to rid the country of them was to prove extraordinarily difficult. They were already a fixed British custom, not lightly to be set aside, and the landed interests both Whig and Tory championed them. A number of Whigs, it is true, favored a reduction of the duty and its transference to a fixed charge; but free trade, with no Corn Laws at all, was considered a will-o'-the-wisp.

Two men, both textile manufacturers, Richard Cobden and John Bright, made it otherwise. Richard Cobden, moderately wealthy, was, in every sense of the word, a self-made man. Protracted travel in both the United States and Europe and the constant study of economic institutions as living realities had convinced him that England ought to buy in the cheapest and sell in the dearest market. He looked forward with misgiving to the increase in England's population and to the growing strength of England's economic competitors. Cheap bread he believed essential to the country's welfare; for it would improve the condition of the working classes and give them more money with which to buy British manufactured goods. At the same time the repeal of the Corn Laws would, in his opinion, stimulate agriculture in the United States and thus give the Americans more money with which to buy from British firms. Only the landlords had received the advantages of protection, and they had not passed these down to the laborer or to the farmer but had kept rents high.

Cobden believed in following Adam Smith to his logical conclusion by allowing the natural laws which supposedly governed economics to operate unhindered. Poverty and suffering among the people, he believed, were caused primarily by interference with these laws; once remove this and the country would prosper. These ideas were not new; but the energy, the skill, and the moral fervor with which they were preached by Cobden and Bright gave them an unwonted vitality and freshness. These two men were leaders of the so-called "Manchester school," and their views were particularly acceptable to the cotton manufacturers of that great Lancashire factory center, who realized that cheaper bread would make it possible to pay a lower minimum wage to their workers. The organization of the Anti-Corn-Law League in 1838–1839 and its subsequent development were Cobden's great achievement. His "fresh and sanguine temper" made the whole enterprise throb with energy. "He had none of the fastidiousness which is repelled by the vulgarities of a proselytizing machine." He mapped out his campaigns in minute detail, pressing forward on half a dozen fronts. He not only enlisted the middle class but also obtained aid from workingmen and even from some aristocrats. None excelled Cobden when it came to raising money, writing pamphlets, and directing missionaries.

The League carried on a war on two fronts: the Chartist front and the conservative front. It was necessary to wean the workmen from O'Connor's agitation; to convince them that the ballot, the vote, and the other four points of the charter were not as important—at least for the time being—as cheap bread; and, above all, to persuade them that the League, financed by the manufacturers of England, was not their natural enemy. At the same time the support of at least a part of the landed aristocracy had to be secured if repeal was to be accomplished. The squires had to be made to feel that their continued monopoly of agriculture was uneconomic, unjust, and wrong.

It was fortunate for the League, under such circumstances, that it had money. In the year 1843 alone its financial status was so satisfactory that it had sufficient funds to publish nine million tracts and to send out eight hundred persons on missionary tours. The following year £100,000 was added to its treasury. In 1845–1846, as the climax approached, no less than £525,000 poured into its coffers.

The League was fortunate also in possessing an extraordinarily good orator in John Bright. He was of Quaker descent and industrial background; few in England have ever surpassed his spoken word for simplicity and directness of diction, pugnacity, and moral fervor. After Cobden spoke, Bright modestly remarked, "I used to get up and do a little prize fighting." Cobden gave the facts, ferreted out conditions, exposed fallacies, laid foundations; Bright stirred the conscience and steeled the will. It was never a question of pounds, shillings, and pence where Bright was concerned. "I be protected and I be starving," said an agricultural laborer. That was a clearer indictment to the popular mind than any fine-spun argument.

> "Child, is thy father dead?"
> "Father is gone!"
> "Why did they tax his bread?"

That was the theme of the League in appealing to the poor—that the poor paid and the rich reaped the profits; and it could depend upon Bright to convince the people of this. Proclaiming himself on the side of the poor, Bright's scathing indictments of the callous rich caught the ear of the workingmen and drew them from the Chartist camp to the support of the League. True, Bright and his fellow manufacturers, with a few exceptions, opposed the factory acts, opposed efforts to put down the international slave trade, and opposed giving encouragement to the oppressed peoples of the Continent; but few remembered these matters in the heat of the free-trade combat. Some, however, have charged the League with hypocrisy. That Bright had a blind spot in regard to certain aspects of social reform was undoubtedly true; but that did not mean that he, Cobden, and the League were merely trying to make themselves richer, for they probably thought in all sincerity that free trade would be good for the whole country as well as for Manchester. Nevertheless, most of the Lancashire manufacturers probably considered their contributions to the League a good investment.

As for the Chartists, they were hopelessly outclassed by the League. Some of them were against the Corn Laws, others in favor of them. O'Connor made such a poor showing in a debate with Cobden that it was whispered he had been bribed to betray his own cause. The Chartists, not knowing how to answer the League's speakers, howled them down—tactics which helped the League and hurt the Chartists.

The landed aristocracy, meanwhile, did its best to frighten the missionaries of the League away from the countryside. Even convinced free traders in the Commons, like Macaulay, refused to appear on League platforms. It was felt somehow that the League was extraconstitutional, if not unconstitutional. What was this organization which was attempting to dictate to Parliament? asked the gentlemen of England. The answer of *The Times* was caustic and contemptuous. It spoke of Cobden, Bright, and their allies as "capering mercenaries who go frisking about the country; as authors of incendiary claptrap; as peripatetic orators puffing themselves into an easy popularity by second-hand arguments."

Time and tide, however, worked in the League's favor. In 1841 the long period of Whig ascendancy came to an end, and the Tories, who were now beginning to be called Conservatives, returned to power, only to face the "hungry forties." Unemployment was rife, the price of bread high. The economic depression in England arose from causes larger than the Corn Laws; but politically a scapegoat was needed, and the Corn Laws provided one. "When two millions of one's brother men sit in workhouses, and five millions, as is insolently said, rejoice in potatoes, there are various things that must be begun, let them end where they can." At the head of the Tory party was Peel, now prime minister, who was pledged to maintain the Corn Laws; but he was a businessman, who recognized facts when he saw them. Bad harvests in England and the potato famine in Ireland precipitated a crisis. Conditions were bad enough in England; but far more serious was the situation in Ireland, with the failure of the potato crop upon which the peasants in many parts were almost completely dependent for sustenance.

The story of the famine of 1846 in Ireland seems almost unbelievable; yet the sober British census of 1851 describes it as follows: "Agriculture was neglected and land in many places remained untilled. Thousands were supported from day to day upon the bounty of outdoor relief; the closest ties of kindred were dissolved; the most ancient and long-cherished usages of the people were disregarded; food the most revolting to human palates was devoured. . . . The disorganization of society became marked and memorable by the exodus of over one million of people, who deserted their homes and hearths to seek shelter in foreign lands, of whom thousands perished of pestilence and hardships endured on shipboard. . . . Generally speaking, the actually starving people lived upon the carcasses of diseased cattle, upon dogs and dead horses, but principally upon the herbs of the field, nettle tops, wild mustard and water cresses, and even in some places dead bodies were found with grasses in their mouths."

# The Victorian Compromise

In the face of this crisis something had to be done. Peel, convinced by Cobden that repeal of the Corn Laws was inevitable, resigned. Russell and his Whigs had their golden chance, but did not take it. The overwhelmingly Tory House of Lords would throw out any repeal bill emanating from the Whigs, who, besides, had no stomach for a new struggle with the Lords. The Whigs pretended that they could not form a new ministry, "passed back the poisoned chalice" to Sir Robert, and prepared to rejoice in Tory recriminations.

There followed the "great betrayal" of 1846. Sir Robert Peel had become a free trader and was determined to give the nation what it wanted—free trade. Furthermore, he felt that this semiradical League's constant talk of rich versus poor was not a good thing for the possessing classes, and that the sooner it accomplished its purpose the sooner it would disband. He realized that by this the Tory party might be broken up for the time being; but he was a statesman, who saw beyond the political exigencies of the moment to the future needs of England. Furthermore, he was sure that the Tory Lords would do the bidding of Tory leadership in the Commons.

Thus Peel, the gifted leader of British conservatism breached the ramparts of his own class and proposed to abolish the Corn Laws. His motion passed the Commons with the assistance of the timid Whigs; and it passed the Lords because the Duke of Wellington said that it must. "Rotten potatoes have done it," he said; "they put Peel in his damned fright." The Duke, old and deaf, did not care about the Corn Laws one way or another; but he did know that the government had to be carried on. Thus the Corn Laws were repealed in 1846.

This repeal is significant in British history. It meant the rise to power of Benjamin Disraeli. This curious interloper in that first club of Europe, the House of Commons, had hitherto scarcely been noticed by the aristocracy. Disraeli determined to make himself their leader, and in one speech he became famous. He drove the rapier of his vitriolic scorn into Sir Robert Peel with unerring skill and drew unto himself the support of the country squires, who knew little of economics or politics, and little about anything except hunting and that Peel was no longer their man. They were tongue-tied by custom, but they knew a leader when they saw one. As for Disraeli, he seemed never to think the issue one of economics, of the greatest good of the greatest number, or even a question which concerned all England. Instead all he seemed to see was what he considered the betrayal of the country gentlemen, who had made England great in the past and were the bone and sinew of all that was best in the nation. He gave them his loyal and romantic devotion, and at the same time, as their leader, found his way into high office.

Again, the repeal marked a serious schism in the Tory party. The majority, the privates, followed Disraeli; the officers,—the "Peelites," as they were nicknamed,—few in number but brilliant in intellect, among whom there stood Gladstone, remained true to the fallen leader. There were now really two Tory parties instead of one, and this marked the beginning of a long period of Whig-Liberal rule.

The repeal of the Corn Laws was also a signal victory for laissez faire over its last redoubtable enemy, the protective tariff. The factory acts, of course, were a standing proof that laissez faire was never to be adopted in its entirety, and the survival of customs duties on commodities other than grain was another. Nevertheless, free contract, free sale, free trade, were henceforth to be the rule rather than the exception for the rest of the century.

In this connection the repeal of the Corn Laws was significant because it registered the finality of the last shift from an agricultural to an industrial economy in England. For years her agriculture had been gradually growing less important; and from now on, England was to become more and more an essentially industrial country.

In addition, the repeal staved off for more than a generation the birth of a British labor movement. The year 1848 came and went, and Europe was aflame with revolution. In England there was no revolt, because, for the time being, the repeal of the Corn Laws improved economic conditions. Business increased, wages rose, and unemployment diminished; and although this was not entirely the result of the repeal, the majority thought it was.

Another bulwark of the Victorian Compromise was Lord Palmerston. This bluff peer was for many years the guiding spirit in British foreign relations, and he was the most popular man in public life in nineteenth-century England. Others might command greater respect, but not one could arouse the widespread affection which Englishmen felt for "Pam." He seemed an embodiment of the things that were essentially English—a regular John Bull or British lion. A "statesman-aristocrat of sporting proclivities," Palmerston had all the background of family, wealth, and education which England still looked for in her leaders; he had, too, wit, joviality, undisciplined exuberance, and a frequent rough arrogance which won the multitude. A gay bachelor until well past fifty and the owner of blooded horses which sometimes won races, he was a thorough man of the world. Yet, with all that, he was a tireless and painstaking worker who did not shrink from the drudgery of administrative routine. However much he might bluster, he knew his facts. Those who dealt with him were impressed by his remarkable mastery of details. With reports pouring into the Foreign Office at the rate of a hundred a day, he boasted that he read them all, "down to the least important letter of the lowest vice-consul." He was blessed with unusual vitality; the cares of office, which drove some statesmen to premature graves, left Palmerston at seventy-five still "springy and elastic" and looking "as if he did not care one straw for any man or thing on earth."

That last quality, perhaps, was what endeared him most to the Britons of his day and made him politically indispensable. He was always conscious of English superiority in all things. England was not in a modest mood, and for that reason the people rejoiced at his arrogant tone used all too freely even toward the great powers of Europe. They were pleased, too, when he declared that British subjects, wherever they might go, should have the same claim to protection which ancient Rome had given her citizens. They cheered his application of that theory even when the claims to British protection were as diluted as those of the Portuguese Jew born at Gibraltar, for whom a fleet was sent to Greece to collect questionable claims, or of the Chinese vessel which helped to bring on a war because of an insult to her British flag which she no longer had the right to fly. It was a risky sort of belligerent patriotism which kept the army and navy in a nervous state of constant expectancy; but the public enjoyed the prestige which it supposedly reflected upon the nation. It did not seem to detract from Palmerston's popularity that he paid relatively little attention to internal problems which, however fundamentally important they might be, were decidedly less spectacular.

A review of Palmerston's public career gives an opportunity to outline the political shifts of more than half a century. Entering public life fresh from Cambridge in 1807, Palmerston was a Tory until after Canning's death. For two years he was a junior Lord of the Admiralty; then he was promoted to Secretary for War, and remained in that office until 1828, when, with other Canningites, he "mutinied" against Wellington. Never essentially a party man, he joined forces with Grey's Whigs, and might thereafter be called a conservative Liberal. When Grey came into power in 1830, Palmerston assumed charge of foreign relations, which henceforth were to be his absorbing specialty. Except for the five months of Peel's first Conservative ministry (1834–1835), he remained steadily in office in the Liberal ministries of Grey (1830–1834) and Melbourne (1834–

1841). His "longest vacation" from office occurred during the second Peel ministry (1841–1846); then he returned to the Foreign Office in the Liberal ministry of Lord John Russell (1846–1852). Just before that ended, however, Palmerston was dismissed for a glaring indiscretion and remained out of office during the ten-month Conservative ministry headed by Lord Derby (whose grandfather had started the celebrated horse races), with Disraeli at the Exchequer as the real leader (February–December, 1852). This "stop-gap government without a majority and without a policy" quickly gave way to a Conservative-Liberal coalition under Lord Aberdeen (1852–1855), in which Palmerston, considered too dangerous at the Foreign Office, was Home Secretary. The coalition proved inadequate as a war government, and the need for more aggressive leadership brought Palmerston into power in 1855 as Liberal prime minister. He held that office, interrupted only by a brief second Derby-Disraeli ministry (1858–1859), until his death ten years later.

As prime minister, even as Home Secretary, Palmerston could not keep his hands off foreign affairs, so that for nearly thirty years he had a commanding voice in England's international relations. His problems covered a wide range, from the pine forests of Maine to the hongs of Canton; but his attention was centered particularly upon the Continent, where numerous delicate situations arose from the various crops of revolutions and the breakup of the Metternich system, along with the perennial crises in the Eastern Question.

Since Canning had done, as we have seen, much to procure independence for Greece and the Latin-American republics, it was fitting that Palmerston, as his avowed disciple, should assist prominently at the births of the new kingdoms of Belgium and Italy and encourage elsewhere those who sought new constitutions, modeled, of course, upon England's. "As long as England shall ride pre-eminent on the ocean of human affairs," he told Parliament, "there can be none whose fortunes shall be so shipwrecked, there can be none whose condition shall be so desperate and forlorn, that they may not cast a look of hope towards the light that beams from hence; and though they may be beyond the reach of our power, our moral support and our sympathy shall cheer them in their adversity."

Palmerston had a strenuous initiation in his first application of this principle, when he took over the Foreign Office late in 1830. The Belgians a few weeks before had revolted against the Dutch, with whom they had been united at Vienna in order to provide a strong buffer state against French aggression in the north. The Belgians now sought independence, which they had never before enjoyed; for the provinces gathered together by Burgundy late in the Middle Ages had belonged to Spain, Austria, France, and Holland in turn. As we have noticed, England had a particularly vital interest in the region, and time and again had fought to prevent its falling into French hands (see pages 406, 552). Now that seemed likely again. France certainly had designs upon Belgium, and might absorb her if she became free; on the other hand, if the antirevolutionary powers—Austria, Prussia, and Russia—had their way, and supported the Dutch king in recovering Belgium, France might fight and thus plunge Europe into a general war. Palmerston steered a clever and careful course in his "diplomatic defense of the Low Countries," with the result that a gathering of the powers at London in 1831 agreed that Belgium should become an independent kingdom, with her neutrality perpetually guaranteed by the five great powers. That was intended as a safeguard against absorption by France. Leopold of Saxe-Coburg-Gotha, uncle of the future Queen Victoria, had recently declined the Greek crown, but now accepted the Belgian one. The new country was provided with a limited monarchy modeled closely after the English pattern. It took eight years of persuasion and armed pressure from England and France to bring both the Belgians and the Dutch finally to terms. In 1839 the representatives of the powers—England, France, Austria, Russia, and Prussia—gathered again at London and signed a final treaty in which they agreed to guarantee Belgian neutrality. Palmerston had done what he could to prevent Belgium from falling into hostile hands, but he remarked that the treaty was only parchment and might be broken. Just seventy-five years later England gave the violation of that treaty as her reason for plunging into the greatest of wars, while a German statesman referred to the 1839 agreement as a "scrap of paper."

Many years later Palmerston was also to play an active role in supporting the unification of Italy. Metternich had called it a "geographical expression," and Austrian influence was strong among the varied states of the peninsula. Austrian whitecoats had crushed the revolts of 1820 and 1830, and even the more serious ones in 1848. By that time Piedmont (Sardinia), which led the opposition to Austria, realized that a free and united Italy could be achieved only with outside aid. The only two nations who might be of help were England and France. To gain recognition as a nation, Piedmont allied herself with them in the Crimean War against Russia, simply in order to have the Italian situation discussed at the peace conference. Both nations were impressed, and England gave assurances of moral support. In 1859, during a war between Piedmont and Austria, France gave something much more tangible by invading

Italy and inflicting two bloody defeats upon the Austrians; then the French emperor, Napoleon III, suddenly stopped short, with the Austrian defeat only half completed. In the peace treaty, however, Piedmont was able to annex Lombardy, the first step in the unification of Italy. Palmerston and Russell, the foreign minister, did much to secure the second step by throwing England's weight behind the proposal that the little states of central Italy be permitted to vote upon their future political status. The other powers reluctantly agreed, and the votes went heavily in favor of union with Piedmont. Soon after came the formation, in 1861, of the kingdom of Italy, a limited monarchy under the ruler of Piedmont, with a constitution on the English model. The new king expressed unbounded gratitude to England, which had not spent a shilling or lost a man in the Italian cause, whereas the French outpouring of blood and treasure was offset by the fact that French troops still guarded the Papal States at Rome and deprived Italy of her natural capital. Palmerston and Russell, more interested in freeing Italy from Austrian control than in uniting her, had no enthusiasm for the third step in her unification, when the dramatic raid (1860) of the Italian patriot Garibaldi and his "Redshirts" brought into the new kingdom the southern part of the peninsula, Naples and Sicily, and thus paved the way for a sixth great power in Europe. Italy was now unified, with the exception of Venetia, which she was to gain from Austria in 1866 during the Austro-Prussian War, and Rome, which she was to seize from the Pope when France was occupied with the war against Prussia in 1870.

During the long interval between Belgian and Italian independence Palmerston had his hands full with the Eastern Question, which, as we saw, had come into prominence with the Greek situation in Canning's time (see page 593). The Ottoman Empire continued to disintegrate under constant pressure from outside, with England continually trying to check that process. It was pointed out at the time, however, that it is extremely difficult to maintain the status quo in a decomposing carcass. Canning's imperious cousin, several times ambassador at Constantinople, did what he could to resist Russian encroachments. There was France to worry about, too; and one of Palmerston's diplomatic masterpieces came in 1840 when the ambitious ruler of Egypt, backed by France, marched northward in a successful attack upon his Turkish overlord. Palmerston and the British fleet intervened, and Turkey was saved from an especially grave threat of dismemberment.

"Pam's" popularity rose to its greatest heights during the Crimean War (1854–1856), when England and France supported Turkey in fighting Russia. The war was one of the most stupid and useless in

# The Victorian Compromise

which England ever took part. Its origin was not particularly Palmerston's fault; for the nations had drifted toward war during the period when he was out of office. The fact that ministries were shaky and short-lived, and that England had five different foreign secretaries in fifteen months, probably helped to encourage the Czar to proceed with his ambitious designs against Turkey. He told the British ambassador that Europe had a very sick man on its hands and that it would be well to make plans about the disposal of his estate. That reference to Turkey put England on guard; possibly Palmerston, had he been in power, might have saved the situation by one of his vigorous dramatic gestures. As it was, England joined in nearly a dozen ineffectual efforts for peace, while Russian troops occupied Rumania, and Russia demanded of Turkey full control over the Balkan Christians. Confident of British support, Turkey refused and late in 1853 went to war with Russia. After a Turkish fleet had been annihilated, England early in 1854 entered the war, acompanied by France, which had a particular and rather trivial grievance against Russia.

The allies, having blundered into the war, continued to blunder through it. They concentrated their efforts in a military and naval attack upon the strong Russian naval base at Sebastopol, on the Crimean peninsula, which juts into the Black Sea. The scene of action was far distant, and the army poorly led, poorly organized, and insufficiently supplied with food and clothes. There were several bloody battles; but the Russians, snugly ensconced, had for a long time little difficulty in driving off the French and British attacks, and the allies lost heavily in men and morale. They made no progress before winter set in, with bitter cold and heavy storms. The commissariat having broken down, there was no hay for the horses, no medicine for the sick, no overcoats for the men. According to *The Times*, "incompetency, lethargy, aristocratic hauteur, official indifference, favour, routine, perverseness and stupidity reign, revel and riot before Sebastopol." At home the ill-assorted coalition ministry under Aberdeen, who did not approve of the war anyway, made little headway in the face of "party anarchy."

In these circumstances there was a general outcry for "Pam." He was over seventy; but he was a fighter, and England clamored for leadership more aggressive than Aberdeen's. Bright and Cobden believed "Pam" a dangerous demagogue, but the public fed upon his noisy patriotism. So Palmerston became prime minister and sent recruits, supplies, and munitions to the Black Sea. Finally Sebastopol fell, after allied efforts in which the French outshone the British. As far as England was concerned, the principal tangible results from her only major conflict between Waterloo and the Boer War arose from her own shortcomings. Tennyson's poem "The Charge of the Light Brigade" commemorated one more instance of British valor in a suicidal military blunder; Florence Nightingale's work on behalf of the sick and wounded, in the face of glaring military neglect, was a step toward the founding of the Red Cross; and an eventual thorough overhauling of the nation's military administration obviated some of its gravest defects. The Treaty of Paris, which ended the war in 1856, among other terms neutralized the Black Sea, from which Russian and Turkish warships were to be barred; but it did not push Russia back from the Balkans and the route to India as decisively as England had anticipated. Twenty years later, as we shall see, the Eastern Question would once more draw British diplomacy and British warships into the defense of the decadent Turk.

From now on, except for sixteen months of Conservative government, Palmerston remained prime minister for the rest of his life, with "Little John" Russell as his foreign minister. In the field of diplomacy they had still further concerns. In 1861, just one month after the formation of the kingdom of Italy, a four-year civil war broke out in the United States between the populous industrial and commercial North and the slave-holding, cotton-growing South. England was bound to be concerned in such a conflict. The factories of Lancashire depended on Southern cotton, just as Flanders had once depended on English wool. The South was eager for British recognition of the Confederacy as an independent state, and hoped that the royal navy might break the Northern blockade, which was slowly strangling Southern economic life. At the same time the North was England's best foreign customer, and Northern grain was beginning to feed Englishmen, though the aggressive Yankees of the North had been giving England a close run in the early fifties with a merchant marine almost equal to the British in size and decidedly superior in quality. English sympathies were divided. The upper classes saw in the Southern planters the closest American approach to the English landed aristocracy; the commercial classes saw a possible chance to weaken a lively business rival. On the other hand, the radicals Cobden and Bright, together with the factory workers of Lancashire, saw in the North the champion of the same democratic principles for which they were contending in England. Whatever their private sympathies may have been, Palmerston and Russell steered a fairly correct and neutral course, hoping for peace but ready for trouble if it should come, though their actions frequently seemed pro-Southern in the eyes of the United States minister at London.

# The Victorian Compromise

Matters came to a crisis late in 1861, when a Northern cruiser stopped the British mail steamer *Trent* on the high seas and removed two Southern diplomatic agents en route to England. This, without question, was a breach of international law on the part of the North, and it was small wonder that British troops were rushed to Canada. The North, still losing battles at that time, could not risk the danger of British intervention. Palmerston and thirteen colleagues drafted a strong note which might have meant war; but Victoria's husband, as his dying act, toned it down. The North disavowed the *Trent* affair, and the crisis passed. In the whole matter of the blockade there was an amusing problem; for the situation of the Napoleonic period was reversed (see page 573). Each side could throw back the other's old arguments, but hesitated to speak too strongly; for both could foresee that some other time England would again probably be the blockader and the United States the neutral. In one way England did help the South. The Northern minister kept protesting about a mysterious vessel "No. 290" which was approaching completion in a British shipyard. Palmerston and Russell may have been innocent in the matter; but, at any rate, "No. 290" was allowed to slip away to sea and, renamed the *Alabama*, began to make flaming wrecks of Northern merchantmen. The dread of the *Alabama* and her consorts sent up insurance rates on Northern shipping so that it was handicapped in competing with the British. Scores of United States vessels were transferred to British registry. That was a final blow to the American merchant marine, which had recently begun to decline. Later, when the *Alabama* claims were arbitrated, the United States received heavy damages from England. When President Lincoln proclaimed the freedom of the slaves, the English attitude toward the conflict began to change. The tide of war turned in the summer of 1863, and the North emerged victorious in 1865.

In the meantime there were difficulties within Palmerston's cabinet. The Liberal party had become a more compact unit in 1859 with the final adherence of the former liberal Conservative followers of Peel. Its three leaders had each come into the Liberal camp from a different direction: Palmerston was a former Canningite Tory; Russell, an old Whig; and Gladstone, the Chancellor of the Exchequer and future leader of the party, a Peelite. There were enough conservative elements in the party to prevent, for the time being, any radical extension of the franchise beyond the 1832 basis. Palmerston himself, so far as he was interested in such matters, did not want to extend it to more than a few of the more intelligent and thrifty; Parliamentary reform was not to come until after his death. He and Gladstone, however, did lock horns on the rival issues of free trade and military preparedness. Gladstone, a financial genius, was carrying to completion the free-trade policy commenced by Huskisson and continued by Peel (see pages 596, 639). In 1860, through the negotiations of Cobden, a free-trade treaty was arranged with France. Gladstone wanted to go farther and repeal the duties on paper, arguing that, since paper was the raw material of books and newspapers, this constituted a tax on knowledge. Interested in economy, peace, and the extension of the franchise, Gladstone had scant interest in or sympathy for the diplomacy and threats of war which had always meant so much to Palmerston. The old prime minister, on the other hand, saw that the repeal of the paper duties meant a considerable loss of revenue at the very time when, in his opinion, England needed to spend heavily for ironclads and forts to protect herself against what he considered the dangerous ambition of the French under Emperor Napoleon III to follow in the first Napoleon's path in extending French influence. At any rate, victory for the time being rested with Palmerston: the House of Lords, fearful of higher income taxes, retained the paper duties. Gladstone was furious, but his day would come. He knew, and the Liberal party knew, that the country loved Palmerston. A new election in 1865 entrenched "Pam," now eighty-one, still further in power; but before the year was out he was dead.

Another explanation of the static quality of the Victorian Compromise may be found in the growing prosperity which characterized English economic history in the middle decades of the last century. England was reaping the rich rewards of her long head start in the Industrial Revolution. The "workshop of the world" was turning out enough textiles, metals, and other manufactures to supply not only her own growing needs but most of the needs of other nations as well. British ships were gaining added profits by distributing these wares, and the surplus capital accumulated in these industrial and commercial pursuits was being lent abroad to bring back still further riches in the form of interest. In deliberately devoting herself to industry, England, in the repeal of the Corn Laws, had shown a readiness to sacrifice agriculture, but for the time being did not have to pay the price; not until the last quarter of the century would overseas foodstuffs bring hardship to rural England.

The significance of these facts can be quickly visualized by an examination of the statistics of British commerce for the century. The most striking feature is the importance of cotton. Cotton goods formed the most valuable single article of export throughout the period, while raw cotton led the imports until finally overtaken by

# The Victorian Compromise

FOREIGN TRADE OF THE UNITED KINGDOM, 1820–1910

(Showing principal articles of export and import in millions of pounds sterling)

### EXPORTS

|      | Total | Cotton Goods | Other Textiles | Iron, Steel, etc. | Coal | Re-exports |
|------|-------|--------------|----------------|-------------------|------|------------|
| 1820 | 48    | 16           | 6              |                   |      | 10         |
| 1830 | 69    | 19           | 8              | 2                 | .1   | 8          |
| 1840 | 116   | 24           | 11             | 4                 | .5   | 13         |
| 1850 | 197   | 28           | 18             | 9                 | 1    | 21         |
| 1860 | 164   | 52           | 26             | 20                | 3    | 28         |
| 1870 | 244   | 71           | 43             | 33                | 5    | 44         |
| 1880 | 286   | 75           | 38             | 40                | 8    | 63         |
| 1890 | 328   | 74           | 47             | 45                | 19   | 64         |
| 1900 | 354   | 69           | 42             | 57                | 38   | 63         |
| 1910 | 534   | 105          | 52             | 85                | 37   | 103        |

### IMPORTS

|      | Total | Cotton | Wool, Silk, Flax, etc. | Grain and Flour | Meat | Dairy Products | Sugar | Tea |
|------|-------|--------|------------------------|-----------------|------|----------------|-------|-----|
| 1820 | 32    | 2      |                        | 1               |      |                | 5     | 2   |
| 1830 | 46    | 8      | 4                      | 3               |      | .3             | 7     | 3   |
| 1840 | 67    |        |                        |                 |      |                |       |     |
| 1850 | 100   | 21     | 9                      | 12              | 1    | 1              | 10    | 5   |
| 1860 | 210   | 35     | 28                     | 32              | 3    | 6              | 12    | 6   |
| 1870 | 303   | 53     | 34                     | 36              | 7    | 11             | 17    | 10  |
| 1880 | 411   | 42     | 40                     | 66              | 26   | 19             | 22    | 11  |
| 1890 | 420   | 42     | 40                     | 56              | 32   | 21             | 18    | 9   |
| 1900 | 523   | 40     | 33                     | 62              | 46   | 32             | 20    | 10  |
| 1910 | 678   | 71     | 46                     | 77              | 48   | 41             | 25    | 11  |

foodstuffs. The chancellor might well have changed his woolsack for a bolt of calico had he desired to be up to date in symbolizing the mainstay of British prosperity. Fashions had something to do with the flourishing condition of the textile industry during the middle decades, when England was sending forth nearly three billion yards of cotton cloth a year. With huge hoop skirts several feet in diameter, supported by numerous petticoats and much other underwear, the woman of the fifties and sixties wore enough material to clothe perhaps ten women in the scant styles of the nineteen twenties. That naturally meant a lively business for the plantations of Georgia and Alabama, for the factories of Lancashire, and for the busy seaports of Liverpool, New York, and New Orleans. The spindles and looms of Lancashire were creating wealth; in 1860, for instance, out of £35,000,000 worth of raw cotton, England exported £52,000,000 worth of cotton cloth, yarn, and thread in addition to meeting the heavy domestic demands within the British Isles. Up to 1870, it will be noted, the value of cotton exports showed a rapid increase; for the rest of the century, however, it remained fairly stationary. The substitution of the bustle for the hoop skirt was not altogether to blame; rival factories in Germany, the United States, and elsewhere, as we shall see, were cutting into the demand for the products of Lancashire. Woolen cloth, England's principal offering to the world of commerce for several centuries past, lagged far behind its lighter and cheaper rival. In 1860 the woolen exports stood at £16,000,000, less than a third of the value of the cotton exports, followed by linen (chiefly from Ireland) at £6,600,000, silk at £2,400,000, and finished apparel at the same amount.

The sudden boom in iron and steel exports, noticeable in 1860, arose from the invention, four years earlier, of a process for producing steel cheaply in large quantities. Steel was more generally useful than cast iron, which was brittle, or wrought iron, which could not be poured into molds; but its manufacture was slow and expensive until Henry Bessemer, the son of a French refugee, discovered the simple process of blowing the proper amount of carbon out of the iron by means of blast furnaces. For a while England enjoyed a lead in steel manufacture. Prices tumbled, and orders poured in from all directions, particularly for railroad material. Closely associated with the production of iron and steel was the making of machinery, for which also there was a heavy foreign demand. At the beginning of the Industrial Revolution, England had forbidden the export of machinery, as we have seen, desiring to keep its mysteries to herself; but the secrets had leaked out anyway, and Huskisson had removed the restrictions. England took her profits while she could, even though the products of the exported machines might later compete with her own. Unlike cotton, the raw materials for her iron and steel industry did not have to be imported; they were dug out of England's own soil in the "Black Country."

So too was coal, which gradually increased in importance as an export. Some nations, such as Italy, had little or no coal, and England was ready to supply their deficiency at a price. The coal exports were more important than their value indicated; for they gave British shipping a useful outward cargo. As in the case of iron and steel, Germany and the United States would gradually enter into keen competition in coal.

Among the imports, sugar and tea were examples of the good old "colonial wares" which had long figured prominently in British commerce, and they remained fairly steady throughout the century.

# The Victorian Compromise

Far more significant were the import figures for the foodstuffs formerly produced by England herself: grain and flour, meat and dairy products. The statistics reveal the gradual effect of the repeal of the Corn Laws in 1846. In 1830, when England was still feeding herself with agriculture well protected, the imports of these foodstuffs amounted to only £3,500,000. Four years after Peel's great act, they had risen to £14,000,000; but a combination of circumstances kept British agriculture in fairly good condition until the late seventies, when bad crops at home coincided with good crops in the United States, while the invention of the refrigerator ship flooded the market with American beef and Australian mutton. By 1880 Britain's bill for food imports had risen to £111,000,000. The landlords at last were feeling the effects of industry's political victory, and England was lapsing into that state of dependence upon foreign food which was to render her dangerously vulnerable to blockade. But in Palmerston's day that all lay in the future, and, for the time being, agriculture had little ground for complaint.

A final important item in England's foreign commerce was her "entrepôt" trade in re-exports. Tea from China, for instance, would be brought to London and reshipped to Spain; wine from Spain would likewise be carried by way of England to Brazil or New Zealand; and in such instances England would be the richer from commissions, insurance, freight, and the like.

Geographically the distribution of British foreign trade in 1860 is interesting when compared with the figures for the previous century (see page 468). The United States stood first both in imports and in exports; England had a heavier trade with New York than with any other foreign port; and the well-beaten ocean trail between New York and Liverpool became the most important of sea routes, while both those ports steadily crept up on London, the busiest seaport of the world. Thanks to cotton, imports from the United States amounted to more than the total for the whole British Empire, with a total of £44,000,000 as against £42,000,000. England was particularly interested in the extent to which various regions purchased her manufactures. Out of the total exports of British products (not including re-exports) of 136 (in millions of pounds sterling), the United States stood first with 21.6, which was exactly half the total for the whole British Empire, including India's 16.9, Australia's 9.2, Canada's 3.2, and South Africa's 2.0. The British West Indies, once the pride of the empire, had dwindled to 2.4. The principal European customers were Germany, 13.3; Holland, 7.5; France, 5.2; Turkey, 5.2; Spain, 4.8; and Italy, 4.5. The value of Canning's diplomacy was shown by the Latin-American total of 10.8.

# A History of England and the British Empire

By 1860 imports were running ahead of exports, but certain "invisible" items indicated that the balance was not "unfavorable," as the old mercantilists would term it. One extremely rich foreign source of British wealth was the interest on capital lent abroad. If one wanted to finance a railroad, a revolution, or a government bond issue in outlying regions, it was generally necessary to consult the Barings, the Rothschilds, or other great private bankers whose influence earlier in the century we have already noticed (see page 596). It has been estimated that by 1825 British foreign loans totaled about £100,000,000; by 1850, £300,000,000; by 1870, £800,000,000, and by 1885, more than £1,000,000,000. Railroads were a particular favorite with investors; it was estimated that in 1857 England had invested £80,000,000 in United States railroads alone, about a quarter of the amount invested in British railways. In such a case the profits of the loan were not limited solely to the interest, for much of the money would probably be spent in England for iron, steel, and machinery.

Marine freight constituted another very important "invisible" source of wealth from foreign trade; for about three fifths to two thirds of England's foreign commerce was carried in her own ships, even after the repeal of the Navigation Acts in 1849. With some bulky commodities like coal and timber, the freight often amounted to more than the original value of the article. The British merchant marine in 1860 consisted of 25,000 sailing vessels totaling 4,000,000 tons, and 2000 steamers totaling 400,000 tons. Some 171,000 officers and seamen manned these ships.

Both merchantmen and warships were in the midst of a thoroughgoing transformation in the middle years of the century. In 1800 wooden sailing vessels were universal, but by 1900 they had been crowded out of all important business by steel and steam. After the successful run of Fulton's *Clermont* up the Hudson in 1807 (see page 508), steamboats had been rapidly adopted for river and harbor work and for other short runs where relief from dependence on the winds was vital. By 1820 steamers were linking England with Ireland and France. On the high seas, however, there was generally plenty of wind, and sailing vessels held their own much longer. They were even brought to their highest peak of perfection at this period by the Americans, with their New York–Liverpool packets and their clippers to California and China.

Regular transatlantic steam navigation dates from 1838, when, within a few hours of each other, the *Sirius* and *Great Western* arrived at New York from British ports. The following year Parliament granted to a Nova Scotian, Samuel Cunard, an annual subsidy

# The Victorian Compromise

of £55,000 to carry the mails from Liverpool to Halifax and Boston, later to New York. That was the beginning of the line celebrated for its long record of safety, regularity, and profit. Shortly afterward another famous British line, the Peninsular and Oriental, cut the time of communication with the East, carrying mails by steamship through the Mediterranean to Alexandria and thence by land to Suez, on the Red Sea, whence other steamships continued the trip to India and China. Then came the screw propeller, safer and more powerful than the early paddle wheels, and the iron hull, which relieved shipping of the limitations imposed by the size of timbers, and which allowed more cargo space because the sides of the ship did not have to be so thick. The introduction of iron in her ships gave England a great advantage over the United States, which had been able to build wooden ships much more cheaply because of the great forests close at hand. England had had to import ship timber; but she had plenty of iron at home, and on the Clyde near Glasgow she had clever builders. The first iron screw steamship on the transatlantic run, the *City of Glasgow*, was built in 1850. For long after that, sailing vessels continued to carry the bulk of the ordinary freight, but gradually they were supplanted by steel "tramps." The steamship could make more runs in a year, with greater regularity; and that offset the fact that coal cost money, while wind was free. In the British merchant marine, steam tonnage caught up with sail tonnage in 1883; but, as the average steamship was larger than the sailing vessel, it was not until 1904 that the former overtook the latter in numbers.

Naval warfare was even more profoundly changed by steam and iron. Both came slowly; for the Admiralty was conservative, and, since England had a larger navy than any other nation, she was not eager to introduce changes which would render her large fleet obsolete. The paddle wheel was too vulnerable for warships, and it interfered with the broadside batteries; but the screw propeller met those objections and consequently was introduced into the wooden ships of the line. In the meantime a former Napoleonic colonel was responsible for the introduction of explosive shells instead of solid shot in naval guns. From the navies the cry went up, "For God's sake, keep out the shells!"; and various nations began to experiment with armor plate. In 1859 the French launched the *Gloire*, the first regular armor-plated warship. For the only time in the century following Trafalgar the British were worried about their naval supremacy. There were skeptics in high naval circles; "Don't talk to me about ships of iron—it's contrary to nature," declared one dockyard official; Palmerston in 1861 told the Commons not to "suppose that iron ships will wholly supersede those of wood." By that time, however, England had her iron *Warrior* as an answer to the *Gloire;* and the days of wooden warships, like the days of Lord Palmerston, were virtually over.

England, once convinced, could afford to build plenty of the new ironclads; for, from all this widespread economic activity, England was rich. The middle class reaped the major profit; but the condition of the poor did improve: real wages, or the amount of goods which money wages would buy, increased; unemployment decreased, and goods and commodities beyond the reach of the laboring class in 1830 were familiar to it thirty years later.

In consequence optimism continued, and the Victorian Compromise remained popular for a long time. Statistics seemed to prove Macaulay correct when he laughed at Southey's rose-covered cottage and praised the steam engine and economic independence. Could the working-man pull himself up by his own bootstraps and by so doing abolish both ignorance and poverty? By 1865 more Englishmen were of that opinion than four decades earlier.

# CHAPTER XXII

## Imperial Apathy

### 1783-1874

WITH the loss of the thirteen colonies England also lost, for a full ninety years, most of her enthusiasm for empire. This apathy stands in sharp contrast both to the aggressive zeal with which the elder Pitt had sought overseas acquisitions in the Seven Years' War and to the new imperialism of the late nineteenth century. During this intervening period the British government showed official initiative in extending the colonies only on rare occasions. It did, to be sure, take steps to improve relations with the remaining possessions, and it now and then acquired strategic points as naval bases; but the colonies of settlement were under a cloud. In the disillusionment which followed the breakup of the Old Empire, colonies were likened to fruit which dropped off when it became ripe, or to ungrateful children who ran away from home as soon as they were big enough. Why, then, men asked, should further British blood and treasure be wasted in gaining and defending overseas lands? Even toward the end of the ninety years there was an influential group of "Little Englanders" talking in that same vein. One Colonial Secretary even expressed the hope that Canada would become independent and that the separation would be a friendly one. England had no desire to spend another £110,000,000 in a vain attempt to hold unwilling members within the imperial family.

Even after the loss of the most populous of the colonies of settlement, England still had a respectable overseas empire left in 1783. Jamaica, Barbados, and more than a dozen lesser islands in the West Indies were scarcely started on their long decline from sugar prosperity; and they were far more profitable than the other remaining American holdings of Canada, Newfoundland, Hudson Bay, and the Maritime Provinces of Prince Edward Island and Nova Scotia (with its new offshoot, New Brunswick), Bermuda, and the Bahamas. Outside of America there was Gibraltar, still guarding the Mediterranean; the pestilential Gold Coast in Africa; lonely St. Helena, far down in the South Atlantic; and, finally, India, where the new province of Bengal represented the first step inland from the seacoast. Compared with the remains of the other old colonial empires,

[ 655 ]

these were impressive. For although Spain's vast holdings in America still loomed large on the map, they were soon to break loose in revolution; Holland had only the rich Spice Islands, together with Ceylon, the Cape, and a few lesser possessions; while Portugal had Brazil and some titles to African territory. The former extensive French colonial empire had dwindled to little more than a few sugar islands in the Caribbean and two tiny, bleak, rocky islands off Newfoundland.

In spite of official and popular apathy, the world map was to become more and more colored with British red during these ninety years. The spoils from the Napoleonic Wars were taken mainly for strategic purposes: the Cape of Good Hope; Ceylon; part of Guiana; Mauritius, in the Indian Ocean; Malta (a base to replace lost Minorca), as well as the Ionian Islands, in the Mediterranean; Trinidad and a few more islands in the West Indies (see page 582). During the course of that long period other new regions also came under the British rule: Australia and New Zealand in the South Seas; the Straits Settlements, guarding the passage from the Indian Ocean to the Pacific; Hong Kong, taken as a foothold for the China trade; Sierra Leone, founded for free Negroes on the Guinea coast; British Columbia, in western America; and various lesser scraps of empire here and there around the globe. The Colonial Office might keep saying, "Go slow"; but hardy settlers none the less kept pushing across the plains of Canada, and in Africa inland from the Cape. Governors-general in India, in spite of similar advice, kept saying that it was a matter of "go ahead or get out." Traders clamored for the protection of the flag as they extended their activities into new fields. The empire meantime experienced a new phenomenon in the rapid spread of missionary endeavors to convert the heathen.

Except for India, which had its own particular form of control, overseas affairs were directed from what came to be called the Colonial Office. For thirty years after the American Revolution this colonial administration was a rather neglected part-time job of a cabinet minister busy with other duties. There was also a committee of the Privy Council, which, like its predecessors, often changed in its makeup. Later there was a regular Colonial Secretary in the cabinet, with a regular Colonial Office. The actual management of most of the details fell into the hands of a few permanent officials, who followed the routine with little imagination. When reformers attacked the system later, they pointed out that, as far as the colonists were concerned, some one of these underling officials represented imperial authority. Parliament, wrote one of the reformers, "exercises, in fact, hardly the slightest control over the administration or the making of the laws for the colonies. In nine cases out of ten it merely registers the edicts of the Colonial Office in Downing Street. . . . In some back room—whether in the attic or in what story we know not—you will find all the mother country which really exercises supremacy and really maintains connexion with the vast and widely scattered colonies of Britain. We know not the name, the history, or [the] functions of the individual into the narrow limits of whose person we find the mother country shrunk." But this anonymity was a general characteristic of the British Empire. As we have noticed before, it was not, like Colbert's French colonial empire, the work of a few spectacular individuals, but, rather, the cumulative achievement of a large number of common-sense men. It was, then, these forgotten undersecretaries, checking up on colonial legislation, reading colonial petitions, and handing out lucrative colonial sinecures, who managed the vast organization, rather than their chiefs in the cabinet, whose names, like those of Sydney and Melbourne, won immortality on the maps of the new regions.

This colonial machinery did not differ much from that of the Old Empire; but shortly after the American Revolution a new influence became active in the spread of British influence overseas. This was the missionary.

It has been remarked that the "three C's" of colonization have been commerce, conquest, and conversion. With the British Empire commerce has always far outranked the other two motives. The element of conversion had been more conspicuously lacking in the Old Empire than in the early colonizing activities of the Catholic powers,—Spain, Portugal, and France,—where the Jesuits and other orders had actively converted the heathen. Wholesale conversions had been conducted by Saint Francis Xavier in the Portuguese East; by Spanish missionaries in America, where the Jesuits in Paraguay and the Franciscans in California even set up states with conversion as the primary motive; and by the French Jesuits in New France, where some of them suffered martyrdom in their futile conversion of the Hurons, who were annihilated by the Iroquois. Religion, to be sure, had considerable to do with the founding of New England; but the Puritans were interested chiefly in their own worship, with scant thought for the souls of the natives. A few missionaries like Eliot and Brainerd had worked among the American Indians, but they were the exception rather than the rule.

In the middle of the eighteenth century, we recall, Wesley and others had reacted against the empty formalism of the Church of England and had brought in the evangelical idea of conversion to Christ as the result of an emotional revival. This had led to Methodism and also to an evangelical movement within the Anglican Church (see page 526). As by-products of this new spirit came various humanitarian movements, such as the abolition of slavery and also the urge to go out and save the souls of the heathen.

British missionary activity is generally considered to have begun in 1792 when William Carey, cobbler, Baptist preacher, naturalist, and linguist, published his *Enquiry into the Obligations of Christians to use Means for the Conversion of the Heathens*. A sermon which he preached that year led to the formation of the Baptist Missionary Society, and Carey himself went out to India for forty years of remarkable work, which included extensive translation of the Bible into various dialects. It is significant that the East India Company refused him passage on any of its ships because it did not want "any interference with the religion of the natives." Within a few years the missionary movement had spread with remarkable rapidity. Representatives of various faiths soon formed the London Missionary Society; then came the Scottish Missionary Society; and by 1799, the Church Missionary Society, limited to Anglicans. The societies continued to multiply; before long there was a "London Society for Promoting Christianity among the Jews." The movement grew until missionaries were numbered by the thousands. While the saving of souls was their prime motive, they did extensive work as teachers and doctors. They also labored, with ultimate success, to stamp out barbarous customs. In India they helped to put an end to "suttee," whereby widows, either voluntarily or under the pressure of custom, were burned alive on their husbands' funeral pyres, and an end also to the sacrifice of infants in the Ganges. In the Fiji Islands they tried to bring humane ideas to the old chief who had set up eight hundred and fifty-two headstones, each for a human being he had eaten; and they interfered to prevent the strangling of another chief's principal wives when he died. In New Zealand too they fought against cannibalism, so that the practice finally died out. Their reports told of constant tribulations and setbacks, but every now and then came the triumphant report "The natives are fully clothed and in their right minds." In most of the tropical regions where they worked, the natives had gone in a happy state of near nudity until it became a pious act to force them into flowing raiment of cotton. It is even said that some of the Lancashire manufacturers contributed liberally to the missionary societies because this pious concealing of nakedness meant a tremendous new market for English textiles. As far, however, as the government was concerned, the missionaries were often regarded as liabilities rather than assets; for even though the Colonial Office might favor them from time to time, the officials and settlers out in the colonies frequently found their activities an embarrassment. At any rate, the missionaries played their part in extending the imperial frontiers.

With these general considerations in mind, we shall turn to one region after another to see how it was affected during these years of intermediate empire. By the time they had passed, it could be said that "the sun never sets on the British flag"; and we shall now trace the course of that flag from the South Seas westward to Canada.

Almost simultaneously with the loss of the American colonies a new part of the world was opened to British imperialism in the South Seas, as the southern Pacific is called. Those waters and islands had been discovered long before by Spanish, Dutch, and even English explorers; but little attention had been paid to them because they seemed to offer scant prospects of commercial profit. Widespread interest in the South Seas dates from the three voyages of Captain James Cook, between 1768 and 1779. He was originally commissioned in the navy and sent out in the little *Endeavour* on a scientific mission. His primary object was an astronomical observation at Tahiti, in the South Pacific; but two naturalists were sent along to study the flora and fauna of the Pacific. After successfully observing the stars at Tahiti, and also noticing the idyllic charm of the native existence there, Cook pushed westward to New Zealand. Then, early in 1770, he continued to the eastern coast of Australia, which he explored for nearly its whole length, finally returning through the East Indies and home by way of the Cape of Good Hope. In 1772 he went out on a second voyage, and spent three years crossing and recrossing the South Pacific to disprove the theory of a great southern continent. On his third voyage—during which American and French warships had instructions from their governments, although it was a time of war, not to molest him, because of the scientific value of his work—he passed through. Bering Strait in search of a northwest passage, and then returned to the Hawaiian Islands, which he had named for the unworthy admiralty chief, Lord Sandwich. There he was killed in a minor scuffle with the natives. His journals, when published, quickened popular interest in the South Seas, not only in England but in France as well.

Within ten years of Cook's death his explorations bore fruit in the first colonization of Australia. This smallest of the continents, or largest of the islands, almost exactly equal in size to the present United States, had been visited several times previously, particularly by the Dutchman Tasman in 1642, but Holland had seen no possibility of profit in a colony there. A considerable part of Australia was desert, its northern tip reaching nearly to the equator, and the natives were perhaps the most backward on the face of the earth. The south-eastern corner, however, was a promising, temperate region, suitable as a "white man's country." Sir Joseph Banks, who had accompanied Cook on his first voyage, was particularly impressed with the possibilities of what he named Botany Bay, in the district which Cook, because of superficial resemblances, called New South Wales.

In 1787 the British government took one of its few positive steps toward extending colonization in this period by establishing a penal colony there. For more than a century it had been customary to commute death sentences to transportation to the colonies. The southern American colonies had received a large number of criminals, but now that outlet was shut off. The prisons became congested, and even the overflow prisons in old ships moored in the Thames were crowded. An experiment with transporting some of the convicts to the fever-ridden Guinea coast of Africa had resulted in wholesale death. News reached England that France was preparing to send an expedition to the South Seas, possibly with colonization in mind. Botany Bay seemed to offer a chance to kill two birds with one stone : prison congestion would be relieved, and England might secure a strategic foothold in the new region of interest. But there was no intention of establishing a normal colony of settlement. Accordingly, a naval captain in the spring of 1787 headed for Botany Bay with an expedition which included about seven hundred and fifty convicts and some marine guards. They arrived early in 1788, but quickly determined to move to the next bay to the northward, where the settlement named for Lord Sydney, the minister in charge of colonial affairs, came into being. Six days later the French expedition appeared on the scene. Whatever its intentions may have been, it departed after an exchange of greetings and was never heard from again.

The convicts were of all sorts : desperate criminals, men and women convicted of minor delinquencies, and not a few innocent persons who had been convicted wrongfully. The old country washed its hands of them, but it did not simply turn them loose in the new world. It was customary, after the transported men had finished serving their term as prisoners, to assign them as laborers to the free settlers, who followed later. From then on they were known as "emancipists"; and while still on parole, an intermediate step toward freedom, they were called "ticket-of-leave men."

The difficulties inherent in such a system were obvious. Many prisoners escaped to the wilds and became bushrangers. Lawlessness was prevalent. "In 1833, when the population was about 60,000, there were sixty-nine death sentences. . . . If the same proportion held good in the British Isles today, it would mean more than 1000 sentences of death every week." Even when lawlessness and crime lessened, there were other troubles; for what free settler, for instance, wanted an emancipist or ticket-of-leave man for a son-in-law?

Only very gradually did New South Wales shake off its original status as a penal colony and develop into a normal colony of settlement. In 1888, at the centennial celebration of the founding of Sydney, the toast was offered, "We left our country for our country's good"; but Australian historians have been active in demonstrating that the original convict stock died out and that the first families of Australia are descended from the honest sheep-raisers who followed them. The government continued to think of New South Wales simply as a dumping ground for criminals for a half century; but before the colony had been long started, a captain of the guards noticed that the land seemed suitable for sheep-raising, and sent back for some merino sheep, whose wool commanded a high price because of its fineness. From that day dates Australia's main source of livelihood. The woolsack became as symbolic of the basis of prosperity in modern Australia as it had been in medieval England. A free population, composed partly of soldiers of the guard whose enlistments had expired and partly of direct free immigrants from England, gradually overshadowed the convicts. During the early years of New South Wales the colonial governor was a naval or army officer with almost dictatorial power. One appointment was a serious error: the same Captain William Bligh, whose crew on the *Bounty* had set him adrift in those same seas, again provoked mutiny and was deposed by the colonists. Gradually, however, the government was changed to that of a regular crown colony.

From the first settlement at Sydney, which soon became the capital of this premier colony of New South Wales, explorers went forth in every direction. They crossed the blue mountains to the west; they traveled north to what is now Queensland; they went south to the present state of Victoria and by sea to Van Diemen's Land (Tasmania). Everywhere near the coast the land seemed fertile, so that the prospects were bright that Australia might provide for England's surplus people (see map, p. 732).

Soon the question of governing these regions which lay far distant from Sydney became a pressing one. This was solved by making three new colonies out of the more remote settlements, and by separating them altogether from New South Wales. The first to split off from the mother colony was Van Diemen's Land, an island which had a much more disturbed history than New South Wales, since the proportion of transported men to free settlers within its borders was much larger and since the aboriginal tribes were much more troublesome. For a long time administered from Sydney, the island gained practical self-government in the twenties, with a lieutenant governor of its own who was immediately pestered to death by the unruly colonists. The British government insisted that the free settlers pay for the upkeep of the transported men, since their presence meant cheap labor; the colonists insisted that transportation be ended, or at least that the home authorities should support the police and the jails. In this long battle the colonists won. In 1853 transportation to Van Diemen's Land was stopped. To get rid of the historic connection of that system with their island the colonists changed its name to Tasmania, after its Dutch discoverer, who had himself originally named it for governor Van Diemen of the East Indies.

Victoria was another offshoot of New South Wales. Far to the south of Sydney, so far that it was impracticable to communicate with it except by sea, lay Melbourne, which had been founded by a British hero of Bunker Hill. Melbourne waxed prosperous, attracting to its hinterland numerous immigrants, who were none too pleased with their dependence on Sydney, and who refused to elect their allotted membership to any legislature which met in that distant town. Victoria therefore became a separate colony in 1851.

Northward a third colony was formed, where the inhabitants of Brisbane, like those of Melbourne, found it inconvenient to look to distant Sydney for their law courts and their government. In 1859, in accordance with their desires, Brisbane, with a huge and unpopulated hinterland still farther to the north, was made into the colony of Queensland.

Then followed the settlement of Western Australia, begun by a number of wealthy Englishmen who colonized the region around the Swan River on a very extensive scale. Western Australia, with its capital at Perth, was opened in 1829. Estates were granted on a mammoth scale, which meant that the settlers were too widely scattered. There were no roads, no commerce, no neighbors, and not enough laborers to work the vast estates. Further handicapped by poor soil and deficient rainfall, Western Australia fell upon hard times, and after twenty years of ill luck was rescued only by the restoration of convict labor, which the settlers had first detested and then heartily desired. The population now increased rapidly; but the rest of the Australian colonies threatened boycott unless convict ships ceased to trouble Australian waters. The British government yielded to pressure, and the convicts were withdrawn. The colony immediately slumped, and misfortunes continued to dog its history.

There remained South Australia, forever associated with Edward

# Imperial Apathy

Gibbon Wakefield, who had a theory of colonization which was very popular in the middle of the century. This theory involved three proposals: land should be sold by the crown at a fairly high price and should never be given away; the proceeds should be applied to a colonization fund to pay the traveling expenses of future immigrants; and self-government should be given to the latter in their new home. Wakefield's economics seemed logical. Free land meant a scattered settlement, no laborers, no wage-earners, and no money for new immigration. If the land were held at a fairly high figure, it was argued, the laborers would save money to buy land of their own. A society, orderly and conservative, capable of self-government, would result, and an immigration fund, steadily augmenting, would bring in a constant flow of new settlers.

So popular were Wakefield's ideas, and so successfully were they pressed in England, that the Colonial Office approved of a settlement planned in accordance with them. This developed into the colony of South Australia, with its capital at Adelaide. The experiment was not a success. The Colonial Office had been unwilling to give Wakefield's company full control of the new colony because it suspected that among the promoters were radicals and republicans. Therefore the granting of land titles was left to the company's commissioners, but the government of the colony remained under the crown. There was friction between commissioners and the governor. Too many settlers dashed to Adelaide before farms could be surveyed; and to keep them alive, public works had to be started on a scale which the company could ill afford. Badly managed, the colony was rescued from insolvency only by the able administration of Sir George Grey, whom we shall see on several other occasions rescuing colonies in distress.

In 1851 boom days suddenly came to Australia. Just as the keen eye of an army captain had laid one foundation of Australian prosperity by deciding that the land looked good for sheep-raising, so now a prospector, fresh from the mad gold rush in California, decided that there might be gold in the hills of New South Wales. He was right: gold was found not only at Bathurst but also in various other parts of Australia. All normal work stopped. Sheep-raisers, storekeepers, clerks, and laborers all dashed to the gold fields to try for sudden riches. The clipper ships, which had been built for the California gold rush, now brought new hordes of adventurers to Australia, and for a while there was difficulty in absorbing the wild swarm of riotous newcomers. But, as in the case of California, prosperity and increased population resulted. There were barely a quarter million colonists in Australia at the beginning of 1851; within a decade an additional half million had joined them. The colony of Victoria alone jumped in five years from 70,000 to 333,000 inhabitants. The discovery of gold, it was said, "precipitated a colony into a nation." It did not quite do that, for the days of the Australian Commonwealth were still far distant; but it did so increase the wealth, the importance, and the population of the six separate colonies that within a period of ten years one after another was granted self-government—all but Western Australia. The charters which granted these privileges were drawn up in general agreement with the principle of responsible government, which will be described in more detail in the case of Canada (see page 684). Western Australia was kept in leading strings until 1890, her scanty and scattered population not seeming to warrant such a degree of freedom.

By the time of the Australian gold rush, British colonization was making rapid and successful progress on the large, beautiful twin islands, twelve hundred miles to the southeast, named by Tasman for the Dutch province of Zealand. Cook had visited them in 1769 and had noted the fertility of the valleys among the mountains. With their temperate and healthful climate, they were ideally suited for what they eventually became, the most characteristically British of all the overseas colonies of settlement. But New Zealand was far from that in the first quarter of the nineteenth century. Several thousand lawless whites had drifted to the islands,—whalers, traders, escaped convicts, and other unregulated and irregular elements,— held down by no law or authority and engaged in high-handed transactions with the native Maoris. Whereas the Australian natives represented the lowest form of physical and social development, the Maoris, like the American Indians, were among the strongest and most self-reliant of the races encountered by European civilization, and were well able to look out for themselves in the matter of fighting. A third group in those early days were the missionaries, who were trying to save the natives from the white man's rapacity for land and who were also working to curb the Maori taste for human flesh. The home government long resisted the efforts to bring New Zealand under the British flag. Originally the islands had been placed under the jurisdiction of the governor of New South Wales, but later England tried to free herself from even that slight implication of governmental responsibility. So New Zealand went its lawless way until the actual planting of regular English settlers necessitated more definite control. Even then it was to take the threat of French annexation to bring New Zealand definitely into the empire.

The colonization of New Zealand was carried on by middle-class British citizens under the spell of Wakefield's teachings. That restless and influential writer, displeased with the way in which his plans had been put into operation in South Australia, had withdrawn from that enterprise and started another, the New Zealand Company, to colonize New Zealand in the way in which a colony should be properly started.

The missionaries had great influence with the Colonial Office, and they considered that the white colonization of New Zealand would seriously hamper their labors. But, company or no company, it had proved impossible to prevent escaped convicts from reaching New Zealand from Australia; and Wakefield pointed out that it was better to have a settlement which could be controlled rather than one which was irresponsible. Still, the Colonial Office refused to sanction the enterprise; and the New Zealand Company began to do business without a charter, dispatching a ship to New Zealand to make treaties with native chiefs for the purchase of land. Thereupon the British government swung into action, sending out an officer who, early in 1840, hoisted the British flag and signed a treaty with the natives whereby the sovereignty of New Zealand passed to the crown, in return for which Her Majesty guaranteed the Maoris full ownership of their land unless they chose to sell it. The company meanwhile had become popular in England. Important persons, like the brother-in-law of Gladstone, and Lord Durham, the colonial reformer, were interested in its success. The rumored threat of a French settlement won over many of its enemies. Therefore in 1841 the company received a charter.

The occupation of New Zealand went on apace during the next ten years. Wakefield secured the support of the religiously inclined by suggesting that subcompanies be formed to buy tracts of land from his company to establish semireligious settlements. In accordance with this idea a number of Scottish Presbyterians made their home in Otago province, founding the city of Dunedin, now famous as the point of departure for the exploration of the South Polar regions. The adherents of the Church of England, supported by the Archbishop of Canterbury and many other bishops, bought the land around Canterbury. While this was happening, Nelson and Wellington were founded, directly under the auspices of the company itself.

Wakefield and his associates had made New Zealand; but the company as a business organization was not to last long. It got into trouble with the civil authorities; with its own settlers, a number of whom arrived before the purchased land was surveyed; and with the native chiefs, who found that the land which they had sold for a song was resold at a much higher rate by this business corporation. Within a decade the affairs of the company were wound up; but in the interim New Zealand was put on a firm foundation.

# A History of England and the British Empire

The man who did this was Sir George Grey, who previously had gone to the rescue of South Australia. His unfailing tact and firmness stood New Zealand in good stead during these formative years, and, thanks to him, serious war did not break out with the Maoris until the colony was able to withstand the attack. New Zealand was given a generous measure of self-government in 1853. Shortly after came two wars with the Maoris, who were stalwart fighters and who did not propose to see their tribal lands occupied by the whites, even if papers were signed to this effect. The backbone of their resistance was broken in 1864, and the rebellious chiefs were fined heavily. Since that time the Maoris have stayed on their reservations and have even slightly increased in number.

This deliberately planned and regulated but unofficial colonization produced excellent results. The growth was steady, but not abnormal as it had been in Australia, and the colonists were for the most part substantial and hand-picked. In 1841, the year after New Zealand was taken officially into the empire, there were 6000 settlers; three years later, 15,000; and by 1865, at the end of a quarter century, the total had risen to 172,000. Of all England's dominions since the loss of the thirteen colonies, New Zealand had the most purely homogeneous British stock. Partly for that reason and partly because of its isolation, it was to become one of the most loyal of all the overseas lands.

Working westward from the South Seas, where England was laying the foundations of two great colonies of settlement, we come to the spread of British power in India, the most important of the colonies of exploitation. When we last saw India during the years of the American Revolution, Warren Hastings was at work organizing on a stable basis the government of Bengal, which Clive had acquired in 1757 as England's first step away from the seacoast toward the interior (see page 470). Hastings did remarkable work in spite of grave handicaps; but on his return to England in 1785 he, like Clive, was faced by a bitter attack in Parliament for alleged unethical and highhanded acts, particularly in extorting large sums from natives by force. Burke led the Commons in a demand for impeachment, and another brilliant Irish orator, Sheridan, joined in heaping moral invectives upon "perhaps the greatest Englishman who ever ruled India." Thereupon Hastings was impeached on twenty-two counts. The trial before the House of Lords dragged on from 1788 until 1795, when he was finally acquitted on all counts. Unlike Clive, he bore the sustained attack resolutely, thoroughly convinced of his own rectitude. The trial, however, left him financially

[ 666 ]

impoverished, and he retired quietly to the country, cheated of the peerage and other honors which his work in Bengal had certainly merited.

Just before Hastings returned from Calcutta, Pitt pushed through Parliament an India Act much more thoroughgoing than North's Regulating Act of 1773. That earlier legislation, we recall, had asserted Parliament's authority over the East India Company, but had not devised adequate machinery for exercising that control. Politics continued to encroach upon trade in India to such an extent that it seemed increasingly unwise for a trading organization to have command of a situation involving foreign complications and other considerations of national importance. Pitt's act of 1784 accomplished the desirable end of preserving the nominal authority of the East India Company while giving actual control of policy to the cabinet. The Court of Directors of the Company still kept up the appearances of rule, retaining in their hands the extensive patronage and management of the commercial affairs; but in all other matters the important decisions were to be made by a political Board of Control, dominated by its president, who was to be a member of the cabinet. That office went to Pitt's friend Dundas, the political boss of Scotland whom we noticed mismanaging military affairs in the war with Revolutionary France (see page 556). He, to all intents and purposes, was the Board of Control. The act of 1773 had stipulated a governor-general at Calcutta, with authority over Bombay and Madras. This was continued, but the governor-general was given increased authority. To prevent a repetition of the difficulties encountered by Hastings, the governor-general was still to have a council, but he might disregard it if he saw fit. This act of 1784 remained the basis of British rule in India until the end of the East India Company in 1858. By that time most of the Company's original justification for existence had gone; for in 1813 it lost its commercial monopoly, except the China trade, and that also was taken away in 1833.

The first governor-general sent out under the new act was Lord Cornwallis. Georgian England sometimes showed a strange sense of reward and punishment. Clive and Hastings, who laid the foundations of British power in India, came back to face humiliating attacks. Cornwallis, on the other hand, who had lost the American colonies by allowing himself to be trapped at Yorktown, was sent to Calcutta to succeed Hastings, and later he became lord lieutenant of Ireland. At any rate, Cornwallis did a much better job at Calcutta than he had done at Yorktown. He rounded out the work which Hastings had commenced in the administration of Bengal. In particular, he placed the land revenue on a permanent basis. This was the chief form of taxation in India; for the land in theory all belonged to the state, which collected rent amounting roughly to a quarter of the annual income. The new regulation relieved the natives of the capricious rapacity of the native tax-collectors, whose rates had often fluctuated violently from year to year. Regular rates were determined as permanent, and the Company could count upon some £2,750,000 a year from Bengal.

Cornwallis was also given an opportunity to retrieve part of the military reputation he had lost in Virginia. One of the two hostile native powers which threatened England's foothold in India was the state of Mysore, in southwestern India. It had been seized by a Mohammedan adventurer who had fought Hastings and whose son, Tippoo, now challenged Cornwallis. The governor-general moved against Mysore and was successful in the field; and Tippoo gave half his territory to the British to save his capital, Seringapatam, from being stormed. Unlike those who came before and after him, Cornwallis had no trouble with the other hostile element, the powerful Hindu confederacy of Maratha chieftains, whose various allied states formed a broad band across central India. This had been a particular menace to Bombay, which had foolishly provoked the confederacy into action in Hastings's time. He had sent Bengal troops to the rescue, and for twenty years thereafter the Marathas had been relatively quiet. England had further trouble ahead, however, both with Mysore and with the Marathas. Cornwallis returned to England in 1793 to gain further honors; and for five years little happened in India, for his successor was definitely instructed not to intervene in the affairs of the native states.

Then, in 1798, the future Marquess Wellesley arrived in Calcutta with a deliberately aggressive policy which aimed at nothing short of making British power paramount in the Indian peninsula. There was a particular excuse for immediate action; for French intrigue was once more active at Mysore and among the Marathas, as it had been in Hastings's time. French officers were training their native troops, while Napoleon's Egyptian campaign was a distant threat against British rule in India. The new governor-general magnified the dignity of his office, engaging in constant pageantry to impress the natives; but India was impressed even more deeply by the spectacular success of British arms. Armies closed in on Mysore from two directions in 1799; Seringapatam was captured, and Tippoo died fighting valiantly to stem the final rush. Then Wellesley's younger brother, a colonel who was to win fame later as the Duke of Wellington, inflicted some smashing defeats on the Marathas. They were brought partly under British influence, but would require further beatings. Wellesley also put pressure on several native rulers to place their states under British protection. Before he was called back in 1805, because the Company considered his policy too costly and aggressive, British rule or influence had extended over more than a third of India. This third included not only Bengal and certain lands stretching westward up the Ganges, but also all the eastern coast and all the southern part of the peninsula. Whatever the authorities at home might desire, Wellesley had committed England to his policy of dominating all India. The huge central block of Maratha territory still remained relatively independent; but a third Maratha war, waged under another governor-general, finally brought that too under England's influence (see map, p. 461).

(see map, p. 461)

As established at that time the British *raj*, or rule, in India has consisted partly of direct rule over certain territory and partly of indirect control over numerous native states. Bengal was the original example of the direct rule. Today British India, which includes about 60 per cent of the territory and 80 per cent of the population of all India, comes under this direct rule. The officials of the East India Company at first, and later of the crown, administered the region under direct rule, collecting taxes, dispensing justice, maintaining army and police, and performing the other necessary functions of government. The land tax, which we have just noticed in Bengal, has been the principal financial support of this entire region, although in sections later acquired the British did not tie themselves to a permanent limitation of the rate, as Cornwallis had done in Bengal. The tax, which might amount to a quarter of the peasant's annual income, was heavy, but no heavier than under native rule; and the British gave far more in return.

Native princes still maintain all the outward pomp and circumstance of rule in the protected states under indirect control. Altogether, there are some seven hundred of these, of which the largest is Hyderabad, part of the old Deccan whose *Nizam*, or ruler, was brought under British influence by Wellesley's threats. The British arrangements with these princes were fairly uniform. A British political "resident" remained in constant attendance as an adviser and as a check upon their actions. Their armies also were under British supervision and sometimes were officered by Englishmen. They were forbidden to make outside alliances or to employ foreign officers or advisers without British consent. In case of misbehavior or misrule such rulers were subject to deposition, and England has thus removed several, including the Gaekwar of Baroda and the Maharaja of Indore, two of the most powerful of the princes. Within these limitations native rulers have been free to tax and to judge their subjects as they pleased. Several of the Indian princes are reckoned among the wealthiest men in the world, because of their fabulous store of wealth in its most concrete form—gold, silver, and rare jewels. The system of indirect control has been of mutual advantage: the British suzerainty is a guarantee to the prince against the old violence of intrigue and revolution, and England is relieved of the direct burden of administration and the menace of such potential enemies as old Mysore and the Maratha Confederacy. The native princes' subjects, however, have had fewer of the civilizing benefits of the West than have those in British India.

The close of the third Maratha war, in 1818, brought a temporary lull in fighting, and for a while attention was concentrated upon improving the condition of the Indian people, principally within the region of direct control. Lord William Bentinck, governor-general from 1828 to 1835, made particular progress in this respect. The old Hindu practice of suttee (see page 658) had been attacked by the missionaries for some time and was finally prohibited by decree in 1829. Bentinck also stamped out the evil practices of the Thugs, assassins who engaged in wholesale killings as part of the worship of Kali, a goddess of death and destruction. During his beneficent administration Thomas Babington Macaulay, later famous as historian, poet, and essayist, came out to Calcutta in an official capacity as adviser. His advent is noteworthy for his famous "minute," or memorandum, on education in which he recommended the use of the English language in Indian education. Macaulay knew nothing of Oriental tongues and despised them. The adoption of his advice by the British introduced the future leaders of the Indian peoples to English history as well as to English literature, thus giving the Indians a common tongue as well as nursing them in the traditions of English liberty, a lesson which they were to apply later to their own land, to the annoyance of their teachers.

Those brown-skinned students might become the future leaders of India, but the immediate masters were the excellent young Britons of the Indian civil service. Few governmental bodies in history have maintained a higher quality of personnel. Ignorant and lazy appointees might safely be sent by the Colonial Office to fill Caribbean sinecures; but even when Dundas, that past master of patronage, was distributing Indian jobs among his deserving Scots, he picked first-rate material. The responsibilities were tremendous. Many officials were needed to administer regions under British direct control; others served as residents at the courts of native princes. Force, tact, and character were necessary in either case. Frequently a youth in his twenties might be the only white man within a radius of fifty miles or more, and the success of British rule in that region might depend upon his quick thinking or force of personality in an emergency. The Indians, with their ancient culture, were keen to sense a man's true character, and no small part of Britain's success in India depended upon the intrinsic worth of her responsible representatives there. For in the last analysis England could not rule by force: she had only some fifty thousand white troops and a smaller number of civil officials to maintain ascendancy over a vast region which even then was approaching its present population of three hundred million. There were about a quarter of a million sepoy troops, to be sure; but they, in turn, depended upon the leadership of their few white officers. Consequently the quality of the Indian civil service was of the utmost importance.

Much constructive work was done during the quieter years of the second quarter of the nineteenth century, but even in that period there were some wars. The governors-general were extending their operations beyond the borders of India proper even before wars with Sind and with the fierce Sikhs of the Punjab had carried the British raj into the northwest corner. Lord Amherst, nephew of Lord Jeffrey, had sent forces to conquer part of the old Indo-Chinese kingdom of Burma, across the Bay of Bengal from Calcutta; and later expeditions extended British authority in that region which Kipling celebrated in his "Mandalay." But to the northwest of India lay tougher fighting men than the Burmese. These were the Afghans, who were to inflict more than one humiliating reverse upon British arms.

The Himalayas, the loftiest mountains in the world, gave India magnificent natural protection all across its northern frontier. But there were several narrow passes in the northwest through which Alexander the Great, the Moguls, and other invaders had entered India in the past. Beyond those passes lay Afghanistan, a land of rough mountains and rough men. And now the specter of Russian invasion arose before British officials at Calcutta and at London—a specter which was to haunt British policy for many years to come. During the Napoleonic period Russia had started a southward drive. After absorbing the province of Georgia, south of the Black Sea, she had carried Russian expansion to the southeast and had occupied the oases in the desert north of Afghanistan. Now a mixed force of Russians and Persians was attacking Herat, in western Afghanistan. To British eyes this seemed to threaten a continued advance to the Himalayan passes and the valley of the Indus beyond. Russia, with her tremendous man power, was always magnified as a menace, and against her huge armies up there in the hills Britain's chief defensive force, the royal navy, would be of no avail. Kabul, the Afghan capital, became a center of intrigue. The old *amir*, or ruler, of the Afghans was a refugee in India, and the new ruler, Dost Mohammed, had vast troubles not only with his outside enemies but also with his unruly tribesmen. To complicate matters, he was quarreling with the Sikhs, the puritanical and warlike Hindus who lived in the Punjab, a part of northwest India not yet under British control. The British governor-general considered it more desirable to remain the friend of the Sikhs than to assist the distant amir at Kabul. Thereupon Dost Mohammed suddenly turned from England to Russia. His intrigues with the Russian bear led to the first Afghan war (1838–1842) and to the occupation of his capital by Anglo-Indian troops.

The British found it easy to occupy Afghanistan, but unpleasant to stay there. The Afghans were ill-disposed to the foreigner and unwilling to obey their old ruler, whom British arms had restored. The venture was exceedingly expensive. The British marked time as they watched a nasty revolt threatening their army stationed outside Kabul. Trusting to the guarantees of the rebels, they began to retreat in the winter of 1841. Some forty-five hundred fighting men and twelve thousand camp followers were caught in the narrow defiles of the Afghan mountains. But one man survived to tell the tale; the rest were victims either of the snow or of Afghan knives and bullets.

A new governor-general, just arrived in Calcutta, was eager to avenge the disaster. To do this, and to rescue the garrisons still left in Afghanistan, he sent a punitive expedition to Kabul, burned the bazaars, and returned to India with some sacred gates supposedly rifled from India centuries before. Afghanistan evidently was a dangerous hornet's nest. It was to remain a buffer state between British and Russian expansionist ambitions; and forty years later, in a second Afghan war, the story of murder, disastrous retreat, and punitive expedition would be repeated.

Year after year the British continued to add bits of territory, particularly in the northwest. They adopted toward the protected native princes a policy resembling the old feudal escheat, whereby a vassal's fief was taken over by the suzerain if he died without heirs or if he seriously misbehaved. The large protected state of Oudh, on the upper Ganges, was liable to absorption in British India on both counts. It had been badly misgoverned, and there was no regular heir; for the British "doctrine of lapse" did not recognize the old Indian practice of adopting heirs. Its annexation in 1856 aroused widespread grumbling among the Indians. That same year the son of George Canning, about to sail for India to take up his duties as governor-general, made a prophetic remark at a farewell banquet of the Company directors. "I wish for a peaceful term of office," he said. "But I cannot forget that in the sky of India, serene as it is, a small cloud may arise, no larger than a man's hand, but which, growing larger and larger, may at last threaten to burst and overwhelm us with ruin."

The next year the British raj in India was shaken to its foundations. The repeated annexations of territory were not the only causes of native unrest. Macaulay's system of English education contributed something to the ferment. The Hindus, with a religion centuries older than Christianity, resented the energetic labors of the missionaries. Native minds were mystified and worried by surveys for irrigation to improve the water supply, while the belching locomotives of India's first railway, built in 1854, heightened the apprehension. India was a conservative country, skeptical of innovations. There was, moreover, a legend that British rule would last just a century, and it was exactly a hundred years since Clive had seized Bengal in 1757.

The immediate source of trouble lay among the sepoys, that quarter of a million of native troops trained in European methods and commanded by British officers. The proportion of sepoys to white troops in India had been increasing until it had become nearly six to one. The Crimean War had brought with it rumors of British decline. The Afghan war had wounded the religious susceptibilities of many sepoys. Now orders came that the sepoys might not re-enlist without agreeing to serve across the salt water, an act which the Hindus believed would cause them to lose caste and jeopardize the future of their souls. The spark which set off the explosion seemed extremely trifling to European minds. During the Crimean War the British army had replaced the inefficient old smoothbore "Brown Bess" muskets (see page 449) with Enfield rifles, which, although still muzzle-loaders, were far more accurate and effective. The rifle cartridge consisted of a paper pouch, containing the powder charge, fastened to the bullet, which was greased so that it could fit into the narrow bore. In order to load, the soldier held the bullet in his teeth, tore off the paper, poured in the powder, and then rammed in the bullet. The new rifles were issued to the sepoys, but word spread among them that the bullets, which must be held in the mouth, were greased with beef or pork fat. That aroused both the Hindus, to whom the cow was sacred, and the Moslems, to whom the pig was unclean. They scented a plot to discredit them with their own religions and then make Christians of them.

Part of a cavalry regiment at Meerut, near the old Mogul capital at Delhi, refused to accept the cartridges in April, 1857. Thereupon they were arrested and sentenced to ten years' imprisonment. The other sepoys at the station rose in revolt, freed the prisoners, and shot most of the officers. The commanders of the white troops there lost a chance to nip the Sepoy Mutiny in the bud. The whole valley of the upper Ganges was quickly aflame. At Delhi the sepoys and the mob killed most of the English, and a revival of the Mogul Empire was proclaimed. The British, taken unawares, were temporarily paralyzed, shut up in their cantonments. The most horrible atrocities occurred at Cawnpore, a border post of Oudh on the Ganges, where some four hundred English and eighty loyal natives, protected merely by a rough embankment, held out for three weeks in June against thousands of sepoys led by the Nana Sahib, the "archvillain of the Mutiny." Finally they surrendered, upon Nana's promise of safe conduct; but just as they were getting into their boats the entire garrison was massacred. Some two hundred women and children were spared for the moment; but later, as relief was approaching, they too were hacked to pieces and thrown down a well, which came to rival in tradition the Black Hole of Calcutta. The white garrison at Lucknow, the capital of Oudh, was more fortunate. Caught unprepared, the force of less than a thousand redcoats, assisted by loyal sepoys and civilians, fought for two whole months behind a rambling line of defenses strung out for over a mile. "Do not negotiate, but rather perish by the sword" was the word sent them; and they had nearly reached the end of their resistance when the distant sound of Highland bagpipes told them of Sir Henry Havelock's timely arrival with reinforcements.

The mutiny collapsed as rapidly as it began. Had all India, or even all the sepoys, joined the revolt, British dominion might have disappeared overnight. But most of the native princes remained loyal; and the Sikhs, those stout soldiers of the Punjab who had been conquered only twelve years before, showed their appreciation of kind British treatment and joined in the suppression of the insurrection. In spite of the moderation of the governor-general, British vengeance rested heavily on the mutineers. Thousands were hanged, and many were blown to bits from the mouths of cannon,—a particularly terrible punishment, as the Hindus believed that the bodies could never be reassembled for the future life.

One particular victim of the Mutiny was the East India Company. Its prerogatives had been gradually shorn from it at various times since the days of North and Pitt. Now, in 1858, the "Honourable John Company," chartered by Queen Elizabeth on the last day of the sixteenth century, ended its existence. The British government took over responsibility for India in the name of the crown. The president of the Board of Control now became the Secretary of State for India, and the governor-general was hereafter known as viceroy. The essential features of the system of rule, however, continued in much the same manner as before, and Indian history was uneventful for some time to come.

The commercial interests in England welcomed the news that expansionist wars would cease in India now that the British raj extended over the whole peninsula. In that period, when England was definitely skeptical about the economic value of most of the other overseas possessions, there was little question about the importance of India in British trade. India's earlier role of furnishing England with finished cotton goods (see page 331) was now completely reversed, and about one tenth of England's total exports went to India, which consumed, in particular, roughly one third of the Lancashire cotton cloth. Indian railroads, too, consumed British iron; altogether, India was becoming a market essential to England's whole economic system.

The East India Company had long linked India with China, where it had had a monopoly of the British trade. From early in the seventeenth century the English had tried to obtain a share in the lucrative China trade from the Portuguese and the more enterprising Dutch; but not for some time were they able to establish trade relations with the Chinese. With its eventual establishment of a permanent post at Canton, the English East India Company had soon gained most of the trade. The Company's "Country" ships carried tea, silks, and "china" ware from Canton to India, whence they were sent to England. China, however, remained indifferent and almost hostile to this outside intercourse, except for a brief interlude about 1685. The foreigners found all Chinese ports closed except Canton, where they were forced to deal through the medium of specified Chinese "hong" merchants and were hindered by numerous other restrictions. China regarded herself as the "Middle Kingdom," or center of the universe, to which the outside "barbarians" brought tribute. The Chinese remained unimpressed by the achievements of the Western nations, and showed no interest when the British made diplomatic efforts to open more ports to commerce. In 1792 Lord Macartney was sent on such a diplomatic mission. Carried up the river on a craft bearing the inscription "tribute-bearer to the Emperor," he had to follow the emperor into the interior; and even when he found him, he was refused an audience unless he would perform the humble bowing gesture of kowtow. That was a bitter pill for a proud British peer; but he finally agreed to do it if a Chinese official of equal rank would kowtow before a picture of George III. Even then, however, he received no trade concessions;

and Lord Amherst, on a similar mission a few years later, was not even permitted an audience.

The East India Company, however, continued to do a thriving business through Canton. Instead of having to bring silver or furs to exchange for tea, as the Americans usually did, it sent Indian opium instead, although from 1800 opium importation was forbidden by the Chinese government. The Company's monopoly of this India-China trade came to an end in 1833. Other British merchants, and Americans as well, were permitted by England to carry Indian opium to China, and in consequence the unruly crowd of foreigners gathered at Canton grew restive under the old and strict regulations that had been enforced upon the servants of the East India Company. The Chinese announced that the newly arriving British merchants must select a "head man" to do their negotiating with Chinese merchants. England, although fully aware what the Chinese meant, tried to use this situation to open direct diplomatic relations with the government; but in vain. Meanwhile opium was coming into China in increased quantities; and the Chinese, disturbed at the debauching of the people by increased smuggling, without warning ordered their officials at Canton to confiscate all the drug they could find. Chests of British opium, grown in India, to the value of several millions were thus destroyed. In addition, the mandarin at Canton, infuriated by the inability or unwillingness of an English captain to turn over to Chinese justice one of his crew, launched a fireship against the British fleet. Swiftly came the reprisal. Canton was bombarded; several Chinese forts were captured; and the Chinese, awakened at last to the effectiveness of Western methods, were compelled to yield. In the Treaty of Nanking, which ended this "Opium War" in 1842, China ceded to England the island of Hong Kong, just below Canton. It has remained a British colony. Shanghai and some other "treaty ports" were opened to British and American trade. At these ports extraterritoriality, by which foreigners were to be under the jurisdiction of their own laws and courts, was established because of the strange methods of Chinese justice. The Chinese naturally resented this concession, which Europeans had long enjoyed in Turkey. This treaty also contained the "most favored nation" clause, by which China promised England a share in any privileges granted to other foreign nations. As this clause was also incorporated by France, the United States, and other powers in their later treaties, it did much to facilitate future foreign-trade expansion in China.

There was less justification for England's action in the second war (1858–1860). As a result of continuous piracy on the Chinese coast, bad blood between the Chinese and British continued. It reached the boiling point when the *Arrow*, manned by Chinese and flying the British flag as a result of former British registry, was seized by Chinese officials. A sharp British ultimatum, only partly met, brought on a new war. The French, enraged at the murder of a missionary, co-operated as allies of the British. The war dragged on until French and British soldiers finally marched on Peking and sacked the Imperial Palace in reprisal for the firing on a flag of truce by the Chinese and their brutal kidnaping and torturing of French and British negotiators. The treaty gave England and other nations a further entering wedge in Chinese trade.

Between those two Chinese wars an American naval squadron had made two visits to Japan and had persuaded her to end her hermit isolation; and, just as the United States shared in the advantages England had won in China, so did England share in the American concessions gained in Japan. Thus were laid the foundations of the Far Eastern problem, which was to become the center of imperial attention at the end of the century.

Shortly after 1815 England had taken steps to safeguard the route between India and China. During the Napoleonic Wars, England had seized the Dutch Spice Islands, in the East Indies, and a very able colonial administrator, Sir Stamford Raffles, governed Java in masterly fashion. The islands were restored to Holland after the peace, but Raffles felt that England should have a foothold in that region. Castlereagh and the East India Company were not favorable to his projects, but certain British commercial interests supported them. He cruised along the Malay coast, looking for a proper site, and finally hit upon the island of Singapore, at the tip of the Malay Peninsula. It was ceded in 1819 by a native sultan; and the surrounding "Straits Settlements" soon became a British colony, subordinate at first to the East India Company. Raffles had chosen the site of Singapore wisely; for, commanding the passage from the China Sea into the Indian Ocean, it became the foremost trading center of that part of the East and a naval base of high importance.

In 1869 India was suddenly brought physically much closer to England by the opening of the Suez Canal. This hundred-mile ditch through the sand, connecting the Mediterranean with the Red Sea, proved a much simpler engineering feat for the Frenchman Ferdinand de Lesseps than the projected canal at Panama, where he later met failure. The initiative in the digging of the Suez Canal was French, but England was the nation most vitally concerned. By eliminating the lengthy trip around Africa, it radically shortened the sea route to India and the Far East, the voyage from London to Bombay, for instance, being reduced from 11,220 to 6332 miles. Though the French financed and dug the canal, we shall see that before it had been open six years England was to gain control of it by a master stroke (see pages 705–706), which was the opening gun in England's revived active imperialism after the century of apathy.

The opening of the Suez Canal robbed the Cape Colony, at the southern tip of Africa, of most of the strategic value for which England had taken it from Holland during the Napoleonic Wars. As long as shipping had had to make its way around Africa, the Cape of Good Hope was naturally a point of importance for the refitting of Indiamen and for naval control on the important sea route (see map, p. 751). Discovered by Dias in 1488, the Cape had been shunned as a land post by the Portuguese; but in 1652 the Dutch had taken possession of it and established Cape Town. The climate was favorable to a "white man's country," and gradually a rather informal colony of settlement developed at the Cape. Dutchmen as well as French Huguenots, who gradually adopted Dutch speech and ways, came out in considerable numbers. In spite of the commercial traditions of both groups, many became farmers, or *boers*, and slaughtered the native Hottentots in order to take their lands. These Boers have ever since remained the most numerous European element in South Africa. There were about twenty-five thousand of them when England took over the Cape in 1795. It was restored by the Peace of Amiens, but was seized again in 1806. British title was confirmed at the peace in 1814, and the Cape has remained part of the British Empire (see page 582). At that time the future of the colony did not seem bright. The Boers were disgruntled, and there was frequent fighting with the native Kaffirs. England soon made one of her few official efforts to send out free colonists. A number of discharged soldiers and sailors had settled in and around Cape Town. To strengthen the British element and to offset the Boers, some four thousand well-selected British settlers, including many artisans, were taken to the Cape at government expense and planted to the northeast of Cape Town. That settlement had a lasting influence in giving a distinctive British tone to that particular section of the Cape Colony, in spite of the general Boer preponderance in South Africa.

Many of the Boers soon withdrew to the interior. They had developed an antagonism to governmental control even in the days of the Dutch East India Company's rule, with its exasperatingly minute regulations. They were already ill-disposed toward their new British overlords when, in 1833, Parliament freed all the slaves in the British colonies (see page 617). The Boers were infuriated by this action, the more so as the payment granted in compensation for their slaves could be collected only in London, and since they felt, furthermore, that it was wholly inadequate. Selling their real estate for what it would bring on the spot, a large number of them placed their belongings in oxcarts and started to "trek" away from the British. The exodus was not conducted as a mass movement. Some went one way, some another: to the north beyond the Orange River, farther to the north beyond the Vaal River, and to the east, to the region which Vasco da Gama had called Natal because he sighted it on Christmas Day. But Natal lies on the sea, and to it had already come the seafaring British. There was sharp fighting, and the Boers, disgusted, would not remain. Taking their oxcarts once more, they went into the interior, leaving their lands to be incorporated in 1843 into the colony of Natal.

The British government was in a quandary at this Boer removal. All these scattered white men were technically British subjects. As such, it was Britain's duty to defend them from the warlike natives. It was also Britain's duty, on the other hand, to defend the natives from the highhanded Boers. The expense of doing this, however, would be great; and since the Boers cared nothing for the British connection, why not let them go their own way? Consequently, in 1852, England formally proclaimed the independence of the South African Republic (the Transvaal), a vast region beyond the Vaal River. Two years later the Boers remaining in the region between the Orange and the Vaal River were likewise given independence as the Orange Free State. The political setup of South Africa was at last definitely outlined: two British colonies (the Cape and Natal) occupying the coast line, and the two Boer republics in the interior, the latter surrounded by a ring of native African tribesmen.

The two British colonies made headway slowly. Sir George Grey, of Australian and New Zealand fame, making his rounds as a governor throughout the British world, helped somewhat in settling troubles with the native chieftains. Representative institutions were established at the Cape in 1854; and responsible government came there in 1872, rather against the wishes of the inhabitants, who did not like the withdrawal of imperial troops which it implied. Just at the time when the opening of the Suez Canal was robbing South Africa of the strategic significance for which it had been added to the empire, diamonds and then gold were discovered in the lands of the Boers. That aroused an entirely new interest in the region and was to result in violent conflict between Briton and Boer.

Following the course of empire across the Atlantic, we find part of England's overseas possessions actually falling backward instead of going forward during this middle period. These were the West Indian sugar islands, which had been the brightest colonial jewels of the crown in the days of the old empire. Those few dots on the map had, as we saw, enjoyed a heavier trade with England than the whole thirteen colonies or the ports of the East India Company. They had devoted themselves to raising sugar, and the old mercantilist regulations had given their sugar a profitable and protected position in British trade (see page 468). Then, beginning in 1783, the Caribbean islands had sustained a series of shocks which ruined their old prosperity. The granting of independence to the United States had knocked askew the old triangular trade which had been of mutual value to the mainland and island colonies. Rival sources of cane sugar developed in Spanish Cuba and in the United States, while European scientists, during the days of the Continental System when "colonial wares" were cut off, had learned to make sugar from beets. The British trend toward free trade during the second quarter of the nineteenth century robbed the British sugar islands of their old preferential position. Perhaps the heaviest blow of all was the abolition of slavery, in 1833. The Negroes did not like to work on the plantations; they did not relish working anywhere and now were beyond coercion. In the smaller colonies they continued to work on the planters' land, for they had to live; but in colonies like Jamaica, where there was much free land, "they deserted the estates and lived in their own villages, supporting themselves by primitive subsistence agriculture." The planters tried to offset this labor shortage by importing several hundred thousand natives from India, a fact that did not favor the growth of responsible government.

In 1865 a Negro revolt broke out in Jamaica which alarmed both planters and Parliament. Up to this time Jamaica and the other islands had enjoyed representative government, with elected assemblies such as the thirteen colonies had had before the Revolution (see page 467). The following year, at a time when many other colonies in the British Empire had just advanced to a still further stage of self-government, Jamaica lost even that. The elected assembly was abolished, and the island was ruled by a governor and council. The same thing happened in most of the other British West Indian islands; little Barbados, however, like Bermuda and the Bahamas (just outside the Caribbean), still maintains today its elective assembly, which has continued steadily for nearly three hundred years.

Finally we come to Canada, England's experimental laboratory in the development of colonial self-government. The American Revolution taught England a lesson she did not forget. Henceforth she governed more wisely her remaining colonies of settlement. From 1774 to 1867 a series of constitutional innovations in Canada illustrated the adaptability and flexibility of the British colonial system and developed features which were soon extended to the other principal colonies of settlement within the empire.

The term "Canada" until 1867 referred only to the present provinces of Quebec and Ontario. The rest of British North America now included in the Dominion of Canada was under separate governments. There were in the east the Maritime Provinces of Nova Scotia, New Brunswick, and Prince Edward Island; on the Pacific was British Columbia (which came into being in 1858 after a gold rush); while the vast region lying between those eastern and far-western possessions was loosely held by the Hudson's Bay Company. Newfoundland, which included part of Labrador, then as ever since played a lone role.

On the eve of the American Revolution, as we recall, England had shown good sense in handling the Canadian situation. Canada at that time was limited to the French colony around Quebec, its population almost completely French Catholics except for a few English adventurers. The same Parliament that in 1774 passed the Boston Port Bill, which goaded New England into revolt, passed also the Quebec Act for the government of that new province which had been wrested from France only a few years before (see page 474). This was a wise measure, although it was denounced by the strongly Protestant New Englanders as another of Parliaments "intolerable" acts. The French settlers were allowed, we recall, to keep their Catholic religion and their old French civil law. That satisfied them to such an extent that they continued, in general, loyal to England throughout the Revolution.

Within ten years, however, conditions had been radically altered in those northern provinces which remained within the empire. Large numbers of "United Empire Loyalists," those "Tories" from the thirteen colonies who chose to stay under the old flag, had migrated northward. England generously demonstrated that loyalty was appreciated; for lands were granted to them, and they were compensated for at least part of the losses which they had suffered during the Revolution. Perhaps thirty-five thousand of these Loyalists went to Nova Scotia, where the western part adjacent to Maine was turned into a special haven for them and renamed New Brunswick. Perhaps six thousand more trekked overland across New York to lay the foundations of what is now Ontario. A third group of these loyal Americans, numbering about one thousand, made their homes on the banks of the St. Lawrence in the present province of Quebec.

Pitt sponsored the Canada Act of 1791, to settle the problems rising from this migration. After its passage two colonies were created, Upper and Lower Canada, the former to include settlers in the new region to the west of the rapids of the St. Lawrence beyond Montreal, the latter those in the lower valley of the St. Lawrence, from Montreal and Quebec to the sea. Pitt's idea had been to separate as much as possible the English-speaking people in Upper Canada from those of French blood farther down the river. Representative government was now introduced. Upper and Lower Canada were organized on the model of the original thirteen American colonies, with a governor as executive, appointed by the crown, and with a legislature which consisted of two chambers: the upper an appointed council; the lower an elected assembly. In Upper Canada provision was made "for the support and maintenance of a Protestant clergy" by setting aside for that purpose large areas of land (the clergy reserves). In Lower Canada the Roman Catholic Church retained its privileged position.

The new constitution, by splitting Canada in two, relieved an awkward situation, but it still left causes for friction. As before 1776, it was not always easy for an assembly elected by the people to agree with a governor appointed from England. The English minority in Lower Canada, moreover, felt itself at the mercy of the French Canadians, and the English majority in Upper Canada was displeased with the fact that between it and the sea was a colony dominated by Frenchmen through which passed its only commercial outlet, the St. Lawrence. The War of 1812, between England and the United States, in which both English and French Canadians fought hard against the invaders from the south, temporarily lessened this friction (see page 574); but with its conclusion trouble between the two Canadas broke out again.

Nor was it simply a question of colony against colony or colony against mother country. The United Empire Loyalists and other early settlers in Upper Canada were none too friendly toward more recent newcomers there,—Irish, British, and American,—and they formed what was called (without very good reason) the "Family Compact," to try to keep the government in their own hands. They were willing to divide the church lands between the Presbyterians and the Church of England; but the numerous Methodists, left out in the cold, were resentful. William Lyon Mackenzie, ancestor of the twentieth-century Canadian statesman Mackenzie King, was the leader of the malcontents. His newspaper hinted at the possibility of secession from the empire, and irate supporters of the "Family Compact" sacked the office where it was published. Mackenzie, however, got himself elected mayor of Toronto, after being five times elected to the legislature, and five times expelled by the "Compact" party.

In Lower Canada a feud arose between the legislative assembly, controlled by the French, and the upper house, the legislative council, nominated by the governor. It began over the payment of judges' salaries, but widened in many directions. Louis Papineau, Speaker of the Assembly, sponsored a large number of resolutions granting to that body many rights not recognized by Pitt's Act. He did not simply demand financial control but insisted on an elected legislative council, and even elected representatives on the executive council of the governor. The imperial government would not yield in the matter of these many resolutions, and Papineau and his party finally came to open rebellion against the crown.

The Canadian rebellion of 1837 was a trifling affair from a military point of view: the adherents of Papineau were quickly put to rout with slight loss of life, and in the upper province an attack by Mackenzie on Toronto proved a fiasco. Nevertheless, the fact that there was fighting at all seemed ominous to English statesmen. Still remembering the American Revolution, they desired to avert another such forcible dismemberment of the empire. In the following year Lord Durham, an advanced Whig known as "Radical Jack," who had been active in drawing up the Reform Bill of 1832, was sent to Canada to diagnose the ills of the colony.

His lordship was given a vague though extensive commission. He was to be "Governor-in-Chief of all the British North American Provinces except Newfoundland, and High Commissioner for special purposes in Upper and Lower Canada." Though he was in North America for only five months, his mission is famous in the annals of the empire. He suffered so grievously from ill-health that he was able to accomplish but a small part of what he attempted. In addition, he got into grave difficulties with the Colonial Office for illegally exiling participants in the rebellion to Bermuda. Nevertheless, his official report on the affairs of British North America, made to Parliament in 1839, is a monumental landmark in British constitutional history. Within a year of its appearance Gibbon Wakefield, who had accompanied Durham to Canada, wrote that "it has gone the rounds from Canada through the West Indies and South Africa to the Australias, and has everywhere been received with acclamations." Wherever and whenever the British have inaugurated self-governing colonies and dominions, this report has been considered a bulwark of British liberty because it suggested and advocated the principles upon which dominion development was to rest.

# A History of England and the British Empire

The importance of the document lay in its recommendation of *responsible government*. There had been "self-government" or "representative government" in the British Empire ever since the House of Burgesses was established in Virginia in 1619, but the actions of the colonial assemblies were limited by the executive power of the governor and by the authorities in England (see page 467). Responsible government meant the dependence of the executive on an elected legislature, as in England. Durham recommended that colonial governors should be instructed to select their ministers from those men who could command a majority in the lower and popular branch of the legislature. The governors, he argued, should be told that they should not look to London for advice or assistance on any domestic questions but were to act in the self-governing colonies as the crown acted in England, holding themselves above the political battle. Authority, under his scheme, would lie with the popularly elected colonial assemblies. The only powers to be reserved for the imperial Parliament were over foreign relations, trade between the colonies and Great Britain, intercolonial trade, and the public lands.

When once the imperial government had been convinced of the soundness of Durham's ideas, they conceded to the colonies an even wider freedom than he had suggested. But it took nearly a decade to make them realize that the doctrines of the report were not too revolutionary. This was mainly the work of a group of eminent British-American statesmen. In Canada the fight for responsible government was carried on by Robert Baldwin, a man much more moderate but no less determined than the fiery Mackenzie (who was now a fugitive in the United States), with the aid of Louis Lafontaine, a French-Canadian leader of similar views. In Nova Scotia the hero of the battle was Joseph Howe. In any analysis of the winning of responsible government for the British colonies Howe deserves a special word. As leader of the democratic group in the assembly of Nova Scotia he worked long and hard to compel the governor to select his advisers from men who were supported by a majority in it. He harassed governor after governor, and in a famous series of open letters to the Colonial Secretary put forward with complete courtesy yet unanswerable logic the case for responsible government. At last, after the Whigs had come into power in England in 1846, the British government made the desired concession. The new Colonial Secretary, Earl Grey, instructed the governors of the colonies in America to rule through the medium of ministries commanding the confidence of the assemblies, "since it cannot be too distinctly acknowledged that it is neither possible nor desirable to carry on the government of any of the British provinces of North America in opposition to the opinion of the inhabitants." Within a few years responsible government was the rule throughout British North America.

In Canada it was inaugurated during the governorship of Lord Elgin (1847–1854). The two Canadas had again been united in 1840. This was the result of a recommendation of Durham, who had mistrusted the French Canadians and desired to ensure an English majority in the legislature; but the latter idea was defeated by a provision of the Act of Union which allotted equal representation in the new parliament to the two old sections of the province. As Upper Canada soon had more people than Lower Canada, yet only the same number of members in parliament, the old jealousies revived; and ultimately the political situation became a complete deadlock in which men began to think of a federal system as a way out. In the meantime, however, Elgin, a man of great intelligence and attractive personality, accustomed the Canadians to the workings of the new system of government and, by his frank acceptance of the principle that real power must rest with ministers backed by a majority in the Canadian parliament, won their confidence and cemented the connection of Canada with the mother country. At the same time he aided the economic life of the colony by negotiating a Reciprocity Treaty with the United States, and thus introducing a period (1854–1866) of relatively free trade across the border, which is regarded as having been advantageous to both countries.

Responsible government spread quickly through the other large colonies of settlement. In 1855 it was extended to Newfoundland and to the four Australian colonies of New South Wales, Victoria, South Australia, and Tasmania. New Zealand received it a year later, while Queensland had it from its beginning as a separate colony in 1859. Cape Colony, however, did not accept it until 1872. In each of these colonies the executive power now lay, as in England, in the hands of a premier and cabinet responsible to the popularly elected legislature. Self-government was almost complete. The colonies could regulate their own trade, even to the point of erecting tariffs against the mother country, which Canada did very early. The only important reservation was the natural and necessary one that the control of foreign affairs should still lie with the imperial government. The governor became more and more a mere representative of the dignity of the crown, playing little part in the real business of ruling.

The next step in the evolution of the new imperial system was the federation of groups of neighboring colonies into larger units, communities large enough to develop a true national spirit and assume national responsibilities. This was later to take place in Australia and South Africa, but again the pioneer was Canada. The idea of uniting British North America was not a new one, and the political deadlock in the province of Canada brought it into the front of men's minds. Its realization, however, was occasioned in great part by the American Civil War, a conflict which made bad blood between Britain and the United States. The *Trent* affair, at the end of 1861 (see page 647), showed how serious was the danger of war, and the fact that the troops then sent to Canada had to be transported overland to Quebec and Montreal in sleighs proved the necessity of an intercolonial railway. It appeared desirable to coalesce all the colonies and present a united front to the Yankees. By 1864 the situation seemed so serious that two bitter political enemies in Canada, John A. (later Sir John) Macdonald and George Brown, patriotically united in a coalition government on the platform of federating British America. At the end of the war abortive attacks on the provinces by Irish "Fenians" from the United States gave point to their arguments and added to Canadian alarm. The result was the British North America Act, passed by the British Parliament in 1867, and the consequent organization of the Dominion of Canada in the same year. There were originally four provinces: Ontario (the old Upper Canada), Quebec (the old Lower Canada), Nova Scotia, and New Brunswick. Prince Edward Island did not join until 1873; and Newfoundland preferred to remain separate, as a self-governing colony (later termed, like Canada, a dominion), down to 1933, and since as a crown colony.

The dominion form of government was a federation, like that of the United States. Provincial self-government and provincial legislatures were provided; but, unlike the American constitution, that of the dominion gave to the central government all powers not expressly reserved to the provinces. The capital was placed at Ottawa, and the Canadian parliament meeting there was to consist of two houses: a Senate, nominated by the governor-general (acting, naturally, on his ministers' advice), and a House of Commons, chosen by popular vote. Special political and religious reservations were made for the protection of the French inhabitants of Quebec. The British cabinet system, already familiar to Canadians, continued in use.

One of the first questions to be taken up by the new Dominion parliament was in regard to the wide expanses of British North America outside the Dominion. Thousands of miles to the west, on the Pacific shore, lay British Columbia, with a population of about ten thousand; and between it and Ontario were untouched fertile prairies to which the Hudson's Bay Company held title. Parliament was worried by the possibility of the northward expansion of the United States into this unoccupied land, and perhaps even feared that the Hudson's Bay Company, which was accustomed to bring in its supplies by way of St. Paul, Minnesota, might so far forget its British allegiance, in its desire for profits, as to sell some of this land to the United States. British Columbia would then be forever separated from Canada. Consequently the parliament in 1869 bought out the rights of the Hudson's Bay Company for £300,000, and in 1870 admitted to the Dominion a portion of the purchased land (the only settled part) as the province of Manitoba, while providing for the territorial government of the rest. British Columbia meanwhile applied for admission to the federation on one condition, that a railway should connect the Pacific with the Atlantic. This was promised in 1871. Finally, owing to the political genius of Sir John Macdonald, whom we have seen as the architect of the confederation, and to the financial genius of Donald Smith (Lord Strathcona), the Canadian Pacific Railway was completed in 1885, a date which marks the real beginning of Canadian nationalism from the standpoint of economics and geography.

England was perhaps not entirely unselfish in granting such generous extensions of self-government to her colonies. During the middle years of the nineteenth century there were in the British Parliament many prominent "Little Englanders" who looked forward to the day when the colonies of settlement might withdraw from the empire, and, far from deploring such an event, they were anxious to make the separation as peaceful as possible. Self-government, in their opinion, would help to prepare the colonies for independence.

The reasons for such an attitude were largely economic. The mercantilist system of the Old Empire had bound the colonies closely to the mother country in matters of trade. Under the Navigation Acts they had been permitted to import only from England and had been required to limit their exports of certain "enumerated" articles to England as well (see page 383). Adam Smith, in his *Wealth of Nations*, had attacked this system, and during the second quarter of the nineteenth century England had made rapid advances toward free trade (see page 595). Huskisson's modifications of the Navigation Acts in 1825 had thrown open the colonies to foreign trade, and they were no longer forced to purchase for their outside needs from the mother country. The Manchester school (see page 636), looking at the colonies from the economic standpoint, considered them liabilities rather than assets. Their meager trade, it seemed, did not offset the heavy cost of defending and administering them. India, which was absorbing fully a tenth of England's exports, was a different matter; but in the colonies of settlement—Canada, Australia, New Zealand, and South Africa—the imperial game did not seem worth the candle in the eyes of the "Little Englanders." They could point to the former thirteen colonies as a demonstration that the actual bond of empire was not necessary for profitable trade. One politician cited the following pertinent statistics: "In 1844 we exported to the United States produce and manufactures to the value of £8,000,000, an amount equal to the whole of our real export trade to all our colonial dominions, which we govern at a cost of £4,000,000 a year; while the United States costs us for consular and diplomatic services not more than £15,000 a year, and not one ship of war is required to protect our trade with the United States."

The most definite of the "Little Englanders'" grievances against the colonies was that they would not pay for their own protection. England was ready to provide naval defense, but felt that they might at least pay for the redcoats maintained within their borders. England's efforts in 1764 to make the thirteen colonies pay for similar protection by regular troops had been the first step toward the American Revolution (see page 467). It was estimated in 1847 that about one third of England's military costs went for these colonial garrisons, and that of every seventeen shillings which the British taxpayer spent in taxes one shilling went to keep redcoats in the colonies. The Indian forces were paid out of Indian revenue, but the troops in Canada, Australia, New Zealand, and South Africa were a direct burden on England. Those garrisons gave the "Little Englanders" a talking point against the whole colonial relationship. One British peer summed up the attitude in a study of the system: "One by one, the last rags of the commercial system have been torn away. We receive no tribute; we expect no commercial advantage in the ports of our colonies that we do not hold by merit and not by favor; yet we undertake the burden of defending them against attack. It is on this ground that certain politicians exclaim against colonies; that they denounce them as useless expense and would do away with them altogether." In 1869 the Colonial Secretary in the Liberal cabinet remarked: "Our relations with North America are of a very delicate character. The best solution of them would probably be that in the course of time and in the most friendly spirit the Dominion should find itself strong enough to proclaim its independence." This view, of course, was not universal, even among the Liberals. Lord John Russell, who was far from being a "Little Englander," sarcastically declared: "When I was young it was thought the mark of a wise statesman that he had turned a small kingdom into a great empire. In my old age it appears to be thought the object of a statesman to turn a great empire into a small kingdom." After a quarter century of anti-imperial agitation the colonial garrisons were finally removed. Quebec had had a garrison of soldiers ever since Wolfe had taken the city; but on a November day in 1871 the last regiment marched down from the citadel with the band playing "Auld Lang Syne," boarded the troopship, and dropped down the river. Halifax, like the Cape, was so important as an imperial naval base that a detachment of redcoats was left there for defense; but Newfoundland, New Zealand, and Australia, with heavy hearts, saw their garrisons withdrawn, and in general the self-governing colonies were left to shift for themselves.

Thus, ninety years after Yorktown, Englishmen still felt but little enthusiasm for the idea of empire. Young Benjamin Disraeli, the coming Conservative leader, had once remarked, "These wretched colonies will all be independent in a few years, and they are a millstone round our necks." And yet, within a few years, this same Disraeli would be leading England into a revival of imperial enthusiasm which would color still more of the world map with the British red.

# CHAPTER XXIII

## Gladstone and Disraeli

### 1865-1880

THE death of Palmerston, in 1865, ushered in a new era in British politics, that of Gladstone and Disraeli. For fifteen years these two men were to dominate the public arena, almost to the exclusion of their contemporaries. Under their leadership, party strife broke forth with a fury which recalled the days of the Reform Bill. Political labels had a meaning once more; the Victorian Compromise perceptibly weakened; and men grew angry and heated over issues made all the more vivid by these two personalities, both forceful, determined, and powerful, but in no other respect alike.

William Ewart Gladstone had been before the public eye somewhat longer than Benjamin Disraeli. Wealth, social influence, an impressive appearance, superb health—all were Gladstone's. Like Peel he was a darling of the gods, early destined to high command; like Peel he was the ambitious son of a wealthy and capable business man; like Peel, again, he had won highest honors as a student at Oxford and had entered the House as an infant prodigy. Gladstone was the nominee of the Duke of Newcastle. His seat had not been bought, as Peel's had, since the Duke of Newcastle was not a boroughmonger who sold Parliamentary seats, but a patron who handed them out. Gladstone had been a loyal follower of Peel from 1832 until that statesman's death. He had not been a slavish disciple; for he had deserted his commander when the latter endowed a Catholic seminary in Ireland with state funds. In general, however, his tremendous admiration for Sir Robert had kept him within the ranks of the Tory party until the breakup of 1846 (see page 639).

Only by very slow stages did Gladstone, the great English Liberal of the nineteenth century, gradually separate himself from his former political allies. The slant of his mind was always toward the middle course. He preferred, other things being equal, to be a liberal Tory rather than a conservative Liberal. But other things had not proved equal. The leadership of the Liberal party was much easier for him to attain than that of the Conservative; for after the repeal of the Corn Laws the county squires would not willingly follow a Peelite.

# Gladstone and Disraeli

To return to the Conservative fold after that, it would be necessary for him to return as a prodigal. Gladstone was a proud man; he would not go back in such a way.

Meanwhile the Liberals beckoned to him. Although hitherto opposed to political reform, he was genuinely liberal at heart in all that had to do with civil and religious liberty. He had defended Roman Catholic and Jew with warmth and been a stanch upholder of "peace, retrenchment, and reform." Although he had opposed Palmerston's Chinese policy, he was at one with him in regard to Italian unification (see pages 643, 676). Gladstone therefore willingly agreed to serve in Palmerston's cabinet in 1859, perhaps because of their joint Italian sympathies. He was, nevertheless, somewhat suspicious of Palmerston, while at the same time the latter was reproached for including a man of Gladstone's views in his cabinet.

The passing of time divorced Gladstone still further from the Conservatives. A masterful man, he took umbrage at what he considered the insolence of the House of Lords in rejecting his paper-tax repeal bill (see page 648). He loved Oxford, which he represented in Parliament, with passionate devotion; but he could not stomach the petty Anglicanism of the majority of his university constituents, who surveyed all life through ecclesiastical prisms. Furthermore, he was not immune to flattery. John Bright and other left-wing Liberals had picked him out as their man, and had assured him that he had it within his power to rise high in the Liberal party. After Oxford rejected him as her candidate in 1865, and South Lancashire, a manufacturing constituency, returned him to the Commons, he was henceforth to lead the Liberal forces.

Such had been Gladstone's past. It was evident that he had not quite lived up to the brilliant promise of his youth. It had taken him more than thirty years to find himself. He was methodical, honorable, just, a hard worker, and conspicuously a success in matters of finance; but his mind worked slowly. After Bright he was probably the finest orator of the century. He was also a man of violent passions, largely swayed by his feelings. He thought always that his mind determined what he did—or his conscience. There seems, however, no clear and logical clue to this strange man's career unless one considers him as controlled by his emotions.

The character of Benjamin Disraeli is in some ways less puzzling. He was evidently not the darling of the gods—at least, not of English gods. Behind him was neither wealth nor social influence. A Jew (D'Israeli was the family name), he did not attend either public school or university. That such a man, particularly in view of his unsuccessful early career, could rise to the command of the aristocratic Conservative party seems on the surface to defy explanation. The young Disraeli was a failure in business. His first try for a seat in the Commons was rebuffed by the electorate. When he eventually won a seat, his first speech was laughed at by Whigs and Tories alike. This man, so flamboyant, so un-English in clothes, in manner, in speech, and a novelist to boot—surely he could not look forward to a political career! Nevertheless, Disraeli had, in the first place, a very clear and definite idea, which steadily grew into a conviction, namely, that the British aristocracy must and could weld all classes in the country into one national body under its control and leadership. The poor, the weak, the lowly, yearned for this leadership and were entitled to it. Secondly, although Disraeli was bright, witty, and adroit in managing men, he was not a profound thinker. The aristocracy instinctively recognized that they could depend upon his loyalty. To Disraeli the English country gentlemen were identical with England. With them lay his heart. He could laugh and jest at all other things, and appear cynical, unscrupulous, and a charlatan to many who never fathomed the man. Profoundly ambitious, highly imaginative, conscious of his own ability in debate and of the inability of his aristocratic followers to speak for themselves, he was willing to lead them to victory.

These two men, originally both Tories, had found themselves on different sides at the time of the Corn Law fight. Disraeli had attacked Peel on that occasion, believing it both undesirable and dangerous for England to permit her agricultural classes to decay; and Gladstone had followed Peel. Disraeli, gradually settled in the saddle as Conservative leader, disliked Gladstone, considering him pompous, a trifle dull, and something of a prude. Gladstone, out in the cold politically, disliked Disraeli, considering him flippant, somewhat unprincipled, and a traitor to the great Peel. Only intermittently, however, before 1866 had the two men crossed swords.

From then on, the duel between them was bitter and continuous. Disraeli first drew blood, within one year defeating the Liberals and within another climbing to the premiership—"the top of the greasy pole" (1868). Twelve months later he was displaced by Gladstone, who in turn became prime minister (1868–1874). Once more Gladstone went out, and Disraeli came in (1874–1880). In the last encounter (1880) Gladstone won, and the battle doubtless would have lasted longer had Disraeli not died in 1881. This long-contested fight, however, meant more to England than the clash of personalities. A victory for Gladstone meant a victory for the Liberals, and a victory for Disraeli was a Conservative triumph. Therefore an analysis of the two parties at this time is essential.

# Gladstone and Disraeli

The Liberal party of 1865–1880 was composed of two main wings. The first, numerically the smaller, consisted of the Whig landlords, who by temperament, economic interest, and class prejudice were much like the Tory landlords. Their presence in the Liberal party was largely a matter of tradition, since they had never seen fit to break their old party ties. These men were liberal in matters of trade, commerce, and the civil rights of British subjects, but they were not enthusiastic about democracy and were largely content with the Victorian Compromise. Their wealth and social position offset to a considerable degree the fact that they were in a minority. The more aggressive, stronger wing of the party was dominated by the manufacturing and commercial interests. Their representatives in the Commons were, first and foremost, advocates of laissez faire. They were not averse to an extension of the suffrage to include the more intelligent workingmen. Some of them, like Bright, even believed that every man should vote as a matter of natural right. They tended to think of the natural political alignment in England as one not of rich versus poor but of landlord versus manufacturer, or country versus city. Any increase in the vote of the urban dwellers, from this point of view, tended to increase their political influence. Added to these two main groups of Liberals were two others of slightly less importance. One included those Nonconformists who wished to break the hold of the Church of England upon education (see page 699). Another consisted of scattered radicals who, too few to form a party of their own, took refuge under the Liberal banner.

The Conservative party was more homogeneous. The overwhelming majority of its membership was drawn from the landed gentry and those of the middle class socially and economically dependent on it, such as small-town merchants, butchers, grocers, and innkeepers. To this was added a minority group of the upper middle class, destined to grow rapidly in numbers,—men of wealth and position in the business world who looked forward to buying estates and becoming country gentlemen. Also included in the Conservative ranks, as far as cheering went (for they had no vote before 1867), were a few workingmen who were Conservative more because they disliked the middle-class Liberals, with whom they came in intimate business contact, than because of any special love of the gentry, with whom they had no dealings. The majority of the House of Lords, the officers of the army and navy, and Society, spelled with a capital "S," were all overwhelmingly Conservative.

In 1866 the opening gun of the new party war was fired for the Liberals by Gladstone, who proposed to lower the franchise requirements for Parliamentary voting. His bill was moderate in scope, seeking to give the vote to the more skilled workingmen, which would raise the theoretical political power of labor in the boroughs from approximately one fourth of the votes cast to about two fifths. This, Gladstone argued, would come about if voting eligibility were based on his proposed lowered standard rental. The act once passed, he planned to introduce another providing for a more equitable distribution of Parliamentary seats. By this scheme the number of unimportant or semi-rotten boroughs would be still further reduced, and new seats would be created for cities which had increased rapidly in population during the preceding thirty years.

Ever since the Reform Bill of 1832 there had been gestures in this direction. Disraeli himself had played with the idea, having at one time suggested a vertical instead of a lateral yardstick. In other words, he had proposed that classes as such be given votes in Parliamentary elections,—so many to the unskilled workers, so many to the shopkeepers, to the landed proprietors, etc. Lord John Russell also had once introduced a moderate reform bill for the Whigs, and Palmerston had given it his support; but it had never been pressed to a vote, neither party really regarding reform of this description as a very serious issue.

The Liberal party now came out officially in favor of a change. The redistribution of seats under the act of 1832 had been inadequate, even then, and by 1866 the inequalities were glaring. The success of the North in the American Civil War seemed to demonstrate to many in England that democracy had justified itself across the Atlantic. The working classes in England had shown a decided advance in literacy. They had also gone in for savings banks, and their trade unions were under conservative leaders. There was no longer any fear of Chartism; but the trade unions here and there were growing restive and were demanding an extension of the suffrage. Gladstone and his Liberals considered it better to give in to their demands before they became too articulate.

The wily Disraeli, meanwhile, decided to await events. He knew that the Palmerstonian Liberals, for the most part the old Whig element, would be apt to balk at Gladstone's bill. If the Liberals quarreled among themselves, Her Majesty's opposition, of which he was the shining light, might sail back into power. This was what occurred. The devoted followers of "Whiggery" revolted against the new leader of their party. Although they were not sufficiently numerous to defeat the second reading of Gladstone's bill, they did hold down the government's majority to five votes. This was not enough, as Gladstone well knew, if his bill was to escape amendment and successfully run the gantlet of the House of Lords, which was ever willing to throw out Liberal bills passed by only a narrow margin in the Commons. Gladstone's enemies, however, did not need to call in the help of the Lords; they defeated the bill on an amendment. Therefore, in June, 1866, into office trooped the triumphant Conservatives with Lord Derby, their nominal head, as prime minister, and Disraeli as leader in the House of Commons.

The next year, 1867, saw strange sights, both within and without Parliament. The English people, hitherto indifferent to these Parliamentary skirmishes, suddenly became vociferous in their demand for Parliamentary reform. The days of 1831 and 1832 returned. Huge mass meetings throughout northern England, fanned into fury by the voice of Bright, reflected in no uncertain way the nation's will; a mob even pulled down the fence around Hyde Park in London.

Disraeli did not care about Parliamentary reform, one way or another, but he did intend that his party should rule England. Therefore he decided that the Conservatives should adopt reform as their child and undermine Gladstone's popularity with the working classes by stealing his thunder. They would lower the franchise requirements of their own accord, and in that way they might retain office. With unerring skill and patience Disraeli, having persuaded the Conservative party to adopt this idea, introduced a reform bill of his own. It was much more radical in a way than Gladstone's, since it discarded property rights and income altogether as a yardstick and proposed to give the franchise to every male householder in the British boroughs. To counter this radical step toward universal suffrage, however, Disraeli proposed that two votes should be given to certain citizens: clergymen, university graduates, men who owned government securities, and those who paid direct taxes of more than twenty shillings a year.

Gladstone was enraged. He felt that he had been tricked by an unscrupulous politician. Yet there had been nothing whatever in Disraeli's past record to indicate that he was opposed to an extension of the franchise. Falling upon Disraeli's bill with fury, Gladstone proposed amendment after amendment and attacked the "fancy franchises," which gave a double vote to certain classes. In every instance Disraeli yielded gracefully; for to him the "fancy franchises" were only devices, not a matter of principle. Disraeli had only one principle in this—that every man who paid taxes should vote. Since one could not occupy even a hovel without paying the poor rate assessed against it, this was equivalent to household suffrage, which, according to Disraeli, was more intelligent than to draw an imaginary line between £10 householders and £7 householders. The "fancy franchises" were deleted from the bill one by one; but in forcing these concessions Gladstone made no dent in the Conservative armor. In 1867 Disraeli's bill became law, and its author, upon the resignation of Lord Derby early in 1868, prime minister.

This second Reform Bill of 1867 was more revolutionary than that of 1832. It extended the franchise in the counties, and it all but made manhood suffrage universal in the boroughs, thus making Great Britain, to all practical purposes, a political democracy. The act of 1832 had shifted the balance of political control toward the middle class, the upper stratum of which was so interlinked with the aristocracy as to continue England's aristocratic tradition, modified but unrevolutionized. The act of 1867 shifted the balance again to the left, this time toward the working classes. It remained to be seen how far the latter would go in making use of their new privileges. Disraeli was confident that the working man would prefer Conservatives to Liberals; Gladstone was as confident of the reverse. Almost everyone approved of what had taken place, except a few like Thomas Carlyle, whose pamphlet, *Shooting Niagara*, bewailed this grant of the vote to ignorant and unthinking men. He believed that once the upper classes gave up their control of the government they could never regain it.

Disraeli was not long to enjoy his triumph. His redoubtable enemy almost immediately launched a successful attack on him from a new angle, Ireland. The woes of that unhappy island continued to be many and vexatious. The close union brought about by Pitt in 1801 had not proved felicitous. The Irish, apart from Ulster, were sullen, poverty-stricken, and ill-disposed toward England. Gladstone rushed to their relief. His approach, a religious one, was typical of the man. He was a devout Anglican, but it seemed to him entirely wrong that the Church of Ireland, an Anglican body closely allied with the Church of England, should be a state organization in that Roman Catholic island. Therefore he moved in the Commons that this ecclesiastical body should cease to exist as a branch of the government. The motion was carried, and Disraeli was defeated. He appealed to the country, confident that the workingmen to whom he had given the vote only the year before would stand by him. Their answer was, No! Once more, in December, 1868, the Liberals came back into power, with a majority of one hundred; and Gladstone, now for the first time prime minster, began his great ministry (1868–1874).

First on the Liberal program was the pacification of Ireland, for which Gladstone held that three things were necessary: an attack on the political and financial status of the Church of Ireland, the reform of the Irish land law, and, finally, the reorganization of Irish education. He began with the Church of Ireland, whose services, it must be remembered, were not attended by most of the Irish people, who crowded into their little Roman Catholic chapels, leaving the stately edifices of the Establishment almost exclusively to the land-lords. The Church of Ireland was wealthy, being in possession of some £16,000,000. Gladstone proposed to take half this sum and devote it to charity and education, leaving the other half to a re-organized Church, divorced altogether from the government. The bill to this effect was pushed through the House of Commons with-out any determined opposition from Disraeli; for the latter realized that some time must elapse before Gladstone's popularity in the country would wane. The House of Lords, however, showed fight. The queen and the bishops were incensed, but they could do nothing with Gladstone save attempt to rescue something for the Church in the way of pounds, shillings, and pence. Gladstone was willing to make financial concessions for the sake of peace, and consequently the Irish Church received a larger share of its own endowment than he had intended to leave it. The Lords grumbled loudly at the violation of property rights, but they were afraid to challenge Glad-stone's large and fresh majority in the Commons. From now on, the Church of Ireland was disestablished and therefore ceased to be a branch of the British government.

Next came the more difficult question of the Irish land, most of which was owned by absentee landlords charging exorbitant rentals. "Rack-renting," as this abuse was called, was made easier by the fact that, with practically no industries in Ireland in which the peas-ants might find alternate employment, they had to stay on the land for their livelihood. The landlords had the whip hand with their rigid monopoly of the one thing desired in Ireland, land; naturally they took advantage of this, leasing land only from year to year. Since the peasants were generally in arrears, eviction for nonpayment of rent was frequent. The land was divided and subdivided into tiny strips until profitable cultivation became almost impossible, and Ire-land became more and more vulnerable to famine. Furthermore, outside of Ulster the land was rented unimproved, without dwelling houses, barns, stables, pigpens, or even drainage. The peasants real-ized the futility of trying to better their material condition when any such indication of improvement would mean a rise in rent.

Various remedies were proposed for this situation. John Stuart Mill, the economist, advocated for the landlord's protection a fixed rent, to be set, guaranteed, and collected by the government. To the peasant he would ensure fixity of tenure, as a guarantee against eviction. John Bright, aside from Gladstone the most important man in the Liberal party, urged peasant proprietorship, by which the government would buy out the landlords and then let the peasants gradually pay the government for their individual bits of land. This proposal of land purchase was to prove the eventual solution; but, like Mill's idea, it was too radical for Gladstone, who favored a third method, "Ulster custom."

Ulster alone of the Irish provinces had escaped economic blight, and in Ulster there prevailed a custom more binding than most laws. It was this: "If the landlord refused to renew a lease or insisted upon evicting a tenant, he was under obligation to pay for improvements made by the latter, also a further sum for intangible damages accruing to him [the tenant] for being disturbed in his occupation." Gladstone took this as the nucleus of his land law of 1870, making legal throughout all Ireland what was merely a custom in one corner of it. That he succeeded in winning the approval of Parliament for such a measure was little short of miraculous. Both houses of Parliament were composed of well-to-do men whose property was largely derived from agricultural rents. Now they were invited to declare that the Irish peasants had certain legal rights to the soil simply because they tilled it. Only the gravity of the Irish economic crisis, the prestige of the recent Liberal victory, and the indomitable will of the prime minister made the members of Parliament accept such a law.

The outcome, as far as Ireland was concerned, was disappointing. The landlords soon found a convenient loophole. They could not dispossess their peasants without paying compensation; but there was nothing in the law to prevent their raising rents. Nevertheless, the law set a valuable precedent: from now on, it would be easier to modify property rights. Quite evidently an owner of agricultural land could no longer do with it exactly as he saw fit,—not, at least, in Ireland.

Gladstone, postponing, for the time being, the question of Irish education, turned his hand to English reforms. One of the first to receive his attention was higher education. He broke the monopoly still possessed by the Church of England, which closed fellowships and professorships in the universities to all but Anglicans. From now on there were to be no such religious tests at Oxford and Cambridge.

He next endeavored to put elementary education on an intelligent footing. Parliamentary appropriations for schooling had hitherto been very meager indeed, partly because of the excellence of a few privately endowed schools, partly because of the prevalent theory of laissez faire, which assumed that the less government interfered with the life of the people the better for all concerned, and, perhaps more important, because of religious strife. The English people refused to divorce religion from education; yet they could come to no common agreement as to the kind of religious instruction to be given to their children. Gladstone's ministry proposed to solve this difficulty by giving subsidies to the existing voluntary schools and at the same time to set up new national "board" schools in which there should be instruction in the Bible but no other religious teaching. This was the basis of the Education Act of 1870, for which W. E. Forster, of Gladstone's cabinet, was largely responsible. It was not displeasing to the Conservatives, since the majority of the voluntary schools were controlled by the Church of England. But Gladstone's Nonconformist following did not approve of church schools' receiving funds raised by general taxation and looked askance at "Bible teaching"; for this might include Anglican doctrines.

Gladstone, however, would yield little to his old allies. He was too good a businessman to build new schools all over England when existing voluntary schools might suffice in many places. Therefore the only compromise he would make was to protect the consciences of the Nonconformists by accepting an amendment to his bill which excluded "every Catechism and formulary distinctive of denominational creed" and which at the same time provided that religious instruction should come at the commencement or the close of the school day, thus making it possible for conscientious objectors to withdraw their children from such instruction. "We must educate our masters" was the cry of England after the general enfranchisement of 1867. Gladstone thus began that process three years later. During the next twenty-one years elementary education was made compulsory and then free. In the short space of ten years the average school attendance jumped from about 1,100,000 to 4,000,000, an assurance that there would be less illiteracy among the coming generation.

Other reforms followed. One of the most beneficial had to do with the civil service, which before Gladstone's day had been the happy hunting-ground of the sons of influential men, many of whom were not qualified to occupy the posts which wealth and family position secured for them (see page 437). The civil service, with the exception of the Foreign Office, was now placed on a competitive basis, and examinations were held for government positions.

In due course came the reform of the British army. The Liberals cut down the strength of the regular army temporarily by twenty thousand men, withdrew garrisons from overseas posts, changed long-term enlistments into short ones (early in the century a recruit had the choice of signing for twenty years or for life), organized a proper reserve, and abolished the purchase of commissions. "Purchase," an old British custom dating back to Stuart days, had not worked badly in practice. Most of the officers did not stay long in the service, and after buying a captaincy or a majority they ordinarily retired to spend the greater part of their active life as country squires. The commissions were bought, but not outright: it was necessary first to be recommended as worthy of promotion. The system, of course, had its abuses,—such, for example, as its discrimination against officers who were poor. On the other hand, it made for rapid promotion; for the common practice of retiring as captains or majors left vacancies by which many distinguished officers might rise to high rank much earlier than if they had had to wait for dead men's shoes (see page 448).

Gladstone's resolve to end this old custom stirred up no small storm in British society. The army had been a preserve of the upper classes, and these classes generally desired that it should remain so. The Lords determined to kill Gladstone's bill abolishing purchase, but they were completely foiled by the prime minister's tactics. To the surprise of everyone he had purchase abolished by royal warrant and not by statute. The royal warrant belonged to the same general type of non-Parliamentary legislation as the earlier ordinances, proclamations, and Orders in Council. Gladstone's procedure was entirely legal, since purchase had been originally started by royal warrant; but to many the prime minister's action seemed the reverse of democratic. Disraeli had been firm for purchase, because his friends and allies liked it. The controversy, moreover, seemed to him foolish; for even after purchase went into the discard, the upper classes would still control the army as long as an officer's pay barely sufficed for the upkeep of a polo pony.

A final reform of importance was the ballot. Time after time, radicals had proposed to substitute secret for open voting in Parliamentary elections. British opinion, however, had felt that there seemed something almost un-English about the secret ballot, which might imply that a man was ashamed of how he voted. Gladstone himself had opposed this before 1867, on the theory that voting was a public trust and that the trustees of the public weal, those who had the franchise, should show to all the world how they proposed to exercise it. Now that almost every adult, at least in the boroughs, could vote, the old argument no longer held. Furthermore, before 1867, with the franchise limited to those who had money, there was little danger of intimidation. Once let the poor vote, and the secret ballot was needed to protect them. An open vote against the candidate of an employer might mean a job lost. In this step Gladstone ran counter to the House of Lords once more. In 1871 it threw out the ballot bill because it was "dangerous," "incoherent," and "contradictory." This made Gladstone angry, and he tried again the following year. If the Lords rejected this bill, he promised to dissolve Parliament and to hold an election on the issue. The Lords did not want this to happen, and, espying signs of growing weakness in Gladstone's popularity, they decided that it was the better part of wisdom to await the rising tide. Consequently the ballot was at last adopted.

By 1873 the popularity of the prime minister was obviously waning, partly because of his very conciliatory foreign policy. He did not wave the Union Jack as Palmerston had done. He had protested against Russia's violation of the Treaty of Paris (1856) in reinstating her warships on the Black Sea during the Franco-Prussian War of 1870–1871; but he had done so quietly, and Russia had ignored his protest. In that Franco-Prussian War, France was quickly beaten by the efficient Prussian army; her emperor, Napoleon III was captured; her Second Empire fell; and at the close of the war, with bloody civil strife in the streets of Paris, the Third Republic slowly emerged. The war was also the final step in the unification of Germany. The Prussian chancellor, Bismarck, had accomplished this through his successful wars against Denmark and Austria, which had resulted in putting Prussia in the latter's dominant position in northern Germany; and now, by this war against the French, he had brought the South Germans, Austria's recent allies, into complete union with Prussia. Thus, along with Italy, another new state and a much stronger one, the German Empire, took her place among the great powers under the rule of the king of Prussia. During all this, again without blare of trumpets, Gladstone preserved strict neutrality while at the same time he ensured the neutrality of Belgium.

Nevertheless, many felt that he was too pacifistic in all these matters; and when, in addition, his submission of the *Alabama* claims of the United States government to arbitration resulted adversely for Britain, angry patriots stormed at their prime minister. In these claims the United States government insisted that Great Britain had been negligent in enforcing international law in regard to Confederate privateering in the Civil War. Some of the Confederate ships had been built in Great Britain, and the United States felt that the British government might have stopped such action on the part of its citizens if it had earnestly desired to do so. The *Alabama*, for instance, was built near Liverpool, and, despite protests from the United States, the British government did nothing to prevent her sailing until it was too late. Upon Gladstone's agreement to arbitrate, an international court, consisting of an Italian, a Swiss, a Brazilian, an Englishman, and an American, met at Geneva in 1871. The United States tried to claim indirect damages, such as added insurance issued on cargoes, etc.; but the British refused to consider such costs. Actual depredations, brought about by several cruisers, were taken under judgment; and the court decided in favor of the United States in respect to those losses occasioned by the rebel cruisers, *Alabama* and *Florida*, and to some extent in respect to those caused by the *Shenandoah*. Great Britain was directed by the court to pay $15,500,000 in gold, which she promptly did. This case was important both because it preserved Anglo-American friendship and because it set a precedent for international arbitration. Many Britons, however, were much humiliated by the decision, British jurists were displeased with it, and Gladstone's enemies made much of it.

Meanwhile, in addition, each reform measure placed on the statute books had antagonized some special interest. The Nonconformists were up in arms over the Education Act. The Irish Land Act had alienated many of Gladstone's old Whig adherents. The man in the street was somewhat disconcerted by the multiplicity of reform bills. A slip here and a slip there—a foolish tax on matches, ill-advised and premature temperance legislation—all combined to lessen Gladstone's grip on the electorate. In 1874 came defeat on a third Irish bill, which would have set up a national university in Dublin, neither Catholic nor Protestant but broadly national. It was a good idea, but the bill was absurd in certain particulars. When Gladstone agreed to include in it, for the sake of religious harmony, a proviso forbidding university lectures in philosophy and modern history, the bill was doomed, and he was defeated.

The Great Ministry had come to an end. Gladstone had been progressive but not radical. Proportional representation, woman's suffrage, further extension of household suffrage to the counties, salaries for members of Parliament, the disestablishment of the Church of Wales—all these had been proposed during his premiership, and none had been supported by him. He had spoken guardedly but with evident disapproval of women's voting: he did not like the idea of women's flocking to the polls and taking part in purely masculine activities. He did not approve of paying salaries to legislators; if the individual constituencies wanted to pay salaries, there was nothing to prevent their doing so. In his opinion the government of England was strong and fine because people of wealth, refinement, and leisure gave their time freely to the nation without thought of pecuniary reward. In the last analysis the Great Ministry had been the active agent of the middle class. As such it left its permanent mark on British history and freed the government of the country from much which hampered an efficient and intelligent democracy. In 1874 its work was finished, and so, apparently, was Gladstone's. Few could have imagined that he would live to head three other British governments, and continue to be a power in the land for twenty years.

The Parliamentary election of 1874, which brought Disraeli back for the second time as prime minister, marked a change in English policy in two ways: it led to an active intervention of the state on behalf of the poor, something new in nineteenth-century England, and also to a more aggressive colonial and foreign policy.

Gladstone, as we have seen, had been primarily interested, apart from Ireland, in the welfare of the middle class. The ballot was, of course, in the interest of the poor, and so was his education bill; but with these two exceptions practically nothing had been done during the long reign of the Liberals to brighten the lot of those who had to toil with their hands for a living. It would not be fair to say that the Liberals had had no philosophy at all in regard to labor. They had a most positive belief in self-help, rugged individualism, and *laissez faire*. They thought that every workman had within himself the possibility of rising from the ranks, and if he did not do so it was assumed to be his own fault. All that the state could do, in their opinion, was to remove restrictions which impeded individual initiative.

Disraeli, on the other hand, wanted to impose restrictions, to improve the condition of the working class by positive rather than by negative legislation. He thought it possible to accomplish what Macaulay had said was impossible: to raise the level of a whole class by enacting laws. A passing witticism of Disraeli's, a Latin phrase which he used in regard to a certain public-health act,—*sanitas sanitatum, omnia sanitas,*—might be said to express his idea of social legislation. In other words, public health in the widest sense of that term was a moral obligation binding on the state. What the working class asked for, in Disraeli's opinion, was "better, healthier, more humanizing conditions in their own daily life. They wanted sanitary and commodious homes; they wanted regulations of their occupations so as to minimize risk to life and health; and to prevent excessive toil for their women and children; they wanted freedom of contract and equality before the law with their employers; they wanted encouragement and security for their savings; they wanted easy access to light and air and all the beneficent influences of nature."[1]

[1] W. F. Monypenny and G. E. Buckle, *Life of Benjamin Disraeli* (6 vols.; 1910–1920), Vol. V, p. 363. By permission of The Macmillan Company and John Murray.

These wants Disraeli considered just, and by a long series of laws enacted over a period of years he did much to secure them.

Among the more important statutes of this description enacted by the Conservatives were an "Artisans' Dwellings Act," a "Consolidating Factory Act," a "Rivers Pollution Act," and a number of laws regulating trade-union activities, the treatment of merchant seamen, and the enclosure of public lands. The Conservatives took a genuine interest in the housing of the poor. The ramshackle tenements, the foul courts, the back-to-back houses, and other warrens in which the very poor lived were private property and therefore sacred in the eyes of a middle class dominated by the concept of *laissez faire*. The Conservatives broke with this doctrine by giving permission to municipalities throughout the country to destroy unsanitary houses and to erect suitable ones. They also extended and consolidated in 1878 the various factory acts hitherto passed. They were likewise responsible for making the rivers cleaner by a law declaring manufacturers responsible for the condition of waters flowing from their establishments and by regulating sewage conditions. The Conservatives were more enlightened in their attitude toward trade unions than the Liberals. Gladstone had sided more with employers than with employees on the question of union labor, but the Conservatives did the opposite. By two separate bills they reversed the historic Liberal interpretation of "breach of contract," hitherto regarded as a breach of the criminal law when perpetrated by a union, and likewise the orthodox Liberal interpretation of "conspiracy" as applied to strikes. Employers and employees were now put on a basis of legal equality in these two respects, whereas hitherto the law had always favored the former. Furthermore, a private bill introduced for the protection of merchant seamen was supported by the Conservatives, obliging all merchant vessels flying the British flag to treat seamen decently in regard to food, quarters, and safety. Finally, the government reversed the historic development known as the enclosure of public lands and commons. They not only forbade enclosures in the future but took steps to redeem public lands for public use by taking over Epping Forest and making it a public park. Grass, light, air, playgrounds for all—these were matters of real importance to Disraeli.

The old-line Liberals were displeased with these measures, which they dubbed "Disraeli's sewage policy." Government, according to their way of thinking, should concern itself with politics, with constitutions, with affairs of state. Disraeli went on his way undisturbed, developing what afterward became known as "Tory democracy." This meant the protection of the physical as well as the spiritual welfare of the many through intervention on their behalf of a wide-awake and alert aristocracy devoted to the interests of all classes—not selfishly intent on the interests of one.

Meanwhile Disraeli changed English policy in a different direction—toward more interest in the British Empire and toward a more spirited foreign policy. He declared that he was interested in the self-governing colonies and looked forward to a time when their bonds of union with the mother country should be drawn closer. He took, however, few active steps in that direction, and as far as the empire was concerned his premiership was important principally in so far as it had to do with India and those sections of Greater Britain occupied by alien races directly subordinate to London.

Disraeli, it has been said, was the first modern statesman to pursue a frankly imperialistic policy. In his youth his imagination had always been fired by the East, and the older he grew the more interested he became in England's Eastern realm. Such a new outside interest, moreover, would help to take England's mind from her threatening economic ills in the world depression of the middle seventies. Whatever the cause of the depression, its effect had been heightened by the industrial and agricultural expansion of the United States in the years following the Civil War. England's agriculture was never again to be as prosperous, after 1879, as before, and England's manufacturers now saw Germany also rising as a possible competitor. The Continent, as well as the United States, was moving toward higher protective tariffs. Cobden's old dream of world peace through free trade seemed far distant, and a reaction was setting in against the ideas of the Manchester school. Disraeli, although no economist, felt the breath of the impending changes, and, always the opportunist, knew how to turn them to account.

A first step toward a more aggressive foreign policy was the purchase in 1875 of a large block of Suez Canal shares for the British government. These shares belonged to the ruler of Egypt, the Khedive Ismail, who was a nominal vassal of the Sultan of Turkey. His predecessor, Said, had received them in return for the grant of a franchise to the French company which completed the canal in 1869 under the supervision of a French engineer, and for providing enforced Egyptian labor in its construction. Ismail was now bankrupt, and the French bankers were not eager to advance more money to the spendthrift monarch. Disraeli saw his chance: without consulting Parliament he asked the great Jewish banking house of Rothschild for nearly £4,000,000 with which to purchase Ismail's canal shares. When questioned as to the security, he replied, "The British Government." Disraeli received the money, bought the shares, informed the queen that they belonged to the British crown, and then sought Parliamentary sanction for what he had done. It was an audacious act, but Parliament approved. The shares were to prove immensely profitable, although they did not give Britain actual control of the canal company. The purchase was to lead to the British occupation of the Nile valley (see page 716).

Disraeli's next advance in imperialism was to make Victoria Empress of India. He knew the queen would be pleased with this title. There were peculiar bonds of sympathy between women and this aged prime minister whose career since its beginning had been constantly aided by them. His sister had nourished his early ambitions; the wealthy, sentimental, and elderly widow who became his wife had done much to smooth his path; and now another widow, Victoria, strong-minded yet withal very feminine, had shown herself his friend. He would do something to soften her grief and loneliness. And while pleasing his sovereign, Disraeli planned also to please India, which had been for centuries a source of English wealth and renown overseas. He would give to the Indian princes and the Indian people, accustomed to imperial magnificence, an empress, and impress them with England's majesty and power. The proclamation of the new title at a superb Indian durbar, he thought, would gratify India, the queen of England, and himself. To many this seemed melodramatic and absurd. "Queen of England" was a sufficiently glorious title for any woman, so the Liberals said. The title of "Empress" seemed to suggest an aggressive imperialism which might endanger world peace. The queen, as well as Disraeli, however, was not to be thwarted; and consequently it came about that Victoria wrote after her name "*Regina et Imperatrix.*" The Suez shares and the Indian imperial title were the two most conspicuous episodes in Disraeli's imperialism, which ended the long period of imperial apathy. Further aspects of this development will be considered later in their special relation to other imperial problems.

In Europe the pot of Balkan politics was seething; and here Disraeli threw the weight of his country's influence against Russia. That country had been defeated in the Crimean War (see page 645), but it had not taken her long to recover her old ambitions in the Balkans. She had helped Rumania to gain virtual independence; and in 1870, when Europe was distracted by the Franco-Prussian War, had defied England successfully in repudiating the clauses of the 1856 treaty which forbade her to fortify Sevastopol and maintain warships in the Black Sea. She continued to stir up unrest among the other Balkan Slavs. When they finally revolted, Russia was ready to act.

# Gladstone and Disraeli

The first of these later revolts came in 1875 in the northern provinces adjacent to Austria, who, with some of the other powers, sought to bring pressure upon the Turks to reform and behave. Disraeli, however, failed to co-operate. He was apparently pro-Turk primarily because he was anti-Russian. He may perhaps have had a certain admiration for the Turks and a lack of faith in the rising Balkan nationalism; he certainly felt the necessity of keeping clear the way to India and was ever-watchful lest Russia gain an outlet into the Mediterranean, which was strategically though not legally a British lake. Disraeli prevented effective concerted international action at this time and even concentrated a British fleet in Turkish waters as a token of support.

The Turks, encouraged by that example, went further in their misbehavior in 1876, in the Bulgarian massacres. The Bulgarians were the last of the subject nationalities in the Balkans to rise against their Turkish masters. Europe, indeed, scarcely knew of the existence of such a people before rumors began to arrive that their revolt had been suppressed with terrific slaughter. "Coffeehouse babble," said Disraeli, unwilling to have his confidence in the Turks destroyed. The rumors, however, were based on fact. Instigated by the Sultan, the bashi-bazouks, or irregular troops, had slain men, women, and children by the thousands. That was too much for Gladstone. "Let the Turks," he wrote, "now carry away their abuses in the only possible manner, namely, by carrying off themselves. Their zapatiehs and their mudirs, their bimbashis and their yuzbachis, their kiamakams and their pashas, one and all, bag and baggage, shall, I hope, clear out from this province they have desolated and profaned." A considerable part of the English people agreed with him. It became more difficult for Disraeli to continue his pro-Turkish attitude, but he remained stubbornly and bitterly anti-Russian.

The Balkan situation grew still more complicated in the summer of 1876, when Serbia and Montenegro, autonomous, though not independent of Turkey, declared war on that country. A conference of the powers, including England, assembled at Constantinople to bring pressure for reform upon the new Sultan, Abdul Hamid II, later to be known as "Abdul the Damned" and the "Sultan Assassin." When the indignant representatives opened their session, however, the wily Sultan informed them that on the previous day Turkey had already become reformed. He produced a new constitution, of liberal design, which, he said, would give Turkey the proper kind of government. There remained nothing for the exasperated conference to do, though, as many foresaw, the new constitution was not to remain in force a year. Turkey still felt secure in her English support.

In 1877 Russia declared war and invaded the Balkans. The Turks put up a gallant and stubborn defense, but by the end of January, 1878, the Russian army was at the gates of Constantinople. Lord Beaconsfield, to use Disraeli's new title, took instant and militant steps against the Russian advance. The British fleet was ordered to advance on Constantinople, while Parliament voted a heavy war grant. For a few days things were tense. Russia, however, was in no condition to take on England as an added foe, and suspended hostilities. A few weeks later the Russians made peace with Turkey at San Stefano, just outside Constantinople. The terms called for a "Big Bulgaria" which would have given Russia indirect control over a considerable part of the remaining Turkish territory in Europe. Such a solution was unpalatable both to England and to Austria. Beaconsfield dramatically ordered a large force of Indian troops to Malta.

Thoroughly dissatisfied with the terms of San Stefano, which would leave Russian influence too close to Constantinople, Beaconsfield demanded a thorough reconsideration of the whole Near Eastern and Balkan questions at an international conference of the powers. Austria joined him in this, and Russia grudgingly consented. Bismarck, declaring that he was acting as an "honest broker," seeking nothing for himself, invited the congress to meet at Berlin and presided at its meetings there in 1878. Beaconsfield was a striking figure at the most important congress of European states since the Congress of Vienna. Even Bismarck admitted the influence and success of "the old Jew." Beaconsfield had already secured agreements on the most significant questions before the congress assembled; and the final terms, embodied in the Treaty of Berlin, included the results of that previous bargaining. In these terms two matters were of particular interest to England. Bulgaria, partly free from Turkish rule, emerged only a third as large as the huge state created by San Stefano; this had a military importance in keeping Russia farther away from Constantinople. Britain, moreover, secured the island of Cyprus for a naval base in the eastern Mediterranean. As for the other terms, Serbia, Rumania, and Montenegro were recognized as completely independent of Turkey, and Austria was granted the military occupation of two adjacent provinces; while Russia had nothing to show for her expenditure of blood and treasure except some minor gains in Europe and the region east of the Black Sea.

At the time seemingly it was a victory for England. Years later Lord Salisbury, Beaconsfield's lieutenant at Berlin, who succeeded him as head of the Conservatives, admitted that in backing Turkey "we put our money on the wrong horse." By that time Turkey had become still more disreputable in the eyes of western Europe through her wholesale massacres of Armenians; the new Balkan nations had enjoyed a vigorous growth when finally freed from Turkish rule; and British statesmen had become less concerned about Russia's Near Eastern menace to the route to India, as Russia had become more threatening in the Middle East and the Far East. The close relationship between England and Turkey, which had lasted a full half century, dissolved, in fact, quickly after Berlin; and Germany soon stepped into the vacant place as supporter of the Turks. We shall see that, in the World War, England was to be the ally of Russia and was to fight three major campaigns against her former Turkish protégés.

Few realized those implications in 1878 when Beaconsfield, returning to London, said proudly, "I bring peace with honor." Without war England had heightened her prestige in the Near East. The Russian Bear had been thwarted. There was now less danger that the route to India would be outflanked by the Czar's progress in the Balkans. And for all this the patriotic and dramatic old Jew, Benjamin Disraeli, earl of Beaconsfield, received the thanks of the queen-empress and the adulation of the people.

Two years later Beaconsfield was repudiated by the British electorate, his old rival Gladstone coming out of semi-retirement to defeat him at the polls and to take his place as prime minister. Gladstone had thought to retire in 1874; he was through with active political life. He had intended to devote his remaining days to literature, religion, and scholarship. Now suddenly this man, who cared little about foreign affairs, came back into power on the heels of Beaconsfield's brilliant diplomatic victory!

Two reasons account for this unexpected turn of events: the economic situation, and the character of Gladstone. During most of Disraeli's second premiership, British commerce, industry, and agriculture were in the doldrums following a lively boom which had reached its peak in 1872, immediately after the Franco-Prussian War. In that year the exports of British products (not including re-exports) reached a total of £256,000,000, the highest in English history up to that time. They had fallen to £192,000,000 by 1878, the year of Beaconsfield's triumph at Berlin, and were slightly lower in 1879, the black year in which English agriculture, in hopeless competition with grain from the United States, sustained a blow from which it never recovered. The world by that time was so closely knit together economically that trouble in one country tended to drag down others as well. The United States, England's best single customer, had undergone a severe financial crisis in 1873, and her purchases of English goods dropped from £40,000,000 in 1872 to £14,000,000 in 1878, accounting for nearly half of England's slump. The empire, on the other hand, was actually buying more at the latter date than at the former. A time might come when the new imperialism would develop new markets for British products; but in the meantime there were dark days for shipowners, manufacturers, landlords, and all those whom they employed. As British trade fell off, the era of budget surpluses did likewise. It had been easy enough for Gladstone to balance the budget in prosperous years. Now times were hard, and governmental expenses, instead of decreasing, were mounting. Therefore it was not difficult to accuse Beaconsfield of extravagance and to persuade the unthinking that he was responsible for deficits and financial gloom.

The second reason was Gladstone himself. His nature was too imperious and too masterful to enable him to stay quiet for long. Furthermore, he was stung to the quick, as a Christian, as a humane Englishman, and as an old Canningite by the Bulgarian massacres. The religious people of England in general and the Nonconformists in particular were indignant at the thought that England might justly be blamed for these massacres. Gladstone believed and made many Englishmen believe that if England had not supported the infidel in 1875 the infidel would not have slaughtered Bulgarians one year afterward. The imperialistic and pro-Turkish character of Beaconsfield's foreign policy was perhaps the principal reason for Gladstone's return to the arena.

Although Gladstone was no longer the official head of the Liberal party, popular attention was focused on him rather than on Lord Hartington, its nominal chief. When Beaconsfield appealed to the country in 1880 for a vote of confidence, it was the personality of Gladstone which turned the tide against the Conservatives and restored the Liberals to power. Gladstone was an old man, now past seventy; but the British traditionally admire activity on the part of their elder statesmen, and in 1880 witnessed a remarkable demonstration of it. Gladstone spoke as he had never spoken before, sweeping through northern England and Scotland like a prophet of Israel. He addressed meetings from railway carriages, thus greatly shocking Queen Victoria. He made the British ashamed of their lust for military glory. He belittled the acquisition of Cyprus, as an island which England did not need or want. He blamed Beaconsfield for the loss of British lives in Afghanistan and Zululand (see pages 714, 725), and accused his opponent of marring the proud record of Canning, who had supported the liberties of the oppressed. Intermittently he spoke of finance,—of how well off he (Gladstone) and the Liberal party had left the British treasury, and of how empty it now was, owing to neglect and extravagance.

So ran the campaign, with Beaconsfield taking little part in it. Hitherto it had not been customary for leading statesmen to make appeals to wide audiences outside their own constituencies. Political strife, so the prime minister thought, should be decided in the halls of Parliament, not in public forums. He too was old and very tired. He had never cared for public meetings, and now he let the others talk. The people, he was sure, would vote for him again; he had done much for them.

In the election Gladstone triumphed. The queen did not wish to send for him; but it was evident to all that he, and not Hartington, had won the election. Hartington could not form a cabinet which did not include Gladstone, and the latter would not serve under Hartington. The queen bowed to the inevitable, and in 1880 Gladstone became prime minister for the second time.

The long and dramatic duel between Gladstone and Disraeli was now about to close. The fierce encounters across the table in the House of Commons between the fiery, imperious Scot and the cynical, debonair Jew had already come to an end in any case because of the latter's withdrawal to the Lords. But Beaconsfield, never particularly robust, had been in failing health for several years, and seemed to have no further zest for honors. For a year and a half he lived in semi-retirement, gave wise counsel to his lieutenants, and made one last speech in the Lords. As Chatham in the eighteenth century denounced the approaching dismemberment of the British Empire, so now the dying Disraeli made a supreme effort to defend the empire he loved. India, the romantic East, and the fear of Russian intrigue held him in thrall; but more romantic yet in his eyes, and more idolized, was London. "My Lords, the key of India is London. The majesty of sovereignty, the spirit and vigor of your Parliaments, the inexhaustible resources of a free, ingenious, and determined people—these are the keys of India." But imperialism was out of favor for the moment, and so was its champion, Disraeli; he had written his allotted sentences upon the page of history.

# CHAPTER XXIV

## *The New Empire*

### 1874-1914

A STRIKING change in the attitude of the average Briton toward his empire came in the last quarter of the nineteenth century. It was heralded by the delivery of Sir John Seeley's lectures on the expansion of England, which, although not published until 1883, gave the impression that Englishmen were uniquely, if not divinely, appointed to rule over Negroes in Africa and brown men in India. It culminated two or three decades later as Rudyard Kipling poured forth poem after poem praising the pluck and daring of Britons overseas, and emphasizing their "dominion over palm and pine." Indifference and apathy gave way to enthusiastic zeal. In Africa, in Asia, in Canada, and in Australia, to say nothing of old England, there came a rebirth of imperial feeling, in respect both to the self-governing colonies of European stock and to those of exploitation; and this was soon translated into action by an enlarged empire acreage and a new empire unity.

Not only England but other great European powers were now turning to empire-building. The principal causes of this general change were these: the triumph of Germany over France in the Franco-Prussian War, of 1870, which ended, for the time being, the more important territorial controversies in western Europe, and which permitted the attention of both peoples and governments to be focused on Asia and Africa; nationalism, which led some countries to seek new lands to gratify national pride by coloring the map; the unparalleled growth of European population, which led to a panic-stricken competition by the Continental powers for unoccupied or thinly settled regions abroad; the increase in wealth which the Industrial Revolution had created, making possible the expenditure of considerable sums for geographical research and missionary activity; and perhaps, most important of all, that same surplus wealth seeking new investments overseas. In England the natural reaction against the unheroic teachings of the Manchester school also contributed to the change in feeling.

There was a double-headed stimulus for such investments: raw materials and new markets. The American Civil War had shown

# The New Empire

Europe's dependence on American cotton, and Europe wanted both to be independent of American cotton and to have cheaper cotton. Palm oil, crude rubber, and, later, petroleum were sought eagerly. New markets also were needed for the textiles, hardware, and other commodities produced in Europe. And as this happened the screw propeller and the tramp ship enormously facilitated transoceanic trade just at a time when surplus capital, piled high in England as a result of the Industrial Revolution, demanded new outlets. The questions of who should sell to the millions of China and to whom should fall the undeveloped lands of Africa perplexed the chancellories of Europe as well as British statesmen. Businessmen looked to politicians for the answer. One thing was evident to the public opinion of the period: the flag must protect the investor as a patriotic duty.

Almost every European country of major importance participated in the new imperialistic enterprises. Russia pushed forward toward the borders of Afghanistan and also toward the Pacific. France energetically set up claims in Africa and expanded across the Sahara, from north to south and from west to east, absorbing a large part of northwest Africa, a conquest which looked well on the map even if it was not especially valuable. Germany, a new contender in the colonial field, commenced in the eighteen eighties to earmark colonies, where opportunity offered, in Africa, China, and the South Seas. Belgium found herself the inheritor of the Congo basin, mainly as the result of King Leopold's misconduct, that monarch having been appointed a kind of international trustee for civilization over the Congo. Italy, also entering the competition late, ran into a hornet's nest in Ethiopia (Abyssinia), and was forced for the time to be content with Eritrea, on the inhospitable coast of the Red Sea, and part of Somaliland. Finally, England, in addition to entrenching herself firmly on her Indian frontiers, now aimed at ultimate control from "Cape to Cairo" and carved out a great and largely new African empire. In the north she was to hold sway over Egypt and the Sudan. In the east, British East Africa was to stretch inland to the great lakes. In the west, Nigeria was destined to grow until, next to India, it became the largest administrative unit in the empire not possessing responsible government. In the south a new dominion was to arise, and still another potential dominion—namely, Rhodesia—was to be born.

Benjamin Disraeli has been popularly credited with being the prophet, if not the founder, of the new empire. His imperial interests were extensive, although, as we have already noted, they lay primarily in the Orient and he neither understood nor appreciated the great colonies of settlement. It is true, nevertheless, that the initial wave of popular enthusiasm came during his second ministry. That wave receded, for the time being, with Gladstone's victory in 1880, which might be regarded as the last successful protest of the ideas of the Manchester school against the incoming tide of economic and national imperialism. Gladstone, however, was able only to check and not to stop what Disraeli started. Therefore it is only logical that we commence the story of the New Empire by tracing it in those regions in which the influence of Disraeli pushed forward an imperialistic program.

One of these was Afghanistan, on the northwestern Indian frontier, where it so happened that the amir at Kabul was displeased with what he termed "the dry friendship of the English," as he wanted an alliance which would guarantee to him his shaky throne. Not having been able to secure this, he veered toward the Russians, who for three decades had slowly but surely been absorbing the oases to the north. Tashkent, Khiva, Bokhara, Samarkand, and Khokand successively had fallen into their hands, and Merv was threatened. This seriously alarmed many Englishmen, including Lytton, the new viceroy of India, who suggested that the amir receive a British mission. The latter declined; if he did so, he said, he must also welcome one from Russia. Two years later (1878) it was noted that Russians were greeted at Kabul. Lytton instantly demanded that a British envoy be received; but the amir said that a recent death in the family made such a visit inopportune. Nevertheless, the British envoy advanced and was stopped at the frontier. The second Afghan war followed.

Once more the British-Indian army marched toward Kabul; once more Afghanistan agreed to accept British advice. England was to control Afghanistan's foreign relations as well as to patrol various Afghan passes. A resident was to be located permanently at Kabul and a subsidy paid the amir. This British victory was premature, the British resident and all his staff being promptly murdered by the Afghans shortly after their arrival. The British reoccupation of the country followed. If Lytton, and Disraeli his backer, had had their way, Kandahar and the southern portions of Afghanistan would have remained British. With the triumph of the anti-imperialists in Gladstone's victory in 1880, the British soldiers left Afghanistan. This did not mean that that country ceased to be a bone of contention between England and Russia. Even the pacific Gladstone later was aroused to the point of making warlike speeches and of calling out the reserves. Not until 1895 and the centering of Russia's interest in the Far East was the problem of Afghanistan temporarily settled to the satisfaction of both European countries (see page 827).

# The New Empire

In view of this British advance in India it is remarkable that Indian affairs did not attract much Parliamentary attention. More time was consumed at Westminster in wrangling over the desirability of a man's being allowed to marry his deceased wife's sister than in debate about India. The Liberals, it is true, were more or less inclined to adhere to Gladstone's motto, "masterly inactivity," and the Conservatives were likely to be the more aggressive in their Indian policy; but this divergence of views was only relative. Despite much flag-waving, Disraeli's imperialism did not greatly change the Indian scene; nor, on the other hand, did Gladstone's professed pacifism. Despite the grumbling of the Tories that the "Grand Old Man" was a "little Englander," there is no evidence to show that he ever thought of cutting India loose, to say nothing of envisaging self-government there. The empire spread, in the Indian peninsula, first here, then there, haphazardly, mainly without direction or planning. Parliament seemed quite content, for the most part, to trust its viceroys to act justly and in Britain's interest.

We turn now to Africa, by this time a renewed source of interest to Europeans. The Dark Continent had attracted much attention in the late fifteenth century, as we saw, when the Portuguese were seeking a way to India; but from then on, until the last quarter of the nineteenth century, Africa had figured mainly in popular imagination as the place where Negro slaves had been obtained. As we have seen, there had been some experimentation with colonies of settlement at the southern tip (see page 678). In Egypt and also in Algeria, French enterprise had been active in the middle of the nineteenth century; but Africa as a whole, until the sixties and the seventies, had been largely a land apart, vast, unknown, vague, mysterious.

During these two decades came the more important explorers, a few of them French or German, but the majority English. Dr. David Livingstone, a famous medical missionary, explored the basin of the Zambezi, and then disappeared from civilization into the heart of the African bush in the direction of what afterward was recognized to be Africa's longest lake, Tanganyika. In search of him the *New York Herald*, in 1869, sent out Henry M. Stanley, its star reporter, a British-born American who had fought on both sides in the American Civil War. Stanley succeeded in rescuing Livingstone and in finding what his predecessor had looked for in vain, the source of the Congo. Afterward, by descending the entire course of that river to the Atlantic Ocean, Stanley opened up central Africa to the European.

Meanwhile Speke and Grant, two Englishmen, had already discovered Lake Victoria (or Victoria Nyanza), the main source of the Nile. On their way north to civilization they met, going south, Sir Samuel Baker and his wife. The Bakers found Lake Albert (or Albert Nyanza), into which flowed Lake Victoria by a stream which Baker named the Somerset Nile. Later Stanley was to map out Lake Victoria, and to identify the famous Mountains of the Moon, to its west, and the Kagera River, the ultimate source of the Nile, which flowed into Lake Victoria.

This special interest in the Nile was caused largely by spectacular events in Egypt. The Khedive, Said, had permitted French capital and a French engineer to build the Suez Canal, and then the Khedive Ismail, being in need of money, had sold his shares in the Suez Canal Company to England, through the instrumentality of Disraeli (see page 705). This gave England, to all practical purpose, a half partnership in the development of Egyptian resources. The inevitable followed. The ambitious and extravagant Khedive borrowed too much money in Europe, mainly from French and English bankers, who floated Egyptian bonds for him; and soon he was unable to pay the exorbitant rates of interest on the bonds. "None of the Egyptian loans cost less than 12 per cent per annum, and some cost more than 13½ per cent per annum." The debt rose in twelve years from £3,000,000 to £91,000,000. The situation was impossible, and Egypt was bankrupt. The international bankers then brought pressure on their governments, to good effect. It was suggested to Ismail that the financial control of his country be assumed by the two powers in question (the "dual control"), an Englishman to collect the revenues, a Frenchman to disburse them. In 1877 this division of financial authority was arranged, with the Khedive's approval. Gladstone thundered in Parliament, but to no avail. Europe heartily approved, especially Germany, where Bismarck was always glad to distract France's attention from Alsace-Lorraine, the two provinces which he had annexed in 1871 at the close of the Franco-Prussian War. All seemed propitious for this international experiment in the liquidation of a bankrupt country.

Then, just as Beaconsfield died, the Egyptian scene was darkened by a storm cloud. Gladstone, pacifistic if not a pacifist, was left to deal with it. Beaconsfield was no more, but the seed which he had planted in Egypt was to bear astonishing fruit.

The bombardment of Alexandria by the British navy in 1882, and the seizure of the Suez Canal and of Cairo in the same year by the British army, were the result of a military revolt, brought about by favoritism shown in the Egyptian army to Turks and Circassians. As the revolt spread it changed from an anti-Turkish protest to an antiforeign uprising. The new Khedive (for Ismail was deposed in 1879) was weak in character and in brains, and appealed to the dual control for assistance. Not receiving it, he yielded to the rebel ringleader, Arabi Bey, appointed him minister of war, and summoned a council of notables. The latter interfered with the dual control, with the cry of "Egypt for the Egyptians!"; and matters went from bad to worse. The Khedive and Arabi intrigued against each other; riots broke out in Alexandria; and the warships of France and England converged on that port. The French soon sailed away, and the safety of the British fleet was endangered by the construction of earthworks on shore. The British admiral demanded that work on these fortifications be discontinued; the Egyptians kept on constructing them. The warships bombarded and then destroyed Arabi's batteries. Fiercer antiforeign riots followed, Europeans lost their lives, and Arabi threatened to blow up or to block the Suez Canal. The British reply was instant. Troops drawn from India and England were placed under General Wolseley, who seized the canal, marched on Cairo, exiled Arabi, and mastered the country.

It proved easier to enter than to leave Egypt. The Egyptian government had long been paralyzed. Foreign bondholders had to be considered, European residents had to be protected, a nasty outbreak of the plague had to be fought—and there was the Sudan! The Sudan comprised the unknown, undefined, and largely waste land to the south of Egypt. Never a part of the old historic Egypt, it had been conquered by the Khedive Ismail, who fondly believed that if he ended slavery there he would be acclaimed in Europe as an advance agent of civilization. Egyptian garrisons were located in the Sudan all the way from Wadi Halfa, at the Second Cataract of the Nile, southward to the great lakes of central Africa, and east and west from Ethiopia to the Sahara. As anarchy came to an end in Egypt it broke out in the Sudan. A prophet known as the Mahdi headed an insurrection which grew steadily through 1882 to 1884. Unless the Mahdi were smashed, not only would the Sudan be lost to civilization but the thousands of Egyptian soldiers who comprised its garrison would be massacred. Since England for the time being was responsible for the government of Egypt, upon her fell the obligation of rescuing these soldiers.

To do that, and to evacuate the Sudan, recourse was had to Charles George Gordon, one of England's most popular military heroes. His ancestors had fought for Prince Charlie in the "Forty-five" and for King George before Quebec. He himself had been in the Crimean War, and had won the name of "Chinese Gordon" because of his work as commander of the miscellaneous defenders of Shanghai during a time of rebellion (see page 742). He was familiar with the Sudan; for he had served there as governor-general under the Khedive and had made himself unpopular with the influential slave-traders by his rigorous measures against their traffic. Now the English newspapers demanded that he be sent to Khartum, capital of the Sudan. He was temperamentally unfitted for a task which consisted of withdrawing and retreating. Matters had not yet come to such a pass that fighting was unavoidable, and the British officials in Egypt would have preferred for this delicate situation someone more diplomatic and less audacious. Nevertheless, Gordon was sent to Khartum, where he arrived in February, 1884.

He probably could have carried out his mission of withdrawal had he begun at once, for the Mahdi had not yet laid siege to Khartum. But Gordon did not intend to withdraw; he planned to stay there and save the city. Within two months he was cut off from Cairo by the Mahdi's dervishes and began to call for a relief expedition. By May it was obvious to most people that such a force must be sent. But, hoping against hope, the anti-imperialistic Gladstone delayed sending it until autumn. The Mahdi in the meantime pressed hard on Khartum, where, with food supplies dwindling, Gordon was withstanding the siege in magnificent fashion. The commander of the relief column, at last realizing that the slow hauling of boats around the Nile rapids involved too much delay, and awakening to Gordon's peril, sent part of his troops hurrying overland. Late in January, 1885, the vanguard came in sight of Khartum—just too late. Over the Sudan capital flew the green flag of the Mahdi, whose dervishes only two days before had captured the city and murdered Gordon.

The Sudan was lost, but the British were still faced with the problem of what to do with Egypt. It had to be protected from the Mahdi, that was certain; and that would take time. Had Turkey, whose Sultan was the hereditary overlord of Egypt, been able or willing to assume responsibility for it, the British would probably have left the country altogether. The Turks, however, taking French advice, refused to give any guarantees. Europe shrugged her shoulders. The international financial obligations of the Egyptian government were now over £100,000,000; and the drop in cotton prices, coincident with the recovery of the Southern states after the American Civil War, seemed to preclude the economic recovery of Egypt. England was to get out of these troubles under the clever management of a member of her great banking family, the Barings. This was Sir Evelyn Baring, afterward Earl of Cromer, consul general at Cairo from 1883 to 1907.

# The New Empire

Cromer's work (for we shall refer to Baring by his later title) was carried on under peculiar circumstances. The Turkish Sultan, as head of the western Mohammedans, was always an important factor in Egypt, and in addition received a yearly tribute as overlord. The Khedive appointed and dismissed all officials, supposedly formulated policies, and signed and enforced decrees. The Caisse de la Dette, or international commission representing European bondholders, still retained control of certain taxes and from the receipts subtracted interest charges. In addition, by the "capitulations," or customary privileges granted foreigners, consular courts and mixed tribunals had jurisdiction over criminal cases in which Europeans or Americans were involved; and, more serious yet, the capitulations forbade the levying of any direct tax on foreigners. Finally there was Cromer, British consul general. All he did was to *advise* the Khedive, and anyone might do that. But British troops paced the streets of Cairo, and that was sufficient reason for the new Khedive to accept Cromer's suggestions.

The choice of an Egyptian prime minister, the appointment of the Egyptian cabinet, the desirability of new legislation, the wisdom of selecting various Englishmen as advisers to the heads of the financial, judicial, and educational departments, the nomination also of an Englishman as sirdar of the Egyptian army—upon matters such as these the Khedive consulted with the consul general. To a resourceful mind the situation gave an opportunity to embark on an extensive program. And Cromer did so. His first definite accomplishment was to redeem Egypt from bankruptcy. He did this by adding to the Egyptian debt and by spending the money on irrigation. The magnificent but half-completed dam on the lower Nile, the work of French engineers, was finished, and at the First Cataract of the Nile, at Aswan, a second great dam was constructed which made possible, through the new irrigation, two crops a year in place of one. The "three C's"—courbash, corvée, corruption—now drew Cromer's attention. The courbash, or whip of rhinoceros hide, which was freely used on native workers, was banished. The corvée, compulsory and unpaid labor on the canals, was done away with. Political corruption, for which Egypt was notorious, almost disappeared. The consul general kept an eagle eye upon his civil service. Carefully recruited in the United Kingdom, where Cromer was said to have accepted men only from Oxford, Cambridge, or Trinity College, Dublin, it was well paid and highly honored. The rehabilitation of Egypt on the material side went on rapidly under its direction.

In the interim Egypt began slowly and painfully to reconstruct her army. The cowed and beaten forces which had feebly resisted the occupation were without pay, without officers, without discipline. These defects were remedied primarily by Colonel Herbert Horatio Kitchener. When the latter became sirdar, or commander in chief of the Anglo-Egyptian forces, in 1892, things began to hum. No married officer might hope to serve under Kitchener. One sick leave might be obtained from the sirdar, and only one. The army was Kitchener's life; it must be that of his subordinates also. To every native Egyptian battalion he assigned three British soldiers, two to serve as bimbashis, or majors, one as a noncommissioned drill sergeant. For the black battalions attached to Egypt's army the number was increased to four. With these few whites Kitchener was content. They were all young. The sirdar in 1898 was only forty-eight years old, and but one English officer in the Egyptian army touched half a century.

The Sudan after Gordon's death had been given over to ten years of frightful anarchy. It was a hornet's nest ever threatening Egypt, and Cromer determined upon its recovery. This time the British resolved to undertake the task scientifically. The campaign was left in Kitchener's hands, and he planned one to last from two to three years, pushing on slowly southward by railway, telegraph, steamboat, and camel corps. By 1898 his army came in contact with the dervishes, the soldiers of the new Mahdi, who were annihilated in a great battle at Omdurman. The sirdar occupied Khartum, and then, with a number of gunboats and several hundred men, sailed up the Nile five hundred miles to Fashoda. Here the British expansion from north to south met the French expansion across northern Africa. Kitchener was in a hurry; for the French, under Captain Marchand, had already reached the Upper Nile, having come in a northeasterly direction from the French Congo. The French had planned for this Marchand expedition to meet another, which was to come across Abyssinia from French Somaliland; but the latter never arrived. Marchand, however, was flying the tricolor at Fashoda, and Kitchener was determined to oust him. The French could claim priority; the British, that they were acting for Egypt, to which the Sudan belonged in theory. Kitchener's force, moreover, was overwhelmingly superior. Consequently France was unable to support her claims, and Marchand lowered the tricolor in 1898. This dramatic clash of imperial ambitions produced excitement at Paris and London, and it might have had serious consequences had not the French backed down.

Kitchener, after this episode at Fashoda, returned to Khartum and completed the annexation of the entire Sudan conjointly to England and to Egypt. The flags of these two nations were to fly, side by side, at equal elevation. England realized that it would not do to annex the region to Egypt alone, since if this were done the obnoxious capitulations would apply to the Sudan. On the other hand, England had no exclusive right to the country. The reconquest of it had been planned by Englishmen, and the Egyptian troops had been British-led; but the Egyptian treasury had paid the bill, and Kitchener's army was composed for the most part of Egyptians. Hence there was to be a condominium (joint rule): a governor-general would administer the Sudan in the name of both countries.

Progress in the Sudan, however, was somewhat less rapid than it had been in Egypt. There was little money to spend and a vast region to govern. To tempt back the old inhabitants, to restore law and order, to introduce new agricultural methods, to improve navigation, to make taxation and justice equitable—these were a few of the problems. The joint rule was succeeding to a remarkable degree, principally through the agency of young British residents scattered through the Sudan and armed with independent administrative powers, when the World War broke out.

To Egypt the twentieth century brought discontent. This did not have its origin in economic troubles; one could not criticize Cromer effectively on that score. What made Cromer unpopular and what led to his recall was the growth of Egyptian nationalism, a movement partly religious, partly political, directed toward the expulsion of foreigners and toward Egyptian independence. The British gave in to it in part, and substituted a less autocratic Englishman for Cromer, who, although just, had been unbending in his relations with the Egyptians. The result was, however, that Egypt became more restless than ever. Since the reformers were divided into two factions, the new consul general advised the Khedive to recognize one of them by appointing its leader to head the government. The appointee was promptly murdered; and ex-President Theodore Roosevelt of the United States, emerging at this time from hunting big game in the jungle, proclaimed in a public speech in Cairo that the British should either withdraw or else rule Egypt with a firm hand. The nomination of Kitchener as consul general indicated that they chose the latter course.

Whether Kitchener would have succeeded where Cromer had failed is problematical. Tackling his new work with speed and dispatch, he came to the rescue of the poorer peasantry by a law which made it impossible for usurers to seize their land. He also increased the number of elected members in the Egyptian legislative council and gave slightly increased powers to that assembly. Before it was possible to judge fairly of his work, however, the World War brought it to an end.

We turn now to South Africa, where, as we have seen, two British colonies—Cape Colony and Natal—were firmly rooted on the sea-coast, and two Boer (Dutch) republics,—the South African Republic (Transvaal) and the Orange Free State—were entrenched in the interior (see page 679).

The Boers, particularly those in the Transvaal, continued restive throughout the century. They ran into all kinds of difficulties with the natives and with the British missionaries, who sponsored actively and not always wisely the cause of the Negro. The Transvaal (South African Republic) seemed powerless to control even its own citizens, who did as they wanted, paid taxes or not as they chose, and on the slightest provocation either resisted their own authorities or, driving their cattle before them, sought homes even more remote. As for the inhabitants of the Free State, they likewise were unhappy. The newly discovered diamond mines, they thought, lay within their boundaries, but Cape Colony disputed this claim. The question was arbitrated, and the Cape was given the mines. The Free Staters felt a new grievance.

Thus lay the situation when Disraeli became prime minister in 1874. His Colonial Secretary, Lord Carnarvon, was eager to federate all South Africa on the Canadian model. To do this he sent out the historian Froude to persuade the inhabitants of South Africa, both Boer and British, that they should follow Canada's precedent. Admirable as such an idea was, its chance of success depended on public opinion. This, it is evident, was not favorable. Carnarvon tried to force the issue. His commissioner, Shepstone, in 1877 suddenly annexed the Transvaal, basing his action on the anarchy which was apparent and on a petition signed by a number of its citizens requesting annexation.

This hasty performance of Carnarvon's ended what little chance there had been for the voluntary federation of South Africa. The Boers in the Cape, it must be remembered, still outnumbered the British there, and to them, as well as to the Boers in the Transvaal, this annexation seemed an act of tyranny. The new British governor was unpopular, and so was his tiny army. Loud and vociferous in their complaints, the Boers refused to co-operate, nor would they pay taxes.

Among those who listened was Gladstone, now in the midst of an election campaign. The South African policy of Disraeli proved an easy target for his scorn, and upon Gladstone's return to office in 1880 the Boers expected immediately to recover their liberty. The prime minister's time, however, was occupied with many matters; his missionary supporters were opposed to complete independence for

SOUTH AFRICA AT THE TIME OF THE BOER WAR

the Negro-hating Boers; and so he delayed action. Not so the Boers, who attacked the British garrisons and who terribly mauled the British army at Majuba Hill in 1881.

Gladstone knew that, although it was possible to subdue the South African Republic, such action would be expensive, and also unjust if the original annexation had been consummated without the consent of the inhabitants. He therefore made a convention with the rebels by which their independence was restored, with a string attached. They were at liberty to manage their own affairs as they saw fit, but suzerainty was reserved for England. A vague word, "suzerainty," and destined to cause trouble later.

While the British guns boomed at Alexandria, a young Englishman was busily at work in South Africa laying the foundations of a colossal fortune. Cecil Rhodes was both a son of Oxford and a son of the frontier. Rough in manner, as well as in act, he was a dreamer and an idealist. He sought money and he found it; but the end in view was neither paltry nor selfish. What he wanted was to extend north and south throughout Africa a broad path of empire, all the way from the Cape to Cairo—not empire in the old sense of that word, ruled and administered from London, but empire in the sense of self-governing, liberty-loving states, bound to one another and the motherland by ties of language, religion, blood, and common political institutions.

Rhodes's first endeavor in this direction was through orthodox political channels, the legislature of Cape Colony. As a member of that body he tried to interest first the Cape and then England in Bechuanaland, that indeterminate region, unoccupied except for its scattered Negro tribes, which lay between German Southwest Africa and the Transvaal. He knew that the Boers regarded Bechuanaland as coming legitimately within the range of their interests,—at least the eastern part of it; also he suspected that unless Britain acted quickly the Germans would stretch out their hands across this territory until it joined that of the Boers. This once done, it was "good-by" to any all-red line on the map of Africa from Cairo to the Cape. Bechuanaland, in Rhodes's opinion, was the "Suez Canal" to the interior; it must be under British control.

Rhodes found politics slow and irksome. He tried to get the Cape to take Bechuanaland, but the Cape saw nothing save added expense in that region. Shifting his efforts from Cape Town to London, he had better luck. Great Britain, largely through his insistence, did consent to annex the southern part of Bechuanaland as a crown colony and to throw a protectorate over the rest. To accomplish this much of his dream took many years, however, and consequently the impetuous and dictatorial Rhodes sought for quicker ways to his end. One of them might be to fill his purse to overflowing. This he did, both through the diamond mines at Kimberley, which he organized into a syndicate, and through the Consolidated Goldfields, Ltd., the most important of the mining corporations which in the early nineties were exploiting the newly discovered gold deposits of the Transvaal.

With Bechuanaland earmarked for the empire, Rhodes turned his attention to south-central Africa. Here was a vast undulating plateau of grassy pasture and woodland through which flowed the Zambezi. This no-man's land stretched for hundreds of miles, all the way from the great lakes in the north to the Limpopo River and the Transvaal on the south. To the east was Portuguese East Africa

(Mozambique), with boundaries ill-defined; to the west, the Kalahari Desert; and beyond it, Portuguese Angola. The Portuguese colonies, low-lying and malarial, seemed of trifling consequence. The unoccupied interior, on the other hand, Rhodes thought should be pounced upon speedily for the British Empire.

It did not seem feasible to him to gain these ends by appealing either to the Cape or to the imperial Parliament. He therefore set his money to work and sent his agents northward to the court of Lobengula, king of the Matabele, a fierce-fighting branch of the Zulus, to bribe, bully, or cajole that monarch into signing away his land. Others were engaged in this same task; but Rhodes's men had more champagne and rifles wherewith to please Lobengula. Consequently the latter sealed the bond with his elephant tusk, and Rhodes, delighted, took his hard-earned contract to London.

Next followed the fight for a charter. Rhodes was a suspicious character to many of the orthodox imperialists. He had stoutly defended the rights of the Cape against imperial interference, and he was a self-made man who did not exactly belong to the official ruling class. But again his money stood him in good stead. He subscribed handsomely to the cause of the Irish Nationalists and won their favor; and he interested a number of philanthropic noblemen in his scheme and in himself. Thus he got his charter; organized the British South African Company, the last of the great chartered companies for imperialistic enterprises; and returned to Cape Town, there to direct its activities.

From the British settlements at the Cape to what afterward became Rhodesia was a long journey. The railroad went only a small part of the way, and from there one had to follow the old missionary trail the whole length of Bechuanaland until one passed beyond the Transvaal. Thence it was necessary to hew one's way through swamp, forest, and desert many weary miles. Detours had to be taken if the fierce Matabele warriors were to be avoided; and soldiers were essential to guide and to protect the settlers, who must be equipped before they would commence their trek. Rhodes bent himself to the task. Already by 1891 Salisbury, the capital of Rhodesia, tactfully named for the Conservative prime minister, "showed the beginnings of a busy little town," with some four hundred European inhabitants whose food and supplies had been sent overland 1700 miles by the company.

Meanwhile Rhodes had become prime minister of the Cape Colony and a privy councilor of the queen. As such he might be interested legitimately in the plight of the British miners in the Transvaal gold fields. These miners had not entered the territory of the South

African Republic unwanted; the Boers had been glad to receive them, for they enriched the republic. The Boers, however, had not counted on there being so many miners. By 1895 they outnumbered the adult Boers, and the city of Johannesburg had a population of about one hundred thousand. The Boers were unwilling to admit the miners —these *Uitlanders* (or foreigners), as they called them—to citizenship in their republic; nevertheless, they taxed them unmercifully, and of the money thus raised little was spent on the local government of Johannesburg. Dynamite was heavily taxed, and so was coal; but the city in which and around which the miners lived was deficient in respect to water supply, lighting, schools, fire department, and other equipment customarily regarded as part and parcel of urban civilization. The miners, in their distress, turned to their friend Cecil Rhodes, and he determined to come to their rescue. The British government could do nothing, since the Transvaal was autonomous, if not completely independent. Consequently Rhodes, impatient, adopted a new plan. By means of his money he would stir up a rebellion of the miners; by means of his political influence he could obtain permission for the police of the South African Company to patrol that strip of Bechuanaland through which his new emigrants came and went to and from Rhodesia. Rhodes foresaw that if anarchy once broke out in "Jo'burg," which was not far from the frontier, its British inhabitants would petition for armed protection, and then the British patrols could dash straight from the border to their succor. Once the British flag flew over Johannesburg the chances were excellent that it would remain there.

And so this man, who had so unselfishly labored for South Africa's good, forgot he was Her Majesty's premier of the Cape, forgot his old ties of friendship with those of Dutch blood, and plunged headlong to disaster. His plot exploded prematurely. Dr. Jameson, in charge of his police on the border, drove at Johannesburg as planned; but he never reached that city. Instead, he was captured by the Boers. The Jameson raid was a fiasco; and Cecil Rhodes, it was evident to many, had disgraced himself and also his country.

This affair ended all hope of reconciliation between Boer and Briton. European public opinion was anti-British. The German emperor, Victoria's grandson, William II, went so far as to send a message of sympathy to the president of the Transvaal, old "Oom Paul" Kruger. This German interference tended to make the British sympathetic toward Rhodes; but even if the British government had put Rhodes in prison for his share in the raid, instead of merely depriving him of his privy councilorship, it is doubtful if the suspicious Boers would have forgiven that attempted coup d'état. Besides, the memory of Majuba was still strong among them: there they had beaten the British once, and they felt that they could do it again. They bought arms and ammunition on a large scale, paying for them with money made from the Uitlanders; and as they did this the British government made the cause of the latter its own.

Powerful in the cabinet of Lord Salisbury, prime minister at this time, was his Colonial Secretary, Joseph Chamberlain (see page 796), who determined to force the issue. The Boers gave way somewhat. They promised larger appropriations for local government, and agreed to lower their franchise requirement from a ten years' residence to one of seven; they would lower it even to five if England would relinquish all claim to sovereignty over their republic. This Chamberlain would not grant, and by the summer of 1899 a deadlock was reached. British troops came pouring into South Africa, and the Boers decided that it was now or never. They gave an ultimatum to the British, received no answer, waited a certain time, and then declared war.

The Boer War (1899–1902) shook the empire to its foundations. It found Britain without a friend in Europe. Even Britons themselves were sadly divided as to the justice of their cause. The British army was shown to be in a pitiful plight as far as military technique was concerned. British prestige was to suffer grievously from the fact that fifty thousand Boers—for that was the total man power of the two republics—could stand off the mighty resources of the British Empire for three years. In only one way was it a comfort to loyal subjects of the queen: it proved that Canada, South Australia, and New Zealand stood steadfastly by the motherland.

During the autumn of 1899 the Boers were victorious. Invading Natal, they defeated the main British army at Colenso. Then they bottled up the British garrisons at Ladysmith and at Mafeking. The next year favored the British. Lord Roberts in command, with Kitchener as chief of staff, swept through the Transvaal and the Free State, the latter country being allied with the Transvaal. He relieved the garrisons, and captured both Bloemfontein, the capital of the Free State, and Pretoria, the capital of the Transvaal. Apparently the war was over. Roberts returned to England, leaving Kitchener to complete such "mopping-up" operations as were necessary.

But the war was not over. The British had a quarter of a million soldiers in South Africa, while the Boers at no time during the war mustered fifty thousand, old men and boys included; but the Boers were ably led by General Louis Botha, in command of the Transvaalers, and by General Christian De Wet, heading the men of the

Free State. For nearly a year and a half more they kept up the fight. South Africa was a huge region which the Boer knew and the Briton did not. A guerrilla warfare was suited to the psychology and equipment of the Boer farmers, who were capital horsemen and dead shots. Such informal fighting reduced military discipline to a minimum and permitted frequent if dangerous visits home. It has always been the most difficult type of opposition for regular troops to overcome. Rapid mobility, surprise attacks, and quick escapes left the conventional fighters bewildered and wondering from what direction the next blow would descend. Thus the Boers fought on, month after month, a losing war; and all the while their ranks were thinning fast by death and capture. They could not even afford to win victories if they lost many men in the process.

Meanwhile Kitchener came to a new decision. He would make of the entire country one gigantic net, burn down Boer farmhouses, ruin crops, herd women and children in refugee camps, build blockhouses but a thousand paces apart, lace barbed wire and trenches between them, and by a number of swift, sharp drives redeem more and more land from the Boers until, either captured or exhausted, they gave over the fight. These methods won out. By the summer of 1902 the war was practically ended. Only six thousand soldiers were left to the Free State and ten thousand to the Transvaal. The British were agreeable to a negotiated peace, promising a degree of self-government within the empire. For a time, however, it looked as though the Boers would not accept. De Wet was for continuing the war; but Botha pointed out to the soldier delegates that further resistance was madness, and to his pleas were added those of young General Smuts, of whom history was to hear much in later days.

In accordance with the peace terms, the Boers were to lay down their arms and to recognize the sovereignty of the British crown. They were not to be deprived of their personal liberty or property. Military government was to be succeeded at the earliest date by civil, and, as soon after as it was feasible, representative institutions were to be introduced. The Dutch language was placed on a parity with English in the schools and courts. No indemnities were to be levied to pay the cost of the war; on the contrary, the British government granted £3,000,000 to assist the people back to their farms.

Lord Milner, who had gone to South Africa as High Commissioner before the war, was governor of the two new crown colonies, the Transvaal and the Orange River. He quickly spent this £3,000,000 granted him by Parliament in buying food, purchasing livestock, rehabilitating a desert land. He borrowed ten times that sum on the surety of the British government and spent it wisely and well. He then tried to entice the Boer leaders into accepting nominations to a legislative council; but warily they refused. They wanted Milner solely responsible. The latter made an unfortunate blunder in importing Chinese coolies to work in the gold mines. This act created an uproar in England, and was one of the main causes which led to the ousting of the Conservative party there in 1905 (see page 801), a political turnover which resulted in the speedy triumph of self-government in the two conquered colonies.

Milner had approved a new constitution for the Transvaal. It provided for a popularly elected legislature with control over the purse, but the governor and the executive officials were to remain appointed. One of the first acts of the triumphant Liberals in London was to suspend this constitution. In place thereof they conferred responsible government, long enjoyed by the Cape, upon both the Transvaal and the Orange River Colony. This was a brave act inasmuch as Britain's late enemies were likely to triumph at the polls; for many of the miners had scattered during the war, and a Boer majority was inevitable.

We have already studied the process by which the various self-governing colonies north of the United States became welded together into the Dominion of Canada (see page 686). In Australia, as we shall shortly see, another dominion had just been formed. In South Africa the four British colonies were now to merge into a union. These federations and mergers within the empire are important because they reflect the political sagacity and experience of the English-speaking peoples and offer a hopeful model for other and wider federations. Therefore, rather than break the continuity of the South African story, we shall take them up here, describing the South African, the Australian, the New Zealand, and the Canadian situation, and the relations of these commonwealths one to another and to the mother country in the days before the World War.

The Union of South Africa was inaugurated in 1910 under the leadership of Louis Botha, late commander in chief of the Boer army. He had been the first premier of the new colony of the Transvaal, and was now to be the first premier also of the new dominion. He was trusted by Boer and Briton alike. He had proved an excellent fighter; at the same time his moderation, good sense, strong character, and wise judgment had been demonstrated again and again throughout the war. Unlike the Canadians and the Australians, the men of South Africa preferred a rather centralized state. The four colonies —the Transvaal, the Orange River Colony (soon to revert to the old name, "Orange Free State"), Natal, and Cape Colony—retained their political identity and certain local administrative powers; but, aside from these, almost all important matters were left to the Union Parliament, which was to meet in Cape Town. The only real concessions to local feeling were the constitutional retention of the right to vote by colored men in the Cape, and the location of the executive offices of the government at Pretoria and of the judiciary at Bloemfontein, the capitals of the Transvaal and the Free State respectively. Four problems promptly put the political tact and acumen of Botha to the test: the relations of Boers and Britons, the treatment of the Negroes and Hindus, and the labor troubles in the mining districts.

The South African party, which Botha headed, naturally was composed of men of Boer blood, some of moderate mind, some the reverse. Botha's own preference was for moderation—for letting bygones be bygones and for working in harmony with the British. It proved difficult for him to do so. Many of his old soldiers resented his favoring immigration from England, and thought it wrong for their old commander to attend, as he did, imperial conferences in London. They looked askance at his accepting an honorary generalship in the British army. Under the leadership of General Hertzog some of the Boers repudiated Botha's leadership. The Free Staters had been bitter-enders in a war which was none of their choosing, and now they forced the issue. The South African party endorsed Botha, and Hertzog, discomfited, withdrew the minority of the Boers, organizing the National party under his leadership.

There was much more unanimity of opinion in regard to the Negro. The blacks outnumbered the whites in every province of the Union, the ratio being two to one in the Free State, three to one in the Transvaal, nearly four to one in the Cape Colony, and almost ten to one in Natal. Both Boer and Briton considered this a threat to white supremacy, and Botha's determination to segregate the races met with the approval of his parliament. Land was given the Negroes, and provision was made to prevent its alienation. A special form of government was adopted for these allotted tracts, somewhat paternalistic in character, putting them partly under Negro supervision, partly under that of white inspectors.

There were likewise a large number of Hindus in South Africa, imported to work on the sugar plantations. They were British subjects; but they were discriminated against, a special head tax being levied against them, free movement within the country being checked, and free immigration being prohibited. The Indian Nationalists in India complained bitterly of the ill-treatment of their brothers in South Africa, and Gandhi (see page 928), then a young lawyer, intervened on their behalf. Botha soothed troubled feelings by passing an immigration law which did not mention Indians by name but which excluded them none the less. Gandhi, however, sought the removal of other restrictions, and led a pilgrimage of Indians from Natal to Pretoria. The Hindu leader was placed in prison and then released. With the peculiar chivalry which frequently characterized his career, Gandhi suddenly ceased from agitation. He thought it unfair to perplex Botha further, in view of new difficulties which confronted the premier in relation to labor. A strike broke out which involved both miners and railway employees. Revolutionary socialism was behind it, and the red flag flew over Johannesburg. Botha struck at that city with a hastily organized force, seized the ringleaders, and put them on a ship bound for England. This act presumably was illegal; and British opinion, both Liberal and Conservative, denounced it heartily, since sound constitutional guarantees of British liberty were thrown to the discard. But the South African party stood united behind its premier; and there was nothing England could do, inasmuch as the Union was a dominion and therefore self-governing.

During the Boer War, in 1901, Australia also became a federated dominion. The birth had been long delayed, but it was inevitable. Commercially it was absurd that six different colonies, with separate railway systems and separate tariffs, should hold aloof from one another in this isolated all-British continent. Politically it was evident that both Germany and the United States were extending their sway in Pacific waters. These countries, perhaps, were not much to be feared; but the men of Sydney and Melbourne had no intention of permitting swarms of little yellow men from Japan, whose power also was growing, to dig in upon Australia's northern shores. This they could better prevent by standing shoulder to shoulder in a firm union.

The making of a constitution was a long-drawn-out affair, lasting many years; for the Australian constitution-makers had more complicated problems to face than those which confronted the American constitutional convention in 1787. Not only were the widely scattered Australian colonies divided into both large and small states, like the American colonies in the eighteenth century, but railways had already been constructed on different gauges, and a whole network of intricate economic problems had appeared which did not confront the men who wrote the constitution of the United States. None the less, the form of government drawn up in the antipodes more closely resembled the American prototype than any other British constitution. It provided for a strong upper house, the Senate, to represent the Australian states rather than the Australian popula-

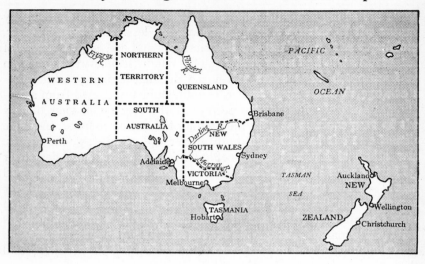

AUSTRALIA AND NEW ZEALAND

tion, and it provided, on the model of the United States, for a supreme court, the permission of which was necessary before appeals could be made to the Privy Council in England on cases arising from purely Australian disputes. In one major respect, however, it followed British precedent rather than that of the United States by adopting responsible government, which the separate colonies had long enjoyed (see page 664). There was to be a premier, who must be supported by a majority vote in the Australian parliament. The constitution once adopted, Australian nationalism grew apace, and Australians for the first time began seriously to consider the extent to which they were prepared to stand alone and the extent to which they would unify their national policy with that of England and of the other dominions.

Canada, as we have seen, had completed federation as far back as 1867, thus becoming the first of the dominions. Certain adverse circumstances, which could not be overcome simply by drawing up a constitution, no matter how comprehensive or intelligent, still kept Canada from complete unity. In two respects, one geographic and the other racial, there still remained work to be done. Means of communication were needed from east to west to counterbalance the gravitational pull of the United States from north to south, and it was also highly desirable that racial antagonism between the French minority and the British majority be reduced to a minimum.

Canadian statesmen, as we have noticed (see page 687), long wrestled with the problem of linking the Atlantic and Pacific coasts

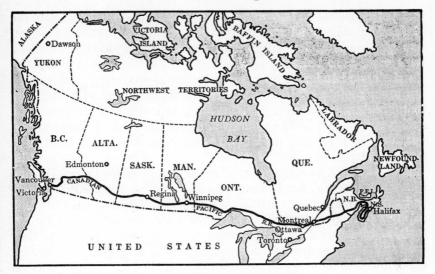

THE DOMINION OF CANADA

with a Canadian railway until it was pushed to completion under the vigorous and determined premier Sir John Macdonald. The first such transcontinental line had been opened in the United States in 1869; but Canada was far from being as wealthy as her southern neighbor, and the final spike of the Canadian Pacific Railway was not driven in, at a lonely spot in British Columbia, until late in 1885. This famous corporation, although privately controlled and operated at that time, became virtually a semipublic enterprise. It built hotels, sold farms, established transpacific and transatlantic steamship lines, and advertised extensively in Europe for emigrants. It became perhaps the greatest single agent of Canadian nationalism.

Probably the most important service of the Canadian Pacific was the opening of the prairie regions which, as we recall, had been taken over from the Hudson's Bay Company in 1869. At that time there were barely 12,000 people in Manitoba, which became a province the following year, and only a handful in the remainder of the vast territory from which the provinces of Alberta and Saskatchewan were to be carved in 1905. By 1901 the total population of the prairie regions had risen to 419,000; then came a tremendous influx which brought the number by 1911 to 1,327,000, about a third of the total population of Canada. Some of the newcomers were from the old Canadian provinces, some from the British Isles, some from the Continent, and many from the United States. Manitoba, Alberta, and Saskatchewan still offered virgin fields to the pioneers who flocked to this last frontier. As in the Dakotas and other states to the south, they devoted themselves principally to the raising of wheat, which became Canada's chief source of wealth. In 1867 Canada had furnished less than 3 per cent of the British grain imports; by 1914 she had overtaken seven other grain-producing regions and furnished more than 30 per cent, standing in second place, just behind the United States. Without the transcontinental railway communication such a development would have been out of the question; the grain at least, and perhaps the provinces too, would have gone to the United States.

The French Canadians, the other serious problem facing Dominion statesmanship, were clannish and exclusive, refusing to adopt the English language or British ways. They were Roman Catholics and insisted upon Catholic schools, wherein French should be the language of instruction. Increasing very rapidly in numbers, they were spilling over from their original province of Quebec into Ontario, and also into the prairie provinces, farther west, where friction speedily arose with their British neighbors.

Fortunately for the Dominion, these racial difficulties were held in check through the wisdom and adroitness of a famous Canadian prime minister of French extraction, Sir Wilfrid Laurier, who headed the government from 1896 to 1911. Gracious and learned, speaking with equal facility in French or English, this competent statesman succeeded in making the French and the British work together for the good of Canada. He straightened out the school question and brought about a working agreement with the papacy on disputed issues. Throughout his career he succeeded in dampening the fiery enthusiasm of the more extreme French Canadians, bent on quarreling with their British compatriots.

So popular, indeed, was Laurier that he might have continued indefinitely as prime minister had he not sought Canadian agreement to a reciprocity tariff agreement with the United States in 1911. For twelve years just before the confederation of 1867 the two countries had drastically lowered the duties on each other's wares; but since that time the tariff walls had grown higher and higher, particularly in the United States. In 1911 the Congress at Washington proposed free trade in many Canadian and American products, with low duties on the rest. Twenty years earlier, Canada might have welcomed such reciprocity, but in the meantime she had become actively interested in protecting her own growing industries. Canadian manufacturers were influential through their contributions to the campaign funds of the Conservatives, who staged a bitter fight when Laurier appealed to the country in a general election on the issue.

# The New Empire

Patriotism became mixed with economics in the campaign. The Conservatives argued that reciprocity might be the first step toward annexation by the United States, and injudicious remarks by some high officials at Washington increased Canadian prejudice on that point. Loyalty to the empire was stressed by the Conservatives, who managed to carry the day, bringing Sir Robert Borden into office as prime minister and ending the fifteen-year Liberal government of Laurier.

In addition to South Africa, Australia, and Canada, there were two other Dominions, New Zealand and Newfoundland. Self-government in both dated back many decades. Newfoundland, it is true, was both poor and small; but, thanks to the work of John Cabot, it prided itself upon being England's oldest colony, as far as discovery was concerned. Since they had no separate provinces to be brought together, New Zealand and Newfoundland did not require any such federation as took place in the other three. The five dominions all belonged in the same category: they all possessed responsible government, and were clearly autonomous in all domestic matters. There still remained, however, the question of imperial federation, to bind these scattered groups of overseas Britons into a more compact relationship.

In the summer of 1897 Queen Victoria's diamond jubilee was celebrated at London; and although it was primarily a tribute to the beloved queen, it was also a graphic portrayal of the magnitude of her empire and of the triumphant progress of Greater Britain. The jubilee parade was led by a thousand men from beyond the seven seas in uniform: Dyak police from North Borneo, Maoris from New Zealand, Hausas from West Africa, mounted riflemen from the Cape Colony, armed men from Hong Kong (some of them European, some Sikh, some Chinese), black fighters in the employ of the Royal Niger Company, mounted Zaptiehs from Cyprus, a contingent of Rhodesian horse, men of Australia clad in brown, and Canadians in the varied uniforms of thirty military organizations. The colonial premiers in sober black were, however, perhaps the most significant feature, symbolizing as they did the spread of British liberty beyond the sea. To these colonial premiers Joseph Chamberlain made definite overtures on the question of imperial federation, which had been discussed academically in one way or another earlier in the century; but he was rebuffed. The premiers gathered in London had no power to negotiate with the British government; and if they had possessed power they would not have utilized it, for any change in the status quo presumably would have meant a sharing of the burden of defense, and therefore an increase in taxation, which their respective democracies would have resented.

Chamberlain, being a determined man, summoned a new conference in 1902, immediately after the Boer War. If imperial federation was not to be had in the field of politics, he would try that of economics; and the conference over which he presided did commit itself in favor of imperial preferential tariffs. Chamberlain's own party, however, the Conservatives, was shortly to go down to defeat on this matter. The colonies had long been used to tariffs, and it was quite to their way of thinking that the empire should become more united commercially. Such a doctrine, however, ran counter to the free-trade tradition now firmly established within England, and in the election of 1906 the British electorate, impressed by the Liberal slogan "Your food will cost you more," refused to abandon free imports.

At the next imperial conference (1907) the idea was aired again. The more doubtful the British at home felt about Chamberlain's idea, the more acceptable did it become overseas. Australia, New Zealand, Cape Colony, and Natal did their best for the cause of inter-imperial tariffs. Once again they were defeated, owing to lack of support in England, with the Liberals in power now; and without the concurrence of the British government, of course, nothing could be done.

In 1911 came the last and the most important of these conferences before the World War. A definite effort on the part of New Zealand to reorganize the entire constitutional machinery of the empire through the creation of a super-Parliament was rejected, partly because the scheme was loosely drawn and impracticable. For the first time, formal consultation between Downing Street and the dominions in regard to foreign affairs occurred when Sir Edward Grey took the dominion premiers into his confidence on recent foreign policy and promised to continue to do so in the future. The conference saw also the beginning of a determined drive for military and naval preparedness that was to continue until 1914. Decided strides were made in regard to naval co-operation in particular; in this, New Zealand, as the most isolated, was the most enthusiastic of the dominions. That country had hoped to have the Pacific patrolled by an all-dominion fleet, of New Zealand, Australian, Canadian, and South African ships. When this did not meet the approval of the Admiralty, New Zealand cheerfully offered to contribute a battleship to be used as the Admiralty directed. South Africa was the least interested in regard to dominion naval affairs, since it was the poorest of the dominions and since the memories of the Boer War still rankled.

# The New Empire

Premier Botha was willing to endorse only a small subsidy, and South Africa would not go beyond that.

Meanwhile the Australian flag made its debut on the high seas; for Australia proudly demanded her own fleet. She insisted that naval vessels for which she paid must be stationed in Australian waters and that, although they might be built in England and manned by officers and crews trained in the royal navy, their control and direction must be determined by her parliament and not by England's. As far as Australia was concerned, the aroused interest in naval and military preparedness at this time was caused by Asiatic rather than by European complications. Europe was far distant, but Japan was near. In consequence the Australians adopted universal, compulsory military service—the first Anglo-Saxon nation to take that step—but limited it to home defense (see page 871).

Canada began naval activity by following Australian precedent, and then shifted to a different policy. The Canadian Liberal party, which was in power, was dubious about building warships at all; and if Canada were to build them, it preferred that they should form a Canadian fleet, under Canadian control, rather than be a mere contribution to the royal navy. Many Liberals dreaded lest Canada be drawn, willy-nilly, into the dangerous maelstrom of European rivalries. Consequently the Canadian government bought two small cruisers for the Dominion, stationing one on the Pacific and the other on the Atlantic. Then, in the same year as the conference, Laurier's fifteen-year Liberal ministry, as we saw, was defeated, and the Conservative party came into power in Canada, waving the Union Jack.

London was jubilant at this change in parties. The new Canadian premier, Sir Robert Borden, was immediately informed that a naval crisis confronted the empire, as Germany was competing with England in the building of warships, and that help was needed from the dominions. Borden instantly promised three large battleships for the royal navy, a promise he was to have difficulty in fulfilling. The proposal was bitterly fought by the Canadian Liberals, who maintained that the scheme menaced Canadian autonomy. The French Canadians were particularly recalcitrant. The Conservative majority in the House of Commons at Ottawa finally approved the bill, only to have it rejected by the Liberal majority still surviving in the Senate. Borden did not choose to hold a new election on this issue, and the World War began before anything effective was done.

Chamberlain's proposals thus were rejected, one after another. Neither in armament nor in political co-operation nor in economic policy were the dominions and the mother country to be drawn really closer at this time. Inertia was apparently too strong. Chamberlain's efforts, however, had not been wasted. Although they produced no immediate institutional results, their sentimental influence for unity was strong, both in England and in the dominions. Each had been given an opportunity to see the others' point of view and to appreciate the spirit of the empire as a whole. These preliminary endeavors were no doubt partly responsible for the magnificent and very tangible co-operation which the dominions were soon to demonstrate in the World War, when the achievements of the Anzacs at Gallipoli, the Canadians at Ypres, and the South Africans in handling their local troubles disproved the German contention that the British Empire was simply a "rope of sand" which would crumble away under the first strain.

Despite the proclamation of Victoria as Queen-Empress, the control of India did not center in London. A member of the British cabinet, it is true, held the portfolio of Indian affairs, and a council exclusively British assisted him. Theoretically India was a direct imperial charge. To this great dependency, however, the British Parliament paid slight attention. At Westminster ministries might rise or fall; but India remained a place apart. A peculiar sanctity was attached, seemingly, to the India Office in London. It was not so much above criticism as beyond it; and Indian policies were seldom debated in the House of Commons. That august body, as a general rule, did not receive the yearly report of the Indian government until the close of the annual session—too late to discuss it at any length, even if it had chosen to do so.

Nor could one say with fairness that the real government of India centered in the viceregal office. The viceroy, appointed for five years, and his executive council comprised the government of India. Even they, however, did not pretend to administer India. Policies they could and did determine; but the real administration depended on the district officers and the Indian civil service. There were several hundred of the former, and they were all British. To their charge were delivered the administration of justice, the collection of taxes, and the enforcement of the laws. They alone came into direct contact with the native population, the practical government being in their hands. Their esprit de corps was excellent, they worked hard and efficiently, their salaries were high, their accomplishments noteworthy, corruption was unknown among them, and they had triumphantly upheld justice, peace, and order for several decades. Yet there were some who criticized the system, because of its wholly British make-up. The Indian civil service also consisted largely of Britons and was entirely recruited in Britain. Indians might receive appointment to

# The New Empire

it, but the examinations were held in London and could be taken only by men between the ages of twenty-one and twenty-four. Furthermore, the examinations were of such a character as virtually to limit success in them to graduates of the British "public schools" and universities. The occasional Indian who passed them and received an appointment almost never rose to the higher ranks.

To this exclusive and also expensive government by foreigners the nineteenth-century Indian nationalists took exception. They complained about the size of the Indian army and attributed the increase in the number of famines in India to British rule, oblivious of the fact that before its advent famine was semichronic and frequently unrecorded. They did not plead for democracy: what these nationalists wanted was India for the Indians.

Before the coming of Lord Curzon as viceroy in 1899, however, these critics of the British "raj" were not particularly vociferous; and it is to the record of his term as viceroy that we should turn if we would understand the rapid growth of Indian unrest in the twentieth century. From many points of view the appointment was excellent. The Indian post had been the constant dream of Curzon's youth, and throughout his early manhood he had placed himself in training for it. He not only knew India thoroughly but knew all Asia as well. Time after time he had gone there, not as a sightseer but as a student. He had held long conferences with Chinese officials in Peking; he had been closeted with the amir of Afghanistan; he had made his way through Russian Turkestan; and the geography of northwest India was as familiar to him as his own English county. Furthermore, Curzon had sat in the House of Commons as Undersecretary of State for Foreign Affairs, and the complexity of British world policy had been his daily concern. Now from 1899 to 1905 he governed India and accomplished much, safeguarding and extending the frontiers, as well as overhauling the educational, economic, and sanitary administrations. But he repressed also every Indian impulse toward self-government, quarreling the while with his own British colleagues. This course of action compelled him eventually to retire, a defeated man, the chosen target for radical criticism throughout the British world.

In frontier policy Curzon was aggressive. Toward the Afghan border he created a new Indian province, the Northwest Frontier Province, which lay in the semi-no-man's-land on the borders of the Punjab, a region over which Great Britain claimed suzerainty. Within this area Curzon's plan was to entice, cajole, and bribe the tribesmen to friendship with Britain. To the south and west of the new province lay Baluchistan, and beyond that country Persia.

# A History of England and the British Empire

European access to India was possible from this direction by land and by sea; for Baluchistan was adjacent to the Gulf of Oman, and the Persian Gulf, still further to the west, opens into that body of water. Here the French, the Germans, and the Russians were all busily engaged in intrigue; and, one after another, Curzon checkmated them. Turning then to the north and the east, the viceroy cast his eye on Tibet, a strange, isolated state ruled by a religious order of peculiar characteristics, and probably less penetrated by Europeans than any other similar region in the world. To forestall the Russians in Tibet, he dispatched thither an expedition which forced its way to Lhasa, the capital, and made the monastic head of the state, the Lama, sign a treaty. According to this treaty, British approval was necessary before any foreign agency might be stationed at Lhasa.

Curzon meanwhile devoted much care to combating India's three major physical evils: famine, malaria, and bubonic plague. He fought famine by spending large sums of money on irrigation projects, and so effectively were they carried out that in the early twentieth century Britain could claim credit for over forty thousand miles of canals, which irrigated some twenty-three million acres. He fought malaria by establishing schools, the graduates of which were sent all over India urging the people to kill mosquitoes and eat quinine. He fought the plague by publicly submitting himself and his entire staff to vaccination, and by starting a campaign against rats, the fleas of which were responsible for the dreaded disease. Few men ever interested themselves more in the poor of India than did this British aristocrat.

Despite these achievements the viceroy was widely criticized by both British and Indians. The British disliked his cold disdain, and objected to his disciplining English soldiers in India. The Hindus became his bitter enemies, primarily because of his partition of Bengal, the nucleus of British India, won by Clive in 1757. That province was a large country in itself, with a population of about eighty million. Hitherto the government of Bengal had been highly centralized, and its administration, under the control of a lieutenant governor, had become top-heavy. The pressure of business was great, the climate of Calcutta was bad, and the more distant districts were neglected. Reform was in order; and the viceroy took the shortest steps to secure it by dividing Bengal and making two separate provinces where there had been one. But to the patriotically inclined Bengalis, who were essentially one race and spoke one language, the old Bengal had been a sacred motherland, even if it had never been a nation in the technical sense of that word. In England their protest at first was considered but a little storm; but in India, on the anni-

# The New Empire

versary of the partition, it was written that "thousands and thousands of Indians rub dust on their foreheads; at dawn they bathe in silence as at a sacred feast; no meals are eaten; the shops in cities and the village bazaars are shut; women refuse to cook; they lay aside their ornaments; and men bind each other's wrists with a yellow string as a sign that they will never forget the shame."[1]

Curzon's reforming zeal stirred such a hornet's nest among the Hindus that he was recalled in 1905 and was succeeded by Lord Minto. The Secretary of State for India in the new Liberal cabinet was John Morley (soon to be Lord Morley), a distinguished author, who took a more active part in the direction of Indian affairs than was usual in his office. A series of so-called Morley-Minto reforms were steps toward self-government; but they were not of a startling character. Indians were placed on the legislative council, and one was even nominated to the viceroy's executive council. In provincial councils they were given a majority of seats, and they were enabled there to pass resolutions condemning the government. These reforms, however, did not satisfy the Indian nationalists, who were growing steadily in number. Popular demonstrations evinced popular discontent. The British sternly suppressed these; but they rescinded the partition of Bengal, and tried to flatter Indian opinion by making Delhi the capital of all British India.

But whether the capital was at Calcutta or Delhi, or whether Bengal was partitioned or not, the rise of Indian nationalism seemed inevitable. The victory of the Japanese army in Manchuria in the Russo-Japanese War, of 1904–1905, was one cause: were not the Russians Europeans, and had not even the British been afraid of the Russians? The spread of British education, with its emphasis on English history and literature, was another cause, carrying with it, as it did, a passionate devotion to political liberty. The Indians were quick to draw analogies between the India of their own day and England in the days of Cromwell. A third explanation of this phenomenon would seem to have been the general wave of unrest in all semidependent countries against European control, whether French, British or Russian. Young Egypt, young Turkey, young India—everywhere nationalism was making headway fast.

There still remain to be considered important concessions, for the most part commercial, won by England in China, and the great stretches of central Africa joined to the empire through the partition of the Dark Continent.

[1] H. W. Nevinson, *The New Spirit in India* (1908), p. 169. By permission of Harper & Brothers and of the author.

# A History of England and the British Empire

It happened that anarchy was brewing in China at the time of the second British war, 1858–1860 (see page 676). Known as the Taiping Rebellion, this disturbance centered in the valley of the Yangtze and threatened the lives and property of foreigners living in the city of Shanghai, which had been opened as a treaty port in 1842. The European and American inhabitants there, in co-operation with Chinese officials, organized a miscellaneous force for defense, at first commanded by an American and then by an Englishman, Major Charles George Gordon, later to die at Khartum. This "Ever-Victorious Army," composed mainly of Chinese, crushed the Taipings within a few years. The end of the rebellion saw the British, as well as other foreigners, firmly entrenched in Shanghai. Side by side with the old Chinese town of that name there now grew up rapidly a modern European and American city. It was built originally on poor and swampy ground leased to the foreigners at a nominal rent; but it soon outdistanced the old Chinese city, though this was much more favorably located. The new Shanghai became autonomous in all municipal matters, with separate courts, police force, and taxation. Before the end of the century it began to vie with Hong Kong as the center of British commerce in the Far East.

The break-up of the Chinese Empire was retarded throughout this time by the abilities of Li Hung Chang, sometimes known as "the Bismarck of the East." His character bore only slight resemblance to that of the famous German except that his perception was acute in all that concerned politics. By yielding here and there to the British, French, and Japanese in Burma, Indo-China, and Korea, by playing off one faction against another, and by announcing reforms which generally existed on paper only, he staved off disaster for many years. One reform, at least, went beyond the paper stage; for he was instrumental in the appointment of an Englishman, Robert Hart, as chief of the Chinese customs service. Hart, who became Sir Robert for his services, organized a unique force of customs inspectors. Englishmen, well paid, with assured tenure, and appointed in accordance with strict civil-service regulations, administered under his direction the collection of all customs duties at Chinese ports, a fact which added greatly to England's prestige in the Orient.

In the last years of the century the Far East became the scene of an imperialistic scramble which for the moment eclipsed the partition of Africa. It was occasioned by the short, decisive war in 1894–1895 when Japan, who had "gone Western" with remarkable speed and thoroughness, soundly whipped backward China. That Sino-Japanese War opened Europe's eyes to two new factors which were to make the Far Eastern situation a matter of increasing concern:

the rising power of Japan and, even more important at the moment, the tempting weakness of China. It had not been surprising that England and France could defeat China in the middle of the century; but when the Chinese were so decisively beaten by another Oriental nation, only a tenth their size, it was a different matter.

The scramble of the nations for China's wealth revealed some of the new devices of economic imperialism. There was no formal partition of China among the powers; her nominal sovereignty, like that of Egypt, was preserved. Instead the powers secured "spheres of interest," concessions, and leased ports. A sphere of interest was a particular region in which a foreign power had been granted prior rights to furnish capital for the development of railways and mines. A concession was similar in nature, but was usually limited to a specified railway or mining property rather than extended over a whole district. Whereas "treaty ports" had been opened to the commerce of various outside nations, a leased port became for a period (ninety-nine years was the common length of time) the private preserve of a particular power which might, if it desired, fortify it as a naval base. The spring and summer of 1898 saw the scramble at its height. France leased Kwangchowan, and secured a sphere of influence in the far south, adjacent to her possessions in Indo-China. The center of the scramble, however, was in north China, around the waters of the Yellow Sea, just east of Peking. Two peninsulas jut into those waters: Liaotung from the north and Shantung from the south. Russia secured a considerable sphere of interest in Manchuria, and leased Port Arthur and another port at the tip of the adjacent Liaotung peninsula. Germany's sphere of interest was the Shantung peninsula, with a lease of Kiaochow on its southern side. England was not anxious to obtain more actual territory in China than she possessed in Hong Kong; but, to prevent the Russians and Germans from controlling all north China, she apologetically joined in the scramble and leased Weihaiwei, at the tip of the Shantung peninsula, a port which she never fortified but which she considered might come in handy sometime as a naval station. Once started, England did not stop with that. She secured additional territory near Hong Kong, as well as a sphere of interest in the Yangtze valley and further concessions. Her heavy investments in China were to give her a vital interest in the Far Eastern situation. The United States, meanwhile, was becoming interested in the Far East through her acquisition of the Hawaiian Islands and, as a result of her victorious war with Spain in 1898, the Philippines. She took no direct part in the Chinese scramble, advocating instead, as most favorable to her own interests (since she was late on the scene), an "open door" policy. This was directly opposed to any possibility of partitioning China and was designed to give all nations equal rights in her economic exploitation.

During the previous twenty years the European powers had been dividing up central Africa in a more thoroughgoing fashion, usually directly annexing territory for their empires without the polite disguises of spheres of interest, concessions, or leases. Europe's interest in central Africa had been aroused by Stanley's explorations, and further stimulated by a conference held in 1876 and presided over by the Belgian king. This led later to the International African Association, organized ostensibly to explore central Africa, to obtain scientific information, and to suppress the slave trade. Stanley, who had recently cut across Africa from east to west,—from Zanzibar through the lake country to the Congo and the sea,—was now employed by the association, and by 1884 he had mapped out for it in the heart of Africa some nine hundred thousand square miles which one year later were to be recognized as the Congo Free State. This quasi-international state, under the control of the Belgian king, started the major rush of the European powers for African loot.

On the eastern coast the principal contenders were the English and the Germans, who were just entering the imperial field. Out of their rivalry were to arise German East Africa (later Tanganyika) and British East Africa (later Kenya), as well as two other British possessions, Uganda and Zanzibar. Until that time the entire region from Portuguese East Africa to the Gulf of Aden supposedly belonged to the sultan of Zanzibar. That potentate had tried to lease all his land to a British merchant at Zanzibar in 1877, but England would have none of it. Thereupon Dr. Karl Peters, a very energetic German promoter of imperial expansion, intrigued at Zanzibar with native chieftains and signed innumerable treaties; and in 1885, almost before the British realized it, the German East African Company was born, claiming some sixty thousand square miles, lawfully acquired.

The British Foreign Office now entered the fray, since it would never do for Germany to control the entire east coast. Thereupon a bargain was struck: the Germans were to keep to the south, the British to the north; and to mark their respective spheres of influence a line was to be drawn from the sea straight northwest, bisecting the shores of Lake Victoria at one degree south latitude. The Imperial British East African Company was formed to exploit the land reserved for British enterprise. As a business concern it was not successful; for though it had some hundred and seventy thousand

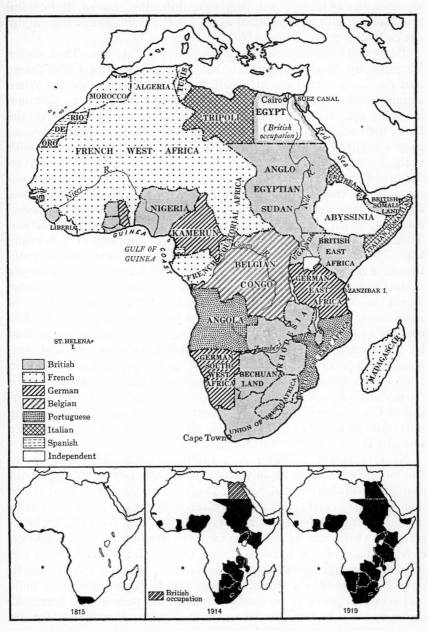

AFRICA IN 1914, WITH INSET SHOWING THE SPREAD OF BRITISH
TERRITORY IN AFRICA

square miles at its disposal, they were difficult of access, and capital was limited. But as a political agent for the extension of the empire the company proved invaluable.

Particularly important was its activity in Uganda. That native kingdom lay roughly between Lakes Victoria and Albert, the Congo and the Nile. The Germans made bold efforts to obtain it. When Peters reached there, he found disorder, with French, German, English, and Moslem missionaries contesting for the souls of the black men and with the sons of the late king at each other's throats. Peters secured a general treaty of friendship for Germany with various native chiefs and then hurried back to report his progress. Meanwhile a modern conquistador, one Captain Lugard, in command of the troops of the British East African Company, also penetrated Uganda with some fifty Sudanese soldiers and likewise obtained a treaty, which placed the country under his company's protection. Then he too left Uganda, disappearing into the bush on a hunting trip. The company offered to retain control if the government would finance a railway from the coast; but Lord Salisbury, prime minister at the time, would advance only a meager £20,000 to survey the route. When the company declared that it could not afford to remain, missionaries raised in England a large sum to retain its protection. The company remained temporarily, insisting that it must be subsidized by the government; but the latter refused. The government suggested, however, that it would buy out the company, and did this in 1895. Five years before this all Anglo-German controversies over Africa had been settled, the Germans acquiescing in the British control of Uganda and in a British protectorate over Zanzibar, obtaining in return the island of Heligoland, in the North Sea, which they were to make into a superbly fortified naval base.

Next came the building of a railway. Constructed largely by Indian coolies, it rose rapidly from the malarial coast to a splendid plateau several thousand feet in height, and therefore good white man's country even though it was directly under the equator. Farming on a large scale began here even before the World War, large tracts of thousands of acres having been granted to immigrants on easy terms. This led to forced labor, disguised, it is true, under the form of a hut tax. The savage warriors of this region, it was explained, must learn the habits of civilization; and if roads were to be built and schools opened it was only fair that the people who benefited thereby should be taxed for these improvements. Fortunately for the British capitalist planters, there was only one way to pay for the hut tax—to work on the plantations. Even by this device, however, it was difficult to secure sufficient labor. According to one British owner of some hundred and fifty thousand acres, the trouble was that the natives were able to save too much, and as a result, "after working a comparatively short time, a man was able to get his first wife. He then settled on the land and produced enough to get another, and as a result of a year's work he established himself on a farm for life without any necessity to work for anyone again, which was wrong and could be done nowhere else on earth."[1]

On the low, swampy, malarial west coast is Nigeria, next to India the largest dependency directly subject to the British crown. It dated back to 1879 and the formation of the United African Company, a successful business enterprise which exploited the lower Niger valley. Reorganized twice, this corporation, later known as the Royal Niger Company, received a charter in 1886; and to its charge was delivered the British protectorate proclaimed the preceding year over the Niger delta and a considerable distance up that river. For fourteen years the company continued its role as political overlord and extended its sway far into the interior, at one time claiming no less than five hundred thousand square miles, an area somewhat reduced in 1898 by Anglo-French agreement. By the end of the century the company could boast that it had an army of its own, commanded by that celebrated empire-tracker Lugard, now a colonel; that it had rid the country of slave raids; and that it kept trade and communication open all the way from the ocean to Sokoto. Having done this, it sold all its war material and administrative buildings to Great Britain and retired from the political field.

The Colonial Office now divided Nigeria into two large divisions, Southern Nigeria and Northern Nigeria. The first, in which was included the old British colony of Lagos, to the east, was already pacified, and could look out for itself with slight advice from London. The second, Northern Nigeria, two thirds of the whole, was a much wilder region, where tribal lands were but recently acquired and where discipline was lacking. The company had clung closely to the rivers, and had warily stood aloof from the fierce Moslem tribes of the interior, as much Caucasian in blood as Negro. The Hausas, pure Negroes, had been driven headlong before these tribes, and a reign of terror had resulted. Lugard, now Sir Frederick, was sent to end it. Speedily three chieftains submitted to his rule, and shortly afterward a fourth, an old slaver who had boasted that he would die like a cat with a slave in his mouth. In two years only one tribe, the Fulani, entrenched in their walled town from which they had forced all

---

[1] Report of Native Lands Commission, Nairobi, 1912–1913, p. 209.

Northern Nigeria to pay tribute, were defiant; but in 1903 Lugard subdued them also. New emirs, friendly to the British, were installed, and wandering tribes of robbers were brought to heel.

The form of government set up in Northern Nigeria was indirect, as the British preferred to rule through the native chiefs. All non-official Europeans, such as missionaries and traders, were refused admittance to the region, while British residents were placed over the various provinces, some the size of England or Scotland, into which the land was divided. These residents were not expected to interfere with the workings of the barbaric customs of criminal justice beyond forbidding that suspected criminals be forced to drink poison, that people be thrown to crocodiles, or that the bodies of twin babies, believed to be fathered by the devil, be forced into gourds. Unlike the system in British East Africa, the land was not declared freehold but was left in tribal holdings. The reason for this preservation of native rights here, and not in East Africa, is not clear, unless it was because the wretched climate made Nigeria less favorable for white settlement. By making it a definite law that no land in Northern Nigeria could be bought, sold, or alienated, since it all belonged to the crown, the British maintained what to all intents and purposes was a kind of native African feudal system here. In 1914 Northern and Southern Nigeria were united under the governorship of Lugard, recalled from Hong Kong for this post. Administratively, however, the distinction between them continued, because the indirect rule was retained in the northern part.

Comprising, as it did, roughly a quarter of the earth's land surface and a quarter of the world's population, the British Empire was impressive indeed from the quantitative standpoint. On every continent portions of the world map were colored in the British red, and more than four hundred million subjects at home and overseas owed allegiance to George V. The following figures, compiled from sources which sometimes disagree in details, are designed to indicate at a glance some distinctive features of the empire on the eve of the World War. They afford a contrast between the mother country, the dominions, and a few selected dependent possessions in regard to population, area, and commerce.

The dominions, it will be noticed, had some two thirds of the land, while the rest of the empire had nine tenths of the people. The distribution of the white men in the overseas possessions is particularly significant. Fourteen million lived in the dominions; the remaining million upheld British power and prestige among the third of a billion brown, yellow, and black peoples. To many Englishmen the

| POPULATION, AREA, AND COMMERCE OF THE UNITED KINGDOM AND BRITISH EMPIRE (1911) | | | | | | |
|---|---|---|---|---|---|---|
| | Population in Thousands | | | Area in Thousands of Square Miles | Commerce in Millions of Pounds Sterling | |
| | Total | White | Colored | | Imports | Exports |
| England . . . . . | 32,045 | | | 50 | 617 | 505 |
| Wales . . . . . . | 2,025 | | | 7 | | |
| Scotland . . . . . | 4,760 | | | 30 | 47 | 49 |
| Ireland . . . . . | 4,390 | | | 32 | 16 | 1 |
| Canada . . . . . | 7,206 | 7,098 | 108 | 3,603 | 114 | 64 |
| Australia . . . . . | c. 4,620 | 4,455 | c. 165 | 2,974 | 66 | 79 |
| South Africa . . . | 5,973 | 1,276 | 4,697 | 473 | 41 | 60 |
| New Zealand . . . | 1,064 | 1,008 | 56 | 103 | 19 | 19 |
| Newfoundland . . | c. 245 | 245 | ? | 162 | 2 | 2 |
| India . . . . . | 315,156 | 136 | 315,020 | 1,802 | 137 | 164 |
| Nigeria . . . . . | 17,100 | 1 | c. 17,099 | 336 | 6 | 6 |
| British East Africa . | 4,038 | 5 | 4,033 | 246 | 1 | 1 |
| Straits Settlements . | 252 | 7 | 245 | 1 | 46 | 39 |
| British West Indies . | 1,728 | ? | ? | 12 | 8 | 9 |
| Total dominions . . | c. 19,098 | 14,070 | c. 5,028 | 7,315 | 246 | 226 |
| Total dependent . | 369,342 | c. 1,000 | c. 368,342 | 3,988 | 232 | 242 |
| Total empire . . . | 388,440 | c. 15,070 | c. 373,370 | 11,303 | 478 | 468 |
| Total United Kingdom | 45,370 | | | 121 | 680 | 557 |

customs statistics meant more than the figures for area and population. In respect to foreign trade the free and unfree portions of the empire were about equal. The importance of Raffles's act in establishing Singapore is evident in a comparison of the trade of the Straits Settlements, with their scant population and scantier area, with that of Nigeria, whose inhabitants outnumbered all the white men of the dominions. Those who recall the eighteenth-century trade statistics will appreciate the marked decline of the West Indies, which had once overshadowed all colonial rivals (see page 468). Every year the British collected such statistics in vast quantities, and published them with the calm assurance that Germans, Frenchmen, Italians, and Russians could not produce such tangible evidence of imperial success.

But there were other aspects of empire which were less tangible. Canada, India, Nigeria, and St. Helena might all be colored in uniform red on the map, but there the resemblance ceased. Unity and homogeneity, both in structure and in spirit, were completely lacking among the scores of separate units involved in Britain's "dominion over palm and pine." It has been contrary to English nature to attempt to jam everything into a rigid mold, as we have seen; and the empire reflected that attitude. The little problems of the crown colonies need not detain us; the major developments were along the two separate lines of settlement and exploitation. The dominions were the logical fruition of the initial settlements in Virginia and Massachusetts. From the House of Burgesses and the *Mayflower* Compact there had been a steady development in self-government by men who had carried with them a strong sense of the basic rights of Englishmen; before long the dominions would be emerging as full partners rather than as possessions of the mother country. But while some Englishmen had been setting out for Jamestown and Plymouth, others had been sailing eastward to carve out fortunes in India. Exploitation had spread into other distant lands, where, for better or for worse, millions became subject to British rule, with practically nothing to say about the manner in which they were governed. On its good side this rule of the white minority meant order, efficiency, discipline, and comparative peace. In the words of Rudyard Kipling, imperialism's poet:

> The 'eathen in 'is blindness bows down to wood an' stone;
> 'E don't obey no orders unless they is 'is own;
> 'E keeps 'is side-arms awful: 'e leaves 'em all about,
> An' then comes up the Regiment an' pokes the 'eathen out.

> *All along o' dirtiness, all along o' mess,*
> *All along o' doin' things rather-more-or-less,*
> *All along of abby-nay, kul, an' hazar-ho,*
> *Mind you keep your rifle an' yourself jus' so!* [1]

Some of the ruling caste, of course, exhibited a tendency, to a greater or less extent, toward harshness, brutality, arrogance, and exploitation, which were resented by these colored races. The native African, forced to work on coffee plantations or in gold mines in order to pay a hut tax for the benefits conferred by British civilization, did not appreciate the latter; nor did most of the Indians warm to those aliens from overseas under whose arbitrary rule they lived. In another poem, "The White Man's Burden," Kipling helped to soothe some of those whose consciences were troubled by the rumored

---

[1] Rudyard Kipling, "The 'Eathen," from *The Seven Seas* (1896). By permission of Doubleday, Doran and Company, The Macmillan Company of Canada, Limited, Methuen & Co., Ltd., and Mrs. Rudyard Kipling.

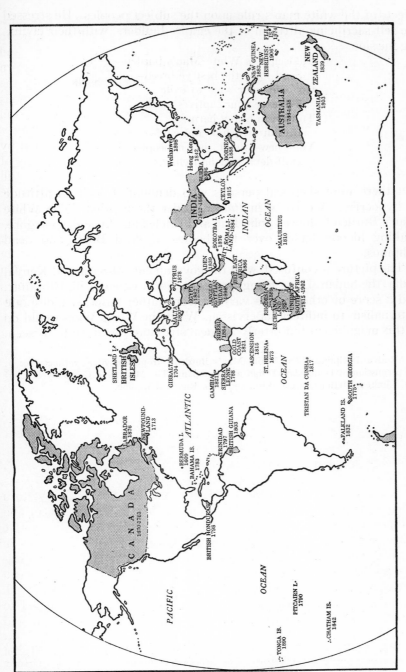

THE EXTENT OF THE BRITISH EMPIRE IN 1914

effects of the white man's rule upon the subject peoples. He stressed the self-sacrificing altruism of the empire-builders, with their civilizing mission.

> Take up the White Man's burden—
> Send forth the best ye breed—
> Go bind your sons to exile
> To serve your captives' need;
> To wait in heavy harness,
> On fluttered folk and wild—
> Your new-caught, sullen peoples,
> Half-devil and half-child.[1]

But there were skeptical persons who denounced such an attitude as hypocrisy. A cartoon in *Punch,* under the caption "The White Man's Burden," showed John Bull and Uncle Sam, knee-deep in gore, shaking bloody hands over the bodies of dead Boers and dead Filipinos.

The picture is confused, with the governments of Sarawak, Kenya, India, the Sudan, Hong Kong, Jamaica, Sierra Leone, Fiji, Gibraltar, and a score of other places varying from rather strict, semidespotic paternalism to indirect supervision. What the World Wars would do to this magnificent but utterly illogical structure remained to be seen.

[1] Rudyard Kipling, "The White Man's Burden," from *The Five Nations* (1903). By permission of Doubleday, Doran and Company, The Macmillan Company of Canada, Limited, Methuen & Co., Ltd., and Mrs. Rudyard Kipling.

# CHAPTER XXV

## The Rise of Irish Nationalism

### 1880-1914

IN IRELAND, England found her thorniest problem and met with her greatest failure. The royal standard might fly over Dublin Castle, the sons of Erin might enlist in British regiments, the Irish might be elected to the English Parliament, and the king's writ might run from Cork to Derry; but this did not make a United Kingdom while in village church, in hut and cabin, in Dublin tenement, and in desolate Donegal there were hostile hands and hostile hearts. Economic distress and awakened nationalism were the interlocking causes of this hatred. Times were very bad in nineteenth-century Ireland, and nationalism was nowhere more rampant or more bitter. Gladstone, in his great ministry, had improved the church situation in Ireland; but his efforts in connection with land and education had failed to bring satisfaction (see page 697). There still remained basic considerations which were to torment Ireland and worry England for many years to come.

The Irish peasants lived so close to starvation that any abnormal conditions of rainfall or of climatic change brought acute misery. The famine of 1846, as we have seen, had helped to bring about the repeal of the Corn Laws (see page 638); but it did not brighten the Irish scene, and the misery which it caused was very unusual, even for Ireland. There was but one *great* famine. On the other hand, outside of Asia, in no country was there more squalid and protracted poverty in the nineteenth century than in Ireland. Overpopulation, or too exclusive reliance on the potato, or perhaps landlordism was to blame. At any rate, in 1841 Ireland had had more than eight million inhabitants; in 1851 it had only six and a half million. About a quarter of a million had died of starvation or its effects; the rest had emigrated, chiefly to the United States. This emigration continued, so that by the end of the century Ireland had less than four and a half million inhabitants.

Gladstone had realized, although somewhat dimly, that something must be done, and he had tried to alleviate the situation by his first land act. Since that had not raised the economic level in Ireland to any appreciable degree, he tried again during his second ministry

(1880–1885). This second land bill involved the principles of the "three F's": fair rent, fixed tenure, free sale. Rents were to be fixed by judicial bodies for periods of fifteen years each; peasants were guaranteed against eviction, except in certain circumstances, such as failure to pay rent; and if they chose to leave their holdings, they had the right to sell to the newcomer such permanent improvements as they had made. These measures of 1881 were radical, and in a sense revolutionary, since rents were now to be determined by a judge instead of by the law of supply and demand—unquestionably a serious infringement of the rights of private property. The bill passed the Commons after considerable difficulty, and the Lords after more. It would not have passed at all if Ireland, with widespread agrarian agitation, had not been more disorderly than she had been since the days of O'Connell (see page 610). Thus the British Parliament broke, as far as Ireland was concerned, with approved economic dogmas and adopted a semisocialistic principle. The legal owner now could no longer do what he wished with his own property, and the man who rented it obtained new legal rights by the mere act of occupancy. In other words, dual ownership of a sort was now to prevail in Ireland.

The law, however, did not satisfy the Irish. One reason was the expense and difficulty of enforcing it. A second objection was that land values were continuously declining in the open market in the last two decades of the century, and in consequence tended to drop below the price fixed by the courts. Peasants, therefore, who had contracted to pay a given rate for fifteen years were soon placed in an impossible position. More important was the fact that this legislation came too late.

The Irish peasants were already in the grip of a nationalistic fever which could not be allayed by such economic medicine. The relations of Ireland to England had changed sharply since Gladstone's first ministry, and for the worse. In 1874 a cultivated Irish gentleman, Isaac Butt, had organized a new political party pledged to obtain a separate legislature for Ireland. Promptly it had won more than fifty seats at the first Parliamentary election, a fact which vastly encouraged all who sought self-government for Ireland. Butt's followers were given a fair hearing, and they discoursed with eloquence and learning on Ireland's wrongs.

They did this annually, and apparently were content to do nothing more until there arrived in their midst Charles Stewart Parnell. "The Uncrowned King" was of different fiber. A man of intense passion and icy manner, he had acquired with his mother's milk hatred for England. He determined to make trouble and succeeded. His method was simple. He advised the Irish members of Parliament to object to everything, make speeches, amendments, more speeches, more amendments. "Refuse all invitations, don't try to make yourself popular, make yourself disliked, have no truck with the enemy, make him want to get rid of you, and above all else make it impossible for the Commons to transact business." The English, he thought, would ultimately grow so disgusted with this performance that they would set up a separate parliament in Dublin.

Parnell, assisted by one other Irishman, put this theory into practice. Butt tried to discipline his unruly colleagues; but one by one the Irish Nationalists were won over to the new tactics. Parnell succeeded Butt as their leader. He began to stage the famous "Irish nights" in the House of Commons, in which the Irish Nationalists refused to obey the speaker and continued with their orations until removed by the sergeant-at-arms. And since they had to be removed one by one, and since they returned as soon as permitted, thereupon to engage immediately in the same procedure, endless time was wasted, and British nerves began to fray. Yet the English did not want to adopt closure (arbitrary closing of debate); such a French precedent was contrary to the spirit of English traditions. Consequently they left the Commons pretty much to the Irish Nationalists, who thought nothing of debating all night, and the succeeding day as well. In the last analysis, in order to carry on Her Majesty's business something had to be done with these surly and truculent fellows who made a point of talking for hours about the petty activities of some unknown magistrate in County Galway.

Meanwhile there was Michael Davitt, who, unlike Parnell, was peasant-born. Embittered and prematurely aged by eight years in a British prison, this Irish agitator went to America. There he saw much of the Fenians, those "physical force" Irish who thought to free their native Ireland by fighting. Davitt was a revolutionary, but did not believe in this method. He preached a different doctrine, which was summed up in his motto "The land for the people." To secure it, he returned to Ireland and started a Land League, to compel the landlords to sell and the government to buy. He and the league asserted that the peasants had already paid in exorbitant rent more than the value of the land, and he urged the peasants to wrest it from its legal owners, the landlords. The league grew fast, and soon an alliance was made between its founder and Parnell.

With Parnell's becoming president of the league, the combination became a powerful one; for the agrarian program was thus identified with the political. Parnell made the peasants conscious of the fact that they were Irishmen, with an economic as well as a political grievance. "In his own stern, calculating way he rubbed hard and goading facts into their heads, and fixed their minds with inexorable deliberation on the relentless features of their case, their bitter need, their appalling outlook." He kept reiterating in one way or another to the Irish peasants that they must show the landlords that they intended to hang on to their homesteads and not again allow themselves to be dispossessed as they had been in 1847.

Parnell did not depend on this support of the Irish peasant as his only source of strength. He also sought aid from the Irish in the United States, where he made a triumphant tour in 1879–1880. He was feted everywhere; and, what was more important to him, he raised large sums of money for his cause. The British government, alarmed at his activities, set a spy upon his tracks; but he was too clever to be caught in treason. He came close to urging violence in his endeavors to win over the "physical force" Fenians to this "new course" of combined agrarian and political agitation; but he did not advocate it, for he knew that the Irish could not successfully fight the British with bayonets. As he stated in a speech in Brooklyn, "We ask you to keep the people of Ireland from starving to death. An armed expedition in Ireland means its destruction."

In addition to the obstructionist tactics in Parliament, Parnell also began to practice, through the instrumentality of the Land League, another method that tended toward violence. At this time very bad crops had led to an unusual number of evictions—over a thousand, it is said, in the first six months of 1880 alone. Parnell himself kept cleverly within the law, but that he and Davitt between them were mainly responsible for the Irish reaction to the British defense of property rights none can gainsay. The leaders of the league advised that the peasants make life hot for the landlords by refusing to pay the rent demanded or by refusing to pay any rent at all, by caring for evicted peasants, by maiming cattle, and by burning barns. The peasants were urged also to make life intolerable for anyone who was sufficiently daring and disloyal to Ireland to take the crofts, or small farms, of the dispossessed: they were to shun him "as if he were a leper." This process, which was to be used repeatedly against landlords as well as peasants, was to add to the language a new word, "boycott," derived from the name of one of the first victims, a landlord's agent. The more the British resorted to coercion in these disorders the more the league resorted to violence. The passage of Gladstone's second land act did not stop this agrarian agitation; for Parnell realized that if the "three F's" were to find favor in Ireland, both Irish nationalism and he (Parnell) would suffer an eclipse. Consequently he saw to it that Gladstone's law did not succeed. This was not difficult, as the redcoats had already been brought into action through the boycotting by the league.

Gladstone, very much perplexed, tried to counteract the league's work by alternating force with remedial legislation. He clapped Parnell into jail. This apparently did no good; it only increased Parnell's popularity. He had coercion bills passed, had civil liberties suspended, had Ireland ruled by a kind of martial law. He appealed to the Pope and to the Irish people—all to little avail. Meanwhile a Ladies' Land League proved even more extreme than its masculine counterpart, which had been suppressed.

Then Gladstone again turned to a milder policy. Parnell was released from prison, and the coercion acts were repealed. Lord Frederick Cavendish was sent as chief secretary to Ireland to administer the new policy. His lordship, together with another prominent official, was promptly murdered in a public park. Although Parnell and his leading henchmen denounced these Phoenix Park murders, the British turned back to coercion at once, as was natural under such circumstances. Trial by jury was ordered suspended for three years, and the police were given greater freedom of search and arrest. At the same time the land act was somewhat amended. Parnell meanwhile organized the National League in place of the suppressed Land League, with the avowed purpose of securing home rule. Agrarian disorders did not end, but they decreased noticeably.

Then Parnell, discovering that after this nothing else was to be gained through Gladstone, began to dicker with the Conservative party. By swinging his votes in their favor on a nonparty issue, he helped the Conservatives to oust Gladstone's second ministry in 1885. Parnell saw that, unless one of the old parties gained an overwhelming plurality at the coming election, the Irish members could make a farce of constitutional government in England by continuing to vote first for one party and then for the other. The new election resulted exactly as Parnell had hoped, with Gladstone and the Liberals having a plurality over the Conservatives but not the majority for which Gladstone had pleaded to make them independent of the eighty-six Parnell votes.

Gladstone, entering his third ministry (February to July, 1886), was seventy-six years old, and his leadership could not last long. For some time skeptical remarks about it had been made by the younger generation of Liberals, who fretted under his discipline and whose ideas on economics were far more radical than his. Throughout the campaign he had refused to commit himself on the Irish question; but once elected he declared for home rule and a separate legislature for Ireland, just as many who had studied his past record had expected. Apparently Gladstone wanted to settle the Irish problem once and for all; in one way or another he had been concerned with it for well-nigh twenty years.

The first of the Irish home-rule bills, in 1886, proposed for Ireland a parliament composed of one house but of two orders, one representing population, the other property. Under ordinary circumstances these two orders would meet and vote together. Either one meeting separately could exercise a veto which would suspend a bill until a new election was held. The Dublin parliament was to control the Irish executive, thus introducing responsible government, and it was to have full powers except on such matters as were reserved for the crown. Among the latter were foreign affairs, the army, the navy, customs and excise duties, and, for the time being, the constabulary. Ireland was to contribute one fifteenth of the total expenses incurred by the British Parliament for imperial purposes. The Irish members were to be withdrawn from the Westminster Parliament, and an Established Church in Ireland was to be forbidden.

The mere announcement of these main outlines of the home-rule bill of 1886 created a whirlwind of opposition from all sides, not only among the Conservatives but among Gladstone's own Liberals. Among the serious objections marshaled against the bill was the fact that if judges in Ireland were appointed in accordance with it, by an executive who was responsible to the Dublin parliament, it would be useless to keep the constabulary under British control. Presumably, the objectors argued, Irish judges would be unwilling to sentence violent and incendiary Irish Nationalists to jail, so that their arrest by the constabulary would be futile. Another objection was that the Irish would be taxed without representation because of the exclusion of their members from the Westminster Parliament on the setting up of their separate parliament in Ireland. Many of the insurgent Liberals stressed this danger, pointing out that such a situation had proved fatal in the American colonies and undoubtedly would be equally fatal to an amicable understanding between England and Ireland. One of these, Joseph Chamberlain of Birmingham, principal heir to the Liberal leadership, said that he favored home rule all around, in the sense of imperial federation throughout the empire, but not this bill, which called for separate parliaments with divided authority. Others, in arguing against the bill, insisted that, since neither party had campaigned on the issue, the electorate had not had any inkling that it was voting for home rule in returning the Liberals, and that on such a momentous matter as breaking up the United Kingdom, as created by Pitt (see page 564), the people should make the decision. Others wondered why Gladstone was coupling this bill with

a new land bill, which he planned to introduce as a companion measure, and in which he proposed to buy out all the landlords in Ireland
by using the credit of the British treasury. Many felt that if English
money was to be thus spent, it should be used for the benefit of English peasants or Scottish crofters, and assuredly not in Ireland, where,
with the establishment of a separate parliament, England would have
no security for her money. So argued Gladstone's opponents, and not
the least vociferous among them was the Protestant majority in Ulster. Resenting the whole idea of home rule, this group threatened
revolt at the possibility of being under the control of a Catholic parliament in Dublin.

As the debate wore on, it became evident that the Liberal party
would break in two over the home-rule bill. The enemies of home
rule, nevertheless, feared that the enormous prestige of Gladstone,
assisted by the phalanx commanded by Parnell, might be enough to
carry the bill through the Commons; and consequently they left no
stone unturned to defeat it. Particularly, they capitalized the religious antipathies, citing the situation of the loyal British citizens of
Protestant Ulster. "Ulster will fight, and Ulster will be right," cried
the inflammatory Lord Randolph Churchill, descendant of the famous
Duke of Marlborough and father of the later statesman Winston
Churchill. Ulster itself, meanwhile, made ready to fight; and as it
did so, many of Gladstone's Nonconformist adherents prepared to
desert him in order to support it.

As a result of this widespread agitation the bill was lost, ninety-
three Liberals voting against it. Gladstone appealed to the country.
Thereupon the Liberal opponents of home rule hastily organized a
party of their own, the Liberal Unionist, and entered the electoral
battle in combination with the Conservatives. This coalition won a
handsome victory, with a safe majority over both Gladstonians and
Parnellites. Home rule was not to be at this time.

The chief reason for its failure lay in the inheritance of animosity,
fear, hatred, and contempt which blinded men's eyes and steeled
their hearts, destroying faith and confidence. Many of the objections raised against the bill were weighty and intelligent, but they
might very likely have been solved in course of time by patient
compromise and good-will. Nationality and religion summarize the
failure. It was natural that the midnight murders, the boycottings,
the maiming of cattle, and the intimidations which had characterized
social disorder in Ireland should bulk large in the minds of Englishmen. They had no clear understanding of the desperation and
squalor of the Irish scene, nor could they visualize half-starved
peasants driven out of "man-pens" by men in red. With their own

ordered lives reflecting the queen's peace, they could not see why it should be different in Ireland. Lord Salisbury, now Conservative prime minister for the second time (1886–1892), compared the Irish to Hottentots, and in his frank and savage way thus expressed what many millions felt in England. In the matter of Catholicism, the Spanish Armada, Tudor glories, and Stuart treacheries might belong to history, but that did not prevent their influencing votes in 1886. There were many in England, especially among the Nonconformists, who felt profound suspicion of the Roman Catholics, while the Protestants in Ireland had been "top dog" too long to relinquish their ascendancy. These elements feared the outcome, if home rule passed, of having both schools and taxes under Catholic control.

The victorious Conservatives, assisted by their allies, the Liberal Unionists, now turned to two seemingly contradictory methods in order to crush Irish nationalism: economic reform, to "kill home rule with kindness," on the one hand, and the suppression of disorder on the other. The first of these involved land purchases on an extensive scale, to inaugurate peasant proprietorship. Evictions were made more difficult, and rentals, it was agreed, were to be revised every three years. Arthur Balfour, chief secretary for Ireland, in 1887 worked hard to redeem the congested districts in the west of Ireland. He introduced light railways, built docks and bridges, gave away seed potatoes, and tried to revive the fishing industry. At the same time, his hand fell heavily on Ireland as this policy was supplemented by the other—unadulterated coercion. The Crimes Act (a name used also for some of the earlier coercion acts), which was passed by the Conservatives, was made the permanent law of Ireland. It gave magistrates and police extensive powers; stipulated that certain criminal cases be tried in London; and authorized the chief secretary at Dublin Castle to suspend all constitutional guarantees whenever he considered it desirable. As a result Balfour proscribed the National League and put several Irish members of Parliament in prison.

Meanwhile the Irish Nationalists had been continuing their propaganda. They organized in the latter part of 1886, without Parnell, a "Plan of Campaign" whereby the peasants were to decide for themselves what rent they could pay and, if the landlords would not accept the proffered payment, were then to continue their old terrorist methods. Despite the efforts of Balfour the economic situation remained bad. Cheap food imported from overseas spoiled the Irish market in Great Britain, and the synthetic manufacture of fertilizers in Germany ruined the Irish exportation of kelp. Opportunity for Irish labor to work in British fields diminished as British farmers began to use new agricultural machinery. These facts added grist to

Parnell's mill. But, above all, the appeal to Irish patriotism was kept alive and warm through the agency of the Irish Nationalist party, a perfect political machine, responsive to Parnell's will.

Something now happened which for the first time aroused deep sympathy for the Irish leader in the land he hated. The London *Times* did Parnell a grave injustice by accusing him of having approved the Phoenix Park murders in Dublin. A Parliamentary commission investigated the charge; for Parnell refused to trust himself to an English jury in a libel suit. The newspaper, it was proved, had based its charge on letters which it had hastily assumed were genuine, but which turned out to be forgeries. Parnell was guiltless, and for a time a remorseful British public made a hero of him.

This fact, coupled with Gladstone's militant advocacy of the Irish cause, did much to hearten the friends of home rule. Englishmen who had voted against Gladstone in 1886 were now changing their minds. It became evident to many that the Irish question was as far from a settlement as ever and that the Irish cherished an undying hatred for "bloody Balfour," whom they accused of going too far in supporting the brutal behavior of police and constabulary. It is barely possible that, had an election followed immediately, Ireland perhaps might have obtained home rule.

All this good-will that Parnell had won in England soon went glimmering, however, when one Captain O'Shea brought suit for divorce, naming Parnell as co-respondent. The suit was undefended; for Parnell had long lived with Mrs. O'Shea and had had a child by her. Gladstone's mail-bags were now full of letters denouncing Parnell and demanding that the Liberal alliance with him be brought to an end. Gladstone was a man of the world, but not so most of his followers. Very prominent among them were the Nonconformists, whose preachers now thundered their anathemas in the name of the Lord. Gladstone then privately sought Parnell's resignation from the House of Commons and, when Parnell refused, told the Irish Nationalists that nothing could be done for them as long as they kept Parnell as leader. The effect upon the Irish M. P.'s was electric. They tore at one another's throats, the majority denouncing Parnell and only the minority remaining loyal to him. Randolph Churchill's earlier statement, "The Irish do not stick together," had come to pass. Gone now was the united block of Irish Nationalist votes in the House of Commons. Divided into Parnellites and anti-Parnellites, the Irish could not agree; and the English, fearing them less, scorned them the more.

Nevertheless, when the election of 1892 was held, Gladstone again won a victory by a narrow majority. He was returned to power for his fourth ministry, and in 1893, in his eighty-fourth year, he introduced his second home-rule bill.

This bill bore a marked resemblance to that of 1886, but there was one major difference. The principal constitutional difficulty in the earlier act had been concerned with the withdrawal of the Irish representatives from the British Parliament to their own at Dublin. To avoid this Gladstone invented so-called "in and out clauses." These would keep the Irish in the British Parliament, but would forbid their voting on domestic legislation and would thus allow their voting only on imperial matters. The Dublin parliament was to consist of two houses, according to this bill. When it was demonstrated that this plan was too complicated, Gladstone changed it and proposed that the Irish M. P.'s should vote on all questions.

The second fight for home rule was a lost battle from the beginning. Even counting the Irish votes, Gladstone's majority in the Commons was only forty. The Liberals, moreover, were not enthusiastic about Ireland's cause, and most of them supported it only as a compliment to Gladstone. The crux of the matter lay in the Irish contention that they were a nation, which neither Liberals nor Conservatives were willing to admit. Probably no compromise could have saved home rule at this time. The men who had opposed it in 1886 on the specific ground that Irish members were to be withdrawn from the British Parliament now fought it because the Irish were to remain there, and these same men would probably have opposed a separate parliament for Ireland under any circumstances. It apparently made no difference in the result whether or not Ulster was excluded from the bill. After many bitter scenes the bill passed the Commons by a close vote, but met defeat in the House of Lords. In rejecting it the Lords performed a popular act and one that had apparently been counted upon by some of the members of the Commons who had voted for the bill. The schism in the ranks of the Irish Nationalists made it impossible for them to obstruct Parliament seriously any longer. It was apparent that there had been no real change of heart in England, and this time home rule seemed dead.

The cause of the Nationalists looked desperate in 1893, with disunion in their ranks and discouragement in Ireland. Long after Parnell's death his followers continued to quarrel over him and formed within the ranks of the Nationalists what were to all intents and purposes little subparties of their own. In England the political situation brought fresh disaster to Nationalist hopes. Gladstone had resigned in the year following the rejection of his home-rule bill; and a year after that the general election of 1895 brought in Lord Salisbury as Conservative prime minister for the third time (1895–

# The Rise of Irish Nationalism

1902). In addition, the Unionists (the new name adopted by the Conservative-Liberal-Unionist alliance) had a tremendous majority. The foes of home rule had triumphed with this victory at the polls, and, what was worse, its former friends among the Liberals had grown lukewarm. Lord Rosebery, the Liberal leader, had no use for the idea, and as a practical issue it disappeared from the Liberal program.

Slowly there came to the fore a new spokesman for Ireland. John Redmond, stanch follower of Parnell in defeat or victory, had been in Parliament since 1881. He was slow of speech and slow of thought; but he spoke with seriousness and dignity in the Commons as became the representative of the Irish people, and the Nationalists trusted him as their Parliamentary chairman. He might have followed Parnell's methods and have sought to gain his ends by nuisance-making or he might have adopted more revolutionary tactics, such as sedition and mutiny; but he did neither. He simply continued to din into British ears Irish aspirations and Ireland's plight. Ireland within the empire was what he sought—a free nation within a free commonwealth.

As the twentieth century opened, a new hope appeared within Ireland itself for that "most distressful country." Many Irishmen began to realize that consciousness of power, so characteristic of the English, came in no small measure from pride in England's past. Ireland too had traditions, not simply of defeat and disaster but of victory. Why not make them live again, give tone and color to the past, brew some new magic based on self-respect and ancient glory? These Irishmen wanted their land to resurrect her native culture, and become self-reliant by looking to her own strength.

There were two ways of doing this. One was to revive the old Gaelic (Celtic) language. Much to the annoyance and also to the amusement of the British, this was done. Teachers sprang up everywhere. Witnesses in the law courts, who knew English perfectly well, swore that they spoke only Gaelic. Newspapers began to publish Gaelic columns. Railway companies were asked for tickets in Gaelic and were petitioned to mark their stations in that tongue. Bank managers found cheques endorsed in Gaelic. Literary men were found who insisted that Ireland's Gaelic language antedated Greek and in certain respects was superior to it. Another way was for Irishmen to reorganize their own economic life without England's assistance. Sir Horace Plunkett was particularly active in this direction. Owing largely to his efforts the Irish began co-operative buying, co-operative dairying and butter-selling, and even co-operative banking on the minute scale successfully put into operation by co-operative peasant banks in Germany.

# A History of England and the British Empire

After 1895 came ten years of Conservative ascendancy. Lord Salisbury was prime minister until his retirement, due to ill-health, in 1902, when he was succeeded by his nephew, Arthur Balfour, of whom we have heard as chief secretary for Ireland. These years were not unfruitful for Ireland. Balfour, we recall, had wanted to "kill home rule with kindness," and the Conservative party at the end of the nineteenth century set out to do so. Its first effort in this direction was the Irish County Council Act of 1898. This revolutionized local government. Before this law was enacted, the Irish grand juries, which were for the most part composed of the local gentry, the landlords, had taken charge of local roads, public buildings, local poor rates, and various other administrative matters. Since the grand juries were appointed by the sheriffs, and since the sheriffs in turn were appointed by Dublin Castle, it is evident that local government had been in the control of an aristocratic caste. By the new statute it was placed under local county councils elected under the Parliamentary franchise.

The Conservatives then went further, inaugurating peasant proprietorship on a grand scale. The effect of this innovation was excellent, as far as economics was concerned. The peasants were encouraged to buy their own land, since the government offered to sell it to them at a figure below the old market value and at a very low rate of interest. The new land law, coupled with the reforms of Plunkett and the general rise in the price of agricultural products which followed the gold discoveries of the Klondike and of South Africa, worked wonders. Emigration declined greatly; Ireland, instead of losing her sons and daughters, began to gain in population; and a period of prosperity opened such as the island had not witnessed since the eighteenth century. In fact, "no country in the world has ever had such advantages from beneficial legislation as Ireland had for a period of thirty years" before the outbreak of the World War.

Meanwhile, politically, there was no change in the Irish situation. Prosperity or no prosperity, the demands of the Nationalists at Westminster were in no way abated. The Irish were as keen as ever for a parliament of their own. The renaissance of the British Liberal party, with its victory in 1905–1906 (see page 801), did not for the time being affect the situation at all; for the twentieth-century Liberals were wary of the Irish question. Their party had been twice defeated on home rule, and they did not court further disaster. Also, their victory was so astonishingly complete that they did not need the Irish votes. Nevertheless, Redmond consistently supported the Liberals. He knew that the real lion in the path was the House of

Lords, and he surmised that in the course of time the Liberals would come into conflict with that august body on some other question and that that would be Ireland's chance.

So it proved. The Lloyd George budget (see page 809) was thrown out by the Lords, and the Liberals, appealing to the country, secured, if one counted the Irish Nationalist votes on their side, a majority for the budget and for the Parliament Act which followed. The Irish once more thus held the balance of power. Whether any formal bargain was now struck between them and the Liberals, as the Conservatives hinted, is doubtful. A bargain was scarcely necessary, since it was obvious to all that Irish votes were necessary and that they would not be given unless the Irish members were given something in return. At any rate, the Liberal party once more embraced the cause of Ireland.

In 1912 Asquith (prime minister, 1908–1916) introduced the third home-rule bill. This created a parliament in Ireland and granted autonomy to a limited extent; but it by no means gave Ireland a status comparable to that of the dominions. To the British government were reserved important constitutional and administrative functions. These included not only those naturally expected—the army, navy, and foreign affairs—but also many of a more domestic nature, such as the control of the Royal Irish Constabulary, land settlement, old-age pensions, the National Insurance Act, the collection and, to some extent, the levying of taxes. The parliament established was to be of two houses: a Senate nominated in the first instance by the government, and a House of Commons elected by popular vote. A ministry, exclusively Irish, was provided for, dependent on the new parliament. After making a goodly number of safeguards with regard to religious liberty and the veto power of the crown, the bill granted the new Irish government control over all domestic matters not specifically reserved to the British government. It likewise provided for the presence in the British Parliament of forty-two Irish members instead of the hundred-odd given by Pitt's Act of Union. Thereby it neither excluded the Irish altogether, as did the first home-rule bill, nor continued their excessive representation, as did the second.

The fight over this bill, which lasted two full years, was extraordinarily complicated. In addition to the old difficulties argued about long and fiercely in 1886 and 1893, there were new ones, mainly of a financial nature. Gladstone's proposed financial settlements were simple as compared with those set up by this bill. The British had sunk a lot of money in Ireland in the twentieth century, and naturally they did not propose to lose it. A tremendous amount had been pledged for the land settlement, and the old-age pension law (see page

[ 765 ]

804) had added greatly to Britain's liabilities in Ireland. Consequently Asquith's bill proposed the collection of Irish taxes by British officials, the deduction of what was due Britain, and the turning back of what was left to the Dublin parliament. As one Tory opponent of the bill put it, "the British go to the Irish taxpayer in the sole capacity of tax-collector, and the Irish government is the fairy godmother distributing gifts which have been collected by the British ogre."

The bill met opposition, however, less upon grounds of finance than because of Ulster. That province again threatened fight. It had done so successfully in 1886; it would have repeated that threat in 1893 if that had been necessary; and once more it stood ready to wreck any attempt to separate it from the United Kingdom. At the time of the third home-rule bill, however, Ulster was Protestant by only a narrow margin. Five of the nine Ulster counties even had a Catholic majority, and the slight majority of the Protestants in the entire province was the result of their concentration in the remaining four counties of the northeastern section. At the same time, within Ulster itself were most of the factories of all Ireland and some two thirds of all the Protestants in the island. The men of northeastern Ulster, content with the status quo, bitterly opposed home rule. Ulster was more prosperous than the rest of Ireland, and they feared heavier taxes and crippled industries from a parliament at Dublin. They were alarmed lest the Roman Catholic south, with its numerical majority, attempt reprisals for the long years of Protestant oppression in centuries past. This fear outweighed the fact that Irish Nationalism had been nonsectarian, and that its leaders, Butt and Parnell, had both been Protestants. The Ulstermen, moreover, were proud of their British citizenship, and considered, not without reason, that the British electorate would refuse to sustain Asquith if he tried to deprive them of it. Of these reasons the first was perhaps the most logical; but it received the least attention. Uncompromising and free-spoken as the men of Ulster were, they did not like to base their case upon the purse. Even to them it seemed of less importance than religion or British citizenship. "You may call it what you like," to quote one of their M. P.'s; "we in the north of Ireland believe that a Parliament in Dublin would be dominated by the Roman Catholic Church; and the Roman Catholic Church being what it is, we do not believe, to use a colloquial expression, that the Protestants would have a fair show." This was the temper of the Protestant Ulstermen. The Conservative leaders, recognizing and perhaps capitalizing this determination to remain British, promised them that they should neither be left in the lurch nor forced out of their country. It was, of course, possible to mutilate Ireland by making Ulster separate, but in that case there were many Catholics to be safeguarded in Ulster. It was likewise possible to give Ulster a position of special dignity and power in the new Ireland. The Irish Nationalists would have reluctantly agreed to the latter, but not the Ulstermen. Another alternative was the exclusion of Protestant Ulster from the jurisdiction of the new Dublin parliament; but neither the Irish Nationalists nor the Unionists would accept that compromise. In fact, the Unionists made it clear that they would agree to nothing except the complete defeat of the bill.

A covenant was signed publicly in 1912, by thousands of Protestant Ulstermen, to resist in every way any effort to enforce home rule. "We stand by one another," it read, "in defending for ourselves and our children our cherished position of equal citizenship in the United Kingdom and in using all means that may be found necessary to defeat the present conspiracy to set up a Home Rule plan in Ireland." The open Bible, the Union Jack, and this Ulster covenant became the symbols of Ulster's resistance.

In January, 1913, the House of Commons passed the home-rule bill, and the Lords promptly rejected it. Some months later the bill was again approved by the Commons, to be rejected by the Lords. The latter's veto power, however, had been clipped by the recent Parliament Act (see page 816), and if the Commons passed the bill once more it would become law.

Meanwhile, the Ulster Protestants, thinking that there was no time to waste under the circumstances, began to arm and to drill in preparation for fighting home rule to the death. Soon they had an army of considerable size. This hypothetical rebellion of Ulster obsessed men's minds. There had been no overt act; the home-rule bill was not yet on the statute books. These men of Belfast were British citizens; had the British Parliament any right to deprive them of that citizenship? Men forgot that Ulster sent fewer Unionists to Parliament than Nationalists, that the Catholic minorities in Ulster had as good a claim to self-determination as the Protestant minorities in all Ireland, that Ulster had always been an integral part of Ireland. The appeal of the Ulstermen was at once subtle and direct: they wanted nothing, they asked for nothing, except to remain the loyal British citizens they had been for centuries; and British public opinion tended to favor them.

When the Government of Ireland Bill came up in Parliament for the third time early in 1914, Asquith, realizing that apart from the Nationalists his majority in Parliament was slender, proposed a compromise. He suggested that every separate county in Ulster should determine by plebiscite whether or not it chose to enter the new Ireland. If it voted for exclusion, for six years it was to remain a part of Great Britain; and if, after that period, which would cover the term of two stated Parliamentary elections (1915 and 1920), the British Parliament did not intervene, the counties were to be included in Ireland and not in Great Britain. Redmond, as the Irish Nationalist leader, reluctantly agreed; but Sir Edward Carson, a south-of-Ireland barrister, who was Ulster's spokesman, remained adamant. Nevertheless, in May, 1914, the bill passed the Commons, and, receiving the royal assent in September, home rule became law.

During the spring and summer, however, much else was to happen. Very early in the spring there were hints that military force might be used to bring Ulster to terms, and a minor crisis occurred when various army officers resigned to avoid such duty. The Ulster volunteers were cutting telegraph wires, bringing ashore ammunition, and distributing it through the province. Southern Ireland followed Ulster's lead in turning to arms. For a long while many had chafed there at Redmond's pacific attitude and his trust in England. Sir Roger Casement, a Protestant, and other eager advocates of home rule now organized national volunteers and sought to arm them. Redmond was reluctantly forced to recognize the necessity for this act. Enlistments in the south grew rapidly, and by summer the national volunteers outnumbered those of Ulster. Because of the tense situation the king in July called a conference of political leaders in Buckingham Palace, and Carson and Redmond faced each other. Before them hung a great map of Ulster. The division might have been made; but neither side would yield County Fermanagh or County Tyrone, where the Nationalist majority was very slight. King George's efforts were futile; and the day after the conference a parade of armed men, Ulster volunteers, marched through Belfast, with no one interfering. The next day His Majesty's troops fired on National volunteers engaged in gun-running near Dublin. Civil war seemed about to begin.

A week later Redmond rose in the House of Commons. A blacker cloud than Ulster was close at hand—the World War. And so the Irish chieftain, with a magnificent gesture of friendship and generosity, pledged Ireland's help in fighting Germany. The operation of the new act was suspended during the war, and home rule was to rest in abeyance. Catholic Ireland, it appeared, would fight for England and trust to the future. Yet before the war was half over, Dublin was to be in revolt.

# CHAPTER XXVI

## *What the Victorians Thought*

$\text{V}$ICTORIAN thought was conditioned in a matrix peculiarly its
own. It was nourished and grew to maturity in a bourgeois
world where the tempo and quality of cultural achievement depended
on the approval of middle-class Englishmen. It was formed in the
hurly-burly which marked the onward sweep of the Industrial Revolution, and was profoundly affected by the development of the natural
sciences. Geology, and more particularly biology, seemed to demonstrate the truth of a new theory of the universe. An intellectual
revolution was born as the Industrial Revolution reached a climax.
Either by itself was sufficient to change the currents of life and
thought. Together the perfected steam engine and the theory of
evolution changed profoundly the currents of life and thought.

Science, in the broadest meaning of that word, is the main key
to Victorian thought. Applied science—namely, the invention of
engines and power machinery—increased the prestige and power of
the middle class; pure science—specifically, the conclusions of geol-
ogists and biologists as to man's origin—changed the Victorian conception of the universe. Pure and applied science together, directly
or indirectly, colored Victorian literature, religion, art, and philosophy.

Science in industry, manufacturing, transportation, and shipping
made the Industrial Revolution the most obvious and the most universal material factor in the life of Victorian England. Some idea of
the attitude of thoughtful men toward all these changes may be
gained by a study of six influential writers: John Stuart Mill, the
foremost English economist of the nineteenth century; Thomas
Carlyle, spokesman for eternal truths; John Ruskin, art critic;
Charles Kingsley, blunt yet sentimental Anglican clergyman; Cardinal Manning, of the Roman Catholic Church; and William Morris,
the English socialist.

John Stuart Mill (1806–1873) was brought up in extraordinary
fashion by his father, James Mill, a fanatical disciple of Bentham
and his utilitarian ideas (see page 626). From the age of three the lad
was drilled on lists of Greek words. His education continued to consist in "storing the mind" with Latin, logic, economics, and history.

Novels, music, and physical games were under the ban. The boy's exercise was to walk with his father, who utilized these occasions to discuss with his son his outside reading. The aged Mr. Bentham was delighted: a philosopher was being created.

Happily the young Mill tore himself loose from this discipline, learned to read poetry and to enjoy it, and fell in love. He became an editor, wrote books, and entered Parliament. A comfortable income from the old East India Company, which he served for more than thirty years, kept him from financial worries. Native ability, hard work, and a fondness for abstract truth made him famous as a logician, an economist, and an authority on political values and ideas. He gave to the science of economics a human touch.

Mill was, for his time, perhaps the foremost apologist and defender of the middle class, and of the Industrial Revolution which filled its pockets. He did not, however, unreservedly uphold the contemporary economic structure of society; he was even in favor of changing it. In certain respects he was an advanced thinker and a radical. He approved of the organization of workers into trade unions for purposes of collective bargaining. "In that contest of endurance between buyer and seller [of labor]," he wrote, "nothing but a close combination among the employed can give them even a chance of successfully competing against the employers." So clearly did he recognize the inequalities of existing society that he even had a kind word to say for the communists of the Continent, afterward called the Marxian Socialists (see page 782), who advocated in one form or another the transfer of the ownership of capital from the few members of the bourgeoisie, or middle class, to the many members of the proletariat, or propertyless class, and who were at this time practically unknown in England. He went so far as to state, in his *Principles of Political Economy*: "If, therefore, the choice were to be made between Communism with all its chances, and the present [1852] state of society with all its sufferings and injustices; if the institution of private property necessarily carried with it as a consequence, that the produce of labour should be apportioned as we now see it, almost in an inverse ratio to the labour—the largest portions to those who have never worked at all, the next largest to those whose work is almost nominal, and so in a descending scale, the remuneration dwindling as the work grows harder and more disagreeable, until the most fatiguing and exhausting bodily labour cannot count with certainty on being able to earn even the necessaries of life; if this or Communism were the alternative, all the difficulties, great or small, of Communism would be but as dust in the balance." It would be almost impossible to believe that the author of these sentiments was a stanch believer in the private ownership of wealth were it not for the use of the word "if," repeated three times. Mill believed that private property was desirable, but he looked forward to a time when it would be diffused among many more people. This advocacy of better distribution of wealth, however, involved nothing in the way of a change in the ownership of the fundamental basis of wealth. In his opinion this improved distribution could be accomplished by peasant proprietorship, by heavy taxes on land, and by inheritance levies. He believed with all his heart and soul in that watchword of Victorian England, "progress." Sufficiently realistic to admit the existence of class lines in England, he nevertheless did not think that there was a class struggle or that antagonism between classes was inevitable. If a better distribution of economic goods were brought about, all would be well, in his opinion. "It is only in the backward countries of the world," he wrote, "that increased production is still an important object; in those most advanced what is needed is better distribution."

In his theories regarding the production of wealth Mill's economic conservatism, however, matched his liberalism in other fields. Distribution of wealth could and ought to be regulated by society, but production of wealth, he thought, was determined by natural law. The first section of his *Principles* is devoted to production, and none could convict him of heresy here. Like his contemporaries in England, he was under the spell cast by Malthus (see page 627) and believed that goods, food, wealth of all kinds, were strictly limited, with always the latent danger of a race between population and production. His economics was thus one of scarcity rather than abundance. The poor should limit their numbers; they would do this of their own accord, he was convinced, once they were better educated. "Given education and just laws the poorer class would be as competent as any other class to take care of their personal habits and requirements."

Consequently, to Mill the prevalent idea of laissez faire in business was a good principle, if not carried to extremes. He clung fast to self-interest as the dynamo of human activity. If every man were allowed to follow his own interests unhindered, society as a whole would be benefited. Free competition aroused such self-interest. "All tendencies on the part of the public authorities to stretch their interference, and to assume a power of any sort which can easily be dispensed with, should be regarded with unremitting jealousy."

In consquence, from Mill's point of view, it was very necessary to affirm that individual liberty was the wellspring of progress. He feared that governmental encroachment on the lives of individuals would make society static. "Whatever theory we adopt," he wrote, "respecting the foundation of the social union, and under whatever political institutions we live, there is a circle around every individual being which no government, be it that of one, of a few, or of the many, ought to be permitted to overstep." Mill insisted that that circle should be generously defined and sacredly guaranteed. There had never been "more necessity for surrounding individual independence of thought, speech, and conduct with the most powerful defenses, in order to maintain that originality of mind and individuality of character which are the only source of real progress, and of most of the qualities which make the human race much superior to any herd of animals."

One might summarize his views thus: governments could and should intervene in the distribution of economic goods; but in all matters which concerned production, governments should keep strictly aloof, since any tampering with economic laws in regard to production would bring inevitable disaster. Private property, to Mill, was one great foundation of personal rights, and laissez faire, within reason, was another. This was the democratic, liberal reaction to the Industrial Revolution.

Thomas Carlyle (1795–1881) was a Tory, a democrat, and a religious revivalist, all in one. He hated the Industrial Revolution and he fought Benthamism, laissez faire, and individualism tooth and nail. His Toryism did not mean conservatism, as popularly understood. He was not content to stem the social and political tide, smoothing out the inevitable readjustments in the life of the British people. Nor did his Toryism consist in romantic musings on the past. Rather was it a vital faith in certain truths, absolute and eternal, which had been forgotten, and which must be remembered if England were to live.

He was democratic, but at the same time he hated Chartists and scoffed at their demand for universal suffrage. He was a democrat in the same sense as was his fellow Scot, Robert Burns, when he wrote, "A man's a man, for a' that." Neither rank, nor wealth, nor brains, nor blood, but inherent character determined manhood to his mind. He was also a revivalist; but that did not mean that he was High, Low, or Broad Church, Catholic or Nonconformist, or even Christian. He did not go to church, nor did he hold with creeds; but no one in the length and breadth of Britain had greater faith in the Almighty than did this vitriolic and impassioned writer.

Carlyle, son of a stonemason, was destined for the Kirk. He went to Edinburgh University, taught school and disliked it, found himself unable to stomach any of the numerous brands of Presbyterian theology, and so gave up the idea of the ministry to become a free-lance writer. Not until he was past forty did the world of letters begin to notice this fiery, independent, and hard-working Scot. Meanwhile he lived a life of bitter poverty, shared by a talented wife; wrote voluminously and well for reviews and periodicals, as chance offered; and on a rough and lonely farm at Craigenputtock compiled *Sartor Resartus* (first published in a periodical, 1833–1834), now renowned throughout the English-speaking world but at the time attracting little attention. In 1837 appeared his *French Revolution*, which established his reputation, and in 1843 *Past and Present*, a clear criticism of Victorian England. Two years later came *Oliver Cromwell*, and between 1858 and 1865 *Frederick the Great*.

Of these major writings, two, *Sartor Resartus* and *Past and Present*, are interpretative of the Industrial Revolution in its broadest sense. The former is the more philosophic. It purports to be an explanation of the writings of a Professor Teufelsdröckh of Weissnichtwo, who elaborates a philosophy of clothes. The style is boisterous and gusty, and the meaning obscure to most people. Its contents cannot be analyzed in a few paragraphs, but its message to an England confused and baffled by the advent of the Industrial Revolution may be glimpsed.

Teufelsdröckh regards human society as defunct. "Call you that a Society," cries he again, "where there is no longer any Social Idea extant, not so much as the Idea of a common Home, but only of a common over-crowded Lodging-house? Where each, isolated, regardless of his neighbour, turned against his neighbour, clutches what he can get and cries, 'Mine!' and calls it Peace, because in the cut-purse and cut-throat Scramble no steel knives, but only a far cunninger sort, can be employed? Where Friendship, Communion, has become an incredible tradition; and your holiest Sacramental Supper is a smoking Tavern Dinner, with Cook for Evangelist? Where your Priest has no tongue but for plate-licking: and your high Guides and Governors cannot guide; but on all hands hear it passionately proclaimed: *Laissez faire*; Leave us alone of *your* guidance, such light is darker than darkness; eat you your wages, and sleep!" A partial answer to this lies in the popular fallacy that the end of life is happiness. "Foolish Soul! What Act of Legislature was there that *thou* shouldst be happy? A little while ago thou hadst no right to *be* at all. What if thou wert born and predestined not to be Happy, but to be Unhappy! Art thou nothing other than a Vulture, then, that flyest through the Universe seeking after somewhat to *eat*?; and shrieking dolefully because carrion enough is not given thee?" One way out of this false, muddy swamp of evil is to reverence all that is most worthy in human life. "Two men I honour," says Carlyle, "and no third. First, the toilworn Craftsman that with earth-made Implement laboriously conquers the Earth and makes her man's. Venerable to me is the hard Hand; crooked, coarse; wherein notwithstanding lies a cunning virtue, indefeasibly royal, as of the Sceptre of this Planet. Venerable too is the rugged face, all weather-tanned, besoiled, with its rude intelligence; for it is the face of a Man living manlike. . . . A second man I honour and still more highly: Him who is seen toiling for the spiritually indispensable; not daily bread, but the bread of Life. . . . Not earthly craftsman only, but inspired Thinker, who with heaven-made Implement conquers Heaven for us! If the poor and humble toil that we have Food, must not the high and glorious toil for him in return, that he have Light, have Guidance, Freedom, Immortality?—These two, in all their degrees, I honour: all else is chaff and dust, which let the wind blow whither it listeth." Carlyle was at once democratic and aristocratic. The honest worker was to be exalted and honored; but he in turn was to seek leadership outside of himself and was to exalt, honor, support, and obey the leader.

Although *Sartor* was not well received in England, it was popular in the United States, owing to the influence of Ralph Waldo Emerson, the American philosophical writer. Carlyle felt encouraged; and he and his wife moved to London, there to depend entirely on the slender reed of literature. When the tide set in his favor, he turned his attention to Oliver Cromwell as a worthy subject for a biography. But his attention was diverted by the contemporary condition of his own country. England was on the eve of the Corn Law repeal, and politics hummed (see page 635). Carlyle found himself pulled first to the right and then to the left: he sympathized with some of the Tories, but he had long been in loose connection with certain of the Radicals. Before *Cromwell* could be written, he must unburden his soul on the England of his own day.

Therefore *Past and Present* was written quickly, at white heat, but as the fruit of long thought and passionate feeling. To Carlyle there were two Englands: not, as in Disraeli's *Sybil,* an upper England of the possessing classes and a lower England of the disinherited, but an England past and an England present. England past had been crude beyond belief; but at least it had been in one respect intelligent: there had been Englishmen then who had obeyed and Englishmen who had ruled, in honor bound to help and to protect those under them. Gurth, the thrall, hard though his lot might be, was assured, under this code of life, of Cedric's protection. England present was given over to Midas worship. Between man and man there was only payment, either cash or credit. The indolent aristocracy refused to accept the responsibility of "noblesse oblige." The "millocracy," the manufacturers, worked hard, but for themselves only, and they too refused to accept responsibility for human lives. Carlyle addressed himself to both classes with vigor. "I say," he told the landed aristocracy, "you did *not* make the Land of England; and by the possession of it, you *are* bound to furnish guidance and governance to England! That is the law of your position on this God's-Earth; an everlasting act of Heaven's Parliament, not repealable in St. Stephen's or elsewhere!" And again: "My lords and gentlemen — why, it was *you* that were appointed, by the fact and by the theory of your position on the Earth, to 'make and administer laws,'—that is to say, in a world such as ours, to guard against 'gluts'; against honest operatives, who have done their work, remaining unfed! I say, *you* were appointed to preside over the Distribution and Apportionment of the Wages of Work done; and to see well that there went no labourer without his hire, were it of money-coins, were it of hemp gallows-ropes: that function was yours, and from immemorial time has been; yours, and as yet no other's."

And then, turning to "millocracy," Carlyle launched his scorn at one Plugson, of St. Dolly Undershot, a mythical cotton manufacturer. "The blind Plugson; he was a Captain of Industry, born member of the Ultimate genuine Aristocracy of this Universe, could he have known it! These thousand men that span and toiled round him, they were a regiment whom he had enlisted, man by man; to make war on a very genuine enemy: Bareness of Back and disobedient Cotton-fibre, which will not, unless forced to it, consent to cover bare backs. Here is a most genuine enemy; over whom all creatures will wish him victory." Plugson wins; and then what happens? The manufacturer says to his men, "Noble spinners, this is the Hundred Thousand we have gained, wherein I mean to dwell and plant vineyards; the hundred thousand is mine, the three and sixpence daily *was* yours: adieu, noble spinners; drink my health with this groat each, which I give you, over and above!" Plugson, like the landed gentry, in the last analysis felt no obligation toward his employees beyond cash payment. Yet Carlyle had more sympathy for Plugson than for the game-hunting squire, more than for Sir Jabesh Windbag, the politician. Plugson would work, at any rate, and to Carlyle work was all but synonymous with religion. Plugson, Carlyle thought, might amount to something, if he would only realize that he was a God-appointed leader of men, not simply a collector of coin.

*Past and Present* made few specific proposals for bettering society. Carlyle refused to write a chapter on the as yet unrepealed Corn Laws, which he considered too absurd to survive much longer. He favored more stringent factory acts, high standards of living, the encouragement of emigration, and large sums for education. All these remedies he hinted at, but not in any detail. Carlyle was a preacher who left practical details to others, because his heart was absorbed in his one great theory of life: that some were born to rule, others to obey, and that great men of heroic mold must arise, seize power, and prove worthy of it. In fairness to him, however, it must always be remembered that hero worship meant nothing to him unless those men who were influenced by it were themselves heroic.

John Ruskin (1819–1900) represents the reaction of the artist to the Industrial Revolution. Ruskin was a childlike, petted, talented, and lovable person for whose influence in Victorian England it is rather difficult to account. His father was a frugal wine merchant who left his large fortune to his only son. After leaving Oxford, the young Ruskin traveled extensively and expensively, particularly in Italy, and wrote voluminous essays on painting, sculpture, and architecture. As time went on he came to know almost everyone who was worth knowing in contemporary England, and was extraordinarily popular with the middle classes as the prophet of new principles of beauty and aesthetics.

> I paints and paints,
> Hears no complaints,
> And sells before I'm dry,
> Till savage Ruskin
> Sticks his tusk in,
> And nobody will buy.

Thus ran the lament of the unhappy artist in *Punch* of whom the critic Ruskin disapproved. He did not confine his disapproval to mere artists but told businessmen how to run their affairs, professors what to teach, writers how to write, architects how to build houses, economists the why and the wherefore of their science, workmen how to use their spare time, women how to conduct themselves, and clergymen how to interpret the will of God.

Ruskin objected to the Industrial Revolution because it was physically ugly and carried with it a sense of false spiritual values. He felt that the pursuit of money-making belittled man. "In a community regulated by laws of demand and supply, but protected from open violence, the persons who become rich are, generally speaking, industrious, resolute, proud, covetous, prompt, methodical, sensible, unimaginative, insensitive, and ignorant. The persons who remain poor are the entirely foolish, the entirely wise, the idle, the reckless.

# What the Victorians Thought

the humble, the thoughtful, the dull, the imaginative, the sensitive, the well-informed, the improvident, the irregularly and impulsively wicked, the clumsy knave, the open thief, and the entirely merciful, just, and godly person." Inasmuch as the elder Ruskin bequeathed his son more than £150,000, this statement might appear unfilial. But to do Ruskin justice, he did not merely denounce, but gave away most of his fortune, devoted a generous share of his talents and energy to the education of Englishmen, poor and well-to-do alike, and wasted both time and money in idealistic attempts to improve the physical well-being of the depressed classes.

In 1869 Ruskin was appointed to the Slade Professorship of Art at Oxford. Never did that university have a more popular lecturer. Crowds came to hear him interpret the painters of the Renaissance; but it made no difference whether he lectured on Botticelli, the principles of drawing, birds, Alpine flowers, or religion. His appeal to youth was magnetic and diversified: young Arnold Toynbee drew from him the inspiration to establish university settlements, that the educated might live among the lowly; and young Cecil Rhodes was inspired to paint the map of South Africa red.

His *Munera Pulveris* is one of the strangest books ever published. There is much in it about Dante, Horace, Shakespeare, Homer, and Plato, and very little about economics. "The high ethical training of the nation," Ruskin wrote, "implies perfect Grace, Pitifulness and Peace; it is irreconcilably inconsistent with filthy or mechanical employment." As for the latter, criminals "should at once be set to work at the most dangerous and painful forms of it, especially to work in mines and at furnaces." As far as agriculture went, "a large part of it should be done by the upper classes; bodily health and sufficient contrast and repose for the mental functions being unattainable without it." All the rest of the stupid and uninteresting work in the world should be assigned as a kind of probationary discipline to those destined to go higher up the ladder, or else allotted to those incapable of higher things. Ruskin, quite evidently, was not a democrat in the Carlyle-Burns sense. In fact, he seems to have been something of a snob, redeemed by a simple and childlike devotion to charitable organizations like St. George's Guild, and by his idealistic though muddled efforts to do something for England. He knew that industrialism was injuring England, and his conscience was troubled; but he did not think himself out of the morass. And so it may have been with the majority of his contemporaries, who flocked to hear his lectures and read his books.

Charles Kingsley (1819–1875) is the best-known clerical writer on the subject of the Industrial Revolution, and his economic ideas typify those held by the Broad Church group in the Church of England. In character he was a true John Bull, hale and hearty, pugnacious, and honest. Kingsley began his career in a poor agricultural parish, where he became angry at the way in which agricultural laborers were treated. Excited by the Chartist agitation, he joined with a number of the younger clergy in a "Proclamation to the Workmen of England," counseling against violence, but friendly and full of sympathy. Kingsley wrote many tracts and novels, such as *Yeast, Alton Locke, Westward Ho! Hereward the Wake,* and other contemporary best sellers, and was appointed professor of history at Cambridge and canon of Westminster.

No one was left in doubt as to Kingsley's views. "I assert," he said, "that the business for which God sends a Christian priest into a Christian nation is to preach and practice liberty, equality and brotherhood, in the fullest, deepest, widest, simplest meaning of those great words; that, in so far as he does, he is a true priest, doing his Lord's will, and with his Lord's blessing on him. All systems of society which favor the accumulation of capital in a few hands, which oust the masses from the soil which their forefathers possessed of old, which reduce them to the level of serfs and day-laborers, living on wages and on alms, which crush them down with debt, or in any wise degrade or enslave them, or deny them a permanent stake in the Commonwealth, are contrary to the kingdom of God which Jesus proclaimed." Here was the essence of the Christian Socialism in which he believed. The bishops of the Church of England, for the most part, did not like this preaching, but they were powerless to stop it. By speech and by pen Kingsley drove his message home. For instance, in *Cheap Clothes and Nasty,* he paid his respects to sweatshop methods in the tailoring trade. The poor devils who do the sewing by piecework "when they have pawned their own clothes and bedding, will use as substitutes the very garments they are making. So Lord —'s coat has been seen covering a group of children blotched with smallpox. The Rev. D— finds himself suddenly unpresentable from a cutaneous disease, which is not polite to mention on the south of the Tweed, little dreaming that the shivering dirty being who made his coat has been sitting with his arms in the sleeves for warmth while he stitched at the tails. The charming Miss C— is swept off by typhus or scarlatina, and her parents talk about 'God's heavy judgment and visitation.' Had they tracked the girl's new riding habit back to the stifling undrained hovel where it served as a blanket to the fever-stricken slopworker, they would have seen *why* God had visited them."

In *Yeast,* Kingsley portrayed the degradation of English village life. Lancelot is listening to the talk of the laborers. "To his astonishment he hardly understood a word of it. It was half-articulate, nasal, guttural, made up almost entirely of vowels like the speech of savages. . . . Here and there he could distinguish a half sentence. An old shrunken man . . . was drawing figures in the spilt beer with his pipestem, and discoursing of the glorious times before the great war, 'when there was more food than there were mouths, and more work than there were hands.' . . .

" 'But I say, vather,' drawled out some one, 'they say there's a sight more money in England now than there was afore the war time.'

" 'Eees, booy,' said the old man; 'but *it's got into too few hands.*' "

Finally, in *Alton Locke,* Kingsley pictured an English factory town. An aged Scot is showing the sights to a young poet. "Well—but—Mr. Mackaye, I know nothing about these poor creatures."

"Then ye ought. What do ye ken anent the Pacific? [Alton Locke had been writing poems about the South Sea islands.] What is maist to your business?—thae bare-backed hizzies that play the harlot o' the other side o' the warld, or these—these thousands o' bare-backed hizzies that play the harlot o' your ain side—made out o' your ain flesh and blude? You a poet! True poetry, like true charity, my laddie, begins at hame. If ye'll be a poet a' a', ye maun be a Cockney poet; and while the Cockneys be what they be, ye maun write, like Jeremiah of old, o' lamentation. . . ."

"But all this is so—so unpoetical."

"Hech! Is there no the heeven above them there, and the hell beneath them? and God frowning, and the deevil grinning? No poetry there! Is no the verra idea of classic tragedy defined to be, man conquered by circumstance? Canna ye see it there? And the verra idea of the modern tragedy, man conquering circumstance?—and I'll show you that too—in mony a garret where no eye but the gude God's enters, to see the patience, and the fortitude, and the self-sacrifice, and the luve stronger than death, that's shining in thae dark places o' the earth."

All this created a sensation at the time. The Christian Socialists were of some prominence socially, and were regarded with more approval than dismay by the ruling classes, probably because they were harmless. Their remedy for England's troubles lay in co-operative shops, manufacturing enterprises in which workmen supplied the capital or had it given to them by charitable men of wealth, and in substituting the blessed word "association" for the evil term "competition." The Christian Socialists did some good by calling attention to the leaky roofs of thatched cottages and by pointing out that sewage was something which concerned society; but they did not succeed, as Kingsley had hoped, in convincing many people that Christianity and Socialism should be married. The fact that Kingsley and his friends were almost exclusively Broad Churchmen, ultra-liberal in their theology, antagonized both the High and the Low wing of the Church of England. Furthermore, the Church as a whole was on the defensive at this time against the tendency of German scholarship to weaken belief in miracles and in the authority of the Scriptures. Kingsley and his allies were identified with the new advanced criticism; and partly on that account they were regarded with suspicion by those who held to the old theology, no matter how they might regard the new economics.

Cardinal Manning (1808–1892) ranks with Kingsley as a clerical foe of the Industrial Revolution. Manning did not write much; but since he came to head the Catholic Church in England, his voice, to many, was more authoritative than that of an Anglican priest. Manning's conversion to Catholicism was one of the surprises of the nineteenth century. As an Anglican clergyman, Manning had written bitterly of Newman's desertion of the National Church, and he had seen eye to eye on ecclesiastical matters with his friend Gladstone. Both were High Churchmen, but none the less stanchly Anglican— heartily in favor of the learning of the Church Fathers, which the Oxford Movement revived, but hostile to Roman Catholicism. Then Manning was unexpectedly converted, becoming an ardent Roman Catholic and an enemy of religious liberalism and of all English Catholics tinctured with it. Newman, whom he had attacked as a renegade Anglican, he now scorned for maintaining independent views as a Catholic. With the majority of English Catholics the new convert was unpopular; but the Pope, Pius IX, nevertheless appointed Manning a cardinal, believing that English Catholics needed discipline and that Manning was the one to exercise it. The new cardinal drew tight the ecclesiastical reins, and stifled practically all discussion in Catholic circles.

But in all that had to do with economics Manning was radical. His first charge in the Catholic Church had been to look after the London poor; and now that he was head of the Church in England he found that the great majority of his flock consisted of Irish immigrants, the poorest of the poor, ignored by the trade unions, and without guidance or hope. Cardinal Manning was prepared to give both. He delivered a celebrated lecture on the *Rights and Dignities of Labor,* which echoed the Marxian socialistic theory that all wealth comes from labor. He said that all men were entitled to work and that society must provide it for them. In a letter to a friend he wrote,

# What the Victorians Thought

"There is the absolute necessity of raising up and easing the labor of men in such a way that their lives may be human lives. . . . Long hours render . . . domestic life impossible." He went on, in a magazine article, to proclaim the doctrine that a starving man might legally steal the necessities of life. Saint Thomas Aquinas, who was unknown and forgotten by the average nineteenth-century Englishman, was his authority for this statement; for the medieval saint had maintained that goods by nature are held in common, and that they are owned by individuals only because men will work better if they can secure title to them. Since, however, in essence these goods are communal, a man is not guilty of larceny if he takes his share from the common store to save his life. This doctrine seemed strange to many people, who thought that what the cardinal proposed amounted to little less than sheer anarchy. Sixteen years later, however, Pope Leo XIII issued his *Rerum Novarum* in defense of the rights of workmen. Manning's influence beyond the borders of his own Church was impaired partly by his autocratic temper, his stern belief in discipline and authority, and his dislike and distrust of trade unions. It should be remembered to his credit, however, that he took a prominent part in housing and educational reform, and that at the time of the great strike of London dockers (see page 794) his was the most influential voice in England in favor of those downtrodden men.

William Morris (1834–1896) was the best-known English socialist of the late Victorian period. Apparently he never went to church, and in all his many volumes there is no indication that he was influenced by the Christian example. Yet few men have ever loved their fellows more than this great, red-bearded man, born a gentleman yet by choice a craftsman. Morris was poet, novelist, painter, designer, architect, furniture-maker, and socialist—all in one. He was well-to-do, went to Oxford, became a friend of Burne-Jones and Rossetti, the "Pre-Raphaelite" painters, wrote easy-flowing poetry, and decided that the Industrial Revolution had made England ugly. He founded a firm to make beautiful things, such as murals, stained glass, metalwork, and furniture. The enterprise prospered. Its founder, believing only in handmade articles, had ideas about wall paper, chintzes, and chairs. Morris also wanted to substitute simplicity and honesty for ostentation, and to seek after the beautiful in all things.

Literature supplanted furniture as his ruling passion. He wrote long poems on early medieval and Icelandic themes, and became interested in old manuscripts and in all that had to do with books, the art of printing, and the designing of new fonts of type. Rough,

A History of England and the British Empire

hearty, full-blooded, warm-hearted, his interests eventually included a solicitude for the way in which the contemporary English lived.

> Hark, the wind in the elm-boughs, from London it bloweth,
> And telleth of gold, and of hope and unrest;
> Of power that helps not; of wisdom that knoweth,
> But teacheth not aught of the worst and the best.

That wind lured him to London and into politics, first as a Liberal, then as a Socialist.

He was not the same kind of socialist as the "Utopian" Robert Owen (see page 588), but followed rather hazily the new socialism of the German economist Karl Marx, which had just begun tardily to make its influence felt in England. Unlike the "Utopian" socialism, which aimed to establish a new organization of society, with more equitable opportunities for all, through the example of ideal communities, this was called scientific, because Marx stressed an "economic interpretation" of history which emphasized the influence of economic factors upon historical events. According to Marx, the age-old struggle between different social classes was at last converging into a two-sided conflict between the bourgeoisie, who owned capital, and the proletariat, who owned nothing but their own labor. With the growth of industry since the Industrial Revolution, Marx declared, capital was becoming concentrated in fewer and fewer hands, while at the same time the proletariat was steadily increasing in numbers. Marx did not want to end the private ownership of personal things, but attacked the private ownership of capital, or the wealth—such as land, mines, and factories—that is used to produce more wealth. Believing in an inevitable class struggle, he called on the workers to unite under an international revolutionary organization for the purpose of overthrowing the capitalistic organization of society. The *Communist Manifesto,* which he wrote in collaboration with another German economist, Engels, in 1848, but which stirred little comment in that year of revolutions, concludes with this ringing call: "The proletarians have nothing to lose but their chains. They have a world to win. Working men of all countries, unite!"

Morris considered himself a revolutionary socialist; but what he really wanted was to make the life of the poor clean, sweet, and beautiful. He hated railway trains, steamships, and the Industrial Revolution, commerce, ledgers, and the stock exchange, and he worshiped old England, old inns, old songs, and the old leisure. He loved his fellow men and had faith in their capacity to slough off capitalism and all its works. Lacking a wide knowledge of economics, Morris wanted to end a social system in which the people who did the most

[ 782 ]

work had the hardest lot while the very wealthy, as a rule, did nothing at all, and to create a society characterized by honest craftsmanship and simple living. This he would achieve not by dividing the wealth of England but by ending surplus production and the fierce competition to create new markets, often for absurd, ostentatious, and useless goods. He at first joined the Democratic Federation (later the Social Democratic Federation), the English organization of Marxian socialists, but soon quarreled with its founder and England's foremost Marxian, William Hyndman (see page 795). Hyndman wanted to build up a political party, but Morris wanted revolution to attain the ends of socialism. Even today Morris would be classified as a left-wing socialist, using "left" to mean radical in contrast to "right," or conservative. He had scant patience with the idealistic Fabian Society of socialists, with its noted membership, which wanted to introduce social changes piece by piece through gradual legislation. This did not mean that Morris wanted actual bloodshed or advocated shedding blood to bring about a reorganization of society, but that, as he wrote, "no program is worthy the acceptance of the working classes that stops short of the abolition of private property in the means of production. Any other program is misleading and dishonest."

Seceding from the Social Democratic Federation, Morris founded another, the Socialist League. This in turn fell a prey to dissensions, and Morris quit it to found the Hammersmith Socialist Society, which held meetings in a renovated stable in the rear of his home. Strange meetings they must have been, with the fiery young Bernard Shaw disputing with the now elderly Morris. Never a fluent speaker, Morris was so deadly in earnest that he insisted on addressing street meetings, waving red flags, publishing militant poems, subsidizing socialist magazines, and spreading propaganda until his death.

The best book of propaganda written by him was his *News from Nowhere*, a naïve and delightful work, every page of which reflects the personality of the writer. No character in this book has any use for money, and only the very old have ever heard that there ever was such a thing. There is practically no machinery, and everything in use is made by hand. Everyone works for the sheer lusty pleasure of exercising his muscles or for the joy of creation. Life is without crime, without meanness, and without hurry.

Though Morris was, indeed, a socialist, he was not interested in spreading his doctrines to other countries: he thought only of his own beloved England. In his own words, he was "careless of the metaphysics of religion, as well as of scientific analysis, but a deep lover of the earth and the life on it."

# A History of England and the British Empire

And what wealth then shall be left us
when none shall gather gold
To buy his friend in the market,
and pinch and pine the sold?

Nay, what save the lovely city,
and the little house on the hill,
And the wastes and the woodland beauty,
and the happy fields we till.

With the possible exception of Mill, all six of the authors quoted regarded the social results of the Industrial Revolution as highly unfortunate, but there were few authors and thinkers of any degree of eminence who thought otherwise. Samuel Smiles, in his *Lives of the Engineers*, had huge numbers of readers, and his pages teem with the blessings conferred on man by power machinery; but Smiles takes no rank at all in English letters. One might cite Macaulay; but that historian refers only here and there in his book reviews to the new golden age, which, without knowing very much about it, he was inclined to regard as a marvelous era. Mention might be made of Herbert Spencer (see page 787); but he more properly fits into the intellectual picture of Victorian life as the prophet of evolution. The conclusion, therefore, may be reached that to thoughtful and cultured Victorians the steam engine was a tribulation as well as a blessing, and that, as to the changes which followed in its wake, they were perplexed in mind and troubled in conscience.

The theory of evolution filled the imagination and perturbed the thought of the Victorians quite as much as did the Industrial Revolution. This period was one of scientific activity, with many eminent names such as Faraday and Lister; but it was the theory of evolution that changed a static Newtonian world into a world of continuous change and development. Evolution was primarily associated with the life and work of Charles Darwin (1809–1882). After his day, man's belief in fixed, scientific laws, such as the law of gravitation, was broadened by a belief in evolution, modification, and adaptation to environment.

This change in thought was not brought about suddenly by Charles Darwin. More than twenty years before Darwin published his famous *Origin of Species*, Sir Charles Lyell inferentially had hinted at evolution in his geology, and for years Darwin had been studying, in minute detail, fossils, barnacles, coral reefs, and pigeons. Slowly scientists had laid the foundations for the Darwinian theory; but of this the lay world knew nothing, and it awoke with a start when it read Darwin, who revolutionized man's entire conception of the universe. Galileo's telescope had done something of this sort when it demonstrated that the sun, not the earth, was the center of all things. That revelation had been a shock to man's pride and a blow to his theology. Slowly he had adjusted himself to this new idea, which did much to shape and to fortify the belief in natural law which pervaded and dominated the thought of the seventeenth and eighteenth centuries. Yet although the earth might be a pitiful gob of mud whirling in space, man, as king upon it, was alone possessed of an immortal soul, and saved from original sin by the death of Christ on Calvary! Then came Darwin; and if what he taught was true, Genesis—the Biblical account of creation—was a myth. If life had developed slowly and gradually into a myriad of species out of earlier and simpler forms, it was dubious whether a Divine Creator had made every species of living thing and, separately and above all, man.

Darwin did not prove, in the sense that two and two make four, that the different species of animal life developed out of earlier forms. He did, however, amass a great deal of evidence to show the probability of such a thesis; and when the biologists applied it to man and drew attention to the similarities between man and the other mammals, the profound implication of this hypothesis had tremendous repercussions in both literary and religious circles. This new idea seemed to destroy all hope for the survival of the individual after death. If man, and the dog, and the pig were all derived from earlier and more elementary forms of life, it would be rather difficult to designate the particular stage in evolution when the soul was acquired. Furthermore, if man survived after death, it was only logical to suppose that lesser forms of life should continue to exist also. The new theory, in effect, removed man from his pedestal as a divinely created being and made him only one among other animals. Nearly every thoughtful person in Victorian England was interested in evolution and its implications, and the great majority of nonfiction writers sooner or later had something to say on the subject. This is true of Huxley the biologist, Spencer the philosopher, Matthew Arnold the poet and critic, and Tennyson the poet laureate.

Thomas Henry Huxley (1825–1895) was the foremost exponent of evolution. "Darwin's bulldog," to use Huxley's description of himself, acted as the interpreter of the gentle biologist to a hostile and skeptical world. The layman reading Darwin's *Origin of Species* is soon bewildered by technicalities and scientific terms, but in Huxley's prose Darwin's conclusions are set forth simply and clearly.

Entering the royal navy as a surgeon at the age of twenty-one, Huxley was assigned to a ship outward bound to make surveys in

Australian waters. The youthful doctor made such a careful study of tropical marine life that he was rewarded with election to the Royal Society. He resigned from the navy, and finally accepted a chair at the London School of Mines. His rise in the world of science was rapid, for the whole gamut of the biological sciences engaged his attention. He was a devoted worker and the author of a steady stream of scientific articles ; before he was thirty-five he was one of three whom Darwin consulted about the publication of *The Origin of Species*. "If I can convince Huxley," said Darwin, "I shall be content."

Huxley thus became Darwin's popularizer and defender before the British public. At an Oxford meeting of British scientists in 1860, Bishop Wilberforce, suave, authoritative, and powerful, attempted to drown Darwin's theory in a flood of sarcasm. "And now," said the bishop in triumphant conclusion, "do you trace your monkey ancestry on your father's side or on your mother's?" "I would rather," replied Huxley, "be descended from the humble ape than to trace my ancestry to one who used his ability and position to discredit and to crush those who sought after truth."

Huxley called himself an agnostic, that is, one who refuses to affirm or deny the existence of God ; and probably he would prefer not to be remembered as a religious man. That he was devoted to the discovery of truth, that he sacrificed his health to this end, that his family life was simple and above reproach—all this is beyond question. Few men have led a more idealistic life than this exponent of what was, to him, a veritable Reformation. Huxley had the utmost confidence that the only key to a better world was science. He thought of science as a prerequisite to life, very much as a man of the Renaissance regarded the study of the classics. Science was neglected in the schools of England ; and he felt that once it was given its proper place, civilization would slowly and steadily become purified, vitalized, and worthy. In his inimitable lecture on *Evolution and Ethics* one sentence sums up Huxley's whole philosophy of life: "Let us understand, once for all, that the ethical progress of society depends not on imitating the cosmic process, still less in running away from it, but in combating it." In other words, man's first duty is to fight nature, and to do this he has one weapon—science. Man cannot escape his past; he is tied down by traditions, by a physical heredity which is as much of a handicap as the load of foolish ideas which he carries in his head. But the fight is not hopeless, and much may be done "to change the nature of man himself. The intelligence which has converted the brother of the wolf into the faithful guardian of the flock ought to be able to do something towards curbing the instincts of savagery in civilized man." Ethics demands that nature be fought and mastered, or at least held at bay, not accepted as un-avoidable fate in the manner of the Hindus. Ethics "demands self-restraint; in place of thrusting aside, or treading down, all competi-tors it requires that the individual shall not merely respect, but shall help his fellows; its influence is directed, not so much to the survival of the fittest, as to the fitting of as many as possible to survive. It repudiates the gladiatorial theory of existence." Science, man's only shield and buckler, his real helmet of salvation, would thus equip man to wage the struggle for life.

Herbert Spencer (1820–1903) was the philosophic interpreter of biological evolution. In his *Synthetic Philosophy* he applied Dar-winian theories to social institutions in order to explain their develop-ment. As a boy Spencer was stubborn and refractory, and made slight use of such meager educational advantages as his lower-middle-class environment offered. He disliked the classics and refused to study them. He served as a civil engineer on a railway-construction project. Abandoning this work for journalism, he wrote many ar-ticles for the reviews, and in 1850 published his first book, *Social Statics*. Within ten years his reputation had secured him several thousand dollars raised in the United States as advance payment for the great philosophy, not yet written. Its ultimate publication, beginning in the sixties, was hailed as an occasion of importance. Yet if the recognition was world-wide, the glory was short: the *Synthetic Philosophy* is now all but forgotten. The stately volumes in which it is enshrined gather dust in libraries, and their author is no longer a guide to the thought of mankind.

If that semi-science known as "sociology" has a father, it is Spencer. He believed it was possible to study humanity in the same way that Darwin studied pigeons, if only one were sufficiently rigid in excluding personalities, and were at the same time sufficiently exact in weighing verifiable fact. He set out to extract the quintes-sence of all knowledge and to deduce therefrom one single evolu-tionary law underlying all phenomena. Huxley said of him, "If Spencer ever wrote a tragedy it would be the slaying of a beautiful deduction by an ugly fact." Yet Spencer never avoided facts; indeed, he employed others to seek out and to classify more facts, with which his books are stored. The philosopher demonstrated to his own satis-faction that there was such a thing as a social science. It embraced all human relationships, showed how religion originated and how the idea of immortality arose, and explained institutions like marriage, the family, war, kingship, priesthood, and private property. It took the biological principle of adaptation to environment and boldly applied it both to prehistory and to recorded history.

Spencer was first and foremost an individualist. "All socialism," he stated, "involves slavery." Evolution proved the case for laissez faire; he widened the application of this theory from economics to almost every form of human activity, believing that any interference with the individual was spoon-feeding the multitude and that "a creature not energetic enough to maintain itself must die."

So widespread was Spencer's influence throughout the Anglo-Saxon world that Justice Holmes, of the United States Supreme Court, considered that the ideas of Spencer's *Social Statics* had become embedded in the decisions of that august body. Indeed, the majority of those educated in his day in both England and the United States were thoroughly imbued with Spencer's sturdy individualism; and for him this at least may be said: he renewed for many faith in the potentialities of individual freedom, and also a hope that history offered possibilities for discovering laws governing conduct. If he attempted the impossible, in one respect at least his philosophy was noteworthy: "to him we owe the best synthesis of his times." For science was then making glorious strides, and to Spencer's contemporaries it held the promise of a new Jerusalem here on earth.

Matthew Arnold (1822–1888) was probably the most celebrated of the many in England who wished to apply evolutionary principles to religion. Just as the study of primitive forms of life by Darwin and Huxley led to biological evolution, and speculation concerning primitive social and political ideas made many believe with Spencer in social and political evolution, so did the detailed analysis of the Bible, and of the literary materials used in its composition, lead to an evolutionary interpretation of religion. It was Arnold's brilliant role to popularize this scholarship.

Arnold was the son of the famous Dr. Arnold, headmaster of Rugby, a clergyman so broad-minded as to hold that some parts of the Bible were not inspired. The boy went beyond his father in this direction, and in the second half of the nineteenth century became the center of a storm of religious controversy in England. His interests were numerous: he wrote a number of essays on comparative literature, and many beautiful poems; served as professor of poetry at Oxford; and later became an authority on secondary education. Throughout his life he was fascinated by the Bible, and his *Literature and Dogma* has become a landmark in the interpretation of the Scriptures.

Arnold believed that people had been taught to accept the Bible too literally by theologians not "conversant enough with the many different ways in which men think and speak so as to be able to distinguish between them, and to perceive that the Bible is literature;

and that its words are used, like the words of common life, of poetry and eloquence, approximately, and not like the terms of science, adequately." In other words, the creeds of the Church had little to do with either Jesus or the Bible. "What is called theology," he said, "is in fact an immense misunderstanding of the Bible, due to the junction of a talent for abstract reasoning combined with much literary inexperience." Arnold wished to cast aside the vast theoretical superstructure of religion and return to the original wellspring of inspiration: the secret of Jesus. He was convinced that a large part of what passed for religion was "a kind of fairy tale which a man tells himself, which no one, we grant, can prove impossible to turn out true, which no one, also, can prove certain to turn out true." Arnold believed in neither prophecy nor miracles. "It can hardly be gainsaid," he wrote, "that to a delicate and penetrating criticism the chief literal fulfillment by Christ of things said by the prophets was the fulfillment such as would naturally be given by one who nourished his spirit on the prophets, and in living and in acting their words." Miracles, in his opinion, were comparatively insignificant in estimating the worth of Christ's message, and Christianity probably would have been better off without the rumor of their occurrence. "To profit fully by the New Testament," he continued, "the first thing to be done is to make it perfectly clear to oneself that its reporters could and did err. . . . To know accurately the history of our documents is impossible, and even if it were possible we should yet not know accurately what Jesus said or did." Arnold's book started a fight which still continues, especially in the various Protestant churches, including the Church of England. Men still seek the answer to the question whether religious revelation is fixed, final, irrevocable, and eternal, or evolutionary in character, slowly emerging from misty clouds of ignorance, superstition, and custom, and only partially revealing man's relation to the Eternal.

And last of all there was Alfred, Lord Tennyson (1809–1892), whose poetry, more than that of Rossetti, Arnold, or even Browning, reflected the quintessence of Victorian ideals. Tennyson was poet laureate by royal patent, and uncrowned king of poetry by the consent of much of the Anglo-Saxon world. He has borne the brunt of the anti-Victorian attack. Assaults have been made upon his old-maidishness, wherein delicacy has been interpreted as hypocrisy. Objections have been raised to the long theological discussion in *In Memoriam*, and the *Idylls of the King* have been criticized as merely a fanciful and romantic escape from the drab environment of industrialism. To all this there is some truth: the Victorians were perplexed by their environment, and they sought and found another world in Tennyson's poetry. *In Memoriam,* written to commemorate Tennyson's friend, Henry Hallam, is inordinately long; but the Victorians did not mind, for it must be remembered that to doubt the immortality of the soul on biological grounds was a subject in which Tennyson and his friends were passionately interested, and was something new in Victorian England.

Tennyson's reputation was not made rapidly. His first poems were published in 1827, but it was some time before he became famous. He was made poet laureate in 1850. Then, seeking privacy, he went to live on the Isle of Wight, where his home promptly became a Mecca for all English-speaking people. Those who came without letters of introduction hid behind trees for long hours to catch a glimpse of the huge, shambling figure; those with letters held their breath while Tennyson read his poetry aloud, as was his daily custom, his "deep bucolic voice . . . booming and chanting with sudden lifts and with disconcerting hisses and whispers."

The poet remained here twenty-two years, and then, to rid himself of the crowds, sought refuge in rural Sussex. Although old, he was still active, and for two more decades poems poured forth from his new retreat, while his fame increased. "His birthdays took upon themselves the solemnity of a national festival; his compatriots would send him presents of honey and garden chairs and rolls of tweed; they christened lakes after him in New Zealand; explorers would select the most remote of hyperborean cliffs for the honor of the poet's name; rosarians would employ it to give a final lustre to their choicest blooms; his every moment, his every action, his clothes, his tobacco, were canvassed and proclaimed in the illustrated journals."[1] But Lord Tennyson (for he finally accepted a peerage) was not spoiled. Childlike he was and more childlike he became. The evening of his life was both dignified and happy.

His contemporary popularity is not to be accounted for purely on poetic grounds. He was a master of poetic technique, but other Englishmen had written poetry quite as good without eliciting such universal praise. He was patriotic and his *Ode on the Death of the Duke of Wellington* has possibly never been equaled, as an expression of national pride and sorrow; but his name overshadowed that of his contemporaries (with the exception of Browning) primarily because what he wrote coincided nicely with what middle-class England chose to believe and feel.

The English middle class always had laid stress on the value and sanctity of the family as an institution. The children of the aris-

---

[1] Harold Nicolson, *Tennyson* (1923), p. 196. By permission of Houghton Mifflin Company and Constable and Company, Ltd.

tocracy, largely educated away from home, introduced to society at an early age, adventurous, knowing much of good and evil, often did not feel the same regard for intimate family ties as did the children of the middle class. Nor did the children of the working class worship the family; they were thrown on their own resources too early. The middle-class family, however, lived at home and loved the home.

> Not learned, save in gracious household ways,
> Not perfect, nay, but full of tender wants,
> No Angel, but a dearer being, all dipt
> In Angel instincts, breathing Paradise.

Thus did the laureate, writing of his mother, appeal directly to the middle class, which was still moral in the old-fashioned sense. Lack of charity, lack of understanding, narrowness of vision, it might, perhaps, justly be accused of; but none could doubt that it had risen by hard work and sobriety. Therefore it demanded, and found, sobriety in its poet.

> Authors—essayist, atheist, novelist, realist, rhymster, play your part,
> Paint the moral shame of nature with the living hues of art.
> Rip your brothers' vices open, strip your own foul passions bare;
> Down with Reticence, down with Reverence—forward—naked—let
>   them stare.

The middle class thoroughly believed in the Victorian compromise. It did not seek to advance too rapidly along political paths; neither did Tennyson.

> . . . our slowly-grown
> And crown'd Republic's crowning common-sense,
> That saved her many times.

Freedom, precedent, and settled ways of government expressed his ideas and those of his readers.

The middle class, also religious, was bewildered by biology. It did not believe in a material universe; it was troubled about the future life, and it demanded a message which would quiet and soothe its religious doubts. The poet laureate also was troubled about these things. He was not a theologian, nor did he concern himself with the Church Fathers; but he wished to reconcile religion with evolution. His solution has been called a compromise, a bit of logic-chopping, "a pathetically inadequate formula"; but it satisfied the majority of his own day. According to Tennyson, "God must exist, because the human heart felt an instinctive need for his existence. The soul must be immortal, because any other solution was unthinkable."

> By night, into the deeper night!
> The deeper night? A clearer day
> Than our poor twilight dawn on earth—
> If night, what barren toil to be!
> What life, so maim'd by night, were worth
> Our living out? Not mine to me.

To "cling to faith beyond the power of faith" was not always easy; and at times Tennyson seemed to have his doubts, as when he wrote of the stars:

> Innumerable, pitiless, passionless eyes,
> Cold fires, yet with the power to burn and brand
> His nothingness into man.

Then always came assurance:

> But such a tide as moving seems asleep,
> Too full for sound and foam,
> When that which drew from out the boundless deep
> Turns again home.

The foregoing eleven writers offer a fair résumé of Victorian thought. Many of the Victorians, of course, did not think at all. The squires, with their "view halloo," read Surtees rather than Huxley, sparing themselves any mental exercise. The vogue of the novel was at its height in Victorian times, but novels were read for pleasure rather than for enlightenment. The middle class grew indignant with Dickens over the treatment of Oliver Twist, shed tears of laughter over Pickwick, and tears of sorrow over Little Nell. It enjoyed Thackeray, smiled at Captain Costigan, approved the dignity of Colonel Newcome and Major Pendennis, and appreciated the cleverness of Becky Sharp; but all this did not involve thinking about what was right and just in the world, let alone speculating on the eternities. There were also the Pre-Raphaelite brotherhood, with their poems, paintings, and ideas; but most of the Victorians preferred to share Browning's robust belief that "God's in his heaven, all's right with the world."

Later writers, inoculated with Marxian doctrines, have not regarded the Victorians highly. Since capitalism in all the vigor of its early manhood characterized the Victorian day, that in itself is a signal for many to flay the bourgeoisie,—a pleasant pastime. One may point to the jerry-built slums of Glasgow, Birmingham, and Manchester, to the ostentatious furniture, to the somewhat crude and

# What the Victorians Thought

literal paintings of Watt (who covered canvas by the square yard), to Holman Hunt's sickly-sweet representations of the Christ, in order to justify an indictment of Victorian England. "I found myself," wrote Edward Carpenter, the poet, "—and without knowing where I was—in the middle of that strange period of human evolution, the Victorian age, which in some respects, one now thinks, marked the lowest ebb of modern civilized society: a period in which not only commercialism in public life, but cant in religion, pure materialism in science, futility in social convention, the worship of stocks and shares, the starving of the human heart, the denial of the human body and its needs, the huddling concealment of the body in clothes, the 'impure hush' on matters of sex, class-division, contempt of manual labor, and the cruel barring of women from every natural and useful expression of their lives, were carried to an extremity of folly difficult for us now to realize."[1]

Even Carlyle could find no harsher words than these to fling at his fellow Victorians. Yet, during the long and wonderful reign of the good queen, a little island set the pace for all mankind in industry, in law, in elevating the character and the dignity of the poor, in the advance of science, in spreading the Christian religion and Parliamentary institutions in all parts of the earth. Distant lands were peopled with Anglo-Saxons, and the dread of war grew less. If one compares representative Victorians with famous Britons of earlier or later times, it is difficult to find in any age in English history a similar galaxy of distinguished men and women; and in view of their accomplishments not only in economic achievement but also in literature, in science, in political and social morality, one must give highest rank to the Victorians.

[1] Edward Carpenter, *My Days and Dreams* (1918), p. 320. By permission of George Allen & Unwin, Ltd.

# CHAPTER XXVII

## The End of Laissez Faire

### 1880-1914

IN 1886 a mob, led by men with red flags, broke the windows of the Carlton Club, looted shops in Piccadilly, turned respectable people out of their broughams in Hyde Park, and terrorized the fashionable West End of London.

One year later came "Bloody Sunday," a rough-and-tumble contest in Trafalgar Square between unemployed workingmen and the police. Law and order triumphed, but at the price of calling out the military. "No one who saw it," wrote a contemporary, "will ever forget the strange and indeed terrible sight of that grey winter day, the vast sombre-coloured crowd, the brief but fierce struggle at the corner of the Strand, and the river of steel and scarlet that moved slowly through the dusty swaying masses when two squadrons of the Life Guards were summoned up from Whitehall."[1]

Two years afterward the strike of the London dockers, fifty thousand unskilled longshoremen led by John Burns, a self-educated Scottish engineer, tied up all shipping at the empire's metropolis. Destitute and ignorant though they were, these men had the courage, the pertinacity, and the discipline to win their strike. The extra penny an hour became theirs, and England realized, as she never had done before, the pitiful way of life of her lower classes.

These demonstrations heralded something new. Within thirty years democratic England was to appreciate the inadequacy of the Victorian compromise made by the middle class and aristocracy and was to adjust herself to the changed conditions. Leaving the affairs of the empire, diplomacy, and Ireland during these years for consideration elsewhere, we shall deal here with the relation of domestic British politics to the demise of laissez faire and to the birth of the Labor party.

We must, however, consider first the years of Gladstone's second ministry (1880–1885), just before these outbursts, when industry and commerce were recovering very slowly from the severe slump of the late seventies which had driven Disraeli from office (see page

[1] J. W. Mackail, *Life of William Morris* (1899), Vol. II, p. 191. By permission of Longmans, Green & Co.

# The End of Laissez Faire

709), and agriculture was not recovering at all. Under the strain of the prolonged depression, shipyards lay idle, factories closed their doors, farmers could not pay their rents, and agricultural laborers flocked to the cities to swell the ranks of those already without work. To be sure, factory hours were shorter than in the earlier part of the century because of the factory legislation, and the working-man could buy more goods with his money because of the decline in prices. But all this was of no use to the penniless unemployed. England was the richest country in the world, but thousands of home-less, hungry men were tramping the streets of her cities.

Gladstone said that the bad times were only temporary and that the government could do nothing. After refusing to consent to the investigation of economic conditions by a royal commission, he soon changed his mind and ordered such a report. The commission proposed only two highly conservative remedies: cheaper manufacturing costs and new markets. Apparently the alliance between the middle class and the aristocracy, firm in its belief in laissez faire, could think of nothing better and had faith in Macaulay's idea: "Our rulers will best promote the improvement of the nation by strictly confining themselves to their own legitimate duties, by leaving capital to find its most lucrative course, commodities their fair price, industry and intelligence their natural reward, idleness and folly their natural punishment, by maintaining peace, by defending property, by dimin-ishing the price of law, and by observing strict economy in every department of the state. Let the government do this: the people will assuredly do the rest."

Some thought otherwise. Hyndman, the leader of the English Marxian socialists, insisted that workingmen must strive for political power and for the abolishment of private productive property. Tele-graph and postal service, gas, and water were already state or muni-cipal monopolies, and he wanted the government to continue in this direction by nationalizing industry upon a large scale. To persuade the conservative trade unions that this was necessary, Hyndman started the Social Democratic Federation. In this way, he hoped to build up an effective political party to obtain his socialistic aims, but his federation accomplished relatively little. Added to his voice was that of Henry George, an American with unorthodox economic ideas. His pet theory of a single tax only, and that on land, was per-haps obscure, but his indictment of contemporary England left a sting. "So long as all the increased wealth which modern progress brings goes but to build up greater fortunes, to increase luxury, to make sharper the contrast between the House of Have and the House of Have Not, progress is not real, and cannot be permanent."

# A History of England and the British Empire

More influential yet, in the long run, was the Fabian Society. It was organized in 1883 for the purpose of educating the public about socialism, which it wanted introduced gradually, by legislation and without class war. Its membership was never large; but among the brilliant young writers who worked for it were Sidney and Beatrice Webb, H. G. Wells, and George Bernard Shaw. The pamphlet literature poured forth by the Fabians was vigorous, provocative, and in many instances the result of careful research. It did much to make socialism respectable in England.

This socialistic attack on the old order and on the gods of laissez faire had its echo in Parliament among the Liberals in the person of Joseph Chamberlain and among the Conservatives in the less radical Lord Randolph Churchill (see page 759). "What ransom will property pay," asked Chamberlain, "for the security which it enjoys?" and although "ransom" was afterward toned down into "insurance," the earlier word was not forgotten. Chamberlain was rising rapidly in popular favor, both within his own party and without. Gladstone had been compelled, for expediency's sake, to include him in his second ministry, although he disliked him as a pushing stranger and a Birmingham manufacturer of screws, whose ideas on religion were unorthodox and who at one time had been in favor of republicanism. Chamberlain had not hesitated to publish what he called an "unauthorized program," which was anathema to old-time radicals like Bright, let alone to Gladstone. This program incorporated many socialistic schemes such as heavy graduated taxes on the income of the wealthy, municipal public works, and free educational facilities for the poor. In addition, it called for the purchase, by condemnation if necessary, of agricultural land, and its resale in small allotments. "Three acres and a cow" was to be the new slogan, the minimum to which British workers were entitled by simple justice. Could it be possible that the British Liberal party would listen to such novelties?

Confronted by this split in his own party,—between the old Whig element and the old radicals, on the one hand, and the adherents of Chamberlain and the new radicals on the other,—Gladstone found a way to heal it temporarily by further political reform, upon which, at least, all types of Liberal thought were agreed. In 1884 he pushed through Parliament the third Reform Bill, which gave to the agricultural laborers in the counties what the second Reform Bill, in 1867, had given to the industrial workers in the towns—virtual household suffrage. Those peasants, who until recent decades had been the most numerous element in England's population, had won no political rights for themselves. Now they received the vote, simply as a measure of justice, to grant them rights equal to those that the factory workers

# The End of Laissez Faire

had gained within the first century of the Industrial Revolution. In
1832 about one adult male in thirty was entitled to vote; in 1867
somewhat more than half the adult males were enfranchised; now, in
1884, four out of five were given the ballot. This was virtually manhood suffrage. Those left out, such as young men living in their
fathers' houses, servants, and others, who did not maintain separate
households, would receive the vote in the fourth Reform Bill, in 1918,
and by that time women too would be enfranchised. In 1885 this
third Reform Bill was supplemented by a further redistribution of
seats, which ended the remaining rotten boroughs and increased the
House of Commons to 670 members, with 465 from England, 103
from Ireland, 72 from Scotland, and 30 from Wales.

The English party system seems to function best with two rival
parties of about equal strength. There were long periods, however,
when one party enjoyed predominance, such as the Whig ascendancy
from 1714 to 1760 and the Tory ascendancy from 1770 to 1830. Between the first and second reform bills, as we saw, the Whig-Liberals
were in power about three quarters of the time. Never were the rivals
so closely balanced in power as in the half century between Gladstone's first appearance as prime minister, in 1868, and the fusing of
the parties into a coalition during the World War, in 1916. Each
enjoyed twenty-four years of power. The Liberals were in the saddle
during the four ministries of Gladstone (1868–1874, 1880–1885,
February–July, 1886, 1892–1894), that of his successor Rosebery
(1894–1895), and then, after a long Conservative interlude, those of
Campbell-Bannerman (1905–1908) and Asquith (1908–1916). The
Conservatives began with Disraeli (1874–1880), and then came the
three ministries of Salisbury (1885–1886, 1886–1892, 1895–1902),
followed immediately by that of his nephew, Balfour (1902–1905).
This close balance explains the marginal importance of a group like
Chamberlain's Unionists or Parnell's Irish Nationalists, whose members could swing the majority from one party to the other.

Party overturns came in unusually rapid succession in 1885 and
1886, while business was undergoing another sharp decline. Within
a period of fifteen months each party fell twice from office. Gladstone's second ministry ended in June, 1885, when he was defeated
on the budget by a few votes, Parnell and the Irish, we recall, desert-
ing to the Conservatives. The Tory champion Lord Salisbury, who
was descended from Cecil, Elizabeth's famous minister, and who had
been Disraeli's right-hand man at Berlin, formed his first ministry.
This was overthrown early in 1886 as the result of a general election.
Gladstone was back in power for the third time, but only for six
months. Then another general election broke the Liberal party in

two, Chamberlain and the anti-home-rule Liberals joining forces with the Conservatives (see page 759). This second time Salisbury's ministry, thus reinforced, was to last six years.

The Irish home-rule bill of 1886, for the time being, continued to distract the attention of the public from the main economic issue of the abandonment of England's old policy of hands off trade, commerce, and industry. The bill did more than that; for it disastrously weakened the cause of the reformers by drawing their leader, Chamberlain, over toward the Conservative camp. Chamberlain hated Irish Nationalists more than he did English landlords; and since he had to co-operate with the latter in order to defeat the former, his zeal for social reform lessened. He and his fellow rebels from the Liberal ranks organized their own party and called themselves Liberal Unionists. The emphasis was on the second word, since their group was composed primarily of old Whigs, conservative Liberals who detested home rule but had scant enthusiasm for reform. Brilliant, eccentric Lord Randolph Churchill tried hard to commit the Conservatives to a strong labor program. But he was in poor health, and when, disgusted by military extravagance, he resigned from the Conservative cabinet, to die shortly afterward, there was no one to take his place. Salisbury, the Conservative prime minister, was at heart no reactionary; but his interest lay primarily in foreign affairs, and political pressure from the working classes was not yet sufficiently powerful to force his hand.

In the rival Liberal camp the prospects for a strong reform stand were no brighter. The social-reform Liberals were without a natural leader; for most of them had followed Gladstone rather than Chamberlain on the Irish question. Just as Salisbury was preoccupied with foreign affairs, so Gladstone, old and venerable, had his heart set on one thing and one only—home rule for Ireland. He did not like the new ideas. The new sort of reform, he felt, would put an end to the old retrenchment, while obliquely it attacked rugged individualism and the sacred rights of private property. In benighted Ireland he was reluctantly prepared to sacrifice property rights, but not in progressive England.

The tide against laissez faire, however, had set in, and the logic of the situation made it necessary for both political parties to bid for the votes of the workingmen, who were more and more influenced by socialistic ideas. Chamberlain, in allying himself with the Conservatives, had not forgotten all his old enthusiasms. He did secure a part of his "unauthorized program" in an act facilitating the purchase of small holdings, and in another doing away with all school fees for the children of the poor. In 1888 the creation of County Councils removed most of the burdens of local administration in the rural districts from the justices of the peace to popularly elected bodies. The "J. P.'s," who had virtually controlled English local government from Tudor times, retained their functions as magistrates only (see page 248). Chamberlain went even further, and in the next election campaign advocated old-age pensions. He did so, however, frankly as an individual, not as the head of the Liberal Unionists; for no important party in the nineteenth century would commit itself to such wild heresy.

The Liberals, however, stole Chamberlain's thunder. The social-reform group had not given up their interest in his "unauthorized" program, and they were strong enough, in fact, to commit the Liberal party to their "Newcastle Programme." This was a curious mixture: it demanded, among other things, home rule, a leash for the House of Lords, disestablishment of the Anglican Church in Wales and of the Presbyterian Church in Scotland, local option for the liquor traffic, payment for members of the House of Commons, district councils, parish councils, small agricultural allotments, and abolition of plural voting. "It is an absurd programme, an impractical programme, a dishonest programme," thundered Chamberlain. Nevertheless, when the time came for a general election, the Liberals carried the day, and Gladstone was brought into office for his fourth and last ministry (1892–1894). It was noticed, as significant of the popular demand for reform, that the Liberal candidates who stuck closest to the Newcastle program made the best showing at the polls. Had Gladstone been willing to extend more than a perfunctory blessing to these ideas, his majority in the Commons would apparently have been substantially larger.

This fourth Gladstone ministry did scarcely anything for social reform. The prime minister, we recall, put his heart into his second home-rule bill; and when that was defeated by the Lords in 1893 (see page 762), it was evident to all that he was too old, too deaf, and too blind to carry on much longer. The following year he resigned because of a new quarrel with the Lords and friction within his own cabinet. The Grand Old Man was eighty-five and had four more years to live. His successor, the Earl of Rosebery, essentially a Whig aristocrat who owed his promotion to good manners, family position, and the favor of the queen, proved a disappointment. He was credited with three ambitions in life, to become prime minister, to win the Derby, and to marry an heiress—all of which he realized. His fifteen and a half months in office (1894–1895) were sterile of achievement.

In 1895 the Unionists (a term now applied to Conservatives and their Liberal-Unionist allies) returned to power. They had a thumping majority over both Liberals and Irish Nationalists combined, and they were to keep it for ten years. This period in English politics (1895–1905) is sometimes referred to as that of the Cecil dynasty, owing to the influence of the two Cecil descendants—Lord Salisbury and his nephew and successor as prime minister, Arthur Balfour, later Earl Balfour. No. 10 Downing Street was even jokingly called the "Hotel Cecil." It was a period of changes in British foreign policy, of vital importance in the empire, and of economic reforms in Ireland (see Chapters XXVIII, XXIV, XXV); but as far as social reform in England was concerned it was comparatively barren.

Victoria died early in 1901, surviving by only three weeks the nineteenth century, with which her sixty-four-year reign is so intimately associated in England. She had won the enthusiasm of her subjects once more in her later years, and the whole empire had joined in lavish tribute to her in the jubilees marking the fiftieth and sixtieth anniversaries of her accession. She was succeeded by her eldest son as Edward VII (1901–1910); he was already nearly sixty and a grandfather. Edward was the most popular occupant of the throne since Charles II. Dignified, robust, and kindly, he was a thoroughgoing man of the world and sportsman. Throughout his long wait as Prince of Wales his mother had denied him any role in the government more serious than the purely ceremonial appearances which she herself neglected almost completely during most of her widowhood. Edward had consequently managed to enjoy life thoroughly in unofficial ways, and many of the gayer places in France knew him well. He and his charming Danish wife were very much liked, and, in spite of all lack of apprenticeship, he made an able king during his few remaining years of life.

Next in influence to the two Cecils in the Unionist party was Joseph Chamberlain, now colonial secretary. The fact that so important a personality chose of his own free will this post once considered of minor importance was an indication of the trend of the times. He had not abandoned his early ideas of social betterment, but he sought to realize them now through trade expansion, imperialism, and colonial federation rather than through direct intervention of the government in the affairs of the poor. What England needed more than anything else, thought Chamberlain, was prosperity. This could be attained, in his opinion, only by abandoning free trade, knitting closer the economic ties of empire, establishing preferential duties on colonial products, and defending British manufacturers from foreign dumping by a protective tariff. England no longer enjoyed the long lead in industrial development which had made free trade safe in the middle of the nineteenth century. Behind high tariff walls the United States, Germany, and other nations were building up their own industries so successfully that they not only were becoming less dependent upon British textiles, metals, and coal but were actually invading free-trade England with their own products (see pages 650, 832). With the surplus resulting from a protective tariff, Chamberlain felt, England could pay for old-age pensions and the relief of the distressed classes.

Chamberlain's campaign against free trade was initiated directly after the Boer War. Balfour, having succeeded his uncle as prime minister in 1902, had not much interest in economic questions. Primarily concerned with upholding the prestige of the Conservatives, he dodged the issue raised by his energetic colonial secretary as long as he could, since influential members of the party opposed the new plan. Chamberlain thereupon resigned in 1903, to press his campaign for protective tariffs with greater vigor. Almost immediately the Unionists fell to quarreling among themselves. Certain of them, warm-hearted adherents of Chamberlain and open advocates of protection, were known as "whole-hoggers." Others, the "little-piggers," taking their cue from Balfour, were willing to consider a tax on imported food as part of a scheme of imperial federation, if and when the latter had been ratified by a general election. Others, the "free-fooders," refused to have anything to do with any scheme which involved a tax on bread.

These dissensions among their rivals caused joy among the Liberals, who rallied to the defense of free trade and the cheap loaf. The temporary economic boom made protectionist warnings less significant. British exports were increasing—£349,000,000 in 1902, £371,000,000 in 1904, and £460,000,000 in 1906; while unemployment was on the decline. The Liberals, also, had other strings to their bow: the unsatisfactory conduct of the Boer War and the financial scandals connected with it, Balfour's ultra-Anglican and unpopular Education Act, and the importation of Indian coolies into South Africa. But none of these rivaled in tactical importance the new heresies of Chamberlain. He was the bête noire of the Liberal party, which he had ruined in 1886 by "betraying" Gladstone; now, it was feared, he would "betray" the memory of Cobden and Bright!

The Liberals made the most of their opportunity. Balfour's majority in the Commons began to dwindle away; and at the end of 1905 he resigned, bringing to an end the Cecil decade of Conservative rule and paving the way for a decade of Liberal control. The new Liberal prime minister was Sir Henry Campbell-Bannerman, a Scot nearly seventy years old. In his cabinet were three men destined to achieve prominence in the next ten years: Herbert Henry Asquith, Chancellor of the Exchequer, who would succeed to the premiership in 1908; David Lloyd George, temporarily in a minor position, who would replace Asquith at the Exchequer and ultimately, in the midst of war, as prime minister; and Sir Edward Grey, who was to handle British foreign relations during the critical prewar years.

Early in 1906 a general election established the new cabinet more firmly in power. The country returned about 380 Liberals, with about 50 Laborites (of whom 29 were of the new Labor party) and 80 Irish Nationalists as their potential allies, with only about 130 Conservatives and 25 Liberal Unionists in opposition (the figures vary slightly in different sources). Under this Liberal leadership Parliament was to enact legislation of tremendous social and political significance. In securing the support of the Laborites and Irish the Liberals assumed the obligation of promoting important legislation desired by those two groups.

The most significant immediate result of this election was the arrival at Westminster of the Laborites. They invaded the staid precincts of the House of Commons wearing cloth caps instead of silk "toppers,"—an ominous portent to the fast-dying Victorians, accustomed to considering government as the private preserve of the wellborn and the well-to-do. The Labor party—according to Ramsay MacDonald, one of its early leaders—was born in 1900 as the result of a conference at which there met representatives chiefly of the trade unions, the Fabian Society, Hyndman's Social Democratic Federation, and the rival Marxian group, the Independent Labor party. It had, therefore, a socialistic tinge. The conference had been planned at the Trade Union Congress the preceding year, "to devise means of increasing the number of Labor members" in Parliament. The socialistic organizations supplied the intellectual material of the new organization, and the trade unions most of the membership. There were some twelve hundred and fifty trade unions, with a total membership of about two million. Hitherto the trade unions, which had been legalized in 1871 and in 1876 (see page 704), had not been actively engaged in politics; but the "Taff Vale decision" in 1901 was to make them change their minds and push to rapid completion the plans for the new party's organization, which, as we have just seen, elected nearly thirty members in 1906.

Taff Vale was an isolated valley in Wales in which there had been a railway strike on a short line which carried coal for the navy. The strikers were sued for picketing, that is, posting members near the scene of the strike in an endeavor to keep new workers from taking jobs as strikebreakers. Naturally this practice often involved in-

# The End of Laissez Faire

timidation. The case had been carried to the House of Lords, which, when acting as the court of highest appeal, consisted of the Chancellor and the few law lords. They handed down a decision that made trade unions financially liable for offenses committed by their agents in such disputes. Employers might now sue trade unions as legally responsible bodies if any damage were done. The Taff Vale decision eventually cost the Amalgamated Society of Railway Servants, which had no direct responsibility for this local strike, no less than £23,000 in damages and about as much again in costs. Consequently, to secure a reversal of this decision by Parliamentary act, the trade unions made common cause with the two socialistic groups in the Labor party. These developments were not overlooked by the older parties, to whom the workingman's vote was a matter of real importance.

Upon meeting Parliament, the new Liberal prime minister declared that underlying every proposal of his government would be a policy of social reconstruction "looking toward a greater equalization of wealth and a destruction of the oppressive land and liquor monopolies." Asquith, who was Chancellor of the Exchequer at the time, hinted strongly at radical measures as he made an even more direct attack on social and economic maladjustment. "Property," he declared, "must be associated in the minds of the people with the ideas of reason and of justice." The Liberals were evidently preparing to embark on a new course. Constantly spurred on by the Laborites, they enacted a whole series of laws which, from the standpoint of nineteenth-century liberalism, were socialistic in character and revolutionary.

One of the first of these laws was the "Workmen's Compensation Act" of 1906, which increased the scope and made more stringent the provisions of two earlier acts (1880 and 1897) that had already established the principle of employers' liability for compensation to injured workmen. Before these acts a workman injured in the course of his work could gain compensation only by suing his employer for damages, an expensive and lengthy process; but the principle of employers' liability made the employer legally responsible for such injuries to his workers unless the latter might be proved to have been willfully careless. The new statute of 1906 extended this employers' liability for compensation, not only in industrial accidents but also in many occupational diseases, to most workers who received less than £250 a year. Under this law a worker received about half his usual wages for the duration of his injuries or illness, while in case of death his dependents received a sum about equal to three years' wages. Nearly six million workers were protected under this act, and in 1912, for instance, compensation totaling more than £3,000,000 was granted in nearly 3600 cases of death and more than 424,000 cases of injury or illness.

A companion piece of labor legislation, the Trades Disputes Act, became a statute on the same day. This reversed the Taff Vale decision; for it granted unions the right "peaceably to persuade," or the right to picket, and also the right to boycott as long as these activities did not involve violence. The funds of unions, moreover, were safeguarded against suits such as those allowed by the Taff Vale decision.

A hot contest preceded the passage of the old-age pension bill in 1908, providing, with certain stipulations as to minimum residence and income, a pension, on a sliding scale, of between one and five shillings a week at the age of seventy for every British subject of good character, not criminal, insane, or receiving poor relief at the time, in the United Kingdom. Its coming had been prophesied in the budget speech of Asquith the year before. In that address, while carefully explaining that he was not a socialist, he said that if the state intervened at the beginning of life's journey in matters of education, it was only logical that it should do so when an individual "spent out with a life of unrequited labour finds himself confronted in old age, without fault or demerit of his own, with the prospect of physical want and the sacrifice of self-respect." This was completely at odds with the nineteenth-century idea that the individual, if compelled, could and would provide for his own old age, and it was a distinct abandonment of one of the most fundamental tenets of laissez faire. There were no provisions, as in the earlier German law, whereby prospective beneficiaries contributed in part to their own pensions. Balfour pointed out how extraordinarily difficult it would be to prove the birth date of many of the poor in the United Kingdom, to say nothing of providing proof as to character; furthermore, there was the problem of funds with which to pay these pensions. But these arguments had scant effect upon the Labor members and the Liberals of the new persuasion, who were worried about Labor's hold upon the constituencies and fearful lest a new party should spring up on the left to undermine their own. The majority in the Commons seemed to see little difference between a major general's pension and a laborer's. The Laborite Will Crooks was quick to answer the objection as to the character of the individual pensioned. "A man of seventy," he said, "with nothing in the world to help him is going to cut a pretty shine on five shillings a week, whether his character is good or bad. What could he do with it? It is not enough to keep him in decency, and he would be well punished for not taking care, if he had to live on five shillings a

# The End of Laissez Faire

week. Who are you, to be continually finding fault? Who amongst you has such a clear record as to be able to point to the iniquity and wickedness of an old man of seventy? I said before, and I repeat it, if a man is foolish enough to get old, and if he has not been artful enough to get rich, you have no right to punish him for it. It is no business of yours. It is sufficient for you to know that he has grown old." The bill became law, and by 1912 nearly a million aged people were enjoying its benefits at a total cost of about £12,000,000, about half of what was spent that year for naval construction and repairs. Later the amount of pension was doubled and those with less meager incomes than the original minimum were made eligible.

In the midst of the Liberal social legislation a Parliamentary committee in 1909 issued in forty volumes a report embodying a three years' study of poor relief. Its wealth of statistical material revealed the unevenness of the distribution of wealth in England. One eighth of the population enjoyed nearly half the wealth; the other half was divided among the remaining thirty-nine million inhabitants. About one third of the employed adult workmen earned less than twenty-five shillings a week, while barely a quarter of them received more than thirty-five shillings. These meager wages were barely enough for existence, even when they came in regularly, while there was no chance to set up a reserve to tide the worker through emergency periods when illness or unemployment might cut off his earnings. At a cost of about £15,000,000 a year the public was supporting some six hundred thousand fairly permanent paupers, in addition to many others who needed poor relief for shorter periods. The committee were divided in the conclusions which they drew from their findings, and consequently their recommendations to Parliament were divided into a majority and a minority report. The former was mild in its advocacy of changes, but the latter contained what at the time seemed very radical suggestions for social security. The Poor Law of 1834, which had supplanted the Elizabethan legislation, had dealt with poverty as an accomplished fact and was concerned primarily with the best method of treating those who were already poor (see page 622). The minority report boldly advocated methods for preventing poverty by alleviating some of its chief causes, such as sickness and unemployment. It consequently became a program for further important progress in social legislation along the line already started with workmen's compensation and old-age pensions.

A moderate attack on unemployment, advocated in the majority report, quickly passed into law with the establishing of the Labor Exchanges Act in 1909. The more technical manufacturing became, the more skill was required. As a result, young men were in constant demand, and it became increasingly difficult to obtain work for the older and unskilled men. Following the German example, the government established several hundred public labor exchanges. These would prevent, it was thought, the wandering of the unemployed here and there in search of work, since they would serve as clearinghouses for information as to where opportunities, if any, might exist throughout the United Kingdom. The government would also, if necessary, advance to the worker the cost of transportation to his new job. At once such exchanges began to be established, with a central office in London and with district offices in the other cities and smaller towns, while much of the work was done through the co-operation of local voluntary committees and the trade unions. The project was successful to a moderate degree and served to ameliorate unemployment. By 1912 the labor exchanges filled about a half million vacancies, roughly one third of the applications for employment.

Sweated labor also engaged the attention of Parliament in 1909, resulting in the passage of the Trade Boards Act. "Sweated" was an adjective applied to the unskilled labor conditions characterized by very low wages, excessive hours, and those unsanitary working conditions about which Charles Kingsley had written (see page 778). To lessen these evils, trade, or minimum-wage, boards, with a membership consisting of representatives of employers, workers, and government, were established throughout England for the purpose of fixing a minimum rate of wages. This rate was to be voluntary for a while, after which it became compulsory upon employers. Only certain trades were specified as coming under the act, especially those which had to do with the manufacture of ready-made clothing, where women in particular, lacking unions to protect them, were often working very long hours for less than fifteen shillings a week. Inspectors were to be appointed to enforce the decisions of the local boards. The bill, the government's spokesman asserted, was "at once an experiment and a revolution—a new step in social progress." "This is the first occasion," he went on to say, "certainly in modern Parliamentary times, in which any government has proposed machinery, first for deciding and secondly for enforcing a legal rate of wages. To that extent the proposal is new—to that extent the proposal is a revolution." In older Parliamentary times, we recall, the English government, in the Statute of Laborers and in the Elizabethan Statute of Apprentices (see pages 186, 302), had set up machinery for deciding and enforcing a legal rate of wages; but those earlier acts were designed to keep wages down by establishing a maximum, and the machinery for enforcement had consisted of justices of the

# The End of Laissez Faire

peace from the employer class, without the representation or participation of the workers. The bill aroused much opposition. The tariff reformers now saw their chance to argue for a protective tariff. The bill, they said, would simply drive business out of England; only behind a protective tariff wall would it be possible to cope successfully with sweated labor. Germany had introduced reforms of this sort, but she had high tariffs. The argument was not a bad one, but it was not heeded. The majority in the Commons was ready to trust that England could still compete with Germany and at the same time establish a minimum-wage law. In 1912, after a serious coal strike, this principle was extended to the miners as well, even though they were not exactly a sweated industry and had their strong unions to protect them.

Health, as the poor-relief committee had demonstrated, was one of the major factors in poverty; and as a third important piece of social legislation in 1909 Parliament passed the Housing and Town Planning Act. According to the census of 1901, millions were living in tenements of only one or two rooms. The industrial towns, as we saw (see page 498), had grown in mushroom fashion, with dingy houses, back to back and devoid of ventilation. Cellars and basements were crowded with human inhabitants. Open spaces, parks, commons, and amusement centers were lacking. In such towns it was easy to demonstrate that the average "age of death of the gentry and professional classes was 44; of the tradesmen, 27; and among the laborers, only 19." To remedy this situation was beyond the power of private initiative, and, in the opinion of the Liberal government, the strong arm of the state was needed. John Burns, the labor leader, who was now in the ministry and president of the Local Government Board, was largely responsible for the passage of the bill. He argued that England was not so destitute of land that the workers should be housed in tenements without back yards and gardens, so important as playgrounds for the children. This Housing and Town Planning Act forbade the construction of back-to-back houses in the future; gave increased powers to the medical officers; and made landlords legally responsible for the condition of their houses, not only when renting them but at all times. The demolition of certain dwellings was made mandatory, and opportunity to build better ones with state aid was assured. Municipalities were authorized to condemn certain areas and to create open spaces in accordance with such aesthetic and sanitary programs as they should see fit to adopt. Parliament also passed several lesser acts for the promotion of health and child welfare.

Finally, to crown the whole program of social legislation, there

# A History of England and the British Empire

was the National Insurance Act, providing insurance against sickness and unemployment. It was more radical than any of the other bills in the program and potentially more costly. Though proposed in 1909, it did not become law until late in 1911, because of very important complications which we shall consider shortly. Sickness, it was pointed out, probably accounted for about 30 per cent of pauperism. The sick workers lacked funds for doctors' bills and hospital charges, to say nothing of supporting their families during the period of enforced idleness. There was already a certain amount of private insurance against illness through mutual "friendly societies" and trade unions; but a large part of the workers who needed insurance most were unprotected. The act made sickness insurance compulsory for most workers (nearly fifteen million) receiving less than £160 a year. Unlike the old-age pension system, where the government alone carried all the cost, the worker, his employer, and the government each contributed a few pence each week toward the insurance. In the event of illness the worker received not only doctor's services and hospital care but also for the support of himself and his family a specified amount a week for the first six months and a smaller weekly sum thereafter. There were, of course, objections to a measure as radical as this. Not only were wage-earners to be docked of their pay without their consent, but doctors were virtually dragooned into serving on boards, a circumstance which they asserted broke their personal relations with their patients and which meant that their fees would be lowered, although payment would be guaranteed. Society was up in arms. Many ladies of social prominence, objecting to a law which made it obligatory for them to paste stamps weekly in the insurance books of their servants, solemnly agreed to discharge their servants and to do their own cooking; but they thought better of it very shortly.

With the unemployment portion of the national insurance policy the government proceeded more slowly. The bill likewise called for contributions by worker, employer, and government, and provided, after one week of unemployment, for the payment of some six or seven shillings a week for a specified period. There were certain restrictions and limitations, including the stipulation that there would be no payments for unemployment arising from the workers' own misconduct or from strikes, lockouts, or similar labor disturbances. Also, if a man had seldom been unemployed, he might obtain at the age of sixty his own contributions to the fund, as well as the interest that had accumulated at a small percentage. Whereas sickness insurance was extended to all trades, unemployment insurance had a modest start with about two and a half million workers in the engineering and building trades, where the seasonal nature of the work increased the risk of unemployment. Under such auspices began the great experiment which became the blessing or the curse of contemporary England,—the "dole," as it is called in popular parlance,—under which the postwar government would later support, with little or no contribution on their part, millions of unemployed in continual idleness.

Thus, in the six years after they had come into power at the end of 1905, the Liberals had carried through an economic program breath-taking in its nature, which was entirely contrary to the laissez-faire liberalism of the nineteenth century. In the three great measures of workmen's compensation, old-age pensions, and national insurance they had helped to dispel some of the major worries which had continually hung over those who toiled with no economic margin of safety. Measures for housing, health, and child welfare had also been passed to improve the laborers' living conditions. The Trades Disputes Act had strengthened the position of the trade unions, and the labor exchanges had to a minor degree relieved unemployment. This program, clearly following the German example, was the new Liberal answer to the economic ills of modern industrial society.

The effect of these measures was not limited to the workers for whose benefit they were designed. The rich had to bear most of the added financial burden, and the House of Lords, in trying to defend the interests of the upper classes, was shorn of most of its power. When, in 1867, the extension of the franchise to labor had made England a democracy, some had called it a "leap in the dark" and "shooting Niagara." For a while things had continued pretty much in their old course; but now, after forty years, the upper classes were beginning to feel the effects of that abdication of their traditional political control. Since command of the government depended upon a majority of the popular vote and since there were many poor men for every rich one, the result was sooner or later inevitable, once labor appreciated its potential power. At any rate, ballots were less deadly than bullets, and England was spared the more violent forms of class struggle.

Matters came to a head in 1909 with the "Lloyd George Budget," which has been called the most important single event in English history between the defeat of home rule in 1886 and the outbreak of the World War. When Asquith replaced the dying Campbell-Bannerman as prime minister in 1908, his office as Chancellor of the Exchequer was filled by Lloyd George, the most prominent Welshman since Henry Tudor. Asquith, Grey, and others of the Cabinet were statesmen of the old school; but Lloyd George, short, dynamic, quick-witted, and persuasive, had the power of appealing to the masses, a useful quality in a democratic government, although his opponents might call him a demagogue. One of the principal duties of the Chancellor of the Exchequer is the preparation of an annual budget, listing the estimated revenues and expenditures for the coming year and attempting, in peacetime at least, to balance the income and costs of government. The problem in 1909 was to find an additional revenue of about £14,000,000 for old-age pensions, labor exchanges, and the projected national insurance, as well as for the construction of new warships necessary to keep a lead in the costly naval race with Germany (see page 841).

Three principles were adopted by Lloyd George in formulating his remarkable proposals: the burden of taxation should fall on all classes; the wealthy should pay more than they had in the past; and the taxes suggested should bring in a steadily increasing revenue in the future. The first principle he made to operate through higher import or excise duties on tobacco and drink. The second he fulfilled by increasing the income-tax rate, distinguishing between "earned" and "unearned" income; by an additional supertax on incomes of over £5000; by an increase in the "death duties," or inheritance taxes; and by taxes on automobiles and gasoline. In accordance with the third principle, he clapped a tax of 20 per cent on the increase of urban land values and at the same time levied a special tax on unimproved agricultural land.

The nature of these changes in government finances is indicated when we contrast the most significant items of the budget of 1908 with those of 1912, as given on the opposite page.

A chorus of protests broke forth against the budget, which many called a step toward socialism. There were charges that it would make whisky more expensive without increasing the tax on champagne, thus discriminating against the workingman; but on the whole the complaints came from the wealthier classes, upon whom would fall the heaviest burden of the new taxation. It was said that capital would flee the country, that resources needed in time of war would be cut down, that playgrounds would be destroyed. Some declared that it proposed the impossible in trying to distinguish between earned and unearned income. The budget was further denounced for discouraging private enterprise, thus leading to lower wages and increased unemployment,—in fact, to the ruin of England.

The major attack, however, was against the land taxes, because Lloyd George proposed to take one fifth of the so-called "unearned increment." By this was meant the economic rent or the increase of value that came to the owner of land through circumstances other

| BRITISH REVENUE AND EXPENDITURES, 1908 AND 1912 (In million pounds) | | | | | |
|---|---|---|---|---|---|
| *Revenue* | | | *Expenditure* | | |
| | 1908 | 1912 | | 1908 | 1912 |
| Total . . . . . . . | 151 | 188 | Total . . . . . . . | 152 | 188 |
| Customs . . . . . . | 29 | 33 | Navy . . . . . . . | 32 | 44 |
| Excise . . . . . . . | 33 | 38 | Army . . . . . . . | 26 | 28 |
| Income tax, etc. . . . | 33 | 44 | Debt service . . . . . | 28 | 24 |
| Death duties, etc. . . . | 18 | 25 | Education . . . . . | 17 | 18 |
| Stamp tax (documents) | 7 | 10 | Law and justice . . . | 4 | 4 |
| Land-value duties . . . | | .4 | Public works . . . . | 3 | 3 |
| | | | Old-age pensions . . . | | 12 |
| | | | Health insurance . . . | | 2 |
| | | | Unemployment and labor exchanges . . | .1 | .8 |

than his own work. This proposition was in some ways similar to that of the "single tax" on the whole unearned increment, made by Henry George, the American, who thought that such a tax would make it unnecessary to levy any other taxes. It seemed unfair to both these men, for instance, that a man who owned land in London should watch it soar in value through the years solely because thousands of new people came there to live and work. Such a man might never do a day's work in his life, while the labor of other people increased his income. This unearned wealth of his, according to Lloyd George, was to be distinguished from that of a businessman, for example, who created his wealth as the result of initiative, risks, and hard work. In many cities large areas owned by a few proprietors, such as the Dukes of Bedford and Westminster in London (see page 480), were leased on long terms during which the owners did practically nothing to improve the value of their holdings. When a lease fell due, it was seldom renewed except at a large increase in annual rent; and when new houses were erected upon the land, they were erected at the expense of the lessee, who, in addition, frequently had to pay an extra amount for the option of renewing his lease. Under these circumstances Lloyd George felt it only right and proper that the owner of the ground should make a special contribution to the state.

It was proposed also to lay a duty upon undeveloped land. In the cities were many who virtually escaped taxation by leaving their land undeveloped, while throughout the country private parks, since they were unproductive, escaped taxation. The new budget put a small tax upon the value of all such undeveloped land unless it was useless for agricultural purposes or unless it was a park to which the public had access. It has been asserted that in this land policy Lloyd George's motives were social rather than financial. From the latter standpoint the immediate results were comparatively negligible, for they yielded only about the equivalent of the expenses of the royal family; but Lloyd George was interested in breaking up the abnormal concentration of English land in a very few hands. There was the possibility that the nuisance effect of these new measures might lead landowners to dispose of some of their holdings and thus provide home sites for the general public.

To overcome the united Liberal-Labor-Irish Nationalist probudget majority in the House of Commons was impossible, and the budget passed with a safe majority. The House of Lords, however, was another matter. It lay within the power of the Conservative peers, who comprised over four fifths of the Upper House, to throw out the budget, provided that body dared, contrary to custom, to refuse assent to a money bill. The Lords had already defeated, early in the life of this Parliament, several Liberal measures, particularly those dealing with the liquor trade and with education; and they had only grudgingly accepted the Liberal social-reform legislation. The time now seemed ripe to them for a rally in defense of the old order, and they determined to fight the budget. Possibly this was an unwise move, since before the hated land taxes could be levied it would be necessary to determine the value of all the land of the United Kingdom,—a gigantic and complicated "Domesday Book." The Lords were angry, however, and especially angry at Lloyd George, the Welsh lawyer and pro-Boer agitator, whom they considered nothing but an inflammatory demagogue.

Lloyd George had made a speech at Limehouse, in the slum section of London, which, for a Chancellor of the Exchequer, in the opinion of the Lords, exceeded the bounds of English propriety. He had given instances and named names, and the Lords did not like that. The Duke of Northumberland, he considered, had tried to gouge the public. He mentioned a London tenant of the Duke of Westminster's. When the lease expired, an increase of £4000 a year was demanded by His Grace; and in addition the tenant had to pay £50,000 and promise to put up at his own expense certain costly buildings according to specifications supplied by the duke's architects. This was a customary procedure with ground landlords in London, but Lloyd George declared that this was not business but blackmail. It was not customary for a Chancellor of the Exchequer to talk thus, and the Lords determined to chastise him.

It was a dangerous procedure. Liberal feeling against the Upper

# The End of Laissez Faire

House had been growing steadily more bitter since the later days of Gladstone, who had prophesied a battle between the two houses of Parliament. The reason was that the House of Commons had adjusted itself to the democratic consequences of the Parliamentary reforms acts, while the House of Lords had not. In the eighteenth century, as we saw, there had been little friction between the two houses (see page 437). The members of both were for the most part landed aristocrats, while some of the peers, through their control of boroughs, could dictate to their henchmen in the Lower House. On the whole, the members of the Lower House were fairly insensitive to the political views of the particular constituencies which had elected them; those who had paid for their seats enjoyed a special independence of action. By the last quarter of the nineteenth century that situation was changed. The rotten boroughs were fast being eliminated; the electorate had been greatly expanded; party organization had been strengthened and perfected; and popular newspapers kept the public in close touch with the political situation. This change decidedly lessened the influence and importance of the individual members of the House of Commons. The cabinet seemed to be growing more dependent upon the votes of the public than upon the votes of the House of Commons. "What is outside Parliament seems to be fast mounting, nay to have already mounted, to an importance much exceeding what is inside," wrote Gladstone in 1880. The cabinet, supported by the electorate, seemed no longer the servant but the master of the Commons, and government policy therefore became more sensitive to popular control. Consequently, when friction arose between Lords and Commons, it was not an even contest between the free opinion of two groups of six hundred and odd men each. On one side the House of Commons was directly sensitive to the views of an electorate of several millions; on the other side the Lords were responsible to no one, vote as they might. Most of them owed their seats to the accident of birth, and the ability which had won peerages for their ancestors was by no means always passed on to the later generations. As long as that irresponsible group enjoyed a final veto upon anything which the House of Commons passed, democratic government seemed to many imperfect.

As far back as 1885 there had been talk of "mending or ending" the House of Lords, and more recently the Liberals had passed a resolution through the Commons to the effect that "in order to give effect to the will of the people as expressed by their elected representatives, it is necessary that the power of the other House to alter or reject bills passed by this House should be restricted." But the matter had been dropped for the time being.

# A History of England and the British Empire

Now, with the Lloyd George budget sent up from the Commons for the approval of the Lords, the time had come for a final reckoning. The fact that it was a budget seriously complicated the situation. Even in the later Middle Ages, we recall, it was acknowledged that finance was a special function of the Commons, and "money bills," or financial measures, always originated in the Lower House. It had become a well-established custom that the Lords might not alter a money bill. They had, to be sure, the theoretical right to throw it out altogether, but even that power had not been exercised for many years. The Lords felt that this was more than an ordinary money bill; that it had been sharp practice on the part of Lloyd George to include the authorization of such revolutionary and "socialistic" principles in a bill which enjoyed special privileges as a finance measure.

During the autumn of 1909 the Lords debated the measure. Interference with financial measures was highly dangerous, as Lord Rosebery, the former Liberal prime minister, pointed out to the peers. "My Lords," he said, "I think you are playing for too heavy a stake on this occasion. I think that you are risking, in your opposition to what I agree with you in thinking is an iniquitous and dangerous measure, the very existence of a second chamber. . . . The House of Lords has lived on menaces ever since I can recollect, and yet it seems to be in a tolerably thriving condition still. . . . The menaces addressed to you now come from a wholly different school of opinion, who wish for a single chamber and who set no value on the controlling and revising forces of a double chamber. . . . 'Hang consequences,' said my noble friend, Lord Camperdown, last night. . . . That is a noble utterance, a Balaclava utterance. Nothing more intrepid could be said. But the truest courage in these matters weighs the consequences, not to the individual but to the state, and thinks not once but twice before it gives a vote which may involve such enormous constitutional consequences." But the Lords acted otherwise. Their point of view on the budget was not surprising. It struck at landholding, and their body had been identified with landholding ever since the days of the witan and the Great Council, before there even was a House of Commons. It struck also at wealth, and their ranks included many of the men who would be liable for the heaviest income taxes and death duties in the whole kingdom. They were, moreover, Conservatives by a great majority. In November, 1909, they rejected the budget, over three fourths of them voting against it, and Asquith promptly asked King Edward to dissolve Parliament.

The general election early in 1910 weakened the Liberals' hold on the House of Commons. Many of the independent voters who had

# The End of Laissez Faire

contributed to their huge majority in 1906 did not favor their radical trend, and they returned with only a few more seats than the Conservatives. That meant that they would be dependent upon the Laborite and Irish Nationalist votes, and they would receive those votes only if they sponsored the measures desired by those two minorities. The new House promptly passed the Lloyd George budget again. This time the Lords, sensing the rising demand for a limitation of their powers, passed it also.

It was too late; for the Commons were by that time discussing a proposed "Parliament Bill" which would make it impossible for the Lords to delay for more than one month any bill certified by the Speaker of the Commons as a finance measure. This bill would also place upon the statute books any other sort of bill passed by the House of Commons three successive times with or without the approval of the Lords, provided that two years intervened between the second reading of the bill at its first passage and the final reading at its last. In other words, the legislative power of the House of Lords would be whittled down to a "suspensive veto" on nonfinancial measures; if the Commons remained persistent for two years, the Lords could be ignored. It was evident that if this bill became law, the British constitution would be profoundly modified.

In the violent disputes aroused by the bill the Conservatives pointed out that since the Lords could do no more than delay certain bills, it meant, in the last analysis, single-chamber rather than the old bicameral government. They considered the Lords as the defenders of British democracy; for the Upper House performed the valuable constitutional function of saying to the Commons, "Stop! Look! Listen!" and thus serving as a check upon precipitate action. The Conservatives felt that the Commons should not control absolutely and in every particular the destinies of the country. The Liberals, with their Irish and Laborite allies, replied that the Parliament Bill provided a quite sufficient check, since the two-year delay should be long enough for public opinion to manifest itself upon one side or another. The Liberals also pointed to the way in which the party situation was perverted by the constant heavy Conservative majority in the Lords: Conservative measures from the Lower House were passed almost automatically, whereas Liberal bills were rejected, modified, or twisted out of shape.

In addition to the disputed power of the Lords in connection with legislation there was the fundamental question of the composition of their membership. Many objected to the pressure "to revise at ten days' notice the constitution of eight hundred years," but the pleas of the Lords that they were taken unawares and lacked sufficient time to reorganize was laughed out of court. Asquith, referring to the sudden efforts of the Lords to reform themselves, quoted Dr. Johnson's remark that "nothing concentrates a man's mind so much as the knowledge that he is going to be hanged." As a matter of fact, the Lords had dallied with the idea of reforming themselves for several decades, and numerous proposals, including the restriction of membership to only a hundred of the hereditary peers, had been made. But before 1910 there had been no indication that they had any serious intention of reforming themselves; and now, under fire, they would have to defend their House as it was, "One-sided, hereditary, unpurged, unrepresentative, irresponsible, absentee . . . with all its anomalies, all its absurdities, and all its personal bias."

All through the late summer and the autumn a committee of four members from each party tried to iron out the differences, but in November they admitted failure. The Lords had not passed the Parliament Bill and their substitute measure had not been acceptable to the Commons.

Meanwhile Edward VII had suddenly died in the spring, after a reign of only nine years, and his conscientious, level-headed, and serious son had ascended the throne as George V. Asquith now secured from the new king an agreement to dissolve Parliament and, for the second time that year, to hold a general election. In the January election the principal issue had been the Lloyd George budget; now it was the Parliament Bill. The results were almost identical: Liberals and Conservatives were practically tied. The balance of power rested with the Irish and Labor members, and the Irish wanted to break the Lords' vote because it would clear the way for home rule.

Once more, early in 1911, the House of Commons passed the Parliament Bill, and the die-hards in the Lords were determined to defeat it. The new king, however, followed the precedent of 1832 and agreed to create as many new peers as should prove necessary to pass the bill in the Upper House. This forced the issue; and in early August, with many members abstaining from voting, the Lords reluctantly passed the measure by 131 to 114 votes, and the Parliament Act became the law of the land. Originally a bill might be defeated in any one of its three stages: during its passage by the Commons, during its passage by the Lords, or by royal veto. There had been no royal veto since 1707, so that now, with the curtailment of the power of the Lords, legislative power lay directly in the hands of the Commons. The Parliament Act also changed the maximum duration of a single Parliament. In 1694 the Triennial Act had set it as three years; in 1716 it had been extended to seven, and so had continued for nearly two centuries until now it was reduced to five.

# The End of Laissez Faire

Nothing definite was done concerning the membership of the House of Lords; that would be the subject for numerous future debates. The abolition of the absolute veto of the Lords opened the way for Irish home rule and the disestablishment of the Welsh Church. Both finally became law in 1914, after being three times passed by the Commons and three times rejected by the Lords; and both were suspended during the war.

Though its legislative functions were radically curtailed in 1911, the House of Lords still maintained the highest position in the English judicial system, which had been quite thoroughly overhauled during the preceding forty years. For centuries England had left almost untouched the legal machinery established during the Middle Ages (see pages 100, 148). By a series of Judicature Acts between 1873 and 1910, this had all been co-ordinated into an orderly system. The three old common-law courts of King's Bench, Common Pleas, and Exchequer were merged into the King's Bench division of the High Court of Justice; the second division of the High Court was Chancery; the third division comprised the Probate Court and Divorce Court (the business of both of which had once been handled by the Church) and the Court of Admiralty. As in medieval times, the justices of these courts not only sat in London but also went on circuit to preside at assizes, as had the itinerant justices of Henry II. Cases might be carried from these divisions of the High Court of Justice to the Court of Appeals and from there, as a last resort, to the House of Lords. In its capacity as a supreme court, the Lords did not depend upon the decisions of the regular hereditary peers, unless they were judges or ex-judges; the legal business was handled by the Chancellor and a few "law barons" who were nonhereditary peers, fairly close counterparts of the justices of the Supreme Court of the United States. It was this little group which had rendered the Taff Vale decision.

On the very day when the Lords passed the Parliament Bill, the House of Commons voted for a measure which affected itself: its members were to be paid salaries of £400 a year. This arose from a dispute with the Lords, acting in their judicial-appeal capacity. Their "Osborne Judgment" in 1909, like their earlier Taff Vale decision, was a blow at trade unions; for it made it illegal to assess union members with a "political levy" for the salary of Labor M. P.'s and, indeed, forbade them to engage in politics at all. If they paid their members, it was contended, they might control their votes, and the independence of the Commons would be threatened. As a matter of fact, the Labor members were required to take a pledge to vote as the party directed. Furthermore, it was argued that men might seek election to Parliament to make money rather than to serve the state. Yet if the unions did not pay their representatives, many Laborites would be driven out of public life by lack of funds. The party balance was so close that the Liberals needed the Labor votes; consequently the House of Commons, not without vigorous opposition, passed the salary measure. Thus one more of the old Chartist demands was realized. It was recognized that such a law tended to alter the character of the House, and succeeding decades were to witness surprising changes from the manners developed in the days when members were gentlemen with independent means.

Meanwhile, England was confronted with a new question, that of woman suffrage. Since the Industrial Revolution the position of women had been changing; the new conditions made it necessary for them to be more independent economically, as the average family could no longer support or find room in the home for dependent aunts, cousins, and sisters. Also, as we have seen, the number of women in industry had been steadily increasing. In education they were admitted to take examinations at the University of London in the late sixties, not long after at Cambridge, and finally at Oxford, where eventually separate colleges were established for them. Agitation for the enfranchisement of women had been proceeding quietly ever since the middle of the nineteenth century, but without gaining many converts. John Stuart Mill had been the only man of importance to advocate with any warmth votes for women. In 1903, however, Mrs. Emmeline Pankhurst and her daughters, Sylvia and Christabel, decided on a change in tactics. The Women's Social and Political Union, which they sponsored, determined to wake up England. Its members, not content with signing and circulating petitions, began to interrupt public meetings and to heckle politicians and statesmen in order to draw public attention to their cause. Such conduct in England, on the part of women, was unheard-of, and the suffragettes, as they were called, were derided and denounced. This served only to stiffen their determination. For five years preceding the World War they alternately amused and angered the British public, annoyed and worried the British Parliament. Year by year the women grew bolder. They padlocked themselves to the grillwork of the visitors' gallery in the Commons, concealed the key, and shouted "Votes for Women!"; they climbed public statues and repeated the trick; they laid siege to Parliament Square; they put chemicals in mail boxes, broke the display windows of Bond Street stores, smashed porcelains in the British Museum, and slashed a Venus at the National Gallery. They refused to pay fines, but went to prison and became martyrs.

# The End of Laissez Faire

The cabinet was divided on the suffrage question and sparred for time, pleading that its social legislation must come first. The women replied that suffrage was not a party issue but simply one of right and justice, and insisted that they must have the vote immediately. The government finally suggested a franchise and registration bill to overhaul the election laws. If this were amended to give the women the vote, well and good. A direct measure granting woman suffrage they would not introduce, since to do so would alienate many of their supporters. The women, in turn, accused the government of trickery and doubled the number of outrages, burning railway stations and cutting telephone and telegraph wires.

Meanwhile, the suffragettes discovered a new method of propaganda: they went on hunger strikes as soon as arrested. The authorities resorted to force. They did not dare let the prisoners starve, and therefore they poured milk down rubber tubes through the women's noses. The public resented this brutal treatment and the suffragettes bravely persisted. Finally Parliament hastily passed a law releasing prisoners on "license," or parole, with the proviso that they might be reincarcerated if they renewed their agitation. This was the famous "Cat and Mouse Act," which made the confusion worse. The nuisance effect of these pioneer suffragette activities was not, as we shall see, to be the decisive factor in the suffrage victory in 1918.

To the disgust of many, Labor's success had seemingly gone to its head during this period. Far from being content with workmen's compensation, old-age pensions, national insurance, and the other social measures which had been passed in their behalf, the working-men continued to clamor for more, both inside Parliament and outside. Within ten years the total membership of the trade unions had jumped from two to four millions, while the process of consolidation and amalgamation had resulted in fewer and more powerful unions, better prepared than ever for concerted action. Though trade was brisk, wages had not kept pace with the increased cost of living. Other nations, as well as England, were experiencing labor disturbances in these same years.

The Laborites did not consider the payment of members an adequate reply to the Osborne Judgment. The Trade Union Act of 1913 extended the scope of the term "trade union" and declared the right of the unions to use their funds for political purposes, though any member might be free to refuse to pay.

The public was aroused by the tremendous epidemic of strikes in 1911 and 1912. Many of these were no longer local affairs. Through the new solidarity of the unions, it was possible to call a strike of all the workers in a particular activity, and even to secure sympathetic strikes of the workers in other fields. Three great labor groups were in a particularly advantageous position to make their influence felt through their capacity to tie up the nation's business: the railway men, the dock workers, and the coal miners; and all three went on strikes during these troubled years. The railway men struck for the principle of the "closed shop," in which no one was to be employed unless he had a union card. For two days all transport was paralyzed. The government did its best to conciliate both sides, but satisfied neither. The most that the railway unions could obtain was the right to elect their representatives on conciliation boards which were to decide disputes between employers and employees. The dock laborers and others in the Transport Workers' Federation also struck without marked success. More was achieved when a million coal miners began a strike, the greatest which England had yet seen. They were able, as we saw, to secure from Parliament inclusion in the minimum-wage provisions of the Trade Boards Act. In the spring of 1914 these three great unions formed a "triple alliance" for common action whenever the three should agree. This was paving the way for labor's strongest weapon, the general strike. Some trade unionists, who felt that Parliamentary socialistic legislation was too slow a method of getting what they wanted, were disposed to listen to the new doctrine of syndicalism, as taught in France, with its advocacy of violence as the best weapon by which the unions might gain their aims. Even during the dark days of both World Wars labor would not hesitate to strike.

All things considered, England, on the eve of the world conflicts, was in a singularly nervous state. The government's home-rule policy (see page 767) had produced a serious danger of civil war in Ulster; the suffragettes were on the rampage; the trade unions were staging more extensive strikes; and conservative folk of both political parties were much alarmed over the condition of England. The old country seemed going to the dogs. No wonder the German observers thought the chances were good that England would stay out of a Continental war.

# CHAPTER XXVIII

# The End of Splendid Isolation

## 1878-1914

THE great powers of Europe between 1879 and 1907 aligned themselves in two rival groups. Germany, Austria, and Italy quickly formed the Triple Alliance, while France, Russia, and England later joined forces in the Triple Entente. England was the last of the six powers to take sides; for the others had all formed definite alliances long before the British put an end to the "splendid isolation" which had characterized their foreign relations since the days of Canning. The growth of the two alliances had tremendous historical consequences, for this international rivalry led in 1914 to the greatest war the world had seen. It is therefore important to study the workings of the Foreign Office, in Downing Street, during those same years in which we have already traced England's domestic problems and her relations with Ireland and the empire, in order to understand how she was gradually drawn into the system which led to such terrible results.

The story goes back to the international congress at Berlin in 1878, whence Beaconsfield returned with Cyprus in his pocket, with Russia blocked in her expansion toward the Straits, and with German relations exceedingly cordial (see page 708). England's position in Europe seemed safe and pre-eminent. Her interventions in the Near East, where her eyes were upon India and the Suez Canal rather than upon the Continental consequences of Turkey's decline, had scarcely impaired her general policy of isolation; and her triumph at Berlin had been complete.

For more than half a century, under Canning, Palmerston, and other foreign ministers, England had held aloof from intimate, long-standing contact with any of the Continental powers. She perhaps flattered herself that she could act as the "balance wheel of Europe" by interfering only when the equilibrium seemed threatened or when her own particular interests seemed involved. England cherished no such permanent enmities as the Franco-German or the Russo-Turkish; at the same time she had no permanent allies, save little Portugal. It is significant that between 1800 and 1918 England was engaged in war with practically every important country, at one time as ally and at another time as enemy. This insular policy gave her constant freedom of action, and, with the royal navy as strong as it was, she was in a position to speak with authority.

Of the five great Continental powers, Russia came nearest to being regarded as a constant enemy of England during the nineteenth century. With a population far greater than that of any of the other powers, Russia's potential strength seemed tremendous. Only in quantity, however, was Russia impressive. The economic, social, and political changes which were transforming western Europe had left her relatively untouched. Socially her population consisted, until late in the century, almost exclusively of the two medieval classes: a small, wealthy aristocracy and a vast, ignorant peasantry. With her agricultural economy, Russia had little in the way of a middle class; for industry was negligible. The Czar ruled as an absolute autocrat, without constitutional checks, and was engaged in a policy of harsh repression after a brief period of reform. In spite of her already vast area, Russia was continually seeking further territorial expansion, with the particular desire for at least one ice-free port on the open sea. Unlike most of the other nations, the Russians could reach their objectives by land; and this made it the more difficult for England to oppose them when the interests of the two nations clashed in the Near East, the Middle East, and, shortly, in the Far East.

If Russia was England's chief object of immediate hostility, friction with France, her traditional foe of the past, still existed. Smarting under the humiliation of 1871, when Germany had taken from her the provinces of Alsace and Lorraine, France wanted revenge and feared further German aggression. There was the constant painful realization that for every two Frenchmen there were three Germans. France was the most democratic of the Continental powers, with responsible government similar to the English system. The Third Republic, however, lacked prestige. France had changed her form of government frequently during the past century, and ministries were short-lived, so that more than once, because of a cabinet crisis, France was not in a position to take a strong hand. France had a moderate commercial and industrial development, although she was still predominantly an agricultural country. French colonial ambitions were centered in North Africa, where Algeria, taken in 1830, was the principal colony, although the Third Republic had other colonial interests in Indo-China and elsewhere.

Germany was forging ahead more rapidly than any of the other powers. Under the presiding genius of her "Iron Chancellor," Prince Otto von Bismarck, Prussia had whipped Denmark, Austria, and

# The End of Splendid Isolation

France in rapid succession, and the king of Prussia had become head of the new German Empire, proclaimed at Versailles in 1871. Then Bismarck dropped his blood-and-iron policy and sought to dominate the Continent by shrewd diplomacy, backed by the best army in the world. Until his forced retirement in 1890, he was the most influential man in Europe,—more successful, however, in his foreign relations than in his encounters with socialists and Catholics in his own country. Germany's government was autocratic; for Bismarck's tenure of office depended solely on the emperor, who not only appointed the chancellor but also controlled, as king of Prussia, either by influence or by appointment, the upper house of the legislature. Nevertheless, the consent of the lower house, popularly elected, was necessary for new expenditures, such as naval construction. About 1878 England liked Germany better than any of the other powers; for the two peoples had much in common, and Victoria's prejudices were strongly pro-German. But with remarkable energy and thoroughness the Germans were making rapid strides in industry and commerce, which, in conjunction with their later colonial and naval ambitions, would eventually bring them into conflict with British interests.

England's path was frequently to cross those of Russia, France, and Germany in various parts of the world, but with the other two powers, Austria and Italy, she would have much less concern. Austria —or, more properly, since 1867, the Dual Monarchy of Austria-Hungary—was slipping back while Germany advanced. The illogical, heterogeneous assortment of lands and races under Hapsburg rule lacked national unity. Austria was in no enviable situation, threatened as she was by the mutterings of her discontented minorities, and worried by the rising tide of nationalism in the Balkans, where, like Russia, she too had ambitions. Italy, once she was united, about 1860, considered herself a first-rate power, but was scarcely accepted at par by the others. She lacked the resources and prestige of the other five; her foreign policy, as we shall note, was dubious and tricky; and her imperialistic ventures were to yield little more than sandy wastes which no one else desired.

The diplomacy of the period, in its major aspects, was largely the concern of the great powers. The lesser nations of Europe played only minor roles. Across the seas, however, the United States and Japan were rapidly rising and, as we shall see, were gradually to be accepted as world powers.

The two great alliances, whose later aggressive rivalry would finally lead to war, were strictly defensive at the outset. Bismarck sought to remove as many sources of international friction as possible. He told Austria that her future lay not in Germany but in the Balkans. Disturbed by French animosity, he sought to isolate France and to encourage her expansion in North Africa, hoping that thus she might forget Alsace and Lorraine. This policy was more successful at Vienna than at Paris, and Bismarck consequently turned more and more toward Austria. Fearful lest France make an alliance with either Russia or Austria against Germany, he organized the "League of the Three Emperors" (Germany, Austria, Russia), thus linking together the three eastern autocratic powers in a common agreement to preserve the status quo. Ever since the days of Castlereagh and Canning, as we recall, the three conservative eastern powers, Prussia, Austria, and Russia, had tended to act in concert; but the events of 1877–1878 had demonstrated that the conflicting ambitions of Russia and Austria in the Balkans made it almost impossible for any country to be on intimate terms with both. At Berlin, Bismarck had seemingly tried to act the "honest broker" between the two; but since the results of the congress had been far more favorable to Austria than to Russia, the latter country felt aggrieved and blamed Bismarck for what had happened. Thus, realizing that he would soon be forced to choose between Russia and Austria, the German chancellor now came to the conclusion that Austria was the safer ally.

The first step in what was to be the Triple Alliance came in 1879, when Bismarck drew Austria into closer relationship. The treaty was not as favorable to Germany as he apparently would have liked; for Austria was unwilling to help Germany against France if that would leave her own eastern frontier exposed to Russia. What he wanted was an ally who would come to his aid against France; what he got was a pledge that if Russia should attack either Germany or Austria, the other would come at once to the aid of her ally, but that if either should be attacked by a power other than Russia (which, of course, meant France), the other need give only "benevolent neutrality" unless Russia should come into the conflict. This was at first only a five-year agreement, subject to renewal, and was to be kept secret unless its announcement might seem threat enough to prevent war. Three years later Italy rounded out this Triple Alliance. It was formerly believed that Bismarck deliberately drew Italy into the alliance by encouraging France to seize Tunis. It is true that the Italians were furious about the seizure of that coveted land in North Africa, but it has been demonstrated that Italy herself sought admission to the alliance and that Bismarck agreed only reluctantly. He knew that Italy wanted support for her colonial ambitions, and he foresaw, as later events demonstrated, that "her promise will have no value if it is not in her interest to keep it." Thus was this triangular

# The End of Splendid Isolation

alliance completed, with Germany at its principal angle, and the Austro-Italian its weak side because of the traditional enmity of those nations and because Austrian holdings stood in the way of Italian expansion, particularly at the north of the Adriatic. This alliance had the advantageous position, in the eventuality of war, of occupying a central strip in Europe from the Baltic to the middle of the Mediterranean. As long as Bismarck remained in power, he held in check the attempts of the Italians to use the alliance to further their African ambitions and of the Austrians to extend their influence in the Balkans. He kept it the purely defensive alliance which had been his original object in bringing Germany and Austria together.

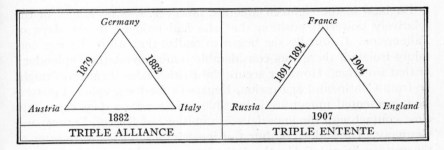

While Bismarck had decided upon Austria rather than Russia for close partnership, he did his best, as long as he was in office, to keep on friendly terms with St. Petersburg. The old "League of the Three Emperors"—of Germany, Austria, and Russia—was kept alive for a while, and he drew up a "reinsurance" treaty with Russia in his desire to prevent a Franco-Russian alliance which would catch Germany with potential foes on two sides. He was successful in this until 1890, when the new German "Kaiser," the energetic and erratic William II, "dropped the pilot" who had steered Germany to her commanding position and took matters into his own less steady hands. Almost immediately the "wire to St. Petersburg" was pulled down.

In the course of the four years after Bismarck was thrust out of the picture, his fears of a Franco-Russian alliance came true. As a result of negotiations which lasted from 1891 to 1894, the French and Russians arrived at a defensive alliance. France had felt completely isolated and was now comforted by the prospect that if German troops should start for Paris, the Russians would start for Berlin. The terms of the 1894 agreement stipulated that France or Russia would support her ally with all available forces in case either were attacked by Germany or if Germany supported an attack by Italy or Austria. This alliance was cemented by huge French loans which Russia used for railways, particularly the Trans-Siberian, and for industrial development, as well as for purely military and naval purposes. This was the first step in what was to become, with the subsequent inclusion of England, the Triple Entente.

In 1894, however, it seemed highly improbable that within twenty years England would unite with France and Russia, her most active colonial rivals and her former enemies, against Germany, a power with whom she had previously been on friendly terms. During the years in which the five Continental powers had been drawing together, England had remained in her "splendid isolation," and much was to happen before she finally staged her "diplomatic revolution."

England in the eighteen nineties, however, was no longer in the relatively powerful position that she had enjoyed in the days of Palmerston. Gradually she began to realize that while she was certainly isolated, there was considerable doubt about the "splendor" of that isolation. However secure the British Isles themselves might be from Continental aggression, England's far-flung colonial possessions presented numerous vulnerable points where they came into close contact with the imperialistic ambitions of Russia, France, and Germany. The sudden outburst of imperialism in the last quarter of the century, stimulated by the desire for new markets, for new sources of raw materials, for new regions to gratify national pride on the world map, and, above all, new countries in which to lend money and build railways, was leading, as we have seen, to a feverish scramble in Africa, at its height about 1885, and in China, beginning ten years later (see pages 744, 742). At every turn England began to encounter the advances of one of the three Continental rivals. England's vast empire, her commercial success, and her sea power excited envy, while her calm assumption of superiority exasperated those who were less sure of themselves. If Russia, France, and Germany should ever all join forces against her, England's position would indeed be serious. Fortunately for her, Alsace-Lorraine stood in the way of that, but the possibility caused concern.

Africa, north, central, and south, was presenting numerous causes of imperialistic friction. England and France had disputes over Madagascar, but these paled into insignificance in comparison with hard feeling over Egypt. The French had not been in a position to join England in the bombardment of Alexandria in 1882; none the less they resented their neighbor's success in the Egyptian enterprise. For over twenty years they kept inquiring when the British were going to retire from their anomalous position on the Nile, but they received no satisfactory answer. In 1898 there came a dramatic climax when

# The End of Splendid Isolation

the paths of empire crossed at Fashoda. That at least cleared the air, for the French gave up the idea of challenging England by force. In central and southern Africa Bismarck had refrained for a while from colonial activity, but he finally yielded to pressure and, once involved, played an energetic part. In 1884–1885 Germany became an African power almost overnight, and the Liberal ministry in England, inclined to be passive in foreign and colonial matters, was deceived or defied in the German acquisition of Cameroons and German Southwest Africa. Gladstone, however, officially welcomed Germany as a great colonial power, invoking God's blessing on her new enterprise. Then, as we have seen, a joint Anglo-German agreement in 1890, involving Zanzibar and Heligoland, ironed out points of difference. After Bismarck's retirement, however, events in South Africa strained Anglo-German relations nearly to the breaking point when the Kaiser sent his telegram of congratulation to President Kruger of the Transvaal (see page 726), and the Boer War, which followed a few years later, rendered England's international position even more acute.

Russia was not involved in the African scramble, but she gave England grave concern in Asia. For the half century leading up to 1878 Anglo-Russian rivalry, as we have seen, had centered in the Turkish situation in the Near East (see page 708). From about 1880 to 1895 the storm center was the Middle East, north of India, and then it moved on to the Far East. The Middle Eastern troubles arose from Russia's steady pressure southward into the desert regions of Turkestan, where she occupied the chief cities and oases. About 1880 an energetic Russian commander pushed on toward Afghanistan, but the British forestalled him by invading, for the second time, that rough buffer state. There was a time, in the middle nineties, when Briton and Russian stood facing one another on the bleak Pamir plateau, in central Asia, and the nations seemed on the verge of war; but diplomacy intervened, England yielded slightly, and the Russians soon shifted their activities farther eastward toward China (see page 743).

England had minor imperialistic encounters with France for influence in the independent kingdom of Siam, which lies between French Indo-China and British Burma, and with France and Germany in the islands of the Pacific; but these were completely overshadowed by the sudden emergence of the Far Eastern question, which became acute with the surprising victory of Japan over China in 1894–1895. This not only revealed the remarkable development of Japan, recently emerged from medieval isolation, but also, by revealing the weakness of China, whetted the appetites of England's three imperialistic rivals, particularly Russia. The Russians had gradually pushed out through Siberia to the Pacific and now saw their chance to extend southward into Manchuria and to gratify their long-cherished desire for an ice-free port. Russia, backed by France and Germany, forced Japan to yield the Liaotung Peninsula, with Port Arthur, the strongest port in China, and then, in 1898, Russia leased it for herself. In the course of four months Russia, Germany, and France, as we have seen, had all leased Chinese ports and had secured spheres of influence for themselves, while England, in self-defense, had leased Weihaiwei (see page 743). The whole situation was distasteful to England. For many years she had enjoyed some three quarters of the foreign trade of China, and she resented the idea that certain portions of it should be staked off for the exclusive use of her rivals.

The Far Eastern situation had brought England's three rivals into concerted action and pointed out more clearly than ever the danger of her isolation. The year 1898 saw a combination of events significant in England's foreign and colonial relations. In the course of those twelve months—during which, incidentally, Gladstone and Bismarck both died—the Chinese ports were distributed among the powers; Kitchener whipped the Mahdi at Omdurman and met Marchand at Fashoda; the United States fought Spain and thereby became a Caribbean and Pacific power; and Germany passed her first important law for a strong navy.

England was worried. Ever since 1886, except for the brief period of Liberal government (1892–1895), the control of her foreign policy had rested in the competent hands of Lord Salisbury, who undertook that burden in addition to his position as Conservative prime minister. Thus far he had been extraordinarily successful in preserving his country's "splendid isolation." The same shrewd skill which had enabled William Cecil to steer England through the problems of Elizabeth's reign had cropped out in this descendant, whom some have considered a match for Bismarck in diplomacy. A keen realist, able to size up men and motives and thoroughly alive to what he considered England's best interests, this aristocrat had guarded those interests well. He had been cautious in commitments. He had, to be sure, agreed to a Mediterranean pact of a distinctly local nature, but all ideas of a general alliance had found him very skeptical. Nevertheless, Salisbury was open to conviction; and there were men of influence in his own cabinet, especially Joseph Chamberlain, his colonial secretary, who thought that the time had come to abandon "splendid isolation" and to cast about for an ally, Russia, Germany, and the United States being the first three objects of their attention. Now in January, 1898, Salisbury approached Russia, not with the

# The End of Splendid Isolation

slightest idea of an alliance (since he still opposed any such project) but with the suggestion that England and Russia come merely to a friendly understanding about "spheres of preponderance" in Turkey and China. A few weeks later his proposal met with a sharp rebuff with the leasing of Port Arthur by Russia. At the end of March, as we shall see, Joseph Chamberlain, who had been actively urging that steps be taken for an alliance, proposed an Anglo-German one. The Germans, however, quickly passed their naval law, an act not pleasing in British eyes.

England's only real friend during that troubled time was the United States, for the two had a common interest in resisting the Russian, French, and German advances in China. England's former thirteen colonies by that time had a population more than double that of the mother country. For many years the Americans had been so busy pushing westward across the plains to the Pacific that they had turned their backs on outside affairs; but now that task was completed. The army was fighting its last Indian battle, and the frontier, by official statement, no longer existed. The United States was ready to play her part in the outside world. England welcomed her appearance, though as late as 1895 the Americans had "twisted the British lion's tail" by invoking the Monroe Doctrine in a border dispute between Venezuela and British Guiana. For several years to come, however, England performed constant favors for the United States and asked little that was definite in return. During the brief war of 1898, in which the United States took away most of Spain's remaining colonial possessions, Continental opinion was bitter against the United States; but England favored the American cause. The British naval attaché, it is said, navigated the American transports on their way to attack Cuba. But England was more interested in the Pacific aspects of the war, hoping that if the Americans gained the Philippines as a definite foothold in the Far East, they would give stronger support to England's desire for equal trading rights in China. After the Americans had defeated the Spanish naval forces in Manila Bay, a German squadron of superior force arrived on the scene and behaved in a threatening manner. The British naval commander thereupon made it clear that if trouble developed he would stand by the Americans. Back in England, Chamberlain was advocating an alliance with the United States as well as with Germany. It was a significant indication of England's isolation and American friendship that the American ambassador was the only representative of the powers to attend a dinner tendered to Kitchener later that year upon his return from his triumphs in the Sudan. The Anglo-American understanding soon bore fruit. The American Secretary of State,

John Hay, secured general, but rather half-hearted, international agreement to the "open door" policy of equal trading rights in China, which England had been trying to maintain singlehanded against the Russians, French, and Germans in 1898. The English, in gratitude, virtually recognized the Caribbean as an "American lake," withdrawing most of their naval force and modifying an old treaty of 1850, which provided for joint Anglo-American construction of a canal, so that the Americans might have the exclusive right to construct the Panama Canal. There was no alliance between Britain and the United States; but in the Pacific, at least, they were united for common action.

Still further to strengthen her hand in the Far East, England in 1902 formed an alliance with Japan. In case of an attack upon either of them in China or Korea by two powers (which implied Russia supported by France), the ally would give support. The alliance was to be renewed more than once. In 1905 the terms were extended to India, and the stipulation was made for mutual support if either of the two signatories were attacked by even a single power. Hardly anyone realized in 1902 the potential strength of Japan, and, after all, the pact was strictly regional. The alliance did much to increase the prestige of Japan, and it added to England's security in Asiatic waters; but England was still worried about her European isolation. The Boer War had humiliated her. Universally unpopular on the Continent, she realized that if her army had such difficulty in subduing fifty thousand farmers, it would have slight chance of victory against a major European opponent. The desirability of a Continental ally was increasingly apparent.

In consequence Britain made overtures to Germany. These were semiofficial in character; but there were several of them between 1898 and 1901, for the most part put forward by Joseph Chamberlain, who did not have behind him a unanimous cabinet. But Chamberlain was enthusiastic and persistent. He approached the German ambassador at London, he discussed the matter with the Kaiser when he came to England, and he made his hopes public in a speech at Leicester. "There is something more," he said, "which I think any far-seeing Englishman must long have desired, and that is that we should not remain primarily isolated on the continent of Europe; and I think it is evident the moment that aspiration is formed—it must have appeared evident to everybody—that the natural alliance is between ourselves and the great German nation."

But this diplomatic kite was not welcomed in Germany. On the practical merits of the proposal Germany felt that she would gain less than England; for the royal navy would be of little help if the

# The End of Splendid Isolation

Russians should invade East Prussia. The British, however, kept on making informal offers. The Germans did not reject them directly. They were willing, perhaps, to consider a guarantee of the British Empire if England would join the Triple Alliance and bring Japan in with her. The British had no intention of doing this. They did not consider themselves suppliants, and they were angry. It did not help matters to have the Kaiser write to Edward VII that his ministers were "unmitigated noodles." Chamberlain began to lose hope. Even his intimation that England would turn to France if rejected by Germany made no impression on the German Foreign Office. The Germans were confident that British rivalry with France and Russia was so deep-rooted that such a partnership was out of the question. They felt that England needed an ally and would ultimately come to them on Germany's terms. After the first rejection of Chamberlain's proposals there was probably little hope of an Anglo-German alliance. Germany's refusal of the proffered alliance was one of the significant steps in the approach to the World War. Outside of purely diplomatic considerations, however, there were several factors which tended to promote ill-feeling between the two nations. Prominent among these was the mutual popular antipathy, particularly strong in Germany, as well as commercial rivalry and the beginning of naval rivalry.

The German foreign minister wrote in 1899 that German feeling was far more anti-English than English feeling was anti-German. Part of this German dislike had its roots in the past and was based on jealousy. The Germans had a feeling that, successful as they might be, the British regarded them as parvenus and pushers. England, moreover, was already well entrenched in the colonial, naval, and commercial fields, where the Germans had ambitions of their own. In order to prepare the popular mind for the naval measures of 1898 and 1900, while the discussions of an alliance were in progress, there was a deliberate stirring up of anti-British feeling. The press was often violent in its denunciations. The Boer War intensified this feeling, and the attacks grew more bitter. When a speaker in the Reichstag was called to order for referring to Chamberlain as "the most accursed scoundrel on God's earth," he received hundreds of congratulatory telegrams. Such things naturally led to counterattacks by the British press and public. Kipling, about this time, was referring to "the Goth and the shameless Hun." In such an atmosphere the public was in no mood to welcome proposals for an alliance.

England, meanwhile, was becoming increasingly aware of two German threats which were eventually to overshadow the French and Russian disputes out on the fringes of the empire. Germany's growing commercial and naval activity seemed to jeopardize things far more vital to England than the Sudan or Manchuria. Ever since Trafalgar, England had been virtually undisputed "mistress of the seas"; for more than a century, too, thanks to her early start with the Industrial Revolution, she had been the "workshop of the world." Wherever British traders or warships had gone, they had been masters of the situation. And now Germany was challenging England, it seemed, in both these fields that had been so distinctively her own. Germany's colonial activity was no particular cause for British concern. Her increasing exports, her merchant marine, and, above all, her navy were a different matter.

The German commercial rivalry, which began to be serious about 1880, the contemporary activity of the United States, and the later activity of Japan were triple blows at British industry and commerce. With high protective tariffs the newcomers shielded infant industries against British goods and began to supply their own domestic needs. They then began to challenge British supremacy in markets of the outside world, and finally they managed to flood the markets of free-trade England herself with their goods. For the time being, the American threat was less serious than the German; for, though the total American exports were about equal to the German, some two thirds of them were grain, meat, and raw cotton, which did not compete with England as did Germany's manufactures.

In industrial and commercial matters England had had the field to herself for so long that she had not kept up to the minute in methods of production and sale. The British had pride in the traditions of their firms and the quality of their products, but considered it undignified to push their wares too vigorously. The Germans, with their remarkable capacity for thoroughness and detail, co-ordinated factories, railways, steamships, and finance to challenge England in one world market after another. By cutting production costs and deliberately sacrificing quality, they could turn out articles more cheaply. Their experts carefully analyzed the needs and desires of particular markets and reported, for instance, that cheap knives with colored handles and poor blades would sell better than the conventional British knives, with their somber black handles and excellent blades. That was typical of a thousand experiments, and the Germans were ever ready to introduce new articles and create new tastes. In the markets of the world appeared a new phenomenon, the German traveling salesman, or drummer, persistent, aggressive, and able to speak the language of the region. German banks offered liberal credit terms to overseas buyers, and German consuls actively aided the nation's commercial interests. The Hamburg-American, North German Lloyd, and other lines, often subsidized by the government, radiated from Hamburg and Bremen in every direction and, in co-operation with the government-owned railways, offered through freight rates much lower than the British. Altogether, their energy and methods were reminiscent of Hanseatic and Dutch activity centuries before.

During the last quarter of the century, while British export totals remained fairly static, the Germans forged rapidly ahead. In many Continental nations Germany actually began to sell more goods than England; for the Germans had the advantage of direct rail communication, which eliminated the cost of loading and unloading ships. The most extreme case was Russia, where, by 1913, Germany was selling four times as much as England. Outside Europe there was scarcely a country where Germany actually went ahead of England; but in the United States, Latin America, and elsewhere the Germans were steadily creeping up on the British total. As foreign markets fell off England increased her proportion of trade with her own possessions, where the German inroads were less marked, although the United States ran far ahead of England in trade with Canada. Even at home England encountered the rivalry. In order to check the German forging of British trade-marks, Parliament required that all imports should be stamped with the country of origin. "The workshop of the world" soon discovered, to its amazement, that it was being flooded with a wide range of articles marked "Made in Germany," even to that most English of objects, the cricket bat. England, in fact, was Germany's best customer. The progress of the rivalry is indicated in the tables on the next page.

There is some dispute as to the extent to which their commercial rivalry promoted hostility between England and Germany. On the eve of Chamberlain's first proposals of alliance one English author, in a volume entitled *Made in Germany*, aroused popular apprehensions and declared that Germany was "battling with might and main for the extinction of her [England's] supremacy"; and another, shortly afterward, stated that "if Germany were extinguished tomorrow, the day after tomorrow there is not an Englishman in the world who would not be the richer." Some Germans, on the other hand, charged England with a desire to crush their commercial development by force, as they had once crushed the Dutch. Those, however, were irresponsible opinions. The diplomatic historians, who draw their conclusions from the archives of Downing Street and the Wilhelmstrasse, are inclined to discount the influence of the commercial friction; for the foreign ministers, perhaps too proud to soil their hands with anything so prosaic as exports, rather neglected the

| EXPORTS OF DOMESTIC PRODUCTS, UNITED KINGDOM, GERMANY, AND UNITED STATES (In millions of pounds sterling) | | | | | | |
|---|---|---|---|---|---|---|
| | 1860 | 1872 | 1885 | 1890 | 1900 | 1913 |
| United Kingdom | 135 | 256 | 213 | 263 | 291 | 525 |
| Germany | c. 40 | 124 | 145 | 170 | 237 | 509 |
| United States | 74 | 110 | 144 | 168 | 274 | 362 |

| IMPORTS INTO UNITED STATES FROM UNITED KINGDOM AND GERMANY (In millions of pounds sterling) | | | | | | |
|---|---|---|---|---|---|---|
| | 1860 | 1872 | 1883 | 1890 | 1900 | 1913 |
| United Kingdom | 27 | 50 | 37 | 39 | 32 | 59 |
| Germany | 3 | 9 | 11 | 19 | 19 | 34 |

subject. At any rate, the competition tended to increase popular, if not official, antipathy in both countries.

That threat to England's prosperity was serious enough, but coupled with it came what appeared to be a threat to the security of England herself and her empire. In 1890 Captain Mahan, an American naval officer, coined the phrase "sea power" and, in a brilliant study, demonstrated its influence in the spread of England's power on the seas and in the lands beyond the seas. Sea power, which meant the ability to go where one pleased in wartime while preventing one's enemy from doing likewise, was suddenly made to appear very desirable. At the time Mahan wrote, British sea power was fully taken for granted. England, ever since the days of the Bourbon "family compact," had maintained her navy on a "two-power" basis, large enough to handle any two rivals that might combine against it. As long as France and Russia remained the runners-up for naval power, England felt that she could manage the situation, believing that, ship for ship, her navy was decidedly superior in quality. Suddenly the Germans appeared as ardent disciples of Mahan's teachings. A well-organized and aggressive Navy League, financed at first by the Krupp munitions concern, which saw prospects of huge orders, stirred up propaganda and soon had nearly a quarter of a million members. The Kaiser, who "liked tall ships as an earlier Hohenzollern had liked tall soldiers," supported the idea. The master mind

# The End of Splendid Isolation

and guiding force was the old sea dog Admiral von Tirpitz. In 1898, close upon Chamberlain's first proposals of alliance, the Reichstag voted to construct, over a period of years, nineteen battleships and numerous cruisers. In 1900, while the proposals for alliance were still under way, a more ambitious naval law was passed. Its preamble, probably the work of Tirpitz, declared that "Germany must have a battle fleet so strong that, even for the adversary with the greatest sea power, a war against us would involve such dangers as to imperil his position in the world." It provided for thirty-four battleships in sixteen years, together with a large number of cruisers and lesser craft. Before Germany's naval spurt she had only fourteen battleships to England's fifty-four. This new program would jeopardize British naval supremacy unless England should lay down new keels even faster than Germany.

Failing to secure an alliance with Germany, England turned to the alternative policy which she was to continue until the World War, a double policy of strengthening the royal navy and of making approaches to Germany's rivals. To provide for possible naval contingencies, the British in 1903 began building a new base on the east coast of Scotland, at Rosyth, and commenced a new building program calling for four capital ships every year. In 1904 they began to concentrate the fleet in home waters. Tirpitz found a doughty rival in Sir John Fisher, another tough old sailor, and the two persistently pushed their plans which led to the costly "naval race," of which we shall hear more.

After unsuccessful endeavors to end her "splendid isolation" through approaches to Russia and Germany, England finally turned toward France. Delcassé, the French minister of foreign affairs, was even more anxious than England to bring about a friendly understanding. The French, to be sure, had many grievances against England, particularly in Africa, where the memory of Fashoda was still fresh. Fashoda, however, had demonstrated that it was next to impossible to thwart England on the Nile; France therefore determined to make terms. Furthermore, Edward VII did not relish the pushing ways of his nephew the Kaiser, who was reported to have called his uncle an old peacock! King Edward, of course, was not the British government; but he was influential and he was pro-French, in marked contrast to Victoria's prejudices in favor of everything German. Paris accepted this fact. Utilized by his cabinet as a harbinger of good will, Edward did much to reconcile the boulevards to the strange notion of an Anglo-French entente. And as he did so the president of the French Republic was cheered in London. Thus was a new friendship suggested, planned, and finally consummated.

# A History of England and the British Empire

What England wanted was a friend on the Continent and a free hand in Egypt, where French influence still interfered with Cromer's plans for the rehabilitation of that country. France wanted many things, but particularly did she want Morocco, the westernmost of the old Barbary States. The French had been in Algeria since 1830 and had made Tunis a protectorate in 1881. If the whole or a part of Morocco could be absorbed into her colonial empire, it would be rounded out well as far as northwestern Africa was concerned. There proved no irreconcilable difficulty here.

In 1904 England paved the way for the Triple Entente by aligning herself definitely with France, which had already been allied with Russia for ten years. As in the other stages of the Entente, a bargain was made. In this "Entente Cordiale," or friendly understanding, Lord Lansdowne, who succeeded Salisbury as Foreign Secretary, agreed to accept the then-existing political status of Egypt, and France promised not to interfere in anything that England might do in that country. In return, France stated that she recognized the existing status in Morocco, and England agreed to give her a free hand there. The lesser agreements ended the centuries-old disputes relative to the Newfoundland fisheries, drew new boundaries between British and French colonies in Africa, led Britain to withdraw certain claims over Madagascar, arranged spheres of influence in the hinterland of Siam, and provided for joint rule over the New Hebrides, in the Pacific. Wherever the Union Jack and the tricolor flew throughout the world, understanding and friendship were now to take the place of suspicion and hostility. All that was made public, but not the secret agreements by which mutual promises of diplomatic support were given in case England or France sought to extend her power in Egypt or Morocco.

This Entente Cordiale was to become a momentous landmark in British history. A prominent member of the British cabinet of 1914 stated after the war that George III began the destruction of the British Empire and that Edward VII consummated it when he tied his country to the chariot wheels of Franco-Russian imperialism. Whether this statement will prove true or not, the Entente ultimately did far more than end colonial friction and reverse the course of Anglo-French relations. By her "diplomatic revolution" England forsook her "splendid isolation" and lost much of her old freedom of action. She had definitely aligned herself with the Continental systems. She was not a member of the Dual Alliance between France and Russia, nor was she likely to become one. While, unlike the other nations in the alliance systems, she did not make (except in her alliance with Japan) formal agreements as to what she would do in case of war, her "friendly understandings" were to prove more binding when the crisis came than Italy's pledged word. When this new English entente with France was shortly extended to Russia, the new triangular arrangement was to surpass in wealth and population the rival Triple Alliance, and so would upset the delicate balance between Europe's armed camps.

The ink of the Anglo-French agreement was no sooner dry than France took action. Within a year she offered to assist the sultan of Morocco in making needed reforms, promised him money to make them, and sent a mission to his capital, Fez, to arrange for spending it. Thereupon the Kaiser landed at Tangier, publicly congratulated the sultan upon his independence, and warned him to be on his guard lest he lose it. The question of Morocco, Germany declared, concerned Europe as a whole, and she insisted that an international conference be held to determine its status. Delcassé now lost his head; for he preferred war to the projected conference, which, he feared, might retard French projects in Morocco. He went so far as to intimate that England was ready to fight and was prepared to land one hundred thousand men in Schleswig-Holstein to cut the Kiel Canal. This was denied by the British Foreign Office, and in 1905 Delcassé resigned. Germany won a temporary victory; for early in 1906 a conference assembled in the Spanish town of Algeciras, near Gibraltar, to discuss Moroccan affairs.

At the end of 1905, just before the conference met, the coming of the Liberals into power brought Sir Edward Grey to the Foreign Office, where he was to remain for more than ten years. Lean, aloof, and dignified, Grey belonged to one of the foremost families of the English aristocracy, a family with a prominent career of public service. He had been a champion tennis-player and was an enthusiastic fisherman and lover of birds. Though the Germans might later call him "Liar Grey," his integrity was apparently above reproach. Yet, with all the fine qualities characteristic of his class, Grey had his shortcomings. An amateur in politics, he was prone to rely strongly upon the permanent officials of the Foreign Office. He knew less than Salisbury had known of the Continental point of view; for he preferred fishing to travel. He was too prone to consider others as honorable as himself,—an unfortunate trait in view of the motives of certain allies of the near future who well merited suspicion. He shared with many previous British foreign secretaries a tendency to meet immediate situations by compromise rather than to formulate a far-reaching policy which took possible consequences into account. Grey accepted fully the new Anglo-French agreement made by his Conservative predecessor, Lansdowne, and was no sooner in office than he gave it full support.

# A History of England and the British Empire

The French emerged victorious from the Algeciras Conference. By making a prior agreement with the Italians, France won them to her side. Secretly, Italy agreed not to obstruct France in Morocco if the French would consent to Italian absorption of Tripoli. From this time Italy was to have a foot in both armed camps; for although she still remained publicly a member of the Triple Alliance, she flirted secretly with France. Spain also was bought off by France in advance, with prospects of a share of Morocco. Russia, from her position in the Dual Alliance, and England, from hers in the Entente Cordiale, sided with France. That left only Austria to support the isolated Germans. Although the conference formally acknowledged the independence of Morocco, France got what she wanted; for she was given control over the policing of Moroccan ports, and a predominant position in an international bank which was to reorganize Moroccan finances. The calling of the Algeciras Conference had been a diplomatic victory for Germany; the results of the conference, a sharp defeat.

In 1907, the year after Algeciras, England and Russia drew closer together to round out the Triple Entente. There was behind them, as we have noted, a long record of hostility and rivalry in Near East, Middle East, and Far East. Russia had rebuffed Salisbury's proposal for an understanding in 1898, and England had allied herself with Japan to offset Russian influence in the Far East. The defeat of Russia by Japan in 1904–1905 had somewhat changed the picture. England now had less to fear from Russia; so, too, had Germany. England seems to have taken the initiative in 1907, in fear of a Russo-German alliance. Russia, repulsed in the Far East, was glad to compound her disputes with England in the Middle East in order to have a free hand in the Near East. The Anglo-Russian agreement, like the Dual Alliance of Russia and France and the Entente Cordiale of France and England, was sealed with a bargain. Its terms were limited to the Middle East. The British and Russians both agreed to stay out of Tibet. Afghanistan was recognized as a British sphere of influence. Persia was virtually partitioned between the two powers. In regard to other matters the agreement was not specific at all. There were no military or naval commitments, and the opening of the Straits at Constantinople, the project closest to the heart of the Russian foreign minister, was hinted at vaguely and indirectly. It boded ill for the future that that foreign secretary was Isvolski, one of the men who probably did most to bring on the World War.

The most important part of the bargain was the offering up of Persia as a sacrificial lamb. The independence of Persia was recognized as a matter of form; but that having been done, Russia and

# The End of Splendid Isolation

England divided the country into three zones without consulting the Persians. Russia received the most important and valuable zone,— including the capital, Teheran,—as a sphere of influence for economic exploitation. South of this there was to be a neutral zone. Still further south and east, England received her share, a desert waste of scant economic value but useful because it protected the approaches to India. Theoretically, there was to be an "open door" policy in Persia; actually the door was closed in the face of Germany. Following hard upon the conclusion of this agreement came the strangling of Persian independence at the hands of Russia, with England somewhat sorrowfully sacrificing the good of Persia for the exigencies of European politics. The Persians did not take their strangling quietly. They stirred up a revolution, exiled their pro-Russian Shah, and attempted to rule themselves. To assist them with their tangled finances, they imported an American, W. Morgan Shuster. He was harassed by Russian and British interference from the first, and was finally driven out of the country by a Russian ultimatum to Persia, backed by England. His vehement public protest caused Grey considerable embarrassment in Parliament; for this seemed a far cry from the policies of Canning and Palmerston. Grey expostulated with Russia in private, but in public he had to defend the good faith of England's new ally. Russia, feeling that England needed her alliance, exploited that fact to the limit, and punished Persia for employing Shuster by invading northern Persia, by blowing up the citadel at Tabriz, and by a general massacre.

The Persian situation showed England how far she had gone from the "splendid isolation" of a few years before. By her action in 1904 and 1907, rival alliances had at last been developed, but they were fast to lose their original defensive nature. There never could be an exact balance of power, and, as the years went on, jealousy developed as prestige was involved. If a member of one group gained something anywhere in the world, the other group felt it necessary to secure compensation. England soon found that she was tied up to two decidedly ambitious nations. In those tense years there were a series of incidents any one of which might have plunged Europe into war.

Morocco furnished one of these with the "Agadir affair," in 1911. French influence had grown apace in that "land of the peacock's tail" since Algeciras. Difficulties with Germany had supposedly been ironed out when, in 1911, a palace revolution at Fez caused the French to dispatch a military force to the Moroccan capital, alleging that the Europeans were in danger there. A similar situation had given the British control of Egypt in 1882, and there was a feeling at Berlin that if the French forces occupied Fez they might not withdraw in the near future, and Morocco would become a French protectorate. The Germans recognized a coup d'état when they saw one. After hinting in vain that they might accept compensation elsewhere, they sent a gunboat, the *Panther*, to Agadir, an obscure Moroccan port on the Atlantic. If France was going to tear up the Treaty of Algeciras, Germany was determined to have something for herself, either in Morocco or elsewhere.

That brought England into the field. She did not want a German naval base in that part of Africa lying athwart her sea lanes. Grey immediately demanded assurance from the German government that it had no intention of occupying Agadir. Before word could come back from Berlin, Lloyd George, then Chancellor of the Exchequer, delivered a speech in threatening vein at the Mansion House. It was an official speech, made after consultation with the prime minister and foreign secretary. Appealing to national honor, he declared that "Britain should at all hazards maintain her prestige amongst the great powers of the world" and that if she were to be treated "as if she were of no account," peace at such a price would be an intolerable humiliation. German public opinion was inflamed. The British cabinet ordered the fleet to make ready, while France and Germany also were preparing for emergencies. War seemed imminent. Cooler heads, however, prevailed. What Germany really wanted, it seems, was not Agadir, as the English believed, but a portion of the French Congo. Upon receiving from France a region of little economic value but of considerable extent as an addition to Cameroons, she agreed to let the French have their way in Morocco. Thus the Triple Alliance had saved its face; the *Panther* had been used for blackmail purposes.

By 1912 England had drifted far into the Franco-Russian camp. To the east and to the west she had connived with Russia and France and had supported them in their inroads on Persian and Moroccan independence. From the German point of view, this action of England's meant that she was actively participating in the encirclement of Germany by a ring of enemies. From the English point of view, Britain was compounding her differences with France and Russia while at the same time taking out insurance policies against a restless and militant neighbor who threatened her peace.

The main cause of England's hostility lay in the continued naval rivalry, rather than in the coldness with which Germany held aloof from proffered friendship or in annoyance at the excitable and often irritating Kaiser. England had given Germany an excellent chance to catch up in the naval race by laying the keel of the *Dreadnought* in 1905. Ever since the old wooden ship of the line had given way to

# The End of Splendid Isolation

the ironclad, about 1860 (see page 653), warships had been undergoing constant evolution toward increased size, fire power, defensive strength, speed, and cost. At the turn of the century, when the naval race began, the British battleships carried four twelve-inch guns and twelve six-inch guns, with armor plate from seven to nine inches thick. The race for "bigger and better" ships had already made some progress in tons, guns, plates, and knots when the British began work on the *Dreadnought*. She measured about seventeen thousand tons, had an eleven-inch armor belt, could travel at twenty-one knots, and cost about £1,600,000, the price of Nelson's whole Trafalgar fleet. But the distinctive feature, which made her a landmark in naval architecture, was that she was an "all-big-gun" ship. The former secondary batteries of six-inch guns were discarded, and she was given ten twelve-inch guns. Consequently, in an action she could stay out of range of the lesser guns of the older ships and would have a tremendous advantage in hitting power. So important was her influence that battleships have since been designated as predreadnoughts, dreadnoughts, and superdreadnoughts. When Germany started the naval race, England, as we saw, had enjoyed a heavy advantage in battle strength. The *Dreadnought*, by rendering all earlier battleships obsolete, wiped out that heavy British advantage and gave the rivals a fresh start. The British, however, knew that the idea of the "all-big-gun" ship was in the air and did not want to be caught unprepared. Though the *Dreadnought* was at sea in a year and four days after her keel was laid, it normally took two or three years to complete a battleship. Consequently, plans and programs had to be arranged far in advance. It was nearly four years more before Germany had her first two "dreadnoughts" at sea; and by that time England had five, as well as three battle cruisers which had the size and gun power of dreadnoughts but sacrificed some armor protection for extra speed. The score of the dreadnought race was as shown in the table on the next page.

The story behind those statistics, however, is not so quickly told. English fear of the German navy was in part fanciful, in part justified. Englishmen resented the German challenge to British naval supremacy. The Liberal party, in control since 1905, was historically pledged to peace, retrenchment, and reform. The new reforms of Asquith and Lloyd George made retrenchment no longer possible, but social reform on a large scale might still be had without too great a strain on the exchequer, provided that additional money need not be spent for the fleet. Public opinion would not permit England to lose control of the seas, and rightly; for, pride apart, England's absolute dependence upon an overseas supply of food and other essentials made

| DREADNOUGHT AND BATTLE–CRUISER STRENGTH OF ENGLAND AND GERMANY | | | | | | |
|---|---|---|---|---|---|---|
| *Dreadnought and Superdreadnought Battleships* | | | | | | |
| | 1906 | 1908 | 1910 | 1912 | 1914 | 1916 |
| England . . . . | 1 | 1 | 5 | 12 | 18 | 29 |
| Germany . . . | | | 2 | 7 | 13 | 17 |
| *Battle Cruisers* | | | | | | |
| England . . . . | | | 3 | 4 | 9 | 10 |
| Germany . . . | | | 1 | 2 | 4 | 5 |

it imperative. Germany, as the World War was to demonstrate, could fight four years with her fleet completely cooped up; England could not have lasted four months. If rising German naval expenditure were not countered by increased British expenditure, England would no longer be mistress of the seas. That was obvious. These facts, more than anything else, had driven the peaceful Grey into the arms of France and Russia.

Truculence on the two sides balanced fairly well. Fisher secretly proposed to the king in 1908 that he "Copenhagen" the German fleet; in other words, seize or sink it without a declaration of war, as England had twice done to the Danes a century before (see pages 562, 570). The Germans, so far as we know, made no similar suggestions, but steadily continued to augment the striking force of their navy. In 1908 they began, apparently, to anticipate their program for 1909–1910, whereupon the British laid down superdreadnoughts, which implied guns of 13.5 inches or more. England, though forced to beg ships from the dominions, managed to keep a safe lead at heavy cost. Between 1900 and 1913 the naval budget nearly doubled.

Both governments meanwhile started negotiations which might end or at least slow down this naval race. The British gave up their time-honored two-power standard and insisted only on a 3–2 ratio over any given nation. The Germans were willing, under certain circumstances, to retard their building program. Winston Churchill, First Lord of the Admiralty, suggested a "naval holiday" during which no construction would be carried on by either side. The Germans would not hear of this. They would, however, negotiate on the basis of a political pact. Their price was England's promise of neutrality in a Continental war, and the British shied away from that suggestion. They were already too far involved with France to risk such a pledge.

# The End of Splendid Isolation

The last of these efforts at compromise was made in 1912, when Lord Haldane, War Secretary, visited Berlin. He was handed the forthcoming German estimates and was told that, if England would agree to keep out of a war on the Continent in which Germany might happen to become involved, the estimates might be reduced. Haldane could not promise, and the negotiations fell through. The British Admiralty was horrified when it examined the German figures, which would give the German navy a position of near equality with the British by 1915.

This was not to be endured. From the English point of view, the German government was trying to browbeat England into a political agreement, using the projected naval increase as a club. Therefore England increased her own appropriations once more and drew closer to France. A new exchange of letters followed between Grey and the French ambassador at London. France wanted to transform the Entente Cordiale into a definite alliance such as she had with Russia. England, on the other hand, wanted to retain freedom of action. Grey stated explicitly that both nations were left completely free to take any line of action they might think desirable in case of war. Their military and naval experts, however, were to consult together. As a matter of fact, they had been doing this secretly for six years, but now, for the first time, most of the British cabinet learned of it. They divided on the advisability of these staff consultations. The particular point at issue was the proposed transfer of part of the British Mediterranean ships to the North Sea to increase the force opposed to Germany, while the French would move their Atlantic fleet from the Channel to the Mediterranean, thus leaving their western coast unprotected unless the British were to guard it. This, it was pointed out by opponents of the policy, seemed to mean that, however much Grey might talk about freedom of action, England would be in honor bound to protect the French coast in case of a Franco-German war. If that was the case, the exchange of letters was not far from an alliance.

There was no question about the readiness of the British navy, which was still the strongest in the world; but the British army was far smaller than those of the other European powers. England and the United States, alone of the great nations, still clung to the small professional armies which had once been common among all countries. They had not adopted the conscription of all able-bodied men of certain ages which, we recall, had been inaugurated in Revolutionary France and then had been made into a system by Prussia when she had been forced to agree, after her defeat by Napoleon, to reduce her army to forty-two thousand men. The Prussians had escaped from that dilemma by the clever ruse of training their army intensively for a few months and then conscripting another batch for training until, while still keeping their standing army small, they had built up a large reserve of trained men. This law remained on the statute books, but was not revived in full force until about 1860, and then helped to give Prussia her victories over Austria and France. Thereupon the system of compulsory, universal military training was adopted by France, Austria, Russia, Italy, and most of the other Continental nations. This accounts for the large number of trained men who were instantly mobilized on the Continent when the World War broke out. Every officer and common soldier knew exactly where he was to report as soon as mobilization was declared. Usually called to the colors at about twenty, he served three years, more or less, in the active army and then passed through a series of reserve groupings, with occasional training, until well into middle age. Sometimes lack of money made it impossible to train all eligible men in this way, and many might be put into an untrained reserve for special duties. Such a general system was quite ideal from the purely military point of view; but the worker was delayed in getting a good start in life, and the productive wealth of a country was decreased by the placing of large numbers in a nonproductive occupation. Russia, moreover, lacked equipment for her full force. Between 1911 and 1913 France and Germany were steadily increasing their active forces.

| ARMIES OF THE GREAT POWERS, 1911 (In hundred thousands) | | | | | | | |
|---|---|---|---|---|---|---|---|
| | England | France | Russia | Germany | Austria | Italy | United States |
| Standing army | 2 | 8 | 12 | 8 | 3 | 3 | 1 |
| Trained reserves | 1 | 23 | 38 | 40 | 16 | 12 | 2 |

The British regular army was of excellent quality, composed as it was of professionals; but it was only about 250,000 strong, one half stationed in the British Isles and the other half in India or elsewhere beyond the seas. In addition, there were some 130,000 reserves. During the three years before the war the size of the army was debated in thousands of British homes. It was recognized that an expeditionary force might have to be dispatched to France in case of an invasion by Germany, but no one could tell how large it would have to be. The government had planned its size at 160,000 and felt that that was enough. At a time when the armies on the Continent were increasing very rapidly, the British standing army was actually re-

# The End of Splendid Isolation

duced by 8000 men. To provide for eventualities, Lord Haldane, the War Secretary, announced the creation of a body of "territorials," or trained militia, more than 200,000 strong. These, with the reserves, it was felt, would be enough to keep the expeditionary force at full strength and could serve as a framework for a new army. Some, however, felt that this was decidedly not enough and that England should adopt conscription on the Continental model. Foremost among these was the aged Lord Roberts, hero of the Afghan and South African wars and, even more than Kitchener, the first soldier of England. So vehement was his voice and so great his popularity that an army as well as a navy scare spread throughout the country. To the dismay of the Liberal government, the old soldier stormed up and down, back and forth, throughout the country picturing the menace of a sudden German attack, the inadequacy of the territorials, and the need for conscription. But forced military service ran counter to English tradition, and nothing happened. When the war finally broke out, however, there were many who declared that if Roberts's advice had been heeded, Germany would have realized that England was in earnest and would have hesitated long before invading Belgium. Germany did not take the British army seriously as it was; Bismarck was reputed to have remarked some time before that if the British sent over an expedition he would ask the police to arrest it.

Meanwhile in the Balkans events were moving rapidly toward the crisis which precipitated the war. Neither Germany nor France nor England was primarily concerned with these events except as they involved Austria and Russia. England's sole concern was the control of Constantinople, and the anti-Russian tradition was still too strong in England to permit British support of Russian policy in any Balkan quarrel. But, as tension increased, every country became more and more convinced that it could not be safe without allies, and to keep its allies it felt forced to support their interests even in quarters where its own were not at stake.

Russia and Austria had been engaged in fierce competition for control of the Balkan situation since 1878. Unfortunately for the peace of Europe, their foreign policies fell into the hands of men more reckless than capable. Their intrigues produced a series of crises between 1908 and 1914, when they finally dragged their more cautious allies with them into war. Particularly conspicuous was the Russian foreign minister Isvolski, a tireless intriguer whose wife was a close friend of the Russian empress. He was a man with one great aim—the opening of the Straits to Russian warships. Toward that end he bargained with one nation after another and planned for the war which Russia might wage when she had recovered from the

[ 845 ]

Japanese defeat. He had played a prominent part in arranging the Anglo-Russian agreement of 1907, and later, as ambassador at Paris, he helped to turn the Franco-Russian alliance from a defensive into an aggressive one.

When the Young Turk revolution drove old Abdul-Hamid from his throne in 1908, Isvolski saw a chance to take advantage of Turkey's temporary weakness. He made some sort of agreement with the Austrian foreign minister that Russia would approve Austria's annexation of Bosnia-Herzegovina if Austria would approve Russia's opening of the Straits. Without notifying him in advance, Austria seized the provinces, and Isvolski, furious at being let down, determined on revenge. He went to London for British support, but was received coldly. Surprised and perplexed at the attitude of his new ally, he could not obtain even sympathy. The utmost crumb of comfort that he could carry away was an assurance that in the future (time unspecified) the British cabinet might consider it desirable to change the status of the Straits, provided Turkey consented. Russia then revived with full force a pan-Slavic policy in the Balkans, a new version of the old religious excuse for interference. Serbia received Russian backing in her intrigues to join to herself the South Slavs in Austria-Hungary. Austria felt compelled to take strong measures to protect herself against disintegration. It was out of this situation that the war would come, and Isvolski would say, "It is *my* war!"

The two fierce Balkan wars of 1912 and 1913 likewise affected England only indirectly. The alliance of the Balkan states of Serbia, Bulgaria, Greece, and Montenegro, which decisively defeated Turkey in the first of these wars, nearly brought Russia and Austria to blows. England joined hands with Germany on that occasion to preserve international peace. Trouble developed over the peace terms, partly because Austria insisted on the formation of a new state, Albania, to keep Serbia from becoming too large and Serbia then compensated herself with a considerable part of Macedonia, which her ally Bulgaria expected. A second war broke out, with Bulgaria in a hopeless fight against her former allies, who were joined by Rumania and even by Turkey. But through all this Anglo-German relations took a turn for the better as London and Berlin worked to restrain their turbulent eastern allies. The peace negotiations, in which the powers participated, were held at London.

There had been, it is true, some heartburnings in England over the Berlin-Baghdad railway which was being built under German auspices. With the Trans-Siberian and the Cape-to-Cairo, it was one of the three great rail projects of the new imperialism. When Turkey first granted the provisional concession, in 1899, England seemed "well disposed to Teutonic penetration in the Near East"; but very soon after Germany had rejected the offers of alliance, and even before the definite concession was obtained in 1903, England's attitude changed sharply. The merchants feared a loss of trade in Turkey and in Mesopotamia, which had been a particular British preserve. The imperial strategists saw a threat to the security of India. Before much progress had been made, England secured a protectorate over a little state on the Persian Gulf which blocked a railway terminus there. Russia and France opposed the project for some time; but in 1912 Russia suddenly came to terms with Germany on the subject, and so, too, did the French and British. England secured for herself a monopoly of the river trade between Basra, the junction point of the Tigris and Euphrates, and the Persian Gulf. The formal agreement between England and Germany had been initialed by June, 1914, and Germany was to build the railway as far as Baghdad. A considerable portion of the road was already completed.

Diplomacy had at least settled that old dispute to the mutual satisfaction of all concerned, but the general international situation in early 1914 was still full of danger. In the successive crises in Morocco and the Near East the powers had shown more and more readiness to run risks in order to hold their allies and to maintain the prestige of their group. Anglo-German relations might be improved for the moment, but England's allies were being drawn into a more aggressive alliance by Isvolski and Poincaré, the French president. Armies were being rapidly increased in size, and any remote incident might drag all Europe into conflict.

Thus stood the situation in June, 1914, when Francis Ferdinand, heir to the Austrian throne, and his morganatic wife were murdered by a young Serb at Sarajevo, in Bosnia. The murder brought about a conflict between Austria and Serbia which Grey insisted was no concern of England's. According to him, England would assist in maintaining the peace of Europe in every honorable and peaceful way, but the British government would not under any circumstances threaten to intervene with force of arms on either side of the dispute. She would gladly act as mediator between Austria and Serbia or between Austria and Russia, now rushing to the defense of her brother Slavs of Serbia. Such was the position the British took in June and held until after Germany declared war on Russia.

Only through indirect causes did England become involved in the World War, and the same statement holds true, to a somewhat less degree, for Germany and France. The main cause of the war was the long-standing quarrel between Russia and Austria as to who should control the Balkans. Serbia was a pawn in the game. Whether

Serbia started the war by conniving at the plot which ended in the death of the Archduke, or whether Austria started it by her untimely ultimatum to Serbia, or whether Russia started it by commencing mobilization on such a scale as to impel Germany into the conflict are mooted points of European rather than of British history. As far as England is concerned, Sir Edward Grey threw all his efforts into trying to keep the war from commencing and then from spreading.

Matters were moving fast during the week before England's declaration of war on August 4. Most of the exacting demands made upon Serbia by the sharp Austrian ultimatum of July 23 had been accepted; nevertheless, on July 28, Austria declared war. Thereupon the two systems of alliances began to fall into line. Russia, interfering on behalf of the Serbs, commenced the mobilization of her immense army. Because of the alliance situation the Russian general staff had made a double mobilization plan whereby troops were to gather on the German frontier as well as on the Austrian. Germany, aware of this, took no chances. As soon as it was certain that Russian mobilization had begun, Germany gave Russia twelve hours to stop it on July 31. Russia continued; so on August 1 Germany declared war. The Germans, like the Russians, had a double mobilization plan. When troops headed for the Russian frontier, others went toward the French border; and at this crisis such an involved plan was very difficult to correct. By August 3 France too was in the war.

Grey's first step to keep Europe out of war had been the suggestion of direct conversations between Vienna and St. Petersburg. Poincaré, the French president, disapproved of that, saying they would be dangerous. Just what he meant by his statement never was specified. Grey next proposed that the four neutral powers, France, Germany, Italy, and England, mediate between Russia and Austria. France would not agree, lest it appear that she was not supporting Russia; Germany, likewise, had a similar attitude concerning Austria; for she had taken the very grave responsibility of assuring her ally that she would stand behind her in any action she might take. As Austria and Serbia approached war Grey proposed a conference of the ambassadors of the neutral powers at London; but Germany refused, fearing that Italy was too undependable and that Russia would gain too much time with her mobilization. Grey still persisted, and, after several communications with the German ambassador at London, informed him on July 29 that "as long as the conflict remained confined to Austria and Russia, England could stand aside; but if Germany and France should be involved, then the situation would be immediately altered, and the British government would be forced to rapid decisions."

# The End of Splendid Isolation

Grey, of course, might have used much stronger language. There was nothing at all in the nature of a threat until the last communication to the German ambassador, which came too late to be of effective service. It might be said that Grey had a chance to notify Germany that, unless she called off Austria, England would stand by Russia in case of eventual war. On the other hand, he might have told France that, while England had made what amounted to definite commitments to France, she was less closely bound to Russia, and that unless France compelled her ally to cease mobilizing, England would refuse to be drawn into any resultant general war. Finally, he might perhaps have appealed direct to Austria as an old friend, demanding the acceptance of the Serbian reply to the Austrian ultimatum, or at least a pledge to refrain from overt act. Sir Edward did none of these things. Any one of the three might have stopped the war—perhaps. Grey, of course, had no authority to act in this highhanded way, and had he asked permission from the cabinet, presumably it would have been refused. A more daring and more unscrupulous Foreign Secretary might have taken a chance, running the risk of having his good name damned forever; but Sir Edward was not a man of that type.

With France in the war, the next question was whether England was bound to follow her. The ambiguous military and naval arrangements which had been made between the two countries in 1912 were not known to the British public, although the cabinet had been informed of them. They were, however, suspected, and before the war several efforts were made to find out whether they existed. Asquith, the prime minister, challenged on the subject in 1913, declared, "This country is not under any obligation, not public and known to Parliament, which compels it to take part in a war."

But now a European war was on. The French ambassador pleaded again and again with Grey for definite support, but the utmost he could learn was that England was undecided. It was true that the Atlantic coast of France lay unprotected because of the 1912 arrangements. But did this involve England in the war? Was there a debt of honor which England owed France? All the morning of August 2 the cabinet debated. At noon a message arrived from the Conservative leaders telling the Liberal government that "It would be fatal to the honor and security of the United Kingdom to hesitate in supporting France and Russia." The cabinet thereupon came to a decision. It assured the French ambassador that "if the German fleet comes into the Channel or through the North Sea to undertake hostile operations against the French coasts or shipping the British fleet will give all the protection in its power." Before knowledge of the German ultimatum to Belgium reached England, she gave this pledge.

# A History of England and the British Empire

England was not yet at war, and it is barely possible that she might never have been if the Germans had kept out of Belgium. Through neutral Belgium, however, lay the road to the least fortified boundary of France, and so Germany chose that way on the excuse of military necessity. Palmerston's treaty of 1839 came to life. Germany sent an ultimatum to Belgium requesting that German troops be allowed to enter France by that route. The same ultimatum went to the adjacent little neutral duchy of Luxemburg, which merely protested against the German advance and did not fight. Belgium might not have fought either, had she not been so bound up with French interests. As it was, the Belgians rejected the German ultimatum and began a stubborn resistance to the invaders.

Before the actual invasion of Belgium, Grey did little to prevent it. Germany had sought previous information about England's attitude and had received only evasive replies. A prompt and militant intimation to Germany on August 1 that England would fight if German troops set foot on Belgian soil might possibly have prevented their doing so. Grey did not want war, but if war came he wanted England to enter it on the side of France. The invasion of Belgium gave him a popular and moral reason for fighting; without it he would have found it difficult to show Parliament that war was necessary. The threatened invasion of Belgium, wrote Lloyd George, "set the nation on fire from sea to sea. . . . Before then the cabinet was hopelessly divided. After the German ultimatum to Belgium the cabinet was almost unanimous." On Tuesday, August 4, the German troops were already invading Belgium when England presented her ultimatum to Germany that an invasion must not be attempted. As a result, at midnight, England declared war upon Germany.

England had plunged into the war for the avowed purpose of saving Belgium. She asserted that she was in honor bound to do so; but as far as a strictly legal interpretation of the treaty of 1839 went, she was pledged simply not to violate Belgium's neutrality. She had been a guarantor of Luxemburg's neutrality as well, but she had not prepared to fight over its violation. The difference lay in Britain's own interests: Luxemburg did not involve them; Belgium, as always, did. It was the old story: England dared not stand by when a great power menaced the Low Countries. This had been for centuries a cardinal point of English policy. In the sixteenth century England had opposed Spain in the Low Countries; in the days of Louis XIV and of Napoleon she had fought the French there, even without neutrality treaties. Now she was ready to fight Germany. A considerable part of her bloodiest fighting would be on Belgian soil.

# The End of Splendid Isolation

Thus, after what seemed an almost unbelievably sudden crisis, a stunned and astonished world found the two great alliance systems aligned against each other in the greatest war history had yet seen. Italy alone had held aloof and would later join the Entente powers— England, France, and Russia—along with Serbia, Belgium, and other nations. Turkey and Bulgaria, both disgruntled by the Balkan situation, joined the so-called Central Powers, Germany and Austria. The war, in the course of its four devastating years, was to become a world-wide contest, with the United States, Japan, and many other overseas nations coming in on the side of the Entente. As for the question of responsibility for starting the war, it is generally conceded on the basis of postwar revelations that one cannot draw the line between black and white in this matter. Austria's and Russia's shares seem greatest, however, with Germany and France somewhat less responsible. England made sincere efforts for peace; but they would doubtless have been more effective had they been more vigorous and definite.

# CHAPTER XXIX

## *Britain in the First World War*

ENGLAND and her empire were taxed to the limit of human and material resources in the First World War, which surpassed all previous conflicts in its magnitude and in its direct influence upon the people of almost the entire world. Lasting from midsummer of 1914 to the late autumn of 1918, the fighting centered in Europe but spread to Asia, to Africa, and to distant seas. Armies were reckoned by the millions, instead of by tens or hundreds of thousands as in earlier wars. Altogether, some sixty-five million men were mobilized, including more than six million from the British Isles and an additional three million from the dominions, India, and other parts of the empire. At least ten million men were killed in the war, and nearly a million of them came from Britain and the empire. Ammunition and supplies of every sort were expended with unheard-of lavishness. The direct cost of the four years' fighting has been estimated at nearly two hundred billions of dollars. The bravery and dogged determination of the British on land and sea played a major part in the ultimate victory of the Allies.

The war was fought in several separate theaters of operations, called "fronts." The most important was the western front, where the British, the French, the Belgians, and later the Americans faced the Germans in Belgium and northern France. Next came the eastern front, where the Russians opposed the Germans and Austrians on their common frontiers. Later, the Italian front saw the fighting of the Italians and Austrians between the Alps and the Adriatic. Another theater of action was the Balkans. England conducted three separate campaigns against the Turks: at the Straits, in Mesopotamia, and in Palestine. Russia also fought the Turks far out in the Caucasus. In the fighting in Africa, the Far East, and the South Seas most of the German colonies were quickly seized, some troops in German East Africa alone holding out until the end of the war. Finally, there was the sea. So far as England is concerned, interest centers in the western front, the Turkish operations, and the sea; but we shall have to keep in mind the constant interplay between the various fronts, and the ways in which they affected one another.

# Britain in the First World War

The two sides were so evenly matched that almost until the very end the outcome was in doubt. Each side had its distinct advantages. The Central Powers (Germany and Austria), as their name implies, had the help of "interior lines" whereby they could operate as a single unit against enemies who had to operate from different directions. They occupied the strip through middle Europe from the Baltic to the Adriatic and, after Turkey and Bulgaria joined them, across Europe from the Rhine into western Asia. They could, for instance, quickly shuttle troops and munitions from the French to the Russian front, while Russia was almost completely cut off from her allies. To offset this military advantage, the Allies controlled the seas; for the British navy was the largest afloat. The Allies were able to draw men, munitions, and supplies from beyond the seas and at the same time to shut off the Central Powers from similar aid. This was naturally a tremendous asset. From the standpoint of quantity, the Allies had an advantage in man power; but the great Russian hordes were largely untrained and unequipped, while the British, with their little regular army, needed considerable time to whip a large one into shape. As far as quality went, Germany was generally supposed to have the best army in the world, with the French a close second. The war demonstrated that, unit for unit, the British, Germans, French, and Americans made more efficient soldiers than the Austrians, Russians, and Italians.

The war did not affect the vast armies alone. The whole populations of the principal belligerents were caught in its grip. It was literally a war of nations. Not merely did armies fight armies, but peoples opposed peoples, whether in front-line trenches or at home. The older men, the women, and the children remaining behind had to be taken into account more than ever before. They took up tasks hitherto performed by able-bodied men, and the armies at the front depended upon them to "carry on." Women toiled even in the munitions factories and on transportation systems. The morale of this "home front," moreover, was of prime importance. All the countries were flooded with propaganda designed to bolster up the spirits of one's own side or to undermine the enemy's. The terrific stress of the four years strained the morale of most of the leading belligerents almost to the breaking point. When a country collapsed, as several did, the home front generally cracked before the army went to pieces. Thus Russia was to go out, followed by Turkey, Bulgaria, Austria, and finally Germany. In such an endurance contest the grim doggedness of the British character was no small element in the final Allied victory. It was significant of the difference in national reactions that while the *Illustrierte Zeitung* and *L'Illustration* refrained from picturing dead countrymen during the war for fear of depressing the national spirit, the *Illustrated London News* every week published the pictures of dozens of officers killed in action. This seemed to make the British fight harder.

Sir Edward Grey and his Foreign Office had been unable to prevent the conflict; after August 4 the burden was shifted to the Admiralty and the War Office, with their respective political heads and fighting leaders. The First Lord of the Admiralty was Winston Churchill, a kinsman of the Duke of Marlborough, brilliant, versatile, and by some considered unstable. Associated with him as professional First Sea Lord was Admiral Fisher, while Admiral Jellicoe at the last moment was placed in command of the Grand Fleet. The Secretary of State for War was, contrary to peacetime custom, not a politician but one of Britain's most celebrated soldiers, Lord Kitchener. He had built his reputation in the Sudan and South Africa, as we recall; but many soon felt that his mind had grown too rigid to adapt itself to the rapidly changing conditions of the new large-scale fighting. The first commander in chief in France, Sir John French, proved inadequate and soon gave way to Sir Douglas Haig, who was to hold that crucial post for the remainder of the war. Finally, in the matter of individuals, there was David Lloyd George, the dynamic Chancellor of the Exchequer in Asquith's Liberal cabinet. He was to grow steadily more influential as the war progressed.

The gray-steel fighting ships of the royal navy went quietly to their posts even before Britain entered the war on August 4, and quickly began to exercise their superiority in an effective if unspectacular manner. They formed one of the two most powerful fighting machines in the world; but for the moment all eyes were centered upon the other one—the German army, whose gray-clad regiments were steadily advancing toward Paris.

All the various general staffs had drawn up elaborate plans during the preceding years. The German plan was largely the work of the late Count von Schlieffen. He knew that when the Germans marched toward Paris, the Russians would start for Berlin. He realized that Germany's trump card was speed. Her army could mobilize faster and maneuver more rapidly than her neighbors' forces. At the same time, France was quicker at mobilization than Russia, with the creaking, corrupt machinery of the Czar's vast empire. Consequently the plan of the German staff was to put France out of the fight in a quick campaign before Russia was ready; then the Russians could be handled at leisure. This idea of concentrating their efforts on one front at a time was to be tried by the Central Powers throughout the war, as they could take advantage of their interior lines. One small

German army would be able to hold off the Russian forces while seven attacked France.

Von Schlieffen had been responsible for the decision to attack through Belgium and had thus helped to bring England into the war. The Germans might have crossed the frontier directly into eastern France without violating neutrality, but there the French had a series of powerful modern fortresses which would have slowed up the attack and nullified the German advantage in speed. He therefore planned to hold that eastern end of the French line lightly and to drive through Belgium with an irresistibly strong right wing, so as to encircle the French and to crush them from the rear. The French had only antiquated fortresses behind the frontier of neutral Belgium; they had planned new defenses there, but had been held back by the terrific cost. Von Schlieffen died shortly before the war began, and his successor, Von Moltke, the nephew of the famous Von Moltke, who had directed Prussia's forces in the wars against Austria and France, foolishly modified his plan just enough to cause its failure. Ignoring Von Schlieffen's dying injunction to "keep the right wing strong," Von Moltke weakened it in order to bolster up less essential parts of the line. The seven German armies in the west were numbered from right to left, and the brunt of the work fell on the First Army, under Von Kluck, and the Second, under Von Bülow.

The great German military machine went crashing into Belgium according to its fast schedule, which called for arrival at Paris within six weeks. The Belgians put up a brave resistance; but their forts at Liége and Namur were battered to pieces by heavy howitzers, and the invasion schedule was not delayed by more than a day or two. The French, slowly realizing that the main German attack was coming through Belgium instead of from the east, rushed troops to the threatened area.

There they were joined by the British Expeditionary Force, which had been hurried across the Channel to Le Havre. Whatever the Kaiser may have thought about Britain's navy, he is reported to have sneered at her "contemptible little army." The British, calling themselves the "old contemptibles," fell in on the French left in an effort to stem the tide. There were not many British—barely one hundred thousand in a war where other nations were mobilizing men by the millions; but they were the flower of the old regular army and gave an excellent account of themselves. On August 23 they had their baptism of fire around the Belgian mining town of Mons. It was familiar ground in British military history, less than thirty miles from Waterloo and close by Marlborough's battlefield of Malplaquet. But the German right wing so far was irresistible. The British, stubbornly fighting, made a stand near the French frontier and then retreated more than a hundred miles to the southeast of Paris. They had lost some fifteen thousand men, and Sir John French felt that his exhausted troops needed a complete rest and reorganization before they would be fit to fight again.

But that was not to be; they were to have a crucial position in one of the decisive battles of world history. The French and British retreat had abandoned the richest industrial section of France to the enemy, and on September 3 the French seat of government was moved from Paris to the southwest coast. Then the German plans went wrong in spite of their magnificent military machine; for the High Command lost adequate contact with the armies in the field. Thanks to the foolish weakening of the right wing, Von Kluck believed that his First Army lacked sufficient force to swing west of Paris as he was supposed to do in order to roll up the Allied left flank. Instead, he headed southeast of Paris; by September 5 some of his units were barely twenty miles from the French capital. This exposed his own flank to the enemy and left a gap of twenty miles between his forces and Von Bülow's Second Army.

The Allies were quick to seize the advantage. The French and British stopped their discouraging retreat. Joffre, the French commander, gave the word for a firm stand near the river Marne. It happened that, out of nearly two million men in the Allied line, the British were directly opposite the gap between the two German armies; but it was not certain that Sir John French would throw in his tired men. On September 5 Joffre hurried to British headquarters and made an impassioned plea for co-operation: "I intend to throw my last company into the balance to win a victory and to save France. It is in her name that I come to you to ask for British aid, and I urge it with all the power that is in me. I cannot believe that the British army, in this supreme crisis, will refuse to do its part—history would judge its absence severely. Monsieur le Maréchal, the honor of England is at stake." There was a pause; then Sir John, in a low voice, said, "I will do all I possibly can." The fierce fighting of the next four days, in this first battle of the Marne, wrecked the German hopes of speedy victory. The British threw themselves into the gap, while the French on either side fought desperately. Finally the Germans fell back to a strong position thirty miles in the rear. By a close shave the initial advantage of Germany's speed had been destroyed, part of northern France regained, and Allied morale restored.

Now came the "race to the sea." Both sides began to extend their lines toward the north to get around each other's flanks. If the Germans could have reached the Channel ports first, they might still have rolled up the French left flank and have threatened England; but the British, French, and Belgians prevented this movement by severe fighting. At Ypres the old British regular army was nearly wiped out, but the line held.

"Open warfare," with maneuvering from place to place, was now over for a long time on the western front. There were no more flanks left to turn on either side since the rival armies stretched from the North Sea to Switzerland. As winter set in, the enemies faced each other in two solid lines of trenches, nearly five hundred miles in length. As the armies could no longer get around each other, they tried to go through. The next four years consisted of these rival attempts to break through the opposing lines. At times, after terrific losses, the lines bent a few miles; but they were never to break decisively until the last days of the war, in 1918.

It was in holding or attacking such trench lines that most of the military efforts of England as well as of France were to be spent. A new and unaccustomed type of fighting resulted. The war on the western front, in fact, became a gigantic siege. Elaborate trench systems were formed as the two sides "dug in," and in front of each barbed-wire entanglements were erected. Thus the foes rested, a few hundred yards apart, week after week and month after month, with frequent lesser raids and occasional major efforts to break through. There was no place for cavalry in such warfare, but artillery, heavy and light, took on increased importance. The heaviest burden in work and in casualties, however, fell on the infantry, who, when not soaking or freezing in the mud, were exposed to the deadly effectiveness of the new weapons. The conventional plan for a "break-through" called for a preliminary effort to blast out the enemy lines with heavy artillery. Then the quick-firing field artillery would lay down a "rolling barrage," providing a curtain of shells just ahead of the infantry, who would go "over the top" to attack the enemy lines at the "zero hour," frequently just before dawn. Then such of the enemy as managed to survive the high-explosive shells and the barrage would cut loose with the *rat-tat-tat* of the machine guns, which too often mowed down the advancing infantry in regular swathes. It was planned that, after the infantry had captured the enemy positions, cavalry would be let loose to exploit the success. Ammunition and men were spent lavishly to gain a few square miles of shell-torn waste; but the cavalry stage never came.

One effect of the new weapons was to make fighting less individual and personal. In the older days one actually saw at close quarters the foe, into whose stomach one pushed a pike or a bayonet. Even with the Brown Bess musket, fire was withheld until one saw the whites of the enemy's eyes. But now the killer and the killed frequently never saw one another as individuals. The artillery fired their high explosives and their shrapnel on distant objectives, where they could not distinguish their victims, while machine gunners would spray a whole line of advancing infantry. Even at close grips the bayonet was rarely used; it was more common to hurl an explosive hand grenade. Millions of Britons, Frenchmen, and Germans were to go through year after year of that muddy and bloody hell. Frequently those who escaped death or wounds had their minds unbalanced by shell shock; and delousing was a routine practice for those who left the front lines. The most spectacular novelty in fighting methods was the development of aviation, which, though still in its infancy, took over the old scouting functions of cavalry and made possible the bombing of positions far in the enemy's rear. Poison gas and tanks would be used later, as the war progressed.

England's portion of the western front lay in and around her old familiar fighting ground, Flanders and the adjacent parts of Belgium and northern France. This was the obvious sector for British activity; for men and munitions could be shipped easily across the Channel, and, protecting the coast as it did, it was the part which England was most vitally interested in defending. Whatever lack of imagination there may have been from time to time on the part of the British High Command, there was never any question of the resolute and stubborn courage of the rank and file or of the officers who led them in action, any more than there had been at Fontenoy or Bunker Hill. Of all the sectors in this portion of the western front the one most famous in British annals is the Ypres Salient, which year after year saw desperate fighting. In that small corner of "Flanders fields [where] the poppies blow" there now lie buried a quarter of a million soldiers of King George. 6

While the western front was being formed in the autumn of 1914, there was activity in many other places. On the eastern front the Russians drove a deep wedge into Austrian territory, but in East Prussia brilliant German strategy led to the routing of two great Russian armies by small German forces. Serbia repulsed an Austrian attack. Japan came into the war in August and quickly took Kiauchow. In the autumn Turkey joined the Central Powers.

The royal navy meanwhile had swung into action. Well did the British know how to name their ships—*Audacious, Repulse, Courageous, Indomitable, Black Prince, Warrior, Invincible, Inflexible, Valiant, Iron Duke, Vengeance*; these names bespoke the fiber and tradition of the navy. Its task in this war was tremendous: to guard England, to patrol all oceans, to sweep the German merchant marine

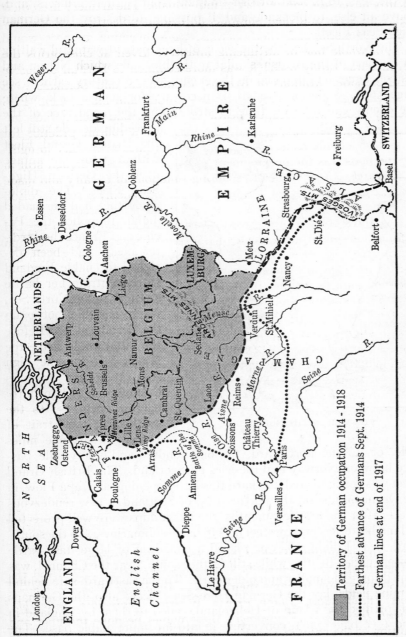

THE WESTERN FRONT

Territory of German occupation 1914 - 1918

••••••• Farthest advance of Germans Sept. 1914

— — — German lines at end of 1917

off the seas, to protect British shipping from German cruisers, and, above all else, to blockade and, if possible, to destroy the German High-Seas Fleet.

The North Sea became the scene of long, patient watchful waiting on the part of the British, similar to the blockade which Nelson and his colleagues had imposed on the enemy fleets a century earlier (see page 566). Superior strength is necessary for such a task, where the enemy can take his time to strike; and the naval race of the preceding decade still left the British Grand Fleet with a 3-to-2 advantage over the German High-Seas Fleet. The diplomacy that had persuaded Japan to police the Pacific and France the Mediterranean had been designed to enable England to concentrate her battle strength in the North Sea, where it could bottle up the German ships. Before the latter could leave the North Sea for the high seas, they had to pass through one of two fairly narrow openings: to the southward, the Strait of Dover, twenty-one miles wide, or, to the northward, the one-hundred-and-ninety-mile passage between Norway and the isles off Scotland. The British Grand Fleet was concentrated, to guard this latter opening, at Scapa Flow, in the Orkneys, just off the northern tip of Scotland, a new rendezvous where, after the first few months, the battleships were well protected by land batteries, and by steel nets to baffle submarines. To the southward, near Edinburgh, was placed a squadron of large, fast battle cruisers under Beatty, while still farther south, near the Channel, was a third force of smaller and older craft. To the eastward, safe behind its mine fields, lay the German High-Seas Fleet; also, the Germans had fortified the island of Heligoland, ceded to them by England in 1890 (see page 746), converting it into an impregnable base. The British had no intention of risking their big ships by venturing in after the Germans. Jellicoe had secured Admiralty consent to the passive

THE WAR IN THE NORTH SEA

# Britain in the First World War

strategy of making the defense of England the first consideration. He was later to be bitterly criticized for this; but his responsibility was tremendous, for, as someone remarked, no one else was in a position to lose the war in a single afternoon. The Germans, on the other hand, knew that in a general encounter they would be badly outnumbered. Each side therefore watched the other warily, waiting for a misstep. So it went for month after month, with only two minor encounters before the full forces met in action in 1916.

Out on the high seas there was more activity. It is said that before the war a British admiral had maintained a world map upon which was marked daily, according to wireless and cable dispatches, the position of every German merchantman and warship as well as of every British naval vessel, so that the British might swoop down upon the enemy as soon as war should be declared. Before August, 1914, was over, the German flag had all but disappeared from the high seas. A few fast ships raced into neutral ports, and a few cruisers escaped; but the remainder felt the full force of British sea power.

When the war began, ten regular German cruisers were at large. The *Goeben* and *Breslau* eluded the numerous British and French naval forces in the Mediterranean in a bold dash from Sicily to safety at Constantinople. The other eight represented a real menace to the British, because they were in distant waters, where they could not only snap up merchantmen but also overpower many of the smaller and older warships with which the British were patrolling remote stations and trade routes. In naval encounters only extreme luck or skill on the part of the weaker craft could offset such enemy advantages in speed, armor, and guns; and Jellicoe was jealously concentrating Britain's best fighting ships in the North Sea. The eight German cruisers had lively adventures before they were finally run down. The *Königsberg* sank a weak old British cruiser off Zanzibar, but was soon chased into an African river, where she ran aground. The *Karlsruhe* destroyed sixteen Allied merchantmen in the West Indies before she blew up at sea. The *Emden* wrought nearly three months of havoc in the Indian Ocean; in addition to sinking numerous freighters, she disguised herself with a false fourth funnel, to look like a British cruiser, and ran boldly into the port of Penang, where she demolished an unsuspecting Russian cruiser and a French destroyer. Early in November her gallant career was ended by the superior guns of an Australian cruiser. The principal British anxiety, however, was occasioned by the powerful squadron of five cruisers with which Admiral von Spee escaped from the Asiatic station just before the Japanese seized the German base at Kiaochow. Early in November, 1914, grim news reached England. Admiral Craddock,

"One-Eyed Chris," had been sent out to catch Von Spee. With two cruisers, the *Good Hope* and *Monmouth*, he encountered the five German ships off Coronel, on the Chilean coast. The British did not have a chance: silhouetted against the setting sun, they were helpless targets for the celebrated gunnery of the Germans. After an hour's unequal fight Craddock and every one of his sixteen hundred and fifty men were at the bottom of the sea; only two Germans were even wounded. Revenge, however, came the following month. Against Jellicoe's protests, three fast and powerful battle cruisers were detached from the Grand Fleet. One hurried to guard the entrance to the Panama Canal; the other two caught Von Spee at the Falkland Islands, as he came around into the South Atlantic. The German admiral, realizing that this time he was hopelessly outclassed, signaled his squadron, "It is my wish and belief that you will conduct yourselves with a gallantry equal to that of Admiral Craddock and his men off Coronel." Outranged, but fighting stubbornly, the *Scharnhorst, Gneisenau, Nürnberg*, and *Leipzig* went down with Von Spee and twenty-one hundred men; the *Dresden* alone escaped, to be trapped the following spring off the coast of Chile. The surface of the high seas was at last swept clear of the enemy's warships; beneath the surface, however, they were already challenging British sea power with their submarines.

Each side had its successes and failures in 1914. Germany had shoved the Russian "steam roller" out of East Prussia, and had come within a few miles of taking Paris and winning the war. Her troops were in possession of northern France, Belgium, and part of Poland. Turkey had joined the Central Powers, cutting off Russia from easy communication through the Mediterranean with England and France. On the other hand, Germany had not achieved the quick, decisive victory she had hoped to win with her rapid mobilization and movement. The first battle of the Marne had determined that it was to be a long war. Austria had been badly beaten by both Serbia and Russia. Japan had joined the Allies. The sea was dominated by the British, and the German High-Seas Fleet was bottled up at Kiel.

In 1915 the Germans stood on the defensive on the western front, while they successfully concentrated on the Russians in the east. The British and French launched several drives on the western front; but instead of achieving a "break-through," they met with only local victories, their heavy casualties being out of all proportion to their meager gains of a few square miles. The principal British attacks that spring were made at Neuve-Chapelle, in a vain hope of capturing the industrial and railroad center of Lille, and, in conjunction with the French, in the second battle of Ypres, (which the men called "Wipers").

# Britain in the First World War

In mid-May, while the latter battle was in progress, British political and military circles were shaken to their foundations by a correspondent's dispatch which somehow escaped censorship and appeared in the *Times*. It declared that "our want of an unlimited supply of high explosive shells was a fatal bar to our success." Those few words not only led to an amazing increase in munitions output but also, as we shall see, ended the decade of Liberal control. The military authorities, not appreciating the new significance of artillery preparation, had failed to provide adequate material. At Neuve-Chapelle, it is said, the British shot away more ammunition than they had used in the whole Boer War, and, at that, the bombardment was so short there and at Ypres that it failed adequately to smash the enemy barbed wire and trenches, so that the infantry sustained heavy losses. The British artillery, woefully deficient in heavy guns, was reduced to two shells a day. The author of that celebrated dispatch later wrote that he should never forget the looks on the faces of the British soldiers when they came out of the trenches after long hammering by the German artillery, to which the British guns could make little reply. "It was a look of utter and complete weariness," he said, "and it haunted me." England had vast industrial potentialities; but they needed arousing and co-ordinating. That task fell to Lloyd George, the dynamic little Welshman who gave up his post as Chancellor of the Exchequer to take the new post of Minister of Munitions. He drew big industrialists to his side as assistants; he made hurried trips to France to find just what was needed; he aroused the populace in general and labor in particular to a pitch of enthusiasm for the production of war materials. Until regular plants could be built, it was necessary to improvise machinery. Lloyd George tells of one great plant, devoted to the manufacture of high explosives, where the raw material was passed "through machines originally used for coal-crushing, stone-pulverising, sugar-drying, paint-making, sugar-sifting." The T.N.T. was ground between rollers of a flour mill and mixed in a bread-making plant. Whenever the industrialists objected that some project was impossible, Lloyd George told them it must be done, and it was; when the military authorities sent in estimates of their needs, he multiplied them several times, and by the day they were ready the army always needed still more. Women by the tens of thousands engaged in this work, in spite of the imminent peril of explosion or of having their faces turned yellow by the fumes. In the spring of 1915 the supply of shells had fallen to seventy-five thousand; by June, 1916, more than nineteen million shells had been completed. Prepared under such circumstances, they were not all good shells—some burst too soon, while others did not burst at all; but they were of tremendous consequence in England's later military efforts. Nor were shells the only problem of the ministry of munitions: heavy artillery, rifles, small-arms ammunition, grenades, trench mortars, and much else were needed and were provided.

The Germans, just before the second battle of Ypres in the spring of 1915, introduced a new element into warfare. Allied troops were suddenly beset by a cloud of poisonous chlorine gas, released from cylinders and blown down on their lines by the breeze. Hundreds writhed in agony, giving the Germans almost a clear field into Ypres for a moment; but the Canadian division on the British right hung grimly on. The Germans were not ready to follow up their advantage; and again the line held. When the enemy tried gas again, the Allies had crude masks for protection, and before long used gas themselves. From that time on, both sides used it freely, particularly in artillery shells. It put many men out of action, but killed relatively few.

Aside from the western front, the major efforts of the British in 1915 were concentrated in the first of three attacks on Turkey. The operations, called by the name of Dardanelles on the naval side and Gallipoli on the military, marked an effort to open the Straits between the Mediterranean and Black Seas, to capture Constantinople, to open up communication with Russia, and to hit at Germany through the back door. The opening of the Straits would be a particular godsend to Russia, with her meager industrial development, unable to turn out sufficient shot and shell for her huge armies. As long as the enemy held Constantinople, munitions could reach Russia only with the greatest difficulty: either through the White Sea, frozen most of the year, to Archangel, whence a narrow, single-track line ran southward, or by way of North America and the Pacific to Vladivostok, whence they would have to be carried over the Trans-Siberian Railway. With free access to the Black Sea, England and France could furnish Russia with manufactures and receive Russian wheat.

The advocates of this offensive were called "Easterners," as opposed to the "Westerners" who believed that every effort should be concentrated on the western front. The two principal Easterners were the Chancellor of the Exchequer and the First Lord of the Admiralty. Both Lloyd George and Winston Churchill had the imagination and the foresight to prophesy correctly a long-drawn-out and inconclusive contest in the west. Both had a flair for the dramatic and saw the possibility of striking the Central Powers where they were weakest, in the region where the racial troubles of the polyglot Austrian Empire and the chaotic Balkans offered a rare opportunity for intervention. Lloyd George, however, favored an expedition to Salonika, to secure Greek support in the Balkans, while Churchill favored the forcing

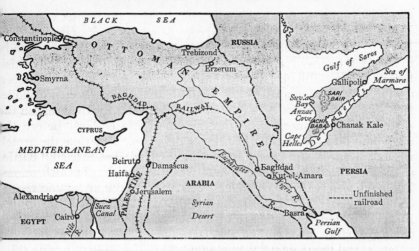

THE SEAT OF THE BRITISH TURKISH CAMPAIGNS

•f the Dardanelles. The French were not captivated by such ideas. This was natural as long as the Germans were at no great distance rom Paris. The majority of the military in both France and England vere Westerners, who were apt to dwell upon the difficulties of waging ι distant campaign and who were apprehensive lest the Allies be eft with insufficient reserves for holding the lines in France. Kitch-ner, however, was won over to the Easterners' point of view, and vas willing to take a chance if the risk was not too great. He swung he cabinet in favor of Churchill's proposed attack on the Straits ·ather than Lloyd George's Greek scheme. He thought that the nitial weight of the enterprise should be borne by the navy rather han by the army. Lord Fisher, the professional head of the navy, :onsented, but without enthusiasm. It was arranged that old British ind French warships should be used for the forcing of the Darda-1elles; a British army would then occupy the Gallipoli peninsula, and ι joint military and naval advance would secure Constantinople.

Early in 1915 the expedition went on a mission of death. The vhole affair, both military and naval, proved a ghastly and expensive ·ailure. Three times in this fatal year did fortune provide a favorable )pportunity for British arms: in February, again in March, and ïnally in July. Had the attack been pressed hard on any one of these hree occasions, victory presumably would have followed. But the ,oldiers and sailors pulled at cross purposes.

In February the British fleet, to which only one new battleship ιad been added, began the bombardment of the outer forts of the )ardanelles. Assisted by several French vessels, it made good progress. The Turkish forts were rendered useless, the Turks withdrew and sailors and marines landed and completed the work of destruction For six miles the Straits were cleared. By March the fleet was ready to attack the inner forts. There were only twenty thousand Turkish troops on the Gallipoli Peninsula at this time, and it could have been captured with comparative ease had British troops been available But Kitchener did not even appoint a commander for the army in the eastern Mediterranean until the middle of March, just before the navy moved to the attack of the inner defenses. This time the attack was not so successful. Some forts were silenced; but three old battle-ships were destroyed and a fourth was crippled by Turkish mines The navy was ready to recommence action, but the army said that it could not be ready before the middle of April. This infuriated Fisher and led to a slackening of naval co-operation. The navy could probably have rushed the Dardanelles in March without as-sistance, and the vigorous young naval chief of staff kept urging this; but the admirals refused to sacrifice their ships, even if these were old, without sufficient military support.

In April the army was finally ready. Its supplies had been packed without forethought, and precious weeks were wasted in Egypt while they were re-sorted. At last the time came for the death grapple for the Gallipoli Peninsula. It was fifty-two miles long, seventeen miles at its broadest, and only three and a half miles at its narrowest. There were no harbors; landing was difficult, and the terrain was precipi-tous. And the number of Turkish troops on the peninsula had risen from twenty thousand to sixty thousand. Liman von Sanders, the German general in command, had taken full advantage of the British military delay to fortify his positions.

The British, also numbering some sixty thousand, struck in two places, at the tip and also further to the north, on the side away from the Dardanelles, at Anzac Bay. (The name "Anzac," derived from "Australian and New Zealand Army Corps," has forever linked Gal-lipoli to the distant dominions in the South Seas.) The British landed with heavy losses, but they could not advance. The Turkish lines held stiffly. Cramped and crowded into their two widely separated areas, the British were compelled to dig themselves in as best they might and wait for reinforcements. They had lost nearly twenty thousand men in securing their tenuous grip on Turkish soil, and for a time it looked as though they must withdraw. Instead they clung desperately to their slippery advance posts, grimly determined to extend them. So far Gallipoli was more a defeat than a victory and was so recognized in England.

Kitchener and Fisher quarreled. Fisher resigned, and in a political reorganization of the cabinet Winston Churchill was replaced by Balfour in the Admiralty. Men wondered what would be the next move at the Straits. In May the New Zealanders struggled to capture the heights. A place called the "Daisy Patch" was made crimson by their blood, but the heights remained uncaptured. During the summer British submarines made a series of daring forays, diving under the mines and sinking one Turkish ship after another in the Sea of Marmara, approaching close to Constantinople itself. Then came the heart-rending conflict at Suvla Bay, on the north side, above Anzac. The British troops at Gallipoli now numbered one hundred and twenty thousand, and the Turks had been reinforced to about the same strength. Several times in this bloody encounter the British were on the point of gaining their objective, the permanent occupation of the hilltop of Bulair, which controlled the neck of the peninsula. But the Turks also were brave, and they had a skilled leader in one Mustafa Kemal, of whom more would be heard after the war. The battle continued for two days. The British had gained a little land; but the Turks had regained Bulair, so that the victory was theirs. "Then, as the pitiless sun beat down on the Anzacs in their narrow bit of conquered territory, disease stalked abroad. The trenches of the foe were but a few feet distant; the dead in many cases only half-buried; and myriads of flies, attacking dead and living alike, brought with them dysentery, typhoid, and other fevers. Thirst was added to their sufferings, since drinking water there was none, except the precarious supply brought up by donkeys from the launches. And sometimes, heavy weather made these keep their distance, days at a time, from the beach. . . . Then broke the winter and a great snow storm, a new sight to Australian eyes. And sentries were found frozen at their posts, and soldiers who a short time before had been blistered by the heat, now were tormented by the cold."

The navy finally planned a new offensive, but its offer came too late. The government was satiated with Gallipoli and determined to abandon the whole unsavory affair. In the last days of 1915 the bloody peninsula was abandoned to the Turks. The British had anticipated heavy losses in withdrawing, but the army and navy cooperated so efficiently that not a man was killed. Had the two forces worked as well together earlier in the year, Constantinople without doubt would have fallen into British hands, and the later course of the war might have been greatly altered.

The Allies had had great hopes when Italy joined them in the spring of 1915. Though a member of the Triple Alliance for more than thirty years, Italy had long realized that most of the land she wanted belonged to Austria. The Allies could make generous promises of such territory; naturally the Central Powers would not. Consequently, after sharp bargaining, the Italians deserted their former allies and entered the war on the other side. It was hoped that by attacking Austria from the rear the Italians could relieve the pressure on Russia, but the nature of the mountainous frontier made it extremely difficult for Italy to accomplish anything.

Meanwhile the Central Powers were meeting with success in the Balkans. The British failure at the Straits helped to throw Bulgaria into the arms of Germany and Austria. Serbia was overrun and put out of the fight. The Central Powers now had direct communication from Berlin and Vienna to Constantinople and the eastern Mediterranean. The British and French tried to remedy the Balkan situation by sending an expedition to Salonika, but for three years it accomplished nothing.

Poison gas was not the only novel and, in outside eyes, unethical weapon used by the Germans against the British in 1915. Just two weeks after the gas attacks at Ypres the great Cunard liner *Lusitania* was torpedoed and sunk close to the Irish coast by a German submarine. Some eleven hundred men, women, and children were drowned, including more than a hundred from the United States.

This was the German answer to the British blockade, which was already depriving Germany of many essential overseas supplies. The royal navy relentlessly patrolled the two entrances to the North Sea and sent neutral vessels—American, Scandinavian, Dutch, and the rest—into British ports, to be searched for materials which might find their way to Germany. Against lively protests from the United States and other neutrals, the British steadily extended the list of contraband articles, adding oil, copper, rubber, and foodstuffs to the old conventional list of war materials. In the latter days of the war this starving process caused intense suffering among the German noncombatants, especially the old and very young. The Germans asserted that three quarters of a million died as a result. This application of sea power by the British undoubtedly played no small part in bringing about the final victory.

In the submarine, or U-boat, the Germans realized that they had a weapon which might inflict an even more deadly blockade upon England than she was inflicting upon them. Whereas Germany could receive supplies by land, England was absolutely dependent upon overseas wheat and meat, to say nothing of oil. If the steady procession of supply ships could be shut off from England for even a few months, she might easily be starved into submission. Early in the war a single submarine had sunk three old British cruisers in rapid succession. With merchantmen, however, a serious problem arose.

An ordinary surface warship, in halting a tramp, could take its crew aboard before destroying the ship or sending it into port with a prize crew. The U-boat, on the other hand, had no room for extra passengers; and frequently it dared not wait for the merchant crew to take to the lifeboats, for a single shot from the victim might sink the submarine. Consequently the Germans usually waited with only the periscope above water until they sighted their prey. Then they would fire the fatal torpedo without warning and withdraw, leaving the crew to save themselves as best they might. The Germans would probably have used surface vessels if they could; since that was out of the question, they resorted to the U-boat. In February, 1915, they declared all approaches to the British Isles a war zone and announced that they would "seek to destroy every hostile merchant ship which enters the War Zone, and it will not always be possible to obviate the dangers with which the persons and goods on board will be threatened. Neutrals are therefore warned not to risk crews, passengers, and goods on such ships." They even published a special notice in the New York newspapers giving warning as the *Lusitania* was about to sail. The great liner was not armed, but she was heavily loaded with munitions. That, however, in the eyes of Americans as well as Englishmen, did not justify the wholesale slaughter of noncombatants. Their death was much more spectacular than that of German soldiers killed by Yankee bullets, and it did much to blacken Germany's case in the United States and to make England fight the harder. The Germans had used their weapon too soon; for they had barely two dozen U-boats at the time. Under protests from the United States, they gradually relaxed this undersea warfare, to revive it ruthlessly early in 1917.

Altogether, the position of the Central Powers was further improved by the events of 1915. The British attack on the Straits had resulted in tragic failure, while, for want of munitions, the drives on the western front had accomplished little. Russia had suffered a terrific defeat, though her line was still intact. The Balkans had come more thoroughly under the control of the Central Powers, who now had a clear route of communications across Europe into Asia. Italy's entrance on the Allied side had not accomplished the desired results.

"Warfare of attrition is being employed against us," remarked a prominent Frenchman toward the end of that year. Attrition, or the wearing down of man power, seemed the only recourse left to the rival armies on the western front. Brilliant maneuvering was giving way to wholesale slaughter, in the hope that one's own human reserves would last longer than the enemy's. Huge forces were shattered against strong positions by both sides and were repulsed with terrific losses. The names of Verdun and the Somme will always be associated with the conspicuous applications of this brutal policy; for, though casualties among British, French, and Germans in those huge 1916 drives were reckoned by hundreds of thousands, the western front still existed much the same as before.

England was barely adjusting herself to the demands of the new warfare in munitions when she realized that she must increase her supply of men also, to meet the changed conditions. At the outset many had expected that England would play in this war her old familiar role, guarding the seas, furnishing money and supplies to her allies, and maintaining a small, efficient army, such as Wellington's had been, on the Continent. Whatever his shortcomings may have been in respect to munitions and other matters, Kitchener had the foresight or the luck to predict that this war would be entirely different—that it would last four years and that England must think of military forces in terms of millions rather than of tens or hundreds of thousands. His great contribution to British military success was his organizing of the nation's man power in time. The initial call for volunteers had met with an amazing response; and by the time the old regular army was melting away, late in 1914, in the "race to the sea," the first hundred thousand of Kitchener's new army was ready to take its place. By the summer of 1916 "K" had expanded six divisions into seventy. The last one sailed for France on the very day on which the cruiser *Hampshire*, bearing Kitchener to Russia, struck a mine off the Orkneys, carrying the silent old soldier to the bottom.

So far, England had filled her ranks by volunteering, and men had readily enlisted to the call "Your King and Country need you." The unfortunate part of the volunteer system in a protracted war, however, is that it tends to draw off the best elements in the population while the least desirable hold back. The lengthening casualty lists in 1915 led to a widespread demand that these latter be forced to bear their share of the terrible burden on the western front. Before resorting to compulsion, England made a final effort, in Lord Derby's plan, to swell the numbers through the volunteer system. Every man of military age was asked to express his readiness to serve, with the understanding that the unmarried men would all be called before the married ones. The latter enrolled in large numbers, but more than a million bachelors held back. Thereupon, not without violent protests, Parliament, early in 1916, passed a conscription act drafting all able-bodied men between the ages of eighteen and forty-one. Though all free Englishmen had been regarded as liable for militia service in time of danger, for centuries—ever since the days of the Saxon fyrd and the Assize of Arms—England had been able to raise her armies by the volunteer system, though the old naval press gang had constituted a rude and informal sort of conscription. Following England's example, Canada, New Zealand, and Newfoundland later passed similar conscription acts. Australia refused to do so, but maintained a splendid volunteer record. In certain places the temper of the population made conscription inadvisable: in Ireland for reasons which we shall see shortly; among the French Canadians of Quebec; and in South Africa, where the loyal Boers had been busy keeping the rebellious ones in check.

Ample cannon fodder was needed for the grim work of 1916. The Germans started the wholesale attrition of the year in February. Having decided to concentrate their attention on the western front this year, they surprised the French by a terrific bombardment of Verdun, the key position of the Allied right flank, hoping to blast their way to a "break-through." The French somehow managed to weather the initial storm, rallied to the cry of "They shall not pass!" and mowed down the Germans, who kept pushing into the fight long after reasonable prospects of victory had gone. The Germans and French each lost about 350,000 men in five months around Verdun.

Even heavier were to be the casualties in the battle of the Somme, where the Allies attacked near Amiens at the beginning of July. This time the British bore the main Allied burden. They held seventeen miles of the twenty-five-mile front of attack, which was directed against one of the strongest positions in the German line. The British would have preferred to strike in Flanders, farther westward, where they might have rolled the German right against the sea; but the French preferred the Somme, where the French and British sectors joined.

The battle of the Somme was the most stupendous in British military annals. Preparations had been made for months. There was no lack of artillery, nor of shells, nor of railway lines to feed the cannon. Haig, the new British commander, had provided, seemingly, for everything: new roads for trucks, causeways across swamps, miles upon miles of communication trenches, hundreds of thousands of fresh troops. Unfortunately, he and his staff had not provided any new ideas of attack. "Ingenuity of execution," it has been remarked, "was sacrificed to the immensity and elaboration of the preparation." The Germans knew what the British were doing and turned their defenses into the strongest link of their western line. Into the chalky soil they had dug line after line of trenches on the ridges which the British would have to ascend. Bombproofs, deep cellars, pits, and quarries were linked up by passages sometimes thirty feet beneath the surface. Protected by their mines, machine guns, and concrete emplacements and redoubts, they awaited the attack.

# A History of England and the British Empire

It came at 7.30 on the morning of July 1, after a seven-day torrent of artillery fire, in which the British expended nearly two million shells produced by Lloyd George's feverish stimulation of munitions production. The British emerged in close lines which advanced slowly, for each man bore more than sixty pounds of equipment. The German machine-gunners caught them before they had advanced far; whole rows of khaki-clad corpses were later found lying where they had been mowed down. On that first day 60,000 British soldiers were killed, wounded, or made prisoner—60 per cent of the officers and 40 per cent of the men in the infantry attack. That was the heaviest single day's loss in British military history; whole wars, such as the American Revolution, had been fought with fewer total casualties. Yet the British fought on; within five days they had advanced one mile on a front of five or six. By the end of the month, at the cost of 171,000 men, they had gained two and a half miles, but on a narrower front. In October came heavy rains, which turned the low-lying terrain into a sea of mud, in which hundreds of thousands of men floundered. To carry on the contest further was impossible. The Germans had been thrust back only a few miles by England's greatest effort. The troops had fought with dogged heroism, but the battle had demonstrated that "bravery was more common than brains." The total casualties were about 500,000 for the Germans, 410,000 for the British, and 190,000 for the French. Attrition at Verdun and the Somme, therefore, had used up about 850,000 Germans and 950,000 of the Allies. France was so thoroughly exhausted that thereafter the British took over increased responsibilities.

While the British attack at the Somme was unimaginative on the whole, toward the end the British did introduce a novel instrument which was later blamed by the Germans as one cause of their final defeat. This was the tank, an armored car, moving by caterpillar tractor and armed with machine guns or light artillery. It was designed to assist the unfortunate infantry in their unequal struggle against the combination of machine guns and barbed wire; for the tank could waddle over trenches and crush out machine-gun nests. The War Office had twice rejected the idea. A plan submitted in 1912 was later found pigeonholed with the comment "This man's mad"; when a general proposed it in 1914, the army would do nothing, and Churchill had some tanks built from Admiralty funds. There were not enough at the Somme to be effective; but the Germans neither imitated them nor found a sure way to stop them, and by 1917 they helped score a British victory. As part of the successful secrecy with which they were prepared, they were labeled "tanks" in transit, to disguise their real purpose; and "tanks" they remained. 13

# Britain in the First World War

A month before the battle of the Somme began, England had fought the greatest naval battle in history; but its result was indecisive. The battle of Jutland, fought off the Danish coast on May 31, 1916, was the one occasion during the four years of watchful waiting in the North Sea when the rival navies clashed in full force.

The Germans had put to sea, hoping to fall with their full force upon a part of the British. Each side had a squadron of battle cruisers, a new type which was a cross between a battleship and a cruiser. It had the size and gun power of the former, combined with the speed of the latter. The battle cruiser looked like a battle-ship and could hit like one, but its high speed was obtained, particularly by the British, at the expense of defensive armor. Behind Von Hipper, with his German battle cruisers, came Scheer with the High-Seas Fleet of battleships and lesser craft. Behind the dashing Beatty, with the British battle cruisers, came Jellicoe with the Grand Fleet.

There was not enough breeze that last afternoon in May to sweep away the heavy mist, but the ships no longer needed wind. The dreadnoughts could make at least twenty knots; the battle cruisers, twenty-five; the destroyers, thirty. The farthest units were over a hundred miles apart when the first shots were fired at 3.48 P. M.; by 6.15 all had joined in the fight—252 ships, of which 151 were British and 101 German. Of the total, however, more than half were little destroyers; the capital ships were fewer than at Trafalgar.

The action started with a running fight of the two battle-cruiser squadrons, speeding at twenty-five knots and exchanging heavy blows which their weak armor could not withstand. Flotillas of little torpedo boats darted between the cruiser lines to launch torpedoes. Hipper knew that he was leading Beatty into a trap, speeding southward to join Scheer's High-Seas Fleet. The German battleships came up, and the outnumbered British now turned northward, retreating until the dreadnoughts of their own Grand Fleet arrived to turn the tide. There were brief, furious, confused encounters in the mist and smoke; then the Germans cleverly turned in their tracks and headed for home, eluding, during a long night chase, their British pursuers, who missed them by a narrow margin. The point-blank firing of Trafalgar had given way to longer ranges. The British battle cruiser *Invincible* was sunk in seventeen minutes by shells from a German rival eight to ten miles away; two other British battle cruisers also went to the bottom. Torpedoes sank an old German pre-dreadnought battleship and two lesser cruisers; several other cruisers and numerous destroyers perished under a hail of shells. The British suffered heavier material damage than the Germans.

# A History of England and the British Empire

England was dumfounded by the news of Jutland, for an Admiralty censorship made it sound worse than it really was. It was one thing to suffer military defeats, but to come out of the first major naval battle since Trafalgar with a suspicion of defeat was a real shock. Jutland has been fought over and over by writers and critics ever since. As far as the actual tactical aspects of the fighting went, the outnumbered Germans had inflicted heavier losses and had maneuvered brilliantly. But the British could point out that the Germans considered themselves lucky in escaping to their home base, from which they never again emerged during the war. Once the British main fleet had come into action, there was no thought for the Germans but retreat. Strategically the British could claim that negative victory. The Admiralty had not forwarded to Jellicoe information which would have been of great value to him in closing on the Germans; moreover, he was not free to pursue the Germans back into their mine fields to annihilate them. His prime mission was to keep the North Sea clear, and he still had a fleet which could accomplish that.

Jutland and the Somme were not all that Englishmen could hope, but they were at least not as humiliating as the news which came in from Mesopotamia a few weeks before Jutland. England's first attack on the Turks had failed at Gallipoli, but the British had managed to withdraw their forces skillfully. Now, in their second Turkish campaign, a whole British army had been forced to lay down its arms to the Turks in Mesopotamia.

The capture of General Townshend at Kut-el-Amara resulted from the stupidity of the government of India. Ever since the end of November, 1914, British-Indian troops had been in possession of Basra, the seaport of Mesopotamia, some forty miles below the junction of the Tigris and Euphrates, in order to protect the near-by Anglo-Persian oil wells. Then the idea came to advance on Baghdad, the Mesopotamian capital, far up the Euphrates. The proposal had been steadily vetoed at London. The enemy were not numerous; but the distance from Basra was great (some two hundred and fifty miles or more), transportation difficult, the climate abominable, the undertaking risky in the extreme. The Indian government, however, begged for an opportunity to show its prowess. From start to finish it mismanaged the expedition, which was poorly equipped respecting almost all necessities, such as wire-cutters, water carts, tents, mosquito netting, and clothes, and for months had no airplanes at all. River transportation was utterly inadequate, and the medical scandals, which resulted in nameless suffering and unnecessary death, were almost beyond belief. General Townshend, in command of the

# Britain in the First World War

Anglo-Indian troops, drove for his objective in the fall of 1915; reached the ancient city of Ctesiphon, close to Baghdad; and was driven back down the river to Kut-el-Amara, in December, where he was told to entrench himself and await reinforcements. They never arrived; and after a defense of one hundred and forty-seven days Townshend surrendered. Had the British in high command in India shown any respectable initiative, however, the expedition could easily have captured Baghdad, and Great Britain would not have lost prestige throughout all the Moslem world, as she did by this ill-starred adventure.

In addition to Verdun, the Somme, Jutland, and Kut, the year 1916 saw activity also on the eastern front. In spite of their handicaps from lack of munitions, the Russians made a last magnificent spurt of energy, and were pushing the Austrians hard when German troops were sent to the rescue. Those same Germans quickly put out of the fight Rumania, who had just entered the war on the Allied side.

In the meantime England was having weighty problems at home. It had taken many months for the British civilian to awaken to the seriousness of the war. School histories had taught that England was in the general habit of winning her wars; the temporary shock of the long retreat from Mons was dispelled by the "miracle of the Marne." There was great faith in the huge Russian "steam roller"; rumor led to the general belief that Russian troops were being hurried through England to the western front; someone had seen them shaking the snow from their boots on station platforms and jamming slot machines with kopeks. Rigid press censorship held back much of the true situation. "Business as usual" was the popular slogan in this initial period of optimism.

As 1915 came on, the temper changed. In spite of their keen pre-war rivalry, the British and Germans had generally entertained a high respect for each other. Now deliberate efforts were made on both sides to develop hatred of the enemy. Exaggerated reports told of German murder, mutilation, and rape of defenseless civilians in Belgium, as more accurate accounts told of the destruction of priceless historical structures. In the last weeks of 1914 a German naval force bombarded two east-coast towns, with heavy loss of civilian lives, a foretaste of later air raids which were more successful in killing noncombatants than in destroying munition plants. On top of that, there was poison gas, the *Lusitania*, and the shooting, on charges of espionage, of the English nurse Edith Cavell in Belgium. The German, obviously, was not a sportsman; and gradually, as casualty lists grew longer, Englishmen developed a lively hate which made life miserable for harmless naturalized Germans and even those with

[ 875 ]

German names. Strange to say, the men over in the trenches did not share this general hatred. "Tommy" was often more irritated by his noble allies than he was by "Fritz." The nervous excitement of 1915 at least stirred England out of her early optimism and made her ready for strenuous efforts. By 1916 the "home front" had settled down to a grim, determined realization of the mighty task ahead, an attitude which the soldiers had long before reached.

Then came Ireland. Home rule, it will be recalled, had for the third time passed the Commons in May, 1914; and Ulster's attitude had brought threats of civil war until the outbreak of the World War had caused home rule, like other domestic problems, to be set aside for the time. England's treatment of the Catholic Irish in the early part of the war had not been tactful. Kitchener did not trust the Irish, south of Ulster. Irish Unionists, rather than Irish Nationalists, had been placed in charge of recruiting. The formation of an Irish division had been delayed, and of the officers appointed less than one in five were Catholics. The donations of flags and standards made by Irish women had been rejected. Meanwhile, to Ulster the War Office had been most gracious. The Ulstermen had been permitted to keep their prewar organization intact and, like the Welsh and Scots, to wear distinctive insignia. The commander of the Ulster Volunteers announced, without reprimand, that, when the war was over, his force would be ready to "relegate home rule to the devil."

Under such circumstances Sinn Fein (literally, "We Ourselves") made fast headway. This was a movement which aimed at the withdrawal of Irish members from the House of Commons, the boycotting of the English government, and, above all else, complete self-government for Ireland; home rule was no longer enough for those extremists. Once more, as in the days of Philip II, Louis XIV, and the French Revolution, the Irish looked to England's enemies for deliverance. Plans were made by this active Sinn Fein minority for a general uprising throughout Ireland and for the seizure of Dublin, while the Germans would provide arms and ammunition and raid the east coast of England. British vigilance nipped the plans in the bud. On Good Friday in 1916 a German submarine landed on the Irish coast Sir Roger Casement, who had won knighthood for excellent work in Africa. He and a companion were immediately caught. A tramp steamer which slipped out of Germany with munitions was stopped by the British and blown up by her own crew. The east-coast raid amounted to little. The general uprising, in view of Casement's capture, was no surprise. The most serious trouble came in Dublin, where on Easter Monday a week of Sinn Fein revolt broke out. The insurgents seized the greater part of the city, including the post office and most of the railway stations. They also proclaimed a republic. Dublin Castle, however, was not captured, nor did the people of the city rise. Instead the British army came. The fight was decently but fiercely waged. The British, tightening up their lines and receiving reinforcements, soon proved to the rebels that resistance meant only death. The rebels surrendered at discretion. The people of Ireland, most of whom had taken no part in the matter, breathed easier and made no resistance to the imprisonment of nearly two thousand men. Considering the nerves of the English, made taut by protracted war, and now strained further by what they considered a treacherous stab in the back, it may seem surprising that only fifteen rebels, including Casement, were executed. The trials and executions, which had been left to the military authorities, were, however, carried out in an unfortunate manner. The executions came at intervals covering a period of nine days, and the announcement of the trial was made simultaneously with that of the execution. No one knew how many more victims were to follow. Possibly, men felt, the British army intended to work through the entire list of victims in its secret trials. This situation produced a wave of disgust, fear, and rage among the volatile Irish. Prisoners who were hissed in the streets by their fellow countrymen at the beginning of May were heroes by the end of the month. Sinn Fein had been almost dead, and the manner of the English reprisals had revived it. Pearse, the poet-president of the "Irish Republic," had built better than he knew. By throwing his life away he had made Sinn Fein and, incidentally, the Irish Free State, which would arise after further bitter fighting following the war.

May, 1916, was indeed an evil month for England: in Ireland, rebellion; in Mesopotamia, the loss of an entire army; at sea, the failure of the Grand Fleet to do a decisive job at Jutland; while the terrible butchery at the Somme lay close in the future. The British buckled down to the war in dead earnest. By this time women were taking over more and more of the jobs formerly monopolized by men, not only in munitions plants but in transportation, in offices, and in many other fields of activity. Perhaps it was a relief from the crushing anxiety over husbands, brothers, sons, or sweethearts across in France, where the chances of returning alive and unmaimed were only about even.

English politics also felt the impact of the war with a moderate change in the spring of 1915 and a more thoroughgoing one at the end of 1916. The Liberal party, at the outbreak of the war, had been in the saddle, we recall, ever since the close of 1905, and since 1908 the ministry had been under the leadership of the fair-minded and scholarly, but slow-moving, Asquith. In August, 1914, the Conservatives announced that they would bury the hatchet of party controversy, so that England might present a united front to her tremendous problems. Disputed domestic issues were set aside, and for a while all went well. In the spring of 1915, however, the munitions situation, coupled with an Admiralty dispute between Churchill and Fisher, brought the long Liberal ascendancy to an end. Under the leadership of Asquith a coalition government was formed, with numerous Conservatives included in the cabinet. By the end of 1916, when the terrible casualty lists from the Somme had arrived, there was increased clamor for change. The British were nobly doing their best to win the war, but many questioned whether all their sacrifices were producing the proper results. With all his admirable qualities, Asquith lacked the quick power of decision and the popular appeal for a war leader; with all his other faults, Lloyd George had, as his munitions experience showed, the ability to inspire co-operation and to get results. England needed an "organizer of victory" such as the elder Pitt had been in the Seven Years' War; and the dynamic little Welshman, with his agile if not profound mind, seemed to come closer to that than any other man. By some clever and perhaps unscrupulous political maneuvering, Asquith was ousted in December, 1916, to be succeeded as prime minister by Lloyd George in another coalition ministry, in which the Conservative element was even stronger.

Accompanying this political shift came an important, though temporary, constitutional change through the formation of the War Cabinet. For the time being, the normal workings of the cabinet system were set aside. The cabinet, we recall, had been composed of men most of whom served also as department heads. The group had gradually grown in size until it was about double the original eleven of Walpole's day. Most of the cabinet members engaged in three separate functions: the formation of policy in cabinet meetings, the direction of their various departments of the government, and the guiding of legislation in Parliament (see page 432). With all the additional burdens imposed by war conditions, the two dozen cabinet members could not efficiently meet all these conditions. The group was too large for immediate and decisive action upon the manifold problems which arose daily and sometimes hourly. Such department heads as the First Lord of the Admiralty and the War Secretary, moreover, could ill spare the time for cabinet meetings, much less for sitting through debates in the Lords or the Commons.

The answer to this situation was the creation of the War Cabinet, a little group of five men including the prime minister. Parliament and the rest of the old cabinet virtually abandoned to them the power of deciding the major questions of what Britain should do. They became a policy-making body, all but one being relieved of departmental and Parliamentary duties. This, as can readily be seen, was a radical constitutional departure from the traditional workings of responsible government. Though still in theory responsible to Parliament, the War Cabinet had a free hand and used it. Parliament lapsed, not without some murmuring at the outset, into a subordinate role as long as the war lasted, enacting what the War Cabinet advised, with only minor changes and only occasional protests. Of these five, two were Englishmen, one a Welshman, one a Scot, and one a native of Canada; from the party standpoint, three were Conservatives, one a Liberal, and one a Laborite. Next to the prime minister, probably the most influential member was Bonar Law, leader of the Conservatives. The rather colorless son of a poor New Brunswick parson, he was a master of Parliamentary tactics. As Chancellor of the Exchequer, he alone of the five held a departmental portfolio, and he alone represented the War Cabinet in the House of Commons. The other members were the proud, cold, and brilliant Lord Curzon, former viceroy of India; Lord Milner, who had handled the civil end of affairs in South Africa before and during the Boer War and was called the most capable administrator in England; and, in strange company with those peers, Arthur Henderson, son of a Scottish workingman, and a one-time workingman himself until he became a trade-union leader and found his way into politics. The War Cabinet certainly speeded up the conduct of the war, and no small part of its success was attributable to the compelling personality of the new prime minister. Lloyd George called himself a drummer boy. He deserved that title, for he awoke his countrymen. Quick, facile, buoyant, he began each day as though all problems were new and fresh. He was not bound by tradition; he could change his mind instantly; he knew how to grip the imagination of his people. For three years he was to be England's hero. After the war crisis was over, however, Parliament was to get rid of the little War Cabinet and revert to the old type, even before it got rid of Lloyd George.

The years of prewar propaganda for imperial co-operation bore sudden fruit in the Imperial War Cabinet, a temporary enlargement of the regular War Cabinet through the addition of representatives from the dominions and India. Twice this body gathered for several months during the war and once just after its close. General Smuts, the former Boer leader, was particularly active, being sent on delicate diplomatic missions and holding a responsible air post as well. Prime Minister Hughes of Australia toured up and down Great Britain with his vigorous message "It is a battle to the death. . . . And we shall win." While the policy-making part of the old cabinet was being compressed into the small War Cabinet, the departmental functions were greatly enlarged. New departments, such as food control, were formed until the ministry numbered about a hundred department heads, many of them businessmen who served without salary and who were frequently rewarded with peerages or knighthood. An unofficial element, meanwhile, was becoming constantly more powerful in English political circles. As the influence of the House of Commons declined, the importance of the great voting population increased, and their views of political matters depended largely upon what they read in the newspapers. This gave immense political power to such men as Lord Northcliffe, who owned and controlled many papers, including the venerable and authoritative *Times,* and the future Lord Beaverbrook, another New Brunswick minister's son like Bonar Law, who played an active part in the fall of the Asquith government. Their support or opposition was more effective than a hundred speeches in Commons; for they could do much to mold public opinion.

The War Cabinet and conscription were not the only wartime breaks with tradition—there were the "Doras" also. Initials were very much in vogue. B.E.F., R.A.C., H.E., V.C., G.H.Q., Anzac, and scores of other alphabetical combinations were in constant use; but probably none had more significance than the abbreviation for the Defense of the Realm Acts. The first of these had been passed in the opening days of the war "to prevent persons communicating with the enemy or obtaining information for that purpose or any purpose calculated to jeopardize the success of the operations of any of His Majesty's Forces, or to assist the enemy." From that initial act there grew up, by means of royal proclamations and Orders in Council, such a mass of regulations that they filled a four-hundred-page volume. Suspected offenders could be arrested, tried before a secret court-martial and sentenced to execution without the usual benefits of habeas corpus or jury trial. From spy-hunting the "Doras" extended into almost every sphere of English activity: industry, commerce, and transportation were minutely regulated; mail and news were censored; food, drinks, amusements, lights, sounds, and much else came within the wide embrace of these administrative laws, which set up a jurisdiction outside the regular courts, and which, beyond their general broad authorization, were not Parliamentary statutes. Some of the more liberal elements protested that the government was acting in excess of its authority. A test case was carried to the House of Lords, the highest court of appeal, which upheld the

# Britain in the First World War

"Doras," though one law baron rendered a dissenting report in which he said much about Star Chamber and certain clauses of Magna Carta. History had repeated itself: just as the French Revolution had caused the government of the younger Pitt to swing from liberal reform to harsh reaction, so now, close upon the ultrademocratic prewar legislation of the Liberals came a drastic curtailment of the normal and traditional freedom of the subject. Two other great democracies, France and the United States, however, went fully as far if not farther along similar lines during the war.

The drag of war had set in by the end of 1916. The Germans and French were badly exhausted by the terrific attrition at Verdun and the Somme. Germany, fresh from her conquest of Rumania, made guarded proposals for a peace conference. Lloyd George spurned them. "To enter," he said, "on the invitation of Germany, proclaiming herself victorious, without any knowledge of the proposals she has to make, into a conference is to put our heads into a noose. Before we can consider such an invitation we ought to know that she is prepared to accede to the only terms on which it is possible for peace to be obtained and maintained—complete restitution, full reparation, effectual guarantee." 14 S.P.

Those words had a note of confidence in them pleasing not only to England but to the dominions as well. The latter, contrary to the hopes and expectations of Germany, were a comfort to the motherland. The Union of South Africa not only had helped conquer the "German Southwest" adjacent to her borders but had suppressed a Boer revolt within her own and was sending troops to German East Africa and even to France. Although the French Canadians held back, the Britons in Canada responded in magnificent fashion and performed many prodigies of valor at Ypres. The Anzacs, the men of Australia and New Zealand, had fought valiantly at the Dardanelles and were now winning laurels in France. The Australian casualties were abnormally high in proportion to the numbers engaged. Little Newfoundland was the only dominion represented at the opening of the Somme, where most of its small force was wiped out. India and other parts of the empire also shared in the difficult imperial task.

For the Allies 1917 was the blackest year of the war. England was the first to suffer. The Germans, with no desire for a repetition of Verdun, decided to rest on the defensive on land, hoping to win the war by a cheaper and easier method than military drives. On the first day of February they began a policy of unrestricted submarine warfare. Their U-boats, as we know, had been active since 1915, when the *Lusitania* was sunk, but hitherto they had shown some respect for neutral rights. Now they began to sink at sight every ship inside a danger zone surrounding the British Isles. It was a clever plan, and it nearly succeeded. With England thoroughly dependent upon outside regions, there was a reasonable prospect that she would quickly be brought to her knees; for Allied shipping was being sunk at the rate of fifty vessels a week. The ocean floor just south of Ireland was strewn with the sunken hulks of torpedoed tramp steamers. This was a black crisis for England; but she met it resolutely, and "seamen torpedoed again and again were ready to sign on as usual." Gradually, before it was too late, England built up a defense against the U-boats: destroyers accompanied the convoys of merchantmen, ever alert for the telltale periscopes. By summer the rate of sinkings had begun to fall off.

Just as the German advance through Belgium in 1914 had brought England into the war, so now the unrestricted submarine warfare added the United States to Germany's enemies. The Germans had foreseen both those possibilities, but had considered the immediate advantages worth the risk. They had laughed at the "contemptible" little British army; they showed even less respect for the small force of American regulars. They felt that the United States, with her military unpreparedness, could not train enough soldiers to make any difference and could not get them across the Atlantic anyway. Consequently they had not been worried by the frequent notes of protest from Woodrow Wilson, the president of the United States, who was re-elected in the fall of 1916 on the slogan "He kept us out of war." American ships, cargoes, and lives were lost, and early in April, 1917, the United States declared war on Germany. At first it was expected that her participation would be limited pretty much to munitions and financial assistance, but she was to do more. Her navy co-operated with the British in the war against submarines, and her shipyards began to turn out steamships faster than the U-boats were sinking them. It was a full year, however, before the United States army was in condition to play an active part in Europe; and in the meantime the Allies were in desperate need of man power, for one member of the Entente had collapsed.

In March, just before the United States entered the war, a revolution in Russia overthrew the Czar's government. The Russian soldiers had been fighting with magnificent bravery; but they finally became tired of trying to pull down barbed-wire entanglements with their bare hands and meeting German machine guns with clubbed rifles. Moreover, they rightly suspected treachery in high places. The revolution, under liberal auspices, was so orderly at first that the Allies took it as a good sign and felt that Russia might make even greater efforts. But the army discipline went completely to pieces when the death penalty for insubordination was abolished and soldiers debated whether or not to obey orders. In a final flare-up of energy the Russians did advance once more against Austria in the summer, but once again the Germans pushed them back.

In November a more radical revolution occurred in Russia. The first revolution had been a moderate affair; but now the most extreme group, the Bolshevists, or majority wing of the Marxian socialists, seized control of the government and began at once to achieve by force a "dictatorship of the proletariat." At last the economic doctrines preached by Karl Marx's followers since the middle of the last century, and feared for years by the conservatives of Europe, were to be put into practice. So radical in their methods were these Bolshevists that many socialists in other countries disowned them, and popularly they have since been known as "Communists" or "Reds." In Russia, as in France in 1793, a reign of terror now developed in which members of the middle, "capitalistic," class were hunted as well as the aristocrats. The Bolshevists believed in class war,— workingmen of all lands against the owners of capital; but as far as the present war was concerned, they wanted peace and were ready to stop fighting at once. In December they agreed to an armistice, which was later confirmed by the Treaty of Brest-Litovsk. Russia withdrew from the war, ceding considerable territory to Germany. The Central Powers now had a vast new region from which to draw supplies, and, still more important, Germany was enabled to release some six hundred thousand men for a concentrated effort on the western front the following year.

The British had expected to accomplish much on the western front in 1917. They had assembled once more a vast quantity of munitions and men, but their blow fell on empty air. Hindenburg and Ludendorff, now in chief command of the Germans, had decided that the irregular trench lines in the western half of the front were not worth holding; so they withdrew quietly to a shorter and more powerful "Hindenburg Line," some distance in the rear, leaving their old positions defended by only a skeleton force. When the British attacked, they pushed this aside and made rapid, almost unopposed gains until they suddenly came up against the concrete defenses, or "pill boxes," of the Hindenburg Line, where, after a month of fighting, Haig realized the futility of further effort. Later in the year the British blew up Messines Ridge with a million pounds of high explosive, and then staged a successful surprise attack with tanks at Cambrai; but in each case they made only local gains.

At that, the British were more successful in battle than their allies; for not only was Russia out, but France and Italy came close to defeat. The French, under Nivelle, launched an ambitious "drive to end the war" by a blow at the middle of the western front. The Germans, however, were forewarned and repulsed it with terrific losses. The brilliant capture of Vimy Ridge by the British and Canadians scarcely compensated for this reverse. The French had hoped for so much from their drive that its failure led to profound depression. Serious mutinies broke out along the French front, and "defeatism" reared its head in Paris until stamped out by "the Tiger," old Georges Clemenceau, the new premier. To prevent the Germans from striking a fatal blow at the demoralized French, the British throughout the summer kept up a series of attacks against the Passchendaele Ridge, in Flanders. This third battle of Ypres, fought in a sea of liquid mud, lives in British memories as the most horrible of the war. Meanwhile things were even worse in Italy. In October a combined German and Austrian force struck the Italians, who within three weeks lost all they had gained in two and a half years. Only the chance rising of a river saved them from further disaster; and Italy had to be bolstered up by her Allies, although, when her people found themselves fighting in defense of their own soil, they showed a new courage.

Only from Asia could the Allies draw any real comfort. There the British were engaged in two campaigns against the Turks. One force invaded Mesopotamia, where Townshend had been captured in 1916, took Baghdad, and continued onward toward the valuable Mosul oil fields. In the meantime England's third scene of action against the Turks was Palestine, where a British force under Allenby advanced from Egypt across the Suez Canal in a "last Crusade." They found valuable allies in the Arabs, who had been roused against their Turkish masters, with promises of independence, by T. E. Lawrence, a young archaeologist whose exploits were among the most dramatic of the war. Allenby, an old cavalryman, waged a brilliant campaign amid scenes where Old Testament kings and medieval Crusaders had fought. In December, Jerusalem fell to the British. Its fall had little military significance, but the moral effect was considerable when everything else looked black for the Allies.

The Allied situation grew even more desperate in the early months of 1918. The transfer of troops from the Russian front gave the Germans a tremendous advantage in man power over the tired French and British in the west. Ludendorff assembled "by far the most formidable fighting force the world had ever seen." It was a case of now or never; for the American troops were landing fast.

On March 21, 1918, the German blow fell upon the British, near the old Somme battlefield, close to where their lines joined the French.

[ 884 ]

# Britain in the First World War

Could the Germans once break through here and reach the main railway line at Amiens, the two allies would be separated and the British thrown back on the Channel. One weak British army caught the blow from a German force twice as strong. The new German "infiltration" tactics honeycombed the British line. Within two weeks the Germans had pushed forward forty miles, the biggest gain since trench warfare began. The French rushed to the aid of the British, and, although the Allied line bent ominously, it did not break. In the midst of the crisis the Allies realized the peril of divided command. The various nations accepted the supreme control of a Frenchman, Ferdinand Foch, as Allied generalissimo. Having failed by a narrow margin to capture Amiens, Ludendorff next struck at the British left, near the coast, in a vain attempt to gain the Channel ports. Then, late in May, he outwitted Foch by a surprise blow at the middle of the western front. It caved in, and within three days the Germans had advanced thirty miles to the Marne and were only fifty miles from Paris.

Now that this war is long over and won, the final Allied victory may seem to have been a foregone conclusion. But in June, 1918, the Allied premiers reported, "As there is no possibility of the British and French increasing the numbers of their divisions, there is great danger of the war's being lost unless the numerical inferiority of the Allies can be remedied by the advent of American troops." About six hundred thousand troops from the United States were then in France, and they kept coming at the rate of about a quarter million a month. Both the Germans and Allies, however, had been skeptical of the effectiveness of these hastily trained soldiers; they might prove as worthless as the Portuguese, who had melted away when first attacked. But, while the Germans were smashing through to the Marne, an American regiment staged an efficient local offensive, and two American divisions had been thrown into the gap to stem the German advance. Once the Americans demonstrated that they too could fight, discouragement gradually began to settle upon the Germans. They had felt that they might eventually overcome the outnumbered British and French, who were as weary as themselves; but now, with fresh millions of fighters available to the Allies, they were fighting against time, and they must hurry or else lose all chance of winning.

Twice more Ludendorff strove to break through. The Marne salient, the pocket in which the Germans found themselves, was deep, but none too broad. To widen it, the Germans struck at its western corner without effect. Finally, on the fifteenth of July, they drove at its eastern side in their last desperate offensive, the second battle of the Marne. As they did so, Foch launched a counterattack from the opposite side of the salient. The Americans and French hurled the Germans back. There, around Soissons, the tide of war turned. The German chancellor later wrote: "We expected momentous events in Paris for the end of July. That was on the fifteenth. On the eighteenth even the most optimistic among us understood that all was lost. The history of the world was played out in those three days."

Ludendorff, however, reserved his superlative tribute for the performance of the British to the westward three weeks later. Once having seized the offensive, Foch gave the Germans no respite. All along the line the French, British, and Americans hammered relentlessly. The British, who had been carrying an increased burden on the western front ever since 1916, had developed high efficiency. In the morning mists of August 8 a force, largely British, Canadian, and Australian, preceded by four hundred and fifty tanks and supported by two thousand guns, smashed the Amiens salient created in those grave March days. Ludendorff called that "the black day of the German army." With the old salients flattened, the Allies drove on against the main lines of the German defenses—the British in the west, the French in the center, and the Americans in the east. The British soldiers were tired—they were no longer the gay enthusiasts who had gone into the Somme battle in 1916; but they were still doggedly determined, and they were veterans who knew their business. The battles which they fought in this last campaign, led by crack assault divisions from Canada and Australia, constitute a classic of the warfare of that day.

Meanwhile Germany's allies, one by one, gave up the fight: Bulgaria at the end of September; Turkey, where Allenby had continued his smashing, at the end of October; and Austria a week later. The German army as a whole did not collapse. In most cases it fought stubbornly and heroically in its long retreat. But behind the army the German population revolted. They had been promised victory in the spring, but only longer casualty lists resulted. The privations caused by the Allied blockade had sapped their morale. They were disillusioned, and President Wilson's "Fourteen Points" made them more ready to give in. Early in November the German High-Seas Fleet received orders to go out and battle the British; the sailors mutinied, and revolt spread through Germany. The Kaiser, William II, abdicated and fled the country. The Germans immediately signed an armistice, and on November 11, 1918, the fighting ended—only to be resumed some twenty years later.

Of the six great powers which had formed the alliances in prewar days, England had been the only one to maintain her morale unimpaired throughout the four long years. Russia had collapsed completely; Austria had been ready to give up the fight long before the war was over, and Germany had finally caved in; while in 1917 both France and Italy had shown dangerous signs of cracking. The British, though sometimes sore disturbed, had kept their chins up from beginning to end, not only in the trenches but at home and out on the fringes of empire. The old Saxon heritage of infinite capacity to take punishment had stood them in good stead.

The terms of the armistice, drawn up in a railway dining-car in a French forest, put Germany at the mercy of the Allies on land and sea pending the settlement of peace terms. Military equipment and supplies were handed over to the victors, and regiments were disbanded. The Allies stationed armies of occupation along the Rhine and continued their relentless blockade of starving Germany. The German High-Seas Fleet, which had not seen action since Jutland, steamed abjectly to Scapa Flow, where some time later it disappeared beneath the waves, scuttled by its own crews.

The Germans had not, however, made an unconditional surrender. They were not in condition to fight another winter, but, on the other hand, the Allies had pushed beyond their railheads and could not immediately invade Germany. The Germans were clearly defeated, but they were counting on the terms given them when they laid down their arms. These were first mentioned when their chancellor, in October, requested peace of President Wilson of the United States on the basis of his already published Fourteen Points, which were to be very important as a basis of the peace settlement. They included open diplomacy, freedom of the seas, reduction of military and naval armaments, removal of economic barriers, fair settlement of colonial claims, evacuation of Russian territory invaded during the war, a restored and compensated Belgium, restoration of Alsace-Lorraine to France, a readjustment of the Italian frontiers, self-determination for the peoples of Austria-Hungary, the Balkans, and Turkey, an independent Poland with an outlet to the sea, and the creation of a League of Nations. The President had then passed this German request to his allies, who accepted it with two qualifications. The point about the freedom of the seas must be omitted, and, furthermore, what the Germans were to pay must be defined more sharply. Consequently it was stated that the compensation to be made by Germany for the restoration of invaded territories must also include all damage done to the "civilian population of the Allies and their property by land, by sea, and from the air." This qualification was deemed essential in order that Great Britain might obtain compensation for the damage done by the U-boats and by German air raids. These terms were accepted by the Germans, who thus thought that they had struck a bargain.

In January, 1919, the Allied representatives assembled, just as the representatives of the powers had gathered at Vienna a century earlier. They had the double and somewhat contradictory purpose of making a lasting settlement and one which would at the same time meet the particular desires of the victors. The peace conference was opened in the old palace at Versailles, and there the final treaty with Germany was signed. The name "Versailles" is often incorrectly applied to the whole work of the conference. Practically all the negotiations were carried on in Paris, and the treaties with the other defeated nations—Austria, Hungary, Bulgaria, Turkey—were signed in other Paris suburbs. In one respect the personnel of the conference departed from precedent. The Germans and their allies were not permitted to take part. At Vienna, Talleyrand had played an active role for defeated France, but at Versailles the representatives of the Central Powers had nothing to say about the terms until they were called in to sign them. It was a victors' peace, but in retrospect it seemed mild.

As usual, the real power of making important decisions lay in the hands of a very few men. In 1814 there had been five great powers: England, France, Austria, Russia, and Prussia. Now the last three empires had recently crumbled in ruins, and in their places were three others: the United States, Italy, and Japan. Before long, Japan, realizing that she could have relatively little to say in such a conference, dropped out, and then Italy withdrew when some of her Adriatic ambitions were thwarted. That left a "Big Three" to dominate the conference: Clemenceau, the old French premier; Lloyd George, the British prime minister; and Wilson, the president of the United States. When disputed matters came up, they listened to the spokesmen for both sides, consulted their staffs of experts, and then made their decisions. Like Metternich at Vienna, Clemenceau represented the victorious nation which had borne the heaviest brunt of the fighting; for the Germans had been on French soil from beginning to end. He was a realist, and he put his faith in definite measures which would prevent a recurrence of such a war. To him that meant a Germany too weak to be dangerous. Wilson, in contrast, was an idealist, even more than Czar Alexander had been a century before. He wanted practically nothing for his own country and was intent upon a peace settlement that would not provoke another war. His particular desire was for a League of Nations in which the various peoples might work together for the preservation of peace. Finally, there was Lloyd George, a clever opportunist, who got all that he could for England and who threw his weight sometimes on the side of Clemenceau and sometimes on that of Wilson. These three men were in no small measure the authors of the final settlement. As far as words went, it was a peace treaty; but the world now knows that it did not make for peace.

As far as the basis of the Fourteen Points was concerned and the prearmistice agreement with the Germans, the Allies kept their word only where it suited their own interests. There was, for instance, Wilson's idea of the "self-determination of nations," the keynote of the conference and a principle very different from the Vienna keynote of "legitimacy." "Self-determination" referred to conquered peoples and to minority nationalities, such as those in the Austrian and Turkish empires in particular. It meant that such peoples were to have the right to decide by what country they should be governed. But it was carried out only in those cases where it would weaken the defeated nations or particularly please or reward one of the victors; otherwise the pleas of the nationalists were not heeded. The same treatment held for the rest of the Fourteen Points. Lloyd George was inclined to bargain, Wilson was outmaneuvered, while Clemenceau fought single-mindedly for a stronger France at the expense of as weak a Germany as possible. His steel will secured some of the harshest terms for the defeated nations. None of the German allies, moreover, had bargained, as Germany had done, before their armistices. Consequently only Germany could claim the protection of the Fourteen Points, although they included generalities which applied to half of Europe.

In territory Germany lost two small sections of land to Belgium; Alsace-Lorraine to France; the northern part of Schleswig to Denmark; considerable territory to Poland in the east; and the cities of Danzig and Memel. In the land ceded to Belgium, plebiscites were taken; that is, the people voted as to whether or not they wished to remain German, in accordance with the idea of "self-determination," although the Germans might legitimately take exception to the way the plebiscites were held. In Schleswig-Holstein also there were plebiscites, but in this instance only the northern section left Germany. No plebiscites were held in Alsace and Lorraine, but few have considered this fact a violation of the peace terms. In the east, however, the justice of the disposition of the German territory was open to question. In the Fourteen Points the Allies had promised Poland, which had disappeared from the map in 1795 (see pages 555, 581), that she should be an independent country, with an outlet to the sea. The outlet to the sea might be interpreted to mean either an extension of Polish territory through a "corridor" which would bisect Prussia or else merely docks and warehouses in a German seaport, to which Polish exports and imports might be freely sent, immune to any German tax. The conference accepted the former definition, and with some reason, since apparently many of the people in the corridor in 1918 were of Polish extraction. Danzig, however, at the end of the corridor, one of the important German seaports, was also taken from Germany; but, instead of being given to Poland, it was placed under the League of Nations as a "free city." Several other districts in dispute between Germany and the new Poland were granted plebiscites, largely through the intercession of Lloyd George, who was much more generous to the enemy in the Polish question than either Clemenceau or Wilson. To be sure, in Silesia the plebiscite returns were juggled to give the coal mines there to Poland, but that was less the fault of the treaty than of the way in which it was executed. The placing of Memel, in the extreme northeast corner of Germany, under the League of Nations, to serve as a seaport for the new republic of Lithuania, was clearly a breach of the Allies' word, since none could question the Teutonic character of Memel's inhabitants. Other treaty terms which affected Germany were the opening of the Kiel Canal to the navigation of all nations; the demilitarization of the left bank of the Rhine, where Germany was forbidden to have fortifications or to station military forces; and the placing of the rich industrial Saar Valley under the League of Nations, with its coal going to France for fifteen years, at the end of which a plebiscite was to decide whether the valley should belong to France or to Germany (see page 925).

Yet, with all those various nibblings at her frontiers, Germany escaped lightly compared with her erstwhile ally Austria-Hungary. If that country had been primarily guilty in starting the war in 1914, she was now severely punished. The former territory of the conglomerate Hapsburg empire found itself under seven different flags, split up in the name of self-determination, which proved a very convenient formula for this purpose. Austria and Hungary became separate little countries only a fraction of their former size; the new republic of Czechoslovakia was carved out in the north; Serbia, doubled in size by a grant of former Hapsburg land and the inclusion of Montenegro, became the kingdom of Yugoslavia; Rumania likewise was greatly increased in size by new Danubian lands; Galicia became part of the new Polish republic; and considerable territory around the Adriatic went to Italy.

The Italians, we recall, had bargained sharply before they threw in their lot with the Allies in 1915, and now they were insistent upon payment in full. They had stipulated a large amount of Austrian

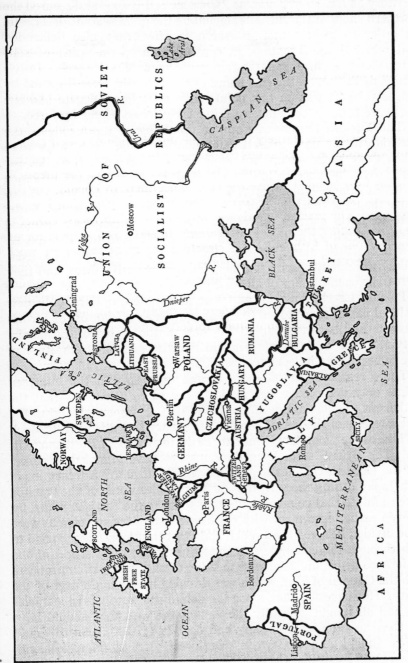

POSTWAR EUROPE

territory as *Italia Irredenta*, or "Unredeemed Italy," and secured the northern shore of the Adriatic, including the great seaport of Trieste. In order to protect their northern frontier, they also demanded and received the Trentino, in contradiction to the spirit of self-determination since some 250,000 Germans lived there. Italy's claims to Fiume, on the east shore of the Adriatic, were disputed by Yugoslavia. It was on this point that the Italian delegate had left the peace conference in anger. Later Italy seized Fiume by force.

The Turkish Empire was broken up almost as thoroughly as the Austrian in the name of self-determination. The Arab states were taken away, to be set up separately, while Greece was rewarded for her tardy adherence to the Allied cause by large grants in Thrace and Asia Minor. This "porcelain treaty" of Sèvres, however, was to prove the most short-lived of the various peace pacts; for the Turks were to settle matters differently. Bulgaria, which had sustained losses of territory in the Balkan wars just before this world war, now lost a little more. The Straits (the Bosporus and the Dardanelles) were neutralized; Turkey was not to fortify them, and they were to be open to ships of all nations.

Poland, Czechoslovakia, and Yugoslavia were not the only new national names to be added to the map of Europe. Out of the former Russian Empire were carved the new Baltic states of Lithuania, Latvia, and Estonia, while Finland likewise escaped from Russian rule to become an independent republic.

There remained the German empire overseas. In the Fourteen Points only one pledge was made in regard to colonies,—that the settlement of colonial questions should be fair, impartial, and to the best interests of the native peoples. In theory this was kept, through the idea of the "mandate," but only at the insistence of President Wilson. The British seem from the outset to have intended to parcel out the German colonies among the Allies, since, by a treaty made with Japan during the war, the Pacific colonies north of the equator were to fall to that country, and those south to the British; while, by an even earlier agreement with the French, the African colonies were to be divided between the French and British. Lloyd George tried to rush through the colonial settlement during the early stages of the conference by calling a surprise meeting of all the dominion premiers with the Council of Ten, which was drawing up the main lines of the treaty. He suggested that, since the dominions were all democracies and had all fought manfully throughout the war, they should have the German colonies that they had captured: the Union of South Africa should annex German Southwest Africa; New Zealand, Samoa; and Australia, German New Guinea. This plan was opposed to the Fourteen Points and was vetoed by Wilson. In consequence the principle of the mandate was invoked. Originally suggested by the British Labor party as a way to detach certain sections of the Turkish Empire from the "terrible Turk," it now seemed a solution of the colonial impasse. Instead of the direct annexation of the colonies by the victor nations, this plan placed them under the League of Nations. Then the League was to entrust the colonies to certain of the victor nations, which would administer the regions as trustees for the League. The League would retain the actual title and would require annual reports for each mandate, with the authority to call the mandatory power to account if conditions warranted such action. As a result of the acceptance of the mandate principle, Great Britain received German East Africa, renamed Tanganyika; sections of Togoland and Kamerun (the major parts of these colonies falling to France as mandates); and the island of Nauru (important for its potash). The Union of South Africa was made the mandatory power over German Southwest Africa; Australia, over the Bismarck archipelago and the German Solomon Islands; and New Zealand, over Samoa. The rest of the German colonies in Africa went to France, and those in the Pacific to Japan, as mandates.

Likewise, some of the former Turkish lands became mandates and were divided between Great Britain and France, Great Britain receiving the Arab states of Mesopotamia and Palestine, and France receiving Syria. All mandates were classified according to their potential possibilities of eventually becoming independent states. One of the so-called "Class A" mandates, Iraq, part of Mesopotamia, since the war has been promoted to the status of an independent kingdom under a native Arab king. Other Arabs have been bitter, however, that the freedom promised them when they aided the Allies against the Turks has materialized only in the cases of Hejaz, which became a kingdom under British protection during the war, and Iraq, which attained that status later. No one was more disheartened over this broken promise than "Lawrence of Arabia," who felt that he had betrayed the Arabs when he found himself powerless to redeem that pledge.

Returning to the Treaty of Versailles, we find that its economic clauses proved not only cruel but impossible to enforce. The Germans could not have complied with them even if they had tried to do so. Although the influence of Lloyd George was often thrown toward leniency in other parts of the peace settlement, he was principally to blame for these clauses. He had pledged himself to two contradictory proposals. Having signed the agreement with the Germans, limiting their liability for damages to that done the civilian population of the

Allies from the air, on land, and on sea, he afterward promised the British electorate that the enemy should pay for the whole cost of the war. At the same time, it must be said in fairness to him that in the last stages of the conference, when the full severity of the terms imposed upon Germany had become obvious, it was he alone who made a real effort to alleviate them. He seems to have infuriated the French by this stand, and apparently he was not supported by Wilson. One of the junior members of the British delegation wrote at the time: "Cannot understand Wilson. Here is a chance of improving the thing, and he won't take it. Lloyd George, however, is fighting like a little terrier all by himself." It was this rather belated move on his part that resulted in a number of minor concessions, including the plebiscite in Upper Silesia.

Lloyd George's difficulties in this matter of the amount that Germany was required to pay were largely the result of the British Parliamentary election of 1918. None had been held during the war, and one was overdue. The Coalition War Cabinet had done wonders in whipping up British public opinion and in modernizing Britain's superb industrial machinery during the conflict, and it thought that it could depend upon a grateful people to return it enthusiastically to office. Instead, the British were too busy welcoming back their men to care about politics. The War Cabinet was popular, but the mild and conservative addresses of Lloyd George and Bonar Law evoked little interest. Then Lord Northcliffe, owner of the London *Times*, and Hughes, the Australian premier, stirred up trouble by suggesting that Lloyd George planned to let the Germans off with an easy peace. Lloyd George began to threaten the Germans as he violently denied this charge. The more he did so, the more he was applauded. Even "Hang the Kaiser!" became a popular slogan. The prime minister assured the people that the Germans ought to pay heavily, even up to the whole cost of the war. It was popularly believed that a hundred billion dollars would be none too much for Germany to pay. How she was to do this nobody knew, but that did not matter to the war-weary man in the street. In this connection, as in certain other matters, the populations of the Allied countries were more to blame for the harshness of the peace terms than were many of their political leaders. Worn by the long agony of the war, and hysterical from the influence of four years of propaganda, they shouted for revenge; and a politician who spoke of generosity to the defeated would have been pushed from power on the instant.

Weighed down by these commitments to the electorate which had returned his coalition ministry to office, Lloyd George met the opposition of President Wilson at Paris. The French did not care how high

# Britain in the First World War

an assessment was levied against the Germans. But Wilson insisted that the obligation of Germany had been limited specifically in the amendment to the Fourteen Points which the Allies had accepted. According to this, one prominent British financial expert carefully estimated that the Germans were due to pay in the neighborhood of $10,000,000,000 for actual damage caused by their armies, their submarines, and their aircraft. Of this he estimated the British share to be $2,750,000,000. If this comparatively reasonable amount had been written into the treaty, the presumption is that it would have been paid within a few years. Lloyd George, however, had the British electorate to propitiate. Consequently, when Wilson would not agree to have the enemy pay the so-called entire cost of the war, he accepted the suggestion of General Smuts of South Africa that military allowances and pensions paid to Allied soldiers were a just charge against the Germans. The argument for this inclusion of pensions was that the Allied armies were largely composed of civilians, temporarily in uniform, who, when discharged, reverted to their original status, thus coming within the German obligations. Premier Hughes of Australia, it is said, demanded that the Germans should make good the difference between the pay of every Australian soldier and the money he would have received in civilian life. On the other hand, one of the delegates from the United States protested: "We are not here to consider as a novel proposition what reparations the enemy should in justice pay; we have not before us a blank page upon which we are free to write as we will. We have before us a page, it is true, but one which is already filled with writing, and at the bottom are the signatures of Mr. Wilson, of Mr. Orlando, of M. Clemenceau, and of Mr. Lloyd George."[1] This strong reminder of their original agreement with the Germans did not hold weight even for Wilson, who eventually signed with Lloyd George for the expansion of the reparations. Once the pensions were included, the bill could be made out for any figure desired.

The treaty was handed to the Germans for their signatures before the amount of the reparations had been decided, despite the prolonged discussion of figures. They were compelled to sign the pact and thus present the victors with what amounted to a blank check. In addition, they had to accept, along with the other harsh terms, a clause by which they acknowledged on the part of themselves and their allies full responsibility for beginning the war. This "war guilt" clause was a peculiarly bitter pill. But it had to be swallowed along with the rest of the treaty; for the Allied blockade had con-

[1] J. M. Keynes, *A Revision of the Treaty* (1919), p. 157. By permission of Harcourt, Brace and Company, and Macmillan & Co., Ltd.

tinued without letup through the months of negotiations, and the
defeated nations were starving.

The amount of reparations as finally presented in 1921 was some
$32,000,000,000,—a reduction from the $56,000,000,000 originally
planned, but still an impossible figure. The Germans, moreover,
were left with almost no resources with which to pay. Their wealth,
before the war, had come largely from their foreign trade, including
their investments overseas and their splendid mercantile marine;
from their coal and iron deposits, which were the material foundations of their economic life; and from their closely knit internal
transportation system. All these sources of wealth were ruined by
the treaty. All their concessions and investments overseas were
taken from them; all their shipping over fifteen hundred tons, half
of their ships between fifteen hundred and five hundred tons, and a
quarter of their tiny fishing trawlers were confiscated. The rich iron
deposits of Lorraine and the coal of the Saar Valley and of Upper
Silesia were gone. In addition to this loss of coal fields, Germany
had to deliver annually, as part of the reparation settlement, thousands of tons of coal to the Allies. With thirty thousand freight cars
and five thousand locomotives delivered to the victors, the internal
transportation was badly impaired. These facts, coupled with the
raising of high tariff barriers throughout the world in the postwar
years, were to make it impossible for the Germans to fulfill the
Versailles terms.

Thus was peace supposedly established. There was only one ray
of hope, and that none too bright—the League of Nations. The
League was a victory for Wilson, who had yielded on others of his
Fourteen Points in order to secure this regular machinery for future
international co-operation. Its member nations were to be banded
together in a formal organization in order to remove the menace of
war by means of joint action. The Covenant, or constitution, of the
League stipulated three separate bodies: the Council, the Assembly,
and the Secretariat. The Council was to consist of five permanent
members, representing the leading powers, together with four (later
nine) nonpermanent members chosen from time to time by the Assembly. It was to meet regularly four times a year, and might be
summoned in special session. It was to exercise the executive functions of the League, to direct investigations, and to supervise the
work of the League's commissions. The Assembly was to be composed of the representatives of all the member states, each having
one vote, and was to be the "instrument by means of which the
nations of the League" were to "confer, advise and deliberate" in
annual session. The Secretariat was to consist of a Secretary-General

and a staff of assistants, whose functions were to be largely administrative. The quarters of the League were to be at Geneva, Switzerland. Membership was to be open to all nations specified in the Covenant, which originally excluded the defeated countries, and to any other nation whose admission should be approved by two thirds of the Assembly. Any member might withdraw from the League upon two years' notice.

The particular significance of the new organization lay in the provisions for preventing future wars. Article Ten of the Covenant stipulated that the League undertook "to respect and preserve as against external aggression the territorial integrity and existing political independence of all members." All international disputes likely to cause war were to be submitted to arbitration or to judicial investigation, machinery for which was established in the Permanent Court of International Justice, popularly known as the World Court, meeting at the Hague. The members who refused to abide by the decision of the World Court or who unlawfully resorted to war would be punished by the League through "sanctions" involving the severance of all trade and financial relations. The Council might also recommend to the member states collective military or naval action to be taken against an offending nation to enforce obedience. As further efforts to maintain international peace, the League was to work for the limitation of armaments "to the lowest point consistent with national safety," the restriction of private manufacture of munitions, the abrogation of all earlier treaties incompatible with the Covenant, the publication of all future treaties, and the rigid enforcement of international obligations. Upon the effectiveness with which it could uphold those provisions in general, and Article Ten in particular, the future prestige and usefulness of the League would depend.

The League, in addition, was entrusted with several international functions such as supervision of the mandates, of plebiscites in disputed regions, of free cities like Danzig, and of the Saar Valley. The League was to undertake also, through its various commissions and bureaus, numerous nonpolitical humanitarian functions, such as the promotion of labor legislation, child welfare, and health, together with the suppression of slavery and the traffic in "white slaves" and narcotics.

England and each dominion received a vote in the Assembly, though the vote of the British Empire was occasionally to be divided on disputed questions. England received also a permanent seat on the Council, and an Englishman was the first Secretary-General of the League. Although General Smuts, the former Boer leader, drew up a considerable part of the actual terms of the Covenant, the

League was generally recognized as the particular creation of Woodrow Wilson. It was consequently a serious blow when his political opponents in the United States Senate kept his country from membership in the League. The opportunity for all the smaller nations of the world to voice their opinions freely in an international gathering was something quite new in history. But the actual domination of the League tended to rest not with the Assembly but with the Council, where the great powers—France and England in particular—were apt to use the League as an instrument for enforcing the Treaty of Versailles in their own interests, just as Metternich had utilized the Quadruple Alliance a century before.

Altogether, England and Europe were about to enter into a postwar period which would bear numerous resemblances to that which had followed the Napoleonic struggle. Men wondered if the machinery set up by the League would be sufficient to maintain peace in the face of a determined effort for war. In the bitter dissatisfaction of the vanquished with the peace settlement were dangerous seeds of future revolt. Many people saw the need of stronger safeguards than those furnished in the League Covenant if the new map of Europe, as created in 1919, was to be kept intact. Others felt that such a crazy patchwork could not last under any circumstances and that any League of Nations entrusted with its defense would eventually collapse. The Vienna settlement had stabilized Europe sufficiently so that there was no world conflict for a century, but that of Versailles lasted only twenty years.

# CHAPTER XXX

## Between the Wars

### 1919-1939

THE war was over, with England and her allies victorious. Once more an enemy lay crushed, with her sea power broken and her colonial empire at Britain's mercy. But again, as after Waterloo, the fruits of victory were quickly to turn sour. Their price had been high and had imposed a cruel strain on British resources and British morale. Britain faced hard years ahead, which in many ways resembled the aftermath of her struggle with Napoleon. Lloyd George talked bravely of making England a land fit for heroes; but in 1919, as in 1815, England had to recognize the disheartening reality that there were no jobs for her returning soldiers.

Economically Britain was to find herself in serious straits. The national debt had increased more than twelvefold in five years, and the interest burden was staggering. Her foreign trade, always the foundation of her prosperity, was diminished. Factories were closed, the mining industry was paralyzed, and ships lay idle in British harbors. Many of her former Continental customers were no longer in a position to buy British goods. Russia, in particular, was in the throes of revolution, and Germany also, while temporarily ruined as a trade rival, was out of the picture as a purchaser. New rivalry came from two overseas nations which had taken advantage of England's wartime distractions to invade some of her old markets. The United States had gone ahead of England in exports and was maintaining that lead, while Japan, supplanting England in many an Asiatic market, saw her exports rise from the equivalent of one twelfth of England's in 1913 to the equivalent of more than half by 1934. To make matters worse, money difficulties, aggravated by the financial clauses of the peace settlement, diminished the sum total of international trade, a very vital matter to a nation so dependent upon exports and shipping as Great Britain. Every one of her immense key industries was badly shaken.

For the British coal trade, one of these key industries, the general postwar shift to oil-burning ships was a calamity. Furthermore, the coal trade was facing the competition of the forced coal deliveries from Germany provided for by the peace treaty. Naturally, France and Italy, obtaining free coal in this way from Germany, did not continue to buy so much from England as formerly. Another threat in the former markets was the increased use of coal from the United States, where the deposits were larger and nearer the surface than the British and where the mining machinery was more modern. The war, moreover, had overstimulated the British mining industry, and new mines had been opened. The industry, while under government control for the period of the war, had granted the miners a seven-hour day as the consequence of their striking during that period of crisis. Now it seemed either that many mines must be closed or that the miners must work longer hours at lower wages.

The merchant marine, another important activity, felt keenly the slump in the coal trade. While, as we have seen, British coal exports were not so valuable as textiles or steel, they had furnished bulky cargoes which kept many ships busy (see page 650). The merchant marine had grown enormously during the last year of the war, partly as a result of the feverish efforts to meet the heavy transportation demands and to offset the submarine losses. At the end of the war, many merchant ships which had formerly flown the German flag were handed over to England. This increase in ships, however, soon was to prove a boomerang. No longer were there American armies to be transported overseas, with their necessary food and supplies, nor was a constant flow of munitions needed. Other nations also had increased their merchant marines, so that, at a time when England had more shipping than ever before in her history, there were more rival bottoms to compete for the diminished cargoes. As ship after ship was tied up in dock or anchored permanently in harbor, silence inevitably descended upon the great shipyards at Belfast, at Glasgow, and on the Tyne.

Since the American Civil War the cotton mills of Lancashire, stronghold of the greatest of the key industries, had not faced such a crisis. Not only did half of England's cotton spindles become idle soon after the peace, but they remained so, largely because of Asiatic competition. While the British were fighting in Flanders, the Japanese began to turn out in vast quantities cheap cotton goods wherewith to capture old British markets. Scarcely a trade secret concerning cotton manufacture remained; for the wily Japanese had ferreted them out, and they had at their command an enormous supply of laborers, intelligent, amenable to discipline, and, above all, content to work for a few pennies a day. That was what made the Japanese competition so much more deadly than that of the Germans before the war. The Germans at least had to pay their workers enough to live according to European standards; the Japanese could live on a small fraction of that. Cheap labor meant cheap goods,—so cheap, in fact, that the British were undersold in market after market. Particularly grave was the situation in India. On the eve of the war India was buying more British goods than any other two regions combined, and those purchases were chiefly cotton goods. During the war years Japanese shipments into India jumped ninefold and continued to gain, whereas British shipments of cotton goods to India in 1934 were only a fifth of what they had been twenty years earlier. Japan by that time had overtaken England in the production of cotton cloth and also of rayon, the silklike substitute. In India and China, moreover, British capital had erected new textile factories which benefited certain wealthy British subjects but paid no wages to British operatives. India, soon to become self-governing in fiscal matters, did not improve conditions when she clapped a very high tariff upon English as well as other imported cotton goods.

Some of the less orthodox economists asserted that this bad industrial situation was made worse by the government's adherence to traditional banking methods. Unlike Germany and France, England did not depreciate her currency but after a few years returned to the gold standard. This tended to keep both prices and wages down; but it benefited the investing class and those upon fixed incomes, since their financial returns remained static as far as figures went while their purchasing power increased with the fall in prices. It made more difficult, however, competition against foreigners for such little international trade as remained; for British gold-standard prices were high in comparison with the depreciated currencies of other nations. On the other hand, history has shown more than once the worse penalties that ordinarily have accompanied an inflated currency.

The economists might argue either way in regard to this question of the gold standard and depreciated currency, but there could be no argument in regard to the lamentable extent of unemployment. England, having adjusted herself to the role of "workshop of the world," had a larger proportion of her population engaged in industry than the other nations, so that, when the demand for her products fell off, she was in a more vulnerable position than a country like France, which was still half agricultural. There were a million unemployed at the beginning of 1921, and two million a year later. Then, after a brief improvement, came the world depression beginning in 1929; and unemployment jumped to a peak of nearly three million at the beginning of 1933. Population increasing annually at the rate of 3 per cent, foreign trade well under the 1914 standards, a poverty-stricken working class and a drastically taxed middle class and aristocracy characterized Britain for many years thereafter.

To remedy this situation, the scope of the insurance laws concerning unemployment was expanded, and the laws were repeatedly modified in the postwar years (see page 808). A specified sum a week was paid to unemployed men, and a somewhat smaller sum to women. At first regarded as a temporary palliative, this practice soon became so habitual that the "dole," as it came to be called by its enemies, eventually ceased to be insurance. In theory, however, the government continued to borrow against its insurance assets to make the payments. As time went on, the dole had a demoralizing effect. After years without work, men gradually lost the will to work, as well as the old British readiness, when things went wrong at home, to migrate oversea. Other proposals were made, involving large outlays for housing projects, road-building, and further naval construction in the hope of encouraging employment; but the tangible results of these experiments seemed inconclusive, and the expenditure for them meant more taxation.

The financial burden which fell upon those who still had money was terrific. Austen Chamberlain, one of the two capable sons of Joseph Chamberlain, was Chancellor of the Exchequer, and in his budgets he put into practice his theory that England should pay as she went along, without further burdening future generations. The budget for 1920 called for a total national revenue of £1,425,000,000, nearly nine times as much as the Lloyd George Budget, which had seemed excessive only eleven years before (see page 809); and the nation was not so rich as it had been in 1909. The interest on the war debt alone came to more than double the whole 1909 budget. There was a drastic rise in the income-tax rate, and persons with even moderate incomes had to pay into the treasury a tax running up to 25 per cent, in addition to local taxes, or "rates." Supertaxes on the larger incomes made the proportion even greater. The "death duties," as well as the local rates, out of which the poor funds were drawn, were so heavy that scores of old landed estates which had been in the possession of single families for generations were being sold by their owners, who could no longer afford to keep them and pay the enormous taxes.

Altogether, it was evident that England, which had been the foremost industrial nation of the world, must recover her foreign trade or else lose her position as a world power. A general economic revival in Europe seemed essential before such recovery could be accomplished, and consequently British statesmen bent their efforts to straightening out the economic tangle left by the peace settlement. In conference after conference Lloyd George tried to undo his own work at Paris and to persuade France to lessen the claims upon Germany.

# Between the Wars

France, however, in those postwar years was torn between the desire to have reparations paid and the fear of a Germany that would be sufficiently strong and prosperous to pay them. France, moreover, not being primarily an exporting nation, was not in such dire economic straits as England at this time. Lloyd George succeeded, after strenuous efforts, in having a world economic conference meet at Genoa in 1922, but it was doomed to failure when the French refused to have the reparation question considered there. All that the conference accomplished was the mutual cancellation of indebtedness by Germany and Russia, who were both penniless anyway.

Meanwhile, the coalition government, re-elected in 1918 (see page 894), was becoming increasingly unpopular. Ostensibly there were three political parties. The Conservatives, commonly known by their old name of Tories, were divided into two factions, the "die-hards" and the moderates. The old Liberal party likewise was split. One section, the followers of Asquith, who was not in the coalition government, had no use for the adherents of Lloyd George, who was a coalitionist. Finally, the Labor party had its moderate and radical wings, which were to divide in 1929. Of those who remained in opposition to the coalition, the Asquith Liberals in particular kept up a running fire of criticism of the peace treaty, which by 1922 was rather generally recognized as unjust to Germany and as injurious to England's interests. These Asquith Liberals, together with the Laborites, who were growing constantly in numbers as the economic clouds darkened, began to win by-elections (elections held in individual constituencies to fill vacancies occurring between general elections). At the same time, the Conservatives, who comprised the bulk of the ministerial forces, were becoming restive under their Liberal prime minister, Lloyd George, and wanted to return to regular party rule.

This coalition, of which everyone now seemed to be wearying, had been re-elected in 1918 by more voters than any preceding government because, in the closing year of the war, the fourth Reform Bill had been passed. Not only had the bill given the suffrage to all male citizens over twenty-one who had been resident in a Parliamentary division for at least six months, by including the small group which had been left without the vote in the third Reform Bill, of 1884, but—a striking novelty—it at last had extended the franchise to women. This was not so much a concession to Mrs. Pankhurst and her troublesome suffragettes as it was a recognition of the splendid accomplishments of women in many difficult spheres of activity during the war. It came almost simultaneously with the granting of woman suffrage in the United States, Germany, Russia, and elsewhere. There was, however, a joker in the British act. There were about two million more women than men in England, partly as a result of war casualties. Some of the alarmists foresaw a danger of "petticoat rule." Consequently the minimum age for women voters was set, not at the conventional twenty-one, but at thirty, possibly in the hope that many might stay away from the polls rather than admit that they had reached that age. This situation lasted for ten years until, in 1928, the fifth Reform Bill, or "Flapper Franchise Act," gave the vote, under the usual residence requirements, to all women who had reached the age of twenty-one. The granting of universal manhood suffrage in 1918 realized the fifth of the six old Chartist demands, and the "Flapper Act" rounded out the movement which had begun in 1832. There were certain other provisions in the 1918 act. All elections were to be held on a single day, instead of being spread out over a longer period as before. "Plural voting," moreover, whereby an individual might be entitled to as many as a dozen votes, was restricted to a maximum of two votes. A university graduate, for example, might still have a second vote as the holder of a degree.

Women were now eligible also to membership in the House of Commons. The first to be elected was Lady Astor, a native of Virginia, whose husband, the son of an expatriate American millionaire, sat in the House of Lords. For many years, by her vivacious personality and pungent wit, Lady Astor was to enliven Parliamentary sessions in her verbal encounters with Labor members. The House of Lords, however, refused to admit even women who held peerages in their own right.

The year 1919 saw also the end of the War Cabinet and the return to the old system. Lloyd George had wanted to retain the efficient little group (see page 878); but the House of Commons objected strongly, and the cabinet of some twenty members, most of them heads of departments and participating in Parliamentary debates, was resumed.

Not only economic woes worried the coalition ministry; the perennial Irish question once more flared up. Easter week of 1916 still lived in Irish memories, and, outside of Ulster, Sinn Fein was carrying practically every parliamentary seat. Sinn Fein would have nothing to do with England, even refusing to permit its representatives to attend Parliament or to allow taxes to be paid in Ireland. It boycotted British law courts, setting up its own judicial bodies and enforcing their decisions. Coercion from the British met with bloody resistance. Between Irish and British actual war arose, none the less war for there being no pitched battles. The officials of the crown and

# Between the Wars

of the Irish republican (Sinn Fein) army were both guilty of the ensuing orgy of cruelty and bloodshed. In order to back up their constabulary, the British introduced an auxiliary police force into Ireland. These "Black and Tans," wearing the old army khaki with black hats, were venomously hated by the republicans. To wear their uniform soon became foolhardy, and to wear it after dark without friends at hand was to invite death. On a recruiting poster inscribed "Join the Royal Air Force and see the world," someone scrawled, "Join the Royal Irish Constabulary and see the next world."

Throughout 1920 and into 1921 this sanguinary strife continued. The government vowed that it would never yield to the "murder gang"; but British liberal opinion was demanding conciliation, and suddenly Lloyd George asked for a conference with the rebels. He agreed to give Ireland dominion status, with entire control of her own finances, police, and law. In return, he demanded that free trade continue between the two islands, that England retain her right to recruit soldiers in Ireland, that the latter country assume a proportion of the United Kingdom's debt, and that Ulster receive permission to make separate arrangements. It proved difficult, however, to deal with the Sinn Fein representatives; for, scorning the substance of self-government, they held out for the symbols of complete Irish independence. The British then whittled down their own terms by withdrawing their claim to enlist Irishmen in the British army and their insistence on free trade. As a result a treaty was finally signed by the rebels late in 1921 and was ratified by an Irish election. Thus the Irish Free State came into being, Ulster remaining outside. The "troubles," however, were not over. The war between Irishman and Briton was now succeeded by another war, no less bitter and murderous, between the Irishmen who accepted the treaty settlement and those "Irreconcilables," led by Eamon de Valera, who refused to do so. By 1924 the moderate party had won a decided victory and was able to turn to the task of civil organization in the new state. This task was carried out with complete success, and without any interference from Britain, under the administration of President Cosgrave, a capable, steady, unspectacular man with a level head and a capacity for hard work,—a very fortunate choice for the position.

The Irish Free State now emerged from chaos. The army was greatly reduced; old-age pensions were cut down; arrears of back taxes were ruthlessly collected; and a protective tariff was instituted. Cosgrave, in 1932, finally gave place to De Valera, who adopted a bitter anti-British policy. The economic dependence of Ireland upon her larger neighbor, however, made it necessary for even this fierce republican to be somewhat conciliatory, and Ireland continued within the empire. England, on the whole, was glad to be thus largely rid of the vexing problem.

In the meantime Ulster was going its separate course as "Northern Ireland." Though it had a parliament of its own for domestic business, it continued to send members to the House of Commons of the "United Kingdom of Great Britain and Northern Ireland."

The year 1922 was a landmark in naval history because the "Mistress of the Seas" admitted a partner to her supremacy—at least on paper. At the Washington Naval Conference she formally agreed that the United States might maintain a navy as large as her own. For nearly two centuries the royal navy had been maintained on a two-power basis; when German rivalry arose, England had still managed to keep a 3-to-2 advantage. When, in 1919, Germany's surrendered fleet had disappeared beneath the waters of Scapa Flow, scuttled by its own crews, England, anxious to relieve the crushing burden of taxation by a naval holiday, had suspended most of her naval construction. Then she realized to her extreme annoyance that the two Pacific rivals, the United States and Japan, were building navies of maximum size. These were the same two powers which, as we just saw, were also becoming serious commercial rivals of England. In 1916 the United States had suddenly taken steps to build a navy "second to none." The motives for that step, beyond the World War fears, were not altogether clear; but a beginning had been made, and when the war was over, the Americans drew up still more ambitious plans. There was no question about their ability to pay for the largest navy in the world if they saw fit, and their new program called for battle strength considerably superior to England's. Japan, which likewise had been spared the financial exhaustion of the European nations, was also building up a large fleet, presumably to sustain her aggressions in China. England resented and regretted the new naval competition into which she was forced by what she considered the artificial and unreasonable desire of the United States and Japan for navies approaching her own in size. Yet, with her eighty thousand miles of sea lanes to guard and her dependence upon overseas regions for many of the necessities of life, she could not afford to let command of the seas pass into other hands.

By her concessions at the Washington Naval Conference in 1921–1922, however, she co-operated to make this competition less costly. At this meeting the chief maritime powers stabilized their battleship strength, thus checking the most expensive form of that rivalry. The ratio of 5–5–3 was established for the battleship strength of England, the United States, and Japan, respectively, with 1.75 for France and for Italy. Thus England submitted to the abandonment of her time-honored supremacy by recognizing the United States as a potential equal, securing in return an agreement that the United States would not carry through her program to outbuild England. The United States, on her side, was pleased to see a limit placed upon the battle-ship strength of Japan. The Japanese, for their part, gained security through the agreement that neither British nor Americans would build or strengthen any naval bases within striking distance of Japan. Another feature that gratified the United States was the abrogation of the Anglo-Japanese alliance, with its naval stipulations, dating back to 1902 (see page 830). England did this partly to please the United States and partly to please the dominions, three of which had interests in the Pacific. In its place, England, France, Japan, and the United States signed a four-power pact to preserve the status quo in the western Pacific. The Washington Conference was a step toward limitation of armaments, but it still left opportunity for unlimited building of cruisers, submarines, and other craft. The whole arrangement, moreover, was later denounced by the Japanese, who resented their inferior status.

Not simply naval rivalry but other and more serious complications in foreign affairs were worrying Britain by 1922. Four years had passed since the war to "make the world safe for democracy," and in Europe democracy seemed to be losing ground all along the line. There was a growing tendency toward autocratic reaction of the sort which, as we recall, had prevailed in Europe in Metternich's day. Before the war, nation after nation had been copying England's form of limited monarchy. After the war, to be sure, republics on a similar model of responsible government, with presidents instead of kings, had been set up in Germany and Austria, as well as in some of the new countries such as Poland, Czechoslovakia, Estonia, Latvia, Lithuania, and Finland; but the new states did not play an important role in the general situation, while the German republic, established after the Kaiser's flight in 1918, lacked prestige and strength. In Italy, where the cabinet and parliament had proved themselves unable to cope effectively with a threatened communist revolt, one Benito Mussolini had formed a "Fascist" party, and with his "Black Shirts" was making his famous "March on Rome" in 1922. Although Italy remained a monarchy, he was soon dictator, thanks to vigorous methods and to the general fear of communist disorder. Once this forceful, bull-like man was in the saddle, Europe saw the beginning of the repressive, strongly state-regulated, rabidly nationalistic and antisocialistic movements in support of law, order, and the continuation of capitalistic society that characterized the postwar years, when

the economic situation and the fear of the spread of Russian radical
doctrines continued to harass Europe. Mussolini gave Italy certain
increased efficiency; but, as in the other Fascist regimes of this sort,
liberalism and liberty were lost in the complete subordination of the
individual to the state.

In Russia revolution ran a bloody course. The radical Marxian
group—the Bolshevists, Communists, or "Reds," as they were called
—maintained the control which they had seized in November, 1917.
They had triumphed over the counterrevolutionary "White" armies,
which had received more than moral support from England and her
former allies. A little Anglo-American military force, for example,
had operated in frozen futility around Archangel. The Bolshevists
under Lenin were now building up a state on the basis (supposedly)
of Marx's doctrines. The old autocracy of the Czars was giving way
to a new, and perhaps equally rigid, dictatorship of the proletariat
which amounted, actually, to a dictatorship of the well-organized
Communist party. The new masters of Russia, like the leaders of the
French Revolution, sought to spread their doctrines to other lands and
to supplant capitalism with communism.

Change was coming also to the Near East. Turkey had a dictator
in Mustafa Kemal, the vigorous leader of the Turkish nationalists,
who had ousted the Ottoman Sultan and become president of the
new republic. He was now busily tearing to pieces the part of the
peace settlement that had partitioned his land. That might mean
trouble for England. But at least she was freed of the old embarrassing fact that the ruler of Turkey had been caliph, or spiritual head, of
all Mohammedans, for at that time there were more Moslems than
Christians among the subjects of King George; and there was little
doubt that a strong, rejuvenated Turkey supplied the best solution for
the "Eastern Question" which long had vexed Europe. Dictatorship,
then, was established in Italy, Russia, and Turkey, and would spread
before long to other lands.

In the Middle and the Far East also the postwar period was not
tranquil. China, a republic since 1911, was torn with constant civil
strife, while Japan, with her expanding population and avowed need
for territory, and Russia, with her communism, were dangerous
neighbors for that weak, divided country with her tempting resources.
Iran (Persia), where, we recall, British influence had been strong not
long before, was growing more nationalistic, and in 1921 overthrew
her government, which was thought too pro-British. Elsewhere, in
one region after another, both within the far-flung British Empire
and all about its boundaries, that same spirit of nationalism was
fast germinating.

France, meanwhile, as distrustful of Germany as ever, was acquiring allies for herself in such a successful manner that some have called the postwar decade the period of the "ascendancy of France." Belgium, now no longer neutral by international treaty, and Poland, into which France poured money for the equipment of an army that might be used against Germany or Russia as occasion demanded, were her close allies; while a new alliance, the "Little Entente," in Central Europe, also was decidedly pro-French. This latter group, composed of Czechoslovakia, Rumania, and Yugoslavia, had profited greatly in the peace settlement, where the ramshackle Austro-Hungarian Empire had been split seven ways in the name of self-determination. The once-proud Austria was prostrate, having been stripped down to "a capital and its suburbs." Hungary, surrounded by the watchful, hostile Little Entente, was in as serious a plight. The League of Nations was supposed to be Europe's guarantee of peace, but apparently the old system of alliances was springing up anew. England had somewhat the attitude she had held under Castlereagh a century before: she recognized the need for co-operation and a united front. France, however, seemed aspiring to such influence as Metternich had once wielded, so that this time the old principle of the balance of power inclined England to a more lenient attitude toward the defeated enemy.

Lloyd George, whose prestige had been hurt by his failure at Genoa and who had not redeemed himself elsewhere, intervened in Turkey in 1922. Mustafa Kemal was strenuously resisting the humiliating terms imposed·upon Turkey by the Treaty of Sèvres as part of the Paris peace settlement. In particular, he was ousting the Greeks from the territory in Asia Minor given them as a reward for their tardy support of the Allies. This fighting reached a cruel climax in a terrible massacre at Smyrna in the summer of 1922. Kemal then started northward for Constantinople. The French and Italians, rather than fight, withdrew speedily; but Lloyd George, feeling that Britain's vital interests in the Near East should be defended, sent troops to Çanakkale (Chanak), on the Asiatic side of the Dardanelles. Neither the war-weary British public nor the dominions, to whom he appealed for support, relished the thought of another Gallipoli; and the Turk, unopposed, had his own way.

This "Chanak affair" helped to terminate the six-year coalition ministry of Lloyd George in the autumn of 1922. The spell of the little "Welsh wizard" was weakening, and the Conservatives, who formed the bulk of his support, grew restive at his autocratic actions. A five-year general election would be due the following year. Consequently, at a significant meeting at the Carlton Club, the majority of the Conservatives determined to operate thereafter as a separate party rather than through the coalition. Lloyd George resigned at once. The king requested Bonar Law to form a Conservative ministry, and the general election shortly afterward established the Conservatives in power with a moderate majority. The Liberal party went to pieces; for Asquith's and Lloyd George's followers were not on speaking terms. The electorate swung largely either to the Conservatives or to the Laborites, with the result that for the first time in history His Majesty's Opposition was the Labor party.

The remainder of George V's reign saw frequent ministerial changes. Bonar Law died after eight months and was followed by the Conservative Stanley Baldwin. After another eight months, Baldwin gave way, early in 1924, to the Laborites under Mac-Donald. After nine months Baldwin and the Conservatives returned to power, from November, 1924, to June, 1929. Then Labor, under MacDonald, was again in the saddle until August, 1931, when, under his leadership, a "National" coalition government, chiefly Conservative, was formed. In the summer of 1935 Baldwin succeeded him, becoming prime minister for the third time, until in 1937, under George VI, he was followed by another Conservative, Neville Chamberlain.

Between the wars the Conservatives were thus definitely the predominant party, with three separate ministries under their own name in addition to the Lloyd George and three National coalitions, which relied principally upon them for support. Along with this Conservative strength went the eclipse of the Liberals and the steady rise, despite an apparently serious setback, of the Labor party. The Liberals, we recall, were divided in 1916 when Asquith's followers refused to participate in the coalition government under Lloyd George, and this hurt them materially. Not once were the Liberals the majority party, and usually even their place as the official opposition party was taken by Labor. In their two ministries the Laborites did not at any time have a majority in the Commons, and in both they had to depend upon the Liberals as allies.

Bonar Law, Canadian-born, the first native of a dominion to be prime minister, had long been a Conservative leader. He had been a prominent opponent of home rule, a member of the War Cabinet, and a delegate at Versailles. He was already mortally ill, and died in the spring of 1923. There had been no question about his leadership of the party, but now three important candidates were in line as his successor. Austen Chamberlain had served both before and after the war at the Exchequer, where his solid rather than showy qualities had been useful. He had also been Secretary of State for

India and, for a time, a member of the War Cabinet. He had reasonable hopes of heading the party, but was passed by as punishment for his loyalty to the Lloyd George coalition. Lord Curzon, the proud ex-viceroy of India, member of the War Cabinet and more recently Foreign Secretary, was well qualified by ability; but he was not a popular figure. Moreover, no peer had served as prime minister since the resignation of Salisbury, in 1902, and, in the new democratic age, leadership in the House of Commons seemed necessary. Thus the choice fell upon a less conspicuous man, Stanley Baldwin, who had been president of the Board of Trade and who, in the existing cabinet, was serving as Chancellor of the Exchequer. Exceedingly shrewd, unassuming in manner, and possessed of an even temper and a fund of common sense, Baldwin summed up in his qualities much that was characteristically British. In his inherited position as head of one of the largest iron, steel, and coal combinations in the kingdom, he had behind him years of practical business experience. At the same time, as a small landowner, he had been a country gentleman as well, an excellent judge of livestock, with experience as a local magistrate. Sound rather than brilliant, he answered the country's desire for strength and security in that troubled period. Austen Chamberlain was temporarily out of office, but his brother Neville served at the Exchequer in this first Baldwin ministry.

The Conservative prime ministers were, each in his turn, to find the serious foreign situation as difficult to manage as Lloyd George had found it. In 1923 the new Turkish government, which Lloyd George had tried to oppose at Chanak, secured at Lausanne a revision of the 1919 Sèvres treaty. Turkey was permitted to reoccupy the lands granted to the Greeks.

England made a concession in that matter in order to preserve what she could of her vital interests in the Mosul oil fields, on the upper Tigris. Oil was becoming what masts and ship timber had been in earlier days, a strategic economic factor in colonial and foreign policy, important partly because of general commercial needs and even more so because of naval and air dependence upon it. England had to look to outside lands for her oil, as she had earlier done for naval masts. This had influenced her dealings with Iran just after the war, and now affected Turkish relations.

With their capital moved inland, far beyond the reach of British naval guns, which more than once had bullied Constantinople, the Turks were to continue their progress. By 1936 the Lausanne treaty of 1923 would go the way of the Sèvres treaty of 1919, and Turkey would once more secure international permission to fortify the demilitarized Straits. One of the reasons for England's having to back down in the face of Turkish demands in 1923 was the withdrawal of French support. Early in that year the French sent military forces to occupy the valuable Ruhr mining region, alleging minor defaults in Germany's reparation payments. The British protested strongly, but in vain, at this French action. England—for the time being, at any rate—could apparently do little in this troubled international situation, although many were quick to criticize Baldwin for what they called insufficient firmness in the Ruhr matter, as they had criticized Lloyd George for being too precipitate at Chanak.

At home Baldwin was baffled by the continued increase in unemployment; and apparently Joseph Chamberlain's old plan of protective tariffs seemed to him the best remedy. Bonar Law, however, had promised not to bring up this question of protection, and consequently Baldwin seemed to feel that he must ask for a mandate from the electorate for his project. He might have remained securely in power for some time to come had he not requested this general election late in 1923.

In the election, fought over protection, the Conservatives won the largest number of seats but failed to obtain a majority. Although they had about sixty-five more members in the Commons than the Laborites, and nearly a hundred more than the Liberals, these two combined had about ninety more than the Conservative total. The Labor party under such circumstances could form the ministry if the Liberals would support them. Had the Liberals combined with the Conservatives, they might still have kept Labor from office. They did not do this, however, partly because they were too proud to play second fiddle to the Tory interests and partly because they were inclined to feel that if Labor were given its chance they might return to power on its heels. Consequently, in January, 1924, the socialist Ramsay MacDonald became prime minister in the first Labor ministry. This seemed revolutionary, with the Labor party pledged as it was to a capital levy and to the nationalization of industry on socialistic lines; but, as it turned out, there was no serious cause for alarm. MacDonald proved "safe"; for, although his goal was socialism, he moved toward it at a walking pace. He had, moreover, insufficient support to attempt it at once, even had he so wished, because the bulk of his following was composed of trade-unionists, who were only very mildly socialistic, and his majority in the House of Commons, being dependent upon the Liberals, was, of course, uncertain. MacDonald and his ministry set out to prove to the country that a Labor government was respectable and not too radical. The skies therefore remained unclouded. No exodus of capital occurred. The first Labor budget won general praise, and businessmen breathed more easily.

# Between the Wars

To be sure, taxes were not lowered, except for the impost on cheap cinema tickets; but it was generally admitted that no government could have reduced taxes at this time.

The Labor leaders who came into power were of two types. Some, such as MacDonald himself, Snowden, and Webb, had long furnished intellectual guidance to the Labor movement, while others, such as Henderson and Thomas, had risen actually from the ranks of labor itself to influential trade-union leadership. MacDonald, a man of nearly sixty, and known for his personal charm, was the son of a laborer in a Scottish fishing village. He had made his own way in the world through diligent self-education and had been a clerk, a teacher, a journalist, and a writer on socialism. He had been active in building up the Independent Labor party, to which he had belonged since 1894, and for some years before the war he had been a prominent Labor member of the Commons. He opposed the declaration of war and then gave up his position as party leader in Commons. He would not serve in the armed forces and was widely denounced. He lost his seat in the election of 1918, but four years later was again elected to Parliament and became leader of the Labor party there. Philip Snowden, the new Chancellor of the Exchequer, lean, frail, and a brilliant orator, had been another pioneer of the Independent Labor party thirty years before. Likewise, Sidney Webb, later Lord Passfield, president of the Board of Trade, had been one of the early leaders of the Fabian Society and with his wife, Beatrice, had written extensively on labor problems. On the other hand, Arthur Henderson, the new Home Secretary, son of Glasgow working parents, had been at one time an apprentice molder at Newcastle and later a power in north-country labor circles. He had already tasted high office as a member of the War Cabinet. John Henry Thomas, another cabinet member, was a Welshman who had once cleaned locomotives and had risen to leadership of the great railway union. Later he would win the unenviable distinction of being the first cabinet minister in British history to lose his office charged with divulging official secrets. There were also a few peers in the new Labor cabinet for duties in the Lords, including a former viceroy of India and a one-time governor of Jamaica.

MacDonald, who was Foreign Secretary as well as prime minister, won general approval by winning over the French to a new plan for clearing the reparation muddle. This so-called "Dawes Plan," named after one of its framers, an American, was a temporary solution which facilitated the withdrawal of the French army from the Ruhr valley. MacDonald also suspended work on the great naval base at Singapore to avoid antagonizing Japan. At the meeting of the League of Nations in 1924 he signed the Geneva protocol by which the signatory nations agreed to accept as compulsory the jurisdiction of the World Court on any questions that seemed to be leading to war; but, as we shall see, his action was not sustained, and the work of the conference came to little. Although he thus did what he could for international peace, his own pacifism was not especially in evidence; for he slightly increased the navy (which, however, was much smaller than it had been in 1914) and refused to yield to either Indian or Egyptian Nationalists.

His attempt to draw Russia (the Union of Soviet Socialist Republics) into the circle of friendly powers led to the downfall of his ministry. He wanted to increase the sale of British goods abroad, and to this end was ready to aid Britain's potential customers. Having already tried to help Germany through the Dawes Plan, he now wanted to arrange by treaty the floating of a Russian loan in the British market, the interest and repayment of the bonds to be guaranteed by the British government. In return, the Soviet government was to pledge, among other things, to abstain from revolutionary propaganda in England. Sharp and shrill was the outcry from all sides, Conservatives, Liberals, even some Laborites, objecting strenuously to this project. England, as we have seen, had aided the counterrevolutionary "White" forces in Russia, and many Englishmen had no desire for relations with Russia as long as the Bolshevists remained in power. Besides, the fact that the Bolshevists hoped that their revolution was only the beginning of a world revolution against all capitalistic powers was not conducive to friendliness. Also, as some of the Laborites pointed out, sympathy on their part with the aims of the Russian revolution was a different matter from a loan to the Russian government.

The treaty never came up for ratification in Parliament because of the appearance in a communist newspaper in England of the following: "Form committees in every barracks, aerodrome and ship. Let this be the nucleus of an organization which will prepare the whole of the soldiers, sailors and airmen not merely to refuse to go to war or to refuse to shoot strikers during industrial conflicts but will make it possible for the workers, peasants and soldiers, sailors and airmen to go forward in a common attack upon capitalism." The editor was arrested, but the case was dismissed by the attorney general. Parliament was incensed, and the explanation of the attorney general, that the article had been intended merely to persuade soldiers and sailors to refuse to do police duty in strikes, failed to satisfy not only the furious Conservatives but also the Liberals, whose friendship with Labor was wearing thin. As a result, the Liberals voted against MacDonald, and this defeat ended the first Labor ministry within its first year.

# Between the Wars

In the next general election (1924) the Conservatives triumphantly returned to power with a big majority. During the campaign they had advocated a protective tariff and had stressed the injury done to imperial interests during MacDonald's ministry by the repeal of Baldwin's duties, which had given preference to dominion products. These Conservative arguments had less to do with their victory, however, than the weak spots in their opponents' armor. To be sure, MacDonald's term had been short, and his majority in Commons uncertain; but more had been expected of Labor than had been accomplished. MacDonald talked, during the campaign, of cooperation, community interest, and the common welfare, as well as of the need to give socialism a real chance; but that did not fill mouths, house people, nor lessen the number on the unemployment dole. With the income tax still standing at five shillings in the pound (25 per cent), his plan to lend millions to the Soviets naturally reacted badly against him. But his defeat was caused chiefly by a mysterious letter which was sprung upon the people a few days before election. It was supposedly written by Zinoviev, the Russian president of the Third International (the communist revolutionary organization), and advocated preparation for revolution in England. Although this letter did not diminish the total Labor vote, it so alarmed the Liberals that they flocked to support Conservative candidates. In effect, they almost killed their own party without diminishing to any great extent the number of Labor seats in the Commons. Their seats were reduced to 40, while Labor retained about 150, and the Conservatives increased their total to over 400.

Thus the genial Stanley Baldwin began his second ministry (1924–1929). Winston Churchill, once a famous Liberal, who had also been a coalitionist, now made a new party shift and, surprisingly enough, went over to the Conservatives, serving at the Exchequer in the new cabinet. The versatile Churchill had previously held six other cabinet posts,—Board of Trade, Home Office, Admiralty, Munitions, War and Air, and Colonies,—besides finding time to write several valuable books on the war and the postwar period. Austen Chamberlain returned to the cabinet also as Secretary for Foreign Affairs.

Under the latter the ministry achieved its most notable work. The Geneva protocol was not ratified by Parliament. Chamberlain opposed it because, in his opinion, it made the League of Nations into a superstate, thus endangering the British Empire's freedom of action in crises. As he said, the British Commonwealth of Nations was an older body, and he felt that its safety must not be jeopardized by such an agreement. This rather lessened England's influence in the League. Nevertheless, Chamberlain consistently strove for peace, as Mac-

Donald had done,—particularly for a more friendly feeling between France and Germany. In this he was fortunate to have as allies two ministers, Briand in France and Stresemann in Germany, who likewise were working for peace. The culmination of the efforts by these three men was the seven pacts signed at Locarno in 1925, at a conference of the powers. The main achievement of this meeting was the mutual guarantee of frontiers by France and Germany in the Rhine region. By this the nations pledged themselves not to invade each other's territories, and to keep the boundaries as established at Versailles, with the left bank of the Rhine as a demilitarized zone in Germany. Belgium and Germany signed similar pledges. Britain and Italy guaranteed the pledges to the extent of promising aid in case of violation of the agreements. Other pacts signed here provided for the arbitration of disputes in other areas; but Britain did not share in the arrangements about Germany's eastern boundaries. Thus peace seemed more secure in the region of England's traditional interest. A significant result of Chamberlain's work and another favorable aspect of the situation was the paving of the way for Germany's entrance into the League of Nations the following year. Lady Chamberlain was decorated along with her husband for her tactful handling of the difficult meetings between French and Germans at Locarno— an unusual recognition in British annals.

At home the crippled mining industry became the focus of discontent. In 1925 the operators announced that wages must be cut in the less profitable mines. The desperate miners appealed to their fellow trade-unionists with success. The railway unions promised to handle no coal in case of a strike. Baldwin, to stave off anything of the sort, consented to a temporary subsidy to the industry in order that the existing scale of wages and the seven-hour day might be continued until a royal commission should have had time to investigate. This action merely postponed the storm that burst upon England in 1926. The commission reported that, if the industry were to survive, there must be either "a sudden contraction" of it to a smaller size or else "an immediate lowering of the cost of production." In the former case thousands of miners would lose their jobs; in the latter, either a longer day or lower wages or both would be necessary. Thereupon the government refused to continue the subsidy; the miners insisted upon "not a penny off the pay, not an hour on the day"; and the trade unions declared a general strike.

The trade-unionists called this a "sympathetic strike" to help the miners. All railway men, all those in iron, steel, and building trades, and all printers stopped work. Baldwin, denouncing the strike as an attempt to "set up an alternative government," summoned the country to resist. He enlisted thousands of special constables and called for volunteers to deliver food. The middle class rose almost to a man to the support of the authorities, running the railways after a fashion, distributing food, and so on, with determination and vim. The strike failed ignominiously; in eight days it was broken. There had been virtually no violence on either side—a circumstance to which Englishmen pointed with considerable pride.

Although the general strike was ended thus quickly, the embittered miners kept up the struggle within their own industry for seven months, assisted somewhat by British public charity and by funds raised, it was said, in Russia. Slowly they drifted back to work. Their hours were uniformly increased to seven and a half, while their wages were lowered in some localities but left as before in others. Many mines, particularly in South Wales, were now abandoned altogether, with a consequent increase in the number of permanently unemployed.

The crisis of 1926 led to much bitter feeling, reflected even among the clergy. In particular, Lloyd George reopened the old rift in the Liberal party. He demanded a renewal of the coal subsidy and attacked the strike policy of the government; whereupon Asquith, now Earl of Oxford and Asquith, urged the party to disown the "Welsh wizard," and, failing in this, retired in disgust from the nominal headship of the party. The Tories, meanwhile, were demanding a frontal attack upon trade unions and were pressing Baldwin hard to this end.

In 1927 they succeeded in passing an act against trade-union activity. This Trade Disputes and Trade Union Act was the first setback the influential trade-union movement had received in many years. It made the general strike illegal, forbade intimidation of strikebreakers, excluded government employees from membership in such organizations, and otherwise limited union activities. Henceforth, therefore, a worker would be breaking the law if he threw down his tools to remedy difficulties in any line of work other than his own. Many felt that this prohibition of the general strike would be hard to enforce and that consequently it irritated the trade-unionists to little purpose.

In other domestic matters Baldwin himself showed that he was far from being a "die-hard" Tory. He not only kept the extreme Conservatives in check (as, for instance, in their desire to strengthen the House of Lords) but also made friendly gestures to Labor, in particular, with a new pension law for widows. Although he was unable to do much about the economic crisis, the budget of 1928 was a determined effort toward improving conditions. One thing that stood in the way was the impasse caused by the insistence of businessmen that lower wages were essential for competition in the world market and by the refusal of the trade unions to consider them. Winston Churchill, turning in another direction, proposed through his budget that the burdensome local "rates" (taxes) be largely taken from industry and agriculture by means of a new tax upon petrol (gasoline). In connection with this, poor relief was to be made easier for the communities, in spite of the reduction in their local rates, by being administered over larger areas, with aid from the national treasury where needed. Another move toward better economic conditions was the removal of the tax on tea; but, all in all, the ministry was content with making only a few reforms. A slight improvement in trade persuaded Baldwin and his followers that all England needed to do was to sit tight and wait for better times.

Consequently, when a Parliamentary election again came due in 1929, the Conservatives used the slogans: "Safety First!" and "Trust Baldwin!" Little difference was apparent in the platforms of the Liberals and Laborites; for the former boldly promised to abolish unemployment in a year's time by a huge loan to be spent on public works, such as roads and housing. Lloyd George's unkept promises of the past, however, as well as the charges of corruption that had been made against his postwar ministry, were too well remembered, and the Liberals won less than one tenth of the seats. The Conservatives came through fairly well, with about 260 seats; but Labor outnumbered them, with over 285.

As a result, Ramsay MacDonald began his second Labor ministry (1929–1931) under much the same circumstances as his first. Again Labor could form a ministry only with the support of the Liberal "rump," as it had no real majority in the Commons. Again a Labor ministry was forced to follow a cautious course because of this insecure majority. Again it was to accomplish more in foreign affairs than at home.

At an international conference at the Hague in 1929, arrangements were made for easing somewhat the reparation burden on Germany. Under the chairmanship of another American, Owen D. Young, a commission evolved a second plan for the reparation payments, to supersede the Dawes Plan, which had proved inadequate in some ways. Snowden, again Chancellor of the Exchequer, insisted that the British share in the payments be increased in the new scheme; but, although he received some concessions, basically the Young Plan was little changed. At the Hague, also, MacDonald, with the cooperation of Briand and Stresemann, who had worked with Chamberlain at Locarno, effected a compromise to facilitate the removal of the Allied troops from the Rhine region, where they had been since 1918.

# Between the Wars

MacDonald also turned again toward Russia. Lenin, the founder of the new Russia, had died some years before, but his work was continued under the virtual dictatorship of Stalin. England had had no official connection with Russia for three years, because of alleged communist agitation; but MacDonald re-established friendly relations.

Another step in the limitation of armaments was attempted at a conference of the naval powers at London in 1930. Only partial success attended this effort to extend the 5–5–3 ratio established for battleships at the Washington Conference. Great Britain, the United States, and Japan agreed to accept that same ratio for many smaller forms of naval craft. The special interests of France and Italy, however,—particularly the French desire for greater strength in the Mediterranean, and Italy's insistence upon parity with France,—prevented further extension of this principle. The conference met failure in other respects, especially in regard to submarines. The latter were considered far more desirable by the smaller naval powers than by the larger, because of the damage they could inflict at relatively low expense. The parity of the United States with Britain was recognized in all classes of warships as well as in the great battleships. Arrangements were made for another conference in 1935.

These various efforts in behalf of better understanding among the nations did not materially change the ominous aspect of the world situation. The spread of Russian communism was still actively feared in many quarters, while its antithesis, Fascist dictatorships on the Italian model, were soon to spread with increased momentum. Revolution had been rearing its head in this postwar decade from South America to Greece, although not as frequently as in the similar Metternich era. In 1931, at the close of the MacDonald ministry, Spain revolted against her monarchy; but the new republic found difficulty in retaining control as the opposing forces of communism and Fascism swept over this land along with most of the rest of Europe. Meanwhile Japan threatened world peace by aggressive and successful moves against China and defied the protests of the League and the powers against this dismemberment of China.

Unemployment presented an insuperable snag to this second Labor ministry as to its predecessors. Snowden believed firmly in a balanced budget and other orthodox financial ideas. In his opinion, increased taxation was the only way to balance the budget. Furthermore, he made it clear that the government had no surplus for additional social legislation. As a result of his stand for sound finances, friction rapidly increased within the ranks of the Labor party. The more conservative elements, including MacDonald, supported Snowden, while the more radical—called by their enemies "the wild men of the Clyde," because their leaders represented Glasgow constituencies—threatened revolt from the party. MacDonald, formerly one of the leading lights of the old Independent Labor party, felt compelled to resign his membership.

Meanwhile, by 1931, after a period of relative improvement in economic conditions, England was feeling the effects of the world-wide "economic blizzard" which had spread rapidly after the crash of securities in the United States in the autumn of 1929. The world was so closely linked together economically that the depression was contagious. Revenues in England continuing to decline, Snowden admitted that the budget for 1931 could not be balanced. The danger was met temporarily by making three quarters of the income tax payable in January and one quarter in July; but even with revenue thus anticipated, the deficit would be enormous by 1932. Snowden and MacDonald were prepared to insist upon immediate drastic economies as the only way out of the situation; but before they had time to make them, the storm broke. The Bank of England was in danger of failure, in spite of hurried loans from New York and Paris bankers, because of heavy withdrawals of gold in exchange for currency. This financial threat, along with the precarious state of the budget, made a crisis of the first magnitude in August, 1931.

MacDonald and Snowden, agreeing that the prime consideration was the saving of the Bank of England and the pound sterling, prepared to make a drastic cut in unemployment insurance. This had been advised by a Parliamentary committee appointed a few weeks earlier, just before the adjournment of Parliament, to investigate ways of reducing governmental expenditures. At this juncture there came word from the bankers that the further essential financial aid of some eight million pounds would not be forthcoming unless the cabinet could reduce expenditures to meet prospective income. The majority of the cabinet, however, although desiring economies, refused to sacrifice the dole. The trade unions made it evident that they too opposed such a measure, as did also the majority of the Labor members of the Commons, which was not in session during the emergency. Obviously, if he followed British party precedents, MacDonald could not continue in office when most of his party were against him.

Time pressed. MacDonald parleyed with Liberal and Conservative leaders to find some way out of the impasse. King George, it was reported, used his influence to bring about a solution. An unusual one was found. MacDonald resigned as Labor's prime minister, only to be immediately recommissioned by the king to deal with the emergency as prime minister of a so-called "National government."

ND WALES

# Between the Wars

Some considered this a departure from precedent, since MacDonald, although deposed by his party, remained as prime minister. King or no king, however, MacDonald could not have remained in power had he not retained a majority in the Commons. The new cabinet, virtually a coalition, had ten members, of whom four, including the prime minister, had been in the previous ministry; four, including Baldwin, were Conservatives; and two were Liberals.

The new government at once set to work. When Parliament reconvened, it gave the ministry a vote of confidence of 311 against 251. The bulk of the support was Conservative; thus MacDonald kept his position "on the strength of his enemies" rather than on that of his erstwhile friends. A 10 per cent cut in unemployment insurance was effected; drastic cuts were made in the salaries of all servants of the crown, from cabinet ministers, judges, and admirals to schoolteachers, policemen, and bluejackets. By October the budget was balanced. Yet day by day the ominous depression of the pound sterling in foreign exchange continued. Finally, to prevent bankruptcy, the government "went off the gold standard"; in other words, it suspended the customary regulation that the Bank of England redeem, upon demand, its paper money with gold. In order to secure the approval of the country for this drastic step and to gain a free hand in applying other remedies, the National government appealed to the country.

This electoral campaign of 1931 proved one of the most exciting in British political annals. On the side of the government were Mac-Donald, with his few loyal followers from the Labor party, together with the Conservatives under Baldwin, urging, as always, tariffs as the remedy. Some Liberals, moreover, under Sir John Simon, head of the 1926 commission to India and a member of the existing ministry, were prepared to swallow the prospective tariffs in their support of the government. Other Liberals, under Sir Herbert Samuel, another cabinet member, and chairman in 1925 of the commission on the mining industry, likewise supported the National government, although vehemently opposed to protection. MacDonald, a lifelong socialist, was thus appealing to the electorate, not as the chieftain of the Labor party which had twice put him in power and the bulk of whose members now repudiated him, but as the head of a coalition of which the Tories were the mainstay. Against the government was the rump of the Liberal party, under Lloyd George, and, more important, the Labor party itself, under its new leader Arthur Henderson. The panic that had swept over England in 1924 because of the Zinoviev letter was as nothing to the financial fear which now gripped the heart of nearly every English man and woman who had saved a pound or two ahead. MacDonald shouted to them that their money would be worth nothing if Labor should win, and dramatically waved German paper money with a face value of millions of marks which had shrunk to the buying value of a few pennies in the recent drastic inflation of that currency. In vain did the trade-unionists and the greater part of the Labor membership of the Commons denounce as absurd such prophecies of disaster and call the election a Tory trick to frighten people. In vain did they charge that bankers in the United States were dictating British policies. The scare succeeded far better than the one of 1924, for the coalition was given an overwhelming vote of confidence. The Conservatives triumphed to the extent of 470 seats, more than three quarters of the total number. The National Liberals (followers of Simon and Samuel) and MacDonald's still loyal following of National Laborites added another seventy-odd government seats in the Commons, while in opposition were left only 52 Laborites and the four Liberal members of Lloyd George's own family: himself, his son, his daughter, and his son-in-law. Wales had stood by its "wizard" when no other part of Britain would.

Thus it looked as if the Labor party had collapsed and all the painful work of years had been lost. Yet a third of adult Britain had voted for Labor candidates. The reason that this 30 per cent of the electorate had gained less than 9 per cent of the seats in the Commons was that in most constituencies the candidate with the most votes was elected whether he received a majority of the votes cast or merely a plurality or even one more vote than those the runner-up received.

Whether MacDonald had proved a traitor to his cause, as this dissenting third of Britain seemed to feel, or whether he and Snowden had shown wisdom and genuine patriotism in the crisis remained a debatable point. Yet if MacDonald had defied the angry "old Lady of Threadneedle Street," the Bank of England, to do her worst, the economic ills of England would probably have been intensified, commercial credit would have been shattered, and banks and factories would have closed their doors.

MacDonald remained prime minister, with a coalition cabinet in which were Neville Chamberlain at the Exchequer. Baldwin as Lord Privy Seal, Simon as Foreign Secretary, and Samuel as Home Secretary. Immediately they set to work on the four major questions listed by MacDonald for first consideration: tariffs, reparations, war debts, and disarmament.

At last, after the long discussions of the recent years, the insistent Conservative clamor for protective tariffs was to succeed. MacDonald had no choice; for evidently the majority felt that England must abandon free trade if she was to remain a capitalistic nation. Consequently, within one year the work of Huskisson, Peel, Cobden, and Bright was reversed, and a tariff wall, though a low one, was constructed. At first it was not intended to affect most foodstuffs; but the Conservatives, traditionally the spokesmen of the agricultural interests, and the Imperial Economic Conference at Ottawa (see page 939) saw that it did so. Existing commercial agreements with certain countries, such as Denmark and the Argentine, made it difficult to tax all food imports, but various ways of accomplishing this were found. Quotas, for instance, were adopted, and in the case of the cattle industry direct bounties were granted in 1934 to home producers.

The abandonment of free trade was, on the whole, popular. The "Simonite" Liberals accepted it quietly, but the "Samuelite" Liberals were not pleased. They decided to retain their seats in the cabinet, but to oppose protection—a curious breach in the traditional English constitutional practice of cabinet responsibility. In fact, one prominent newspaper went so far as to declare that MacDonald had now broken up the cabinet system as well as the party system. Both systems, however, survived these episodes unscathed. Eventually, with the acceptance of the Ottawa pacts and the taxation of food, four Samuelite Liberals resigned from the cabinet. With the Simonite Liberals supporting the government, the Samuelites thus largely in opposition, and the Lloyd George family in a huddle in the corner, the speedy demise of the old Liberal party was anticipated.

The reparations assessed against Germany at Versailles (see page 896), together with the war debts, particularly the amounts that the Allies had borrowed from the United States during the conflict, were logically linked together in the British view. If Germany could not pay the Allies what she owed, then, Britain and her allies felt, it was understandable if they did not pay the United States. Because of the world-wide depression, President Hoover, of the United States, declared a year's moratorium, or suspension, on reparation and war-debt payments; and at the close of that year (1932) the powers met at Lausanne to revise the Young Plan, its provisions being no longer feasible under the current economic conditions. This meeting resulted in the virtual cancellation of reparations, upon certain lump-sum payments from Germany. The Allies now optimistically expected that the United States would cancel the war debts, since Germany was not paying the reparations. Furthermore, if the Allies were to pay the Americans, they presumably would have to ship more goods to the United States than they would take in return; and this was extremely difficult unless the latter lowered her tariffs or the Allies decreased their purchases of American goods, both of which measures would be injurious to the trade of the United States. The Americans, however, would not cancel the war debts; the laconic President Coolidge had once expressed their sentiments in remarking of the Allies, "They hired the money, didn't they?" When this attitude became obvious, the British, with pride in their financial past, paid the usual installment, but stated that it was to be considered not as a payment of interest but as a reduction of the principal of the debt. The French had already ceased to make payments. After another failure to come to terms with the United States, Britain twice paid a relatively small sum, purely as a "token payment," or an acknowledgment that she recognized the debt. Thereafter the National government decided to cease payments altogether. Meanwhile all the other foreign debtors of the United States, except Finland, had done likewise.

The government made little headway in the matter of naval and military disarmament. The naval question mainly concerned relations between England, the United States, and Japan in the Pacific. British and American admirals continued to hold radically different views in the matter of cruisers: the former wanted many small ones to guard England's far-flung responsibilities, while the latter, having few overseas bases, wanted a few large ones with wider cruising radius. Since a compromise of sorts had been reached on this point at London, the chief source of dispute was now the Japanese insistence on the abrogation of the 5–5–3 ratio among the three powers as determined at Washington. Britain, fairly content with this ratio, tended to side with the United States in favor of its retention, but was more inclined to find some middle ground acceptable to Japanese pride. This proved impossible, as neither the United States nor Japan was willing to compromise; and eventually Japan denounced the Washington treaty, which she considered humiliating to her national dignity. In the naval conference held in 1935 at London, Japan refused to budge an inch in her demand for equality, while the United States was equally insistent in her desire for larger ships. The Japanese abandoned the conference in disgust, leaving England, France, and the United States to sign a treaty of a sort. Practically all that this treaty achieved was to leave the maximum displacement of battleships at thirty-five thousand tons and to provide for the exchange of naval information among the three signatories, any one of whom was left at liberty to build as many battleships or submarines as seemed desirable.

No progress was made in disarmament on land. Germany had weathered the postwar chaos, we recall, with a republic which, after its first years, was headed by the steady old general Hindenburg. In 1933 she came under the dictatorship of Adolf Hitler. An Austrian by birth but an ex-corporal in the German army, Hitler headed the

# Between the Wars

National Socialist German Labor party, called Nazi for short. The German Nazis, or Fascists, in many respects resembled Mussolini's followers, since in both Italy and Germany the new dictatorships represented an avowed determination on the one hand to hold in check the great capitalists and on the other to blot out revolutionary socialism. Both, moreover, were violently nationalistic. Taking complete control of Germany in 1933, the Nazis focused popular interest in that country against Marxian socialists, Jews, and the Versailles "Dictate," as they chose to call the treaty. Germany was increasingly incensed at the limitations imposed upon her while her former enemies, who had indicated at Versailles a willingness to disarm, had failed to reduce their forces. In 1933 she withdrew from the League of Nations and proceeded toward rearmament. Before long, Hitler's proposed air program was causing concern in many quarters, while the rumors of his plan for general rearmament grew increasingly ominous. Hitler also worried the other powers by his apparent designs upon the independence of Austria; for her union with Germany would greatly strengthen his hand. Austrian political troubles, which had been acute for some time, with one faction favoring the Nazi idea and another as strenuously opposing it, came to a climax in the summer of 1934 with the assassination of the anti-Nazi Austrian chancellor. Finally, in March, 1935, Hitler, probably encouraged by the return of the Saar region to Germany as the result of a plebiscite, openly repudiated the Versailles treaty by announcing the rearmament of his country.

The British government had long been disturbed by the situation on the Continent, particularly by this prospect of German rearmament. In fact, Baldwin, during MacDonald's absence in Canada the preceding summer, had referred significantly to the Rhine, rather than the Channel or the North Sea, as England's first line of defense. After more of such propaganda for better protection of England, the ministry, early in 1935, announced to the House of Commons a new policy calling for an increase of about 40 per cent in England's defenses. This came some ten days before the official repudiation, by Hitler, of the arms clauses of the Versailles treaty, and was undoubtedly the result of rumors that that step was pending. The air force, in particular, was to be greatly enlarged; for England was visualizing more and more the dangers from the air, which threatened her formerly secure insular position. England had done more, probably, than any other European power since the war for the cause of disarmament and had kept her own forces at a relatively low level; this was the sequel.

England, however, was not showing a definitely hostile attitude toward Germany, although she protested against Hitler's arms proclamation and attended the conference at Stresa, Italy, in April, 1935, with France and Italy. There the three powers discussed the situation created by Hitler's declaration, but abstained from any drastic measures. England made few commitments at the conference. Three months later, apparently without consulting France, she entered into a naval understanding with Germany which brushed aside one more of the Versailles limitations. By this agreement, Germany was to be free to build ships as she chose, provided that she built up to only 35 per cent of the British strength. Such a percentage would virtually put Germany on an equality with France on the seas.

Meanwhile the prestige of the National government, now in its fourth year, was somewhat diminished. It might or it might not have saved the country in 1931, but that year was in the background. It had stimulated business to a certain extent by fiscal reform and had brightened the prospects of agriculture by direct governmental intervention and subsidy. Nevertheless, the "depressed areas" remained: shipping, shipbuilding, steel, coal, and cotton showed little improvement. To aid these industries, the government was planning to spend two million pounds; but little could be accomplished by a sum of that size. Already the Cunard–White Star Line, recently formed by a merger of the two famous companies, was building a ship of maximum size; but whether it would be profitable or not was another question. With another election legally due not later than 1936, the Labor party began to show signs of life. At the party conference its more radical members made an effort to commit it to a frontal attack upon the House of Lords. The more conservative majority voted that down, but pledged the party to the nationalization of banking, transportation, and certain key industries. The National coalition also prepared to go to the country. Although its Liberal and Labor membership had become insignificant, it refused, for strategic reasons, to admit this and continued to urge that the domestic crisis required a coalition in which all patriotic Britons should stand shoulder to shoulder against a socialistic Labor party.

There now intervened the silver jubilee of King George, a social event not without political importance. Celebrated throughout the British world, it was a manifestation of national unity of thought and feeling. Inevitably the occasion recalled Queen Victoria's two great jubilees; but this twenty-fifth anniversary of the accession of the queen's popular grandson was celebrated in different spirit. There was no pride of conquest nor dream of dominion, but rather a sense of thanksgiving for the traditions of freedom in the British world and for the devotion to duty manifested by a king who had led Britons through the trials of the war and the hard days of the peace. The jubilee, together with a slight decline in unemployment and a general improvement in the economic situation, created an atmosphere so favorable to the National government that it considered calling the general election at that time. This was not done; but there was a cabinet shuffle in which MacDonald, exhausted and ill, resigned to take a subordinate position in the cabinet, and Baldwin for the third time became, in June, 1935, England's prime minister.

As this was happening the skies grew dark. An international crisis, which had been hanging fire for some months, became so serious that not only England but the whole British world was once more faced with imminent danger of war. Before considering this ominous threat we shall review briefly, as we have the home situation, the years between the wars in greater Britain beyond the seas.

Two beasts, the lion and the unicorn, are represented on the royal standard as upholders of the British crown. The lion, on the one hand, typifies physical might and power, while the unicorn, on the other, may be called a symbol of strength founded rather upon gentleness. The empire as it evolved after the First World War may be said in certain aspects to partake of both characteristics; for while the effect of self-determination, as preached at Versailles, was steadily in the direction of the unicorn, the lion was still far from dead.

During the war the British had promised to introduce self-governing institutions in India. The Government of India Act, passed in 1919, created a legislature for all British India, though not for the protected native states. There was a lower house with fairly high financial requirements for electors, and an upper house with much higher requirements. The latter body was carefully safeguarded from any excess of democratic zeal: of its sixty members, twenty-seven were nominated by the viceroy, and it remained within the power of the viceroy to issue any ordinance which he might deem necessary for the safety of India. A novel feature of the new government was the "dyarchy" (the word means "double government"). This was a constitutional gadget which applied only to the eight provinces of British India. In accordance with this, certain governmental functions, such as education, sanitation, and forestry, were "transferred," that is, placed under officials who held office at the will of the elected legislators; while other functions, such as the judiciary and finance, were "reserved," or left under the control of members of the civil service responsible only to the British officials. In short, a degree of responsible government was now allotted to the Indian provinces, but the degree was limited. The new scheme was to be tried out for a period of ten years, after which the British promised to consider further steps in the way of self-government.

Mohandas Gandhi, the "Mahatma" (or Holy One), was one of the most troublesome characters in the history of the empire, although by many he was considered a saint. For years he was to be a thorn in the flesh of the perplexed rulers of British India. Gandhi, a high-caste Hindu, studied law in England and practiced in South Africa (see page 730), where the treatment of his fellow Indians distressed him greatly. He tried to improve their condition by the same methods with which he was later to plague the British officials in India. During the Boer War he did some excellent work in organizing a Red Cross unit. Returning to India in 1914, he helped to raise recruits for the British army during the First World War; for, although a Nationalist, he was then friendly to the British "raj." In time, however, he was antagonized by the harsh treatment meted out to his fellow Nationalists, and in 1920 he put himself at the head of the movement for "swaraj," or home rule. He advocated a policy of passive resistance to combat British authority—the same method he had tried in South Africa. He urged his followers never to engage in violence under any circumstances, but to show their disapproval of British control by educating their own children, by submitting their disputes to their own law courts only, by buying no British goods, and by having nothing to do with the strangers within their gates. In particular, Gandhi encouraged "swadeshi," a movement which, in opposition to modern industrialism, urged the use of handmade goods, such as homespun cloth, as a protest against the manufactured articles of the British. Consequently Gandhi taught the Indians to resurrect their spinning wheels and to make their own cloth. If he had succeeded in uniting the Indians in this non-co-operation, Britain would indeed have been hurt in a vulnerable spot, the Indian market.

Gandhi taught nonviolence; but his disciples made bonfires of British cloth, and the Mahatma was put in jail. As this happened insurrections broke out at Amritsar and Delhi. In the former city a British general ordered shot down, without warning, several hundred persons in a mob which had gathered in defiance of prohibitions. Thus was the growth of Indian nationalism accelerated. Gandhi, released from jail, became practically dictator of the Indian Nationalist Congress; but his followers continued to find difficulty in living up to his precepts, and they beat a number of policemen to death. The Mahatma, in humiliation, suspended the non-co-operative campaign, but the government of India sentenced him anew to jail.

For a short time it seemed as though India might pass through the ten-year experimental period without further outbreaks. The Mos-

ems, nearly one quarter of the entire population, did not take kindly
to swaraj, and the Hindus, despite their leader's admonitions, were
not altogether disinclined to co-operate in executing the new reforms.
The first elections to the new legislature returned a majority of
moderates, but those in 1924 showed an increase in radical strength.
The Swarajists who rejected the Mahatma's advice to refrain from
voting had a plurality in the lower house, and they demanded immediate home rule, except in regard to the army, the navy, and
foreign affairs. The British would have none of this, and in revenge
the Indian assembly threw out the budget for India. Thereupon
the viceroy, in accordance with the 1919 act, certified that a state of
danger existed; and the budget was put into effect without legislative
approval.

India became progressively more restive during 1926–1928, and
the British cabinet, aware that changes would soon be due in the
Indian constitution, sent out a Parliamentary commission headed by
Sir John Simon, the leader of the National Liberals, to report upon
the affairs of India. The commission was composed entirely of Englishmen, and, though this was natural enough in an investigation on
behalf of Parliament, the Indians were much affronted. They decided
to boycott the commission, and wherever it went it was greeted by
cries of "Go back, Simon!" Its findings were delayed. At this
time Gandhi won back his old supremacy among his people by an
act which combined religious faith and political daring. In 1929 the
viceroy, Lord Irwin, asserted that, regardless of the Simon report,
Britain was pledged ultimately to grant dominion status to India.
Gandhi thereupon offered to cease civil disobedience and non-co-
operation provided that the salt tax were halved, political prisoners
released, and the salaries of British civil servants in India slashed.
When these conditions were refused, he began a "march to the sea."
This was a religious pilgrimage to break the law publicly by obtaining salt, a government monopoly, without paying for it. It was a long
journey, taken on foot in short stages; and the entire Western world
as well as India watched the Mahatma's progress. The sea was at last
reached; the salt scooped up; the law defied. The Mahatma then
advocated the seizure of the salt works; and his followers, rushing
upon the forbidden salt, were struck down by the police.

The Simon commission finally reported in favor of a further decentralization of India, making it a federation of states. Special
exceptions were made of Burma, which was to be detached from India
altogether, and of the North-West Frontier Province, which was to remain under more direct British control. Responsible government was
to be introduced into the separate Indian provinces, but it was not

to apply to the All-India legislature meeting at Delhi. The federation was to be open to the native states, should they care to join. This report was unsatisfactory to the Indian Nationalists, who were determined to secure either complete independence or, at the least, dominion status. Riots and cloth-burning began again. Gandhi, once more released (he was always being sent to prison or being released), had a long and futile conference with the viceroy.

Next, round-table conferences were proposed at which native princes, Hindus, Moslems, and Englishmen might sit together in London, there to iron out their differences. To the second, after much persuasion, came Gandhi, wearing only a loincloth, and accompanied by several goats to provide his diet of fresh milk. The conferences met in 1930 and 1931, in the midst of the political and financial crises in Britain. Nothing was accomplished. The British were willing to make further compromises, suggesting responsible government for the All-India legislature provided there were a number of safeguards in respect to finance, the army, and international relations. Hindus and Moslems alike objected to these safeguards. The Indians quarreled with one another over the basis of representation, the Moslem minority insisting that representation be based on religious belief, and the Hindus standing fast for electoral districts on the basis of population. Over this old bone of contention the Moslems now found unexpected allies in the lowest-caste Hindus, the "untouchables," some five millions of outcasts and scavengers, who, fearing the treatment that they might receive from the high Brahman caste of their own religion, joined with the Moslems in demanding representation on the basis of creed. The British, finding the Indians unable to agree, decided to end the farce, and promised to assume responsibility themselves for the new constitution.

Meanwhile, during Gandhi's absence, a "Red Shirt" movement arose among Moslems for the nonpayment of taxes. Camps were established, parades were held, and finally force was necessary to quell these "Red Shirts." In the Central Provinces the Indian Nationalist Congress assumed the right to say what, if any, rent should be paid to landlords. Further imprisonments followed. In Bengal two young girls murdered a British official, and the British found it necessary to suspend all legal rights there. On his return Gandhi sought an interview with the viceroy, the Earl of Willingdon, who refused to discuss his actions with the Mahatma because the latter was the head of a nonconstitutional body, the Indian Nationalist Congress. Consequently Gandhi declared the truce with the British at an end and renewed the civil-disobedience campaign, whereupon he was once more clapped in jail. The government's firmness cowed

he agitators, and the violence which had marked Irwin's viceroyalty
vas much less in evidence under Willingdon.

The British now proceeded to draw up their own form of government for India on the basis of a legislature providing for representa-
ion according to religious belief. Gandhi maintained that this was
in insult to the untouchables, since it perpetuated caste lines; and
o show his disapproval he began to fast to death. The leaner he grew
he more worried grew public opinion in India. To prevent his death
f possible, a hurried compromise was effected which accepted communal representation in modified form.

The new British plan finally emerged definitely in 1934. Following the idea suggested at the round-table conference, it provided for
an Indian federation with responsible government in both central
and provincial legislatures, with safeguards. In other words, England presented India with the name of responsible government, but
retained in large measure the substance of power—control of finance,
the army, international relations. Altogether, this was something
quite different from dominion status. Nevertheless, the new Government of India Act, passed in 1935, seemed a long step forward. It
ended the ingenious but impractical experiment of the dyarchy, enlarged the provincial electorate, gave really responsible government
to the provinces (except for certain emergency police powers left in
the hands of the governors), opened the door for the native states to
enter the federation, and increased very decidedly the power of the
central legislature at the expense of that of the viceroy. No longer
might the viceroy in effect control the upper house by nomination;
for virtually all its members were now chosen by the princes or by
the provincial legislatures, as in the case of the lower house.

The constitution apparently pleased few. The majority of Indians
denounced it bitterly, but they would probably have received in that
way any British constitution for India. The British Labor party also
was against it for its failure to realize even approximately Lord
Irwin's promise of eventual dominion status. On the other hand,
from the Conservative view, the autonomous powers implied in dominion status were proving risky enough even in Ireland and South
Africa, where the controlling element consisted of white men rather
than brown; what such self-government might mean if granted to
the hostile and divided peoples of India was not pleasant to imagine.
The Conservatives felt that the constitution, even as it was, granted
too much and did not take into sufficient account the complicated
racial and religious differences, deep-rooted and fundamental in
India, nor the poverty and ignorance of the masses. In fact, Baldwin
had to use all his prestige and personal popularity and to warn, "We

# A History of England and the British Empire

shall lose India within two generations unless these reforms are passed," in order to secure the passage of the bill by Parliament. The responsibility of initiating the constitution was given in 1935 to the new viceroy, the Marquess of Linlithgow, an able and distinguished authority on India and Indian life, who had played an active part in the commission responsible for the constitution.

"His Majesty's Government view with favour the establishment in Palestine of a national home for the Jewish people"—thus declared the British government in 1917. For such a stand Balfour, the former prominent Irish Secretary and prime minister (1902–1905), was largely responsible. He was at the time Foreign Secretary, after having previously held the Admiralty post as Churchill's successor. Two years later Great Britain officially assumed the responsibility for Palestine as mandatory power, or trustee, for the League of Nations.

Palestine was designated as a Class A mandate, that is, one that would probably in course of time be in a condition to be allowed independence (see page 893); but although the country became sufficiently prosperous to warrant self-government, other factors stood in the way. Enormous sums of money were poured into it from Jewish sources, and Jerusalem prospered as never before in its history. Tel Aviv, a Jewish city, grew up near Haifa, on the Mediterranean; orange groves dotted the landscape; a university was opened; huge electric works in the Jordan valley supplied light and power; and oil was pumped six hundred miles through the desert. These facts, however, did not settle deep and nasty racial antipathies. The Arabs, outnumbering the Jews by more than three to one, considered Palestine theirs, while the Jews, basing their claims on more ancient history and on the British promise of 1917, believed it belonged to them. The British, trying to steer an even course between these racial hatreds, pleased neither side.

Self-governing institutions consequently were not established because Arab and Jewish leaders refused to co-operate. England made the effort more than once, and was rebuffed, the Arabs wanting representation on the basis of population, and the Jews, since they were a decided minority, holding out for racial equality. When opportunity offered, as occasionally it did, for a massacre of their enemies, the Arabs were quick to take advantage of it. When punished by British soldiers or the police, they complained bitterly to the League of Nations of British tyranny, while the Jews loudly lamented the failure of the British to protect them on such occasions.

The Jewish inhabitants, taking naturally to politics, divided into three groups, one stanchly orthodox and interested in the Hebraic revival along Old Testament lines; another ultramodern, with a strong socialistic slant; and the third with Fascist tendencies. The Arabs stood aloof. The British High Commissioner, compelled to govern through a nominated council, was unable to please all factions. If the tariff was lowered in order to encourage the importation of building materials, the Arabs groaned about the land tax. If the land tax was reduced to aid the Arab farmers, the Jews complained about discrimination; and all this might be done in four languages, Hebrew, Yiddish, Arabic, and English. Yet probably there should have been enough wealth for all: the climate was fair; irrigation did wonders with the soil; every immigrant had to bring with him a considerable sum of money, which meant an abundance of capital; and the sacred places of the Bible were visited yearly by thousands of pilgrims with money to spend. Yet had the British withdrawn, the Arabs would have driven the Jews into the sea. Jerusalem was holy ground to Arabs as well as to Jews and Christians, and it was Arab efforts, in part at least, which had wrested it from the Turks during the war; on that account the Arabs felt all the more strongly that the land was theirs. Furthermore, they despised the Jews on racial grounds and feared them for economic reasons. The showing made by England's high commissioners was, on the whole, most creditable. A glare of publicity had been thrown upon Palestine by the Jewish press and by the Jews of all countries; yet no major mistake could be laid at the door of the British save perhaps the original promise to make a Jewish home on what had become Moslem land.

A steadily increasing grievance of the Jews was the British restriction on their immigration into Palestine. In 1930 England virtually suspended it altogether when she canceled twenty-four hundred immigration permits because of Jewish discrimination against landless Arabs. The German persecution of the Jews after Hitler became dictator led the British to lower their restrictions temporarily, so that thousands of exiled German Jews rushed as quickly as they were provided with funds to this land, which was neither Jewish nor Arab nor British. The more that came, the more trouble the Arabs raised. A Royal Commission in 1937 was futile. As war approached in 1939, Britain severely restricted immigration.

Not only in Palestine but in other Arab lands there was smoldering discontent between the world wars. An aroused spirit of nationalism and an increasing determination to form one great independent Arab state kept these lands and peoples restless. Palestine, heavily fortified by Britain, was in too strategic a position in the eastern Mediterranean for the British to feel that they could loosen their hold, but the more purely Arab mandate of Iraq, in Mesopotamia, was allowed a freer status. Whereas one third of the 1,200,000 inhabitants of Palestine were non-Moslems, all but 8 per cent of the 2,800,000 in Iraq were Mohammedans, chiefly Arabs, so that the troublesome question of the Jews was not present here. Nevertheless there was constant friction, with occasional armed outbreaks. The British, at the outset, had inclined to keep a considerable part of the control in their own hands. In 1921 Britain agreed to the establishing of a limited constitutional monarchy with a parliament, and with Feisal, who had fought under Allenby and Lawrence (see page 884) as king. Feisal's father, supposedly an Arab descendant of the Prophet, was for a short time king of Hejaz, in Arabia. Iraq prospered under this change, and the new government made such progress that in 1932, at Britain's recommendation, the mandate was ended, and Iraq was admitted as a member of the League of Nations. She thus became a nominally independent state, although Britain still maintained an air force there and exercised a certain control over the new nation's foreign relations.

The British likewise granted at least nominal independence to Egypt. In 1915 Britain had declared a protectorate over Egypt in place of the previous "temporary occupation" (see page 719). The Egyptians were not asked to fight against Germany; but they were urged to enlist in labor battalions, despite the protests of Egyptian Nationalists. Their leader, Zaghlul Pasha, hastened to Versailles in 1919; but the "Big Three" paid no more attention to his pleas than to those of the other disregarded nationalists in Persia, Ireland, or Korea. He returned home such a bitter enemy of England that he was exiled. Thereupon trains were derailed and rioting broke out. A royal commission was sent to Egypt under Lord Milner, whose stiff manner as a high commissioner had irritated South Africa before the Boer War, and who, as a leading Conservative, had been a member of the inner circle of the War Cabinet and a delegate at Versailles. The commission's reception was similar to that given the Simon Commission in India. Nevertheless, Lord Milner got in touch with Zaghlul and drew up a treaty which provided for Egyptian independence, with four reservations: British troops were to remain in Egypt to guard imperial communications; the Egyptians were to appoint English financial and judicial advisers; England was to retain the right of re-entry to protect foreigners; and the Anglo-Egyptian Sudan was to be left for further negotiations. The treaty was unpopular in both countries; and when England attempted to strengthen these four qualifications by further definition, Zaghlul induced Egypt to reject it. Once more he departed into exile, to the accompaniment of re-

# Between the Wars

ewed rioting. Finally, in 1922, England declared Egypt an independent country. Fuad, the Khedive, was promoted to be king, "the
first sovereign ruler of Egypt since Cleopatra." England clung to
qualifying reservations, however, in regard to defense, the rights of
foreigners, and the Sudan. Instead of "responsible government with
safeguards," as in India, the slogan here was "independence with
reservations."

Under Fuad, Zaghlul returned as prime minister of Egypt. He had
no intention of allowing British troops to stay permanently in Cairo
nor of surrendering Egyptian claims to the Sudan. The British asserted that their line of communications with the Sudan must be kept
open, and that it was impossible to substitute the internationalized
canal zone for Cairo as a station for their troops. As for the Sudan,
Britain made it clear that she would never agree to abandon either
the British capital invested in irrigation projects there or the natives
under her protection; for British officials were dubious regarding the
ability of the Egyptians to control the warlike Sudanese tribesmen.

Thus matters stood in 1924 when Sir Lee Stack, the governor-
general of the Sudan, was murdered in the streets of Cairo. The
British promptly dispatched an ultimatum more drastic than that
sent by Austria to Serbia in 1914. Not only must a large indemnity
be paid and all Egyptian troops withdrawn from the Sudan, but in
case of noncompliance England threatened to cut off Egypt's water
supply. Egypt yielded, and for four years there was comparative
peace. In 1928, however, England once more intervened, sent warships to Alexandria, and threatened a reoccupation unless certain
distasteful bills were withdrawn from the Egyptian legislature. A
year later came a new treaty, providing for an alliance between England and Egypt. In this the British agreed to withdraw their soldiers
to the neighborhood of the Suez Canal, and the Egyptians promised
to employ only English advisers in the training of their troops. Again
the Egyptian Nationalists rejected the olive branch. Meanwhile a
conservative revolution was taking place in Egypt, a new constitution being adopted with more power given to the king.

King Fuad was generally suspected of playing the political game
as the friend of England. Whether he did or not, antiforeign and,
particularly, anti-Christian agitation continued. Although Sir Austen
Chamberlain, as Foreign Secretary, stated in 1927 that Britain had
made her last concessions, three years later the MacDonald government made more. England, it seemed, asserted only a form of Monroe Doctrine over Egypt, and, although British troops stayed within
striking distance of Cairo, there was no military occupation. In the
Sudan a joint agreement regulated the use of the Nile waters.

In 1936 this theory could not well be sustained. The Ethiopia war (see page 941) made the Egyptian situation so ominous tha British troops were rushed to Egypt, and as this happened the Egyp tians elected a large Nationalist majority to their legislature. Kin Fuad died; his successor was his inexperienced young son, and th hopes of the Nationalists rose high. They found the British concilia tory. A treaty was signed by which Britain, in return for the accept ance by Egypt of a British military commission, promised to evacuat Cairo and Alexandria and to station her troops in the Suez Cana zone only. In addition, the Egyptians secured the right to share i the defense and administration of the Sudan.

With one exception, as far as the dominions were concerned, th British lion had retreated so far into the background as to be vir tually invisible. In 1933 Newfoundland fell upon evil days; for th world depression proved a last straw to this island, long a prey t political dissension and to economic hardship. This dominion there fore requested British intervention, and asked to be reduced to th status of a crown colony. A very friendly lion, out of compassion intervened, advanced the much-needed money, and assumed respon sibility for this colony.

Canada, New Zealand, Australia, South Africa, and the Irish Free State meanwhile grew more nationally-minded in the postwar years Aside from the Free State (not yet born), they had sent their own soldiers to the war, paid for their maintenance, signed the peace treaty, and joined the League of Nations as individual states. After 1919, with the exception of New Zealand, which was less nationally-minded than the others, the dominions showed a tendency to follow a line somewhat aloof from British foreign policy.

New Zealand, of all the dominions, showed herself most devoted to the imperial tie. The two islands of this dominion, being relatively small and completely isolated, were more dependent upon the mother-land than the sister dominions. At the Imperial Conference of 1921 New Zealand alone pleaded the cause of closer constitutional unity; and again in 1922, when Lloyd George cabled the dominions for sup-port in his efforts to make Turkey abide by the Treaty of Sèvres, New Zealand alone offered immediate assistance, whereas Canada and South Africa were noncommittal and Australia qualified her provisional support with "if circumstances permit" (see page 909).

Canada showed a greater inclination toward independent action. She established a new imperial precedent when she sent her own min-ister to Washington and received a minister from the United States at Ottawa in exchange. This settling of American diplomatic relations in America was more convenient than dealing through the British Foreign Office at London. Once started, the practice spread: Canada exchanged diplomatic representatives with France and Japan also, and the other dominions followed suit. The premier of Canada publicly affirmed that his country was not bound by the Treaty of Lausanne, made between England and Turkey in 1923, because Canada was not represented at the conference. So great an impression did this make in London that England expressly stated in 1925 that the Locarno pacts did not obligate any of the dominions unless they chose to ratify.

In South Africa the current of popular opinion veered from the British tie in a different spirit; for beneath Canada's attitude of independence there was a very genuine sentiment of loyalty to the crown. In the first postwar election in South Africa the old Boer irreconcilables, headed by General Hertzog, won a plurality of seats in the legislature of the Union. The general was kept out of office only because the ultra-British Unionist party submerged itself in the South African party, composed of moderate Boers friendly to England. This compromise did not last; for Hertzog, still a bitter enemy of England, pleaded with the Boers of the South African party to join his Nationalist party. He also made an agreement with the dominion Labor party by which the two parties, if they had together a majority at the next election, would form a joint ministry, with the understanding that Labor would not insist upon socialism nor the Nationalists upon secession. The coalition won; and in 1924 Hertzog became prime minister, a post which he was to hold for many years. At the time of the Imperial Conference of 1926 the ultimate secession of South Africa from the Commonwealth seemed a possibility. Yet the friendly attitude of England toward dominion ideas at this conference did much to reconcile Hertzog, though his subsequent career still showed a good bit of the old anti-British animus. At that time the Union adopted a flag of its own; and only after terrific protests were raised did it consent to permit a tiny Union Jack, one twenty-seventh of the whole flag, to be incorporated in the design. In other ways South Africa stressed its aloofness: not willing, like Canada or Australia, to use the British seal, it chose one of its own; and it went so far as to amend the wording of its constitution so that it referred to the Union as "a sovereign independent state." In 1935 another evidence of South Africa's nationalistic stand was obvious from the hot dispute with Britain over the three native protectorates of Basutoland, Bechuanaland, and Swaziland. Originally England had planned to let the Union control them; but the anti-Negro policy of the Hertzog government made her reluctant to give up her trusteeship for these black folk. The Union drew the color line sharply, with special discrimination against the Negroes in the mining industry, even establishing separate post offices for white persons and Negroes. In 1934 a British commission reported that the Union government as then constituted was technically not the same as that provided for in the Union constitution and that therefore Great Britain was under no obligation to turn over the protectorates. In 1936, when Italian aggression against Ethiopia threatened the security of the Suez Canal, and England turned her attention to the longer but safer route around the Cape, the Union government offered to extend naval facilities in South Africa, but set the transfer of these protectorates to the dominion as the price for this concession.

The friendly Imperial Conference of 1926, which had tended to tone down Hertzog's anti-British attitude, helped to attach all the dominions more closely to one another and to the mother country. Joseph Chamberlain's earlier efforts to bring closer co-operation between Britain and the dominions had produced few tangible results; but in the First World War the dominion premiers had several times participated in an imperial War Cabinet, we recall. Dominion sensibilities had already been taken into account before the conference was held when the British cabinet established a Secretaryship of State for the Dominions, thus creating a Dominion Office apart from the Colonial. When the conference met, "it refused to lay down a constitution for the empire." On the other hand, for the first time it clearly defined the relations of the dominions and Great Britain. The dominions were, it asserted, together with the mother country, "autonomous communities within the British Empire, equal in status, in no way subordinate one to another in any aspect of their domestic or external affairs, though united by a common allegiance to the Crown, and freely associated as members of the British Commonwealth of Nations." There was nothing new in this definition; for everybody had understood before this that the dominions were practically free. None the less, this formal acknowledgment of complete equality cleared the air of any possible suspicion of British domination and also paved the way for the construction of a true system of co-ordination. The committee on intra-imperial relations indicated in outline how this might be done. Treaties in the future might be signed by all the dominions, by several of them, or by one. All were to be signed in the name of the king, but none were to be negotiated save by the governments concerned. In the dominions the governors-general were no longer to be considered as representatives of the British government but as the personal representatives of the crown. No longer were official communications from the British government to pass through these governors to the dominion govern-

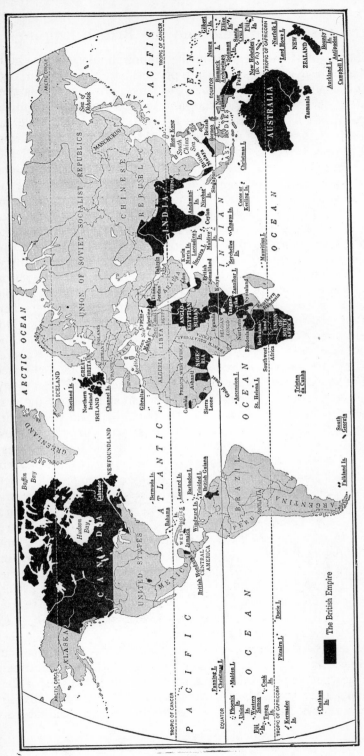

THE BRITISH EMPIRE IN 1937

■ The British Empire

ments, New Zealand alone excepted. Instead, the governments would communicate through recognized semidiplomatic channels provided by the appointment of dominion high commissioners to London and British high commissioners to the dominion capitals. Between the dominions and Great Britain there was thus to be absolute equality, in status if not always in function.

One slight flaw remained in this settlement, the Colonial Laws Validity Act of 1865, which was a statute of the British Parliament and therefore could not be repealed by an imperial conference. This act proclaimed invalid any law passed by a British colony that conflicted with a law passed by the British Parliament. In 1931 Parliament ended this one remaining vestige of imperial authority by the Statute of Westminster, which repealed the law of 1865 and definitely stated that "no act of the British Parliament shall apply to any dominion unless the latter requests it."

The Imperial Economic Conference of 1932, at Ottawa, was intended to be the British answer to the world depression. The more enthusiastic participants looked forward to free trade within the Empire-Commonwealth, but, for the time being, sought reciprocal agreements to lower tariffs within the empire while retaining or raising those against the non-British world. Since most of the dominions had built up industries by protective tariffs, they were unwilling to jeopardize them; but some concessions were made, and a number of intra-imperial trade pacts were concluded. Preferential rates given to British goods were automatically increased by raising dominion tariffs against countries outside the Commonwealth. Britain in turn placed a tariff against foreign wheat and other agricultural products. These advantages were refused to the Irish Free State. Another conference, in 1937, in London, continued these economic discussions.

The Irish Free State, immediately upon her formation in 1922, had shown her distaste for partnership in the Commonwealth by registering her treaty with Britain with the League of Nations, thereby implying that the treaty was not an intra-imperial one but a pact concluded between independent countries. Membership in the League gave the Free State a chance which she sometimes seized to act against British interests. Nevertheless, there was little real friction until 1932, when Cosgrave's government of moderates was defeated in an election and the extremist De Valera became president of the Free State. The oath of allegiance to the king, as stipulated in the Anglo-Irish treaty, now provided a convenient point of attack. Temporarily thwarted by the Irish senate in his efforts to end this hated bit of symbolism, De Valera did succeed in virtually abolishing the office of governor-general. After completely ignoring the representative of the crown, he changed the title to "Seneschal" and nominated an obscure workingman for the post. Another bone of contention was the matter of finances. It had been agreed that while, in return for the acknowledgment of Ulster's rights to a disputed boundary, no part of the British national debt was to be assumed by the Free State, the Free State obligated itself, nevertheless, to pay the land annuities due for money advanced in the past by the British treasury for the purchase of small homesteads (see page 764). Under De Valera the Free State, now Eire, refused to pay these annuities. Great Britain offered to arbitrate, but insisted that the arbitrator be chosen from within the Commonwealth. To this De Valera would not agree. Ireland ceased to pay, and Britain proceeded to raise the money by increasing the British tariff against Ireland, to the distress of the Irish agricultural interests, much of whose income had come from selling dairy products to England. The Irish electorate, however, continued to support De Valera. In 1935 he succeeded in passing a law defining Irish citizenship, which was so drawn as to make it appear that a citizen of Eire was no longer, ipso facto, a British subject. A year later he proposed a new constitution whereby not only would there be no longer a governor-general, but even the constitution would be of that type which "the Irish people would themselves choose if Britain were a million miles away." Ireland became, therefore, the weakest link in the Commonwealth chain, though an essential one since the island lies athwart England's lines of communication. By 1939 the Irish republican army was engaging in bombing outrages, both at home and in England.

Of the dominions, then, Canada, New Zealand, and Australia seemed more attached to the Commonwealth than ever. From time to time there might be grumbling, but their loyalty was vital and deep. A common language, a large share of common blood, and a common devotion to the crown bound them together. To a lesser degree the same was true of South Africa; circumstances would decide whether that dominion stayed in or slipped out of the Commonwealth. Eire, on the other hand, was not unlikely to wash its hands of all British connection at the slightest provocation. Yet under modern conditions, with dominion status giving them what amounted to complete independence and with Britain's might standing between them and possible foreign foes, even these latter countries would probably think twice before they left the empire.

Meanwhile another European war seemed to be drawing England inevitably into its orbit. Baldwin, on assuming the premiership in June, 1935, was immediately confronted with a problem of the utmost delicacy. With conditions in Germany approaching a dangerous pass and with Japan too in defiant mood, Italy started on a career of aggression. Confident of the friendship of France and England and of their dependence on her help in keeping the Germans out of Austria, she took the offensive in Africa. She wanted the old native kingdom of Ethiopia (Abyssinia), to round out her colonies of Eritrea and Italian Somaliland. Her excuse for attacking this country, as so often in the annals of imperialism, was that the Ethiopians were raiding across the border into her lands. Mussolini's bold statement of his intentions in regard to Ethiopia, a member of the League of Nations, made it necessary for that organization to take some action to protect its weak member. The League, having already lost prestige by its failure to take action in the case of Japanese aggression against China in Manchuria in 1931, and by the withdrawal from membership first of Japan and then of Germany, had to do something to stop Mussolini if it expected to continue to function. England was seriously concerned; for not only did Ethiopia border upon the Anglo-Egyptian Sudan, but Lake Tana, in Ethiopia, the headwaters of the Blue Nile, was essential for the irrigation of the Sudan. Furthermore, it was widely believed that Mussolini was but taking the first step in a grandiose plan of controlling the Mediterranean. At the same time it was clear that the British public, alarmed by the German rearmament, was more devoted to the League of Nations than it had ever been before. A "peace ballot" lately conducted by the League of Nations Society had rolled up a tremendous vote in favor of the application of sanctions against any aggressor nation. Thus urged on both by danger to British interests and by an aroused idealism, Baldwin's cabinet decided to support Ethiopia through the League.

Throughout the summer of 1935 Anthony Eden, the minister in charge of League of Nations affairs in the cabinet, hurried from one European capital to another in behalf of the interests of both the League and England. The League met, and exhausted every means of reconciling Italy and Ethiopia. With the cessation of the summer rains, the Italian troops began the invasion, England and the League still marking time. The British garrisons at Malta and in Egypt were strengthened, and the Admiralty sent south their most powerful warships. The Channel was virtually without protection; and although England kept her two largest battleships safely off Gibraltar, she brought into the Mediterranean a fleet overwhelmingly superior in tonnage, if not in speed, to the entire Italian navy. Then the League, acting under British advice, voted for economic sanctions, which meant virtually an economic boycott of Italy. Mussolini was furious;

for Italy depended on other nations for many war materials, particularly petroleum.

In England most people apparently approved this policy of the government. A handful of Tory die-hards objected, perhaps because they feared that any weakening of Mussolini might lead to a communist victory in Italy; and a group of conscientious pacifists feared that sanctions might lead to war. The war scare gave Baldwin a superb opportunity to hold in November, 1935, the Parliamentary election which must legally have come by 1936 at the latest. The result was a foregone conclusion: Liberals, Laborites, and Conservatives all were agreed in favor of sanctions. This carried with it approval of a strong navy and air force; for England could not rely upon the League to defend her, even though she might get into difficulties as the defender of the League. The government therefore received its vote of confidence, and also public approval of rearmament. Even Labor did not oppose this program beyond criticizing Baldwin for not having warned Mussolini earlier, and pointing out the continued gravity of economic conditions at home. The election resulted in 431 supporters for Baldwin, almost all Conservatives, with 185 in opposition. Labor managed to increase its membership by a large percentage, but the Liberals shrank to a mere shadow of their former strength. England seemed to be returning to the old two-party system, with the Conservatives opposed by Laborites instead of by Liberals. Yet the government continued to call itself National. This was to be the last election for ten years.

Soon afterward Sir Samuel Hoare, the Foreign Secretary, came to an understanding with the French government whereby Italy might be permitted a free hand in a considerable part of Ethiopia. A cry of shame went up in press and Parliament. Hoare resigned and was succeeded by Eden. Nevertheless Baldwin, despite the election results, was unwilling to press the Italians hard without French support, and this was not noticeably forthcoming. The League applied sanctions, but not very stiff ones, the Italians continuing to import the all-important petroleum. During the winter of 1935–1936 and the following spring England and Italy continued to glare at one another, while the British fleet stayed ready for action off the coast of Egypt. But nothing serious occurred. The triumphant Italians, entering the Ethiopian capital, made it obvious that Italy could not be dislodged from Ethiopia without war. Hoare, whose compromise had been rejected with scorn, now seemed vindicated; and he returned to the cabinet as First Lord of the Admiralty. Shortly afterward England reluctantly gave up her policy of sanctions against Italy, thus tacitly recognizing the latter's conquest of Ethiopia.

# Between the Wars

With England and Italy at swords' points, Hitler had seen his chance. Quickly and decisively he moved German troops into the demilitarized Rhine valley. France demanded the support which England had promised at Locarno for such an eventuality, but England was lukewarm in this. Germany was apparently not hostile to Britain; but if Germany destroyed the Treaty of Versailles she might change the balance of power in Europe. The British realized also that a triumphant Hitler might soon come knocking at the door for a return of Germany's colonies; and in the background was the possibility that Hitler and Mussolini might combine, and even perhaps join with Japan in a united front.

Altogether, the international situation was deteriorating rapidly. Whereas the twenties had witnessed a constant series of efforts toward peace, the thirties brought a never-ending recurrence of crises. The seven major powers seemed to fall into three groups: the troublemaking "have-nots," Germany, Italy, and Japan; the peace-desiring "haves," eager to maintain the status quo, which suited them, England, France, and, less closely involved, the United States; and in a mysterious class by itself, the Union of Socialist Soviet Republics. The "have-nots," with their undemocratic, totalitarian governments, seemed ready to disturb the peace if that alone would make possible the realization of their ambitions. During 1936 they drew together in an Anti-Comintern Pact, allegedly aimed against communism. Germany and Italy first formed the so-called "Rome-Berlin Axis," to which Japan adhered a few weeks later. On the other hand, England and France knew that they had nothing to gain by war and everything to lose. The various crises, therefore, drew them closer together, until they made a regular alliance in 1938. France had irritated everyone, including England, by her development of power during the twenties; now, although international relations were growing hourly more dangerous, she had begun to relax her guard. The United States, secure, across the oceans, from these crises, stayed fairly aloof, while Russia was the great enigma. The latter, already possessing vast territory and resources, was possibly looking for more; and the widespread distrust of her government and her economic setup made her still not quite respectable internationally.

These repeated aggressive actions of the "have-nots" placed England and France in a cruel dilemma. They had the choice of trying to nip them in the bud by force or threats of force or of trying to preserve the peace by "appeasement." Collective security by the united action of all the powers through the League of Nations was daily becoming less likely. The small nations were naturally afraid of the covetous eye of Axis neighbors, and the larger ones never seemed to be ready to stand firm at the same time. In 1931 the United States sought to check the Japanese in Manchuria, but the others would not follow her; in the case of Ethiopia, as we saw, France was not ready to support England on sanctions against Italy; and England held back when France, in her turn, might have stamped down reviving German armament. In the savage civil war begun in Spain in 1936 all three were inclined to a hands-off policy even when they saw active aid from Italy and Germany ensuring victory to the reactionary rebels, while Russia stepped into the picture to help the Loyalist side. The Axis powers took full advantage of this hesitant attitude by never pushing their aggression far enough at any one time to force war. In England some demanded action against the Axis before too much should be lost; Anthony Eden was among these, but was overruled by the so-called "appeasers."

Under the circumstances it seemed best to rearm, rapidly, extensively, and expensively. Parliament authorized the strengthening of the royal navy all the way from battleships down to fast little torpedo boats. In addition, the old pre-Suez sea route around the Cape of Good Hope was to be put into condition. The army was to be increased, and gas masks were to be produced for civilians. Particularly, however, the air force was to be expanded. The British no longer enjoyed their old insular security, as Hoare warned them; for the new conditions in the air made the island kingdom terribly vulnerable. Consequently thousands of fast fighter planes were a major part of this expansion program. Altogether, in the budget for 1936–1937, Parliament voted an increase of 30 per cent for national defense over the large appropriation of the year before and of some 400 per cent over that of 1911; yet this was to be far below the 1937–1938 budget and those of the years thereafter.

King George V, who, through his kindliness and quiet wisdom, had given his people dependable leadership during some of the most critical days in British history, did not live to witness these final feverish reminders of 1914. He died in January, 1936, sincerely mourned by the whole empire and by many beyond its limits. His eldest son and successor, Edward VIII, had long been popular throughout the world as the informal, charming, and sports-loving Prince of Wales, who nevertheless had taken his duties conscientiously and, in his almost constant travels, had made himself familiar with the lives and problems of his future subjects in all walks of life. Although the tremendous expenditures for armaments made it necessary that the condition of the depressed classes of the country take a subordinate place in the government's plans, those classes were not

# Between the Wars

forgotten by their new king. This was made clear, for instance, by Edward at the launching of the new superliner named for his mother, when he asked, "How do you reconcile a world that has produced this mighty ship with the slums we have just visited?" And again, on a visit to the forlorn region of abandoned mines in south Wales, he was stirred to promise that something should be done.

Altogether, in spite of economic ills and threats of war, it seemed as if England were entering a reign full of promise, with one of the most popular kings in all her history and one determined to improve the conditions under which his half-billion subjects lived. Yet before ten months had passed, the swift series of developments in a December week were to result in his voluntary abdication, the first of its kind in English history. According to Prime Minister Baldwin, no constitutional crisis (although many called it that) caused Edward's decision, but rather it was Edward's wish to marry the woman of his choice, an American, though she had been twice divorced and was therefore, in the cabinet's opinion, unacceptable to the British peoples. Forthwith his brother ascended the throne as George VI.

In the spring of 1937, as soon as King George and his queen were duly crowned at Westminster, Baldwin voluntarily relinquished the prime ministership to Neville Chamberlain, who was at the time Chancellor of the Exchequer. Tall, gaunt, and somber, Chamberlain had shown ability in finance, but he lacked the dynamic vigor of his father and even more the adroit diplomatic skill of his brother. The government still went under the name of "National," although, like the two preceding ministries, it was essentially Conservative.

About this time Japan suddenly intensified her drive against China, which, as we saw, had been spasmodically underway for six years. Dispensing with a declaration of war, she launched a determined attack into China proper, which brought her closer to British holdings than her earlier invasion of Manchuria. The British interests around Shanghai alone suffered a billion-dollar loss, while further damage was inflicted upon their wealth elsewhere, and Britain's prestige was dealt a severe blow. She failed, however, once again to take any decisive action.

Bloodshed in China and in the continuing bitter struggle in Spain was soon overshadowed by the German menace in central Europe. Hitler began to make it clear that he intended to join to Germany all contiguous areas occupied by German people. Austria, first on his list, was predominantly German, and ever since 1919, when she had been whittled down to an abnormal status of "a capital and its suburbs," many of her people had wanted union with the northern neighbor. Italy had prevented such action in the 1934 crisis (see pages 890, 925); but now, in March of 1938, no one lifted a hand to stop Germany from occupying Austria.

Democratic Czechoslovakia came next on Hitler's program. Although she had been an example of the self-determination of peoples, an unfortunate exception had been made in including the Germans of the Sudeten Mountains, which formed a powerful and final strategic barrier between Germany and the approach to the Danube valley. France had promised to protect the Czechs, and Russia had agreed to aid France if the latter was attacked. Thus matters lay when Hitler's proposal to annex the Sudeten region as part of his all-German policy came to a crisis in September, 1938.

Three times within two weeks Chamberlain flew to Germany to reason with Hitler. His missions to the mountain lair at Berchtesgaden and to Godesberg were fruitless. Finally, at Munich, war was averted by a conference of Hitler, Chamberlain, the French premier, and the Italian foreign minister; but the Russians and the intimately concerned Czechs were not invited. Hitler had his way at the price of a humiliating acceptance by the others of his taking over of the Sudetenland. Hitler's statement that this was the end of what he wanted in territory was the one encouraging note in the meeting. Chamberlain returned to England, announcing that he had achieved "peace in our time." The House of Commons upheld his action by a vote of 266 to 144; but many in the nation felt shocked and humiliated at his acquiescence in a dictator's terms. Eden had already resigned, months before, in anger over appeasement.

But this was not the end of German aggression. Up to this point Hitler could argue the old doctrine of self-determination as he concentrated upon essentially German regions; now matters took a new and infinitely graver turn. In the spring of 1939, a year almost to a day after their entrance into Vienna, German troops marched into non-German Prague, the capital of the republic of Czechoslovakia, which had lost its Sudeten lands in the preceding autumn and which now virtually ceased to exist. No longer could any nation feel safe from German ambition; Poland, in particular, was aware of her peril in view of the bitter German resentment concerning the corridor to Danzig, which cut East Prussia from the rest of Germany.

The unjustifiable attack upon the Czechs ended appeasement in England. Sir Edward Grey had been criticized for not taking a firm and vigorous stand in the 1914 crisis (see pages 850–851). Heavy pressure from labor, from Eden, from Churchill, from Lloyd George, and from many others now pushed Chamberlain into very specific declarations. In a momentous speech before the Commons in the last hours of March, 1939, he flatly declared, "In the event of any action which threatened Polish independence and which the Polish government accordingly felt it vital to resist with their national forces, the Government would feel themselves bound at once to lend to the Polish government all support in their power." These were fighting words, and they were to be put to the proof before the year was out.

But to Hitler, after his victory at Munich, they apparently did not sound too serious; within the month he denounced his non-aggression pact of 1934 with Poland and also his naval agreement of 1935 with Britain. His Axis partner, Italy, meanwhile invaded Albania across the Adriatic.

England pursued her new vigorous course of developing a peace front. To Rumania, to Greece, and to other anxious nations, she extended guarantees similar to that given to Poland. France stood with England in this policy, and together they began to integrate plans for a possible war. During that troubled spring England decided upon compulsory military service, although there was some opposition from labor. George VI and his queen, who had visited France the summer before, now spent several weeks in Canada and the United States, building up good will for their troubled country, the first time that a reigning British sovereign had crossed the Atlantic.

Russia, the enigma, shocked the peace front in August, as she suddenly made a commercial agreement with Germany and followed it four days later with a nonaggression pact. This startling reversal of policy ended British and French expectations that they could rely again, as in 1914, upon Russia's military strength to help keep Germany in line. Russia had some cause for this action: she had not been invited to Munich; Poland had refused to let Russian troops defend the Polish-German frontier; and the French and British had been exceedingly dilatory in sending a military mission to Russia to discuss terms of co-operation. This was Russia's answer, even while that mission was actually in Moscow.

Hitler was now free to deal with Poland, and he wasted no time. After a hasty ultimatum, which Poland did not have time to act upon, his troops launched an attack upon her in the early hours of the morning of September 1; and the Second World War was under way.

England sent a note saying that either hostilities must be stopped at once or she would carry out her pledge to Poland. When no answer had come from Germany by Sunday morning, September 3, Chamberlain solemnly broadcast to the nation that Hitler could be stopped only by force; that the situation had become intolerable; and that England was resolved to keep faith with Poland, standing by her pledged word. At noon Parliament received the formal announcement of the state of war. The French declaration followed a few hours later.

# CHAPTER XXXI

## *"There'll Always Be an England"*

THE SUPERLATIVES used to describe the First World War are inadequate for the magnitude of its successor, a quarter-century later. For the British it was a tragedy from which even "total victory" seemed unlikely to bring back the prestige and power that had long been theirs. A new and stronger mistress of the seas and air, the United States, emerged from the holocaust; while in Europe, the balance of power, endangered by Nazi Germany, tended to be even more out of alignment with the growing dominance of the other great power of the postwar era, Soviet Russia.

The conflict itself lasted a year and nine months longer than the first war, which then had seemed to tax human endurance to the limit. For six whole years, almost to a day, from September 3, 1939, to September 1, 1945, the British were at war. Whereas in the earlier conflict the British always had had several allies, in this they stood almost alone during one terrible year, with France surrendered and with neither Russia nor the United States yet allies. In the direst peril since the Armada, the island kingdom was blasted by the German air force in a rain of destruction upon its old and young, its women and children, its homes and factories. Little short of miraculous did it seem to those beyond the seas, who watched this dread assault, that, despite all this, no army of the foe set foot upon the shores of Britain.

Yet with all the accelerated horror that science brought to warfare, Britain's dead were fewer than half of those in the First World War, even with some 60,000 civilian victims of air power, of whom there had been but a few in the first war. Winston Churchill vowed that this time England would not let war wipe out a whole generation of her young men; and that did not happen again. But capital, built up over the generations, was blasted into rubble. Not only was property destroyed at home, but England's Victorian heritage of invested wealth across the seas was dissipated in the desperate rush for armament credits.

This was, geographically, far more a world war than its predecessor. Whereas the bulk of Britain's fighting during every year of

# "There'll Always Be an England"

the other war had been along the trench line of the western front in Europe, this time the whole long middle years of the contest found the major fronts in the sandy wastes of North Africa or in the distant jungle terrain of Malaya, Burma, and New Guinea. In fact, for three of the six years, England was unable to attain a foothold in western Europe. Only at the very beginning and at the end of this war were British armies to be found there on their centuries-old battleground (see page 407). The major war theaters this time were the Mediterranean, the Pacific, and southeastern Asia, primarily because Britain's former allies, Italy and Japan, were on the Axis side.

Technologically, this second war was fought in a state of almost constant transition; the unheard-of and the fantastic in 1939 were commonplace by 1945. To be sure, tanks and poison gas had been developed in the earlier contest, along with new submarine techniques and the elementary use of aviation; but by and large the forms of ships and weapons changed relatively little during those four years. This time, however, soldiers and sailors were having to try out one strange gadget after another, and never knew, from day to day, whether the enemy had found something better. To mention but a few of the scientific miracles: Fighter planes of amazing speed and bombers of ever-increasing range and capacity made aviation constantly more effective and more important. Carriers at sea brought the power of this new arm close to enemy shores and into every phase of naval fighting. On land, tanks, coupled with motorized infantry and artillery units, were used in conjunction with planes to enable ground forces to hit harder and faster. Whole air-borne divisions in gigantic gliders or transport planes and specially trained parachute troops radically increased the mobility of armies. Amphibious warfare, with newly devised landing craft, enabled navies to put men and equipment ashore even in shallow water. Rockets greatly extended fire power, both afloat and ashore. Radar, it was finally revealed, was an almost human "seeing eye" for both offense and defense in sea and air warfare. And finally, a stunned world saw the sudden end of the war with the atomic bomb, frightful in its original destructive form and carrying threats of infinitely far worse to come.

Actually, the Second World War consisted of two fairly distinct contests: one with Germany and one with Japan. Britain and later Russia were intent upon the defeat of Germany, which was accomplished by May, 1945. The fighting in North Africa, in Italy, and elsewhere in Europe all pointed to that end. Italy, which came in late on the German side, surrendered early. In the Pacific war Japan attacked the United States and Britain, and thereby extended her private Asiatic fight with China, which had been in progress intermittently since 1931 and more steadily since 1937. The Japanese came into the war in December, 1941, sixteen months after its outbreak in Europe, and surrendered some five months later than the Germans. The bulk of the fighting in the Pacific fell to the United States. British forces were involved to a considerable extent, with portions of the empire overrun by the Japanese, but Britain had to concentrate her main strength against the enemy nearer home.

Although most of the nations of the world came in on the Allied side at one time or another, the main burden of the fighting, as before, was carried by a few countries. Even as early as January, 1942, there were twenty-six Allies, or United Nations as they came to be formally called, and that number had nearly doubled by 1945; but a good many were belligerents in little more than name. Nations invaded by the enemy and represented by token governments-in-exile were on the list. From some of these, fighting men, and even ships, escaped to join the Allies, while from within, underground movements did what they could. Of the major Allies, Britain alone was in the war from start to finish, and with her stood most of her empire. Eire was neutral. Probably the greatest British contribution was the firm stand during that terrible year in which Britain fought alone. Russia played an invaluable role by wearing down German man power in a bloody war of attrition at appalling cost to herself, as well as to the Germans. The Americans, with their tremendous offerings of men, ships, and material, sustained most of the Pacific war and also contributed heavily to the blows against Germany and Italy. But France collapsed in the first year, and China was able to do no more than drag through, under crushing handicaps. On the Axis side Germany took the worst punishment, Italy lasted only three years, and Japan surrendered before her home islands were invaded.

This war represented another turning point in military annals. According to the American military attaché at Berlin, who witnessed Hitler's invasion of Poland in the first weeks of the war, a revolution had occurred in military science. The last war, as we recall, degenerated into a gigantic siege because the weapons of defense were developed beyond the power of those of attack; and the eventual break-through was achieved only after years. At the same time, so close was the balance that men died by tens of thousands, both charging and defending the trench systems of that day. Now, for the first time, motorized, armored equipment and aviation were synchronized with the old infantry and artillery to return warfare to

a mobile and offensive status. In this development of new techniques and weapons the Germans were not handicapped, like their
rivals, by having usable, too-good-to-scrap, yet obsolescent material
on hand, because Versailles had stripped them of all major armament. Strategy, more reminiscent of the days of Marlborough and
the Napoleonic Wars than of the last war, thus caught the Allies
napping from Poland to France in that first year. This new *Blitzkrieg*, or "lightning war," struck with special surprise because the
French and others had drawn opposite conclusions from their studies
of that stalemate on the western front in the previous war; their
faith was in ever more powerful defenses against which no attack
would succeed. They built, accordingly, the Maginot line at a cost
of some two million dollars a mile, and hoped to sit out the next war
in safety, while the enemy did the dying under their defensive fire.

This new *Blitzkrieg* struck Poland before dawn on the morning of
September 1, when swarms of German planes swept over the border
to smash the Polish air force, still grounded at its airfields. The
Polish troops, drawn up along the frontiers to fight the conventional
defensive action, next were pierced at one place after another by the
*Panzer* mechanized forces. Those fast tanks and motorized carriers
of infantry and guns then dashed behind the lines to disrupt headquarters and communications. Droves of planes bombed constantly
the jammed roads, bridges, and railroad centers to isolate reserves.
The frantic Poles fought bravely but were helpless in the destruction
wrought by this new type of warfare; the best they could do was to
pray for the usual autumn rain to bog down the German motors, but
no rain came.

Sixteen days later a new enemy, Russia, moved into hapless
Poland from the east. Already most of her army was surrounded by
the Germans; Warsaw, the besieged capital, surrendered before the
month was out. Poland was divided between her German and Russian conquerors. An almost complete news black-out closed down,
through which, later in the war, began to leak terrible tales of the
fate meted out to the Poles in general, and in particular to the Jews
among them.

Neither England nor France, though they had gone to war on
September 3 to save Poland's independence, could prevent its destruction. British planes dropped a few bombs around the Kiel
Canal, and the French attacked German outposts; that was about
all. Thereupon Hitler, declaring that he had "no war aims against
Great Britain," suggested that since Britain's original purpose in
declaring war had not been accomplished, hostilities might well

be ended at this time. England rebuffed this peace feeler and others which followed.

The war went on, but for the six months after the fall of Poland it was pretty much a war in name only. Daily the Basel express ran between the near-by bristling guns of the French Maginot line and the German West Wall. The guns were fired only occasionally, and seemed aimed to do a minimum of damage. German loud-speakers worried the French with an uncanny knowledge of their troop movements, and taunted individual French soldiers by name about their girls' affairs with civilians at home. The Royal Air Force flew frequently far over Germany to let loose, not bombs, but showers of pamphlets warning the Germans that they did not have a chance. Characteristic of the sarcastic attitude toward this type of warfare was the yarn about the R.A.F. flyer who was reprimanded by his squadron leader for dropping his whole sack at once instead of scattering the leaflets: "But, my dear fellow, you must be more careful. You might have hurt someone." The Americans began to talk about the "phony war"; others dubbed it *Sitzkrieg*.

At sea, where England, as usual, was primarily concerned, there was less of that tendency to pull punches. Each side picked up its maritime offensive about where it had dropped it in the fall of 1918. On the whole, familiar features were repeated with certain variations, as each side applied the lessons it had learned and utilized new devices. Once again the royal navy swept most of the German merchant marine off the seas, as superliners rushed to safety. A rigid blockade was resumed to strangle German imports and exports (see page 860). Both sides laid mines freely, with Germany's new magnetic mine causing concern until the British found ways to neutralize its effects. The struggle of U-boat against convoy was picked up almost where it had been dropped; for unlike the long delay before, the British lost no time in establishing convoys to safeguard their merchantmen (see page 882). One disconcerting factor was the improvement in the U-boats, which rather nullified the effectiveness of the new submarine detectors and other devices of the royal navy. The submarines, larger and with a wider cruising range, used detectors, too, and no longer had to keep their periscopes in sight. Enemy surface raiders were at large. The airplane brought many new complications, even menacing merchantmen in port. Altogether the sea lanes were more threatened than before; and the threats were to become more extensive as the war engulfed the Mediterranean and the Pacific.

In the opening months, through March, 1940, the British losses from U-boats were decidedly moderate compared with what they had been in 1917 and what they would be again. On the first day of the war the westbound passenger liner *Athenia* went down off the coast of Scotland; and the carrier *Courageous* was sunk on patrol off southwestern Ireland shortly afterward. Four weeks later a bold U-boat slipped into the great naval base at Scapa Flow and sank the battleship *Royal Oak*.

Surface raiding by the enemy was a cause of much anxiety to the royal navy that year. Germany, stripped of her fleet and forbidden at Versailles to build any warships over 10,000 tons, had not thrown off the restrictions in time to have enough capital ships for a full-dress naval battle like Jutland; this meant that she no longer had to conserve battle strength but could scatter her units to break up convoys. Within that tonnage, moreover, she had three so-called "pocket battleships," a type of supercruiser with guns which could outrange those of any ordinary cruiser and with speed enough to run away from any battleship. This was the same combination which had made American superfrigates so effective in the War of 1812 (see page 573). As in that war, some of the most powerful capital ships of the royal navy now had to be on convoy patrol and lesser warships had to cruise in groups. Yet these three ships proved singularly ineffective as commerce raiders and did not approach the havoc wrought in the first war by the ordinary German cruiser *Emden*. The pocket battleship *Graf Spee* had only nine freighters to her credit when she was crippled by three British cruisers, traveling together for safety, off South America in December, 1939. Her 11-inch guns should have been able to sink all three of them, but they boldly slid in close enough to use their guns of shorter range. The admiral for whom she was named had gone down fighting in those same South Atlantic waters, but she sought neutral refuge in the Uruguayan port of Montevideo (see pages 861–862). Uruguay, following international law, ordered her to leave within the brief prescribed period or be interned. After calling Hitler by transatlantic telephone, her captain ordered the ship abandoned and scuttled. Except for the distant war between Russia and little Finland, that was the principal dramatic event of the six strange months of *Sitzkrieg*.

Beyond the seas the members of the British Commonwealth of Nations, with one exception, quickly joined the mother country in the war, although there were some marked differences in the reaction toward this step. In 1914, dominion or crown colony, all had been regarded as automatically at war after England's own declaration, and had no further say in the matter themselves. In 1939 that held true again in the scattered units of the dependent empire, such as Jamaica, St. Helena, Hong Kong. The dominions, however, were now a different story. They, we recall, had signed the peace treaties in 1919 separately, and the Imperial Conference in 1926 had made their independent status definitely clear (see pages 936, 938). Yet when Britain went to war, they all had various ideas about the technicalities of their status.

In Australia and New Zealand the old relationship was more or less assumed, and war was declared immediately by executive action. The Australians heard Chamberlain's announcement of war by radio; an hour later the dominion prime minister broadcast the decision "Great Britain has declared war and, as a result, Australia is also at war." New Zealand's answer came through with similar speed. Thus the two dominions "down under" were at England's side before the war was more than a few hours old.

Canada and South Africa, on the other hand, did not take belligerency for granted and waited for action by their dominion parliaments. The Canadian parliament had been summoned for September 7; in the two-day debate at Ottawa a few radicals and French Canadians railed against being dragged into an imperialistic struggle, but another French Canadian made the most spirited plea for war. The decision was never in doubt; war was voted by a chorus so overwhelming that the actual votes were not counted. South Africa's decision had come a few days sooner, but only after sharp dissension. Prime Minister Hertzog, whose anti-British attitude we have seen before, presented to the Assembly a motion for neutrality, but it was voted down, 80 to 67. Instead, by a similar vote, a motion, made by the pro-British Smuts, was passed, calling for participation. Hertzog asked for an appeal to the country, but the governor-general refused, and accepted Hertzog's resignation. Smuts was called in as prime minister and at once proclaimed a state of war.

The rapid adherence of those four dominions had far more than a sentimental importance, for they contained nearly one third of the white population of the British Commonwealth, as compared with barely one fourth in the previous war. If we leave out Southern Ireland and the dark-skinned people of South Africa, the United Kingdom had numbered some 41 millions in 1914 and the four dominions barely 14 millions (see page 749). Now, as against the United Kingdom's 47 millions, the dominions totaled nearly 22 millions (Canada, 11; Australia, 7; South Africa, 2; and New Zealand, 1½).

Although in the dominions the question arose as to whether their forces should be used overseas on distant missions, their military and naval response was immediate. By the spring of 1940 Australian and New Zealand troops had reached the Middle East, where the Anzacs had gone before, and Canadians had arrived in England. Canada, whose navy heretofore had been negligible, suddenly began to build one in earnest to patrol the North Atlantic. It undertook also a tremendous program of training its own airmen, along with some from Britain and the other dominions. The small New Zealand cruiser *Achilles* had helped to defeat the *Graf Spee*, and several Australian cruisers were patrolling the western Pacific.

India presented a special problem, since Indian Nationalists vigorously opposed any possibility that India be dragged into war or made to use its resources in the war without the consent of the Indian people. Nevertheless, India was legally in the war the very first day by action of the viceroy, who proclaimed that "a state of war exists between His Majesty and Germany." The Nationalist protest was repeated vehemently and coupled with a demand for independence; but to no avail, as we shall see. Indian troops were quickly dispatched to various danger spots of the Middle and the Far East—from North Africa and Aden around to Singapore and Hong Kong. Troubled days lay ahead with the chronic friction, ever growing worse, between India and the British raj (see page 993).

One government, still somewhat legally within the perimeter of the British Commonwealth, did not participate, the Irish Free State, or Eire. Northern Ireland (Ulster) was, of course, automatically in the war as part of the United Kingdom. But Eire, as we have seen, had been going its own way more definitely than ever since De Valera had become president (see page 939). He had already announced, early in 1939, that Eire had decided to be neutral in case of war, adding later, "We know, of course, that should the attack come from a power other than Great Britain, Great Britain, in her own interests, must help us repel it." And when war did come, Eire stuck to neutrality from first to last. On September 3 its neutrality was acknowledged by the various combatants; the German minister remained and Britain, to fill the abandoned equivalent of a governor-general in this recalcitrant dominion, sent over a "British Representative in Ireland."

This Irish decision for neutrality would handicap England severely in combating the submarine menace. In 1938 the British had appeased Eire by abandoning the south-coast naval bases, which had been centers of antisubmarine activity in the last war. Their lack would be keenly felt in the coming contest, for the "Southwest Approaches," off the Irish coast, were again to be one of the happiest hunting grounds of the U-boats. Air bases likewise were denied to the British.

Meanwhile, at home, the British were undergoing a trying "ordeal by suspense" during those months of waiting. The nightmare of air attack had hung over the nation for at least six years, ever since Germany had begun to develop her air force; and now it came closer. Planes were designed and constructed; rings of airfields were built to protect London and other cities; and the fliers of the Royal Air Force underwent the rigorous training that was to pay dividends later.

England's preparations did not stop with planes, airfields, and pilots. The whole nation went feverishly to work on detailed plans for civilian defense against the expected fury. Some two million civilian volunteers, men and women of all ages and of all social strata, commenced tedious, and often arduous, training as air-raid wardens, plane-spotters, fire-fighters, demolition corpsmen, extra police, motor-transport drivers, first-aid assistants, stretcher-bearers, hospital and rescue workers of every sort: all the vast army needed to warn of air attack and to help a city dig itself out after one. Parliament authorized more than two million steel air-raid shelters for use in courts and gardens, and thousands of homemade ones were built, while the London subway tunnels were to prove a haven for thousands of sleeping families night after night. Ample underground quarters, powerfully protected by concrete and every other conceivable means, were built eighty feet under Whitehall to serve as an impregnable "nerve center" where the War Cabinet and the heads of vital services could carry on. Precious historical documents and art treasures were hidden in distant regions; some found safekeeping in America.

The civilian volunteers most closely connected with the military were the aircraft warning observers and others of the Royal Observer Corps. Ten days before the war began, some thirty thousand of these men and women took up their posts along the coasts and at other vantage spots to watch for approaching planes. Their task was to telephone warnings of any enemy planes to the secretly located filter stations. There the route would be plotted from the reports of successive spotters; the nearest airfield and antiaircraft batteries hastily notified; and the probable target alerted. Every minute, almost every second, counted in sounding the alarm for the defensive fighter planes to take to the air, and for the civilian workers to fight the fires, dig out the victims, render first aid, evacuate families, and attend to all the endless bitter aftermath of a raid. Earlier warning

# "There'll Always Be an England"

f the approach of planes, even before they came into sight, was
given by an electronic device, long kept a secret. This was radar,
later extensively developed for naval use, and was one of the silent
heroes of those dark days. It did not do away with the need for the
potters, however, because it did not have their ability to recognize
whether a plane was friend or foe.

A few days before the declaration of war the lights went out all
over England and stayed out until the last year of fighting. This
rigid black-out was designed to make night bombings more difficult
by preventing raiders from finding their targets easily. Through
some two thousand nights the British lived in darkness; for many
that was perhaps the most nerve-wearing restriction they endured.
It made nights dangerous too, even without raids; during the *Sitzkrieg*, for example, motor accidents on blacked-out roads caused
more casualties than military action.

Evacuations from the cities began. Whole families later moved
out to less vulnerable places than London or the great industrial
centers; but at first the mass evacuation chiefly concerned the children. Some of these were sent to America, but plans for such a
distant migration of children on a large scale were postponed when
a submarine sank a westbound ship with child refugees aboard. In
the spring of 1940, evacuees in quiet, remote villages began to drift
back to their unbombed towns.

The U-boat threat to shipping made it advisable to ration food,
even as the fear of bombs led to civilian defense. The British had not
forgotten their hunger pangs in the First World War, and now they
saw to it that the specter of starvation should not haunt them again.
Grain was no longer the acute need, for the government had laid in
a huge reserve and farmers had planted extra acreage as well; but
other foods for a balanced diet had to be imported still. With
U-boats already at work, food-rationing went into effect in January, 1940.

Shipping space, however, was not the whole story of rationing.
Winston Churchill, First Lord of the Admiralty, a cabinet post that
he had held for a while in the other war, explained that the need for
foreign credits was another reason for rationing:

We are rationing ourselves because we wish to save every ton of imports,
to increase our output of munitions . . . to maintain and extend our export
trade, thus gaining the foreign credits wherewith to bring more munitions of
war. We mean to regulate every ton that is carried across the sea and
make sure that it is carried solely for the purpose of victory. We must grow
more food and accommodate ourselves as much as possible to eat the kind
of food we can grow.

# A History of England and the British Empire

The impact of rationing, which was to be extended to clothing, will be treated later, as will the drastic, new internal legislation which followed quickly the end of those quiet months.

But the dreaded raids did not come; German planes occasionally flew over England, as British planes were flying over Germany. Early in 1940 a civilian in the Orkneys was killed during an air raid on Scapa Flow, but no bomb fell on England proper during the *Sitzkrieg*.

On April 9, 1940, the *Blitzkrieg* was turned against western Europe, seven months after its tryout in Poland. In a single day a stunned world saw the Nazis seize Denmark and invade Norway. Both had remained neutrals in the first war. The occupation of Denmark was a matter of hours; except for the palace guard in Copenhagen, the helpless people did not resist. Norway was a different story, for the sea lay between, and supposedly England was mistress of that.

The Germans had planned their simultaneous invasions with amazing detail. Naval forces, which eluded the British, seized six of Norway's chief ports at one stroke. There they were instantly reinforced by troops who had lain hidden in the holds of innocent-looking freighters. Well-planned collaboration with the Germans by a Norwegian "fifth column" caused confusing orders to paralyze most of the defense forces, though they managed to sink several German cruisers. Quickly airfields were seized, and more troops, planes, and some mechanized equipment came over from Germany. The Norwegian army, such as it was, put up what fight it could.

It looked at first glance as if the royal navy should have been able to save Norway. Its attention was focused there, for it had, against Norway's protests, entered her territorial waters, on the day before the invasion, to mine them. The port of Narvik, in the far north, was captured and a few confused encounters were fought; but with air control, the Germans were not wholly dependent on the sea for the conquest of this sparsely populated and weakly prepared land. Within a week the British did get an expeditionary force off to Norway, but it was "a boy sent to do a man's work." Twelve thousand British troops, without proper air coverage or antiaircraft guns, landed north and south of Trondheim; but German planes and armored equipment made short work of their attempt to struggle inland. By May 1 they had been evacuated and were homeward bound, in failure. One ray of light in this Norwegian tragedy was the fortunate escape of most of Norway's excellent merchant marine, a godsend to England in her coming dependence on shipping.

# "There'll Always Be an England"

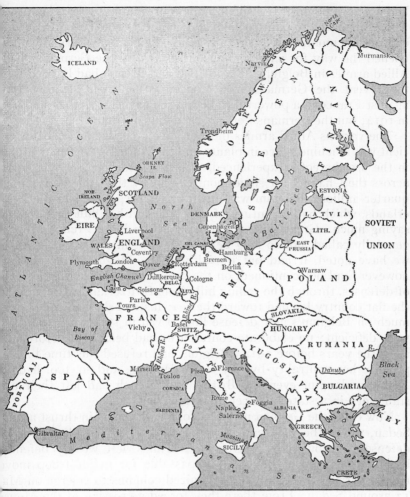

WESTERN AND CENTRAL EUROPE IN 1940

Nine days later, on the very day, as we shall see, that England was changing prime ministers, the *Blitzkrieg* was launched with tremendous force toward France. The Netherlands, Belgium, and Luxembourg were the first victims of that campaign, which Hitler promised his armies would "decide the fate of the German nation for the next thousand years." Three days later Winston Churchill, England's new leader, warned the House of Commons, "I have nothing to offer but blood, toil, tears, and sweat."

The Netherlands was overrun and surrendered in four days; Rotterdam was leveled in a merciless bombing, such as the world

had not seen before. The supposedly impregnable Belgian fortress c
Eben Emael fell to paratroopers and engineers who had practiced it
capture for months on a carefully made duplicate in Germany. Thi
opened the way for an advantageous attack by the Germans on th
Allied armies in Belgium. The British and French had hurried ther
to prevent the Germans from concentrating their striking forc
against France in a powerful right-wing movement, as they had don
in 1914; but the Germans were not repeating old plans (see page 855)

The various Allied armies did not have a chance against this eff
cient war machine, since in planes and tanks they were deficient, an
in the use thereof inexperienced. England had been sending troop
across the Channel for some months, and by this time had about
quarter-million. Belgium was much better prepared than the Netl
erlands, which had a century of peace behind her, but that was nc
saying much. Great faith was placed in the large French army,—
generally called, not so long before, the best in the world,—but, a
we have noted, it had put its faith in the Maginot line. Franc
however, had not continued, on the same scale, that powerful serie
of defenses, through the rolling hills from Switzerland to Sedan, int
the flat country beyond toward the sea; instead she had relied ovei
much on Belgium's new defense line. Even in staff work the Allie
were deficient; no elaborate conferences had been held beforehanc
as in the years before 1914. Belgium had refused this time to com
promise her neutrality by any such planning, and so, too, had th
Netherlands; but even the British and French had left their ow
staff work in a state of uncertainty and flux.

Now came the German master stroke with the main thrust aroun
Sedan, where the west end of the Maginot line joined the weake
defenses. Through the Forest of Ardennes, left weakly defende
because the French thought it impassable for major troop move
ments, hurried two German mechanized columns to emerge on Ma
13 around Sedan. From there they forced a crossing of the Meuse
and began to disrupt everything behind the main Allied lines.

Another race to the sea was on; and this time the Germans wo
(see page 856). With unsurpassed speed their *Panzer* divisions
preceded by clouds of Stuka bombers, swept in a great arc, first t
Soissons on the Aisne, then, turning right, toward the valley of th
Somme. Disregarding Paris they were intent only on separating th
French divisions from their Belgian and British allies. Reaching th
Somme the Germans followed its course almost to the Channel
Turning north they rushed on Calais and continued up the coast
thus drawing an iron ring around the Belgian and British armies. I
the "Battle of the Pockets," as this was called, the British and Bel

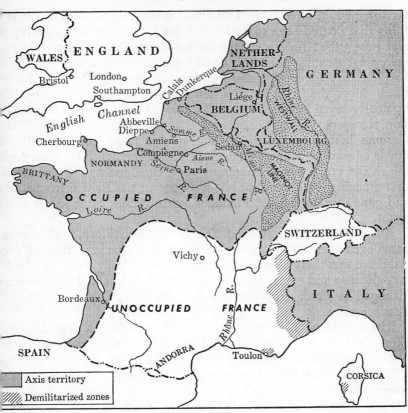

THE INVASION COAST

ians, with some French, were trapped in one large pocket; the rest of the French, in a number of smaller ones. The Belgians surrendered, exposing the British flank; it seemed as though the British must do likewise, since the French commander was powerless to break through to their aid. With fresh German forces pressing on hem from east, west, and south into an hourly constricting pocket round the coastal town of Dunkerque, escape was apparently impossible.

The "miracle of Dunkerque" it was called, that astonishing evacuation of 335,000 troops from a seemingly hopeless trap on exposed eaches. Never had the royal navy saved the British army from more certain annihilation; and of the rescued this time, a third were 'rench allies. But the navy could not have done it had not Britain's utnumbered Royal Air Force been concentrated here to provide a air "umbrella" against the mighty *Luftwaffe*; and neither navy nor

air force could have ferried all those soldiers home had not every
thing that floated been rushed across the Channel. Between May 2
and June 3 the strangest mongrel assortment of vessels probably eve
seen plied steadily back and forth from Dunkerque to the coast c
England through enemy-infested waters, while air battles raged over
head. More than two hundred units of the royal navy were joine
by nearly seven hundred other craft, from Cunarders down to excur
sion steamers, fishing boats, and many private motorboats. Wit
German bombs and shells falling around them, the interminabl
queue of waiting soldiers waded out shoulder-deep to be hauled int
the rescue craft, which came and went, time and again, throughou
that amazing week. All but about 30,000 of the British troops, wh
had gone over to the old Flanders battleground, came safely hom
again.

But only the men returned. Their tanks, artillery, and in many
cases even their rifles were left behind, and precious little of such
ordnance was there at home. England was virtually stripped of mili
tary defense and would have been almost helpless had the German
managed to land. For the moment, however, Germany chose t
attack France.

The defeat of British arms was none the less a stunning one
When the last troops were ferried home from Dunkerque, the British
had no foothold in the whole of western Europe, save for isolated
Gibraltar, at the mercy of the uncertain Spaniards. But worse was t
come; within three weeks France surrendered to the Germans. The
French collapse surprised the world in 1940, as had the valian
French rally at the battle of the Marne in 1914 (see page 856)
Since this is British history,—and since for three years to come no
British army was able to land in western Europe for anything more
than hit-and-run raids,—there is no need here to examine the strange
causes of that French weakness, nor the details of German strategy
that effected the quick surrender.

In Hitler's renewed drive into France itself, the Marne wa
quickly passed; the Maginot line enveloped and attacked from the
rear; and Paris declared an open city, to fall undamaged to the
enemy. The disorganized French forces fled southward, disputing
the roads with hordes of frantic civilians under the machine-gun fire
of low-flying German planes.

Meanwhile, in the week after Dunkerque, Mussolini threw Italy
into the war. As in 1915, Italy had waited until she thought she had
picked the winning side. Confident that France was falling and that
England would soon follow, she hoped by this "stab in the back" to
annex some French territory with a minimum of effort and danger.

# "There'll Always Be an England"

In those dark days of May and June began the ministry of Winston Churchill. He was to remain at the helm until the Germans had surrendered, five years later. It was the Norway fiasco that caused England "to change horses in the middle of the stream." For months the Laborites and even some of the Conservatives had been growing increasingly impatient with what they considered the inept leadership of Neville Chamberlain. His government, although called "National," was essentially Conservative, for the Laborites and Liberals had declined to join his ministry when he had reorganized it on the first day of war. Now the discontent was unleashed in the House of Commons. One Conservative quoted Cromwell's dismissal speech to the Long Parliament: "You have sat too long here for any good you have been doing. Depart, I say, and let us have done with you. In the name of God, go." By the narrow margin of 281 to 200, Chamberlain escaped a formal vote of censure, but he resigned nevertheless a few days later, on May 10.

In Winston Churchill, his successor, England had a superlative war leader without whom she might never have weathered the storm. The new prime minister, we recall, had already sampled eight different cabinet posts and more than one political party in his colorful but far from tranquil political past (see page 915). He had been the champion of Edward VIII, the only one of consequence. "Brilliant, versatile, and by some considered unstable" had been the earlier verdict; in these fearful days the brilliance and versatility remained, but "tough, forceful, dogged," were now better words for this vigorous and undaunted leader of forlorn hopes. In his late sixties he still had the fresh vision which had caused him to cut military red tape to have tanks built from Admiralty funds in 1914, and the flair for the dramatic in strategy that had resulted disastrously at Gallipoli (see page 864). His mastery of "the arrogance and splendor of Elizabethan language," which had long enlivened Commons debate and made him a writer of distinction, now made his speeches unforgettable.

Under him the Laborites and Liberals consented to join in a real coalition government. The small War Cabinet, which, we recall, was introduced in 1916, had been revived by Chamberlain and was retained by Churchill (see page 878). This small group, which eventually numbered nine, included several Laborites, of whom more will be heard later. In particular, Clement Attlee served as Lord Privy Seal and also as the leader of Commons until he became deputy prime minister, while Ernest Bevin, that autumn, became Minister of Labor and National Service. Churchill, with his old desire to have his word in high strategic councils, kept the role of Minister of

Defense himself and was also inclined to take over many of the fun<br>
tions of Foreign Secretary as well. He continued to dominate tl<br>
latter post, to which Anthony Eden returned when Lord Halifa<br>
went to the Washington embassy in 1941.

The week before France collapsed, Churchill flew to Tours, tl<br>
temporary capital, to discuss the French request for release from tl<br>
agreement not to make a separate peace. After this conference can<br>
the amazing proposal from England that the two nations link then<br>
selves in a Franco-British union with a single war cabinet, joint orgar<br>
for defense, and joint foreign, financial, and economic policies. But a<br>
was over in France; old Marshal Pétain, the defender of Verdun i<br>
1916, became premier, and France sued for peace. Most threatenin<br>
to England of the severe terms was the German occupation of thre<br>
fifths of France, including Paris, the industrial north, and the who]<br>
west coast. And most discouraging with respect to any future uj<br>
rising against the conquerors was the retention in Germany of tl<br>
two million French prisoners of war, who incidentally would k<br>
unable to breed little Frenchmen for a future war. As for the u<br>
occupied two fifths of France, Pétain set up a government at tl<br>
fashionable resort Vichy, and Pierre Laval, an unscrupulous form<br>
premier, saw to it that the co-operation with the Germans wa<br>
close.

Yet not all Frenchmen were out of the war. In the French coloni<br>
empire and on the seas were elements far from Vichy's control. Th<br>
French navy was England's immediate concern. It contained som<br>
powerful units; it would be bad enough if these were subtracted fror<br>
the Allied sea forces; it would be still worse if they were potenti<br>
enemies, for that would require units of the royal navy to watc<br>
them. The armistice terms stipulated that these ships should not b<br>
used by the Germans or Italians, but such a stipulation was not t<br>
be trusted.

A few days after the surrender England wisely raised a standar<br>
to which might rally those Frenchmen who wanted to keep on fight<br>
ing. She went further and recognized the new "Free French" go<br>
ernment, an exile group headed by General Charles de Gaulle, whos<br>
prewar writings on mechanized warfare had been neglected by a<br>
save German readers. Thus every general, admiral, or colonial go<br>
ernor in Africa, Syria, Indo-China, and the Caribbean could follo<br>
his conscience or his interests, and still pride himself upon being<br>
loyal Frenchman. Some stood apart, however, and joined neithe<br>
Vichy nor the new Cross of Lorraine.

With the French navy Britain felt she must take a rather hig<br>
hand, in view of its threat to her precarious situation on the sea

# "There'll Always Be an England"

ome French warships accepted her invitation to come over to Brit-
h ports; others refused. The latter was the case with the powerful
uadron at Oran in Algeria. On July 3 a British fleet appeared off
at port, and when the French admiral ignored an ultimatum,
ritish gunfire sank or crippled most of his ships. The Vichy gov-
nment broke diplomatic relations with England at once, but within
e week another French squadron, at Alexandria, agreed to demili-
rize itself to avoid the fate of the Oran ships. Not everything went
smoothly, however; at Dakar, on the previous day, the governor
cided for Vichy and beat off a British naval force accompanied by
ree French troops. This Dakar fiasco hurt British prestige, but it
as not all loss; a daring boat crew had immobilized the great battle-
ip *Richelieu* by blowing out her stern during the encounter. Mean-
hile, at Toulon, safe from British interference, were still a goodly
mber of strong warships.

But the French navy was a minor worry. With the French coast
enemy hands, Germany's navy could no longer be cooped up in
e North Sea, with its two narrow entrances; submarines and sur-
ce vessels now had many new bases, which in many cases were
ose to England. Worst of all, no longer did the planes of the *Luft-
affe* have to fly three hundred miles to reach their objective, but
ey could take off from just across the Channel to threaten the sea
pproaches and the very heart of England. Guns from that French
ast could actually throw shells into Dover; and once again, as in
apoleon's time, an invading army could mass in French ports. In
is dreadful year other grave complications, to be considered
ortly, came from the vastly increased responsibilities of the navy,
eakened at Dunkerque, and from now hostile Italy, athwart the
ort route to the Far East and too close for comfort to Britain's
terests in the Middle East.

To most outsiders it seemed next to impossible that England could
ng survive. Churchill, however, refused to be dismayed; and the
ay after the last men arrived from Dunkerque he told his fellow
ountrymen:

We shall go on to the end . . . we shall defend our Island, whatever the
ost may be, we shall fight on the beaches, we shall fight on the landing
rounds, we shall fight in the fields and in the streets, we shall fight in the
ills; we shall never surrender, and even if, which I do not for a moment
elieve, this Island or a large part of it were subjugated and starving, then
ur Empire beyond the seas, armed and guarded by the British Fleet, would
arry on the struggle.

# A History of England and the British Empire

Two weeks later he concluded another speech with these words:

> Let us therefore brace ourselves to our duties, and so bear ourselves tha
> if the British Empire and Commonwealth last for a thousand years, me
> will say, "This was their finest hour."

Once again England was keyed to meet destruction; but the sum
mer days came and went after Dunkerque, and still the German
paused. The first bomb on England herself had long since explode
harmlessly in a field near Canterbury the day before the German
plunged into Holland and Belgium. Scattered raids had followe
and with gradually increasing intensity, but they were mild com
pared with what was to come.

Hitler, for some reason, was giving England a respite; yet he wa
not idle. Thousands of boats and barges were being gathered b
the Germans all along the Dutch, Belgian, and French "invasio
coasts," just as Napoleon and other French leaders had hopefull
prepared in the past. The British too worked fast; secretly pipe line
were run out from their beaches, through which oil could be pumpec
which, ignited, would turn the waters into a fiery inferno to preven
landings. But the invaders never got so close as that to England'
shores. The British fliers bombed the assembled barges across th
Channel; but what apparently stopped the Germans was their reluc
tance to send forth their landing barges until the *Luftwaffe* con
trolled the skies over the Channel and could beat off any naval an
air attacks by the defenders. Consequently the first phase of th
aerial battle of Britain would be for control of the Channel and th
southeast coast.

The storm struck on August 8, 1940. Hundreds of German plane
launched a terrific, all-out attack on shipping and ports and airfield
along the southeast coast. Thus began the epic battle of Britain—
three months of a fiery trial that defies description; after that cam
seven months of intensive night bombings to wear down still furthe
the heroic survivors.

Yet the enemy found no easy victory. Adequately warned an
superbly manned, the Royal Air Force took a tremendous toll. O
August 15, for instance, out of more than a thousand German planes
158 were shot down by the defending fighters and 17 more by anti
aircraft fire; the R.A.F. lost only 34 planes, and half the fliers wer
saved. Nor were the Germans able to gain their objective, air mas
tery to safeguard an invasion. For all their terrific losses, they wer
not able to smash enough of the well-scattered airfields to halt th
angry swarms of fighters, which rose day after day to meet th
oncoming *Luftwaffe*.

# "There'll Always Be an England"

In this crucial test the R.A.F. was seriously outnumbered by Marshal Hermann Göring's *Luftwaffe*, but it made up for that deficiency by the quality of its fighter planes and their pilots. For the moment, the offensive Bomber Command was a secondary consideration; its great days would come later when England would carry the air war to Germany. Now the British pinned their defensive hopes on two splendid types of fighters, the Spitfires and the Hurricanes. Capable of traveling some 350 miles an hour, easily maneuverable and very well armed, these single-seater monoplanes were more than a match not only for the slow and lightly armored bombers, but also even for the fast Messerschmitt fighters. The Germans had concentrated on a tactical air force, designed to co-operate with the tanks and other ground forces as part of their *Blitzkrieg* technique. Their dive bombers had served their purpose well against the Poles, Dutch, Belgians, and French. They were not, however, so well adapted for the work ahead over Britain. Man for man, moreover, the pilots of the R.A.F. were better trained than the German fliers.

After a month of pounding the southeast coast, the Germans, early in September, made their first great daylight raid on London itself; thereafter the capital sustained thirty-eight such attacks throughout September and into October. Naturally, the destruction was horrible. The bombs themselves and the fires which followed destroyed docks, factories, railroads, and electric and gas installations, together with thousands of homes. If the Germans hoped to break British morale, they failed. From the wreckage and debris, volunteers pulled out the dead and rushed the wounded to such hospitals as survived the bombings, while others tried to fight the fires amid broken water mains. At the same time, millions kept up their daily routine at office or store, all with amazing fortitude and cheerfulness.

The Spitfires and Hurricanes fought on far overhead. In the first three months of the battle of Britain the *Luftwaffe* lost 2375 planes and their crews; the R.A.F. counted its losses in the hundreds, only 375 pilots and a somewhat larger number of planes. On September 15, when the Germans sent over the greatest of their attacks, they lost 185 of their planes. Ten per cent was reckoned as the heaviest loss that an air force could sustain and still keep going. The Germans could not keep up this rate of loss, and by the end of October they had abandoned daylight raids, which meant also the abandonment of immediate invasion. The R.A.F., in its sturdy planes, had saved England; "never in the field of human conflict was so much owed by so many to so few," Churchill declared. They fully deserved the nation's gratitude; so, too, did the thousands who spread the warnings, manned the antiaircraft guns, and cleared up the wreckage, along with the millions of others who refused to be dismayed.

Though the invasion crisis was past, the *Luftwaffe* was not through with England. It turned to night bombing, which the British fighters could not intercept as efficiently. Throughout that winter and the following spring, night after night was made hideous with the sirens, the antiaircraft fire, the falling of bombs, and the ruddy glow of fire. The City, London's financial district, was almost wiped out by a terrible shower of incendiary bombs on December 30, with St. Paul's Cathedral spared almost miraculously amid surrounding wreckage. Birmingham and the ports from Southampton to Plymouth and Bristol and Liverpool were visited and revisited. Coventry was devastated by the first of the so-called saturation raids, eleven hours of bombing by successive trips of four hundred planes in mid-November. Finally, when Germany turned to new attacks in Crete and Russia, the raids died down.

German bombs killed 23,767 civilians in 1940 and 20,881 in 1941; thereafter the score fell off to 3236 in 1942 and 2367 in 1943. A still larger number were seriously injured, to say nothing of an appalling casualty list resulting from accidents in the black-out. Whatever the actual figures were, the people of England went through those years of war never knowing from one moment to the next when death might descend upon them from the skies. The terror from the air, as will be seen, revived in 1944 with the German use of "robot bombs" fired from the Continent.

Meanwhile, in the battle of the Atlantic, the bright outlook of March, 1940, had turned black by the middle of June; the *Blitzkrieg* had made the incredible happen to British sea power. With the whole western coast of Europe, from the North Cape to Spain, in German hands, the Mediterranean too, as we shall see, had become another perilous sea lane. No longer did the enemy U-boats have to use German bases; they had their choice of harbors from Norway to the Bay of Biscay. What was worse, these included ports just across the Channel. And not only submarines, but planes were now utilizing those same bases to blast shipping in British ports and even to menace it several hundred miles at sea. Nor was that all; destroyers, the most valuable vessels for escort work, were sadly lacking. In contrast to the 781 in use by the Allies during the latter part of the first war, England had fewer than 150 available after Dunkerque. As a result, the convoy system deteriorated; and the attempt to substitute seaplanes for destroyers was helpful only within a comparatively short distance from shore. Antisubmarine defense was further badly handicapped, as we saw, by the neutrality of Eire.

From the toll of 98,000 tons sunk in March, there was a rapid rise to 538,000 tons in June, the month of Dunkerque. Yet, as in 1917, a steady flow of oil, food, munitions, and other essentials must pour into England, or she was finished. And to the rescue, once again, came the United States, not only to be the arsenal of democracy, but also to see that those precious cargoes reached their destination. This time that did not mean just the comparatively short Atlantic shuttle, but the far reaches of the Pacific, and halfway round the world by Africa to the Middle East.

Churchill had closed his speech after Dunkerque with the hope "until, in God's good time, the New World, with all its power and might, steps forth to the rescue and the liberation of the old." He had in mind, of course, the United States, where he had cultivated a close community of interest with President Franklin Delano Roosevelt, who was to prove England's most useful supporter beyond the seas. Much earlier than President Wilson, in the first war, Roosevelt began to place America's abundant resources at England's disposal in her hour of need, in spite of the determination, at this time, of a large portion of the American public not to be drawn into another war "to save the British Empire."

Most Americans, however, were prepared to go a good way in that direction so long as they did not become involved in a "shooting war." Their forthcoming actions were not entirely unselfish, for the amazing events of May and June made them fear the elimination of that bulwark of the Atlantic, the royal navy, and they could imagine such dire possibilities as the Germans in Bermuda and Newfoundland. Congress authorized a tremendous "Two-Ocean Navy" in July and compulsory military service in September. In the latter month, one of the worst in the battle of Britain, the nation had gone far enough on the road to war to accept the presidential announcement that fifty overage destroyers had been given Britain in exchange for long-term leases of eight western-Atlantic colonial bases. These stretched from Newfoundland to British Guiana, with sites in Bermuda, the Bahamas, Jamaica, Antigua, St. Lucia, and Trinidad included.

The fifty destroyers helped, but they were not enough to restore relative security on the all-important Atlantic. During the winter months the sinkings dropped toward 300,000 tons, which was roughly two ships a day; but with the spring of 1941 they rose again. They did not reach the high toll of April, 1917; yet the situation was fully as gloomy because the longer duration of this crisis meant a greater total drain on shipping. The home waters were gradually made comparatively secure by the planes of the Coastal Command and the swarms of hastily built corvettes; but the German answer was to move out into mid-Atlantic, beyond the range of the shore-based planes. New tactics, which proved more deadly, caused the U-boats to hunt in groups instead of alone. These "wolf packs" tore into shipping with devastating effect.

That spring saw a new threat on the North Atlantic. The mighty battleship *Bismarck*, suspected of being the most powerful warship afloat and reputedly unsinkable, was missing from her Norwegian base and apparently bent on commerce-raiding or worse. Spotting her at last between Greenland and Iceland, the royal navy gave immediate chase. Its greatest ship, the *Hood*, went down in the ensuing battle, and the new battleship *Prince of Wales* withdrew badly mauled. Later, however, the *Bismarck* was cornered by the determined British, who called in everything they had for the pursuit, and at last she was sunk by the combined pummeling of naval guns and torpedoes, four hundred miles from the French coast.

In August, 1941, Churchill met with Roosevelt on warships off the coast of Newfoundland. They laid down general principles, reminiscent of the Fourteen Points, as the basis for peace. This Atlantic Charter emphasized to the world the growing unity of Britain and the United States.

With Britain's stormy North Atlantic life line in such peril, the United States quietly and gradually stretched neutrality to and beyond the limit. British warships were allowed to seek haven for repairs in American navy yards. American forces occupied Greenland, at first secretly, and relieved the British in Iceland, where the British had sent troops earlier to circumvent a possible German seizure. More and more of the Atlantic patrolling was taken over by the United States navy. In the autumn of 1941 American destroyers were being fired upon south of Iceland. In return, orders were sent American naval vessels to "shoot at sight." It was war, except in name.

All in all, the situation on the high seas, thanks to this American co-operation, began to show a constant improvement. The man in the street, however, was unaware of this because the British stopped publishing the statistics of monthly tonnage losses after July, and he still read of U-boat attacks and sinking merchantmen. In November, Churchill announced that the average losses for the four months through October had been only 180,000 tons, as earlier in the war, in contrast to the half-million average of the preceding four months. But the spread of the war to the Pacific, in December, was to force a relaxation of the thoroughgoing precautions of the elaborate convoy system and to bring, as we shall see, worse dangers to the sorepressed Atlantic shipping.

Not only on the seas did the United States help with those all-important cargoes for the battle fronts. Britain was in desperate financial straits and hard put to it to pay for the essential supplies. More quickly than before, the United States once more assumed England's old role of "Paymaster of the Allies." When the war broke out, it looked as if this time the United States might be going to avoid the pitfalls that had brought her into war in 1812 and 1917. Her new neutrality acts, passed in the hope of keeping out of future wars and in disillusion over past war profits and unpaid foreign loans, were reminiscent of the days of Embargo and Nonintercourse (see page 573). Not only was the sale of war supplies, either directly or indirectly, to belligerents prohibited, but loans also were barred, and by the Neutrality Act of 1935 and its modifications American vessels were forbidden to enter any war zone. Four years later, with the outbreak of war in Europe, the sale of munitions to belligerents again was allowed, but the belligerent must pay for them without aid of loans, must take possession of them in the United States, and must transport them in non-American vessels. This was blatantly aid to Britain alone, since Germany could never get by the British navy to take advantage of it. By 1941 not even this cash-and-carry arrangement served Britain's needs, for she was running short of cash. Try as she would to ship tweeds, heirlooms, and Scotch whisky westward to pay for the planes, guns, and munitions that she had ordered, they were not enough. Then she took a step which was to be one of the heaviest prices she would have to pay in the war. For a century England had been investing her surplus capital beyond the seas; when the war began, this Victorian inheritance amounted to some fourteen billion dollars, the dividends and interest from which were a vital part of the British economy. The war was to see all that spent; and England would actually be owing several billions to her former overseas debtors.

By this time the United States was too far committed to her old role of being England's arsenal to refuse aid in this new financial crisis. She did not repeat her heavy loans, still unpaid, of the first war, but took the more realistic attitude that if a friend needed money which was unlikely to be repaid, it was better to get credit at the outset for generosity than to whistle vainly for repayment at the end (see page 923). This policy also might give the donor more control than he would have if the recipient felt that he was spending his own money. Lend-lease, as it was called, empowered United

States government agencies "to manufacture in arsenals, factories, and shipyards under their jurisdiction . . . any defense article for the government of any country whose defense the President deems vital to the defense of the United States," and "so sell, transfer title to, exchange, lease, lend or otherwise dispose of, to any such government any defense article." This made outright gifts possible not only to England, but to the other belligerents who needed material. By mid-1942 the rate of expenditure was already eight billions a year. Out of the 42 billion dollars of lend-lease supplies and services furnished by the United States by July 1, 1945, to the various recipients, about two thirds went to the British Empire and one quarter to the Russians.

Lend-lease was not altogether a one-way affair. England, Australia, New Zealand, and India, for example, furnished munitions and supplies to American forces quartered there. This "reverse lend-lease" from the British Empire amounted to over five billion dollars' worth, which was about 95 per cent of the total reverse lend-lease from all nations. The United Kingdom supplied about 70 per cent of this; Australia and New Zealand, about 18 per cent (returning almost as much as they received); India, about 9 per cent; and the rest came in small amounts from South Africa and colonies as scattered as Fiji and Nigeria. Canada, which had its own separate arrangement with the United States, was not included in lend-lease transactions. This reciprocal aspect of lend-lease relieved shipping and made for better co-operation. The latter was needed, for sour tales came of British use of lend-lease material to compete with Americans in export markets and in other objectionable ways.

Britain's third major problem in 1940–1941 lay in the Mediterranean and North Africa, where Italy had become a threat. The usual trade route to India and the East by way of Gibraltar and Suez naturally was blocked. Luckily, the old pre-Suez detour around Good Hope was available, but its added length cut the number of round trips a year that the all-too-scarce ships could make (see page 944). England had to use that roundabout run to supply not only her forces in the Far East, but also those in Egypt and other parts of the Middle East. Later many supplies to Russia had to go around that tip of Africa to the Persian Gulf ports. The bulk of this armament, of course, came increasingly, as the months passed, from the United States; it was 14,000 miles from New York around the Cape to the Persian Gulf or to Suez, in contrast to the 3000 of the North Atlantic shuttle and even to the 9000 via Panama across the Pacific to Australia.

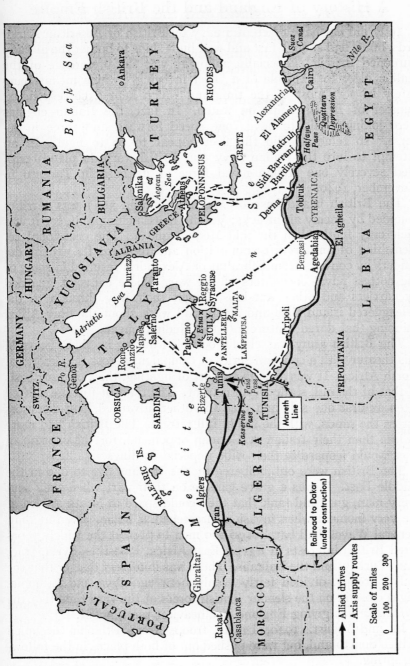

THE MEDITERRANEAN AND NORTH AFRICA

# A History of England and the British Empire

Italy did not have much of a navy by British or American standards, but it had enough fast and well-built ships to bother the already burdened British. Especially annoying was the preference of the Italian navy for the role of a "fleet in being," which meant lying safely in port most of the time and which kept a corresponding number of British ships on watch. In fact, the Italian engines were jokingly said to have "one speed forward and three in reverse," so reluctant did the fleet appear to be to fight. In an attempt to lure the Italian navy out, British torpedo planes crippled severely one Italian naval force at its base in Taranto in November, 1940.

The British island base of Malta (see page 566) was terribly pounded by enemy air attacks; yet the British clung to it, for it was their only foothold in the mid-Mediterranean. The occasional replenishing of antiaircraft ammunition and food for its valiant defenders by convoys from Gibraltar or Alexandria resulted in some of the hottest naval encounters of the war. These convoys, guarded by carriers and other warships, fought their way through to the beleaguered island time and again, and were about the only Allied shipping that dared venture into the Mediterranean.

The British army was chiefly occupied during its three years in this theater with a constant series of campaigns across the deserts of North Africa. It was a fantastic sort of fighting, the very antithesis of that of the old, static western front. The tides of fortune shifted often as first one side and then the other advanced long distances across the sands, with the foe in full retreat. The British had more to lose than their Italian or German opponents, for the capture of Suez would jeopardize their wide imperial holdings.

The British were outnumbered by the Italians five to one in the Middle East. It was a grave gamble on their part when they sent every man, gun, and tank that they could spare to North Africa at the very moment when invasion threatened at home. Even at that, General Wavell had barely 100,000 men to protect the widely separated British interests in Egypt, East Africa, Palestine, Syria, Iraq, Iran, Turkey, and the Balkans. There was imminent danger that the Italian troops, divided fairly evenly between Libya and Ethiopia, might close in on the slender British forces at the very time that the *Luftwaffe* was giving England her heaviest punishment.

In mid-August, 1940, Italian troops from Ethiopia occupied British Somaliland, but were pushed out of both places in the following spring.

The North African fighting proper began when Italy's Libyan army crossed the frontier into Egypt in September, 1940. After penetrating fifty miles to Sidi Barrani, they stopped to dig in; and here they sat for three months, until in December the British fell upon them in a surprise attack.

Then followed the first of the great North African chases. While the demoralized Italians fled along the coast road, trying to hold own after town, the British tanks led a hot pursuit. The great northward bulge of the coast at Bengasi gave the British their chance; cutting two hundred miles across trackless desert, they reached El Agheila at the foot of the bulge barely two hours ahead of the fleeing enemy in February, 1941. The little British force of only 30,000 men bagged some 135,000 Italian prisoners and themselves lost only 604 men in their whirlwind campaign, which gave them eastern Libya.

Then, as happened often for both sides in this disheartening desert fighting, the North African picture suddenly turned black for the British. Crises in the Balkans and elsewhere to the eastward drew off troops that the British could ill spare; and the retreat-hungry Italians were replaced by crack German troops. The lightning winter desert campaign was undone before summer. Eastern Libya, so quickly gained, was lost even more quickly in a counterdrive by the German *Afrika Korps* and some Italians under the brilliant Rommel, a master of mobile warfare. He had been able to get a considerable force to Africa while the royal navy was busy with the Balkan situation; but he failed to capture the port of Tobruk, where an Australian division withstood an eight months' siege. Before long, however, he too was slowed down, by German needs elsewhere.

Meanwhile, Hitler's move to the eastward had made the Balkans a trouble-spot of the first order. Italy had already staged an invasion of Greece, in the preceding fall, only to be badly mauled by the heroic Greek defense. At the same time, the British had moved into Crete. Some weeks later the way was cleared for Hitler's eastward projects when Hungary, Slovakia, and Rumania joined the Axis; and in March of 1941 Bulgaria also came in.

Then, in April, as in the preceding April, Hitler sprang a sudden offensive, with Yugoslavia and Greece the victims. Yugoslavia put up one of the bitterest fights the Germans had met, though to no avail; but Greece added to Britain's troubles.

Britain had promised to defend Greece, as she had promised Poland; but she was in no state to keep this pledge either. Any effective British resistance was obviously out of the question at this time; yet political considerations prevailed against the hopeless military outlook, and Wavell was ordered to send to Greece some 76,000 of the troops he needed to consolidate his desert victories. The way

was clear for their transport across the Mediterranean because of a
recent smashing naval victory over the Italians at Cape Matapan,
but on land inevitable defeat awaited them at the hands of the
Germans. The loss of 30,000 soldiers was the cost to the British, and
Greece succumbed quickly.

Late in May came another German demonstration of new military
ideas. With Crete 180 miles from the Greek mainland, which they
occupied, and with the British navy in control of the intervening
waters, German air-borne troops, arriving by parachute, glider
and transport, descended upon the island and wrested it from the
British. The latter fought bitterly and lost some 13,000 more men,
as well as several cruisers and destroyers, which too could ill be
spared.

The unfortunate scattering of Wavell's forces did not end here,
however, for it began to look as though German intrigue were paving
the way for further jumps into western Asia. In late spring, while
some of his troops were clearing the Italians from Ethiopia, a revolt
had to be put down in Iraq. In early summer Wavell's forces joined
with Free French forces in clearing out the pro-Axis Vichy government in Syria. Later they co-operated with the Russians to save the
situation in Iran. By that time Wavell had gone to India, where he
became viceroy.

On top of all the bad news from the Middle East that spring of
1941, a most providential stroke of luck befell England on June 22,
when Hitler turned on Russia. Almost exactly a year after the
French surrender the British finally gained an ally. Hitler, on the
other hand, now had the two-front war that he had always feared,
and eventually would find the going harder. The *Luftwaffe* soon
eased its bombing of Britain to seek new targets, and in the long
run the Russian campaigns were still more helpful through their
attrition of German man power.

Three years later Churchill declared:

It is the Russian Army that has done the main work of tearing the guts
out of the German Army. In the air and on the ocean and seas we can maintain ourselves, but there was no force which could be called into being except
after several years that would have been able to maul and break the German
Army and subject it to such terrible slaughter and manhandling as has fallen
upon the Germans by the Russian Soviet Armies.

The lightning campaigns up to that invasion of Russia had killed
and wounded few men compared with the toll of the First World
War; the casualties had been largely prisoners. Now, at terrific cost

to themselves, the Russians performed the grim task of eliminating millions of Germans, a task that otherwise would have fallen to the British and the Americans.

Russia had been doing her share of annexing territory since 1939. Her pact with the Germans on the eve of the war, as we saw, had given her eastern Poland. In November, 1939, she had attacked her small neighbor Finland, which put up such a gallant resistance that the outside world drew erroneous conclusions about Russian military efficiency. The following May, Russia had quietly annexed Lithuania, Latvia, and Estonia, her former Baltic provinces. A month later she had moved into two Rumanian provinces.

In retrospect Hitler's attack on Russia, like Napoleon's long before, stands out as his most ghastly military blunder. Up to then, his campaigns had easily made him master of western and central Europe. His "intuition" has been credited with the success of many of the brilliant moves at which his professional soldiers had shaken their heads. This time it led him too far; but it must be recalled that military experts in many lands expected another swift victory for him.

There is no room here to follow the Russian campaigns except as they affected England's situation. In brief, the Russians "traded space for time" and did not check the Germans until they were almost at Moscow and Leningrad and had overrun most of the Crimea. Then winter set in, and the Germans were not prepared for that. *Blitzkrieg* gave way to months of grim slaughter.

By the time snow and cold had bogged down the Germans in Russia, the United States had changed from an informal to a formal ally, on December 7, 1941. Japan had struck simultaneously at the British and the Americans in various parts of the Pacific and eastern Asia; in the next few days the Americans were at war with Germany and Italy also.

The Japanese, allies in the First World War, had been working aggressively to spread their power in the Far East. They had begun to wrest Manchuria from China in 1931, without serious protest from the Western powers. In 1937 they launched a strong attack on China proper, after withdrawing from their agreements for naval disarmament. When the war in Europe began, they occupied the China coast and temporarily forced England to close the Burma Road, the only remaining route of any importance by which British and American supplies could reach China. In mid-September, 1940, they secured permission from Vichy France to send troops, ships, and planes to strategically located Indo-China. A week later Japan formally joined Germany and Italy in an Axis military alliance.

As was their wont, the Japanese struck first and declared war afterward. Early on the Sunday morning of December 7 their planes from a carrier force swooped down upon the great American naval base at Pearl Harbor in Hawaii. They wiped out most of the American planes before the latter could rise to meet the attack, and sank or crippled the battleships of the Pacific fleet, to say nothing of other ships and installations. Within a few hours they had achieved their purpose: the United States navy would not interfere with their plans elsewhere for some time to come. That same day they attacked also the Philippines and the little crown colony of Hong Kong.

Three days later two mighty British warships, the battle cruiser *Renown* and the battleship *Prince of Wales*, which had fought the *Bismarck* in the spring, went to the bottom under the blows of Japanese bombs and torpedoes. These great ships had been hurried to the British naval base of Singapore, in anticipation of trouble. That base was supposedly impregnable to attack, with the royal navy to brush off any approach from the sea and with the Malay jungles behind it, considered impassable. But the sea dog who commanded those warships failed to secure air protection; and this second naval disaster within a week further expedited the Japanese progress southward.

To the further consternation of the British and Americans, the impossible kept happening. The base itself was in Japanese hands by February 15. With the naval part of the Malayan defense plan out, the rest of it was to prove equally ineffectual. On the day after Pearl Harbor, Japanese soldiers were already approaching the upper neck of the long Malay Peninsula; and they were such well-trained jungle fighters that the thick tangle ahead did not daunt them. Whenever the British defenders tried to form a defense line across the peninsula, the Japanese simply cut in behind them and forced their retreat. Unlike the Americans in the Philippines, who were receiving valuable aid from native soldiers whom they had trained, the British had scorned, until the last minute, to rely on the Malayans for support; and naturally they received none. And without air coverage the British found themselves helplessly exposed to Japanese reconnaissance and bombs. By the end of January the mainland was abandoned and only Singapore island was left. In contrast to the antiquated efforts of the army, the royal navy had equipped its base with big guns and the most modern of fortifications; but all that bristling armament pointed seaward—and the enemy came from the defenseless rear. Singapore fell in February. An army of some 100,000 British, Australian, and Indian troops, which had previously sustained relatively few casualties, was captured by only 30,000 Japanese.

# "There'll Always Be an England"

Well could Churchill call it "the greatest disaster to British arms which history records." For centuries it had been understood that if the British army got into a jam, the royal navy would extricate it. Except for Yorktown it had performed this service regularly, even to Norway and Dunkerque in this war. It was understandable that nothing could save the diminutive Hong Kong garrison, whose surrender on Christmas Day had been followed by the bayoneting of prisoners and the raping of Englishwomen. But for a city which was world-famed as a naval base to surrender with a large army quite intact was indeed something new in British annals. Yet the royal navy could scarcely be blamed, when, within ten weeks, seven of its capital ships had been sunk or seriously damaged, losses comparable to those of the Americans at Pearl Harbor. Furthermore, an army of 100,000 might have been expected to be able to handle 30,000 of the enemy.

All this served merely to clear the way for the prime objectives of the enemy; what the Japanese really wanted were the rich British and Dutch possessions at the southeast corner of Asia—Malaya, Java, Sumatra, Borneo, and the rest. With the American fleet at Pearl Harbor immobilized for the moment and the British base at Singapore in her hands, Japan had practically within her grasp vast reserves of oil, which she had lacked, together with the lion's share of the world's rubber and tin supply and much other rich plunder. While the getting was good, the Japanese would pick up whatever else they could, to protect the approaches against counterattack; they might even threaten Australia and India. Their propaganda told the sullen native subjects in those regions how much more fortunate they would be as partners in Japan's "Greater East Asia Co-Prosperity Sphere" than under the heel of the arrogant white man.

The Australian prime minister saw the fall of Singapore opening the battle for Australia; Java, the next great prize, lay between, but was already ripe to fall. During late January and February, 1942, a small force of British, American, and Dutch cruisers and destroyers in those waters fought a desperate delaying action in the Strait of Macassar and the Java Sea, but were overwhelmed. Japanese air superiority continued; and Port Darwin, at the northeast tip of Australia, toward which refugees from Java were heading, was almost demolished. Java was not the only rich island to fall; Sumatra, Borneo, and many others were overrun by the swarming Japanese advance.

In Australia the people were both alarmed and disgruntled. They felt that England was letting them down and demanded the return of their troops sent up to Suez two years before. This was done; and by the time these troops reached home in late March, American

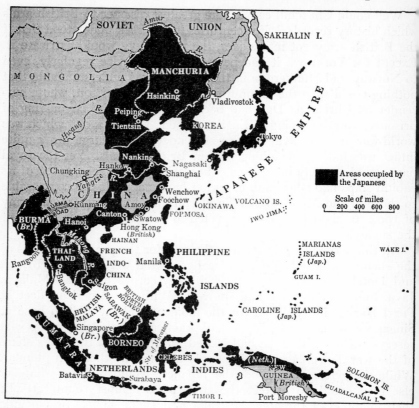

JAPANESE CONQUESTS AT THEIR GREATEST EXTENT, 1942

forces, under the American general MacArthur, the designated Allied commander of the Southwest Pacific Area, were already there to defend the dominion. Danger was closer then, for the Japanese were already in New Guinea.

The seemingly irresistible onward march of the little yellow men was not only island-jumping. They were spreading westward into Burma, with India just beyond, even before they were halfway down the Malay Peninsula. If the Malays were apathetic, the Burmese showed definite hostility to the British rule. By early March, Rangoon was gone; the British were out of southern Burma; and Mandalay was to be next. With Singapore theirs, the Japanese navy now moved out into the Gulf of Bengal to threaten the shipping lanes to Calcutta and Madras. Early in April, Ceylon was raided, and two British cruisers and a carrier were sunk. There seemed no limit to the distances the Japanese victors might travel; in anticipation of the worst, the British quickly sent an expedition to seize the distant French island of Madagascar, off the coast of Africa.

The Pacific war became, by the spring of 1942, primarily the responsibility of the United States navy, together with the air forces, and to a lesser degree the army of the United States. Although Australians and New Zealanders co-operated in all this, there is no room here to follow it play by play. Gradually the Japanese were slowed down and finally checked during 1942. Having broken the Japanese naval code, the Allies were able to anticipate their moves. A drive toward Australia was smashed early in May in the battle of the Coral Sea, a carrier fight in which the ships never came within a hundred miles of one another. Just a month later the Japanese navy was further severely crippled in the battle of Midway. There was still a danger, however, that the Japanese occupation of the Solomon Islands might endanger the southern supply route between the United States and Australia. In early August the Americans moved in there with a desperate minimum of force; the next night the Japanese sank three American cruisers and one Australian cruiser; but the Solomons fight went on, with the enemy sending a constant succession of expeditions to recover the islands. Beaten back or smashed in constant minor and occasional major engagements, they finally gave up the attempt in November. From that point the Japanese fleet showed that it was past its peak.

Meanwhile, based on Australia, the Australians and Americans were fighting bitter battles in New Guinea jungles to check the enemy approach there. Slowly they succeeded in doing this; and with that defensive work finally in hand, the time came for counterdrives toward Japan. One of these, led by MacArthur, was to approach northward past New Guinea and adjacent islands toward the Philippines, while the other was to be a drive by the United States navy through the islands of the Central Pacific, capturing some, and by-passing others. Eventually the two would meet. Any former British or Dutch territory recovered in the process was to be immediately restored.

Two weeks after Pearl Harbor, Churchill arrived in Washington. Germany and Italy had declared war on the United States, and he wanted to be sure that the present concentration on the Pacific would not cause the Americans to slacken their support of the war in Europe. His visit marked the beginning of a formal integration of British and American war-planning, which already was well developed on an informal basis. From this meeting would follow a series of conferences on major policies by the leaders of the two nations, sometimes with others present, such as Stalin of Russia and Chiang

Kai-shek of China. A permanent mechanism for translating those policies into action also was to be evolved. Less immediately tangible, but important for future possibilities, was the signing of a military alliance by the United Nations, on January 1, 1942. Henceforth the war was to be definitely a global war. The signers of this "Declaration of Washington," which contained many of the broad war aims of the Atlantic Charter of the previous August, included, besides Britain and the United States, Russia, China, the British dominions, many of the governments in exile from Holland to Yugoslavia, many of the Latin-American republics, and various other nations. The United Nations soon included double these original twenty-six.

It was indicative of Britain's weakened position that, though Washington was more than once the site of these major conferences of leaders, London never was. Other factors were involved, of course, such as the bombing of London and Stalin's refusal to budge far beyond his borders, which brought conferences to remote Tehran and Yalta; but nonetheless Britain no longer was the dominant power. Yet Churchill seldom came away from such gatherings without getting a good deal of what Britain wanted. He persuaded the Americans to give priority to Europe in their war plans; he kept lend-lease supplies flowing freely; and his adamant refusal to commit British forces to a repetition of the "sombre mass slaughters" on the western front of the first war made good his promise that England should not have another "lost generation." (Both he and Roosevelt, after consultation with their professional advisers, felt themselves competent to make the final military and naval decisions. Those two men were the core of the united decisions; Stalin generally played a lone hand, and the other participating nations carried little weight.

Out of such conferences came the general approval of major operations to be launched months later. To preserve secrecy, these were always referred to by nicknames, such as "Torch" (North African landings), "Husky" (Sicilian invasion), "Avalanche" (invasion of Italy), and "Overlord" (invasion of Normandy). The next step fell to the Combined Chiefs of Staff, set up at Washington. This group consisted of the heads of the American land, sea, and air forces, known as the Joint Chiefs of Staff, sitting with representatives of the corresponding British group. They worked out further details of what, when, and where. Their decisions were binding on the armed forces of both nations, whose appropriate staffs then developed the overwhelming amount of detailed planning which necessarily preceded such tremendous undertakings.

In addition, the British and Americans agreed upon over-all combined command in each major theater of war. An operation such as

# "There'll Always Be an England"

Gallipoli in 1915 had shown what trouble might arise when the army and navy of the same nation were simply enjoined to co-operate with each other; the difficulties were naturally multiplied when more than one nation participated, as Marlborough, Wellington, and Haig had learned to their cost. Instead, therefore, one man was given actual command over all land and sea forces of both nations in a particular theater or area. This control was a more tangible one than Foch had been given in 1918 (see page 885). Thus ultimately an American admiral (Nimitz) commanded the Pacific Ocean Areas; an American general (MacArthur), the Southwest Pacific Area; a British admiral (Mountbatten), the Southeast Asia Command; and a British general (Wilson), the Mediterranean area, relieving an American general (Eisenhower), who eventually was promoted to command the European Theater of Operations. If the top layer was British, the next layer would contain some Americans, and vice versa. This integration was essentially an Anglo-American arrangement; some of the smaller nations came under this leadership, but the Russians and Chinese were linked simply by Allied missions. Outside the purely military field, other joint groups controlled shipping, economic resources, and other essentials. Altogether, it was a unique venture in Allied integration, and it must be reckoned as one of the important causes of final victory.

The summer of 1942 marked the low ebb of the fortunes of the Allies; and it followed months of seeing their enemies victorious east and west, on Russian plains and African deserts, in the jungles and swamps of southeastern Asia, and among the clustered islands of the East Indies. September 1, 1942, the exact middle day of the six-year war, found the conquering Germans far across Russia at the Volga and far across North Africa into Egypt; the Japanese navy was pounding at the Solomons, and the Japanese army was at the gates of India; the precious supplies for those hard-pressed Allied fronts faced worse jeopardy than ever before on sea lanes near and far. Had the two German drives joined, as looked all too possible at this grim moment, they would have forced the British out of the Middle East, and presumably could have swept on toward India to meet the Japanese swarming toward them. In these weeks Britain and the United States were faced with possible loss of the war, and Russia seemed on the verge of surrender. Churchill flew to Moscow to plan with Stalin a way out of their desperate plight.

Yet that fall of 1942 marks the turning point toward total victory for the sore-pressed Allies. In the Solomons, as we have seen, the Japanese navy lost its offensive power; in Russia and Egypt the turning point was thorough and dramatic. In Northwest Africa the United States and Britain staged their first major invasion. Only in southeastern Asia did the tide fail to turn in favor of the Allies. Henceforth the course of the war will be followed in less detail because Britain's part was overshadowed by that of Russia and the United States, in contrast to the previous years, when she carried the bulk of the burden.

In Russia the Germans, though checked in the winter months of 1941–1942, had been on the march again soon after and headed toward the oil of the Caucasus, which they needed badly. In August, 1942, after a victorious sweep, they reached the distant industrial city of Stalingrad on the Volga. If that fell, all Asia seemed before them, as well as the Middle East, with the chance to unite with Rommel. Week after week, they stormed and pounded until little was left of Stalingrad but a mass of rubble. Yet the Russians doggedly held their ground; finally a relieving army doomed the German attackers, but Hitler ordered them to stand to the last man. Blasted by Russia's crack artillery, they had lost a third of a million men when their pitiful remnant surrendered in February, 1943. The Stalingrad stand gave the war on that front to the Russians. From then on they were able to push steadily westward to recover their devastated lands.

In North Africa the German reverses were as complete, but for the time being were less deadly. In the spring of 1941 Rommel had rapidly recovered eastern Libya, which the British had wrested from the Italians. For a whole year the fortunes of war had shifted back and forth in Libya, with some of the coastal towns being taken and retaken time and again. Late in May, 1942. Rommel started a major drive, which quickly assumed dangerous proportions. In one surprise action he nearly wiped out the whole British tank force with his heavy guns. Tobruk, which had withstood an eight months' siege at the time of his previous attack, now was taken with surprising ease. Crossing the Egyptian frontier, Rommel pushed on until, early in July, he reached the little railroad station of El Alamein, only seventy-five miles from Alexandria. A state of near panic developed as German patrols began to push still closer to the heart of Britain's vital interests in that region; secret papers were burned at headquarters lest they fall into enemy hands, and hasty plans were made to evacuate the whole Suez area. All through midsummer it seemed possible that at any moment Rommel's tanks might bring disaster.

The royal navy, during those tense weeks, strengthened the army's tight supply situation. Both sides had been short of supplies, but Rommel had been aided by being nearer his source. Now the

# "There'll Always Be an England"

royal navy was able to threaten his short supply run across the Mediterranean from Germany via Italy. At the same time, a steady stream of tanks, trucks, guns, and troops for the British was beginning to reach the Red Sea by way of the long run around Good Hope from America or England.

A change in command may have played its part also. Almost always England's stock of good admirals has been far more plentiful than that of adequate military commanders. At sea Admirals Cunningham and Somerville had been handling the Mediterranean naval situation with masterly skill; but on land North Africa, like Norway, Flanders, and Malaya, had been a graveyard for British military reputations. One commander after another had been tried, and the general who had routed the Italians so completely in 1941 had been killed in action. Now General Sir Harold Alexander was given the over-all Middle East Command and General, later Field Marshal, Sir Bernard Montgomery, who wore a jaunty beret constantly and neither smoked nor drank, became field commander in charge of the Eighth Army. This combination was to be heard from again, in Europe.

In October the British were able at last to smash at Rommel. Their planes gained mastery of the air; their sappers cleared paths through the deadly fields of land mines; and then, with a great assemblage of artillery and tanks, carefully camouflaged against aerial detection, they hit the German lines in full force. After a few days of furious fighting, in which many of his tanks were destroyed, Rommel started westward in one of the famous retreats of history. The British pounded steadily along at his heels, but they could not catch the "desert fox" as they had trapped the Italians; he kept ahead of them in the 1400-mile pursuit. We shall hear of him again shortly.

In early November, as this retreat was under way, and far across the world the Japanese fleet was withdrawing from the Solomons offensive, the Americans and British made their highly spectacular and "top secret" landings in force on the northwestern coasts of Africa. Simultaneously, and with complete surprise, a tremendous armada of 700 warships and transports landed a mighty army in French North Africa: British forces at Algiers, Americans at near-by Oran inside the Mediterranean, and other Americans at Casablanca on the Atlantic coast of Morocco. Much depended upon the very uncertain attitude of the French leaders in Africa. After much melodramatic negotiation, Algeria did not resist, but fighting was necessary for the Americans at Casablanca. Some of the ships came from Britain, others directly from American ports; yet the secret of the enormous preparations for this gigantic undertaking had been perfectly kept. It came as a stunning surprise to the world; more important, it caught the enemy unawares.

These North African landings were the best that the United States and England could do at the moment in answer to Stalin's clamor for a "second front" to relieve the pressure on Russia. The possibility of a direct crossing from England into France, which Stalin most desired, had been considered, but adequate forces were not available. Churchill announced that this new stroke, in Africa, would expose "the soft underbelly of the Axis" to Allied attack.

It had been hoped that these landings would quickly eliminate this front and release troops for a new offensive elsewhere. Unfortunately, the Allies did not consider themselves strong enough to occupy Tunisia at once, when the taking would have been easy. With Rommel steadily racing toward that goal, other Germans slipped across the Mediterranean to occupy Tunis and Bizerte. The advancing Allies still hoped to trap Rommel between themselves and the pursuing British forces; but in February, 1943, he turned on his pursuers. Complicated operations finally forced the surrender of Tunis and near-by Bizerte in May, and more than a quarter-million crack German troops were captured. Thus, at long last, the three years of North African fighting came to an end.

Before this surrender Churchill and Roosevelt had held another meeting, in January, at Casablanca, near the battle fronts. Churchill at last accepted the plan for a second front in France, but saw to it that the Americans agreed to furnish most of the troops. It was at this conference that the drastic words *unconditional surrender* and *no negotiated peace* were hurled at the enemies of the United Nations.

The battle of the Atlantic, we recall, had been going better at the time of Pearl Harbor; but the months thereafter were among the grimmest for the Allies. The United States found herself confronted with a two-ocean war without a two-ocean navy. Five weeks after she entered the war, the Germans launched a terrific, all-out U-boat attack on shipping in general and on oil tankers in particular. Boldly they did much of this sinking in American coastal waters within sight of the shore. The United States was caught without adequate small patrol vessels; her destroyers, as we saw, had already been busy for sometime out at sea. So serious was the lack of such small craft for this sort of inshore warfare that she had to borrow some from the British. As the antisubmarine patrols were improved in that region, the Germans moved down into the Caribbean, and the old Spanish Main was ablaze with burning vessels.

Naturally these sinkings reduced still further the number of cargo vessels. Already the lengthening of the sea lanes with the spread of the war to the Far East had cut that tonnage. Such long hauls inevitably meant fewer trips: a vessel could make only about one third as many round trips to Australia via Panama from New York, for instance, as it could across the North Atlantic, and less than one quarter as many to the Persian Gulf. Congested ports in these out-of-the-way places and inadequate facilities further tied up tonnage.

Into this emergency stepped the tremendous shipbuilding program of the United States; Britain was already building to capacity. In contrast to the situation in the first war, these new American cargo ships were to be at work on the seas long before peace came. Welding and preassembling made it possible to build more ships faster on fewer ways. In contrast to the average of ten to twelve months in the first war between laying the keel and delivering a steel freighter, it was a matter of weeks and even of days this time. Though several hundred ships were lost from enemy action during the war, this unprecedented shipbuilding program gave the United States, at the end of the war, the world's largest merchant marine, 5529 seagoing merchant ships against 1401 in 1939. Britain too had built many freighters, and, in spite of her far severer losses, the end of the war found her in second place with 2347 ships, only 545 fewer than she had had in 1939, when she occupied first place. And during hostilities these rapidly built ships kept the supplies reaching the distant fronts, despite all the enemy could do by undersea, surface, and air attack.

Not until the fall of 1942 was the latest U-boat offensive checked to any extent. In this war, when things became too hot, the U-boats shifted their hunting grounds; thus, from the waters just west of Britain, they had moved into the Greenland-Iceland region, then from the coastal waters of Canada and the United States to the Caribbean and beyond. Incidentally, the great expedition to North Africa was scarcely molested, thanks to secrecy, until after the transports had landed their troops.

By the spring of 1943 the end of the submarine story was in sight. By May the toll of U-boats sunk by the Allies began to mount, as the merchant sinkings fell off. The use of little escort carriers, which could give protection even on the hitherto bad Iceland stretch, drastically reduced losses. Danger still lurked on the icy run from the United States to Murmansk, beyond the North Cape on the open Arctic. This shortest way for supplies to the Russian front was so perilous that altogether about one fourth of the vessels that risked it were lost. Some of its danger was eliminated when superior forces of the royal navy trapped and sank the German battleship *Scharnhorst* as she was trying to raid a convoy in the last days of 1943. Later another powerful threat was removed when the giant *Tirpitz*, formidable sister ship of the *Bismarck*, which had long lain sheltered in a Norwegian fiord, was sunk by British bombers.

The first half of 1943 brought rumblings of restlessness in England. There was a general lull in the fighting as Britain and her allies shifted from the defensive to the offensive. Compared with the first war, when the armies remained in pretty much the same positions on the western front for four years and the hostile fleets lay at their bases across the North Sea for months on end without exchanging a shot, this second conflict had been packed with dramatic action all around the world. The British had experienced a series of dangerous crises, which had reached a climax in the preceding fall. The North African landings in November had aroused high hopes of a speedy major counteroffensive, which the stubborn German stand in Tunisia delayed for six months. All this contributed to a general and quite understandable sense of letdown in England, an irritation which was accentuated by the wholesale shifting of laborers to new places and new jobs because industrial effort was changing from defensive to offensive munitions.

While the feeling of acute danger, with its attendant spirit of heroic determination, had declined as the raids of the *Luftwaffe* grew less frequent, most of the wartime discomforts continued unabated. The black-out was still just as black as during the battle of Britain, but the novelty had worn off. For some those long, dark evenings meant increased opportunity for home life; others used them otherwise, and religious leaders began to deplore the decline in morals.

The nation too was becoming heartily tired of "Woolton pie," a nourishing but unexciting concoction of potatoes, cauliflower, turnips, carrots, and oatmeal, with a pastry top and gravy. It was named for the peer who had been doing a most effective job of adjusting Britain's diet to her food supply. The nation had become infinitely more self-supporting in foodstuffs than it had been in 1917. Four million grassy acres, including parks and golf courses, had come under the plow; the new Women's Land Army, eventually a half-million strong, was producing huge quantities of potatoes, barley, Brussels sprouts, and other crops which nutrition experts had recommended. England did not go hungry, but there were nostalgic yearnings, not only for steaks and chops, but for eggs, fish, tomatoes, oranges, and onions as well. Sugar and tea were scarce. Clothing too was severely rationed, alike for a duke and a docker, the queen and a charwoman.

A large portion of the population, moreover, had been uprooted from its familiar surroundings. More than a quarter of London's millions had abandoned the metropolis by mid-1941, while the exposed southeastern counties and the great industrial centers likewise had fallen off. Remote and quiet communities like York, Oxford, and Salisbury were struggling to accommodate swarms of newcomers. Some, including the evacuated children, began to return after the aerial *Blitz* had subsided, but the millions of damaged or demolished homes checked that process. Also, the policy of scattering industries around the country anchored large numbers of workers to new communities. These readjustments of population, with their attendant friction, were complicated by the increasing presence of overseas troops all over Britain, Canadians from the start and, by 1943, the advance guard of a million and a half Americans, who would use England as a staging area for the next year's assault on the Continent.

Along with black-out, rationing, and transplanting went a concentration of governmental power which made the "Doras" of the last war seem tame in comparison (see page 880). The Emergency Powers Act, passed a week before the war began, had re-enacted that former permission to govern by decree, rather than by legislation, during the emergency.

The radical novelty was the Emergency Powers Defense Act, introduced by Attlee in May, 1940, while the British army was retreating toward Dunkerque. The time had come, he said, to mobilize to the full the whole resources of the country. It gave the government "complete control over persons and property, not just some persons in some particular class of the community, but all persons, rich or poor, employer or employed, man or woman." The Minister of Labor was empowered to direct any person to perform any service required and to prescribe wages, hours, and conditions of labor. Employers could be told what to produce, and excess profits were eliminated. Even banks and finance in general came under this sweeping control. Conscription for the armed services had been introduced just before the war; now every adult civilian of working age likewise was placed at the government's disposal. Ernest Bevin, as Minister of Labor and National Service, administered both military conscription and these new powers. The inclusion of women in the compulsory category was a complete novelty. By the end of the war a very large proportion of British women were engaged either in the armed services as "Wrens" (navy), "Waafs" (air force), or "Ats" (army); in full-time civilian defense; or in industry.

Industrial unrest began to be evident in 1943, with the first strikes since 1939. The trade-unions had pledged themselves not to strike, and legislation forbade the practice. Nevertheless, scores of unofficial strikes sprang up, primarily among the coal-miners, but also among aircraft workers, bus-drivers, shipyard workers, and others. Some of the Conservatives felt that Bevin, who had organized a great trade-union himself, was not sufficiently severe in handling the strikes. On the other hand acrimonious debates occurred in Parliament when the government refused to let the postal workers unionize.

The nation in general, and labor in particular, were beginning to give attention also to reconstruction in the postwar world. Lloyd George, during the first war, had promised that peacetime England should be "a land fit for heroes," but it had proved anything but that; this time, even with the war in full swing, millions began to give thought to the future (see page 899). In mid-February, 1943, the Commons took up a sweeping report on social insurance made public ten weeks before by Sir William Beveridge, who proposed to "abolish want . . . from the cradle to the grave." When the government wanted to postpone definite action, the Labor party threatened a revolt and mustered 119 votes against 335 in a demand for immediate action. Churchill, a month later, tried to calm labor with a "Four-Year Plan" for reconstruction, but widespread dissatisfaction at the delay continued. In November, 1943, this feeling produced a new post; Lord Woolton, who had administered the food problem, was created Minister of Reconstruction, with a seat in the war cabinet. Labor, in the meantime, had decided to remain in the coalition while the war with Germany lasted.

That question of discussing postwar reconstruction raised distant echoes in some of the dominions, where the Beveridge report had been read with keen interest. The liveliest discussions occurred in Australia, where the political balance between the Labor party and the two anti-Labor parties was very close. In the very month that the Beveridge report appeared, a constitutional convention at Canberra discussed the extension of the wartime emergency powers of the federal government into peacetime in order to carry through a reconstruction program; the proposal was defeated by a narrow margin in a referendum in 1944. The question arose also in Canada and New Zealand, where the right-wing parties considered it inappropriate to devote much time to social reform with the war in full swing.

Linked with that were questions involving the nature and extent of the war effort. Except for the die-hard Afrikander element in

South Africa, the question of supporting the war did not arise. The Australian Labor party, however, was opposed to sending the dominion's armed forces, even the volunteers, outside the Southwest Pacific and, as we recall, drew back the Australians from the Middle East when the Japanese menace grew acute. New Zealand, with its tradition of ultraloyalty, which some termed a "mother complex," toward Great Britain, allowed its division to proceed from North Africa on up into Italy, despite occasional mutterings. Canada, which had refrained from conscripting the French Canadians in the first war, put through a modified conscription for home service, with only volunteers to go overseas (see page 871). Later, after a referendum permitted foreign service for conscripts, some of the drafted "Zombies" rioted in protest. In South Africa, with its ticklish political situation, the original limitation of its troops to African service was finally relaxed.

Although they constantly protested their undying devotion to the mother country, the dominions seemed to be growing more aware of their nationhood during the war. More and more they took external relations into their own hands, made their own combinations among themselves and with outsiders, and, except for South Africa, tightened their links with the United States. An outward symbol of this was the rapid growth of the various dominion diplomatic corps, which had begun just after the first war, when ministers were exchanged between Ottawa and Washington (see page 936). Canada, by 1944, had missions to twenty-four different countries, and its envoys to the United States, Russia, China, and Brazil had been elevated to the rank of ambassador. The Pacific dominions had had no direct foreign representation before the war, but in 1940 Australia decided to find out for itself what was going on, and exchanged envoys with Washington, Tokio, and Ottawa. Two years later New Zealand sent its first diplomat to Washington.

Australia, particularly jealous of its international status, clamored unsuccessfully for direct representation on the Combined Chiefs of Staff, while Canada kept a military mission at Washington to consult with them. Canada entered into a joint defense agreement with the United States and arranged its own substitute for lend-lease. Australia and New Zealand, early in 1944, drew up at Canberra an agreement for co-operation in regional defense.

Later, when the United Nations began to take form, Prime Minister Curtin of Australia was the outstanding exponent of the rights of the smaller nations, as opposed to domination by the great powers. It was also significant that a Canadian, tired perhaps of hearing that England fought alone between the fall of France and the entry of

Russia, referred to his dominion as "Great Britain's strongest ally" during that period. Not until the spring of 1944 did England finally summon a conference of the dominion prime ministers—Mackenzie King of Canada, Curtin of Australia, Smuts of South Africa, and Fraser of New Zealand. Curtin's proposal of an Empire Secretariat was rejected.

Whatever the sentimental implications of those diplomatic developments might be, there was an implied practical threat to England's postwar prosperity in the rapid development of war industries in the dominions. Previously the dominions had drawn a considerable part of their manufactured needs from Britain, but during the war all four developed industrially. This, of course, was of immediate valuable assistance to the imperial war effort, but England, already beginning to think in terms of "export or die," might suffer if those war plants were to be converted to the peacetime manufacture of planes, automobiles, and other products of her own industry. Canada already had a moderate industrial development, and Australia, starting almost from nothing, built plants to equip an armored division, yards to turn out warships and merchantmen, and much else. The industrial efforts of New Zealand and South Africa were more modest, yet far beyond any they had made before.

The military efforts of the dominions were magnificent and contributed mightily to the final victory. It is out of the question to recount all their accomplishments here. The North African desert campaigns and other fighting in the Middle East depended to no small extent upon the Australians, New Zealanders, and South Africans, along with Indian troops. The South Africans were the mainstay of the operations which cleared the Italians out of Ethiopia and Somaliland. The Australians, finally called home, contributed a major part of the ground forces which fought the Japanese in the jungles of New Guinea. The New Zealanders, as we saw, would continue into Italy. The Canadians, after long training in England, also would play an important role in Italy and then in the final great drive against Germany; they had already made a bloody raid on Dieppe and were represented in the defense of Hong Kong. The dominion navies likewise had relieved the royal navy of some of its burden. Canadian warships ultimately took over half the escort duty in the North Atlantic. Of Australia's little navy, the *Perth* disappeared in Sunda Strait under heavy fire during the loss of Java; the *Sydney* likewise slipped from view in flames after challenging a disguised German raider; and the *Canberra* was sunk with three American cruisers at Savu Island. The surviving vessels, with the New Zealand navy, carried on in the Pacific fighting. Fliers from all the dominions were constantly active, operating either from England or from other bases throughout the world. Tens of thousands of them had been trained in Canada in the Commonwealth Air Training Program; still others were trained at home. Preliminary casualty totals showed that 77,710 soldiers, sailors, and airmen from the four dominions were killed in the war (Canada, 37,476; Australia, 23,365; New Zealand, 10,028; and South Africa, 6840).

India also made a heavy contribution. Indian troops, it must be remembered, not only fought well in North Africa and in Italy, but helped to make possible the daring exploits of General Wingate in North Burma in 1943, the defeat of the vicious Japanese thrust at the American life line through the upper Brahmaputra valley to China in 1944, and the reconquest of Burma in 1945. India's economic contribution to the war effort, meanwhile, was, like that of the dominions, so extensive that even before the end of hostilities the financial ledger, for the first time in history, showed Britain in debt to India also.

This did not mean that the majority of Indians approved the war; quite the contrary. So densely populated was India, so illiterate and isolated were many of its people, that millions did not even know there was a war. Many millions more, however, did know; and probably a large part of them either belonged to or sympathized with the Indian National Congress, that extralegal organization, not recognized by the Indian constitution, which claimed, under the leadership of Gandhi and Nehru, to speak for India, and which opposed the war, as was noted earlier. Nevertheless, since the viceroy's cabinet was exclusively appointed by him without prior approval of the Indian legislature, and since the latter was only partially elected anyway,—and that, too, by a very narrow franchise,—the peoples had no option but to submit to war. Such control of local affairs as did remain in their hands in this far from democratic government, did not affect the war one way or another.

The Indian National Congress agreed to co-operate in winning the war, but at a price, immediate and complete independence for India. Since Gandhi, however, was a pacifist, who openly stated that he would not oppose the Japanese by force, and since many Moslems, among them India's best fighting men, rejected independence under the domination of the Congress, Britain dared not yield. What the Moslem League demanded was not only independence, but the separation of the predominantly Moslem provinces from the rest of India.

Britain compromised; Sir Stafford Cripps was sent to India with the promise of dominion status after the war and, for the time being, further representation in the viceroy's cabinet. The Indians might even have their own minister of defense in it and thus have an active share in the war, a share, that is, in preparing and in mobilizing for it. The war itself would be waged by a British commander in chief, untrammeled by political control. The Congress refused this offer; so also did the Moslem League. Cripps returned to England, and in August, 1942, the Congress summoned all Indians to revolt.

The British promptly threw the leaders into jail and suppressed the revolt which followed. This proved something more than a sit-down strike, something less than civil war. There were only a few thousand British troops in India, but they had machine guns and planes. They used both; with them they soon restored order.

The Japanese, as we have seen, were busy elsewhere in 1942. They did not interfere in India except by long-distance radio, and by inviting the Indian rebels to visit Tokyo, and, in Burma, by drilling a handful of Indian Nationalists for a coming war of liberation.

The inability of the British in India to imagine their danger and incompetence tided them over this crisis, as it had over so many others in their past history. As things stood, all of near-by Burma but its northern tip was lost; Japanese planes skimmed over the Bay of Bengal; disaffection was rife; the Nationalist Congress was in revolt. But this did not ruffle Wavell, sent from his North African command to be the new viceroy. He reorganized the Indian army, prepared to invade Burma, and actually did so on a small scale in 1943.

This British counterthrust into Burma was led by General Wingate, whose romantic career parallels in many ways that of General Gordon, England's erratic roving soldier of the nineteenth century (see page 717). Wingate introduced something new in warfare. His long-protracted hardening of raw recruits into tough, resilient units was not new, nor was the painstaking, minute drill in geographic lore upon which he insisted. What he did that was novel was to plan a campaign in which commissariat and munitions for several thousand air-borne infantry were transported entirely by plane and to articulate the planes so closely with the offense that they replaced railroads, motor trucks, and bullock trains to make movement rapid, despite rain, forest, and jungle. His new type of British soldier, moreover, became better trained in jungle tactics than the Japanese.

The immediate task in this counterattack was to sever enemy communication lines. These ran north and south through Burma, following the river valleys. Most important of all such lines was the railroad from Mandalay to Myitkyina; to reach it Wingate's men had to drive west-east, over high mountains, down through deep valleys, roughing it over bridle paths or no paths at all.

Wingate's guerrillas succeeded in demolishing the Mandalay railroad in seventy-five places and in dynamiting three steel bridges. They ambushed munition trains and captured supply dumps. Scattering to right and left, they always escaped capture. They were fed and supplied throughout by aerial transport, the R.A.F. flying some 50,000 air miles in their support. With each column went an R.A.F. officer in radio contact with planes. Guided by smoke signals by day, by flares by night, from the skies planes dropped gasoline, munitions, food, rum, clothes, even spectacles and false teeth, whatever, indeed, the portable radio ordered.

By the time that Wingate's men returned to India, they had raided on foot over 1000 miles, had penetrated to the east of the Irrawaddy River, and had disrupted communications over an important strategic area of 10,000 square miles in North Burma. Their feats proved that a small army could be fed, clothed, and armed by air, even in the tropics.

Britain, however, had very little to spare for such costly fighting in Burma. Lord Louis Mountbatten, sent out to head the Southeast Asia Command, flew to the capital of Chiang Kai-shek to confer with him and with the American general Stilwell. This was merely preparatory; until airfields in great number could be built and equipped in India, both for the R.A.F. and for the United States Tenth Air Force, no large-scale offensive against the implacable Japanese foe was feasible in the humid-hot malarial jungle of that dysentery-ridden land of Burma.

The British, in fact, had all they could do in 1944 to repel a Japanese attack on India. This was directed against Imphal, capital of a tiny Indian state, tucked away amid the hills on the borders of North Burma and India. North from Imphal for some 174 miles a highway led to Dinajpur on the Calcutta-Ledo railway. Once the Rising Sun reached Dinajpur, the American route to China would have to revert to the jungle, and the Chinese-American-British forces in the upper tip of Burma would be isolated. All that would be necessary then for the Japanese would be a holding action, while their troops, assisted, they hoped, by revolting Indians, swung down the Brahmaputra valley into Bengal, perhaps to stage another Singapore at Calcutta.

Against Imphal the Japanese hurled 80,000 picked troops and besieged it for over two months. Surging on north, they surrounded for eighteen days a British force at Kohima; if they had only by-passed it, they might have reached the strategic railroad. Fortunately for the British, it was much easier for them to reinforce their troops under General Slim than it was for the Japanese to send fresh troops up narrow mountain passes from the southeast.

The tide of battle turned with dramatic swiftness. The British Imperials drove the adversary into headlong flight, like thistledown before the wind, counting more than 50,000 Japanese dead. How many more of the original 80,000 perished in the jungle of sickness or by the knives of irate tribesmen, we do not know. Before the year was out, General Slim was back on the frontier of India, where he had buried his guns in the retreat from Burma in 1942. From now on it would be the British Empire, not Japan, that would take the offensive in Burma.

The British and Americans, by the middle of 1943, were ready to advance against the Continent. Three full years had gone since Dunkerque, and no British army had stood on European soil, except for the brief fiasco in Greece and occasional commando raids at Dieppe and elsewhere on the French coast. With American industry getting into its stride and with the enemy cleared from North Africa, Italy was next on the list. This was by no means what Stalin wanted as a second front, but it was the most the British and Americans dared now attempt; and it would be something to put Italy out of the war.

In the early hours of July 10, some three thousand strange-looking vessels, under heavy naval escort, were crossing the Mediterranean from North Africa to Sicily. Crowded aboard were 160,000 men, half British, half American, and their equipment, ready to be disgorged by these new landing craft directly upon the beaches ahead. A terrific gale struck. Disaster threatened this unwieldy armada; but the wind subsided in time for the seasick armies to land safely under the protection of naval guns. From these amphibious landings on the southeast corner of Sicily, they overran the whole island in thirty-eight days, and took 100,000 Italian and German prisoners. The rest of the German troops seemed trapped at Messina, but they staged a Dunkerque escape across the strait to Italy.

On the very day in early September that the first British troops crossed to the toe of Italy, that nation surrendered. Mussolini had fallen from power in July. One Axis partner was through; but bitterly disappointing were the results. The surrender did not end the Italian front; the worst fighting lay ahead. While the Allies were delaying in Sicily, the Germans took over in Italy. They were to persist in a stubborn rear-guard action northward to the very last days of the war.

# "There'll Always Be an England"

The southeastern part of Italy fell quickly to British air-borne troops. By October the great air base at Foggia was in British hands, a base that not only made fighter protection available for Allied military operations, but, more important, laid Austria and southern Germany open to bombing raids for the first time. A bloody amphibious landing, chiefly by Americans, had been made at Salerno, just below Naples, which was taken shortly afterward. Meanwhile, most of the Italian navy (some ships were seized by the Germans) came into Allied hands; this released Allied warships from watchdog duty in the Mediterranean and helped to save cargo vessels the delaying detour around the Cape of Good Hope.

Some think that the Allies would have been better off if they had been content with such useful gains. Instead, they doggedly kept on in a painful progress up the peninsula, a British army under Montgomery on the right, and an American on the left, under the over-all British command of Alexander. It took months and heavy casualties to dislodge the Germans from their perfect defense positions in the jagged Apennines and behind swift rivers. To pass Cassino, where Saint Benedict had begun Western monasticism in the sixth century, was costly and long-drawn-out. Rome was not entered until June, 1944, only two days before the great invasion of France.

Although large bodies of troops were withdrawn from Italy for the landing in Normandy, the slow push northward was not abandoned. Allied forces in this theater were called a "demonstration of the solidarity of the United Nations"; they comprised "Americans, British, Canadians, French, New Zealanders, South Africans, Poles, Indians, Brazilians, Italians, Greeks, Moroccans, Algerians, Goums, Senegalese, and a brigade of Jewish soldiers." There were even Japanese, who had been born in the United States. Florence and Pisa fell; but the Germans stood firm behind their powerful "Gothic line," guarding the Po valley. Not until April, 1945, when Germany was about to collapse at home, were the Allied troops able to sweep into that valley. But in spite of its disheartening aspects, this campaign helped to make possible the success in France by keeping a quarter-million of the best German soldiers too busily engaged in Italy to aid in the defense of the fatherland.

England had not been idle during those years when she had no armies in the European theater; her air force was dealing out increasing punishment ever closer to the very heart of Germany. Early in the war Marshal Göring had promised the German people that no bomb would fall on Berlin; but even before the end of 1941 hundreds of bombers from Britain were proving him a false prophet. The destruction wrought by the *Luftwaffe* in London, Coventry, and Bristol seemed mild, indeed, as the Allies constantly stepped up their raids upon German cities and military targets.

While tactical bombing involved co-operation with the ground forces, and carrier warfare at sea was tied in with surface vessels, strategic bombing was the airmen's own private show. Cities hundreds of miles from the nearest British regiment or warship were laid in ruins by the planes of the R.A.F. Experts carefully studied the industrial and transportation systems of Germany in order to make every bomb do the maximum damage in softening up the enemy. Some air enthusiasts predicted that these attacks alone would be enough to bring Germany to her knees. That did not happen, but continuous bombing left the Germans greatly handicapped when the Allied ground forces finally came to grips with them.

The R.A.F., we recall, had concentrated its first efforts on the production of fighter planes to drive back the *Luftwaffe* in the battle of Britain. As those assaults slackened in mid-1941, British emphasis shifted to bombers for the aerial counterattack. In November of that year, four hundred planes raided Berlin; but the Germans had their first real taste of the horrors to come when, late in the following spring, a thousand planes in ninety minutes dropped three thousand tons of bombs on Cologne. The casualties of that single night of horror were about equal to the total in England during the whole year of 1940. Such night saturation attacks became the conventional R.A.F. formula.

Within three months American bombers based in England joined the offensive with a different technique. Their giant, multimotored, well-armored planes, with their excellent bombsights, went in for daylight precision bombing of specific factories or other key targets. By mid-1943 a round-the-clock schedule gave the Germans little respite: by night the R.A.F. would leave a saturated city in a sea of flames; the next day the Americans would single out specific objectives for destruction. Even bad weather did not always give much rest to the bombed, for most of the raiders came from British bases, where a device called "Fido" burned away the fog from air strips. With the clearing of North Africa and the landings in Italy, Axis installations beyond the range of British-based bombers came into the danger zone.

From time to time target priorities changed. Attention at first was concentrated upon submarines and planes, together with the plants that built them. Germany's synthetic oil production next was systematically cut down to about a fifth of its capacity; and the great steel works of the Ruhr were laid waste. Pilots hunted out locomotives, railroad yards, and other key links in the transportation system until that system was frequently and badly disrupted. Plants where secret weapons were in production or in blueprint suddenly disappeared. And so it went, month after month.

To defend the homeland, Germany weakened her air force on the Russian front. Many Allied bombers did not return from their flights over Germany, for the German antiaircraft flak was effective and the enemy fighter planes, sometimes firing rockets, took their toll. In one wild week the *Luftwaffe* went all out in a desperate defense against the incessant terror from the skies, and lost far more planes than it could afford. But the never-ceasing punishment went on.

Early in 1944, as the invasion date grew closer, the bombings took on an even intenser fury. Hamburg almost disappeared; the heart of Berlin was gutted. Preparatory tactical bombing wiped out bridges and disrupted all routes by which the Germans could bring reinforcements to the threatened invasion areas. The R.A.F., which had saved England in 1940, now shared with the American air forces the credit for thus crippling Germany. As Churchill put it, "He who sows the wind shall reap the whirlwind."

During these months tireless preparations were completed for the invasion. Far more than in North Africa, Sicily, or Italy, landing on the exceedingly well-fortified coast of France presented problems of the gravest sort; and failure could not be risked. American troops had been pouring overseas at the rate of 150,000 a month to join in training, especially amphibious, with the British and Canadians. American industry, now in high gear, was making amazing production records. Down on the south coast of England huge concrete and steel caissons were assembled to be towed across the Channel to make artificial ports. Engineers were building underwater oil pipe lines to France. All this—and infinitely much else planned in the minutest detail—was guarded with the utmost secrecy as the ground, air, and sea forces rehearsed again and again for perfect correlation in invasion tactics. Not even the accelerated bombings hinted at the landing site, for it was not singled out for special softening until the very last hours. Meanwhile, all along the invasion coast from Calais to Brittany, worried Germans waited anxiously behind their mined beaches, artillery-protected cliffs, and elaborate concrete defenses for this new war machine to select its point of attack.

June 6, 1944, was D-Day; the British and Americans landed in force upon the shores of Normandy. The final drive to victory and Berlin was under way. The establishment of beachheads was of unsurpassed difficulty, though effected in masterly fashion. A storm, lashing the Channel, had held the invasion flotilla in port. But at last, in the dark hours long before daylight, the terrific bombing of the German defenses began, as paratroopers and other air-borne troops were dropped in the rear of the fortifications. The Germans were set for landings farther northward, and the surprise was complete. Some eleven thousand Allied aircraft of every sort crowded the skies over the Channel as the invasion proceeded as planned. The main armies filled some four thousand landing craft, and were convoyed across by eight hundred warships. As this immense fleet neared France, the battleships and cruisers stood in to give the shore defenses the further punishment by big guns that can be more devastating than bombing. The soldiers stormed ashore with guns and tanks under the protective screen of fire from bombing planes and naval guns. Yet there was bloody fighting on the beaches, and the casualties were heavy. But at every point bitter conflict won a foothold for the invaders. Slowly, in the days that followed, the enemy were pushed back from the shore, and the beachheads were joined. Reinforcements were brought in on an average of nearly 40,000 a day to reach a million within the first twenty days, even though the worst June gales in forty years wrecked half of the artificial port installations.

As in Sicily, the British and Americans had shared the initial attack in almost equal numbers. Afterward the Americans took over an ever-increasing share of the invasion. Ultimately almost three quarters of the total forces were from the United States, with part of the remainder from Canada. Montgomery was in charge of all ground forces, with the American general Eisenhower the Supreme Allied Commander; against them, for a while, was Rommel, the "desert fox" of North Africa.

Nine days after D-Day, Germany struck back with a new and highly destructive air assault against England. Small robot bombs without pilots, jet-propelled from bases on the French coast, descended upon southeast England in general and on London in particular. Each carried a ton of high explosive, causing extensive damage, especially to buildings. They came without warning at any hour, day or night, and with such speed that they were not heard until they had passed by. Fighter planes, barrage balloons, and anti-aircraft fire brought down many, but some 2300 of them landed. It was a nerve-shattering ordeal for the weary people; more than four thousand were killed, and a million homes were damaged. In September the advancing armies captured the major robot bases, and England breathed more freely.

# "There'll Always Be an England"

Through June and well into July the fighting was stubborn and savage in the battle of Normandy. The demolished port of Cherbourg did not fall to the Americans until nearly three weeks after the landings, while the British fought against similar difficult resistance around Caen. The battle of Normandy ended shortly after the taking of Caen, with the spectacular break-through of American armored divisions. They tore through France, separating two German armies and forcing their retreat to their own borders, much as the Germans, we recall, had split the Allies in their onrush in France in 1940. Paris was freed late in August, and by the middle of September two American armies had crossed the German border. On their right another American army, which had been landed in southern France, was moving steadily up toward the Rhine. It had met its chief resistance at the ports of Marseille and Toulon, where the French fleet had long before been scuttled by its crews to prevent its seizure by the Germans. Meanwhile, the British and Canadians, advancing up the Channel coast, were capturing the robot bomb emplacements and were moving into Belgium over those old battlefields where for centuries Englishmen had died. They captured Antwerp with its docks intact. The greatest air-borne operation of the war landed British and American troops in Holland, by a plan to turn the enemy right flank in order to advance over easy level country into the heart of Germany.

It looked as though final victory were coming before snowfall; then various misfortunes bogged down the onrushing offensive. The lightning advance of the American armored divisions had to be halted until supplies caught up with them. An adequate port was needed; Antwerp was useless until the lower Scheldt was cleared, and there was stubborn fighting there. And at Arnhem the Germans successfully checked the air-borne offensive mentioned above. The Siegfried line, or West Wall, and the broad Rhine still guarded much of their front.

Suddenly, just before Christmas, the Germans counterattacked with fury against a thinly held American sector in the Ardennes. For a few desperate days they seemed to have their old offensive power back; a break-through to Liége and even Antwerp threatened. The American losses were heavy. Forces from the north and other American troops from the south rushed to the rescue, closed in, and relentlessly pushed the enemy back and out of the salient. This "Battle of the Bulge" gave the Germans a six weeks' respite, but it cost them most of their remaining armored force.

By late winter the Allied forces were ready for the grand assault which would carry them across the Rhine itself. On the extreme left in Holland were the Canadian First Army and the British Second Army; on the extreme right, toward the Swiss border, was the French First Army. In the center, comprising nearly three quarters of the total strength, stood the Americans.

Early in March, 1945, a lucky stroke gave a quick foothold on the far bank of the river. An American armored patrol rushed the great Ludendorff Bridge at Remagen, almost midway in the line, before the Germans could blow it up. In great force the American First Army poured across the bridge; the Germans had to hurry troops from all directions in an effort to stop them, thus dislocating their carefully planned defense behind their river. During the last ten days of the month violent air preparation cleared the way for the other armies to cross.

The Canadians mopped up the rest of the Netherlands, while the British sped ahead to take Bremen and Hamburg. The main objective lay in the vital industrial region of the Ruhr, where the British co-operated with the Americans to trap a huge German force.

It had become pretty much a rout in the west by the first of April; and in the east the Russians were pushing German forces steadily ahead of them into Germany. The gap between the two fronts narrowed daily, until later that month Russian and American patrols met at Torgau. To the Russians was granted the costly honor of the assault on Berlin.

The end came during the first week of May. On May 2 the Germans in Italy surrendered, and on May 5 those in northwest Germany, Holland, and Denmark; finally, two days after that, the Germans made a complete and unconditional surrender at Reims. The two men who had led their nations to disaster disappeared in those last days. Hitler, in the final Russian assault on Berlin, apparently married his mistress, and together they committed suicide. Mussolini and his mistress were captured by fellow countrymen and shot on the spot, and their battered bodies were hung by the heels in a public square of Milan.

The United States took V-E (Victory-in-Europe) Day in her stride; her mind was still on the war with Japan. London and the rest of Britain, however, went wild at the news of Germany's surrender. So far as the British were concerned, the imminent menace of years at last was gone; the distant fighting on Pacific islands was almost forgotten in the sense of overwhelming relief.

Churchill soon suffered as the victim of that attitude. Labor had agreed to co-operate in his coalition government while the war lasted, but had not specified which war. He had promised that England would throw her full resources against Japan, but the Labor party was unwilling to wait for the outcome of that contest. They had recognized his unique value as a war leader, but felt that he was not sufficiently sympathetic toward their ideas of social reform to give them the reconstruction which they had been seriously thinking about for some time.

In view of the growing opposition, Churchill secured a dissolution of Parliament late in May. Until the appeal to the country could be made and its results known, he set up a provisional "caretaker" government in place of the wartime coalition. After the general election, the first in ten years, weeks elapsed before the votes of distant soldiers and sailors could be counted; not until late June were the results made public.

Labor had won a smashing victory. From only 163 seats it had jumped to 390 out of the total of 640 in the House of Commons. With this clear majority, it would not longer be dependent upon Liberal support, as MacDonald had been. Churchill kept his seat in Commons and headed the Opposition.

Only time would tell what this would mean to the British way of life. In addition to its long-range social reconstruction, the party's immediate plans called for such socialistic measures as the nationalization of mines, utilities, and the Bank of England. Such other projects as the stimulus of export trade and the mass building of homes in the bomb-ravaged nation would probably have found a place on the program of any ministry at this time, however conservative in viewpoint.

The leaders of the Labor party were still a mixture of old-school-tie intellectuals and former workmen who had come up the hard way (see page 913). Like Ramsay MacDonald, Clement Attlee, the new prime minister, represented the intellectual side of the labor movement, and so, too, did the head of the Board of Trade, Sir Stafford Cripps, a brilliant lawyer, of whom we heard in connection with the 1942 mission to India. Attlee was an obvious choice to head the government; he had been leader of the Opposition for five years before he joined the coalition cabinet in 1940 as Lord Privy Seal and later as Deputy Prime Minister. Son of a London lawyer, he had won honors in history at Oxford. Keenly interested in social work, he had lived among the poor in East London, and at times had worked at the docks. He became "an enthusiastic convert to socialism," and joined the Fabian Society and the Independent Labor party (see pages 796, 802). He taught at the London School of Economics for nine years, which were interrupted by the First World War. In that, he saw service in France, Gallipoli, and Mesopotamia, and rose to major. By 1922 he began to hold a series of junior political posts, and in 1935 became head of the Opposition. Now, at sixty-two, he was well versed in the ways of government. Less colorful and less eloquent than Churchill, he was thoroughly respected for his sincerity and integrity.

From the ranks of labor itself came his Foreign Secretary, Ernest Bevin, big, ruddy-faced, and vigorous. Son of a West Country farmer, he had been an orphaned farm hand at ten. Later, as a truck-driver in Bristol, he joined the Dockers Union and soon showed that he was a born labor organizer. His master stroke came in 1922, when he merged thirty-two unions into the powerful Transport and General Workers Union. In 1936 he became head of the central council of the trade-unions, the highest position in British organized labor. During the coalition War Cabinet, as we saw, he had been Minister of Labor and National Service. Another self-made man in the new ministry was Herbert Stanley Morrison, son of a London policeman, who had started as errand boy, become an authority on local government, served in the second MacDonald ministry, organized London's air-raid precautions, and been Home Secretary in the coalition War Cabinet. Now he was made Lord President of the Council and leader of Commons. Nine of the new ministry had been miners; one of the new Lords of the Admiralty was a former stoker in the royal navy.

As this change of government took place, another conference of the leaders of the Big Three was going on at Potsdam on the edge of ruined Berlin. But it was not the old triumvirate: President Truman was there instead of President Roosevelt, who had died in April; now Churchill, in the midst of the negotiations, relinquished his place to Attlee; only Stalin was left of the original three. The plans for the control of Germany drawn up at this meeting were harsh in the extreme and made the severe terms of 1919 seem mild indeed (see page 889). Germany was to be permitted no government of her own for the time being; she was to be divided into four zones to be occupied and ruled separately by Britain, Russia, the United States, and France; her industries were to be stripped to a bare subsistence minimum to permit her a standard of living far lower than she had had; and her war-making potential was to be completely destroyed. An innovation in international relations was the plan to put her leaders on trial for their lives as war criminals, her army and navy commanders, even her diplomats, and perhaps even her industrialists. The world had been particularly angered and shocked by the deliberate and efficient murder in concentration camps of millions, especially Jews of many nationalities and Poles, but also Russians, Frenchmen, anti-Nazi Germans, and others.

# "There'll Always Be an England"

The Potsdam Conference did not pretend to deal with the final peace settlement, nor did the San Francisco gathering of representatives from more than fifty United Nations during the late spring. That was left to the future. In the meantime, the United Nations tried hard to draw up a workable organization to keep the peace and to settle international disputes without war. It was much on the order of the old League of Nations, but every effort was made to avoid the pitfalls which had wrecked that earlier international organization for peace.

A somber realization came over Englishmen during these months; London was now overshadowed in influence by both Washington and Moscow. It was one thing that the United States, Britain's former transatlantic colonies, now was hailed as mistress of the seas and air, outstripping her in population, wealth, and much else besides. At least, the two nations still spoke the same language in more senses than one and had behind them over a century and a quarter of peaceful settlement of disputes. Russia was a different matter. She seemed bent on exploiting her hard-earned gains. It was ironic that she was now accomplishing the very thing which England had gone to war to prevent Germany from doing: the domination of Poland and of most of central and eastern Europe. In Greece, the one Balkan state not yet under her sway, British troops were intervening, and Churchill had spent the previous Christmas Day in Athens in efforts to check the spread of Russian influence. Elsewhere too the Lion and the Bear were already growling; future prospects were not pleasant.

Through all this the distant war with Japan was heading fast toward victory. Britain's contribution to it was to be mainly on land and in Burma, while the Americans were making their spectacular advances across the Pacific. In North Burma and from the air also, American assistance was substantial; but of the ground troops in Burma in 1945, only about 25,000 were Americans, whereas about 250,000 came from Britain, some 470,000 were Indian, with some 30,000 each from British West Africa and British East Africa. Chinese forces engaged were approximately 125,000. The fighting there in 1944 had proved costly to the British, both from enemy action and from the execrable climate. There were 40,000 casualties and no fewer than 237,000 cases of illness, which necessitated the evacuation of the sick to hospitals far in the rear of the front.

But fighting in Burma reached its climax the next year with the capture of Kipling's Mandalay, which had become Japan's main base. Late in February, General Slim, commanding the Fourteenth

British Army, led it to victory in ways reminiscent of Montgomery's exploits in North Africa (see page 985). As Slim drove at Mandalay from the north, he simultaneously rushed a mechanized force eastward for a surprise attack eighty miles south of his main objective. While a Chinese-American force, assisted by British troops, drove from Lashio in the northeast to assist in the siege of Mandalay, an additional brigade was flown intact to support the mechanized force mentioned above. Thus it was that when the Burmese capital fell and the Japanese were forced to evacuate, they found themselves outflanked in the south and overwhelmed in the north. The most severe fighting in Burma ensued, as the Mikado's men tried frantically to break through to the south. The line held; and in little over a week Slim's men had killed over 10,000 of the best Japanese troops in that area, and had acquired six air strips far from mud and monsoons, the top of the railroad corridor, the main automobile routes, tons of Japanese war material, and, most important of all, a springboard from which to drive south.

There was still Rangoon to capture, eight hundred miles down the pestilential valley of the Irrawaddy. Time was precious; for unless Slim took Rangoon before the middle of May, the monsoon would stymie operations on land and write finis to the war in the sky. He, therefore, took the long chance. Disregarding his flanks, he drove his truck-borne infantry and tanks south. All April the enemy did his best to stay that onward rush; but so fast did it crash through that frequently Japanese headquarters heard of British victories only days after they had occurred. In one instance, Slim's tanks "ran down Jap policemen directing traffic at the crossroads."

The terrain was now flat and open, well suited for rapid movement. May 1, and Rangoon was close at hand. From the sea amphibious British landings drove ashore, and British paratroopers dropped down on the lowlands of the Irrawaddy delta. Rangoon was surrounded, north, south, and west. The foe had had enough and too much. Within two days he fled. "Slim had beaten the enemy and the monsoon." Japan had suffered her severest worsting on the Asiatic continent; and Burma, approximately the size of Germany, had been rewon for the empire.

The real threat to Japan, however, was coming by sea. Being an island kingdom, like England, she was very vulnerable. Germany had known, in both world wars, that if she won the battle of the Atlantic, victory might well be hers; to cut off an island from its essential supplies means surrender sooner or later. What the U-boats failed to accomplish against England, the United States navy, with modest help from other Allied warships, succeeded in doing to Japan.

# "There'll Always Be an England"

As this was essentially an American effort, it, like the Russian victories, need be mentioned but briefly here. The desperate days of 1942 had long since passed in the Pacific, where the tremendous industrial output of the United States was furnishing an overwhelming superiority in ships, planes, rocket guns, and all sorts of other tools for victory; and skilled leadership was making the most of these material assets.

Two separate drives were placing the Mikado's home islands in deadly peril. American and Australian forces, land, sea, and air, were "climbing the ladder" of the coast of New Guinea and adjacent islands. The American Pacific Fleet, with air and ground forces, was slashing across the Central Pacific. Some islands were captured and others by-passed, with their garrisons left to "wither on the vine." Once Saipan and the other Marianas were taken in mid-1944, the giant B-29 bombers were based only seven hours from Tokyo, Yokohama, and other inflammable targets; and they began to pound them regularly.

The autumn of 1944 saw the two drives joined with landings in the Philippines. Japan's communications with her stolen riches in Malaya, Java, Borneo, and the rest were now in serious jeopardy. In March, 1945, the costly capture of tiny Iwo Jima, only 775 miles from Japan proper, enabled fighter planes to accompany the bombers on their raids of the home islands. By that time some capital ships from the royal navy had joined the American fleet. The German surrender, in early May, came during the bloody assault on Okinawa, still closer to Japan.

In the secret councils of the combined command tremendous forces were being assembled for the "Olympic" invasion of the southern island of Japan proper, planned for the fall of 1945, and to be followed by the "Coronet" attack on the main island early in 1946. In view of the desperate resistance on Iwo Jima and Okinawa, these final drives, it was feared, might take a million lives.

But "Olympic" and "Coronet" were not used. Amazing events early in August, 1945, stunned the world. B-29's and carrier-based planes were inflicting terrible destruction upon Japan's cities and the remnants of her fleet, but that was nothing compared with what happened to the industrial city of Hiroshima on August 6. The heart of that populous city was wiped out by a single bomb of a new and revolutionary nature. That one bomb flattened a wide area and killed more people than the entire total of civilian victims of air power in England during the whole war. Scientists had known for some time of the tremendous force which might be released by splitting the atom; and during the war both sides had been racing to translate that power into a practicable weapon. With utmost secrecy the combined efforts of hundreds of scientists, chiefly American and British, finally produced a workable atom bomb. Some of these bombs were rushed by fast cruiser to the Marianas; and Hiroshima was selected as the unlucky target. Three days later a second such bomb wrought similar annihilation in the port of Nagasaki. Between those two bombs Russia declared war upon Japan and launched an attack upon Manchuria.

Thus came the end of the Second World War. Peace negotiations culminated in a cessation of hostilities less than a week later. The formal signing of unconditional surrender by the Japanese took place on September 1 in dramatic ceremonies on the deck of the American battleship *Missouri* in Tokyo Bay. Nine of the United Nations, among them the three dominions of Australia, Canada, and New Zealand, signed the document that closed the Second World War.

Britain had weathered this second catastrophe of the twentieth century, but grave problems of peace clouded the hour of triumph. The terrible potentialities of the atom bomb sobered the whole world in that moment of victory. At home Britain's economic future looked grim. Along with labor's plans for social reconstruction went the realization that England must "export or die." The nation had to tighten its belt and endure even shorter food rations than those of wartime. With all that, Britain's millions faced the uncertain future with the same undaunted fortitude which had carried them through the battle of Britain and earlier crises of their history. However dark the prospect might look, they could still sing, as they had when German bombs were falling on London, "There'll always be an England."

# CHAPTER XXXII

## *Austerity and Experiment*

ONCE again, victory in a great war was to bring stress and strain to Britain. The years following the defeat of Napoleon in 1815 and of the Germans in 1918 were, at their worst, but mild previews of the sheer dreariness that had to be endured after World War II (see pages 586, 899). Behind much of the trouble that besieged the unhappy island lay Britain's inability to pay for what she needed from beyond the seas.

In earlier times, much of the outside world had owed money to Britain; now, with roles reversed, Britain was in debt to much of the outside world. Largely because of that, the fifty million Britons were forced to forego, year after year, many of the things that make life more pleasant. For the same reason, it was necessary to cut down the size of the once-great Royal Navy and the other armed forces. And, partly as a result of that, the British Empire-Commonwealth began to disintegrate. Those difficulties would probably have beset Britain whether Conservatives, Liberals, Labor, or even a divine-right king had been in power. But, further to complicate the picture, the British government for the first six postwar years was in the hands of the Labor party, which was determined to carry out its socializing, nationalizing, leveling policies, come hell or high water.

Some of these postwar problems had their roots back in the mid-Victorian period. In 1850 Britain still had what the Mercantilists had termed a "favorable balance of trade," with exports exceeding imports. Ten years later, British exports no longer paid for the imports, and the gap between them grew wider as the "workshop of the world" drew more and more of its food from beyond the seas (see pages 648 ff.). There was no cause for alarm then, however, because Britain had ample "invisible" means of paying for the surplus imports. Part of those consisted of the earnings of shipping, of banking, and of insurance; in later days the spending of foreign tourists would also contribute. Behind those special sources of revenue, moreover, lay rich resources from money invested beyond the seas—the so-called "Victorian heritage." For more than a century, we remember, the Barings, the Rothschilds, and other British bankers had been financing ventures of every sort in foreign lands (see page 652). There had been a particular boom of this overseas investment of British savings around the turn of the century, "building railroads in Canada and the Argentine, docks in West Africa, oil refineries in Persia, office buildings in Shanghai, and tin smelters in Malaya." In 1913 the total value of these holdings amounted to some £4 billion ($20 billion), yielding an annual income of £200 million ($1 billion) or more. That in itself was enough to pay Britain's heavy bill for food imports.

Never again, however, was the situation to be that good. During World War I, when Britain was hard pressed for funds to buy American munitions, a quarter of that total was liquidated to meet the pressing needs. Despite that heavy cut, the "Victorian heritage" by 1939 had climbed back to £3.6 billion ($14.4 billion). By that time, however, with exports shrinking, the interest and dividends from those overseas investments could pay for only half the food imports.

Then, during World War II, Britain's account with the outside world went "into the red." By 1945 she owed outsiders more than they owed her. Once again in this war it had been necessary to liquidate a heavy share of the "Victorian heritage," with the British government requiring private investors to turn over, in exchange for government securities, their marketable stocks and bonds to be sold in New York to build up the needed "dollar exchange." A third of these assets were sold this time (see page 971). On top of that, Britain ran deeply into debt, not only within the Commonwealth, but with some foreign nations as well. This debt, coupled with the sale of the securities, meant a total "disinvestment" of some £4.2 billion ($16 billion). Britain now owed some £112 million ($448 million) a year in interest alone to outside regions, outweighing the income from the meager remnant of her once-great overseas investments almost four to one. Now and then during the postwar years, it again became necessary to dispose of more of those distant holdings. On one occasion, when Britain sacrificed her Argentine rail holdings to pay for meat, a London newspaper cartoon showed a butcher telling his customer: "In the future, Mrs. Jones, every time you eat a sausage say to yourself 'Wallop! There goes another British-owned railway in Buenos Aires.'"

One must dip into the mysteries of foreign exchange a bit to appreciate the further complications caused by the new wide gap between the American dollar and the British pound sterling. In the old days, before 1914, most of the nations of the world were on the gold standard, and there were no artificial barriers to prevent them from using the London money market as a sort of clearing house to keep their accounts straight. If they wound up owing more than was coming to them, they could ship gold to make up the difference. The relationships of the various currencies to gold and to each other remained virtually unchanged year after year. Everyone knew that in terms of American dollars the pound sterling was worth about $4.87, the German mark about 24 cents, the French franc and the Italian lira about 19 cents, and so on. After World War I, things were never the same again. One nation after another went off the gold standard. Even Britain had to take that step reluctantly in 1931. This meant, we recall, that the Bank of England no longer was required to redeem its paper money, on demand, in gold (see page 921). New strange patterns, even including barter, took the place of the old free exchange of the London money market.

Gradually the American dollar began to achieve a unique commanding position in the world of international finance, even though it, too, was no longer redeemable in gold. It had been taken off the gold standard in 1933, and was reckoned at only about 62 cents. The United States, however, had a great many assets that made its dollar desirable, including a large share of the world's gold supply buried at Fort Knox in Kentucky. Its vast natural resources and its tremendous industrial plant gave it a surplus of materials which other nations wanted and needed; but there was comparatively little that they had which the United States needed in return. Unlike Britain, there was ample meat, wheat, and much else within its spacious borders. To complicate matters further, it protected many of its industries by tariff walls, which made it difficult, of course, for other nations to repay their debts in manufactures. Consequently, there arose around the world a clamor for "dollar exchange," which was very hard to come by. The world's currencies were divided into the "hard," which meant principally United States and Canadian dollars, and the "soft" ones, which included the pound sterling and almost everything else.

Back around 1930, when she went off the gold standard, Britain had organized the so-called "sterling area," consisting chiefly of herself, the elements of her Empire-Commonwealth except Canada, and a few other nations. To avoid running into debt to outsiders, trade was encouraged within this group as far as possible. Could Britain have developed as completely a "self-sufficient empire" as the Mercantilists had sought in the seventeenth century, all might have been well; but, unfortunately for her, things were required from the United States that neither Australia, South Africa, India,

Malaya nor the other sterling regions could produce. To make this "sterling area" more effective in the postwar situation, Britain established a "dollar pool," with herself acting as the banker. In this the various members would deposit what they received from sales to the Americans, and from it they might draw what they needed for purchases from the United States and Canada. It was rather like one of those joint bank accounts, in which it sometimes happens that one party does most of the depositing and the other most of the withdrawing. Malaya, for instance, was able to contribute heavily from its sales of rubber and tin; this helped Britain to acquire dollar exchange to meet her own needs.

Britain tried several means of solving this severe dollar exchange shortage in order to procure what she needed from America. The first method, called "earning dollars," necessitated a drastic increase in the nation's exports, particularly to dollar areas. The second step, "saving dollars," meant cutting down purchases from America, and from that came the grim years of austerity for the average Briton. The third step consisted of getting loans or gifts of dollars from the United States or Canada. All three of these methods went along with each other through the first six postwar years.

The most satisfactory way out of the difficulty, naturally, would have been the stimulating of exports. This was a field in which England had led the world in the early days of the Industrial Revolution, with her textiles, iron, steel, and coal. Gradually, we recall, other nations had made inroads upon the widespread markets of the "workshop of the world," with the result that there had been a serious slump between the two world wars (see pages 921 ff.). It was estimated in 1945 that Britain would have to export at 175 per cent of the 1938 rate in order to pay for her imports, now that not enough was left of the "Victorian heritage" to close the export-import gap. During these postwar years there was constant exhortation to meet that goal, with varying success in different industries. The record was least satisfactory in coal and most successful probably in motors.

Coal had been one of the mainstays of the Industrial Revolution in England. It had not only helped to turn the wheels of industry at home, but it had also been a valuable article of export. Britain had exported large quantities to Italy, Brazil, and other countries that had lacked their own supply, and had maintained bunkerage depots in seaports all around the world to keep ships moving. These steady outward cargoes had been one of the things that had made British tramp shipping so profitable. In 1913 Britain had produced 287,000,000 tons of coal, of which 94,000,000 tons were exported.

# Austerity and Experiment

This amounted to 55 per cent of all world exports. By 1938 production had dropped to 227,000,000 tons, with only 46,000,000 exported; in 1945, with World War II still dislocating industry, production was down to 182,000,000 tons, with a mere 8,000,000 exported. To many minds this seemed a first-rate opportunity to revive a trade that had once been so profitable, and thereby build up much-needed exchange.

There were, however, difficulties in the way. The general shift to oil-burning ships around the time of World War I and the competition that arose from American coal mines had been two major factors in seriously damaging the profitable returns from the British mines. As a result, the crippled industry became the center of labor unrest in the mid-twenties, as the hard-pressed operators tried to cut costs (see pages 899, 916). And it had continued to be a troublesome sore spot in the national economy. Some mines had been abandoned; others had been worked for a century or more, so that it was now necessary to dig very deep; in others, the seams were too narrow for effective operation; and machinery and equipment were too often obsolete. Boys who might normally have gone into mining in the thirties had avoided the "sick industry," which naturally meant somewhat of a short labor supply. Those still in mining, aware of these factors and of the good chances for employment in less disagreeable surroundings, were inclined to be recalcitrant with little fear of discharge or wage cuts. A proposal to bring over 100,000 displaced Polish miners was opposed by the trade unions. To complicate matters further, the unions demanded the same pay for a five-day week that they had been getting for six days' work. Their new employer under the Labor government, the National Coal Board, allowed this, although it brought higher coal prices. In spite of better pay, the curse of absenteeism continued to lie heavy over the mines; and the men, now offered time and a half to work a sixth day, would not do so. Early in 1947 a coal shortage paralyzed industry for several weeks. Later that year, 40,000 miners in Yorkshire staged a 35-day strike that cost some 570,000 tons of coal.

The effort to "earn dollars" from coal was, consequently, hardly a success. Output increased slowly from 212,000,000 tons in 1946 to 222,000,000 in 1951. In that latter year, Britain exported only 7,800,000 tons, which was more than offset by the 8,700,000 tons imported from the United States and elsewhere, a real case of "coals to Newcastle," even if the cargoes did not go to that particular port.

At the opposite extreme, the manufacture of automobiles and trucks boomed until Britain became the principal exporter of what had been practically an American monopoly. The British were able to turn out efficient cars at a reasonable price and with moderate gasoline consumption. Aggressive salesmanship on their part found markets for the Austin, the Hillman Minx, and various other cars even in the United States. In steel, a more typically British field, Britain produced in 1950, just before the industry was nationalized, 16,200,000 tons, which was an all-time record. Textiles responded more slowly. Labor had been dislocated, and wages had not been attractive enough to lure large numbers back to the spindles and looms.

The principal articles of export in 1949, along with the principal articles of import, are indicated in the following table, in millions of pounds sterling:

### BRITISH EXPORTS AND IMPORTS, 1949

#### (In millions of pounds sterling)

| EXPORTS | | IMPORTS | |
|---|---|---|---|
| Vehicles (including ships and aircraft) | 314 | Grain & flour | 183 |
| Machinery | 279 | Dairy products | 176 |
| Cotton yarns & manufactures | 159 | Seeds & nuts for oils & fats | 172 |
| Iron & steel manufactures | 127 | Meat | 146 |
| Woolens, etc. | 104 | Wool, raw | 130 |
| Chemicals, drugs & dyes | 86 | Beverages & cocoa preparations | 123 |
| Electrical goods & apparatus | 79 | Cotton, raw | 121 |
| Nonferrous metals & mfrs. | 64 | Oils, fats & resins | 112 |
| Coal | 50 | Wood & timber | 100 |
| Pottery & glass | 49 | Fresh fruit & vegetables | 95 |
| Cutlery | 45 | Nonferrous metals & mfrs. | 93 |
| | | Tobacco | 52 |

| | 1945 | 1946 | 1947 | 1948 | 1949 | 1950 | 1951 |
|---|---|---|---|---|---|---|---|
| Total Imports | 1,103 | 1,297 | 1,787 | 2,076 | 2,272 | 2,609 | 3,915 |
| Total Exports | 396 | 911 | 1,137 | 1,646 | 1,843 | 2,256 | 2,707 |
| Excess of Imports | 707 | 386 | 650 | 430 | 429 | 353 | 1,208 |

These figures sum up the difficulties of the export-import race. The export totals might climb in a most encouraging manner, but the imports always kept well ahead of them. The "invisible services," such as banking, shipping, and insurance, might make up some of the export deficit, but there was still indebtedness left, especially to the dollar area. One factor was that the general trend

# Austerity and Experiment

f postwar international trade was unfavorable to Britain, since the prices of some raw materials that she had to import increased much more rapidly than the prices which could be obtained for manufactured exports. Another dilemma was that, while the United States and Canada furnished nearly 20 per cent of the imports, they took only 7.6 per cent of British exports in return. Britain's best customers—Australia, South Africa, India, and Ireland—were within the sterling area; and that, of course, was no help in the crucial dollar situation.

In September, 1949, the government took a drastic step to improve the export situation. The pound sterling, once rated at about $4.87, had been stabilized at $4.08 for the past ten years. Now it was suddenly devalued to $2.80. This move cut the price of British exports in America 30 per cent, which it was hoped would increase their sale. Devaluation, however, was a two-edged weapon. The British themselves would now have to pay more of their devalued pounds to purchase needed American goods. The foregoing table shows that the export-import gap had widened rather than narrowed with the inflated figures of 1950 and 1951. Within a month after Britain reduced the value of the pound, twenty-eight other countries, including most of her Commonwealth, had followed her example in adjusting their currencies downward.

Hand in hand with "earning dollars" by exportation had to go the unpleasant task of "saving dollars" by reducing imports from the hard money countries. One way of doing this—and the least painful—was to grow as much food as possible at home. England had let her agriculture slump in the 1870's, we recall, and had become so dependent upon overseas foodstuffs that in World War I what she grew in a year provided food enough for only a few weeks (see pages 649 ff.). That was what made Britain so vulnerable to submarine attacks on shipping in both world wars. During the second one she had extended her agricultural acreage and produced a much larger proportion of her necessary food (see page 988). This process was further extended in the postwar years, with more than half of the government's food subsidies going to domestic agriculture. By 1950, Britain was raising 40 per cent of her food, which was excellent progress in view of past performance.

This left still 60 per cent of the food supply, along with a host of other imported goods, to be kept in check by the hard road of austerity. This meant that the consumption of meat, bread, gasoline, tobacco, and much else had to be low. Newspapers, too, felt the pinch when they had to be cut to four pages to save newsprint imports. Even amusements were curtailed in the form of American

movie films, another item on which dollars could be saved. As i
that were not austerity enough, clothing and liquor—both in deman
overseas as popular British products—had to be conserved for ex
port to "earn dollars." The depressing impact of all this was in
tensified, as will be noted later, by crushing taxes.

The first disheartening shock, with the coming of peace, was th
request of the Labor government for five more years of controls
this involved the continuation of wartime rationing of many com
modities (see page 957). The people had put up with the discom
forts of rationing when submarine-infested seas were the cause o
the shortages, but they had been buoyed up then also by the ex
pectation that the war was not going to last forever. Except for th
relaxation of the "blackout" to a "dimout," the first postwar year
brought relatively scant relief from wartime deprivations. The
vexatious regulations and red tape continued, with the food and
clothing rations, and the endless standing in line in "queues." "The
Briton's life," stated one writer in 1946, "is still an interminable
sequence of eating dull food, standing in queues and going home
to a shabby house or apartment." And, six years later, another
writer pointed out that you still had to "put your name down" and
wait tediously for an interminable number of things, even though
the actual "queueing up" had almost disappeared. The meagre
supplies for home consumption, the high taxes, and the exorbitant
cost of average comforts made for an inexpressible weariness among
the people as a whole.

As far as food was concerned, the government subsidies kept
those prices down, so that few went hungry. In fact, for much of
the period, more was spent on food subsidies than on the Navy and
the Air Force. In theory, all economic groups felt equally the impact
of the national struggle to keep food imports as low as possible.
Opinions differed as to whether or not people were getting proper
nourishment, though it was officially claimed that the national health
was better than in prewar days. No one, however, disputed the
poor quality, lack of variety, and general drabness of the fare.
Housewives, struggling to make appetizing meals under such handicaps, could scarcely have been pleased when the Economic Secretary
of the Treasury referred to them as "not to be trusted to buy the
right things. . . . In the case of health and nutrition, just as in
the case of education, the gentleman in Whitehall really does know
better what is good for people than the people know themselves."
Fresh fruit, canned goods, meat, and butter were among the strictly
rationed goods. Bread, obviously the basis of these restricted diets,
was added to the list in 1947 for the first time in English history.

# Austerity and Experiment

fter that black year, there was some gradual relaxation in much
f the rationing. Yet even at the end of 1952, when the meat ration
as to be raised a bit, it still was not quite enough for a person to
uy a pound of ground beef a week.

The restrictions on clothing were also vexatious. It seemed a
it incongruous that the nation whose spindles and looms had for
ore than a century and a half supplied the world with wearing
pparel should now have to ration it. Morale was not helped by
10p windows well stocked with clothes marked "For Export Only."
'he forty-two coupons a year were not just for wearing apparel but
1cluded household equipment, such as sheets and towels, as well.
f a man spent his coupons just on himself, they would buy about
ne suit, one shirt, one pair of shoes, and one pair of socks a year.
Make Do and Mend" was the watchword of the day. Already
habby from the lean war years, the public became increasingly tired
f an allowance far too short to meet bare replacement needs.

In the matter of the so-called "luxury" items, soaring prices were
ounted upon to curb demand. In one year's analysis of dollar ex-
enditures, it was found that 12 per cent had gone abroad for tobacco
nd 4 per cent for movie films. The tobacco supply was thereupon
lrastically curtailed, with the result that at the beginning of 1947,
or instance, a package of twenty cigarettes cost the equivalent of
orty-five cents, just about double the American price; and before
he year was out, a package was seventy cents. Pipe tobacco rose
n price in the same way. There was a rush for preparations to
nake it easier to stop smoking. In the same spirit, a 75 per cent
evy was laid upon the profits from American movie films. In the
natter of gasoline (petrol), the end of the war had brought an in-
:rease in the allowance for so-called pleasure driving, but that was
vithdrawn by 1947. The price of beer increased to the equivalent
f twenty-three cents a glass, and its quality was poor. Scotch
whiskey, an export item of importance, brought fantastic prices or
was diluted in content. The long-standing British passion for travel
likewise was rudely curtailed by the rigid restriction on the amount
f cash which could be taken out of the country and the necessity
f buying exchange for each particular currency.

It began to look to the British people as though there might never
be an end to going without, as the situation grew gradually worse
into 1947. In a Christmas broadcast that winter of 1946–1947 General Slim, the hero of Burma, declared, "We are dissatisfied, restless,
uncertain. We were more at peace inside ourselves when we were
at war." A few days later, one newspaper referred to the weariness
from "forever making do and mending in a way of life that is drab,

grubby, undersoaped, and starved of color." Scarcely had the Ne
Year started when things grew worse. Storms and continued co
gave England the worst winter since 1894; for weeks on end th
sun did not shine. The Minister of Fuel had gambled on mil
weather with the coal supply; instead of the usual 14 million ton
distributed, there were only 10 million. It was necessary to shut o
electric power for several weeks; mills closed down; two millio
were unemployed; the export goals suffered a heavy setback; an
in homes throughout the land the lack of facilities for lighting an
heating accentuated the long-accumulating discontent. "England i
bitterly cold and coldly bitter," snapped one commentator. B
spring a big league of housewives was protesting, and cabinet minis
ters were being booed. Slowly, in 1948, conditions began to improv
somewhat; and coronation year, 1953, saw most controls relaxec

The third possibility for solving the dollar problem was to receiv
financial relief from beyond the seas, which meant the United State
in particular. The British were understandably somewhat resentfu
about the Americans, who seemed to have so much more than th
British, who had borne the heavier wartime burden. Nevertheless
the former Thirteen Colonies were the one real source of hope ii
these times of trouble; and they had, we recall, come to Britain'
aid even before entering the war. Altogether, the British had re
ceived more than two thirds of the billions spent by the United State
on Lend Lease (see page 971). Scarcely was the war over, however
and Labor at the helm, when Washington announced that Lend Leas
was to terminate immediately. That news created consternation ii
London, which then began to look for a substitute form of finan
cial aid.

Consequently, an Anglo-American agreement was made in Decem
ber, 1945, and approved by Congress the following summer. Thi
agreement provided for a loan of $3,750,000,000 at a low rate o
interest, which was expected to be enough to enable Britain to mee
her dollar obligations until 1951. At about the same time, Canada
loaned an additional $1,250,000,000. This made a total of five
billions available for Britain; but it proved to be insufficient. Insteac
of lasting the expected five years, the United States' funds were
virtually gone by mid-1947, and once more it was necessary to gc
to Washington, hat in hand.

At this point the United States initiated a new policy to deal with
the situation. The Secretary of State, General Marshall, proposec
in June, 1947, that the United States contribute financially to the
democratic nations of Western Europe to put them on their feet ir
order to keep them from economic and social distress, which, in turn

ight lead to Communism. By the next year Britain was the prin-
pal beneficiary of this "Marshall Plan," as she had been of Lend
ease. By the end of 1950 affairs in Britain had taken a turn for
ıe better, and the government announced that it could get along
ithout further Marshall Plan help. The estimate was premature,
owever, and Britain once more turned hopefully to Washington.
inancial aid was only one aspect of the close Anglo-American rela-
onships in the postwar world, as will be seen.

During these dismal postwar years the Labor party was going
ght ahead with its plans to change the British way of life. This
as not, we recall, the first time the party had been in power, but
ıe first clear majority it had had in Commons to push through its
rogram (see page 1003). Neither the dislocations, the wreckage,
nd the dilapidated condition of war-torn Britain, nor the staggering
osses in manpower and economic resources were to stop the Labor
overnment from attempting much and achieving a fair amount.
.nd all this added tremendously to the already smothering financial
oad on the nation. Through the increased taxes and subsidies, more-
ver, the leveling theories of the Laborites could be carried out,
1aking the rich ever poorer and the very poor better off, with the
ull weight crushing the middle, white-collar classes.

In its manifesto of 1945, the Labor party proclaimed itself "a
ocialist party and proud of it. Its ultimate purpose at home is the
stablishment of the Socialist Commonwealth of Great Britain—
ree, democratic, efficient, progressive, public spirited, its material
esources organized in the service of the British people." Such a
ocialistic state, according to the *Encyclopœdia Britannica*, implies
"the collective common ownership and collective control of the
neans of production and exchange." This was one of the teachings
of Marxian socialism (originally called communism). On its tenets,
we recall, the Socialist Soviet Republics of Russia had been founded,
although the Russian Communists later diverged radically from the
gospel both of Marx and of their own Lenin (see pages 783, 883).
The more radical Labor theorists hoped that some day all the fruits
of privately owned capital investment (the economic rent from land
and mines, the interest on bonds, stocks, etc., and profits from business enterprises) might be altogether discarded as relics of a defunct
nineteenth century laissez-faire economy. And when that day arrived all individual income would be on a salary or wage basis.

In the meantime the government began to take over industries—
to nationalize them—as a major step in ending the private ownership of capital. Simultaneously controls were stiffened over such

rents, interest, and profits as remained in private hands. Imports of many sorts were put under close regulation, and overseas agricultural experiments were attempted. Various projects for social betterment included free medical service, the extension of the required school age, and state-built houses with regulated rent.

Nationalization was instituted in finance, in certain key industries in the overseas communication field, and in transportation. Actually this was not as revolutionary as it seemed. Already there was government ownership of the telephone and telegraph, operated by the post-office officials; the British Overseas Airways Corporation financed by the state with a virtual monopoly of air transportation and the British Broadcasting Corporation, with control of all domestic radio communication. Many docks and harbors, along with most public utilities, were owned by public trusts, while the supplying of electric voltage in bulk was under similar ownership and operation.

First to be nationalized, in 1946, was the Bank of England. That hardy "Old Lady of Threadneedle Street," dating back to 1694 would seem the last stronghold that Labor would dare approach but its nationalization was accomplished without much hue and cry Actually, it had long been accustomed to submit to the dictates of the Treasury.

Next it was the turn of coal. It is not easy to estimate the exact ways in which nationalization influenced these various fields. At any rate, as we have seen, coal did not make the hoped-for come-back, nor did hoisting the Union Jack over the pits make that disagreeable occupation more popular with the rank and file of workers Overseas cables and radio communications were also taken over at this time. Then came the nationalization of transportation facilities, including railways, long-distance trucking, London busses, and the like.

Steel was next on the program, but the experiment with coal cast something of a shadow over the pledge to nationalize steel. To many it seemed the better part of wisdom to leave well enough alone. Unlike coal, this industry had been highly successful under private ownership. Also, the technical problems in steel were far more complicated than those involved in taking over coal mines or railways. Yet the Labor government was well aware that it could scarcely claim Britain had become a socialistic state while such a major industry, upon which depended a host of other industries, flourished in private hands. The government bill for its nationalization, therefore, went to the House of Commons.

At this point the proposed nationalization of steel was to lead to another step, although a minor one, in England's constitutional de-

elopment. By the Parliament Act of 1911 the House of Lords could
old up for only two years a non-financial bill that the Commons
ad passed three times; then it automatically became law (see
age 815). The steel bill was delayed so long in Commons that the
abor leaders realized that the House of Lords could hold up the
ill until after the election, due in 1950; and Labor might have lost
s Commons majority in that election. Labor, therefore, utilized
s present majority to amend the Parliament Act; the Lords' right
ɔ hold up bills of which they disapproved was reduced to one year.
n this way, the bill to nationalize steel became law before the elec-
ion. Even so, a compromise had to be made to get it through Com-
ions. Attlee's government promised not to inaugurate nationalization
ntil after the election, so the Conservatives agreed to the passage of
he bill, while, of course, planning to repeal it promptly if returned
o office.

The need to curb imports, already noted, led to a series of special
ontrol devices between 1945 and 1950. A Raw Cotton Commission
vas authorized to buy all cotton imported into England. The war-
ime Ministry of Food was continued to buy all imported meats,
ivestock, cereals, eggs, sugar, and tea. The Board of Trade was
ɔut in charge of all imports of chemicals, flax, hides, molasses, paper,
ɔlastics, timber, wool, sulphuric acid, and, for a short time, rubber.
A Ministry of Supply supervised all imports of iron, steel, manga-
iese, aluminum, and radioactive substances.

The Overseas Development Act carried experimentation out into
:he colonial field. In Africa the state undertook to utilize waste land
:o grow ground nuts (peanuts) on a mammoth scale, with the idea
ɔf crushing them into vegetable oil. This bright scheme was spon-
;ored by John Strachey, Minister of Food, who got the government
to back the plan, 3,250,000 acres of bush land in East Africa, mainly
in Tanganyika, being set aside for this purpose. By 1952, it was confidently expected, 609,834 long tons of ground nuts would be harvested annually. The Treasury allotted £24,000,000 for these nuts.
For 1948, the crop was to be 56,920 tons; for 1949, the estimate was
227,676 tons. Some £23,000,000 had been spent for the experiment
by 1949; but the harvest in 1948 was only 1,566 tons, and in 1949
it rose to a mere 7,150. Everything had gone wrong with the experiment: the land proved poor for ground nuts, proper machinery
was not available and the native laborers misused what there was,
the embankment of a railway into the venture washed away, and so
it went.

Another fiasco, though on a smaller scale, was the attempt of the
government to go into the poultry business in West Africa. In this

instance, £825,000 was spent; theoretically, the state-owned chicken were to produce 20,000,000 eggs a year. Instead only 38,000 eggs were laid, which were imported for the home market at a total cost to Britain of £20 per egg!

Nationalization of industry continued to remain a Labor idea, but, as time passed, less and less stress was put upon it. The key place in the Labor program went instead to the social welfare serv ices, whereby Labor planned to end poverty and unemployment.

The National Health Services Act went into effect in 1948. It was the pride of Aneurin Bevan's heart. That fiery miner—not to be confused with Ernest Bevin, the Foreign Secretary—had fought vigorously since the coal strike of 1926 for unadulterated and immediate socialism; and now, as Minister of Health, he was doing all he could in his sphere to achieve that end. Free medical and dental services were made available to everyone living in Britain. Those who still wanted to pay for medical treatment were allowed to continue to do so. Doctors were not compelled to join the national service, but those who did were paid by the state. People could still go to the doctor of their choice if he was able to take on that number of patients. Doctors could not be ordered to understaffed or congested districts, but they might be "negatively directed" by having their pay increased if they moved thither.

The British Medical Association at first fought these proposals tooth and nail, arguing, among other points, that relations between physician and patient would be threatened. After a very few concessions from the militant Bevan, it withdrew its opposition; but individual doctors continued to be very critical. They asserted that the quality of service was lowered, partly because of the larger number of patients, partly because of the excessive amount of required paper work. Apparently dentists objected less, perhaps because so many of them were making a better living than before. Almost a mania to have teeth extracted seemed to seize a large section of the population. At the same time, in this accelerated use of the dentist's chair, where the pay was now by the job rather than by the time taken to do it, the quality of the work probably suffered.

It did not help Britain's financial woes that the free spectacles and dentures proved so popular—and also the free prescriptions. Many were said to be going to the doctor for written prescriptions for such remedies as aspirin, instead of continuing to buy them themselves at the drugstore. The state thus had the apothecary as well as the doctor to pay. Even wigs were provided for the bald; and since one only had to be in Britain to be eligible, Frenchmen were said to be crossing the Channel to obtain theirs from John Bull.

# Austerity and Experiment

The National Insurance Act, which went into effect the same day as the National Health Act, rounded out what Prime Minister Attlee called "the most comprehensive system of social security ever introduced in any country." It was by no means the first such plan to safeguard the masses against the causes of insecurity—sickness, accident, unemployment, and old age. Bismarck had tried to "kill" the German Socialists "with kindness" by introducing the first such major program in the 1880's. Britain had made further advances in the proposals that led to the Lloyd George Budget of 1909; and the United States in the 1930's had followed a similar path with its "New Deal" legislation. But Sir William Beveridge, under Churchill's ministry in 1943, had gone still further with his plan to insure the populace against life's hazards "from the cradle to the grave" (see page 990). And now the Labor government was putting his ideas into effect.

Everyone above school age was required to make a single weekly payment that made one eligible for all the benefits, as circumstances might arise. For men, this amounted at the outset to a payment of the equivalent of $1.00 matched by 85 cents from the employer; for women, the respective figures were the equivalent of 85 and 66 cents. There were seven general benefits: (1) the equivalent of $5.30 a week while unemployed, with extra for dependents; (2) the same amount when laid up by illness; (3) a maternity benefit of the equivalent of $16.32, at the birth of each child, plus $7.34 a week for 13 weeks in the case of working mothers; (4) a widow's benefit beginning at the equivalent of $7.34 a week plus $2.44 a week for each child of school age for 13 weeks, with $6.83 a week thereafter, as long as the child remained in school; (5) a "guardian's allowance" of $2.48 a week for any family with an orphan in it, one of whose parents had been insured; (6) retirement pensions of $5.30 a week for men over 65 and $3.26 for women over 60, if actually retired from work; and (7) a "death grant" of $81.60 for adults and from $12.24 to $30.60 for children. This last item, coupled with the maternity benefit, literally fulfilled the promise of insurance "from the cradle to the grave."

There was also a special setup in the act for Industrial Injuries Insurance, which took the place of the old Workmen's Compensation Acts. Men made an additional payment of about 7 cents and women about 5 cents; this was matched by the employers in equal amounts. These payments made them eligible for injury, disablement, and death benefits.

The weekly premiums paid barely 30 per cent of the cost of the insurance program at the outset and 9 per cent came from local "rates." The huge remainder of the cost, some £825 million ($3 billion), was one more drain on the overstrained national Excheque But, however expensive all this new social legislation might be, th people liked it too well for any political party to dare attack it i principle.

In the same general spirit were the likewise costly improvement in the nation's educational system. The so-called "school-leavin age" was raised from fourteen to fifteen years. The hope was ex pressed that eventually children would be required to remain a school until sixteen. More money was granted for the building o new schools, the training of new teachers, and for free school lunche and milk. Increased provisions were made for adult education. Th universities received financial grants, and university scholarship were set up by the state for unusually promising students.

Some action had to be taken in connection with housing, wit 460,000 houses completely destroyed by bombing or fire an 3,500,000 damaged during the war. Public housing, along wit town planning, were old issues in British politics and a good dea had been done about them before Labor rode to victory. But nov with Bevan in the driver's seat, and with new houses needed i almost astronomical numbers, matters were speeded by state action A board was established to dictate what new buildings would b built and how land would be used. Reluctant landlords found them selves forced to sell at a low valuation. If a landowner wanted t keep his property for future development value, he still could, bu he was then faced with a development tax whether or not he buil on it or otherwise developed his land. And if his decision was t build, he ran into Bevan's restrictions on speculative building an on houses for individual ownership. Bevan gave priority to house for rent rather than for sale, because he felt they served the interest of the poor better. He also had a low ceiling price put on the cos of private housing when allowed, and no house that cost more thar that could be legally constructed. Local authorities had to certify moreover, that there was a surplus of labor and materials befor granting a permit for a private dwelling. And those local board were under orders to build quantities of low-cost rental units, witl the government bearing three fourths or more of the constructior costs as well as subsidizing the future rents. It was inevitably a bitter pill for many a citizen to swallow, when he was, perhaps, pay ing interest on his own mortgaged home, taxes on that home, anc then had to help with further taxes to subsidize state-built house occupied by those who had never saved, as he had, to make a dowr payment on a house of their own.

# Austerity and Experiment

And, with all that, the number of housing units still was insufficient. To be sure, Bevan pointed with pride in 1950 to the fact that the new housing completed since 1945 more than replaced in numbers those destroyed by war. But, as his political opponents were quick to demonstrate, this was misleading, because quonset and aluminum huts, repaired dwellings, and temporary structures such as service camps had all been counted. Actually only a little more than half of the new units could be classified as permanent dwellings. Meanwhile the population had jumped ahead so far that these were not nearly enough, so the housing problem was still unsolved.

These social and economic changes would have been costly experiments even for a government operating well "in the black," but to the overstrained finances of postwar Britain they meant more taxes for an already over-burdened people. Government bonds had largely paid for what was taken over. Also, the ever widening mesh of controls necessitated an army of inspectors and officials. All this added up to an ever greater indebtedness.

The drastic income taxes from the war were kept without much change. They were just about as high already as the traffic could bear, with a normal tax of 45 per cent and with surtaxes running up to 98 per cent on the few incomes of £100,000 or more. Death duties were increased; they became so high that they could not normally be paid out of income, and capital assets had to be sold to meet them. Taxes on profits rose to an unprecedented height. The tax on dividends went up from 5 per cent in 1945 to 12½ per cent in 1946, and to 25 per cent the next year. The purchase (sales) tax on all luxury or near luxury goods was also increased, and ran frequently from 20 to 70 per cent. And on top of all this, the government imposed a "once-in-a-lifetime" sort of "capital levy." As with the death duties, most taxpayers had to sell capital assets to pay it. It was no wonder that the peers and landed gentry were selling their estates or turning them over to the state.

And with all this, the overall picture of British life was changing. Back in the days of the English Civil Wars there had been a radical sect known as the "Levelers" who proposed to make the "lowest" men in England equal with the "greatest" (see page 352). Nothing came of their program, but now the postwar years saw rapid progress toward that goal. Politics has sometimes been described as a means of transferring money from the pockets of one group into those of another; and something of that sort was happening in Britain. The result seemed to be that very poor folk, at least for the time being, were better off than ever before, while the very rich were practically disappearing, and the middle class was being crushed as well. A

graphic example was the drop in the number of Britons with n
incomes of £6,000: from 7,000 in 1938–1939 to 70 in 1945–194
While the condition of the laboring classes did improve, with a 20 p
cent increase in the purchasing power of their wages, the salarie
of white-collar workers and executives fell off 17 per cent. Profi
from investments went down 27 per cent. Taxes were so heavy o
the people of the so-called middle class that they were in danger o
being liquidated as a group. Postwar costs of their standard of livin
were prohibitive, pushing them down towards a grubby sort o
existence. On the surface, this was not always apparent, with Bri
ishers traveling in Europe still, and with the famous and expensiv
public schools crowded as never before. But, in reality, many of th
upper-middle-class group were now living on capital rather tha
upon income, spending what they had while they still had some t
spend. And that was hardly a good augury for the future stabilit
of the nation.

In the Empire-Commonwealth, as at home, these were difficu
years for the mother country, and disheartening to those Briton
who had so long been able to boast of an "empire upon which th
sun never sets." In Asia and Africa the Labor government had t
face an irresistible trend towards self-government or even independ
ence. Since the relinquishing of many of the old imperial power
was to prove unavoidable, it was perhaps fortunate that the liquida
tion was in their hands. Winston Churchill had once angrily an
nounced that he had not become prime minister to preside over th
dissolution of the empire. With him in office at this time instead o
Attlee, British resources might have been unduly strained had h
attempted to hold some of the reluctant regions, which probabl
would have been lost in any event.

This sharp diminution of the Empire-Commonwealth, that ha
covered a quarter of the earth's surface and included a quarter o
the earth's population, did not show on the map the extent of th
actual loss of British control. Palestine, Burma, and Ireland alon
severed all connection with the Commonwealth. The vast India
Empire did not; but Britain's hold upon it became only a fair
shadow of the old *raj*. Ceylon remained, but as a dominion. Else
where in Asia many difficulties, some large and others small, kep
cropping up to plague the path of empire. In Africa, trouble de
veloped all the way from "the Cape to Cairo."

Imperial headaches were not the lot of Britain alone. The Frenc
and Dutch empires also suffered the effects of the postwar reactio
against imperialism, and fared less well than the British. The Dutc

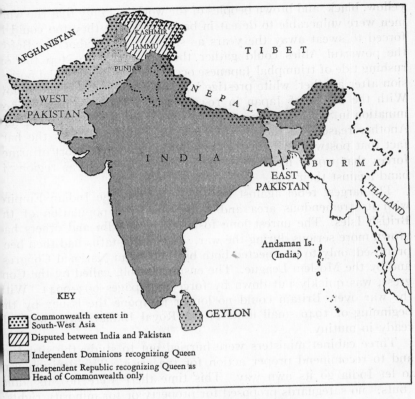

**KEY**

- ▨ Commonwealth extent in South-West Asia
- ▨ Disputed between India and Pakistan
- ▨ Independent Dominions recognizing Queen
- ▨ Independent Republic recognizing Queen as Head of Commonwealth only

POSTWAR CHANGES IN THE BRITISH EMPIRE

were to lose their rich empire in Indonesia; and the desperate fight of the French in Indo-China was at one time killing off officers faster than the military schools could produce them. The United States voluntarily and quickly relinquished the Philippines after the war.

There were various reasons behind this upheaval in the long-standing colonial systems. Since the turn of the century there had appeared, we recall, signs of growing nationalism both among the self-governing dominions and also in India and other subject lands. Some concessions were made to meet the situation, particularly between the two World Wars. The Japanese had been among the pioneers in the growing reaction against European imperialism. Then during World War II came their attack on Pearl Harbor, their seizure of Singapore, and their swift, spectacular conquest of Southeast Asia and the Pacific islands. They showed to all the

yellow, black, and brown peoples of the world not only that the whi
men were vulnerable to defeat in battle, but that they too could l
forced to sweat away the years as starving slave laborers. Befo
the powerful Allies could gather their resources to stop the o
rushing tide of triumphal Japanese occupation of one colonial posse
sion after another, white prestige had suffered an almost fatal blo
With the defeat of Japan in 1945, there was a widespread dete
mination in Southeast Asia to resist the return of the white master
Another reason for the disintegration of the empire was the har
fact that postwar Britain simply could not afford the sort of arme
forces that would have been able to keep her overseas regions i
hand against their will.

The largest rebel against the old order was the Indian Empir
with its tremendous area and eight times the population of th
British Isles. The unrest long fostered by Gandhi and others ha
grown more serious during the war. Dominion status had then bee
promised, only to be rejected both by the Indian National Congres
and by the Moslem League. The ensuing revolt, called by the Cor
gress, was quickly put down by force (see pages 993–994). Wit
the war over, Britain could no longer postpone the issue; by th
beginning of 1946 small units of the Royal Indian Navy were a
ready in mutiny.

Three cabinet ministers were hurried out to study the situatio
and to recommend proper action for the crisis. The decision wa
to let India go its own way. This time there were no "ifs" an
"buts," no safeguards proposed for property or for minority rights
the date was set, June, 1948, after which Britain refused to accep
any responsibility for India whatsoever.

In the mid-nineteenth century the "little Englanders" had bee
ready to let Canada, Australia, and New Zealand go because the
cost more than they seemed worth to the mother country; but n
one suggested in those days that India be given back to the Indians
It was far too valuable an outlet for the textiles of Manchester an
the iron of Birmingham to risk losing. In 1946, however, India n
longer "paid"; in fact, quite the reverse, for it had become th
creditor of Britain to the tune of heavy sums. No longer were ther
profits to offset the responsibilities, inseparable from that enormou
stretch of territory with its bitterly divided peoples.

A certain sense of responsibility still lingered nonetheless—a tra
dition so ingrained and long-standing as the "white man's burden'
did not die instantly. It had been predicted—and by an Indian—
that, if the British ever withdrew, such chaos would ensue tha
"within a year, there would not be a virgin or a rupee in all India

# Austerity and Experiment

om Cape Comorin to the Himalayas." And now, with that day
: hand, a particular reminder of responsibility existed in the fears
: the minority Moslems of being subjected to Hindu control.

The situation resembled that in Ireland, where the Protestants
. Ulster in the northern part stubbornly and successfully resisted
.clusion in the Irish Free State, with its Catholic majority (see
age 768). The Moslems in northern India, only about a fifth of
.e whole population, were equally determined not to participate in
single Indian government that had a Hindu majority. In this
:and they had an able and insistent leader, Mohammed Ali Jinnah,
.ll, lean, and ascetic, and, like Nehru, the Hindu leader, educated
. England.

Britain offered to assist the Indian National Congress and the
Ioslem League in drawing up a constitution for a united India,
.ut no agreement could be reached. The Moslem stand was ada-
.ant against inclusion in a Hindu-controlled India. There was riot-
.g with many lives lost. Gandhi reluctantly agreed, rather than
ritness further bloodshed, to the division of India into two countries.
.he British, finding no compromise possible, moved up the date of
heir departure one year, to 1947.

Boundary commissions made the division, while Parliament hastily
.assed the Indian Independence Bill. India, composing most of the
ubcontinent, had an area of some 1,246,880 miles with a population
.f approximately 325,000,000. Delhi was its capital. The scattered
.ocation of the Moslem population resulted in a strange arrange-
.ent for Pakistan in the north. West Pakistan included the old
.egion of the Northwest Province out as far as the Khyber Pass.
.ast Pakistan, with a thousand miles of Hindu territory intervening
.etween the two sections, was carved out of eastern Bengal, but did
.ot include the great city of Calcutta. The port of Karachi, at the
.ead of the Arabian Sea, was made the capital of the new state.
.ltogether, Pakistan was granted some 337,524 square miles for its
.opulation of approximately 75,000,000. The state was handicapped
.y its geographical separation, which made administration very com-
.licated, and by its lopsided economy. It was primarily agricultural,
.with ample production of grain, cotton, and a major part of the
.vorld's jute supply, but it had little industry or mineral resources,
.uch as India had in abundance.

By the Indian Independence Act of 1947 Britain renounced all
.ontrol, and both India and Pakistan became, for the time being,
.elf-governing dominions. The several hundred independent native
.tates, in which 25 per cent of the total population of old India lived
.n approximately 45 per cent of its land area, were allowed by this

[ 1029 ]

act to adhere to either Pakistan or India. The Earl of Mountbatte
the last Viceroy of India, became the Governor General in each
the new dominions. The words "Emperor of India" were droppe
from the title of King George VI, while the traditional "India Office
became a bureau in the "Commonwealth Relations Office."

In August, 1947, the old British *raj* thus came to an end, ju
one hundred and ninety years after Clive's victory at Plassey ha
opened the way for the spread of English rule over the huge countr
Some of the Anglo-Indians—the "pukka sahibs" of whom Kiplin
wrote—remained on under the new regimes. This was particularl
true in Pakistan, which lacked trained personnel for its more re
sponsible governmental and business positions, since in the old In
dian empire such jobs, when not held by the British, had usuall
gone to Hindus. The other Britons sadly returned home, preferrin
a lean existence on pensions rather than service under the ne
brown leaders.

Except in a few places, especially the Punjab, the British with
drawal did not produce quite the dire conditions that had bee
feared. The relations between the two new states, however, wer
not happy in the years following the liberation.

In the Punjab, in the north, there was a ghastly readjustment fo
months. It was divided between the two states, with part of it adde
to Pakistan and part to the new India. In Pakistan's section Mos
lems massacred Hindus and Sikhs by the thousands, while acros
the line in India's territory, local Moslems in their turn were mur
dered by Hindus and Sikhs. Such slaughters caused a mass migra
tion of millions of Moslems from the Indian section into Pakista
and of Hindus and Sikhs in the opposite direction. Each fleein
horde of desperate, homeless families left a grim trail of corpses i
its wake—men, women, and children dead from violence, hunger
or exhaustion. Likewise in Bengal, to the eastward, Hindus tryin
to escape to Calcutta from the countryside that was now easter
Pakistan were slain by Moslems. And in that big city, largely Hind
in population, Moslems were killed in retaliation.

Gandhi struggled to calm the bitterness in Calcutta, and i
January, 1948, entered his last fast in protest against the slayings
He ended it five days later, when the leaders of both sides pledge
to keep the peace. His efforts to bring about better understanding
with the Moslems and his desire to abolish untouchability in the ol
Hindu caste system had made him hated by some of the orthodo
aristocratic Hindus. Shortly thereafter he was killed by a national
istic fanatic of high caste.

The assassination of Gandhi centered the direction of India mor

# Austerity and Experiment

than ever in the hands of Jawaharlal Nehru, the first prime minister of India. Cultured, polished, a graduate of Harrow and Cambridge, Nehru was a gifted writer and historian. Like Gandhi, he had frequently been imprisoned by the British, particularly during World War II's civil disturbances.

Another bone of contention between the new states was the distribution of the native states. For the most part, the choice between Pakistan and India was undisputed. The native rulers, seeing the handwriting on the wall, generally preferred to accept the good pensions offered them rather than offer resistance. In some cases, however, the Hindu-Moslem line was not clear-cut. Of the larger states, only in Hyderabad did the Moslem ruler, with some 16,000,000 Hindu subjects, threaten to fight. He had an ancient treaty in which Britain guaranteed his throne; but his defiance was short-lived when India sent an army against him.

More serious was the case of Kashmir, the border state that controlled mountain passes into Afghanistan, Tibet, and China. In this Hindu-Moslem impasse the Hindu ruler wanted to join India, but his Hindu subjects were only a small aristocracy, the population at large being some 80 per cent Moslem and mostly illiterate. To prevent the ruler from having his way, Moslem tribesmen from the wilds of Pakistan invaded Kashmir, massacring, looting, and abducting women. Nehru, upon an appeal from the ruler, countered by sending in an army, 15,000 strong. Only heavy pressure from the United Nations prevented this incident from expanding into war between the two states; but the efforts of various intermediaries to achieve a permanent settlement met with almost no success.

In the meantime, in Ceylon, south of India, Parliamentary government was introduced in December, 1947, by the Ceylon Independence Act, which provided that the island would have full dominion status by February, 1948. Burma, over across the Bay of Bengal, established itself as an independent nation in January of that same year. The Attlee government had hoped that Burma would be willing to agree to dominion status, but the opposition to the British was strong, and the country was torn by internal strife. Consequently, it was allowed to go with no particular objection. Actually, like India, it did not "pay" enough to be worth an attempt to hold it.

But however easily the British might let most of southeastern Asia change its status, Singapore and Malaya were a decidedly different matter. Malaya did "pay"—and well; its rubber and tin were creating new millionaires at Singapore by the hundreds and were giving Britain's sterling area its chief source of the essential dollar exchange. The holding of Malaya was no simple task, for

Communism had invaded its jungles and rubber plantations so successfully that rubber production was threatened. The "hit and run" guerrilla tactics of these Communists were hard to combat in the jungles; but the British spared no efforts to maintain their hold on the vital area. They built up a force of some 35,000 regular and colonial troops, 25,000 trained Malay police, and 50,000 special constables. By 1952, they seemed to be slowly but successfully gaining the upper hand.

The proverbial flexibility of British imperial policy never received a greater strain nor produced a stranger compromise than occurred in January, 1950, when India formally proclaimed itself an independent republic. India seemed to want to have its cake as well as eat it, as far as Britain was concerned. It severed its allegiance to the crown, but recognized that crown as a symbol, or link, uniting free, independent nations in the Commonwealth. Thus India became independent, but nevertheless still remained in the Commonwealth of Nations. As India was no longer a dominion, it obviously ceased to have a governor general; but Britain appointed a Commissioner General for all Southeastern Asia.

The Commonwealth was also shrinking nearer home. Two years before, Ireland severed its last remaining ties with the British Crown and Commonwealth. Its dominion status had long been wearing thin. As the Republic of Eire, it had remained neutral, we recall, in World War II and had otherwise conducted itself as an independent nation, but it was still classified as a dominion. Now its Parliament repealed the External Relations Act, whereby Eire had been represented by the British Foreign Office in those nations where it did not send its own ambassadors or ministers. At the same time, it took a lone stand in refusing even to join the other nations of the west in the North Atlantic Pact. Nonetheless, the following year Britain unilaterally defined British citizenship as falling into three categories: United Kingdom citizens, Commonwealth citizens, and Irish citizens!

In Palestine, that mandate of the defunct League of Nations, the thirty years of British rule were also fast running out. The British were not sorry to relinquish the Jewish national home to which Balfour had committed the nation in 1917. Responsibility for it had conflicted with their much wider concerns with the Arab world; and, as we know, the Arabs had persistently and bitterly resented the intrusion of the Jews into what had been their lands for centuries. The presence of the British garrisons alone had kept Arab and Jew from flying at one another's throats; and small thanks was Britain to get for trying to keep the peace. Usually it was the Jewish colonists the British had protected from Arab outbreaks, but now, after World War II, the British found themselves faced by hostile Jews, determined to be rid of British control (see pages 932 ff.).

The main postwar troubles revolved about Jewish immigration policies, which had long been one of the chief problems of the administrators of the mandate. The Labor party, when not in office, had criticized the way this immigration had been held to a mere trickle since 1939, but now Bevin continued to stand by the Arab point of view. This traditional attitude of the Colonial Office was strengthened by Britain's need for Arabian oil. Britain contended that she had kept her promise to admit Jewish immigrants up to the absorptive capacity of the land, but that to go beyond it would be unfair to the Arabs. By 1944, the Jewish minority had risen to nearly one third of the population. The Jews, however, pointed to the progress their coming had meant for Palestine: their city of Tel Aviv, their flourishing orange groves, the hydroelectric possibilities of the Jordan Valley, and the potentialities of the desert lands south of Jerusalem, inhabited by only a few, wandering Arab tribes.

In most postwar situations Bevin found himself in close agreement with the successive American secretaries of state, but a wide rift opened between the two nations over Palestine. There was widespread sympathy for the Jewish stand in the United States, with its substantial Jewish population, and little realization of the Arab side of the matter.

With the defeat of Germany came a rush towards Palestine of Central European Jews who had survived Hitler's gas chambers. No other country wanted them and most of them wanted no other country. This new pressure against immigration restrictions brought the whole Palestine problem to a head. Aided by the Jewish underground, wholesale smuggling of these refugees was organized. The British intercepted most of the ships headed for Palestine with the European Jews, whom they then placed behind wire fences on Cyprus. Now it was the Jews who began a campaign of increasing violence and terror within Palestine, aimed mainly against the British. There were three main categories of armed Jewish extremists, differing in their degree of radicalism and in the violence of their tactics. Bridges and trains were dynamited; the bombing of a hotel killed numerous British officers; British personnel were ambushed and killed; others were kidnapped and held as hostages.

As the terror accelerated, the British officials worked hard, during the last months of 1946, to find some compromise by which Jew and Arab might achieve a peaceful solution. Failing in this attempt, Britain referred Palestine to the United Nations. There an independent Jewish state was recommended, but then no agreement could be reached on the terms of partition. Just six weeks after giving up India, Britain washed her hands of this trouble spot by announcing in September, 1947, her intention of withdrawing from Palestine. The outbreaks of violence persisted as the British prepared to leave.

In May, 1948, the independent state of Israel came into being. The quickness of the United States in recognizing the new government annoyed the British. It soon became a member of the United Nations. But peace did not come to it, as Jews and Arabs began to fight each other. To the general surprise, the Jewish army proved better than was expected; when the Egyptians sent their army in on the Arab side, the Israeli threw back the attack. Most Britons breathed a sigh of relief to be no longer embroiled there; they felt well rid of a place that had cost them more than 300 lives and £100,000,000.

The serious unrest in Asia was no great surprise, but the British had scarcely anticipated the troubles that developed rapidly in Africa. From the "Cape to Cairo," quite literally, spread bitter hatred of all that was British. In the north, the retention of Suez and the Sudan was threatened. In the south, an ugly attitude showed itself in the great dominion of South Africa. But the worst shock came from the violence of native attacks against British settlers in central Africa, where the Negroes had been heretofore among the most docile people of Britain's overseas lands.

In Egypt the trouble that erupted after the war was not a new story but the continuation of anti-British feeling that went back a good many years. The need to have troops concentrated in that strategic area during both world wars had tended to deepen that nationalistic attitude. Egypt had not been a part of the empire, of course, since 1922, when Britain ended her protectorate there and acknowledged the independence of the Egyptian kingdom (see page 934). The adjacent Suez Canal and the Sudan, however, were still very much the concern of Britain, as well as of Egypt. The canal was, as always, a vital link in Britain's overseas communications, and the Sudan had been under a nominal joint control by Britain and Egypt, but mostly British, since 1899. Serious anti-British riots early in 1946 jeopardized the Anglo-Egyptian Treaty of 1936, which had continued, we recall, some few of the military privileges that Britain had enjoyed since 1882 (see page 936). Britain now had to relinquish most of those; she abandoned the Cairo citadel, where she had had a garrison stationed, and the naval dockyard at Alexandria. She withdrew her forces to the canal zone. There they were involved in fighting in 1951, after Egypt had tried to interfere with British commerce. As for the Sudan, Egypt demanded that Britain clear out of it completely; eventually, in 1953, the British would agree to a trial of self-government in the Sudan, with an ultimate decision on its final status to be made at the end of three years.

Down at the other end of Africa, Britain had cause to regret that General Smuts was no longer premier, for he had, as we know, long kept that dominion loyal to the mother country. In the general election of 1948 his party went down to defeat, and he was succeeded by Dr. Daniel Malan of the Afrikander Nationalist Party. A dour Calvinist, Malan hated the British only a little less than he hated the Negroes. Immediately South Africa's strange racial situation was subjected to new stresses. Among the white minority there were more Boers, or Afrikanders, than Britons; Smuts had managed to hold power by a coalition of the more moderate Boers with the British (see page 937). Malan, like Herzog before him, was able to win with the slogan "British hands are still red with Boer blood." He then proceeded to utilize his premiership to foster racial discrimination, a matter in which Boers and Britons had long disagreed. This race question involved the treatment, not only of the Negroes and mulattoes, but also of the Indians, of whom, we recall, there were many. The British in the Cape and Natal had been less illiberal than the Afrikanders in the Transvaal and Orange Free State. Malan represented the feeling of a large proportion of those Boers when he began to launch a campaign to enforce a policy of "apartheit," which carried to much greater extremes the spirit of "segregation" and "Jim Crow" laws in the southern United States. In violation of the South African constitution, the "colored" people in the Cape province, who had long been able to vote, were now disenfranchised. Malan's party also passed a new nationalization law, which discriminated against not only the Indians living in the Union but also British immigrants, who now had to live there a number of years before being able to vote. Despite the loud outcries against such irregularities, Malan sought to perpetuate the existing control of his Nationalist party by having drastic changes made in the constitution. It was believed that he contemplated for South Africa a status somewhat like India's—an independent republic, yet remaining in the Commonwealth for economic reasons. The Nationalist "Jim Crow" restrictions were bringing passive resistance from the Negroes; and that, in turn, brought them imprisonment. Yet the 1953 election continued Malan in his position of premier.

In Kenya, the former British East Africa, which had a good climate for its many white settlers, one of the ugliest native uprisings in many years caused bloody scenes by the close of 1952. A Negro sect, known as the Mau-Maus, suddenly began a reign of terror, swooping down upon one British farm after another to torture and slaughter any whites they might find. The extreme secrecy of its membership not only made it difficult to suppress but added to its terror; the gentle cook of many years' devoted service was as likely as not to be the one who unlocked the door to the murderers and helped them destroy the family.

This appalling uprising took on a still grimmer aspect with the possibility that it might spread through the whole of central Africa. There in the possessions of Britain, France, Belgium, and Portugal lived a quarter of a million white Europeans in the midst of 150 million blacks.

Already, in 1948, Britain had made some concessions to the rising tide of nationalism and anti-imperialism among these hitherto most acquiescent of colonial subjects. The Gold Coast, an old crown colony on the Guinea coast, which had become prosperous through successful cultivation of cocoa, became the first laboratory of Negro colonial self-government. By the close of the war a United Gold Coast Convention was clamoring for home rule; and, by 1948, disputes over cocoa prices led to some fairly severe rioting in the colonial capital. A parliamentary commission hurried down from London, with the result that the Gold Coast was given a new constitution with popular elections. Then there entered upon the scene a flamboyant youth just back from college in the United States and England. This young Negro, Kwame Nkrumah, loudly demanded immediate self-government and spread about his half-digested ideas about Marxian socialism until the British jailed him. Proclaiming him a "martyr," his improvised party swept to victory in the general election. The British governor of the Gold Coast, known as "a wise old Africa hand," then appointed Nkrumah a virtual prime minister.

That example was not lost upon either the blacks or the whites throughout Africa. The great colony of Nigeria was starting out on the same path, with a leader who predicted that within a century Black Africa would have crushed the armies of Europe and brought the United States to the verge of extinction, while black missionaries would be preaching the gospel of peace in "darkest Europe." Down in South Africa, Malan voiced the apprehension of many other whites when he declared, "If other African native territories demand with the same success what the Negroes in the Gold Coast have gained, it means the expulsion of the white man from everywhere between South Africa and the Sahara."

One of the most orderly of these new developments was the effort to unite Northern and Southern Rhodesia and Nyasaland into a dominion; and there, too, the voice of the black folk was heard. Plans had been on foot for some time to make such a Central African Dominion. One difficulty was that Southern Rhodesia already had achieved responsible government to a considerable extent and feared that federation with two crown colonies would mean losing some of the prestige and comfort of that position. Another obstacle was that the Negroes wanted an equal share in the government. A parley of the three territories failed to result in agreement, because the whites were willing at this time to talk only in terms of a "partnership" with the Negroes. Under this plan the whites would be the senior partners, with the Negroes only junior partners until the latter were sufficiently educated to be raised to a full partnership, but no details were offered as to when and how that might occur. Census figures revealed the magnitude of the problem: in Southern Rhodesia 128,000 Europeans to 1,726,000 Africans, in Northern Rhodesia 35,000 to 1,640,000, and in Nyasaland only 3,500 to 2,430,000.

Britain's manifold difficulties, along with the weakening of her armed forces, led even lesser nations to snap at the heels of the sick lion. In March, 1948, an expedition from Chile, with its president aboard, and a squadron of five ships with five admirals from Argentina appeared at the edge of Antarctica to challenge British control of some islands in her Falkland Island Dependencies. A British cruiser was rushed to the scene; her crew defeated the Argentinians at soccer; and the affair quieted down. At about the same time, restless forces in Guatemala threatened to seize Belize in British Honduras. Another British cruiser landed marines and averted the danger.

Two months before, however, two dominions took small countermeasures in this widespread slackening of imperial controls. In order to obtain weather stations, Australia and South Africa each annexed a lonesome little island far down toward the Antarctic Ocean.

Along with the political disintegration of the empire and her economic ills, Britain was caught in the tangled and seething aftermath of the war in her foreign relations. The major concern of Britain—and all the other democracies—was the ever-threatening hostility of the Union of Socialist Soviet Republics. Peace treaties were still to be negotiated with the defeated nations, and British troops had to help make up armies of occupation, particularly in Germany. In the Middle East danger developed in the rising surge of nationalism, especially in Iran and Egypt, where Britain faced bitter hatred in the Mohammedan world. In the Far East there were similar undercurrents, with Russia, as always, very much in the picture. And it was here that, in 1950, war broke out in Korea. Although President Truman called it merely a police action by the United Nations, and although every effort was made to keep it localized, it was nonetheless war in its intensity and its casualties—and it was in constant danger of spreading like fire around the world.

Even in the weeks before V-E Day, in 1945, Britain and the United States became aware of an attitude in their ally, Russia, that boded ill for the future. As time went on, it grew increasingly apparent that Stalin had driven some extremely sharp bargains both at Yalta, that spring, at the conference with Churchill and the dying Roosevelt, and at Berlin, that summer, when he met Attlee and Truman. Despite its already tremendous area and population, and the need of repairing its war damages, Russia appeared in western eyes to be dangerously ambitious. It seemed bent on obtaining all the new territory and population it could get, aiming ultimately perhaps at world conquest at the expense of the "capitalistic, imperialistic democracies." In the Far East, Russia's reward for its belated and unneeded aid against Japan was privileges in Manchuria and some island territory. In Europe it shared the rule of Germany and Austria. But that was not enough for the Communists; they gained control in one helpless "satellite" after another: Poland, Rumania, Bulgaria, Hungary, Czechoslovakia, Albania, and, for a while, Yugoslavia.

Out of that situation came two new phrases in the vocabulary of the democracies, signifying new experiences in international relations: the "iron curtain" and the "cold war." The "iron curtain" denoted the barriers which the Russians raised to shut off themselves and their satellites from contact with the western world. The master minds of the dominant Politburo in the Kremlin at Moscow were aware that a full realization of what life was like in the democratic countries would be pretty sure to cause serious discontent among the peoples in their sphere. The meager economic existence under the Soviets would make British austerity seem mild inconvenience; and there was ever present under that domination the terror of surveillance by a police state—the threat of the concentration camp. The "iron curtain" frontiers had to be guarded not only to keep out knowledge of western conditions, but also to keep in those distressed wretches who might long to escape to the democracies.

The phrase "cold war" was applied to the never-ending manifestations of hostility which the Russians in those postwar years applied with keen ingenuity in one area after another, and also to the counter measures taken by the democracies, in their turn, against such aggression. Behind it all was the realization that the cold war might, at any moment Russia saw fit, turn into a real, major, shooting war. Whether or not the Russians really planned "World War III," the democracies had to strain themselves to try to be ready if it came. The terrible possibilities of the atomic bomb, to say nothing of the still more devastating hydrogen bomb, meant that such a war might well be the end of civilization. The democracies had hoped that their head start with the atomic bomb might give them some years of relative security to get ready. Traitors passed on some of the Anglo-American secrets to the Russians, however, and enabled the latter to develop their own atomic weapons much more speedily than had been anticipated.

Britain found that now she had to be content with second place among the democratic nations arrayed against these Communist threats. Leadership had definitely passed to the United States, which alone had the wealth and power to face the Russians on something like equal terms. It was not easy for a nation like Britain to accept that secondary role, especially when her leaders could remember when she herself had so recently exercised commanding influence. One particular concern on the part of the British was shared by some of her neighbors in western Europe. If a wrong decision were made in Washington, the United States itself was fairly safely protected against the consequences by thousands of miles of ocean on each side, whereas Britain, France, Holland, and other nearby nations would at once be in extreme peril if the Russians should start to roll westward. Consequently, time and again, London would try to tone down some of the more drastic moves planned in Washington.

Russia's attitude was to severely limit the effectiveness of the United Nations as an organization. It had come into being in the summer of 1945, just as World War II was ending in the Pacific (see page 1005). Both in its purposes and in its organization it resembled its late predecessor, the League of Nations. Its two principal bodies, the General Assembly and the Security Council, were in general similar to the Assembly and Council of the old League. The General Assembly consisted of representatives of all the member nations—fifty-one in number at the outset. It met once a year. The real direction, however, lay in the smaller Security Council, which had five permanent members in the United States, Britain, Russia, France, and China, along with six short-term representatives from the rest of the membership. Four lesser groups were the Economic and Social Council, the Trusteeship Council, the International Court of Justice, and the Secretariat. Affiliated with the United Nations were a number of specialized groups, such as the United Nations

Educational, Scientific, and Cultural Organization (UNESCO), the World Health Organization, the International Monetary Fund, the International Labor Organization, and so on. Whereas the League of Nations had had its headquarters at Geneva, the United Nations eventually selected New York City as its base.

Fundamentally, the United Nations was one more effort to achieve "collective security" through the curbing of aggression, an aim in which the League of Nations had proved ineffectual in the 1930's. It was hoped this time that by giving authority to the Security Council to call upon members of the United Nations for armed forces to oppose disturbances of the peace aggression might be arrested. But there was a fatal weakness in the Security Council; it had been agreed when drawing up the organization that any majority decision of the Council in matters of a "substantive," as opposed to a "procedural," nature should include the votes of all the five permanent members. In other words, the veto of any one permanent member would be enough to prevent any positive action by the Council. Quickly, Russia began to abuse this power, vetoing all sorts of measures.

With Russia thus in a position to nullify effective action by the United Nations, the democracies began to draw together in various other international organizations which were not handicapped by the veto. Some of these were economic, some military. Their major purpose was to unite the nations of Western Europe so that they might be able to check an attack by Russia's huge armed forces. The first essential was to help those nations achieve a more satisfactory economic condition, not only to support such military expenses as might be necessary, but also to prevent such distress among the people as might throw them into the hands of the Communists. The number of persons already favoring Communism in France and Italy were too numerous for comfort. The United States took the initiative in many of these moves, frequently paying a considerable part of the costs and sometimes assuming the leadership. Britain co-operated in some, but not in all. One of the first steps was the setting up of the Organization for European Economic Control in 1947. In this the sixteen recipients of United States Marshall Plan aid, already mentioned in connection with its help to Britain, could discuss how such aid might be distributed to the best advantage. Early in 1948 representatives of Britain, France, Belgium, the Netherlands, and Luxemburg (the last three united in a customs union known as "Benelux") met at Brussels and signed a fifty-year treaty "for collaboration in economic, social, and cultural matters and for collective self-defense." This so-called "Western Union" or

# Austerity and Experiment

"Brussels Treaty Organization" then began to prepare military plans. In 1949, those same nations, plus Denmark, Ireland, Italy, Norway, and Sweden, formed a "Council of Europe" with a consultative assembly. Out of this movement came discussions of a sort of supergovernment or political federation. When matters reached that stage Britain objected and declined to agree to any impairing of her sovereignty.

The chief military step was the creation in Washington, in 1949, of the "North Atlantic Treaty Organization (NATO)," consisting, at the start, of the United States, Britain, Canada, France, Italy, Norway, Denmark, Iceland, Portugal, and the "Benelux" countries. Its purpose was "to promote stability and well-being in the North Atlantic Area," with the members "resolved to unite their efforts for collective defense for the preservation of peace and security." A formal military organization with a "supreme commander" was established, followed by a similar naval setup. There was no strong objection when an American was named supreme military commander; but, when the sea command came up, the British protested loudly at the idea of having another American in overall command in a sphere where their Royal Navy had so long been dominant. The United States Navy, on the other hand, opposed a British admiral for supreme command partly because, in its opinion, the British had not sufficiently developed naval aviation and amphibious warfare to utilize them fully. An American admiral was finally given the top post, with British admirals under him in charge of the waters around Britain; in the Mediterranean, however, each side was left pretty much in command of its own forces. In the top military post Dwight D. Eisenhower, the former Allied Supreme Commander, did much by his effective persuasiveness to move the somewhat reluctant nations to agree to the burdens involved in building forces strong enough to meet the Russians. Later they would lose some of their enthusiasm and the movement would be in danger of bogging down.

Among other movements for international co-operation was the so-called Schuman Plan, whereby Germany and France were to pool their coal and steel resources. Britain refused, however, to participate in this enterprise.

By the Potsdam agreement Germany had been divided into zones, with the country as a whole under an Allied Control Council, made up of the commanders-in-chief of the four armies of occupation (see page 1004). Britain's portion in northwestern Germany included the industrial regions of the lower Rhine valley, the great port of Hamburg, and the state of Hanover, whence had come England's royal line. Still potentially the richest section, with the largest population

[ 1041 ]

and the most factories, this area had also suffered the greatest ruin from Allied bombing. The result was an impoverished population, for whose sustenance Britain was responsible. Russia had the eastern part of Germany, with about a quarter of its population. The United States' share was a generous section of southwest Germany, while the French were reluctantly granted a small area adjacent to France. Berlin, the former capital, lay well within the boundaries of the Russian portion, but the city itself was divided among the four powers, each with its own sector.

Such a four-nation setup would have been a drag upon the effective handling of the chaotic German problem under any circumstances. The situation in Japan was very different, with a single American general empowered to manage the whole show without having to defer to other points of view. In Germany, from first to last, Russia refused to co-operate in any reasonable manner. No sooner was the Potsdam agreement signed than the Russians drew a veil of silence over their zone in eastern Germany. Neither British, French, nor Americans were allowed there. In the city of Berlin, a constant succession of petty annoyances made it obvious that Moscow proposed to force the evacuation of that city by the three western powers.

Russia pressed hard for the dismantling of the factories still standing in the British zone. At the same time it demanded an equal voice in the control of the Ruhr steel mills, also in that section. Britain went slowly in the dismantling of the factories, because she did not want this sector to be a continued drag on her slender resources. Her policy of denazification, also, was too mild to suit the Russians or, to some extent, the French and Americans, but she realized that German production would be hamstrung if all former Nazis, both big and little, were excluded from positions of responsibility in industry. Altogether, Britain was soon being accused by Russia of favoring her former enemies at the expense of her allies.

Early in 1948 the Russians walked out of the Allied Control Council. Shortly afterwards they produced one of the most spectacular incidents of the cold war. In the Potsdam agreement for the garrisoning of Berlin by the four powers nothing had been stipulated about the transmission of supplies to the troops there. With Berlin within the Russian zone, the British, Americans, and French assumed naturally that the right to station troops included the right to feed them. Suddenly the Russians prohibited all rail and motor travel into Berlin; this obviously would force the evacuation of the city by the other three powers. To circumvent this attempt, the Americans and British began to use aviation to supply the isolated sections of the city. This "Berlin airlift," which was primarily American, with the British assuming about a quarter of the huge task, proved successful after a most trying winter and at tremendous cost. For 15 months, some 300 planes made about 275,000 individual flights; they carried some 2,000,000 tons of supplies, including even coal, for the troops and the residents of the blockaded zones. At the same time, the western powers retaliated with a counter blockade, which cut off much-needed industrial supplies from Russia's eastern Germany. Russia at last lifted the ban on surface travel, as the airlift continued to prove its effectiveness as a surprisingly adequate substitute.

As far as Britain was concerned, the expense of the airlift was one more serious drain on the fast-emptying Exchequer. A further heavy outpouring of her money was buying the necessities of life for the fast-growing population in her zone in the northwest of Germany. A constant stream of refugees poured in there from eastern Germany, the Baltic states, and Communist Czechoslovakia. To be sure, the other two western powers had their refugee problems also, but it was Britain's lot to be burdened with probably the most restive and overcrowded part of a war-torn land, within whose shrunken boundaries were crammed several million more people than in 1939.

By the time the Berlin blockade was lifted in 1949, two separate Germanies had emerged. It had become evident that the Russians had no intention of agreeing to any German peace treaty unless the western powers abandoned Berlin, ceased to demand a plebiscite in which they would share the supervision, and allowed Russian participation in the management of the Ruhr; and none of these proposals would the British, French, and Americans accept. In the meantime, the British and Americans had long since united their two zones economically. Now those two, with the French region, were joined formally into a new German Federal Republic, which was proclaimed in May, 1949, and became effective in September. The Allied military government gave way to an Allied High Commission, under civilian high commissioners of Britain, the United States, and France, with sovereign powers. A month afterwards, Russia set up a German Democratic Republic in its eastern zone; this new state had only 17 million inhabitants, as compared with 47 million under the western "Bonn" government and 3 million in Berlin, still divided among the four powers. Under Allied guidance and with a shrewd president, the German Federal Republic assumed more and more of the status of a normal, independent state. But the tension remained, as Germany continued under the control of the victors some eight years after its defeat.

# A History of England and the British Empire

The same general situation that prevailed in Germany was duplicated in Austria, where detachments of the British army also formed part of the occupation forces. The Russians, on one pretext or another, kept refusing to agree to peace terms, and conditions remained unsettled. Italy, after long wrangling, fared better and received a peace treaty. It left much to be determined later, however, particularly in regard to Libya and the port of Trieste. Italy agreed to pay Russia $100,000,000 and, at Russian insistence, also some $125,000,000 to Yugoslavia. British detachments, however, still remained in the former Italian colonies until their future might be determined. Also, a small Anglo-American force garrisoned Trieste, neither awarded to Yugoslavia as the Russians demanded, nor left in Italy as the British and Americans favored.

In the Far East there developed the most critical situation of all, with the result that actual shooting broke out in Korea between the two fronts of the "cold war." The powers had watched with mixed emotions and uncertain policies while Communist adherents within China gradually took over the whole country from Chiang Kai-shek and his Nationalist party, thus inevitably aligning that country, not only ideologically but politically, with Russia. Chiang Kai-shek was forced to set up a government-in-exile on the island of Formosa.

Here, as in Palestine, the British and Americans differed in their partisanship. The British had heavy financial stakes in China, especially in internationalized Shanghai and their own colony of Hong Kong, close to Canton, commercial capital of southern China. Consequently, Britain formally recognized the new government, hoping, perhaps, to continue as much business as possible and to avoid an attack on Hong Kong. The United States was annoyed at this action, since it had decided, after considerable uncertainty, to continue to recognize the Nationalist government.

In the meantime, the United Nations was taking armed action against aggression in Korea. This was something new in international relations and was hoped to be an augury of peaceful settlement of international difficulties in a foreseeable future. The earlier League of Nations, we recall, had failed largely because it did nothing to implement the provisions in its charter for stopping aggression when Japan, Italy, and Germany began their conquests in the thirties (see pages 897, 941–942).

Korea, a strategic, oft-disputed peninsula on the Pacific coast of Asia, had been definitely annexed by Japan in 1910. As a Japanese possession at the close of World War II, its administration had been taken from Japan, and it had been divided into two parts at the arbitrary line of the thirty-eighth parallel, with a Russian sphere of influence in the north and an American one in the south. In the American zone a Republic of Korea was soon set up, but the Russians refused to allow the country to be united under it. In June, 1950, prompted probably by the Russians, a North Korean army crossed the border and invaded South Korea. The United States led the move in the United Nations for immediate action to deal with this first instance since the recent war of flagrant aggression against a neighbor. Normally, in a case like this, Russia could have killed any such move by the use of its veto in the Security Council. It so happened at this crucial moment that the Russian representative was deliberately boycotting the Council sessions over another matter. As a result, the Security Council, when hastily summoned, authorized immediate armed opposition to the invasion of South Korea. The United States rushed ships, planes, and troops to the scene; and the North Koreans were temporarily stopped, as they swept down the peninsula, by American soldiers from nearby Japan. Britain, which had supported the United States in the Security Council, made the next heaviest contribution, with some 14,000 ground troops and some 10,000 men in her naval forces in those waters. These troops were to be the nucleus of what was to be known, by 1952, as the Commonwealth Division—with Canada, Australia, and New Zealand joining Britain in this United Nations action. The bulk of the troops and the supreme commander, however, were American.

This deployment of British forces was the source of no little friction within Attlee's own ranks. Many were inclined to feel that Britain had become too prone to follow along with the United States, especially in the Far East. Britain had so much more at stake there, with her investments in China, and the very existence of Hong Kong depended on trade with the Chinese mainland. The British feared that the Americans were "trigger-happy," apt to drag them into an Asiatic war which might spread and spread until it became worldwide.

The United States was to continue to bear the brunt of the Korean task, suffering more than 125,000 casualties in the next three years. By the late fall of 1950 it looked as though success were in sight; the United Nations forces had pushed the North Koreans up to the Yalu River, which marked the boundary of Soviet Manchuria. Then suddenly the Chinese Communists joined the fight, and it was the Allies' turn to retreat. Eventually the front became stabilized approximately at the thirty-eighth parallel, while localized fighting and armistice negotiations dragged on and on in a sort of stalemate. Fearful of provoking Russia into "World War III," although it was

# A History of England and the British Empire

already the main supply source for the North Koreans, or even of goading Communist China into such a major war, the United Nations refrained from bombing the Communist airfields and supply bases beyond the Yalu River in Chinese territory. When the United States contemplated such action the British sought strenuously to prevent them from doing anything drastic, for fear of reprisals.

A third major center of foreign complications was the Balkans and the Middle East. Since the beginning of the nineteenth century those lands of the old Turkish Empire had been a source of tension, with Russia a threatening neighbor on one side and the conflicting interests of Britain and other western powers on the other. Early in this century Persia, later renamed Iran, had become an additional danger spot in the explosive Middle East (see pages 593, 838). And it was in Persia that Britain's worst difficulties were to occur at this time. Her troubles with Egypt over Suez and the Sudan, as well as the relinquishment of Palestine, have already been noted in connection with the empire.

Britain's first concern in the eastern Mediterranean developed during the last months of the war, when Russian forces were over-running the Balkans. Had Russia obtained a hold upon Greece, as it did over Rumania, Bulgaria, and Yugoslavia, it would have had air and submarine bases for the future, penetrating far into the Mediterranean and threatening British interests throughout that region. Ally though Russia was, Churchill rushed British troops to Greece and went to Athens himself at Christmas, 1944, to counteract Russian influence. As a result, Britain was in Greece when peace came that spring (see page 1005). The anti-Soviet government of the Greek king was inefficient and weak, but it was approved by a plebiscite carefully executed under Allied supervision. Communist guerrillas were active in Greece, and such bands were also constantly crossing the border from Yugoslavia and Bulgaria. These were kept at bay by the British troops garrisoned there. Britain also had a strong personal interest in protecting Turkey against any threats of Russian aggression, as she had so often in the past.

Gradually these responsibilities became more than Britain could afford. The United States took them over in 1947, thus releasing British troops from duty in Greece. At the same time, the powerful Sixth Fleet of the United States Navy was stationed in Mediterranean waters.

The British were grateful for that, but, as already noted, American support, for political reasons, of Jewish ambitions in Palestine was a different matter. The reaction of that American policy upon the Moslems of the Middle East was a serious threat to British interests there, and as such was deeply resented. As early as 1945, a so-called "Arab League" had been organized. It was, of course, the phenomenal development of the new oil fields in Arabia and the Persian Gulf region that gave added significance to every aspect of that tangled situation and made what happened there of vital interest to the western world, with its insatiable need for oil. Russia, too, was too close for comfort, with the ever-present possibility that it might grasp the chance to fish in troubled waters. A fanatic, with the title of Grand Mufti of Jerusalem, was tireless and fairly successful in his efforts to stir up anti-British feeling throughout the Moslem world. Several pro-British statesmen in the Middle East were assassinated. One of these was perhaps Britain's staunchest ally, King Abdullah of Jordan, who had the most effective Arab military force, trained by a British brigadier known as "Glubb Pasha."

The most serious Middle Eastern trouble came not from the Arabs but from other Moslems, their neighbors in Iran. The country had long been divided between Russian and British spheres of influence (see page 838), and its people lived in constant fear of Russian aggression. The outbreak in 1951, however, was a direct conflict between Iran and Britain over the rich oilfields in the south.

Back in 1914, when the navies of the world were changing from coal to oil, Winston Churchill, then First Lord of the Admiralty, had arranged for the Admiralty to purchase a controlling interest in the wealthy Anglo-Persian (later Anglo-Iranian) Oil Company. Ultimately that company developed the greatest refineries in the world at the port of Abadan. The Iranians, however, became dissatisfied because their government was not getting as generous royalties in their contract with the Anglo-Iranian company as the 50 per cent royalties that American companies were paying for the operation of oilfields in Saudi Arabia.

In March, 1951, the pro-British, "strong man" premier of Iran was assassinated, and shortly afterward the Iranian Parliament passed an act taking over all the oil properties of the Anglo-Iranian Oil Company. Britain's efforts at negotiation, as well as those of the United States as mediator, proved fruitless in view of the excited attitude of the Iranians. Early that fall Iran ordered the last British technicians out of the country, and a British cruiser bore them away from Abadan. The Iranians did not know how to refine the oil; they owned no tankers in which to deliver it to customers overseas; mountains made it difficult to pipe the oil to Russia; but that made no difference, the oil business henceforth must be an Iranian industry. Gradually, however, they began to realize that they had cut off the nation's main source of revenue. Ultimately that realization might make them more ready to make a compromise settlement with the British; at least Britain was working towards that solution.

A century earlier, faced with such situations, Britain did not hesitate, compromise, and cajole; instead the government got quick results by "letting the British lion roar." Palmerston, for instance, would have rushed fleets and regiments to the critical spot to overawe the troublemakers. The very fact that Britain's strength could so easily be turned against them, normally kept other nations from annoying the British in those days. In the mid-twentieth century, however, Britain could not afford enough of those instruments of power to deter unfriendly action or to punish it—and the nations of the world, both large and small, were well aware of the relative impotence of the British lion. Like her neighbors in Western Europe, Britain had to wrestle with the constant problem of whether to spend her limited funds for "guns or butter."

For a while, the Labor government hoped to be able to achieve its socialistic goals by economizing on the armed forces. In the grim days of 1947 the Home Fleet, which in earlier days had numbered sixty-seven vessels, was for a while reduced to one cruiser and four destroyers! Not a single battleship was available for active service; there was nothing larger than light aircraft carriers in both the Mediterranean and the Pacific. Early in 1948 Churchill stormed in the House of Commons, "Britain has always floated upon her Navy. Well, the great Indian Empire has gone down one drain and now the Admiralty proclaim that the Royal Navy has gone down another. . . . Can you wonder that . . . we are checked by Chile and abused by Argentina—and fired at by Guatemala?" There was, of course, in this emergency the knowledge that the United States Navy was strong enough—galling though it was to British pride—to take over those tasks in which the two nations had a common interest.

But no other friendly nation had a big enough army to underwrite Britain on land; it was, therefore, not so easy to cut down the Army budget. Several divisions had to be maintained as occupation troops in Germany. Some 40,000 British soldiers were eventually needed to fight in Malaya. Although heavy forces had been withdrawn from Palestine, as well as those troops formerly needed in India, Egypt, Greece, and other regions, considerable forces were still stationed in Austria, Trieste, the Suez Canal Zone, Iraq, Gibraltar, Malta, Cyprus, Libya, and Hong Kong.

With the Korean crisis in 1950 and the North Atlantic Treaty Organization drive for armament, further economizing on the military budget was out of the question. Resentfully the Laborites had to allow the military program to overshadow the outlay for social

# Austerity and Experiment

welfare. The contrast is shown by the following figures, which do not include interest on the national debt and normal civil expenditures. One must, of course, take into account the 30 per cent inflation by the devaluation of the pound in 1949:

| BRITISH BUDGETS, 1947–1952 | | | | | | |
|---|---|---|---|---|---|---|
| (In million pounds sterling, adjusted to nearest million) | | | | | | |
| | 1947 | 1948 | 1949 | 1950 | 1951 | 1952 |
| Total Budget | 3,187 | 3,176 | 3,375 | 3,455 | 4,196 | 4,230 |
| Army | 384 | 347 | 292 | 299 | 449 | 521 |
| Navy | 194 | 163 | 187 | 193 | 278 | 375 |
| Air Force | 182 | 187 | 202 | 223 | 329 | 468 |
| Defense, misc. | 125 | 56 | 60 | 65 | 87 | 116 |
| Total Defense | 885 | 753 | 741 | 780 | 1,143 | 1,480 |
| National Insurance-Assistance | (159) | 128 | 197 | 200 | 218 | 145 |
| National Health Service | 2 | 146 | 249 | 374 | 379 | 371 |
| Food Subsidies | 333 | 320 | 410 | 402 | 403 | — |
| Education | 168 | 198 | 225 | 243 | 252 | 259 |
| Housing | 47 | 58 | 60 | 61 | 60 | 60 |
| Total Social | 709 | 850 | 1,141 | 1,280 | 1,312 | 836 |

The "cold war" was cutting down on the "butter" to provide the "guns," but even at that the British, for all their austerity, had far more of the pleasant things of life than did most of the poor wretches beyond the "iron curtain." Above all, they lived in a land where the rights of the individual were still respected and safeguarded. It was in the hope of preserving such a way of life that the expenditures for the armed forces were allowed to creep up each year.

The Labor party remained in power the full five years, until a new election was due in 1950. This was an unusually quiet campaign. Foreign affairs played little part in it, and, even regarding controversial domestic issues, neither side was particularly aggressive. Contributing factors were the curtailment of radio time for political purposes by the British Broadcasting Company and the strict limitation of election expenses.

Attlee's strategy was to point to the recent accomplishments of his party and to stress the grim unemployment of the thirties as the nation's fate, should his party lose. The tory-baiting "Nye" Bevan was kept as much as possible in the background. Further nationalization was soft-pedaled, although the sugar and cement industries were mentioned as next on the list, with shipbuilding, chemical production, and life insurance to come sometime in the future. Labor's two alluring slogans were "Fair Shares for All" and "Full Employment"; and it was constantly reiterated that the poor now had better food, higher wages, steadier jobs, and a higher standard of living than before the war.

The popularity of the social-welfare measures kept the Conservative party leaders cautious, too. Their strategy had to be to accept, in general, what Labor had done, and then to argue that they could do it more effectively and more cheaply. They promised to repeal the nationalization of steel, but otherwise only urged more decentralization and more elastic controls. They blamed the continuing housing shortage on the way private builders had been hamstrung by Bevan's restrictions on building materials. Their frontal attack was against Labor's financial policy, claiming it was leading straight to economic collapse, which had only been postponed by the American loan of 1946 and Marshall Plan aid, soon due to run dry. Britain's desperate efforts to sell widely in the world market had been stymied by the way production costs had mounted under Labor; and the Conservatives pointed to the rapid rise in the price of nationalized coal as against the lesser rise in the price of steel before it was nationalized. They reminded the people that it was taxes that were having to make good the deficits in the coal industry, in railways, and much else.

Also in the campaign was the Liberal party, strong in financial strength, though long a minor party, and contesting nearly 500 constituencies. It had no hope of winning many seats, but if it could even double its current eleven seats in Commons, and if the election proved close, it might hold the balance of power as it had done in the MacDonald Labor ministries. The Communists were in the campaign, too, with 100 candidates, but they elected no one, losing even the two seats they already had.

Labor won the election in February, 1950, and returned to office for what was to prove to be a brief stay of twenty months. Their victory was a very slim one. Instead of the 390 seats of the past five years, they won only 315; this gave them such a small majority that even the slightest revolt within their own party might turn them out of office. The Conservatives now had 294 seats, but this increase was cold comfort when their hearts had been set on victory. As for the Liberals, the old party of Bright, Cobden, and Gladstone seemed, at long last, ready to give up the ghost, with but 9 seats left. From the beginning it was obvious that Attlee's second Parliament would probably not last out its five-year term. If things went well, he might call a new election in hopes of securing a more adequate working majority in Commons. If the political skies should become overcast, his hold on Commons was too slender to save him from having to resign or dissolve Parliament for a new election.

The latter proved to be the case for both international and domestic reasons. These were the months when, as we have seen, Britain's most prosperous overseas investment, oil, met disaster in Iran; when Egyptian hostility threatened Suez and the Sudan; when Malaya and its rubber plantations were aflame; and when open fighting "to stop aggression" was undertaken by the United Nations in Korea. To people with the horror of the German bombs so fresh in their memory, the Korean war was particularly disquieting as a possible prelude to World War III. At home, too, all was not going smoothly: for one thing, the nationalization of steel was running into snags. Within the Labor party itself there was growing dissension. It had lost two of its ablest leaders: Ernest Bevin, who had been conservative enough to please even the tory-minded, was dead, and Sir Stafford Cripps, Chancellor of the Exchequer and generally admitted to be a financial wizard, was dying in Switzerland.

Into this vacuum in the party's leadership rushed Bevan, who had been recognized for some time as the head of the left-wing Laborites. For two decades there had been enmity between Bevan and Bevin, both of whom had risen from the ranks of labor in contrast to Attlee and Cripps, who represented the intellectual side of the Labor movement (see pages 1003–1004). Compromise with capitalism, or with any conservative ideas whatsoever, was not in Bevan. His hates were many, from Bevin to Churchill. During the war, he had called the latter "turgid, wordy, dull, and prosaic"—a "bloated bladder of lies." Now Bevan charged that his precious National Health Act was menaced in the new budget of Cripps's successor as Chancellor of the Exchequer; for one thing, henceforth the recipient was going to be required to pay for half the cost of new dentures and spectacles. He was violently opposed to any cuts in social welfare in the search for additional funds for the stepped-up rearmament. He resigned his post within a week of the announcement of the budget, and a handful of Labor members of the Commons sided with him.

Attlee felt that this split between the radical and the moderate wings of the party was more than his narrow majority in Commons could stand. Consequently, he dissolved Parliament, although it had still almost four more years to run. The election was held in the fall of 1951.

The Labor party thus entered this campaign with disunity within its ranks. Bevan suspended his attack on increased armament for the duration of the campaign, but made it evident that this was only a postponement. Attlee tried to avoid this cleavage between left and right, with the result that his campaign was colorless and conciliatory. Little that was new was promised, as Attlee and his wife took to their battered car to tour the countryside. Labor had done well in trying times, he kept saying, and unemployment under the Conservatives in the thirties must not be forgotten. That was about all; he shied away from the issue of nationalization for fear of alienating the Liberal vote, which both parties were wooing. Two and a half million had voted the Liberal ticket twenty months before, though only nine seats had been won. A clear-cut issue was lacking until Churchill brought foreign policy into the campaign. That gave Labor its slogan, "Keep the Peace with Attlee." Both parties had been pretty much as one in support of the United Nations, in continuing rearmament and conscription, and in the defense of British interests overseas; but this anti-war cry appealed to many, especially to the Liberals.

In the Conservative campaign Churchill blamed the Laborites for the difficulties in the Middle East. He referred to the Iranian oil seizures as laying Britain "flat on the face as though she was a booby and a coward." He was outspoken on the necessity for Britain and the United States to stay bound together in mutual interest. The Conservatives were inclined to be somewhat overconfident, with the nation in such a sorry plight after six years of Labor's rule. There was full employment, but little else to give comfort to men and women who had been on short rations for over a decade.

When it came to remedial measures, however, the Conservatives still dared not repudiate the welfare state. Their contention, in the main, was the same as twenty months before; they promised to stay the advance of socialism and to put the nation on a firmer foundation in both domestic and foreign affairs. When Laborites argued that, if the nation was as near economic collapse as was claimed, rearmament must be curtailed, Churchill pointed to the increased danger from Russia and the impairment of Anglo-American unity invited by such a course. In East Anglia American bombers were poised for flight; what was the best way to keep them grounded? As election day approached this question tended to overshadow domestic issues.

The Conservatives won the election in October, 1951, but the returns showed again a badly divided country. It was not a clear-cut victory; the Conservatives won 321 seats to Labor's 294, with only 6 Liberals left. The Conservatives thus had only 6 more votes to bolster their small majority than Labor had had. The schism in the

# Austerity and Experiment

Labor party was threatening to grow worse, for in spite of the party's defeat, Bevan and his left wing group had personally triumphed: they were all re-elected and by increased majorities.

Winston Churchill at seventy-seven undertook his second ministry with his accustomed courage. Anthony Eden was again Foreign Secretary. The task ahead was a formidable one, and about all that Churchill could do was to play for time, as he took office in the face of almost insoluble situations at home and abroad. With the fighting going on in Korea, in Malaya, and at Suez; the unsettled disputes with Iran and Egypt; the seething undercurrents elsewhere in Asia and Africa; and the ever-present shadow of a hostile Russia, international skies had seldom, if ever, been darker for Britain. Even Iraq, long closely linked to Britain and graduated from mandate to kingdom through British sponsorship, was beginning to press for higher royalties for oil extracted from its Mesopotamian fields. On the Continent plans for a European army were still in the blueprint stage, with neither Churchill nor British public opinion indicating any intention of doing more than support its creation by words; a fact that irked France and annoyed the United States.

Churchill almost immediately announced his intention of going to Washington. There he had had successes in the past, and it was the only quarter of the globe whence shone a ray of hope. He thereupon postponed the opening of Parliament until the end of January to give himself time for the trip. He attended to a few stop-gap measures in the bad home situation. Gold reserves were declining again, so he clamped tighter controls on the leakage of gold. Imports were further restricted, and the food ration cut.

In Washington Churchill found that he had to make some concessions. He yielded to American insistence on an American admiral to command the naval forces of the North Atlantic Treaty Organization. He promised to give the United States "prompt and effective" support if a truce were arranged in Korea and broken by the Communists. For that pledge he was angrily accused by Bevan and his left-wing cohorts of changing British foreign policy without warrant. He found that his countersuggestion, that the United States send a token force to Suez if the British endeavor to placate Egypt bogged down, was not kindly received. He did achieve his main objective— steel for British rearmament. He was also able to ease the dollar situation by persuading the United States to agree to take some of Britain's stores of tin and rubber.

Early in February, 1952, the death of King George VI brought to the throne his daughter, England's second Queen Elizabeth, the fifth queen regnant. Her marriage in 1947 to Philip Mountbatten, lieutenant in the Royal Navy and related to the royal house of Greece, had been almost the sole bright spot in that dreary year. Elizabeth had won the hearts of the Britons with her unusual charm. Because of King George's failing health, the young couple had already taken on a fair share of the ceremonial duties that have become the chief function of royalty; and they were on the way to Australia, in the king's place, when the news of his death brought them home from Kenya. The very fact of having a queen again seemed to bring cheer to the people; for, except for Mary Tudor, England had prospered under her queens. Two of her greatest eras had been symbolized in the reigns of the first Elizabeth and Victoria. The pageantry of the coronation in June, 1953, seemed to dramatize the link between the glorious past and the ever-changing present. In the midst of medieval ritual was proclaimed the new royal title, which reflected the latest weakening of Britain's ties with her old "dominion over palm and pine": "Elizabeth the Second, by the Grace of God of the United Kingdom, Canada, Australia, New Zealand, South Africa, Pakistan, Ceylon, and her other realms and territories Queen, Head of the Commonwealth, Defender of the Faith."

# SOVEREIGNS OF ENGLAND

| | Sovereigns | Basis of Title |
|---|---|---|
| | **IMPORTANT BEFORE CONQUEST** | |
| 871–899 | ALFRED | Wessex line |
| 1017–1035 | CANUTE | Conquest |
| 1042–1066 | EDWARD (Confessor) | Return to Wessex line |
| 1066 | HAROLD | Son of Earl Godwin ; elected by witan |
| | **NORMANS** | |
| 1066–1087 | WILLIAM I | Conquest |
| 1087–1100 | WILLIAM II (Rufus) | 2d son of William I |
| 1100–1135 | HENRY I | 3d son of William I |
| 1135–1154 | STEPHEN | Son of daughter of William I |
| | **ANGEVINS — PLANTAGENETS** | |
| 1154–1189 | HENRY II | Son of daughter of Henry I |
| 1189–1199 | RICHARD I | Eldest surviving son of Henry II |
| 1199–1216 | JOHN | Next surviving son of Henry II |
| 1216–1272 | HENRY III | Son of John |
| 1272–1307 | EDWARD I | Son of Henry III |
| 1307–1327 | EDWARD II | Son of Edward I |
| 1327–1377 | EDWARD III | Son of Edward II |
| 1377–1399 | RICHARD II | Son of eldest son of Edward III |
| | **LANCASTRIANS** | |
| 1399–1413 | HENRY IV | Son of 4th (3d surviving) son of Edward III |
| 1413–1422 | HENRY V | Son of Henry IV |
| 1422–1461 | HENRY VI | Son of Henry V |
| | **YORKISTS** | |
| 1461–1483 | EDWARD IV | From Edward III through his 3d and 5th sons |
| 1483 | EDWARD V | Son of Edward IV |
| 1483–1485 | RICHARD III | Younger brother of Edward IV |
| | **TUDORS** | |
| 1485–1509 | HENRY VII | From 4th son of Edward III through Beaufort line |
| 1509–1547 | HENRY VIII | Son of Henry VII |
| 1547–1553 | EDWARD VI | Son of Henry VIII |
| 1553–1558 | MARY (I) | Elder daughter of Henry VIII |
| 1558–1603 | ELIZABETH I | Younger daughter of Henry VIII |
| | **STUARTS** | |
| 1603–1625 | JAMES I | From daughter of Henry VII through Scottish line |
| 1625–1649 | CHARLES I | Son of James I |
| 1649–1660 | INTERREGNUM | (Commonwealth and Protectorate) |
| 1660–1685 | CHARLES II | Elder son of Charles I |
| 1685–1688 | JAMES II | Younger son of Charles I |
| 1688–1702 | WILLIAM III AND MARY (II) | Mary, elder daughter of James II |
| 1702–1714 | ANNE | Younger daughter of James II |
| | **HANOVERIANS** | |
| 1714–1727 | GEORGE I | From James I through Hanoverian line |
| 1727–1760 | GEORGE II | Son of George I |
| 1760–1820 | GEORGE III | Son of eldest son of George II |
| 1820–1830 | GEORGE IV | Eldest son of George III |
| 1830–1837 | WILLIAM IV | 2d son of George III |
| 1837–1901 | VICTORIA | Daughter of 4th son of George III |
| 1901–1910 | EDWARD VII | Son of Victoria |
| 1910–1936 | GEORGE V | Son of Edward VII |
| 1936 | EDWARD VIII | Eldest son of George V |
| 1936–1952 | GEORGE VI | 2d son of George V |
| 1952– | ELIZABETH II | Daughter of George VI |

# BRITISH MINISTRIES

A = First Lord of the Admiralty; BT = President of the Board of Trade; C = Colonial Secretary; D = Minister of Defense; DPM = Deputy Prime Minister; E = Chancellor of the Exchequer; F = Foreign Secretary; H = Home Secretary; Ind = Secretary for India; Ire = Secretary for Ireland; L = Minister of Labor; PC = Lord President of the Council; PMG = Postmaster General; PS = Lord Privy Seal; S = Secretary of State (eighteenth century); Scot = Secretary for Scotland; T = Minister of Transport; W = War Secretary

| | *"Prime Minister"* | *Other Prominent Cabinet Members* |
|---|---|---|
| 1721 | WALPOLE | TOWNSHEND (S), STANHOPE (S), NEWCASTLE (S) |
| 1742 | WILMINGTON | CARTERET (S), NEWCASTLE (S) |
| 1744 | PELHAM | NEWCASTLE (S) |
| 1754 | NEWCASTLE I | |
| 1756 | DEVONSHIRE | PITT (S) |
| 1757 | NEWCASTLE II | PITT (S) |
| 1761 | BUTE | G. GRENVILLE (S) |
| 1763 | G. GRENVILLE (also E) | |
| 1765 | ROCKINGHAM I | GRAFTON (S) |
| 1766 | CHATHAM (PITT) | TOWNSHEND (E), SHELBURNE (S) |
| 1767 | GRAFTON | NORTH (E), SHELBURNE (S) |
| 1770 | NORTH | SANDWICH (A), GERMAIN (C) |
| 1782 | ROCKINGHAM II | FOX (S), SHERLBURNE (S) |
| 1782 | SHELBURNE | PITT (E) |
| 1783 | PORTLAND I | FOX (S), NORTH (S) |
| 1783 | PITT I (also E) | W. GRENVILLE (F), DUNDAS (Ind, W) |
| 1801 | ADDINGTON | |
| 1803 | PITT II (also E) | CASTLEREAGH (W) |
| 1806 | W. GRENVILLE | FOX (F) |
| 1807 | PORTLAND II | CANNING (F), CASTLEREAGH (W), LIVERPOOL (H) |
| 1809 | PERCEVAL (also E) | CASTLEREAGH (F), LIVERPOOL (W) |
| 1812 | LIVERPOOL | CASTLEREAGH (F), CANNING (Ind, F), PEEL (H), HUSKISSON (BT), ROBINSON-GODERICH (E) |
| 1827 | CANNING (also E) | HUSKISSON (BT) |
| 1827 | GODERICH | HUSKISSON (W) |
| 1828 | WELLINGTON | PEEL (H) |
| 1830 | GREY | PALMERSTON (F), MELBOURNE (H), DURHAM (PS) |
| 1834 | MELBOURNE I | PALMERSTON (F) |
| 1834 | PEEL I | WELLINGTON (F) |
| 1835 | MELBOURNE II | PALMERSTON (F), RUSSELL (H) |
| 1841 | PEEL II | ABERDEEN (F), DERBY (W), GLADSTONE (W) |
| 1846 | RUSSELL I | PALMERSTON (F) |
| 1852 | DERBY I | DISRAELI (E) |
| 1852 | ABERDEEN | PALMERSTON (H), CLARENDON (F), GLADSTONE (E) |
| 1855 | PALMERSTON I | CLARENDON (F), GLADSTONE (E) |
| 1858 | DERBY II | DISRAELI (E) |
| 1859 | PALMERSTON II | RUSSELL (F), GLADSTONE (E) |
| 1865 | RUSSELL II | CLARENDON (F), GLADSTONE (E) |
| 1866 | DERBY III | DISRAELI (E) |
| 1868 | DISRAELI I | |
| 1868 | GLADSTONE I (also E) | BRIGHT (BT) |
| 1874 | DISRAELI II | DERBY (F), SALISBURY (Ind, F), CARNARVON (C) |
| 1880 | GLADSTONE II (also E) | J. CHAMBERLAIN (BT) |
| 1885 | SALISBURY I (also F) | R. CHURCHILL (Ind) |
| 1885 | GLADSTONE III (also H) | ROSEBERY (F), MORLEY (Ire) |
| 1886 | SALISBURY II (also F) | R. CHURCHILL (E), BALFOUR (Scot, Ire) |
| 1892 | GLADSTONE IV (also PS) | ROSEBERY (F), ASQUITH (H) |
| 1894 | ROSEBERY (also PC) | ASQUITH (H) |
| 1895 | SALISBURY III (also F to 1900) | LANSDOWNE (F), J. CHAMBERLAIN (C) |
| 1902 | BALFOUR | LANSDOWNE (F) |
| 1905 | CAMPBELL-BANNERMAN | GREY (F), LLOYD GEORGE (E) |
| 1908 | ASQUITH | GREY (F), LLOYD GEORGE (E), W. CHURCHILL (A) |
| 1916 | LLOYD GEORGE | BALFOUR (F), BONAR LAW (E)—War Cabinet |
| 1922 | BONAR LAW | BALDWIN (E) |
| 1923 | BALDWIN I | N. CHAMBERLAIN (E) |
| 1924 | MACDONALD I (also F) | SNOWDEN (E), HENDERSON (H) |
| 1924 | BALDWIN II | A. CHAMBERLAIN (F), W. CHURCHILL (E) |
| 1929 | MACDONALD II | SNOWDEN (E), HENDERSON (F), MORRISON (T) |
| 1931 | MACDONALD III | BALDWIN (PC), SIMON (F), N. CHAMBERLAIN (E), ATTLEE (PMG) |
| 1935 | BALDWIN III | MACDONALD (PC), HOARE (F, A), N. CHAMBERLAIN (E), EDEN (F) |
| 1937 | N. CHAMBERLAIN | SIMON (E), EDEN (F), HALIFAX (F), HOARE (H) |
| 1940 | CHURCHILL I (also D) | ATTLEE (DPM, PS), HALIFAX (F), EDEN (F), BEVIN (L), MORRISON (H) |
| 1945 | ATTLEE (also D) | BEVIN (F), MORRISON (PC), CRIPPS (BT, E) |
| 1952 | CHURCHILL II | EDEN (F), BUTLER (E) |

# SUGGESTED BOOKS FOR FURTHER READING

FOR THE student who desires to follow up particular subjects in English history, the following suggestions contain the titles of some of the books most likely to prove useful. Many excellent works have been omitted deliberately because their detailed or controversial treatment seems to adapt them to the needs of the advanced scholar rather than to those of the college undergraduate. There is, moreover, no space here for a detailed bibliography, nor is one necessary since several very comprehensive bibliographical aids are available in most college libraries.

Foremost among these aids, for the more prominent works, is *A Guide to Historical Literature* (ed. W. H. ALLISON et al., 1931), with brief, authoritative estimates of the various titles. Valuable for their greater detail are the bibliographies of English history edited by C. GROSS, for the period to 1485; C. READ, 1485–1603; G. DAVIES, 1603–1714; and, in preparation, D. J. MEDLEY, 1714–1789; as well as *A Bibliography of British History, 1700–1715* (ed. W. T. MORGAN; Vol. I, 1934). More compact are H. L. CANNON, *Reading References in English History* (1910), and W. T. MORGAN, *A Guide to the Study of English History* (1926). The most comprehensive textbook bibliography is in W. E. LUNT, *History of England* (1928), pp. 822–881. Useful critical bibliographies will be found in each volume of the *Political History*, the "Oman Series," and the new *Oxford History*, described below. For references to particular individuals or subjects the brief bibliographical notes attached to articles in the *Dictionary of National Biography, Encyclopaedia of the Social Sciences*, and *Encyclopaedia Britannica* may be found serviceable.

# I. *General Works*

This section is devoted to works which cover more or less the whole period of English history. Books more limited in their time scope are listed under subsequent sections for particular periods (to 1066; 1066–1485; Tudor period; Stuart period; 1714–1815; and since 1815). These general works, of course, should be consulted in connection with the studies of the limited periods.

The best single-volume general history by an English author is G. M. TREVELYAN, *History of England* (1926). Like his numerous other works, it is an admirable combination of scholarship, interpretation, and style. Three co-operative series, with each volume by a different author, and sometimes uneven in quality, give more detailed treatment: *The Political History of England* (ed. W. HUNT and R. L. POOLE; 12 vols., 1905–1910); *A History of England* (ed. C. W. C. OMAN; hereafter referred to as "Oman Series") (8 vols.; 1904–1934); and the projected *Oxford History of England* (ed. G. N. CLARK; 14 vols., 1934–    ). Authorship is still further divided in *Social England* (ed. H. R. TRAILL and J. S. MANN; 6 vols.

in 12; new ed., 1909), with separate sections in each period on political, religious, social, economic, cultural, military, and other aspects. Certain chapters or sections are devoted to English history in the *Cambridge Medieval History* (8 vols.; 1911–1936) and *Cambridge Modern History* (14 vols.; 1902–1912).

## GENERAL WORKS IN SPECIAL TOPICS

CONSTITUTIONAL AND LEGAL. Most useful for the whole period is G. B. ADAMS, *Constitutional History of England* (new ed., with additional chapters by R. L. SCHUYLER, 1935). Also valuable are W. R. ANSON, *Law and Custom of the Constitution* (2 vols. in 3; new ed., 1909); F. W. MAITLAND, *Constitutional History of England* (1908); D. J. MEDLEY, *Student's Manual of English Constitutional History* (6th ed., 1925); and, with a wealth of detail, T. P. TASWELL-LANGMEAD, *English Constitutional History* (9th ed., 1929). The most comprehensive legal study is W. S. HOLDSWORTH, *History of English Law* (9 vols.; 1903–1926). For briefer treatment see E. JENKS, *A Short History of English Law* (1912), and H. POTTER, *Introduction to the History of English Law* (1926).

ECONOMIC AND SOCIAL. For brief, general works see E. P. CHEYNEY, *Introduction to the Industrial and Social History of England* (new ed., 1920); C. DAY, *History of Commerce* (new ed., 1928); F. MILNER, *Economic Evolution in England* (1931); and A. P. USHER, *Introduction to the Industrial History of England* (1920). For the period to the end of the eighteenth century the standard authority is E. LIPSON, *Economic History of England* (3 vols.; 1915–1931); it has in many ways supplanted the old authority, W. CUNNINGHAM, *Growth of English Industry and Commerce* (rev. ed., 2 vols. in 3; 1915–1921). For agriculture see R. E. PROTHERO (LORD ERNLE), *English Farming, Past and Present* (4th ed., 1927), and N. S. B. and E. C. GRAS, *Economic and Social History of an English Village, A.D. 909–1928* (1930).

RELIGION. The best brief study is H. O. WAKEMAN, *Introduction to the History of the Church of England* (new ed., 1920). For more detail consult the co-operative work *History of the English Church* (ed. W. R. W. STEPHENS and W. HUNT; 9 vols., 1899–1910). For particular subjects or individuals see the *Encyclopaedia of Religion and Ethics* (ed. J. HASTINGS et al.; 13 vols., 1908–1927) and the *Catholic Encyclopaedia* (ed. C. G. HERBERMANN et al.; 16 vols., 1907–1914).

LITERATURE, ETC. The most satisfactory brief studies are C. G. OSGOOD, *The Voice of England* (1935), and E. H. LEGOUIS and L. CAZAMIAN, *A History of English Literature* (2 vols.; 1927). A lengthy co-operative work of uneven quality is the *Cambridge History of English Literature* (15 vols.; new ed., 1933). For science see *Studies in the History and Methods of Science* (ed. C. J. SINGER; 2 vols., 1917–1921) and L. THORNDIKE, *A History of Magic and Experimental Science* (2 vols.; 1929).

MILITARY. The standard work is J. W. FORTESCUE, *History of the British Army* (13 vols. in 20; 1899–1930). For a brief sketch of various aspects of military development see R. G. ALBION, *Introduction to Military History* (1929).

NAVAL AND COLONIAL. See section 3, Tudor Period.

SCOTLAND, IRELAND, AND WALES. For Scottish history the standard work is P. H. BROWN, *History of Scotland* (3 vols.; 1902–1909); for a livelier account see A. LANG, *History of Scotland* (4 vols.; 1900–1907). The most satisfactory brief Irish surveys are R. DUNLOP, *Ireland from the Earliest Times to the Present Day* (1922), and P. W. JOYCE, *Short History of Ireland* (1911). For Wales see J. E. LLOYD, *History of Wales* (2d ed., 1912).

# Bibliography

SOURCE COLLECTIONS. For assembled selections from the original sources consult E. P. CHEYNEY, *Readings in English History* (new ed., 1922); A. B. WHITE and W. NOTESTEIN, *Source Problems in English History* (1915); and S. E. WINBOLT and K. BELL, *English History Source Books* (21 vols.; 1913–1927). For source collections in particular subjects see G. B. ADAMS, and H. M. STEPHENS, *Select Documents of English Constitutional History* (new ed., 1910); D. J. MEDLEY, *Original Illustrations of English Constitutional History* (1910); A. E. BLAND, P. A. BROWN, and R. H. TAWNEY, *English Economic History, Select Documents* (1914); R. B. MORGAN, *Readings in English Social History* (5 vols.; 1921–1922); and H. GEE and W. J. HARDY, *Documents Illustrative of English Church History* (1896).

REFERENCE WORKS. The standard work for British biography is the *Dictionary of National Biography* (ed. L. STEPHEN and S. LEE; 63 vols., with various supplements; 1885–1900). There are a slightly revised edition (22 vols.; 1908–1909) and a brief single-volume epitome (1914). For maps consult W. R. SHEPHERD, *Historical Atlas* (7th ed., 1929). *Ploetz's Manual of Universal History* (new ed. by H. E. BARNES, 1933) is a very useful outline of dates and events. Much information for the later period is to be found in the annual editions of the *Annual Register* (since 1759), the *British Almanac* (1828–1914), the *Statesman's Year Book* (since 1864), and *Whitaker's Almanack* (since 1868).

## II. *Works Listed by Periods*

### 1. TO 1066

NARRATIVE AND GENERAL. The period is covered in the three general series by the following: *Political History*, Vol. I (T. HODGKIN), *To 1066*. "Oman Series," C. W. C. OMAN, *England before the Norman Conquest*. *Oxford History*, R. G. COLLINGWOOD and J. N. L. MYRES, *Roman Britain and the English Settlements*; F. M. STENTON, *Anglo-Saxon England*.

The hazy problems of prehistory and racial backgrounds, in England and elsewhere, are treated in G. C. MacCURDY, *Human Origins* (2 vols.; 1924); H. F. OSBORN, *Men of the Old Stone Age* (1915); W. Z. RIPLEY, *Races of Europe* (1910). These are on the whole more satisfactory than the volumes dealing with prehistory in Britain alone.

For the Roman period the best works are R. G. COLLINGWOOD, *Roman Britain* (new ed., 1932); F. J. HAVERFIELD, *Romanization of Roman Britain* (1906) and *Roman Occupation of Britain* (1924); and T. R. HOLMES, *Ancient Britain and the Invasions of Julius Caesar* (1907).

The modern views on Anglo-Saxon England, taking into account archaeological research, are embodied in R. H. HODGKIN, *A History of the Anglo-Saxons* (2 vols.; 1935). Prominent older accounts, somewhat modified by later research, are J. R. GREEN, *The Making of England* (1882) and *The Conquest of England* (1883), and the first three volumes of E. A. FREEMAN, *History of the Norman Conquest* (6 vols.; 1867–1879). More specialized studies are E. HULL, *The Northmen in Britain* (1913); T. D. KENDRICK, *A History of the Vikings* (1930); L. M. LARSON, *Canute the Great* (1912); B. A. LEES, *Alfred the Great* (1915); C. PLUMMER, *Life and Times of Alfred the Great* (1902); G. SHELDON, *The Transition from Roman Britain to Christian England* (1932); and M. W. WILLIAMS, *Social Scandinavia in the Viking Age* (1920). Two celebrated histories written during the period and edited for the Everyman edition are the VENERABLE BEDE'S *Ecclesiastical History of the English Nation* (1910) and the *Anglo-Saxon Chronicle* (1913).

CONSTITUTIONAL AND LEGAL. W. A. MORRIS, *The Constitutional History of England to 1215* (1930), and F. POLLOCK and F. W. MAITLAND, *History of English Law before the Time of Edward I* (2d ed., 1899), are sound studies covering this and part of the succeeding period.

# A History of England and the British Empire

ECONOMIC AND SOCIAL. Divergent views concerning the importance of Roman and Saxon influences upon the development of the manor are found in H. L. GRAY, *English Field Systems* (1915); F. SEEBOHM, *The English Village Community* (4th ed., 1890); and P. G. VINOGRADOFF, *The Growth of the Manor* (2d ed., 1911).

RELIGION. The most useful general works are T. ALLISON, *English Religious Life in the Eighth Century* (1929), and S. J. CRAWFORD, *Anglo-Saxon Influence on Western Christendom, 600–800* (1933). Of numerous biographies the most satisfactory are G. F. BROWNE, *Augustine and his Companions* (2d ed., 1897); J. B. BURY, *The Life of St. Patrick* (1905); and J. A. ROBINSON, *The Times of St. Dunstan* (1923).

LITERATURE, ETC. The best general surveys are S. A. BROOKE, *English Literature from the Beginning to the Norman Conquest* (new ed., 1907), and M. L. W. LAISTNER, *Thought and Letters in Western Europe, A.D. 500 to 900* (1931). For special topics see *Beowulf* (tr. C. B. TINKER, 1910); W. W. LAWRENCE, *Beowulf and the Epic Tradition* (1928); *The Cædmon Poems* (ed. C. W. KENNEDY, 1916); *The Poems of Cynewulf* (ed. C. W. KENNEDY, 1910); and *Old English Poetry* (tr. J. D. SPAETH, 1922).

## 2. 1066–1485

NARRATIVE AND GENERAL. *Political History*, Vol. II (G. B. ADAMS), *1066–1216*; Vol. III (T. F. Tout), *1216–1377*; Vol. IV (C. W. C. OMAN), *1377–1485*. "Oman Series," H. W. C. DAVIS, *England under the Normans and Angevins*; K. H. VICKERS, *England in the Later Middle Ages*. Oxford History, A. L. POOLE, *The Twelfth Century*; F. M. POWICKE, *The Thirteenth Century*; M. V. CLARKE, *The Fourteenth Century*; E. F. JACOB, *The Fifteenth Century*. A good brief survey is F. M. POWICKE, *Medieval England, 1066–1485* (1931).

A delightful and valuable volume on the Normans in England and on the Continent is C. H. HASKINS, *The Normans in European History* (1915). For the Crusades see T. A. ARCHER and C. L. KINGSFORD, *The Crusades* (1895); D. C. MUNRO, *The Kingdom of the Crusaders* (1935); R. A. NEWHALL, *The Crusades* (1927); and, for Richard's work in particular, *Chronicles of the Crusades* (tr. J. A. GILES and T. JOHNES, 1848).

Among the more useful biographies for the period are F. M. STENTON, *William the Conqueror* (1908); A. S. GREEN, *Henry the Second* (1888); L. F. SALZMAN, *Henry II* (1914); T. I. JARMAN, *William Marshal* (1930); S. PAINTER, *William Marshal* (1933); C. BÉMONT, *Simon de Montfort* (new ed., E. F. JACOB, 1930); E. JENKS, *Edward Plantagenet* (1902), with special emphasis on the legal reforms; T. F. TOUT, *Edward the First* (1893); A. M. MACKENZIE, *Robert Bruce, King of Scots* (1934); R. VERCEL, *Bertrand of Brittany, a Biography of Messire Du Guesclin* (tr. M. SAUNDERS; 1934); R. P. DUNN-PATTISON, *The Black Prince* (1910); J. H. WYLIE, *History of England under Henry the Fourth* (4 vols.; 1884–1898) and *The Reign of Henry the Fifth* (3 vols; 1914–1929); C. L. SCOFIELD, *Life and Reign of Edward the Fourth* (2 vols.; 1923); K. H. VICKERS, *Humphrey, Duke of Gloucester* (1907); J. GAIRDNER, *History of the Life and Reign of Richard the Third* (3d ed., 1898). Cf. also the biographies listed under religion.

Among the studies of particular aspects of the period are G. M. TREVELYAN, *England in the Age of Wycliffe* (new ed., 1904), an excellent work; E. C. LODGE, *Gascony under English Rule* (1926); C. W. C. OMAN, *The Great Revolt of 1381* (1906); C. L. KINGSFORD, *Prejudice and Promise in Fifteenth-Century England* (1925). A first-hand picture of the earlier part of the Hundred Years' War is found in J. FROISSART, *Chronicles* (of England, France, etc.), in various editions, full or abridged.

CONSTITUTIONAL AND LEGAL. MORRIS, and POLLOCK and MAITLAND, are valuable for this period as well as the preceding one. Good studies of English feudalism are J. H. ROUND, *Feudal England* (1895), and F. M. STENTON, *The First Century of English Feudalism* (1932). The standard work on its subject is W. S. McKECHNIE. *Magna*

# Bibliography

*Carta* (2d ed., 1914). Important for the origins of Parliament are C. H. McILWAIN, *The High Court of Parliament and its Supremacy* (1910); D. PASQUET, *Essay on the Origins of the House of Commons* (tr. R. G. D. LAFFAN. 1925); and A. F. POLLARD, *The Evolution of Parliament* (1920). Useful studies in administrative history include J. F. BALDWIN, *The King's Council in England during the Middle Ages* (1913); R. L. POOLE, *The Exchequer in the Twelfth Century* (1912); J. H. RAMSAY, *History of the Revenues of the Kings of England, 1066–1399* (2 vols.; 1926); T. F. TOUT, *Chapters in the Administrative History of Mediaeval England* (6 vols.; 1920–1933). For the baronial experiments see R. F. TREHARNE, *The Baronial Plan of Reform* (Vol. I, 1932).

ECONOMIC AND SOCIAL. Good general surveys include M. BATESON, *Mediaeval England* (1904); E. POWER, *Medieval People* (1924); and L. F. SALZMAN, *English Life in the Middle Ages* (1926). For the manor and agriculture, in addition to GRAY, SEEBOHM, and VINOGRADOFF mentioned for the preceding period, see G. G. COULTON, *The Medieval Village* (1925); N. J. HONE, *The Manor and Manorial Records* (1906); and N. NEILSON, *Medieval Agrarian Economy* (1936). Among the best works on the towns and industry are C. GROSS, *The Gild Merchant* (2 vols.; 1890); S. KRAMER, *English Craft Gilds* (1927); L. F. SALZMAN, *English Industries of the Middle Ages* (new ed., 1923); and C. STEPHENSON, *Borough and Town* (1933). Medieval London is well described in M. R. HOLMES, *Mediaeval England: London, the Treasure House* (1934). The standard works on the Black Death are C. CREIGHTON, *History of Epidemics in Britain* (1891), and F. A. GASQUET, *The Black Death of 1348 and 1349* (2d ed., 1908). For conditions during the latter part of the period consult A. ABRAM, *English Life and Manners in the Later Middle Ages* (1913) and *Social England in the Fifteenth Century* (1909); H. S. BENNETT, *The Pastons and their England* (1922) and the original *Paston Letters*, in the Everyman and numerous other editions. Also important are N. S. B. GRAS, *The Early English Customs System* (1918), and G. UNWIN, *Finance and Trade under Edward III* (1918).

RELIGION. For the general background of the Church there are two useful volumes in the Berkshire Studies: S. BALDWIN, *The Organization of Medieval Christianity* (1929), and S. R. PACKARD, *Europe and the Church under Innocent III* (1927). Important works for the situation in England in particular are Z. N. BROOKE, *The English Church and the Papacy from the Conquest to the Reign of John* (1931), and F. A. GASQUET, *Henry III and the Church* (1905). The best works on English monasticism are F. A. GASQUET, *English Monastic Life* (6th ed., 1924), and A. SAVINE, *English Monasteries on the Eve of the Dissolution* (1909). The beginnings of the mendicant orders in England are admirably related in A. JESSOPP, *The Coming of the Friars* (7th ed., 1895). The outstanding religious biographies for the period are S. DARK, *St. Thomas of Canterbury* (1927); F. M. POWICKE, *Stephen Langton* (1928); F. S. STEVENSON, *Robert Grosseteste* (1899); and H. B. WORKMAN, *John Wyclif* (1926). A delightful and valuable first-hand account of the inner workings of a great monastery is *Jocelin of Brakelond*, in various editions.

LITERATURE, ETC. Two general surveys are C. S. BALDWIN, *Three Medieval Centuries of Literature in England, 1100–1400* (1932), and W. H. SCHOFIELD, *English Literature from the Norman Conquest to Chaucer* (1906). Stimulating and important volumes by an eminent medievalist are C. H. HASKINS, *The Renaissance of the Twelfth Century* (1927), *The Rise of the Universities* (1923), and *Studies in the History of Medieval Science* (2d ed., 1927). Also important for the education of the period are A. F. LEACH, *The Schools of Medieval England* (1915), and H. RASHDALL, *Universities of Europe in the Middle Ages* (new ed., 3 vols., 1936). A valuable analysis of the general intellectual background is H. O. TAYLOR, *The Mediaeval Mind* (2 vols.; 4th ed., 1930). Among the principal works on the period of Chaucer are G. G. COULTON, *Chaucer and his England* (1921); W. A. NEILSON and K. G. T. WEBSTER, *Chief British Poets of the Fourteenth and Fifteenth Centuries* (1916); and R. K. ROOT, *The Poetry of Chaucer* (1922). The architectural development is treated in F. BOND, *Gothic Architecture in England* (1905); C. H. MOORE, *Mediaeval*

*Church Architecture in England* (1912); and E. S. PRIOR, *History of Gothic Art in England* (1900). For a concise general survey of art and architecture in England and other lands, see S. REINACH, *Apollo: An Illustrated Manual of the History of Art throughout the Ages* (new ed., 1935).

MILITARY. The standard work for the period is C. W. C. OMAN, *History of the Art of War in the Middle Ages* (2 vols., 2d ed., 1924). For a more limited field see R. A. NEWHALL, *The English Conquest of Normandy, 1416–1424* (1922).

## 3. TUDOR PERIOD, 1485–1603

NARRATIVE AND GENERAL. Two of the best volumes in the *Political History* are V (H. A. L. FISHER), *1485–1547*, and VI (A. F. POLLARD), *1547–1603*. The period is covered in the "Oman Series" by A. D. INNES, *England under the Tudors*, and in the *Oxford History* by J. D. MACKIE, *The Earlier Tudors, 1485–1558*, and J. B. BLACK, *The Reign of Elizabeth, 1558–1603*. The best brief survey of the period is C. READ, *The Tudors* (1936). The most ambitious detailed study, very readable but often inaccurate, is J. A. FROUDE, *History of England from the Fall of Wolsey to the Defeat of the Spanish Armada* (12 vols.; new ed., 1899); the remainder of the Tudor period is ably covered by E. P. CHEYNEY, *History of England from the Defeat of the Spanish Armada to the Death of Elizabeth* (2 vols.; 1914–1926).

Biographies of the first Tudor include F. BACON, *Historie of the Raigne of King Henry the Seventh* (new ed., 1902); J. GAIRDNER, *Henry the Seventh* (1899); and G. TEMPERLEY, *Henry VII* (1914). The standard life of his son is A. F. POLLARD, *Henry VIII* (new ed., 1905); there are also some popular books emphasizing his wives. Also important are M. CREIGHTON, *Cardinal Wolsey* (1888); R. B. MERRIMAN, *Life and Letters of Thomas Cromwell* (2 vols.; 1902); A. F. POLLARD, *England under Protector Somerset* (1900); and J. M. STONE, *History of Mary I, Queen of England* (1900), which has a strong bias in favor of Mary. The best biography of Elizabeth, which "displaces all earlier short lives," is J. E. NEALE, *Queen Elizabeth* (1934). Studies of her ministers include M. A. S. HUME, *Great Lord Burghley* (1898); A. CECIL, *Life of Robert Cecil, First Earl of Salisbury* (1915); C. READ, *Mr. Secretary Walsingham and the Policy of Queen Elizabeth* (3 vols.; 1925). A popular work on the later years of the reign is G. L. STRACHEY, *Elizabeth and Essex* (1928). Mary Stuart has been a difficult subject for impartial treatment; possibly the most satisfactory life is T. F. HENDERSON, *Mary Queen of Scots* (2 vols.; 1905). For the setting of England in the international background see P. SMITH, *The Age of the Reformation* (1920).

CONSTITUTIONAL AND LEGAL. The most useful works are F. M. G. EVANS, *The Principal Secretary of State . . . 1558 to 1680* (1923); K. PICKTHORN, *Early Tudor Government* (2 vols.; 1934); and J. R. TANNER, *Tudor Constitutional Documents* (1922).

ECONOMIC AND SOCIAL. A valuable co-operative work, containing chapters on many aspects of Tudor life, is *Shakespeare's England* (ed. W. RALEIGH, S. LEE, and C. T. ONIONS; 2 vols., 1917); also useful is L. F. SALZMAN, *England in Tudor Times: an Account of its Social Life and Industries* (1926). The best work on the early enclosure movements is R. H. TAWNEY, *The Agrarian Problem in the Sixteenth Century* (1912). Other pertinent studies are E. M. LEONARD, *Early History of English Poor Relief* (1900), and W. NOTESTEIN, *History of Witchcraft in England* (1911). Several works dealing with the commerce of the period are listed in the maritime section.

RELIGIOUS. A useful study of the background is R. S. ARROWSMITH, *Prelude to the Reformation* (1923). F. A. GASQUET, *The Eve of the Reformation* (3d ed., 1905) and *Henry VIII and the English Monasteries* (new ed., 1906), were written by a future Catholic cardinal, whereas J. GAIRDNER, *The English Church in the Sixteenth Century* (1904), has

# Bibliography

been called "coldly Protestant." A new study is G. CONSTANT, *The Reformation in England* (Vol. I, 1934). Also important are A. F. POLLARD, *Thomas Cranmer and the English Reformation* (1904); C. H. SMYTH, *Cranmer and the Reformation under Edward VI* (1926); and W. H. FRERE, *The English Church in the Reigns of Elizabeth and James I* (1904). The influential contemporary work J. FOXE's *Acts and Monuments* (popularly known as the *Book of Martyrs*) has appeared in many editions since its original publication in 1563.

LITERATURE, ETC. *Shakespeare's England*, already mentioned, has valuable chapters in this field. Some of the foremost men are described in S. LEE, *Great Englishmen of the Sixteenth Century* (1904). For the earlier period the principal books are L. D. EINSTEIN, *The Italian Renaissance in England* (1902) and *Tudor Ideals* (1921), and F. SEEBOHM, *The Oxford Reformers: John Colet, Erasmus and Thomas More* (new ed., 1914). There are excellent lives of Erasmus by E. EMERTON (1899), J. HUIZINGA (1924), and P. SMITH (1923). For More there are R. W. CHAMBERS, *Thomas More* (1935), and E. M. G. ROUTH, *Sir Thomas More and his Friends* (1934). J. Q. ADAMS, *A Life of William Shakespeare* (1923), is perhaps the best biography.

MARITIME (NAVAL, COLONIAL, COMMERCIAL). Inasmuch as England's maritime activity was not important before Tudor times, the general works are included at this point before those dealing with the Tudor situation in particular. The most ambitious general naval history is the co-operative work *The Royal Navy* (ed. W. L. CLOWES; 7 vols., 1897–1903). For briefer treatment the most useful studies are G. CALLENDER, *The Naval Side of British History* (1924); D. HANNAY, *Short History of the Royal Navy, 1217–1815* (2 vols.; 1898–1909); and B. TUNSTALL, *Realities of Naval History* (1936). The most useful relatively brief survey of colonial history is J. A. WILLIAMSON, *Short History of British Expansion* (2 vols. in 1; new ed., 1930). H. E. EGERTON, *Short History of British Colonial Policy* (5th ed., 1918), is the best in its field. More extensive are two co-operative works: the *Cambridge History of the British Empire* (ed. J. H. ROSE, A. P. NEWTON, and E. A. BENIANS; 8 vols., 1929–    ), the first volume dealing with the "Old Empire" to 1783; and the *Historical Geography of the British Colonies* (ed. C. P. LUCAS; 7 vols., 1888–1923). A series of interpretative lectures, important in reviving imperial enthusiasm, is J. R. SEELEY, *The Expansion of England* (2d ed., 1895). For commercial history see especially the general works by DAY and LIPSON, already mentioned. The general European and overseas situation up to 1789 is ably treated in W. C. ABBOTT, *The Expansion of Europe* (2 vols. in 1; new ed., 1924).

The general Tudor maritime activity is treated in C. P. LUCAS, *The Beginnings of English Overseas Enterprise* (1917); J. A. FROUDE, *English Seamen in the Sixteenth Century* (new ed., 1917); and J. A. WILLIAMSON, *Maritime Enterprise, 1485–1558* (1913). Important contemporary collections of maritime narratives are R. HAKLUYT, *The Principall Navigations . . . of the English Nation*, and S. PURCHAS, *Purchas his Pilgrimes*, both of which have appeared in various editions. For the "sea dogs" the standard works are J. S. CORBETT, *Drake and the Tudor Navy* (2 vols.; 1898) and *The Successors of Drake* (1900). On the commercial side valuable studies are W. FOSTER, *England's Quest of Eastern Trade* (1933); W. E. LINGELBACH, *Merchant Adventurers of England* (1902); and A. J. GERSON, E. V. VAUGHAN, and N. R. DEARDORFF, *Studies in the History of English Commerce in the Tudor Period* (1912). For the general international background see L. B. PACKARD, *The Commercial Revolution, 1400–1776* (1927), and G. F. VON SCHMOLLER, *The Mercantile System* (tr. W. J. ASHLEY; 1896).

FOREIGN POLICY. J. R. SEELEY, *Growth of British Policy* (2 vols., 1897), analyzes, in a rather discursive manner, the evolution of English foreign policy in the sixteenth and seventeenth centuries.

IRELAND. Detailed treatment will be found in R. BAGWELL, *Ireland under the Tudors* (3 vols.; 1885–1890).

# A History of England and the British Empire

## 4. STUART PERIOD, 1603–1714

NARRATIVE AND GENERAL. *Political History*, Vol. VII (F. C. MONTAGUE) *1603–1660*; Vol. VIII (R. LODGE), *1660–1702*; Vol. IX (I. S. LEADAM), *1702–1760* "Oman Series," G. M. TREVELYAN, *England under the Stuarts*, a particularly useful account. *Oxford History*, G. DAVIES, *The Early Stuarts, 1603–1660*, and G. N. CLARK, *The Later Stuarts, 1660–1714*. The period has been covered also by a succession of detailed works of the scope of FROUDE, but on the whole more accurate. The most ambitious of these is S. GARDINER, *History of England* (with various subtitles) (18 vols.; new ed., 1901–1903), covering the years 1603 to 1656; it is continued by C. H. FIRTH, *Last Years of the Protectorate, 1656–1658* (2 vols.; 1909). One of the classics of English history is T. B. MACAULAY, *History of England from the Accession of James II*, for the period 1685–1697. Originally published between 1849 and 1861, it has gone through numerous editions, usually in five volumes. It is written in the grand manner, and, despite its strong Whig prejudices, it has been called "one of the most brilliant and popular pieces of historical writing in any language." A decidedly worthy continuation, by Macaulay's grand-nephew G. M. TREVELYAN, is *England under Queen Anne* (3 vols.; 1930–1934).

For the disturbed middle years of the century there is a valuable Royalist first-hand account in the EARL OF CLARENDON's *History of the Rebellion*, which, like his *Life*, has passed through several editions. The most interesting life of Cromwell is by J. BUCHAN (LORD TWEEDSMUIR) (1934); also useful are the biographies by C. H. FIRTH (1900) and J. MORLEY (1900); while copious source material with pungent comment is found in T. CARLYLE, *Letters and Speeches of Oliver Cromwell*, published in several editions (usually three volumes) since its original appearance in 1845.

The Restoration period has only recently begun to receive adequate scholarly treatment. Two works of particular value are A. BRYANT, *King Charles II* (1932), and D. OGG, *England in the Reign of Charles II* (2 vols.; 1934). An invaluable and delightful source account for the period is the diary of SAMUEL PEPYS, mentioned in the text, which has been translated and published in numerous editions; most complete and valuable is the edition by H. B. WHEATLEY (9 vols.; 1893–1899). Foremost among the biographies of Pepys is A. BRYANT, *Samuel Pepys* (Vols. I–II, 1933–1935). The less lively diary of JOHN EVELYN likewise has numerous editions, especially by H. B. WHEATLEY (4 vols.; 1879) and by A. DOBSON (3 vols.; 1906). Also useful is H. D. TRAILL, *Shaftesbury* (1888). The best party history for the period is K. FEILING, *History of the Tory Party, 1640–1714* (1924). William III has been treated in such detail by Macaulay that few others have dealt particularly with his reign.

The reign of Anne, on the other hand, has received marked attention of late. In addition to Trevelyan's volumes there is W. S. CHURCHILL, *Marlborough, his Life and Times* (Vols. I–IV, 1933–1936), in part an effort to whitewash the author's illustrious ancestor. Military studies of Marlborough will be noted later. On the political side there are W. M. MORGAN, *English Political Parties and Leaders in the Reign of Queen Anne* (1920), and W. S. SICHEL, *Bolingbroke and his Times* (2 vols.; 1901–1902).

CONSTITUTIONAL AND LEGAL. For contemporary statements of the conflicting political theories see *The Political Works of James I* (ed. C. H. MCILWAIN, 1918); T. HOBBES, *Leviathan*; and J. LOCKE, *Treatises on Government* (in various editions). Also valuable are J. N. FIGGIS, *The Theory of the Divine Right of Kings* (new ed., 1914), and G. P. GOOCH, *Political Thought in England from Bacon to Halifax* (new ed., 1923) and *English Democratic Ideas in the Seventeenth Century* (2d ed., 1927). In addition to the works on Parliament mentioned in the medieval section see W. NOTESTEIN, *Winning of the Initiative by the House of Commons* (1925).

ECONOMIC AND SOCIAL. MACAULAY's third chapter and the opening chapters in TREVELYAN's *Stuarts* and *Anne* contain excellent surveys of the various aspects of English life, as does A. BRYANT, *The England of Charles II* (1935). Useful works in nar-

# Bibliography

ower fields are A. M. ANDRÉADÈS, *History of the Bank of England* (1909), and E. TROTTER, *Seventeenth Century Life in the Country Parish* (1919).

RELIGION. Prominent works on Puritanism are H. H. HENSON, *Puritanism in England* (1912), and G. B. TATHAM, *Puritans in Power* (1913).

LITERATURE, ETC. A helpful introduction is B. WILLEY, *The Seventeenth Century Background* (1934). More specialized are B. DOBREE, *Restoration Comedy* (1924) and *Restoration Tragedy* (1929); T. S. ELIOT, *John Dryden* (1932); W. RALEIGH, *Milton* (1900); and A. E. TAYLOR, *Francis Bacon* (1926).

MARITIME (NAVAL, COLONIAL, COMMERCIAL). Contemporary commercial theories are well expressed in J. CHILD, *A New Discourse of Trade* (1693), and T. MUN, *England's Treasure by Foreign Trade* (new ed., 1895). Naval studies include J. CORBETT, *England in the Mediterranean* (2 vols.; 1904), and R. BEADON, *Robert Blake* (1935). Naval, colonial, and commercial problems are discussed in R. G. ALBION, *Forests and Sea Power: The Timber Problem of the Royal Navy, 1652-1862* (1926). Naval and commercial considerations are combined in G. N. CLARK, *The Dutch Alliance and the War against French Trade* (1923). Outstanding works in the colonial field include C. M. ANDREWS, *The Colonial Period of American History* (Vols. I-II, 1934-1936); G. L. BEER, *The Old Colonial System* (2 vols.; 1912); A. P. NEWTON, *Colonising Activities of the English Puritans* (1914) and *The European Nations in the West Indies, 1493-1688* (1933); and H. L. OSGOOD, *The American Colonies in the Seventeenth Century* (3 vols.; 1904-1907). There are also very numerous works dealing with particular American colonies.

MILITARY. The make-up of the Civil War forces, as distinct from their operations, is ably handled in C. H. FIRTH, *Cromwell's Army* (1902). Marlborough's military career is well treated in C. T. ATKINSON, *Marlborough and the Rise of the British Army* (1921), and F. TAYLOR, *The Wars of Marlborough* (2 vols.; 1921), as well as in CHURCHILL'S work already mentioned.

FOREIGN RELATIONS. SEELEY's *Growth of British Policy*, mentioned in connection with the Tudor period, continues to be useful. For the Continental background see L. B. PACKARD, *The Age of Louis XIV* (1929).

SCOTLAND AND IRELAND. There is an excellent general picture of Scotland about 1700 in the second volume of TREVELYAN'S *Anne*. The romantic side of Scotland in the Civil War period is ably portrayed in J. BUCHAN (LORD TWEEDSMUIR), *Montrose, a History* (1928). Also useful are A. V. DICEY and R. S. RAIT, *Thoughts on the Union between England and Scotland* (1920), and W. L. MATHIESON, *Politics and Religion in Scotland, 1550-1695* (2 vols.; 1902) and *Scotland and the Union, 1695-1747* (2 vols.; 1905). The principal work on Ireland in the period is R. DUNLOP, *Ireland under the Commonwealth* (1913).

## 5. EIGHTEENTH CENTURY, 1714-1815

NARRATIVE AND GENERAL. *Political History*, Vol. IX (I. S. LEADAM), *1702-1760*; Vol. X (W. HUNT), *1760-1801*; Vol. XI (G. C. BRODERICK and J. K. FOTHERINGHAM), *1801-1837*. "Oman Series," G. ROBERTSON, *England under the Hanoverians*. Oxford History, B. WILLIAMS, *The Establishment of the Hanoverians, 1714-1760*, and G. S. VEITCH, *The Reign of George III, 1760-1815*. A comprehensive work, on the scale of FROUDE, GARDINER, and MACAULAY, is W. E. H. LECKY, *History of England in the Eighteenth Century* (new ed., 7 vols., 1913), originally written between 1878 and 1890. It gives particular emphasis to social, economic, philosophical, Irish, and American aspects; the portions on Ireland and the American Revolution have been published separately. The

# A History of England and the British Empire

latter part of the period is well handled in G. M. TREVELYAN, *British History in the Nineteenth Century, 1782–1901* (1922).

Useful works dealing with the earlier part of the period are J. MORLEY, *Walpole* (1889), and C. PETRIE, *The Stuart Pretenders* (1933). For the middle part the political situation is discussed in D. A. WINSTANLEY, *Personal and Party Government . . . 1760–1766* (1910) and *Lord Chatham and the Whig Opposition* (1912). The best biographies of the elder Pitt are A. VON RUVILLE, *William Pitt, Earl of Chatham* (3 vols.; 1907), and B. WILLIAMS, *Life of William Pitt, Earl of Chatham* (2 vols.; 1913). A delightful picture of social and political conditions is to be found in G. O. TREVELYAN, *The Early Life of Charles James Fox* (new ed., 1908). The Wilkes troubles are treated in H. W. BLEACKLEY, *Life of John Wilkes* (1917), and W. P. TRELOAR, *Wilkes and the City* (1917). The best studies of Burke are by A. COBBAN (1929) and J. MORLEY (1867). *The Correspondence of King George the Third, 1760–1783* (ed. J. FORTESCUE; 6 vols., 1927–1928), contains much of interest.

For the later part of the period one of the foremost works is J. H. ROSE, *Life of William Pitt* (2 vols.; 1924), originally published in 1911 as *William Pitt and the National Revival* and *William Pitt and the Great War*. A briefer life of the younger Pitt is LORD ROSEBERY, *Pitt* (1892). Some of his contemporaries and successors are discussed in J. W. FORTESCUE, *British Statesmen of the Great War* (1911). The intellectual and reform ferment of the period is treated in W. P. HALL, *British Radicalism, 1791–1797* (1912), and R. COUPLAND, *Wilberforce, a Narrative* (1923). For diplomatic, naval, and military aspects of the period see below. The Continental background is well treated in C. BRINTON, *A Decade of Revolution, 1789–1799* (1934), and J. H. ROSE, *Life of Napoleon I* (new ed., 1922).

CONSTITUTIONAL AND LEGAL. A general study of value is T. E. MAY, *Constitutional History of England . . . 1760–1860*, continued in a new edition to 1911 (3 vols.; 1912). E. and A. G. PORRITT, *The Unreformed House of Commons* (2 vols.; 2d ed., 1909), is an invaluable study of the subject. Useful analyses of the workings of the old political system are W. T. LAPRADE, *Public Opinion and Politics in Eighteenth Century England to the Fall of Walpole* (1936), and L. B. NAMIER, *The Structure of Politics at the Accession of George III* (2 vols.; 1929). For political theory see H. J. LASKI, *Political Thought in England from Locke to Bentham* (1920).

ECONOMIC AND SOCIAL. Two of the best surveys of the modern period are G. H. PERRIS, *Industrial History of Modern England* (1914), and G. SLATER, *The Growth of Modern England* (1932). The working out of economic principles is ably handled in C. R. FAY, *Great Britain from Adam Smith to the Present Day* (1928). The technological side of the Industrial Revolution is best explained in A. P. USHER, *Introduction to the Industrial History of England*, mentioned in the general works. The leading study of the social consequences of the movement is J. L. and B. HAMMOND, *The Town Labourer, 1760–1832* (1917), while other aspects of change are given in their volumes on *The Village Labourer* (new ed., 1920) and *The Skilled Labourer* (1919). Also useful on the same subject is W. BOWDEN, *Industrial Society in England towards the End of the Eighteenth Century* (1925). Prominent among the studies of particular industries are T. S. ASHTON, *Iron and Steel in the Industrial Revolution* (1924); S. J. CHAPMAN, *The Lancashire Cotton Industry* (1904); G. W. DANIELS, *Early English Cotton Industry* (1920); and J. U. NEF, *Rise of the British Coal Industry* (2 vols.; 1932). Biographical sketches of many of the leaders in the movement will be found in S. SMILES, *Lives of the Engineers* (3 vols.; 1862–1868). The foremost work in economic theory is ADAM SMITH, *Wealth of Nations*, in the Everyman and other editions, while the prevalent doctrines are discussed in E. F. HECKSCHER, *Mercantilism* (tr. M. SHAPIRO; 2 vols., 1935). For general social surveys, apart from the purely economic, the foremost works are *Johnson's England: An Account of the Life and Manners of his Age* (ed. A. S. TURBERVILLE; 2 vols., 1933), similar in arrangement to *Shakespeare's England*; J. B. BOTSFORD, *English Society in the Eighteenth Century as Influenced from Oversea* (1924); F. J. F. JACKSON, *Social Life in England, 1750–1850* (1916); and A. S. TURBERVILLE, *English Men and Manners in the Eighteenth Century* (1926).

# Bibliography

RELIGION. The principal works are the *Journal of John Wesley* (ed. N. CURNOCK et al.; 8 vols., 1909–1916) and C. T. WINCHESTER, *Life of John Wesley* (1906).

LITERATURE, ETC. *Johnson's England*, already mentioned, is useful in this field; also L. STEPHEN, *English Literature and Society in the Eighteenth Century* (1904) and *History of English Thought in the Eighteenth Century* (2 vols.; 3d ed., 1902). For particular aspects see J. B. BLACK, *The Art of History, a Study of Four Great Historians of the Eighteenth Century* (1926); J. W. KRUTCH, *Comedy and Conscience after the Restoration* (1924); and C. B. TINKER, *The Salon and English Letters* (1915) and *Nature's Simple Plan* (1922). Among the best biographies are J. BOSWELL, *Life of Samuel Johnson* (various editions); W. CROSS, *The Life and Times of Laurence Sterne* (1925); C. VAN DOREN, *Swift* (1930); W. P. TRENT, *Daniel Defoe, How to Know Him* (1916); S. A. SHELLABARGER, *Lord Chesterfield, a Man of the World* (1935); and G. R. S. TAYLOR, *Mary Wollstonecraft* (1911). For the later part of the period see H. N. BRAILSFORD, *Shelley, Godwin and their Circle* (1913), and E. DOWDEN, *The French Revolution and English Literature* (1897).

MARITIME (NAVAL, COLONIAL, COMMERCIAL) AND MILITARY. A classic analysis of the imperial and naval situation is A. T. MAHAN, *The Influence of Sea Power upon History, 1660–1783* (32d ed., 1928); also useful is A. H. BUFFINTON, *The Second Hundred Years' War, 1689–1815* (1929). For colonial history, particularly for the period before 1763, see H. L. OSGOOD, *The American Colonies in the Eighteenth Century* (4 vols.; 1924–1925); G. L. BEER, *British Colonial Policy, 1754–1765* (1907); O. M. DICKERSON, *American Colonial Government, 1696–1765* (1912); A. L. BURT, *The Old Province of Quebec* (1933); C. WITTKE, *History of Canada* (1928), a general history; G. M. WRONG, *History of Canada* (3 vols.; 1929–1935), to 1783; J. B. BREBNER, *New England's Outpost, Acadia before the Conquest of Canada* (1927); A. LYALL, *Rise and Expansion of British Dominion in India* (5th ed., 1910), a general history; and F. W. PITMAN, *The Development of the British West Indies* (1917), particularly for the early eighteenth century. The middle period of the Anglo-French duel for empire is well treated in J. S. CORBETT, *England in the Seven Years' War* (2 vols., 1907); F. PARKMAN, *A Half-Century of Conflict* (2 vols.; new ed., 1903) and *Montcalm and Wolfe* (2 vols.; new ed., 1903), for Canada; R. PARES, *War and Trade in the West Indies, 1739–1763* (1936); and G. FORREST, *Life of Lord Clive* (2 vols.; 1918), for India.

One of the first important works to present the new interpretation of the American Revolution was G. O. TREVELYAN, *The American Revolution* (4 vols.; new ed., 1905–1912); also valuable for background and causes are C. M. ANDREWS, *Colonial Background of the American Revolution* (1924); H. E. EGERTON, *Causes and Character of the American Revolution* (1923); C. H. MCILWAIN, *The American Revolution* (1923); C. L. BECKER, *The Eve of the Revolution* (1918); and R. L. SCHUYLER, *Parliament and the British Empire* (1929). For the naval and military aspects of the war, consult, in addition to MAHAN and FORTESCUE, T. S. ANDERSON, *The Command of the Howe Brothers during the American Revolution* (1936), and W. M. JAMES, *The British Navy in Adversity* (1926). The fighting is briefly analyzed in R. G. ALBION, *Introduction to Military History*, already mentioned. For imperial aftereffects consult H. T. MANNING, *British Colonial Government after the American Revolution, 1782–1820* (1933), and C. H. VAN TYNE, *The Loyalists in the American Revolution* (1902).

For the naval side of the conflict with France from 1793 to 1815 the best work is A. T. MAHAN, *The Influence of Sea Power upon the French Revolution and Empire* (2 vols.; 10th ed., 1898). There is a readable brief life of Nelson by A. F. FREMANTLE (1933), and a more comprehensive life by MAHAN (2 vols.; 2d ed., 1899). Special aspects of this war and the American Revolution are treated in ALBION, *Forests and Sea Power*, already mentioned. For commercial aspects pertinent studies are W. F. GALPIN, *The Grain Supply of England during the Napoleonic Wars* (1925); E. F. HECKSCHER, *The Continental System* (1922); and F. E. MELVIN, *Napoleon's Navigation System* (1919). The best treatment of relations with the United States during this time is H. ADAMS, *History of the United States* (3 vols.; new ed., 1929). The best brief treatment of Wellington is P. GUEDALLA, *Welling-*

# A History of England and the British Empire

*ton* (1931), called *The Duke* in British editions; for more detailed works consult C. W. C. OMAN, *The Peninsular War* (7 vols.; 1902–1934), and FORTESCUE, already mentioned, who also deals with the earlier fighting of the period.

FOREIGN RELATIONS. The most useful work for the period following the American Revolution is the *Cambridge History of British Foreign Policy, 1783–1919* (ed. A. W. WARD and G. P. GOOCH; 3 vols., 1922–1923). An interesting study in the earlier period is B. WILLIAMS, *Stanhope: A Study in Eighteenth Century War and Diplomacy* (1932). For the peace settlement in 1814–1815 see W. A. PHILLIPS, *The Confederation of Europe* (2d ed., 1919); A. W. WARD, *The Period of Congresses* (1919); and C. K. WEBSTER, *The Congress of Vienna, 1814–1815* (new ed., 1934), and *The Foreign Policy of Castlereagh, 1812–1815* (1931).

## 6. SINCE 1815

NARRATIVE AND GENERAL. *Political History*, Vol. XI (C. G. BRODERICK and J. K. FOTHERINGHAM), *1801–1837*; Vol. XII (S. J. LOW and L. C. SANDERS), *1837–1901*. "Oman Series," J. A. R. MARRIOTT, *England Since Waterloo* and *Modern England, 1885–1932*. Oxford History, E. L. WOODWARD, *The Age of Reform, 1815–1870*, and R. C. K. ENSOR, *England, 1870–1914*. G. M. TREVELYAN'S *British History in the Nineteenth Century, 1782–1901*, already mentioned, is useful. An ambitious detailed study, covering the periods 1815–1841 and 1895–1915, is E. HALÉVY, *History of the English People* (5 vols.; 1924–1934). Older comprehensive works are S. WALPOLE, *History of England . . . from 1815* (6 vols.; new ed., 1910–1913) and *History of Twenty-five Years, 1856–1880* (4 vols.; 1904–1908).

Except for M. HOVELL, *The Chartist Movement* (1925), the principal general works on the earlier part of the period take the form of biography. Foremost among these are A. ASPINALL, *Lord Brougham and the Whig Party* (1927); H. C. F. BELL, *Lord Palmerston* (2 vols.; 1936); F. K. BROWN, *Life of William Godwin* (1926); P. GUEDALLA, *Palmerston* (1927), as well as his *Wellington*, already mentioned; J. L. and B. HAMMOND, *Lord Shaftesbury* (1923); J. A. HOBSON, *Richard Cobden, the International Man* (1919); J. MORLEY, *Life of Richard Cobden* (10th ed., 1903); G. M. TREVELYAN, *Lord Grey of the Reform Bill* (1920) and *Life of John Bright* (1925); and G. WALLAS, *Life of Francis Place* (4th ed., 1925). There are good biographies of Queen Victoria by E. F. BENSON, (1935), E. SITWELL (1936), and G. L. STRACHEY (1921). *The Letters of Queen Victoria* (ed. A. C. BENSON, G. E. BUCKLE, and LORD ESHER; 9 vols., 1908–1932) contain much of value.

The years from 1846 to 1895 are covered in detail by H. W. PAUL, *History of Modern England* (5 vols.; 1904–1906); another comprehensive work is R. H. GRETTON, *Modern History of the English People, 1880–1910* (2 vols.; 1913). The most comprehensive biography of Gladstone is J. MORLEY, *Life of William Ewart Gladstone* (new ed., 1921); briefer accounts are P. GUEDALLA, *The Queen and Mr. Gladstone* (1933), and W. P. HALL, *Mr. Gladstone* (1931). For Disraeli the fullest account is W. F. MONYPENNY and G. E. BUCKLE, *Life of Benjamin Disraeli* (6 vols.; 1910–1920); a shorter life is A. MAUROIS, *Disraeli* (1928). Other prominent biographies for the middle part of the period are G. CECIL, *Life of Robert, Marquis of Salisbury* (4 vols.; 1921–1932); J. L. GARVIN, *Life of Joseph Chamberlain* (Vols. I–III, 1932–1934); and S. LEE, *King Edward VII, a Biography* (2 vols.; 1925–1927).

The reign of George V up to 1935 is the subject of two works: J. BUCHAN (LORD TWEEDSMUIR) *The People's King* (1935) (called *The King's Grace* in the British editions), and D. C. SOMERVELL, *The Reign of King George V* (1935). Covering much of the same period, and written by a versatile statesman, is W. S. CHURCHILL, *The World Crisis* (5 vols.; 1923–1928). Analyses of postwar England include C. F. G. MASTERMAN, *England after the War* (1923), and A. SIEGFRIED, *Post-war Britain* (1924); while W. DIBELIUS, *England* (1930), presents an interesting objective German view, taking historical background into account. A collection of somewhat iconoclastic biographical sketches of leading figures is offered by A. BEGBIE, *Mirrors of Downing Street* (new ed., 1922). More formal biography

# Bibliography

'ncludes LORD HALDANE, *Autobiography* (1929); LORD RONALDSHAY (later LORD ZETLAND), *Life of Lord Curzon* (3 vols.; 1928); and J. SPENDER and C. ASQUITH, *The Life of Herbert Henry Asquith, Lord Oxford and Asquith* (2 vols.; 1932). Works on the World War will be found in a special section.

CONSTITUTIONAL AND LEGAL, ETC. Three important contemporary analyses of the British constitutional system are W. BAGEHOT, *The English Constitution* (new ed., 1872); S. J. M. Low, *Governance of England* (new ed., 1915); and a study by a distinguished American educator, A. L. LOWELL, *Government of England* (2 vols.; new ed., 1912). Leading works on political theory include E. BARKER, *Political Thought in England from Herbert Spencer to the Present Day* (1915); C. C. BRINTON, *English Political Thought in the Nineteenth Century* (1933); W. L. DAVIDSON, *Political Thought in England . . . Bentham to J. S. Mill* (1915); and H. J. LASKI, *Liberty in the Modern State* (1930). The foremost work in its field is S. and B. WEBB, *English Local Government* (4 vols.; 1906-1922). Also useful is C. SEYMOUR, *Electoral Reform in England and Wales . . . 1832-1885* (1915). For constitutional source material consult *English Constitutional Documents since 1832* (ed. E. M. VIOLETTE, 1936).

ECONOMIC AND SOCIAL. The general works by FAY, the HAMMONDS, PERRIS, and SLATER, mentioned in the preceding section, continue useful. The standard work for the period following that covered by LIPSON is J. H. CLAPHAM, *An Economic History of Modern Britain* (Vols. I-II, 1926-1932). The most useful collection of statistics for the century 1815-1914 is in *Commerce and Industry* (ed. W. Page; 2 vols., 1919). A co-operative work, with chapters on various social aspects, is *Early Victorian England, 1830-1865* (ed. G. M. YOUNG, 1935). Other valuable general surveys are C. R. FAY, *Life and Labour in the Nineteenth Century* (1933), and J. L. and B. HAMMOND, *The Age of the Chartists, 1832-1854* (1930). For special topics important works include C. J. H. HAYES, *British Social Politics* (1913), a study of the social legislation of 1906 to 1911; B. L. HUTCHINS and A. HARRISON, *History of Factory Legislation* (2d ed., 1911); W. T. JACKMAN, *Development of Transportation in Modern England* (2 vols.; 1916); L. H. JENKS, *Migration of British Capital to 1875* (1927); S. and B. WEBB, *English Poor Law History* (3 vols.; 1927-1929) and *History of Trade Unionism* (new ed., 1920). For a very important original statement of economic theory see J. S. MILL, *Principles of Political Economy* (ed. W. S. ASHLEY, 1926).

RELIGION. A good general survey of modern developments is W. L. MATHIESON, *English Church Reform* (1923). For the Oxford movement see R. W. CHURCH, *The Oxford Movement* (new ed., 1904), and C. SAROLEA, *Cardinal Newman and his Influence on Religious Life and Thought* (1908). Also important are ST. J. G. ERVINE, *God's Soldier: General William Booth* (2 vols.; 1934), for the origins of the Salvation Army; and B. N. WARD, *Dawn of the Catholic Revival in England, 1781-1803* (2 vols.; 1909) and *The Dawn of Catholic Emancipation* (3 vols.; 1911-1912).

LITERATURE, ETC. General surveys include E. BERNBAUM, *Guide through the Romantic Movement* (1931); O. ELTON, *A Survey of English Literature, 1780-1880* (4 vols.; 1924); G. P. GOOCH, *History and Historians of the Nineteenth Century* (1913); *The Social and Political Ideas of Some Representative Thinkers of the Victorian Age* (ed. F. J. C. HEARNSHAW, 1923); D. C. SOMERVELL, *English Thought in the Nineteenth Century* (1929); and H. WALKER, *Literature of the Victorian Era* (1921). Outstanding among the numerous biographies are A. BRYANT, *Macaulay* (1932); O. BURDETT, *The Brownings* (1929); J. BUCHAN (LORD TWEEDSMUIR), *Sir Walter Scott* (1932); L. F. CAZAMIAN, *Carlyle* (1932); G. M. HARPER, *William Wordsworth* (2 vols.; 1923); J. W. MACKAIL, *The Life of William Morris* (new ed., 1922); E. NEFF, *Carlyle and Mill* (1924); H. G. NICOLSON, *Tennyson* (1923); G. SAINTSBURY, *Matthew Arnold* (1899); J. A. SYMONDS, *Shelley* (new ed., 1925); *Ruskin the Prophet* (ed. J. H. WHITEHOUSE, 1920); A. WILLIAMS-ELLIS, *The Tragedy of John Ruskin* (1928).

# A History of England and the British Empire

FOREIGN RELATIONS. The whole period to 1919 is ably covered in the *Cambridge History of British Foreign Policy*, already mentioned. A brilliant brief summary is G. P. GOOCH and J. H. B. MASTERMAN, *Century of British Foreign Policy* (1917). Excellent studies for the beginning of the period are C. K. WEBSTER, *Foreign Policy of Castlereagh, 1815–1822* (1925), a continuation of his 1812–1815 study, and H. W. V. TEMPERLEY, *Foreign Policy of Canning, 1822–1827* (1925), a continuation of the preceding. BELL'S *Lord Palmerston*, already mentioned, is valuable for the next period. Also important in the middle years are E. D. ADAMS, *Great Britain and the American Civil War* (2 vols.; 1925); D. JORDAN and E. J. PRATT, *Europe and the American Civil War* (1931); and P. KNAPLUND, *Gladstone's Foreign Policy* (1935). The diplomatic background of the World War is ably covered in its broadest aspects by S. B. FAY, *Origins of the World War* (2 vols.; 1928), and R. J. SONTAG, *European Diplomatic History, 1871–1932* (1933). Somewhat more specialized are G. L. DICKINSON, *The International Anarchy, 1904–1914* (1926); EARL GREY, *Twenty-five Years* (2 vols.; 1925); R. J. S. HOFFMAN, *Great Britain and the German Trade Rivalry, 1875–1914* (1933); W. L. LANGER, *European Alliances and Alignments, 1871–1890* (1931) and *The Diplomacy of Imperialism, 1890–1902* (2 vols.; 1935); H. G. NICOLSON, *Portrait of a Diplomatist* (1930); G. M. TREVELYAN, *Grey of Fallodon* (1937); and E. L. WOODWARD, *Great Britain and the German Navy* (1935). Useful for background is J. A. SPENDER, *Fifty Years of Europe* (1933).

FIRST WORLD WAR. The most useful survey, with special emphasis upon British aspects, is C. R. M. F. CRUTTWELL, *A History of the Great War, 1914–1918* (1934); his brief *Role of British Strategy in the Great War* (1936) also is good. The most complete accounts, published under official British auspices, are the numerous volumes of the *History of the Great War, based on Official Documents*. Two of England's foremost statesmen during the war have written full and interesting, but not unbiased, accounts: CHURCHILL'S *World Crisis*, already mentioned, and the *War Memoirs of David Lloyd George* (5 vols.; 1933–1936); the latter in particular has a strong antimilitary bias. For the western front see J. CHARTERIS, *Field Marshal Earl Haig* (1929); A. D. COOPER, *Haig* (1935); F. B. MAURICE, *The Last Four Months* (1919); and, for actual fighting conditions, S. L. SASSOON, *Memoirs of an Infantry Officer* (1930). For the Dardanelles-Gallipoli operations see I. S. M. HAMILTON, *Gallipoli Diary* (2 vols.; 1920), by the British military commander; J. MASEFIELD, *Gallipoli* (new ed., 1927); W. D. PULESTON, *The Dardanelles Expedition* (1927); and *The Naval Memoirs of Admiral of the Fleet Sir Roger J. B. Keyes* (Vol. I, 1935). Naval activities in the North Sea are described by the British commander LORD JELLICOE in *The Grand Fleet, 1914–1916* (1919); the clearest and most vivid account of Jutland is L. GIBSON and J. E. T. HARPER, *The Riddle of Jutland* (1934). The remarkable work of the Arabs is told by the leader T. E. LAWRENCE in *Revolt in the Desert* (1927) and *The Seven Pillars of Wisdom* (new ed., 1935); also in *The Letters of Gertrude Bell* (ed. LADY BELL; 2 vols., 1927). For the "home front" see H. L. GRAY, *War Time Control of Industry: the Experience of England* (1918).

PEACE SETTLEMENT (1919). Perhaps the best account of the peace settlement is H. G. NICOLSON, *Peacemaking, 1919* (1933). Important for their early questioning of the fairness and wisdom of the settlement are J. M. KEYNES, *Economic Consequences of the Peace* (1920) and *A Revision of the Treaty* (1922); also useful is F. H. SIMONDS, *How Europe made Peace without America* (1923).

EMPIRE. *The Cambridge History of the British Empire*, already mentioned, is a thorough and reliable general authority, with special volumes for the various major parts of the empire since 1783; there are general accounts in Volume II, 1783–1870, and Volume III, 1870–1914. Useful general surveys of the workings of the different parts are E. JENKS, *Government of the British Empire, as at the End of the Year 1917* (1918), and the *Oxford Survey of the British Empire* (ed. A. J. HERBERTSON and O. J. R. HOWARTH; 6 vols., 1914). General imperial conditions in the middle years of the century are discussed in P. KNAPLUND,

# Bibliography

*Gladstone and Britain's Imperial Policy* (1927), and W. P. MORRELL, *British Colonial Policy in the Age of Peel and Russell* (1930). The new imperialism is discussed, and in the main disapproved, in J. A. HOBSON, *Imperialism, a Study* (1905), and P. T. MOON, *Imperialism and World Politics* (new ed., 1932). General discussions of the modern problems of the empire include J. BRYCE, *Modern Democracies* (2 vols.; 1921); L. CURTIS, *The Problem of Commonwealth* (1916); C. W. DILKE, *Problems of Greater Britain* (4th ed., 1890); W. Y. ELLIOTT, *The New British Empire* (1932); W. P. HALL, *Empire to Commonwealth: Thirty Years of British Imperial History* (1928), for the years 1897–1927; R. JEBB, *The Imperial Conference, a History and a Study* (2 vols.; 1911) and *The Britannic Question, a Survey of Alternatives* (1913); A. B. KEITH, *Imperial Unity and the Dominions* (1916); and A. E. ZIMMERN, *The Third British Empire* (1926). For participation in the World War see *The Empire at War* (ed. C. P. LUCAS; 5 vols., 1921–1926).

In addition to these works on the empire as a whole there are many useful books dealing with particular parts of the empire.

For Canada the brief general survey by WITTKE, already mentioned, continues useful; also Vol. VI of the *Cambridge History of the British Empire*. Much of value will be found in some of the volumes of two ambitious co-operative series: *Chronicles of Canada* (ed. G. M. WRONG and H. H. LANGTON; 32 vols., 1912) and *Makers of Canada* (ed. W. L. GRANT; 12 vols.; new ed., 1926). A valuable detailed account is A. SHORTT and A. G. DOUGHTY, *Canada and its Provinces* (23 vols.; 1914–1917). More specialized in their scope are R. L. BORDEN, *Canada in the Commonwealth* (1929); W. P. M. KENNEDY, *The Constitution of Canada* (1922), the best outline of the subject; W. R. LIVINGSTON, *Responsible Government in Nova Scotia* (1930); C. P. LUCAS, *Lord Durham's Report on the Affairs of British North America* (3 vols.; 1912); J. L. MORISON, *British Supremacy and Canadian Self-Government, 1839–1854* (1919); C. NEW, *Lord Durham* (1929); J. POPE, *Memoirs of Sir John Alexander Macdonald* (2 vols.; 1895); O. D. SKELTON, *Life and Letters of Sir Wilfred Laurier* (2 vols.; 1921); and C. P. STACEY, *Canada and the British Army, 1846–1871* (1936), a valuable study in the adjustment of dominion responsibility.

For Australia and New Zealand the best short histories are E. JENKS, *History of the Australasian Colonies* (3d ed., 1912); A. W. JOSE, *History of Australasia* (new ed., 1926); and the *Cambridge History of the British Empire*, Vol. VII. Also useful are R. C. MILLS, *The Colonization of Australia, 1829–1842, The Wakefield Experiment in Empire Building* (1915); E. SWEETMAN, *Australian Constitutional Development* (1925); and B. R. WISE, *The Making of the Australian Commonwealth, 1889–1900* (1913).

For Africa in general see H. H. JOHNSTON, *History of the Colonization of Africa* (2d ed., 1913), written by an official who did much to extend British power there. For South Africa the most useful accounts are the *Cambridge History of the British Empire*, Vol. VIII; R. I. LOVELL, *The Struggle for South Africa, 1875–1899* (1934); D. REITZ, *Commando* (1929), a vivid picture of the Boer War, continued in his *Afrikander* (1933) (called *Trekking On* in the British edition); and B. WILLIAMS, *Cecil Rhodes* (1921). For Egypt the leading accounts are B. M. ALLEN, *Gordon and the Sudan* (1931); V. CHIROL, *The Egyptian Problem* (1920); LORD CROMER, *Modern Egypt* (2 vols.; 1908); LORD LLOYD, *Egypt since Cromer* (2 vols.; 1933–1934); and LORD ZETLAND, *Lord Cromer* (1932).

For India a good general account, in addition to LYALL, already mentioned, is E. THOMPSON and E. GARRATT, *The Rise and Fulfilment of British Rule in India* (1934). The *Cambridge History of the British Empire*, Vol. IV., carries the story to 1858. For the earlier part of this period see T. R. HOLMES, *History of the Indian Mutiny* (5th ed., 1913), and L. J. TROTTER, *History of India from the Earliest Times to the Present Day* (2 vols.; 3d ed., 1911). More recent problems are discussed in D. H. BUCHANAN, *The Development of Capitalistic Enterprise in India* (1934); V. CHIROL, *India Old and New* (1921) and *India* (1926); R. CRADDOCK, *The Dilemma in India* (1930), for a reasoned and intelligent Tory viewpoint; E. A. HORNE, *Political System of British India* (1922); C. ILBERT, *Government of India* (1922); K. MAYO, *Mother India* (1927), an extreme attack on Indian practices; and D. G. MUKERJI, *My Brother's Face* (1924) and *Disillusioned India* (1930), giving an Indian point of view.

# A History of England and the British Empire

For the West Indies see L. J. RAGATZ, *The Fall of the Planter Class in the British Caribbean* (1928).

Among the more objective accounts of modern events in Ireland are E. BARKER, *Ireland in the Last Fifty Years, 1866–1916* (new ed., 1919); ST. J. G. ERVINE, *Parnell* (1925); R. M. HENRY, *The Evolution of Sinn Fein* (1920); R. McNEILL, *Ulster's Stand for Union* (1922); J. O'CONNOR, *History of Ireland, 1798–1924* (2 vols.; 1925); W. A. PHILLIPS, *Revolution in Ireland, 1909–1923* (1923); J. E. POMFRET, *The Struggle for Land in Ireland, 1800–1923* (1930); and W. B. WELLS, *John Redmond, a Biography* (1919).

In addition to the foregoing serious works on British history, numerous works of historical fiction of the sounder type may be useful in helping to recreate the atmosphere of earlier times. No attempt is made to enumerate them here, but a complete account of the chief works up to its time of publication will be found in E. A. BAKER, *A Guide to Historical Fiction* (1914).

SECOND WORLD WAR. Overall accounts include C. B. FALLS, *The Second World War, a Short History* (1948); J. F. C. FULLER, *The Second World War, 1939–1945, a Strategical and Tactical History* (1949); R. W. SHUGG and H. A. DEWEERD, *World War II, a Concise History* (1946); and W. P. HALL, *Iron out of Calvary* (1946). The most ambitious project is W. S. CHURCHILL, *The Second World War* (1948 ff.) which contains many of the wartime prime minister's official papers; each volume has its special title, such as *The Gathering Storm, Their Finest Hour, The Grand Alliance*, etc. Naval works include SIR W. M. JAMES, *The British Navies in the Second World War* (1947); JOHN CRESSWELL, *Sea Warfare, 1939–1945* (1950) and *Generals and Admirals: The Story of Amphibious Command* (1952); and RUSSELL GRENFELL, *The Bismarck Episode* (1949) and *Main Fleet to Singapore* (1951). The official Canadian studies are C. P. STACEY, *The Canadian Army, 1939–1945* (1948); G. N. TUCKER, *The Naval Service of Canada: Its Official History* (2 vols., 1952); and JOSEPH SCHULL, *The Far Distant Ships* (1950).

POSTWAR BRITAIN. Two important economic surveys are KEITH HUTCHISON, *The Decline and Fall of British Capitalism* (1950) and G. D. N. WORSWICK and P. H. ADY, ed., *The British Economy, 1945–1950* (1953). Among the political studies, of varying permanent importance, are: G. D. H. COLE, *A History of the Labour Party from 1914* (1948); R. B. McCALLUM and ALISON READMAN, *The British General Election of 1945* (1946); H. G. NICHOLAS, *The British General Election of 1950* (1951); ERNEST WATKINS, *The Cautious Revolution* (1950); QUINTIN HOGG, *The Case for Conservatism*. The views of four prominent members of the Labor government are presented in: C. R. ATTLEE, *The Labour Party in Perspective—and Twelve Years Later* (1949); SIR STAFFORD CRIPPS, *Democracy Alive* (1946); H. S. MORRISON, *The Peaceful Revolution* (1949); and ANEURIN BEVAN, *In Place of Fear* (1952). Three useful small "Pelican" volumes are: E. M. HUBBACK, *The Population of Britain* (1947); KENNETH MACKENZIE, *The English Parliament* (1950); and FERDINAND ZWEIG, *The British Worker* (1952).

POSTWAR COMMONWEALTH. Useful general studies are C. E. CARRINGTON, *The British Overseas: Exploits of a Nation of Shopkeepers* (1950); ERIK ESTARIK, *Changing Empire: Churchill to Nehru* (1950); R. P. DUTT, *The British Crisis of Empire* (1950); and SIR READER BULLARD, *Britain and the Middle East*. The books on India, of varying value, include JAWAHARLAL NEHRU, *Independence and After* (1950); KINGSLEY DAVIS, *The Population of India and Pakistan* (1951); ANDREW MELLOR, *India since Partition* (1950); RICHARD SYMONDS, *The Making of Pakistan* (1950); PERCIVAL SPEAR, *India, Pakistan, and the West* (1949); and LOUIS FISCHER, *The Life of Mahatma Gandhi*. Works on Africa include GEORGE PODMORE, *Africa, Britain's Third Empire* (1949); S. G. MILLIN, *The Peoples of South Africa* (1951); F. J. PEDLER, *West Africa* (1951); HENRY GIBBS, *Twilight in*

# Bibliography

*South Africa* (1950); and ALAN WOOD, *The Ground Nut Affair* (1950). Three Palestine works are BERNARD JOSEPH, *British Rule in Palestine* (1948); F. E. NEWTON, *Fifty Years in Palestine* (1948); and RICHARD CROSSMAN, *Palestine Mission* (1947). Other subjects are covered in G. RAWSON, *Australia* (1947); H. SHEARMAN, *Anglo-Irish Relations* (1948); and M. J. MACMANUS, *Eamon de Valera* (1946).

# Index

# Index

# Index

# Index

# Index

# Index

# Index

# Index

# Index

# Index

722, 729; Orange Free State (Orange
River Colony), 679, 722, 728, 729;
Transvaal (South African Republic), 679,
722 ff., 725, 728, 729; diamond and gold
mines, 679, 722, 724; responsible government, 679, 685, 729; federation, 686, 722,
729 f.; Majuba Hill, 723; Bechuanaland, 724; Rhodesia, 725; British South
African Company, 725 f.; Jameson's
Raid, 726; Kruger telegram, 726; Boer
War, 727 f.; conditions after Boer War,
728 ff., 749, 928; in First World War,
871, 879, 881; and the Peace Settlement,
892, 893; between wars, 936, 937 f., 940;
in Second World War, 954, 972, 992, 997;
postwar, 1035
South African War, see Boer War
South Sea Bubble, 429 f., 438
Southey, Robert, 605 f.
Spa Fields riot, 589
Spain, in the 15th and 16th centuries, 218,
229, 236 ff., 253 f., 262, 277 f., 280, 286 f.,
290 ff., 296 ff.; extent and wealth of colonial empire, 232, 254, 274, 278, 291, 299,
429; and Elizabeth, 287, 290 f., 296 ff.;
monopoly of trade within colonial empire, 291 ff., 429, 440, 449 f.; in the 17th
and 18th centuries, 309, 384 f., 405, 406,
462; and the early Stuarts, 319, 321 ff.,
337; and the American Revolution, 472,
475, 476, 477; and the French Revolution, 551 ff.; and Napoleon, 574 ff.;
Congress of Vienna and Metternich
period, 581, 584 f., 591; loss of American
colonies, 362, 591 ff., 656; War with
United States, 743; since 1914, 919, 944,
962
Spanish America, see Latin America
Spanish Netherlands, see Low Countries
Spanish Succession, War of the, 412, 414 ff.,
423 ff.
Spencer, Herbert, 784, 785, 787, 788
"Spheres of interest," 743, 828
Stalin, Marshal Josef, 981, 982, 983, 986,
996, 1004, 1038
Stalingrad, 984
Stamford Bridge, battle of, 60
Stamp Act, 467 f., 469
Standard, battle of the, 94
Stanhope, Lord, 430
Stanley, Edward George, 14th Earl of
Derby, 642, 695

Stanley, Edward G. V., 16th Earl of Derby,
870
Stanley, Henry M., 715 f., 744
Star Chamber, Court of, 239, 315, 317 f.,
328, 340 ff.
Statutes, 148, 199. See also under separate
names
Steam engine, see Railways
Steamships, 508, 509, 652 f.
Steele, Sir Richard, 423, 513, 519 f.
Stephen of Blois, 92 ff.
Stephenson, George, 508, 607 ff.
Sterne, Laurence, 521 f.
"Sterling area," 1011 ff.
Stirling Bridge, battle of, 166
Stockmar, Baron, 625
Stockton and Darlington Railway, 607 f.
Stonehenge, 5
Strafford, see Wentworth, Sir Thomas
Straits Settlements, 656, 677, 749
Strathcona, Lord, see Smith, Donald
Stresa, conference at, 926
Strikes, 502 ff., 807, 819 f., 900, 916 f.,
990, 1013
Strongbow, see Clare, Richard de
Stuart line, 308, 426, 452
Stuart, Arabella, 309, 311
Submarine warfare, in First World War,
868 f., 881 f.; in Second World War,
952 f., 955 f., 957, 965 f., 986 f.
Succession, Acts of, 266, 309
Sudan [See also Egypt], 717 f., 720 f., 827,
934 ff., 941, 1035
Suez Canal [See also Egypt], 677 f., 705 f.,
716, 935, 936, 938, 941, 972, 984, 1034,
1048, 1053
Suffolk, see Pole, de la
Suffrage [See also Reform Bills], 200, 314,
818 f., 903 f.
Sugar Act, 468
Supremacy, Act of, 265 f.
Surrey, Earl of, see Howard, Henry
Sussex, 15, 353
Sweden, 237, 309, 337, 386, 406, 440, 554
Sweyn, 50, 52
Swift, Jonathan, 423, 513, 520

Tacitus, 7
Taff Vale Decision, 802 f., 817
Tanganyika, 744, 746, 893, 1021
Taranto, 974
Tehran, conference at, 982

# Index

# Index